T0340030

A COURSE IN ENVIRONMENTAL ECONOMICS

Theory, Policy, and Practice

This unique graduate textbook offers a compelling narrative of the growing field of environmental economics that integrates theory, policy, and empirical topics. Authors Daniel J. Phaneuf and Till Requate present both traditional and emerging perspectives, incorporating cutting-edge research in a way that allows students to easily identify connections and common themes. Their comprehensive approach gives instructors the flexibility to cover a range of topics, including important issues – such as tax interaction, environmental liability rules, modern treatments of incomplete information, technology adoption and innovation, and international environmental problems – that are not discussed in other graduate-level texts. Numerous data-based examples and end-of-chapter exercises show students how theoretical and applied research findings are complementary, and will enable them to develop skills and interests in all areas of the field. Additional data sets and exercises can be accessed online, providing ample opportunity for practice.

Daniel J. Phaneuf is Professor of Agricultural and Applied Economics at the University of Wisconsin-Madison. He has been Managing Editor of the *Journal of Environmental Economics and Management*, and is currently Editor in Chief of the *Journal of the Association of Environmental and Resource Economists*. He is a member of the US Environmental Protection Agency Science Advisory Board and also serves on the board of directors for the Association of Environmental and Resource Economists. His many research articles have appeared in top field and general economics outlets, and he has won awards for his graduate and undergraduate teaching in environmental economics and econometrics.

Till Requate is Professor for Economic Policy at Kiel University, Germany. He was previously Professor for Environmental Economics and Director of the Interdisciplinary Institute of Environmental Economics at Heidelberg University. He is currently Managing Editor of the *Journal of Environmental Economics and Management* and Associate Editor of *Resource and Energy Economics*, and was Chairman of the German Association of Environmental and Resource Economists. He won the European Association of Environmental and Resource Economics' Erik Kempe Award for the best paper in 2004 and the German Society of Health Economics' best paper award in 2013. His research articles have appeared in top field and general economics outlets.

A COURSE IN ENVIRONMENTAL ECONOMICS

Theory, Policy, and Practice

Daniel J. Phaneuf

University of Wisconsin-Madison

Till Requate

University of Kiel, Germany

CAMBRIDGE UNIVERSITY PRESS

CAMBRIDGE
UNIVERSITY PRESS

University Printing House, Cambridge CB2 8BS, United Kingdom

One Liberty Plaza, 20th Floor, New York, NY 10006, USA

477 Williamstown Road, Port Melbourne, VIC 3207, Australia

314-321, 3rd Floor, Plot 3, Splendor Forum, Jasola District Centre, New Delhi - 110025, India

103 Penang Road, #05-06/07, Visioncrest Commercial, Singapore 238467

Cambridge University Press is part of the University of Cambridge.

It furthers the University's mission by disseminating knowledge in the pursuit of
education, learning and research at the highest international levels of excellence.

www.cambridge.org
Information on this title: www.cambridge.org/9780521178693
10.1017/9780511843839

© Daniel J. Phaneuf and Till Requate 2017

First published 2017

A catalogue record for this publication is available from the British Library

Library of Congress Cataloging in Publication data
Names: Phaneuf, Daniel J. (Daniel James), author. | Requate, Till, 1957– author.
Title: A course in environmental economics : theory, policy,
and practice / Daniel J. Phaneuf, Till Requate.
Description: New York, NY : Cambridge University Press, 2017. |
Includes bibliographical references and index.
Identifiers: LCCN 2016044938 | ISBN 9781107004177 (hardback) |
ISBN 9780521178693 (pbk.)
Subjects: LCSH: Environmental economics.
Classification: LCC HC79.E5 P5125 2017 | DDC 333.7–dc23
LC record available at https://lccn.loc.gov/2016044938

ISBN 978-1-107-00417-7 Hardback
ISBN 978-0-521-17869-3 Paperback

For Tammo, Finja, and Silke – D.P.
For Sabine and Frederik – T.R.

Contents

Figures

Tables

Preface

This book grew out of discussions we had more than ten years ago, when we were both teaching graduate courses in environmental economics at our respective universities in Germany and the United States. Though our interests and skills were different – Requate is a theorist/experimentalist, and Phaneuf an empiricist – we both had the sense that there was something missing in the textbooks we used for our classes. Specifically, while there are a variety of excellent undergraduate and some Master's-level textbooks, there was not a single obvious choice for instructors teaching at the advanced graduate level. For environmental policy design, the classic book by Baumol and Oates (1988), *The Theory of Environmental Policy*, had become dated. For non-market valuation, Freeman (2003) and Freeman et al. (2014), *The Measurement of Environmental and Resource Values*, was (and remains today) an authoritative and obvious choice, but its emphasis is on concepts rather than empirics. As such, there was no single volume suitable for advanced study that presented the theoretical, empirical, and policy aspects of the field as an integrated narrative. As a result, we felt that our students were seeing the trees but not the forest, i.e. they were learning environmental economics as a collection of disjointed topics, but failing to appreciate how the topics fit together into something greater than the sum of their parts. We felt that a textbook for graduate students was needed that: (a) presented the field's canon on environmental policy design and non-market valuation using a single notational convention; (b) included contemporary and advanced topics missing in other sources; (c) reflected the increasingly empirical nature of environmental economics; and (d) conveyed the excitement and dynamism of a growing field. This book is our attempt to meet that need.

Our vision for the book is best explained by discussing its organization. We have divided the material into four parts. In Part I, we set the stage by placing environmental economics in its historical context. This is accomplished by reviewing the field's roots in neoclassical welfare theory and the theory of externalities (Chapter 1), and its close relationship to environmental policy and environmental science (Chapter 2). In Chapter 3 we close Part I by laying out our basic modeling framework for the first half of the book. We define the environmental externality problem and optimal solution, and introduce a variety of environmental policy instruments, which are potentially suitable for decentralizing the social optimum. We also begin to establish criteria that we will use to evaluate their performance. A main conclusion from Part I is that the portfolio of economic-incentive based policies that we introduce – e.g. emission taxes, cap and trade programs, emission subsidies – are equivalent in their economic efficiency properties.

Our Part I conclusions set up an important benchmark for Part II of the book, in which we add real-world complexity to our description, and investigate the conditions under which the equivalence of the above-mentioned policy tools breaks down. We also study circumstances in which alternative (or complementary) policy instruments are preferred, and when second-best optimal solutions need to be implemented. More specifically, the first several chapters in Part II cover the traditional sub-field of policy design. In Chapters 4 through 9, we consider a range of generalizations and extensions that add nuance to our comparisons of policy instruments. Examples of specific topics include the role of uncertainty in policy design (Chapter 4), considerations related to competitive and non-competitive output markets (Chapters 5 and 6), the role of other, non-environmental distortions in formulating environmental policy (Chapter 7), complications related to spatial considerations and other institutional features (Chapter 8), and the particular problems associated with non-point source pollution (Chapter 9). A common theme in these chapters is that context matters. We show that the equivalence of different economic-incentive based policies holds only in special cases, meaning that effective policy design requires careful consideration of multiple (often competing) factors. These chapters also illustrate how, in its focus on policy-specific challenges, environmental economics has matured beyond an application of the theory of public goods and externalities to the environment.

The last four chapters of Part II cover themes that move beyond the standard suite of policy design topics. For example, in Chapter 10 we provide a detailed treatment of liability rules as an alternative to emission regulations for environmentally risky activities. This is followed in Chapter 11 by a comprehensive discussion of environmental technology development, adoption, and diffusion. In Chapter 12 we discuss several topics that are specific to international environmental problems, including transboundary pollution and international trade. Finally, we close Part II in Chapter 13 by addressing dynamic aspects of externalities – notably models for stock (accumulating) pollutants, and their connection to climate change and non-renewable resource policy.

Throughout Parts I and II of the book, we use conceptual representations of cost and utility functions to characterize policy solutions. Implementation of policy solutions in most instances requires empirical estimates of pollution abatement costs and damage functions, which derive from firms' and households' underlying technology and preference structures. In Part III we turn our attention to the traditional sub-field of non-market valuation, which includes theoretical and empirical tools used to measure the costs and benefits that result from changes in environmental quality. We begin by describing the theoretical basis for applied welfare analysis (Chapter 14), and then discuss the specific assumptions that are needed to calculate non-market values using only observed behavior (Chapter 15). These assumptions give rise to the so-called revealed preference models. In Chapter 16 we present a review of discrete choice econometrics – a class of empirical models that plays a large role in many areas of non-market valuation. These initial Part III chapters provide the conceptual and empirical backgrounds needed for studying the specific techniques and applications that follow. These include recreation demand (Chapter 17), property values (Chapter 18), stated preference methods (Chapter 19), and health valuation (Chapter 20).

We complete the book in Part IV by examining themes related to the practice of environmental economics. Our main task is to discuss, across two chapters, a handful of topics connected to cost-benefit analysis. These include conceptual issues such as discounting and the use of integrated assessment models (Chapter 21), and applied issues related to benefits transfer and estimating abatement cost functions (Chapter 22). We then close the book in Chapter 23 with observations on the increasingly empirical nature of environmental economics, discussions on themes we have not covered, and identification of topics that we believe provide important opportunities for future research.

A distinguishing feature of the book is that we have used a single notational scheme across the four parts of the book in order to connect the various topics and minimize the cost of entry into each new concept. We have also included numerous numbered examples, which we use to describe relevant empirical research, provide intuition with specific functional forms, or place our discussions in the context of a specific policy. A variety of exercises are included at the end of most chapters, which, depending on the chapter's content, are analytical, numerical, empirical, or literature based.[1] In some cases, advanced material or proofs are included in appendices that follow the main content of a chapter. The book's website (www.phaneuf-requate.com) houses data for the empirical exercises as well as supplemental information and errata.

Finally, we have included a "further reading" section at the end of each chapter. It is here that we identify the original source material our discussion has drawn on, and highlight related and in some cases recent research contributions to the area. We have used this approach for two reasons. First, we wrote using a narrative format rather than a review article format, meaning we tried to avoid breaking the flow of description with a large volume of parenthetical references. Thus our citations in the main body of the chapters are usually reserved for attribution of specific ideas, identification of classic sources, and acknowledgment when we have used published material as a model for our textbook presentation. Second, we wanted to have a specific section in each chapter that would serve as a literature-organizing vehicle, where we could classify different areas of inquiry that fit under the chapter's broad themes. We emphasize that our further reading sections are designed to be illustrative rather than comprehensive, and so we have not included citations to many (or even most) of the relevant papers. That said, a book this long that unfolded over many years will undoubtedly have failed to give proper credit in many places, and so the book's website will include expanded versions of our further reading sections, which will be updated periodically.

There are many ways that instructors and students can make use of this book. One possibility is to use the content as the basis for a lecture-based survey of the field. For Master's level survey classes, the early sections in most chapters are accessible and provide the basic canon, while more advanced topics, covered in the later sections, can be skipped. For PhD level survey classes, instructors will have more flexibility to cover the advanced sections and the more technical chapters. A second possibility is to use chapters in the book as background reading for discussion classes focused on contemporary research. For example, students exploring new research at the health-environment nexus may benefit from an initial review of our revealed preference, stated preference, and health valuation chapters. As these different uses suggest, the book does not have

---

[1] When relevant, the difficulty of individual exercises is indicated using asterisks. One, two, or three asterisks denote basic, intermediate, and advanced problems, respectively.

to be read linearly. A course on environmental policy design could focus on Part I and selected chapters in Part II, while a course on non-market valuation could start directly with Part III and incorporate some material in Part IV. Finally, the book can serve as a reference for the collection of theoretical predictions and empirical methods that environmental economists use in their day-to-day research and teaching.

In terms of technical preparation, readers should have a good understanding of core microeconomic theory. This includes familiarity with consumer demand theory, the theory of the firm, standard duality methods, and general equilibrium concepts. Basic knowledge in game theory, including the concepts of Nash and sub-game perfect equilibria, is useful. In a few instances we use more advanced tools, including mechanism design in Chapter 4 and dynamic optimization in Chapter 13. In these cases we have tried to introduce the needed tools along with the specific concept. Topics that require techniques beyond what is listed above are identified and references provided, but not discussed in detail. Nonetheless, some of the end-of-chapter exercises provide opportunities to explore the advanced areas. For several of the analytical and numerical exercises, familiarity with computational software packages such as Matlab or Mathematica is necessary.

Readers should also have a good understanding of basic econometrics and applied methods. Familiarity with linear regression models and discrete choice econometrics is needed for our applied chapters and to appreciate many of the empirical examples we use throughout. Since discrete choice methods are not always taught in core econometrics classes, we have included a chapter on this subject, which can serve as a point of entry for the interested reader. Experience with applying basic regression and discrete choice models using software tools such as Stata or R is necessary for completing the applied end-of-chapter exercises.

To close the preface, we would like to share a few personal notes and express thanks to the many people and institutions that supported our efforts during the writing of this book. In retrospect, our feeling is that the book was harder to write than expected. Our early plans envisioned translating our respective lecture notes into a narrative, but we quickly discovered that the task of surveying a dynamic and growing field required more than that. As we worked, we became convinced that the book needed to have substantial breadth to represent the range of themes that have occupied environmental economists. At the same time, we did not want to sacrifice depth, since our goal was to provide a genuinely advanced treatment of topics in the field. These two objectives largely explain the book's length and the time it has taken to write. They are also the likely explanations for any limitations that may be present in the final product. Challenging though it was, writing the book was enormously satisfying intellectually, and we are grateful for the opportunity the publisher and our institutions have given us to pursue this work.

A defining characteristic of any multi-year project is that the list of people and organizations to whom thanks is owed is long. We are unable to list here the names of many colleagues and students who read drafts, provided reviews, reacted to ideas, and gave encouragement, but we want to extend our collective thanks for their input. In addition, we have accumulated and presented the ideas in this book, but most of them originated with other people. As such we want to thank the many economists, past and current, who have shaped the field and driven its progress. We also want to acknowledge the authors, reviewers, and publishers of the journals that we have edited during many of our writing years. Our editing work at *Journal of the Association of Environmental and Resource Economists* (*JAERE* – Phaneuf) and *Journal of Environmental Economics and Management* (*JEEM* – Requate/Phaneuf) has complemented our writing by keeping us abreast of the field's development, expanding our understanding of different topic areas, and introducing us to researchers around the globe.[2]

We would also like to explicitly recognize the institutions that have supported our efforts: North Carolina State University and University of Wisconsin-Madison (Phaneuf), and University of Heidelberg and University of Kiel (Requate). Phaneuf also acknowledges generous support from the NCSU Kriz Faculty Study Leave Endowment, which partially funded his sabbatical visit at the University of Kiel.

---

[2] At the time of writing, Requate is the Managing Editor for *JEEM* and Phaneuf is the Editor in Chief for *JAERE*. Phaneuf served as *JEEM*'s Managing Editor from 2011 through 2013.

Notational Conventions

The following describes the notation conventions that we generally maintain throughout the book.

STRUCTURAL FUNCTIONS

$D(\cdot)$:	Household pollution damage function
$C(\cdot)$:	Firm abatement cost or general cost function
$\Pi(\cdot)$:	Firm profit function
$U(\cdot)$:	Household or individual direct utility function
$V(\cdot)$:	Household or individual indirect utility function
$P(\cdot)$:	Inverse demand function
$E(\cdot)$:	Household expenditure function (also industry emission level; see below)
$f(\cdot), g(\cdot)$:	Technologies

QUANTITIES

x:	Scalar or vector of consumer demand or firm output levels
p:	Scalar or vector of market prices for x
z:	Scalar consumer good or firm output level; often the numeraire good
l:	Scalar or vector of firm factor input levels
w:	Scalar or vector of firm factor input prices. Also used for household wage rate
y:	Household, individual, or firm income level
e:	Firm level pollution emissions
E:	Industry level pollution emissions (also household expenditure function; see above)
q:	Scalar or vector of an environmental good or quality level
s:	Scalar or vector of agent characteristics
Capital letters:	aggregate outcomes
Lower-case letters:	agent level outcomes

BEHAVIORAL FUNCTIONS

$x(\cdot)$: Ordinary (uncompensated) demand scalar or vector
$h(\cdot)$: Compensated demand scalar or vector
$\pi^q(\cdot)$: Compensated inverse demand function for quality
$\theta^q(\cdot)$: Uncompensated inverse demand function for quality
$l(\cdot)$: Firm's factor demand function

POLICY PARAMETERS

τ: Pollution tax
ς: Pollution or other subsidy
σ: Price of a pollution allowance in a pollution rights market
α: Relative standard
L: Supply of pollution allowances in a pollution rights market

INDEXES

$i = 1,\ldots,I$: Index of households or individuals
$j = 1,\ldots,J$: Index of firms; also used as index of consumer choice elements in later chapters

OTHER SYMBOLS

$\varepsilon, \eta, \kappa, \nu$: Parameters of structural, behavioral, or econometric functions. Also used for elasticities or response functions
ξ: Unobserved attribute of a quality-differentiated consumer good
β, θ, γ: Symbols commonly used as known or unknown parameters of a model; often the targets of estimation
ρ: State of the world probability. Also used for consumption discount rate
π: General probability

PRONOUNS:

he: Economic agent
she: Analyst or regulator
it: Firm or household

PART I

Economics and the Environment

In Part I of the book, we present three chapters that set the stage for our detailed study of the field. Our first objective is to discuss the intellectual and policy roots of environmental economics. In Chapter 1, we review several key results from welfare economics, which provide the normative criteria that we will use to distinguish different market and policy-influenced outcomes. We also review the basic theory of public goods and externalities, which provides the basis for the design and evaluation of environmental policy. In Chapter 2, we turn to a discussion of how environmental policy evolved out of the environmental movements of the 1960s, and how policy needs were, and continue to be, important drivers of research in the field. With this as motivation, we review several different environmental problems and policy initiatives, and discuss the multidisciplinary aspects of work in environmental economics. Finally, in Chapter 3, we describe our baseline model of environmental costs and benefits, which we use to introduce concepts and notation, define a suite of policy options, and establish the evaluation criteria that we will use in later chapters.

Part I of the book also introduces the contributions to the field of two influential thinkers. Arthur Cecil Pigou was a British economist who, working in the early twentieth century, explored market failures through externalities, and made suggestions on policy interventions. An environmental tax is often referred to as a Pigouvian tax in recognition of his work. Likewise, an environmental policy that seeks to balance marginal benefits from reducing pollution with the marginal costs of abatement, is often referred to as the Pigouvian paradigm. More generally, the Pigouvian paradigm is associated with an interventionist approach to solving environmental problems. This is in contrast to the Coasian paradigm, which is named after the University of Chicago economist Ronald Coase. In an influential paper, Coase (1960) argued that externality problems, of which environmental problems are one example, arise from an incomplete definition of property rights. He suggested that if property rights were clearly defined, private negotiations would lead individuals to the correct outcome, without the need for intervention. Given this, the Coasian paradigm is associated with a non-interventionist approach to solving environmental problems. As we will see in Part I and throughout the book, the Pigouvian and Coasian traditions continue to be useful bookends for understanding debates over environmental policy.

CHAPTER 1

Environmental Economics and the Theory of Externalities

Our aim in this book is to provide a comprehensive treatment of graduate level environmental economics in a single volume, using a style of presentation that integrates the many sub-areas of inquiry that have come to define the field. To this end we begin in this chapter by introducing the field of environmental economics via its roots in neoclassical welfare theory and the theory of externalities. Environmental problems and policy challenges stem, of course, from human uses of the environment and natural resources. This statement alone does not provide the basis for our study, however. Rather, it is the way that humans use the environment and the impact this use has on the well-being of others that interests us and defines the field. Our starting point therefore is the notion that one person's interactions with the environment can have direct and unsolicited effects on another person, without compensation or other recognition of the impact. To use the classic example, a factory owner whose plant sits next to a laundry impacts the launderer by dirtying the air he needs to produce clean linen. The launderer suffers as a result of the actions of the factory owner, without recourse or compensation. A contemporary example involves the leaching of nitrogen fertilizer from agricultural fields into underground aquifers, from which surrounding communities draw drinking water. Users of groundwater for drinking suffer due to the actions of the farmer, again without recourse or compensation.

These two examples serve to illustrate the types of problems considered in environmental economics and hint at both the positive (describing what is) and normative (describing what ought to be) aspects of study. From a positive point of view, we might be interested in understanding how existing institutional structures lead the self-interested factory owner and farmer to undertake actions that have negative consequences for others. From a normative perspective, we might be interested in suggesting policy interventions that help mitigate these consequences. In either case we are dealing with a potential misallocation of resources that affects the level of well-being that members of society can obtain. It is in this sense that environmental economics falls under the rubric of welfare economics and the theory of externalities, dealing specifically with the failure of market economies to properly account for the environmental ramifications of economic activity. As an aside, we are also dealing with behavioral interactions between humans and the natural environment, or humans and environmental policy. In this sense, environmental economics is also closely tied to both the broader environmental and public policy sciences. In the remainder of this chapter we focus on developing the welfare theoretic basis for environmental economics. We delay discussion of the field's links to policy and environmental science until the next chapter.

1.1   MARKET FAILURES

The starting point for developing the welfare-theoretic basis for environmental economics is the definition of a normative criterion that we will use to judge the desirability of different economic outcomes. The criterion we use is Pareto optimality, which has both virtues and weaknesses as a normative basis for policy recommendations. Its virtue is its simplicity, illustrated by the following definition.

Definition 1.1
An economic outcome is said to be Pareto optimal if a reallocation of resources cannot make at least one person better off without making another person worse off.

From this it follows that there is the potential for a Pareto improvement if one person's well-being can be improved without decreasing that of another person. A second virtue is the lack of income distribution judgments imbedded in the criterion. By saying nothing about whose well-being matters more, Pareto optimality sidesteps the tricky issue of equity and fairness among economic agents, focusing instead on efficiency – making the economic pie as large as possible, regardless of how it is sliced. This virtue, however, is also a vice, in that outcomes that favor a small number of people while leaving many in need can be judged optimal based on the relatively weak Pareto condition. The trade-off is clear: by saying nothing about income distribution, Pareto optimality as a normative criterion has the potential for admitting rather perverse outcomes into the "desirable" category.

This weakness in the normative criterion is partially offset by the statement of the first and, more directly, second fundamental theorems of welfare economics. Informally, the first welfare theorem states that if markets are complete and perfectly competitive, a decentralized price system coupled with self-interested behavior provides an allocation of resources among society's individuals that is Pareto optimal. The second welfare theorem states the converse of this. If markets are complete and perfectly competitive (and certain regularity conditions hold), any Pareto optimal allocation can be supported by a price system arising from an appropriate redistribution of income, via lump sum taxes and transfers. The appeal of the first and second welfare theorems is obvious: if the conditions are met, society can achieve the largest size pie (efficiency) simply by allowing the free market to function. If society perceives some inequity in how individuals fare in the market system (how large a slice of pie some are getting), simple transfers of income can be used to appropriately adjust the distribution of well-being to something more palatable.

Besides the obvious difficulty in arranging suitable transfers of income, the problem with the first and second welfare theorems is that their conditions are often not met. The two examples from above are cases in point. There is no market intervening between the factory owner and launderer to sort out how much dirty air will be allowed in the vicinity of the linen. Likewise, there is no market determining the "proper" quantity of nitrogen that ends up in local drinking water. These missing markets arise from the absence of well-defined property rights for clean air and potable groundwater. Without property rights, there can be no self-interested owner who makes decisions on how much air and water contamination to allow, and for what price, meaning the factory owner and farmer are not obliged to pay for their use of the environment as an input. In these two examples, we cannot conclude from the first welfare theorem that the free market leads to an efficient allocation. Thus, rather than using the fundamental welfare theorems as justification for non-intervention in markets, environmental economists use them as a point of departure for understanding when free markets are unlikely to deliver efficient outcomes. Judging the validity of the first welfare theorem's result involves establishing the extent to which its conditions hold, which takes us to the theory of externalities and public goods.

For environmental problems, complete markets are the exception rather than the norm, owing to the related problems of externalities and public goods. There are several ways to define an externality using either informal description or formal mathematics. We rely on the following definition from Baumol and Oates (1988, p. 17) to motivate our analysis.

Definition 1.2
An externality exists when agent A's utility or production function depends directly on real variables chosen by another agent B, without an offer of compensation or other attention given to the effect on A's well-being.

A key aspect of the definition rests on the notion of *real* variables. The examples of the laundry and factory owner and farmer and water consumers are externalities in that real outcomes – smoke emissions and nitrogen leaching, respectively – directly impact the production or utility functions of the victims. We can contrast this with a different type of interaction in which, for example, the factory owner's demand for labor drives up the wages the launderer must pay his workers. Here again the launderer is impacted by the factory owner, but the interaction has an indirect path that is filtered through the labor market, and manifests itself only through the price of labor. This latter type of interaction is not an externality according to our definition.

Many externalities in environmental economics have a structure that is similar to that of public goods. Public goods, by definition, are goods that are at least partially non-rival and non-exclusive. Non-rival means multiple people can simultaneously enjoy the services of the good; non-exclusive means that none of these people can be *prevented* from enjoying the services of the good. It is via the latter characteristic that public goods cause problems for the conditions of the first and second welfare theorems. If a good is non-exclusive, a meaningful competitive market price cannot arise in a decentralized system, since individuals can have the good for "free" even if they do not elect to "buy" some positive amount of it. For example, it is possible to use the services of National Public Radio in the United States, even if one does not make a contribution to the annual fund drive. This is the classic *free rider* problem associated with public goods. Thus public goods, like externalities, lead to a type of missing market situation that violates the conditions of the first and second welfare theorems. This is relevant for environmental economics, in that many environmental problems and their solutions share characteristics of public goods (or bads). For example, smog exists frequently in Mexico City due to unfortunate combinations of geography, weather and vehicle traffic – and it broadly affects people with respiratory problems. Efforts to reduce smog in the city would benefit these same people, regardless of their contribution to the control effort. In this sense, air pollution is a public bad, and a reduction in air pollution is a public good. As such, voluntary efforts to improve air quality will lead to its under-provision, since people have incentive to free ride rather than actively contribute.

The definitions and examples of externalities and public goods highlight the importance of these concepts for understanding environmental problems. The failure of the fundamental welfare theorems to hold in the presence of externalities and public goods provides the analytical starting point for the study of environmental economics. Before using these concepts in a formal analysis, however, we consider the following intuitive description of market failure in an environmental context.

1.2 DESCRIPTIVE EXPLANATION OF MARKET FAILURE

We illustrate the concepts of Pareto optimality and market failure via the familiar parable of a small, isolated, and primitive island economy. To begin, suppose there is a single person R living on the island who extracts resources, engages in production, and consumes goods provided directly by the natural system, as well as those he produces himself using the island's resources. For concreteness, suppose further that the island contains a small grove of slow-growing timber, which provides the only source of wood for constructing shelter and consumer goods, as well as habitat for the island's only game animals. In this initial setup, there can be no externalities and any observed outcome is efficient according to our Pareto criterion, since R's actions by definition affect only his own well-being. This is worth elaborating on. Person R can elect to cut the stand of timber and eat the entire population of game animals immediately, and the outcome will still be considered optimal. While outside observers might object to the removal of an entire animal population and clear cutting a forest on moral grounds, our normative criterion considers only the human society's well-being based on its members' preferences. For the single person society, this criterion admits only the well-being of the individual *as he defines it* – and therefore any observed outcome will be Pareto optimal.

This is of course an uninteresting case from the perspective of economics, but it serves to illustrate how the concept of an externality is directly tied to human interactions and consumer sovereignty, and is thus an amoral concept, as opposed to a moral concept based on higher order judgments of right and wrong. To illustrate the economic concept of an externality, suppose now that the island is inhabited by a second person F. With this step, a number of interesting economic problems present themselves. These include issues of specialization, exchange, ownership of property, income distribution, and the potential for externalities. Suppose that R and F agree to joint ownership of the grove of trees. Suppose as well that they are different in their preferences, in that R does not much care for meat, but would like to have a large shelter, while F does not mind sleeping outside, so long as he can eat meat every day. In this setup, the two men see different, and competing, uses for the shared grove of trees: R's large shelter will require a reduction in habitat for game animals, thereby decreasing the quantity of animals available to F. In the language from above, it is now the case that self-interested behavior on the part of both people will not lead to an efficient outcome – the externality has caused a market failure. Without some type of coordination, R will over-cut trees and F will be left to suffer without his daily meat.

In the island parable, the solution to this problem is obviously some type of coordination between the two people. This might take one of two forms. First, suppose R was the first to arrive on the island and as such has established undisputed control over the grove of trees. Person F might offer something to R – perhaps advice and help on constructing his shelter out of stone rather than wood – in return for his agreement to leave the grove of trees in place. In this scenario, the conditions of the first welfare theorem hold, in that the clear division of property rights leads to an *exchange mechanism* (bartering over advice and labor) for the resource that formerly had a missing market. As such, the negotiated outcome is efficient, and it will have come about through non-cooperative market-like coordination. Second, R and F might engage in cooperative or collective decision-making as a household or clan might, voluntarily weighing both sets of preferences to arrive at an agreed upon division of uses of the grove. In the special case where their preferences are identical, the collective agreement would only require mutual restraint, to avoid over-use of the common resource. In the case of heterogeneous preferences, the collective decision will reflect the men's sense of equity and their negotiating skills. Regardless, the cooperative agreement balances the competing uses of the grove, and provides an efficient allocation of the resource. Both coordination strategies – non-cooperative/market and cooperative/collective – serve to "internalize" the externality, allowing R and F to reach an efficient outcome. The two approaches can, however, result in substantially different distributions for the two men's well-being.

How is this parable relevant for environmental economics as a whole? Most types of environmental problems result from a failure of coordination due to missing markets, incomplete property rights, and/or the inability of affected individuals to make collective decisions. The solution to environmental problems often involves designing coordination mechanisms that can work at the scale of the problem at hand. We begin to formally analyze this type of coordination failure (and potential solutions) for a modern economy in the next section.

1.3 A FORMAL MODEL OF EXTERNALITIES

Consider a simple modern economy with two individuals, a dirty good, a clean good, and labor as the only factor of production. Define the utility function for each person by $U_i(x_i,z_i,E)$ for $i=1,2$ where x_i and z_i are consumption levels of the two goods and E is an exogenous (to the individual) level of pollution emissions. Production of x causes the emissions. Define the production function for x by $x=f(l_x,E)$ where both labor input l_x and emissions E have a positive marginal product. This setup treats emissions as an input, implying that a reduction in pollution reduces the output of x, by decreasing a productive factor. While it is also possible to develop the model by treating x and E as joint products, this approach reduces notational clutter. The clean good z is produced using only labor according to the production technology $z=g(l_z)$. Labor employed in the economy is constrained by the work time endowment l such that $l_x+l_z=l$.

1.3.1 Pareto Optimality

Our first task is to derive the conditions for a Pareto optimal allocation of resources in this economy. This involves finding the consumption levels, factor allocations, and pollution amount that maximizes one person's utility in a way that makes the other no worse off than a given benchmark. The allocation must also obey the inherent technology and factor endowment constraints. The problem is given analytically by

$$\max_{x_1,x_2,z_1,z_2,l_x,l_z,E} U_1(x_1,z_1,E) + \lambda_u \left[U_2(x_2,z_2,E) - \bar{u}_2 \right] + \lambda_x \left[f(l_x,E) - x_1 - x_2 \right]$$
$$+ \lambda_z \left[g(l_z) - z_1 - z_2 \right] + \lambda_l \left[l - l_x - l_z \right], \tag{1.1}$$

where we are maximizing person 1's utility subject to the constraint that person 2 obtains at least utility level $\bar{u}_2$. For clarity of exposition, we state and interpret the first-order conditions for maximization in stages. Beginning with the consumption levels we have

$$\frac{\partial U_1(\cdot)}{\partial x_1} = \lambda_x, \quad \frac{\partial U_1(\cdot)}{\partial z_1} = \lambda_z \tag{1.2}$$

and

$$\lambda_u \frac{\partial U_2(\cdot)}{\partial x_2} = \lambda_x, \quad \lambda_u \frac{\partial U_2(\cdot)}{\partial z_2} = \lambda_z, \tag{1.3}$$

from which we can derive the expression for *efficiency in consumption* as

$$\frac{\partial U_1(\cdot)/\partial x_1}{\partial U_1(\cdot)/\partial z_1} = \frac{\lambda_x}{\lambda_z} = \frac{\partial U_2(\cdot)/\partial x_2}{\partial U_2(\cdot)/\partial z_2}. \tag{1.4}$$

From this we see that efficiency in consumption requires that the solution to Eq. (1.1), denoted $\{x_1^*, x_2^*, z_1^*, z_2^*, l_x^*, l_z^*, E^*\}$, must be such that the marginal rate of substitution between goods is equal for both individuals. Taking derivatives with respect to labor we obtain

$$\lambda_x \frac{\partial f(\cdot)}{\partial l_x} = \lambda_l, \quad \lambda_z \frac{\partial g(\cdot)}{\partial l_z} = \lambda_l, \tag{1.5}$$

which implies that the shadow value of the marginal product of labor for each of the goods should be equal to the shadow price of labor. This is the *efficiency in production* condition. From these expressions, and the result in Eq. (1.4), we can also state the condition for *efficiency in exchange*

$$\frac{\partial U_i(\cdot)/\partial x_i}{\partial U_i(\cdot)/\partial z_i} = \frac{\lambda_x}{\lambda_z} = \frac{\partial g(\cdot)/\partial l_z}{\partial f(\cdot)/\partial l_x}. \tag{1.6}$$

This shows that for an allocation to be Pareto optimal, it must be the case that the slope of the production possibility curve is equal to the slope of each person's indifference curve.

Finally, we complete the Pareto optimal characterization by analyzing the first-order condition with respect to emissions

$$\frac{\partial U_1(\cdot)}{\partial E} + \lambda_u \frac{\partial U_2(\cdot)}{\partial E} + \lambda_x \frac{\partial f(\cdot)}{\partial E} = 0. \tag{1.7}$$

The intuition of this condition is best shown by a simple transformation. Dividing both sides of the expression by λ_x, and substituting the first and third terms in Eq. (1.2), leads to

$$-\frac{\partial U_1(\cdot)/\partial E}{\partial U_1(\cdot)/\partial x_1} - \frac{\partial U_2(\cdot)/\partial E}{\partial U_2(\cdot)/\partial x_2} = \frac{\partial f(\cdot)}{\partial E}, \tag{1.8}$$

which has a clear interpretation. While a reduction in E increases utility for both people directly, it decreases utility indirectly, since a smaller quantity of x is available for consumption. The amount of utility decrease is dependent on the intensity of individual preferences for x. As such, the optimum emission level should balance the utility cost of emissions against the utility benefit of x. This trade-off is shown in Eq. (1.8). The terms on the left represent each person's marginal willingness to give up x for reduced E in consumption, while the term on the right is the physical cost in x of reducing E. Since a reduction in E benefits both people, the marginal cost in x of a reduction in E needs to be compared to the *sum* of both people's marginal willingness to give up x to have the reduction. When the marginal cost is equal to the marginal willingness to pay for reduced E (both as measured in x), the outcome is efficient.

Equation (1.8) also serves to illustrate the symmetry in particular cases between externalities and public goods. Although we have described E as an externality, a reduction in E also has the characteristics of a public good. The benefit that person 1 receives from a reduction in E does not impact or interfere with person 2's benefits, and neither person can be prevented from enjoying the reduction. Viewed in this light, Eq. (1.8) is also the Lindahl-Samuelson condition for the efficient allocation of a public good.[1]

Finally, it is worth emphasizing that $\{x_1^*, x_2^*, z_1^*, z_2^*, l_x^*, l_z^*, E^*\}$ is just one of many possible Pareto efficient outcomes, since it is conditional on a particular reference level of utility for person 2. A different maintained division of utility among the two agents – i.e. a different distribution of well-being – would lead to a different solution generally, and a different optimal level of pollution in particular.

1.3.2 The Competitive Market

The Pareto optimum conditions provide a baseline against which other potential allocations can be assessed. It is reasonable to ask if the free market outcome meets the Pareto criteria, when the output and factor markets are competitive. To study this, suppose p_x and p_z denote the prices of x and z, respectively. In addition, let w denote the price of

---

[1] The condition is named after the work by Lindahl (1919, 1958) and Samuelson (1954a, 1954b).

labor, and y_i income for person i. Acting as price takers, the individuals maximize utility, and the firms maximize profits. The utility maximization problem for each person i is

$$\max_{x_i, z_i} U_i(x_i, z_i, E) + \lambda_i \left[y_i - p_x x_i - p_z z_i \right], \tag{1.9}$$

with first-order conditions

$$\frac{\partial U_i(x_i, z_i, E)}{\partial x_i} = \lambda_i p_x$$

$$\frac{\partial U_i(x_i, z_i, E)}{\partial z_i} = \lambda_i p_z, \quad i = 1, 2. \tag{1.10}$$

From this we can derive the condition for efficiency in consumption as

$$\frac{\partial U_1(\cdot)/\partial x_1}{\partial U_1(\cdot)/\partial z_1} = \frac{p_x}{p_z} = \frac{\partial U_2(\cdot)/\partial x_2}{\partial U_2(\cdot)/\partial z_2}. \tag{1.11}$$

The profit maximization problem for firm z is

$$\max_{L_z} \left\{ p_z g(l_z) - w l_z \right\}, \tag{1.12}$$

which leads to the first-order condition $p_z \partial g(\cdot)/\partial l_z = w$. Of more interest is the behavior of the firm that produces x. In the market situation, the firm selects both its labor and emission inputs to maximize profit, treating emissions as a free factor of production. The profit maximization problem is

$$\max_{L_x, E} \left\{ p_x f(l_x, E) - w l_x \right\}, \tag{1.13}$$

and the first-order conditions for a solution are

$$p_x \frac{\partial f(\cdot)}{\partial l_x} = w$$

$$p_x \frac{\partial f(\cdot)}{\partial E} = 0. \tag{1.14}$$

Two observations arise from equations (1.12) through (1.14). First, for the market solution, efficiency in labor use and efficiency in exchange are met, in that the value of the marginal product of labor in producing both goods is equal to the wage rate, and the slope of the production function is equal to the slope of each person's indifference curve (the price ratio). Second, and more importantly for our purposes, the condition for an efficient allocation of emissions is not met. The condition for E in Eq. (1.14) is different from Eq. (1.8). The unregulated free market provides no mechanism that encourages the firm that produces x to treat E as scarce, or to account for the impact of its choice on consumers. Instead, the firm emits pollution until the value of the marginal product of pollution is zero – the pollution price the firm faces. Given that the externality is in effect a missing market, and complete markets is a condition for the first fundamental welfare theorem to hold, it is unsurprising that the competitive market equilibrium is not Pareto efficient.

1.3.3 Market Intervention

Much of environmental economics is concerned with designing policy to correct this type of market failure. The intellectual starting point comes from Pigou (1920, 1932), who suggested that if the government can correctly compute and impose a fee (subsequently to be known as the Pigouvian tax) which the polluting firm must pay for each emission, decentralized market behavior will lead to the Pareto optimal result. To see this, define

$$\tau^* = -p_x \left[\frac{\partial U_1(\cdot)/\partial E}{\partial U_1(\cdot)/\partial x_1} + \frac{\partial U_2(\cdot)/\partial E}{\partial U_2(\cdot)/\partial x_2} \right], \tag{1.15}$$

and suppose firm x is required to pay τ^* for each unit of pollution emitted. The firm's modified objective function is now

$$\max_{L_x, E} \left\{ p_x f(l_x, E) - w l_x - \tau^* E \right\}, \tag{1.16}$$

and the first-order conditions are

$$p_x \frac{\partial f(\cdot)}{\partial l_x} = w$$

$$p_x \frac{\partial f(\cdot)}{\partial E} = \tau^* = -p_x \left[\frac{\partial U_1(\cdot)/\partial E}{\partial U_1(\cdot)/\partial x_1} + \frac{\partial U_2(\cdot)/\partial E}{\partial U_2(\cdot)/\partial x_2} \right]. \tag{1.17}$$

Comparing condition (1.8) to (1.17), we see that the market outcome conditions do indeed match the Pareto optimum conditions, when pollution is priced at τ^*. This suggests that the government can, in principle, intervene in the market to provide the proper incentive for the polluting firm to internalize the externality. The proper intervention depends, however, on a particular distribution of income. This is apparent from Eq. (1.17), which makes clear that the correct emissions tax depends on solutions to the individuals' utility maximization problems, which are themselves functions of the income (and more generally, endowment) distribution. Changes in income or factor endowments will therefore lead to different tax and emissions levels, which will still be Pareto efficient. This application of the second fundamental welfare theorem is easily overlooked when we refer to "the" optimal pollution level.

The idea of a Pigouvian tax is further illustrated in panel A of Figure 1.1, which relates levels of E to the marginal benefit and marginal cost of additional E. The marginal benefit is reflected in the value of the marginal product of E in producing x (denoted VMP_E), which is the firm's factor demand for E. Without the tax, the firm chooses emissions level $\hat{E}$, where the value of marginal product is zero. The cost of pollution is the marginal utility loss of additional E, denoted by $MUC1_E$ and $MUC2_E$ for the two people, measured as the value of additional x that is needed to compensate for the loss due to E. Because E is non-rival, the total marginal utility cost of additional pollution is found by summing the costs to the individuals, which results in the curve we have labeled MUC_E. The vertical summation of these curves further connects the notion of an externality to the public good (bad) case. Intuitively, MUC_E represents the two individuals' collective marginal willingness to accept compensation in exchange for additional E. The efficient level of pollution is found by balancing the firm's value of E in production, against the non-market cost of pollution to the individuals. The point E^*, where the marginal willingness to accept and the value of the marginal product are equal, is the optimum amount. The polluting firm can be induced to emit at this level if they face an emission fee in the amount τ^*.

Panel B of Figure 1.1 illustrates how the externality and Pigouvian tax can also be viewed from a public good perspective. As described above, pollution emissions E are a bad. We can, however, define its mirror image – the elimination of pollution – as a good. Let $A = \hat{E} - E$ be the units of pollution removed, where $\hat{E}$ is the baseline emissions level shown in panel A. Using this notation, we have $E = \hat{E} - A$, which can be substituted into the households' and firm's utility and profit functions in equations (1.9) and (1.16), respectively. The level of abatement (pollution removal) A is found by differentiating with respect to A, and the optimality conditions are reflected in the figure. The only difference from panel A is that the curves now slope in opposite directions. For the firm, increased abatement implies a marginal cost, because it involves reduction of a productive input. For the households, increased abatement corresponds to fewer emissions, and so it is a benefit. The firm's curve, labeled MC_A, is the marginal cost of providing abatement, and the curve labeled MUB_A is the households' collective marginal willingness to pay (demand) for abatement. Because abatement is a public good, demand is found by summing the individual households' marginal willingness to pay curves. The optimal abatement level is labeled as A^*, which is linked to panel A by the relationship $A^* = \hat{E} - E^*$. The Lindahl-Samuelson optimal price per unit for abatement is τ^*, of which person 1 should contribute τ_1^* and person 2 τ_2^*, so that $\tau^* = \tau_1^* + \tau_2^*$.

Figure 1.1 and Eq. (1.17) serve to foreshadow many of the themes we will discuss in the balance of the book. From the perspective of designing environmental policy, Eq. (1.17) establishes a shadow price of emissions that a polluting firm must face if its emissions are to be efficiently reduced. *How* the environmental authority imposes this shadow price on firms via environmental policy – e.g. emission taxes, pollution permits, standards – is our theme as we begin the book. From the perspective of policy implementation, Eq. (1.17) also illustrates the measurement challenges faced by environmental authorities. The shadow price of pollution is a function of individuals' preferences for the environment, which are not directly observable. The conceptual and empirical techniques necessary for measuring preferences are considered later in the book.

1.4   POINTS GOING FORWARD

Our approach in this book will adhere fairly strictly to the neoclassical economic paradigm as we explore the design and implementation of environmental policy. Even in a

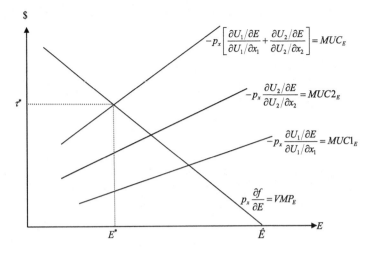

Panel A

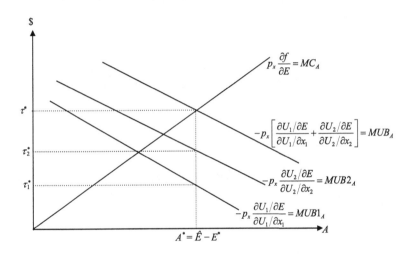

Panel B

Figure 1.1 Efficient pollution level and Pigouvian tax

book written by economists for other economists, this approach requires some further explanation. There are a variety of ethical positions one might take when discussing the relationship between humans and the natural environment. The economic approach is notably anthropocentric, in that there is no presumption of an "intrinsic" value for nature. Instead, nature is attributed value only in so far as it contributes to human well-being and human valuation. This is less restrictive than it sounds; a point to which we return in later chapters. Nonetheless, it is in contrast to other normative criteria described in philosophy, ethics, and literature, for example, that place the natural world on something like equal footing with human well-being. These alternative criteria certainly have appeal, and often appear much more elegant, moral, and well-argued than the economist's weak and amoral efficiency criterion. The amoral nature of the efficiency criterion, however, allows economists to contribute to environmental policy in ways that disciplines with greater advocacy paradigms are unable to do. By taking no explicit position on the moral nature of pollution, economists are well-positioned to provide objectivity and dispassionate analysis in an area that, arguably, could benefit from more of each.

Within the economics paradigm, the concepts of consumer sovereignty and opportunity cost are paramount, and they were on display in our modeling exercise above. Pollution emissions were "bad" because they decreased individuals' utility, not because the environment is endowed with an extra-anthropocentric value. We should be clear that this perspective does not preclude an individual person from viewing the environment as intrinsically valuable. It does, however, require that we acknowledge that preference heterogeneity may cause some to regard the environment differently than others. This is a non-trivial point, since in a world of scarcity, something must be given up to obtain something of value. In our simple model, the opportunity cost of an improved environment is decreased availability of the dirty good. The size of this decrease, and the importance of its loss, depend on current and future technology, individual preferences, and the availability of substitutes. Economic solutions to environmental problems require that we gauge the magnitude of the opportunity cost of pollution reduction and the potential gains from intervention, and design and evaluate policies that balance the two. The study of environmental economics is by and large concerned with these two themes, around which we divide the components of this book.

1.5   SUMMARY

Baumol and Oates (1988, p.1) began their classic treatment of the theory of environmental policy by stating, "When the environmental revolution arrived in the 1960s, economists were ready and waiting." By this they meant that a large, coherent body of existing theory could be readily brought to bear on the specific challenges of designing environmental policy. As they go on to say, and nearly four decades of research in environmental economics is testament to, there was more to it than that. Nonetheless, an understanding of neoclassical welfare theory is an essential starting point for understanding the field of environmental economics. As such, our objective in this chapter has been to provide an intuitive, rather than fully formal, review of key concepts.

To summarize briefly, neoclassical welfare theory begins by defining a weak normative criterion, Pareto optimality (or Pareto efficiency), which lies at the heart of environmental economics. Pareto optimality describes an allocation of resources which, if shuffled, cannot make one person better off without harming another. This is a convenient benchmark, since complete and perfectly competitive markets lead to Pareto efficient outcomes (the first fundamental welfare theorem) and any particular Pareto efficient outcome can be obtained via suitable lump sum income transfers (the second fundamental welfare theorem). The key ingredient is complete and perfectly competitive markets, the absence of which is the basis for examining the theory of market failures – instances when an unregulated, free market may not reach a Pareto efficient outcome. In this chapter we have defined externalities and public goods as the causes of market failure most relevant for environmental economics. This is because unregulated polluting behavior by one group of agents that directly affects the utility or profit of another, without consent or recourse, is a specific example of an externality. In addition, the cleanup of pollution (and ambient environmental quality generally), to the extent that it is non-excludable, shares many characteristics with public goods. It is in this sense that welfare theory and the theory of externalities and public goods are the basis for much of environmental economics.

If an externality causes a market failure, our analytical model suggested the government may be able to intervene to improve the outcome. Though our stylized example of a Pigouvian tax is far from operational from a policy perspective, it is illustrative of the challenges a realistic policy needs to overcome. Specifically, the incentive structure that a polluting agent faces needs to be altered by policy, in a way that causes him to explicitly account for his emissions. An efficient intervention depends on the government knowing many things, including the preferences and production technologies among all the involved agents. To a large degree, the field of environmental economics is about identifying when environmental market failures exist, studying the properties of different intervention options, and estimating the specific functions that are needed for policy implementation. This book is concerned with telling the story of environmental economics as it has developed to meet these basic challenges.

1.6 FURTHER READING

Most of the material in this chapter is drawn from our respective lecture notes, which have evolved over several years of teaching environmental economics to Master's and PhD level students in Germany and the United States. Motivation for including much of the basic welfare theory material comes from Baumol and Oates (1988), and some of our definitions and discussion points are based on their presentation. For a much more complete discussion of public goods and externalities, see Cornes and Sandler (1996). For a full discussion of neoclassical welfare economics, see Feldman and Serrano (2006). For an intuitive and accessible discussion of how neoclassical welfare economics and market failures provide the basic motivation for environmental economics as a field, see Fullerton and Stavins (1998). Classic references on the efficient allocation of public goods include Lindahl (1919, 1958), Bowen (1943), and Samuelson (1954a, 1954b). Pigou (1920, 1932) is a classic reference on internalizing externalities through taxation. An additional classic, on the separation of efficiency and distribution in public goods problems, is Bergstrom and Cornes (1983).

EXERCISES

1.1 * Our model of pollution in this chapter assumed that emissions are a pure private bad, and that people have no ability to protect themselves from the adverse consequences of exposure. In reality, individuals can often take private action to mitigate the effective level of pollution. For example, one can stay inside during high ground-level ozone alerts. Consider a generalization of our model in which effective emissions are $\varepsilon(E, d_i)$, where $\partial\varepsilon(E, d_i)/\partial E > 0$ and d_i is the amount of time person i devotes to defensive action, such that $\partial\varepsilon(E, d_i)/\partial d_i < 0$. The utility function for person i is now $U_i[x_i, z_i, \varepsilon(E, d_i)]$, and the labor constraint in the economy is $l = l_x + l_z + d_1 + d_2$. The production side of the economy is unchanged.

(a) Derive and interpret the Pareto optimum conditions for this economy.

(b) Consider a free market, competitive economy in which each person is endowed with an amount of time T. The person sells time in the labor market at wage w, earns income to spend on x and z, and also uses time (at an opportunity cost of w) to defend against pollution. Under these assumptions each person's maximization problem is given by

$$\max_{x_i, z_i, d_i} U_i[x_i, z_i, \varepsilon(E, d_i)] + \lambda_i[w(T - d_i) - p_x x - p_z z].$$

Derive the conditions for a competitive equilibrium. How do they compare to the Pareto optimum? Is a Pigouvian tax necessary? If so, what form does it take? Is this different from Eq. (1.15)? Is some sort of intervention also necessary to assure the efficient level of defensive effort?

1.2 ** From Figure 1.1 it is clear that the marginal utility cost of pollution for each person at the optimum is

$$MUCi_E = -p_x \frac{\partial U_i/\partial E}{\partial U_i/\partial x_i}\bigg|_{E=E^*}.$$

(a) Consider a proposal to use the revenue from the Pigouvian tax to compensate people for damages. In particular, each person i would receive $p_e = MUCi_E$ for each unit of E. How does this affect the efficiency of the outcome in the regulated, competitive economy examined in the chapter?

(b) What if there are defensive possibilities, as considered in exercise 1.1? Specifically, each person would be compensated according to $p_e\varepsilon(E, d_i)$, where p_e in this case is a fixed per unit value. Can we draw general conclusions from this about the wisdom of compensating victims of externalities at the margin?

Environmental Problems and Policy Issues

In Chapter 1 we illustrated how the field of environmental economics has its roots in neoclassical welfare theory. From a theoretical perspective most contemporary topics in the field continue to fit into the historic paradigm of the failure of the first welfare theorem, missing markets, externalities, and public goods. Describing environmental economics in such purely theoretical terms, however, ignores the importance that practical policy issues have played and continue to play in the development of the field. Indeed research in environmental economics, perhaps more so than other fields in economics, is driven by the needs of the policy-making community.

Because of this link it is useful from the outset to understand how environmental economics developed in parallel with the growth of the environmental movement and the coming of national-level environmental policy. In the first section of this chapter we therefore provide a brief review the social, policy, and research themes from the last four decades that together helped to define the field. We follow in section 2.2 with a review of contemporary environmental problems that motivate current research, focusing on the causes and consequences of water, air, and land pollution in a variety of contexts. The environmental science discussion from this section transitions in section 2.3 to explore the relationship between economics and ecology. In both sections our review is selective and heuristic, with a focus on qualitative description rather than summarizing actual (and soon to be outdated) environmental trends. In the final section we review several policy examples in order to illustrate how the environmental and behavioral elements connect, thereby creating the need for environmental economics in policy design. These examples also provide specific context for the more abstract discussions that are used later in the book.

2.1 EVOLUTION OF ENVIRONMENTAL POLICY AND ECONOMICS

Concerns about environmental externalities are not new. For example, during the thirteenth century coal became commonly used in England as a heating fuel, and the consequences for air quality were dire enough that in 1306 King Edward I banned its use in London, albeit to little effect. Nonetheless, modern environmental awareness arose in developed countries in the 1960s as a result of the pollution consequences of the postwar economic expansion. By the late 1960s environmental conditions in many industrial countries had deteriorated enough – and perhaps as importantly, their populations had become wealthy enough – that electorates began demanding national-level responses to pollution problems. Several well-known events have been identified as major drivers of changing public opinion. For example, the 1969 Cuyahoga River fire in Cleveland, Ohio, covered somewhat sensationally by the news magazine *Time*, was a rallying point in the United States that helped spur the passage of the Clean Water Act in 1972. Americans old enough to watch television in 1971 are also likely to recall the iconic "Crying Indian" advertisement, in which a Native American man weeps while looking over a polluted, littered landscape while a narrator advises that "People start pollution. People can stop it." The environmental movement in Germany gained momentum in the late 1970s, when commentators coined the term *Waldsterben* to describe the large-scale and highly visible dieback of forests in the country. Widespread public protests led to strict sulfur dioxide emission standards for German electricity generating plants and contributed to the rise of the Green Party in German politics. By the 1980s most developed countries had established national environmental ministries that were responsible for administering regulations targeting a variety of air, water, and land pollutants.

The field of environmental economics – as distinct from resource economics – developed simultaneously with the environmental movement of the 1960s. While important contributions occurred earlier, the field began an expansion in the 1970s that has continued to this day. The inaugural issue of the *Journal of Environmental Economics and Management* (*JEEM*), the first scholarly journal dedicated to publishing research in the field, appeared in 1974. In an opening editorial the journal editors commented that:

> [The journal] is meant to provide a focused outlet for high quality research in the rapidly growing area of environmental economics … Major stress will continually be on the interactions between human social decision and process, and the natural environment, and not on strictly human resource issues or on natural environmental issues devoid of a substantial management pertinence. (Kneese and d'Arge, 1974, p.1)

Thus from the early days of the field, scholarship priorities were closely tied to management and policy issues. While the major environmental statutes were being debated in the United States and Europe, economists published research in *JEEM* and other outlets on cap and trade instruments, subsidizing pollution control investments, the economic value of air pollution improvements, and optimal emission taxation, to name but a few examples. These environment-specific analyses built on the well-developed theory of externalities and further developed the Pigouvian approach to internalizing pollution damages. This research seemed to offer practical prescriptions for the policy challenges the environmental movement brought to the forefront. The Pigouvian insights notwithstanding, however, economics as a discipline had little influence on how the early environmental regulations were designed. In the United States the Clean Water Act's stated goal was the complete elimination of pollution discharges into the nation's waterways – an objective clearly at odds with the notion of trade-offs inherent in economic thinking. More dramatically, the early US Clean Air Act Amendments explicitly forbade consideration of costs in prescribing actions that would protect human health from air pollution, as did the US Endangered Species Act in determining which species should be protected. These examples help illustrate that the field of environmental economics developed simultaneously with the environmental movement, and its topics were largely motivated by the environmental policy concerns of the day. Its influence on the actual design of national-level policy was, however, minimal.

In retrospect one can identify two reasons for this lack of influence, in spite of the appearance of a relevant body of research output. First, on the political side, the early environmental movement was a visceral, emotional response to problems that seemed to transcend the financial topics that were seen as the realm of economics. Thus policy makers and the public they represented were arguably not ready for the detached, trade-offs-focused advice economists were apt to give. Second, and as importantly, research in environmental economics had not yet developed the empirical and conceptual nuance to be transferred to the policy arena wholesale. For example, while economists were prepared to offer the Pigouvian tax as a way to regulate pollution emissions, the methods needed to actually estimate its magnitude were in the early stages of development. Thus the early large-scale experiments in environmental regulation unfolded during the 1970s and 1980s with only minimal input from economists. During this time environmental economists instead developed much of the conceptual basis for the field that we now see as critical for providing policy advice and evaluating policy performance under the actual circumstances in which it is implemented. Much of this book is dedicated to tracing this development.

By the 1990s the environmental policy process in developed countries had matured, as had the field of environmental economics. Environmental conditions were improving in many dimensions, and regulators began focusing on fine-tuning existing regulations and designing new regulations to tackle heretofore unaddressed challenges. Environmental economics became more mainstream, and with this the number of economists researching environmental problems (and training students to do so) increased dramatically. Two decades of research results also meant economists were better positioned to provide meaningful policy advice. As a result, the ideas long debated in academic journals regarding the advantages of economic incentive approaches to pollution regulation began to be noticed by policy makers – to the point that the use of, for example, cap and trade approaches to emission reductions are now commonly discussed. Likewise cost-benefit analysis for environmental rule making has become more accepted (though still controversial) as the tools available for measuring the non-market value of environmental changes have matured. The general acceptance of economics as relevant for environmental policy meant that research topics became even more closely aligned with policy needs. For example, the 1989 *Exxon Valdez* oil spill in Prince William Sound, Alaska, motivated two decades of research on how compensation for non-market environmental damages can be estimated for litigation purposes.

Our discussion thus far of the connections between environmental policy and environmental economics has focused almost entirely on the developed country context. This is because most of the problems that occupied environmental activists and spurred environmental regulation were "rich-country" issues – i.e. problems that have salience only after a certain level of income is achieved. During the rise of the environmental movement in wealthy countries, developing-country environmental issues remained closely connected to poverty alleviation goals, and hence their study was primarily the job of development economists. For example, access to safe drinking water was (and continues to be) the main health problem in many developing countries. Water pollution problems were therefore viewed primarily as a threat to productivity and income growth rather than for their amenity consequences. Similarly, a major air pollution problem in many developing countries is access to clean fuel for cooking. Wood-burning cook stoves expose family members preparing food to highly localized particulate matter, which can lead to substantial health problems. Finally, some aspects of the environmental movement in developed countries were in direct conflict with the poverty and disease alleviation goals of developing countries. For example, the pesticide DDT is an inexpensive and effective method for controlling malaria by eliminating disease-carrying mosquitos in poor, tropical countries. Nonetheless, following publication of Rachel Carson's book *Silent Spring* in 1962, which discussed the ecological dangers of indiscriminate pesticide use, there was a concerted effort among environmentalists to ban the use of DDT. These efforts ultimately were successful and helped to bring back populations of many endangered birds, but it may have made the fight against malaria more difficult. These examples show how water, air, and land pollution can have different consequences and require different policy responses in developing and developed country contexts.

The globalization of the past two decades, however, has coincided with mounting concern about global pollution problems, and so environmental economists are increasingly engaged with developing country and cross-border environmental issues. In this context an important issue is international trade and factor mobility, where concerns about pollution-intensive production migrating to developing countries with less stringent environmental regulations have led many to claim that globalization is harming the world environment. This "race to the bottom" reasoning was one of the factors driving the anti-globalization protests that occurred at the 1999 World Trade Organization meeting in Seattle. The potential for "carbon leakage" is a related topic. Carbon leakage relates to the possibility that carbon reductions from countries pledging to reduce emissions are offset by an increase among non-pledging countries, due to the migration of carbon-intensive activities away from the participating countries. Since developing countries have been slow to agree to carbon reductions on equity grounds, economists have become interested in the carbon emissions trajectories of countries such as China, India, Brazil, and Indonesia. Deforestation in the latter two countries, which increases net carbon emissions and reduces biodiversity, is also a developing country topic that has attracted the attention of environmental economists. Finally, climate change more broadly has the potential to create large-scale shocks to agricultural productivity, the location of economic activity and migration patterns, and human health in both developed- and developing-country contexts. Thus environmental economics and the environmental policy issues studied by economists have become more global and the focus has expanded from the initial emphasis on environmental problems in wealthy countries.

As we will convey in this book, environmental economics today is a mainstream, vibrant field with a large body of core material that continues to be relevant for policy design, scholarly research, and the overlap between the two. Environmental economists are key contributors to debates on climate change policy, distributional issues related to pollution and environmental policy, the health consequences of pollution, international trade and the environment, hazardous waste policy, agricultural sources of degradation, and other contemporary topics. In later sections we will discuss these policy issues in more detail.

2.2 MAJOR POLLUTANTS AND POLLUTION PROBLEMS

Pollution types can be physically categorized based on the affected media (water, air, land), the sectors responsible (e.g. manufacturing, agriculture, electricity generation, mobile sources), and the source type (point and non-point). Water, land, and air are quite broad categories that need to be defined with more precision when discussing actual pollutants, but they provide a useful top-level organizing rubric. This is likewise the case for polluting sectors. Point and non-point sources refer to the extent to which the source of specific emissions can be identified. For example, the nitrogen discharged into a water body from a particular municipal wastewater treatment plant is a point source because the emissions can be measured and attributed to the facility. In contrast, the nitrogen contained in fertilizer that runs off a farmer's field into the same water body is a non-point source because the emissions and their consequences cannot be measured and attributed to the individual farmer.

It is also useful to categorize pollution based on how humans are impacted. The possible channels include health, productivity, amenity, and preservation consequences. Health impacts are measured as the extent to which mortality and morbidity risks and outcomes are affected by pollution, while productivity impacts describe the dependence of income-earning opportunities on environmental conditions. An example of the latter is commercial fishing's dependence on the quality of fish spawning habitat. By amenity consequences we mean the extent to which people's leisure and aesthetic experiences are directly impacted by environmental changes. Examples include the reduced swimming, boating, and fishing opportunities associated with water pollution and the damage to local vegetation and wildlife caused by an invasive species. Preservation consequences refer to indirect ways in which people are affected by environmental changes, such as the utility loss felt by a reduction in the population of giant pandas or the utility gain from knowing that a national park will be available for future generations. When discussing the human impacts of particular pollutants, it is useful to distinguish between developing country, developed country, and world contexts. In developing countries the main concern is usually how resource degradation directly affects the health and productivity of local residents, with amenity and preservation channels being relatively less important. Developed countries have by definition reached a level of per-capita income at which normal-good type services, such as amenity and preservation aspects of the environment, also play a major role. Global pollution problems blend elements of all of the impact channels, with additional emphasis on the distributional consequences of both the pollution problems and potential interventions.

In the following subsections we elaborate on pollution problems from each of these perspectives, using the affected media as our main organizing vehicle. We note at the start that it is beyond our scope to provide an exhaustive overview of environmental science, and we do not attempt to summarize the enormous volume of actual pollution data and trends. Our intent is to provide a self-contained and concise overview of environmental terms and concepts, in order to provide context for the more abstract discussion that follows in later chapters.

2.2.1 Water Pollution

Water pollution is a broad notion that includes the degradation of freshwater surface waters, groundwater, and oceans and coastal areas. Common surface water problems include: (a) organic pollutants that may contain disease-causing bacteria, often resulting from the discharge of untreated municipal wastewater, sewage, or other organic material; (b) excess loading of nutrients such as nitrogen and phosphorus, usually resulting from agricultural and urban storm water runoff; (c) heavy metals like lead and mercury, usually generated as by-products from manufacturing and electricity generation; and (d) non-organic solids and sediments from construction sites and agricultural erosion. To this list we can also add increased acidity of surface waters from precipitation containing sulfuric acid, a by-product of coal-fired electricity production, and changes in water temperature resulting from cooling water intake and discharge at manufacturing and power facilities. Groundwater problems occur when fertilizers, pesticides, and chemicals leach into underground aquifers from agricultural and manufacturing operations. Groundwater can also be contaminated by hazardous chemicals such as arsenic or radon – both from natural occurrence and leaching from mining and manufacturing. Finally, oceans and coastal areas are vulnerable to accidental oil spills, "dead zones" resulting from nutrient pollution carried by rivers, direct discharges of municipal wastewater, and solid waste disposal. In addition, ocean acidification is a consequence of higher levels of dissolved carbon dioxide in ocean waters.

The physical effects of water pollution are as varied as its sources. When organic materials are discharged into surface water they consume dissolved oxygen while decomposing; the depletion of oxygen (hypoxia) leads to stress and mortality for aquatic organisms. For this reason organic water pollution is often measured by its BOD (biological oxygen demand) – i.e. the oxygen that is needed to break down the effluent. Nutrient pollution has a similar impact. Excess nitrogen and phosphorus cause accelerated algal growth, which reduces water clarity and leads to changes in the ecological balance of lakes and streams. Some types of algae are also toxic to humans, causing skin rash and sickness from contact or ingestion. When nutrient-induced algal blooms decompose they consume dissolved oxygen so that, like organic pollution, nutrient pollution often results in low oxygen (hypoxic) conditions leading to fish kills in lakes, streams, estuaries, and coastal areas. Ocean dead zones, such as the seasonally occurring hypoxic areas in the Gulf of Mexico and several Baltic Sea regions, are particularly salient examples of the consequences of nutrient pollution.

Sediments and other non-organic solids cause reduced water clarity and ecological changes in receiving water bodies. For example, lakes receiving sustained nutrient and sediment pollution become increasingly eutrophic, with decreased species diversity, increased weed levels, and rough fish displacing game fish populations. Sediment loads also enable the accumulation of heavy metals in streambeds and lake bottoms. Among heavy metals mercury is of particular concern, because it enters the food chain and accumulates in top-level predator fish tissue. Since many of these fish are commercially and recreationally harvested, fish consumption is a potential cause of mercury poisoning in humans. Other pollutants change the ecological structure of receiving waters more directly. Acidification of lakes and streams from precipitation holding sulfuric acid can dramatically alter the ability of receiving waters to support aquatic life. Likewise water temperature increases from cooling water discharges affect the ability of cold-water fish to survive in rivers that are used for this purpose. The main health problems related to water quality are due to the biological and chemical contamination of surface water and groundwater that is used for drinking. Some of these contaminants, such as cancer-causing agents and diarrhea-causing bacteria, may constitute threats to life; others lead to more minor or temporary symptoms.

Water pollutants and the physical changes they cause have the potential to affect human well-being through several channels. In developed countries most of the impacts flow through amenity and preservation channels. For example, oil spills have dramatic and wide-ranging impacts on beaches, fish populations, marine mammals, and birds. These impacts are often felt mainly through the loss of preservation or existence services, since most people do not directly experience the consequences of oil spills – particularly when they occur in remote locations, as was the case with the *Exxon Valdez* spill. Nutrient, sediment, and organic pollutants affect how lakes, streams, and coastal areas can be used for recreation or enjoyed as scenic areas, while heat and acidification damage fish and other aquatic populations that may be important for recreation or preservation purposes. The health impacts of water pollution in developed countries tend to be less pronounced. By the start of the environmental movement in the 1960s, populations in developed areas such as the US and Western Europe generally had full access to treated drinking water, and so widespread problems with waterborne diseases were never part of the movement narrative in these areas. Health policy related to drinking water has instead focused on health-enhancing refinements, such as defining appropriate standards for carcinogenic contaminants such as arsenic, and preventing and managing localized shocks to drinking-water quality. Efforts have also focused on distributing information to help vulnerable populations such as children and pregnant women avoid inadvertent exposure to low-level contaminants.

The situation in developing countries is almost completely reversed. In many areas access to safe drinking water is limited, meaning households need to undertake in-home treatment and/or spend productive time on its provision to avoid exposure to disease-causing bacteria. Even in areas where piped water is available, it is often the case that contaminants are present. For example, well testing in the late 1990s revealed that 57 million people in Bangladesh were drinking water with arsenic concentrations above the World Health Organization recommended standard (Bennear et al., 2013). In other areas, sickness from waterborne bacteria is common even when defensive actions are taken and, for vulnerable sub-populations such as infants and the elderly, repeated exposure can be fatal. Indeed the World Bank (2002) estimates that 3 million children die from preventable water-related diseases each year. Thus the consequences of water pollution in developing countries are felt primarily through health and labor productivity channels. The problems often arise and persist due to institutional failures that prevent collective action attempts to provide sanitation and treated drinking water.

2.2.2 Air Pollution

Air pollution can be roughly grouped into three categories: hazardous, conventional, and climate changing. Examples of hazardous air pollutants include chemical compounds such as asbestos, lead, mercury, benzene, arsenic, and fluorides. These are so-named because they are known or thought to be carcinogenic (or toxic in other ways) and they have no agreed-upon safe threshold level. Hazardous air emissions can occur, for example, during building construction or demolition, chemical manufacturing, or aluminum production.

Conventional air pollution is almost entirely the result of the combustion of fossil fuels for electricity generation, transportation, and home heating. The primary pollutants include gasses such as sulfur dioxide (SO_2), nitrogen oxides (NO_X), and carbon monoxide (CO) as well as particulate matter (PM). Sulfur dioxide emissions come mainly from coal-fired electricity generation. The amount of sulfur contained in coal varies widely across deposits, and determines the amount of SO_2 that is potentially emitted upon combustion. Nitrogen oxides are also attributable to electricity generation, since NO_X is emitted any time that nitrogen and oxygen are present together during high-temperature combustion. For a similar reason NO_X is also produced during internal combustion in automobile engines, meaning that road transport is the second major contributor of this pollutant. In many areas it is the primary local concern, since during warm weather seasons vehicle emissions of NO_X react with sunlight and volatile organic compounds (VOCs) – the latter also emitted during road transport – to produce ground-level ozone (O_3), which is the main component of urban smog. Finally, PM is a general term for a complex mixture of non-gaseous airborne pollutants that include nitrates, sulfates, metals, dust, and many other elements, but that consists primarily of non-combusted carbonaceous particles. Incomplete combustion of fossil fuels during electricity production and transportation are major sources of PM, though forest fires and wood burning for heating and cooking are also important contributors in some areas.

Climate-changing pollutants are of two types. Greenhouse gasses such as carbon dioxide (CO_2), nitrous oxide (N_2O), and methane (CH_4) are natural components of the earth's atmosphere whose presence at appropriate concentrations is necessary for life on the planet. They are not pollutants in the narrow sense of the word. However, emissions from human activities increase their concentration in the atmosphere, thereby changing the planet's heat absorption capacity and impacting the climate system. Carbon-based fuels such as coal, natural gas, and oil emit CO_2 upon combustion, making CO_2 the primary greenhouse gas (GHG) and energy consumption its main source. Reducing carbon emissions is a particularly difficult problem given the enormous reliance on fossil fuel energy in modern economies. Nitrous oxide and methane are secondary greenhouse gasses. Agriculture is the primary source of N_2O emissions, which result from fertilizer use and the breakdown of livestock waste. Methane has three primary sources. It is the main component in natural gas, and so emissions result from natural gas production and leakages in storage and transportation. Agriculture is also a source of methane emissions through rice and cattle production. Finally, landfills emit methane when solid waste is broken down.

The second type of climate-changing pollutants are those that erode the stratospheric ozone layer, which shields the planet from the sun's ultraviolet rays and makes life on earth possible. Ozone depletion mainly results from the use of chlorofluorocarbons (CFCs) as refrigerants (e.g. for air conditioning) and as aerosol spray propellants. The manufacture and use of CFCs has declined due to the discovery of effective substitutes and the scientific consensus about their effect on the ozone layer.

Conventional and hazardous air pollutants affect human well-being mainly through their impact on health, though there are also significant ecological impacts. Particulate matter is increasingly recognized as the most important of the four primary conventional threats. Concentrations of PM are usually categorized as PM_{10} and $PM_{2.5}$ – concentrations of particles that are smaller in diameter than 10 and 2.5 micrometers (μm), respectively. Particles smaller than 10 μm are able to pass through the nose and throat and hence enter the lungs directly, causing an increased risk of respiratory and cardiac diseases following chronic exposure. People with pre-existing conditions, as well as the young and elderly, are particularly susceptible to PM-related health problems such as heart attacks, aggravated asthma, and decreased lung function. As noted above, emissions of NO_x from road transport are the precursor to ground-level ozone, making NO_x the second primary conventional threat. In addition to causing photochemical urban smog of the Los Angeles type, exposure to ground-level ozone can irritate and damage lung tissue. As with PM, children, the elderly, and people with pre-existing conditions such as asthma are especially susceptible to ozone-induced health problems. High local concentrations of SO_2 are the third most important primary threat. Acute exposure can lead to shortness of breath, chest tightening, and death in extreme cases. Industrial smog of the type made famous by the London "pea soups" of the 1950s derives from high near-ground concentrations of SO_2 generated by coal combustion. The 1952 London Fog that killed 4,000 people in four days is an extreme example of the health effects of sulfur dioxide. While the SO_2 problems in most developed countries now derive indirectly from its contribution to PM, many cities in Asia continue to have concentrations that can generate direct health effects.

The non-health impacts of conventional and hazardous air pollutants can be large in some contexts. Sulfur dioxide emissions are the primary cause of acid rain, which can lead to acidification of lakes and streams. Acid rain is also responsible for the *Waldsterben* phenomenon in Germany and Scandinavia, and for forest and vegetation diebacks more generally in other parts of the world, including the northeast US and southeast Canada. In urban areas sulfur emissions cause building corrosion. Primary examples include the pollution-related damage to Germany's Cologne cathedral and the monuments in Washington, DC. Finally, air pollution in general reduces visibility. A dramatic example is the Great Smoky Mountains National Park in the United States, where the National Park Service reports that visibility from the mountain vistas has decreased by as much as 80 percent during the summer months.[1]

Greenhouse gas emissions are important because of their ability to change the earth's climate. Observed and expected changes include higher temperatures, more frequent extreme weather events, changing precipitation patterns, and rising sea levels. These have the potential to flood coastal areas, change agricultural production possibilities, increase the prevalence of disease, and disrupt natural systems, to list a few examples. The range of climate change consequences for human well-being is vast and uncertain, and the incidence of climate change damages will be felt disproportionately across developed and developing countries.

Air pollution causes similar health-related problems in both developed and developing countries, though the extent and source of the specific concerns varies considerably. In the United States and Western Europe, air quality was at its worst in the early 1970s and began improving thereafter. For example, the US Environmental Protection Agency reports that total emissions of the principal air pollutants decreased by 53 percent

---

[1] www.nps.gov/grsm/naturescience/air-quality.htm.

between 1970 and 2005, while GDP increased 195 percent over the same time period. Improving air quality in developed nations is the result of regulations, changes in technologies, and shifts in the composition of the economies in these countries away from manufacturing. Policy challenges in the developed countries are now focused on eliminating pollution "hotspots" and debating the merits of further pollution reduction measures. In contrast to developed countries, air pollution in many developing countries has increased substantially in recent decades. This is particularly the case in China, where growth in manufacturing has been fueled by the country's abundant sources of coal-based energy. As a result, 14 of the 20 most polluted cities in the world are in China (World Bank, 2013), which contributed to an estimated 1.2 million premature deaths in the country in 2010.[2] Pollution in urban areas in other parts of the developing world is mainly attributable to vehicle emissions, which are high due to the large number of older and poorly maintained vehicles used on highly congested roads.

2.2.3 Land Pollution

For our discussion here we use the concept of land pollution broadly to include (a) dumping of conventional, hazardous, and radioactive waste materials; and (b) the alteration of landscapes that reduces recreation or preservation services, damages biodiversity, and destroys carbon sinks. The first of these is more conventionally thought of as pollution and it includes, for example, topics related to municipal solid waste, past and future releases of hazardous materials into the environment, and the risks associated with nuclear energy. Examples of problems related to municipal solid waste are NIMBY (not in my back yard) related amenity effects from landfill location decisions as well as end-user incentives for waste reduction and recycling. Additional issues related to industry include the deployment of production technologies that allow for recycled inputs, and the extent to which the design of products facilitates the reuse and recycling of materials at the end of the product's lifetime.

Prior to large-scale environmental regulations many industrial operations accumulated and stored hazardous waste on-site. In the US, the best-known example of this is the Love Canal incident, where a neighborhood and school in upstate New York were built atop a site previously used as a dumping ground for chemical waste. Proximity to the site resulted in a large increase in the incidence of birth defects, miscarriages, and cancer among local residents, ultimately leading to the site's evacuation. Other examples are smaller in scale and less dramatic. Many cities have "brownfields" – areas that in the past housed factories, gas stations, dry cleaners, auto repair shops, or other large- and small-scale industrial enterprises – that contain residual hazardous waste material that must be remediated before redevelopment. The cleanup of large- and small-scale hazardous waste areas is a policy objective for environmental agencies at national and lower levels based on the health risks they might convey, as well as the negative amenity effects for local residents. To reduce the development of new contaminated sites, agencies have also taken steps to implement "pollution prevention" policies, whereby

---

[2] "Early Deaths Linked to China's Air Pollution Totaled 1.2 Million in 2010", *New York Times*, April 3, 2013, p. A9.

entities working with hazardous chemicals find ways to eliminate the need to discharge hazardous waste.

Concerns about nuclear power focus on the potential for catastrophic malfunctions leading to widespread radiation release, and the transportation and long-term storage of radioactive waste. Following the Fukushima nuclear disaster in Japan in 2011, in which a tsunami caused equipment failures and the large-scale release of radioactive material into populated areas, several countries began re-evaluating their reliance on nuclear energy. For example, Germany has announced its intent to close all of its nuclear reactors by 2022. Germany's actions are complex in that the potential for radioactive land pollution needs to be balanced against the potential for increased air pollution if nuclear power is replaced by fossil fuel generation, or sharply increasing electricity prices if a larger share of renewable energy sources are employed.

Landscape alteration is usually not classified as pollution per se, but as it can have profound effects on the environment we include it in our discussion here. The main large-scale example of landscape change is the loss of tropical rainforests in South America, Africa, and Southeast Asia. Deforestation is caused by expanding agriculture and timber harvesting, and its consequences include lost biodiversity and increased atmospheric carbon via the elimination of carbon sinks. For example, tropical forests in Indonesia have been cleared and replaced by palm oil plantations at a rate that is fast enough to make Indonesia the world's third largest contributor of carbon emissions after China and the United States. Biodiversity losses from clearing at this scale can be large, because an estimated 50 percent of the world's plant and animal species live in tropical forests. An effect of lost biodiversity is the reduced potential for discovering new pharmaceuticals, in that many existing medicines were derived from rainforest plants. At a smaller spatial scale, landscape alteration can have consequences for scenic amenities and recreation opportunities as well as biodiversity consequences when species exist only in specialized areas or habitats.

2.2.4 Pollution Problems and Economics

The descriptions of water, air, and land pollution provide an overview of the environmental topics that are relevant for our later discussion. They also foreshadow many of the features that we will focus on in studying the economic approach to environmental problems. Perhaps most importantly, the examples demonstrate the role of context in framing the problem. Populations affected by pollution of a common medium can differ in their income levels, how they interact with the resource, and the ways in which pollution affects their well-being. For economic policy analysis it is therefore necessary to examine the institutions, preferences, characteristics, and baseline environmental conditions that are relevant for the economic agents bearing the costs and enjoying the benefits of a proposed action. Related to this, the previous discussion demonstrates the large variability in spatial scale of different environmental problems. For problems like climate change, the spatial scale may be the entire planet, and the impacted agents the world population. For local or regional problems, such as conventional air pollution, outcomes might reasonably be different across different populations.

2.3   ECONOMICS AND ECOLOGY

As a policy-focused field, environmental economics is closely related to environmental policy and science, and a working knowledge of elements of both is necessary for research in the field. Perhaps less obviously, environmental economics is also closely connected to the discipline of ecology via the use of ecosystems as an organizing principle and ecosystem services as a type of commodity produced by the environment. In this section we discuss these connections.

The taxonomy of pollution problems described in the previous section is useful for organizational purposes, but it implies there are boundaries between the various media that do not exist in reality. Ecologists favor a paradigm in which the various media are examined in a more holistic way, as part of an integrated system. The unit of analysis for this is an ecosystem, which is a spatial unit describing a collection of entities – plants, animals, soils, microorganisms, hydrological and landscape features, etc. – that exists and interacts in complex, interdependent ways. Depending on the context, an ecosystem can be as large as the entire planet or as small as a local wetland. Regardless of the spatial scale, using an ecosystem as the unit of analysis encourages consideration of the multiple media that are affected by a single pollution event, though the variation in the potential boundaries of an ecosystem introduces other challenges.

Defining environmental problems via their effect on ecosystems is also useful for classifying issues that do not fit easily into the water, air, and land taxonomy used in the previous section. A prime example of this is invasive species. Ecosystems evolve over long periods of time, with each individual component filling a specific niche and a general balance being maintained in predator/prey relationships. Human activities related to trade over long distances have the potential to introduce non-native species into ecosystems, where they may disrupt this balance and cause large changes in how the ecosystem functions. For example, the sea lamprey is a parasitic eel-like fish native to Europe that was introduced into the lower Great Lakes in the United States and Canada through commercial ship traffic. The sea lamprey feeds by attaching itself to large fish using its suction-like mouth; the victim fish eventually dies from blood loss or infection. Lake trout in Lake Michigan and Lake Superior were decimated by the sea lamprey, which grew in population due to the absence of a natural predator in the Great Lakes ecosystem. With lake trout – the top-level predator fish – removed, prey fish populations exploded, including populations of the non-native alewife. Thus over a relatively short time period, the introduction of sea lampreys changed the types and population sizes of multiple fish species in the Great Lakes. Other examples of invasive species that are dramatically changing ecosystems include the hemlock woolly adelgid, which is an East Asian insect that is destroying hemlock forests in eastern North America, and Asian milfoil, which is an aquatic weed clogging freshwater lakes in many areas of the United States.

An ecosystem is a stock concept. The flow of services that an ecosystem provides are known as ecosystem services. For our purposes, it is useful to think of these services as generating value in the anthropocentric sense that we are using in this book. Thus a riverine wetland is an ecosystem, and its ability to provide flood protection, wildlife habitat, sinks for excess nutrients, and other services useful to humans is what generates value. An action that degrades the ecosystem's ability to provide these services causes economic losses by diminishing the flow of valuable ecosystem services.

The ecosystem and ecosystem service concepts are useful to environmental economists in several ways. For organizational purposes, ecosystems as spatial units can help determine the appropriate spatial scale of an economic analysis. For example, to study threats to water quality we should work at the spatial scale of a watershed, which will allow for a comprehensive accounting of factors affecting water quality within the study boundaries rather than using a political unit (such as a county) that may cut across, include, or exclude physically relevant areas.

For conceptual and applied purposes, the notion of an ecological services production function is helpful. This is a function that maps indicators of an ecosystem's health into the quantity and quality of the ecosystem services it provides. This allows us to trace potentially measurable indicators of ecosystem quality – for which it is cumbersome to define household preference for – into services that we can imagine including as an argument in a utility function. For example, brackish coastal wetlands are critical breeding areas for several species of ocean game fish. The size of an undisturbed coastal wetland is therefore an indicator for the potential breeding success and size of the fish population, and the size of the population determines angling catch rates – a service provided by the ecosystem that enters an angler's utility function.

2.4 POLICY EXAMPLES

In this section we describe in additional detail four examples that illustrate the range of ways in which topics we will study in this book are linked to specific policy questions.

2.4.1 Sulfur Dioxide

Sulfur dioxide provides a good starting point in that concern about SO_2 emissions from electricity generation date back to the start of the environmental movement. As noted above, emissions arise primarily from coal-fired electricity plants, which release effluent through smoke stacks high into the atmosphere. Prevailing winds carry the pollution over long distances so that the ecological and human health impacts of emissions operate at the regional and continental scale. The ecological damages from SO_2 arise when emissions react with other compounds in the atmosphere to form sulfuric acid, which returns to earth as acid rain. Acid rain poisons lakes and streams and causes the unsightly dieback of forests and other vegetation. These ecological effects were widespread in Europe and North America in the 1970s and 1980s and were the impetus for national-level regulations in many countries. Subsequent to the initial round of regulations in these countries, the health impacts of SO_2 emissions became better appreciated – particularly as regards the contribution of SO_2 emissions to particulate matter concentrations.

The policy problem related to SO_2 emissions is relatively straightforward to describe. Sulfur dioxide emissions are an example of a point source pollutant that is relatively easy to observe and measure from a finite number of large coal-burning electricity plants. Emissions cause ecological damage and negatively impact human health. Ecological damage generates economic losses through diminished recreation and preservation services, while the latter generates losses via the utility and productivity impacts of higher mortality and morbidity. Thus the external costs of sulfur dioxide emissions are felt by populations that are downwind from emissions sources. Absent regulation, the electric utilities do not consider these external costs, and a market failure results in which the level of emissions is higher than the Pareto optimal level. Utilities have several physical options available for reducing emissions. Different coal deposits vary substantially in their sulfur content and so emissions can be reduced by switching or blending fuel sources. Sulfur can also be "scrubbed" from emissions by installing and operating smokestack abatement equipment. Finally, coal-fired electricity can be phased down and replaced by cleaner natural gas generation or renewable sources. These options are roughly ordered by costliness (fuel switching is the least expensive) and effectiveness (switching to renewable energy eliminates all emissions). The policy problem involves (a) determining the amount by which emissions should be reduced; (b) designing a mechanism to achieve the reduction; and (c) establishing how the incidence of abatement costs will be shared amongst the affected parties.

Retrospectively studying sulfur dioxide emission policies is useful because in many ways it is the prototype pollution problem used by economists to illustrate the benefits of economic approaches to environmental policy. In addition, as an early target for regulation there are several examples of national-level programs that provide a variety of policy regimes that can be compared. For example, in Germany the problem was addressed using technology and performance standards – an approach we will label as "command and control" in later chapters. Emissions were quickly and dramatically reduced by mandating that utility managers retrofit their plants with sulfur-scrubbing technologies. In the United States the problem was addressed by setting up the world's first large-scale "cap and trade" program, which gave utilities the flexibility to comply with the regulation by fuel blending, scrubbing, or purchasing emission rights on a well-functioning market. Here too dramatic reductions were achieved, though they were more gradual and less uniform across different regions of the country. In general, the German program was more costly to implement than the American program, though Germany's rapid and spatially uniform reductions in emissions provided greater environmental benefits. In later chapters we discuss the theoretical explanations for these differences.

2.4.2 Nutrient Surface Water Pollution in the US

As noted above, surface water nutrient pollution results primarily from municipal wastewater discharge, agricultural runoff, and storm water runoff from urban areas. Beginning in the early 1970s, the United States invested heavily in wastewater treatment facilities and other point source controls, mainly via the mandated technology standards set up by the 1972 Clean Water Act. Most of the remaining problems in the United States (and other developed countries) are therefore the result of non-point sources – particularly agriculture. This has led to challenges in obtaining additional pollution reductions given the difficulty associated with regulating emissions that cannot be attributed to a particular source (the defining feature of non-point source pollution) and the reluctance of governments to compel agricultural producers to adopt pollution-reducing measures.

In the United States, non-point source nutrient pollution from agriculture has mainly been addressed using voluntary measures, whereby farmers can enroll in programs that compensate them for changing land use or production practices to minimize water pollution. The primary federal program of this type is the Conservation Reserve Program (CRP). The CRP pays farmers to take marginal or environmentally sensitive land out of production for a contracted time period. Other conservation programs encourage the installation of grass strips ("buffer zones") between fields and water bodies, the use of conservation tillage practices, and precision agriculture to minimize the use of fertilizer. Under these types of institutional arrangements pollution reduction efforts are undertaken by individual farmers, but the costs are borne by taxpayers. In other contexts local regulations have assigned responsibility for reducing nutrient pollution to the industrial or municipal point sources, but has allowed them to contract with farmers to implement land use changes that provide a similar pollution reduction, albeit for lower cost. These two approaches provide examples of property right schemes whereby the primary polluter (the farmer) has the right to pollute and must be compensated to do otherwise. It is in contrast to the SO_2 examples above, in which the polluters (coal-fired utilities) were expected to bear the upfront costs of pollution abatement – likely to be shared subsequently by consumers in the form of higher prices.

The responsibility for water quality regulation in the United States has historically been divided between the states and the federal government. On occasion this arrangement has resulted in conflicts over trans-boundary problems and spatially varying quality levels. These conflicts illustrate a general issue related to the level of government that should be responsible for environmental protection in federal systems. When pollution effects are geographically larger than the jurisdiction responsible for regulating emissions, the regulating agency may not consider the pollution damages occurring outside its area of authority. This argues for assigning responsibility to the level of government that operates at or above the spatial scale of the environmental problem, in order to assure that the full extent of pollution damages is considered when the regulatory target is set. In contrast, the preferences of residents and the costs of providing environmental quality are likely to vary substantially across the federal landscape, which suggests that some degree of local decision-making is necessary for achieving economically efficient trade-offs.

2.4.3 Hazardous Waste in the US

As noted above, hazardous waste is a legacy of industrial activities that in many cases occurred before widespread environmental regulations were adopted. To prevent the introduction of new hazardous waste sites, the Resource Conservation and Recovery Act (RCRA) was enacted in the United States in 1975. This required that firms acquire a permit for storing or disposing of hazardous waste and participate in a "cradle to grave" tracking system that helps federal authorities to determine compliance with safe handling regulations. To deal with existing hazardous waste sites, the Comprehensive Environmental Response, Compensation, and Liability Act (CERCLA) was passed in 1980. CERCLA is primarily known for the "Superfund" that it created to partially finance the remediation of hazardous sites. The provisions of the law are complex in that they allow different parties – including current and past owners as well as persons responsible for the waste disposal – to be potentially liable for cleanup costs. Thus when a financially solvent, responsible party can be found, it can be made liable for the costs of remediation. In cases when a responsible party cannot be found and cleanup is deemed necessary, the costs are covered from a fund (the Superfund) that was originally financed by a tax on chemical manufacturers and the petroleum industry. This tax was allowed to lapse in the mid-1990s, so that publicly financed remediation now relies on general tax revenues. To prioritize sites for evaluation and cleanup the National Priorities List (NPL) was created, which ranks sites based on an index of their toxicity.

A second initiative in the United States related to hazardous waste is the Toxic Release Inventory (TRI), which requires US facilities in several industries to annually report the quantities of over 650 otherwise unregulated chemicals that are released into the environment during their operations. The Superfund and TRI programs illustrate two quite different approaches to environmental policy: one based on direct liability laws, and the other based on the indirect effects on a polluter's behavior due to public response to disclosure of its emissions.

The hazardous waste policies are also noteworthy for the way in which they convey benefits. Exposure to toxic materials can cause sickness and fatality, and so one component of the benefits of remediation is conveyed locally via the reduced health risks faced by surrounding populations. A second component of the benefits of site cleanup is amenity driven. Often remediation results in redevelopment to a more favorable land use, which may serve to boost the property values in surrounding neighborhoods. Because remediation is usually enormously expensive, estimating the magnitudes of these benefits is of some interest for understanding the efficiency of hazardous waste policy.

2.4.4 Climate

Climate change is the quintessential example of a large-scale spatial and temporal externality. Fossil fuel use and deforestation anywhere in the world contribute to the stock of greenhouse gasses in the atmosphere, meaning the cause and effect of emissions are separated by long distances – both physically, and amongst communities of people. Furthermore emissions today will have their primary effect in the future, meaning the actions of today's generation impact the well-being of future generations. Climate change also illustrates the equity dilemmas that can accompany environmental policy. Emissions of greenhouse gasses are associated with income growth, and so most of the current human-caused stock of atmospheric carbon dioxide is the result of past consumption by today's wealthy countries. An effective policy, however, would require that today's developing countries reduce their emissions trajectories, and perhaps their growth potential as a result. Finally, climate change shows that the costs and benefits of an environmental policy can be quite heterogeneous. Different areas of the world will be impacted by climate change differentially, with northern areas benefiting in some dimensions (e.g. longer growing seasons), and many tropical regions suffering disproportionately. The distribution of impacts will also depend on the ability of societies to adapt to the changes. While most developed countries have the institutional and finan-cial resources to organize adaptation efforts, many developing countries do not, particu-larly those in tropical regions.

The policy design challenges associated with climate change are substantial. The absence of an international authority that can compel individual countries to reduce emissions means that any policy response needs to arise from the voluntary participation of individual countries. Thus the study of international agreement-making is relevant for climate economics. The potential for negotiated environmental agreements is illus-trated by the Montreal Protocol, which provided an agreement on eliminating the use of chemicals that deplete the ozone layer. The broad ratification and compliance with the Protocol seemed to bode well for climate negotiations, but subsequent experience has illustrated the difficulty of persuading countries with widely varying interests to accept carbon emission reductions.

Negotiations led to the Kyoto Protocol in the late 1990s, which was never ratified by the US and China (the two largest emitters of carbon dioxide). Kyoto has now largely been replaced by several smaller, regional coalitions that have unilaterally agreed to reduce carbon dioxide emissions. The largest of these is the European Union (EU), which operates the EU Emissions Trading System (ETS) for CO_2 and covers roughly 5 percent of world emissions, though the EU ETS may be overtaken by the Chinese national carbon trading scheme planned for introduction in 2017 (Jotzo and Löschel, 2014; Zhang et al., 2014). Other coalitions are the Regional Greenhouse Gas Initiative (RGGI) in ten Northeast and Mid-Atlantic state in the US, the New South Wales Green-house Gas Abatement Scheme in Australia, the Japanese Voluntary Emission Trading Scheme, and the New Zealand Emission Trading Scheme.[3]

The non-universal nature of membership in these coalitions has brought questions of leakage to the forefront, i.e. the extent to which emissions reduced in a participating country simply reappear in a non-participating country. These challenges suggest that a technology-based solution is likely needed, whereby an alternative source of reliable and inexpensive energy is developed as a replacement for fossil fuels. To encourage the development of renewable energy sources, many countries now have renewable energy portfolios standards that stipulate a percentage of generation that must come from non-fossil fuel sources. Most developed countries also directly subsidize "green" energy production in some way. For example, many European countries use a feed-in tariff system whereby renewable energy suppliers are guaranteed a price that is high enough to cover the larger costs associated with most renewable technologies, compared to fos-sil fuel generation. Tradable green certificate programs have also emerged, whereby an aggregate quota of renewable energy production is collectively met via the exchange of green generation obligations among participating utilities. US states such as New Jersey and European countries such as the United Kingdom and Italy have implemented this approach.

---

[3] At the time of writing, the Kyoto agreement is poised to be replaced by the Paris agreement, which has been ratified by a sufficient number of countries (United Nations Treaty Collection, 2016). The Paris agreement, however, has been criticized for its lack of enforcement mechanisms (Milman, 2015).

2.5 SUMMARY

The arc of environmental economics development overlaps a variety of intellectual, historical, social, and policy themes. We discussed in Chapter 1 how the field has its intellectual roots in neoclassical welfare economics and theory of public goods and externalities. In this chapter we saw that the field's distinctiveness comes from its thematic roots in the environmental movement of the 1960s and the early round of large-scale environmental policy initiatives in the 1970s. The main themes and methodological approaches that came to define the field began their evolution during this era, thereby providing the core canon in use today.

Contemporary topical research in the field is motivated by the ongoing and evolving environmental problems that span local, regional, and global scales. In the past, environmental economics research was focused mainly on domestic, developed country issues. Today the focus is broader, with research themes that overlap into areas that were traditionally classified as development, international, and urban economic themes. Nonetheless the needs of the policy community continue to be paramount in defining specific research topics, meaning researchers in the field need to keep abreast of current policy debates and changes, and be knowledgeable of their historical context.

More generally, working in the field of environmental economics requires basic fluency in several subjects that go beyond standard economics. For example, studying how humans interact with the environment first requires an understanding of the physical pathways in which these interactions occur. Students choosing to pursue environmental economics will therefore be well served by seeking out basic knowledge on the physical, chemical, and biological properties of pollution types they are interested in. Our discussion in this chapter provides only a first step in this direction. Similarly, the field of ecology provides many concepts that are useful to environmental economists, and the notions of ecosystems, ecosystem services, and ecosystem service production functions are now part of the common parlance.

2.6 FURTHER READING

Our discussion in this chapter draws mainly on experience and knowledge gained over several years, and the wide breadth and narrow depth of coverage makes it difficult to identify a shortlist of recommended sources. Categories of useful sources include: (a) undergraduate environmental economics texts, which often include brief summaries of environmental issues and trends; (b) environmental studies texts, which usually seek to place environmental problems into their wider social context; (c) environmental policy texts, which tend to cover the political and legal nuance associated with policy issues; and (d) environmental science texts, which delve more deeply into the chemical, biological, and physical properties of pollution problems. Among the latter, Peirce et al. (1998) provide a comprehensive yet accessible (albeit somewhat dated) overview of the chemical and engineering aspects of environmental science, with chapters that focus on water, air, and land pollution. Among policy sources, Harrington et al. (2004) contains a collection of case studies comparing environmental policy issues and solutions in the United States and Europe.

CHAPTER 3

Introduction to the Theory of Environmental Policy

In this chapter we develop a simple analytical model describing pollution damages in monetary units, the cost of pollution prevention, and the characteristics of an efficient allocation of pollution emissions. We then use this analytical structure to describe the menu of environmental policy instruments and their comparative properties, and discuss the information needs of designing and implementing the policies. The primary purpose of the chapter is to introduce the main themes of study in environmental economics in their simplest form, to be followed in later chapters by more detailed topical discussions. The chapter also derives three main insights that will reappear in various forms throughout the book. First, for optimal environmental policy, the marginal cost of abatement should be equal to the marginal damage of pollution. Second, if pollutants are homogeneous, the cost of removing the last pollution unit should be equal across the different pollution sources. Finally, market-based instruments that provide incentives through prices – notably emission taxes, tradable emission permits, and per unit subsidies on pollution abatement – are the most effective means of decentralizing efficient abatement decisions. These insights are derived by abstracting from several real-world complexities. Specifically, in this chapter we assume full information, fixed pollution technologies that are separable from output technologies, flow (as opposed to stock) pollutants, fully competitive markets, no pre-existing, non-environmental distortions, and no spatial, temporal, or international dimensions. In Part II of the book we consider generalizations of the model presented here, which accommodate these complexities.

In this chapter we also discuss bilateral voluntary agreements for internalizing pollution externalities, which involves presentation of the celebrated Coase Theorem. Finally, our discussion includes several policy examples drawn from the United States and Europe, which provide context for the conceptual discussion in this and subsequent chapters.

3.1 A SIMPLE MODEL OF DAMAGES AND COSTS

Consider an area where a number of polluting firms and affected households are located. For concreteness, suppose the firms are coal-burning electrical plants emitting sulfur dioxide that impacts people living in the area. The firms are output price takers, selling electricity on the national market. People living in the area buy electricity on the national market and therefore do not rely exclusively on the local firms for electricity production. Each of J firms produces a level of emissions e_j, and total emissions are $E = \sum_{j=1}^{J} e_j$.

The model is non-spatial in that we assume all firms contribute uniformly to total emissions in the area. Likewise we assume that all households experience the same aggregate pollution level, regardless of their location in the landscape.

3.1.1 Damage Function

To derive a simple function that summarizes damages from emissions in monetary units, we assume households have utility functions given by

$$U_i(y_i, E) = y_i - D_i(E),\tag{3.1}$$

where y_i denotes the consumer's income level that is spent on market goods, and $D_i(E)$ is the disutility caused by the aggregate level of pollution, which the person takes as given. The preference function is quasi-linear in income and the marginal utility of income is one, allowing us to interpret $D_i(E)$ as the dollar value of lost utility for person i from aggregate emissions. We follow convention and refer to this as the damage function, and assume it is increasing and convex such that $D_i'(E) > 0$ and $D_i''(E) \geq 0$, implying damages are increasing at a constant or increasing rate in E. In Part III of the book we discuss the definition and measurement of the damage function and related concepts in greater detail, including more general ways that environmental quality can affect well-being. For the moment we assume the individual damage functions are known, and that the aggregate damage function is found by summing over the individual disutility functions so that

$$D(E) = \sum_{i=1}^{I} D_i(E),\tag{3.2}$$

where I denotes the number of households in the area.

3.1.2 Abatement Costs

An electricity-generating firm has costs associated with its operation, and it also incurs costs if it is required to reduce sulfur dioxide emissions below its freely chosen level. We assume in this chapter that operating and pollution reduction costs are separable, and focus only on the latter. Specifically, we define the cost of pollution reduction, or the *abatement cost function* for firm j, by $C_j(e_j)$. If the firm is not compelled to reduce its emissions below its freely chosen level $\hat{e}_j$, the abatement cost is zero (i.e. $C_j(\hat{e}_j) = 0$). Conversely, $C_j(e_j)$ is positive for any emission level $e_j < \hat{e}_j$. We also assume that abatement costs are lower when emissions are higher, so that $C_j'(e_j) < 0$ for $e_j < \hat{e}_j$. Since a marginal *reduction* in emissions marginally *increases* cost, the marginal abatement cost function is given by

$$MAC_j(e_j) = -C_j'(e_j) > 0, \quad e_j < \hat{e}_j.\tag{3.3}$$

Finally, we assume the marginal abatement cost increases when emissions are reduced; that is, the abatement cost function is weakly convex:

$$MAC'_j = -C''_j(e_j) \le 0, \quad e_j < \hat{e}_j. \tag{3.4}$$

This assumption is a reasonable approximation of piecewise constant marginal abatement cost functions, and is consistent with empirical observation for many types of pollutants. It is often the case that the initial pollution reductions can be achieved by relatively inexpensive changes in operating procedures, while further reductions require more expensive capital investments and changes in production procedures. Sulfur dioxide emissions from electricity-producing firms fit this pattern. Coal-burning plants can often achieve inexpensive emission reductions by switching from high-sulfur to low-sulfur coal, while large emission reductions are possible only via installation and operation of a comparatively expensive smokestack scrubber. In Chapter 5 we examine abatement costs in greater detail, including cost structures that are not separable in abatement effort, as well as pollution abatement's interactions with output and profits.

3.1.3 Efficient Allocation

Our analysis in Chapter 1 showed that Pareto optimality in the presence of an externality requires a trade-off between the negative impact on consumers and the productive benefits of the externality. Here, emissions from the firms negatively impact consumers, and their control has an opportunity cost to firms, as summarized by the abatement cost function. An efficient outcome is one that balances these two types of cost to the economy. Specifically, the efficient emission level for each firm is found by minimizing the total cost of the externality to society. Because abatement costs and pollution damages are both measured in dollars, the social objective function is

$$SC(e_1,...,e_J) = \sum_{j=1}^{J} C_j(e_j) + D(E), \tag{3.5}$$

where SC denotes the total social cost that is minimized by choosing each firm's emission level. Differentiating Eq. (3.5) with respect to each individual e_j we obtain

$$C'_j(e_j) + D'(E) = 0, \tag{3.6}$$

or

$$-C'_j(e_j) = D'(E) \quad \forall j = 1,...J. \tag{3.7}$$

Equation (3.7) can be used to further show that

$$-C'_j(e_j) = -C'_k(e_k) \quad \forall j = 1,...J, j \neq k. \tag{3.8}$$

The conditions in (3.7) and (3.8) illustrate two fundamental characteristics of an optimal allocation of pollution: for each firm the *marginal abatement cost is equal to the marginal damage* from pollution, and the *marginal abatement costs are equal across all polluters.* A strategy for regulating an environmental externality of this simple type is optimal (economically efficient) if it leads to allocations that satisfy these two conditions.

In Figure 3.1 we graphically demonstrate some of the features of this model. Panel A illustrates the abatement cost function. The top graph shows the abatement cost function for a firm indexed by 1, and the lower graph shows the firm's marginal abatement cost. From the starting point $\hat{e}_1$, the firm bears costs as it begins reducing emissions towards zero. The marginal cost of the initial reduction is small but positive, and increases as the firm's emissions continue to fall. As such, total abatement costs increase at an increasing rate. This can be seen on either the top or bottom graph, where the area under the marginal abatement curve between $\hat{e}_1$ and e_1 is the total abatement cost. For example, area $a+b+c$ in the lower graph is equal to the total abatement cost of achieving the emission level labeled $\bar{e}_1$. Panel B shows a second firm's marginal abatement cost curve, drawn to reflect differing cost structures between the two firms.

Panel C shows total and marginal damage functions under the curvature assumptions we have used. For total emissions E^* total damages are shown on the vertical axis of the top graph, and as area g under the marginal damage function in the lower graph. The two firms' marginal abatement cost curves illustrate the concept of an efficient allocation of pollution abatement. For the pollution amount E^* efficiency is obtained when both firms' marginal abatement cost levels are equal to the marginal damage. In our illustration this occurs for the points e_1^* and e_2^*.

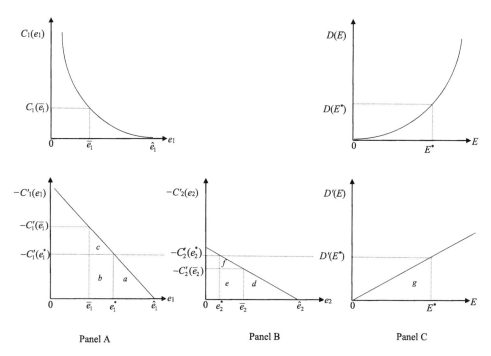

Figure 3.1 Pollution damages, costs, and efficient emission level

3.2 PROPERTY RIGHTS AND THE COASE THEOREM

The usual presumption in environmental policy is that solutions to environmental problems require legislative or executive rule making. There is, however, a long tradition in environmental economics (dating to Coase, 1960) of investigating situations in which the parties to an environmental conflict are able to arrive at an efficient outcome via negotiation, without government intervention. Examining when this approach to environmental policy is feasible helps to set the stage for the more interventionist approaches. To this end, consider a special case of the model with one firm and one affected household such that $I = 1$ and $J = 1$. All pollution damages $D(E)$ are borne by the affected household, the polluting firm incurs abatement costs $C(e_1)$, and all pollution is from emissions by the firm such that $e_1 = E$, where we have dropped the firm and household subscripts for simplicity. Under these conditions a simple assignment of property rights for pollution to either the firm or the household, and subsequent private negotiation between the parties, may lead to the optimal level of pollution. When pollution rights are assigned to the affected household, it has the legal right to zero emissions. Nonetheless, the household may elect to accept payment from the firm in exchange for allowing a non-zero level of pollution. Correspondingly, when the pollution rights are assigned to the firm, it has the legal right to set emissions to its unregulated optimum. The firm may, however, be willing to accept payment from the household to reduce its pollution level. In what follows we consider the efficiency and distributional consequences of these two property rights definitions.

3.2.1 Household Ownership of Pollution Rights

If the household owns the right of zero pollution, the firm can suggest a contract in which the household would accept some pollution in exchange for a transfer payment. Modeling this as a sequential game, the firm first proposes a contract (E, θ) consisting of an emission level E and transfer payment θ. In the second step the household can either accept or refuse the contract. If the household accepts, the firm picks a pollution level no larger than the one contracted. Negotiating the contract, however, is costly and involves transactions costs tr.

We assume both players are fully informed about preferences and technologies, and solve the sequential game for a sub-game perfect equilibrium. During the second stage of the game the household will accept the contract if $\theta \geq D(E)$. If the firm has bargaining power it will offer $\theta = D(E)$ to just compensate the household for the damage suffered. We assume the firm bears the transactions costs, since it must seek out the household and formulate an offer in order to operate. The firm's total cost is given by

$$TC(E) = C(E) + D(E) + tr \tag{3.9}$$

and its choice of E results in the condition

$$-C'(E) = D'(E), \tag{3.10}$$

which matches the social optimal with optimum level denoted by E^*. Importantly, however, this result is only obtained if the extensive marginal condition

$$tr \leq C(0) - \left[C(E^*) + D(E^*)\right] \tag{3.11}$$

holds. That is, the transaction costs must not exceed the gains from negotiation (the difference between social costs at $E = 0$ and social costs at the optimum E^*) for the efficient outcome to be obtained.

3.2.2 Firm Ownership of Pollution Rights

If the firm is endowed with the pollution right, the household can suggest a contract under which the firm will reduce pollution in exchange for compensation. Similar to above, the household first suggests an emission/compensation contract (E, θ) where θ is now a transfer payment from the household to the firm. The firm then decides to accept or refuse the contract and sets its emission level accordingly. Once again solving for a sub-game perfect equilibrium, in the second stage the firm will accept the contract if $\theta \geq C(E)$. Assuming now that the household has bargaining power, it will offer a transfer payment to just compensate the firm for the abatement costs incurred. The household's first stage utility maximization problem is

$$\max_{E} \left\{ y - \left(D(E) + C(E) + tr\right) \right\}, \tag{3.12}$$

and the first-order condition is

$$-C'(E) = D'(E), \tag{3.13}$$

which again matches the social optimum. As above, however, this solution is only obtained if transaction costs are smaller than the potential gains from negotiation:

$$tr \leq D(\hat{E}) - \left[D(E^*) + C(\hat{E}^*)\right], \tag{3.14}$$

where $\hat{E}$ is the firm's initial emission level.

3.2.3 Coase Theorem

The previous two subsections show that if property rights are clearly defined and the affected parties can negotiate, private contracts between rational agents will lead to an efficient pollution abatement level. Importantly, the assignment of property rights does not matter for efficiency, but it certainly affects the distribution of wealth.[1] The efficiency

---

[1] For our special case of quasi-linear utility functions (which rule out income effects) it is also the case that the level of pollution will be the same regardless of the assignment of property rights. For utility functions that include income effects, however, different ownership assignments can lead to different pollution outcomes.

result, however, is contingent on transaction costs not exceeding the potential gains from negotiation. The practical ramification of this is that for some classes of environmental problems, public intervention may not be necessary. In these cases, all that is required is a clear assignment of the distribution of property rights (for example, via courts or a government agency), a forum for negotiation, and an enforcement mechanism. These observations have come to be known as the Coase Theorem, named for the intuition suggested by Coase (1960) in his influential paper. A formal summary is given in the following proposition.

Proposition 3.1 (Coase Theorem)
Suppose party A imposes an externality on party B. Provided transaction costs are sufficiently small, irrespective of the initial allocation of property rights:

(a) *there exists an efficient contract describing a socially optimal level of pollution E^* and a transfer payment θ from one party to the other, which makes both parties at least as well off as without the contract;*
(b) *the efficient contract can be interpreted as the outcome of a sub-game perfect equilibrium of a sequential game, where the non-property right owner suggests a contract to the property right owner, who either accepts or rejects the contract.*

Part (b) of the theorem has been suggested by Schweizer (1988).

3.2.4 Comments on the Polluter Pays Principle

When the conditions for the Coase Theorem hold, efficiency can be achieved via negotiation regardless of the initial property rights regime. While this is clearly an important result, it sidesteps the important social question regarding to whom the rights should be assigned. Environmental policy is often (but certainly not always) debated within the context of the "polluter pays" principle, whereby the entity producing emissions is responsible for bearing the cost of pollution prevention *and* compensating victims for their damages. Thus the polluter pays principle is consistent with assigning property rights to the household in our model, but what of ex post compensation for damages actually suffered? Specifically, is the efficient outcome achieved if the household owns the ex ante right to pollution and is also entitled to compensation for the damages that occur in the event?

In our simple model, ex post compensation for damages does not affect the efficiency properties, but in some ways this is not an interesting test in that households do not have any control over the damages they suffer. In more realistic situations, households can undertake activities to prevent or reduce the impact of an externality. For example, people who experience respiratory problems on days with poor air quality can adjust their schedule to minimize outdoor time. Similarly, a reciprocal relationship can exist between the firm and household if the household's private decisions impact the magnitude of the external damage. The classic example of this is where a household locating near an airport flyway suffers greater external damages from noise than one locating further away. In these cases ex post compensation for damages *will not* lead to the efficient outcome.

To demonstrate why efficiency can fail under the polluter pays principle we describe a generalization to the model used so far. Suppose the damage function for the household is now given by $D(E,x)$, where x is a private market good that mitigates the impact of pollution but otherwise provides no utility to the consumer. We assume $D_x < 0$ and $D_{Ex} < 0$, implying that an increase in x causes both total and marginal damages to fall. The consumer's utility maximization problem in this case is

$$\max_{x} \{y - [D(E,x) + px]\}, \tag{3.15}$$

where p is the market price of x, and the term in square brackets is now the effective damage function. With x a choice variable, the effective damage borne by the consumer is partially under his control. Efficiency in the two agent economy still requires minimization of total abatement cost plus damages, but now involves an efficient mitigation level as well as an efficient pollution amount. The cost minimization problem is

$$\min_{E,x} \{D(E,x) + px + C(E)\}, \tag{3.16}$$

and the first-order conditions are

$$\begin{aligned} -C'(E) &= D_E(E,x) \\ -D_x(E,x) &= p. \end{aligned} \tag{3.17}$$

These equations imply that in addition to the familiar equality of marginal abatement cost and marginal damage, the marginal benefit of private mitigation (as measured by reduced damages) is equal to the marginal cost of mitigation (as given by the market price). Efficiency implies the person should undertake private mitigation so long as the incremental reduction in damage is less than the price of x.

Suppose a regulatory scheme is in place in which the firm must fully compensate the household for all ex post external damages. By definition in this case, the household suffers no adverse consequences from the externality, and hence there is no incentive to spend private resources to mitigate its effect. The household's optimal choice is therefore $x = 0$. The firm's task is to choose its emission level to minimize the sum of abatement cost and compensation to the household:

$$\min_{E} \{C_1(E) + D(E,0)\}. \tag{3.18}$$

The first-order condition for this problem is $-C'(E) = D_E(E,0)$, which clearly does not match the conditions in (3.17). This is not surprising: under ex post full compensation the household suffers no private damages, and as such there is no incentive to engage in private (and costly) mitigation. The level of x is therefore inefficiently small. Nonetheless, the Coase Theorem is still valid. If the household is endowed with the legal right to demand zero emissions (rather than full ex post compensation), there may be an amount of money that it would voluntarily accept to allow some pollution. The generalization of the damage function implies that the willingness to accept will depend on additional factors, including the price of the mitigating good and the technology of the damage function.

Part of what makes the Coase Theorem appealing is the large stock of real-world contexts in which Coase-like solutions may be possible. The following two examples illustrate that bargaining over environmental outcomes is more than a theoretical curiosity, and may even occur at the international level.

EXAMPLE 3.1 (POLICY) In 1988, sellers of the French mineral water brand Vittel noticed a deterioration in their product due to a slow but significant increase in nitrates. The main cause was identified as nutrient runoff from farming operations near Vittel's source springs. Further contamination of the springs would have damaged the Vittel brand's reputation as clean and natural, suitable even for infant feeding. When the problem was first recognized, there were 37 farmers operating in the catchment area. After several unsuccessful attempts to deal with this problem, including ex post water filtration and legal efforts to assign liability to the farmers, Vittel ultimately contracted with each individual farmer to alter his operations. The contracts committed farmers to several measures such as eliminating corn cropping, banning pesticides and nitrogen fertilizers, and limiting livestock numbers per unit of grazing area. In return, Vittel paid the farmers €230 per hectare for seven years, plus a one-time payment of €150,000 per farm. In addition, Vittel offered free technical and other assistance with implementing cleaner production methods.

The Vittel case was relatively complex, but a Coase-like solution was feasible because the affected parties were easily identified and not numerous, and the allocation of property rights was possible at a reasonable cost. Though the transactions costs (borne by Vittel) were non-trivial, these costs and the compensation paid were lower than the damages that may have been incurred by Vittel. For more details on this case see Depres et al. (2008) and the sources cited therein.

EXAMPLE 3.2 (POLICY) Since the 1930s Mines de Potasse d'Alsace (MdPA), a French state-owned producer of potash (used as fertilizer), emitted chlorides (a by-product of potash mining) into the Rhine River. The Rhine is an important inland waterway beginning in Switzerland, running through France and Germany, and emptying into the North Sea in the Netherlands. By the 1970s the Rhine was widely derided as the "sewer of Europe" (LeMarquand, 1977), with multiple polluters and pollutants contributing to damages. Nonetheless, chlorides were the major concern, and MdPA was the largest emitter. In addition, MdPA was thought to have low abatement costs: the by-product chlorides were solid particles that could be deposited elsewhere. In 1972, Switzerland, France, Germany, and the Netherlands agreed to pay MdPA 532 million French francs to reduce its emissions by 1975. After the Swiss contributed 6 percent of the compensation, the remaining costs were evenly divided between France, Germany, and the Netherlands. However, the upstream countries also agreed to pay 100 million francs to compensate the Netherlands, which suffered the majority of pollution damages.

The Mines de Potasse d'Alsace case is noteworthy in that it shows the power of Coasian bargaining in instances when there is no top-level jurisdictional authority, and it demonstrates that negotiations can work in complex cases with multiple polluters and pollution victims. It is also an example of how the Coase mechanism can lead to minimum abatement costs. Although Germany, Switzerland, and other entities in France were also emitters of chlorides, they had an incentive to approach the largest emitter with the lowest marginal abatement cost with an offer of compensation rather than attempting their own reductions. For more on this case see Bernauer (1995) and the sources cited therein.

3.3   ENVIRONMENTAL POLICY INSTRUMENTS

While the Coase Theorem is applicable for many localized externality problems involving a small number of affected agents, most contemporary environmental issues such as air and water pollution concern multiple and spatially diffuse polluters and affected parties. In these cases, private negotiation between parties is likely to be prohibitively expensive (i.e. transactions costs are high), and there is a role for public intervention. In this section we introduce and begin to assess the menu of policy options available to environmental regulators. Using the notation developed above, we describe the constraints on polluters' behavior introduced by each regulation and examine how firms' emissions and abatement costs are affected in each case.

3.3.1 Command and Control

Command and control policies for environmental regulation take their name from the fact that polluting firms are required to carry out a prescribed pollution-reducing action or face a civil penalty. Command and control regulations come in many forms, each of which affects the behavior of polluters in distinct ways. The most common policy types are emission limits, often in the form of generation performance standards (i.e. emission limits per unit of output) or technology standards. Generation performance standards require polluting firms to meet an emission reduction standard (in absolute or relative terms), while technology standards require them to install and operate mandated production and/or abatement technology. Here we focus on absolute emission standards, and delay discussion of relative standards until Chapter 5.

We first consider the theoretically simplest policy in which the regulator requires that all firms emit no more than their socially optimal level e_j^*, where e_j^* is the solution to the system in (3.7). By definition this policy will achieve the efficient level of pollution at minimum total abatement cost. In practice, however, it is not a realistic option. In addition to knowing the social damage function and individual firms' abatement costs, the regulator must implement a discriminatory policy that is unlikely to be legally feasible. Given these limitations a more realistic policy is a *uniform emission standard*. Suppose the regulator sets an emission standard $e_j \leq \bar{e}$ for all firms, where for example $\bar{e} = E^*/J$ and E^* is the socially optimal level of aggregate emissions. If the firms are identical, this policy will meet the conditions for an efficient allocation of emissions. In the more realistic case that firms are heterogeneous, however, the uniform standard will not lead to an efficient result. Consider once again Figure 3.1, where firm 1 has a higher abatement cost structure than firm 2. The regulator can achieve E^* using allocations $\bar{e}_j$ or e_j^* for $j = 1,2$. Note, however, that $-C'_1(\bar{e}_1) > -C'_2(\bar{e}_2)$, which violates the condition in Eq. (3.8). It costs more for firm 1 to eliminate its last emission than firm 2, suggesting it is possible to reduce the sum of the firms' abatement costs by reallocating some abatement effort from firm 1 to firm 2.

The efficiency loss from the uniform allocation can be found by examining the area under the marginal abatement cost functions in the Figure. For firm 1, the total abatement cost of $\bar{e}_1$ is area $a+b+c$, and for firm 2 the total cost is d. As the Figure is drawn, a reallocation of abatement effort to the efficient level will save firm 1 the amount $b+c$, and increase costs to firm 2 by area $e+f$. The dead weight loss from the uniform allocation is therefore area $b+c-e-f$, which is also the efficiency gain available from switching to the optimal allocation of abatement effort.

Figure 3.1 also serves to illustrate that there are potential gains from exchange between the two firms when coordination of abatement effort is possible. Suppose rather than setting emission standards for each firm the regulator sets the aggregate emission level E^*, and then allows the firms to privately determine how to allocate individual emissions via negotiation. For negotiation to take place, an initial allocation of emission rights is needed; each firm might, for example, receive an equal share such that $\bar{e}_1=\bar{e}_2=\bar{e}$, where $2\bar{e}=E^*$. In the course of negotiation, firm 1 would pay up to $c+b$ to increase emissions by the amount $e_1^*-\bar{e}_1$, and firm 2 will accept a payment of $f+e$ or more to reduce its emissions by an additional $\bar{e}_2-e_2^*$. As drawn, $c+b>f+e$, and so it is mutually beneficial to coordinate abatement effort.

This example makes clear that in pollution abatement, as in most other areas of economics, there are efficiency gains from specialization and trade. When institutions allow it, firms with costlier abatement options will voluntarily pay for the right to emit more pollution, while firms with relatively inexpensive abatement options will voluntarily engage in greater abatement effort. The intuition described here forms the basis for policy options based on economic incentives.

As noted above, in reality, standards often take the form of performance (i.e. relative) and technological standards, which impact emissions indirectly. A regulation of this type is illustrated in the following example.

EXAMPLE 3.3 (POLICY) An example of a command and control policy is the approach Germany took to reducing sulfur dioxide emissions in the 1980s. Acid rain linked to emissions of SO_2 from coal-burning utility boilers was causing damage to forests and lakes in northern Europe. In response, German regulators launched the *Ordinance on Large Combustion Plants* (GFA-VO, 1983, 1990), which mainly affected electricity suppliers. The GFA-VO set an SO_2 performance standard of 2,500 mg/m^3 of smokestack releases for all incumbent boilers exceeding a generation threshold. For new plants a more stringent standard of 400 mg/m^3 was assigned, and slightly less stringent regulations were applied to smaller units. In addition to the volume limits, a desulfurization rate of 85 percent was stipulated, which effectively required installation of scrubbers. The total cost of scrubber installation was estimated at €7.3 billion (Jung, 1988). The emission reductions among West German utility boilers totaled approximately 73 percent from 1980 to 1988, and reached 93 percent by 1995. Though these reductions were probably not achieved at least cost, the regulation was considered successful by the general public, since emissions were reduced relatively quickly at low monitoring and enforcement costs.[2]

---

[2] Figures for the German SO_2 example are drawn from Wätzold (2004). For more details on this case see Wätzold (2004) and the sources cited therein.

3.3.2 Emission Taxes

An emission tax (or administered price) sets a fee to be paid by the polluting firm per unit of effluent. While there have been few examples of emission taxes in the United States, European countries have long employed this type of policy. To model firms' behavior under emission taxes, suppose the government charges a tax of size τ per unit of pollution. A polluting firm's total pollution-related cost under taxation is now given by

$$TC_j(e_j) = C_j(e_j) + \tau e_j, \tag{3.19}$$

and cost minimization leads to the first-order condition

$$-C'_j(e_j) = \tau. \tag{3.20}$$

Equation (3.20) shows that the firm's optimal response to the emission tax is to reduce emissions until the marginal abatement cost is equal to the tax rate. Intuitively, the firms will reduce emissions so long as the incremental abatement cost is less than the tax rate; when the cost of abating a unit of pollution exceeds the tax rate, firms will find it optimal to emit and pay the tax. This implies a firm's emission level is a function of the tax rate, which is obtained by solving (3.20) for $e_j(\tau)$. The intuition of a firm's response to an emission tax is shown in panel A of Figure 3.2, where terms with σ and L can be ignored for now. Starting at $\hat{e}_1$, the marginal abatement cost for the initial units of emission is smaller than the tax rate, and so the firm will reduce emissions to the point labeled $e_1(\tau)$. Further emission reductions from this point have higher marginal abatement cost than the tax rate, so the firm will continue to produce $e_1(\tau)$ emissions. In this example the firm bears total abatement costs shown as area a, and pays a tax bill to the government in the amount of area b. What the government does with this revenue turns out to be of some importance, and we return to this topic in Chapter 7. For now we simply note that it is generally *not* the case that the revenue should be paid directly to those who suffer the pollution damages.

If all firms face the same marginal tax rate, Eq. (3.20) also implies that all firms will have equal marginal abatement costs at their chosen emission levels. That is,

$$MAC_j(e_j) = \tau = MAC_k(e_k) \ \forall j \neq k. \tag{3.21}$$

Finally, given the tax rate τ, the aggregate emission level is determined by

$$E(\tau) = \sum_{j=1}^{J} e_j(\tau). \tag{3.22}$$

Panels B and C of Figure 3.2 show these results. Firm 2, which faces the same tax rate τ, chooses an emission level $e_2(\tau)$ by the logic discussed above, thereby equating the tax rate to its marginal abatement level. The curve labeled $E(\tau)$ shows the total emissions from the two firms that arise as the tax rate varies along the vertical axis in Panel C. As (3.22) suggests, it is derived by summing the emissions each firm would choose at each possible tax rate. Deriving aggregate emissions in this way is often referred to as a horizontal summation of the individual firms' marginal abatement cost curves. For the

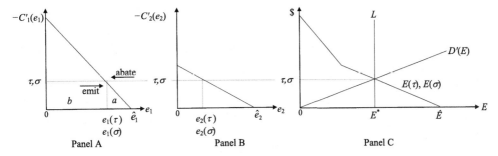

Figure 3.2 Emission taxes and auctioned permits

specific tax rate shown in the graph, $E^* = e_1(\tau) + e_2(\tau)$ is the total emissions remaining after implementation of the policy.

With these results it is possible to analyze how emissions vary with changes in the tax rate. Intuition suggests emissions should decrease with an increase in the tax rate, and indeed this is the case. If we differentiate (3.20) with respect to τ we obtain

$$C_j''(e_j)\frac{de_j(\tau)}{d\tau} = 1, \tag{3.23}$$

or

$$\frac{de_j(\tau)}{d\tau} = \frac{1}{-C_j''(e_j)} < 0, \tag{3.24}$$

from which we can see that $dE(\tau)/d\tau < 0$. Thus higher taxes induce lower total emissions if the marginal abatement cost curves of the individual firms are decreasing in emissions. This implies that, under full information about firms' abatement cost functions, the regulator can achieve any aggregate emission level E by choosing the appropriate tax rate. In particular, there is a tax rate that will lead to the socially optimal aggregate emission level E^*. Imperfect information about the cost function on the part of the regulator suggests that in actuality achieving a certain level of aggregate emissions via an emissions tax is difficult, unless the policy allows for substantial trial and error adjustment of the tax rate. We consider further the ramifications of this uncertainty for the efficiency properties of emissions taxes in Chapter 4.

EXAMPLE 3.4 (POLICY) Sweden was an early user of emission taxes. In response to the acid rain problem described in example 3.2, Swedish regulators replaced SO_2 performance standards with emission taxes in the early 1990s, and later added a nitrogen oxides (NO_X) tax. Sweden's taxes are relatively high, with rates of around \$3,000 per ton for SO_2 and \$4,000 per ton for NO_X aggregates. Around the same time, France also introduced SO_2 and NO_X taxes, albeit at rates that were substantially lower than the Swedish levels. The two countries use their environmental tax revenues in different ways. Sweden refunds NO_X tax revenue back to industry according to market shares, thereby forgoing the opportunity to swap out other distortionary taxes (to be discussed in Chapter 7). France refunds tax revenues indirectly to the polluting firms by subsidizing investment in new abatement technologies (Millock and Sterner, 2004).

3.3.3 Auctioned Pollution Permits

Suppose that rather than charging an ex post fee for each unit of pollution produced by a firm, for a given time period the government auctions off a fixed number of ex ante rights to emit a unit of pollution. For many environmentalists a policy of this type implies an appropriate distribution of property rights in that firms must purchase the right to pollute from the public at large. Denote the number of permits available for sale by L and the auction price that emerges for an emission right by σ. In fact multi-unit auctions of this type are complicated, multiple equilibria are possible, and observed prices need not correspond to their competitive counterparts. Nonetheless, we abstract from these issues and assume that the auction design is such that permits are sold at a unique market clearing price. At a minimum this assumption implies the number of participants in the auction is large.

If firms behave as price takers, the total pollution-related cost for a firm will be

$$TC_j(e_j) = C_j(e_j) + \sigma e_j, \tag{3.25}$$

where the second term shows the payment made by the firm to purchase permits. The first-order condition for cost minimization is $-C'_j(e_j) = \sigma$, suggesting the firm chooses its emission level to equate the marginal abatement cost to the purchase price of a permit. The intuition of this condition mirrors that from the emission tax case, and we can likewise solve for the firm's emission response function, denoted now by $e_j(\sigma)$. Because the firm is effectively purchasing an input when it bids for permits, we can interpret $e_j(\sigma)$ as the firm's factor demand function for permits/emissions. Under this interpretation the total (or aggregate) demand for permits is given by

$$E(\sigma) = \sum_{j=1}^{J} e_j(\sigma), \tag{3.26}$$

and with L permits available for auction, the market clearing price emerges from the equilibrium condition

$$L = \sum_{j=1}^{J} e_j(\sigma). \tag{3.27}$$

Figure 3.2 illustrates the auction market and firms' behavior. Panel C shows the aggregate factor demand for permits/emissions $E(\sigma)$, and the supply of permits, given by the vertical line labeled L. The price σ is determined in equilibrium by the intersection of permit supply and demand. The cost-minimizing, price-taking firms then choose levels of emissions $e_1(\sigma)$ and $e_2(\sigma)$ to equate the permit price to the marginal abatement cost curve.

The similarity between emission taxes and auctioned permits is apparent from a comparison of the equations and figure illustrating firms' behavior under the two policies. Under perfect information, emission taxes and auctioned permits are fully equivalent. This result is summarized formally in the following proposition and illustrated by Figure 3.2.

Proposition 3.2

If the regulator knows the polluting industry's aggregate demand curve for emissions, or equivalently the aggregate marginal abatement cost curve, and if the firms behave as price takers on the permit market, the regulator can achieve an aggregate emission target $\bar{E}$ by:

(a) issuing a total amount of permits for auction $L = \bar{E}$; or

(b) charging an emission tax τ which leads to $\bar{E}$. In this case $\tau(\bar{E}) = \sigma(L)$, where $\sigma(L)$ is the market clearing price in the auction.

Furthermore, with knowledge of the damage function $D(E)$ the regulator can implement the socially optimal emission level E^* using either instrument.

3.3.4 Freely Distributed Transferable Permits

Despite the potentially favorable property rights implied by a system of auctioned permits, most existing tradable permit schemes allocate the majority of pollution rights for free to firms based on historical emissions. Because the initial allocation of permits is a de facto subsidy to existing firms, there are long run and distributional consequences attached to how allocations are made. We study these topics in more detail in Chapters 5 and 8; here we focus on the short run static difference between auctioned permits, emissions taxes and freely distributed permits. Under a system of freely distributed transferable permits, the regulator sets the total amount of pollution and endows individual firms with emission permits totaling the aggregate pollution goal. Thus, while firms do not own the right to unlimited pollution, they do possess the right to emit a specified amount free of charge. Once the initial endowment is made, firms may buy or sell pollution rights, suggesting an individual firm is not constrained by its initial endowment. This setup is similar to the negotiated coordination of abatement effort that was described in section 3.3.1. The main difference here is that a competitive market institution for pollution rights is established, allowing for anonymous transactions between firms rather than negotiated exchanges.

Suppose firm j is endowed with pollution permits denoted by $\bar{e}_j$, and once again let σ be the market price for a pollution permit. The firm's pollution-associated costs are given by

$$TC_j(e_j) = C_j(e_j) + \sigma(e_j - \bar{e}_j), \tag{3.28}$$

and cost minimization implies the firm chooses its emission level according to the first-order condition $-C'_j(e_j) = \sigma$. This condition is clearly identical to the auctioned permit case. Firms reduce emissions up to the point where the marginal abatement cost equals the marginal opportunity cost of an emission permit. This marginal condition is met either through the sale or purchase of permits in the market, depending on the initial endowment and abatement cost structure. The initial endowment is effectively a lump sum transfer to the firm, and does not impact the firm's marginal decisions. Under this system the market equilibrium condition is

$$\sum_{j=1}^{J} e_j(\sigma) = \sum_{j=1}^{J} \bar{e}_j = L, \tag{3.29}$$

and the market price is determined by this condition. Not surprisingly, Eq. (3.29) is equivalent to Eq. (3.27), suggesting that in the short run, freely distributed permits have identical efficiency properties to auctioned permits and emission taxes, but substantially different distributional properties. In particular, this type of permit scheme is cost neutral for the government in that compliance with the environmental objective does not involve auxiliary transfer payments from firms to the government.

The system is illustrated for the case of two firms in Figure 3.3. Here firm 1 is a net buyer, firm 2 is a net seller, and the equilibrium price is σ. When the market clears, firm 1 bears area a in abatement costs, and spends area b in the permit market to purchase $e_1(\sigma) - \bar{e}_1$ permits. Firm 2 spends area $d + e$ on abatement, but recieves area $e + f$ in revenue from the permit market by selling $\bar{e}_2 - e_2(\sigma)$ permits. The industry spends $a + d + e$ on abatement rather than $a + b + c + d$ (the abatement costs without exchange), resulting in savings of $b + c - e = c + f$, where the equality follows from $b = e + f$. Thus the market institution allows firms to coordinate their abatement effort through voluntary exchanges, thereby minimizing the cost of abatement for the industry. Intra-industry transfers – area $b = e + f$ in the diagram – occur based on the initial allocation of permits to firms.

The United States was an early user of flexible trading-based environmental policy. For example, the phase out of lead additives in gasoline was the first national-scale emissions trading program. Though it lasted only from 1982 through 1987, it was considered a successful proof of concept (Newell and Rogers, 2004), and helped set the stage for the larger and more important US sulfur dioxide trading program.

EXAMPLE 3.5 (POLICY) Title IV of the US 1990 Clean Air Act Amendments (CAAA) set up the largest emission trading program used in the US to date. The 1990 CAAA had two purposes: to reduce SO_2 to just over half of the 1980 level, and to achieve the overall target of 8.9 million tons of SO_2 among electricity-generating facilities at the lowest possible cost, through emissions trading. Emission allowances were freely distributed based on a proportion of average emissions between 1985 and 1987. The program was divided into phase I (1995 to 1999) and phase II (2000 and later). Phase I covered 263 of the most-polluting electricity-generating plants, and phase II covered all electric-generating facilities with a capacity exceeding 25 MW, plus smaller units using sulfur-intensive fuels (approximately 3,200 units). While all existing phase I and II sources were endowed with permits, new sources had to buy any needed allowances on the market. Trading was initially concentrated in an EPA-run auction taking place once a year at the Chicago Board of Trade, though the bulk of exchanges shifted relatively quickly to private brokers.

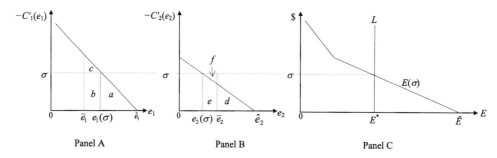

Figure 3.3 Freely distributed transferable permits

One important feature of the US sulfur dioxide market is that unused emission allowances could be shifted to later years (we discuss permit banking formally in Chapter 8), which in theory should reduce price volatility. In the early years, there was nonetheless some volatility in that prices moved between $70 and over $200 per ton. By the end of the 1990s, the price had stabilized at around $150 per ton and the market was relatively thick, with 8.4 million tons of SO_2 exchanged in a 12-month period during 1997–1998. Volatility returned, however, in the early 2000s, when the EPA under President George W. Bush sought to tighten the Title IV SO_2 caps, given the newly appreciated, large human health benefits available from reducing emissions further. Several new regulations, court rulings, and administrative responses caused the permit price to jump to $703 in the 2005 EPA auction, peak at $1,200 later that year, and then begin a decline, with the 2009 auction producing a price of $70 per ton. In recent years the price of an SO_2 allowance has fallen further, to nearly zero. The changing regulatory environment explains this pattern. To pursue additional reductions, the EPA originally sought to work within the Title IV framework, by reducing the number of available permits. The expectation of this caused permit prices to rise. Court rulings subsequently confirmed, however, that congressional action was needed to change the aggregate cap. With this it became clear that new SO_2 regulations would be forthcoming, and prices began to fall. The Bush and later Obama administrations ultimately used their rule-making authority under other aspects of the Clean Air Act to promulgate a series of state- and source-specific targets that effectively eliminated interstate permit trading, and caused the Title IV legislation to become non-binding for most polluters. Though the program remains nominally in place as of this writing, it is no longer an important element of SO_2 control policy, in that the new regulations are responsible for the main restrictions on emissions.

A second important aspect of the program features somewhat in its later demise: the Title IV legislation ignored the spatial dimension of SO_2 emissions (we discuss the role of space in cap and trade programs formally in Chapter 8). Due to heterogeneous weather and geological conditions, the location of emission sources matters for the spatial distribution of atmospheric concentrations of SO_2, and hence the location of damages. Indeed, two separate markets (for eastern and western regions) were considered as an option in the planning phase of the program, but were ultimately dropped.[3]

EXAMPLE 3.6 (EMPIRICAL) The Pigouvian rule requires emission prices to equal marginal damages. Even though measuring marginal damages is a topic that we do not address until Part III of the book, it is informative to compare the emission prices reported in examples 3.4 and 3.5 to approximate estimates of marginal damages. Since damages from SO_2 and NO_X can be quite different across regions, due to different population sizes and geography, estimates differ substantially between countries. For the US, Muller and Mendelsohn (2009, 2012) report mean marginal damages of $1,300 per ton of SO_2. The SO_2 permit prices summarized in example 3.5 are always below this marginal damage estimate, from which one could conclude that the permit allocation was probably too generous. Marginal damage estimates for Europe are available

---

[3] Early discussions of the US sulfur dioxide trading system are provided by Ellerman et al. (2000) and Stavins (1998); Schmalensee and Stavins (2013) provide a recent discussion and updated critique of the program. We have drawn most of our figures from Schmalensee and Stavins (2013) and the references contained therein.

in a non-peer reviewed report submitted to the European Commission. In this, Holland et al. (2005) report much higher values than Muller and Mendelsohn: €16,000 per ton of SO_2, and €12,000 per ton of NO_X. For Sweden, with its comparatively low population, the estimates are €2,800 to €8,100 per ton of SO_2 and €2,200 to €5,900 per ton of NO_X, depending on the estimation approach. Comparing these to the Swedish tax rates reported in example 3.4, one could conclude that Sweden has approximately satisfied the Pigouvian rule. In contrast, France (and most other countries) have under-internalized the damages from SO_2 and NO_X.

3.3.5 Subsidies

Each of the policy instruments we have described thus far assigns responsibility for abatement expenditures to the polluting firms. For a variety of political economy reasons, however, it is often the case that regulators do not want to impose additional cost burdens on firms. For example, in the US and Europe governments subsidize agriculture heavily and have generally been hesitant to tax or directly control pollution from crop and animal production. In agriculture and other areas this has led to policies whereby the regulator provides subsidies to firms for abatement activity. The property rights implied by subsidy systems are the inverse of what we have described above, in that the public at large must now purchase improved environmental quality from polluting firms. Subsidies can involve financing to purchase abatement equipment or can involve direct payments for abated units. In this subsection we describe firm behavior under direct payments.

Under a program of subsidized abatement the firm receives a payment ζ for each unit of pollution abated below some reference level. The reference level can be based on historic emissions or an emission standard; in describing the model we initially set the reference point to $\hat{e}_j$ (the firm's unregulated emissions level). With this incentive scheme the firm's total cost is given by

$$TC_j(e_j) = C_j(e_j) + \zeta(e_j - \hat{e}_j).$$ (3.30)

From this we can see that subsidized abatement is similar to the other incentive-based mechanisms. The amount $\zeta\hat{e}_j$ is in effect a lump sum transfer to the firm that has no impact on marginal decisions. Instead, the firm sets emissions based on the first-order condition $-C_j'(e_j) = \zeta$, from which we can see that the per unit subsidy has the same behavioral effect as an emission tax in that firms choose the emission level that equates marginal abatement cost to the per unit subsidy. This outcome is shown in panel A of Figure 3.4, in which the subsidy ζ leads firm 1 to select emissions $e_j(\zeta)$, for which it receives a subsidy shown by area $a+b$.

The regulator can achieve a particular total emission goal by appropriately choosing the subsidy rate in the same way as the corresponding tax rate is determined in an emission fee program. While the marginal incentive effects for the two policies are similar, the subsidy system is more expensive for the government, with total payments to polluting firms given by $\zeta\sum_{j=1}^{J}(\hat{e}_j - e_j)$. The government can reduce transfers to the industry by reducing the reference emission point below which the firm begins to receive the

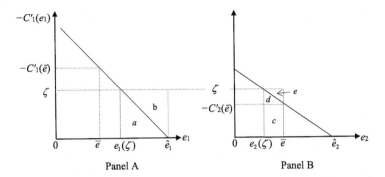

Figure 3.4 Subsidized abatement

subsidy. Panel B of Figure 3.4 shows that the behavior of firm 2 is the same regardless of whether the reference point is set at $\hat{e}_2$ or $\bar{e}$. The only difference is that firm 2 receives a subsidy of area $c+d+e$ rather than the larger amount implied by an $\hat{e}_2$ reference point. However, the change from $\hat{e}_1$ to $\bar{e}$ in panel A will cause firm 1 to drop out of the program, since $-C'_1(\bar{e})>\varsigma$. Thus, to effectively design a pure subsidy scheme the government needs some knowledge of individual firms' marginal abatement curves *and* a willingness to devote perhaps substantial resources to the program.

One solution to these drawbacks is a mixed tax/subsidy scheme whereby the polluting firm receives a subsidy for each unit abated below some standard and pays a tax for all units emitted above the standard. In this case the firm's cost structure is

$$TC_j(e_j) = C_j(e_j) + \zeta(e_j - \bar{e}), \tag{3.31}$$

where $(e_j - \bar{e})$ can now be positive or negative, implying the firm is either paying a tax bill or receiving a subsidy payment. In this case knowledge of the individual marginal abatement cost curves is not needed to induce abatement on the part of the firm, and the potential cost to the public sector is smaller than in a pure subsidy program. Nonetheless, this simple model ignores several potential incentive problems with subsidies, particularly with respect to long run entry and exit. In both the United States and Europe "shadow" firms exist whose primary purpose is to collect subsidies for reducing pollution that otherwise would not occur. We study these long run incentive problems in greater detail in Chapter 5.

3.4 AGGREGATE MARGINAL ABATEMENT COST CURVE

We conclude the analysis in this chapter by defining more precisely the aggregate marginal abatement cost curve, which we alluded to in discussing emission taxes and permits but did not precisely define. By definition, the aggregate marginal abatement cost curve is the horizontal summation of the individual firms' marginal abatement costs, and it reflects the industry marginal and total abatement costs when a cost efficient (i.e. least cost) policy is implemented. The aggregate marginal abatement cost curve tells us the efficient marginal abatement cost level for each firm for any aggregate emission target E.

To develop this concept more formally, suppose firms pay a per unit tax of τ for each unit emitted. From our earlier analysis we know that the firm chooses its emissions according to the rule

$$-C_j'(e_j) = \tau, \tag{3.32}$$

with resulting emission response function $e_j(\tau)$, which we interpret as the firm's demand for emissions. The aggregate demand is the summation of the individual firm demands

$$E(\tau) = \sum_{j=1}^{N} e_j(\tau), \tag{3.33}$$

and the *aggregate marginal abatement cost curve* is derived by inverting (3.33):

$$AMAC = E^{-1}(\cdot). \tag{3.34}$$

The aggregate marginal abatement cost curve allows us to characterize the socially optimal level of emissions in a more direct way. Because the social objective is to minimize the sum of aggregate abatement costs and social damages, the optimal level of pollution given the use of an efficient instrument occurs where the aggregate marginal abatement cost is equal to the marginal damage. This is shown in panel C of Figure 3.2, where the optimal emissions are given by E^* and L for the cases of emission taxes and transferable permits, respectively. Although we do not explicitly address uncertainty until Chapter 4, this definition of the social optimum allows us to foreshadow the information needed for the regulator to implement an optimal policy. Specifically, the regulator needs information on the marginal damage curve and the aggregate marginal abatement curve. Importantly, it is not necessary that the regulator has knowledge of the individual firms' abatement cost curves, except in so far as firm level information is needed to estimate the industry cost structure.

3.5   SUMMARY

Our objective in this chapter has been to introduce the basic concepts of environmental economics, focusing in particular on defining damage functions and abatement costs, the notion of an efficient pollution level, and the menu of policy options one might consider for achieving a target level of pollution. While these core themes will appear throughout the book, our interaction with them here has been highly stylized and simplified. We have assumed that consumer preferences and firm costs are fully known and that they take particular forms, which allowed us to focus narrowly on pollution damage functions and abatement cost functions with intuitive, but not necessarily general, properties. Under our full information assumption real-world notions of future uncertainty, asymmetric information among agents, risk attitudes, and the need to estimate behavioral functions are ignored. Furthermore, our perspective has been static, aspatial, partial equilibrium, and short run in nature. As such we have abstracted from firms' entry and exit decisions, changes in technology over time, interactions between environmental policy and other markets, and the key role that spatial variation plays in environmental policy. Discussion of these and other generalizations occur throughout the book.

The strong assumptions used in this chapter have allowed several key insights to emerge. First, the optimal response to pollution externalities involves a trade-off between the negative consequences of the externality and the cost of its control. The optimal level of pollution is that which equates the damage to society from the last unit of pollution to the marginal cost of its prevention. Second, the minimum total abatement cost for any level of pollution occurs when polluters' marginal abatement cost levels are equal. This suggests that institutions allowing firms to specialize – i.e. engage in more abatement if they are good at it and emit more if they are not – will generally be more cost effective than those that prescribe a particular behavior. Thus a key criterion in distinguishing among policy options is the extent to which each policy option encourages specialization, allowing aggregate outcomes to occur as if they were coordinated, even as firms pursue their own interests.

Policies that use economic incentives – emission taxes, auctioned and distributed permit schemes, and subsidies – will generally be preferred to command and control-type policies based on cost effectiveness, since they result in the equality of marginal abatement costs across all firms in the industry. The economic incentive policies, however, vary greatly in their implied property rights over emissions as well as the direction of transfers between the industry and regulatory agency, and among firms. Although efficiency can be achieved with any of these policies in the short run (and by Coasian bargaining if the conditions apply), they are associated with large variations in ex post income distributions. Furthermore the efficiency equivalence of many of these instruments breaks down when some assumptions are relaxed. In Chapter 4 we will examine how uncertainty in damage and abatement cost curves on the part of the regulator is an example of this.

3.6 FURTHER READING

The presentation in this chapter has drawn heavily on lecture notes from Master's and PhD level classes we have taught, for which there is no main reference. However, among the first papers to study the efficiency of emission taxes (or effluent charges) are Baumol and Oates (1971) and Baumol (1972). Likewise, Tietenberg (1980) and McGartland and Oates (1985) were pioneers in analyzing emissions trading. Hefland et al. (2003), and the references included therein, provide a broad survey of the theory of environmental policy, which includes many topics we have not discussed, including mention of non-convexities, distributional aspects of environmental policy, and voluntary programs. The issue of non-convexities – situations in which damage and/or cost functions do not obey standard curvature conditions – was researched in some detail in the 1970s. See Baumol and Oates (1988, Chapter 8) for an overview, and Starrett (1972) for an original discussion. This older literature has had a reawakening in the context of examining the services provided by ecosystems, where ecological threshold effects and irreversibility are often important considerations. See Dasgupta and Mäler (2003) for a general discussion, and the articles contained in the symposium that they introduce for specific examples. Finally, see Medema (2014) for a discussion of the Coase Theorem in environmental economics.

EXERCISES

3.1 * Show that the allocation which solves the first-order condition from Eq. (3.7) for a social optimum satisfies the second-order conditions.

3.2 * Consider an industry consisting of two firms ($j = 1$ and 2) that produce a consumer good and pollution. The abatement cost and damage functions are

$$C_j(e_j) = \begin{cases} (a_j - b_j e_j)^2 / 2b_j & \forall e_j \le a_j / b_j, \quad a_j, b_j > 0 \\ 0 & \text{otherwise} \end{cases}$$

$$D(E) = \frac{d}{2} E^2 \quad d > 0.$$

(a) Determine the firms' marginal abatement cost curves.

(b) Determine the socially optimal allocation and level of pollution.
    Now let $a_1 = 10$, $b_1 = 1$, $a_2 = 12$, and $b_2 = 0.5$. Suppose the environmental authority aims to establish an aggregate emission level of $E = 16$ units.

(c) What is the unregulated market emission level for each firm?

(d) What is each firm's abatement cost and the aggregate abatement cost if the government requires $e_j = 8$ for each firm?

(e) What is the tax rate the government should charge in order to achieve the target of $E = 16$ units? What is each firm's abatement cost and the aggregate abatement cost if the government charges this tax rate? What is each firm's tax bill?

(f) Suppose instead the government freely issues tradable emission permits, with each firm receiving an initial endowment of 8 units. If the permit market is competitive, what is the market price for permits? How many does each firm buy or sell? What is each firm's total cost (abatement plus net permit expenses)?

(g) Suppose instead the government auctions off 16 permits. What is the competitive auction price? What is each firm's total cost (abatement plus permit expenses)? What are government revenues?

(h) What would be the per unit subsidy needed to achieve a total of $E = 16$ units? What baseline emission level, below which the firms receive a subsidy, should the government set? What is each firm's total cost (abatement minus subsidy receipts)? What is the government expenditure?

(i) Construct a table summarizing the following for each policy option: total abatement cost, total industry cost, and government revenue (expense).

3.3 * In the 1990s, the leader of Germany's Social Democratic Party, Oscar LaFontaine, suggested a type of environmental regulation combining emission taxes with a minimum allowable emission standard. Specifically, each firm would be allowed to pollute an amount $\bar{e}$ without paying the tax. All units exceeding $\bar{e}$ would be subject to taxation.

(a) Determine the firm's objective function.

(b) Explain why this system is inefficient in general and does not provide incentives for least-cost pollution reduction. Under what conditions will this system be efficient?

3.4 ** Consider the basic model shown in section 3.1, but assume the social damage function is linear such that $D(E) = d \times E$ for $d > 0$.

(a) Show that for an efficient amount of pollution, both individual firm and total emissions decrease with an increase in d.

(b) Derive the comparative static relationships between d and the following potential policy variables: emission tax rate, total amount of issued permits, subsidy rate.

Suppose now we have a convex damage function $D(E,d)$ where $D_E(\cdot) > 0$, $D_{EE}(\cdot) > 0$, $D_d(\cdot) > 0$, and $D_{Ed}(\cdot) > 0$. That is, both total damage and marginal damage increase as d increases.

(c) Derive the relationship between d and the variables listed in part (b).

3.5 ** Consider the generalized externality problem. Assume the damage and cost functions are given by

$$C(E) = E - \alpha \frac{E^2}{2}$$

$$D(E, y) = y - \beta \frac{y^2}{2} - \gamma E y, \quad \alpha, \beta, \gamma > 0.$$

(a) Determine the non-regulated level of E if the polluter has the right to pollute.

(b) Determine the level of E under the polluter-pays principle.

(c) Determine the efficient solution.

(d) Determine the payoffs for both parties under no regulation and the polluter-pays principle for $\alpha = 1$, $\beta = 2$ and $\gamma = 3$.

Assume now there are transaction costs of $Tr = 1/240$.

(e) Which contract will the household suggest to the polluter if the polluter has the right to pollute and the household has to pay the transaction costs? What are the final payoffs to both parties?

(f) What will be different if the polluter has to bear the transaction costs?

(g) Which contract would the polluter suggest to the household if the household has the right to a clean environment and polluter has to pay the transaction costs? What are the final payoffs to both parties?

3.6 ** Suppose in a given area there are three power plants, each of which emits SO_2 with different intensities. The abatement cost functions for each firm j are

$$C_j(e_j) = \begin{cases} b_j / e_j, & e_j \le b_j / a_j \\ 0 & otherwise, \end{cases}$$

where $a_j > 0$, $b_j > 0$ for $j = 1,2,3$. The damage function is

$$D(E) = \frac{d}{2} E^2,$$

where $d > 0$.

(a) Set up the conditions for the socially optimal allocation. Can you solve it algebraically?

(b) Let $a_1 = a_2 = a_3 = 1$, $b_1 = 1000$, $b_2 = 640$, $b_3 = 360$, and $d = 1$. Calculate the optimal emission levels for each firm using a numerical software program (i.e. Matlab, Mathematica).

(c) Suppose the government sets an SO_2 tax such that $\tau = 10$. Is the size of this tax optimal?

3.7 ** Consider constant marginal abatement cost for two firms:

$$-C_1'(e_1) = a, \quad e_1 < \hat{e}_1$$
$$-C_2'(e_2) = b, \quad e_2 < \hat{e}_2.$$

(a) Determine the optimal allocation for both firms when the damage function is convex, and when it is linear.

(b) Is it possible to achieve the optimal allocation using economic incentive policy tools in these cases?

3.8 ** Consider the case of J polluters and with abatement cost functions $C_j(e_j)$ and one pollution victim. Abatement costs are ordered from highest to lowest such that $C_1(e_1) > C_2(e_2) > \ldots > C_J(e_J)$. Assume the pollution victim approaches the polluters in order to offer compensation for pollution reductions. Characterize the optimal contract when the polluter pays all transaction costs.

The Design of Environmental Policy

In Part II of this book we focus on the design of environmental policy by considering several generalizations and extensions to the model developed in Chapter 3. We begin in Chapter 4 by examining the effects of uncertainty on policy design. Here we will see that the welfare equivalence of emission tax and cap and trade systems, established in Chapter 3, breaks down under some types of uncertainty. In Chapters 5 and 6 we consider how competitive and imperfectly competitive output markets, respectively, interact with policy design. The focus on competitive output markets also enables an initial look at distributional issues in environmental policy, and our analysis of imperfect competition allows us to introduce second-best policy considerations. Second-best considerations then become the primary focus in Chapter 7, in which we examine how environmental policy interacts with other, pre-existing distortions in the economy, such as income taxes. This yields some important insights that differentiate revenue raising and non-revenue raising policy prescriptions. In Chapter 8, we consider a range of topics that are relevant for the real-world design and performance of cap and trade systems. It is here, for example, that we formally address the spatial and temporal aspects of environmental policy, and consider issues related to monitoring and enforcement. In Chapter 9, we introduce the non-point pollution problem, whereby a potentially stochastic ambient pollution level is observed, but emissions cannot be attributed to individual polluters. We will see that the inability to observe polluter behavior creates challenges for implementing the policy options discussed in the earlier chapters, and explains the relative dearth of economic incentive-based approaches to regulating many types of non-point source pollution.

Taken as a whole, Chapters 4 through 9 cover the main topics related to domestic environmental policy for flow pollutants, and they constitute the core themes in many graduate offerings on environmental policy. In the remainder of Part II, we cover several additional, and in some cases more advanced, topics. We begin in Chapter 10 with a discussion of liability rules. When an economic activity creates the risk of an environmental spill, as with nuclear power production or petroleum transport, liability rules can be designed that incentivize the proper level of accident prevention effort. We study the performance of liability rules under different assumptions about risk reduction effort observability, solvency, organizational structure, and insurance coverage. In Chapter 11 we turn to the critical issue of technology adoption and innovation. We examine the optimal degree of costly technology innovation and adoption, and study how environmental policy incentivizes firms to engage in R&D and adopt cleaner production methods. Borrowing from the industrial organization literature, our analysis in Chapter 11 is static or quasi-dynamic (two or three discrete periods), meaning we do not consider endogenous growth models. In Chapter 12 we examine how international aspects, including transboundary pollution and international trade, affect the design of environmental policy. We consider both cooperative and non-cooperative approaches to policy, and study how trade-related objectives may overlap with pollution policy. Finally, in Chapter 13, we introduce an explicitly dynamic element to abatement costs and damages, so as to study optimal policy for stock pollutants, such as greenhouse gasses. As part of this discussion, we also illustrate the connections between the stock of non-renewable resources such as oil and coal, and carbon emissions from fossil fuel energy sources.

CHAPTER 4
_____

Imperfect Information

In our discussion to this point, we have assumed that there is perfect and symmetric information among all agents involved in the design and execution of environmental policy. This has allowed us to refer to damage and cost functions that are fully observed by the regulator, firms, and households alike. Among other things, the full information assumption helped us establish the equivalency of auctioned permits and emission taxes, and more generally suggested that a particular pollution reduction goal can be obtained using one of several economic incentive instruments – all of which have similar efficiency properties. Though it is pedagogically useful, a perfect information assumption is a clear departure from reality. In this chapter we begin to consider how imperfect information may alter the effectiveness and efficiency properties of the policy instruments.

Imperfect information plays a large role in environmental economics, and as reviewed by Pindyck (2007), it comes in many guises. In this chapter we focus on a particular type of uncertainty: the regulator's inability to fully observe aggregate pollution damage and abatement cost functions. Importantly, we assume for this analysis that firms know their own abatement cost functions with certainty. Once we acknowledge that these functions must be estimated by the regulator (inevitably with error), it is natural to ask about the extent to which estimation error influences the performance of different regulatory approaches. Casual intuition suggests estimation errors will result in imprecise policy, but will not cause us to systematically favor one approach over another. Investigation of the extent to which this intuition holds began with Weitzman's (1974) classic paper, and has continued in various forms to this day. The unifying theme in this large literature is a search for policy instruments that minimize the ex post inefficiencies that occur due to the regulator's uncertainty. A related literature beginning with Kwerel (1977) examines ways that the regulator can design mechanisms that resolve the uncertainty, thereby eliminating ex post inefficiencies. In this chapter we examine these two strands of literature.

In focusing on uncertainty related to abatement cost and damage functions, we abstract for now from other types of imperfect information. Importantly, in what follows we assume that aggregate and firm-level emissions are perfectly observed. Thus we abstract from moral hazard issues that arise when the regulator cannot monitor firms' pollution and abatement outcomes. Furthermore, since abatement costs are deterministic from a firm's perspective, we do not examine their behavior under state-of-the-world uncertainty. Finally, our discussion in this chapter is static in nature; dynamic issues such as irreversibility, learning over time, and discounting are not addressed.

4.1   PRICE VERSUS QUANTITIES

We begin with a comparison of emission taxes and marketable pollution permits under imperfect information. Weitzman (1974) and Adar and Griffin (1976) present similar research designed to determine the conditions under which price instruments such as emission taxes or quantity instruments such as transferable permits will dominate under different types of uncertainty. We follow convention in this area by first examining damage function uncertainty with known abatement costs, and then cost function uncertainty with a known damage function. We examine the efficiency properties of taxes and permits in these cases and establish some qualitative results. Using the method described by Weitzman, we then add structure to the damage and abatement cost functions, which allows us to derive more precise descriptions of the ramifications of the two types of uncertainty. We close our discussion on prices versus quantities by commenting on how current policy and research continues to be influenced by these findings.

4.1.1 Damage Function Uncertainty

Continuing our established notation, define $D(E)$ as the social damage function from aggregate pollution level E, $C(E)$ as the aggregate abatement cost curve, and $D'(E)$ and $-C'(E)$ as the marginal damage and aggregate marginal abatement cost curves, respectively. Denote the optimal level of pollution by E^* and recall that this is defined as the solution to $-C'(E) = D'(E)$. The functions $D(\cdot)$ and $C(\cdot)$ summarize true schedules that, under different scenarios, may be imperfectly observed by the regulator. Functions that are estimated with error are denoted with "~", so that $\tilde{D}(\cdot)$ and $\tilde{C}(\cdot)$ are the estimated abatement cost and damage functions, and $\tilde{D}'(\cdot)$ and $\tilde{C}'(\cdot)$ are their respective derivatives.

Consider first the case where the regulator knows $-C'(E)$ with certainty, but uses the damage function estimate $\tilde{D}(E)$ to choose a policy emission target. Suppose for illustration that the regulator underestimates the marginal damage function so that

$$\tilde{D}'(E) < D'(E) \quad \forall E, \tag{4.1}$$

and that she chooses a policy target $\tilde{E}$ based on the relationship $-C'(E) = \tilde{D}'(E)$. Two related questions arise from the fact that $\tilde{E} \neq E^*$ in general: what is the welfare (efficiency) loss from targeting $\tilde{E}$, and does the size of the loss depend on the instrument choice? The welfare loss is defined as the difference between total social costs realized at $\tilde{E}$ and those that would occur at E^*:

$$WL = \left[D(\tilde{E}) + C(\tilde{E}) \right] - \left[D(E^*) + C(E^*) \right]$$
$$= \int_{E^*}^{\tilde{E}} D'(E) dE - \int_{E^*}^{\tilde{E}} -C'(E) dE. \tag{4.2}$$

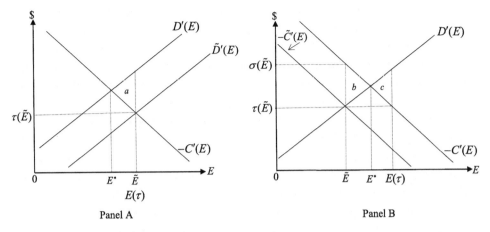

Figure 4.1   Damage and abatement cost curve uncertainty

The welfare loss for our particular case is illustrated by panel A of Figure 4.1, shown as area a. Since the emission level is set too high, $\tilde{E} - E^*$ units of pollution having higher marginal damage than marginal abatement cost are emitted.

Figure 4.1 also shows that, under this scenario, the choice of emission tax versus transferable permits results in the same welfare loss. For the former the regulator sets $\tau(\tilde{E})$, and for the latter she distributes or auctions off an amount $L = \tilde{E}$ of permits. Since the polluting firms choose emissions such that $\tau = -C'(E)$, both policy instruments result in the same ex post level of pollution, and hence the same welfare loss. That the same result holds when the marginal damage function is overestimated is also clear from the Figure. From this we see that damage function uncertainty by itself should not cause the regulator to favor one instrument over the other.

4.1.2 Abatement Cost Function Uncertainty

Suppose now that the regulator knows $D(E)$, but needs to use an estimate of $C(E)$ to set the pollution target. For illustration we assume that

$$-\tilde{C}'(E) < -C'(E) \quad \forall E < \hat{E}, \tag{4.3}$$

which is to say that the regulator underestimates the true marginal abatement cost curve for all policy-relevant emission levels. She chooses the emission target $\tilde{E}$ based on the relationship $-\tilde{C}'(E) = D'(E)$. Thus, the a priori target implies a level of emissions that is too low relative to the optimum. The ex post emission level and welfare loss, however, will depend on the actual policy chosen.

The difference between the tax and permit policies is shown in panel B of Figure 4.1. Under the quantity instrument the regulator supplies $L = \tilde{E}$ permits to the polluting firms, and the permit price $\sigma(\tilde{E})$ emerges at the point where permit supply intersects the true aggregate marginal abatement cost curve. Thus the quantity of emissions is fixed by the regulator, but the price is based on firms' behavior. Under the tax instrument the regulator administratively sets an emission fee $\tau(\tilde{E})$, and firms react by choosing emissions to equate the tax level to their true marginal abatement cost curve. In Figure 4.1 this causes the ex post aggregate emission level to be $E(\tau)$. In contrast to the quantity instrument, here the emission price is set and the aggregate emission level is determined by firms' behavior. Qualitatively, abatement cost uncertainty clearly matters, since the two policies lead to different emission level outcomes. But is there a systematic difference in the efficiency properties of taxes and permits?

In panel B of Figure 4.1 the welfare loss from the quantity instrument is area b and the welfare loss from the tax instrument is area c, which are given analytically by

$$
\begin{aligned}
b &= \int_{\tilde{E}}^{E^*} -C'(E)dE - \int_{\tilde{E}}^{E^*} D'(E)dE \\
c &= \int_{E^*}^{E(\tau)} D'(E)dE - \int_{E^*}^{E(\tau)} -C'(E)dE.
\end{aligned}
\tag{4.4}
$$

Inspection of the Figure and the analytical expressions suggests that we cannot make a general statement about the relative size of the welfare losses – i.e. in some instances $b>c$ and in others $c>b$. We can, however, try to isolate the features of the cost and damage functions that will cause one to be larger than the other. For intuition in this regard consider Figure 4.2. Panels A and B are drawn to reflect the same true and estimated abatement cost functions, as well as the same policy target $\tilde{E}$. The figures differ only in the steepness of the marginal damage curve as it passes through $-\tilde{C}'(\cdot)$ at $\tilde{E}$ (albeit dramatically to make our point). In both cases the regulator distributes $L = \tilde{E}$ to implement a quantity instrument or sets $\tau = \tau(\tilde{E})$ to implement a price instrument. In Panel A the steep, known marginal damage curve restricts the relative gap that can arise between $\tilde{E}$ and E^*, while the unknown marginal abatement cost curve implies the relative size of the gap between $E(\tau)$ and E^* can be large. The tax instrument in this case leads to the higher welfare loss – i.e. $b>a$ – due to the larger resulting distance between the optimal and realized emission level. The opposite is true in panel B. Here the flat marginal damage curve bounds the difference arising between $\tau(\tilde{E})$ and the optimal but unknown emission tax, so that the gap between $E(\tau)$ and E^* is small. In contrast, estimation error

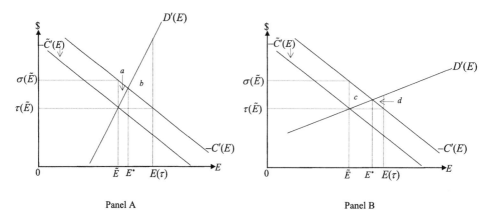

Figure 4.2   Welfare loss with steep and flat marginal damage curves

in the marginal abatement cost curve implies that the relative gap between $\tilde{E}$ and E^* can be large. With a flat marginal damage curve $c > d$, and a tax policy leads to a smaller welfare loss.

This intuition can be made more formal by writing the marginal damage function to include an explicit parameter for its slope. We rewrite the damage function as $D(E, \eta)$, and assume that $D_{E\eta}(\cdot) > 0$. Thus η is a parameter that determines the slope of the marginal damage function. Note that (as implied by Figure 4.2) the optimal pollution level E^* depends on η, which we here denote as $E^*(\eta)$. The following proposition summarizes the consequences of abatement cost function uncertainty when the marginal damage function is known.

Proposition 4.1

Suppose the regulator has an estimate of the aggregate marginal abatement cost curve such that $-\tilde{C}'(E) \neq -C'(E)$. *Consider a pollution target* $\tilde{E}$ *defined by* $-\tilde{C}'(\tilde{E}) = D_E(\tilde{E}, \eta)$, *a class of marginal damage functions* $D_E(\tilde{E}, \eta)$ *running through* $\tilde{E}$, *and a tax level* $\tau(\tilde{E})$. *For larger values of* η, *i.e. a steeper marginal damage curve:*

(a) the gap $|E^*(\eta) - \tilde{E}|$ *becomes smaller and the welfare loss under a permit policy shrinks; and*

(b) the gap $|E^*(\eta) - E(\tau)|$ *becomes larger and the welfare loss under a tax policy increases, where* $E(\tau)$ *is the emission level that occurs under the tax* $\tau = \tau(\tilde{E})$.

This proposition is illustrated by Figure 4.3, for which $\eta_1 < \eta_2$. As the marginal damage curve pivots from $D_E(E, \eta_1)$ to $D_E(E, \eta_2)$, the optimal pollution level moves closer to $\tilde{E}$, and the welfare loss from a permit policy based on $L = \tilde{E}$ shrinks from area $a + b + c$ to area a. Simultaneously the pivot in the marginal damage curve causes the optimal emission level to shift further away from $E(\tau)$, and the welfare loss under a tax policy based on $\tau = \tau(\tilde{E})$ increases from area e to area $d + e$. Thus all else being equal, a flatter marginal damage curve favors a tax approach to regulation, and a steeper marginal damage function favors a permit approach.

4.1.3 Weitzman Theorem

Our discussion to this point has been intuitive more than formal in that we have primarily used graphs to highlight the role of relative slopes in determining the performance of tax and permit policies under uncertainty. We have not yet presented a general result summarizing how slope features of both abatement cost and damage functions determine the second-best optimal policy when uncertainty is present. For this purpose it is necessary to introduce additional structure to the model. Define the damage function by $D(E, \eta)$, where η is now a random variable representing the regulator's uncertainty about the damage function. As usual $D_E(\cdot) > 0$ and $D_{EE}(\cdot) > 0$; we also assume $D_\eta(\cdot) > 0$ and $D_{E\eta}(\cdot) > 0$ so that increases in η shift up both the damage and marginal damage functions. Similarly define the aggregate abatement cost function by $C(E, \varepsilon)$, where ε is a random variable representing the regulator's uncertainty about abatement costs. To our familiar assumptions $-C_E(\cdot) > 0$ and $-C_{EE}(\cdot) < 0$, we add that ε enters the cost function so that total and marginal abatement cost are increasing in ε; that is, $-C_\varepsilon(\cdot) > 0$ and $-C_{E\varepsilon}(\cdot) > 0$.

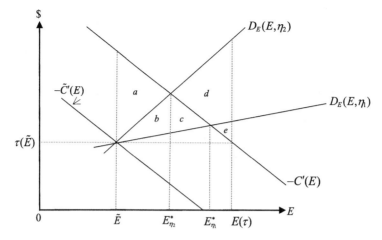

Figure 4.3   Illustration of proposition 4.1

Faced with uncertain damage and abatement cost functions, the regulator's task when designing a quantity instrument is to find the emission target that minimizes the expected sum of abatement costs and damages:

$$\min_{E} EV\big[C(E,\varepsilon)+D(E,\eta)\big],\tag{4.5}$$

where EV is the expected value operator. The emission target $\tilde{E}$ satisfies the first-order condition

$$EV\big[-C_E(E,\varepsilon)\big]=EV\big[D_E(E,\eta)\big].\tag{4.6}$$

To implement the quantity instrument, the regulator issues or auctions off a quantity $L=\tilde{E}$ of permits to the polluting industry. Under such a quantity instrument the expected social cost (*ESC*) at pollution level $\tilde{E}$ is

$$ESC^Q(\tilde{E})=EV\big[C(\tilde{E},\varepsilon)\big]+EV\big[D(\tilde{E},\eta)\big].\tag{4.7}$$

Things are somewhat more complicated under the tax policy. Behavior among polluting firms determines the aggregate emission level under a tax policy according to $-C_E(E,\varepsilon)=\tau$. We can solve this for $E=E(\tau,\varepsilon)$, which is the ex post emission level that arises, given firms' actual costs under a particular tax rate τ. Knowing the response function $E(\cdot)$ but not the value of ε, a rational regulator's objective is to choose τ to solve the problem

$$\min_{\tau} EV\big[C\big(E(\tau,\varepsilon),\varepsilon\big)+D\big(E(\tau,\varepsilon),\eta\big)\big],\tag{4.8}$$

which arises from substituting $E = E(\tau, \varepsilon)$ into (4.5). Her choice of tax instrument $\tilde{\tau}$ satisfies the first-order condition

$$EV\left[-C_E\left(E(\tau, \varepsilon), \varepsilon\right) \times E_\tau(\tau, \varepsilon)\right] = EV\left[D_E\left(E(\tau, \varepsilon), \eta\right) \times E_\tau(\tau, \varepsilon)\right], \tag{4.9}$$

where $E_\tau(\cdot)$ is the partial derivative with respect to τ. Using the condition $-C_E\left(E(\tau, \varepsilon), \varepsilon\right) = \tau$ and substituting into (4.9) we obtain

$$EV\left[\tau \times E_\tau(\tau, \varepsilon)\right] = \tau \times EV\left[E_\tau(\tau, \varepsilon)\right] = EV\left[D_E\left(E(\tau, \varepsilon), \eta\right) \times E_\tau(\tau, \varepsilon)\right], \tag{4.10}$$

from which we can implicitly define the target tax rate $\tilde{\tau}$ by

$$\tilde{\tau} = \frac{EV\left[D_E\left(E(\tilde{\tau}, \varepsilon), \eta\right) \times E_\tau(\tilde{\tau}, \varepsilon)\right]}{EV\left[E_\tau(\tilde{\tau}, \varepsilon)\right]}. \tag{4.11}$$

The expected social cost from pollution under this price instrument is

$$ESC^P(\tilde{\tau}) = EV\left[C\left(E(\tilde{\tau}, \varepsilon), \varepsilon\right)\right] + EV\left[D\left(E(\tilde{\tau}, \varepsilon), \eta\right)\right]. \tag{4.12}$$

Ex post, it is generally the case that $\tilde{E} \neq E(\tilde{\tau}, \varepsilon)$, and so the preferred second-best policy depends on the relative sizes of ESC^Q and ESC^P.

To gain traction on comparing the two expected social cost levels, we approximate the true abatement cost and damage functions using a second order Taylor series expansion around $\tilde{E}$. Define

$$\begin{aligned}
C(E, \varepsilon) &\equiv c(\varepsilon) + \left(K_1 + \varepsilon\right) \times (E - \tilde{E}) + \frac{K_2}{2} \times (E - \tilde{E})^2 \\
D(E, \eta) &\equiv d(\eta) + \left(\Delta_1 + \eta\right) \times (E - \tilde{E}) + \frac{\Delta_2}{2} \times (E - \tilde{E})^2,
\end{aligned} \tag{4.13}$$

where ε and η are zero mean random variables, $c(\varepsilon)$ and $d(\eta)$ are random functions, and $(K_1, K_2, \Delta_1, \Delta_2)$ are constants. Differentiating with respect to E, the implied marginal damage and marginal abatement cost functions from these approximations are

$$\begin{aligned}
-C_E(E, \varepsilon) &= -\left(K_1 + \varepsilon\right) - K_2 \times (E - \tilde{E}) \\
D_E(E, \eta) &= \Delta_1 + \eta + \Delta_2 \times (E - \tilde{E}).
\end{aligned} \tag{4.14}$$

A few things about these functions are noteworthy. First, ε and η summarize the regulator's uncertainty about the marginal damage and cost curves, and they serve as shift factors in the marginal damage and abatement cost curves. Second, if we evaluate the functions at $E = \tilde{E}$, from (4.14) we can see that

$$EV\left[-C_E(\tilde{E},\varepsilon)\right]=-K_1>0$$

$$EV\left[D_E(\tilde{E},\eta)\right]=\Delta_1>0, \tag{4.15}$$

since $EV(\varepsilon)=EV(\eta)=0$ and the last terms drop out when $E=\tilde{E}$. Finally, differentiating the marginal damage and abatement cost approximations with respect to E leads to

$$K_2=C_{EE}(E,\varepsilon)>0$$

$$\Delta_2=D_{EE}(E,\eta)>0. \tag{4.16}$$

The Taylor series approximation allows us to derive a statement for ESC^P-ESC^Q that depends only on terms with known signs. We summarize this finding in the following proposition.

Proposition 4.2 (Weitzman theorem)
For approximations of the abatement cost and damage functions given by Eq. (4.13), and for ε and η independently distributed with expected value of zero, the expected social cost difference between a price instrument and a quantity instrument is

$$ESC^P(\tilde{\tau})-ESC^Q(\tilde{E})=\frac{\sigma^2(\Delta_2-K_2)}{2(K_2)^2}, \tag{4.17}$$

where

$$\sigma^2=EV\left[\left(-C_E(E,\varepsilon)+EV\left[C_E(E,\varepsilon)\right]\right)^2\right]=EV\left[\varepsilon^2\right]>0. \tag{4.18}$$

We provide a derivation of Eq. (4.17) in appendix A, and give an opportunity to consider the case when ε and η are correlated in the end-of-chapter exercises.

This result shows that the welfare loss difference depends on the relative steepness (in absolute value) of the marginal abatement cost and marginal damage functions. Extreme examples can help to illustrate this finding. If the marginal damage function is a horizontal line (i.e. all units of pollution contribute equally to total damages), then $\Delta_2=0$ and $ESC^P(\tilde{\tau})-ESC^Q(\tilde{E})<0$, suggesting a tax instrument will be the preferred choice. In contrast, if the marginal abatement cost is constant, then $K_2=0$ and $ESC^P(\tilde{\tau})-ESC^Q(\tilde{E})>0$. This implies a system of pollution permits will be preferred. The more general case is illustrated by Figure 4.4, where panel A shows a comparatively steeper marginal damage curve, and panel B shows a comparatively steeper marginal abatement cost curve. The efficiency loss from tax and permit policies under both scenarios are shown as areas a, b, c, and d. Note that in each case uncertainty in the marginal damage function (or a shift in its estimate) affects the size of the inefficiencies but not their ranking. Consistent with the Weitzman theorem, the characteristics of the functions in panel A favor a quantity instrument, while those in panel B favor a tax instrument.

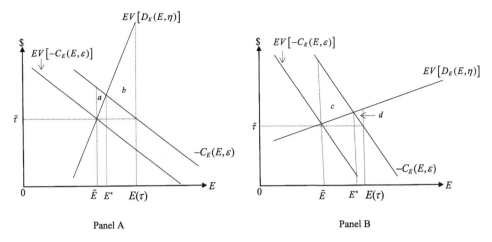

Figure 4.4 Illustration of the Weitzman theorem

4.1.4 Contemporary Policy and Research Relevance

The theoretical results from the 1970s comparing price and quantity instruments continue to have relevance in both policy and research circles to this day. The policy relevance comes from the fact that, while damage and abatement cost functions are almost always unknown, it is often possible to develop intuition on their shapes over the policy relevant range of emissions. Climate change is a good case in point. As discussed by Nordhaus (2007a, p.37) and others, the marginal cost of greenhouse gas abatement is related to the current level of emissions and is therefore sensitive to the degree of reduction, as is the case for most common pollutants. In contrast, the damages from greenhouse gas emissions occur based on the cumulative stock of gasses in the atmosphere; as such the marginal damage from an additional unit of CO_2 emission, for example, is largely independent of how much CO_2 is currently being emitted. This intuition implies that the marginal damage of a particular ton of CO_2 emitted is the same, whether it was the first or last ton emitted in a month. These features suggest that, for climate change, the marginal abatement cost function is likely to be steeper than the marginal damage function, and all else being equal a tax approach to climate change policy is preferred to a permit-based scheme. Several authors (Metcalf, 2009, is a good example) have used this argument in policy debates to support their preference for carbon taxes rather than a system of tradable carbon emission permits. More generally, the Weitzman rule reminds us that the regulator's goal is to fill in the demand for abatement that is missing from the market, and so she should select an instrument that best reflects that demand. If the demand is flat, then a tax does a better job of tracing out the marginal benefit curve; correspondingly, if the demand for abatement is steep the quantity instrument is preferred. The latter implies there is a threshold level of pollution around which the benefits of additional abatement are small and the costs of less abatement are high. The welfare consequences of missing this threshold are high, and so it makes sense to set emissions at that threshold. For the former there is no such quantity urgency, since every emission reduction or increase delivers the same marginal benefit or cost – meaning it is more important to set the price correctly.

4.2 HYBRID POLICIES

Our analysis thus far has considered only linear tax schemes. However, non-linear tax schemes may be preferred when the regulator has imperfect information about firms' abatement cost curves. Non-linear tax schemes are common in other contexts, the best example being progressive income taxes in both Europe and the United States, where the marginal tax rate depends on a person's income. In principle, something similar could be used for environmental policy. Consider again the case of a known damage function $D(E)$ but unknown abatement cost function, and define a pollution tax schedule $\tau(E)$ based on total emissions such that $\tau(E) = D'(E)$. Firm j's pollution-related total cost under this type of policy is

$$TC_j = C_j(e_j) + \tau(E) \times e_j, \tag{4.19}$$

where $C_j(\cdot)$ and e_j are the abatement cost function and emission level, respectively. If we assume that firms cannot influence the tax schedule (i.e. each behaves as a price taker regarding the tax system), the first-order condition for cost minimization results in $-C'_j(e_j) = \tau(E) = D'(E)$ for all firms, suggesting the condition for optimal pollution is met. Intuitively, the regulator and the firms know the marginal damage function, but only firms know their abatement cost functions. The regulator sets the tax rate ex post to the level of marginal damage that occurs based on the observed pollution level. If the industry emits $E > E^*$, a comparatively high emission fee (i.e. far up the $D'(E)$ curve) is assessed ex post, and firms must pay a marginal tax rate that is higher than their marginal abatement cost at E. If the industry emits $E < E^*$ a low emission fee is assessed, but the firms' marginal abatement cost level at E is higher than the marginal tax rate. In either case firms would have been better off at E^*, since it is only at this emission level that the ex post tax will be equal to the marginal abatement cost level.

Though attractive in concept, a non-linear tax scheme as described here is fraught with practical difficulties. Since firms do not know the actual price when making emission decisions, this logic only holds when firms have knowledge of their own *and* their competitors' cost structures. In addition, tax bills based on collective rather than individual behavior tend to be infeasible from a moral and fairness perspective. For this reason research has focused on investigating policies that mimic features of a non-linear tax, but do so without similar barriers to their use. By and large these have taken the form of hybrid policies that combine elements of tradable permit and emission tax instruments. In this section we review theoretical developments in this area.

4.2.1 Safety Valves

Roberts and Spence (1976) suggest a mixed system in which a polluting industry receives an allocation of transferable permits to cover emissions, as well as the option to pay a tax on emissions that are not covered by a permit or receive a subsidy for permits that are not used. By providing a safety valve in the form of the announced prices, the regulator guards against the more extreme consequences of improperly estimating E^* due to abatement cost uncertainty. To see how the mechanism works, consider the following additions to our model. The regulator distributes or auctions off an amount $L = \tilde{E}$ of permits based on the known damage function and her estimate of the aggregate marginal abatement cost function. Denote the price of an emission permit by σ, and the quantity of permits that firm j holds after the permit market clears by $\bar{e}_j$. The regulator announces a tax τ that firms must pay for all emissions in excess of their permit holdings, so that the tax bill is $\tau(e_j - \bar{e}_j)$ if $e_j > \bar{e}_j$. She also announces a subsidy ς that firms receive for each permit they hold but do not use. For $e_j < \bar{e}_j$ the subsidy amount is given by $\varsigma(\bar{e}_j - e_j)$. Under this type of policy firm j chooses e_j and $\bar{e}_j$ to minimize its pollution-related expenses according to

$$\min_{e_j, \bar{e}_j} TC_j = \begin{cases} C_j(e_j) + \sigma\bar{e}_j + \tau(e_j - \bar{e}_j) & e_j \geq \bar{e}_j \\ C_j(e_j) + \sigma\bar{e}_j - \varsigma(\bar{e}_j - e_j) & e_j \leq \bar{e}_j \end{cases}. \tag{4.20}$$

Before examining the firm's optimal behavior, consider the following argument for why, in equilibrium, the permit price must be bounded from above by the tax rate and from below by the subsidy. Suppose instead that $\sigma > \tau$. In this case firms will always choose to pay the emission tax rather than covering emissions with the more expensive permits. Firms will sell their permits (or not bid in the case of auctioned permits), and the permit price will fall at least until $\sigma \leq \tau$. If $\sigma < \varsigma$, firms could earn profit by buying permits at σ and turning them back in for the larger amount ς. This type of arbitrage opportunity will increase the demand for permits, and push the price up at least until $\varsigma \leq \sigma$. So in equilibrium, it must be the case that $\varsigma \leq \sigma \leq \tau$.

This condition suggests there are three types of firm-level outcomes that we can observe. If $\varsigma < \sigma < \tau$, firms set $e_j = \bar{e}_j$, since it is cheaper to cover emissions with a permit than to pay the tax, and holding extra permits to receive ς results in a loss per permit. In this case firms operate such that $-C'_j(e_j) = \sigma$. If instead $\sigma = \tau$, firms operate such that $-C'_j(e_j) = \tau$, and emission levels are not constrained by the original supply of permits. Finally, if $\sigma = \varsigma$ firms operate such that $-C'_j(e_j) = \varsigma$, and there will be an excess supply of permits, resulting in less pollution than the regulator's target. The Roberts and Spence mechanism is hybrid in that in some instances it functions like a price instrument, and in others like a quantity instrument. The tax rate provides a safety valve to polluting firms, in that it assures that emission rights will always be available at a fixed and known price, regardless of the position of the actual or estimated marginal abatement cost curve. The subsidy rate provides a safety valve for the environment, in that emission reductions beyond that implied by L can still be achieved when marginal abatement costs are overestimated by the regulator.

A hybrid policy of this type provides advantages over pure price or quantity instruments when the regulator is uncertain about abatement costs. If she underestimates the aggregate marginal abatement cost curve (and therefore the price of permits), the tax rate serves to cap how high firms' marginal abatement cost levels can climb. If the regulator overestimates the aggregate marginal abatement costs (and therefore the price of permits), the subsidy assures there are still incentives for emissions reductions. These advantages are illustrated in Figure 4.5. Panel A shows three different aggregate marginal abatement cost curves and policy parameters corresponding to $L = \tilde{E}$, τ and ς. By specifying the prices along with the quantity the regulator can achieve an efficient outcome (zero welfare loss) for three possible marginal abatement cost curves. For the

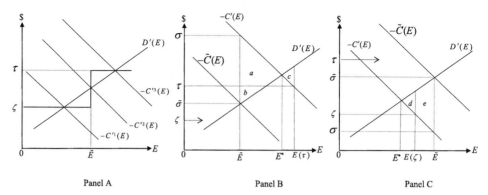

Panel A   Panel B   Panel C

Figure 4.5   Roberts and Spence Instrument

cost function $C^1(E)$, the relevant policy parameter is ς, and firms receive subsidies for reducing emissions below $\tilde{E}$. For $C^2(E)$ the market price of permits lies between τ and ς, suggesting the quantity parameter $L = \tilde{E}$ is in play. Finally, for $C^3(E)$ the tax level determines aggregate emissions in that firms pay τ for each unit of pollution beyond $\tilde{E}$.

The more practical advantages of the hybrid system are shown in panels B and C. Panel B shows a case in which the regulator has underestimated the aggregate marginal abatement cost curve. To implement a pure quantity instrument she would issue $L = \tilde{E}$ and expect a price of $\tilde{\sigma}$ to arise. Once in place, such a policy would result in an actual price of σ and a welfare loss given by area $a+b$. If she instead implements a mixed instrument that also includes a safety valve tax τ, the realized level of emissions is $E(\tau)$ and the welfare loss reduces to area c. The parallel case in which the regulator overestimates the marginal abatement cost function is shown in panel C. If $L = \tilde{E}$ permits were distributed without an accompanying subsidy price ς, there would be a gap of size $\tilde{E} - E^*$ between realized and optimal emissions, leading to a welfare loss shown by area $d+e$. With the subsidy option included, firms accept payment to reduce emissions below the number of permits distributed, leading to aggregate emissions $E(\varsigma)$ and the smaller welfare loss shown as area d. So while the Roberts and Spence mechanism cannot prevent welfare losses from occurring, it does serve to limit their magnitude relative to pure quantity or price approaches.

EXAMPLE 4.1 (POLICY) Discussions about the inclusion of safety-valve-like provisions are common in almost all of the ongoing debates regarding the formation of permit trading schemes for controlling CO_2 emissions. As of this writing the world's largest existing carbon market is in the European Union, where the member states have agreed to limit carbon emissions through the European Union Emissions Trading Scheme (EU-ETS). For example, the EU-ETS has a design feature that, in phase I (2005–08), stipulated a €40 fine for emitting a ton of CO_2 without surrendering an allowance. The fine rose to €100 in 2008 with the onset of phase II. This is not a pure safety valve, however, because an allowance from the next year's allotment must subsequently be surrendered. From the market's founding in 2005 until the time of this writing, the price of an emission unit has generally not exceeded €30, and fines have not been assessed for uncovered emissions.[1] In the

---

[1] There were only a few cases reported where, at the beginning of the first EU-ETS trading period in 2005, some smaller firms held too few permits, because they were not yet familiar with the

United States, a number of carbon trading schemes have been proposed and debated, though not implemented as of this writing. As an example, the carbon control bill from the US 110th Congress – S.1766, the "Bingaman-Specter" bill – stipulated a safety valve price on carbon emissions that would be available one month per year, during the time when emissions and allowances are being balanced. See Murray, Newell, and Pizer (2009) and the citations therein for additional discussion.

4.2.2 Approximating the Marginal Damage Curve

In a coarse sense, the Roberts and Spence Instrument traces out the marginal damage curve using stepwise constant functions. This is most apparent in panel A of Figure 4.5, where the price line that firms face begins at ς, is vertical at $\tilde{E}$, and then levels off at τ. Recall that the non-linear tax scheme discussed above defines the tax schedule to be the marginal damage curve. Thus any policy that connects the effective price that firms pay for emission rights to the marginal damage function will emulate the non-linear tax, and reduce the welfare loss that occurs due to uncertainty about abatement costs. This realization has led researchers to consider generalizations of the price/quantity hybrid instruments that provide finer approximations to the marginal damage function, while avoiding the difficulties of non-linear taxes.

In an appendix to their article, Roberts and Spence themselves suggest a generalized version of their instrument in which a portfolio of permit types $L_1,...,L_N$ is announced, along with corresponding tax levels $\tau_1,...,\tau_N$ and subsidy levels $\varsigma_1,...,\varsigma_N$. As market prices $\sigma_1,...,\sigma_N$ for each permit type emerge, the regulator obtains a stepwise approximation to the aggregate marginal abatement cost curve. From this she determines the optimal (i.e. welfare loss minimizing) permit supply, denoted L_n, from among the N that were announced. Through a system of complicated side payments and purchases, she then adjusts the system so that only type n permits are held by the firms and $\varsigma_n < \sigma_n < \tau_n$. Thus a flexible permit supply system can, in principle, be used to reduce the degree of inefficiency compared to the simple hybrid model. In practice, the Roberts and Spence mechanism is cumbersome to communicate, and likely impossible to implement. Nonetheless, the idea is compelling, and so we proceed by first presenting a simpler approach proposed by Henry (1989), which allows us to develop the intuition of approximating the marginal damage curve with multiple permit types.

Like Roberts and Spence, Henry's (1989) approach uses a flexible supply menu of permits $L_1 < L_2 < ,..., < L_N$, where L_1 and L_N are the lowest and highest conceivable emission levels, respectively. For each interval $(L_{n-1}, L_n]$, an upper threshold price $\bar{\sigma}_n$ and a lower threshold price $\underline{\sigma}_n$ are fixed and announced, where $\underline{\sigma}_{n+1} = \bar{\sigma}_n$. The regulator uses the permit levels and threshold prices in the following algorithm to implement the instrument:

(a) Issue an initial amount of permits L_n based on the condition $-\tilde{C}'(L_n) = D'(L_n)$, and observe the permit market price σ that emerges. If $\underline{\sigma}_n < \sigma < \bar{\sigma}_n$, take no further action.

formal procedures. The volume of such under-compliance by mistake was, however, negligible. (Source: personal communication between authors and EU Commission staff)

(b) If $\sigma > \bar{\sigma}_n$, issue an additional $L_{n+1} - L_n$ permits and observe the new price.

   (i) If $\underline{\sigma}_{n+1} < \sigma < \bar{\sigma}_{n+1}$, take no further action. If $\sigma > \bar{\sigma}_{n+1}$ an additional $L_{n+2} - L_{n+1}$ permits are issued and a new price is observed. This continues a total of K times until either $\underline{\sigma}_{n+K} < \sigma < \bar{\sigma}_{n+K}$, or $\underline{\sigma}_{n+K} > \sigma$.

   (ii) If at iteration K the permit price emerges below the lower threshold such that $\underline{\sigma}_{n+K} > \sigma$, buy back a quantity of permits $(L_{n+K} - L_{n+K-1})/2$ and observe the permit price. Continue buying back permits in smaller increments until $\underline{\sigma}_{n+K} < \sigma < \bar{\sigma}_{n+K}$.

(c) If $\sigma < \underline{\sigma}_n$, buy back $L_n - L_{n-1}$ permits and observe the new price.

   (i) If $\underline{\sigma}_{n-1} < \sigma < \bar{\sigma}_{n-1}$, take no further action. If $\sigma < \underline{\sigma}_{n-1}$, buy an additional $L_{n-1} - L_{n-2}$ back and observe the market price. This continues K times until either $\underline{\sigma}_{n-K} < \sigma < \bar{\sigma}_{n-K}$, or $\bar{\sigma}_{n-K} < \sigma$.

   (ii) If at iteration K the permit price emerges above the upper threshold such that $\bar{\sigma}_{n-K} < \sigma$, issue an additional quantity of permits $(L_{n-K} - L_{n-K-1})/2$ and observe the permit price. Continue issuing additional permits in smaller increments until $\underline{\sigma}_{n-K} < \sigma < \bar{\sigma}_{n-K}$.

Henry's algorithm allows the regulator to incrementally buy and/or sell permits at fixed and known prices in order to adjust the permit supply level to correct errors based on her initial estimate of the industry's costs. Figure 4.6 displays a stylized example of how the algorithm unfolds. Panel A shows how the permit levels and threshold prices trace out the known marginal damage curve in a stepwise fashion. The behavior of firms and the reactions of the regulator assure that the price firms ultimately face lies within the step through which the true but unknown marginal abatement cost curve runs. This is shown in panel B. Two permit levels L_1 and L_2 are drawn along with their respective threshold prices. Based on her best estimate $-\tilde{C}'(E)$, the regulator initially issues L_1 permits. The firms' reaction, based on the true cost curve $-C'(E)$, causes the initial permit price to be $\sigma(L_1)$, where $\sigma(L_1) > \bar{\sigma}_1$. Seeing this, the regulator issues an additional $L_2 - L_1$ permits; this causes the market price for permits to fall to $\sigma(L_2) < \underline{\sigma}_2$. In this example the regulator has over-adjusted, and she now needs to purchase permits

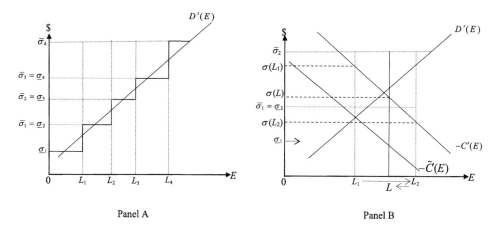

Panel A   Panel B

Figure 4.6   Henry's Instrument

back from the industry. The Figure shows a buyback of $L_2 - L$ permits and a final price of $\sigma(L)$, where $\underline{\sigma}_2 < \sigma(L) < \bar{\sigma}_2$. With this buyback the regulator has reached her stopping point, and the final pollution/permit level occurs at $E = L$. As the Figure is drawn, a small welfare loss still occurs relative to the optimal pollution level, but the iterative algorithm has allowed the regulator to come arbitrarily close to the optimum – without ex ante knowledge of the industry's abatement cost function.

While the Henry algorithm is intuitive, the institutional structure needed to actually implement such a policy is substantial. In particular, multiple points of interaction between the regulator and the polluting industry are needed, and examples of such iterative approaches to environmental policy are almost nonexistent. Unold and Requate (2001) describe a policy that is similar in spirit, but relies instead on financial institutions to adjust the supply of pollution permits to the near-optimal level. They suggest augmenting a system of tradable permits with a system of call (or put) options, with different strike prices to purchase (sell) additional (spare) permits at those prices, in order to mimic the marginal damage curve.

4.3   MECHANISM DESIGN

Our discussion thus far has focused on the design of policies that minimize welfare losses arising from the regulator's uncertainty about firms' abatement cost functions. We have taken uncertainty as given and studied how taxes, permits, and hybrid instruments are best designed conditional on imperfect information. From this perspective, the main objective has not been to learn about firms' abatement costs ex ante (though in some instances this information became available as the policy unfolded), and so we generally did not expect to obtain the ex post social optimum. A good policy was judged by how close it came to the social optimum, and how feasibly it could be implemented.

An alternative perspective for studying the imperfect information problem is mechanism design. Mechanism design is an area of research that grew out of principal–agent problems in which asymmetric and incomplete information among players (e.g. workers, firms, regulatory agencies) with different incentives leads to sub-optimal outcomes. The classic examples are the employee/employer relationship in which workers do not always have incentive to act in the best interest of the firm (moral hazard problem), or a firm offering a wage scheme when it cannot ex ante observe the workers' skills (adverse selection). The objective in these situations is to design "mechanisms" – contracts or regulatory schemes – that align the incentives of all players such that their self-interested actions lead to the preferred group outcome. In many instances this requires revelation of private information by the agents to the principal, and sometimes leads only to second-best outcomes.

In our case, polluting firms are agents who hold private information about their abatement cost functions, without which the regulator cannot design efficient environmental policy. The regulator must effectively ask firms about their abatement costs, and depending on the circumstances, firms may find it optimal to misrepresent *or* truthfully reveal their cost structure. Kwerel (1977) describes how this may play out in the case of simple permit or emission tax schemes. For permit schemes, firms would like to see a generous supply of emission rights, and so they have an incentive to *overstate* abatement costs. As is clear from the models developed earlier in the chapter, the regulator's resulting overestimate of marginal abatement costs causes her to issue a number of permits that is greater than the true social optimum. For tax schemes, firms would like to see an emission fee that is as low as possible, and so they have an incentive to *understate* abatement costs. Through her underestimate of marginal abatement costs, the regulator sets a tax level that is too low relative to what is needed to obtain the true social optimum. Thus, in neither pure tax nor pure permit schemes, do firms have the incentive to fully cooperate.

To obtain the information needed to implement an efficient policy the regulator needs to set a mechanism that manipulates firms' payoff functions to be incentive compatible and individually rational. Incentive compatibility means a firm's best strategy is to reveal its true cost structure, given that other firms do as well, and individually rational means the firm will find it best to participate in the mechanism. A handful of authors have considered environmental policy from the perspective of mechanism design. Examples include Kwerel (1977), Dasgupta et al. (1980), and Montero (2008). In this section we briefly outline Kwerel's approach for motivation. Then we describe in greater detail Montero's mechanism, which does not use the typical mechanism design machinery, but surprisingly leads to a first-best outcome. We close the section by considering mechanism design under fiscal restrictions, which requires consideration of participation and incentive compatibility constraints.

4.3.1 Kwerel's Mechanism

Kwerel (1977) proposes a hybrid instrument in which the regulator auctions off a quantity of permits L, and additionally pays a subsidy ς, which the firms receive for each pollution permit they do not use. In other words, the regulator buys back unused permits at a fixed price ς. If the market for permits is competitive, a particular firm j minimizes pollution-related costs by choosing emissions and permit purchases to minimize

$$
\begin{aligned}
TC_j &= C_j(e_j) - \zeta(\bar{e}_j - e_j) + \sigma \bar{e}_j \\
&= C_j(e_j) + (\sigma - \zeta)\bar{e}_j + \zeta e_j,
\end{aligned}
\tag{4.21}
$$

where as usual $C_j(\cdot)$ is the abatement cost function, $\bar{e}_j$ is the amount of permits bought by firm j, and σ is the permit price. The regulator sets L and ς based on the information she receives from the firms about their abatement costs. In particular, the regulator asks the firms to submit their marginal abatement cost curves and then each firm reports a curve $-\tilde{C}'_j(e_j)$, which may or may not be equal to its true cost curve. The reports from all firms in the industry are used to estimate the aggregate marginal abatement cost function $-\tilde{C}'(E)$, which the regulator then uses to set the policy parameters L and ς according to the rule

$$
D'(L) = -\tilde{C}'(L) = \zeta.
\tag{4.22}
$$

The combination of a permit market and subsidy so structured will lead firms to report their true cost function such that $-\tilde{C}'_j(e_j) = -C'_j(e_j)$, as long as firms believe that all their counterparts will also truthfully report. This allows the regulator to choose the socially optimal permit and subsidy levels $L = E^*$ and ς^*, respectively.

Showing that this is the case is relatively straightforward. First, observe that if all the firms report truthfully, we have $D'(L) = \sigma = \varsigma = -C'(L)$ and a typical firm's objective function is $C_j(e_j) + \varsigma e_j = C_j(e_j) + D'(L)$. Now assume that firms deviate from truth telling, resulting in a permit price $\sigma > \varsigma$. Then there is no advantage to bidding for extra permits, since the cost of doing so exceeds the revenue from returning them unused. So $e_j = \bar{e}_j$ for all firms, the cost minimization problem in (4.21) implies that firm j chooses emissions such that $-C'_j(e_j) = \sigma$, and aggregate behavior leads to $-C'(L) = \sigma$. If instead $\sigma = \varsigma$, Eq. (4.21) reduces to

$$TC_j = C_j(e_j) + \varsigma e_j, \tag{4.23}$$

and individual and aggregate firm behavior implies $-C'_j(e_j) = \varsigma = -C'(L)$. Finally, the case where $\sigma < \varsigma$ cannot exist in equilibrium, since the demand for permits is infinite when such arbitrage profits are available, causing the price of permits to rise to $\sigma = \varsigma$. These three cases imply that the equilibrium pollution permit price under policy parameters (L, ς) is $\sigma = \max\{\varsigma, -C'(L)\}$. Since the regulator has chosen $\varsigma = D'(L)$, we can further note that

$$\sigma = \max\{D'(L), -C'(L)\}. \tag{4.24}$$

Thus firms face a price determined by their true abatement cost functions and the damage function, and they know this to be the case when announcing their cost type to the regulator.

To close the argument, consider now the social optimum $L = E^*$ defined, as always, by $-C'(E^*) = D'(E^*)$. Note that for any permit level $L < E^*$ or $L > E^*$, (4.24) implies the permit price σ will be *higher* than for $L = E^*$. This follows formally from the assumptions $D''(\cdot) > 0$ and $-C''(\cdot) < 0$, but it is most easily seen by inspecting any of the figures shown above that contain $C'(\cdot)$, $D'(\cdot)$, and E^* (e.g. Figure 4.1 Panel A). Because firms' pollution-related costs are an increasing function of σ, costs will be at a minimum when $\sigma = D'(E^*)$. Thus under the assumptions of the model, firms can do no better than to reveal their true abatement cost type to the regulator, so the mechanism is incentive compatible. More to the point, the regulator can achieve an ex post optimal level of pollution without knowing firms' abatement cost functions ex ante.

A drawback of Kwerel's mechanism is that it implements truth telling only in Nash equilibrium, when other equilibria are possible. Suppose for instance that there are two firms and one over-reports its costs. Then it will be optimal for the other firm to under-report its costs in such a way that the aggregate marginal abatement cost curve from reporting, coincides with the true marginal abatement cost curve. Also, as Montero (2008) points out, Kwerel's mechanism only works when permits are auctioned to the firms, and not when they are allocated for free.

4.3.2 Montero's Mechanism

In more recent research, Montero (2008) proposes a mechanism that is more general than Kwerel's, and as such is applicable in a wider range of settings, including when the pollution permit market is not perfectly competitive. In his model the regulator first auctions off a fixed number of permits based on firms' self-reported abatement cost functions, and then she reimburses firms a fraction of the revenue. The auction rules assure that the outcome – i.e. the number of permits made available – is ex post efficient. Furthermore, firms pay a net amount that is equal to their contribution to pollution damages; in this sense it is also ex post equitable from a polluter pays perspective. The combination of generality, efficiency and equity properties, and ease of implementation, makes this mechanism deserving of further study.

For intuition, we first consider the case of a single firm with abatement cost function $C(E)$, where we have dropped subscripts since the single firm is equivalent to the industry. To implement the policy, the regulator informs the firm about the following steps, which are then executed:

(a) The firm submits a marginal abatement cost schedule $-\tilde{C}'(E)$, which in general need not be its true cost structure.
(b) The regulator sells L permits at a price of σ, where L and σ are determined by $-\tilde{C}'(L) = D'(L) = \sigma$. The firm pays the regulator $\sigma \cdot L$ and receives L pollution permits.
(c) The firm receives a fraction of the auction revenues $\beta(L)$, so that an amount $\beta(L) \cdot \sigma \cdot L$ is returned after the auction.

Under these rules the firm decides what form of marginal abatement cost schedule to submit in order to minimize total pollution-related costs, which are

$$TC = C(L) + \sigma L - \beta(L) \cdot \sigma \cdot L. \tag{4.25}$$

Note that the last term in the total cost expression is the revenue returned following the permit auction, and that if we substitute out $\sigma = D'(L)$ based on the mechanism rules, the firm's objective function is

$$\min_{L} C(L) + D'(L) \cdot L - \beta(L) \cdot D'(L) \cdot L. \tag{4.26}$$

Differentiating (4.26) with respect to L leads to the first-order condition

$$\begin{aligned} &C'(L) + D'(L) + D''(L) \cdot L \\ &\quad - \beta'(L) \cdot D'(L) \cdot L - \beta(L) \cdot \left[D''(L) \cdot L + D'(L) \right] = 0. \end{aligned} \tag{4.27}$$

Denote the solution to the costs minimization problem by $\tilde{L}$, and the firm's marginal abatement cost at this level of pollution by $-C'(\tilde{L})$. The firm announces a marginal abatement cost schedule that runs through $-C'(\tilde{L})$.

The regulator's task is to announce $\beta(L)$ in a way that makes the condition in (4.27) match the condition for a social optimum, which is defined as the level of L that makes $C'(L) + D'(L) = 0$. For this, $\beta(L)$ needs to be set so that it satisfies

$$\beta'(L) + \beta(L) \frac{D''(L) \cdot L + D'(L)}{D'(L) \cdot L} = \frac{D''(L)}{D'(L)}, \tag{4.28}$$

since this is the condition that needs to hold if we want (4.27) to collapse to $C'(L)+D'(L)=0$. Equation (4.28) can be viewed as a differential equation in L, which we can solve for $\beta(L)$ to obtain the correct payback function. The solution is (see Montero, p.515)

$$\beta(L) = 1 - \frac{D(L)}{D'(L)\cdot L}, \tag{4.29}$$

which lies in the unit interval by the weak convexity of the damage function. If we substitute (4.29) into (4.26), we see that the firm's pollution-related total cost function is $C(L)+D(L)$, which matches the regulator's objective function. This form of $\beta(L)$ will therefore induce the firm to set its emissions to the social optimum, and announce a marginal abatement cost schedule in the auction-relevant range that allows it to do so. Furthermore, the firm bears both the cost of pollution abatement, and the damages from any remaining emissions.

Examination of the range of values that β might take in special cases helps to further clarify the mechanism. Note that when the damage function is linear (i.e. $D(E)=d\cdot E$) it is optimal for the regulator to set $\beta=0$. In this case the mechanism is effectively an emissions tax set at the constant marginal damage level, which from our previous analysis in section 4.1 we know to be optimal regardless of the abatement cost function. More generally, it will be optimal for the regulator to keep a proportion, but not all, of the revenue she raises through the auction. For a quadratic damage function $D(E)=\delta E^2/2$, for instance, it is easy to verify that (4.29) implies $\beta(E)=0.5$, irrespective of the resulting emission level.

To see why it may pay off for a firm to over- or under-report its true (marginal) abatement costs when the refunding rule is not chosen optimally, we examine two non-optimal refunding levels: full refunding ($\beta=1$) and non-refunding ($\beta=0$). Figure 4.7 illustrates these situations. Panel A displays the case in which $\beta=1$. If the firm truthfully reveals its marginal abatement cost curve to be $-C'(E)$, the regulator issues L^* permits at a price of σ^*. The firm pays area $a+b$ in abatement costs, and the permit expenditures $\sigma^*\cdot L^*$ are fully paid back to the firm. If instead the firm reports its marginal abatement cost curve to be $-\tilde{C}'(E)$, the regulator auctions $\tilde{L}$ permits at a price of $\tilde{\sigma}$. The firm now pays only area a in abatement costs (based on its true cost function), and once again expenditures on permits are fully refunded. Thus, when auction revenues are fully refunded, the firm spends less on regulatory compliance when it exaggerates its abatement costs. The opposite case for $\beta=0$ is shown in panel B. If the firm truthfully reports its abatement cost function, the regulator auctions L^* permits at a price of σ^*. The firm pays area $c+d$ in abatement costs, and spends $e+f+g+i+j+k+l$ to purchase permits, none of which is refunded. If instead the firm reports $-\tilde{C}'(E)$, the regulator sets policy parameters $\tilde{L}$ and $\tilde{\sigma}$. Abatement expenditures based on the actual cost curve are now the larger area $c+d+e+f+g+h$, but the payment for permits falls to area $k+l$. So long as $j+i>h$, the firm pays less in pollution-related costs if it under-reports its abatement cost structure. These two extreme cases echo Kwerel's intuition about firms' incentives under pure price and quantity instruments, and help to illustrate why it is optimal for the regulator to balance the misreporting incentives by refunding some, but not all, of the auction revenue.

Montero's mechanism for multiple firms proceeds similarly to the single firm case. The regulator informs the firms about the auction rules, and then the following steps are taken.

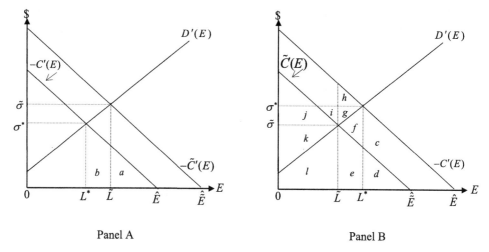

Panel A   Panel B

Figure 4.7   Montero Mechanism with $\beta=0$ or $\beta=1$

(a) Each firm j submits a marginal abatement cost schedule $-\tilde{C}'_j(e_j)$.

(b) For each firm j, the regulator sums the collection of submissions $\{-\tilde{C}'_k(e_k)\forall k \neq j\}$ to obtain $-\tilde{C}'_{-j}(E_{-j})$, which is the aggregate marginal abatement cost function absent firm j, where $E_{-j} = \sum_{k \neq j} e_k$.

(c) For each firm j, the regulator uses $-\tilde{C}'_{-j}(E_{-j})$ to compute a residual marginal damage function for firm j, defined as

$$D'_j(e_j) = D'(E) - \tilde{C}'_{-j}(E_{-j}).\tag{4.30}$$

(d) The regulator clears the auction for each firm by determining the number of permits l_j and the price σ_j for each bidder according to the rule

$$-\tilde{C}'_j(l_j) = D'_j(l_j) = \sigma_j.\tag{4.31}$$

Firm j spends $\sigma_j \cdot l_j$ and receives l_j pollution permits.

(e) Each firm j receives back a fraction of its expenditure on permits according to the rule

$$\beta_j(l_j) = 1 - \frac{D_j(l_j)}{D'_j(l_j) \cdot l_j},\tag{4.32}$$

where $D_j(l_j)$ is the integral of $D'_j(l)$ between 0 and l_j. The firm receives a rebate of $\beta_j \cdot \sigma_j \cdot l_j$.

Montero shows that submitting the true marginal abatement cost curve is incentive compatible in dominant strategies – i.e. firms will find it optimal to submit their true marginal abatement cost function regardless of what other firms do. Showing this analytically involves replacing $D'(L)$ in the single firm case with $D'_j(l_j)$ for each firm in the general case, so that the objective function for firm j is

$$\min_{l_j}\left\{C_j(l_j)+D'_j(l_j)\cdot l_j-\beta_j(l_j)\cdot D'_j(l_j)\cdot l_j\right\}. \tag{4.33}$$

It follows analogously from the single firm derivation that plugging (4.32) into (4.33) results in total pollution-related costs of $C_j(l_j)+D_j(l_j)$, and the firm will announce its marginal abatement cost function based on the condition $-C'_j(l_j)=D'_j(l_j)$. The rules of the mechanism therefore result in each firm's behavior being determined by

$$-\tilde{C}'_j(l_j)=-C'_j(l_j)=D'_j(l_j)=\sigma_j. \tag{4.34}$$

Montero (p.504) explains this condition as "basically informing the firm that, whatever (abatement cost function) it chooses to submit to the regulator, that report, together with the other firms, will be used efficiently." Importantly, Eq. (4.34) suggests it is optimal for firm j to reveal its true cost function, regardless of what other firms do. If other firms for some reason misrepresent their costs, $D'_j(\cdot)$ will be incorrect from an efficiency perspective, but firm j can still do no better than to announce its costs according to (4.34). The mechanism therefore eliminates the role of expectations of other firms' actions, and knowledge of competitors' cost structures, in the decisions of any single firm.

Figure 4.8 illustrates the mechanism and the efficiency consequences of its truth-telling property. The curves $-C'(E)$ and $-C'_{-j}(E_{-j})$ show the industry marginal abatement cost curves with and without firm j, respectively. Note that E is the efficient pollution level and σ is the corresponding efficient price, based on the intersection

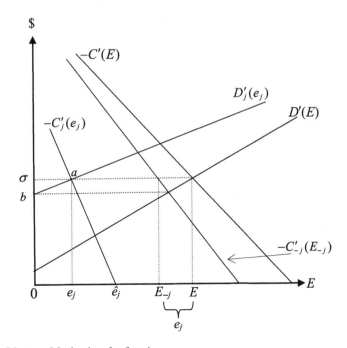

Figure 4.8 Montero Mechanism for firm j

of $-C'(E)$ and $D'(E)$. When $D'_j(e_j)$ is the true contribution by firm j to marginal damages and $-C'_j(e_j)$ is its true marginal abatement cost curve, the two curves by construction must intersect at σ, and all firms face the same permit price in the regulator's auction. In this example, firm j emits e_j units and, based on its pre-regulation emission level $\hat{e}_j$, the firm abates $\hat{e}_j - e_j$ units. Thus the firm bears abatement costs traced out by the points $e_j a \hat{e}_j$, and at the auction pays the area $\sigma a e_j 0$ in permit costs. The reimbursement mechanism, however, implies that firm j receives a refund that results in its total regulation-related expenditures given by the area $b a \hat{e}_j 0$. This is just equal to the sum of the firm's abatement costs, and its contributions to total damages.

4.3.3 Second-Best Mechanism Design

The mechanism described in the previous subsection was compelling for two reasons. First, the optimal allocation could always be implemented in dominant strategies. Second, the regulator did not need information on the range of cost structures among firms in the industry, and so did not need to form prior beliefs on the distribution of technologies. This is noteworthy, in that mechanism design often needs to exploit this type of information, yet only arrives at second-best solutions. It turns out that Montero's mechanism obtains the first-best due to the absence of any fiscal constraints. Specifically, an optimal proportion of the auction revenues is distributed back to firms, which assumes the regulator is authorized to freely use the revenue as part of her policy design. Matters may be different if there is a positive marginal cost of public funds (a topic we address in detail in Chapter 7) or if the environmental policy must be revenue neutral, in the sense that fees collected and subsidies given must balance. In this subsection we examine a special case that illustrates how, given a positive marginal cost of public funds, a second-best incentive scheme can be designed under information asymmetry, which exploits firms' incentive compatibility and participation constraints.

We begin by defining the marginal cost of public funds by λ. This measures the welfare cost of raising one dollar via distortionary taxation elsewhere in the economy – perhaps via labor or consumption taxes. Public funds obtained from environmental policy create the possibility of a tax swap, whereby revenue raised via distortionary taxation could be replaced with revenue obtained by taxing emissions. For example, taxing J firms' emissions at the constant rate of τ produces $\tau \sum_{j=1}^{J} e_j$ in new revenue and, assuming the same amount of distortionary taxation is reduced, an additional welfare gain of $\lambda \cdot \tau \sum_{j=1}^{J} e_j$. In what follows, we consider the optimal second-best mechanism under asymmetric information, when there is the possibility of using the environmental revenue in a welfare-improving tax swap.

Our objective is to characterize a menu of choices consisting of a total fee and emission level, which is presented to the polluting firms, and which maximizes welfare from reducing pollution and raising revenue. In selecting the fee level, the regulator needs to be cognizant of the firm's option to shut down, which would result in no revenue and inefficiently high abatement. To accommodate this aspect, we define the payoff to a firm operating in the industry by B. In addition, we assume there are two types of firms with abatement costs $C(e, s_L)$ and $C(e, s_H)$, where L and H denote low and high cost types, respectively, and s_L and s_H are firm specific factors. We assume that $C(e, s_L) < C(e, s_H)$ and $-C_e(e, s_L) < -C_e(e, s_H)$. That is, type L has lower abatement and marginal abatement costs, for a given level of emissions. Finally, among the J firms in the industry, a fraction χ are low cost types, and a fraction $(1-\chi)$ are high cost types, so that there are $K = \chi \cdot J$ low cost and $J - K$ high cost firms operating. This distribution of types is common knowledge, while a firm's individual type is only known by the firm.

The regulator's objective is to maximize net welfare based on firms' operating payoffs and abatement costs, the pollution damages, and the possibility of a tax swap. Specifically, the objective function is

$$
\begin{aligned}
W = J \cdot B + \lambda \cdot \left(K \cdot T_L + (J - K) \cdot T_H \right) \\
- K \cdot C(e_L, s_L) - (J - K) \cdot C(e_H, s_H) - D\left(K \cdot e_L + (J - K) \cdot e_H \right),
\end{aligned}
\tag{4.35}
$$

where T_L and T_H are the low and high type fees, respectively. The regulator selects e_L, e_H, T_L, and T_H to maximize welfare by offering a menu of choices $\{(e_L, T_L), (e_H, T_H)\}$, where the L and H pairs are designed so as to be selected by the low and high cost firms, respectively. To make sure this occurs, the regulator sets the menu so that the following *incentive compatibility constraints* are satisfied:

$$
\begin{aligned}
B - C(e_L, s_L) - T_L &\geq B - C(e_H, s_L) - T_H \\
B - C(e_H, s_H) - T_H &\geq B - C(e_L, s_H) - T_L,
\end{aligned}
\tag{4.36}
$$

or equivalently

$$
\begin{aligned}
C(e_L, s_L) + T_L &\leq C(e_H, s_L) + T_H \\
C(e_H, s_H) + T_H &\leq C(e_L, s_H) + T_L.
\end{aligned}
\tag{4.37}
$$

That is, the low cost type will never find it optimal to select the high cost type menu, and vice versa.

In addition, assuming that a first best, full information solution would involve positive emissions from both types of firms, the fees T_L and T_H need to be set so as to make sure both types of firms continue to operate. For this, the following *participation constraints* must be satisfied:

$$
\begin{aligned}
B - C(e_L, s_L) - T_L &\geq 0 \\
B - C(e_H, s_H) - T_H &\geq 0.
\end{aligned}
\tag{4.38}
$$

Under asymmetric information about the firms' abatement costs, the regulator maximizes (4.35) subject to the incentive compatibility constraints in (4.37) and the participation constraints in (4.38).

It is common in problems of this type that only one of the participation constraints and one of the incentive constraints are binding, and showing this in our context helps to simplify the regulator's problem. For example, consider the following inequality chain

$$B - C(e_L, s_L) - T_L \geq B - C(e_H, s_L) - T_H > B - C(e_H, s_H) - T_H \geq 0, \qquad (4.39)$$

where the first inequality follows from the low cost firm's incentive constraint (4.37), and the second (strict) inequality follows from the assumption that a higher parameter s causes a higher cost, for a given emission level. The last inequality is simply the high cost firm's participation constraint from (4.38). Note that this last inequality must in fact bind as an equality, since if it did not, the regulator could increase T_H without affecting participation, and thereby increase welfare through a larger tax swap. A similar argument implies that the low cost firm's incentive constraint – the first inequality in (4.39) – must also bind at zero. If it did not, the regulator could increase the low cost firm's fee T_H, and thus raise more fee revenues. With this we can rewrite (4.39) as

$$B - C(e_L, s_L) - T_L = B - C(e_H, s_L) - T_H > B - C(e_H, s_H) - T_H = 0, \qquad (4.40)$$

which implies

$$B - C(e_L, s_L) - T_L > 0. \qquad (4.41)$$

That is, the low cost firm's participation constraint is non-binding.

One can also show that the high cost firm's incentive constraint in (4.37) is always satisfied, if the low cost firm's constraint is binding. In particular, note that

$$
\begin{aligned}
&C(e_H, s_H) + T_H \\
&= C(e_H, s_H) + T_L + C(e_L, s_L) - C(e_H, s_L) + C(e_L, s_H) - C(e_L, s_H) \\
&= C(e_L, s_H) + T_L + \left[C(e_L, s_L) - C(e_H, s_L) \right] - \left[C(e_L, s_H) - C(e_H, s_H) \right] \\
&\leq C(e_L, s_H) + T_L.
\end{aligned}
\qquad (4.42)
$$

The first equality holds by adding and subtracting $C(e_L, s_H)$, and substituting out the expression $T_H = T_L + C(e_L, s_L) - C(e_H, s_L)$, where the latter holds since we have asserted that the first expression in (4.37) is binding. The second equality comes from rearranging terms. The two terms in brackets are the abatement cost differences from moving from low to high emissions, for low and high cost types, respectively. Since we have assumed that $-C_e(e, s_L) < -C_e(e, s_H)$, the difference between the terms in brackets must be non-positive, and negative for $e_L < e_H$.

With the constraint set so reduced, we can simply restate the regulator's welfare maximization problem as follows:

$$\max_{e_L, e_H, T_L, T_H} \left\{ \begin{aligned} &J \cdot B + \lambda \cdot \left(K \cdot T_L + (J - K) \cdot T_H \right) \\ &-K \cdot C(e_L, s_L) - (J - K) \cdot C(e_H, s_H) - D\left(K \cdot e_L + (J - K) \cdot e_H \right) \end{aligned} \right\}, \qquad (4.43)$$

subject to the constraints

$$B - C(e_H, s_H) = T_H \tag{4.44}$$
$$C(e_L, s_L) + T_L = C(e_H, s_L) + T_H.$$

The solutions to this problem, derived in appendix B, are characterized by

$$-C_e(e_L^{sb}, s_L) = \frac{D'(E^{sb})}{1 + \lambda} \tag{4.45}$$

and

$$-C_e(e_H^{sb}, s_H) = \frac{D'(E^{sb}) - \dfrac{K}{(J-K)} C_e(e_H^{sb}, s_L)}{1 + \dfrac{K}{(J-K)} \lambda}, \tag{4.46}$$

where sb denotes "second best," and $E^{eb} = K \cdot e_L^{sb} + (J - K) \cdot e_L^{sb}$ is the aggregate emission level. In addition, we show in appendix B that $e_L^{sb} \le e_H^{sb}$.

Two things are noteworthy about this second-best optimal solution. First, it is apparent that our well-established efficiency rule requiring marginal abatement costs to be equal across polluters is violated. Likewise, marginal abatement costs do not equal marginal damage. Instead, the second-best optimal rule implies that for low cost firms, marginal abatement cost is smaller than marginal damage, meaning the firms pollute more than the first-best efficient level. For the high cost firm, by contrast, it is ambiguous whether marginal abatement cost is larger or smaller than marginal damage.

EXAMPLE 4.2 (NUMERICAL/ANALYTICAL) Consider a situation with two firms, with abatement costs $C(e, s_j) = 0.5 \cdot (s_j - e)^2$, for $j = L, H$, with damage function $D(E) = d \cdot E$. We set $s_L = 12$, $s_H = 15$, $B = 80$, $d = 6$, and $\lambda = 0,25$. The first-best allocation requires $-C_e(e, s_j) = (s_j - e) = d$, implying the first-best solutions $e_L^* = 6$ and $e_H^* = 9$. Substituting $-C_e(e_L^{sb}, s_L) = (s_L - e_L^{sb})$, $\quad -C_e(e_H^{sb}, s_H) = (s_H - e_H^{sb})$, and $\quad -C_e(e_L^{sb}, s_H) = (s_H - e_L^{sb})$ and the parameter values into (4.45) and (4.46), we obtain $e_L^{sb} = 7$, and $e_H^{sb} = 10.5$. With these we can compute the abatement costs $C(e_L^{sb}, s_L) = 0.5 \cdot (12 - 7)^2 = 12.5$ and $C(e_H^{sb}, s_H) = 0.5 \cdot (15 - 10.5)^2 = 10.125$. This allows us to solve for the fee structures using $T_H = B - C(e_H^{sb}, s_H) = (80 - 10.125) = 69.875$, and $T_L = T_H + C(e_H^{sb}, s_L) - C(e_L^{sb}, s_L) = (69.875 + 1.125 - 12.5) = 58.5$. With these computations, total welfare is 58.05. As a comparison, one can show that the second-best optimal linear tax (taking into account the marginal costs of public funds) is $\tau^{sb} = 6.21 > d$, meaning we over-internalize the externality for fiscal reasons. With this second-best linear tax total welfare is 52.06. When the linear tax is set to its Pigouvian level, total welfare is 52.0.

We applied second-best mechanism design[2] to a situation when there is a positive marginal cost of public funds, but there are other situations where these techniques apply.

---

[2] For simplicity we restricted the analysis to the case of two types only. Generalization to a finite number of types is straightforward. For a continuum of types, more advanced techniques such as the calculus of variations are needed.

For example, if there is a budget constraint such that transfer payments between different types of firms must be balanced, or if budget balancing transfer payments must be made between different countries to implement international environmental agreements, the techniques of mechanism design are useful. We explore these additional contexts in exercises 4.13 and 4.14.

4.4   SUMMARY

Our objective in this chapter has been to introduce uncertainty in abatement cost and damage functions, and examine how this generalization changes the efficiency properties of the policy instruments introduced in Chapter 3. By limiting attention to a specific type of uncertainty – the regulator's inability to fully observe the damage function and/ or firms' private abatement cost functions – three fairly robust conclusions emerge.

First, the ex post efficiency properties of emission taxes and marketable permits generally diverge when uncertainty is introduced. This is in contrast to the certainty case, for which the full menu of economic incentive approaches provided similarly efficient outcomes, and varied only in their distributional impacts. The specifics of how taxes and permits (i.e. price and quantities) diverge under uncertainty have been well established in the four decades since Weitzman's (1974) article. When the uncertainty in the damage function and the cost function are uncorrelated it is the case that:

- damage function uncertainty does not affect the relative performance of price versus quantity instruments, and
- abatement cost function uncertainty affects the relative performance based on the fact that ex post pollution levels will differ under price and quantity instruments due to the unknown position of the aggregate marginal abatement cost curve.

The preferred instrument under the latter type of uncertainty depends systematically on the curvature properties of the aggregate damage and abatement cost functions:

- a flat marginal damage curve relative to the marginal abatement cost favors a tax instrument, while
- a steep marginal damage curve favors a permit instrument, all else being equal.

Using linear approximations for the damage and abatement cost functions, Weitzman provides a simple formula relating the efficiency loss under both instruments to the slope parameters for the two functions, and the variance of abatement cost function. From this we learn that the efficiency loss due to uncertainty is absolutely larger when the estimates for the functions are less precise, but that relative efficiency loss between emission taxes and permits depends on the relative slopes of the marginal damage and abatement cost functions:

- If the (absolute value) of the slope of the marginal abatement cost curve is greater than the (absolute value) of the slope of the marginal damage curve, a tax approach minimizes the ex post welfare loss.

- If the opposite holds – i.e. the magnitude of the slope of the marginal damage function is greater – a permit approach is preferred.

A defining characteristic of the Weitzman theorem and related research is that ex post inefficiency remains regardless of whether the correct price or quantity instrument is chosen ex ante. Thus related research has examined the potential for hybrid instruments that mix elements of price and quantity controls to improve on the performance of either alone.

Our second major conclusion regarding uncertainty emerges from our review of Spence and Roberts' 1976 hybrid policy proposal, and subsequent research. Specifically, combining a permit trading scheme with floor/ceiling limits (i.e. safety valves) on the permit price guards against the extreme consequences of a poorly estimated marginal abatement cost function. If abatement costs are higher than expected by the regulator, firms can pay an emission fee to obtain pollution rights beyond the initial permit distribution. If abatement costs are lower than expected, the regulator can secure additional pollution reduction through an effective buy-back of permits. In either case, the efficiency loss is smaller than would occur under a permit or tax only approach. More generally, the ex post efficiency loss can be made arbitrarily small if a flexible system of permit supply can be used to provide price incentives that trace out the marginal damage curve.

Finally, our examination of mechanism design suggests that environmental policy can be formulated in a way that leads to ex post efficiency (as opposed to minimized efficiency loss) if polluting firms have an incentive to truthfully reveal their abatement cost structure to the regulator. Montero's (2008) mechanism is the best example of how a specific set of pollution permit auction rules – in his case payment combined with partial reimbursement – can be used to obtain the first-best pollution outcome under fairly general circumstances, and with favorable equity and institutional features. Obtainment of this first-best result requires that the regulator ignores any fiscal constraints. If fiscal constraints are a concern, and if she is imperfectly informed about the individual firms' abatement costs, the logic of mechanism design incorporating participation and incentive constraints is useful for providing incentives to polluters to reveal their costs, by picking the "right" emission and fee levels, offered in a non-linear emission/fee schedule.

4.5 FURTHER READING

Our discussion in this chapter has followed fairly carefully the original articles on this topic. In the prices versus quantities discussion, our analytical approach is drawn primarily from Weitzman (1974), though our graphical analysis has been motivated by Adar and Griffin (1976). The undergraduate textbook from Keohane and Olmstead (2007) contains a clear verbal description on the policy ramifications of the Weitzman result. The research agenda launched by the original prices versus quantities analysis has focused on examining how specific features of policy design that were left out of the base model, may interact with abatement cost and damage function uncertainty to alter the original conclusions. A non-exhaustive list of specific areas that have been examined include correlated uncertainty (Stavins, 1996), modeling a stock externality (Newell and Pizer, 2003), and dealing with imperfect enforcement (Montero, 2002b). For a survey of more recent research on prices versus quantities see Requate (2013).

Our discussion of hybrid policies draws on many sources, but it is fundamentally based on Roberts and Spence (1976) and extensions thereof. Montero's (2008) discussion of mechanism design as related to environmental economics, drawing on ideas suggested by Kwerel (1977) and also showing their limitations, is particularly useful, and we have borrowed heavily from his original analysis in explaining his models. We also refer the reader to Dasgupta, Hammond and Maskin (1980), who discuss conditions and general features of second-best optimal mechanisms as applied to environmental problems. In addition, there are several papers applying mechanisms to specific environmental regulation problems. Examples include Lewis (1996), Clemenz (1999), and Sheriff (2008), who draws on the seminal (non-environmental) paper on regulation by Baron and Myerson (1982). Finally, Prasenjit and Shogren (2012) examine mechanism design in the context of land conservation.

APPENDIX A: DERIVATION OF WEITZMAN THEOREM RESULT

Recall from (4.15) that

$$
\begin{aligned}
K_1 &= EV\left[-C_E(\tilde{E}, \varepsilon)\right] \\
\Delta_1 &= EV\left[D_E(\tilde{E}, \eta)\right],
\end{aligned}
\tag{A4.1}
$$

and that for the quantity instrument the regulator chooses $\tilde{E}$ such that

$$
EV\left[-C_E(\tilde{E}, \varepsilon)\right] = EV\left[D_E(\tilde{E}, \eta)\right],
\tag{A4.2}
$$

leading to $K_1 = \Delta_1$.

Recall that for the price instrument, firms' behavior results in their equating the marginal abatement cost curve with the tax rate such that

$$
\begin{aligned}
\tau &= -K_1 - \varepsilon - K_2(E - \tilde{E}) \\
&= -K_1 - \varepsilon - K_2\left[E(\tau, \varepsilon) - \tilde{E}\right],
\end{aligned}
\tag{A4.3}
$$

where the marginal abatement cost curve is from (4.14), and we have substituted the behavioral relationship $E = E(\tau, \varepsilon)$ into the equation. Solving for $E(\tau, \varepsilon)$ we obtain

$$
E(\tau, \varepsilon) = -\frac{K_1 + \tau + \varepsilon}{K_2} + \tilde{E}.
\tag{A4.4}
$$

Differentiating (A4.4) with respect to τ leads to

$$
E_\tau(\tau, \varepsilon) = -\frac{1}{K_2}.
\tag{A4.5}
$$

By using this expression for $E_\tau(\tau,\varepsilon)$, we can write the optimal tax rate from Eq. (4.11) as

$$\tilde{\tau} = \frac{EV\left[D_E\left(E(\tilde{\tau},\varepsilon),\eta\right)\right] \times (-1/K_2)}{-1/K_2} = EV\left[D_E\left(E(\tilde{\tau},\varepsilon),\eta\right)\right]. \tag{A4.6}$$

Furthermore, we can substitute (A4.4) into the formula for the marginal damage function in (4.14) and take expectations to simplify the expression, so that

$$\tilde{\tau} = EV\left[D_E\left(E(\tilde{\tau},\varepsilon),\eta\right)\right]$$
$$= \Delta_1 - \frac{\Delta_2}{K_2}(K_1 + \tilde{\tau}), \tag{A4.7}$$

which leads to $\tilde{\tau} = \Delta_1$.

This, along with $-K_1 = \Delta_1$, allows us to simplify (A4.4) to

$$E(\tilde{\tau},\varepsilon) = \tilde{E} - \frac{\varepsilon}{K_2}. \tag{A4.8}$$

Recall from Eq. (4.7) that the expected social cost from the quantity instrument is

$$ESC^Q(\tilde{E}) = EV\left[C(\tilde{E},\varepsilon)\right] + EV\left[D(\tilde{E},\eta)\right]$$
$$= EV\left[c(\varepsilon)\right] + EV\left[d(\eta)\right]. \tag{A4.9}$$

Likewise the expected social cost from the price instrument is

$$ESC^P = EV\left[C\left(E(\tilde{\tau},\varepsilon),\varepsilon\right)\right] + EV\left[D\left(E(\tilde{\tau},\varepsilon),\eta\right)\right]$$
$$= EV\left[c(\varepsilon) + K_1\left(\frac{-\varepsilon}{K_2}\right) + \frac{-\varepsilon^2}{K_2} + \frac{K_2}{2(K_2)^2}\varepsilon^2\right]$$
$$+ EV\left[d(\eta) + \Delta_1\left(\frac{-\varepsilon}{K_2}\right) - \frac{\eta \times \varepsilon}{K_2} + \frac{\Delta_2}{2(K_2)^2}\varepsilon^2\right] \tag{A4.10}$$
$$= EV\left[c(\varepsilon) + d(\eta)\right] - \frac{\sigma^2}{K_2} + \frac{\sigma^2}{2K_2} + \frac{\Delta_2\sigma^2}{2(K_2)^2}$$
$$= EV\left[c(\varepsilon) + d(\eta)\right] + \frac{\sigma^2(\Delta_2 - K_2)}{2(K_2)^2},$$

where the last step uses that fact that ε and η are independent so that $EV(\varepsilon \times \eta) = 0$, and $EV(\varepsilon^2) = \sigma^2$ is the variance of ε. Taking the difference $ESC^P - ESP^Q$ matches Eq. (4.17).

APPENDIX B: CHARACTERIZATION OF OPTIMAL SECOND-BEST SOLUTION

The Lagrangian for the problem is given by

$$
\begin{aligned}
L(e_L, e_H, T_L, T_H) &= J \cdot B + \lambda \cdot \left(K \cdot T_L + (J - K) \cdot T_H \right) \\
&- K \cdot C(e_L, s_L) - (J - K) \cdot C(e_H, s_H) - D\left(K \cdot e_L + (J - K) \cdot e_H \right) \\
&+ \mu_1 \left[B - C(e_H, s_H) - T_H \right] \\
&+ \mu_2 \left[C(e_L, s_L) + T_L - C(e_H, s_L) - T_H \right],
\end{aligned}
\tag{A4.11}
$$

with first-order conditions

$$
\begin{aligned}
\frac{\partial L}{\partial e_L} &= -\left(K - \mu_2 \right) C_e(e_L, s_L) - K \cdot D'(E) = 0 \\
\frac{\partial L}{\partial e_H} &= -\left(J - K + \mu_1 \right) C_e(e_H, s_H) - \mu_2 C_e(e_H, s_L) - (J - K) D'(E) = 0,
\end{aligned}
\tag{A4.12}
$$

and

$$
\begin{aligned}
\frac{\partial L}{\partial T_L} &= K\lambda + \mu_2 = 0 \quad \rightarrow \quad \mu_2 = -K\lambda \\
\frac{\partial L}{\partial T_H} &= (J - K)\lambda - \mu_1 - \mu_2 = 0 \quad \rightarrow \quad \mu_1 = J\lambda.
\end{aligned}
\tag{A4.13}
$$

We substitute (A4.13) into (A4.12) and rearrange to obtain the solution.

To show that $e_L^{sb} \leq e_H^{sb}$, we sum the two incentive constraints in (4.37) to obtain

$$
C(e_L, s_L) + C(e_H, s_H) \leq C(e_H, s_L) + C(e_L, s_H),
\tag{A4.14}
$$

or equivalently

$$
C(e_L, s_L) - C(e_H, s_L) \leq C(e_L, s_H) - C(e_H, s_H).
\tag{A4.15}
$$

Since $-C_e(e, s_H) > -C(e, s_L)$ by assumption, both sides of the inequality must be non-negative, implying $e_L \leq e_H$.

EXERCISES

4.1 * Consider a situation where the true aggregate marginal abatement cost curve is given by $-C'(E) = a - bE$, and the marginal damage function by $D'(E) = d \cdot E$. The regulator believes the marginal damage curve to be $D'(E) = \tilde{d} \cdot E$ with $\tilde{d} < d$.
   (a) Which total emission level will a benevolent but ill-informed regulator choose?
   (b) Calculate the resulting welfare loss for a tax and a permit instrument. Show that this welfare loss is independent of instrument choice.

4.2 * Consider a situation where the true aggregate marginal abatement cost curve is given by $-C'(E) = a - bE$, and the marginal damage function by $D'(E) = d \cdot E$. The regulator believes the true marginal abatement cost curve is $-C'(E) = \tilde{a} - bE$ with $\tilde{a} < a$ (alternatively $-C'(E) = a - \tilde{b}E$ with $\tilde{b} < b$).

   (a) Which total emission level will a benevolent but ill-informed regulator choose?

   (b) Calculate the resulting welfare loss for a tax and for a permit instrument. Under what conditions is the tax instrument better than the permit instrument? What is the resulting emission level under the regulator's choice?

4.3 *** Our derivation of the Weitzman theorem has proceeded by assuming that the uncertainty in the abatement cost and damage functions (ε and η, respectively) are uncorrelated. If we generalize the problem and allow $COV(\varepsilon, \eta) \neq 0$, a slightly different expression for Δ as shown in Eq. (4.17) arises. Consider the case of correlated uncertainty to:

   (a) derive an explicit expression for Δ in the general case. See Weitzman (1974), p.485, footnote 1 for guidance on how our derivation in the appendix must be modified;

   (b) describe how positive or negative correlation in damages and abatement costs augments the purely slope-based arguments from the independence case.

   Stavins (1996) argues that the type of correlation we might expect to see in many situations will lead us to favor quantity instruments, all else being equal. Summarize his arguments, and comment on the extent to which you agree.

4.4 ** Weitzman's research has motivated several subsequent papers examining how features of policy design in specific contexts interact with benefit or cost uncertainty to alter the original model's conclusions. Examples include Newell and Pizer (2003), Montero (2002b), and Quirion (2004). Consider the following for these papers:

   (a) Explain in words the generalization examined relative to Weitzman's baseline analysis, and how the modeling framework is altered to accommodate the generalization.

   (b) Explain how the conclusions regarding the regulator's appropriate choice of a quantity or price instrument are altered by the generalization.

   (c) Summarize any specific examples discussed in the papers in which the generalization is thought to matter for a particular policy or environmental issue.

4.5 * Consider a situation where the marginal damage function is known and equal to $D'(E) = d \cdot E$. The aggregate marginal abatement cost curve is given by $-C'(E) = \tilde{a} - bE$ where $\tilde{a}$ is a random variable uniformly distributed on the interval $[\underline{a}, \overline{a}]$. The regulator wants to apply the hybrid instrument with a supply of tradable permits, a tax rate as an upper valve, and a subsidy rate for nonused permits $\varsigma < \tau$ as a lower valve. Determine the optimal levels for τ, ς and L.

4.6 ** Consider a situation similar to the previous exercise. According to Roberts and Spence, the regulator can set n different levels of tradable permits $L_1 < L_2 < ... < L_n$, subsidy rates $\varsigma_1 < \varsigma_2 < ... < \varsigma_n$ and tax rates $\tau_1 < \tau_2 < ... < \tau_n$ with $\varsigma_2 = \tau_1, \varsigma_3 = \tau_2, ..., \varsigma_n = \tau_{n-1}$. Assume further that ς_1 is chosen such that it corresponds to the optimal emission price when $\tilde{a} = \underline{a}$ and τ_n corresponds to the optimal emission price when $\tilde{a} = \overline{a}$. Further let $E^*(\underline{a})$ be the optimal emission level for $\tilde{a} = \underline{a}$ and $E^*(\overline{a})$ be the optimal emission level for $\tilde{a} = \overline{a}$. Finally, assume that the regulator chooses $E^*(\underline{a}) < L_1 < L_2 < ... < L_n < E^*(\overline{a})$ as well as $\varsigma_1 < \varsigma_2 = \tau_1 < ... < \varsigma_n = \tau_{n-1} < \tau_n$ in equal distances. Calculate the maximum possible welfare loss.

4.7 ** Show that Kwerel's mechanism is not incentive compatible if the regulator allocates the permits for free. Would the firms over- or under-report their marginal abatement costs? Illustrate this graphically.

4.8 * Consider a situation with two firms that have marginal abatement cost functions $-C_1'(e_1) = a - b_1 e_1$ and $-C_2'(e_2) = a - b_2 e_2$. The marginal damage function is known and given by $D'(E) = d \cdot E$. Assume the regulator applies Kwerel's mechanism, but firm 1 reports $-\tilde{C}_1'(e_1) = (a + \varepsilon) - b_1 e_1$. Knowing this, what would be the optimal response of firm 2?

4.9 ** Consider a situation with two firms that incur marginal abatement cost functions $-C_1'(e_1) = a - b_1 e_1$ and $-C_2'(e_2) = a - b_2 e_2$. The marginal damage function is again equal to $D'(E) = d \cdot E$. Assume the regulator applies Montero's mechanism. Determine the optimal allocation and the optimal refunding shares β_1 and β_2.

4.10 ** Consider a situation with J identical firms that have marginal abatement cost functions $-C_j'(e) = a - b e_j$ for $j = 1, \ldots, J$. The marginal damage function is equal to $D'(E) = d \cdot E$. Determine the optimal allocation and the optimal refunding shares $\beta(J)$ of the Montero mechanism and the share of total refunding.

   (a) Show that both individual and total refunding decreases with J.

   (b) Show that both individual and total refunding decreases when the slope of the marginal damage function decreases.

4.11 ** Consider the Montero mechanism with two (or three) firms. Assume that two firms (or two of the three firms) form a bidding coalition. Show that the bidding coalition can do no better than submitting its joint aggregate marginal abatement cost curve.

4.12 ** Modify the problem in example 4.2 by considering an increasing marginal damage function of type $D(E) = dE^2 / 2$.

   (a) Modify the example by assuming that there are K firms of type L and $J - K$ firms of type H.

   (b) Assume now that there are three types of firm with a number K of type L firms, a number N of type M (medium cost) firms, and $J - K - N$ firms of type H, with $s_L < s_M < s_H$. Derive the second-best optimal emission and fee scheme.

   Hint: Show that only the participation constraint of the H-type firm is binding, and that for both the L-type and the M-type firm only one of the incentive constraints is binding. Which one is it?

4.13 *** Consider a regulator's objective formulized as:

$$\max_{e_L, e_H, T_L, T_H} \left\{ JB - K \cdot C(e_L, s_L) - (J - K) \cdot C(e_H, s_H) - D\left(K e_L + (J - K) e_H\right) \right\},$$

subject to the balanced budget constraint

$$K T_L + (J - K) T_H = 0.$$

   (a) Show that at most one of the four constraints (incentive compatibility and participation) can be binding in this case, that the high cost firm's fee is always positive, and, therefore, that the low cost firm's participation constraint is always satisfied (since it receives additional money from the high cost firm).

(b) Derive the optimality conditions for the different cases where either one of the incentive constraints, or the H-type firm's participation constraint, is binding.

(c) Describe a numerical example for each of the three cases.

4.14 *** Consider a situation with two countries that have abatement cost functions

$$C(e, s_j) = 0.5 \cdot (s_j - e)^2$$

for $j = L$ and $j = H$. The countries have identical damage functions $D(E) = d \cdot E$. For each country the parameters s_j are drawn independently from an identical Bernoulli distribution, with probabilities π_L and $(1 - \pi_L)$ for high and low values of s, respectively. The countries do not know each other's abatement cost parameters. Derive the ex ante, second-best optimal contract, such that both countries would agree on the contract. Possible transfer payments between countries must sum to zero. How must the mechanism be modified when $D(E) = 0.5 \cdot d \cdot E^2$?

CHAPTER 5

Competitive Output Markets

Thus far in Part II of the book we have not explicitly considered output markets in our analysis of environmental policy. This simplification has allowed us to derive several useful results based only on firms' abatement cost functions and the social damage function. In general, however, firms have both production costs and abatement costs, and except for "end of the pipe" type abatement technologies, these costs cannot always be separated. Moreover, for some pollutants, such as carbon dioxide emissions from fossil fuels, the only abatement possibility may be to reduce output. To analyze these types of cases, we need a richer model that explicitly accounts for the output market. In this chapter we focus on competitive output markets, and examine whether the results derived so far hold only for the separable case, or if they are indeed general.

In addition to accounting for a larger range of technologies, there are several policy motivations for considering output markets. Political debates on environmental policy often focus on distributional considerations, such as how a policy will impact output prices. Will polluting firms simply pass on higher prices to consumers? To consider this explicitly, attention needs to be given to firms' output cost structure and consumers' demand. Debate also focuses on the impact that policies may have on firms' survival, scale of operation, and employment levels. For these types of questions it is necessary to consider the long-run entry and exit behavior of firms in response to the various policy options. Since entry and exit decisions in competitive markets are driven by zero profit conditions, we need to explicitly consider profit maximization, and therefore output markets.

Furthermore, we have modeled environmental standards in a stylized way, as emission caps for firms. In reality, command and control policies often work quite differently. They may fix emissions per unit of output, or limit quantities of a particular pollutant relative to the total amount of effluent released. These kinds of *relative* or *performance* standards are historically used to regulate vehicle emissions and wastewater disposal. A contemporary example is the European Union's target of producing 20 percent of its energy from renewable sources. To model relative standards and to study their performance, we again need to explicitly account for output levels. Finally, by considering firm profits and consumer preferences for the polluting good, we can expand on the concept of abatement cost by distinguishing between engineering-based abatement costs, and the gross economic costs that arise from lost profit and consumption benefits. We show that when firms can adjust their output level, engineering costs typically overstate the real opportunity cost of pollution reduction, which in general includes both lost profit and lost utility components. Thus, an expanded view of abatement costs allows us to more clearly see the opportunity cost of pollution reduction from the perspective of society as a whole.

By limiting our attention in this chapter to competitive markets and partial equilibrium analysis, we are able to show that the results derived in Chapter 3 for a fixed number of firms continue to hold; in particular, optimal abatement policy is still characterized by the marginal abatement cost equals marginal damage rule. We also show that emission taxes, subsidies, and permits continue to be equivalent in the short run and that the optimal allocation of pollution is characterized by equality of marginal abatement costs across firms. In the long run, however, we find that there are important differences between these policies. When entry and exit are possible we find that taxes and permits can still be effective, though subsidies and standards may lead to sub-optimal outcomes through excessive entry. We also show that relative standards are inefficient in general, including when firms are identical.

5.1 MODEL EXTENSION

In this section we derive a more general statement for firms' cost structure than was used in Chapter 3, beginning with explicit definitions for firms' production and emission technologies. In describing technologies and costs we drop for the moment firm-specific subscripts, though unless otherwise stated we maintain the assumption that firms are asymmetric. Define an individual firm's production technology by $x = f(l_1,...,l_K)$, where x is a scalar denoting units of output produced using the vector of inputs $l_1,...,l_K$ and $f(\cdot)$ is a well-behaved production function. In addition, define the firm's emission technology by $e = g(l_1,...,l_K)$, where e is emissions resulting from the employment of the input vector. In general the curvature of $g(\cdot)$ is not restricted. The technologies for x and e are quite general in that the marginal product of l_k for either or both can be positive, negative, or zero. In particular, an input that reduces emissions may have no effect on output or could, in other instances, negatively or positively affect output. Likewise an input that increases x can also increase emissions, or may be emissions-neutral.

5.1.1 Cost Functions

Based on the technologies described by $f(\cdot)$ and $g(\cdot)$ we can define the firm's cost function as it depends on a given level of output and emissions. In particular, the firm's cost function $C(x,e)$ is derived from the following cost minimization problem:

$$C(x,e) = \min_{l_1,...,l_K} \left\{ \sum_{k=1}^{K} w_k l_k + \lambda \left[x - f(l_1,...,l_K) \right] + \mu \left[e - g(l_1,...,l_K) \right] \right\}, \tag{5.1}$$

where $w_1,...,w_K$ is the vector of factor input prices. For our subsequent discussion it is useful to formally state two assumptions that, in different cases, describe the structure of the cost function.

Assumption 5.1

The cost function $C(x,e)$ is twice continuously differentiable with $C_x(\cdot)>0$, and for any production level x there is an emission level $\hat{e}^x$ such that $C_e(x,\hat{e}^x)=0$. Furthermore

$$
\begin{aligned}
C_e(x,e) &< 0 \quad \forall e < \hat{e}^x \\
C_e(x,e) &\geq 0 \quad \forall e \geq \hat{e}^x,
\end{aligned}
\tag{5.2}
$$

and

$$
C_{xe}(x,e) = C_{ex}(x,e) < 0 \quad \Leftrightarrow \quad -C_{ex}(x,e) > 0, \quad \forall e < \hat{e}^x.
\tag{5.3}
$$

Finally, strict convexity holds so that $C_{xx}>0$, $C_{ee}>0$, and $C_{xx} \times C_{ee} - C_{xe}^2 > 0$.

The condition $C_x(\cdot)>0$ is the standard positive marginal cost condition, while $C_e(x,\hat{e}^x)=0$ says that for each output level x there is a cost-minimizing emission level $\hat{e}^x$ that results when the emission constraint is non-binding – i.e. when $\mu=0$ in Eq. (5.1) – due to the absence of environmental regulation. In Chapter 3 we denoted the unregulated emission level by $\hat{e}$; here $\hat{e}^x$ corresponds to the same concept, but for a specific output level. Given this, (5.2) establishes the familiar characteristics for the marginal abatement cost curve, given by $-C_e(x,e)$. In particular, moving emissions below (or above) the optimal unregulated choice for an output level x increases the firm's cost; this is to say that the marginal abatement cost is positive for the policy-relevant range of emission levels. Equation (5.3) says that marginal cost of production is smaller if the emission level is allowed to rise ($C_{xe}(\cdot)<0$) or equivalently, the marginal abatement cost function shifts up if the output level rises ($-C_{ex}(\cdot)>0$). These assumptions are fairly plausible and have intuitive economic interpretations, including the notion that the non-regulated emission level $\hat{e}^x$ rises with x. To see this, we totally differentiate $C_e(x,\hat{e}^x)=0$ to obtain $C_{ee}(x,\hat{e}^x)d\hat{e}^x + C_{ex}(x,\hat{e}^x)dx = 0$, which we can rearrange so that

$$
\frac{d\hat{e}^x}{dx} = -\frac{C_{ee}(x,\hat{e}^x)}{C_{ex}(x,\hat{e}^x)} > 0.
\tag{5.4}
$$

Throughout the chapter we will often consider production and emission technologies for which it is not possible to reduce emissions except by reducing output. In these cases the following alternative assumption about the cost function is useful.

Assumption 5.2

The cost function $C(x)$ is twice continuously differentiable satisfying $C'(\cdot)>0$ and $C''(\cdot)\geq0$, and emissions depend on x directly according to $e=\delta(x)$, where $\delta'(x)>0$. For some discussions we will use a simplification of the emissions technology in which $\delta(x)=\delta \cdot x$, for $\delta>0$.

Note that under assumption 5.2 the marginal abatement cost function is tied to the firm's profit per unit of output. If p is the output price of x the competitive firm's profit is $\Pi = px - C(x)$, and adopting the simplification that $e=\delta x$ allows us to more readily express profit as a function of emissions, so that $\Pi = p(e/\delta) - C(e/\delta)$. Differentiating with respect to e we obtain

$$\frac{d\Pi}{de} = \frac{p - C'(e/\delta)}{\delta}. \tag{5.5}$$

Since $p - C'(x) = 0$ is the condition for profit maximization with no regulation, $p - C'(\hat{e}^x/\delta) = 0$ implicitly defines the unregulated level of emissions. For $e < \hat{e}^x$ we know that $p - C'(e/\delta) > 0$, since an emission level lower than $\hat{e}^x$ implies the output level is also lower than what is privately optimal for the firm. Under assumption 5.2 the marginal abatement cost function is therefore given by (5.5), where $d\Pi/de > 0$ for $e < \hat{e}^x$. Also, since

$$\frac{d^2\Pi}{de^2} = \frac{C''(e/\delta)}{\delta^2} \geq 0, \tag{5.6}$$

we know that the marginal abatement cost curve is increasing (or at least non-decreasing) in e.

For expositional purposes we refer to the cost function when abatement is possible as Case 1 and the cost function when abatement is not possible as Case 2. The two structures are displayed visually for a single firm in Figure 5.1, where Case 1 is shown on the left two panels. The upper panel relates the total cost of production to emissions, conditional on an output level. The two curves are drawn for two different output levels x_1 and x_2, where $x_1 > x_2$. From these we can see that the unregulated level of emissions for a given output level x_k occurs at the minimum of $C(x_k, e)$, shown here as $\hat{e}^{x_k}$. Emissions smaller or larger than this level will raise the cost of producing x_k, and so at $\hat{e}^{x_k}$ the marginal abatement cost is zero. This is shown in the lower panel, where we have drawn two marginal abatement cost curves for the two output levels. From these we can see that when output increases, the marginal abatement cost curve shifts out.

Graphs for Case 2, when $e = \delta x$ (or $x = e/\delta$), are shown on the right two panels of Figure 5.1. Equation (5.5) suggests that the optimal unregulated choice of e (and hence x) when the output price is p_k is given implicitly by $p_k = C'(\hat{e}^{x_k}/\delta)$. This emission level is shown on the upper panel for two different prices p_1 and p_2, where $p_1 > p_2$. The panel also shows that when emissions are reduced by one unit from any point $e < \hat{e}^{x_k}$, output falls by $1/\delta$ units, costs fall by $C'(e/\delta)/\delta$ and the revenue loss is p_k/δ. Together, these suggest that the firm's opportunity cost of a unit reduction in pollution is the difference between lost revenue and reduced costs, which is shown in the lower panel for the two price levels by the two $d\Pi/de = [p_k - C'(e/\delta)]/\delta$ curves – i.e. the marginal abatement cost functions.

5.1.2 Market Demand

To derive households' benefits of consuming x and the damages suffered from pollution, we once again assume that preferences are quasi-linear, now of the form $U^i = u_i(x_i) + z_i - D_i(E)$. In this definition, x_i is the person's consumption level, $u_i(x_i)$ is the sub-utility function from consuming the polluting good, z_i is spending on all other

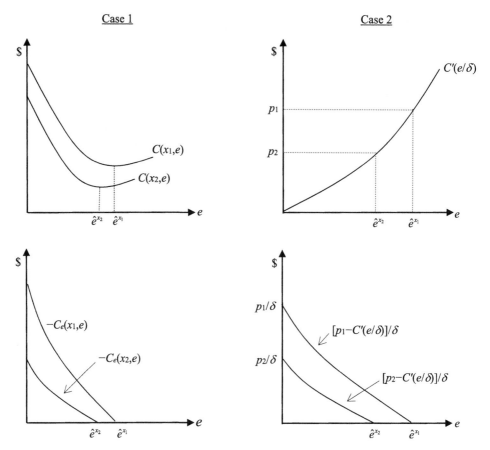

Figure 5.1 Assumptions on abatement costs

goods, and there are $i=1,\dots,I$ consumers in the economy. As in Chapter 3, the quasi-linear preference function allows us to treat $D_i(E)$ as the money-metric damages that person i suffers due to aggregate emissions E, from which we define the aggregate damage function $D(E)$ as the sum of individual $D_i(E)$ functions. Maximizing utility subject to the budget constraint $y_i = px_i + z_i$, where y_i is income and p is the price of x, results in a first-order condition for x_i that is given by $u_i'(x_i) = p$. This defines the inverse demand (marginal willingness to pay) for x function for person i as $p_i(x_i) = u_i'(x_i)$. Note from this that the money-metric gross benefit he enjoys from consuming the polluting good is

$$\int_0^{x_i} p_i(t)dt = u_i(x_i). \tag{5.7}$$

To measure the market benefits, let $X = \sum_{i=1}^{I} x_i$ be the aggregate consumption level, and define $P(X)$ as the market inverse demand curve, which is obtained by horizontally summing the individual inverse demand curves. With this, the money-metric benefit to all households from consuming the polluting good is the area under the market inverse demand function. Thus the damage function $D(E)$ and the market inverse demand function $P(X)$ allow us to fully characterize the benefits and damages to society, brought about by the production and consumption of the polluting good.

5.1.3 Welfare and Social Optimum

Given our assumptions on technology and preferences, the net benefits to society from the polluting good is the difference between the utility benefits of its consumption as reflected by the market inverse demand function, and the private and environmental costs of its production. If the firms' cost functions are given by Case 1, then the net benefits are

$$W(x_1,...,x_J,e_1,...,e_J) \equiv \int_0^{\sum x_j} P(t)dt - \sum_{j=1}^{J} C^j(x_j,e_j) - D(E), \qquad (5.8)$$

where the scripts $j=1,...,J$ index the specific firms and $E = \sum_{j=1}^{J} e_j$ is the aggregate emissions level. If the technologies are such that emissions are directly related to output as in Case 2, the net benefits are

$$W(x_1,...,x_J) \equiv \int_0^{\sum x_j} P(t)dt - \sum_{j=1}^{J} C_j(x_j) - D(E), \qquad (5.9)$$

where $E = \sum_{j=1}^{J} \delta_j(x_j)$.

Our objective in this subsection is to derive the socially optimal allocation of pollution based on (5.8) or (5.9). Specifically, we examine the social optimum in our single industry, short run, and partial equilibrium model by maximizing the net benefit functions with respect to each x_j and e_j. For Case 1, the first-order conditions for the optimum are

$$P(X) = C_{x_j}^j(x_j,e_j), \qquad (5.10)$$
$$D'(E) = -C_{e_j}^j(x_j,e_j), \quad j=1,...,J,$$

from which the solutions x_j^* and e_j^* for $j=1,...,J$ arise. There is nothing surprising about the conditions leading to these solutions. Interpreted individually, the first gives the standard microeconomic theory result that at the social optimum the marginal cost of production should be equal to the marginal benefit of consumption. The second reproduces the result from Chapter 3, confirming that for each firm the marginal abatement cost should be equal to its marginal social damage. Taken together, the expressions in (5.10) imply that both production costs and pollution damages need to be balanced against the consumption benefits of the good to achieve the social optimum. The latter point is nicely illustrated using the social net benefit function for Case 2 in (5.9). Here only the x_j's are choice variables, implying the first-order conditions are

$$P(X) = C_j'(x_j) + D'(E)\delta_j'(x_j), \quad j=1,...,J. \qquad (5.11)$$

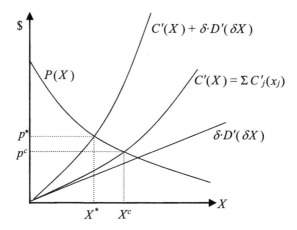

Figure 5.2   Social optimum

The left-hand side is the marginal benefit to households from an additional unit of x from firm j, and the right-hand side is the total marginal cost of an additional unit, divided into its component parts. The first term accounts for the private production costs while the second term accounts for the public pollution cost. Ignoring the pollution cost would imply overproduction by firm j.

For the special case of identical firms with linear emission functions $e = \delta x$, we can develop further intuition graphically. In this case (5.11) becomes

$$P(X) = C'(x) + \delta D'(\delta X), \tag{5.12}$$

and we can define the aggregate marginal cost curve as the horizontal summation of the individual firms' $C_j'(x)$ functions. Figure 5.2 shows the aggregate marginal cost, marginal damage, and inverse demand for X curves. From this we see that in an unregulated market, a competitive equilibrium emerges with output X^c and price p^c. However, when we account for all the social costs of X by vertically summing the marginal cost and damage functions, we see that the social optimum is given by X^* and p^*. Thus the consumption and production of the polluting good is smaller, and the price higher, than in the unregulated case.

5.2   ENVIRONMENTAL POLICY INSTRUMENTS

In this section we compare the performance of the policy instruments described in Chapter 3 using the more general model, and derive additional results specific to the output market. Our main objective is to show that, in the short run, all the earlier results continue to hold. In particular, an environmental regulator can obtain the socially optimal allocation of pollution using emission taxes, subsidies, auctioned permits, or freely distributed tradable permits. In later sections, we examine how this equivalence result breaks down when we allow firms to enter and exit the market.

5.2.1 Taxes

We first consider a competitive firm's choices when faced with an emission tax τ and abatement is possible (Case 1). In this case the profit for firm j is

$$\Pi_j(x_j, e_j) = px_j - C^j(x_j, e_j) - \tau e_j, \tag{5.13}$$

where p is the market price of x that is taken as given. The firm chooses its output and emission levels to maximize profit based on the first-order conditions

$$p = C^j_{x_j}(x_j, e_j)$$
$$\tau = -C^j_{e_j}(x_j, e_j). \tag{5.14}$$

From this, we see the familiar result that the competitive firm chooses output to set its marginal cost equal to the market price. Also, as in Chapter 3, we see that the firm chooses its emissions so that its marginal abatement cost is equal to the tax level. It is clear that if the regulator sets $\tau = D'(E^*)$, she can obtain the conditions for a socially optimal allocation of pollution shown in Eq. (5.10), so long as there is a unique market equilibrium. In this partial equilibrium context, the downward sloping demand function guarantees uniqueness.

Under Case 2 it is still the case that the optimal tax rate is set equal to the marginal damage function. In particular, the firm's profit is given by

$$\Pi_j(x_j) = px_j - C_j(x_j) - \tau\delta_j x_j, \tag{5.15}$$

and the first-order condition is $p = C'_j(x_j) - \tau\delta_j$. If we set $\tau = D'(E^*)$ and assume the competitive market clears, each firm j behaves according to

$$P(X) = C'_j(x_j) + \delta_j\tau = C'_j(x_j) + \delta_j D'(E^*), \quad j = 1, \dots, J, \tag{5.16}$$

which matches the condition in (5.11). For each firm the optimal production level equates the marginal benefit of an additional unit with the marginal cost consisting of private and external components.

This finding is displayed in Figure 5.3 for two industries with identical cost structures, but facing two different inverse demand curves. To show the intuition, we again consider the identical firm case with $e = \delta x$. In both graphs the optimal output level X^* is found at the point where the inverse demand curve intersects the social marginal cost curve, where the latter is defined as the sum of production costs and marginal damages. To reach this point the regulator defines an emission fee in the amount τ, which is equivalent to a tax rate of $\delta\tau$ per unit of output. The tax serves to shift the aggregate marginal cost curve up by an amount sufficient to land output at X^* and the price at p^*. In the two panels, the different price and quantity outcomes are determined by the different shapes of the inverse demand curves, which has ramifications for whether consumers or the industry bear the incidence of the tax.

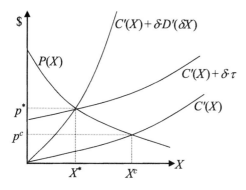 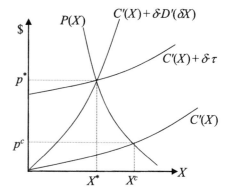

Figure 5.3 Two optimal environmental taxes

Comparative Statics

By explicitly including the output market in our model, we can now consider how an emission tax influences the endogenous variables in the model. In particular, we are interested in how the output and emission levels are affected by an increase in (or introduction of) an emission tax. To derive comparative statics for these effects we consider the situation when all firms are identical (similar results more difficultly obtained hold for asymmetric firms), beginning with the simple case where there are no abatement possibilities (Case 2). The profit maximizing condition for each of the J firms is $P(X)=C'(x)+\delta\tau$, where $X=x \cdot J$. By implicitly differentiating the profit maximization condition with respect to τ we obtain

$$\left[P'(X)\cdot J - C''(x)\right]\frac{dx}{d\tau} = \delta, \tag{5.17}$$

from which we can solve for and sign the comparative static effects as

$$\frac{dx}{d\tau} = \frac{\delta}{P'(X)\cdot J - C''(x)} < 0,$$
$$\frac{dX}{d\tau} = J\frac{dx}{d\tau} < 0, \tag{5.18}$$

since $P'(X)<0$ and $C''(x)\geq 0$. Furthermore, with $E=\delta \cdot X$ we can see that

$$\frac{dE}{d\tau} = \delta\frac{dX}{d\tau} = \frac{J\cdot\delta^2}{J\cdot P'(X)-C''(x)} < 0. \tag{5.19}$$

Finally, since $p=P(X)$ is the market price of the polluting good, we can state the relationship between the equilibrium price level and the emission tax as

$$\frac{dp}{d\tau} = P'(X)\frac{dX}{d\tau} > 0. \tag{5.20}$$

As intuition suggests, the output and emission levels decrease when an emission tax is introduced or increased, and the market price for the polluting good increases. This is not surprising since a higher tax rate raises marginal cost for firms, thereby shifting back the market supply curve and causing price to slide up and quantity down along the inverse demand curve. What is perhaps less obvious is that consumers' share of the tax incidence depends on how elastic the demand curve is. If $P'(X)$ is small in absolute magnitude (demand is elastic) the price increase will be comparatively small, and the tax incidence will be borne primarily by firms and their workers in the form of a smaller market. In contrast, if $P'(X)$ is large in absolute magnitude, demand is inelastic, and consumers have few substitutes available for the polluting good. In this case the incidence will be borne primarily by consumers in the form of higher prices, and the industry will be comparatively unaffected. The demand for an essential commodity like electricity is an example of this. Electricity demand is relatively inelastic, and so an energy tax would mainly be borne by consumers. The demand for a commodity like asbestos (for insulation) is elastic, since it has relatively inexpensive and less-polluting substitutes, and so costs are mainly shifted to the industry. Graphs of these two types of demand structures are shown in the two panels of Figure 5.3, where identical cost curves lead to different incidence burdens, based on the different shapes for the inverse demand curves.

Showing these results is slightly more complicated for Case 1. We once again assume identical firms, each of which maximizes profit according to the first-order conditions

$$P(X) = C_x(x,e)$$
$$\tau = -C_e(x,e). \tag{5.21}$$

When we implicitly differentiate both conditions with respect to τ we obtain

$$P'(X) \cdot J \cdot \frac{\partial x}{\partial \tau} = C_{xx}(x,e) \cdot \frac{\partial x}{\partial \tau} + C_{xe}(x,e) \cdot \frac{\partial e}{\partial \tau},$$
$$1 = C_{xe}(x,e) \frac{\partial x}{\partial \tau} + C_{ee}(x,e) \frac{\partial e}{\partial \tau}, \tag{5.22}$$

or in matrix form,

$$\begin{bmatrix} P'(X) \cdot J - C_{xx}(x,e) & -C_{xe}(x,e) \\ C_{xe}(x,e) & C_{ee}(q,e) \end{bmatrix} \begin{bmatrix} \partial x/\partial \tau \\ \partial e/\partial \tau \end{bmatrix} = \begin{bmatrix} 0 \\ 1 \end{bmatrix}. \tag{5.23}$$

Solving this system using Cramer's Rule results in

$$\frac{\partial x}{\partial \tau} = \frac{C_{xe}(x,e)}{-J \cdot P'(X) \cdot C_{xx}(x,e) + C_{xx}(x,e)C_{ee}(x,e) - C_{xe}^2(x,e)} < 0 \tag{5.24}$$

and

$$\frac{\partial e}{\partial \tau} = \frac{P'(X) \cdot J - C_{xx}(x,e)}{-P'(X) \cdot J \cdot C_{ee}(x,e) + C_{xx}(x,e)C_{ee}(x,e) - C_{xe}^2(x,e)} < 0. \tag{5.25}$$

Interestingly, we can see from (5.24) that a tax increase decreases output more when emissions and output are relatively more complementary. In the special case where $C_{xe}(x,e)=0$, which is unlikely to occur, output and price levels will not be affected by introducing or increasing an emission tax. From our assumptions on the cost and demand functions, the denominator in both (5.24) and (5.25) is positive and the numerators are negative. From these it follows that

$$\partial X/\partial\tau = J\cdot\partial x/\partial\tau < 0$$
$$\partial E/\partial\tau = J\cdot\partial e/\partial\tau < 0 \qquad\qquad (5.26)$$
$$\partial p/\partial\tau = P'(X)\cdot\partial X/\partial\tau > 0.$$

We summarize these results in the following proposition.

Proposition 5.1
Under the assumptions of the model, the introduction (or increase) of an emissions tax leads to:

(a) a decrease in both individual firms' and aggregate emission levels;
(b) a decrease in individual firms' and aggregate output levels; and
(c) an increase in the output price.

The incidence of the emissions tax depends of course on the relative steepness of the marginal cost and demand functions. Thus, as described above for the simple case, while the output price rises, it is not necessarily the case that the tax is completely passed on to consumers.

5.2.2 Permits and Other Instruments

Instead of charging an emissions tax the regulator could make available a number of pollution permits $L=E^*$, either by auctioning or distributing them freely to firms and allowing exchanges. If the permit market is well functioning there is a market clearing price $\sigma(L)$ for each level of permits L. If firms are permit market price takers, their profit maximizing behavior leads to identical conditions as in the emission fee case. In particular, the first-order conditions are

$$p = C^j_{x_j}(x_j, e_j)$$
$$\sigma = -C^j_{e_j}(x_j, e_j), \quad j=1,...,J. \qquad\qquad (5.27)$$

By optimally choosing the level of permits to make available, the regulator can implement the first best. Specifically, by choosing $L=E^*$ the regulator can assure the resulting permit price will be $\sigma(L)=\sigma(E^*)=D'(E^*)$, and the output price equilibrates to $p=P(X^*)$. Similarly, one can also show for the case of freely distributed permits and subsidies that properly chosen aggregate permit or subsidy levels can achieve the first-best, short run outcome (see exercise 5.4).

It is important to note that auctioned and freely distributed permits are fully equivalent here, outside of the obvious property rights differences. This means that under freely distributed permits, the output price change is equivalent to what would occur

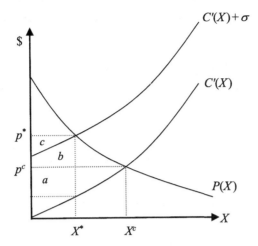

Figure 5.4 Distribution of rents in auctioned versus freely distributed permits

with auctioned permits. This subtlety can be lost in policy discussions. For example, the European Union's CO_2 trading program involved the free distribution of emission permits in the first two program phases (2005 through 2012). Politicians and competition authorities complained that permit costs were being passed on to consumers in the form of higher prices, even though the regulated industries obtained the rights for free. Our model suggests that this argument misses the point. If emissions are limited the marginal cost of production is higher, since $C_{xe}(x,e) < 0$. If demand is not perfectly elastic, this must be reflected in a market price increase, regardless of how emission rights are distributed. A better argument would take a distributional point of view, noting that emission taxes and auctioned permits direct scarcity rents to the government, while freely distributed permits and subsidies leave these rents with the firms. For Case 2, we illustrate the effect on equilibrium price and rents under auctioned and freely distributed permits in Figure 5.4. For simplicity we assume $x = \delta e$ and $\delta = 1$, which allows us to show both emissions and output at the same scale. The Figure shows that the market price must rise when emissions are reduced; if permit (or more appropriately, abatement) costs were not passed on to consumers the output market would not be in equilibrium. The Figure also shows the scarcity rent as area $a + b + c$, which stays with the industry when permits are freely distributed, while under an auctioned permit scheme rents go to the government as auction market revenues.

EXAMPLE 5.1 (NUMERICAL/ANALYTICAL) Consider a linear inverse demand function $P(X) = A - BX$. Assume there are two firms with technologies satisfying assumption 5.2. The cost functions are $C_j(x_j) = 0.5 \cdot c_j x_j^2$ for $j = 1, 2$, where $c_1 \leq c_2$ and the emission coefficients are $\delta_1 \geq \delta_2$, such that $e_j = \delta_j x_j$. The social damage function is $D(E) = 0.5 \cdot d \cdot E^2$. Note that in this setup, firm 1 is the lower cost producer but also pollutes more intensively. The first-order conditions for a socially optimal allocation of production and emissions are

$$A - B(x_1 + x_2) = c_j x_j + \delta_j d(e_1 + e_2)$$
$$= c_j x_j + \delta_j d(\delta_1 x_1 + \delta_2 x_2), \quad j = 1, 2. \tag{5.28}$$

Solving this equation yields the following expressions for output

$$x_1 = \frac{A\left[c_2 + d(\delta_2 - \delta_1)\delta_2\right]}{c_1 c_2 + d\left(c_1 \delta_2^2 + c_2 \delta_1^2\right) + B\left[c_1 + c_2 + d(\delta_1 - \delta_2)^2\right]}$$

$$x_2 = \frac{A\left[c_1 + d(\delta_1 - \delta_2)\delta_1\right]}{c_1 c_2 + d\left(c_1 \delta_2^2 + c_2 \delta_1^2\right) + B\left[c_1 + c_2 + d(\delta_2 - \delta_1)^2\right]},$$

(5.29)

and price:

$$p = \frac{A\left[c_1 c_2 + d\left(c_1 \delta_2^2 + c_2 \delta_1^2\right)\right]}{c_1 c_2 + d\left(c_1 \delta_2^2 + c_2 \delta_1^2\right) + B\left[c_1 + c_2 + d(\delta_1 - \delta_2)^2\right]}.$$

(5.30)

Note from the expressions for output that, if d (the slope parameter for the damage function) is zero or sufficiently small, then the lower cost firm (firm 1) has the larger market share (this can be verified by setting $d = 0$). We can also see that an increase in d shifts production from the low cost (but higher polluting) firm to the higher cost (but more environmentally friendly) firm, and for d sufficiently high, firm 2 will have the higher market share at the social optimum. In Eq. (5.30), we can see the effect of the damage function slope parameter on price. Although d shows up in the numerator and the denominator of p, differentiating the formula with respect to d yields a positive expression. This is easily seen for the symmetric case $c_1 = c_2 = c$ and $\delta_1 = \delta_2 = \delta$, where

$$p = A\left[1 - \frac{B}{B + c/2 + d \cdot \delta^2}\right].$$

(5.31)

The formula for the optimal emission tax is also relatively simply to state in the symmetric case:

$$\tau^* = \frac{A \cdot d \cdot \delta}{B + c/2 + d \cdot \delta^2}.$$

(5.32)

Differentiating the tax formula with respect to d, one can see that the optimal tax rate (marginal damage) is increasing in the damage function slope parameters. Likewise, the optimal tax rate increases with higher demand, since the derivative with respect to A is positive.

Consider instead a tradable permit policy with L permits available, and assume once again that the firms are symmetric. Equilibrium in the permit market requires that $L = 2 \cdot \delta \cdot x$, since emissions for each firm are given by $e = \delta \cdot x$. This shows that each symmetric firm produces the amount $x = L/(2 \cdot \delta)$, and the industry supply is $X = 2x = L/\delta$. From the firms' profit maximizing condition we know

$$C'(x) + \sigma = P(L/\delta) \quad \rightarrow \quad c \cdot (L/2\delta) + \sigma = A - B \cdot (L/\delta),$$

(5.33)

from which we can derive the equilibrium price for emission permits σ as $\sigma = A - L \cdot [B + c/2]/\delta$, which shows that the permit price decreases when more permits are issued.

A final feature to examine is the distributional consequences of free and auctioned permits. To simplify further we assume that $c = 0$, so that $\sigma = A - B \cdot (L/\delta) = A - B \cdot X = p$. Under auctioned permits, profits are zero, since the revenue from selling a unit of the good is equal to the price of permits needed to cover its emissions. Under freely distributed permits, the firms retain the scarcity rents from the policy. A lower L reduces the supply level X, and raises the output price. Rents are maximized at $L = \delta \cdot X^m$, where X^m corresponds to the monopoly output level. Reducing permit supply such that $L < X^m$ therefore reduces the firms' rents.

EXAMPLE 5.2 (EMPIRICAL) Our comparative statics suggest that environmental regulations will decrease the level of output in the regulated industry. A number of empirical studies have sought to test this prediction, in addition to considering the response of employment to specific policies. Greenstone (2002) provides a compelling example. He examines the relationship between the 1970 and 1977 US Clean Air Act Amendments (CAAA) and manufacturing activity. A feature of the CAAA was the establishment of standards for several criterion air pollutants. Each year, individual counties are assigned attainment or non-attainment status for each criterion pollutant. Non-attainment status subjects emitters of the pollutant in the county to greater regulatory oversight, and therefore higher abatement costs. Greenstone examines how output, employment, and capital investment in manufacturing plants in non-attainment counties were affected by the designation, relative to plants in attainment counties. He uses data on nearly 1.5 million plants drawn from the five Censuses of Manufacturing taken during the period 1967 to 1987, and assigns emitter or non-emitter status to each plant for each criterion pollutant, based on industry codes. The plants' locations are merged to the more than 3,000 US counties, and through this an attainment/non-attainment status is assigned for each pollutant emitted by each plant. With these data, comparison of plant outcomes is possible across three dimensions: (a) between plants in different counties with different attainment/non-attainment assignment at a given time; (b) within plants across time, as county-level attainment/non-attainment status changes; and (c) between plants emitting different attainment/non-attainment-designated pollutants in the same county. In his main analyses, Greenstone compares changes in the growth of output, investment, and employment in the four five-year intervals that define his study period. He finds that between 1972 and 1987, non-attainment counties lost nearly 600,000 jobs, $37 billion in capital stock, and $75 billion in output in polluting industries (1987 dollars), relative to attainment counties. These findings match theoretical intuition, in that we have shown that output decreases in the face of regulations. Similarly, it is likely that the demand for factor inputs will fall when emissions are regulated, though the direction of change is theoretically ambiguous. The empirical results suggest that the five-year growth in output is 14.6 percent smaller in plants with carbon monoxide non-attainment, 3.2 percent smaller for ozone non-attainment, and 3.2 percent smaller for total suspended solids non-attainment – all relative to plants in attainment counties. These changes are economically meaningful for the specific counties and affected plants, but their overall magnitude is small in comparison to the aggregate US manufacturing sector.

5.3 STANDARDS RECONSIDERED

Theoretical discussions on environmental standards, or command and control, usually focus on an absolute emission standard of the form described in Chapter 3, in which firms' emissions may not exceed an administratively set level. Implementation and enforcement of this type of standard, however, requires regular measurement of emissions from the polluting sources. For many types of pollution this is prohibitively expensive or even impossible. As a result, environmental standards as implemented often diverge substantially from what we have thus far considered. In this section we examine *relative* (or *generation performance*) standards, a class of policy tools in which polluting sources are regulated based on the concentration of a pollutant in some measurable output.

Use of relative standards is common in both Europe and the United States. For example, automobile and truck emissions are regulated via exhaust pipe tests in which the concentration of gasses such as carbon monoxide (CO), nitrous oxides (NO_x), and sulfur dioxide (SO_2) may not exceed a particular proportion of the total. In addition, compliance with clean-water regulations for wastewater emitters is often based on the ambient concentration of pollutants in the discharged water. Water discharges by mining firms are often checked for acidity levels and metals concentration. In both of these examples no limits are set on total emissions. A transport vehicle that logs twice as many miles in a time period will produce twice the effluent, yet still be in compliance with a relative standard. A mining firm that expands its scale of operation will increase its total wastewater discharge, perhaps increasing emissions of heavy metals into surface water, while maintaining compliance with the relative standard.

To examine the conceptual properties of relative standards, consider a regulation based on emissions per unit of output. Specifically, output and emission levels for a firm must comply with

$$e/x \leq \alpha, \tag{5.34}$$

or $e \leq \alpha x$, in which α is the policy variable. In Case 2, (5.34) is satisfied whenever $\alpha \geq \delta(x)$; conversely, if $\alpha < \delta(x)$ the firm can only comply with the standard by shutting down. The analysis is more interesting for Case 1, when abatement possibilities exist. If (5.34) is binding, profit for a single competitive firm is given by

$$\Pi(x) = px - C(x, \alpha x), \tag{5.35}$$

where substituting $e = \alpha x$ implies that x is the only choice variable. The first-order condition for profit maximum in this is

$$p = C_x(x, \alpha x) + \alpha C_e(x, \alpha x). \tag{5.36}$$

The solution to this problem is the firm's output supply function, which we denote $x(\alpha)$ to make explicit its dependence on α.

To examine the efficiency properties of this type of relative standard, suppose the regulator aims to establish an emission goal for the firm of $e = \bar{e}$, and that she has knowledge of the firm's behavior as summarized by $x(\alpha)$. With this, the regulator can simply set $\alpha = \bar{e}/x(\alpha)$ to achieve the emission goal. For comparison consider an absolute standard of the type we examined in Chapter 3, in which the regulator directly sets $e = \bar{e}$ to achieve the same outcome. In this case the firm's profit function is

$$\Pi(x,\bar{e}) = px - C(x,\bar{e}), \tag{5.37}$$

and the firm's output supply $x(\bar{e})$ is implicitly defined by first-order condition $p = C_x(x,\bar{e})$. If the regulator has properly chosen $\bar{e}$, this will lead to an efficient outcome. If instead the regulator sets the same emission level with the relative standard $\bar{e} = \alpha x(\alpha)$, we get the condition

$$p - \alpha C_e(x(\alpha),\bar{e}) = C_x(x(\alpha),\bar{e}) > p, \tag{5.38}$$

where the inequality follows from the fact that the marginal abatement cost curve $-C_e(\cdot)$ is positive. Comparing (5.38) with the first-order condition under the absolute standard we see that

$$C_x(x(\alpha),\bar{e}) > C_x(x(\bar{e}),\bar{e}). \tag{5.39}$$

From this it follows that $x(\alpha) > x(\bar{e})$ and

$$\begin{aligned} C(x(\alpha),\bar{e}) &> C(x(\bar{e}),\bar{e}) \\ -C_e(x(\alpha),\bar{e}) &> -C_e(x(\bar{e}),\bar{e}). \end{aligned} \tag{5.40}$$

In words, it is the case that total cost *and* the marginal abatement cost are greater under the relative standard than the absolute standard. We summarize this result in the following proposition.

Proposition 5.2
Suppose an environmental regulator sets an emission goal of $\bar{e}$ and uses a relative standard α to obtain it. If there is a single firm or J identical firms, the policy will lead to higher output, higher total costs, and higher marginal abatement cost relative to a comparable absolute standard.

The intuition of this finding is clear. Under the relative standard, a polluting firm can achieve compliance with the regulation not only through the direct reduction of emissions, but also by "diluting" emissions via increased output. The use of a relative standard therefore is preferred only in a second-best setting in which an absolute standard or other more efficient instrument cannot be implemented, for either technical or political reasons. Suppose such technical or political constraints exist, and given a known damage function, the regulator must choose a relative standard to maximize social welfare in the presence of a single polluting firm. The problem faced by the regulator in this case is

$$W(\alpha) = \int_0^{x(\alpha)} P(t)dt - C\big(x(\alpha), \alpha x(\alpha)\big) - D\big(\alpha x(\alpha)\big). \tag{5.41}$$

Differentiating with respect to α leads to

$$\left[P - C_x(\cdot) - \alpha C_e(\cdot)\right] x'(\alpha) - C_e(\cdot)x - D'(\cdot) \times \left(x + \alpha x'(\alpha)\right) = 0. \tag{5.42}$$

Given the firm's optimal behavior as shown in the first-order condition in (5.36), the term in square brackets on the left-hand side of (5.42) is zero. Rearranging the remaining terms to isolate the marginal abatement cost function we obtain

$$-C_e(x,e) = \frac{x + \alpha x'(\alpha)}{x} D'(e). \tag{5.43}$$

Recall that $x'(\alpha)$ summarizes the firm's output reaction to the policy variable, and note that its sign determines whether the marginal abatement cost exceeds or falls below marginal damages in (5.43). While the sign of $x'(\alpha)$ is indeterminate in general, it is intuitive to suppose that $x'(\alpha) > 0$, so that output expands when the standard is relaxed. If this is the case, the optimal policy in an environment that requires use of a relative standard leads to marginal abatement costs which exceed marginal social damage, and as such emissions that are lower than socially optimal.

A second type of relative standard restricts the amount of a particular pollutant relative to a total volume of effluent. For example, nitrous oxides (NO_x) are often jointly produced with more benign emissions such as CO_2, and a regulator may wish to limit the proportion of nitrous oxides contained in the aggregate of the two. In this case we can think of the two pollutants, labeled e_1 and e_2, as arising from a joint production process given by a generalization of the emission technology shown above:

$$(e_1, e_2) = h(l_1, \ldots l_K). \tag{5.44}$$

Suppose that pollutant 1 is subject to regulation relative to total emission of both pollutants. In this case a relative standard can be defined according to

$$\frac{e_1}{e_1 + e_2} \leq \alpha. \tag{5.45}$$

One can verify that, once again, a standard leads to an inefficient result, even if firms are identical. In this case, too, there is little we can say about the comparative statics effects arising from making the standard stricter. Therefore, it is also ambiguous whether or not the second-best optimal standard would lead to marginal abatement costs that are larger or smaller than marginal damage. Note also that relative standards must fail if both emissions cause environmental damage. This is so because setting two kinds of relative standards according to $e_1/(e_1 + e_2) \leq \alpha_1$ and $e_2/(e_1 + e_2) \leq \alpha_2$ are not consistent with each other.

EXAMPLE 5.3 (POLICY) Many countries use performance standards to regulate emissions. This in particularly so for road transport, where upper limits for nitrogen oxides (NO_X), carbon monoxide, and particulate matter concentrations are set in terms relative to use. For example, in 2015 it was discovered that automobile manufacturer Volkswagen had violated the US NO_X certification standard of 0.043 g/km in its small diesel engine cars, as well as the less stringent European standard of 0.08 g/km. Controversy erupted when it became known that Volkswagen had programmed the vehicles' pollution control equipment to operate only during emissions testing, which allowed the standard to be met in laboratory settings. During actual travel, however, the pollution control equipment was left off, and NO_X emissions exceeded the standard by up to 40 times in some tests. Nearly 500,000 vehicles were sold in the US with the "defeat device," and perhaps 8 million in Europe.

5.4 LONG RUN OPTIMALITY OF ENVIRONMENTAL POLICY INSTRUMENTS

Our discussion thus far has assumed that the number of firms is fixed at J, and therefore it has been limited to short run analysis. In the long run, of course, firms may enter and exit the market, and this may impact the optimality properties of the environmental policy instruments we have studied thus far. Basic microeconomic theory demonstrates that under perfect competition, technologically identical firms enter or exit the market until profits are driven to zero, and all firms produce at the minimum point on their long run average cost curve. Furthermore, if firms have non-zero fixed costs and strictly convex cost functions, the socially optimal number of firms is endogenously determined. In what follows we maintain these traditional assumptions while considering the long run impact of environmental policy on a competitive industry. This is a departure from our usual starting off assumption that firms are asymmetric. It is necessary because firm heterogeneity is inconsistent with the long run zero profit condition, in the sense that it is not possible for firms with different minimum average costs to be in the market at the same time, since only firms operating at the smallest minimum cost can survive. To avoid the awkwardness of asymmetric firms with identical minimum average costs, we proceed with the identical firm assumption.

5.4.1 Long Run Social Optimum

We begin by characterizing the long run social optimum for a competitive industry when technologically identical firms are polluters. Define the cost function for the J identical firms as consisting of both fixed and variable costs, so that

$$C(x,e) = \begin{cases} VC(x,e) + F & x,e \neq 0 \\ 0 & x,e = 0, \end{cases} \tag{5.46}$$

where F is the fixed cost of entry and $VC(x,e)$ denotes variable costs. We assume that the curvature properties of $VC(\cdot)$ are similar to what was given in assumption 5.1 above. In the long run, social welfare depends on firms' output and emission levels as well as the number of firms. The optimal values of these three variables are determined by the welfare expression

$$W(x,e,J) = \max_{x,e,J} \int_0^{x \cdot J} P(t)dt - J \cdot C(x,e) - D(e \cdot J), \tag{5.47}$$

where total output is $X = x \cdot J$ and total emissions is $E = e \cdot J$. The first-order conditions that implicitly define the social optimum (x^*, e^*, J^*) are given by

$$P(X^*) = C_x(x^*, e^*)$$
$$D'(E^*) = -C_e(x^*, e^*) \tag{5.48}$$
$$P(x^*)x^* = C(x^*, e^*) + D'(E^*)x^*.$$

The first two equations are familiar; the latter, however, is new and defines the optimal number of firms. Rearranging slightly we obtain

$$P(X^*) = \frac{C(x^*, e^*) + D'(E^*)e^*}{x^*}, \tag{5.49}$$

which has a useful interpretation. In approaching the social optimum, firms should enter or exit the market until the market price reaches the minimum of the average *social* cost curve, where social cost includes the private production as well as the public environmental costs of a unit of the good. Note that the public environmental costs generated by a single small firm are represented by $D'(E^*)e^*$, since for the firm's emissions the damage can be approximated by the product of aggregate marginal damage and the number of emissions. In the following subsections we consider the degree to which the various policy instruments obtain the long run social optimum.

5.4.2 Standards

If firms are identical and their number is given exogenously, our analysis in Chapter 3 suggests that (absolute) emission standards lead to the same result as market-based instruments such as taxes and tradable permits. The advantage of decentralized behavior leading to equal marginal abatement costs, which favors market-based instruments, does not apply in the identical firm case. If the number of firms is determined endogenously, however, emission standards fail to obtain the social optimum even when firms are identical. To illustrate this, suppose the regulator wants to implement the optimal total emission level E^* by setting an emission standard $e = e^*$ for all firms, where $e^* = E^*/J^*$ and J^* is the optimal long run number of firms. In this policy setting, firms can only choose the level of output, which each will do according to the first-order condition $p = C_x(x, e^*)$. Define the zero profit, long run equilibrium that arises from this policy as consisting of $\hat{J}$ firms each producing $\hat{x}$ units of output, where $\hat{J}$ and $\hat{x}$ are implicitly defined by

$$P(\hat{x}\hat{J}) = C_x(\hat{x}, e^*)$$
$$P(\hat{x}\hat{J})\hat{x} - C(\hat{x}, e^*) = 0. \tag{5.50}$$

Note that $\hat{x}$ cannot be equal to the optimal long run level x^*, since according to (5.48) we have

$$P(X^*)x^* - C(x^*,e^*) = D'(E^*) \cdot e^* > 0, \tag{5.51}$$

and therefore

$$P(X^*)x^* - C(x^*,e^*) > P(\hat{x}\hat{J}) \cdot \hat{x} - C(\hat{x},e^*) = 0, \tag{5.52}$$

from which it immediately follows that $\hat{J} \neq J^*$ and $\hat{x} \neq x^*$ when a standard $e = e^*$ is set. In words, the standard causes existing firms to reduce production, which leads to non-zero (but socially optimal) profits in the short run, since rents to the environment are not paid in this policy. The existence of short run positive profits causes new firms to enter the market until long run profits are zero, leading to non-optimal output level, industry size, and total emissions. We summarize this result and its consequences for aggregate emissions and output in the following proposition.

Proposition 5.3
Consider a competitive polluting industry with identical firms and free entry. If the regulator sets an emission cap for each firm equal to the (long run) socially optimal level per firm $e^* = E^*/J^*$, then:

(a) the industry size is larger than the social optimum, i.e. $\hat{J} > J^*$;
(b) each firm produces less than is socially optimal, i.e. $\hat{x} < x^*$;
(c) total output and total pollution are greater than the social optimum.

A formal proof of this proposition is given in the appendix. This is an important result. Conventional wisdom suggests that incentive-based policies such as taxes and tradable permits only hold advantage over command and control regulation when there is heterogeneity across regulated firms, implying the need for specialization in abatement effort. Here we see that this is only the case in the short run, or when the number of firms is exogenously fixed (perhaps due to entry restrictions). Absent these conditions, command and control emission caps *do not* provide optimal incentives in the long run, even in the identical firm case. If the policy were also accompanied by a mechanism in which the environmental damage (the rent to the environment) was appropriated from the firms, long run optimality could be achieved. We return to this point below.

5.4.3 Taxes
If firms are subject to an emission tax, it is straightforward to see that the long run social optimum can be achieved by setting the emission tax equal to the Pigouvian level, such that $\tau = D'(E^*)$. Under this policy each identical firm's profit function is $\Pi = px - C(x,e) - \tau e$, and the familiar first-order conditions $p = C_x(x,e)$ and $-C_e(x,e) = \tau$ arise from profit maximization. In the long run, firms enter the market until profits are zero, implying that

$$px - C(x,e) - \tau e = 0. \tag{5.53}$$

All of these are equivalent to the social optimum conditions in (5.48) when we substitute $p = P(X)$ and $\tau = D'(E^*)$. The difference between taxes and standards in the long run, identical firm case is therefore one of transfers. In the taxes case an amount related to environmental damages is paid by the firms to the regulator, while in the standards case these rents are kept by the firms. Payment of rents for the environmental damage attenuates the effects outlined in proposition 5.3, and maintains the long run optimality of emission taxes in our modeling setup.

5.4.4 Auctioned and Freely Distributed Permits

Rather than charging an emission tax the regulator could instead auction off or distribute a quantity of transferable permits $L=E^*$, where E^* is the socially optimal level of emissions. Consider briefly the auctioned permit case. Once again denoting the market price for permits by σ, the long run market equilibrium with an endogenous number of identical firms is described by

$$P(xJ) = C_x(x,e)$$
$$\sigma = -C_e(x,e) \tag{5.54}$$
$$P(xJ)x - C(x,e) - \sigma e = 0,$$

where $eJ = L = E^*$ permits are available, and the interpretation for each condition is by now familiar. Since the aggregate factor demand for permits is strictly decreasing in the number of permits (see above), a unique market price for permits exists such that

$$\sigma = -C_e(x^*,e^*) = D'(E^*), \tag{5.55}$$

and total demand for permits equals total supply. Unsurprisingly, we see that auctioning an optimal number of permits leads to the long run socially optimal outcome in a manner quite similar to the emission tax case.

In some respects, the freely distributed permits case is more interesting. As described in other contexts, auctioned permits and emission taxes can be difficult to implement politically because they involve transfers from the industry to the regulating authority. It is therefore often the case that permits are freely distributed to the regulated industry, thereby endowing the industry with the right to emit a fixed number of units. In the long run with free entry, this begs the question of which firms will be allocated permits and what the quantity will be. In this sense, the long run case adds an additional equity consideration to the short run challenge of what constitutes an appropriate initial endowment. In practice, it is likely that existing firms would receive a permit allocation at the time the regulation is introduced, and future entrants to the industry would compete without an endowment. Alternatively, a fixed number of permits could be annually divided among the existing firms, originals and new entrants. In the end it does not matter: so long as the number of permits available does not expand with new entrants, the allocation across existing and future firms will not affect the long run optimality of freely distributed permits.

To see this, suppose a total permit endowment L is made available to the industry, broadly defined to include identical existing firms and future entrants. Furthermore denote $\bar{e}$ as the initial allocation to each of the $L/\bar{e}$ existing firms. The profit function for the firms with an allocation is

$$\Pi(x,e) = px - C(x,e) - \sigma(e - \bar{e}), \tag{5.56}$$

and profit for subsequent entrants is

$$\Pi(x,e) = px - C(x,e) - \sigma e, \tag{5.57}$$

where σ is the equilibrium permit price. Note that for $\sigma > 0$ it cannot be the case that both (5.56) and (5.57) are equal to zero. Instead, the exit/entry condition requires that new firms enter until their profits are zero, and this can only happen if they purchase permits from the existing firms. The long run equilibrium therefore is described by

$$\Pi(x,e) = xq - C(x,e) - \sigma e = 0. \tag{5.58}$$

Importantly, this implies that existing firms (i.e. those that received a permit endowment) will sustain long run positive profits according to

$$\Pi(x,e) = px - C(x,e) - \sigma(e - \bar{e}) = \sigma\bar{e}. \tag{5.59}$$

Intuitively, it is the case that operating profits must be zero for all firms that stay in the market. Firms that were originally allocated permits, however, capture the rents from the scarcity value of the fixed quantity factor. Furthermore, if the initial aggregate endowment of permits is chosen optimally such that $L = E^*$, where E^* is described by Eq. (5.48), the freely distributed permit regime will be long run optimal. This is best seen by noting that the first-order conditions describing firms' behavior and the market equilibrium under the freely distributed permit policy match those associated with the auctioned permit policy, implying long run optimality is achieved. The difference, of course, lies in which party – the industry or the regulator – captures the rents flowing from the policy-induced scarcity of the environment. In this sense the equality of auctioned versus freely distributed permits is an application of the Coase Theorem, in that the efficiency result is unaffected by the initial ownership of pollution rights. This is of course a first-best finding; situations in which there may be additional benefits to revenue recycling by the government are the subject of Chapter 7.

5.4.5 Subsidies

To some extent we can view freely distributed emission permits as a type of subsidy to polluting firms, in that a valuable commodity is allocated to individual firms. We saw above that this does not affect the long run optimality of the policy when compared to auctioned permits. Since emission taxes and subsidies were previously shown to be equivalent in the short run, we might expect a similar result to hold in the long run. However, this turns out not to be the case. Unlike a fixed allocation of freely distributed permits, abatement subsidies are inefficient because payments are available to all firms, and can therefore induce excessive market entry. To see this, recall from Chapter 3 that a subsidy policy requires a reference level of emissions, below which firms receive a per-unit subsidy for all units of pollution eliminated. Denote the reference level of emission by $\hat{e}$, where we can think of $\hat{e}$ as the baseline emissions from existing firms. Denoting the per-unit subsidy by ς, a firm's profit level is

$$\Pi(x,e) = P(X)x - C(x,e) - \zeta(e - \hat{e}), \tag{5.60}$$

and the free entry condition implies this expression will be equal to zero. There are two sources of inefficiency inherent in the subsidy regime. The first is the broader issue of subsidy-seeking entry, which is not unique to environmental regulation. Of more direct relevance is the impact that subsidies have on the scale of operation of producing firms, the number of firms, and the aggregate level of emissions. As shown in Chapter 3 a necessary condition for subsidies to be efficient is that the subsidy rate is set optimally so that it equals marginal damages, i.e. $\varsigma = D'(E^*)$. Substituting this into Eq. (5.60) and imposing long run zero profit we have

$$P(X)x - C(x,e) - D'(E^*) \times (e - \hat{e}) = 0. \tag{5.61}$$

Note from (5.61) that

$$P(X)x - C(x,e) - D'(E^*)e = D'(E^*)\hat{e}. \tag{5.62}$$

Recall from Eq. (5.48) that long run optimality requires the left-hand side of (5.62) be equal to zero, which we can see is not the case under the subsidy regime. A subsidy that is equal to marginal damages translates to a de facto decrease in firms' fixed costs. This decreases the scale of individual firms' operation, and leads to socially excessive market entry and industry production. Kohn (1992) shows that even emissions may increase through abatement subsidies. From this analysis, we conclude that subsidies are not an effective long run tool for internalizing externalities when there is free market entry and exit.

5.5   AN EXPANDED EXAMINATION OF ABATEMENT COSTS

In Chapter 3 we defined abatement cost as the cost borne by a firm when it is required to reduce emissions below some pre-regulation level, which we denoted $\hat{e}$. In this section, we broaden the notion of abatement costs by identifying three types of costs that can arise when regulation requires a reduction in emissions. In particular, we distinguish among technical or engineering costs holding output constant, economic costs when output can adjust, and the social cost of abatement. These notions allow us to gain a greater appreciation of the opportunity cost of pollution reductions, and how these costs are distributed among agents.

We begin with technical abatement cost when output is held constant. We can interpret this as an engineering cost concept that arises when a firm reduces emissions by

$\hat{e}^x - e$ while holding output constant at x, where e is the emission target and $\hat{e}^x$ is once again the unrestricted emission level for output level x. Define this cost concept by

$$\breve{C}(x,e) = C(x,e) - C(x,\hat{e}^x). \tag{5.63}$$

This abatement cost concept does not match the economic definition of abatement opportunity cost, since for the latter the firm can adjust its other decisions, including its production level. Nonetheless we can use (5.63) to define the marginal abatement cost function as

$$-\breve{C}_e(x,e) = -C_e(x,e) \tag{5.64}$$

for a given x. For small changes in emissions that hold output constant, it is therefore the case that technical costs accurately represent economic costs. The technical cost of a non-marginal reduction in emissions as given by (5.63), however, overstates the opportunity cost of the reduction by ignoring output adjustments. The opportunity cost of abatement is therefore best represented as forgone profits arising from the emission reduction. Continuing with the assumption of perfect competition, the profit maximizing firm chooses output according to the condition $C_x(x,e) = p$. From this we can solve for the output level conditional on an emission level, which here we denote $x(e)$. Substituting $x(e)$ into the profit function allows us to express profits conditional on a particular emission level by

$$\Pi(e) = px(e) - C(x(e),e). \tag{5.65}$$

With this, we can define the opportunity cost to the firm of the emission reduction as

$$C(e) = \Pi(e) - \Pi(\hat{e}^x), \tag{5.66}$$

where the dependency on the output and input market structures is implicit in this expression. Two points distinguish $C(e)$ from $\breve{C}(x,e)$. First, $C(e)$ is finite as we approach $e=0$, since the firm has the option of choosing $x=0$ and thereby earning zero profit. Second, $\breve{C}(x,e)$ can approach infinity as emissions tend to zero; this is particularly likely if emissions are proportionately related to output.

The discussion of abatement cost in this section has thus far assumed prices do not change when an emission reduction policy takes effect. This may be reasonable for a small open economy in which polluting commodities are also traded on an international market. With no output price change (and the implied perfectly elastic import supply curve) the burden of regulation is completely borne by firms, and society's abatement costs are equivalent to firms' lost profits. In the case of a closed economy, coordinated environmental policy across countries, or for domestically traded polluting commodities the reduction in total output causes output price to rise (recall proposition 5.1 above). The rise in price mitigates the lost profit to firms, and therefore reduces firms' opportunity cost of pollution reductions. The rise in price, however, suggests there is a broader notion of society's abatement costs, from which further insight can be developed. Consider for example the case when there are J identical firms with no abatement possibilities outside of reducing output (Case 2 from above), and $e = \delta x$. From this we can define society's gross abatement cost by

$$SC(e) = \left\{ \int_0^{J \cdot \hat{e}^x / \delta} P(t)dt - J \cdot C\left(\hat{e}^x / \delta\right) \right\} - \left\{ \int_0^{J \cdot e/\delta} P(t)dt - J \cdot C\left(e / \delta\right) \right\}, \tag{5.67}$$

where the first term in brackets is the net benefit from consumption prior to regulation, and the second term is the net consumption benefit under a policy restricting emissions to e. We see from (5.67) that society's gross cost from the regulation consists of the increase in costs to firms as well as the lost consumption value from a reduction in X. Differentiating SC with respect to e we recover the society's (gross) marginal abatement cost function as

$$MSC(e) = -SC'(e) = J \times \frac{P(X) - C'(e/\delta)}{\delta}, \tag{5.68}$$

where $X = J \cdot (e/\delta)$. Comparing this expression with the condition for optimality shown in Eq. (5.11) allows us to develop further intuition. The optimality conditions suggest that marginal abatement cost needs to be equal to marginal damages, so that

$$\frac{P(X) - C'(e/\delta)}{\delta} = D'(\delta E). \tag{5.69}$$

From this we see that optimality can be described as the point where the marginal cost of the regulation, as defined by the lost net consumption benefit, is equal to the marginal benefit. This shows the central role that consumer preferences play in an expanded notion of abatement costs. In particular, whether or not $MSC(e)$ approaches infinity as e goes to zero depends on the extent to which substitutes are available for the polluting good. If substitutes are readily available there will be a finite choke price for the good, so that $\lim_{X \to 0} P(X) = p^{ch} < \infty$. This implies it is at least possible to optimally eliminate all emissions, a necessary condition for which is that the marginal damage of the first unit of pollution is larger than the marginal willingness to pay for the commodity – i.e. $D'(0) > p^{ch}$. An example of this is the use of CFCs as coolants in household refrigerators, for which other affordable and clean chemical coolants are readily available. As a result the optimal level of CFCs for cooling is essentially zero, and this is reflected in the policies of most developed nations. As a counter example, consider the use of household heating oil in cold climates, which may be said to be an essential good such that $\lim_{X \to 0} P(X) = \infty$. In this case the marginal abatement cost is infinitely large if the amount of effluent, and thus consumption, is reduced to zero. For such goods the optimal total abatement level will certainly not involve a complete elimination of pollution.

5.6   SUMMARY

Our objective in this chapter has been to examine how our suite of environmental policy developed in Chapter 3 performs when we generalize the analysis to give specific attention to competitive output markets. Our main findings can be grouped into three areas. First, in the short run when the number of firms is fixed, the basic conclusions from Chapter 3 continue to hold:

- The optimal level of pollution requires that firms' marginal abatement cost functions are equal to marginal damages, and all of our economic incentive policies, when optimally applied, are capable of delivering the efficient result.
- Likewise, command and control policies lead to higher abatement costs for a similar level of pollution reduction in the more general model. By considering the output market we were also able to show this for relative standards, a common type of regulation in which effluent must be less than a given proportion of output.

Second, when firms are able to enter and exit the market, several of our short run conclusions break down. Generally we expect that economic incentive policies only dominate direct standards when cost heterogeneity can provide gains from specialization; for identical firms, direct standards and economic incentives are the same. However, in the long run we saw that standards fail even in the identical firm case. This is because standards provide no means of appropriating a "payment for the environment", and so an efficient standard requires that firms operate so as to earn profit equal to the environmental damage. In the long run positive profits cannot be sustained due to free entry, and so regulating only emissions (as opposed to also entry and exit) cannot lead to long run optimality. In contrast, taxes and auctioned permits require payment for damages, and so the optimal emission level can be obtained with zero profit. Freely distributed permits, somewhat surprisingly, also lead to the optimal emission level since the environmental rents are captured by the original permit-holding firms. Although these firms can maintain non-zero long run profits due to the scarcity value of the permits, as long as no additional permits are issued new entrants can do no better than earn zero profits in the long run. Thus freely distributed permits function similarly to taxes and auctioned permits in the long run, though they have different equity characteristics. Finally, subsidies in the long run are inefficient and can even be counterproductive, since they encourage excess entry and, more generally, subsidy-seeking behavior among firms.

Lastly, examining the output market allows us to consider issues more directly related to equity. We saw, for example, that the burden of an environmental tax is borne partially by consumers and partially by the polluting industry and its workers. If demand for the polluting good is relatively inelastic, we saw that consumers will tend to bear the burden of an environmental tax in the form of higher prices. In contrast, if demand is relatively elastic, firms and their workers will bear most of the burden in the form of a smaller market. Thus efficient policies for different types of polluting activities can have quite different equity outcomes. We were able to further expand on this by decomposing the abatement cost function into its component parts. These included technical abatement costs, which are generally not applicable for considering the economic properties of different policies. Instead, firms' lost profit when output adjustment is considered is the appropriate measure of a firm's opportunity cost of reducing emissions to a particular level. If prices do not adjust after the regulation – perhaps because the commodity's price is set internationally but the regulation is domestic – firms bear all abatement costs in the form of higher production costs and reduced output. If the market price is affected, then consumers share in the burden. In this more general case, the gross opportunity cost of abatement to society is best seen as the lost net benefit of consumption owing to the regulation. This is shared by the industry and consumers based on the elasticity of demand and firms' technology.

All of these findings are derived in a partial equilibrium framework when output markets are competitive and there are no other distortions in the economy. In Chapter 6 we therefore examine environmental regulation when output markets are imperfectly competitive, and consider general equilibrium topics in Chapter 7.

5.7 FURTHER READING

Much of the discussion in this section is drawn from lecture notes from our respective classes. There are a handful of classic and newer articles related to output markets and environmental policy. Spulber (1985) and Carlton and Loury (1980, 1986) are worth reading together, since they arrive at different conclusions regarding the suitability of an emission tax alone for regulating competitive polluting firms in the long run. Zhao and Kling (2000) consider the long run efficiency of auctioned versus freely distributed permits. One of the first papers examining various kinds of standards (including relative standards) on firm behavior is Harford and Karp (1983). Other papers on relative standards include Harford and Ogura (1983), Harford (1984), Helfand (1991), and Holland (2012). Our analysis draws mainly on Ebert (1998), who in particular looks at emissions per output relative standards. Kohn (1992) makes the point that abatement subsidies can increase total emissions. Recent examples of empirical papers looking at environmental policy and employment include Ferris et al. (2014) and Walker (2013). See also the symposium in *Review of Environmental Economics and Policy* (volume 9, issue 2, 2015) on environmental regulation and unemployment.

APPENDIX: PROOF OF PROPOSITION 5.3

Recall from Eq. (5.48) that long run optimality requires $P(x^* \cdot J^*) \cdot x^* = C(x^*, e^*) + D'(E^*) \cdot x^*$. Denote K as the amount firms pay for their emissions, and note that $K = D'(E^*) \cdot x^*$ at the optimum and recall that $K = 0$ under an emission standard. Consider an emissions standard $e = e^*$. The conditions governing a firm's long run behavior are

$$P(xJ) - C_x(x, e^*) = 0$$
$$P(xJ) \cdot x - C(x, e^*) = K, \tag{A5.1}$$

where $K = 0$ for the pure standard policy. Differentiating with respect to K we obtain

$$P'(xJ)\left[\frac{dJ}{dK}x+\frac{dx}{dK}J\right]-C_{xx}(x,e^*)\frac{dx}{dK}=0$$

$$P'(xJ)\left[\frac{dJ}{dK}x+\frac{dx}{dK}J\right]x+\left[P(xJ)-C_x(x,e^*)\right]\frac{dx}{dK}=1. \tag{A5.2}$$

The second equation can be simplified to

$$P'(xJ)\left[\frac{dJ}{dK}x+\frac{dx}{dK}J\right]x=1, \tag{A5.3}$$

via the Envelope Theorem. Substituting (A5.3) into the top equation in (A5.2) and rearranging, we obtain

$$\frac{dx}{dK}=\frac{1}{x\cdot C_{xx}(q,e^*)}>0. \tag{A5.4}$$

This says that when K goes up – e.g. from $K=0$ to $K=D'(E^*)\cdot x^*$ – the output for a typical firm rises, and so output under the absolute standard is too small, which proves part (b). Equations (A5.3) and (A5.4) together show that $dJ/dK<0$, because the sum of the terms in square brackets needs to be negative since $P'(X)<0$. If K rises above zero, the number of firms falls, and so a standard results in a larger number of firms than is optimal. This proves part (a) of the proposition. To show part (c), note that $dE/dK=(dJ/dK)\cdot e^*<0$ and

$$\frac{dX}{dK}=\frac{d(xJ)}{dK}=\frac{dJ}{dK}\cdot x+\frac{dx}{dK}\cdot J<0. \tag{A5.5}$$

Thus, total emissions and total output fall when K rises, so emissions and output are greater under standards than for the social optimum.

EXERCISES

5.1 * Which of the following costs functions satisfies assumption 5.1?
  (a) $C(x,e)=\alpha(x^2/e)+\beta e$
  (b) $C(x,e)=0.5\times[\alpha e-\beta x)]+0.5\times\gamma x^2$
  (c) $C(x,e)=\alpha x^2/e$
  (d) $C(x,e)=\alpha x^2/e+\beta e^2$
  where $\alpha,\beta,\gamma>0$.
5.2 * Consider a firm whose technology satisfies assumption 5.2. The cost function is $c(x)=c\cdot x^2/2$. The output price is fixed and denoted by p. Emissions are proportional to ouput according to $e=\alpha\cdot x$. The firm is subject to an emission tax τ.
  (a) Calculate the optimal output and determine the firm's profit function.
  (b) Determine the firm's marginal abatement cost function (as a function of emissions) when output is the only option to reduce emissions.

5.3 ** Consider the Cobb-Douglas production function with $x = l_1^\alpha l_2^\beta$, where $\alpha + \beta < 1$ and emissions are proportional to input 2, so that $e = d \cdot l_1$, where $d > 0$.
   (a) Denoting the input prices by w_1 and w_2, derive the cost function as it depends on x and e. Show that it satisfies assumption 5.1.
   (b) What happens when $\alpha + \beta = 1$?

5.4 ** Consider a firm with the production function $x = f(l) = l^\alpha$, where $\alpha < 0$ and emissions are proportional to x so that $e = d \cdot x$. Suppose as well that the firm has a separable abatement cost function $AC(e) = \beta(\hat{e} - e)$.
   (a) Derive the overall cost function $C(x,e)$ and examine its properties.
   (b) Suppose instead that the emissions are given by $e = d \cdot l$. Derive the overall cost function for this case, and compare its properties to part (a).
   (c) Suppose instead that the production function is $x = f(l) = \gamma \cdot l$. Derive the overall cost functions for the $e = d \cdot x$ and $e = d \cdot l$ cases.
   (d) Consider the production function in exercise 5.2, with $e = d \cdot x$ and separable abatement cost function $AC(e) = \beta(\hat{e} - e)$. Derive the overall cost function $C(x,e)$ and determine its properties.
   (e) Repeat part (d) using $e = d \cdot l_2$.

5.5 ** Show using the model from section 5.2 that, for an exogenous number of firms, freely distributed permits or subsidies can be used to implement the social optimum.

5.6 *** Consider the model from section 5.4, where the number of firms is endogenous. Derive the comparative static results for emission taxes, auctioned permits, and absolute standards. That is, determine the direction of change for x, e, J, p, X, and E when the level of each policy variable is marginally changed.

5.7 ** Consider instances when a pollution tax is equivalent to an output tax by examining the following:
   (a) Suppose a firm's cost function satisfies assumption 5.2. Show that in this case, an emissions tax is equivalent to a sales tax. Determine the optimal sales tax.
   (b) Suppose now that a firm's cost function satisfies assumption 5.1. Show that it is in general not possible to achieve a first-best allocation by charging a sales tax.
   (c) Determine the comparative static effect from increasing the output tax. Derive signs for the change in firm's output, emissions, and the market price.
   (d) Determine the second-best optimal output tax when firms are symmetric.

5.8 ** To study the impact of market demand on the optimal emissions level, consider a parameterization of the inverse demand curve such that $p = P(X, \alpha)$, where α is a parameter such that $P_\alpha(\cdot) > 0$ and as usual $P_X(\cdot) < 0$. Assume there are J identical firms. Show that the market levels of both total output and total emissions increase when α increases.

5.9 ** Consider the case when the cost function satisfies $C_{xe}(\cdot) = 0$. This can arise for different reasons. Consider the following two possibilities:
   (a) Suppose production and abatement costs (AC) are separable, so that $C(x,e) = \check{C}(x) + AC(e)$. Show that in this case an emissions tax does not affect the output price.
   (b) Suppose that $C_{xx}(\cdot) \geq 0$ and abatement costs are linear. For example, $C(x,e) = c \cdot x + \beta(\delta \cdot x - e)$. Show that the firm's optimal choice for emissions is a corner solution. In particular, show that for $\tau < \beta$ the firm does not reduce any emissions, and for $\tau > \beta$ it reduces emissions to zero.

5.10 *** Show that proposition 5.1 holds for asymmetric firms.

5.11 * Show that in the model with an exogenous number of firms, the second-order conditions for profit maximum are satisfied. Show that these cost functions satisfy assumptions 5.1 and 5.2.

5.12 *** Consider the model in section 5.3.

(a) Derive the firm's first-order conditions for profits maximization when they are subject to the relative standard given by Eq. (5.45).

(b) Derive a rule for the second-best optimal standard of the type given by Eq. (5.45).

5.13 ** In contrast to our analysis in Section 5.4.3, Carlton and Loury (1980) suggest that a Pigouvian tax alone will not lead to a long run social optimum for competitive polluting firms. Using their arguments, show that when the damage function is $D(E,J)$, depending on both emissions *and* the number of firms, an entry tax or subsidy is needed to reach the long run social optimum.

CHAPTER 6

Non-Competitive Output Markets

In the last chapter we introduced the output market to our analysis and used it to extend several of the results we derived in Chapter 3. Throughout we maintained the assumption that all markets were competitive, which allowed us to show that the optimal level of pollution was still characterized by the marginal abatement cost equals marginal damage condition. In this chapter we consider how optimal policy might be different under non-competitive market structures. As we will see, our analysis is complicated by the presence of both market power and pollution-related distortions, and these will cause some of our familiar results to no longer hold. Indeed, the presence of multiple distortions means the regulator's objective is typically to locate a second-best optimal emission tax rate that reflects the relative strength of the two market distortions. The material we present in this chapter will therefore be more technical than what was used in Chapter 5.

What is our motivation for including a chapter on non-competitive markets? Although competitive markets provide a useful starting point for studying environmental policy, non-competitive industries are the primary sources of many regulated pollutants. For example, in both the United States and parts of Europe electric utilities and petroleum refineries tend(ed) to exercise monopoly power at the regional level, pulp and paper production has concentrated in recent decades, and automobile manufacturing is done by a relatively small number of firms in any given country. These examples suggest that non-competitive industries are more than a theoretical curiosity for environmental policy. In response, an enormous literature has arisen that considers the role of market power in all its guises. Researchers have examined output market structures such as monopoly, oligopoly, and monopolistic competition. Homogeneous versus differentiated products, quantity versus price competition, and market power in factor markets have also been considered. In this chapter we limit attention to monopoly and oligopoly output market structures, since these provide useful vehicles for demonstrating the main techniques and conclusions from this larger literature.

The early literature on environmental policy and market power provides additional motivation for studying non-competitive output markets. Papers by Buchanan and Stubblebine (1962) and Buchanan (1969) challenged the Pigouvian point of view outright, by noting that a monopolist distorts the market by producing too little output.

An emission tax on a polluting monopolist would therefore exacerbate rather than mitigate the overall distortion. This viewpoint is nicely articulated by Buchanan when he writes:

> the whole approach of the Pigouvian tradition is responsible for many confusions in applied economics ... Making the marginal private cost as faced by the decision-making unit equal to marginal social cost does not provide the Aladdin's Lamp for the applied welfare theorist, and the sooner he recognizes this, the better. (1969, p.177)

On the relationship between Pigouvian taxes and market structure he notes:

> It is necessary to distinguish, however, between the relevance of market structure for the emergence of an externality and the relevance of market structure for the application of Pigouvian norms ... It is necessary to limit the Pigouvian corrections on the tax side to situations of competition. (1969, p.175)

The later literature began to take a more nuanced approach, which we will use in this chapter. For example, Barnett (1980) recognized that when regulating a polluting monopolist we are in a second-best situation, which requires an adjustment to the Pigouvian rule rather than its outright rejection. He argues that a second-best optimal emission tax will be smaller than its competitive counterpart, since by producing less output the monopolist is also producing fewer emissions – his market power, in essence, already does part of the job of the emission tax. We will see that this intuition is sound, though we will also show that the Pigouvian argument is valid if the regulator has separate instruments for addressing both the pollution and market power distortions. Thus one of the findings from this chapter is that in an ideal regulatory world, tools would be available for separately addressing non-competitive outcomes and pollution externalities.

This chapter is organized as follows. We start by studying the monopoly problem under the two technology types discussed in Chapter 5: situations in which abatement is possible (assumption 5.1) and situations when pollution can only be reduced by reducing output (assumption 5.2). We characterize the regulator's best response under these two situations, and demonstrate the analytical techniques we will use throughout the chapter. We then turn our attention to the more complicated oligopoly case and derive several general results as well as results that hold in special cases. We conclude the chapter by briefly mentioning several generalizations and providing references to further reading.

6.1 MONOPOLY

In this section we examine an industry consisting of a single firm that generates a local pollutant; this latter point allows us to focus on regulation for the single firm/industry. As in Chapter 5, we will distinguish between technologies in which the polluting firm can abate pollution directly (assumption 5.1) and those for which pollution can only be reduced by reducing output (assumption 5.2). In both cases we begin by examining the firm's behavior and then consider the regulator's optimal response.

6.1.1 Taxation When Abatement is Not Possible

We begin with the simplest case in which pollution can only be reduced by reducing output. Specifically, if the firm's technology satisfies assumption 5.2 and pollution is proportional to output so that $E = \delta X$, the monopolist's profit maximization problem given an emission tax τ is

$$
\begin{aligned}
\max_X \Pi(X) &= P(X)X - C(X) - \tau E \\
&= P(X)X - C(X) - \tau \delta X,
\end{aligned}
\tag{6.1}
$$

where $P(X)$ is the market inverse demand curve as described in Chapter 5, and we have used capital letters for output and emissions to stress that the firm and industry are equivalent. The first-order condition for this problem is

$$
P'(X)X + P(X) = C'(X) + \tau \delta.
\tag{6.2}
$$

We denote the solution to (6.2) by $X^m(\tau)$ when we want to explicitly note the dependence on τ, or simply by X^m when the dependence is left implicit. Note that this equation shows the familiar monopolist's behavioral rule in which marginal revenue is set equal to the effective marginal cost and that the latter is smaller than the price.

Throughout the chapter we will be interested in characterizing firms' responses to changes in the emission tax rate. For the monopoly case this task is relatively straightforward, in that there is no strategic behavior to consider. Differentiating (6.2) with respect to τ we obtain

$$
\left[P''(X^m)X^m + 2P'(X^m) - C''(X^m) \right] \frac{dX^m}{d\tau} = \delta,
\tag{6.3}
$$

from which we can solve for the monopolist's quantity response to changes in the tax rate as

$$
\frac{dX^m}{d\tau} = \frac{\delta}{P''(X^m)X^m + 2P'(X^m) - C''(X^m)}.
\tag{6.4}
$$

To sign this expression, it is useful to add the following assumption.

Assumption 6.1

The inverse demand function $P(X)$ is decreasing in X so that $P'(X) < 0$. Furthermore for all $X > 0$ it is the case that

$$
\frac{P''(X)}{P'(X)} X > -1.
\tag{6.5}
$$

This standard assumption on preferences states that the inverse demand function is not too convex. It in particular guarantees that the monopolist's second-order conditions for profit maximization are satisfied and, in a Cournot oligopoly, it ensures that equilibria are unique and stable. Given this we can see that $dX^m/d\tau$ is negative, and so an increase in the tax rate causes the firm to decrease its output.

In Chapter 5 we saw that the regulator's objective in general is to maximize the net consumption benefit from X, taking into account the costs to the firm and environmental damage. In this sense, the first-best outcome X^* is the solution to

$$\max_X \int_0^X P(t)dt - C(X) - D(\delta X),\tag{6.6}$$

which is characterized by the first-order condition

$$P(X^*) = C'(X^*) + \delta D'(\delta X^*).\tag{6.7}$$

To set the stage for the second-best analysis that follows, we consider a modified version of the regulator's problem, in which she selects a tax rate to maximize welfare, conditional on the firm's optimal response to her choice. The objective function from this perspective is

$$W(\tau) = \int_0^{X^m(\tau)} P(t)dt - C(X^m(\tau)) - D(\delta X^m(\tau)),\tag{6.8}$$

and by differentiating with respect to τ we obtain

$$\left[P(X^m) - C'(X^m) - \delta D'(\delta X^m)\right] \times \frac{dX^m}{d\tau} = 0.\tag{6.9}$$

Recall from (6.2) that the monopolist's behavior implies that $P(X^m) - C'(X^m) = \tau\delta - P'(X^m)X^m$. Since the regulator's choice accounts for the firm's response, we can substitute this expression into (6.9); rearranging (and recalling that $dX^m/d\tau$ is non-zero) we arrive at

$$\tau = D'(\delta X^m) + \frac{P'(X^m)X^m}{\delta}\tag{6.10}$$

as a characterization of the optimal tax rate. This is a characterization rather than a solution for τ, since the tax rate is implicitly contained on the left- and right-hand sides of the equation. Nevertheless, (6.10) shows that the regulator can obtain the first-best outcome via her choice of τ, since (6.2) reduces to (6.7) when the optimal tax rate is substituted in. This is possible because the regulator effectively controls both the pollution and output levels via her choice of τ. Equation (6.10) also shows that since $P'(\cdot) < 0$, the tax rate faced by the monopolist is smaller than the marginal damage. We summarize this finding in the following proposition.

Proposition 6.1
If emissions are proportional to (or a monotonic function of) output, and if there is no abatement technology so that emissions can only be reduced by reducing output, there exists an emission tax rate which implements the social optimum. Furthermore, the optimal tax rate is lower than marginal damage.

This result suggests that in this special case, the regulator can effectively address the two market distortions – too little output and the externality – using a single instrument. In extreme instances the optimal tax rate could be negative, implying the regulator needs to subsidize pollution in order to entice the firm to produce more output. This counterintuitive possibility arises as a direct result of the non-competitive environment in which the polluting firm operates. It also illustrates how, in some situations, monopolists and environmentalists may be strange and perhaps reluctant bedfellows.

6.1.2 Taxation When Abatement is Possible

We now consider the more general case described by assumption 5.1, where the firm can deploy abatement technology to at least partially decouple emission reductions from output reductions. In this setup the firm's profit maximization problem given an emission tax is

$$\max_{X,E} \Pi(X,E) = P(X)X - C(X,E) - \tau E, \tag{6.11}$$

with first-order conditions

$$P'(X)X + P(X) = C_X(X,E) \\ -C_E(X,E) = \tau. \tag{6.12}$$

The interpretation of these conditions is straightforward. The first illustrates once again the basic monopoly rule whereby the firm selects its output so that its marginal cost is equal to its marginal revenue. The second condition carries over from the perfect competition case, and suggests that the marginal abatement cost level is set equal to the tax rate. We denote the solutions to (6.12) by $X^m(\tau)$ and $E^m(\tau)$, and will once again occasionally use X^m and E^m to reduce notational clutter.

Recall from Chapter 5 that if the regulator was able to directly determine X and E, she would solve a generalization of Eq. (6.7) in which the optimal output X^* and pollution E^* are characterized by

$$P(X^*) = C_X(X^*,E^*) \\ -C_E(X^*,E^*) = D'(E^*). \tag{6.13}$$

In what follows, we will examine the degree to which the regulator can use a tax instrument alone to achieve this outcome, given the monopolist's optimal response to her choice. For this her problem is formally given by

$$\max_{\tau} W(\tau) = \int_0^{X^m(\tau)} P(t)dt - C\left(X^m(\tau), E^m(\tau)\right) - D(E^m(\tau)), \tag{6.14}$$

where the direct and indirect effects of τ – i.e. the firm's response to the tax level – need to be accounted for. Fully differentiating the welfare function with respect to τ leads to the first-order condition

$$\left[P(X^m) - C_X(X^m, E^m)\right]\frac{dX^m}{d\tau} - \left[C_E(X^m, E^m) + D(E^m)\right]\frac{dE^m}{d\tau} = 0. \tag{6.15}$$

By substituting the behavioral rules $-C_E(X^m, E^m) = \tau$ and $-P'(X^m)X^m = P(X^m) + C_X(X^m, E^m)$ from Eq. (6.12) and rearranging, we can isolate the second-best tax rate as

$$\tau = D'(E^m) + P'(X^m)X^m \times \frac{dX^m/d\tau}{dE^m/d\tau}. \tag{6.16}$$

From this we can see that the optimal tax rate will deviate from marginal damage by a term that depends on the degree to which the monopolist exercises market power, as well as his response to the tax rate.

To establish the signs of $dX^m/d\tau$ and $dE^m/d\tau$, we need to totally differentiate the conditions in (6.12) and solve for the two responses, which after several algebra steps results in

$$\frac{dX^m}{d\tau} = \frac{-C_{XE}(\cdot)}{C_{EE}(\cdot)\left[P''(\cdot)X + 2P'(\cdot) - C_{EE}(\cdot)\left\{C_{XX}(\cdot)C_{EE}(\cdot) - C_{XE}^2(\cdot)\right\}\right]} \tag{6.17}$$

and

$$\frac{dE^m}{d\tau} = -\frac{1}{C_{EE}(\cdot)} + \frac{C_{XE}^2(\cdot)}{C_{EE}^2(\cdot)\left[P''(\cdot)X + 2P'(\cdot) - C_{EE}(\cdot)\left\{C_{XX}(\cdot)C_{EE}(\cdot) - C_{XE}^2(\cdot)\right\}\right]}. \tag{6.18}$$

The curvature conditions stated in assumptions 5.1 and 6.1 together ensure that both of these derivatives are negative. Thus the optimal emission tax in this general case, as in the specific case above, is smaller than marginal damages.

Unlike the specific case above, however, the regulator can no longer achieve the first-best optimum by setting an emission tax alone. This is apparent from the fact that substituting the formula for the optimal tax rate from (6.16) into (6.12) does not cause the firm's behavioral rules to collapse to the conditions in (6.13). This is because the monopolist has two degrees of freedom in selecting both output and emissions, while the regulator has only one instrument – placing her firmly in a second-best world. Suppose, for example, that $P'(X^m)$ is large in absolute value, implying that small changes in quantity lead to large changes in price (i.e. demand is inelastic). In this case the welfare loss from the monopolist's quantity choice may be the dominant distortion and the second-best optimal emission tax level might be primarily influenced by the second term on the right-hand side of (6.16). A higher tax rate in this example will exacerbate the monopoly-induced distortion, more than it solves the pollution distortion.

Note that (6.16) can also be rewritten in terms of elasticities:

$$\tau = D'(E^m) - P(X^m)\varepsilon(X^m) \times \frac{dX^m}{dE},$$

(6.19)

where $\varepsilon(X^m) = -P'(X^m)X^m / P(X^m)$ is the absolute value of the inverse demand elasticity, and dX/dE is the change in monopoly output from relaxing the emission constraint. The formula is useful as it tells us that if demand elasticity is large (i.e. $\varepsilon(X^m)$ is small), the distortion through imperfect competition is small and the second-best optimal tax is almost at the Pigouvian level. If, by contrast, demand is very inelastic, and therefore $\varepsilon(X^m)$ is large, the regulator has to correct for too little output, and set the emission tax considerably below the Pigouvian level.

6.1.3 Regulating Output and Emissions Simultaneously

A second-best optimal outcome is easily avoided if the regulator has two instruments to address the two distortions rather than only the emission tax. We know from the industrial organization literature that a monopolist can be induced to produce the efficient level of output by subsidizing production. The same holds true here. If we tax emissions and at the same time subsidize output we can get the first-best outcome, if the regulator chooses the right level of those instruments. To see this, suppose there is an emission tax τ and a subsidy on output ζ so that the firm's profit is given by

$$\Pi(X, E) = \left[P(X) + \zeta \right] X - C(X, E) - \tau E,$$

(6.20)

with first-order conditions for profit maximization now given by:

$$P(X) + \zeta + P'(X)X = C_X(X, E)$$
$$-C_E(X, E) = \tau.$$

(6.21)

If we set $\tau = D'(E^*)$ and the subsidy so that

$$\zeta = -P'(X^*)X^*,$$

(6.22)

where E^* and X^* are the socially optimal level of emissions and output, respectively, the first-best allocation can be obtained. This is best seen by comparing (6.13) to (6.21), with the optimal values for the tax and subsidy substituted in. This is actually a special case of the Tinbergen (1952, 1956) rule stating that in general one needs as many instruments as there are market imperfections. Since subsidies are often not feasible due to political realities, trade treaties, or other international agreements this policy mix is more of a theoretical possibility than a real option. Thus the second-best analysis is even more relevant from a normative perspective.

6.2 OLIGOPOLIES

We now turn our attention to the challenge of regulating a polluting, oligopolistic industry. Under this rubric researchers have considered a wide range of industry characteristics, including homogeneous versus differentiated products and price versus quantity competition to give two prominent examples. In this section we limit our attention to the Cournot model, in which firms compete by setting the quantity of a homogeneous commodity. The Cournot model is a useful starting point for understanding this literature, and it also allows us to link the perfect competition and monopoly industries that we have already discussed. It also fits some real-world industries, with the best example being the energy sector. Electricity is produced by a relatively small number of firms, who compete to sell their perfectly substitutable output.

In what follows we first examine firms' behavior in this market structure, when there is an emissions tax in place. We then consider how the regulator should set the tax rate to best address the pollution externality, as well as the distortion arising from the non-competitive industry. Finally, we consider an extension of the model in which entry and exit are possible.

6.2.1 Firm Behavior Under Emission Taxes in a Cournot Model

We assume there are J firms that sell a homogeneous product and compete in a quantity-setting Cournot game, where the number of firms is exogenous and fixed. The market price is determined by the inverse demand function $p = P(X)$ that satisfies assumption 6.1, and the firms' technology follows assumption 5.1. Thus, if a firm j is subject to an emissions tax, its profit maximization problem is given by

$$\max_{x_j, e_j} \Pi_j(x_j, e_j, X_{-j}) = P(X)x_j - C^j(x_j, e_j) - \tau e_j, \tag{6.23}$$

where $X_{-j} = (x_1, ..., x_{j-1}, x_{j+1}, ..., x_J)$ is the strategy profile of the remaining $J-1$ competitors. We assume that firms take their competitors' decisions as given and that the resulting Nash equilibrium leads to positive amounts of output $x_j^o(\tau)$ and emissions $e_j^o(\tau)$ for each firm j. These non-cooperative solutions satisfy the following first-order conditions for profit maximization:

$$\begin{aligned} P'(X)x_j + P(X) - C_x^j(x_j, e_j) &= 0 \\ -C_e^j(x_j, e_j) &= \tau, \quad j = 1, ..., J. \end{aligned} \tag{6.24}$$

We assume that the solution is unique and stable, which can be shown to be the case for our model assumptions. The aggregate quantities of output and pollution are given by $X^o(\tau)$ and $E^o(\tau)$, respectively. To limit notational clutter, in what follows we once again drop the explicit dependence on τ when writing the firm and industry optimal quantities of these variables.

It is useful for the discussion that follows to first look at the comparative static effects of a tax increase. For this purpose, we differentiate each of the J pairs of equations in (6.24) with respect to τ to obtain

$$\left[P''(\cdot)x_j^o + P'(\cdot)\right]\frac{dX^o}{d\tau} + \left[P'(\cdot) - C_{xx}^j(\cdot)\right]\frac{dx_j^o}{d\tau} - C_{xe}^j(\cdot)\frac{de_j}{d\tau} = 0$$

$$-C_{xe}^j(\cdot)\frac{dx_j}{d\tau} - C_{ee}^j(\cdot)\frac{de_j}{d\tau} = 1 \tag{6.25}$$

for $j = 1, \ldots, J$. Note that in computing this derivative, care has been taken to distinguish between the aggregate response $dX^o/d\tau$, and the individual firm's response $dx_j^o/d\tau$, in the product rules used. Solving each pair of equations for $dx_j^o/d\tau$ and $de_j^o/d\tau$ yields

$$\frac{dx_j^o}{d\tau} = -\frac{C_{ee}^j(\cdot)\left[P''(\cdot)x_j^o + P'(\cdot)\right]\dfrac{dX^o}{d\tau} + C_{xe}^j(\cdot)}{C_{ee}^j(\cdot)P'(\cdot) - A_j} \tag{6.26}$$

and

$$\frac{de_j^o}{d\tau} = -\frac{C_{xe}^j(\cdot)\left[P''(\cdot)x_j^o + P'(X^o)\right]\dfrac{dX^o}{d\tau} + C_{xx}^j(\cdot) - P'(\cdot)}{C_{ee}^j(\cdot)P'(\cdot) - A_j}, \tag{6.27}$$

where $A_j = C_{xx}^j(\cdot)C_{ee}^j(\cdot) - [C_{xe}^j(\cdot)]^2 > 0$ by the convexity of the cost function. In contrast to the monopoly case, we cannot sign these two firm-level effects. The denominator in both expressions is negative; however, the numerators are indeterminate. We show below that $dX^o/d\tau < 0$, so in (6.26) the first term in the numerator is positive and the second term is negative. Likewise, in (6.27) the first term in the numerator is negative, while the middle and last terms are positive. Thus it can happen that an individual firm will increase or decrease its output and emissions in response to an increase in the tax rate. This is possible because a firm's decisions depend on its competitor's quantity response to the tax, which could lead to an increase or decrease in activity, apart from its direct response to the tax change.

To show that $dX^o/d\tau$ is negative, we note that the sum of the individual expressions in (6.26) is equal to the aggregate response. Adding the J values and rearranging to isolate $dX^o/d\tau$ leads to

$$\frac{dX^o}{d\tau} = -\left[\sum_{j=1}^{J}\frac{C_{xe}^j(\cdot)}{C_{ee}^j(\cdot)P'(\cdot) - A_j}\right]\left[1 + \sum_{j=1}^{J}\frac{C_{ee}^j(\cdot)\left[P''(\cdot)x_j^o + P'(\cdot)\right]}{C_{ee}^j(\cdot)P'(\cdot) - A_j}\right]^{-1}. \tag{6.28}$$

From assumption 5.1 we know that the first term in brackets is positive; likewise, from assumptions 5.1 and 6.1, the second term is positive. The aggregate quantity response to a change in the tax rate is therefore negative. Strategically, individual firms may find it optimal to increase their output when the emission tax is raised, but the industry-wide output falls following the increase.

By contrast, signing the aggregate industry emissions response to a tax change is not possible in general, as summing over the J individual response in (6.27) and rearranging yields

$$\frac{dE^o}{d\tau} = \sum_{j=1}^{J} \frac{C_{xx}^j(\cdot) - P'(\cdot)}{C_{ee}^j(\cdot)P'(\cdot) - A_j} + \frac{dX^o}{d\tau} \sum_{j=1}^{J} \frac{P''(\cdot)x_j^o + P'(\cdot)}{C_{ee}^j(\cdot)P'(\cdot) - A_j}. \tag{6.29}$$

Inspection of the expression shows that the sign of the first term is positive, while the sign of the second term is negative. Thus an increase in emissions following an increase in the emission tax rate is a possibility when firms compete in a Cournot game.

It is possible to derive sharper results when we add the assumption that firms are symmetric – i.e. $C_j(\cdot) = C(\cdot)$ for $j = 1, \ldots, J$. Under symmetry, $dX^o/d\tau = J \times dx^o/d\tau$, and substituting this expression into Eq. (6.26) and solving for $dx^o/d\tau$ allows us to unambiguously sign the comparative static as

$$\frac{dx^o}{d\tau} = -\left[\frac{C_{xe}(\cdot)}{C_{ee}(\cdot)P'(\cdot) - A} \right] \left[1 + \frac{C_{ee}(\cdot)\left[P''(\cdot)x^o + P'(\cdot) \right]J}{C_{ee}(\cdot)P'(\cdot) - A} \right]^{-1} < 0. \tag{6.30}$$

Following from this, we are also able to sign the firm's emission response to a tax change, which under symmetry is given by

$$\frac{de^o}{d\tau} = -\frac{C_{xe}(\cdot)\left[P''(\cdot)x_j + P'(\cdot) \right]J\dfrac{dx^o}{d\tau} + C_{xx}(\cdot) - P'(\cdot)}{C_{ee}(\cdot)P'(\cdot) - A} < 0. \tag{6.31}$$

EXAMPLE 6.1 (NUMERICAL/ANALYTICAL) The potential role of asymmetry in firms' cost functions is nicely illustrated by the following example, in which we examine how profits respond to a change in the tax rate for a duopoly. Suppose the two firms have constant marginal costs c_1 and c_2 such that $c_1 < c_2$. Suppose as well that pollution is proportional to output such that $e_j = \delta_j x_j$ and the inverse demand function if $P(X) = 1 - X$. In this case profits for the two firms are given by $\Pi^j = [1 - 2(c_j + \delta_j \tau) + (c_k + \delta_k \tau)]^2/9$. Differentiating Π^j with respect to τ shows that profits for firm j increase when the tax rate increases if $\delta_k > 2\delta_j$. Thus firm 1 can benefit from a higher tax rate if firm 2 pollutes twice as much per unit of output as firm 1.

6.2.2 Regulator's Problem Under Cournot Oligopoly

We now examine the regulator's problem, which is to choose a tax rate to maximize social welfare subject to the firms' response function. In particular she maximizes

$$W(\tau) = \int_0^{X^o(\tau)} P(t)dt - \sum_{j=1}^{J} C^j(x_j^o(\tau), e_j^o(\tau)) - D(E^o(\tau)), \tag{6.32}$$

where the superscripts "o" once again indicate that the quantities are solutions to the firms' optimal behavior as shown in Eq. (6.24). Differentiating (6.32) with respect to τ, substituting the firms' behavior rules using (6.24), and setting to zero we obtain (again omitting the dependence on τ for simplicity):

$$
\begin{aligned}
0 &= \sum_{j=1}^{J} \left[P(\cdot) - C_x^j(\cdot) \right] \frac{dx_j^o}{d\tau} + \sum_{j=1}^{J} \left[-C_e^j(\cdot) - D'(\cdot) \right] \frac{de_j^o}{d\tau} \\
&= \sum_{j=1}^{J} \left[-P'(\cdot) \right] x_j^o \frac{dx_j^o}{d\tau} + \sum_{j=1}^{J} \left[\tau - D'(\cdot) \right] \frac{de_j^o}{d\tau}.
\end{aligned}
\tag{6.33}
$$

Rearranging to isolate τ, we obtain a characterization of the optimal second-best tax rate as

$$
\tau = D'(E^o) + P'(X^o) \frac{\sum_{j=1}^{J} x_j^o \frac{dx_j^o}{d\tau}}{\frac{dE^o}{d\tau}}.
\tag{6.34}
$$

Note that the optimal second-best tax rate can lie above or below the marginal damage level, depending on the sign of $dE^o/d\tau$. If firms are asymmetric and this derivative is positive, the second-best optimal tax rate could lie above the marginal damage level. If firms are symmetric – or sufficiently similar – the result obtained for the monopoly case follows through, whereby the tax is set below the marginal damage. Specifically for the symmetric case we have

$$
\tau = D'(E^o) + P'(X^o) x^o \frac{dx^o/d\tau}{de^o/d\tau},
\tag{6.35}
$$

which matches the result we obtained in the monopoly case when $J = 1$. We summarize these findings in the following proposition.

Proposition 6.2

For oligopolistic firms whose technology satisfies assumption 5.1, Cournot quantity-based competition implies the following:

(a) *For symmetric firms or firms that are sufficiently similar in their cost structure,*
   (i) *aggregate emissions and output are decreasing in the emission tax rate; and*
   (ii) *the optimal second-best tax rate is smaller than the marginal damage level.*
(b) *For asymmetric firms that are sufficiently different in their cost structure, (i) aggregate output is decreasing in the tax rate, though individual firms may increase output following a tax increase; (ii) it is possible for some tax rate ranges that pollution is increasing in the emission tax rate; and (iii) the second-best tax rate may exceed the marginal damage level.*

Thus, we see that if firms are symmetric or sufficiently similar, we obtain the same results in qualitative terms as in the case of monopoly. If firms are asymmetric, some perverse effects may arise. The intuition is that if the marginal cost differential between firms is different from the difference in emission coefficients, taxation changes the cost structure between the firms, leading to complex strategic responses. This can lead to a situation where one firm gains whereas another firm suffers from a tax increase, or even cause aggregate pollution to rise and the tax rate to exceed marginal damage. For the last two effects to arise, however, asymmetry of firms does not suffice. As Levin (1985) has shown, we also need an inverse demand function which has extreme curvature – i.e. it is either sufficiently convex or sufficiently concave.

6.2.3 Entry and Exit

We now extend our oligopoly model by allowing for free entry. Recall from Eq. (6.24) that the price firms receive is above marginal cost, and so without free entry positive rents are maintained in the industry. When entry is possible these rents attract additional firms, which introduces the possibility of a third market distortion in the form of excess entry. To provide a brief sense of how this might matter, we simplify the analysis so that firms are identical and their technology follows assumption 5.2, with $e = \delta x$. We then introduce a fixed cost of entry F, so that a representative firm's profit is given by

$$\Pi(x, X_{-j}) = P(X)x - C(x) - F - \tau\delta x, \tag{6.36}$$

where x is a typical firm's output, and X_{-j} is the strategy profile of the remaining firms. The assumption of symmetric firms when entry is possible is not as restrictive as it seems. Under free entry, only the firms with the lowest average cost survive, and so it is unlikely that multiple different technologies (with different cost implications) can simultaneously exist. The zero profit condition that governs the size of the industry is

$$P(X)x - C(x) - \tau\delta x - F = 0, \tag{6.37}$$

and firms' Nash equilibrium strategies are determined according to

$$P'(X)x + P(X) = C'(x) + \tau\delta, \tag{6.38}$$

where $X = xJ$ and J is the (endogenous) number of firms.

Continuing the approach used above, we examine comparative static results before characterizing the regulator's optimal tax rate. Differentiating (6.37) with respect to τ leads to

$$P'(\cdot)\left[J^o\frac{dx^o}{d\tau} + x^o\frac{dJ^o}{d\tau}\right]x^o + \left[P(\cdot) - C'(\cdot) - \tau\delta\right]\frac{dx^o}{d\tau} = \delta x^o, \tag{6.39}$$

and differentiating (6.38) we obtain

$$[J^oP''(\cdot) + (J^o + 1)P'(\cdot) - C''(\cdot)]\frac{dx^o}{d\tau} + [P''(\cdot) + P'(\cdot)]x^o\frac{dJ^o}{d\tau} = \delta. \tag{6.40}$$

Gathering terms and solving using Cramer's Rule, we arrive at solutions for the comparative statics given by

$$\frac{dx^o}{d\tau} = \frac{\delta P''(\cdot) x^o}{P'(\cdot)\left[C''(\cdot) - 2P'(\cdot) - P''(\cdot)x^o\right]} \tag{6.41}$$

and

$$\frac{dJ^o}{d\tau} = \frac{\delta\left[C''(\cdot) - 2P'(X^o) - J \times P''(\cdot)x^o\right]}{P'(\cdot)\left[C''(\cdot) - 2P'(\cdot) - P''(\cdot)x^o\right]} < 0. \tag{6.42}$$

From (6.42) we can see that the number of firms decreases if the tax rate goes up. The effect on output from a single firm, by contrast, cannot be signed, in that it depends on the curvature of the inverse demand function. The reason for this ambiguity is that with a fixed J, output falls, since a tax increase raises each firm's costs. However, as J falls, the single firm can increase its market share. Nonetheless, total output (and hence total pollution) falls when the emission tax is increased. We can see this by calculating

$$\frac{dX^o}{d\tau} = J\frac{dx^o}{d\tau} + x^o\frac{dJ^o}{d\tau} = \frac{\delta\left[-2P'(\cdot) + C''(\cdot)\right]}{P'(\cdot)\left[C''(\cdot) - 2P'(\cdot) - P''(\cdot)x^o\right]} < 0. \tag{6.43}$$

We are now ready to look at the regulator's objective, which is to maximize

$$W(\tau) = \int_0^{X^o} P(t)dt - J^o(\tau)C(x^o(\tau)) - D(\delta X^o(\tau)). \tag{6.44}$$

Differentiating this expression with respect to τ yields

$$P(X^o)\left[J^o\frac{dx^o}{d\tau} + x^o\frac{dJ^o}{d\tau}\right] - \frac{dJ^o}{d\tau}C(x^o) - J^o \cdot C'(x^o)\frac{dx^o}{d\tau}$$
$$- \delta D'(\delta X^o)\left[J^o\frac{dx^o}{d\tau} + x^o\frac{dJ^o}{d\tau}\right] = 0. \tag{6.45}$$

Substituting in expressions from the behavioral conditions in (6.37) and (6.38), we can simplify this to obtain

$$J^o\left[-P'(X^o)x^o + \delta\left(\tau - D'(\delta X^0)\right)\right]\frac{dx^o}{d\tau} + \left[\delta x^o\left(\tau - D'(\delta X^0)\right)\right]\frac{dJ^o}{d\tau} = 0. \tag{6.46}$$

Isolating the tax rate and using $dE^o/d\tau = \delta dX^o/d\tau$ we obtain

$$\tau = D'(E) + P'(X^o)X^o\frac{dx^o/d\tau}{dE^o/d\tau}. \tag{6.47}$$

By inspection of this second-best optimal tax formula we obtain the following neat result.

Proposition 6.3

Under symmetric oligopoly with a fixed entry cost[1] where pollution is proportional to output, the second-best optimal emission tax rate:

(a) exceeds marginal damage if the inverse demand function is strictly convex;

(b) is smaller than marginal damage if the inverse demand function is strictly concave; and

(c) equals marginal damage if the demand function is linear.

In cases where the firms' technologies satisfy assumption 5.1, we do not obtain results that are as clear cut. Requate (1997) gives conditions under which the second-best optimal tax rate exceeds marginal damage. If the latter is the case, the market imperfection of excess entry dominates the market imperfection of firms holding down output.

6.3   EXTENSIONS

As noted in the introduction, the literature contains examinations of several additional topics related to market power. In this section we briefly note in survey format a handful of examples, summarizing without derivation the main results, and comparing them to what we have shown above.

A number of papers have considered Bertrand rather than Cournot competition. For example, Lange and Requate (1999) consider a duopoly model in which firms offer differentiated products and engage in price competition. In their model, emissions are proportional to output, and the damage function takes the more general form $D(e_1, e_2)$, so that damages from a given aggregate level of pollution can depend differentially on how it is allocated between the two firms. The authors examine firm-specific tax rates and a uniform tax rate. For the former, a result similar to the Cournot competition case arises in which the second-best tax rate for firm j is smaller than its marginal damage level, by an amount that depends on the own price elasticity for the differentiated product j. If firms are symmetric in the sense that their damage and cost functions are similar, and they face similar own and cross-price demand elasticities, it is likewise the case that the second-best optimal uniform tax rate lies below the marginal damage rate. For asymmetric firms, it can happen that the second-best optimal uniform tax rate lies above the marginal damage rate. Thus, most of the findings from the Cournot case discussed above qualitatively carry over to the Bertrand duopoly case.

Requate (1993b) also studies the case of Bertrand competition for a homogeneous commodity with constant but differential marginal costs. In that case, the first best can always be implemented by an emission tax, whenever it is optimal for only one of two (asymmetric) firms to produce total output. If it is optimal that both firms produce, the first-best allocation cannot be obtained by a uniform emission tax. The reason is that the

---

[1] Note that it does not matter whether the firms incur a fixed cost per production period or a fixed entry cost, or both.

Pigouvian tax can induce the optimal price, but not the optimal overall cost-minimizing production allocation among the two firms. This result carries over to market entry of firms with different technologies (Requate, 1995).

Lange and Requate (1999) also study monopolistic competition with polluting firms. First, they examine the Dixit and Stiglitz (1977) model, with constant marginal cost and emissions proportional to output. Here too they show that the second-best optimal tax rate is smaller than the marginal damage rate, though it approaches the marginal damage function (and hence the competitive outcome) as the differentiated commodities become better substitutes. The same authors then examine a version of Salop's (1979) circular city model, but with the generalization that consumer demand is continuous and elastic. They find, again, that if the number of firms is exogenous, the second-best optimal tax rate is smaller than marginal damage. If market entry is possible, and thus the number of firms is endogenous, the second-best optimal tax rate may be larger or smaller than the marginal damage rate.

In separate analyses related to input markets, David and Sinclair-Desgagné (2005) and Requate (2005) show that if a monopolistic upstream firm offers an abating input or new technology, then the second-best optimal tax rate of the polluting downstream firm will typically exceed marginal damage. This is because the upstream monopolist supplies too little of the abating input, and the regulator needs to stimulate demand among the polluting firms, by raising the emission tax above marginal damage. Requate (2006) summarizes further models of imperfect competition on both input and factor markets.

6.4 SUMMARY

We have studied optimal environmental policy in markets where one or several firms exercise market power on the output market. This causes two market imperfections, and in general calls for multiple policy instruments. In many cases it is not feasible to tackle market power directly. Therefore, the question arises whether environmental policy should account for multiple market imperfections, and in fact it turns out that the Pigouvian rule per se no longer holds in such environments. In most of the models discussed, we found that if the regulator has only one instrument – e.g. an emission tax – the (second-best) optimal emission tax rate is below marginal damage. The reason is that a polluting firm that exercises market power pollutes less than under perfectly competitive conditions. Therefore, a tax below the marginal damage can help to mitigate the market failure related to the too-small output level. In a way, output is subsidized by not fully internalizing the social cost of pollution. As special results we obtained the following.

- In a model of a polluting monopolist with pollution proportional to output, the optimal emission tax rate is lower than marginal damage and leads to the first-best outcome.
- In a model of a polluting monopolist with an abatement technology, the optimal emission tax rate is lower than marginal damage but creates only a second-best optimal outcome.
- If in the latter model the regulator has two instruments, an emission tax and a subsidy on output, the first-best allocation can be achieved.

- In a symmetric oligopoly model of quantity setting firms (Cournot competition), the previous results hold. If by contrast firms are extremely asymmetric, perverse results may emerge in which an increase in the emission tax raises total pollution and the second-best optimal tax rate exceeds marginal damage.

In oligopoly models with market entry, the second-best optimal tax rate may exceed or be less than marginal damage. In that case the regulator has to address three market imperfections: too much pollution per unit of output, price higher than marginal cost, and excess entry. If the dissipation of fixed costs through excess entry is stronger than the under-provision of output, the emission tax rate will exceed marginal damage.

6.5 FURTHER READING

Buchanan and Stubblebine (1962) and Buchanan (1969) were the first to address the non-optimality of the Pigouvian paradigm if polluting firms exercise market power (see also the discussion by D.R. Lee, 1975). Barnett (1980) was the first to discuss second-best optimal tax rules for a polluting monopolist (see also Misiolek, 1980). Requate (1993a) studies regulation of several local monopolies. Levin (1985) was the first to investigate the comparative static effects of emission taxes in Cournot (quantity setting) oligopoly, while Ebert (1992), Katsoulacos and Xepapadeas (1995), and Simpson (1995) characterize the structure of the second-best optimal tax rates, for several cases of quantity-setting oligopolies. Requate (1993c) compares taxes versus permits in a Cournot duopoly while Gersbach and Requate (2004) investigate refunding schemes of emission tax revenues in a Cournot oligopoly.

For price oligopolies, see Requate (1993b), and Lange and Requate (1999) for price-setting firms with differentiated commodities. For models of market entry, see Katsoulacos and Xepapadeas (1995), Requate (1997), and Lee (1999) for the Cournot case, and Lange and Requate (1999) for the prototype price-setting models, notably the Dixit-Stiglitz model and the Salop model. In this chapter we only discussed emission taxes. There is a lot of literature on emission permit markets, which we partly discuss in Chapter 8. For a detailed survey of environmental policy when firms exercise market power, see Requate (2006).

EXERCISES

6.1 Consider a monopolist facing linear demand $P(X) = 1 - X$ and constant marginal costs $c > 0$ (and/or increasing marginal cost $C'(X) = cX$). The social damage function is quadratic of the form $D(E) = dE^2/2$. Emissions are proportional to output, where $E = X$.

(a) * Determine the socially optimal level of production (emissions) and the optimal tax rate.

(b) * For which damage parameters is the tax rate positive (negative)?

(c) * For which damage parameters can the social optimum be achieved with an emission cap?

(d) ** Consider now a cost function $C(X, E) = (\alpha X - \beta E)^2 / 2\beta$ and derive the second-best optimal tax.

6.2 * Show that the monopoly output determined by Eq. (6.2) is a decreasing function of the tax rate.

6.3 ** Show that the monopoly output and emissions determined by (6.12) are decreasing in the tax rate. That is, verify equations (6.17) and (6.18).

6.4 ** Show that an emission tax and an *absolute* emission standard are equivalent instruments to regulate a polluting monopolist if and only if the standard is binding.

6.5 *** Derive a formula for the second-best *relative* standard to regulate a polluting monopolist.

6.6 ** Show that in a symmetric Cournot oligopoly under both assumptions 5.1 and 5.2 (see Chapter 5), profits decrease if the emission tax goes up.

6.7 ** Show that in a symmetric oligopoly where the firms' technologies satisfy assumption 5.1, the first-best outcome can be achieved by a tax on emissions and a subsidy on output. Determine the optimal levels of the tax and the subsidy.

6.8 *** Consider a symmetric oligopoly in which firms' technologies satisfy assumption 5.1. Assume that firms get part of the tax revenues refunded, according to their market shares. The refund share is $0 < d < 1$. A typical firm's profit is thus given by:

$$\pi(x_j, e_j) = P(X)x_j - C(x_j, e_j) - \tau e_j + d\tau E \frac{x_j}{X}.$$

(a) Show that the first-best outcome can be achieved by a tax on emissions and a refunding system according to market share, if the damage from pollution is sufficiently high.

(b) Determine the optimal levels of the tax and the refunding share d.

6.9 ** Consider a Cournot oligopoly facing linear demand $P(X) = 1 - X$ and constant marginal costs $c > 0$ (and/or increasing marginal cost $C'(X) = cX$). The social damage function is quadratic of the form $D(E) = dE^2/2$. Emissions are proportional to output, where $E = X$.

(a) Determine the optimal emission tax.

(b) Suppose instead that the cost function is $C(X, E) = (\alpha X - \beta E)^2 / 2\beta$. Derive a formula for the second-best optimal tax rate.

6.10 *** Show that in a symmetric oligopoly with free entry and firms' technologies satisfying assumption 5.1 the first-best outcome can be achieved by an emission tax, a subsidy on output, and either an entry fee or a quota of auctioned licenses. Determine the optimal levels of those policy tools.

6.11 *** Consider a firm that produces an output using two inputs so that $x = f(l_1, l_2)$. Pollution is proportional to one of the inputs. The polluting firm has market power in the market for l_1. Denote the inverse supply function for l_1 by $w_1(l_1)$. Assume that the polluting firm is subject to an emission tax.

(a) Solve the polluting firm's profit maximization problem. Distinguish the cases where l_1 is the polluting input or clean input, respectively.

(b) Derive the comparative static effects on raising the emission tax rate, again distinguishing the cases when l_1 is the polluting or clean input.

(c) Determine the second-best optimal tax rate for the two cases.

(d) How could the regulator achieve the first-best outcome?

6.12 ** Consider the regulation of J local monopolies for different goods with inverse demand functions $P_j(X_j)$ and cost functions $C^j(X_j,e_j)$. Social damage depends on total pollution $E = \sum_{j=1}^{J} e_j$ and is given by a convex damage function $D(E)$.

(a) Derive an expression for the second-best tax to jointly regulate the J local monopolists.

(b) Show that such a system is equivalent to a system of tradable permits.

CHAPTER 7

Environmental Policy with Pre-existing Distortions

Our emphasis thus far in Part II of the book has been partial equilibrium, in the sense that we have focused only on the polluting sector in our consideration of environmental policy. When studying competitive markets from this perspective, we have consistently found that the optimal pollution level occurs at the point where firms' marginal abatement costs are equal to society's marginal damages. Furthermore, the short run performance of the full suite of incentive-based policies was equivalent. Importantly, the extent to which the different policies raise revenue for the government was important only for equity, and did not play a role in efficiency comparisons. Thus emissions could be taxed or abatement subsidized, and pollution permits auctioned or freely distributed, and the only difference was in who captured the environmental scarcity rents. Things were slightly different in the long run, in that abatement subsidies could cause excess entry and were therefore inferior to emissions taxes. Nonetheless, we found that permit schemes that do not raise revenue perform equally to their auctioned counterparts, so long as total emissions are capped when firms enter or leave the market. The ability to separate equity considerations from efficiency outcomes was touted as an important source of flexibility available to the environmental regulator.

A question we have not yet examined is the extent to which these partial equilibrium results continue to hold when we consider how environmental policy might spill over into other markets. We saw in Chapter 5, for example, that environmental policy raises the output price of the polluting good. This can affect the demand for other consumption goods, impact households' labor supply decisions, and cause changes in real income. More importantly, pollution externalities are usually not the only sources of distortions in an economy. Government revenue is often raised via proportional labor taxes, thereby encouraging the overconsumption of leisure, and causing potentially substantial welfare losses. Other factor input markets are also distorted, as are many product markets through value added taxes or subsidies. It is natural to ask how these pre-existing distortions might interact with environmental policy, causing us to alter the conclusions obtained when such spillover effects are ignored.

Thinking on this topic emerged along two lines. The first focused on the potential for environmental policy to result in a "double dividend". The idea is that emission taxes can be used to fix the pollution externality, which is the first dividend. Since revenue is also raised in the process a tax swap is possible, in which labor taxes can be reduced. The resulting decrease in the labor market distortion is the second dividend. This is an idea with considerable appeal, since it diminishes the need to understand the benefits of environmental policy. If the overall cost of a revenue-raising environmental policy is small or zero due to the second dividend, we only need to know that environmental benefits are positive to justify its implementation. The second line of thinking took a more nuanced view of how environmental policy and pre-existing distortions interact. This gave rise to the "tax interaction" literature from the 1990s, in which formal modeling was used to isolate the multiple pathways through which the costs of environmental policy in a distorted economy might diverge from costs in the first best. Some surprising theoretical insights emerged from this research, which led many to doubt the potential for a double dividend. Topics related to tax interaction and the double dividend continue to be discussed to this day, with much of the work now empirical in nature.

Our objective in this chapter is to carefully examine how interactions with pre-existing distortions might cause us to alter the performance ranking of policy instruments that we established in earlier chapters. The modeling framework that we need for this will necessarily become more complex. For example, we will add a government sector that has revenue needs beyond what can be raised from taxing emissions. Since the government's main source of revenue will be labor taxes, we need to add a labor/leisure component to household decisions. We will also expand the concepts considered. For example, public finance topics such as the marginal welfare cost of public funds and the excess burden from taxation will have a role to play in our analysis. The payoff to this is that some surprising results emerge, which are only apparent from careful modeling. For example, the notion that marginal abatement cost equals marginal damages at the optimum breaks down in a second-best setting. Also, the extent to which a policy raises revenue has efficiency ramifications, which limits a regulator's ability to decouple efficiency and equity characteristics of an intervention. Finally, abatement subsidies are now problematic even in the short run, due to the fiscal burdens they cause.

In the next section we lay the groundwork for showing these effects by extending the model used thus far in Part II to include household labor supply and a government budget constraint. Following our established convention, we then consider the optimal level of pollution in the presence of the government's revenue needs, distinguishing between non-revenue raising and revenue-raising optimal pollution levels. This is followed by sections on policy tools and their performance, and a discussion of generalizations to our basic model that can alter its conclusions. We also review some of the empirical findings that shed light on what types of pollution taxes have the potential for creating a double dividend.

7.1 EXTENDING THE MODEL

We start out by generalizing the model so that consumer utility depends on consumption of the polluting good, damages suffered from emissions, and leisure time. In what follows it will be convenient to simplify the analysis so that there is one representative consumer and one representative firm, which allows us to treat individual and aggregate outcomes as the same. As such we use X to denote consumption of the polluting good, Z for spending on the numeraire, and N to denote hours of leisure time. The utility function is now $U(X,Z,N,E) = u(X,N) + Z - D(E)$, where E is aggregate emissions and $D(E)$ is the damage function.

We assume $u(X,N)$ is strictly concave, so that $u_{XX}<0$, $u_{NN}<0$, and $u_{XX}u_{NN}-(u_{XN})^2>0$. We do not make a specific assumption on the sign of u_{XN}. If $u_{XN}<0$, then consumption of the polluting good and leisure are substitutes. If $u_{XN}>0$, they are complements. The person is endowed with an amount of time T, which he sells as labor or consumes as leisure. Wages earned in the labor market are used to purchase X and Z, so household income is now endogenous in our model. We assume the demand for labor is perfectly elastic economy wide, meaning that the labor demand curve is a horizontal line at the market wage rate w. Absent an income tax, $w \cdot (T-N)$ is the household's income. To establish a point for comparison, note that the consumer's problem when there is no distortion in the labor market is

$$\max_{X,N} U = u(X,N) + Z - D(E) \quad s.t. \quad w(T-N) = Z + pX$$
$$= u(X,N) + w(T-N) - pX - D(E), \tag{7.1}$$

where the second line follows from substituting Z out using the budget constraint. The first-order conditions are $u_X(X,N)=p$ and $u_N(X,N)=w$, which leads to ordinary demand functions $X(p,w)$ and $N(p,w)$, where we have suppressed T as an argument in these functions. Note that these can also be interpreted as compensated demand functions due to the absence of income effects in the specification for utility. To obtain a comparative static relationship between N and p we differentiate the first-order conditions with respect to p to obtain

$$u_{XX}(X,N)\frac{\partial X}{\partial p} + u_{XN}(X,N)\frac{\partial N}{\partial p} = 1$$
$$u_{NN}(X,N)\frac{\partial N}{\partial p} + u_{NX}(X,N)\frac{\partial X}{\partial p} = 0. \tag{7.2}$$

From this system it is possible to express the comparative statics as

$$\frac{\partial N}{\partial p} = \frac{-u_{XN}}{\left(u_{XX}u_{NN}-u_{XN}^2\right)} \begin{array}{c} < \\ = 0 \\ > \end{array}$$
$$\frac{\partial X}{\partial p} = \frac{u_{NN}}{\left(u_{XX}u_{NN}-u_{XN}^2\right)} < 0. \tag{7.3}$$

Note that the denominator for both expressions is positive by the concavity of the utility function, and that $\partial X/\partial p$ is negative by the properties of the utility function. The sign of the numerator for $\partial N/\partial p$ depends on the complement or substitute relationship between X and N, and so is indeterminate in general. If leisure and the dirty good are substitutes, the demand for leisure increases when the price of the dirty good goes up.

The firm's problem is unchanged from Chapter 5. We assume the representative price-taking firm produces X and discharges emissions E. For simplicity, we will work with Case 2 from Chapter 5, so that a firm's problem is to maximize profits $\Pi = pX - C(X)$, where $E = \delta X$. Furthermore, we assume that $\delta = 1$, which allows us to use E and X interchangeably. The cost function $C(X)$ in general has the properties $C'(X)>0$ and $C''(X)\geq 0$; in some instances it will be useful to consider the special case of constant marginal cost, so that $C'(X)=c$ and $C''(X)=0$. Finally, we imagine that the polluting industry's demand for labor is small relative to the wider economy, so that changes in the aggregate demand or supply for the polluting good do not affect the overall labor market. Thus the market wage rate faced by both firms and households stays fixed throughout our analysis. Absent any regulation of emissions, the firm produces at the point where price equals marginal cost.

7.1.1 Optimum with No Labor Market Distortion

Absent other distortions in the economy, the regulator's problem is to choose the level of X, and therefore emissions $E=X$, to maximize the economic surplus from the dirty good. With our quasi-linear utility function, this is equivalent to maximizing the sum of utility and profits:

$$
\begin{aligned}
\max_{X} W &= u(X,N)+Z-D(X)+pX-C(X) \\
&= u(X,N)+\underbrace{w(T-N)-pX}_{Z}-D(X)+pX-C(X) \\
&= u(X,N)+w(T-N)-D(X)-C(X).
\end{aligned}
\tag{7.4}
$$

In order to focus on interactions with markets that are *not* regulated by the environmental authority, we assume throughout this chapter that the regulator does not determine leisure (N). Instead, the consumer selects N, and therefore Z, according to his budget constraint $Z=w(T-N)-pX$ and first-order condition $u_N(X^*,N)=w$, where X^* is the regulator's choice of X arising via her choice of E. In addition, it is useful at this point to conceptualize the regulator's problem as one in which she imposes a quantity standard X, which is then sold by the firm. Given the quantity X^* a market price p^* arises that affects the demand for leisure.

By taking the derivative with respect to X in (7.4) we can express the first-order condition for the social optimum as

$$
u_X(X,N)-D'(X)-C'(X)+\left[u_N(X,N)-w\right]\frac{\partial N}{\partial X}=0,
\tag{7.5}
$$

where the last term is the consumer's indirect response in N to the regulator's marginal adjustment of X. Since the consumer's optimal choice of N results in $u_N-w=0$, the condition reduces to

$$
u_X(X,N)-C'(X)=D'(X),
\tag{7.6}
$$

or marginal abatement cost equals marginal damage. The efficient outcome is illustrated in panels A and B of Figure 7.1. In panel A we have included the demand function $X(p,w)$ and labeled the optimum by X^*. For comparison we have also shown p^c and X^c as the competitive (non-regulated) price and quantity, respectively, and labeled the implied price of the regulated good at X^* by p^*. Relative to the market outcome, there is a lower level of X and the consumer faces a higher price under the social optimum. Panel B shows the efficient level of X in marginal abatement cost (MAC) and marginal damage (MD) space, where $MAC=u_X(\cdot)-C'(X)$ is the opportunity cost of reducing X. For simplicity we have assumed constant marginal damages in both illustrations.

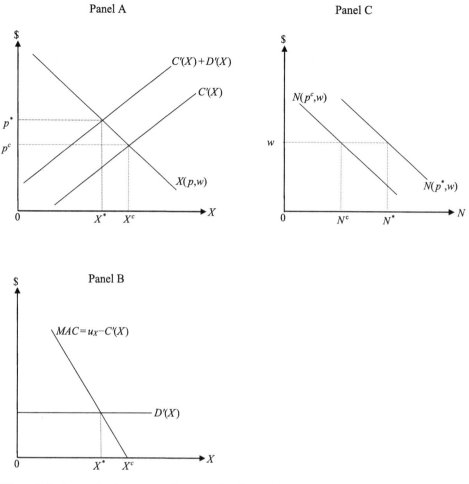

Figure 7.1   Interaction between environmental policy and labor/leisure

In panel C of Figure 7.1 we illustrate how the regulation of pollution has an effect that spills over to the labor/leisure market. In particular, the pre-regulation level of leisure is given by $N(p^c,w)$. After the increase in the price for X (and assuming for the moment that X and N are substitutes), we have $N(p^*,w) > N(p^c,w)$.

The increase in the price of the polluting good causes the demand for leisure to shift out, leading to more leisure consumed and less labor supplied. Thus the regulation of the dirty good affects outcomes in the labor market. However, there are no efficiency ramifications, since the value of the marginal product of labor (i.e. the wage rate) equals the value of forgone leisure in both the pre- and post-policy cases. From this we can see that setting marginal abatement cost equal to marginal damages continues to be optimum in a competitive market, so long as there are no other distortions in related markets.

7.1.2 A Labor Market Distortion

We now examine a situation in which the government needs to raise revenue using a tax on labor to finance a fixed budget of size G. Specifically, there is a proportional tax on

Panel A   Panel B

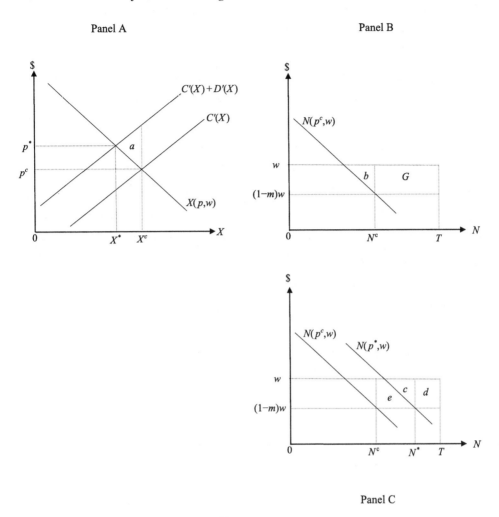

Panel C

Figure 7.2   Tax interaction and revenue effects

labor income given by m, so that the net wage earned by the consumer from supplying labor is $(1-m)\cdot w$. The representative consumer's utility maximization problem is now

$$\max_{X,Z,N} U = u(X,N) + Z - D(E) \quad s.t. \quad (1-m)w(T-N) = Z + pX, \tag{7.7}$$

and the first-order conditions are

$$u_X(X,N) = p$$
$$u_N(X,N) = (1-m) \times w. \tag{7.8}$$

The labor tax causes inefficiency in the labor market in the form of overconsumption of leisure. Indeed, the first-order condition with respect to leisure can be rewritten as $u_N + mw = w$, which illustrates how the income tax is equivalent to a subsidy to leisure. Thus prior to regulation there are two distorted markets: too much X due to the externality, and too little labor due to the income tax. The two distorted markets are shown in Figure 7.2. In panel A, area a is the efficiency loss due to the externality, and in panel B area *b* is the loss due to the labor market distortion. The latter is often referred to as the "excess burden" from the labor tax, and it results because the marginal value of leisure at N^c is smaller than w, its marginal value as labor. Area G shows the amount of revenue the government raises via the tax, which is equivalent to government spending if the government budget balances. Panel C shows how the leisure market interacts with the product market when the regulator sets the quantity X^* in the latter. The shift in leisure demand causes a change in the excess burden from b to c, where the relative sizes of the two are indeterminate. Importantly, there is also a decrease in the tax receipts raised by the government, where now $d < G$ is available for public expenditures. Thus when there is a distortion in the labor market due to an income tax, regulation of a polluting good has efficiency ramifications beyond those directly associated with the externality: it can affect the size of the excess burden and the amount of income tax revenue that the government raises. In such cases it is necessary to consider interactions between the two markets in formulating the optimal environmental policy. As we will show below, it will generally *not* be optimal to set marginal abatement cost equal to marginal damage when there are pre-existing distortions in related markets.

7.2   SECOND-BEST OPTIMAL POLLUTION LEVELS

In this section we derive results describing optimal pollution levels when there is an existing distortion in the labor market. We again assume the government needs to finance a fixed budget of size G, which it can raise by taxing both labor and the firm's emissions. For illustration, we first consider the case when only labor taxation is available, which is equivalent to the government setting a pollution standard. We subsequently examine the more general case where the government can tax emissions along with labor to raise revenue.

7.2.1 Non-revenue Raising Environmental Policy

The regulator's problem when environmental policy does not raise revenue is to choose X (and thereby the emission level E) and the marginal tax rate m to maximize the sum of utility and profit, subject to the government's budget needs. Once again, the government cannot choose the level of labor/leisure in this setup. Instead, the person consumes leisure according to the optimality condition $u_N(\bar{X}, N) = (1 - m)w$, given the regulator's choice $\bar{X}$ of the polluting good. The representative firm sells the fixed quantity $\bar{X}$ at a price p to earn profits $\Pi = p\bar{X} - C(\bar{X})$. The marginal value of the dirty good arises from the consumer's inverse demand function $P(\bar{X}) = u_X(\bar{X}, N)$, which is endogenous via its dependence on the choice variable N. This sets the price the firm receives from the household for selling a unit of the polluting good at $p = u_X(\bar{X}, N)$. Thus p and N are endogenous outcomes that are determined by the household's response to the regulator's choices for the dirty good and m according to

$$u_X(\bar{X}, N) = p$$
$$u_N(\bar{X}, N) = (1 - m)w. \tag{7.9}$$

For later reference we note that differentiating the conditions in (7.9) with respect to $\overline{X}$ leads to

$$u_{XX}(\overline{X},N)+u_{XN}(\overline{X},N)\frac{\partial N}{\partial \overline{X}} = \frac{\partial p}{\partial \overline{X}}$$

$$u_{NX}(\overline{X},N)+u_{NN}(\overline{X},N)\frac{\partial N}{\partial \overline{X}} = 0,$$

(7.10)

which we can solve to obtain the comparative statics

$$\frac{\partial N}{\partial \overline{X}} = -\frac{u_{XN}(\overline{X},N)}{u_{NN}(\overline{X},N)} \overset{\leq}{>} 0$$

$$\frac{\partial p}{\partial \overline{X}} = \frac{u_{XX}(\overline{X},N)u_{NN}(\overline{X},N)-[u_{NN}(\overline{X},N)]^2}{u_{NN}(\overline{X},N)} < 0,$$

(7.11)

where the sign of the first expression is indeterminate because leisure and the polluting good can be substitutes or complements. Combining these expressions with the comparative static result for $\partial N/\partial p$ from (7.3) allows us to express the consumer's optimal response to the regulator's choice of the polluting good as

$$\frac{\partial N}{\partial \overline{X}} = \frac{\partial N}{\partial p}\frac{\partial p}{\partial \overline{X}}.$$

(7.12)

Analytically, the regulator's problem is to maximize the sum of utility and profit, subject to the government revenue constraint, as given by

$$\max_{X,m}\left\{u(X,N)+Z-D(X)+pX-C(X)\right\} \quad s.t. \quad wm(T-N) = G.$$

(7.13)

In addition, we assume for convenience and tractability that government revenues are returned back to the consumer as a lump sum transfer, so that

$$Z = (1-m)\times w\times(T-N)-pX+G.$$

(7.14)

Note that numeraire consumption now consists of net income less spending on X, augmented by the transfer amount G. Furthermore, Eq. (7.14) simplifies to $Z=w\times(T-N)-pX$, so that the tax and transfer mechanisms leave household income unchanged for a given level of N. This formulation of the problem allows us to avoid the complication of modeling government-provided services, while preserving the essential feature of distortionary income taxation.

Substituting out for Z using (7.14), we can reduce the regulator's problem to

$$\max_{X,m} W = u(X,N)+w(T-N)-D(X)-C(X)+\lambda\left(wm(T-N)-G\right),$$

(7.15)

where λ is the Lagrange multiplier, which has an important interpretation. In particular, $-\lambda=\partial W/\partial G\le 0$, which is the marginal welfare cost of public funds. This measures the welfare consequences of each additional dollar of government revenue collected via tax-ing labor, where welfare falls when G increases due to the distortionary effect of the tax.

In maximizing W, we need to account for both the direct effects of the choice vari-ables, as well as the indirect effects associated with the consumer's choice of N. Con-sider first the condition for m

$$\left(u_N(\cdot) - w\right)\frac{\partial N}{\partial m} + \lambda\left(w(T - N) - wm\frac{\partial N}{\partial m}\right) = 0, \tag{7.16}$$

where the terms containing $\partial N/\partial m$ are the indirect effects of m working through lei-sure demand. From the consumer's optimal choice of N we know that $-mw = u_N(\cdot) - w$. Making this substitution and rearranging, we can derive an expression for λ as

$$\lambda = \frac{w\dfrac{\partial N}{\partial m}m}{w(T - N) - w\dfrac{\partial N}{\partial m}m}. \tag{7.17}$$

This form of the first-order condition illustrates the interpretation of λ as the marginal welfare cost of public funds. Note in particular that the numerator is the welfare loss from a change in m. To see this, recall that the excess burden from labor taxation is shown as area b in panel B of Figure 7.2. An increase in m leads to a higher quantity of leisure demand; multiplying this change by wm (the height of the tax wedge) gives the change in the excess burden, which is the additional welfare loss from the increase in m. The denominator is the derivative of tax revenue (i.e. $mw \cdot (T - N)$) with respect to m, which is the increase in revenue that an increase in m provides. The change in revenue consists of the extra revenue resulting from the higher m (the first term) less the loss in revenue that occurs when leisure increases (the second term). The ratio in Eq. (7.17) is therefore the welfare loss per dollar of additional revenue raised, when m increases – i.e. the marginal welfare cost of revenue raised via distortionary taxation.

To gain further insight on the factors that determine the marginal cost of public funds, note that the effect of m on leisure demand is based on the net wage $(1 - m) \cdot w$. Specifi-cally, the demand for leisure in this context can be written as $N(X, (1 - m) \cdot w)$, which implies that $\partial N/\partial m = w(-\partial N/\partial w)$. In addition, $-\partial N/\partial w = \partial L/\partial w$, where $L = T - N$ is labor supply, since leisure demand and labor supply are mirror images in this model.

Next define the labor supply elasticity evaluated at the net wage $(1 - m) \cdot w$ as

$$\varepsilon_L = -\frac{\partial N}{\partial w}\frac{(1 - m)w}{L}, \tag{7.18}$$

from which we see that $(\partial N/\partial m) \cdot m = \varepsilon_L \cdot L \cdot m/(1 - m)$. Substituting this into (7.17) leads to

$$\lambda = \frac{\varepsilon_L m/(1 - m)}{1 - \varepsilon_L m/(1 - m)}, \tag{7.19}$$

which is the expression that Parry (1995) presents for λ. From this we can see that the marginal welfare cost of public funds is small when labor supply is inelastic, and it is zero when labor supply is perfectly inelastic. Thus the more responsive labor supply is to the wage rate, the greater is the distortion from labor taxation. This is the marginal analog to the idea that a more elastic labor supply curve implies a larger excess burden from income taxation. For example, if the leisure demand curve in panel B of Figure 7.2 was steeper, the excess burden shown by area b would be smaller.

Continuing with the regulator's problem in Eq. (7.15), the first-order condition for X is

$$u_X(\cdot) - D'(X) - C'(X) + \left[u_N - w - \lambda w m \right] \frac{\partial N}{\partial X} = 0. \tag{7.20}$$

By substituting out for $\partial N / \partial X$ using (7.12), substituting in $-wm = u_N(\cdot) - w$ from the household's first-order conditions, and then rearranging we obtain

$$\underbrace{u_X(X,N) - C'(X)}_{MAC} + \underbrace{(1+\lambda) \left\{ -\frac{\partial N}{\partial p} \times \frac{\partial p}{\partial X} \right\} wm}_{MIE} = D'(X), \tag{7.21}$$

where the term we have labeled MIE constitutes the departure from the optimal condition shown in (7.6), when there was no distortion in the labor market. This is the *marginal interaction effect* (MIE), and it arises because leisure demand responds to the policy-induced price change for X. If leisure and the polluting good are substitutes so that $\partial N / \partial p > 0$ – i.e. the demand for leisure shifts out when X becomes more expensive – then $MIE > 0$ and the marginal social cost of abatement becomes $u_X(\cdot) - C'(X) + MIE$. That is, the marginal cost of reducing X is larger than when there is no labor market distortion. From this we see that when there is a pre-existing distortion in a related market, the marginal abatement cost equals marginal damage condition no longer holds, even when markets are competitive, and the regulator needs to consider the impact on the labor/leisure outcome when formulating her second-best optimal policy.

Panel C of Figure 7.2 is useful for visualizing the cause of the interaction effect when $\partial N / \partial p > 0$ (when labor and the polluting good are substitutes). Note that $N^* - N^c$ is the increase in leisure that occurs when the price of X moves from p^c to p^*. This is the discrete analog to $(\partial N / \partial p) \cdot \partial p / \partial X$ in (7.21). The increase in leisure causes a loss in labor tax revenue shown as area $e + c$ and given analytically by $(N^* - N^c) \cdot mw$. This revenue loss must be made up by marginally increasing m, if the government revenue requirement is to be met. Recall that the welfare loss per additional currency unit raised via labor taxation is given by λ. Recovering the lost revenue $(N^* - N^c) \cdot mw$ by increasing m therefore has a welfare cost of $\lambda \cdot (N^* - N^c) \cdot mw$. Finally, using $N(p^c, w)$ as the baseline, area $e + c$ is also the increase in the excess burden that arises from the increase in leisure, and so $(N^* - N^c) \cdot mw$ is a direct welfare loss. Taken together, the interaction effect shown in panel C of Figure 7.2 results in a welfare loss of $(1 + \lambda) \cdot (N^* - N^c) \cdot mw$, which is the discrete counterpart to the MIE. Figure 7.3 shows how this type of interaction effect changes the optimal level of X, relative to the baseline when there is no labor market distortion. When leisure and the polluting good are substitutes, the interaction effect

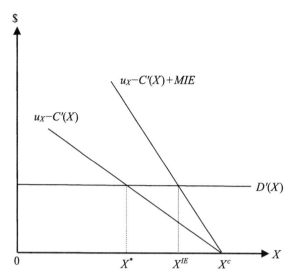

Figure 7.3   Optimal environmental policy with an interaction effect

makes the welfare cost of reducing X higher than when there is no distortion in the labor market, and so the optimal level of the polluting good is X^{IE}, where $X^{IE} > X^*$.

We can express the *MIE* more formally by noting that $\partial p/\partial X = 1/(\partial X/\partial p)$, since p resulting from the regulator's choice of X is monotonically decreasing in X. Substituting this into (7.21) we obtain

$$u_X(\cdot) - C'(X) + (1+\lambda)\underbrace{\left\{ -\frac{\partial N(\cdot)}{\partial p} \Big/ \frac{\partial X(\cdot)}{\partial p} \right\} wm}_{MIE} = D'(X). \tag{7.22}$$

From this expression we can see that the sign and magnitude of the *MIE* depend on three factors: the size of the labor supply elasticity (and hence λ), the complements/substitutes relationship between N and X, and the sensitivity of the demand for X to its price. We summarize our findings on the *MIE* in the following proposition.

Proposition 7.1

Suppose there is a government revenue constraint, and that public funds can only be raised by taxing labor. In this second-best world when the government needs to raise revenue via labor taxes, and cannot raise revenue via emission taxes, the optimal level of pollution is no longer characterized by the marginal abatement cost equals marginal damage condition. Instead, the interaction between the polluting good and the labor market causes social costs to diverge from the first-best case, so that:

(a) *the marginal social cost of reducing X is higher than in the first-best case when X and N are substitutes, and lower when X and N are complements;*

(b) *the optimal level of pollution is larger than in the first-best case when X and N are substitutes, and smaller when X and N are complements;*

(c) *the absolute value of the difference between the first- and second-best pollution levels is larger when labor supply is more elastic, the demand for X is less price responsive, or the strength of the complement/substitute relationship between X and N is stronger.*

The last point can be easily seen when we express the *MIE* in elasticity form as

$$MIE = (1+\lambda)\left(-\frac{\eta_{XN}}{\varepsilon_X}\right)p\frac{m}{(1-m)},\tag{7.23}$$

where we have used the Slutsky symmetry condition to substitute $\partial N(\cdot)/\partial p = \partial X(\cdot)/\partial w$, ε_X is the own price elasticity of X, and η_{XN} is the elasticity of substitution between X and N. The latter are evaluated at the actual price and net wage, respectively, so that

$$\eta_{XN} = \frac{\partial X(\cdot)}{\partial w}\frac{(1-m)w}{X},$$
$$\varepsilon_X = \frac{\partial X(\cdot)}{\partial p}\frac{p}{X}.\tag{7.24}$$

For subsequent analysis, it is useful to further reduce the expression for *MIE*. Using Eq. (7.19) we can derive an expression for $m/(1-m)$ as

$$\frac{m}{(1-m)} = \frac{\lambda}{(1+\lambda)\varepsilon_L}.\tag{7.25}$$

Substituting this expression into (7.23) provides a formula for the *MIE* that depends directly on own, cross price, and labor supply elasticities:

$$MIE = \lambda\left(-\frac{\eta_{XN}}{\varepsilon_X}\right)\frac{p}{\varepsilon_L}.\tag{7.26}$$

The consequences of proposition 7.1 are potentially far reaching, as demonstrated by the following example.

EXAMPLE 7.1 (NUMERICAL/ANALYTICAL) On average, leisure and market goods are thought to be substitutes. In particular, if preferences for leisure and the polluting good are such that $\eta_{XN} = \varepsilon_L$, they are said to be "average substitutes". This follows because a 1 percent increase in the wage leads to an ε_L percent increase in income, and therefore an ε_L percent increase in total, and hence average, consumption spending. If X is an average substitute for leisure, then a 1 percent increase in the wage leads to an $\eta_{XN} = \varepsilon_L$ percent increase in spending on X. In this case, the expression for the *MIE* reduces to $MIE = -\lambda(1/\varepsilon_X)$. If the marginal tax rate is $m = 0.30$ and the labor supply elasticity is $\varepsilon_L = 0.40$, then $\lambda \approx 0.20$. To complete the example, suppose that $\varepsilon_X = -0.50$. In this scenario, the magnitude of the *MIE* is equivalent to approximately 40 percent of the price of the polluting good.

This example suggests that it is empirically plausible for the interaction effect to be large enough to affect the design of an efficient policy. Nonetheless, the extent to which the interaction effect is large in specific contexts depends on the signs and magnitudes of the relevant demand elasticities.

7.2.2 Revenue Raising Environmental Policy

Suppose now that the government can collect revenue by extracting payment for emissions, via an emission tax or by auctioning pollution permits. In this subsection, we proceed using the framework of an emissions tax, so that the government revenue requirement can be met using two taxes according to $G = wm \cdot (T-N) + \tau X$, where τ is the revenue per unit of the dirty good (or equivalently, per unit of pollution) collected by the government. We now conceptualize the regulator's problem as one in which she selects the two tax rates m and τ to maximize social welfare, taking into account the household's and firm's utility and profit maximizing responses to her choices. The firm's profits in this context are given by $pX - C(X) - \tau X$, and government revenue is once again returned to the household as a lump sum payment. This implies that household spending on the numeraire good is given by

$$\begin{aligned} Z &= (1-m) \cdot w \cdot (T-N) - pX + G \\ &= w \cdot (T-N) - pX + \tau X, \end{aligned} \tag{7.27}$$

where the second line follows when we substitute out using the government's budget constraint $G = wm \cdot (T-N) + \tau X$. We continue to assume that the household and firm are price takers, and that markets clear so that X denotes both the quantity demanded and quantity supplied. The endogenous variables in this context are X, N, and p, which are determined conditional on m and τ, according to the following household and firm behavioral equations:

$$\begin{aligned} u_X(X,N) &= p \\ u_N(X,N) &= (1-m)w \\ C'(X) &= p - \tau \end{aligned} \tag{7.28}$$

For later reference it is useful to differentiate the conditions in (7.28) with respect to τ to obtain

$$\begin{aligned} u_{XX}(X,N)\frac{\partial X}{\partial \tau} + u_{XN}(X,N)\frac{\partial N}{\partial \tau} &= \frac{\partial p}{\partial \tau} \\ u_{XN}(X,N)\frac{\partial X}{\partial \tau} + u_{NN}(X,N)\frac{\partial N}{\partial \tau} &= 0 \\ C''(X)\frac{\partial X}{\partial \tau} &= \frac{\partial p}{\partial \tau} - 1, \end{aligned} \tag{7.29}$$

which we can solve to obtain the comparative statics

$$\frac{\partial X}{\partial \tau} = \frac{u_{NN}}{H} < 0$$

$$\frac{\partial N}{\partial \tau} = \frac{-u_{XN}}{H} \begin{array}{c} \leq \\ > \end{array} 0$$

$$\frac{\partial p}{\partial \tau} = \frac{u_{XX} u_{NN} - [u_{XN}]^2}{H} > 0$$

(7.30)

where $H = u_{XX} \times u_{NN} - (u_{XN})^2 - C''(X) u_{NN} > 0$ is the determinant of the Hessian matrix of the linearized system.

The regulator's formal problem is to maximize the sum of utility and profits according to

$$\max_{m, \tau} \{ U(X, N) + Z - D(X) + pX - C(X) - \tau X \} \quad s.t. \quad wm(T - N) + \tau X = G.$$

(7.31)

By substituting out for Z using (7.27), we can simplify the regulator's problems so that it reads

$$\max_{m, \tau} \{ U(X, N) + Z - D(X) + pX - C(X) - \tau X \} \quad s.t. \quad wm(T - N) + \tau X = G.$$

(7.32)

We focus initially on the first-order condition with respect to the emission tax rate τ, which is given by

$$[u_X(\cdot) - C'(X) - D'(X)] \frac{\partial X}{\partial \tau} + \lambda \left[X + \tau \frac{\partial X}{\partial \tau} \right] + \left[\underbrace{u_N(\cdot) - w}_{-wm} - \lambda wm \right] \frac{\partial N}{\partial \tau} = 0.$$

(7.33)

This expression can be usefully rewritten by repeating the manipulations used in the non-revenue raising case, and then dividing through by $\partial X / \partial \tau$, to obtain

$$\underbrace{u_X(\cdot) - C'(X)}_{MAC} + \underbrace{(1 + \lambda) wm \left[-\frac{\partial N}{\partial \tau} \Big/ \frac{\partial X}{\partial \tau} \right]}_{MIE} + \underbrace{\lambda \left[\tau + X \Big/ \frac{\partial X}{\partial \tau} \right]}_{MRE} = D'(X).$$

(7.34)

To match the expression for the *MIE* from the non-revenue raising case, note from the comparative statics in (7.3) and (7.30) that

$$\frac{\partial N}{\partial \tau} \Big/ \frac{\partial X}{\partial \tau} = \frac{\partial N}{\partial p} \Big/ \frac{\partial X}{\partial p},$$

(7.35)

which shows that the interaction effects in the revenue and non-revenue raising contexts have a similar structure.

The new term, labeled *MRE*, is the *marginal revenue effect*. It is so-labeled because $\tau + X/(\partial X/\partial \tau)$ is the amount by which the revenue raised from taxing pollution changes, when X changes. The marginal welfare value of this change in revenue is obtained when we scale it by λ. Thus, we can interpret the *MRE* as the change in the social cost of a unit of X, which comes about due to the increase or decrease in the public funds that need to be raised in the (distorted) labor market, to meet the revenue requirement. Note that at the starting point $\tau = 0$, and the *MRE* is negative because $\partial X/\partial \tau < 0$. This means that the additional revenue raised from taxing the dirty good contributes a negative cost of reducing X, since the revenue that needs to be raised by taxing labor is smaller.

As with any consumption tax, the total revenue collected from taxing X can increase or decrease with a change in the tax rate, depending on how the change in the tax affects the size of the tax base. Thus the *MRE* can be positive or negative at the optimum. To gain insight on the likely sign and magnitude of the marginal revenue effect, it is useful to assume that $C'(X) = c$, so that $p = c + \tau$ and $\partial X/\partial \tau = \partial X/\partial p$. This latter point follows from the comparative statics in (7.3) and (7.30), when $C''(X) = 0$. Making these substitutions, we have

$$MRE = \lambda \left(X \bigg/ \frac{\partial X}{\partial p} + \tau \right) = \lambda \left(\frac{p}{\varepsilon_X} + \tau \right). \tag{7.36}$$

From this it is clear that the *MRE* will be negative when the emission tax is small relative to the price of the dirty good, and/or when demand for the dirty good is inelastic.

EXAMPLE 7.2 (NUMERICAL/ANALYTICAL) Suppose once again that $\lambda \approx 0.20$ and $\varepsilon_X = -0.50$. Assume for illustration that the tax magnitude is approximately 25 percent of the price of the dirty good, so that $\tau \approx 0.25p$. In this scenario the *MRE* is negative, and its magnitude is equivalent to approximately 35 percent of the price of the polluting good.

To study the revenue effect in isolation from the interaction effect, suppose that $\partial N(\cdot)/\partial p = 0$ so that $MIE = 0$. Continuing with the assumption that $C'(X) = c$, in this special case (7.34) reduces to

$$\underbrace{u_X(\cdot) - C'(X)}_{MAC} + \underbrace{\lambda \left(\frac{p}{\varepsilon_X} + \tau \right)}_{MRE} = D'(X). \tag{7.37}$$

Figure 7.4 illustrates the role of the revenue effect when $MRE < 0$ over the range of values for X that are relevant for the policy. We have drawn the demand for X so that it is relatively inelastic, implying ε_X is small in absolute value and causing *MRE* to be a comparatively large negative number over much of the range of values for $X < X^c$. This means that the marginal social cost of reducing X is *smaller*, than in the case when we ignore spillovers into the labor market. On the lower panel, the marginal social cost of reducing X is the vertical summation of the *MRE* and *MAC* curves. The optimal level of the polluting good occurs at X^{RE}, which is smaller than the level equating marginal abatement cost with marginal damages, shown as X^*.

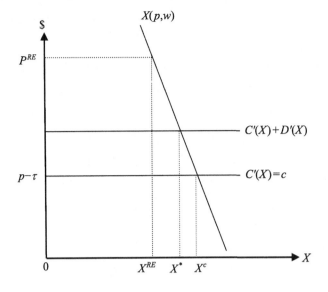

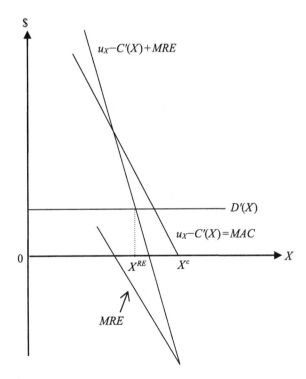

Figure 7.4 Optimal environmental policy with a revenue effect

This happens because a comparatively high amount of revenue per unit of X can be extracted without a large reduction in X. That is, the tax base does not shrink substantially, and so pushing the tax rate above its partial equilibrium counterpart produces more revenue, and therefore a comparatively greater reduction in distortionary labor taxation.

Additional insight on the role of the revenue effect can be obtained by substituting $\tau = u_X - C'(X)$ from the consumer and producer problems in (7.28) into the expression in (7.37), and solving for the optimal tax rate:

$$\tau^{RE} = \frac{D'(X)}{(1+\lambda)} - \frac{\lambda}{(1+\lambda)} \frac{p}{\varepsilon_X}. \tag{7.38}$$

This expression shows that τ^{RE} can be higher or lower than its partial equilibrium counterpart, depending on the size of the marginal cost of public funds and the elasticity of demand for the dirty good. These features of the revenue effect in isolation from the interaction effect are summarized in the following proposition.

Proposition 7.2
Suppose there is a government revenue constraint, and that public funds can be raised by taxing labor and emissions. Suppose as well that there is no interaction effect. The optimal level of pollution in this case differs from the partial equilibrium case via a revenue effect labeled MRE, which measures the welfare effect of the increase or decrease in tax revenue that accompanies a change in the emission tax rate. The MRE:

(a) *is smaller (less positive or more negative) when the demand for X is inelastic;*
(b) *is smaller when the tax rate is small relative to the price of X;*
(c) *lowers the social cost of abatement when MRE < 0, implying the optimal quantity of the dirty good is smaller than the partial equilibrium optimum;*
(d) *raises the social cost of abatement when MRE > 0, implying the optimal quantity of the dirty good is larger than the partial equilibrium optimum.*

In sum, the fact that the regulator can raise revenue by taxing X implies the seemingly separate objectives of controlling pollution and raising revenue in the least distortionary way become confounded. Thus the outcome in the polluting good market need not correspond to the case when pollution is the sole concern. This finding is difficult to grasp for many who are accustomed to single-issue debates, because we need to imagine a multi-tasking government with many objectives rather than a government focused on specific objectives in isolation.

To complete our analysis of the revenue raising environmental policy case, we now state the first-order condition with respect to m for the regulator's problem in (7.32) as

$$(u_N - w)\frac{\partial N}{\partial m} + \lambda \left(w(T-N) - wm\frac{\partial N}{\partial m} \right) + (u_X - D'(X) - C'(X) + \lambda\tau)\frac{\partial X}{\partial m} = 0. \tag{7.39}$$

The first two terms match what we saw in the non-revenue raising case, while the latter term arises from the fact that X is now a choice variable. Once again using the consumer's optimality condition $-mw = u_N - w$, we can rewrite the condition as

$$-wm(1+\lambda)\frac{dN}{dm} + \lambda w(T-N) + (u_X - D'(X) - C'(X) + \lambda\tau)\frac{\partial X}{\partial m} = 0 \tag{7.40}$$

and solve for λ as

$$\lambda = \frac{wm\dfrac{\partial N}{\partial m} - \left(u_X - D'(X) - C'(X)\right)\dfrac{\partial X}{\partial m}}{\left[w(T-N) - wm\dfrac{\partial N}{\partial m} + \tau\dfrac{\partial X}{\partial m}\right]}. \tag{7.41}$$

This expression for the marginal welfare cost of public funds has a nice interpretation. When m increases, a welfare loss occurs both through N (the first term in the numerator) and X (the second term in the numerator). In particular, if $\partial X/\partial m < 0$, which is the case when N and X are substitutes, then an increase in m causes a decrease in both X and the net benefits from consuming X. The denominator is once again the addition to revenue from the change in m. The extra term now has to do with the fact that the tax base for emissions shrinks if $\partial X/\partial m < 0$, since X falls and emissions revenue is lost. Thus the interpretation of λ is the same as in the non-revenue raising case, but there are extra terms determining its magnitude.

7.2.3 Prospects for a Double Dividend?

Having identified the interaction and revenue effects, we are now in a position to examine the prospects for a double dividend arising from regulating emissions. Before proceeding, it is necessary to be clear about what is meant by a double dividend. There are two possibilities. The first, or weak form, simply says that welfare is greater when any revenues raised via environmental policy are used to reduce distortionary taxation rather than refunded in a lump sum fashion. This is always the case, and so the existence of a weak double dividend is not in doubt. The second, or strong form, is much more controversial. It suggests that an emission fee should be set above its partial equilibrium (marginal abatement cost equals marginal damage) level, thereby resulting in more pollution reduction and a larger amount of revenue raised vis-à-vis the partial equilibrium case. The appeal of this is obvious. While it is easy to conclude that reducing pollution is qualitatively good, it is much harder to quantitatively compare the non-market benefits of less pollution to the market losses of reduced output. Policy decisions would therefore be much easier (and politically palatable) if aggressive emission reductions could be set without knowledge of the size of pollution reduction benefits, but with confidence that market losses from the policy would be offset by reductions in the labor tax rate and its associated excess burden.

Under what conditions does a strong double dividend arise in the context of the model we have developed thus far? We have seen that in a second-best world, reductions in the polluting good result in social costs that diverge from the first-best case by an interaction and a revenue effect, so that marginal social cost in the second-best world is

$$\begin{aligned} MSC &= u_X(\cdot) - C'(X) + MIE + MRE \\ &= MAC + MIE + MRE. \end{aligned} \tag{7.42}$$

The strong form double dividend requires that $MSC < MAC$, which is equivalent to $MIE + MRE < 0$. We have seen that this can come about in one of two ways, which we summarize in the following proposition.

Proposition 7.3
Within the context of the model examined thus far, a strong double dividend is defined as an outcome in which the optimal level of the polluting good X^{GE} (where GE stands for general equilibrium) is smaller than its partial equilibrium counterpart X^*, so that $X^{GE} < X^*$. This occurs when the net impact of the interaction and revenue effects serves to reduce the marginal social cost of reductions in X relative to the partial equilibrium case; i.e. MIE + MRE < 0. This can occur in one of two ways:

(a) MIE < 0 and MRE < 0, or MIE < 0 and |MIE| > MRE > 0;
(b) MIE > 0 and MRE < 0 where |MRE| > MIE.

This proposition suggests that a double dividend can arise, but how likely is it that it will? The path in part (a) of the proposition requires that leisure and the polluting good are complements, so that when the price of X increases, the demand for leisure is reduced and labor supply increases. On average, market goods and leisure are substitutes, and so this path to a double dividend cannot be expected to hold for typical cases. Nonetheless, some specific polluting commodities may be complements with leisure; we return to this possibility below when we discuss empirical findings. The more likely path is part (b), where the interaction effect is positive, but it is dominated by a negative revenue effect. In what follows we consider this possibility in more analytical detail.

To simplify the discussion we again use the case in which $C'(X) = c$, so that the *MIE* and *MRE* are given in equations (7.26) and (7.36), respectively, as:

$$
\begin{aligned}
MIE &= \lambda \left(-\frac{\eta_{XN}}{\varepsilon_X} \right) \frac{p}{\varepsilon_L} \\
MRE &= \lambda \left(\frac{p}{\varepsilon_X} + \tau \right).
\end{aligned}
\tag{7.43}
$$

Considering the case in which leisure and the polluting good are average substitutes, example 7.1 showed that the marginal interaction effect reduces to $MIE = -\lambda p / \varepsilon_X$, which is larger than |*MRE*| since $\tau > 0$. This suggests that on average we should not expect a strong form double dividend. Combining the results from examples 7.1 and 7.2 shows this to be the case for the elasticity values used in those calculations.

EXAMPLE 7.3 (NUMERICAL/ANALYTICAL) Suppose once again that $\lambda \approx 0.20$ and $\varepsilon_X = -0.50$, so that the *MIE* is once again approximately 40 percent of the price of the polluting good. For a tax magnitude that is in the range of 25 percent of the price of the polluting good, the *MRE* is negative and its magnitude is approximately 35 percent of the price of the polluting good. That is, $MRE = 0.20(-p/0.5 + \tau) = 0.20(-2p + 0.25p) = -0.35p$. As the tax magnitude increases, the gap becomes larger. If the tax magnitude is on the order of 50 percent of the price of the polluting good, the marginal revenue effect is $MRE = 0.20(-2p + 0.50p) = -0.30p$.

7.2.4 Second-Best Optimal Pollution

Although our discussion suggests a double dividend is unlikely on average, optimal pollution levels and welfare outcomes depend critically on the revenue effect. Therefore, when there are pre-existing distortions in the economy due to labor taxation, the second-best

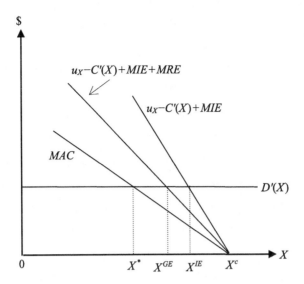

Figure 7.5   Optimal environmental policy with a pre-existing distortion

optimum requires that environmental rents are extracted from firms and used to reduce distortionary taxation. Given this, Figure 7.5 shows how the marginal damage, *MAC*, *MIE*, and *MRE* curves jointly determine the optimal second-best pollution level. We have drawn the Figure to reflect $MRE < 0$ and $MIE > 0$, where the magnitude of the latter is dominant. The optimal pollution level in the face of existing distortions in the labor market is therefore larger than in the first-best case, but smaller than would be optimal absent revenue recycling. Figure 7.5 is typical of how the two effects have been discussed in the literature, but it is not completely general, in that a result in which $X^{IE} < X^{GE}$ is also possible.

7.3   AN EXTENDED EXAMPLE

The theoretical results derived in the previous two sections can be challenging to appreciate in the abstract. To complement our general derivations, we present in this section an extended example using specific functional forms, which is designed to illustrate the mechanisms leading to the interaction and revenue effects, and their potential magnitudes. In this section we assume that the private goods component of the representative consumer's utility function is

$$u(X, N) = \alpha X - \beta X^2 / 2 + \gamma N - \phi N^2 / 2 - \eta X N + Z. \tag{7.44}$$

Note that if $\eta > 0$ consumption of the polluting good and leisure are substitutes, which we refer to as the normal case. When $\eta < 0$ leisure and the polluting good are complements. The firm produces X units of the polluting good and incurs a cost of $C(X) = c \cdot X^2 / 2$. Emissions are equal to output so that $E = X$, and the damage function is $D(X) = d \cdot X^2 / 2$.

The social welfare function is the sum of utility and profit, which according to Eq. (7.15) simplifies to

$$W = \alpha X - \beta X^2 / 2 + \gamma N - \phi N^2 / 2 - \eta X N + w(T - N) - (c + d)X^2 / 2. \tag{7.45}$$

Let $G > 0$ be the government revenue needs. If taxes can be raised in a lump sum way (i.e. without distortion) the socially optimal allocation is determined by

$$
\begin{aligned}
u_X(X,N) = C'(X) + D'(X) \quad &\rightarrow \quad \alpha - \beta X - \eta N = (c+d)X \\
u_N(X,N) = w \quad &\rightarrow \quad \gamma - \phi N - \eta X = w.
\end{aligned}
\tag{7.46}
$$

This linear system can be readily solved for the efficient production/consumption and leisure levels.

Consider now the case where the government uses only a proportional labor tax m to finance the state budget G, so that the representative consumer's net wage is $m(1-w)$. Private utility maximization leads to the consumer's first-order conditions

$$
\begin{aligned}
u_X(X,N) = \alpha - \beta X - \eta N = p \\
u_N(X,N) = \gamma - \phi N - \eta X = w(1-m),
\end{aligned}
\tag{7.47}
$$

which gives us expressions for the polluting good and leisure as

$$
\begin{aligned}
X\big(p, w(1-m)\big) &= \frac{\phi(\alpha - p) - \eta\big(\gamma - w(1-m)\big)}{\beta\phi - \eta^2} \\
N\big(p, w(1-m)\big) &= \frac{\beta\big(\gamma - w(1-m)\big) - \eta(\alpha - p)}{\beta\phi - \eta^2}.
\end{aligned}
\tag{7.48}
$$

From this we obtain:

$$
\frac{\partial N}{\partial p} = \frac{\eta}{\beta\phi - \eta^2}.
\tag{7.49}
$$

The environmentally unregulated equilibrium with a labor tax is therefore characterized by the equation system

$$
\begin{aligned}
\alpha - \beta X - \eta N &= p \\
\gamma - \phi N - \eta X &= w(1-m) \\
cX &= p,
\end{aligned}
\tag{7.50}
$$

where the last equality follows from the firm's profit maximization condition.

7.3.1 Setting an Environmental Standard

If the regulator sets an emission standard $\overline{X}$, the firm has no freedom of choice and the last expression in Eq. (7.50) drops out, while the first two equations jointly determine both the demand for leisure N and the market clearing price p, given that the consumer is restricted to $\overline{X}$ in his consumption of the polluting good. Solving the first two equations conditional on $\overline{X}$ we obtain

$$
\begin{aligned}
p(\overline{X}, m) &= \frac{\alpha\phi - \eta\big(\gamma - w(1-m)\big)}{\phi} - \frac{\beta\phi - \eta^2}{\phi}\overline{X} \\
N(\overline{X}, m) &= \frac{\gamma - w(1-m)}{\phi} - \frac{\eta}{\phi}\overline{X},
\end{aligned}
\tag{7.51}
$$

from which we easily derive

$$\frac{\partial p}{\partial \overline{X}} = -\frac{\left(\beta\phi - \eta^2\right)}{\phi}$$

$$\frac{\partial N}{\partial \overline{X}} = \frac{-\eta}{\phi}.$$

(7.52)

These expressions provide the terms needed to compute the marginal interaction effect (*MIE*) as

$$MIE = (1+\lambda)\left\{-\frac{\partial N}{\partial X}\right\}wm$$

$$= (1+\lambda)\left\{\frac{\eta}{\phi}\right\}wm.$$

(7.53)

7.3.2 Setting an Emission Tax

Consider now the case in which the regulator taxes X and uses the revenues, along with the income tax, to finance G. Assuming that the firm pays the tax, the equilibrium is now characterized by

$$u_X(X,N) = \alpha - \beta X - \eta N = p$$
$$u_N(X,N) = \gamma - \phi N - \eta X = w(1-m)$$
$$C'(X) = cX = p - \tau.$$

(7.54)

Solving the system results in

$$X(\tau,m) = \frac{\phi(\alpha-\tau) - \eta\left(\gamma - w(1-m)\right)}{(\beta+c)\phi - \eta^2}$$

$$N(\tau,m) = \frac{(\beta+c)\left(\gamma - w(1-m)\right) - \eta(\alpha-\tau)}{(\beta+c)\phi - \eta^2}$$

(7.55)

$$p(\tau,m) = \frac{(\beta\phi - \eta^2)\tau + c\left[\phi\alpha - \eta\left(\gamma - w(1-m)\right)\right]}{(\beta+c)\phi - \eta^2},$$

from which we can derive

$$\frac{\partial N}{\partial \tau} = \frac{\eta}{(\beta+c)\phi - \eta^2}$$

$$\frac{\partial X}{\partial \tau} = \frac{-\phi}{(\beta+c)\phi - \eta^2}$$

(7.56)

$$\frac{\partial p}{\partial \tau} = \frac{\beta\phi - \eta^2}{(\beta+c)\phi - \eta^2}.$$

These derivatives allow us to express the marginal interaction and revenue effects as

$$MIE = (1+\lambda)wm\left\{-\frac{\partial N}{\partial \tau}\Big/\frac{\partial X}{\partial \tau}\right\}$$

$$= (1+\lambda)wm\frac{\eta}{\phi}$$

$$MRE = \lambda\left\{\tau + X\Big/\frac{\partial X}{\partial \tau}\right\} \tag{7.57}$$

$$= \lambda\left\{\tau - X\frac{((\beta+c)\phi-\eta^2)}{\phi}\right\}.$$

7.3.3 A Numerical Example

In this subsection we select specific values for the parameters of the utility and cost functions, in order to provide numerical values for the interaction and revenue effects. In particular, we parameterize the system according to:

α	β	γ	ϕ	η	c	d	G	w	T
2.0	0.9	2.0	0.9	0.4	0.1	0.04	0.3	0.1	10.0

Note that "full" income in this economy is normalized to one, in that $wT = 10 \times 0.1 = 1$. Thus $G=0.3$ corresponds to the government sector accounting for 30 percent of the economy, and $d=0.04$ means that the increase in marginal damage from an additional unit of X is equivalent to 4 percent of full income.

Table 7.1 displays the results for allocations, tax rates, distortionary effects, and welfare effects that arise using these parameters. Note that for the first-best allocation (the top row of results) the marginal damage and emission tax rate are the same, there is no interaction or revenue effect, and the marginal cost of public funds is zero. These follow because the pollution externality is the only distortion in the economy.

For the case with only a labor tax (the middle row of results), the tax rate is approximately $m=0.36$, which induces a positive marginal cost of public funds of nearly 0.006. This implies that marginally increasing G by 0.01, so that the government sector takes an additional 1 percent of total income, leads to a marginal welfare loss that is more than half as large as the revenue gain. The marginal interaction effect that arises from the labor market distortion ($MIE=0.016$) drives a gap between marginal damage ($MD=0.054$) and the marginal cost of abatement ($MAC=0.038$), where the latter is presented as the shadow tax in the table. Note that these figures imply $MIE+MAC=MD$. Note as well that the choice of X has not much changed relative to the first-best case, but leisure consumption is 2.5 percent higher. This increase in leisure drives down the marginal utility of X, so that the MAC is smaller than in the first-best case, even though the levels of X are similar. The welfare realized in this case is marginally lower than in the first best case, as predicted by the theory.

The case with both a labor tax and a revenue-raising environmental tax is shown in the third row of Table 7.1. Because pollution tax revenues partially offset the need to tax

Table 7.1 Numerical results

Policy	Welfare	X	N	P	τ	m	MD	MIE	MRE	λ
First-best (lump sum tax)	3.7799	1.3402	1.5155	0.1876	0.0536	0	0.0536	0	0	0
Emission standard with labor tax	3.7792	1.3405	1.5548	0.1716	(0.038[a])	0.3552	0.0536	0.0158	0	0.0057
Emission tax and labor tax	3.7794	1.3353	1.5492	0.1785	0.0449	0.2839	0.0534	0.0126	−0.004	0.0040

[a] This is the shadow tax on emissions, which is equal to the marginal abatement cost at the level of X selected by the regulator. It is the tax that would support the chosen level of X, when tax revenues are not used to reduce labor taxes.

labor, the marginal labor tax rate falls to $m = 0.28$, and the marginal cost of public funds is correspondingly smaller. In addition, the emission tax rate of $\tau = 0.045$ is larger than the shadow tax in the non-revenue raising case, but still smaller than marginal damage $MD = 0.053$. This is because the positive interaction effect still drives a wedge between MD and MAC, but the negative revenue effect $MRE = -0.004$ serves to partially offset this. Since $|MRE| < MIE$ no double dividend occurs – i.e. the emission tax in this second-best world is smaller than when there is no labor market distortion. Nonetheless, the revenue recycling effect is important, and overall welfare is higher than in the case when emission taxes do not offset labor taxes.

7.4 POLICY INSTRUMENTS

Our discussion thus far has suggested that the optimal pollution policy in a second-best world must balance the costs and benefits of pollution reduction, and consider interactions with the existing tax system and government revenue needs. Unlike our analysis from earlier chapters, the latter means that the revenue-raising properties of our suite of instruments will matter for how we rank their performance. In what follows, we describe how each instrument's efficiency properties are altered when we move from the partial to general equilibrium context, when there are pre-existing distortions.

7.4.1 Taxes and Auctioned Permits

Consider first a decentralized emissions tax policy, in which the polluting firm faces a tax per unit of the dirty good so that its profits are $\Pi = pX - C(X) - \tau X$. As usual, the firm maximizes profits by producing X so that $p = C'(X) + \tau$, and the consumer maximizes utility by choosing X so that $u_X(\cdot) = p$. From Eq. (7.42) we can see that if the regulator sets the tax rate so that

$$\tau = D'(X) + MIE + MRE, \tag{7.58}$$

she can assure an outcome in which

$$u_X(\cdot) = p = C'(X) + D'(X) + MIE + MRE, \tag{7.59}$$

which leads to X^{GE}. Not surprisingly, an emission fee can therefore be used to obtain the optimal level of pollution. Also, the regulator collects revenue in the amount of τX^{GE}, which can be used to reduce the burden of labor taxation. Thus the tax approach allows the regulator to obtain the welfare maximizing outcome, conditional on the pre-existing distortions.

The story is nearly identical for the case of auctioned permits. Rather than setting a price for emissions, the regulator sells X^{GE} emission permits, which causes the price of a permit to be $\sigma = D'(X) + MIE + MRE$, and the amount of revenue raised to be σX^{GE}. As in the tax case, a system of auctioned permits allows the regulator to obtain the optimum second-best welfare level.

7.4.2 Freely Distributed Permits and Command and Control

The regulator could also implement environmental policy by freely distributing X^{GE} emission permits to the polluting firm, where X^{GE} is derived from (7.59). While this would lead to the same environmental outcome as in the emission tax and auctioned permit cases, it would not correspond to the welfare maximizing outcome for this policy instrument. This is because the quantity $X^{GE} < X^c$ will cause the output price of X to rise, and leisure demand will adjust accordingly, thereby producing the interaction effect. However, the labor tax revenue lost via the increase in leisure demand will not be offset by revenue collected from the environmental policy, when permits are freely distributed. Thus X^{GE}, which depended on the revenue effect to be welfare maximizing, cannot be optimal when revenues are not collected. If leisure and the polluting good are substitutes, the optimal pollution level when emission permits are freely distributed will be larger than both the partial equilibrium level, and the pollution level when revenue is collected.

This is an important observation. Unlike our findings from earlier chapters, the difference between free and auctioned permits is not merely one of property rights and equity. For similar pollution targets, and assuming that leisure and the polluting good are substitutes, the non-revenue raising permit scheme will have a higher welfare cost than the revenue raising instruments. This logic also carries over to the classic command and control policies. The increase in the firm's costs due to abatement effort leads to an increase in the price of X, setting off the chain of events that produces the interaction effect. Since the firm retains the environmental scarcity rent, no revenue is collected by the government, and no reduction in distortionary taxation is possible. Command and control is worse still when there are multiple, heterogeneous firms. As discussed in earlier chapters, this causes abatement costs to be higher than under policies leading to equal marginal abatement cost levels. Comparatively higher abatement costs imply a larger price increase, and a larger interaction effect – again without the offsetting revenue recycling effect. Thus in the multiple, heterogeneous firm case, command and control is inferior to freely distributed permits, which is inferior to both tax and auctioned permit systems.

7.4.3 Subsidies

An abatement subsidy program is distinguished by its use of payments to polluting firms for their reduction in emissions. We have seen in past chapters that this functions like an emission tax, coupled with a lump sum transfer to firms. In our current analysis, this suggests that a subsidy approach ranks below a tax system and both types of permits systems. As with the other policies, the short run cost of reducing pollution implies an increase in the price of X, from which the interaction effect follows. However, payment to firms as part of the policy implies the government's budget must expand when a subsidy scheme is used, with no corresponding increase in revenue from the policy. Thus additional, distortionary taxation is needed to cover the increased government expenditure. This causes a larger excess burden in the labor market. Viewed from this perspective, the gradation from taxes and auctioned permits, to freely distributed permits, and to subsidies is one of increasing social costs of abatement, because we move from revenue raising to revenue neutral to additional expenditures.

7.5   GENERALIZATIONS AND EMPIRICAL EVIDENCE

The model we have used thus far in the chapter is similar to those that were used early in the development of this literature to show its defining results. Subsequent research in this area has focused on two areas. First, there are several features one can add to the baseline model, which can in some cases alter the key insights that emerge. In the next subsection we discuss one such generalization, and exercise 7.5 provides an opportunity to review additional examples. Second, the importance of interaction and revenue effects in particular contexts depends on parameters that can often be estimated, and so research in this area has progressed to become more empirical. We consider examples of this at the end of this section.

7.5.1 A Generalization

Consider a generalization of our model in which the representative household's utility is given by $U = u(X,N,E) + Z$, where the effect of emissions on utility is no longer separable. This implies that the damage function under the quasi-linear utility function is $D(E) = -u_E(X,N,E)$, which means that the level of damage suffered by the person due to emissions depends on his private choices as well as the shape of his utility function. Under this more general specification for the utility function the household's problem is

$$\max_{X,Z,N}\{u(X,N,E) + Z\} \quad s.t. \quad (1-m)w(T-N) = Z + pX, \tag{7.60}$$

and the first-order conditions absent environmental policy are

$$
\begin{aligned}
u_X(X,N,E) &= p \\
u_N(X,N,E) &= (1-m)w,
\end{aligned}
\tag{7.61}
$$

where we have continued with our assumption that the representative consumer does not account for the effect of X on E when making his private decision. Thus the demand equations for leisure and the dirty good implied by this problem are of the form $X(p,w,E)$ and $N(p,w,E)$, where the non-separability of E means the demand equations depend on the level of emissions. This generalization has a potentially large impact on how we characterize the interaction effect. In what follows we focus on the case in which the regulator selects the level of X directly, and does not collect revenue from emissions.

The regulator's problem in this case is

$$
\max_{m,X} W = u(X,N,E) + w(T-N) - C(X) + \lambda\big[wm(T-N) - G\big],
\tag{7.62}
$$

which is a generalization of the problem in (7.15), rewritten to reflect the new utility function. The first-order condition with respect to m is unchanged from our previous analysis. The condition with respect to X appears similar at first glance, in that the interaction component is derived in the same way as equations (7.20) and (7.21):

$$
u_X(\cdot) + u_E(\cdot) - C'(X) + \underbrace{(1+\lambda)\left(-\frac{\partial N}{\partial X}\right)wm}_{MIE} = 0.
\tag{7.63}
$$

The difference, however, is in the form that $\partial N/\partial X$ takes. In particular, the non-separable utility function implies N is affected by X indirectly through its price, and directly through emissions (recall $E=X$ in our simple model). The analog to (7.12) in this more general framework is therefore

$$
\frac{\partial N}{\partial \overline{X}} = \frac{\partial N}{\partial p}\frac{\partial p}{\partial \overline{X}} + \frac{\partial N}{\partial \overline{E}}.
\tag{7.64}
$$

To see this, note that we can differentiate (7.61) with respect to E to derive

$$
\frac{\partial N}{\partial E} = \frac{u_{NX}u_{XE} - u_{XX}u_{NE}}{u_{XX}u_{NN} - u_{XN}^2},
\tag{7.65}
$$

where the denominator is positive by concavity, and the overall sign of the comparative static depends on the complement/substitution relationship between leisure and the polluting good (u_{NX}) as well as the relationship between the two private goods and pollution (u_{XE} and u_{NE}). Taking this further, the household's first-order condition when the regulator fixes X (and therefore E) is

$$
\begin{aligned}
u_X(\overline{X},N,\overline{E}) &= p \\
u_N(\overline{X},N,\overline{E}) &= (1-m)w,
\end{aligned}
\tag{7.66}
$$

which is the analog to (7.9). By differentiating (7.66) with respect to the regulator's choice variable $\bar{X} = \bar{E}$, we can derive expressions for $\partial N/\partial X$ and $\partial p/\partial X$ that are generalizations of (7.11). Finally, the expression for $\partial N/\partial p$ shown in Eq. (7.3) provides the last term that is needed to confirm that (7.64) holds.

The expression for $\partial N/\partial X$ in (7.64) implies that the interaction effect is given by

$$MIE = (1+\lambda)\left(\underbrace{-\frac{\partial N(\cdot)}{\partial p}\frac{\partial p(\cdot)}{\partial X}}_{+} - \underbrace{\frac{\partial N(\cdot)}{\partial E}}_{?}\right)wm. \qquad (7.67)$$

If leisure and the polluting good are substitutes, the first term in parenthesis is positive, as discussed above. However, leisure demand could be positively or negatively influenced by emissions, depending on the specific context, meaning that the non-separable utility function could exacerbate or mitigate the interaction effect. If E measures an environmental outcome that is a complement to leisure, so that $\partial N(\cdot)/\partial E < 0$, the feedback between the environment and leisure demand will increase the interaction effect. This could happen, for example, if an improvement in the environment makes outdoor recreation more attractive. Conversely, if $\partial N(\cdot)/\partial E > 0$, so that the person consumes less leisure when emissions fall, the interaction effect will be weakened relative to the separable case. This could happen if a reduction in emissions improves health, and thereby reduces sick days (a type of forced leisure). The point of this example is to demonstrate that generalizations of our basic model can lead to theoretical predictions that are more complex and perhaps ambiguous, and therefore help illustrate the extent to which empirical work is needed to understand the implications of pre-existing distortion for environmental policy in specific contexts.

7.5.2 Empirical Research and Policy Implications

Our analysis and examples illustrate the empirical evidence and results that are needed to support the design of environmental policy, when interactions with the distorted labor market are possible. In general there are two complementary categories of empirical work that can contribute to policy design. The first focuses on econometrically estimating the elasticities that determine the direction and magnitude of the marginal interaction and revenue effects in specific policy contexts. The following example illustrates this type of research.

EXAMPLE 7.4 (EMPIRICAL) West and Williams (2007) provide an example of this in their analysis of optimal gasoline taxes in the US. The authors estimate a household level demand system that includes equations for gasoline (the dirty good), leisure, and spending on all other goods. The main targets of estimation include the own price elasticities for gasoline and labor/leisure, along with the cross price elasticity for gasoline and leisure. For two adult households, West and Williams report an own price elasticity of gasoline demand of −0.123, and labor supply elasticities that range from 0.19 for men to 0.34 for women. Importantly, the authors find small but *negative* cross price elasticities for leisure demand with respect to gas price, meaning that leisure consumption falls when the gas price increases – i.e. gas and leisure are found to be complements.

West and Williams show that these estimates imply that the optimal gas tax is approximately 35 percent greater than the marginal damage. In this specific context a double dividend is implied, since the higher tax on the dirty good induces an increase in labor supply.

The second type of empirical work makes use of large-scale computable general equilibrium (CGE) models to predict optimal emission tax levels, which are based on richer and more realistic representation of the economy than is possible with an analytical model. These models are complements to the econometric work noted previously, in that the predictions from numerical analyses are only as good as the parameterizations that are used. Nonetheless, the ability to represent factor markets, multiple pre-existing distortions, overlapping regulations, and other real-world complications make CGE models critical for understanding the design of environmental policy.

Notwithstanding the empirical research that has investigated optimal environmental taxation in different contexts, the most enduring policy impact of the double dividend/tax interaction debate is arguably the recognition that revenue raising is a first order concern when evaluating the performance of different environmental policy instruments. This is often one of the main arguments used by economists in favor of a carbon tax rather than a cap and trade system with freely distributed permits to mitigate climate change. For example, Goulder and Parry (2008) calculate that a $20 per ton tax on carbon dioxide in the US would raise roughly $100 billion annually in the short term. They further suggest that the cost savings from the emission tax with efficient revenue recycling vis-à-vis a similar, non-revenue raising policy is on the order of $30 billion per year.

7.6 SUMMARY

In this chapter we have examined how thinking on environmental policy needs to be adjusted when we consider interactions between the polluting and other sectors of the economy. The labor market is of considerable interest in this regard, given its size and the distortions that typically exist due to income and payroll taxes. We found that if the labor/leisure market is *not* distorted – i.e. there is no labor tax – then the results derived earlier in the book for environmental policy with competitive markets continue to hold. Spillover effects do exist, in that if the environmental policy causes an increase in the price of the polluting good, the cross price relationship between leisure and the polluting good causes the demand for leisure to shift. The direction of the shift depends on whether leisure and the polluting goods are complements or substitutes. Regardless of this, if there is no distortion of the labor/leisure market, the shift does not have efficiency ramifications.

Our analysis demonstrated that things are different when there is a pre-existing distortion in the labor market. The use of a proportional tax on wages to raise revenue for the government means there are two distorted markets. Too much of both the polluting good and leisure are consumed, with the former due to the external environmental cost and the latter due to the marginal disincentive to work when the net (take home) wage is lower. In this situation, we saw that the optimal second-best environmental policy depends on how the environmental policy impacts outcomes in the labor/leisure market, with the impact operating through two potential channels.

For the first channel we identified the *marginal interaction effect*, which arises when the demand for leisure shifts due to the change in the price of the polluting good. If leisure and the polluting good are substitutes the demand for leisure increases, thereby exacerbating the distortion in that market and adding an additional category of cost to the policy. This also causes a loss in labor tax revenue, which must be made good if the government has a fixed budget requirement. The necessary increase in the marginal labor tax rate causes a further welfare loss in the labor market. Thus when leisure and the polluting good are substitutes the interaction effect causes the costs of the environmental policy to be higher than in the partial equilibrium context. When they are complements the effect works in the opposite direction: the increase in the price of the polluting good leads to less leisure (and more labor) consumption, thereby mitigating the distortion in the labor market. In this case the interaction effect causes the costs of the environmental policy to be lower than in the partial equilibrium context.

For the second channel we identified the *marginal revenue effect*, which arises when environmental policy allows for a tax swap whereby labor tax revenue is replaced by revenue raised from taxing emissions. The overall effect of this type of revenue recycling is to reduce the cost of environmental policy, since it reduces the overall distortion in the labor market. At the margin we say that the revenue effect can be positive or negative, depending on the elasticity of demand for the polluting good.

Having identified the marginal interaction and revenue effects as additional factors to consider when designing environmental policy, we examined the extent to which a "*double dividend*" from environmental taxation might be possible. We saw that a *strong double dividend* – i.e. a situation when it is optimal to set an environmental tax *above* marginal damage – is unlikely in general, since on average the marginal interaction effect is likely to increase cost at a magnitude larger than the marginal revenue effect lowers cost. Nonetheless, our numerical and empirical examples showed that special cases do exist, in which a double dividend can arise.

The consequences for real-world environmental policy from the "tax interaction" literature covered in this chapter are potentially large. Most importantly, our results show that revenue recycling can be an important component to consider when evaluating the performance of different policy instruments. Given this, the equivalence we saw in previous chapters between cap and trade with freely distributed permits and emission taxes, for example, breaks down. Indeed, policy instruments that do not raise revenue, but still affect the price of the polluting good, can generate an interaction effect without the corresponding revenue effect, thereby affecting the welfare gains from the policy. Much of the recent empirical and numerical modeling in this area focuses on identifying specific contexts in which the interactions with pre-existing distortions are likely to be of first order importance for policy design.

7.7 FURTHER READING

There are a large number of articles that theoretically explore the implications for environmental policy of pre-existing distortions. Bovenberg and de Mooij (1994) and Bovenberg and Goulder (1996) provide early influential papers, and Parry (1995) provides an accessible, graphics-based presentation of the main predictions. In a series of papers, Bovenberg and van der Ploeg (1994a, 1994b, 1996) explicitly examine the existence of double dividend, under labor market imperfections. The model we have used in this chapter is adapted from Parry (1995) and his follow-on papers. Our examination of the model when environmental quality is non-separable in utility was adapted from Schwartz and Repetto (2000). Goulder (1995) and Bovenberg (1999) provide surveys and conceptual clarifications about competing concepts of a double dividend. West and Williams (2007) provide an empirical analysis of optimal gasoline taxes given interactions with leisure demand, and Anger et al. (2010) and Fraser and Waschik (2013) explore optimal taxation from the perspective of CGE models. Noteworthy generalizations of the basic model structure include Bento and Jacobsen (2007), who consider the impact of fixed factors of production, Parry and Bento (2000), who examine the role of tax favored consumption on environmental policy, and Williams (2003), who considers the links between health effects and optimal taxation. Parry et al. (2012) provide a wide-ranging discussion of environmental taxation that includes commentary on the role of the interaction and revenue effects in policy design and evaluation. Finally, in a recent contribution, Jacobs and de Mooij (2015) generalize the second-best emissions tax framework to address redistribution issues among heterogeneous agents.

EXERCISES

7.1 * Consider the partial model of Chapter 3 with an aggregate abatement cost function $C(E)$ satisfying the usual properties. The regulator charges an emission tax. Assume there exists a marginal cost of public funds denoted by λ, and that the regulator's objective function is $SC(E) = C(E) + D(E) - \lambda \tau E$, where τ is the tax rate.
   (a) Determine the optimal tax rate and show that it can be smaller or larger than the marginal damage, depending on the elasticity of the marginal abatement cost function. Draw two figures to illustrate the different cases.
   (b) Interpret the optimality formula for the tax rate. How can you decompose it using the concepts studied in this chapter? Which effect is missing?

7.2 * Use a software package such as Matlab or Mathematica to program the example described in section 7.3.
   (a) Assume the environmental regulator ignores the impact on the labor market and sets an emission standard X according to the Pigouvian rule. Determine the second-best optimal labor tax and all other endogenous variables. How big is the MIE in this case? For the next two parts, assume that the polluting good and leisure are complements by selecting a negative value for η (e.g. $\eta = -0.4$).
   (b) Assume no emission taxation is possible and therefore no revenues are collected from emission taxes. Determine the second-best optimal combination of the emission standard and the labor tax.
   (c) Assume now that an emission tax is possible. Determine the second-best optimal combination of the emission and the labor tax.
   (d) Try to find parameter combinations where either $MIE < 0$ and $MRE < 0$, or $MIE < 0$ and $|MIE| > MRE > 0$ hold.

7.3 ** Extend the model of this chapter by assuming that there are several firms with (possibly asymmetric) cost functions with increasing marginal costs. Assume first that emissions are regulated by a cap and trade system with freely allocated emission permits.

(a) Write down the equilibrium conditions for a given emission cap and labor tax.

(b) Compute the comparative static effects with respect to the emission cap and the labor tax on all endogenous variables, including the price for emission permits.

(c) Determine the second-best optimal combination of the emission cap and the labor tax.

(d) Assume now that an emission tax is possible. Determine the second-best optimal combination of the emission and the labor tax.

7.4 ** Extend the model of this chapter by assuming that the firm's cost function has the form $C(X,E)$ satisfying assumption 5.1.

(a) Derive the second-best optimal combination of an emission standard (no emission tax revenues) and labor tax.

(b) Assume now that an emission tax with revenue recycling is possible. Derive formulas for the second-best optimal combination of the emission and the labor taxes.

(c) Substitute $C(X,E) = (aX - bE)^2/2b + cX^2/2$ for the cost function $C(X) = cX^2/2$ in the section 7.3 example, and assume all other functions are the same. Determine the second-best optimal formulas corresponding to (a) and (b).

7.5 ** Replicate the calculations of the example in section 7.3 using numerical software such as Mathematica, Mathlab or the like. Do the calculations also for the following parameter sets and interpret your results:

	α	β	γ	ϕ	η	C	d	G	w	T
(i)	2.0	0.9	2.0	0.9	0.4	0.1	0.04	0.3	0.1	10.0
(ii)	2.0	0.9	2.0	0.9	0.4	0.1	0.04	0.5	0.1	10.0
(iii)	4.0	0.9	4.0	0.9	0.2	0.4	0.04	0.6	0.1	10.0
(iv)	4.0	0.9	4.0	0.9	0.2	0.4	0.04	0.8	0.1	10.0
(v)	2.3	0.5	2.3	0.5	0.4	0.1	0.3	0.3	0.1	10.0

7.6 *** Modify the model in this chapter by considering a closed economy with endogenous wage formation. The production sector is now characterized by a decreasing returns to scale production function $F(L,E)$ where E is a polluting input, L is labor, and $F_{LE} > 0$, $F_{EE} < 0$, and $F_{LL} < 0$. Emissions are directly proportional to the polluting input, so that emissions and the polluting input are interchangeable and the damage function is $D(E)$. The household owns the firm and collects its profits.

(a) Set up the conditions for an unregulated competitive equilibrium (no government budget, no regulation of emissions). Assume now that the regulator sets an emission standard E and charges a labor tax m paid by the consumer to finance a fixed budget G.

(b) Conduct a comparative static analysis with respect to E and m on all endogenous variables, including the now endogenous wage rate.

(c) Determine the second-best optimal combination of the emission cap and the labor tax, and derive an expression for the marginal cost of public funds. Assume now an emission tax with revenue recycling is possible.

(d) Conduct a comparative static analysis with respect to the emission tax rate τ and the labor tax m on all endogenous variables.

(e) Determine the second-best optimal combination of the emission and the labor tax. Investigate and interpret the decomposition of the emission tax rate.

(f) Modify the model by assuming the firm has a constant returns to scale production function $F(L,E)$, where profits are zero. Proceed as above. What difficulties do you face and how do you solve them?

7.7 *** [Based on Bovenberg and De Mooij, 1994] Assume now that the consumer consumes a clean and a dirty good, the quantities of which are written as C and D, which generate utility $U(C,D)$. Assume the clean and the dirty good are substitutes. A fixed amount of labor is supplied by the consumer (with elasticity equal zero and no disutility of labor) to a representative firm, which with one unit of labor can either produce one unit of the clean or the dirty good.

(a) Set up the conditions for an unregulated competitive equilibrium (no government budget, no regulation of emissions).

Assume now that the regulator sets an emission standard (i.e. she directly fixes the amount of the dirty good D) and charges a labor tax m paid by the consumer to finance a fixed government budget G.

(b) Conduct a comparative static analysis with respect to D and m on all endogenous variables, including the wage rate.

(c) Determine the second-best optimal combination of the emission standard D and the labor tax m, and also derive the formula for the marginal cost of public funds.

Assume now that an emission tax can be charged on the dirty good with the revenues recycled.

(d) Conduct a comparative static analysis with respect to the emission tax rate and the labor tax on all endogenous variables.

(e) Determine the second-best optimal combination of the emission and the labor tax, and investigate and interpret the decomposition of the emission tax rate.

CHAPTER 8

Institutional Topics in Cap and Trade Programs

Our discussion of environmental policy to this point has generally abstracted from the many ways that institutional and design elements can affect the performance of the suite of policy instruments. For example, while we have distinguished between auctioned and freely distributed permits in cap and trade programs, we have not addressed the many ways that freely distributed permits can be assigned to participating firms. In this chapter we discuss a collection of institutional issues in cap and trade programs, analyzing how design elements that are common in practice may affect performance.

We focus specifically on cap and trade because its theoretical merits have long been stressed by economists, and these efforts have paid off in the sense that emission trading is now part of the common parlance in environmental policy discussions. Indeed we now have experience with two major programs – the US sulfur dioxide program, and the European Union Emissions Trading System for carbon dioxide – and several smaller, regional programs. It is telling, however, that few if any of the existing programs were designed according to the principles described in the theoretical papers. Instead, they combine political compromises, interest group demands, and economic ideas in ways that have on occasion contributed to disappointing performances for cap and trade programs.

In what follows we examine seven topics related to cap and trade programs, and which economists have examined. In section 8.1 we present an analysis that explicitly accounts for differences in the location of polluting firms and the spatial extent of the damages their emissions cause. We show that cap and trade programs can be designed to accommodate the spatial dimension, but that it involves a change in focus from emissions to ambient pollution outcomes. In section 8.2 we address the temporal dimension by considering the merits of allowing polluters to transfer emissions across time by permitting them to bank (or borrow) emissions rights. Both the US SO_2 program and the European Union CO_2 program allow some form of permit banking, and so understanding how this affects behavior in these programs is necessary for evaluating their success. We show that, under some circumstances related to abatement cost uncertainty, some limited forms of banking are welfare improving. In section 8.3 we examine the consequences of market power in the emission permit market. Many programs include both large and small polluters, and others contain a relatively small number of participants. We show that departures from competitive behavior can prevent cap and trade programs from achieving the cost-minimizing allocation of abatement effort and that, in contrast to our Chapter 3 findings, the initial allocation of permits can matter for efficiency. In section 8.4 we consider a general model of transactions costs. Many existing programs have included design elements that make permit exchange more costly by restricting the types of trades that can occur. Other programs include a relatively small number of participants, resulting in thin markets or the need for bilateral negotiations. We find that transaction costs of any type drive a wedge between the marginal abatement costs of potential permit buyers and sellers, meaning the least cost allocation is not achieved, and the initial allocation of emission rights matters for efficiency. In section 8.5 we use a two-period model to show that the way that freely distributed permits are allocated can matter for program performance. Both "grandfathering" (assigning permits based on historic emissions) and "benchmarking" (assigning permits based on past output) can cause departures from efficiency by encouraging polluters to behave strategically in the run-up to a program's start date. In section 8.6 we examine how overlapping regulations can distort outcomes in emissions trading markets. Federal systems and international agreements may cause polluters to be subject to regulations from multiple jurisdictions. We show that in some cases, this can cause cap and trade programs to exhibit "leakage" – a tendency for emissions to go to the region/state/country with the less-stringent regulations. Finally, in section 8.7 we study monitoring and compliance, when monitoring is imperfect and costly. We show that a higher inspection probability induces more compliance, and enhances the price for tradable permits. Since there is always some under-compliance, marginal damage exceeds marginal abatement costs under the second-best optimal inspection probability.

8.1   THE SPATIAL DIMENSION

In previous chapters we treated pollution as a homogeneous, pure public bad. We modeled this by assuming that environmental damage depends only on total emissions, so that the spatial location of pollution sources was irrelevant. This assumption is reasonable for greenhouse gasses, for example, in that climate change damages are independent of where an additional ton of carbon dioxide originates. For some pollutants, however, the distance between emission sources and affected areas matters for damages, as do weather and geographical conditions. For example, the direction of prevailing winds means that sulfur dioxide emissions from coal-fired electricity plants in the American Midwest have strongly affected the New England states and eastern Canada, while areas further west have been much less impacted. Thus for sulfur dioxide and many other pollutants, there is a significant spatial dimension in the distribution of damages. In this section, we present a model that explicitly accommodates multiple pollution sources and receptors at different points in space, and examine how the spatial dimension affects the design of a cap and trade regulatory approach.

8.1.1 A Spatial Pollution Model

We assume there are J polluters located at different points in the landscape, and M receptor regions. The receptor regions are distinguished by how emissions from the pollution sources affect local ambient conditions. Emissions from pollution source j are denoted e_j, and the ambient pollution level at receptor region m is given by A_m, for $m = 1,...,M$. The ambient pollution level at location m depends on the emission levels from the J sources. Formally the relationship is determined by a diffusion matrix

$$H = \begin{pmatrix} h_{11} & \cdots & \cdots & \cdots & h_{1J} \\ \vdots & \ddots & & & \vdots \\ \vdots & & h_{mj} & & \vdots \\ \vdots & & & \ddots & \vdots \\ h_{M1} & \cdots & \cdots & \cdots & h_{MJ} \end{pmatrix}, \tag{8.1}$$

where h_{mj} is a diffusion coefficient that indicates the extent to which an emission from source j affects the ambient conditions at receptor m. Thus the ambient pollution level at receptor m is given by

$$A_m = \sum_{j=1}^{J} h_{mj} e_j, \quad m = 1,...,M. \tag{8.2}$$

Following the framework in Chapter 3, we assume that all polluters incur abatement costs $C_j(e_j)$, where the abatement cost function satisfies the familiar properties $C_j'(e_j) < 0$ and $C_j''(e_j) \geq 0$. The damage function, in contrast, is made more complicated by the spatial dimension. Specifically, we denote local damages at receptor m by $D_m(A_m)$ so that the total social cost from pollution can be written as

$$\sum_{j=1}^{J} C_j(e_j) + \sum_{m=1}^{M} D_m(A_m), \tag{8.3}$$

where A_m is given by Eq. (8.2). The first-best allocation of abatement effort is found by differentiating total costs with respect to each e_j:

$$-C_j'(e_j) = \sum_{m=1}^{M} h_{mj} \times D_m'(A_m), \quad j = 1,...,J. \tag{8.4}$$

This means that the marginal abatement cost incurred by polluter j should be equal to the sum of the marginal damages caused by the marginal emission, where the marginal damages are computed as the diffusion coefficient-weighted slope of each location-specific damage function. We denote the optimal emission levels by $e_1^*,...,e_J^*$ and the optimal ambient pollution levels at the M receptors by $A_1^*,...,A_M^*$.

8.1.2 Decentralization

In order to decentralize this optimal allocation, we introduce ambient pollution permits. For each receptor region the regulator makes available a number of transferable emission permits, denoted by $L_1,...,L_M$. To comply with the regulation, a polluter j must possess $h_{mj} \times e_j$ permits of type m for each of its emissions, for all $m = 1,...,M$. Following our established notation we use σ_m to denote the price of a type m emission permit. Under this scheme, and assuming for simplicity that the permits are auctioned, a polluter j emitting e_j units faces total compliance-related costs of

$$TC_j(e_j) = C_j(e_j) + \sum_{m=1}^{M} \sigma_m \times \left(h_{mj} \times e_j\right),$$ (8.5)

and the first-order condition for cost minimization is

$$-C_j'(e_j) = \sum_{m=1}^{M} \sigma_m h_{mj}.$$ (8.6)

From this it is easy to see that if $L_m = A_m^*$, then M competitive markets for ambient pollution permits will lead to the first-best allocation, and we have

$$\sigma_m = D_m'(A_m).$$ (8.7)

That is, the price for an ambient pollution permit at receptor m reflects the marginal damage from pollution in that region.[1] Note that this general spatial framework nests the non-spatial, single receptor model from Chapter 3 as a special case, in which $M = 1$ and $h_{1j} = 1$ for all j. We can also interpret the spatial model as a firm emitting multiple pollutants – either as spatially differentiated versions of the same effluent, or as unique emission types – and needing to comply with cap and trade regulations for each type.

Implementation of an optimal, spatially explicit system would be difficult. Models are needed that can accurately track the diffusion of emissions to receptor points across the landscape. In addition, transaction costs will increase with the number of receptor points (and hence individual permit markets), and the market design would need to be adjusted when firms relocate. It may therefore be preferable to pursue approximations to the ideal spatial trading system. One option is to assign sources and receptors into a finite number of spatial zones, with diffusion coefficients fixed at the zone rather than source level. In such a system each emitter needs to hold permit types equivalent to the number of zones, which may still imply substantial transactions costs. Another option is to create separate trading zones in which trades may not cross zone boundaries. Thin markets may be a consequence of this. For example, in Orange County, California in the 1970s, 30 different trading zones for sulfur dioxide and nitrogen oxide were created. When the US sulfur dioxide program was in the planning stage, western and eastern trading zones were discussed, though ultimately the regulation was implemented with a single, nation-wide market. Tietenberg (2006, Chapter 4) presents additional details on the spatial aspects of the early cap and trade programs.

8.2   THE TEMPORAL DIMENSION

Cap and trade programs are typically implemented over several years. The largest program to date, the European Union Emissions Trading System (EU-ETS), is unfolding

---

[1] Our simple presentation here ignores the fact that the optimality of a competitive equilibrium with multiple affected regions is not a trivial outcome. Montgomery (1972) addresses this and demonstrates that for the setting examined here the multiple competitive equilibria are efficient.

across several trading phases: phase I (2005–07), phase II (2008–12), phase III (2013–20), phase IV (2021–8) and possible additional phases in the future.[2] The US sulfur dioxide program does not have a legislatively determined end date. These multiple year programs partially admit the possibility of banking or borrowing of emission permits across years of the program. This means, for example, that a pollution permit issued in 2016 could be used in that year or retained to cover compliance for an emission unit in a later year. Correspondingly a firm operating in year 2016 might use a 2017 vintage permit to cover its current emissions, meaning the 2017 permit would not be available in later periods. Most programs to date have allowed at least some form of permit banking. For example, the US SO_2 program allowed unlimited banking, and participants' active shifting of permits into future compliance periods was a defining feature of the program in its early years. The EU-ETS originally allowed banking within, but not across phases; more recently, this has been relaxed to allow limited banking across trading phases. With some limited exceptions (see example 8.1), programs to date have not allowed permit borrowing. This is likely due to the potential political economy problems associated with emission-indebted firms. In this section, we examine the temporal dimension of cap and trade programs using a simple, two-period model. We consider the general case of both banking and borrowing, but focus our normative analysis on the desirability of allowing permit banking in actual cap and trade programs.

EXAMPLE 8.1 (POLICY) In the European Union Emissions Trading System (EU-ETS), banking was initially allowed only in phase I (2005–07). Since firms had banked permits allocated in the first two years, and demand was lower than expected at the end of phase I, this caused the price for emission permits to fall to zero at the end of 2007. Trading across phases was initially disallowed because policy makers feared that member states would not meet their obligations (or burden-sharing agreements) in later phases. A second reason for banning banking was the concern that, if there were an unexpectedly large number of allocations banked for use in later years, member states would need to make additional abatement efforts in sectors not covered by the EU-ETS, in order to comply with annual national-level targets under the Kyoto agreement (Alberola and Chevallier, 2009). Since 2008, however, unlimited and free banking has been allowed across years and trading phases. By contrast, borrowing is only allowed within one year. The reason is neither environmental nor economic, but due to an administrational loophole: the allocation of allowances takes place in February, but the surrender of allowances for the previous year takes place by the end of April. (European Commission, 2016)[3]

8.2.1 A Two-Period Model

We assume there are J firms that operate for two periods. The abatement function is denoted by $C_{jt}(e_{jt})$ where $t = 1,2$ indexes the two periods. Following the convention from Chapter 3, we denote the firm j and time t permit endowment by $\bar{e}_{jt}$, which can be zero as

---

[2] Phase IV is projected, but no definite emission cap is defined yet. The latest information at the time of writing is available in *The EU Emissions Trading System (EU-ETS)*, January 2016. The document is available for download at http://ec.europa.eu/clima/policies/ets/revision/index_en.htm

[3] For more details on the EU-ETS, see Chevallier (2012, 2013).

a special case. In the first period, the firm decides how much to emit and how many pollution permits it will bank or borrow. We use b_j to denote the amount of permits moved through time, where $b_j > 0$ indicates banking and $b_j < 0$ indicates borrowing. Denoting the equilibrium permit price in period t by σ_t, the firm's decision problem is to select e_{jt} and b_j to minimize total compliance costs:

$$\min_{e_{j1}, e_{j2}, b_j} TC = C_{j1}(e_{j1}) + \sigma_1\left(e_{j1} + b_j - \overline{e}_{j1}\right) + \delta\left[C_{j2}(e_{j2}) + \sigma_2\left(e_{j2} - b_j - \overline{e}_{j2}\right)\right], \qquad (8.8)$$

where $\delta = 1/(1+r)$ is the discount factor, and r is the interest rate. The first-order conditions for emissions are

$$\frac{\partial TC}{\partial e_{jt}} = C'_{jt}(e_{jt}) + \sigma_t = 0 \quad \rightarrow \quad -C'_{jt}(e_{jt}) = \sigma_t, \quad t = 1, 2, \qquad (8.9)$$

which shows the familiar condition that marginal abatement cost equals the permit price, albeit for both periods in the two period context. The first-order condition with respect to b_j is

$$\frac{\partial TC}{\partial b_j} = \sigma_1 - \delta\sigma_2 \underset{<}{\overset{>}{=}} 0, \qquad (8.10)$$

where the relationship to zero depends on the equilibrium price formation process. Note in particular that, if $\sigma_1 > \delta\sigma_2$ persists, firms will want to borrow infinitely many permits from the future in order to sell them at today's currently high price, whereas with $\sigma_1 < \delta\sigma_2$, firms will want to bank infinitely many permits today in order to sell them in the next period. Since actions of either type will change the relative permit prices in the two periods, neither $\sigma_1 > \delta\sigma_2$ nor $\sigma_1 < \delta\sigma_2$ can be sustained in equilibrium. Thus the two periods are linked via the equilibrium condition

$$\sigma_1 = \delta\sigma_2 \quad \rightarrow \quad \sigma_2 = (1+r)\sigma_1, \qquad (8.11)$$

which means that the permit price must increase according to the interest rate when banking and borrowing are freely available.

8.2.2 Should Banking Be Allowed?

Equations (8.9) and (8.11) show that permit banking and borrowing in cap and trade programs serve to smooth abatement costs over time. Just as current period trading results in marginal abatement costs that are equal across space, temporal trading implies that discounted marginal abatement costs are equal across time. Thus abatement costs are smaller when firms are allowed to transfer emission permits between time periods. This does not necessarily imply, however, that banking or borrowing lowers overall social costs. If abatement cost and damage functions differ over time, and if the regulator has issued the optimal number of pollution permits in each period to reflect this, then bank-ing or borrowing will temporally shift emissions away from the optimal allocation – i.e. the allocation that minimizes the sum of abatement costs *and* pollution damages. Thus in a perfect-information context, permit banking and borrowing will increase social costs, and therefore should not be allowed.

Matters can be different if there is incomplete information about abatement costs. For example, abatement costs may fluctuate year to year due to regional-scale weather conditions or the business cycle, which may cause demand for the industry's output to ebb and flow. To see that banking can contribute to lower social costs in the uncer-tainty context, we use the aggregate abatement cost function $C(E_t, \eta_t)$ for both peri-ods, where η_t is a random variable defined so that both abatement cost and marginal abatement cost are increasing in η_t (see also section 4.1.3 in Chapter 4). Note that the uncertainty is aggregate, in that its role in the aggregate abatement cost function is to shift all firms' costs in the same direction. We assume for simplicity that the dam-age function is time invariant. More importantly, we assume that the regulator has to commit to the number of permits at the start of the program, prior to the two trading periods and the resolution of uncertainty. In this case, she chooses permit endowments L_1 and L_2 to minimize

$$\bar{C}(L_1) + D(L_1) + \delta\left[\bar{C}(L_2) + D(L_2)\right], \tag{8.12}$$

where $\bar{C}(L_t)$ denotes the expected value of $C(E_t, \eta_t)$. Note that the optimal ex ante per-mit allocations will satisfy

$$-\bar{C}_{E_t}(L_t) = D'(E_t) \tag{8.13}$$

for the two time periods, meaning the regulator issues permits in each period to the point that marginal damage is equal to expected marginal abatement cost.

The resolution of uncertainty in period 1 determines the degree to which the ex ante allocation differs from the ex-post optimal. For example, if η_1 is lower than average the aggregate marginal abatement cost function in period 1 will be lower than expected – i.e. $-\bar{C}_{E_1}(L_1) > -C_{E_1}(L_1, \eta_1)$. In this situation with low marginal abatement cost, it may be socially optimal to abate more in period 1, and simultaneously shift some emissions permits into the second period via banking. The shape of the marginal damage function, however, can limit the amount of banking that is optimal. If the marginal damage curve is steep, so that damages increase rapidly with additional emissions, then excess permit banking can lead to a temporal "hotspot". Thus, under cost uncertainty, the decision of whether or not to allow banking depends on the slope of the damage function, as well as the amount of potential variability in abatement costs. In the appendix we provide an extended example demonstrating situations when permit banking is socially beneficial and harmful.

Rather than a hard distinction between allowing banking or not, hybrid regimes are possible. One possibility is to set a cap on banking, whereby only a given percentage of permits could be transferred to future periods. For example, according to Article 11 of the Icelandic Fisheries Management Act (1990), between 5 and 20 percent (depending on species) of the annual individual transferable fishing quotas (ITQs) can be transferred to the next year. New Zealand allows for both banking and borrowing of up to 10 percent of ITQs from one year to the other.[4] An alternative is to allow banking, albeit with depreciation. This means, for example, that a permit with vintage 2013 can be used to cover one emission unit in 2013 or saved for use in 2014, at which point it will be able to cover $\alpha < 1$ emission units.

8.3   MARKET POWER

In our discussion thus far, we have implicitly assumed that there are many small polluters regulated by a cap and trade program, so that pollution permit markets are competitive and individual firms behave as price takers. This need not be the case in practice. Localized regulations may involve only a few polluters, and large-scale regulations may target an industry with numerous small firms and a few large firms. For example, Rico (1995) provides empirical evidence that the early US sulfur dioxide market involved a few large and many small firms. In an influential paper, Hahn (1984) uses a stylized model with many small firms and a single large firm exercising market power in the market for tradable permits, to show that the initial distribution of permits matters for efficiency. In this section we present a generalized version of the Hahn model that allows for several large firms.

To this end, we divide a set of J firms participating in a cap and trade program into large firms $j=1,...,l$ and small firms $j=l+1,...,J$. We allow the divide point to be exogenous for simplicity, and continue to focus only on the abatement cost functions $C_j(e_j)$. We first examine a system of freely distributed permits so that each firm owns an initial permit endowment, denoted by $\bar{e}_j$, with the aggregate permit supply given by

$$L = \sum_{j=1}^{J} \bar{e}_j. \tag{8.14}$$

A typical firm's total costs can then be written as

$$TC_j(e_j) = C_j(e_j) + \sigma(e_j - \bar{e}_j), \tag{8.15}$$

where σ is the permit market price.

The small firms, also called *fringe firms*, act as price takers, and thus set their marginal abatement costs equal to the market price of permits:

$$-C_j'(e_j) = \sigma, \quad j = l+1,...,J. \tag{8.16}$$

Based on the small firms' first-order conditions, we can solve for emissions as $e_j(\sigma)$; this can also be interpreted as their factor demands for emission permits. Summing

---

[4] For more details on the New Zealand tradable quota system see Newell et al. (2005).

factor demands across all small firms, we obtain the total permit demand for the competitive sector

$$E^c(\sigma) = \sum_{j-l+1}^{J} e_j(\sigma), \tag{8.17}$$

and inverting the competitive sector demand function leads to the competitive sector inverse demand function, which we denote by $\sigma_c(E^c)$. Since the number of emission permits used by the competitive sector is equal to the residual left by the large firms, we can rewrite E^c as

$$E^c = L - \sum_{j=1}^{l} e_j, \tag{8.18}$$

and express the competitive sector inverse demand function as

$$\sigma_c \left(L - \sum_{j=1}^{l} e_j \right). \tag{8.19}$$

Equation (8.19) makes clear that the price ultimately paid by the fringe firms for emission permits will depend on the choices made by the l firms possessing market power.

We now turn our attention to the large firms' choices. By definition, the permit market price is affected by the emission choices of the l firms with market power. That is, the large firms implicitly set the market price for permits by determining the emission rights that are left for use by the competitive sector. Thus the objective function for a large firm j is

$$TC_j(e_j) = C_j(e_j) + \sigma_c \left(L - \sum_{n=1}^{l} e_n \right) \left[e_j - \bar{e}_j \right], \tag{8.20}$$

where $\sigma_c(\cdot)$ is once again the competitive firms' aggregate inverse demand function. Each large firm selects e_j to minimize costs, which affects the equilibrium permit prices. The first-order condition for this choice is

$$-C_j'(e_j) = \underbrace{-\sigma' \left(L - \sum_{n=1}^{l} e_n \right) \left[e_j - \bar{e}_j \right]}_{+} + \underbrace{\sigma \left(L - \sum_{n=1}^{l} e_n \right)}_{-/0/+}, \quad j = 1, \ldots, l. \tag{8.21}$$

Inspection of this condition suggests that if the initial distribution of permits is such that $e_j > \bar{e}_j$ for a large firm, the choice leads to $-C_j'(e_j) > \sigma$. Likewise, if $e_j < \bar{e}_j$ then $-C_j'(e_j) < \sigma$, and it is only when $e_j = \bar{e}_j$ that the efficient outcome $-C_j'(e_j) = \sigma$ occurs. We summarize these findings in the following proposition.

Proposition 8.1

Consider a cap and trade system with a free allocation of permits and a mixture of large firms exercising market power on the permit market and small fringe firms behaving as price takers.

(a) If in equilibrium a large firm is a net buyer (seller), the large firm sets its marginal abatement cost higher (lower) than the permit price.

(b) Only if the large firms obtain an initial permit endowment corresponding to their efficient emission level will permit trading lead to a cost-minimizing outcome.

The intuition for these conditions follows from the incentives of firms with market power. A large firm that wants to *buy* additional permits purchases *fewer* than the efficient amount, in order to keep the permit price low. Thus the net buyer behaves as an oligopsonist, or a monopsonist if $l=1$. A large firm that wants to *sell* unused permits sells *fewer* than the efficient amount, in order to keep the permit price high. Thus the net seller behaves as an oligopolist, or a monopolist if $l=1$.

Figure 8.1 illustrates the monopsony and monopoly cases, where firm 1 possesses market power. The top and bottom panels are identical outside of the position of firm 1's marginal abatement cost curve, which is labeled $-C_1'(e_1)$. The initial endowment for firm 1 is shown as $\bar{e}_1$, and the figures illustrate the optimal choice of emissions e_1 for the large firm. The curve labeled $\sigma(L-e_1)$ is the inverse demand function by the competitive sector. In both panels, the efficient outcome occurs when the marginal abatement costs are equal between the large and small firms – i.e. when $-C_1'(e_1) = \sigma(L-e_1)$. This point is labeled e_1^c, and σ_c denotes the price that would arise in a competitive permit market.

Firm 1's market power distorts the equilibrium abatement allocation. The top panel of Figure 8.1 shows the monopsony case in which firm 1 is a net permit buyer. The curve labelled MC is the marginal cost to firm 1 for each emission right purchased; it consists of both the level price (the first term) and the increase in price that results from the incremental increase in permit demand (the second term). The optimal choice occurs when the marginal abatement cost is equal to the marginal cost of purchasing an emission permit, which is shown as e_1^m in the top panel. The permit price in this case is $\sigma_m < \sigma_c$, meaning that the monopsonist permit buyer selects its purchase level to keep the price lower than would occur in a competitive market. It purchases fewer permits and hence abates more than is optimal, thereby driving a wedge between its marginal abatement cost level and that of the competitive sector. The welfare loss is shown as area $a+b$ in the top panel; it arises based on the fact that aggregate costs would be lower if the large firm abated less and the competitive firms more.

The bottom panel shows the monopoly case in which firm 1 emits less than its endowment, meaning it is a net seller of permits. The curve labeled MR is the marginal revenue that firm 1 receives for each emission right it sells. Note that this is the same curve that was labeled MC in the top panel, but that here attention focuses on the segment to the left of $\bar{e}_1$. This segment shows that marginal revenue consists of the level price less the fall in price that occurs when firm 1 offers an additional emission right to the competitive sector. The optimal choice occurs when the marginal revenue the firm receives for selling a permit is equal to the opportunity cost of the sale, as reflected by the marginal cost of abatement. This point is shown as e_1^m in the bottom panel. The permit price in this case is $\sigma_m > \sigma_c$, meaning that the monopolist permit seller selects its sales level to keep

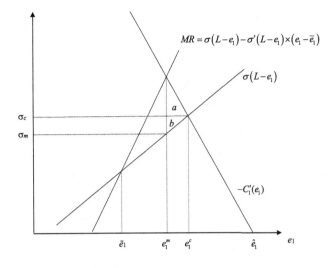

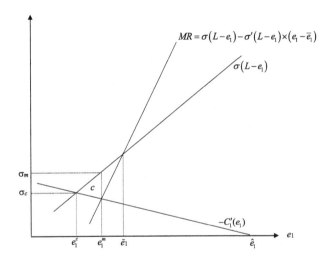

Figure 8.1   Monopsony and monopoly examples

the price higher than would occur in a competitive market. This leads to a welfare loss of area c in the bottom panel, which could be eliminated via a reallocation of abatement effort towards the large firm.

Although it is not shown in the figure, we can also imagine drawing $-C'_1(e_1)$ so that it intersects $\sigma(L-e_1)$ at $\bar{e}_1$. In this case firm 1 is neither a buyer nor a seller, and the equality of marginal abatement costs between the competitive sector and the large firm implies there is no distortion in the permit market. Thus, when the large firm's initial endowment corresponds to its efficient emission level, the potential market power of the large firms does not affect the outcome, since they do not participate in trading. This does not generally imply, however, that large firms should not participate in trade. Since any mutually beneficial trade reduces costs it will improve efficiency – i.e. the final allocation is less inefficient than the initial allocation, even if the final allocation is not cost minimizing. If it is legally feasible and the regulator has sufficient information she should, however, allocate approximately as many permits to the large firms as they will ultimately need in an efficient allocation of abatement effort.

If there is a thin market with only a few relatively large firms, the model outlined above is not appropriate. If there are two firms, the market is a bilateral monopoly. If the firms operate in separate output markets, they have incentive to trade permits efficiently in order to jointly minimize costs.[5] The trading price itself arises via negotiation, and is not relevant for efficiency. The situation is different if the firms also compete on the output market. In this case, the two firms have an incentive to exchange permits in a way that the sum of profits is maximized. We examine this via the following example.

EXAMPLE 8.2 (NUMERICAL/ANALYTICAL) Consider a Cournot duopoly with inverse demand function $P(X) = 1 - X$. Firms incur zero cost of production, and pollution is proportional to output, such that $e_1 = x_1$ and $e_2 = x_2$. In an unregulated Cournot-Nash equilibrium, each firm produces $x^N = 1/3$ and total unregulated pollution is $E^N = 2/3$. Suppose the regulator wants to reduce pollution to $\bar{E} = 0.60$ and issues free permits according to $\bar{e}_1 = \bar{e}_1 = 0.30$. If firms do not coordinate emissions, each will earn a profit of $(1 - 0.6) \times 0.3 = 0.12$, and the sum of profits is 0.24. Higher profits can be obtained via exchange. For example, firm 1 could offer to purchase firm 2's permit endowment for an amount $0.125 > 0.12$. After the exchange, firm 1 will retire 0.10 permits, use 0.5 permits to produce 0.50 units, and earn a profit of $(1-0.5) \times 0.5 - 0.125 = 0.125 > 0.12$. Firm 2 will close down, content with its permit sale profit of $0.125 > 0.12$.

This example demonstrates that both firms can be better off through trade, though at the expense of the consumers. We also see that marginal abatement costs, measured as forgone profits through a marginal emission reduction, differ across firms at the final allocation. This would also emerge under a more general setting with cost function $C^j(x_j, e_j)$. Firms may seek to raise rivals' costs, thereby triggering lower output and higher prices. Through permit trade, firms compensate their rivals for profit losses. For more than two firms, it is less clear how firms will allocate their permits within the industry. Firms may trade permits cooperatively such that the sum of their profits is maximized. However, one can show that the core of such a cooperative game[6] will be empty in general. In other words, a subset of firms may further exchange permits in order to increase their joint coalition profits at the expense of firms outside the coalition. Therefore, there is no clear prediction about the outcome through trade in a thin market with imperfect competition on both the output and the permit market.

The literature studying how permit and output markets may interact is relatively sparse, though there are a few notable papers. Misiolek and Elder (1989) were the first to highlight this strategic opportunity, finding that accumulation of allowances by a dominant firm prevents its competitors from pursuing their optimal production and abatement strategies. Von der Fehr (1993) and Sartzetakis (1997) extend this argument by studying the effects of raising rivals' cost strategies in an oligopolistic setting.

---

[5] See Requate (1993b) for a model of several local monopolists emitting a homogeneous pollutant. See also exercise 8.8.

[6] The core of a cooperative game consists of the set of all allocations in which no coalition can improve its payoff by redistributing their own resources.

8.4 TRANSACTION COSTS

Our discussion thus far has abstracted from the fact that permit trading can involve transaction costs, which may introduce frictions into a cap and trade system. Stavins (1995) was the first to offer a detailed analysis of how transaction costs impact the efficiency of permit trading schemes. He identifies three potential sources of transactions costs: (a) search and information; (b) bargaining and decision; and (c) monitoring and enforcement. Most of these costs arise at the beginning of a new emissions trading program. As the program matures, brokers will offer their services and transaction costs will fall considerably. Bargaining costs typically arise in thin markets, where the absence of a robust market means trades involve bilateral agreements rather than bids and offers submitted to an exchange (see previous section). For the large-scale permit trading programs such as the EU-ETS, emission exchange institutions usually exist which reduce the need for bilateral bargaining. Finally, monitoring and enforcement is not specific to permit trading, but is also necessary for other policy instruments that are emission (as opposed to technology standard) based. Nonetheless, understanding how transaction costs can affect efficiency is useful for understanding the types of institutional arrangements that are likely to promote or inhibit the success of cap and trade programs generally. In this section we present a model that is designed to illustrate how market frictions in the form of transaction costs can affect permit trading markets.

8.4.1 Modeling Transaction Costs

Consider again our familiar model with J firms, each with abatement cost function $C_j(e_j)$ that has the usual properties. Each firm has an initial permit endowment $\bar{e}_j$, and when emitting e_j units, it trades $t_j = |e_j - \bar{e}_j|$ pollution permits. Trading incurs transaction costs $\alpha_j \cdot Tr(t_j)$, where α_j is a (possibly firm-specific) cost parameter, meaning firms bear transaction costs regardless of whether they participate in the market as a buyer or seller. We assume $Tr'(t_j) > 0$, but do not place a priori restrictions on the sign of $Tr''(t_j)$. With these new costs included, the firm's objective function is to select e_j to minimize

$$TC_j(e_j) = C_j(e_j) + \sigma[e_j - \bar{e}_j] + \alpha_j Tr\left(| e_j - \bar{e}_j |\right). \tag{8.22}$$

We first examine behavior when the firm is a net buyer of permits ($e_j > \bar{e}_j$), in which case the cost function can be written as

$$TC(e_j) = C(e_j) + \sigma[e_j - \bar{e}_j] + \alpha_j Tr(e_j - \bar{e}_j). \tag{8.23}$$

The first-order condition for cost minimization is

$$-C'_j(e_j) = \sigma + \underbrace{\alpha_j Tr'(e_j - \bar{e}_j)}_{+} \tag{8.24}$$

and we assume that the second-order condition is satisfied. If the firm is instead a net seller of permits ($e_j < \bar{e}_j$), its cost function is

$$TC(e_j) = C(e_j) + \sigma[e_j - \bar{e}_j] + \alpha_j Tr(\bar{e}_j - e_j), \qquad (8.25)$$

with first-order condition

$$-C'_j(e_j) = \sigma \underbrace{- \alpha_j Tr'(\bar{e}_j - e_j)}. \qquad (8.26)$$

From (8.24), we see that higher transaction costs effectively increase the cost of buying permits, meaning the firm buys fewer permits and abates more, relative to the no transaction costs case. For the seller, (8.26) shows that transaction costs lower the effective return per permit sold, meaning the firm sells fewer permits and abates less, relative to the no transaction cost case. Thus, in the presence of transaction costs, marginal abatement costs do not equalize across firms, and the least cost abatement allocation is not obtained.

In addition, transaction costs impact the equilibrium price of permits. To see this, consider a two firm example, in which firm 1 is the seller and firm 2 is the buyer. The equilibrium (first-order) conditions in this context are:

$$-C'_1(e_1) = \sigma - \alpha_1 Tr'(\bar{e}_1 - e_1)$$
$$-C'_1(e_2) = \sigma + \alpha_2 Tr'(e_2 - \bar{e}_2) \qquad (8.27)$$
$$e_1 + e_2 = \bar{e}_1 + \bar{e}_2.$$

Totally differentiating this system we obtain:

$$-C''_1(e_1)de_1 = d\sigma - d\alpha_1 Tr'(\bar{e}_1 - e_1) + \alpha_1 Tr''(\bar{e}_1 - e_1)de_1$$
$$-C''_2(e_2)de_2 = d\sigma + d\alpha_2 Tr'(e_2 - \bar{e}_2) + \alpha_2 Tr''(e_2 - \bar{e}_2)de_2 \qquad (8.28)$$
$$de_1 + de_2 = 0.$$

We can solve this system to isolate the effect on emissions and the permit price of changes in α_j. Denoting the net trades by $t_1 = \bar{e}_1 - e'_1$ and $t_2 = e'_2 - \bar{e}_2$ and considering the symmetric case in which $\alpha_1 = \alpha_2$ we obtain

$$\frac{de_1}{d\alpha} = \frac{Tr'(t_1) + Tr'(t_2)}{\Delta + \alpha[Tr''(t_1) + Tr''(t_2)]} > 0$$

$$\frac{de_2}{d\alpha} = -\frac{Tr'(t_1) + Tr'(t_2)}{\Delta + \alpha[Tr''(t_1) + Tr''(t_2)]} < 0, \qquad (8.29)$$

$$\frac{d\sigma}{d\alpha} = \frac{C''_2(e_2)Tr'(t_1) - C''_1(e_1)Tr'(t_2) + \alpha[Tr'(t_1)Tr''(t_2) - Tr'(t_2)Tr''(t_1)]}{\Delta + \alpha[Tr''(t_1) + Tr''(t_2)]},$$

where $\Delta = C_1''(e_1) + C_2''(e_2) > 0$ via the assumed cost function curvature. These comparative static results illustrate that an increase in transaction costs causes the seller to emit more, and therefore to sell fewer permits, while the buyer emits less, and thus purchases fewer permits. The price effect can go either way and will vanish for linear and identical marginal abatement and transaction costs. For the case of asymmetric transaction costs, a similar calculation shows that a unilateral increase in the buyer's costs has the same qualitative effect on emissions, but increases the permit price. Likewise, a unilateral increase in the seller's transaction costs decreases the permit price. We summarize these results in the following proposition.

Proposition 8.2

An increase in transaction costs induces buyers to abate more and to emit less, and sellers to abate less and emit more. The trade volume decreases.

Figure 8.2 illustrates our findings for the case of increasing marginal transaction costs, denoted by the dashed lines starting at the initial allocation $(\bar{e}_1, \bar{e}_1)$. Firm 1 is a seller of permits, whereas firm 2 is a buyer. In the absence of transaction costs, the efficient allocation would be (e_1^*, e_2^*) at price σ^*. With transaction costs, there are wedges Δ_1 and Δ_2, respectively, between the new permit price σ^t and the marginal abatement costs, and the trade volumes are lower: $\bar{e}_1 - e_1^t < \bar{e}_1 - e_1^*$, and $e_2^t - \bar{e}_2 < e_2^* - \bar{e}_2$. We also see that the price with transaction costs differs slightly from the price without. If we had $\Delta_1 = \Delta_2$, the marginal transaction costs would offset each other such that $\sigma^* = \sigma^t$. In exercise 8.10, we show that a unilateral increase in transaction cost can have opposite effects, depending on whether a firm is a seller or a buyer of permits.

It is also interesting to examine how a change in the initial endowment affects the allocation of emissions and abatement efforts. To illustrate this, we consider an increase in the initial allocation for the buyer, combined with a corresponding equal decrease in

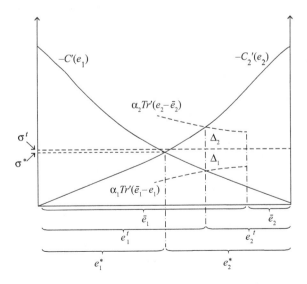

Figure 8.2 Emissions trading with transaction costs

the endowment for the seller. Differentiating the equation system (8.27) with respect to $\bar{e}_1$, keeping total emissions constant, and solving for e_1 and e_2 yields

$$\frac{de_1}{d\bar{e}_1} = \frac{\alpha_1 Tr''(t_1) + \alpha_2 Tr''(t_2)}{\alpha_1 Tr''(t_1) + \alpha_2 Tr''(t_2) + \Delta}, \quad \frac{de_2}{d\bar{e}_1} = -\frac{\alpha_1 Tr''(t_1) + \alpha_2 Tr''(t_2)}{\alpha_1 Tr''(t_1) + \alpha_2 Tr''(t_2) + \Delta}. \tag{8.30}$$

From these formulas we see immediately that the effect on abatement and trading of a change in the initial allocation depends on the curvature of the transaction cost function. Only in the special case of $Tr''(\cdot) = 0$ do we obtain the Chapter 3 result, where the initial allocation of permits does not matter for the equilibrium allocation of abatement effort. The effect on the equilibrium price of permits is ambiguous in general, but will be zero if marginal abatement and transaction costs are linear and constant. We summarize this in the following proposition.

Proposition 8.3

If there are transaction costs in permit trading, an increase in the initial endowment for buyers and an equivalent decrease in the initial endowment for sellers induces permit buyers to increase (decrease) their emissions, and permit sellers to decrease (increase) their emissions, if marginal transaction costs are increasing (decreasing). The allocation of emissions is independent of the initial endowment when marginal transaction costs are constant.

EXAMPLE 8.3 (EMPIRICAL) Much of the appeal of cap and trade programs comes from the invariance property, whereby under textbook conditions the initial allocation of emission rights does not affect the ultimate allocation of abatement effort. We have seen in sections 8.3 and 8.4, however, that actual programs can deviate from the theoretical ideal in ways that could cause the invariance property to fail. With this as motivation, Fowlie and Perloff (2013) empirically test whether the invariance property holds in a typical cap and trade program. They examine the Regional Clear Air Incentives Market (RECLAIM), which was launched in 1994 with the objective of reducing NO_X emissions from point sources in four Los Angeles area counties. RECLAIM covered most large and medium-sized emitters by freely allocating emission rights in 1994 for the duration of the program. That is, annual allocations to participating firms for the years 1994 to 2004 were publicly announced at the start of the program. The aggregate emission cap fell over time to achieve the program goal of a 75 percent reduction from covered sources by 2003. The allocation mechanism, however, provided variation in permit endowments across firms and over time, which Fowlie and Perloff exploit in their analysis. In particular, they observe emissions e_{jt} and permit endowments $\bar{e}_{jt}$ for an unbalanced panel of 361 firms over the ten-year period. With these data, they estimate models of the form

$$\ln e_{jt} = \theta \ln \bar{e}_{jt} + \beta X_{jt} + \delta_t + \alpha_j + \varepsilon_{jt}, \tag{8.31}$$

where X_{jt} is a vector of controls, and δ_t and α_j are year and firm fixed effects, respectively. The primary empirical task is to identify θ, which is the elasticity of emissions with respect to the permit endowment. A finding of $\theta = 0$ provides evidence in favor of the invariance property, while $\theta \neq 0$ implies that the permit endowment has a systematic effect on firms' emissions.

Consistent estimation of θ is made difficult by the fact that permit endowments are based on historic emissions, so that e_{jt} is almost certain to be correlated with unobserved determinants of emissions that reside in α_j and ε_{jt}. To begin to address this, the authors first present results from a fixed effects model, where they find a statistically significant estimate of $\hat{\theta} = 0.49$. This suggests that a 1 percent increase in the permit endowment causes a 0.5 percent increase in emissions – a failure of the invariance property. To address remaining endogeneity concerns, Fowlie and Perloff exploit a feature of the RECLAIM program that provides some random variation in permit endowments among firms. In particular, at the start of the program, participating firms were randomly assigned to one of two compliance cycles. One set received permit endowments on January 1 for use in the subsequent 12 months, and certified compliance for the period January 1 through December 31 (cycle 1). A second set received its permit endowments on July 1 for use in the subsequent 12 months, and certified compliance for the period July 1 through June 30 (cycle 2). This program feature caused cycle 2 firms to have on average 15 percent more permits in the first six months of a calendar year, due to the timing of annual decreases in the aggregate cap. This suggests that assignment to cycle 2 is positively correlated with $\bar{e}_{jt}$, but by virtue of the randomization, assignment to cycle 2 is uncorrelated with ε_{jt}. Using a fixed effects, instrumental variables estimator with assignment to cycle 2 as the instrument for $\bar{e}_{jt}$, Fowlie and Perloff find a statistically insignificant estimate of $\hat{\theta} = -0.11$. With this as their preferred specification, they conclude that, in spite of several design elements that likely increased transactions costs, the RECLAIM program did exhibit invariance to the initial allocation of emission permits.

8.5 INITIAL ALLOCATION SCHEMES

Our analysis in Chapter 3 distinguished between auctioned permits and free distribution systems for allocating the initial pollution rights endowment to firms participating in a cap and trade program. This simple distinction abstracted from several institutional aspects that may affect abatement behavior. For auctioned permits, emission rights can be sold via an ascending or descending bid auction, or by asking firms to submit an entire demand schedule showing how many permits they would buy at each price. Free allocation is usually done according to some historic criterion. Allocation based on historical emissions is usually referred to as "grandfathering", while allocation based on historical output is usually referred to as "benchmarking". If the timing of a regulation is such that firms know that their current emissions will determine their future permit allocation, they will take this into account and behave strategically, by adjusting their current emissions and output. In this section we study different permit allocation schemes, to show how they affect firms' behavior and create distortions.

To examine permit allocations based on historic behavior we need to consider multiple time periods. We use a two-period model along with the cost function set out in

Chapter 5, where $C^{jt}(x_{jt}, e_{jt})$ is the firm j cost function in period $t=1$ or $t=2$, given output x_{jt} and emissions e_{jt}. The cost function satisfies assumption 5.1, so that $-C_e^{jt}(\cdot) > 0$, $C_x^{jt}(\cdot) > 0$, $C_{ee}^{jt}(\cdot) > 0$, $C_{xx}^{jt}(\cdot) > 0$, $C_{xe}^{jt}(\cdot) < 0$, and

$$\Delta = C_{xx}^{jt}(\cdot) \times C_{ee}^{jt}(\cdot) - \left(C_{ex}^{jt}(\cdot)\right)^2 > 0. \tag{8.32}$$

The initial permit endowments are denoted by $\bar{e}_{jt}$ for firm j in period t, and emissions in period 1 may or may not be subject to a cap.

We define a free allocation mechanism using the function $\bar{e}_{j2} = g_j(e_{j1}, x_{j1})$, which maps production and emissions in period 1, to the emissions endowment in period 2. Following Böhringer and Lange (2005c), we work with a linear allocation scheme in which

$$\bar{e}_{j2} = g_j(e_{j1}, x_{j1}) = \lambda_j + \lambda_j^e e_{j1} + \lambda_j^x x_{j1}, \tag{8.33}$$

where λ_j^e and λ_j^x are the firm-specific proportionality factors for emissions and output, respectively. Finally, for simplicity, we assume that output prices are exogenously given and denoted by p_t for each time period. Using this setup, in the following subsections we will distinguish between a closed trading system and an open trading system. In a closed trading system, a single regulatory body distributes permits to all participating firms, while in an open trading system, multiple regulatory bodies distribute permits, which can be traded across jurisdictions. The US sulfur dioxide program is an example of the former, while the EU-ETS, where national governments have some discretion on how they allocate Europe-wide CO_2 emission permits, is an example of the latter. For both cases, we examine and contrast the socially optimal permit allocation and firms' behavior under the allocation rule, taking as given the aggregate emission cap $\bar{E}_t$ each period in the regulator's jurisdiction. Thus the social optima we consider are constrained by an a priori-given emission cap. In the case where emissions are initially non-binding, period 1 can be considered as the pre-trading phase, as in the years prior to 1990 in the US sulfur dioxide trading program or before 2003 in the European EU-ETS.

8.5.1 Closed Trading Systems

In a closed trading system, the social optimum is found by maximizing the discounted sum of industry profits in the two periods, subject to the emission constraint. Specifically, x_{jt} and e_{jt} are selected to maximize

$$\sum_{j=1}^{J}\left(p_1 x_{j1} - C^{j1}(x_{j1}, e_{j1})\right) + \delta\left[\sum_{j=1}^{J}\left(p_2 x_{j2} - C^{j2}(x_{j2}, e_{j2})\right)\right], \tag{8.34}$$

subject to

$$\bar{E}_t = \sum_{j=1}^{J} e_{jt}, \quad t = 1, 2, \tag{8.35}$$

where δ is the discount factor. The first-order conditions for the socially optimal allocation are given by

$$p_t = C_x^{jt}(x_{jt}, e_{jt}) \tag{8.36}$$

$$\mu_t = -C_e^{jt}(q_{jt}, e_{jt}), \quad t = 1, 2, \tag{8.37}$$

where μ_t is the Lagrange multiplier on the aggregate emissions constraints. The interpretation for these conditions is by now familiar: the marginal cost of production should be equal to market price, and the marginal abatement cost should be equal to the shadow value of the emissions constraint. For later reference, we denote $\sigma_t^* = \mu_t$ as the permit price that would arise in a decentralized cap and trade program that, conditional on $\bar{E}_t$, induces the social optimum.

Under the allocation rule given by (8.33), a typical firm j selects x_{jt} and e_{jt} to maximize its two-period profit function

$$\begin{aligned} \Pi = {} & p_1 x_{j1} - C^{j1}(x_{j1}, e_{j1}) - \sigma_1 \times \left(e_{j1} - \bar{e}_{j1}\right) \\ & + \delta\left[p_2 q_{j2} - C^{j2}(x_{j2}, e_{j2}) - \sigma_2 \times \left(e_{j2} - \lambda_j - \lambda_j^e e_{j1} - \lambda_j^x x_{j1}\right)\right], \end{aligned} \tag{8.38}$$

where (8.33) is substituted into the profit function for $\bar{e}_{j2}$, and σ_t is the permit price the firm faces in period t. To understand how the allocation rule affects the firm's behavior, we proceed backwards and first note the profit maximization conditions for the second period:

$$p_2 = C_x^{j2}(x_{j2}, e_{j2}) \tag{8.39}$$

$$\sigma_2 = -C_e^{j2}(x_{j2}, e_{j2}). \tag{8.40}$$

In the first period we have

$$p_1 + \delta\sigma_2 \lambda_j^x = C_x^{j1}(x_{j1}, e_{j1}) \tag{8.41}$$

$$\sigma_1 - \delta\sigma_2 \lambda_j^e = -C_e^{j1}(x_{j1}, e_{j1}). \tag{8.42}$$

We see from (8.39) and (8.40) that in the second period, firms' behavior is socially optimal in the sense that the marginal production cost is equal to market price, and the marginal abatement cost is equal to the permit price. In the first period, however, firms produce more than the efficient amount if $\lambda_j^x > 0$ – i.e. if the allocation of free permits for use in the second period depends on output in the first. They also pollute more than is efficient if $\lambda_j^e > 0$ – i.e. if the allocation of free permits for use in the second period depends on emissions in the first. Thus the allocation scheme functions as a first period subsidy to both output and emissions.

It is clear from (8.41) and (8.42) that the firm's choices for x_{j1} and e_{j1} do not depend on λ_j. In contrast, differentiating the first-order conditions with respect to λ_j^x, and λ_j^e we have

$$\frac{\partial x_{j1}}{\partial \lambda_j^x} = \frac{\delta \sigma_2 C_{ee}^{j2}(\cdot)}{\Delta} > 0, \qquad \frac{e_{j1}}{\partial \lambda_j^x} = -\frac{\delta \sigma_2 C_{xe}^{j2}(\cdot)}{\Delta} > 0 \tag{8.43}$$

and

$$\frac{\partial x_{j1}}{\partial \lambda_j^e} = -\frac{\delta \sigma_2 C_{xe}^{j2}(\cdot)}{\Delta} > 0 \qquad \frac{\partial e_{j1}}{\partial \lambda_j^e} = \frac{\delta \sigma_2 C_{xx}^{j2}(\cdot)}{\Delta} > 0, \tag{8.44}$$

where Δ is given by (8.32). This means that increasing either of the two proportionality factors induces an increase in both output and emissions in the initial period, thereby further exacerbating the inefficiency.

Note that the only way for the regulator to induce the optimal output in period 1 is to set $\lambda_j^x = 0$. In this case, condition (8.41) describing firms' behavior matches (8.36) – i.e. the condition for the socially optimal allocation in period 1. To induce the socially optimal emissions in period 1, the regulator has to set λ_j^e so that the behavioral condition (8.42) coincides with the optimality condition (8.37). For this it must be that

$$\sigma_1 - \delta \sigma_2 \lambda_j^e = -C_e^{j1}(x_{j1}, e_{j1}) = \sigma_1^* \tag{8.45}$$

holds for all firms, meaning that $\lambda_j^e = \lambda^e$ for all j so that

$$\sigma_1 - \delta \sigma_2 \lambda^e = \sigma_1^*. \tag{8.46}$$

In addition we observe that

$$\sum_{j=1}^J \left(\lambda_j + \lambda^e e_{j1} \right) = \bar{E}_2 \tag{8.47}$$

and

$$\sum_{j=1}^J e_{j1} = \bar{\bar{E}}_1 \tag{8.48}$$

must hold. Solving (8.47) for λ^e using (8.48) yields:

$$\lambda^e = \frac{\bar{E}_2 - \sum_{j=1}^J \lambda_j}{\bar{E}_2}, \tag{8.49}$$

which allows us to summarize our findings as follows.

Proposition 8.4

An efficient dynamic allocation scheme in a closed trading system must be of the form

$$g_j(x_{j1}, e_{j1}) = \lambda_j + \lambda^e e_{j1}. \tag{8.50}$$

That is, the allocation rule must be independent of output and linear in emissions. For $\lambda_j = 0$, *the proportionality factor is* $\lambda^e = \bar{E}_2 / \bar{E}_1$.

8.5.2 Open Trading Systems

In an open trading system the local regulator takes the permit price as given when deciding on the socially optimal allocation of output and emissions. In this case, the social objective is to select x_{jt} and e_{jt} for all firms over the two time periods to maximize

$$\sum_{j=1}^{J} \left(p_1 x_{j1} - C^{j1}(x_{j1}, e_{j1}) \right) + \sigma_1 \left(\bar{E}_1 - \sum_{j=1}^{J} e_{j1} \right)$$
$$+ \delta \left[\sum_{j=1}^{J} \left(p_2 x_{j2} - C^{j2}(x_{j2}, e_{j2}) \right) + \sigma_2 \left(\bar{E}_2 - \sum_{j=1}^{J} e_{j2} \right) \right], \tag{8.51}$$

where σ_t is the system-wide permit price in period t that the local regulator takes as given, which can be interpreted as the regulator's opportunity cost of allocating an emission permit to a firm rather than selling it in another jurisdiction. The first-order conditions for the optimal allocation in this case are the same as equations (8.36) and (8.37), with the shadow value of an emission μ_t in (8.37) replaced by the actual market value σ_t. Because the individual firm's behavior is still governed by (8.38), the firm-specific allocation system given by (8.33) once again fails to produce a decentralized optimal allocation of abatement effort.

Böhringer and Lange (2005c) show that the only possibility for equating the social and decentralized conditions in an open trading system is to set $\lambda^x = \lambda^e = 0$. It follows from this that, while in a closed trading system grandfathering proportional to historic emissions is efficient, in an open trading system it is not. Similar to the closed system, benchmarking is never efficient. The authors go on to show that, when some benchmarking or grandfathering is politically necessary, the second-best optimal allocation depends crucially on firms' price elasticity of output, their permit price elasticity of emissions demand, and cross price elasticities between output and permit demand.

EXAMPLE 8.4 (POLICY) During phases I and II of the EU-ETS, member states could choose their own rules on how to allocate country-level emissions. Most allocated allowances for free, based on historical GHG emissions to the emitters – a scheme known as grandfathering. The grandfathering scheme has been criticized for rewarding high emitters and ignoring past efforts to reduce emissions. For phases III, IV and beyond, the European Commission recommends benchmarking, which allocates allowances based on production performance, rather than historical emissions. The recommended benchmark is product specific, and based on the average greenhouse gas emissions of the top 10 percent performing installations in the EU, for that product.

With the one product/one benchmark principle, there is no differentiation based on technology, fuel used, facility size, or location. As a result, GHG-intensive installations would receive fewer allowances, relative to their production, compared to efficient installations. This would incentivize inefficient installations to adopt newer and cleaner technologies. Transitional, harmonized EU-wide rules for free allocation are described in the European Commission's 2011 "Benchmarking Decision" (EC, 2011), and the Commission and member states have taken measures to assure the rules are applied in a consistent way.

8.6 OVERLAPPING REGULATIONS

In this section we examine overlapping environmental regulations, whereby polluters are subject to multiple regulations, perhaps from different jurisdictions. For example, in Europe it is often the case that EU member states set additional regulations, on top of the Europe-wide regulations, such as the EU-ETS. Likewise, China's many experiments with different environmental regulations have often involved layering a cap and trade system on top of existing command and control regulations. In what follows we present a stylized model that is designed to provide some intuition on the performance of these types of overlapping regulations.

The essential insights are best seen via a model with two polluters, which can be interpreted as representing two regions or two member states in a super-national emission trading system. Following the Chapter 3 framework, we denote abatement costs in the two regions by $C_1(e_1)$ and $C_2(e_2)$, where the cost functions have the familiar properties. We assume there is a binding emission cap L for the two regions such that

$$e_1 + e_2 \leq L. \tag{8.52}$$

Once again we let σ denote the competitive emission permit price.

8.6.1 Permit Trading and Emission Taxes

We begin by studying a situation in which emission taxes are added to the existing cap and trade system. We first assume there is an emission tax τ that *both* regions implement, so that the representative firm j in each region faces total costs of the regulation

$$C_j(e_j) + (\tau + \sigma)(e_j - \overline{e}_j), \quad j = 1, 2, \tag{8.53}$$

where $\overline{e}_j$ is the initial permit endowment for region j. The first-order condition for cost minimization is given by

$$-C_j'(e_j) = \tau + \sigma, \quad j = 1, 2, \tag{8.54}$$

which together with (8.52) determines the equilibrium permit price. Differentiating (8.52) and (8.54) with respect to the tax rate gives us:

$$\frac{de_j}{d\tau} = 0, \quad j = 1,2; \qquad \frac{d\sigma}{d\tau} = -1. \tag{8.55}$$

Thus a one unit tax increase leads to a one unit permit price decrease, and the additional tax does not affect the efficiency properties of the regulation. Still, such a tax can play a role if permits were issued for free initially, and the government subsequently wants to claim some of the permit rents.

Matters are different if only one region imposes a unilateral tax on top of the cap and trade program. Suppose, for example, that only region 1 imposes the tax, so that the first-order conditions are

$$\begin{aligned} -C_1'(e_1) &= \tau + \sigma \\ -C_2'(e_2) &= \sigma. \end{aligned} \tag{8.56}$$

It is clear that this system cannot minimize total abatement costs, since the unilateral tax drives a wedge between the marginal abatement costs for the two regions. Differentiating these conditions and (8.52) with respect to τ yields the following comparative statics:

$$\frac{de_1}{d\tau} = -\frac{1}{C_1''(e_1) + C_2''(e_2)} < 0 \tag{8.57}$$

$$\frac{de_2}{d\tau} = \frac{1}{C_1''(e_1) + C_2''(e_2)} > 0 \tag{8.58}$$

$$\frac{d\sigma}{d\tau} = -\frac{C_2''(e_2)}{C_1''(e_1) + C_2''(e_2)} < 0. \tag{8.59}$$

The tax causes a shift of emissions from region 1 to region 2, keeping total emissions constant. We refer to such an effect as emission leakage, and study the phenomenon in more detail in Chapter 12. Note that the permit price decreases when the tax is added, though the change is less than one to one. For example, if the regions are symmetric, starting from a zero tax rate a one currency unit tax increase leads to a 0.5 currency unit decrease of the permit price.

In contrast to an auxiliary tax on emissions, some countries have imposed taxes on output. For example, Germany taxes its electricity producers, which also participate in the EU-ETS. In exercise 8.12 we use a stylized example to show that this policy regime causes output to fall, while emissions stay constant.

8.6.2 Emission Trading and Energy Policies

Similar effects occur if a regional government implements energy-saving programs or subsidizes the use of renewable energy, in that these policies reduce the demand for emission permits. One can interpret this as artificially shifting the marginal abatement cost curve for one region to the left, causing emissions to shift from region 1 to region 2. In addition, the subsidy distorts conservation incentives by making energy less expensive via the subsidy. We examine this type of policy regime in exercise 8.14.

EXAMPLE 8.5 (POLICY) In March 2007, leaders in the European Union committed to becoming an energy-efficient, low carbon economy, and they launched a climate and energy initiative in 2009. With this, regulators set a "20-20-20" target, to be reached by the year 2020. These targets comprise three key objectives: (a) a 20 percent reduction in EU greenhouse gas emissions from 1990 levels; (b) raising the share of EU energy consumption produced from renewable resources to 20 percent; and (c) improving the EU's energy efficiency by 20 percent. How meaningful is this initiative?

While a 20 percent reduction in emissions is more ambitious than previously established levels (ignoring carbon leakage for the moment), the additional goals will make it more costly to reach this target. While setting a more ambitious emission target will increase the share of renewable energy automatically, it will also induce abatement efforts at conventional sources, and energy savings through higher prices. However, the promotion of renewable energy through subsidies such as feed-in tariffs interferes with this by distorting abatement incentives at conventional locations and reducing incentives for conservation. For a detailed model showing these effect, see Requate (2015).

8.7   MONITORING AND COMPLIANCE

To this point in the book, we have worked with models in which firms always comply with environmental policy. This means we implicitly assumed firms were perfectly monitored, monitoring costs could be neglected, and sufficiently high penalties were assessed for non- or under-compliance. In this case, a firm's true emissions always correspond to its allowance holdings (or its emission standard). In this section, we assume instead that firms can under-comply, but are inspected with some probability, and fined if found to be in non-compliance. To build intuition, we start with a representative firm that is subject to an emission standard, and then extend the analysis to multiple firms in a cap and trade system. Our main insight is that a higher inspection probability induces more compliance, and increases the price for permits.

8.7.1 A Simple Model with Monitoring and Punishment

Our representative firm has abatement cost function $C(e,v)$, where v is a technology parameter that shifts the abatement cost function. A larger v increases both abatement and marginal abatement costs, such that $C_v > 0$, $-C_{ev} > 0$, and $\hat{e}'(v) > 0$, where $\hat{e}$ is the unregulated level of emissions, defined so that $C(\hat{e}, v) = 0$. The firm is subject to an emission standard $\bar{e}$, but the regulator does not directly observe whether the firm complies. Instead, she inspects the firm with probability $\pi > 0$ and charges a fee $\Phi > 0$ in the case of non-compliance. Given these, the firm will comply if

$$C(\bar{e}, v) \le C(\hat{e}, v) + \pi \cdot \Phi = \pi \cdot \Phi. \tag{8.60}$$

To see how changes in the inspection probability and fee affect firms' decisions, we define $\tilde{v}$ as the value of v that leaves the marginal firm indifferent between compliance and non-compliance, so that

$$C(\overline{e}, \tilde{v}) = \pi \cdot \Phi. \tag{8.61}$$

Carrying out the comparative statics, we have

$$\frac{\partial \tilde{v}}{\partial \pi} = \frac{\Phi}{C_v} > 0, \qquad \frac{\partial \tilde{v}}{\partial \Phi} = \frac{\pi}{C_v} > 0. \tag{8.62}$$

From this it is clear that a higher inspection probability and a higher penalty both increase the number of compliant firms. We also see that the inspection probability and the fee are substitutes. If inspection is costly, the optimal policy to induce all firms to comply would require setting π arbitrarily low and imposing a penalty Φ sufficiently high, which in the limit implies $\pi = 0$ and $\Phi \rightarrow \infty$. In other words, an optimal combination consisting of a penalty and an inspection probability does not exist. This is a well-known result from other inspection/compliance problems, such as tax enforcement. Therefore, it is often assumed that there is an institutionally determined upper bound for the fee, so that Φ is taken as exogenous.

8.7.2 Incremental Punishment and Costly Monitoring

In this subsection, we generalize two features from the simple model: we allow inspection to be costly, and apply the penalty based on the extent of non-compliance. The latter is needed for fairness considerations – especially when there are stochastic influences on emissions, and/or measurement imprecision that may inaccurately indicate under-compliance. We now specify the penalty function according to $\Phi(e - \overline{e}, \varphi) > 0$ for $e > \overline{e}$, where ϕ is a scaling parameter. We use $u = e - \overline{e}$ to denote the extent of under-compliance, and assume that $\Phi_u > 0$, $\Phi_{uu} \geq 0$, $\Phi_\varphi > 0$, and $\Phi_{u\varphi} \geq 0$. This implies the fee function is linear or convex in the amount of under-compliance, and that a higher scaling parameter implies a higher fee. In addition, we assume that inspection is costly, with cost denoted $I(\pi)$, where $I(0) = 0$, $I'(\pi) > 0$ and $I''(\pi) > 0$.

Under this inspection regime, the firm's expected costs from the policy are

$$EC(e) = C(e) + \pi \cdot \Phi(e - \overline{e}, \varphi), \tag{8.63}$$

where for simplicity we have now suppressed the technology parameter v. The first-order condition with respect to e is

$$-C'(e) = \pi \cdot \Phi_u(e - \overline{e}, \varphi), \tag{8.64}$$

which shows that the firm sets its marginal abatement cost equal to the expected fine for its last unit of pollution emitted. By differentiating the first-order condition, we can show that

$$
\frac{\partial e}{\partial \pi} = \frac{\Phi_u}{-[C''(e) + \Phi_{uu}]} < 0, \quad \frac{\partial e}{\partial \varphi} = \frac{\pi \Phi_{u\varphi}}{-[C''(e) + \Phi_{uu}]} < 0,
$$
$$
\frac{\partial e}{\partial \bar{e}} = \frac{-\pi \Phi_{uu}}{-[C''(e) + \Phi_{uu}]} > 0.
$$
(8.65)

That is, an increase in stringency for any of the three policy parameters induces the firm to reduce its emissions.

8.7.3 Second-Best Optimal Inspection Policy with Costly Inspection

We now consider the regulator's problem, whereby she seeks to minimize

$$
TC = C(e) + D(e) + I(\pi)
$$
(8.66)

for a given firm, taking account of its optimal response to her choices. We noted above that the regulator cannot optimize over both the penalty level and the inspection probability. Likewise, she cannot minimize social costs by choosing both a standard $\bar{e}$ and the inspection probability π. This can be seen by first differentiating (8.66) with respect to $\bar{e}$, yielding

$$
\left[C'(e) + D'(e) \right] \frac{\partial e}{\partial \bar{e}} = 0.
$$
(8.67)

After dividing by $\partial e / \partial \bar{e} > 0$, we obtain the first-order condition for the socially optimal emission level. This implies that emissions are independent of π in the solution to (8.67), and so total social cost is minimized for $\pi = 0$. However, if $\pi = 0$, the firm has no incentive to reduce emissions at all, and social costs optimum is not obtained.

Given this, restrictions on the regulator's problem are needed. One approach is to take the standard as given, and then derive a condition for the second-best optimal inspection probability. For this, we differentiate (8.66) with respect to π to obtain

$$
I'(\pi) = \left(-C'(e) - D'(e) \right) \frac{\partial e}{\partial \pi}.
$$
(8.68)

Since $\partial e / \partial \pi < 0$, the marginal abatement cost must be smaller than marginal damage, meaning the firm's emissions will exceed the standard. We denote the solution to (8.68) by $\pi(\bar{e})$.

As a theoretical curiosity, one can show that lowering the emission standard that conditions the solution to (8.68) will lower total costs, and thus increase welfare. As a consequence, we obtain the paradoxical result that the second-best optimal emission standard with inspection probability $\pi(\bar{e})$ is $\bar{e} = 0$. Formally, this can be seen by differentiating

$$
TC(\bar{e}) = C\big(e\big(\bar{e}, \pi(\bar{e})\big)\big) + D\big(e\big(\bar{e}, \pi(\bar{e})\big)\big) + I\big(\pi(\bar{e})\big)
$$
(8.69)

with respect to $\bar{e}$ and employing the Envelope Theorem to obtain:

$$TC'(\bar{e}) = \left[C'\big(e(\bar{e}, \pi(\bar{e}))\big) + D'\big(e(\bar{e}, \pi(\bar{e}))\big) \right] \frac{\partial e}{\partial \bar{e}} > 0. \tag{8.70}$$

The sign comes from Eq. (8.68) showing that marginal damages exceeds marginal abatement cost, and Eq. (8.65) showing that $\partial e / \partial \bar{e} > 0$. Thus, lowering the emission standard reduces total social costs. This means that the optimal second-best emission standard, given costly inspection, functions like an emissions tax. Unable to meet the zero emission standard, firms pay an expected fee that depends on their overall emissions level. We have referred to this as a theoretical curiosity, since a standard that cannot be complied with is unlikely to be politically infeasible.

8.7.4 Compliance and Monitoring Under Cap and Trade

We now apply our insights on monitoring and compliance in the context of tradable emission permits. Consistent with our established notation, we denote the emissions from firm j by e_j and its initial endowment of permits as $\bar{e}_j$. To this we add l_j, which is the number of permits the firm uses to cover its emissions. In case of under-compliance, we have $e_j < l_j$. A firm's objective function is now

$$TC_j(e_j, l_j) = C_j(e_j) + \sigma\left[l_j - \bar{e}_j \right] + \pi\Phi(e_j - l_j, \varphi), \tag{8.71}$$

which includes the familiar abatement cost and permit expenditure/revenue terms, as well as an expected fine based on the extent of under-compliance. With this there are two decision variables: the amount of pollution, and the number of permits to hold, where the former could be larger than the latter.

The firm's first-order conditions for cost minimization are

$$-C'_j(e_j) = \pi\Phi_u(e_j - l_j, \varphi)$$
$$\sigma = \pi\Phi_u(e_j - l_j, \varphi). \tag{8.72}$$

The condition for e_j (top equation) is the same as under the simple emission standard – i.e. marginal abatement cost is equal to the expected fine. The condition with respect to l_j shows that the firm buys or sell permits to the point where the expected marginal fine equals the permit price. Note that it also implies the familiar result from Chapter 3 that $-C'_j(e_j) = \sigma$.

From the first-order conditions we further see that the permit price depends on the inspection probability and fine. If the inspection probability is zero, the permit price will also be zero, since holding allowances is not necessary. Denoting the firms' optimal choices by $e_j(\sigma, \pi)$ and $l_j(\sigma, \pi)$, the permit market equilibrium is given by

$$\sum_{j=1}^{J} l_j(\sigma, \pi) = L. \tag{8.73}$$

Differentiating (8.72) and (8.73) with respect to π, one can show (by induction) that

$$\frac{\partial e_j}{\partial \pi} = -\frac{J \prod_{k \neq j}^{J} C_k''(e_k)}{|H|} < 0, \tag{8.74}$$

where

$$|H| = J \prod_{j=1}^{J} C_j''(e_j) + \pi \sum_{k=1}^{J} \prod_{j \neq k} C_j''(e_j) > 0 \tag{8.75}$$

is the determinant of the Hessian matrix of the linearized system. In addition, we have

$$\frac{\partial l_j}{\partial \pi} = \frac{C_j''(e_j) \sum_{k \neq j}^{J} \prod_{i \neq k}^{J} C_i''(e_i) - (J-1) \prod_{k \neq j}^{n} C_k''(e_k)}{|H|} \lessgtr 0, \tag{8.76}$$

and

$$\frac{\partial \sigma}{\partial \pi} = \frac{J \cdot \Phi_u \prod_{j=1}^{J} C_j''(e_j)}{|H|} > 0. \tag{8.77}$$

From these comparative statics, we see that a higher probability of inspection decreases the firm's emissions, and increases the permit market equilibrium price. However, a higher inspection rate may increase or decrease the demand for permits for a given firm, depending on the relative slopes of the marginal abatement cost curves among polluters. Note as well that, from (8.73), the $\partial l_j / \partial \pi$ terms must sum to zero.

Similar to the previous subsection, we can derive the second-best monitoring probability (assuming that each firm is monitored by the same probability). In this case the objective function is

$$TC - \sum_{j=1}^{J} C_j(e_j) + D\left(\sum_{j=1}^{J} e_j\right) + J \cdot I(\pi), \tag{8.78}$$

giving a second-best optimal monitoring probability characterized by

$$I'(\pi) = \frac{\sigma - D'(E)}{J} \sum_{j=1}^{J} \frac{\partial e_j}{\partial \pi}, \tag{8.79}$$

implying $D'(E) > \sigma = C_j'(e_j)$. Also in this case, the regulator could increase welfare by reducing the number of permits available. We summarize these findings as follows.

Proposition 8.5

Given a total permit supply L and a penalty function $\Phi(e - l, \varphi)$:

(a) A higher inspection probability leads to fewer emissions and raises the price for tradable permits.

(b) The second-best optimal inspection probability induces marginal damage to exceed marginal abatement costs.

Note that in addition, the regulator can increase welfare by lowering the total amount of permits, with the inspection probability adjusted based on the total permit supply.

8.8   SUMMARY

Over the past three decades the cap and trade approach to environmental regulation has evolved from an academic curiosity to a familiar and often-used policy instrument. This has prompted investigation of the many institutional details that matter for how cap and trade programs actually function in specific contexts. In this chapter we have examined several of these issues, and have demonstrated that the efficiency of cap and trade depends critically on design elements related to spatial and temporal dimensions, market power, transaction costs, permit allocation schemes, and overlapping regulations.

We found that the spatial and temporal dimensions add additional margins over which abatement cost savings need to be balanced against environmental costs. A defining feature of cap and trade programs is that abatement cost savings are generated by the reallocation of abatement effort across polluting sources. The polluting sources, however, are often distributed across the spatial landscape in a way that causes their emissions to have differential effects on ambient environmental quality at different points in space. Thus different receptor regions (i.e. population centers) are differentially affected by emissions from different sources when the effluent is non-uniform mixing. In this case one-to-one trading between the polluting firms can lead to "spatial hotspots", where ambient concentrations are governed by diffusion coefficients that translate emissions from the sources into pollution levels at a receptor. In this case the efficient allocation of abatement effort needs to consider how pollution damages vary amongst receptor regions. Our analysis demonstrated that the solution to this is to create multiple emission permit markets that correspond to the different receptor regions, and require polluting sources to hold permits covering their emissions for each affected region.

Similar to the spatial dimension, abatement cost savings are possible when firms are allowed to transfer emission permits over time via *banking* and *borrowing*. While the notion of temporal cost smoothing has appeal, the extent to which this is optimal depends on the pollution damage function and the information available to the regulator at the time of design. Our analysis showed that, under conditions of certainty in which the regulator has chosen emission caps optimally, permit banking and borrowing is not socially desirable. If by contrast abatement costs are subject to random fluctuations that occur and are resolved after the regulator has set the emission caps, some permit banking and borrowing may be welfare enhancing. In this case the amount of temporal shifting of abatement effort that is ex post optimal will depend on the damage function and the potential for "temporal hotspots".

Market power and transactions costs topics are also related. In the ideal design, cap and trade programs contain many small, price taking firms as participants. In reality, programs may consistent of a small number of firms and/or a mixture of large and small polluting sources. This can create market power situations in which large firms are able to exercise influence on the market price for emission permits, and/or strategic interactions between regulated firms. Our analysis demonstrated that when a subset of firms can influence the permit price, the least cost outcome can only be achieved when the initial allocation of pollution permits corresponds to the large firms' optimal emission levels. An allocation that induces the large firms to engage in trading will create monopoly or monopsony type outcomes that drive a wedge between the marginal abatement costs of the price setting and price taking firms. Thus in contrast to the ideal situation, the allocation of initial pollution rights matters for efficiency when market power can be exercised.

Transaction costs can also affect efficiency when they are large enough to affect the volume of trading. In this case our analysis demonstrated that the additional costs cause polluting firms that wish to purchase permits to buy fewer, and firms that wish to sell permits to sell fewer. This drives a wedge between the marginal abatement costs for buying and selling firms, which causes the cap and trade system to fail to achieve its cost-minimizing allocation of abatement effort. As with the market power case, this implies that the initial allocation of pollution rights can affect the outcome, in the sense that it determines the amount of exchange that is necessary to reach efficiency.

Initial allocations schemes can also influence the performance of cap and trade programs directly. For example, grandfathering and benchmarking are commonly used to determine the initial allocation of pollution permits in programs with free distribution of pollution rights. Grandfathering implies that the allocation is based on historic emissions, while benchmarking implies that the allocation is based on historic output, and/or the most efficient technologies to produce a particular product. The performance of the two allocation approaches depends on whether the cap and trade program is open or closed. In a closed system a single regulator implements the program for a single jurisdiction, while in an open system multiple jurisdictions set up coordinated programs in which permits can be exchanged across jurisdiction borders, meaning that a single permit price arises. Our model showed that benchmarking creates distortions in both systems, in that incentives exist to produce and emit more in early periods in order to secure a more generous permit endowment for later periods. In contrast, allocation according to historic emissions can be efficient in a closed trading scheme, though it still creates incentives to over-emit in early periods when the system is open. On the other hand, benchmarking rewards early action while grandfathering does not.

Overlapping regulations can occur under various federal systems in which firms are subject to national or international cap and trade systems, combined with regional policies such as a local emissions tax or standards on renewable energy production. Overlapping regulations interact with cap and trade systems in a way that allocates emissions away from the region with the extra requirements, thereby affecting efficiency by creating a difference in marginal abatement costs across the regions. This is a form of "leakage" – i.e. the phenomenon in which local regulations induce the migration of emissions to another region – though with a binding emissions cap in place the consequences are limited to a failure to achieve the least cost allocation of abatement.

Finally, imperfect and costly monitoring typically incentivizes firms to under-comply with a standard, or to hold fewer permits than the amount of pollution emitted. Increasing the inspection probability lowers emissions and increases the price of tradable permits. Under second-best optimal monitoring marginal damage exceeds marginal abatement cost.

8.9 FURTHER READING

The seminal paper to address the spatial problem of emissions trading is Montgomery (1972), which carefully establishes the conditions for existence and efficiency of multi-permit markets equilibrium. Rubin (1996) and Kling and Rubin (1997) were the first to rigorously investigate the mechanism of permit markets with banking and borrowing, while Phaneuf and Requate (2002) study how banking impacts investment into pollution abatement technology. Hahn (1984) was the first paper to investigate market power in emission permit markets. Our extension to several firms with market power is taken from Requate (2006). While those papers ignore interactions with output markets, both Misiolek and Elder (1989) and Sartzetakis (1997) discuss strategic manipulation of emission permits markets in order to improve positioning in the output market. The seminal paper on transaction costs in emission permit markets is Stavins (1995), who also reports empirical magnitudes of transaction costs. Böhringer and Lange (2005c) were the first to investigate how free allocation schemes that depend on past output and emissions induce firms to strategically increase output and emissions. In two companion papers (Böhringer and Lange, 2005a, 2005b), they further discuss the advantages of output-based allocation schemes, and trade-offs between efficiency and distributional issues in permit allocation schemes. Both Böhringer and Rosendahl (2010) and Requate (2015) discuss overlapping regulations of emissions trading and green tradable certificates. Finally, Gray and Shimshack (2011) provide an overview of the empirical literature on monitoring and enforcement, and Muehlenbachs et al. (2016) contribute a recent application.

APPENDIX: AN EXAMPLE OF BENEFICIAL AND HARMFUL BANKING

To illustrate the impact of banking on social costs we use a quadratic cost function $C(E) = (\eta_k - bE)^2/2b$, representing the aggregate abatement costs of some polluting sector with two states of the world given by η_L and η_H, where $\eta_L > \eta_H$. The "low" cost state of the world η_L occurs with probability pr and the "high" cost state occurs with probability $(1-pr)$. The damage function is $D(E) = dE^2/2$. There are two periods denoted 1 and 2, and we use δ to denote the discount factor. The aggregate permit endowments in periods 1 and 2 are L_1 and L_2, respectively.

The ex ante socially optimal permit allocation is given by Eq. (8.13). For our specific functional form this becomes:

$$pr(\eta_L - bL_t) + (1 - pr)(\eta_H - bL_t) = dL_t, \quad t = 1, 2, \tag{A8.1}$$

which implies that $\bar{\eta} - bL_t = dL_t$, where $\bar{\eta} = p\eta_L + (1-p)\eta_H$ is the expected value of the random cost parameter. Solving for the quantity of permits we obtain

$$L_t = \frac{\bar{\eta}}{b+d}. \tag{A8.2}$$

Inserting this into the social cost we obtain as expected social cost:

$$SC(L_1^*, L_2^*) = (1 + \delta) \frac{\bar{\eta}^2 \left(\dfrac{b}{b+d} \right)^2}{2b}. \tag{A8.3}$$

We now assume that both banking and borrowing are allowed, and denote by B the amount of banked permits. We also take into account the possibility of depreciation. This means that if the sector wants to bank B units, it is allowed to use only αB banked permits in the next period, where $0 \leq \alpha \leq 1$. If $B < 0$ the firms borrow emissions from the future. Under depreciation, it can only use αB units in the current period when it borrows B from the future.

We begin by considering the second period. In the second period, given the amount of banked (or borrowed) permits, and given a realization of η, market clearing is determined by:

$$\eta_k - b(L_2 + \alpha B) = \sigma_k \qquad k = L, H, \tag{A8.4}$$

where σ_k is the competitive permit price under state of the world k. The expected permit price is therefore given by

$$\bar{\sigma} = \bar{\eta} - b(L_2 + \alpha B). \tag{A8.5}$$

In the first period the firms observe η and decide how many permits to bank or to borrow. If firms bank (borrow) B emission units they can emit $E_1 = L_1 - B$ units in the first period. Banking will occur if marginal abatement costs are lower than expected, i.e. for $\eta = \eta_L$. Due to the non-arbitrage condition (8.11) the firms choose the amount of banking according to

$$-C'(L_1 - B, \eta_L) = \eta_L - b(L_1 - B) = \sigma_1 = \delta\alpha\bar{\sigma} = \delta\alpha[\bar{\eta} - b(L_2 + \alpha B)], \tag{A8.6}$$

and solving for B yields

$$B = \frac{1}{1 + \delta\alpha^2} \left[\frac{\delta\alpha\bar{\eta} - \eta_L}{b} + L_1 - \delta\alpha L_2 \right]. \tag{A8.7}$$

For $\eta = \eta_H$ firms choose the amount of borrowing ($B < 0$) according to

$$-\alpha C'(L_1 - \alpha B, \eta_H) = \alpha(\eta_H - b(L_1 - \alpha B)) = \sigma_1 = \delta\bar{\sigma} = \delta\alpha[\bar{\eta} - b(L_2 + B)]. \quad \text{(A8.8)}$$

Solving this equation for B yields

$$B = \frac{1}{\alpha^2 + \delta}\left[-\frac{\alpha\eta_H - \delta\bar{\eta}}{b}\alpha L_1 - \delta L_2\right]. \quad \text{(A8.9)}$$

Calculating the resulting emissions and inserting these expressions into the expected social cost gives a tedious expression which we omit here.

To see that banking can be beneficial (detrimental) when the damage function is flat (steep), we present a numerical example. We choose parameters

$$\eta_L = 1, \quad \eta_H = 2, \quad pr = 0.5, \quad b = 1, \quad \delta = 1, \quad \alpha = 1. \quad \text{(A8.10)}$$

For $L_1 = L_2 = 0.75$ and $d = 1$ with banking we obtain for the social cost $SC^B = 1.375$, whereas without banking we have $SC^{NB} = 0.563$. If instead we use $L_1 = L_2 = 1.3636$ and $d = 0.10$, we obtain $SC^B = 0.398$ and $SC^{NB} = 1.86$.

We can demonstrate that depreciation will lower the cost somewhat. For example, with $d = 1$ the approximately optimal combination of permit supply and depreciation rate $L_1 = L_2 = 0.78$ and $\alpha = 0.71$, yielding $SC^B = 1.3439$. This is lower than under the no depreciation ($\alpha = 1$) case, but still higher than when banking is not allowed. For $d = 0.1$ the approximately optimal policy is $L_1 = L_2 = 1.5$ and $\alpha = 0.27$, yielding social cost of $SC^B = 0.3863$. In both cases we see that when choosing depreciation, the regulator can extend the number of permits being issued. But as we see, depreciation is not a silver bullet.

EXERCISES

8.1 * Consider a pollution problem with two sources and two recipient regions. Abatement cost functions are given by $C_j(e_j) = (a_j - b_j e_j)^2 / 2b_j$ for $j = 1,2$. The diffusion matrix is given by

$$H = \begin{pmatrix} h_{11} & h_{12} \\ h_{21} & h_{22} \end{pmatrix}$$

and the damage function for receptor m is $D_m(A_m) = d_m A_m^2 / 2$.
(a) Determine how many permits must be issued for each region.
(b) Consider the special case where $h_{12} = h_{22} = 0$, and interpret.

8.2 *** Consider a spatial pollution problem with J pollution sources and M recipients. The regulator is concerned that M different permit markets will cause transaction costs to be too high. She decides to set up two trading regions, one with J_1 sources and the other with J_2 sources. Find a rule to determine the second-best number of permits for each region.

8.3 ** Consider a stylized two-period model with banking. The aggregate abatement cost function in period t is given by $C(E)=(a_t-be)^2/2b$ with $a_1 < a_2$, and the social damage function in both periods is $D(E)=dE^2/2$.

(a) Determine the optimal emission quantities for both periods without banking.

(b) Assume that, starting from these optimal non-banking permit quantities, banking is allowed. Calculate how many permits will be banked and determine the resulting welfare loss.

(c) Determine the second-best optimal amount of permits when banking is allowed.

8.4 *** Suppose that firms can invest in abatement technology prior to permit trading. Firms have abatement cost functions $C^j(e_j,\kappa_j)$, where κ_j is measured in money and lowers both the abatement and marginal abatement cost functions. More specifically:

$$C^j_{\kappa_j}(e_j,\kappa_j) < 0, \quad -C^j_{e_j\kappa_j}(e_j,\kappa_j) < 0 \quad C^j_{\kappa_j\kappa_j}(e_j,\kappa_j) > 0$$

$$C^j_{\kappa_j\kappa_j}(e_j,\kappa_j)C^j_{e_je_j}(e_j,\kappa_j)-\left[C^j_{e_j\kappa_j}(e_j,\kappa_j)\right]^2 > 0.$$

Consider three periods. In period 0 firms select the level of investment κ_j. In periods 1 and 2 firms choose abatement and engage in permit trading. The firm's objective function is then given by:

$$\kappa_j + \delta\left[C^j(e_{j1},\kappa_j)+\sigma_1\left(e_{j1}-\bar{e}_{j1}\right)\right] + \delta^2\left[C^j(e_{j2},\kappa_j)+\sigma_2\left(e_{j2}-\bar{e}_{j2}\right)\right],$$

where δ is the discount factor and (e_{j1},e_{j2}) and $(\bar{e}_{j1},\bar{e}_{j2})$ are emissions and permit endowments, respectively, in periods 1 and 2.

(a) Characterize the firms' cost minimization problem with respect to investment and emissions when no banking is allowed, and then when banking is allowed.

Consider now the polluting sector's aggregate abatement cost function $C(E,K)$, which is assumed to have the same properties as the individual firms' cost functions. Moreover assume the abatement cost functions are constant over time, and let L_1 and L_2 be the aggregate permit endowments.

(b) Determine the sector's optimal investment level in the absence of banking. Investigate the comparative static effects of increasing L_1 and L_2 on the choice of K.

(c) Assume now that banking is allowed. Determine the amount of investment K and banking B.

(d) For the case of banking investigate the comparative static effects of increasing L_1 and L_2 on the choice of K and B.

(e) Assume now social damage is given by a convex social damage function $D(E)$ that is constant over time. Determine the optimal levels of investment and pollution. Show that with competitive markets, the optimal level of investment will be chosen if the supply of permits corresponds to the optimal pollution level and banking is not allowed. What will happen if banking is allowed?

Consider now an extension of the model with aggregate uncertainty. The sector's abatement cost function is given by $C(E,K,\eta)$, where η is a cost parameter that can take values η_L and η_H with probabilities pr and $1-pr$, respectively. Assume also that the firms can increase their investment level in period 1 after observing η.

(f) Assume first that banking is not allowed and L_1 and L_2 are the aggregate permit endowments. Determine the optimal investment level K_0 in period 0. Determine the optimal investment level K_1 in period 1, as it depends on the observed cost parameter η.

(g) Assume now banking is allowed. Repeat the part (f) and compare the levels of investment. Investigate the comparative static effects of L_1 and L_2 on K_1 and B.

(h) For quadratic abatement costs $C(E,K,\eta)=(\eta-E-K)^2/2$ and quadratic damage function $D(E)=dE^2/2$ determine the optimal amount of permit quantities without banking, and the second-best optimal permit quantities when banking is allowed.

8.5 ** Consider $J-1$ small polluting firms with abatement cost functions $C_j(e_j)=(a_j-b_je_j)^2/2b_j$ and one large firm indexed $j=1$ with market power and abatement cost function $C_1(e_1)=(a_1-b_1e_1)^2/2b_1$. Let $\bar{e}_2,\ldots,\bar{e}_J$ be the initial permit endowment for the small firms and $\bar{e}_1$ be the endowment for the large firm. The damage function is $D(E)=dE^2/2$.

(a) Determine the socially optimal allocation.

(b) Consider the case where the initial endowment of the large firm is larger (smaller) than socially optimal. Determine the permit trading equilibrium.

(c) Investigate the comparative static effects of increasing the large firm's initial permit endowment.

Assume now there are two large firms $j=1$ and $j=2$.

(d) Consider the case where the initial endowments of the large firms are larger (smaller) than socially optimal. Determine the permit trade equilibrium.

(e) Consider the case where the initial endowment of one large firm is larger and the initial endowment of the other large firm is smaller than the socially optimal allocation of abatement. Determine the permit trading equilibrium.

8.6 * Consider two polluting firms with marginal production costs $c_1=0$ and $c_2=0.25$. Pollution is proportional to output with emission coefficients $d_1=1$ and $d_2=0$. Inverse market demand is $P(X)=1-X$.

(a) Determine the Cournot-Nash equilibrium in the absence of environmental regulation.

(b) Assume each firm holds an initial permit endowment of $\bar{e}_1=\bar{e}_2=0.375$. Suppose the firms negotiate over permit levels. What is the likely outcome?

8.7 ** Consider two polluting firms with cost functions $C^j(x_j,e_j)$. The inverse demand function is $P(X)$. Firms engage in negotiations about the permit allocation and a transfer price in a first stage, and engage in Cournot competition in the second stage. Derive a condition describing how the firms will trade the permits. Show that marginal abatement costs will eventually not be equal in general.

8.8 ** Consider J local monopolists with cost functions $C^j(x_j,e_j)$ and facing inverse demand functions $P_j(x_j)$. The pollutant is homogeneous and the total supply of tradable permits is L, with each firm holding a permit endowment of $\bar{e}_j$.

(a) Show that a competitive permit market leads to an efficient allocation of permits among the monopolists.

(b) Assume now there are only $J=2$ ($J=3$) such firms. Firms can trade bilaterally with prices being negotiated. Show that firms can do no better than exchanging the permits in a way that produces an efficient allocation.

8.9 * Consider $J=J_1+J_2$ polluting firms, where there are J_1 firms of type 1 and J_2 firms of type 2. The abatement cost functions are given by $C^j(e_j)=(a_j-b_je_j)^2/2b_j$ for types $j=1,2$. The damage function is $D(E)=dE^2/2$, where E is total emissions.

(a) Determine the socially optimal allocation of emissions.

(b) Assume now that there are transaction costs $T_j(t_j)=\phi_t t_j$, where $t_j=|e_j-\bar{e}_j|$. Assume that the regulator has issued a total number of permits that is socially optimal. Type 1 firms (type 2 firms) have an initial endowment smaller (larger) than socially optimal. Determine the trade equilibrium and calculate the welfare loss generated through transaction costs.

(c) Repeat part (a) for $T_i(t_i) = \varphi_t t_i^2 / 2$.

8.10 ** Consider the transaction costs model of section 8.4. Show that a unilateral increase in the seller's transaction costs (increasing α_1) induces the permit price to decrease, while a unilateral increase in the buyer's transaction costs (increasing α_2) induces that price to increase. Show also that the sign effect on emissions is the same as in the case of a uniform marginal transaction cost increase.

8.11 ** Consider J symmetric firms operating in two periods with constant over time cost functions $C^j(x_j,e_j)=(x_j-b_je_j)^2/2b_j+c_jx_j^2/2$. The output prices are exogenous and given by p_1 and p_2 for the two periods. When relevant, emission caps are denoted by $\bar{E}_1$ and $\bar{E}_2$ in periods 1 and 2, respectively.

(a) Assume that first period emissions are unconstrained. Consider an allocation scheme for the second period given by

$$\bar{e}_{j2} = g_j(e_{j1},x_{j1}) = \lambda_j + \lambda_j^e e_{j1} + \lambda_j^x x_{j1}, \quad j=1,...,J, \quad \sum_{j=1}^{J}\bar{e}_{j2} = \bar{E}_2.$$

Determine the firms' emission and output choices in the two periods, as well as the second period equilibrium permit price.

(b) For part (a), verify that the allocation is efficient if $\lambda^e = \bar{E}_2 / E_1$ and $\lambda^x = 0$.

(c) Determine the firms' choice in period 1 when $\lambda^x = x_{j1}\left(\sum_{k=1}^{J}x_{k1}\right)^{-1}$ and $\lambda^e = \lambda = 0$.

(d) Consider now an open trading scheme from the perspective of a particular jurisdiction that takes both output and emission prices as given and uses an allocation scheme

$$\bar{e}_{j2} = g_j(e_{j1},x_{j1}) = \lambda_j + \lambda_j^e e_{j1} + \lambda_j^x x_{j1}.$$

Determine the firms' emission and output choices in the two periods for the cases when there is no emission cap in the first period and when there is a binding cap in the first period.

8.12 ** Consider the energy sector consisting of J firms where energy producers are characterized by their cost functions $C^j(x_j,e_j)$. The firms are subject to an emission trading system with a total emission cap $\bar{E}$.

(a) Assume that an (additional) energy tax on output is introduced. Show that individual and total energy output goes down while total emissions remain constant.

(b) Assume now there are K other firms emitting CO_2. Those firms are characterized by their abatement cost functions $C^k(e_k)$. All $J+K$ firms are subject to the same emission trading system with a total emission cap $\overline{E}$, but the energy sector is subject to an additional output tax. Investigate the comparative static effects of an energy tax increase on emissions and output. Show that emissions move from the energy to the other sector.

8.13 ** Assume there are two regions with a joint emission trading system. The government of region I can influence its abatement costs by investment. The abatement cost function is written as $C^I(e_I,k)+k$ where k is measured in monetary units. Assume that

$$-C^I_{e_I k}(e_I,k) < 0, \quad C^I_k(e_I,k) < 0.$$

The other region's abatement cost function is simply $C_{II}(e_{II})$.

(a) Investigate the comparative effects of a unilateral investment lowering (marginal) abatement costs on emissions in regions I and II and on the permit price.

(b) Determine the unilaterally optimal level of investment in region I.

(c) Determine non-cooperative and cooperative investment levels for both regions.

8.14 ** Assume electricity is generated by three technologies: a base load technology with cost function $C_b(x_b)$ and proportional emission coefficient α_b; gas turbines with cost function $C_g(x_g)$ and emission coefficient $\alpha_g < \alpha_b$; and an emission-free renewable energy source with cost function $C_r(x_r)$. All cost functions are convex, and there is a total emission cap of L. The inverse demand function for electricity is given by $P(X)$.

(a) Characterize the optimal allocation given the emission cap.

(b) Investigate the comparative static effects of lowering the emission cap on quantities, total output, price, and the percentage of renewable energy, denoted by $\beta = x_r/(x_b+x_g+x_r)$.

(c) Assume now that in addition to the emission cap there is a quota for renewable energy. Show that a quota raises the total cost of electricity production.

CHAPTER 9

Ambient Pollution Control

To this point in Part II of the book we have generally considered the regulation of point sources, and with the exception of the spatial problem in Chapter 8, have assumed there is a one-to-one relationship between emissions and the ambient pollution level. This allowed us to measure environmental damages as a function of total emissions. In addition, we have implicitly assumed that emissions from particular sources are perfectly observable, so that responsibility for a given emission level can be assigned to a specific source. In this chapter we turn our attention to ambient pollution problems, in which environmental damage is assessed based on the concentration of effluent in the environment rather than the count of emissions at the polluting source. The ambient pollution problem has two crucial characteristics. First, ambient pollution problems often arise from non-point sources of emissions. A prominent example is agriculture, where nutrient fertilizers, animal waste, sediments, and pesticides can run off fields or leak from waste management systems into surface and groundwater. Emissions of these substances from individual agricultural producers are usually not observable. Rather, the collective consequences of all farmers' emissions in a watershed are reflected in ambient concentrations of effluent in lakes, streams, and wells. Second, in many cases there is not a deterministic relationship between total emissions and ambient pollution problems. Instead, the relationship is stochastic, with randomness coming from weather events and other exogenous shocks beyond the control of polluters and the regulator. Once again considering the agricultural example, nutrient concentrations are generally higher in streams when the water volume is low. Similarly, heavy rains can increase the amount of nutrient and sediment runoff, thereby causing acute spikes in ambient pollution levels.

In this chapter we discuss the challenges associated with regulating ambient pollution levels. We begin in the next section by focusing on the non-point source pollution problem in a deterministic environment, which illustrates how moral hazard – i.e. the inability of the regulator to observe individual polluters' emissions – necessitates the use of an ambient pollution tax in lieu of an emission tax. In section 9.2 we introduce a stochastic relationship between emissions and ambient pollution. We show that, under constant marginal damage, a uniform ambient tax can induce the efficient abatement effort, while under increasing marginal damage a uniform tax is only second-best optimal. If there is increasing marginal damage and if each firm has only a one dimensional effort space to reduce emissions, a system of firm-specific tax rates can implement the first-best allocation. If firms have several choices, then even firm-specific taxes are only second-best optimal. Finally, we examine the case in which a damage function is not known, and instead the regulator wants to assure that an ambient threshold is exceeded only with a small probability. In this case, we will determine a threshold for expected aggregate emission targets that is consistent with a precautionary principle.

The models that we develop in this chapter are simple at the beginning, but increase quickly in their complexity. The fact that the decision environment for both firms and the regulator is characterized by uncertainty means that the socially and privately optimal solutions are functions of the moments of random variables. In addition, the information asymmetries between firms and the regulator mean that socially optimal regulation needs to incorporate firms' expected reaction functions. The complexity of the analytical models reflects the real-world difficulties associated with managing non-point source pollutants, and illustrates the challenge inherent in implementing incentive-based policies. Thus, unlike the tax and cap and trade policies discussed in the point source pollution context, we have little actual experience with implementing the policy solutions discussed in this chapter. There is, however, some experimental evidence on how versions of the policies described here may perform. Rather than providing policy examples or empirical research related to the analytical models, we therefore close this chapter by briefly discussing the experimental literature that has emerged in the wake of the main theoretical predictions.

9.1 DETERMINISTIC NON-POINT SOURCE POLLUTION

In this section we consider the pure non-point source pollution problem under certainty. The crucial characteristic of the problem is that only the ambient pollution level can be observed and measured, while the polluters' individual emissions are unobservable. This implies that individual emissions cannot be the target of regulation, for example by a Pigouvian tax or by a cap and trade system. If only ambient pollution can be observed, a tax on (or subsidy to) polluters must be based on the ambient pollution level.

We begin with the simple model introduced in Chapter 3, in which we ignore output markets and assume that firms' technologies are represented by their abatement cost functions $C_j(e_j)$, which satisfy the assumptions previously outlined. Since we are not considering uncertainty in this section, we also make the simplifying assumption that ambient pollution is equivalent to total emissions, so that $A = E = \sum_{j=1}^{J} e_j$. The social cost function is

$$\sum_{j=1}^{J} C_j(e_j) + D(E), \tag{9.1}$$

where $D(E)$ is the damage function. The first-order necessary conditions for cost minimization then boil down to our familiar conditions

$$-C_j'(e_j) = D'(E), \quad j = 1,...,J, \tag{9.2}$$

so that marginal abatement cost equals marginal damage for all firms. We denote the optimal levels of individual and total emissions by $e_1^*,...,e_J^*$ and E^*, respectively.

The policy design task is to find a mechanism that incentivizes firms to pick their efficient abatement levels. One possibility is to make each firm pay for the total damage created by the J firms. In this case, the objective function for firm j is to select e_j to minimize

$$TC_j(e_j) = C_j(e_j) + \tau E$$
$$= C_j(e_j) + \tau e_j + \tau \sum_{k \neq j} e_k. \tag{9.3}$$

If firm j takes the emissions from the remaining $J-1$ firms as given (i.e. the firm cannot influence the emission decisions of others), then $\tau \sum_{k \neq j} e_k$ is a constant in its objective function. In this case, the first-order condition for firm j is

$$-C_j'(e_j) = \tau, \quad j = 1,...,J, \tag{9.4}$$

and if the tax rate is set such that $\tau = D'(E)$, the instrument leads to the first-best allocation of abatement effort.

The drawback of the objective function in (9.3) is that the compliance cost for each firm is potentially large, and the tax revenues collected are many times the value of damages suffered. There are also non-marginal implications, in that polluting firms may face bankruptcy when presented with such a tax bill. It is clear from the first-order conditions, however, that if each firm pays only the proportion $1/J$ of total damage, there is an inefficiently low level of abatement effort.

Segerson (1988) suggests alternative mechanisms that incentivize firms to engage in efficient abatement. One example is to define the objective function so

$$TC_j(e_j) = \begin{cases} C_j(e_j) + \tau(E - E^*) + F & if \quad E > E^* \\ C_j(e_j) & if \quad E \leq E^*. \end{cases} \tag{9.5}$$

In this case, if $\tau = D'(E)$, the efficient allocation is an equilibrium for any $F \geq 0$. However, there are other, alternative equilibrium strategy profiles $e_1^a,...,e_J^a$ that lead to $\sum_{j=1}^J e_j^a = E^*$. In addition, note that $\tau = 0$ and $F > 0$ can also lead to a "no abatement" equilibrium. The following example demonstrates the possibility of multiple equilibria under the mechanism in (9.5).

EXAMPLE 9.1 (NUMERICAL/ANALYTICAL) Let there be two firms with identical abatement cost functions $C(e) = (10 - e)^2/2$ and let $D(E) = E^2/6$ be the damage function. The efficient allocation in this case is determined by $(10 - e) = 2 \cdot e/3$, so that $e^* = 6$ and $E^* = 2 \cdot e^* = 12$. Suppose that the ambient emission standard is $E^* = 12$, and that $\tau = 0$ and the fine is set as $F = 13$. It is clear from this that $e_1 = e_2 = 6$ is an equilibrium, since $C(6) = 8 < 13 = F$. Thus, upon observing $e_1 = 6$, firm 2 will not wish to change its emission choice of $e_2 = 6$, and vice versa. Suppose, however, that neither firm abates so that $e_1 = e_2 = 10$ – i.e. the point where abatement costs are zero. This is also an equilibrium in which each firm will pay the penalty of $F = 13$. This is because upon observing $e_1 = 10$, firm 2 would need to reduce its emissions to $e_2 = 2$ in order to avoid the fine, and thereby incur abatement costs $C(2) = 32 > 13 = F$. Firm 2 is therefore better off emitting $e_2 = 10$, incurring no abatement costs, and paying the fine. The case is likewise for firm 1. Other equilibria also exist. For example, $(e_1, e_2) = (5,7)$ is an equilibrium since $C(5) = 12.5 < 13 = F$ and $C(3) = 4.5 < 13 = F$. Indeed, all strategy profiles (e_1, e_2) with $e_1 + e_2 = 12$ and $e_j \geq 10 - 26^{0.5} \approx 4.9$ are equilibria since $C(4.9) \approx 13 = F$, implying there is a continuum of equilibria that firms could coordinate on.

An alternative mechanism to implement the efficient allocation would be to charge a tax only on ambient pollution in excess of some threshold. In this case, the objective function is given by

$$TC_j(e_j) = C_j(e_j) + \tau(E - \bar{E}) \quad \forall E \geq 0, \tag{9.6}$$

where $\bar{E}$ is the ambient standard or threshold. Firms will pay a tax if $E > \bar{E}$, and will receive a subsidy if $E < \bar{E}$. However, if the standard is equal to the efficient ambient pollution level and $\tau = D'(E)$, the unique equilibrium induces an efficient allocation, and in equilibrium, no taxes are paid or subsidies received by the firms.

9.2   STOCHASTIC AMBIENT POLLUTION

We now turn our attention to uncertainty in the ambient pollution level whereby the ambient pollution level A is influenced by both aggregate and firm-specific (idiosyncratic) random variables. For the former, ambient pollution depends on a random variable η that reflects, for example, the impact of weather conditions on the concentration of effluent in the environmental media. We write $A = A(e_1, \ldots, e_J, \eta)$ and assume that $A_\eta = \partial A / \partial \eta > 0$, so that a higher value of η implies a higher level of ambient pollution. We also assume that $\partial A / \partial e_j > 0$, which formalizes the idea that higher emissions from any one source cause an increase in ambient pollution. As a special case, the ambient pollution may depend only on total emissions E so that $A = A(E, \eta)$, but generally we assume that different polluting sources can affect ambient concentrations differentially.

Individual firms' emissions are determined by abatement effort and idiosyncratic stochastic factors not under the control of the firm. We capture this idea by writing emissions as $e_j = e_j(l_j, v_j)$, where l_j is a scalar measuring the deployment of an abatement input, or a vector representing a collection of abatement or productive inputs, and v_j is a firm-specific random variable. We begin by assuming that l_j is a single abating input, so that $\partial e_j(l_j, v_j) / \partial l_j < 0$. Furthermore, we define v_j so that $\partial e_j(l_j, v_j) / \partial v_j < 0$.

Since firms are not able to control emissions directly, but can only control abatement effort, we need to depart from our familiar specification of the abatement cost function. In particular, we now write $C_j(l_j)$ to represent the cost that firm j incurs when it deploys abatement effort l_j. We assume that $C'_j(l_j) > 0$ and $C''_j(l_j) > 0$ so that the cost of abatement effort is increasing at an increasing rate in l_j. Although we will refer to $C_j(l_j)$ as the abatement cost function, it is important to stress that its interpretation is different than was used in earlier chapters. The marginal abatement cost function $C'_j(l_j) > 0$ does not refer to the additional cost of reducing an emission unit per se, since the realization of

v_j determines in part the change in emissions induced by a change in l_j. Instead, $C'_j(l_j) > 0$ is the additional cost from employing an additional unit of the abating input, which depending on the outcomes for v_j, may be more or less effective in reducing the ambient pollution level A.

We assume that the random variables $v_1, \ldots, v_J, \eta$ are jointly distributed with the density function $f(v_1, \ldots, v_J, \eta)$. As special cases, we consider contexts in which the vector $(v_1, \ldots, v_J)$ is independent from η, and when all $J+1$ random variables are independent. In the following subsections, we examine optimal abatement and policy decentralization when outcomes for the aggregate and idiosyncratic random variables cannot be observed prior to when abatement action is taken.

9.2.1 The Constrained Social Optimum

To set a benchmark for designing a decentralized policy, we begin by examining the first-best allocation of abatement effort under the information environment implied by the aggregate and idiosyncratic uncertainty. The objective is to minimize the expected social cost from abatement effort and pollution damages:

$$\min_{l_1, \ldots, l_J} ESC = \sum_{j=1}^{J} C_j(l_j) + EV_{v_1, \ldots, v_J, \eta} \left\{ D\left[A\left(e_1(l_1, v_1), \ldots, e_J(l_J, v_J), \eta \right) \right] \right\}, \qquad (9.7)$$

where EV_r is the expectation operator with respect to the $J+1$ dimension random vector $r = (v_1, \ldots, v_J, \eta)$. In what follows, we will often write EV to reduce clutter, with the understanding that the expectation is over all random elements in the damage function.

The first-order necessary conditions for choosing l_j are given by

$$C'_j(l_j) = EV \left\{ D'(A) \times A_{e_j} \times \left(-\frac{\partial e_j(l_j, v_j)}{\partial l_j} \right) \right\}, \quad j = 1, \ldots, J. \qquad (9.8)$$

This condition tells us that the marginal cost of abatement effort – i.e. the additional cost from an additional unit of l_j – should be equal to the decrease in the expected damage that is provided by the additional unit of l_j. Note that the latter is different from the expected marginal damage of ambient pollution, which is simply $EV\{D'(A)\}$.

The right-hand side of (9.8) can be usefully decomposed into the product of the expected marginal damage from the ambient pollution level, and the expected marginal impact of the abating input on ambient pollution, plus a term reflecting the covariance between the two:

$$C'_j(l_j) = EV\left\{ D'(A) \right\} \times EV \left\{ A_{e_j} \times \left(-\frac{\partial e_j(l_j, v_i)}{\partial l_j} \right) \right\}$$
$$+ COV \left\{ D'(A), A_{e_j} \times \left(-\frac{\partial e_j(l_j, v_i)}{\partial l_j} \right) \right\}. \qquad (9.9)$$

The covariance term can be zero, positive, or negative. Additional intuition is possible when we consider special cases. For example, suppose that each v_j is independent from η, meaning there is no relationship between the individual and aggregate uncertainty. In this case the covariance term is positive: the impact of emissions on ambient pollution (the term A_{e_j}) correlates positively with A, and hence $D'(A)$, via the common influence of η. When marginal damage is increasing in A, high draws of η into the environmentally "bad" state of the world cause a larger increase in marginal damage, than low draws into the "good" state of the world decrease marginal damage. The social planner wants to avoid environmental cost spikes that can occur with bad draws of η, and so compensates by deploying more of the abating input in an amount governed by the variance of A, as inherited from the distribution of η.

Note that this discussion implies that independence between the $J+1$ random variables *does not* in general cause the covariance term to be zero. Instead, the covariance term in (9.9) can only be zero when marginal damage is constant, so that $D'(A)$ is deterministic. In this special case, the marginal abatement cost is simply equal to the expected decrease in damages from the marginal increase in l_j.

Suppose instead that η and each v_j are negatively correlated. In this case a high aggregate damage parameter η is associated with low values of v_j, meaning a given level of abatement effort l_j leaves higher emissions, relative to the case when v_j is high. This implies that abatement effort is comparatively ineffective, and so all else being equal, a smaller value of l_j is optimal. The sign of the covariance term in this case is based on two opposing forces. To see this let $\Delta A / \Delta l_j$ denote the second element in the covariance expression in (9.9). There is a negative relationship between $D'(A)$ and $\Delta A / \Delta l_j$ arising from the negative correlation between η and v_j, and a positive relationship between A and $\Delta A / \Delta l_j$ via the common influence of η. If the former dominates, the covariance will be negative and a smaller level of abatement is optimal relative to other correlation structures. Specifically, for environmentally "bad" draws of η and v_j, abatement is ineffective, and so less l_j is deployed, while for environmentally "good" draws, less abatement is needed. The opposite holds when η and each v_j are positively correlated, in that an unfavorable draw of η occurs jointly with a favorable draw of v_j, and the two determinants of the covariance work in the same direction. In this case the abatement effort should be adjusted up, due to the effectiveness of l_j in reducing emissions during environmentally "bad" draws of η. The following extended example illustrates this intuition using specific functional forms.

EXAMPLE 9.2 (NUMERICAL/ANALYTICAL) Suppose there are two firms with abatement cost functions $C_j(l_j) = c_j l_j^2 / 2$ and emissions $e_j = (\hat{e}_j - v_j l_j)$, where $\hat{e}_j$ is the maximum (unregulated) emission level, and v_1 and v_2 determine the effectiveness of abatement activities l_1 and l_2, respectively. Denote $\hat{E} = \hat{e}_1 + \hat{e}_2$ as the aggregate unregulated emission level, and let ambient pollution be given by $A = \eta \cdot (e_1 + e_2) = \eta \cdot (\hat{E} - v_1 l_1 - v_2 l_2)$, where η represents the aggregate uncertainty. We consider two damage functions, given by $D(A) = \delta \cdot A$ and $D(A) = \delta \cdot A^2 / 2$, which represent constant and increasing marginal damages, respectively. The random variables (v_1, v_2, η) are jointly distributed with independence as a special case, and we have $\partial A / \partial e_j = \eta$ and $\partial e_j / \partial l_j = -v_j$.

For the case of constant marginal damage we have $D'(A) = \delta$. According to Eq. (9.8), the first-order condition with constant marginal damage is

$$c_j l_j = \delta EV\left(\eta v_j\right) = \delta \overline{\eta} \overline{v}_j + \delta COV\left(\eta, v_j\right), \qquad (9.10)$$

where $\overline{\eta} = EV(\eta)$ and $\overline{v}_j = EV(v_j)$ are the means of the random variables, and the constant marginal damage δ is deterministic. From this expression, it is apparent that if η and v_j are positively correlated, so that a large positive shock to ambient pollution is likely to accompany a high level of effectiveness for the abating input, the optimal use of l_j is higher. If η and v_j are negatively correlated the opposite holds, and if they are independent we simply have $c_j l_j = \delta \overline{\eta} \overline{v}_j$.

For the case of increasing marginal damage the first-order condition corresponding to (9.8) is

$$c_j l_j = \delta EV\left(\underbrace{\eta(\hat{E} - v_1 l_1 - v_2 l_2)}_{D'(A)} \underbrace{\eta}_{\frac{\partial A}{\partial e_j}} \cdot \underbrace{v_j}_{\frac{-\partial e_j}{\partial l_j}} \right). \qquad (9.11)$$

If (v_1, v_2, η) are independently distributed, we obtain

$$c_j l_j = \delta EV\left(\eta^2\right)\left(\overline{v}_j \hat{E} - EV(v_j^2) l_j - \overline{v}_1 \overline{v}_2 l_k\right), \quad j = 1, 2, \quad k \neq j, \qquad (9.12)$$

which can be solved for the optimal values of l_j. From this we can see that, even under independence, the covariance term in (9.9) is not zero, since both random functions depend on η and v_j. Therefore, the optimal solutions for l_1 and l_2 contain the second moments of the random variables.

Continuing with the independence assumption, additional insights can be gained by starting with (9.11), and carrying out the decomposition shown in (9.9). We first calculate the expectations of the marginal damage and marginal change in A functions:

$$\begin{aligned} c_j l_j &= EV\left(\delta A\right) \times EV\left(\eta v_j\right) + COV\left(\delta A, \eta v_j\right) \\ &= \delta\left[\eta\left(\hat{E} - \overline{v}_1 l_1 - \overline{v}_2 l_2\right)\right] \times \overline{\eta} \overline{v}_j + COV\left(\delta A, \eta v_j\right). \end{aligned} \qquad (9.13)$$

Next, we derive the explicit form of the covariance term:

$$\begin{aligned} &COV\left(\delta A, \eta v_j\right) \\ &= COV\left[\left(\delta \eta \hat{E} - \delta \eta v_1 l_1 - \delta \eta v_2 l_2\right), \eta v_j\right] \\ &= \delta EV\left[\left(\eta \hat{E} - \eta v_1 l_1 - \eta v_2 l_2\right) \times \eta v_j\right] - \delta EV\left[\eta \hat{E} - \eta v_1 l_1 - \eta v_2 l_2\right] \times EV\left[\eta v_j\right] \\ &= \delta EV(\eta^2)\left[\overline{v}_j \hat{E} - EV(v_j^2) l_j - \overline{v}_1 \overline{v}_2 l_k\right] - \delta \overline{\eta}^2\left[\overline{v}_j \hat{E} - \overline{v}_j^2 l_j - \overline{v}_1 \overline{v}_2 l_k\right]. \end{aligned} \qquad (9.14)$$

Combining the two expressions we obtain:

$$
c_j l_j = \delta\left[\overline{\eta}\left(\hat{E} - \overline{v}_1 l_1 - \overline{v}_2 l_2\right)\right] \times \overline{\eta}\overline{v}_j +
$$
$$
\delta EV(\eta^2)\left[\overline{v}_j \hat{E} - EV(v_j^2) l_j - \overline{v}_1 \overline{v}_2 l_k\right] - \delta\overline{\eta}^2\left[\overline{v}_j \hat{E} - \overline{v}_j^2 l_j - \overline{v}_1 \overline{v}_2 l_k\right].
\tag{9.15}
$$

We see that the first and the last terms cancel out, so that (9.15) matches (9.12). Nevertheless, the decomposition is useful, since the first term represents the expected marginal damage. By recalling that $EV(\eta^2) = VAR(\eta) + \overline{\eta}^2$, $EV(v_j^2) = VAR(v_j) + \overline{v}_j^2$, and rearranging the last two terms we obtain

$$
c_j l_j = \underbrace{\delta\left[\overline{\eta}\left(\hat{E} - \overline{v}_1 l_1 - \overline{v}_2 l_2\right)\right] \times \overline{\eta}\overline{v}_j}_{EV(\hat{D}'(A))} + \delta VAR(\eta)\left[\overline{v}_j \hat{E} - \overline{v}_1 \overline{v}_2 l_k\right] + \delta VAR(\eta v_j) l_j,
\tag{9.16}
$$

which shows that the right-hand side of the optimality condition is greater than the expected marginal damage. In case of independence between the random parameters, it is their variances that determine the size of the term added to expected marginal damage. The intuition is that under increasing marginal damage, the environmentally "bad" states of the world are not compensated by the "good" states. The larger is the spread of the environmental parameters, the heavier is their impact in the bad states, and therefore the shadow price of pollution exceeds expected marginal damage.

9.2.2 Decentralization of the Social Optimum

We now turn our attention to the regulator's policy problem, which is to induce an ex ante efficient level of abatement given that emissions are unobservable from her perspective. In what follows, we show that the regulator needs to use firm-specific taxes in which each firm's tax bill depends on ambient pollution. Since no firm can anticipate the ex post ambient pollution level prior to making its decision, it must consider the expected ambient pollution level and therefore minimize expected pollution-related costs.

We first examine the firm's behavior when presented with an ambient pollution tax τ_j, where the subscript j indicates that the tax level is firm specific. The firm selects its abatement effort l_j prior to the realization of the random variables $v_1, \ldots, v_J$ and η, meaning the decision occurs prior to knowledge of its own as well as other firms' value for v_j. Thus the objective is to minimize the expected value of total compliance costs, where the expectation is over the ambient pollution level $A(e_1(l_1, v_1), \ldots, e_J(l_J, v_J), \eta)$. Under this setup, the typical firm chooses l_j to minimize

$$
EV\left[TC_j(l_j)\right] = C_j(l_j) + \tau_j \cdot EV\left[A\left(e_1(l_1, v_1), \ldots, e_J(l_J, v_J), \eta\right)\right].
\tag{9.17}
$$

Since the firm can only influence its own abatement effort, its first-order necessary condition for cost minimization is given by

$$
C_j'(l_j) = \tau_j \cdot EV\left\{A_{e_j} \times \left(-\frac{\partial e_j(l_j, v_j)}{\partial l_j}\right)\right\},
\tag{9.18}
$$

which holds for all $j = 1,\ldots,J$. We denote the solutions to these J equations by $l_1(\tau_1),\ldots,$ $l_J(\tau_J)$. Note that $l_j(\tau_j)$ is *not* a random variable; rather, it is functionally related to the moments of the random variables, which are present via the expectation operator.

The regulator's task is to select the firm-specific tax rates τ_j to minimize the total expected social cost of pollution, where the expectation is taken over the vector of random variables $(v_1,\ldots,v_J,\eta)$. The policy design objective function is

$$\min_{\tau_1,\ldots,\tau_J} \sum_{j=1}^{J} C_j\left(x_j(\tau_j)\right) + EV\left\{D\left[A\left(e_1\left(l_1(\tau_1),v_1\right),\ldots,e_J\left(l_J(\tau_J),v_J\right),\eta\right)\right]\right\}, \qquad (9.19)$$

and the first-order condition for each τ_j is

$$
\begin{aligned}
0 &= \left\{C_j'\left(l_j(\tau_j)\right) + EV\left[D'(A)\times A_{e_j} \times \frac{\partial e_j\left(l_j(\tau_j),v_j\right)}{\partial l_j}\right]\right\} l_j'(\tau_j) \\
&= C_j'\left(l_j(\tau_j)\right) + EV\left[D'(A)\times A_{e_j} \times \frac{\partial e_j\left(l_j(\tau_j),v_j\right)}{\partial l_j}\right],
\end{aligned}
\qquad (9.20)
$$

where we have divided through by $l_j'(\tau_j) > 0$. Using the behavioral equation in (9.18), we are then able to isolate and characterize the optimal firm-specific ambient pollution tax as

$$\tau_j = \frac{-EV\left[D'(A)\times A_{e_j} \times \left(\dfrac{\partial e_j\left(l_j(\tau_j),v_j\right)}{\partial l_j}\right)\right]}{EV\left\{A_{e_j} \times \left(-\dfrac{\partial e_j(l_j,v_j)}{\partial l_j}\right)\right\}}. \qquad (9.21)$$

We can rearrange this expression by applying the covariance formula to the numerator to obtain

$$\tau_j = EV\left[D'(A)\right] + \frac{COV\left[D'(A), A_{e_j} \times \left(\dfrac{\partial e_j\left(l_j(\tau_j),v_j\right)}{\partial l_j}\right)\right]}{EV\left\{A_{e_j} \times \left(\dfrac{\partial e_j(l_j,v_j)}{\partial l_j}\right)\right\}}. \qquad (9.22)$$

Inspection of the optimal firm-specific tax shows that the tax is not equal to expected marginal damage, as may have been anticipated prior to the analysis. This is because the optimal tax needs to account for three factors. First, abatement effort affects ambient pollution only indirectly, and so the tax needs to be adjusted via a term that translates a change in l_j into an expected change in A. This adjustment is reflected in the denominator of the last term in (9.22). Second, the volatility of ambient pollution is driven by draws of the aggregate and firm-specific stochastic parameters. In some contexts a high ambient pollution level may be comparatively more harmful than a low ambient pollution level is beneficial. The numerator of the last term in (9.22) embeds this adjustment for volatility's impact on damages. Finally, correlation amongst the $J+1$ random variables $(v_1,\ldots,v_J,\eta)$ determines the relationship between marginal damage and the effectiveness of abatement effort, which impacts the optimal deployment of abatement. The numerator of the last term in (9.22) imbeds this effect along with the volatility effect.

Inspection of (9.22) also shows that the "tax equals marginal damage" rule applies in the special case when there are constant marginal damages, so that $D'(A)=\delta$. This is because the covariance between the deterministic parameter δ, and the random variable describing the change in ambient pollution when l_j changes, is zero. In this situation, the regulator can use a uniform ambient pollution tax, given by $\tau_j=\tau=D'(A)$, to internalize the externality.

In the following example we use quadratic cost functions and linear or quadratic damage functions to demonstrate the intuition of this section via closed form analytical solutions.

EXAMPLE 9.3 (NUMERICAL/ANALYTICAL) We once again use the ambient pollution and damage functions from example 9.2. Under the constant marginal damage scenario, we know that the uniform ambient tax is simply $\tau_j=\tau=D'(A)=\delta$. The firms' objective function is

$$
\begin{aligned}
EV\big[TC(l_j)\big] &= C_j(l_j)+\tau EV\big[\eta(\hat{E}-v_1 l_1 - v_2 l_2)\big] \\
&= C_j(l_j)+\delta EV\big[\eta(\hat{E}-v_1 l_1 - v_2 l_2)\big],
\end{aligned}
\tag{9.23}
$$

and the first-order condition corresponding to (9.18) is

$$
C'_j(l_j) = -\tau EV\big[\eta(-v_j)\big] = \delta EV\{\eta v_j\}, \quad j=1,2.
\tag{9.24}
$$

If we again assume independence between δ and v_j this reduces to $C'_j(l_j)=\delta\bar{\eta}\bar{v}_j$ for $j=1,2$.

For the quadratic damage function we use (9.21) to derive the specific first-order condition. Plugging our functional forms into (9.21) and assuming independence we obtain

$$
\tau_j = \delta\frac{EV(\eta^2)\big[\hat{E}-EV(v_j^2)l_j -\bar{v}_1\bar{v}_2 l_k\big]}{\bar{\eta}\bar{v}_j}, \quad j=1,2, \quad k\neq j.
\tag{9.25}
$$

Using (9.22) we can decompose the tax into terms reflecting the expected marginal damage and the variance of the random parameters:

$$
\begin{aligned}
\tau_j &= \frac{\delta\bar{\eta}\big(\hat{E}-\bar{v}_1 l_1 -\bar{v}_2 l_2\big)}{\bar{\eta}\bar{v}_j}+\frac{VAR(\eta)\big(\hat{E}-\bar{v}_k x_k\big)}{\bar{\eta}}+\frac{VAR(\eta v_j)l_j}{\bar{\eta}\bar{v}_j} \\
&= \frac{EV(D'(A))}{\bar{\eta}\bar{v}_j}+\frac{VAR(\eta)\big(\hat{E}-\bar{v}_k x_k\big)}{\bar{\eta}}+\frac{VAR(\eta v_j)l_j}{\bar{\eta}\bar{v}_j}, \quad j=1,2, \quad k\neq j
\end{aligned}
\tag{9.26}
$$

Once again, we see that for the case of increasing marginal damage, the firm-specific ambient tax rate exceeds marginal damage.

9.2.3 Uniform Tax

If the regulator cannot assign firm-specific tax rates, and instead must use a uniform (equal across firms) ambient tax, we are necessarily in a second-best world. In this subsection we briefly examine the second-best optimal tax formula. The firm's objective function is

$$EV\big[TC_j(l_j)\big] = C_j(l_j) + \tau \cdot EV\big[A\big(e_1(l_1,v_1),...,e_J(l_J,v_J),\eta\big)\big], \tag{9.27}$$

and its behavior is determined by the first-order condition

$$C_j'(l_j) = \tau \cdot EV\left\{A_{e_j} \times \left(-\frac{\partial e_j(l_j,v_j)}{\partial l_j}\right)\right\}, \quad j = 1,...,J. \tag{9.28}$$

This is similar to Eq. (9.18), albeit with all firms now facing an equal tax. The solutions to these J equations are denoted by $l_1(\tau),..., l_J(\tau)$.

The regulator's task is to select the tax rate τ to minimize the expected social cost from pollution, given by

$$EV\big[SC(\tau)\big] = \sum_{j=1}^{J} C_j\big(l_j(\tau)\big) + EV\left\{D\big[A\big(e_1\big(l_1(\tau),v_1\big),...,e_J\big(l_J(\tau),v_J\big),\eta\big)\big]\right\}. \tag{9.29}$$

Differentiating with respect to the tax rate yields

$$\left\{C_j'\big(l_j(\tau)\big) + EV\left[D'(A) \times \sum_{j=1}^{J} A_{e_j} \times \frac{\partial e_j\big(l_j(\tau),v_j\big)}{\partial l_j}\right]\right\} l_j'(\tau) = 0 \tag{9.30}$$

Substituting the behavior Eq. (9.28) into the regulator's condition for an optimum, we obtain

$$\tau = \frac{EV\left[D'(A) \times \sum_{j=1}^{J} A_{e_j} \times \dfrac{\partial e_j\big(l_j(\tau),v_j\big)}{\partial l_j}\right]}{EV\left\{A_{e_j} \times \left(\dfrac{\partial e_j(l_j,v_j)}{\partial l_j}\right)\right\}}, \tag{9.31}$$

which can be rewritten as

$$\tau = EV\big[D'(A)\big] + \frac{COV\left[D'(A),\sum_{j=1}^{J} A_{e_j} \times \dfrac{\partial e_j\big(l_j(\tau),v_j\big)}{\partial l_j}\right]}{EV\left\{A_{e_j} \times \left(\dfrac{\partial e_j(l_j,v_j)}{\partial l_j}\right)\right\}}. \tag{9.32}$$

Comparing (9.32) to (9.22) we see that the covariance term in the former accounts for the marginal impact of abatement effort of all firms on the ambient pollution level, while under firm-specific taxes, only the covariance between marginal damage and the specific firm's marginal abatement impact on ambient pollution matters.

9.2.4 When Firms Can Observe their Idiosyncratic Shocks

To this point in the chapter, we have assumed that firms can observe neither their own idiosyncratic shock (v_j) nor the other firms' shocks (v_k for all $k \neq j$) before making abatement decisions. In some contexts, it may be more realistic to suppose that the firm can observe its own value of v, but not others'. For example, the impact of fertilizer use by agricultural producers on water quality may depend on things that the farmer can observe on his own land, such as soil type and local topography. If the farmer can observe these states of the world, his emission function $e_j(l_j, v_j)$ is no longer stochastic from his perspective, though the ambient pollution level remains uncertain due to the aggregate shock η and the farmer's inability to observe other producers' emissions. Under this setup, if the firm is faced with a non-uniform ambient tax, it will select its abatement effort to minimize the objective function shown in (9.17). The difference, however, is that the expectation is taken with respect to η and v_k for all $k \neq j$. In this case, the first-order condition determining behavior is

$$
\begin{aligned}
C_j'(l_j) &= \tau_j \cdot EV\left[A_{e_j}\left(-\frac{\partial e_j(l_j, v_j)}{\partial l_j} \right) \right] \\
&= \tau_j \cdot EV\left[A_{e_j} \right] \cdot \left(-\frac{\partial e_j(l_j, v_j)}{\partial l_j} \right), \quad \forall j = 1, \dots, J,
\end{aligned}
\tag{9.33}
$$

where the second line follows from the fact that $e_j(l_j, v_j)$ is deterministic from the firm's perspective. The condition therefore shows that the firm's choice depends on the realized value of its own idiosyncratic (or type) term v_j, and expectations over the values for the remaining firms. If the parameters v_j are drawn from a finite set of outcomes of size N for all firms, then (9.33) is an $N \times J$ dimensional system describing a Bayesian-Nash equilibrium. For some parametric representations of the cost and damage functions the equilibrium outcome from the system can be solved.[1] For the finite outcomes case the optimal firm-specific tax rate can be shown to be similar to (9.22), except that the uncertainty is slightly reduced and the expectation in each firm-specific tax rate is with respect to η and v_k for all $k \neq j$. We do not provide an example of this case because the formulas are tedious and do not offer much additional insight. Nonetheless, we note that observing v_j is beneficial to society, in that the individual firm has no reason to ignore knowledge about its parameter, since it pays a tax proportional to the amount of total pollution. For the case of a uniform tax rate the structure of the second-best optimal tax rate is also similar to (9.32).

---

[1] If the parameters v_j are drawn from a continuum of outcomes, there is typically no general technique to determine the (pure strategy) equilibria, and it is usually not possible to calculate those in closed form, provided they exist at all.

9.2.5 When Firms Have Several Choices

Thus far in section 9.2, we have modeled the firm's choice variable l_j as one dimensional. We might anticipate that a generalization to multiple dimensions, in which l_j is a vector consisting of multiple abating and polluting inputs, does not qualitatively affect our predictions. Perhaps surprisingly, however, this generalization makes a difference in the sense that even with a firm-specific tax the regulator cannot implement the first-best allocation. The reason is that for a K dimensional choice vector $l_j = (l_{j1},...,l_{jK})$ there will be $J \times K$ first-order conditions characterizing the socially optimal allocation. In this case Eq. (9.9) is generalized so it reads

$$\frac{\partial C_j(l_j)}{\partial l_{jk}} = EV\{D'(A)\} \times EV\left\{A_{e_i} \times \left(-\frac{\partial e_j(l_j, v_i)}{\partial l_{jk}}\right)\right\}$$

$$+ COV\left\{D'(A), A_{e_j} \times \left(-\frac{\partial e_j(l_j, v_i)}{\partial l_{jk}}\right)\right\}, \quad \forall j = 1,...,J, \quad k = 1,...,K. \tag{9.34}$$

With $J \times K$ equations we cannot uniquely identify J firm-specific tax rates. The reason is that if a firm can affect the ambient pollution level via K different decision margins, it is equivalent to K different externalities. To incentivize optimal choices for the different inputs, K different instruments are necessary per firm. The second-best optimal, firm-specific tax rates for this generalization are derived in appendix A.

9.2.6 Non-linear Tax Scheme

The previous subsections have shown that decentralizing the first-best allocation of abatement effort using a linear ambient tax scheme involves considerable information requirements for a potential regulator. For the one input case, she must construct J different tax rates, while the multiple input case requires $J \times K$ rates. In contrast, the decentralization problem can be solved relatively easily when a non-linear tax scheme is used in which the tax liability exactly reflects the *damage* amount rather than a scaling of the ambient outcome. In the one input case the firm's objective function under a non-linear tax is

$$EV[TC_j(l_j)] = C_j(l_j) + EV\{\tau(A)\}, \tag{9.35}$$

where

$$\tau(A) = D\big(A\big(e_1(l_1, v_1),...,e_J(l_J, v_J), \eta\big)\big). \tag{9.36}$$

The first-order condition for cost minimization is then given by

$$C_j'(l_j) = EV\left[-D'(A) \times A_{e_j} \times \frac{\partial e_j(l_j, v_j)}{\partial l_j}\right], \tag{9.37}$$

which is exactly equivalent to Eq. (9.8). Note that the non-linear tax also works in the case where the firm has multiple input choices.

9.3 OTHER APPROACHES

The ambient tax schemes developed in the previous sections were derived using the Pareto optimality objective, in which the regulator minimizes the expected social costs given knowledge of the abatement cost and pollution damage functions. In many instances, however, ambient regulations take the form of a threshold that is to be exceeded only in rare instances. A formalization of such a criterion is

$$\Pr\left[A\left(e_1(l_1, v_1),...,e_J(l_J, v_J), \eta\right) > \bar{A}\right] \leq \alpha, \tag{9.38}$$

where α is a precautionary level such as 0.05, meaning pollution should exceed the threshold only 5 percent of the time. An application of Chevyshev's inequality (shown in appendix B) allows us to rewrite the precautionary criterion as

$$EV_{v_1,...,v_J, \eta}\left[A\left(e_1(l_1, v_1),...,e_J(l_J, v_J), \eta\right)\right] = \bar{A} - \frac{\sigma}{\sqrt{\alpha}}, \tag{9.39}$$

where σ is the standard deviation of the distribution of ambient pollution.

If the regulator wants to decentralize an allocation of abatement effort that achieves (9.39) at minimum cost, she needs to charge all firms an ambient tax τ derived from the following objective function:

$$\min_\tau \sum\nolimits_{j=1}^{J} C_j\left(l_j(\tau)\right) + \lambda\left\{EV\left[A\left(e_1(l_1, v_1),...,e_J(l_J, v_J), \eta\right)\right] - \bar{A} + \frac{\sigma}{\sqrt{\alpha}}\right\}, \tag{9.40}$$

where $l_j(\tau)$ is the solution to the individual firm's objective function

$$\min_{l_j} C_j(l_j) + \tau EV\left[A\left(e_1(l_1, v_1),...,e_1(l_J, v_J), \eta\right)\right]. \tag{9.41}$$

Visually, the emission tax shifts the distribution of total emissions to the left as depicted in Figure 9.1.

A problem with this and all of the ambient tax schemes that we have discussed is that, as a collective punishment, it can be considered unethical since firms that pollute only a small amount face the same payment as large polluters. The extent to which this is a problem can be limited by setting an ambient pollution threshold, and designing the ambient tax scheme so that only deviations from this threshold are taxed. Thus the rule formulated in (9.6) for the deterministic case can also be applied when emissions and ambient pollution are random.

There are other instruments discussed in the research literature, and applied in practice, to combat non-point source emissions. Examples include targeting polluting inputs

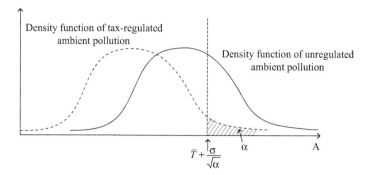

Figure 9.1   The unregulated density function of total emissions (solid line) and the density function under an emission tax

via an input tax, setting command and control rules on certain best management practices, or mixtures of instruments. By definition, these approaches tend to be second best only, though they may be preferred when the information and transaction costs associated with ambient pollution schemes are considered. In most cases cap and trade schemes are not viable for non-point source pollution problems, since individual emissions cannot be observed. Nonetheless, when both point and non-point sources pollute a common environmental resource, opportunities to reduce total abatement costs via exchange may exist (see Horan et al., 2004; and Horan and Shortle, 2005). For example, for agricultural water pollution, policies exist in which point sources such as municipal water treatment plants can contract with agricultural producers to install best management practices (e.g. grass buffer strips between crop fields and waterways), in lieu of abating emissions directly. This requires the specification of a conversion factor, or trading ratio, governing the number of point source emissions that can be offset by specific actions, taken by specific farmers.

9.4   POLICY AND EXPERIMENTAL EVIDENCE

In the last three decades the use of economic incentives in environmental policy making has become sufficiently common that empirical analysis of the performance of economists' recommended approaches has been possible. A notable exception to this trend has been in the area of non-point source pollution control, where the ambient tax/subsidy schemes discussed in this chapter have not been implemented in practice. Instead, a range of command and control and proxy approaches have been the tools of choice. For example, agricultural water pollution is addressed by regulating inputs such as pesticide and fertilizer applications, or by land use measures such as installing grass strips near waterways, or alternative tilling methods. When economic incentives have been employed, they have usually been in the form of the point/non-point source trading mechanisms mentioned in the previous section.

There are three potential explanations for why the ambient tax schemes discussed in this chapter have not advanced much beyond the research stage. The first relates to the core ethical issue noted above. The moral hazard problem implies that all polluters must be held responsible for the entire group's pollution outcome. Thus the possibility exists that a polluter who has behaved in accordance with social objectives could still be financially liable, because of the behavior of others. It is difficult to find parallels to this type of collective punishment approach in contemporary public policy contexts, though incentives based on group outcomes are not uncommon in private organizations. Thus actual implementation of an ambient pollution tax, even one based on deviations from an ambient standard, would need to overcome opposition based on agents' sense of fairness and justice.

A second explanation for the lack of policy examples arises from the fact that agricultural interests in most developed countries have successfully resisted attempts to hold small agricultural producers financially responsible for pollution abatement. As a result, agriculture-related environmental problems are usually addressed using payments to farmers, who voluntarily engage in conservation practices. This political economy reality may make it difficult to experiment with alternative policies that reverse the established property rights structure by introducing payment from, rather than subsidies to, the polluting industry.

The third explanation relates to uncertainty about how the theoretically appealing ambient pollution schemes might perform in practice. The previous sections have illustrated the complexity of both the social planner's problem, and the steps that are needed to decentralize the optimum outcome. What was not clear was the extent to which regulated farmers, acting under real-world time, information, and know-how constraints, will behave in ways predicted by the models. To begin to understand this, an experimental literature has developed that examines how lab and field subjects behave in controlled contexts designed to mimic elements of the non-point source pollution problem.

Spraggon (2002) provides an early and transparent example of this research, which we outline here. In an experimental session involving university students, six identical laboratory subjects select a pollution amount $e_j \in [0,100]$ to maximize a private payoff function $B(e_j) = 25 - 0.002(100 - e_j)$. In addition, total emissions $E = \sum_{j=1}^{6} e_j$ result in public damages, given by $D(E) = 0.3E$. The author examines the performance of four different instruments; among these are the tax/subsidy scheme given by (9.6), as well as a version of (9.6) that only includes the tax side. In particular, the tax payment (or subsidy, when negative) is defined by $\tau(E) = 0.3 \times (E - 150)$, where 150 is the optimal aggregate pollution level, according to the private benefit and public damage functions. The form of this instrument makes clear that each of the six subjects (polluting firms) pays the full marginal damage for each unit of group pollution that is above the standard. As noted above, a unique Nash equilibrium exists for this type of policy; Spraggon shows that the socially optimal choice $e_j = 25$ is also the unique optimal private choice in his experimental setup.

The experiments generally support the theoretical predictions stated in section 9.1. Under the tax and tax/subsidy instruments, the aggregate pollution levels correspond to the optimal levels. To add an element of uncertainty to the setup, Spraggon also considers scenarios in which $E = \sum_{j=1}^{6} e_j + \eta$, where $\eta \sim \text{UNIF}(-40, 40)$. Here too, the two ambient instruments produce pollution outcomes that correspond to the social optimum. At the aggregate level, the evidence therefore shows that ambient instruments can perform as predicted by the theory. Importantly, however, the experiments show that individual outcomes do not always correspond to the optimal choice, meaning even in this simple context, individual agents were prone to decision errors.

More recent studies have added elements of realism to the basic setup described here. For example, Spraggon (2004) and Suter et al. (2009) consider how heterogeneity in the size of polluting firms affects the performance of ambient tax schemes, while Vossler et al. (2006) investigate how communication amongst regulated firms affects outcomes. Following the theoretical framework of Xepapadeas (1991), Camacho and Requate (2012) experimentally compare ambient taxes to collective and random fee punishment rules. Finally, Suter and Vossler (2014) present a field environment with farmers, where the experimental context is tailored to the specific watershed in which they operate.

9.5 SUMMARY

In this chapter we have examined the theory of environmental policy for the non-point source pollution problem. The design of policy in this context is complicated by two defining characteristics of non-point source pollution: moral hazard and stochastic pollution. The first of these arises due to the inability of the regulator to observe the emissions from individual polluters, so that performance cannot be assessed based on individual firms' outcomes. The second arises from the fact that ambient concentrations of pollution are subject to natural variation based on weather and topography. The design of policy that simultaneously accommodates the moral hazard and uncertainty aspects of the problem has been our focus in this chapter.

We first saw that the moral hazard problem implies that we need to design policy that is based on the observed ambient pollution level rather than the unobserved emissions levels. Because the ambient pollution level is determined by the group's behavior, and the contributions of individual members cannot be ascertained, our model showed that efficiency can only be reached when each polluter pays the full marginal damage for each ambient pollution unit in excess of the optimal ambient level. The notion that all polluters pay a tax that is derived from the full marginal damage is a defining characteristic of the ambient tax literature. The fact that tax revenues collected may exceed total damages, and that polluters who have behaved in accordance with social goals can still face a tax liability, have contributed to a dearth of policy examples using this mechanism.

Aggregate uncertainty introduces additional challenges in that the object of taxation – the ambient pollution level – is not fully determined by polluters' choices. Thus while the tax amount is assessed after the resolution of uncertainty, firms' and the regulator's decisions need to be made based on expectations. We demonstrated that the optimal solutions are, in general, functions of both the first and second moments of the stochastic ambient pollution level. For marginal damage functions that are increasing in ambient pollution, the variance of ambient pollution matters, because it determines the likelihood that an extreme event will lead to a spike in marginal damage. Thus the optimal ambient tax is derived from expected marginal damage, as well as the variance of ambient pollution. When marginal damages are constant, the ambient tax reduces to the expected marginal damage level. In both cases the presence of only aggregate uncertainty means that a uniform tax can be used to achieve the efficient allocation of abatement effort.

The addition of firm-specific uncertainty adds additional complexity that requires the use of firm-specific ambient tax rates to achieve the efficient abatement allocation, when marginal damage is not constant. Thus a uniform ambient tax rate can only be second-best optimal, and the correlation structure between the firm-level and aggregate uncertainty determines the relationship between the firm-specific ambient tax rate and expected marginal damage.

Finally, we saw that even firm-specific ambient taxes are only second-best optimal, when firms have multiple input choices that impact ambient pollution. The most general case of moral hazard, multiple inputs, increasing marginal damage, and both firm and aggregate uncertainty combine to produce an unusually challenging regulatory environment. These features of the problem help explain why we have limited real-world experience with ambient tax schemes of the types described in this chapter. Applied research in this area has therefore focused on using laboratory and field experiments to examine the potential for ambient pollution schemes to work as theory predicts.

9.6 FURTHER READING

Besides the seminal paper by Segerson (1988), Meran and Schwalbe (1987) were the first to address the problem of controlling non-point pollution sources. Xepapadeas (1991) suggested two further mechanisms for dealing with non-point pollution problems, notably a collective fine and a random fining scheme. If the ambient pollution level exceeds the level set by a regulator, the whole group of potential polluters is punished under collective fining, while under random fining, one potential polluter is selected randomly for punishment. Horan et al. (2002) study the non-point source pollution problem with stochastic impacts, while Horan et al. (2004) and Horan and Shortle (2005) analyze trading programs between point and non-point sources. See also Shortle and Horan (2001) for a survey on earlier research, and Shortle and Braden (2013) for a recent survey on regulation of non-point source pollution problems.

There have been several experimental evaluations of ambient tax and subsidy mechanisms in recent years. Examples of these include Spraggon (2002, 2004), Cochard et al. (2005), Vossler et al. (2006), Suter et al. (2008), Camacho-Cuena and Requate (2012), and Suter et al. (2009). Reichhuber et al. (2009) conduct a common-pool framed field experiment which is similar to a non-point source pollution problem, as subjects' individual resource exploitation activities cannot be observed.

APPENDIX A: SECOND-BEST OPTIMAL FIRM-SPECIFIC TAXES WITH MULTIPLE INPUTS

In section 9.3, we demonstrated that a firm-specific tax rate will not induce the first-best allocation when polluters have multiple input choices. In this appendix section, we derive the second-best optimal, firm-specific ambient tax, and show that this will not induce the socially optimal allocation. In particular, a multiple input firm's cost minimization problem when faced with an ambient tax scheme is

$$EV\big(TC_j(x_j)\big) = C_j(l_j) + \tau_j \cdot EV\big[A\big(e_1(l_1, v_1), ..., e_J(l_J, v_J), \eta\big)\big],$$ (A9.1)

where $l_j = (l_{j1}, ..., l_{jK})$ is the K dimensional input vector. The first-order conditions for cost minimization are

$$\frac{\partial C_j(x_j)}{\partial l_{jk}} = -\tau_j \times EV\left\{A_{e_j} \times \frac{\partial e_j(l_j, v_j)}{\partial l_{jk}}\right\}, \quad k = 1, ..., K.$$ (A9.2)

Denote the solutions for the J firms by $l_1(\tau_1), ..., l_J(\tau_J)$.

The regulator minimizes total expected pollution-related costs according to

$$\min_{\tau_1, ..., \tau_J} \sum_{j=1}^{J} C_j\big(l_j(\tau_j)\big) + EV\big[D\big(A\big(e_1(l_1(\tau_1), v_1), ..., e_J(l_J(\tau_J), v_J), \eta\big)\big)\big],$$ (A9.3)

and the first-order conditions for τ_j is

$$\sum_{k=1}^{K} \frac{\partial C_j\big(l_j(\tau_j)\big)}{\partial l_{jk}} \frac{\partial l_{jk}(\tau_j)}{\partial \tau_j}$$
$$+ EV\left[D'(A) \times A_{e_j} \times \sum_{k=1}^{K} \frac{\partial e_j\big(l_j(\tau_j), v_j\big)}{\partial l_{jk}} \frac{\partial l_{jk}(\tau_j)}{\partial \tau_j}\right] = 0.$$ (A9.4)

Substituting the behavioral condition (A9.2) we obtain:

$$\sum_{k=1}^{K} \tau_j \times EV\left\{-A_{e_j} \times \frac{\partial e_j(l_j, v_j)}{\partial l_{jk}}\right\} \frac{\partial l_{jk}(\tau_j)}{\partial \tau_j}$$
$$+ EV\left[D'(A) \times A_{e_j} \times \sum_{k=1}^{K} \frac{\partial e_j\big(l_j(\tau_j), v_j\big)}{\partial l_{jk}} \frac{\partial l_{jk}(\tau_j)}{\partial \tau_j}\right] = 0,$$ (A9.5)

which we can rewrite as

$$\sum_{k=1}^{K} \tau_j \times EV\left\{-A_{e_j} \times \frac{\partial e_j(l_j, v_j)}{\partial l_{jk}}\right\} \frac{\partial l_{jk}(\tau_j)}{\partial \tau_j} +$$
$$EV\big(D'(A)\big) \times EV\left[A_{e_j} \times \sum_{k=1}^{K} \frac{\partial e_j\big(l_j(\tau_j), v_j\big)}{\partial l_{jk}} \frac{\partial l_{jk}(\tau_j)}{\partial \tau_j}\right] +$$
$$COV\left\{D'(A), A_{e_j} \times \sum_{k=1}^{K} \frac{\partial e_j\big(l_j(\tau_j), v_j\big)}{\partial l_{jk}} \frac{\partial l_{jk}(\tau_j)}{\partial \tau_j}\right\} = 0.$$ (A9.6)

By rearranging this expression, we can characterize the firm-specific tax rate as

$$
\tau_j = EV\left(D'(A)\right) + \frac{COV\left\{D'(A), A_{e_j} \times \sum_{k=1}^{K} \dfrac{\partial e_j\left(l_j(\tau_j), v_j\right)}{\partial l_{jk}} \dfrac{\partial l_{jk}(\tau_j)}{\partial \tau_j}\right\}}{EV\left[A_{e_j} \times \sum_{k=1}^{K} \dfrac{\partial e_j\left(l_j(\tau_j), v_j\right)}{\partial l_{jk}} \dfrac{\partial l_{jk}(\tau_j)}{\partial \tau_j}\right]}.
\tag{A9.7}
$$

Comparing the characterization here to the optimality condition shown in (9.34) suggests that a single firm-specific tax rate will not lead to the first-best allocation.

APPENDIX B: DERIVATION OF (9.39)

Let X be any random variable with mean μ and standard deviation σ. Then Chebyshev's inequality states

$$
\Pr\left\{|X - \mu| > k\sigma\right\} \le \frac{1}{k^2}.
\tag{A9.8}
$$

In the context of (9.39), we write $E = \sum_{j=1}^{J} e_j(l_j, v_j)$ and $\mu = EV\left[\sum_{j=1}^{J} e_j(l_j, v_j)\right]$. Setting $\alpha = 1/k^2$, Chebyshev's inequality implies

$$
\Pr\left\{E > \mu + \frac{\sigma}{\sqrt{\alpha}}\right\} \le \alpha,
\tag{A9.9}
$$

or equivalently:

$$
\Pr\left\{E > \bar{A}\right\} \le \alpha,
\tag{A9.10}
$$

with $\bar{A} = \mu + \sigma/\sqrt{\alpha}$. Thus if the threshold $\bar{A}$ must not be exceeded with probability α, effort $(l_1, \ldots, l_J)$ must be chosen such that

$$
EV\left[\sum_{j=1}^{J} e_j(l_j, v_j)\right] = \bar{A} - \sigma/\sqrt{\alpha}.
\tag{A9.11}
$$

EXERCISES

9.1 * Consider firms' abatement cost functions $C_j(e_j) = (a_j - b_j e_j)^2/2b_j$ and an ambient damage function $D(A) = \delta A^2/2$, where $A = \sum_{j=1}^{J} e_j$ is the ambient pollution level.
   (a) Determine the optimal emission level.
   (b) Determine the optimal ambient tax and the optimal ambient tax/subsidy scheme.

(c) Determine an optimal collective lump-sum fine, where all firms have to pay a fixed fine F if some ambient pollution threshold is exceeded.

9.2 * Repeat exercise 9.1 using $A = \sum_{j=1}^{J} \alpha_j e_j$ for $\alpha_j > 0$.

9.3 * Show that if in an ambient pollution problem with J polluters each firm pays only $1/J$ of the damage, there will be too little incentive to abate emissions efficiently.

9.4 ** Consider example 9.2. Determine the socially optimal level of abatement input in closed form for the case of independently distributed parameters v_j and η.

9.5 ** Modify example 9.2 by assuming there is only one firm. Assume that both η and $v_1 = v$ can take two values: v_L, v_H, and η_L, η_H. Denote $p_{LL} = \Pr(\eta = \eta_L, v = v_L)$ as the probablity that both parameters take their low values, and similarly define p_{LH}, p_{HL}, and p_{HH}. Define abatement costs by $C(l) = c \cdot l^2/2$ and damages by $D(A) = \delta \cdot A^2 / 2$, where $A = \eta(e^{max} - vl)$ is the ambient pollution level.
   (a) Calculate the optimal level for abatement input and the optimal ambient emission tax rate.
   (b) Consider the following special cases and interpret: (i) $p_{LH} = p_{HL} = 0$, (ii) $p_{LL} = p_{HH} = 0$, and (iii) $\Pr(\eta, v) = \Pr(\eta) \times \Pr(v) = p_\eta \cdot p_v$.

9.6 *** Consider examples 9.2 and 9.3. Assume that social damage is quadratic as in the examples. Following section 9.2.3, assume that the regulator can only set a uniform tax. Determine the formula for the second-best optimal tax rate.

9.7 *** Consider again the case of one firm as in exercise 9.5, but now assume that the firm can observe its parameter v.
   (a) Determine the firm's efficient choice of l for each value v_L and v_H.
   (b) Determine the optimal tax rate for this case.

9.8 *** Consider again examples 9.2 and 9.3, and once again assume that there are two states of the world for each random variable, denoted by v_j^L, v_j^H and η^L, η^H. Denote the probabilities for these by p_v^L and $p_v^H = 1 - p_v^L$, and p_η^L and $p_\eta^H = 1 - p_\eta^L$, respectively. Assume the random variables are all independent.
   (a) For given firm-specific tax rates τ_j determine the firms' equilibrium choices $l_j(v_j^k)$ for $k = L, H$.
   (b) Determine the optimal firm-specific tax rates.
   (c) Derive a formula for the second-best optimal uniform tax rate.

9.9 *** Assume now that each firm has two abatement possibilities represented by the abatement vector $l_j = (l_{j1}, l_{j2})$. The abatement cost function is additively separable and given by $C_j(l_{j1}, l_{j2}) = c_{j1} x_{j1}^2 / 2 + c_{j2} l_{j2}^2 / 2$, and emissions are determined by $e_j = (e_j^{max} - v_{j1}^k l_{j1} - v_{j2}^k l_{j2})$. Once again there are two states of the world $k = L, H$, with probabilities p_v^L and $p_v^H = 1 - p_v^L$. The random variables are independent across firms.
   (a) Determine the socially optimal allocation.
   (b) Derive a formula for the second-best optimal firm-specific tax rates.
   (c) Derive a formula for the second-best optimal uniform tax rate.

9.10 *** Consider a modified version of the model with uncertainty from section 9.2. Assume that the firm is characterized by an output production function $g_j(l_j)$, where l_j is now a single productive input, and emissions are given by $e_j(l_j, v_j)$, where now $\partial e_j(l_j, v_j)/\partial l_j > 0$ (that is, the input is now polluting rather than abating).
   (a) Derive the formula for the optimal firm-specific tax rates.

(b) Derive the formula for the second-best optimal uniform tax. Assume now that l_j is a vector, where some inputs are productive but polluting such that $\partial g_j(l_j)/\partial l_{jk} > 0$ and $\partial e_j(l_j, v_j)/\partial l_{jk} > 0$, while others are costly but reduce emissions so that $\partial g_j(l_j)/\partial l_{jn} < 0$ and $\partial e_j(l_j, v_j)/\partial l_{jn} < 0$.

(c) Determine formulas for the second-best optimal firm-specific tax rates as well as for the second-best optimal uniform tax rate.

9.11 ** Show that a non-linear tax scheme which reflects total damage from ambient pollution also works to decentralize the first-best allocation if a firm has several choices.

CHAPTER 10

Liability

In previous chapters we have focused on environmental problems that are characterized by a flow of emissions or an ambient concentration of pollution that arise from production activities. In these cases, emissions were closely linked to a firm's technology, output level, and abatement activity. In many instances, however, environmental damage is the result of an acute accident that can occur with some probability. In these cases it is the level of accident prevention effort that influences the likelihood that environmental damage occurs. There are several well-known examples of this. In 1989 the oil tanker *Exxon Valdez* ran aground in Alaska's Prince William Sound, causing what, at the time, was the largest discharge of oil into US waters. The size of this spill was eclipsed by the 2010 BP/Deepwater Horizon oil spill in the Gulf of Mexico. Both of these accidents might have been prevented with additional care. In the case of *Exxon*, more could have been invested in training qualified officers to guide the ship; the BP spill occurred in part due to sub-par construction practices. Nuclear disasters such as Chernobyl in Russia, where insufficient maintenance was a culprit, and more recently Fukushima in Japan, where additional safety measures were available but not deployed, are further examples.

The emission- and ambient-based policies that we have previously examined are ill-suited for addressing discrete-event environmental accidents of these types. Instead, policies need to address the incentives that potential polluters have to minimize the likelihood that an accident occurs. In this chapter we focus on such a regulatory environment, where the goal is to achieve a socially optimal level of accident prevention effort. We begin by defining an economically efficient level of accident prevention effort, and then present legal frameworks that provide incentives for private enterprises to deploy the efficient effort. We will see that simple liability rules work well when firms are wealthy enough to pay for any accident-related damages they cause. Things are more complicated, however, when the possibility of bankruptcy exists, in that a firm will behave differently when the amount it is liable for is capped by its current assets. In such cases, a firm's accident prevention effort only provides private benefits if the firm remains solvent, which changes its incentives in ways that lead to an inefficient level of accident prevention effort. After establishing this, we examine the extent to which optional or compulsory insurance is useful when insolvency is possible. We will see that the extent to which a polluter's accident prevention effort can be observed is critical for understanding how insurance markets function, and when insurance provides welfare-enhancing possibilities. Similar to our findings in Chapter 9, the moral hazard that arises when accident prevention effort is unobservable creates regulatory challenges, since liability cannot be tied to prevention effort.

We use a single firm framework to examine the issues just listed. In the latter part of the chapter, we generalize our analysis to examine contexts in which several firms are engaged in environmentally risky behavior. We distinguish between alternative causality, whereby one of many firms is responsible for an accident, and multi-causality, when firms are jointly responsible. We will see that in these cases as well, the extent to which accident prevention efforts are observable is critical for determining the effectiveness of different liability regimes.

The model that we use in this chapter is relatively simple, but the results that we derive often involve complicated proofs. As such we will generally state results and illustrate them with examples, and relegate the formal proofs to the appendices.

10.1 BASIC MODEL

Consider a context in which a firm's activities have the potential to cause an environmental accident that leads to external damages. The accident occurs with probability $\rho(a)$, where a is the level of accident prevention undertaken by the firm. Throughout the chapter we will refer to a as the care level or abatement level. We assume the probability of an accident decreases with additional care at a decreasing rate, and that it converges to zero when care is infinite. Formally these assumptions imply that $\rho'(a)<0$, $\rho''(a)>0$, and $\lim_{a\to\infty}\rho(a)=0$. Finally, we assume for most of the chapter that external damages are fixed and denoted by D. This allows us to write expected damages as $\rho(a)\times D$.

To link the firm's activities to our familiar model of market benefits and costs we denote x as the quantity of output associated with the hazardous activity and $P(x)$ as the inverse demand function faced by the firm. Let $C(x,a)$ be the cost of production as a function of the output quantity and level of abatement. We assume $C_x(\cdot)>0$ and $C_a(\cdot)>0$, so that both additional output and additional care have positive marginal cost. Furthermore we assume that $C_{xx}(\cdot)\geq 0$, $C_{aa}(\cdot)\geq 0$, and $C_{ax}(\cdot)=C_{xa}(\cdot)\geq 0$, so that the cost function is weakly convex in both its arguments. With this the social optimum is found by selecting x and a to maximize

$$SW(x,a)=\int_0^x P(t)dt-C(x,a)-\rho(a)D. \tag{10.1}$$

The first-order conditions are

$$P(x)=C_x(x,a) \tag{10.2}$$

and

$$-\rho'(a)D=C_a(x,a). \tag{10.3}$$

Equation (10.2) is the familiar condition that consumers' marginal willingness to pay equals the marginal cost of output, while (10.3) states that the expected marginal damage equals the marginal cost of increasing care. These are intuitive conditions that follow closely the ideas and assumptions used in earlier chapters.

The analysis that follows requires much in the way of additional concepts, and so we introduce a few simplifying assumptions into our baseline analysis. Specifically, we assume that abatement effort is measured in currency units and that production costs are separable, so that $C(x,a)=C(x)+a$. This implies that the level of output x is independent of the level of abatement, and so the net consumption benefits of x are also independent of a. We denote the maximum net consumption benefits from the perspective of society by

$$b = \max_{x} \int_{0}^{x} P(t)dt - C(x),$$

(10.4)

which allows us to rewrite expected social welfare as a function of only a, so that

$$SW(a) = b - [a + \rho(a)D].$$

(10.5)

Maximizing social welfare therefore boils down to selecting a according to

$$-\rho'(a)D = 1.$$

(10.6)

We use a^* to denote the socially optimal level of care, and denote the expected social cost due to the possibility of an accident by $SC = a + \rho(a) \times D$. Figure 10.1 depicts the expected social cost and its components (upper panel), the first-order condition (lower panel), and the how the optimal care amount is determined.

Note that with this form of the social welfare function, we are implicitly assuming that society is risk neutral. This can be justified if the scale of analysis is such that the impact of a single accident is small relative to the overall size of the economy. For a larger-scale analysis – such as risks associated with the entire nuclear power industry – it might be appropriate to assume some societal risk aversion. The models we present can be extended to this case without qualitative changes in their predictions. For simplicity we therefore maintain the assumption of societal risk neutrality.

A private company engaging in the risky activity can, in contrast, be either risk neutral or risk averse. As in earlier chapters we will refer to the firm as the polluter or the polluting firm, though in this context the accident may or may not happen. Continuing with the simplification that costs are separable and abatement is measured in monetary units, the firm's profit function absent any type of liability regime is $\Pi = px - C(x) - a$. To simplify notation we rewrite profit as $\Pi = v - a$, where

$$v = \max_{x} px - C(x).$$

(10.7)

In subsequent sections we will discuss ways that different liability rules can alter the form of the profit and cost functions; for now we note that without any liability rule the firm's optimal choice is to set $a = 0$, and a market failure results. In order to focus attention on policies that internalize this externality, we assume throughout the chapter that the output market is competitive, so that $v \leq b$.

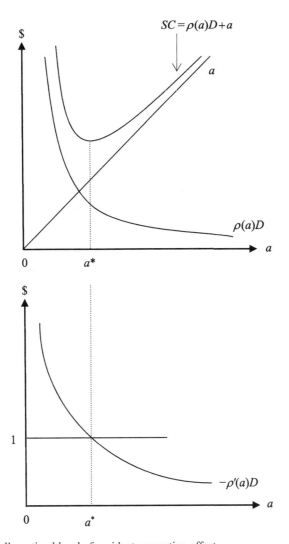

Figure 10.1   Socially optimal level of accident prevention effort

In considering the efficacy of different liability rules, it is useful to define the additional variable k as the value of the firm's assets. This can be important in instances when damages from an accident exceed the firm's net profits. In particular, we define the firm's wealth as $y = k + v$ and distinguish between cases when the firm is solvent ($y \geq D$) and not solvent ($y < D$). For both cases we will study different rules for decentralizing the level of care; the most prominent of these are *strict liability* and a *negligence rule*.

If the firm owner is risk averse, his utility is represented by a concave von Neumann-Morgenstern utility function $U(y - a)$, where $U'(\cdot) > 0$, $U''(\cdot) < 0$, and $U(0) = 0$.[1] While large firms such as BP or Exxon may be considered risk neutral, owners of smaller firms facing the risk of bankruptcy in the event of an

---

[1] If society (the social planner) is risk averse, we add the reasonable assumption that the firm's degree of risk aversion is larger than the social planner's. The results derived below continue to hold if this is the case.

environmental accident may be risk averse. For most of the chapter we will derive our results for the simpler case of risk neutrality, adding more specific focus on risk aversion when we consider insurance as a way a firm can hedge against paying compensation, in the event of an accident.

10.2   LIABILITY RULES FOR A SOLVENT FIRM

We begin by studying liability rules for a solvent firm. By this we mean situations where the polluting firm holds enough wealth to cover both its expenditures on care and any damages it might later be liable for, according to the regulatory regime. Since abatement spending is endogenous this means we assume that $y \gg a + D$ – i.e. damages can be covered regardless of the choice of a.

10.2.1 Strict Liability

Under *strict liability* a firm that causes an environmental accident is fully responsible for the damage that occurs, in the sense that it must pay an amount equal to the value of damages. In this case the expected wealth for a risk neutral firm is

$$E\Pi^{sl}(a) = y - a - \rho(a)D, \tag{10.8}$$

where the *sl* superscript indicates the strict liability regime. Note that (10.8) matches the social welfare function in (10.5) up to a constant. The solvent and risk neutral firm maximizes expected wealth by selecting a such that $-\rho'(a)D = 1$, which is equivalent to the rule for the social optimum. Thus when the solvency condition holds, strict liability is an effective decentralized policy instrument. In addition to efficiency, there are favorable information properties in that the regulator does not need to have information on the polluting firm's level of care, or an ex ante estimate of the potential damages.

   If the owner of the firm is risk averse, his objective function is given by the expected utility of his firm's net wealth:

$$EU^{sl}(a, y) = \rho(a) \cdot U(y - a - D) + (1 - \rho(a)) \cdot U(y - a). \tag{10.9}$$

In this case the first-order condition for the firm's optimal level of a reads

$$\begin{aligned}
-\rho'(a) \cdot \left[U(y - a) - U(y - a - D) \right] \\
- \rho(a)U'(y - a - D) - (1 - \rho(a)) \cdot U'(y - a) = 0.
\end{aligned} \tag{10.10}$$

We denote the level of care chosen by the risk-averse firm owner under the strict liability rule by $a_s^{sl}(y)$, where the subscript s indicates that the solution is conditional on the firm's solvency.

10.2.2 Negligence Rule

Under the negligence rule the regulator sets a due care level $\bar{a}$. This means that if an accident occurs, the firm is only liable for damages if it can be shown that the firm engaged in a level of care lower than $\bar{a}$, and was therefore negligent. The risk neutral firm's objective is therefore to select a to maximize

$$E\Pi^{nr}(a) = \begin{cases} y - (a + \rho(a)D) & a < \bar{a} \\ y - a & a \geq \bar{a}. \end{cases} \tag{10.11}$$

We denote the solvent firm's choice of abatement under the negligence rule by $a_s^{nr}(\bar{a})$, where the *nr* superscript indicates the negligence rule regime. Note that the risk neutral firm will just meet the standard $\bar{a}$, whenever $\bar{a} \leq a^*$. This is because a^* minimizes $a + \rho(a)D$, but the abatement level a^* places the firm in the non-negligent component of (10.11), which it can obtain for the smaller expenditure $\bar{a} < a^*$. If the due care level exceeds a^* the firm compares the expected compliance costs $\bar{a}$ and $a^* + \rho(a^*)D$. In particular, there is a cut-off level $\hat{a} > a^*$ defined by $\hat{a} = a^* + \rho(a^*)D$. If $\bar{a} < \hat{a}$ then the firm operates in the non-negligent part of (10.11) with compliance cost equal to $\bar{a}$, while for $\bar{a} > \hat{a}$ it is optimal to accept negligence in the event of an accident, with expected compliance cost $a^* + \rho(a^*)D$. Figure 10.2 illustrates the case when the firm selects $a = a^* < \bar{a}$, thereby accepting some probability that it will be liable for the amount D in the event of an accident.

If the polluting firm is risk averse the same result essentially holds. Once again there is a cut-off level below which the firm will comply with a standard, and above which it will accept negligence. We summarize our findings for the risk neutral and solvent firm in the following proposition.

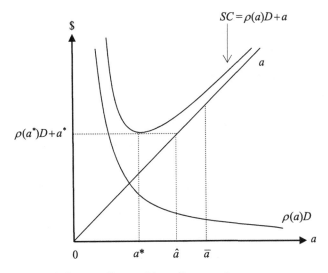

Figure 10.2 Cutoff levels for compliance with negligence rule

Proposition 10.1

Assume a polluting firm is risk neutral and sufficiently wealthy such that $y - a^* - D \gg 0$ (i.e. it can cover all damages in the event of an accident). Then

(a) *under strict liability the polluter will choose the socially optimal level of care a^*;*
(b) *under the negligence rule it will choose the care level $\bar{a}$ if that level is smaller than some cutoff level $\hat{a}$, and it will act negligently otherwise. The cutoff level is defined by*

$$\hat{a} = a^* + \rho(a^*)D. \tag{10.12}$$

The socially optimal due care level is given by $\bar{a} = a^*$.

One might ask why we require $y - a^* - D \gg 0$ as the condition for the proposition rather than simply $y - a^* - D \geq 0$. The reason is that the level of care chosen by the firm is endogenous and if the firm is close to bankruptcy, it may choose a level of care higher than socially optimal, which in turn may lead to bankruptcy. Therefore, for our main result under risk neutrality, the level of wealth should be sufficiently high that bankruptcy is not an issue.

In a more general setup the damage level could depend on how much output is produced. For example, in case of an accident, a large oil tanker will cause greater environmental damage than a small oil tanker, by the simple reason that more oil spills from the large one than from the small one. It is not difficult to extend our model to the case where damage depends on the scale of activity. Exercise 10.4 provides an opportunity to explore this in detail.

10.3   LIABILITY RULES FOR A JUDGMENT-PROOF FIRM

Until now we have assumed that firms with the potential to cause environmental accidents are sufficiently wealthy to cover all damages arising from the risky activity. In many cases this need not be so. For example, a nuclear power plant may not be able to cover all damages in the case of a major disaster. Large companies can also contract risky activities to smaller enterprises, which may not have the resources to pay full damages. In this section we examine cases in which the offending firm may become insolvent in the event of an accident.

To begin we note that from the viewpoint of society, the expected net benefit resulting from the risky activity should be positive in order to justify its implementation. Specifically, the condition $b - a^* - \rho(a^*)D > 0$ must hold in order for the activity to be desirable. Note that this does *not* necessarily imply that $y - a^* - D > 0$. Thus it can be the case that ex ante, the activity is socially desirable, but ex post the firm cannot cover its full liability in the event of an accident. In this situation we say that the firm is judgment proof, which alters the firm's objective functions under the two liability schemes thus far discussed. In particular, since a firm's wealth cannot be negative, under strict liability the private firm's expected wealth is

$$E\Pi^{sl}(a,y) = \rho(a) \cdot \max\{0, y - a - D\} + [1 - \rho(a)](y - a), \tag{10.13}$$

and under the negligence rule we have

$$E\Pi^{nr}(a,y) = \begin{cases} E\Pi^{sl}(a,y) & a < \bar{a} \\ y - a & a \geq \bar{a}. \end{cases} \tag{10.14}$$

Thus the firm's expected profits in both cases are bounded by zero – i.e. it cannot pay out in compensation more than the value of its assets and operating returns. In what follows we use the general expressions $a^{sl}(y)$ and $a^{nr}(y)$ to denote the (potentially) non-solvent firm's choices under the strict liability and negligence rule regimes, respectively.

10.3.1 Strict Liability

We first consider the judgment-proof firm's behavior under strict liability. If the firm is wealthy enough (or D is small enough) that insolvency is not an issue, then (10.13) collapses to (10.8). The more interesting case in this section is when $y < a + D$ for feasible values of a, so that the expected profit function in (10.13) becomes

$$\begin{aligned} E\Pi^{sl}(a,y) &= \rho(a)\cdot 0 + [1 - \rho(a)](y - a) \\ &= [1 - \rho(a)](y - a). \end{aligned} \tag{10.15}$$

Differentiating with respect to a leads to the first-order condition for profit maximization of

$$-\rho'(a)(y - a) = 1 - \rho(a). \tag{10.16}$$

This condition shows that the firm selects a so that the marginal expected benefit of a (the left-hand side) is equal to the marginal cost of a (the right-hand side). Note that the marginal cost of a is smaller than one since, in contrast to the case when the firm is solvent, spending on a lowers wealth *only* in the non-accident state, since all wealth is lost in the accident state regardless of a.

To gain some additional intuition on what (10.16) shows, note that the expression relates to D according to

$$-\rho'(a^{sl}(y)) = \frac{1 - \rho(a^{sl}(y))}{y - a^{sl}(y)} \begin{matrix} < 1 \\ > D \end{matrix}, \tag{10.17}$$

since $1 - \rho(\cdot) < 1$ and $y - a^{sl}(y) < D$ in the non-solvency case. This means that $a^{sl}(y)$ can be smaller *or* larger than a^*, where a^* is determined by the condition $-\rho'(a^*) = 1/D$. The ambiguity is noteworthy in that one might expect $a^{sl}(y) < a^*$ to always hold when bankruptcy is an option. If wealth is small relative to damages, the denominators in (10.17) drive the relationship, and indeed we have $-\rho'(\cdot) \times D > 1$ at the solution, meaning that $a^{sl}(y) < a^*$ as intuition suggests. This is clear from inspection of the lower panel of Figure 10.1.

Consider instead the case in which wealth is such that $y - a^{sl}(y) \approx D$, so that the numerators in (10.17) drive the relationship, implying $-\rho'(\cdot) \times D < 1$ and $a^{sl}(y) > a^*$. In this case the firm spends *more* on care than is socially optimal.

To explore this further, define $\hat{y} = a^* + D$ as the level of wealth coinciding with the socially optimal division between solvency and non-solvency for the firm, and recall once again that by definition $-\rho'(a^*) \times D = 1$. Since payoff in the accident state of the world is zero for wealth $\hat{y}$, the first-order condition in (10.16) determines the firm's choice of a. In particular, we have

$$-\rho'\left(a^{sl}(\hat{y})\right)\left(\underbrace{D + a^*}_{\hat{y}} - a^{sl}(\hat{y})\right) = 1 - \rho\left(a^{sl}(\hat{y})\right). \tag{10.18}$$

Note that $a^{sl}(\hat{y}) \leq a^*$ cannot be a solution to (10.18). This is because $a^{sl}(\hat{y}) \leq a^*$ implies: (a) $\rho(a^*) \leq \rho(a^{sl}(\hat{y}))$; (b) $-\rho'(a^*) \leq -\rho'(a^{sl}(\hat{y}))$, since $-\rho''(\cdot) < 0$; and (c) $D + a^* - a^{sl}(\hat{y}) \geq D$. Using these we obtain

$$-\rho'\left(a^*\right)D \leq -\rho'\left(a^{sl}(\hat{y})\right)\left(\underbrace{D + a^*}_{\hat{y}} - a^{sl}(\hat{y})\right) = 1 - \rho\left(a^{sl}(\hat{y})\right) \leq 1 - \rho\left(a^*\right) < 1, \tag{10.19}$$

contradicting the first-best condition (10.6). Therefore, for wealth level $\hat{y}$, we must have $a^{sl}(\hat{y}) > a^*$ and $\hat{y} - a^{sl}(\hat{y}) < D$. Although it is possible to deploy the optimal level of care, the firm chooses excess care and, if an accident occurs, it will not be able to cover damages. This counterintuitive result arises from the different marginal costs of abatement that the firm faces when it is solvent, relative to when it is judgment proof. For the former, the marginal cost is one since spending on abatement decreases wealth in both states of the world. In the latter case, spending on abatement only affects wealth in the accident state, which is equivalent to a subsidy on abatement at wealth levels close to $\hat{y}$. Thus the cutoff level of wealth that governs the firm's switch from non-solvent to solvent is endogenously based on its choice of a. The potential for excessive care contrasts with Shavell's (1986) original result, from which we have drawn the material in this section. This is because his analysis does not consider how an income effect influences the choice of a, and therefore remaining wealth and the firm's ability to cover damages in the event of an accident. We summarize the impact of wealth in the strict liability case in the following proposition.

Proposition 10.2
Assume that strict liability holds. For different wealth levels the firm's optimal choice is as follows.

(a) For sufficiently small wealth levels $a = 0$.
(b) For an intermediate range of wealth, care is increasing in wealth but is less than the optimal level, so that $a < a^*$.
(c) For some range of wealth in the neighborhood of $\hat{y} = a^* + D$ there will be excess care relative to the social optimum, so that $a > a^*$.
(d) For sufficiently high wealth levels the private choice of care is equal to the social optimum, so that $a = a^*$.

The general proof for this proposition is tedious, and so we omit it. However, the wealth regions corresponding to each care level categories are shown in Figure 10.3. In addition, the following example illustrates the result for a specific functional form.

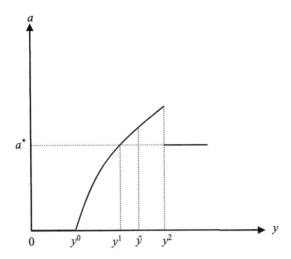

Figure 10.3 Potential for too much care when insolvency is possible

EXAMPLE 10.1 (NUMERICAL/ANALYTICAL) Let the firm be risk neutral with $\rho(a)=\min$ $\{1/a,1\}$, and assume that $y>1$. Under full solvency, the firm solves $-\rho'(a)D=1$, which in this case corresponds to $(1/a^2)D=1$ and $a_s^{sl}=a^*=D^{0.5}$. Under this specification, expected profit as defined by (10.8) reduces to $y-2D^{0.5}$. However, when bankruptcy is possible, the decision corresponds to (10.16), so that $1/a^2(y-a)=(1-1/a)$. Solving for a results in $a^{sl}(y)=y^{0.5}$ and expected profit, as defined by (10.15), reduces to $y-2y^{0.5}+1$. To determine the firm's optimal choice, we equate the expected profit levels under the solvency and non-solvency cases, and compute the level of wealth that endogenously defines the transition point between the two. In doing so, we obtain $y=D+D^{0.5}+0.25$ as the wealth level corresponding to the transition point, which is greater than $\hat{y}=a^*+D=D^{0.5}+D$. On the other hand, $a^{sl}(y)=y^{0.5}<D^{0.5}=a^*$ only if $y<D$. For this example we therefore have

- $a^{sl}(y)<a^*$ for $y<D$;
- $a^{sl}(y)>a^*$ for $D\leq y<D+D^{0.5}+0.25$; and
- $a^{sl}(y)=a^*$ for $y\geq D+D^{0.5}+0.25$.

In this example, the wealth level where the firm switches from too little to too much effort corresponds to the damage amount D. In general, however, the switching level can be larger or smaller than D.

Given that a firm may engage in too much care, one may ask whether a polluter should always be made fully liable, even if it is possible that the firm will be insolvent ex-post, or whether *partial coverage* of the resulting damage may induce a more efficient level of care. It is in fact the case that for some wealth levels, the requirement of partial coverage induces a polluter to select a more efficient care level than under the requirement of full coverage. Since excess care occurs only across a small range of wealth levels it is unlikely to be a policy-relevant issue.

10.3.2 Negligence Rule

In studying the negligence rule, we first consider the case in which the regulator sets $\bar{a}=a^*$. That is, she selects the socially optimal due care level, regardless of the firm's wealth level and potential for insolvency. After characterizing the firm's behavior in this case, we discuss the extent to which welfare might be higher with a care level that explicitly accounts for the possibility of bankruptcy.

Focusing on a risk neutral firm, it is clear that for sufficiently low wealth levels such as $y \approx a^*$, the firm will behave negligently and select spending on care according to (10.15) from the strict liability case. This is because negligent behavior provides a positive expected payoff given by

$$\left[1 - \rho\left(a^{nr}(y)\right)\right] \times \left[y - a^{nr}(y)\right] > 0 \approx y - a^*. \tag{10.20}$$

If instead the firm's wealth is large enough that $a^{sl}(y) \approx a^*$, the expected payoff under negligent behavior will be lower than under compliance with the due care level, so that

$$\left(1 - \rho\left(a^{sl}(y)\right)\right) \times \left[y - a^{sl}(y)\right] \approx \left(1 - \rho(a^*)\right) \times \left[y - a^*\right] < y - a^*. \tag{10.21}$$

Thus the firm will comply with the due care level, and there is a threshold wealth level $\breve{y}$ defining the switch from negligent to non-negligent behavior.

These comparisons show that for wealth levels $y < \breve{y}$, the amount of care from the firm is too low. However, the regulator can increase a by setting a due care level $\bar{a}(y) < a^*$ according to the incentive compatibility constraint

$$y - \bar{a}(y) = \left[1 - \rho\left(a^{sl}(y)\right)\right]\left[y - a^{sl}(y)\right]. \tag{10.22}$$

From (10.21), it is obvious that $\bar{a}(y) \geq a^{sl}(y)$ must hold in the relevant range. Thus if the polluter is sufficiently poor, a due care level lower than the efficient level leads to higher welfare than the efficient due care level. We summarize this result as follows.

Proposition 10.3
If the polluting firm's wealth is low enough that its effort under the strict liability rule will be lower than socially optimal, the negligence rule outperforms strict liability, if the regulator sets the second-best optimal due care level according to

$$\bar{a}(y) = \max\left\{a^{sl}(y), y - \left[1 - \rho\left(a^{sl}(y)\right)\right]\left[y - a^{sl}(y)\right]\right\}. \tag{10.23}$$

Figure 10.4 illustrates the behavior of a risk neutral polluter under the negligence rule with $\bar{a} = a^*$ and the second-best due care level. A drawback of this rule is that the regulator has to know the firm's wealth and individually has to adjust the due care level to the firm's wealth.

10.4   LIABILITY RULES IF INSURANCE IS AVAILABLE

If a firm's declaration of bankruptcy prevents accident victims from being compensated for the damage suffered, mandatory insurance may be a useful regulatory device in much the same way as obligatory automobile insurance is in most developed countries.

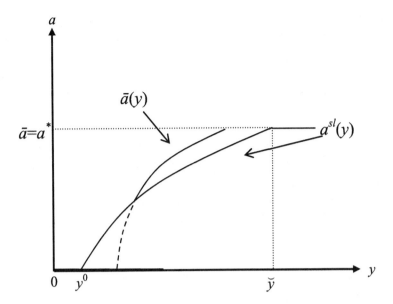

Figure 10.4   Behavior under the negligence rule and the second-best due care level

However, insurance gives rise to moral hazard, in the sense that polluters may engage in less care, since the insurance company will pay for any resulting damages. To study the insurance problem we add additional components to the model developed thus far. We denote by c the level of coverage the polluting firm purchases to cover its possible damages and use π to denote the premium it pays for one currency unit of coverage. An insurance contract is called *actuarially fair* if the premium is equal to the accident probability – i.e. $\pi = \rho$. Actuarially fair contracts will be offered if insurance companies incur no costs and operate in perfectly competitive markets. In what follows we maintain these simplifying assumptions and employ the relationship $\pi = \rho$ throughout.

10.4.1 Risk Neutrality

We begin by studying the firm's decision on how much coverage to buy under the strict liability policy, given its risk attitude. For this it is useful to first consider a simplified version of our model in which the probability of an accident is exogenous, in the sense that it cannot be influenced by care on the firm's part. The polluter's budget constraint is $\pi c \leq y$. For the case of risk neutrality, the firm's insurance decision problem can be written as

$$\max_{c} E\Pi^{sl} = (1-\rho)[y - \rho \cdot c] + \rho \cdot \max\{0, y - \rho \cdot c + c - D\} \quad s.t. \quad 0 \leq \rho c \leq y, \quad (10.24)$$

where we have substituted out for π using $\pi = \rho$. The form of the objective function follows from the fact that the firm pays the premium ρc in both the accident and no accident states, while in the case of an accident, the firm pays damages D but receives an insurance payment of c.

From (10.24) we can see that when the payoff in the accident case is non-positive (i.e. $y - \rho \cdot c + c - D \leq 0$), the firm's objective function reduces to $(1 - \rho)(y - \rho \cdot c)$, which is maximized at $c = 0$. Therefore, a necessary condition for the firm to buy any insurance is that $y - \rho \cdot c + c - D > 0$ – i.e. expected payoff is positive. If this is the case, then the objective function becomes

$$\max_c E\Pi^{sl} = (1 - \rho)[y - \rho \cdot c] + \rho \cdot (y - \rho \cdot c + c - D)$$
$$= y - \rho \cdot c + \rho(c - D) \qquad (10.25)$$
$$= y - \rho D \quad s.t. \quad 0 \leq \rho c \leq y,$$

which is not a function of c. Thus the opportunity to buy insurance does not change the risk neutral firm's behavior, or alter its expected wealth level. We summarize this result as follows.

Proposition 10.4
Under strict liability, if the polluting firm is risk neutral, it will not buy insurance if $y - D < 0$. If the firm is fully solvent it is indifferent between not buying insurance and buying any level of insurance $c \leq D$.

This result that buying insurance is not privately optimal under risk neutrality also holds if the accident probability can be affected by the level of care. If the level of care is observable and can be contracted on, the logic leading to proposition 10.4 continues to hold. If the level of care is not observable, we have a moral hazard problem, which we address in detail below.

10.4.2 Risk Aversion

Proposition 10.4 suggests that the insurance issue is irrelevant when the firm is risk neutral. Consider instead a risk averse firm owner, whose maximization problem under strict liability is

$$\max_c EU^{sl} = (1 - \rho)U(y - \rho \cdot c)$$
$$+ \rho \cdot U\left[\max\{0, y - \rho \cdot c + c - D\}\right] \quad s.t. \quad 0 \leq \rho c \leq y. \qquad (10.26)$$

Standard insurance theory shows that a risk averse agent with sufficient wealth – defined here to mean $y - D \geq 0$ – will purchase full coverage if it is available, meaning he will select $c = D$. This follows from the first-order condition for (10.26) when the firm is solvent:

$$-(1 - \rho)\rho U'(y - \rho c) + (1 - \rho)\rho U'(y - \rho c + c - D) = 0, \qquad (10.27)$$

from which we can see that $U'(y - \rho c) = U'(y - \rho c + c - D)$ and hence $c = D$. The more interesting case occurs when the polluter is insolvent in the event of an accident, so that $y - D < 0$. The main result in this case is given by the following proposition.

Proposition 10.5

If a polluting firm has risk averse owners and its wealth is such that $y - D < 0$, there exists a cutoff wealth level $\hat{y}$ with $\rho D < \hat{y} < D$ such that:

(a) $c = 0$ for $y < \hat{y}$
(b) $c = D$ for $y > \hat{y}$.

That is, the cutoff wealth level determines whether the firm fully insures or does not insure.

The proof is technical but informative, and so we include it in appendix A. However the idea is easy and it mainly works by showing that for $y = \rho D$ buying insurance does not pay, while for $y = D$ the firm is strictly better off when buying insurance. By continuity this holds also in the neighborhoods of $y = \rho D$ and $y = D$, respectively. Therefore, there must be an income level $\hat{y}$ with $\rho D < \hat{y} < D$, where the firm switches from no insurance to insurance. The following example illustrates the result.

EXAMPLE 10.2 (NUMERICAL/ANALYTICAL) We use the utility function $U(y) = y^{(1-g)}/(1-g)$ for $y > 0$ and zero otherwise, with parameters $g = 0.5$, $D = 25$, and $\rho = 0.1$. Assume that $y \leq D$. If the firm does not buy insurance, the owner receives expected utility level $(1-\rho)U(y) = (0.9/0.5)y^{0.5}$. If the firm buys insurance with full coverage, the owner receives the certain utility level $U(y - \rho D) = (y - 2.5)^{0.5}/0.5$. Setting $(1-\rho)U(y) = U(y - \rho D)$, we have $(0.9/0.5)y^{0.5} = (y - 2.5)^{0.5}/0.5$; solving for y yields $\hat{y} = 13.16$ as the point of indifference between buying and not buying insurance. From this we see that $\rho D = 2.5 < 13.16 = \hat{y} < 25 = D$.

We now return to the more general case in which the probability of an accident depends on the firm's level of care, and we distinguish two cases: when the insurance provider can observe the level of abatement effort, and when it cannot. In some instances monitoring may be easy. For example, a polluter can invest in observable equipment such as oil-tankers with a double hull. In other cases, it may be more difficult to observe care, such as when it is based on workers' efforts. In analyzing these two cases we abstract from monitoring costs and consider observable abatement as a discrete concept.

Care is Observable

We start with the case where the level of care is observable, meaning it can be the object of a contract between the polluter and the insurance company. Under the *strict liability* rule we obtain a similar result as for the case of fixed probability – i.e. there is a cutoff level of wealth that delineates the insurance buying and not-buying regimes. For the *negligence rule*, in contrast, the polluting firm will never purchase insurance. These results are formally stated as follows.

Proposition 10.6

<u>Strict liability</u>. *Let y^m be the largest income level for which the risk averse polluting firm selects $a^{sl}(y)$ so that it becomes insolvent in the case of an accident. That is, $y^m = D + a^{sl}(y^m)$. There exists a cutoff level of wealth $\hat{y}$ with $a^* + \rho(a^*)$ $D < \hat{y} < y^m = D + a^{sl}(y^m)$ such that*

(a) $c = 0$ for $y < \hat{y}$
(b) $c = D$ for $y \geq \hat{y}$.

<u>Negligence rule</u>. *If the regulator sets the due care level to the socially optimal level of abatement, the polluting firm will never purchase insurance.*

A formal proof of the proposition is included in appendix B. The intuition behind this result is as follows. If the firm's wealth is such that it can only just cover the insurance premium, its profit in both states of the world will be approximately zero when it selects the first-best care level. The firm therefore prefers a smaller care level that corresponds to positive profit in the no accident case, and zero profit (through bankruptcy) in the accident case. If instead, the firm's wealth is high enough that it can readily pay the insurance premium, it obtains positive profit in both states of the world, and therefore is better off with full coverage, which requires a care level of a^* to obtain. We demonstrate this intuition via the following example.

EXAMPLE 10.3 (NUMERICAL/ANALYTICAL) We once again use the utility function $U(y)=y^{(1-g)}/(1-g)$ with parameters $g=0.5$ and $D=25$, and again let $\rho(a)=\min\{1/a,1\}$. We assume the firm faces strict liability, and first consider the case when wealth is low enough that the firm's expected utility is $EU=[1-\rho(a)]U(y-a)=(1-1/a)(y-a)^{0.5}/0.5$. Setting up the first-order condition for a and solving yields $a^{sl}(y)=0.5((1+8y)^{0.5}-1)$, which leads to expected utility

$$EU(a^{sl}(y),y)=\left[1-\frac{1}{0.5((1+8y)^{0.5}-1)}\right]\frac{\left[y-0.5((1+8y)^{0.5}-1)\right]^{0.5}}{0.5}.$$

Recall the socially optimal care level a^* satisfies $(1/a^2)D=1$, so that $a^*=D^{0.5}=5$. When the firm buys full coverage (contracted on $a=a^*$) it receives the certain utility level

$$U\left(y-a^*-\rho(a^*)D\right)=\frac{\left(y-D^{0.5}-D^{-0.5}D\right)^{0.5}}{0.5}=\frac{\left(y-2D^{0.5}\right)^{0.5}}{0.5}.$$

To find the cutoff level wealth $\hat{y}$, we equate the expected utility without insurance to the certain utility level with insurance:

$$\left[1-\frac{1}{0.5((1+8y)^{0.5}-1)}\right]\frac{\left[y-0.5((1+8y)^{0.5}-1)\right]^{0.5}}{0.5}=\frac{\left(y-2D^{0.5}\right)^{0.5}}{0.5}.$$

Solving for y gives us the cutoff wealth level $\hat{y}=19.13$. Observe for comparison that $a^*+\rho(a^*)D=D^{0.5}+D^{0.5}=10$. Note that for $y=20$, $EU(a^{sl}(20),20)=6.24$, and $U(20-a^*-\rho(a^*)D)=6.32$, so that full insurance provides higher utility for this wealth level. In contrast, when $y=18$, we have $EU(a^{sl}(18),18)=5.79$ and $U(18-a^*-\rho(a^*)D)=5.66$, so that the firm is better off not buying insurance.

Under the negligence rule, the firm will compare the utility of its profit under compliance with the due care level to the utility of profit from behaving negligently. If the firm's wealth is sufficiently low, such that $U(y-a^*-\rho(a^*)D)<(1-\rho(a^{sl}(y)))U(y-a^{sl}(y))$, it will clearly be better off when it behaves negligently, in which case the firm cannot contract for insurance and so will not purchase it. If, by contrast, it is optimal for the firm to comply with the due care level, it will never be liable for any damage, and therefore will again not purchase it.

Unobservable Care

We now consider the more realistic and interesting case where the level of care is not observable by the insurance company. As for the case of observable effort, the polluting firm does not buy insurance if its wealth level is sufficiently low, and it wants to buy insurance if y is sufficiently large. More specifically, if the risk premium is actuarially fair – i.e. $\pi = \rho(a)$ – and y is sufficiently large, the polluter would *wish* to buy full coverage. But with full coverage, the firm would have no incentive to spend on abatement, and would choose $a = 0$. This is the typical moral hazard problem. Anticipating this, the insurance company offers only *incomplete* coverage in equilibrium. In what follows, we develop this notion more formally.

We again use π to denote the insurance premium per currency unit of coverage, and note that it cannot be made explicitly contingent on the level of a selected. Under strict liability, the firm owner's expected utility is

$$EU^{sl} = (1 - \rho(a))U(y - a - \pi c) + \rho(a)U\left(\max\{0, y - a - \pi c + c - D\}\right), \qquad (10.28)$$

where $c \leq D$ is the level of coverage that is exogenously on offer. Once again, if $y - a - \pi c + c - D$ is negative for any c, the firm does not buy insurance.

If the polluting firm is sufficiently wealthy, partial coverage is possible in equilibrium. We assume an insurance company offers coverage c at some premium π per unit of coverage. In this case the firm will select its care level a conditional on c, π, and its wealth to maximize

$$EU^{sl} = (1 - \rho(a))U(y - a - \pi c) + \rho(a)U(y - a - \pi c + c - D). \qquad (10.29)$$

Differentiating this expression with respect to a yields

$$\begin{aligned} -\rho'(a)[U(y - a - \pi c) - U(y - a - \pi c + c - D)] \\ - (1 - \rho(a))U'(y - a - \pi c) - \rho(a)U'(y - a - \pi c + c - D) = 0. \end{aligned} \qquad (10.30)$$

Our assumption of perfect competition in the insurance market implies zero profits for the insurance provider. An equilibrium insurance contract must therefore result in $\pi = \rho(a)$ for the agreed partial coverage amount, where a is now the equilibrium care level arising from the specific contract. Thus while the premium cannot be explicitly written to reflect the (unobservable) abatement level, the process by which the insurance company and polluting firm agree to a mutually satisfactory level of partial coverage pushes the equilibrium premium to the point where $\pi = \rho(a)$.

To see how the level of care changes with the level of coverage offered, we apply the implicit function theorem to (10.30) and obtain[2]

$$\begin{aligned} \frac{\partial a}{\partial c} &= \frac{-\rho'(a)\left[\pi U''(y - a - \pi c) + (1 - \pi)U''\left(y - a + (1 - \pi)c - D\right)\right]}{-EU_{aa}} \\ &+ \frac{(1 - \rho(a))\rho(a)\left[U'(y - a - \pi c) - U'\left(y - a + (1 - \pi)c - D\right)\right]}{-EU_{aa}} < 0. \end{aligned} \qquad (10.31)$$

---

[2] Note that this is the partial effect, where the insurance premium remains constant.

If we assume that the second-order condition of the maximization problem is satisfied, the denominator of each term is positive. Note that the numerator of the first term is negative since $U'' < 0$. The second term is also negative since $y - a - \pi c > y - a - \pi c + c - D$ (coverage is incomplete), and the marginal utility of wealth is decreasing in wealth. Thus, as one would expect, polluters become less careful as insurance increases.

We next examine the impact of a change in partial insurance coverage on the firm owner's expected utility. Differentiating (10.29) with respect to c and substituting $\rho(a) = \pi$ we obtain

$$
\begin{aligned}
\frac{\partial EU}{\partial c} &= \pi U'\left(y - a + (1 - \pi)c - D\right) \cdot \left[(1 - \pi) - c\frac{d\pi}{dc}\right] \\
&\quad - (1 - \pi)U'(y - a - \pi c) \cdot \left[\pi + c\frac{d\pi}{dc}\right],
\end{aligned}
\tag{10.32}
$$

where

$$
\frac{d\pi}{dc} = \rho'(a)\frac{\partial a}{\partial c} > 0.
\tag{10.33}
$$

Looking specifically at $c = 0$ and $c = D$ cases we note that

$$
\frac{\partial EU(c = 0)}{\partial c} = \pi(1 - \pi)\left[U'(y - a - D) - U'(y - a)\right] > 0
\tag{10.34}
$$

and

$$
\frac{\partial EU(c = D)}{\partial c} = -U'(y - a - \pi D) \times D \times \frac{d\pi}{dc} < 0.
\tag{10.35}
$$

Therefore, by the intermediate value theorem, there exists a level of insurance $0 < c < D$ where $\partial EU/\partial c = 0$.

Since perfect competition on the insurance market leads to the best offer for the insured parties, equations (10.30) and (10.31), and the conditions $\partial EU/\partial c = 0$ and $\rho(a) = \pi$, determine the equilibrium contract on the insurance market. Note that the contract is contingent on the level of wealth. This means that for different wealth levels, different insurance contracts will be offered. Thus we make the implicit assumption that wealth can be observed. If wealth can be hidden, matters are more complicated and beyond the scope of this chapter.

Penalties to Enhance Care

Recall that a firm facing bankruptcy in case of an accident would not buy any insurance. Thus insurance is relevant only for the wealthy polluter. However, due to the moral hazard problem the level of care taken by the insured party is less than optimal. Can the regulator take measures to correct this sub-optimal outcome? Suppose she charges a fee F in addition to the damage amount in the event of an accident, so that the expected utility function in (10.29) becomes

$$EU = (1 - \rho(a))U(y - a - \pi c) + \rho(a)U(y - a - \pi c + c - D - F). \tag{10.36}$$

The equilibrium is still given by equations (10.30) and (10.31), and the conditions $\partial EU/\partial c = 0$ and $\rho(a) = \pi$, except that $D + F$ is substituted for D. The analysis of comparative static effect on increasing the penalty F on the endogenous variables a, c, and π is quite tedious, however, and in general the effects cannot be uniquely signed. While the partial effect of increasing the penalty on the level of care is positive, the polluter at the same time demands a higher level of insurance, which in turn lowers the level of care and increases the insurance premium. The normal case, however, is that the resulting total equilibrium effect of increasing the penalty fee on the level of care is positive. Given this, the regulator can in fact induce the efficient level of care by charging a sufficiently high punitive fee, in case of an accident.

10.4.3 Compulsory Insurance

We have seen that firms with sufficiently low wealth do not want to buy insurance. By contrast, wealthy firms want to purchase full insurance, but are not able to due to the moral hazard problem. In this subsection we examine the possibility of compulsory insurance, focusing on a risk neutral firm for simplicity. We consider the cases of full insurance and insurance with a deductible in turn.

Full Compulsory Insurance

If the polluting firm must fully insure all damage, the coverage level is $c = D$. Continuing with the case in which the insurance company cannot observe the care level, the firm's objective function is

$$E\Pi(a) = y - a - \pi D, \tag{10.37}$$

where π is the insurance premium. Since insurance eliminates all risk, the expected profit is a sure value. In addition, with an insurance premium that is independent of care, the firm would choose $a = 0$. Anticipating this, the insurance company sets its premium as $\pi = \rho(0)$. Compulsory insurance therefore leads to an inefficient outcome. In the absence of further care standards, the level of care is too low, and the insurance premium is accordingly too high.

Compulsory Insurance with Deductible

We now assume that the regulator allows for partial insurance $c < D$ and a deductible to be paid by the firm in the event of an accident. This means that, in the case of an accident, damaged parties will receive only partial compensation. We model this by assuming the insurance company offers a contract to the potential polluter that stipulates payments s_A and s_N in the case of an accident (A) and no accident (N), respectively. The payment s_N is the insurance premium $c\pi$ for coverage level c, while s_A is the insurance premium plus the deductible. The expected payoff to the firm is

$$E\Pi = y - a - \rho(a)s_A - (1 - \rho(a))s_N,$$ (10.38)

and taking s_A and s_N as given, the first-order condition for profit maximization is

$$1 = -\rho'(a)(s_A - s_N).$$ (10.39)

This equation is important for the remainder of this subsection. We see that the greater the difference in payments made by the polluting firm in the bad and good states of the world, the larger the level of abatement effort.

We continue by examining the insurance company's profit, which is given by

$$\Pi^{Ins} = \rho(a)(s_A - c) + (1 - \rho(a))s_N = 0,$$ (10.40)

where the zero profit condition comes from our assumption that the insurance sector is competitive. Note that in the accident state of the world, the insurance company pays out the coverage amount c to the injured party. From this we can solve for the premium to be paid in the no-accident state as

$$s_N = \frac{\rho(a)}{1 - \rho(a)}(c - s_A),$$ (10.41)

where a is determined by (10.39). Note from above that the polluting firm's payment in the accident case can be no larger than $y - a$, so that $s_A \leq y - a$. Competition on the insurance market forces insurance companies to offer a low insurance premium, but the premium can only be low if the firm's care level is high. To induce the highest possible care level from the condition in (10.39), the difference between s_A and s_N must be maximized, and so $s_A = y - a$. With this, (10.41) becomes

$$s_N = \frac{\rho(a)}{1 - \rho(a)}(c - (y + a)).$$ (10.42)

In other words, the insurance company covers the difference between the partial compensation c and the firm's remaining wealth $y - a$. Anticipating that the polluting firm will choose the care level a according to (10.39), the insurance company implicitly chooses the care level a as well as the payments s_A and s_N that simultaneously solve $s_A = y - a$ and conditions (10.39) and (10.42).

It is important to note that the higher the compensation required by the regulator, the higher the payment s_N (representing the insurance premium) the insurance company has to charge the firm in the no-accident case, and therefore the lower the difference between s_A and s_N and the lower the care level chosen by the firm. This reasoning suggests that a regulation requiring full insurance of all remaining damages in case of a firm's non-solvency may not be optimal, due to the low incentives for care it provides.

Regulator's Optimal Choice of Compensation

We close this subsection by asking what compensation to the injured party the regulator *should* require, if the damage exceeds the firm owner's wealth – i.e. if $D > y - a^*$. The answer is that a compensation level c should be chosen so that it exactly expropriates all the polluter's wealth in case of an accident. To see this, let $a^*(c)$ be the efficient care level when compensation c has to be paid, so that $a^*(c)$ satisfies $-\rho'(a^*(c)) \times c = 1$. Then the regulator should choose $c = \hat{c}$ that solves

$$c = y - a^*(c). \tag{10.43}$$

We can then summarize our main result as follows.

Proposition 10.7

If $D > y - a^*$, the welfare maximizing compensation to the injured party is given by $\hat{c}$, determined by (10.43), which expropriates all the polluter's wealth.

The proof is given in appendix C. The idea is as follows. One shows that if $c < \hat{c}$, increasing c induces more care. Since for any coverage level $\hat{c} < D$ care is still less than socially optimal, $c < \hat{c}$ cannot be second-best optimal. Similarly, one shows that for $c > \hat{c}$, reducing c induces more care. The proof is a bit complicated since the response by the insurance company to an increase in compensation can have several solutions, and therefore the implicit function theorem cannot be applied. Note that substituting (10.43) into (10.42) gives us $s_N = 0$. Thus the insurance premium is zero, since no additional compensation beyond the co-payment has to be insured. In other words, if there is an accident, the polluting firm pays its remaining wealth $y - a^*(c)$, and the damaged party receives nothing more, since additional insurance would induce a lower level of care.

Proposition 10.7 is important. The result tells us that requiring too much compensation will be counterproductive from an efficiency viewpoint. Recall, however, that if $\hat{c} < D$, and the regulator sets $c = \hat{c}$, victims get insufficiently compensated. Fairness considerations may induce regulators to demand a higher compensation at the expense of less care, and thus at the expense of a higher frequency of accidents. So, as often is the case, there is a trade-off between efficiency and fairness.

10.4.4 Lender Liability

In many cases, firm owners do not possess sufficient wealth to independently finance a project, which likely means that wealth is also insufficient to cover damages from an environmental accident. The policy temptation in this context is to assign liability for damages to the lender. This problem was first studied by Pitchford (1995). Since it is analytically similar to the compulsory insurance case we provide only a brief sketch of the lender liability model in this subsection.

The basic idea is that a project requires an investment of size $I > 0$, and the firm's existing assets k are such that $k < I$. The project can only take place if there is a loan of size $L = I - k$. For simplicity we assume the interest rate is normalized to zero, which allows us to stay within a static framework. We ask whether the lender should be made liable for any damage compensation shortfall in the event when $y = v + k < a + D$.

Suppose that, in the case of an accident, the lender must pay some amount $c \leq D$ in compensation. For the lender's expected profit to be non-negative, he needs to offer contract terms that on average recover the expected compensation payments from the firm owner. Seen in this light, the relationship between the lender and firm is identical to the relationship between the insurance company and firm examined in the previous subsection. The lender will offer a contract to the owner that, in addition to providing the loan, stipulates payments s_A and s_N in the case of an accident (A) and no accident (N). The firm's expected payoff and first-order condition are therefore the same as in (10.38) and (10.39), respectively. The lender's profit function, with the outgoing and incoming loan amounts cancelled out, is likewise given by (10.40). Given perfect competition in the lending market the profit level will be zero, and the same results arise as in the compulsory insurance case with deductible. Thus from an efficiency viewpoint the regulator should not require compensation exceeding the firm's wealth, when using lender liability. In this case the insurance premium is zero, and the care level is as large as possible given the firm owner's wealth.

This equivalence of outcomes begs the question of whether we need lender liability in the first place. The answer may be yes if a firm owner is better able to conceal wealth from a regulator or insurance company than from a lending agency, given the need to secure a loan from the latter. For this reason, lender liability with partial compensation may be a useful regulatory device. A disadvantage of partial compensation is that it must be set ex ante and individually fixed according to the firm owner's wealth. This may cause relatively high transaction costs. In his original article, Pitchford (1995) shows that, under certain conditions a minimum equity requirement is an instrument that works equally well as partial lender liability.

10.5   ALTERNATIVE CAUSALITY

In this section we return to our simplifying assumption that polluters are sufficiently wealthy to cover all damages, and consider situations where several firms may be responsible for an accident, but it is not possible to identify the specific one. For example, an oil spill observed in a coastal area may have come from a number of different nearby ships. We refer to this situation as alternative causality. In this section we extend our model to accommodate multiple potential polluters, and examine the performance of liability regimes under different information contexts.

10.5.1 Model Extension

We assume there are J potential polluters, each of whom spends a_j on accident prevention. The probability that firm j is responsible for an accident is $\rho_j(a_j)$, and for simplicity we assume that the J accident probabilities are independent. If $\rho_j(a_j)$ and $\rho_k(a_k)$ for any k and j are relatively small, so that their products almost vanish, the probability that an accident does not occur can be approximated by

$$\prod_{j=1}^{J} \left(1 - \rho_j(a_j)\right) \approx 1 - \sum_{j=1}^{J} \rho_j(a_j) \equiv 1 - \mathrm{P}, \tag{10.44}$$

where we use P to denote the approximate probability that an accident occurs. Using this approximation, the total expected social cost from abatement and accident damage is

$$SC = \left[\sum\nolimits_{j=1}^{J} \rho_j(a_j)\right] D + \sum\nolimits_{j=1}^{J} a_j, \tag{10.45}$$

and the first-best care levels are determined by $-\rho'_j(a_j) \times D = 1$ for all j. Thus for each polluter the marginal cost of care (equal to one) should be equal to the marginal expected damage from each polluter. In the following subsections we investigate different strategies for decentralizing the social optimum.

10.5.2 Proportional Liability

To begin we consider a rule in which, in the event of an accident, firms must pay a share of the damage according to the conditional probability that the firm has caused the accident. We refer to this as the *proportional liability* rule, and examine its performance under situations of observable and unobservable care levels.

Care is Observable

To determine a firm's liability share we define the *conditional probability* that the firm is responsible for an accident that has occurred by

$$\xi_j(a_1,...,a_J) \approx \frac{\rho_j(a_j)}{\sum\nolimits_{j=1}^{J} \rho_j(a_j)} = \frac{\rho_j(a_j)}{P}. \tag{10.46}$$

According to the proportional liability rule, in the case of an accident, firm j must pay a fraction of damages according to $\xi_j \times D$, and so the firm's total expected cost is based on its liability level, the probability an accident occurs, and its spending on abatement:

$$\begin{aligned} TC_j &= \left(\xi_j(a_1,...,a_J) \cdot D\right) \times P + a_j \\ &= \left(\frac{\rho_j(a_j)D}{P}\right) \times P + a_j \\ &= \rho_j(a_j)D + a_j. \end{aligned} \tag{10.47}$$

Note that the first-order condition for cost minimization is $-\rho'_j(a_j) \times D = 1$ for all j, which matches the social optimum. We summarize this result in the following proposition.

Proposition 10.8

If care levels are observable, under alternative causality the proportional liability rule leads to the first-best level of care for all J polluters.

Care is Unobservable

A problem with the proportional liability rule occurs when care is unobservable, since the regulator needs to use estimates of the accident probabilities to assign liability. In particular, we use $\overline{\xi}_j$ to denote the regulator's ex ante estimate of the probability that firm j's actions cause some future accident. In this case the firm's total expected cost function is

$$TC_j = \overline{\xi}_j D \times \left(\sum\nolimits_{j=1}^{J} \rho_j(a_j)\right) + a_j. \tag{10.48}$$

That is, firm j's expected cost is the product of its (deterministic) share of the liability and the probability that an accident occurs, plus its abatement expenditure. The first-order condition that minimizes expected cost is $-\overline{\xi}_j \rho'_j(a_j) \times D = 1$, which leads to a lower level of care than is socially optimal. We summarize this result as follows.

Proposition 10.9
If care levels are not observable and the regulator applies the proportional liability rule according to a priori given proportions $\overline{\xi}_1,...,\overline{\xi}_J$, each firm's abatement level is less than socially optimal.

Note that since in this case the cost of care is less than socially optimal, under conditions of free entry, more than the optimal number of firms will enter the market. This in turn increases the total probability that an accident occurs.

10.5.3 Collective Liability

The moral hazard problem that arises when care is unobservable is similar to what we encountered in the non-point source pollution context discussed in Chapter 9. In that case we saw that a solution was to have each firm pay the full cost of damages from ambient pollution. The analogy here is to make each firm liable for the entire damage amount. To see that this is efficient, note that firm j's total expected cost under full liability is

$$TC_j = \left(\sum\nolimits_{j=1}^{J} \rho_j(a_j)\right) \times D + a_j, \tag{10.49}$$

and the first-order condition for cost minimization is $-\rho'_j(a_j) \times D = 1$. As was the case for non-point source pollution, assigning responsibility for full expected damage to each firm breaks the moral hazard and leads to a first-best allocation of abatement effort. The same limitations also apply, in that fundamental legal principles are likely to preclude assigning liability to $J-1$ non-responsible parties. Moreover, large damages may cause multiple firms to become bankrupt, and the high potential liability costs are likely to deter entry into the industry. These facts suggest collective liability is unlikely to be a practical alternative for managing environmental accident risks.

10.5.4 Costly Monitoring

We have seen that a proportional liability approach can work when abatement effort is observable, but it leads to under-commitment of effort when care is unobservable. An alternative approach to addressing this moral hazard problem is costly monitoring. In this case firms agree to be monitored at an additional cost of $m_j(a_j)$, which reveals the form of $\rho_j(a_j)$ to the regulator. If firms bear the monitoring costs and all firms agree to be monitored, we can rewrite (10.47) as

$$
\begin{aligned}
TC_j &= \left(\xi_j(a_1,...,a_J)\cdot D\right)\times \mathrm{P} + a_j + m_j(a_j) \\
&= \left(\frac{\rho_j(a_j)D}{\mathrm{P}}\right)\times \mathrm{P} + a_j + m_j(a_j) \\
&= \rho_j(a_j)D + a_j + m_j(a_j).
\end{aligned}
\tag{10.50}
$$

This leads to first-order conditions

$$
-\rho_j'(a_j)D = 1 + m_j'(a_j),
\tag{10.51}
$$

which is a second-best optimum in the sense that firms (and thus society) must pay the monitoring costs to avoid the moral hazard problem and still choose sub-optimal care levels. Nevertheless, this second-best allocation may be superior to a legal system with collective liability, or proportional liability with a priori accident probabilities resulting in low care levels.

10.6   MULTI-CAUSALITY

In this section we once again consider a multiple firm framework, but assume that the damage may be caused by several firms, so that the accident probability is jointly determined by all firms' abatement choices – i.e. we have $\rho=\rho(a_1,...,a_J)$. For example, this may be the case when several chemical firms simultaneously pollute a river, creating a risk that the entire ecosystem collapses. Under such a scenario the expected social cost takes the form

$$
SC(a_1,...,a_J) = \rho(a_1,...,a_J)D - \sum_{j=1}^{J} a_j,
\tag{10.52}
$$

and the first-best allocation of abatement effort is determined by the condition

$$
-\frac{\partial \rho(a_1,...,a_J)}{\partial a_j}\times D = 1, \quad \forall j.
\tag{10.53}
$$

One approach for assigning liability in the multi-causality case is to implement a proportional liability rule where each polluter contributes a fixed share β_j to the total damage. A firm's objective function in this case is then

$$
TC_j = \rho(a_1,...,a_J)\beta_j D - a_j,
\tag{10.54}
$$

and the firm's first-order condition is

$$-\frac{\partial\rho(a_1,...,a_j)}{\partial a_j}\beta_j D = 1. \tag{10.55}$$

By inspection, we see that the care level is too low whenever $\beta_j < 1$. As was the case for alternative causality without monitoring, each firm should pay the full expected damage in order to incentivize the efficient care level.

10.7   EXAMPLES OF ENVIRONMENTAL LIABILITY LAWS

In this section we discuss two major environmental liability rules, in the United States and Europe. In the US, the 1980 Comprehensive Environmental Response, Compensation, and Liability Act (CERCLA) provides an example of a strict liability regime, while in the European Union, the European Liability Directive is a combination of strict liability and negligence rule approaches.

EXAMPLE 10.4 (POLICY) CERCLA is one of the first major nation-wide statutes assigning liability for environmental damage. It was enacted as a response to threats from hazardous waste sites in the 1970s, which entered the public consciousness via several highly publicized events. The most notorious was the Love Canal spill in Niagara Falls, New York, where toxic chemicals dumped decades earlier percolated up near a school and residential areas. The main policy lever in CERCLA is a wide-ranging strict liability rule. When a contaminated site is identified and placed on the National Priority List, potentially responsible parties (PRPs) are identified as candidates for liability. This can include current or past owners of the property, as well as entities that were responsible for transporting and depositing hazardous substances at the site. Liability is joint and several, meaning any party found to bear some of the responsibility can be held fully liable for damages. In this regard, CERCLA has some resemblance to the multi-causality regime described above. In addition, an important feature of the law is that liability can be assigned retroactively, for actions that took place long before the existence of the legislation.

Once liability has been assigned, the responsible parties are required to compensate victims and/or pay for cleaning up the contaminated site. Clean-up can take one of two forms: removal actions and remedial actions. The former is a short run response designed to remove acute exposure risks via prompt action. The latter is a long run, more costly, and often contentious response that is designed to restore the site and prevent the migration of pollutants to other areas. In cases where a responsible party cannot be identified, or the responsible party is insolvent, site remediation is paid from a trust fund known as "Superfund", which was originally supported via taxes on the petroleum industry. In recent years, the Superfund has instead been supported from general revenues, and limits on its endowment have caused delay in cleaning up many sites on the National Priority List. As a result, there is some evidence that the EPA has explicitly sought to identify PRPs with sufficient wealth to finance remediation. In addition, the wide definition of a PRP has had some unintended consequences. For example, investors have in some cases been unwilling to redevelop urban "brownfields" – small-scale contaminated sites with potentially large value in alternative land uses – due to the threat of liability for wider clean-up. Additional details on CERCLA and related regulations can be found in Jenkins et al. (2009).

EXAMPLE 10.5 (POLICY) In 2004, the European Commission launched the Environmental Liability Directive (2004/35/EC) as a general framework for dealing with environmental accidents. This was followed in 2008 by the Environmental Liability Regulation (Statutory Instrument No. 547 of 2008). The fundamental objective of the Directive/Regulation is to prevent and remedy environmental damage, and to provide incentives for operators, who engage in environmentally hazardous activities, to proactively assess their environmental risks and manage them to prevent environmental damage. Environmental damage in this context is divided into three categories: (a) damage to natural habitats and protected species; (b) water damage; and (c) land damage. Airborne emissions can also be subject to environmental liability, if they impact these three categories. Article 1 of the Directive states that environmental liability is based on the "polluter-pays" principle. The regulatory instruments are a combination of strict liability and a negligence rule. In particular, strict liability applies to a set of explicitly listed activities (Annex III of the Directive/Schedule 3 of the Regulation), while a negligence rule applies to all other activities not listed.

The regulations also define remedial measures in cases where damage has occurred. The Directive/Regulation distinguishes three layers of remediation: (a) *primary* remediation, which involves restoring a damaged area and transforming it back into its original state; (b) *complementary* remediation, referring to complementary compensation if complete restoration is not possible or prohibitively expensive; and (c) *compensatory* remediation, meaning that affected parties are compensated for interim losses if the full restoration takes time. Article 9 of the Directive also accounts for multiple-party causation, but relegates rules of apportionment among the parties to member states' national laws. Ireland, for example, explicitly allows for the possibility that each polluter pays the full damage, which is similar to CERCLA and matches a necessary condition for first-best incentives.[3] Unlike CERCLA, neither the Directive nor the Regulation include provision for remediation when the responsible party is insolvent.

There are other similarities and differences between the US and European laws. CERCLA is mainly retrospective, with most applications of the law focused on remediation of long-ago contaminated sites. The Liability Directive/Regulation, by contrast, has a larger focus on proactive incentives for avoiding contamination. There are also subtle differences regarding the role of damage compensation and site restoration between the two laws. With CERCLA, restoration is an option when it is less expensive than compensation, though in practice restoration has been the usual path. With the European

---

[3] See EPA (Ireland) (2011).

rules, the aim is restoration, while compensation is an option when compensation is not possible or is prohibitively expensive.

10.8   SUMMARY

In this chapter we have departed from our usual interpretation of pollution as emissions based, and have instead focused on managing the risk of environmental accidents. In this context a firm's actions generate some probability that an accident will occur, which results in damage to the environment. The firm can, however, engage in a costly accident prevention effort that reduces the probability that an accident will occur. The trade-off between these costs and expected damage – defined as the product of damages and the probability that an accident occurs – gives rise to a socially optimal level of accident prevention care. Our objective in this chapter has been to examine how different regulatory regimes, based on the assignment of liability for damages, succeed in decentralizing the socially optimal care level.

We saw that the most important liability rules include *strict liability* and the *negligence rule*. In the former the firm must pay compensation equal to the amount of damage it causes, while in the latter compensation is paid only if the firm has engaged in a level of prevention effort that is lower than a given due care standard. Our analysis demonstrated that performance of the two rules depends critically on (a) the extent to which the polluting firm remains solvent in the event of an accident; (b) their risk attitudes, and (c) the extent to which care levels are observable. In particular, when the polluting firm is solvent and risk neutral, the strict liability rule is an ideal instrument for inducing the efficient level of care, in that care does not need to be observed and potential damage amount does not need to be known ex ante. While the negligence rule can also be used to induce the first-best care level, the information requirements for the regulator are higher, and care must be observable.

Things are more complicated when a polluting firm may become bankrupt in the event of an accident. Under strict liability the level of care increases with a firm's wealth and may exceed the efficient level over some ranges. For lower wealth levels, however, the firm's private spending on accident prevention will be smaller than the socially optimal amount. We saw that in these cases the negligence rule can be used to induce a second-best level of care that is higher than under strict liability, though still smaller than the first best.

The potential for *bankruptcy* motivated our discussion of *voluntary* or *compulsory insurance* as an accident risk management tool. We saw that risk attitude was an important driver of the extent to which firms will voluntarily purchase insurance. In particular, risk neutral firms will not want to purchase voluntary insurance under either liability regime, while risk averse firms will want to purchase full insurance under strict liability only if their wealth is high enough, and never under a negligence rule. The extent to which a firm will be able to purchase insurance depends on whether or not accident prevention effort is observable. If so an insurance contract can be written conditional on prevention effort, and full coverage will be available. If prevention effort is not observable a *moral hazard problem* exists in that firms will want to purchase full insurance and engage in no environmental care. In this case only partial coverage will be available in equilibrium in the insurance market.

The limitations of voluntary insurance motivated our consideration of compulsory insurance. Here we saw that when care cannot be observed, the requirement of full insurance leads to an inefficiently high premium rate, based on the insurance company's assumption that the firm engages in zero care, and a realized care level of zero, based on the moral hazard problem. Thus compulsory insurance can only be welfare enhancing when it is combined with a deductible and partial coverage. In this case it is optimal for the regulator to set a compensation level smaller than damages, which leads to a second-best optimal care level and the expropriation of all of the polluter's residual wealth in the event of an accident. Thus the liability amount is smaller than the level of damages, which is necessary to achieve the desired level of prevention effort.

We ended the chapter by briefly considering two multiple firm contexts. Under *alternative causality* one of several firms is responsible for the accident, but it cannot be known which one. Under *multi-causality*, several firms jointly affect the probability that an accident will occur. The regulatory solution in both cases is to rely on some form of proportional liability, though we saw that in some situations – particularly when prevention effort is not observable – efficiency requires that each of the polluting firms be made fully liable for the environmental damages. In this regard the problem of multiple firms is similar to the non-point source pollution problem that we examined in Chapter 9.

10.9 FURTHER READING

Posner (1972) offers one of the first general analyses of the economics of law, while Shavell (1987) provides a comprehensive framework for studying the economics of accidents, liability, and compensation. Several themes from that book were published earlier in a series of separate journal articles. Most importantly, Shavell (1980) formalizes the strict liability and negligence rules that have been the focus of this chapter. Since then, Shavell's framework has been extensively applied to issues of environmental accidents and damages. Examples include Endress and Rundshagen (2013), Friehe and Endress (2011), Heyes (1996), Hutchinson and van't Veld (2005), van't Veld (2006), and van't Veld and Hutchinson (2009).

Shavell (1986) analyses liability rules when firms can become bankrupt following an accident. Other authors, notably Schwartz (1985), Beard (1990), Kornhauser and Revesz (1990), and Polinsky and Shavell (1991), have further studied imperfect internalization of external damages caused by insolvency. Beard (1990) accounts for the wealth effect of care costs (an approach we also adopt throughout this chapter), and shows that under strict liability, a risk neutral injurer may select too much or too little care, relative to a social planner's choice.

Another seminal contribution is Pitchford (1995), who asks whether lenders should be made fully or partially liable for potentially occurring damage. Balkenborg (2001) studies the Pitchford model for the case when the lender has bargaining power, and comes to quite different results than Pitchford. The role of insurance in accident liability was first addressed in Shavell (1982) (see also Jost, 1996), although in this chapter we adapted Pitchford's model to analyze the incentive structure of environmental insurance contracts. For further contributions on liability rules in the presence of financial and insurance markets see Boyer and Laffont (1997), and Fees and Hege (2000, 2002). For a comprehensive survey of economic analysis of law in general, see the excellent article by Kaplow and Shavell (2002).

APPENDIX A: PROOF OF PROPOSITION 10.5

From (10.27) we know that if $y - D > 0$ (i.e. the firm is fully solvent), we have $y - \rho c + c - D > 0$ and $c = D$ at the optimum. If $y - \rho D < 0$, the expression $y - \rho c + c - D < 0$ holds for $c = D$, and so the agent's expected utility is $(1 - \rho)U(y - \rho c)$ and his optimal choice is $c = 0$. For $\rho D < y < D$ we must compare the expected utility when $c = 0$ and $c = D$. The polluting firm will not buy insurance if $(1 - \rho)U(y) > U(y - \rho D)$, which is the case for $y = \rho D$. If $y = D$ we have

$$(1 - \rho)U(y) = (1 - \rho)U(D) < U\big[(1 - \rho)D\big] = U(y - \rho D), \tag{A10.1}$$

where the inequality follows from the concavity of $U(\cdot)$. If $y + \varepsilon = D$ for small $\varepsilon > 0$, it follows that $(1 - \rho)U(y) < U(y - \rho D)$ still holds. By continuity of the utility function, there exists a cutoff level $\hat{y}$ so that $(1 - \rho)U(y) > U(y - \rho D)$ holds for $y < \hat{y}$ and $(1 - \rho)U(y) < U(y - \rho D)$ holds for $y > \hat{y}$.

APPENDIX B: PROOF OF PROPOSITION 10.6

Under the strict liability rule the polluter's objective function is

$$
\begin{aligned}
EU^{sl}(a, c; y) = \\
\big(1 - \rho(a)\big)U\big(y - a - \rho(a)c\big) + \rho(a)U\big(\max\{0, y - a - \rho(a)c + c - D\}\big).
\end{aligned}
\tag{A10.2}
$$

It is clear from the objective function that if the polluter selects $c > 0$ such that $y - a + (1 - \rho(a))c - D > 0$, he will buy full coverage for any level of abatement. This is so because once a is determined, the situation is the same as when the accident probability is exogenous. With full insurance, the objective function reduces to

$$EU^{sl}(a, c = D; y) = U\big(y - a - \rho(a)D\big), \tag{A10.3}$$

which is a deterministic value. The expression $\rho(a)$ is the known risk premium conditional on the contracted-on and observable level of a. Anticipating full coverage, the polluter's first-order condition for the choice of a is simply given by $-\rho'(a) = 1$, which leads to the socially optimal level of abatement.

Next we investigate when it will pay for the polluter to buy insurance. For this we again have to compare the expected utility with and without insurance. If the polluter does not buy insurance, his problem reduces to the strict liability case when insolvency is possible. As shown above, when $y \leq a^* + \rho(a^*)D$ the solution is given by $a^{sl}(y)$, which implies:

$$\big[1 - \rho\big(a^{sl}(y)\big)\big]U\big(y - a^{sl}(y)\big) > \big(1 - \rho(a^*)\big)U(y - a^*). \tag{A10.4}$$

By continuity, the above inequality also holds for y greater than but sufficiently close to $a^* + \rho(a^*)D$. Therefore, the polluter will not buy insurance for values of y that are smaller than, or even larger but sufficiently close to, $a^* + \rho(a^*)D$.

Now consider the case where $y = y^m = D + a^{sl}(y^m)$. Here we have

$$
\begin{aligned}
\left[1 - \rho\left(a^{sl}(y^m)\right)\right] &U\left(y^m - a^{sl}(y^m)\right) = \left[1 - \rho\left(a^{sl}(y^m)\right)\right]U(D) \\
&< U\left(\left[1 - \rho\left(a^{sl}(y^m)\right)\right]D\right) \\
&= U\left(y^m - a^{sl}(y^m) - \rho\left(a^{sl}(y^m)\right)D\right) \\
&< U\left(y^m - a^* - \rho(a^*)D\right),
\end{aligned}
\tag{A10.5}
$$

where the first equality follows from the definition of y^m. The first inequality follows from the concavity of $U(\cdot)$. The second equality again is due to the definition of y^m. The final inequality follows from the fact that $U\left(y^m - a^{sl}(y^m) - \rho\left(a^{sl}(y^m)\right)D\right)$ is the utility to the risk averse firm, when it chooses the effort level $a^{sl}(y^m)$, and also buys full insurance. However, with full insurance, $a^{sl}(y^m)$ is not optimal. Rather, a^* is the utility maximizing effort level. Therefore, insurance (with full coverage) is optimal for $y = y^m$. By continuity, the argument holds for y smaller than, but close to, y^m. Therefore, there must be a cutoff level of wealth $\hat{y}$ with $\rho(a^*)D < \hat{y} < y^m = D + a^{sl}(y^m)$, where behavior switches.

Next consider the *negligence rule*. We claim that in this case the polluter never buys insurance. To see this, observe first that for $a \geq a^*$, there is no need to buy insurance, because the polluter meets the due care level. Buying insurance therefore only makes sense for $a < a^*$. To benefit from insurance, $y - a - \rho(a))c + c - D \geq 0$ must hold. Since

$$
-\rho(a)c + c - D = (1 - \rho(a))(c - D) - \rho(a)D \leq -\rho(a)D \leq -\rho(a)c,
\tag{A10.6}
$$

we obtain by concavity of the utility function the following inequality chain:

$$
\begin{aligned}
(1 - \rho(a))U(y - a - \rho(a)c) &+ \rho(a)U(y - a - \rho(a)c + c - D) \\
&\leq U(y - a - \rho(a)D) \leq U(y - a^* - \rho(a^*)D) \leq U(y - a^*).
\end{aligned}
\tag{A10.7}
$$

But this means that the polluter would be worse off with insurance than if he had chosen a^* and not purchased any insurance coverage. QED.

APPENDIX C: PROOF OF PROPOSITION 10.7

Recall that $\hat{c}$ is defined by $\hat{c} = y - a^*(\hat{c})$, where $a^*(\hat{c})$ satisfies $-\rho'\left(a^*(\hat{c})\right) = 1/\hat{c}$. Consider first the case where $c < \hat{c}$, so that the compensation to be paid by the polluter does not expropriate all his wealth. In this case, the insurance company will set $s_A = c$ and $s_N = 0$, and the polluter will choose a care level a according to

$$
1 = -\rho'(a)c.
\tag{A10.8}
$$

Differentiating with respect to c yields $da/dc = -\rho'(a)/(\rho''(a)c) > 0$ – i.e. a higher compensation leads to more care, which is still sub-optimal for $c < D$. Now assume that $c > \hat{c}$.

The insurance company will choose $s_A = y - a$, expropriating all of the polluter's wealth in the event of an accident and, anticipating the polluter's choice of a, will set

$$s_N = \frac{\rho(a)}{1 - \rho(a)} \big[c - (y - a) \big], \tag{A10.9}$$

which guarantees zero profit in expectation for the polluter. The polluter takes s_A and s_N as given, so his first-order condition reads:

$$-\rho'(a)(s_A - s_N) = 1$$
$$\rightarrow \quad g(a,c) \equiv -\rho'(a)\big[(y - a - \rho c)/(1 - \rho)\big] - 1 = 0. \tag{A10.10}$$

There may be several pairs (a,c) that solve $g(a,c) = 0$, and so we cannot simply apply the implicit function theorem and differentiate the above equation with respect to c. Instead, we look at two possible compensation levels, c_1 and c_2 with $c_2 > c_1 \geq \hat{c}$, and let a_1 and a_2 be the largest care levels solving (A10.10), so that $g(a_1,c_1) = 0$ and $g(a_2,c_2) = 0$. We need to show that $a_2 \leq a_1$. Assume otherwise, so that $a_2 > a_1$. From (A10.10), we see that $\partial g(a,c)/\partial c = \rho'(a)\rho(a)/[1 - \rho(a)] < 0$. That is, the direct effect is negative. Therefore, $g(a_2,c_1) > g(a_2,c_2) = 0$. Next, observe that since $c \geq y - a$, we have

$$(y - a - \rho c)/(1 - \rho) \leq \big(y - a - \rho(y - a)\big)/(1 - \rho) = y - a, \tag{A10.11}$$

and therefore

$$g(a,c) \equiv -\rho'(a)\big((y - a - \rho c)/(1 - \rho)\big) - 1 \leq -\rho'(a)(y - a) - 1 \equiv h(a). \tag{A10.12}$$

Differentiating $h(a)$ gives us $h'(a) < 0$. Hence there exists some $\tilde{a}$ sufficiently large, such that $g(\tilde{a}, c_1) < 0$. Since $g(a_2, c_1) > 0 > g(\tilde{a}, c_1)$, by the intermediate value theorem there must exist some value $a_0 > a_1$ with $g(a_0, c_1) = 0$. This contradicts our definition of a_1 as the largest value solving $g(a_1, c_1) = 0$. We have therefore shown that if $c > \hat{c}$, higher compensation levels induce lower care levels, making the situation worse. Therefore, if $y < D + a^*(y)$, the optimal compensation must be equal to $\hat{c} = y - a^*(\hat{c})$, expropriating all the polluter's wealth in case of an accident, but not more or less than that. QED.

EXERCISES

10.1 * Consider the probability functions $\rho(a) = \min\{1/a, 1\}$ and $\rho(a) = 1 + a(a - 2)$. Calculate the socially optimal levels of care for the simple model outlined in section 10.1.

10.2 * Consider a risk averse firm with utility function $U(z) = z^{1-g}/(1 - g)$. Further assume that $D = 5$, $y = 10$, and $g = 0.5$. Calculate the care level chosen by the firm under the strict liability rule for the two probability functions in exercise 10.1. Compare the levels to the socially optimal care levels.

10.3 * Consider a risk averse firm that is regulated by the strict liability rule. Set up the first-order condition for the firm's optimal care level. Show that our assumptions guarantee that the second-order condition is also satisfied.

10.4 ** Consider a competitive firm engaging in risky activity, where damage is a function of output level x. The cost of production is $C(x)$, which is increasing and convex in x. The damage function is $D(x)$ and the cost of care is simply a, as before.

   (a) Determine the socially optimal levels of output and care.

   (b) Determine a competitive and solvent firm's choice of output and level of care under both the strict liability and the negligence rule for an arbitrary due care level $\bar{a}$.

   (c) Assume now that the firm may become non-solvent in case of an accident. Determine the competitive firm's choice of output and level of care under both the strict liability and the negligence rule, for an arbitrary due care level $\bar{a}$.

10.5 * Assume now that production and care cost are not separable, but are instead represented by a joint cost function $C(x,a)$. What assumptions should be imposed on $C(x,a)$? Determine the socially optimal levels of output and care as well as the competitive and solvent firm's choice of output and level of care under the strict liability and the negligence rules, for an arbitrary due care level $\bar{a}$.

10.6 ** Consider the model as in exercise 10.4, but assume the polluting firm has monopoly power on the output market. For this we assume the monopolist faces a downward sloping inverse demand function $P(x)$, resulting in a concave revenue function. Show that the monopolist chooses a sub-optimal level of care.

10.7 * Consider the case of limited liability, where the firm becomes bankrupt in case of an accident. Show that the second-order condition for the firm's first-order condition is guaranteed by our assumptions.

10.8 *** Assume a polluting firm is risk averse and sufficiently wealthy such that bankruptcy is not an issue (i.e. $y - a^* - D \gg 0$).

   (a) Show by examples that under strict liability a polluter may choose too small or too large a level of care, depending on the curvature properties of the utility and probability functions (Hint: use $\rho(a) = \min\{1/a,1\}$ and $\rho(a) = 1 + a(a-2)$).

   (b) Show that under the negligence rule with a due care level $\bar{a}$:

   (i) a polluter will choose the due care level if that level is smaller than the cutoff level $\hat{a}$, implicitly defined by

   $$\rho(a_s^{sl}(y))U(y - a_s^{sl}(y) - D) + [1 - \rho(a_s^{sl}(y))]U(y - a_s^{sl}(y)) = U(y - \hat{a}),$$

   and will act negligently otherwise

   (ii) if $a^* \le \hat{a}$, the optimal due care level is determined by $\bar{a} = a^*$

   (iii) if $a^* > \hat{a}$, the regulator maximizes welfare by choosing a second-best optimal due care level $\bar{a} = \hat{a}$.

10.9 * Assume a polluting firm is risk averse and not sufficiently wealthy to cover the damage in case of an accident (i.e. $y - a^* - D < 0$). Set up the firm's objective function and the first-order condition for the optimal care level.

10.10 *** Assume that the strict liability rule holds and a potentially polluting firm is risk averse. Define $\hat{y}$ implicitly by $\hat{y} = a_s^{sl}(\hat{y}) + D$, where $a_s^{sl}(\hat{y})$ is the solution to the solvent firm's problem and $\hat{y}$ divides wealth into (privately) optimal solvent and insolvent regimes. Characterize the optimal choice for care as a function of wealth. More precisely, show that there exist wealth levels y^0, y^1, and y^2 with $y^0 < y^1 < \hat{y} < y^2$ such that:
  (a) the firm engages in no care so that $a^{sl}(y) = 0$ for $y \leq y^0$, for some $y^0 \geq 0$. More precisely, if $\rho(0) = 1$, then $a^{sl}(0) = 0$ and $a^{sl}(y) > 0$ for $y > 0$. If $\rho(0) < 1$, then $y \leq y^0$;
  (b) $a^{sl}(y)$ is increasing in y for $y^0 < y < y^2$ and:
      (i) $a^{sl}(y) < a^*$ for $y < y^1$
      (ii) $a^{sl}(y) = a^*$ for $y = y^1$, and if the firm is risk neutral, also for $y > y^2$. If the firm owner is risk averse, then for $y > y^2$ the solution $a_s^{sl}(y)$ can be smaller or larger than the social optimum
      (iii) $a^{sl}(y) > a^*$ for $y^1 < y < y^2$;
  (c) the cutoff level of wealth $\hat{y} = a_s^{sl}(\hat{y}) + D$ dividing private solvency and insolvency can be larger or smaller than the socially optimal division.

10.11 *** Assume the *negligence rule* holds and the owner of the potentially polluting firm is risk averse. Assume that the regulator sets the due care level equal to the socially optimal level, so that $\bar{a} = a^*$. Let $y^1 < \hat{y}$ be the smallest wealth level for which $a^{sl}(y^1) = a^*$. Show that there exists some wealth level $\bar{y}$, such that:
  (a) $a^{nr}(y) = a^{sl}(y)$ for $y < \bar{y}$. In particular, the polluter sets $a = 0$ if wealth is sufficiently low
  (b) $a^{nr}(y) = a^*$ for $y \geq \bar{y}$. Here $a^{nr}(y)$ denotes the optimal care level under the negligence rule.

10.12 ** Assume the negligence rule holds. Show that the second-best optimal due care level $a^{nr}(y)$ is given by:
  (a) $a^{nr}(y) = a^*$ for $y \geq \bar{y}$
  (b) $a^{nr}(y) = \bar{a}(y)$ for $y < \bar{y}$

where $\bar{y}$ satisfies

$$\left[1 - \rho\left(a^{sl}(\bar{y})\right)\right] U\left(\bar{y} - a^{sl}(\bar{y})\right) = U\left(\bar{y} - \bar{a}(\bar{y})\right)$$

10.13 ** Draw on example 10.1 to show that for $y = 30$, partial coverage (denoted by c) induces a higher level of welfare than full coverage. Determine the second-best optimal level of partial coverage. Which incentive condition must this level satisfy? Show that for $y = 25$, partial coverage does not induce a higher care level. Determine the cutoff wealth level $\hat{y}$ for which partial coverage enhances welfare for $\hat{y} < y < y^3$, but not otherwise.

CHAPTER 11

Innovation and Adoption of New Technology

Human history has been defined by innovation and technological progress. Economists have for decades recognized that technological progress is critical for increasing general material wealth and the quality of human life. More recently, economists began focusing on the specific role that technological progress plays in the environmental context. In this chapter we synthesize the large conceptual literature related to innovation, technology adoption, and the environment.

The general topic of technology nests several related but distinct sub-areas of environmental economics, and so in this chapter we will look at multiple decision margins from a variety of actors. For example, when subject to environmental regulation, polluting firms can directly invest in R&D (research and development) efforts to reduce their abatement costs. In section 11.1 we study this type of behavior when investment has purely private benefits, and ask if additional efforts by the regulator are necessary to assure an efficient amount of investment in abatement cost reduction. In section 11.2 we generalize the model to allow for investment spillovers, whereby R&D effort by an individual firm creates knowledge that serves to reduce the abatement costs of all firms in the industry. We will show that, while purely private benefits from investment do not result in additional market imperfections, the spillover case produces a second market failure, based on the public good nature of R&D effort. Thus two policy instruments are needed to reach an efficient outcome.

In other contexts, polluting firms do not internally innovate, but instead must decide whether to bear the fixed cost of installing an available (abatement) cost-reducing new technology. We study this context in section 11.3, where we compare private and socially optimal adoption outcomes and discuss the performance of our suite of policy instruments in regulating emissions, and encouraging firms to deploy the new technology. The incentives for technology adoption that the various policy instruments provide have been loosely referred to in the literature as their "dynamic efficiency" properties. We discuss rankings of policies relative to a common environmental starting point, as well as their comparative usefulness for decentralizing the fully efficient outcome.

When a polluting industry faces costly environmental regulation there are opportunities for innovators to profit by developing technologies that reduce the compliance costs faced by the regulated industry. Thus the behavior of agents outside of the polluting industry, who invest resources to discover and sell a new technology to the polluting firms, can also be examined. In section 11.4 we present an economic model of innovation, whereby a monopoly supplier of a potential new technology must decide how much to invest in its discovery, and if successful, how much to charge firms in the polluting industry to license its use. We will see that new complications arise for the regulator when we introduce a monopoly innovator. These include the divergence between the private and social value of the innovation, and what this means for the private versus socially optimal R&D spending, as well as the market power the innovator possesses when he sells the new technology. The additional market imperfections ultimately affect the polluting firms' adoption incentives, and so in section 11.5 we bring together the behavior of the innovator and the polluting firms, and discuss the regulator's options for dealing with the multiple market imperfections that exist in this environment.

We will see that a common theme in the chapter is that, in order to implement a first-best outcome, the regulator often needs to deploy multiple policy instruments, which in actual policy situations is unlikely to be feasible. Throughout the analysis we therefore devote attention to second-best solutions that only use one policy instrument, and compare these to their first-best counterparts.

Before beginning it is useful to present some general terms that have been used in the broader economics literature on technology. Two types of innovations have been defined: process innovations and product innovations. A process innovation is a new way of producing a particular product that reduces costs. A product innovation, by contrast, has to do with consumers. Product innovations can be subdivided into "vertical" and "horizontal". Vertical product innovations are quality improvements for existing goods, while horizontal product innovations increase the variety of products. Obviously, the distinction between process and product innovations is not always sharp. A process innovation in connection with some output good may be based on product innovations for intermediate products.

Environmental innovations can be considered as product innovations, since they may provide higher environmental quality as a product attribute. At the same time, they may be process innovations, since they make it possible to produce a commodity at lower social cost. In this case, when emissions are priced at the true social marginal cost, there is little difference between environmental and non-environmental process innovations. However, non-environmental process innovations are usually driven by market forces, while environmental innovations usually require additional, policy-based incentives.

11.1   THE PRIVATE INNOVATION MODEL

We start by looking at the private innovation activities of a single firm, drawing on the simple environmental-damage-plus-abatement-cost model set out in Chapter 3. We assume that the typical firm can lower its marginal abatement cost by investing in improved abatement technology. Leaving aside the output market, we write a typical firm's abatement cost function as $C(e,\kappa)$, where e once again denotes emissions. We use κ to denote the amount of investment (measured in monetary units) dedicated to lowering both the abatement and marginal abatement cost functions. We make the following assumptions about $C(e, \kappa)$:

(a) $-C_e(e, \kappa) > 0$ for $e < \hat{e}$
(b) $C_\kappa(e, \kappa) < 0$, $-C_{e\kappa}(e, \kappa) < 0$ for $e < \hat{e}$
(c) $C_{ee}(e, \kappa) > 0$, $C_{\kappa\kappa}(e, \kappa) > 0$, $C_{ee}(e, \kappa)C_{\kappa\kappa}(e, \kappa) - [C_{e\kappa}(e, \kappa)]^2 > 0$

As usual, the first property (a) states that marginal abatement costs are positive for emissions below some non-regulated baseline emission level $\hat{e}$. Property (b) is the crucial new assumption in this extension of the model, stating that investment lowers both abatement and marginal abatement costs. Finally, (c) guarantees the overall convexity of the cost function.

With J different firms, the social objective for this economy is to select $e_1, \ldots, e_J$ and $\kappa_1, \ldots, \kappa_J$ to minimize

$$\sum_{j=1}^{J} \left(C^j(e_j, \kappa_j) + \kappa_j \right) + D(E), \tag{11.1}$$

where total pollution is denoted by $E = \sum_{j=1}^{J} e_j$. The first-order necessary conditions for optimal abatement and investment levels are given by

$$-C_e^j(e_j, \kappa_j) = D'(E) \tag{11.2}$$

$$-C_\kappa(e_j, \kappa_j) = 1 \tag{11.3}$$

for all j. Equation (11.2) is the now familiar condition requiring that marginal abatement costs equal marginal damage, while (11.3) implies that the last currency unit invested in decreased abatement should lead to a cost reduction equal to its unit value.

11.1.1 Decentralized Decisions

If the firms are regulated by, for example, an emission tax their total costs are given by

$$TC(e_j, \kappa_j) = C^j(e_j, \kappa_j) + \tau e_j + \kappa_j, \tag{11.4}$$

where τ denotes the emission tax rate. The firm chooses emissions and investment to minimize costs such that

$$-C_e^j(e_j, \kappa_j) = \tau \tag{11.5}$$
$$-C_\kappa^j(e_j, \kappa_j) = 1. \tag{11.6}$$

We see immediately that, if the emission tax is set equal to marginal damage, the first-best abatement and investment decisions can be implemented by our familiar price-based instruments. Similar logic also suggests that the first best can be obtained using tradable emission permits. Accordingly, in this simple model featuring private investment activity – and no positive externalities from a single firm's investment – there is no market failure beyond pollution, and the Pigouvian paradigm prevails.

11.2 INVESTMENT SPILLOVERS

Matters are slightly more complicated when investment spills over to other firms or, to put it differently, when firm j can benefit from firm i investing in abatement cost reductions. For example, κ_j might lead to a knowledge-based improvement that can be directly used by other firms to decrease their abatement costs. We model this by rewriting the abatement cost function as

$$C^j\left(e_j,\left[\kappa_j + \varepsilon\sum\nolimits_{i\neq j}\kappa_i\right]\right) = C^j\left(e_j, K_j\right) \tag{11.7}$$

where the parameter $\varepsilon \geq 0$ represents the degree of technological spillover measuring how much of one firm's investment activity contributes to other firms' cost reductions, and $K_j = \kappa_j + \varepsilon\sum\nolimits_{i\neq j}\kappa_i$ is firm j's *effective investment*. We assume that $C(e,K)$ has the same curvature properties as $C(e,\kappa)$, simply replacing κ with K in assumptions (a)–(c) above.

Total social costs with investment spillovers are now given by

$$\sum_{j=1}^{J}\left\{C^j\left(e_j,\left[\kappa_j + \varepsilon\sum\nolimits_{i\neq j}\kappa_i\right]\right) + \kappa_j\right\} + D(E), \tag{11.8}$$

and the first-order conditions for a first-best allocation are

$$-C_e^j(e_j, K_j) = D'\left(E\right) \tag{11.9}$$

$$-C_K^j(e_j, K_j) = 1 + \varepsilon\underbrace{\sum\nolimits_{i\neq j}C_K^i(e_i, K_i)}_{(-)}. \tag{11.10}$$

Note that the right-hand side of (11.10) is smaller than one, meaning in the social optimum that each firm's last currency unit of spending on investment should provide less than one unit's reduction in private abatement cost, since this spending also helps to reduce other firms' abatement costs. Clearly, an individual firm will ignore the positive spillovers provided to other firms, so besides regulating pollution, a first-best policy needs to address a second market failure by subsidizing investment. If firms are identical such that $C^j(e_j, K_j) = C(e, K)$ for all $j = 1,\ldots,J$, the optimal subsidy rate per dollar invested that will lead to the social optimum is

$$\varsigma = -(J - 1) \times \varepsilon \times C_K(e, K). \tag{11.11}$$

For asymmetric firms an individual subsidy rate may be necessary to obtain the first best, though when J is large and each firm is small, the optimal subsidy can be approximated by

$$\zeta \approx -\varepsilon \sum\nolimits_{j=1}^{J} C_K^j(e_j, K_j). \tag{11.12}$$

11.2.1 Second-Best Optimal Environmental Policy

Suppose now that subsidies are ruled out, but the environmental regulator wants to account for the positive spillovers. For simplicity, we assume that firms are symmetric so that in equilibrium, effective investment for each firm is given by $K=[1+(J-1)\varepsilon]\kappa$. In this second-best scenario with an emission tax as the only instrument, the regulator minimizes social costs as given by (11.8), subject to the behavioral conditions

$$-C_e(e, K) = \tau$$
$$-C_K(e, K) = 1. \tag{11.13}$$

To understand the second-best optimal allocation, it is useful to derive the signs of the comparative static effects resulting from a small variation in the policy instrument level. We do this by totally differentiating the conditions in (11.13) with respect to the tax rate, yielding

$$-C_{ee}(e, K)\frac{de}{d\tau} - C_{eK}(e, K)[1+\varepsilon(n-1)]\frac{d\kappa}{d\tau} = 1 \tag{11.14}$$

and

$$-C_{eK}(e, K)\frac{de}{d\tau} - C_{KK}(e, K)[1+\varepsilon(n-1)]\frac{d\kappa}{d\tau} = 0. \tag{11.15}$$

Solving this equation system for $de/d\tau$ and $d\kappa/d\tau$ using Cramer's Rule yields

$$\frac{de}{d\tau} = \frac{-C_{KK}(e, K)}{C_{KK}(e, K)C_{ee}(e, K) - [C_{Ke}(e, K)]^2} < 0 \tag{11.16}$$

and

$$\frac{d\kappa}{d\tau} = \frac{C_{eK}(e, K)}{C_{KK}(e, K)C_{ee}(e, K) - [C_{eK}(e, K)]^2} > 0. \tag{11.17}$$

To obtain the second-best optimal tax rate, the regulator differentiates (11.8) with respect to the tax rate, while accounting for the behavioral response of both e and κ to the choice of τ:

$$J[C_e(e, K) + D'(e \cdot J)]\frac{de}{d\tau} + J\{C_K(e, K) \times [1 + \varepsilon(J-1)] + 1\}\frac{d\kappa}{d\tau} = 0. \tag{11.18}$$

Using the behavioral conditions from (11.13) we obtain

$$[-\tau + D'(E)]\frac{de}{d\tau} + C_K(e, K)\varepsilon(J-1)\frac{d\kappa}{d\tau} = 0, \tag{11.19}$$

and isolating the tax rate on the left-hand side we arrive at

$$\tau = \underbrace{D'(E)}_{(+)} + \underbrace{\varepsilon(J-1)C_K(e,K)}_{(-)}\underbrace{\frac{d\kappa/d\tau}{de/d\tau}}_{(-)},\tag{11.20}$$

where the signs on the right-hand side terms follow from the model assumptions and equations (11.16) and (11.17). From this expression, it is clear that τ is larger than $D'(E)$ in the second-best optimum, meaning the regulator internalizes the investment spillovers by over-internalizing pollution damages. Instead of rewarding investment with a subsidy, the regulator punishes emissions more severely. In order to reduce their tax burden, firms will choose a higher investment level than under the Pigouvian rule, which then positively spills over onto the other firms.

Note that positive spillovers are not specific to environmental improvements. They occur in connection with almost every product cost reduction or quality improvement innovation. What is special here is the complementary relationship between abatement and investment. Accordingly, investment and the positive spillovers can be indirectly addressed by increasing the price of emissions.

11.3 DISCRETE ADOPTION DECISIONS

Thus far we have interpreted private investment either as private R&D with deterministic outcomes, or as the degree of adoption of some existing technology. In many cases, technology adoption is a yes/no discrete decision involving fixed investment costs. Since large fixed costs are involved in such investments, the question is not *how much* an individual firm should invest to lower its abatement costs, but rather *how many* firms should adopt the cleaner, but costly new technology. In this section, we first investigate the investment decision made by a single firm, and then look at the optimal adoption rate as it depends on fixed costs. We also examine how different policy instruments perform under different circumstances.

11.3.1 Additional Model Features

Instead of assuming a finite number of firms, we now consider a continuum. This has several advantages, as we will see below. The assumption is particularly appropriate if we want to model firms as small, and unable to influence environmental policy. More specifically, we assume that the set of firms is represented by the $[0,1]$ interval and that each firm is characterized by a firm-specific parameter $\chi \in [0,1]$. For simplicity, we further assume that initially all firms have identical technologies represented by the abatement cost function $C_0(e)$. Each firm can invest so as to adopt the new technology, leading to a new abatement cost function $C_1(e)$. To obtain the new technology, however, a firm must pay a firm-specific fixed cost denoted $F(\chi)$. Both abatement cost functions (for the old and the new technology) satisfy the familiar assumptions from Chapter 3: $-C'_j(e) > 0$

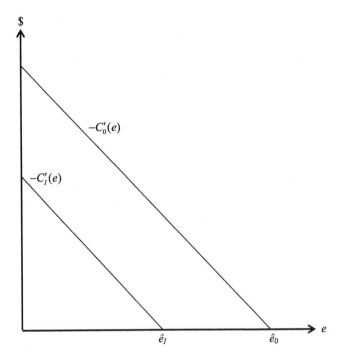

Figure 11.1 Marginal abatement cost curves with old (0) and new (*I*) technologies

and $C''_j(e) > 0$ for $j = 0, I$ when $e \leq \hat{e}_j$. For simplicity, we assume that the new technology provides lower abatement cost and lower marginal abatement cost, plus non-increasing maximum unregulated emission levels.[1] Formally this means that

$$C_I(e) < C_0(e),$$
$$-C'_I(e) < -C'_0(e), \quad \forall e < \hat{e}_0, \tag{11.21}$$

where $\hat{e}_j$ denotes the unregulated emission level for technology j. We also assume that $\hat{e}_I \leq \hat{e}_0$. These assumptions are displayed in Figure 11.1, which illustrates the two marginal abatement cost curves. For the firm-specific fixed cost we assume $F'(\chi) > 0$ and

$$\chi F''(\chi) + F'(\chi) > 0. \tag{11.22}$$

The latter will be satisfied if $F(\cdot)$ is convex or at least not too concave; the former means that firms' fixed costs increase as we move left to right along the unit interval. Including

---

[1] This assumption is convenient but not completely inconsequential. Complications arise when the old and new marginal abatement cost curves cross, which can affect the conclusions we draw in this section. For pedagogical purposes we proceed with this assumption, and refer the interested reader to Perino and Requate (2012) for a treatment of the more general case.

firm heterogeneity in this way is useful because it adds smoothness to the model that is not present when there are a finite number of symmetric firms. Assuming that firms differ in their fixed adoption costs is the simplest way of introducing this heterogeneity, without unduly complicating the model.

11.3.2 Adoption Incentives Under Different Policy Instruments

We now study how firms behave under different policy instruments. We leave time issues out of most of this section by assuming that the regulator makes a long-term commitment to the level of her policy instrument. In all cases, we assume that firms make their decisions sequentially. In a first step they decide whether or not to adopt the advanced technology, and in a second step they decide how much to emit and, in the case of permit markets, how many permits to trade. We start with emission taxes, proceeding from there to tradable permits and finally to emission standards.

Emission Taxes

Recall from Chapter 3 that under an emission tax, firms choose an emission level that equates marginal abatement cost with the tax rate, so that $-C'_j(e) = \tau$ for both $j = 0$ and $j = I$. We denote the emission level occurring under the old and new technologies by $e_0(\tau)$ and $e_I(\tau)$, respectively. Recall that our model assumptions imply $e_0(\tau) \geq e_I(\tau)$. Thus for a firm with parameter χ, it will pay off to adopt the new technology only if

$$C_I\left(e_I(t)\right) + \tau e_I(\tau) + F(\chi) < C_0\left(e_0(t)\right) + \tau e_0(\tau). \tag{11.23}$$

If a firm exists that is indifferent between the two technologies, we identify it using $\tilde{\chi}$ and note that

$$C_I\left(e_I(t)\right) + \tau e_I(\tau) + F(\tilde{\chi}) = C_0\left(e_0(t)\right) + \tau e_0(\tau). \tag{11.24}$$

An indifferent firm only exists if the tax rate is neither too low (in which case no firm will adopt the new technology) nor too high (in which case all firms will adopt the new technology). Since $F'(\chi) > 0$, it is the case that all firms with $\chi < \tilde{\chi}$ will adopt the new technology, so long as $\tilde{\chi}$ does. Therefore, $\tilde{\chi}$ also represents the share of adopting firms. In what follows we refer to $\tilde{\chi}$ interchangeably as the index for the indifferent firm, and the overall share of technology-adopting firms. To see how the adopting share changes with an increase in the tax rate, we differentiate (11.24) implicitly with respect to τ and use the Envelope Theorem to obtain

$$\frac{d\tilde{\chi}}{d\tau} = \frac{e_0 - e_I}{F'(\tilde{\chi})} > 0. \tag{11.25}$$

Thus as intuition suggests, a higher tax rate induces more firms to adopt the new technology. We summarize this result in the following proposition.

Proposition 11.1

When a new technology is available and pollution is regulated with an emissions tax,

(a) no firms will adopt the new technology if the tax is sufficiently low;

(b) all firms will adopt the new technology if the tax is sufficiently high; and

(c) for an intermediate range of tax rates, a partial share $0 < \tilde{\chi} < 1$ will adopt the new technology, and increasing the emission tax will induce a higher share of firms to adopt.

In Figure 11.2 we illustrate the cost savings for different tax rates. Area $a+b+c$ represents the variable cost savings under tax rate τ_1 while under a higher tax rate τ_2 the variable cost savings are represented by area $a+b+c+d+f$. Note, for example, that if $a+b+c < F(\chi) \leq a+b+c+d+f$, the firm will adopt the new technology under the higher tax τ_2, and will stay with the old technology under the lower tax τ_1.

Tradable Permits

Under tradable permits, firms choose their emissions in the last phase to equate marginal abatement cost with the competitive price of permits. By virtue of our continuum model, firms are small enough that the permit price does not change if one additional

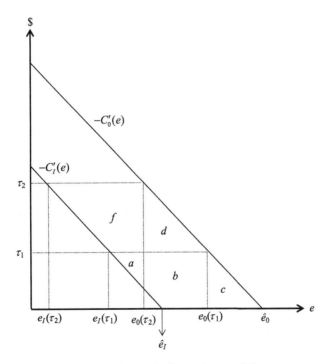

Figure 11.2 Cost savings from technology adoption under two different tax rates

firm adopts the new technology. Accordingly, the firms' behavior on the permit market in the last stage is characterized by

$$-C_j'(e) = \sigma, \quad j = 0, I, \tag{11.26}$$

where σ is the permit price and $e_0(\sigma)$ and $e_I(\sigma)$ denote emissions for the non-adopting and adopting firms, respectively. Once again interpreting $\tilde{\chi}$ as the share of adopting firms, market clearing on the permit market is determined by

$$L = \tilde{\chi}e_I(\sigma) + (1 - \tilde{\chi})e_0(\sigma). \tag{11.27}$$

Before examining how many firms adopt the new technology in equilibrium, it is useful to derive the relationship between σ and $\tilde{\chi}$. For this purpose, we differentiate (11.27) with respect to $\tilde{\chi}$, and use the implicit function theorem to obtain

$$\frac{d\sigma}{d\tilde{\chi}} = \frac{e_0 - e_I}{\tilde{\chi}\dfrac{de_I}{d\sigma} + (1 - \tilde{\chi})\dfrac{de_0}{d\sigma}} < 0. \tag{11.28}$$

Differentiating (11.26) with respect to σ leads to $de_j/d\sigma = (-C_j''(e_j))^{-1} < 0$, which establishes that the expression is indeed negative. This result is formally stated in the following proposition.

Proposition 11.2
When a new technology is available and pollution is regulated with a tradable pollution permit instrument, the equilibrium permit price decreases as more firms adopt the new technology.

With this result we are now able to examine what determines the share of firms adopting the new technology in equilibrium. Consider first the case of auctioned permits, where firms have to pay for all the permits they hold. If the marginal firm $\tilde{\chi}$ is indifferent between adopting and non-adopting we have

$$C_I\big(e_I(\sigma)\big) + \sigma e_I(\sigma) + F(\tilde{\chi}) = C_0\big(e_0(\sigma)\big) + \sigma e_0(\sigma). \tag{11.29}$$

Clearly such an indifferent firm can only exist if the total number of emission permits issued is neither too large nor too small, implying the emission permit price is neither too low nor too high.

Under freely distributed or grandfathered permits each firm χ receives an initial endowment of permits denoted by $\bar{e}_\chi$. For the indifferent firm in this case we have

$$C_I\big(e_I(\sigma)\big) + \sigma\big[e_I(\sigma) - \bar{e}_\chi\big] + F(\tilde{\chi}) = C_0\big(e_0(\sigma)\big) + \sigma\big[e_0(\sigma) - \bar{e}_\chi\big]. \tag{11.30}$$

By inspection, we see that the value of the initial endowment $\sigma\bar{e}_\chi$ cancels out on both sides, so that (11.30) is equivalent to (11.29). Thus the incentives for adoption are equivalent under both auctioned and free permits.

How do changes in the aggregate allocation of permits affect technology adoption decisions? To derive the comparative statics, we differentiate the equation system consisting of (11.26), (11.27), and (11.29) with respect to L. Using Cramer's Rule and the result from (11.28), we obtain

$$\frac{d\sigma}{dL} = -\frac{C_0''(e_0)C_I''(e_I)F'(\tilde{\chi})}{C_0''(e_0)C_I''(e_I)[e_0 - e_I]^2 + F'(\tilde{\chi})[(1 - \tilde{\chi})C_I''(e_I) + \tilde{\chi}C_0''(e_0)]} < 0 \qquad (11.31)$$

$$\frac{d\tilde{\chi}}{dL} = -\frac{C_0''(e_0)C_I''(e_I)[e_0 - e_I]}{C_0''(e_0)C_I''(e_I)[e_0 - e_I]^2 + F'(\tilde{\chi})[(1 - \tilde{\chi})C_I''(e_I) + \tilde{\chi}C_0''(e_0)]]} < 0 \qquad (11.32)$$

and

$$\frac{de_j}{dL} = \frac{de_j}{d\sigma}\frac{d\sigma}{dL} = -\left(C_j''(e_j)\right)^{-1}\frac{d\sigma}{dL} > 0, \quad j = 0, I. \qquad (11.33)$$

From these results we see that increasing the total emission cap leads to decreasing permit prices and hence to lower rates of technology adoption. A small firm's adoption incentive can also be visualized in Figure 11.2 by substituting different emission permit prices for the tax rates. Summarizing our observations, we obtain the following.

Proposition 11.3
When a new technology is available and pollution is regulated with a tradable pollution permit instrument:

(a) *no firm will adopt the new technology if the aggregate emission target is sufficiently large;*
(b) *all firms will adopt the new technology if the aggregate emission target is sufficiently small; and*
(c) *for an intermediate range of aggregate emission caps a partial share of firms $0 < \tilde{\chi} < 1$ will adopt the new technology. Relaxing (strengthening) the emission cap leads to a smaller (larger) share of firms adopting the new technology and to a decreasing (increasing) permit price.*

Emission Standards

Finally, we investigate adoption incentives provided by an emissions standard where we again use $\bar{e}$ to denote the uniform emission standard applied to each firm, irrespective of its technology. Since firms have no choice in deciding their emissions level we can immediately look at the marginal firm that is indifferent between adopting and non-adopting. This is the case if

$$C_I(\bar{e}) + F(\tilde{\chi}) = C_0(\bar{e}). \qquad (11.34)$$

To look at the impact of relaxing the emission standard, we differentiate (11.34) with respect to $\bar{e}$ to obtain

$$\frac{d\tilde{\chi}}{d\bar{e}} = \frac{C_0'(\bar{e}) - C_I'(\bar{e})}{F'(\tilde{\chi})} < 0, \qquad (11.35)$$

where the sign follows from the assumption in (11.21) stating that the marginal abatement cost of the new technology is below that of the old technology. Equation (11.35) says that relaxing the standard induces a smaller share of firms to adopt the new technology and, correspondingly, that tightening the standard leads to higher technology adoption. Analogous to the earlier propositions we state the following result.

Proposition 11.4

When a new technology is available and pollution is regulated with a uniform emission standard:

(a) *no firm will adopt the new technology if the standard is too lax;*
(b) *all firms will adopt the new technology if the standard is sufficiently tight; and*
(c) *for an intermediate range of emission standards a partial share of firms $0 < \tilde{\chi} < 1$ will adopt the new technology. Relaxing the standard leads to a lower share of adopting firms.*

Figure 11.3 shows the variable cost savings under an emission standard. Area a displays the variable cost savings $C_0(\bar{e}_1) - C_I(\bar{e}_1)$ under emission standard $\bar{e}_1$, while area $a+b$ represents the cost savings under the more stringent standard $\bar{e}_2 < \bar{e}_1$.

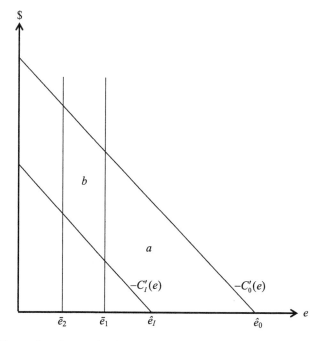

Figure 11.3 Cost savings from technology adoption under two emission standards

11.3.3 Ranking of Policy Instruments

In the early literature on adoption incentives, a central question focused on what instrument provides stronger incentives to invest in advanced abatement technology. However, a general statement such as "taxes provide stronger incentives to adopt new technology than tradable permits" has little meaning, since the strength of the incentive depends not only on the choice of the policy instrument, but also on its stringency. To compare different policy instruments, we need a common reference point for the stringency levels. For example, we might choose a stringency level that induces identical aggregate emissions under different policy instruments before technology adoption takes place. Let $\bar{E}$ be an aggregate emission target in a situation where all firms have the original technology 0, and let $\tau_0 = \tau(\bar{E})$ be the tax rate that induces total emission level $\bar{E}$, again when all firms still have technology 0. Furthermore, let $L_0 = \bar{E}$ be the corresponding quantity of tradable permits, and $\sigma_0(L_0)$ the equilibrium permit price that arises before technology adoption. By construction in this full certainty case, we have $\tau_0 = \sigma(L_0)$. Finally, we use $\bar{e}$ to denote the corresponding emission standard. Since the total mass of firms is equal to one, the individual emission standard is numerically equal to the aggregate standard, i.e. $\bar{e} = \bar{E}$. From the previous discussion it is clear that if the aggregate emission target is sufficiently lax, no firm will adopt the new technology under any of the three policy instruments. We therefore assume that $\bar{E}$ is sufficiently stringent, so that when the new technology becomes available, at least some of the firms will find it worthwhile to adopt it. More specifically, condition (c) in propositions 11.1, 11.3, and 11.4 applies.

For the tradable permit policy we use $\sigma_I(L_0)$ to denote the equilibrium permit price that arises after some subset of firms has adopted the new technology. By proposition 11.2, it decreases after adoption, so that $\sigma_I(L_0) < \tau_0$. It therefore follows from (11.25) that

$$\tilde{\chi}\big(\sigma_I(L_0)\big) < \tilde{\chi}(\tau_0), \tag{11.36}$$

meaning that fewer firms adopt the new technology under the tradable permit policy than under the tax policy.

We can visualize these different incentives by means of Figure 11.4. Under the tax instrument, the adopting firm reduces emissions from $e_0(\tau)$ to $e_I(\tau)$, achieving a variable cost saving represented by area $a+b+c+d+f$. Under permits, by contrast, the marginal firm faces a lower equilibrium price σ_I and therefore achieves a variable cost saving represented by area $a+b+c$ only. Comparing an emission tax to an emission standard, it is also easy to see that the tax provides higher investment incentives than the standard. Figure 11.5 shows the variable cost savings. The variable cost savings under an emission standard are represented by area a, while under an emission tax the variable cost savings are represented by area $a+b$.

By contrast, a comparison between tradable emission permits and an emission standard is ambiguous. This is illustrated by Figure 11.6. Here, the variable cost saving under an emission standard is given by area $a+c+d$, while under tradable permits it is given by area $b+c+d$. The comparison between areas a and b depends on the specific functions.

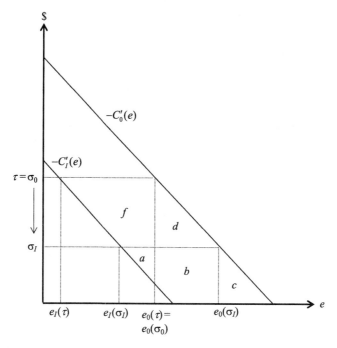

Figure 11.4   Comparison of adoption incentives under an emission tax and cap and trade

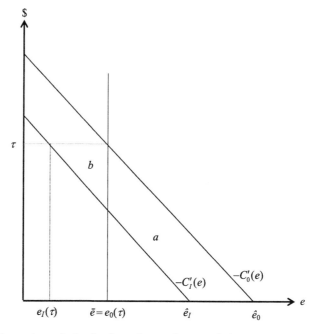

Figure 11.5   Comparison of adoption incentives under an emission tax and emissions standard

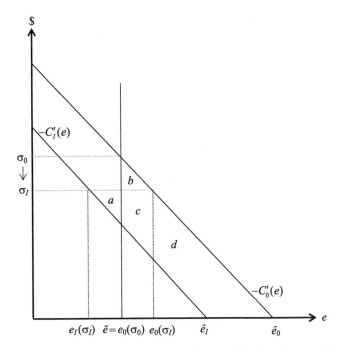

Figure 11.6 Comparison of adoption incentives under cap and trade and an emissions standard

EXAMPLE II.I (NUMERICAL/ANALYTICAL) The ambiguous comparison between an emissions standard and tradable permits is clear when we let $C_0(e) = 0.5 \times (10 - e)^2$, $C_I(e) = 0.5 \times (5 - e)^2$, and $F(\chi) = 4\chi$. For an aggregate emission cap of $\bar{E} = 7$ we obtain $\chi^{per} = 0.52$ under tradable permits and $\chi^{es} = 0.625$ under an emission standard. By contrast, for $\bar{E} = 7.2$ we have $\chi^{per} = 0.48$ and $\chi^{es} = 0.375$.

We summarize these comparison results in the following proposition.

Proposition 11.5
Assume that all three instruments – taxes, tradable emission permits, and uniform emission standards – lead to the same aggregate emission level before adoption of the new technology. Then taxes will induce a higher share of adoption than either tradable emission permits or standards, while the ranking between standards and tradable emission permits is ambiguous and depends on the stringency of the original emissions target.

It is worth noting that if a particular emission level is desired, the permit instrument is the best instrument to achieve this target. The emissions do not change through technology adoption, except for special cases where the permit price drops to zero. Firms (and consumers) benefit from the technology adoption through decreasing emission permit prices (and thus lower product prices, although this is not modeled explicitly). In the absence of policy adjustment, environmental quality does not improve. The tax, by contrast, induces lower emissions. Thus, environmental quality improves and consumers benefit from this adjustment, but absent a change in the tax level, firms (and consumers) do not benefit from lower prices. The extent to which lower prices or lower emissions are preferred requires that we pay explicit attention to the damages from emissions and the costs of adopting the new technology. We know from Chapter 3 that the optimal emission target depends on both the marginal pollution damage and the marginal abatement cost. Thus if the marginal abatement cost changes, the optimal pollution level will change as well. In the next subsection, we therefore study the optimal degree of technology adoption, including the optimal aggregate emission target.

11.3.4 The Socially Optimal Degree of Technology Adoption

The rankings in the previous section were conditional on a specific emission target. In this section we look at the total social cost when a new technology is available by examining optimal adoption. Since the firms are ordered from lowest to highest adoption costs along the unit interval, it is clear that if some but not all firms adopt the new technology, those that do so will have the lowest costs. The socially optimal solution will therefore be characterized by a marginal firm $\tilde{\chi}$ adopting the new technology (implying an optimal adoption share $\tilde{\chi}$) as well as emission levels e_0 and e_1 assigned to the firms with old and new technology, respectively. The total social cost is therefore given by

$$SC(\tilde{\chi}, e_1, e_0) = (1 - \tilde{\chi})C_0(e_0) + \tilde{\chi}C_1(e_1) + \int_0^{\tilde{\chi}} F(\chi)d\chi + D(\tilde{\chi}e_1 + (1 - \tilde{\chi})e_0), \qquad (11.37)$$

where $\tilde{\chi}C_1(e_1)$ and $(1 - \tilde{\chi})C_0(e_0)$ represent the total variable abatement costs contributed by the adopting and non-adopting firms, respectively, and $\int_0^{\tilde{\chi}} F(\chi)d\chi$ is the total fixed adoption cost among all adopting firms. Total emissions are given by $E = \tilde{\chi}e_1 + (1 - \tilde{\chi})e_0$.

To obtain the socially optimal allocation, we differentiate (11.37) with respect to emissions e_0 and e_1 and the share of adopting firms $\tilde{\chi}$. For an interior solution in adoption share, this yields the first-order conditions

$$\begin{aligned} -C_1'(e_1) &= D'(E) \\ -C_0'(e_0) &= D'(E) \end{aligned} \qquad (11.38)$$

and

$$C_1(e_1) + F(\tilde{\chi}) - C_0(e_0) = D'(E)[e_0 - e_1]. \qquad (11.39)$$

Equation (11.38) contains the usual conditions stating that for both the adopting and the non-adopting firms marginal abatement costs should be equal to marginal damage. The third condition is new and states that the total cost difference for the marginal firm operating with the new versus the old technology must be equal to its emission reduction multiplied by the marginal damage. That is, the socially optimal adoption level balances the reduced damages contributed by the marginal firm with the abatement cost consequences of technology adoption.

For further insight and intuition on the new condition, we define the aggregate marginal abatement cost curve $MAC(E, \tilde{\chi})$ for an arbitrary fixed share of adopting firms $\tilde{\chi}$. This curve is derived by horizontally summing the individual marginal abatement cost curves when all firms – the adopting and non-adopting enterprises – equalize their marginal abatement costs. A marginal increase in $\tilde{\chi}$ leads to an incremental shift of the aggregate marginal abatement cost curve to the left. Equation (11.39) provides the condition for the optimal position of the aggregate marginal abatement cost curve, which we denote by $MAC(E, \tilde{\chi}^*)$. Rearranging yields

$$F(\tilde{\chi}) = C_0(e_0) - C_1(e_1) + D'(E)[e_0 - e_1]. \tag{11.40}$$

The right-hand side of (11.40) represents the reduction in variable social costs – including damage costs – that occurs when the aggregate marginal abatement cost curve shifts to the left. The left-hand side represents the additional fixed cost of shifting the aggregate MAC curve to the left. The optimum adoption level trades off these marginal variable emissions and fixed adoption costs to determine $\tilde{\chi}^*$.

Figure 11.7 illustrates these optimality conditions for a damage function with increasing marginal damage, and several aggregate marginal abatement cost functions. The curve on the far right labeled $MAC(E,0)$ shows the situation when no firms adopt the new technology, and correspondingly $MAC(E,1)$ on the far left shows the curve when all of the firms adopt the new technology. For each of the four curves we can imagine

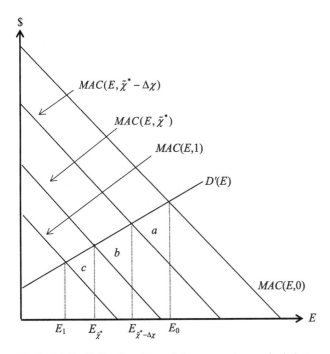

Figure 11.7 Optimal position of the aggregate marginal abatement cost function

the conditionally optimal emission level implicitly defined by $MAC(E, \tilde{\chi}) = D'(E)$. Shifting the aggregate abatement cost curve from $MAC(E,0)$ to the interior curve $MAC(E, \tilde{\chi}^* - \Delta\chi)$, and reducing emissions to the conditionally optimal level, provides benefits equal to area a in the form of reduced damages and variable abatement costs. Obtaining this shift costs

$$\int_0^{\tilde{\chi}^* - \Delta\chi} F(\chi)d\chi < a \tag{11.41}$$

in additional fixed costs, where in this example the savings in pollution damages and abatement costs from the shift are larger than the fixed costs, when $\tilde{\chi}^*$ is the optimal adopting share. A further marginal increase in the share of adopting firms provides variable cost reductions of the amount b and an incremental increase in fixed costs given by

$$\int_{\tilde{\chi}^* - \Delta\chi}^{\tilde{\chi}^*} F(\chi)d\chi = b, \tag{11.42}$$

where the equality follows from $\tilde{\chi}^*$ being the optimal share of adopting firms. Thus area b is the graphical equivalent to the left- and right-hand sides of Eq. (11.40). Finally, a shift in the aggregate marginal abatement cost curve to $MAC(E,1)$ provides variable cost savings given by area c, but adds fixed costs equal to

$$\int_{\tilde{\chi}}^1 F(\chi)d\chi > c, \tag{11.43}$$

which is larger than area c in this example. This illustrates that full adoption is inefficient in this context, because the additional fixed costs of all firms deploying the new technology exceed the damage and abatement costs savings it provides. Note from the Figure that the case of increasing marginal damages makes it more likely that partial adoption is optimal. In particular, the damage avoided via the last (i.e. highest fixed cost) firms installing the new technology is small relative to what is provided by the emission reductions following the initial installations.

The conditions discussed in the example are for an interior solution, but the optimal solution can also be full or zero adoption, depending on the level and slope of the marginal damage curve and abatement cost differences. Full adoption is optimal if for the values of e_0 and e_I that satisfy Eq. (11.38) we have

$$F(1) \leq \underline{F} \equiv C_0(e_0) - C_I(e_I) + D'(e_I)[e_0 - e_I], \tag{11.44}$$

in which case total emissions are given by $E = 1 \times e_I$, since the total mass of firms is normalized to one. By contrast, no adoption is optimal if

$$F(0) > \overline{F} \equiv C_0(e_0) - C_I(e_I) + D'(e_0)[e_0 - e_I], \tag{11.45}$$

in which case total emissions are given by $E = 1 \times e_0$. Note that if marginal damage is constant we have $\underline{F} = \overline{F}$. With these corner solution results stated, we can now characterize the social optimum via the following proposition.

Proposition 11.6

Let $\underline{F}$ and $\bar{F}$ be defined by the right-hand side of (11.44) and (11.45), respectively.

(a) If the firm indexed $\chi=1$ (i.e. the highest adoption cost firm) has $F(1) \leq \underline{F}$, the entire industry should adopt the new technology.

(b) If the firm indexed $\chi=0$ (i.e. the lowest adoption cost firm) has $F(0) \leq \bar{F}$, no firm should adopt the new technology.

(c) In all other cases partial adoption is optimal.

The proof is left as an exercise. It works by setting up a Kuhn-Tucker problem with non-negativity constraints $\chi \geq 0$ and $1-\chi \geq 0$ and verifying that $\chi=0$ for $F(0) \geq \bar{F}$ and $\chi=1$ for $F(1) \leq \underline{F}$.

We can gain further insight into the socially optimal allocation by parameterizing the social damage function with a shift parameter η, as we did in Chapter 4. We write the damage function as $D(E,\eta)$ and assume $D_{\eta}(E,\eta)>0$ and $D_{E\eta}(E,\eta)>0$ – i.e. that both damage and marginal damage are increasing in the parameter η. Then by replacing $D'(E)$ with $D_E(E,\eta)$ in (11.39), and differentiating this equation with respect to η (applying both the Envelope Theorem and the implicit function theorem), we obtain

$$\frac{d\tilde{\chi}^*}{d\eta} = \frac{D_{E\eta}(E,\eta)[e_0 - e_I]}{F'(\tilde{\chi}^*)} > 0. \tag{11.46}$$

Similarly, we can differentiate $\underline{F}$ and $\bar{F}$ from (11.44) and (11.45) with respect to η to obtain

$$\frac{d\underline{F}}{d\eta} = D_{E\eta}(e_I,\eta)[e_0 - e_I] > 0$$
$$\frac{d\bar{F}}{d\eta} = D_{E\eta}(e_0,\eta)[e_0 - e_I] > 0. \tag{11.47}$$

We summarize the findings from these derivatives as follows.

Proposition 11.7

As marginal damage increases:

(a) the optimal share of adopting firms is (weakly) increasing; and

(b) the fixed cost boundaries for which complete adoption or no adoption is optimal are strictly increasing.

11.3.5 Decentralization of Optimal Solution

We are now ready to ask how the first-best allocation can be decentralized. For this we need to define the timing and the order of moves between the regulator and the firms. There are two major possibilities: ex ante and ex post regulation. Under ex ante regulation, the regulator moves first by choosing the policy instrument and committing to its level. Under ex post regulation, the regulator chooses the policy instrument first, observes the rate of technology adoption, and then adjusts the level of her instrument accordingly.

Ex Ante Optimal Regulation

We first examine the case where the regulator anticipates the new technology – including its variable and fixed adoption costs – and sets her policy level accordingly. For the case of an emission tax, the Pigouvian level

$$\tau^* = D'\left(\tilde{\chi}^* e_I^* + (1-\tilde{\chi}^*)e_0^*\right) \tag{11.48}$$

is an obvious candidate for the optimal charge, where $(\tilde{\chi}^*, e_0^*, e_I^*)$ denote the optimal adoption and emission rates derived above. Given this tax rate, a firm with specific parameter $\chi \in [0,1]$ will adopt the new technology if

$$C_I\left(e_I(\tau^*)\right) + \tau^* e_I(\tau^*) + F(\chi) \leq C_0\left(e_0(\tau^*)\right) + \tau^* e_0(\tau^*) \tag{11.49}$$

or, expressed differently by rearrangement, if

$$C_I\left(e_I(\tau^*)\right) + F(\chi) - C_0\left(e_0(\tau^*)\right) \leq \tau^*\left[e_0(\tau^*) - e_I(\tau^*)\right], \tag{11.50}$$

where $e_0(\tau^*)$ and $e_I(\tau^*)$ satisfy the familiar cost minimization rule for each technology choice:

$$\begin{aligned}
-C_I'\left(e_I(\tau^*)\right) &= \tau^* \\
-C_0'\left(e_0(\tau^*)\right) &= \tau^*.
\end{aligned} \tag{11.51}$$

The right-hand side of (11.50) is the difference in tax liability under non-adoption and adoption options. If this difference is larger than the abatement cost difference at the optimal choices under the new and old technology, it is in the firm's interest to adopt the new technology.

Firms will not adopt the new technology if the inequality in (11.49) is reversed. It is now clear that if the tax rate is set at the level τ^*, then the firm with fixed cost parameter $\chi = \tilde{\chi}^*$ is indifferent between adopting the new technology or not. Formally, for the indifferent firm, we have

$$\begin{aligned}
\tau^*\left[e_0(\tau^*) - e_I(\tau^*)\right] &= C_I\left(e_I(\tau^*)\right) + F(\tilde{\chi}^*) - C_0\left(e_0(\tau^*)\right) \\
&= D(E^*)[e_0^* - e_I^*],
\end{aligned} \tag{11.52}$$

where the second equality follows from (11.39). Since $F'(\chi) > 0$, all firms with fixed cost parameter $\chi < \tilde{\chi}^*$ will find it strictly better to adopt the new technology in that

$$C_I\left(e_I(\tau^*)\right) + F(\chi) - C_0\left(e_0(\tau^*)\right) < C_I(e_I^*) + F(\tilde{\chi}^*) - C_0(e_0^*). \tag{11.53}$$

For all firms with fixed cost parameter $\chi > \tilde{\chi}^*$ the inequality (11.53) is reversed, and it does not pay to adopt the new technology.

Under a regime of tradable permits, both auctioned and freely distributed, an analogous argument holds. As in the previous chapters, we use σ^* to denote the (competitive) price for emission permits. Then under a system of auctioned permits it will pay for a firm with fixed cost parameter χ to adopt the new technology if and only if

$$C_I\left(e_I(\sigma^*)\right) + \sigma^* e_I(\sigma^*) + F(\chi) \le C_0\left(e_0(\sigma^*)\right) + \sigma^* e_0(\sigma^*). \tag{11.54}$$

If the regulator issues a total amount of permits $L = E^*$ equal to the optimal aggregate emission level, and if there is a unique equilibrium on the permit market, then the competitive permit price will be equal to the optimal tax rate, and thus to the optimal marginal damage – i.e. $\sigma^* = \tau^* = D'(E^*)$. This must be the case since the firms' individual demand curves for permits are downward-sloping, so the aggregate demand curve must be downward-sloping as well, implying that emission permits $L = E^*$ will lead to $\sigma^* = \tau^*$. We summarize our findings in the following proposition.

Proposition 11.8
If a new technology is available and the regulator anticipates the new technology including its costs, then the first-best allocation can be implemented by setting an ex ante optimal tax rate, or by issuing an ex ante optimal number of emission permits.

We have already established that it does not matter whether permits are auctioned or issued for free. Clearly, emission standards do not induce a first-best allocation, if partial adoption is socially optimal. The first-best allocation requires that firms' emission levels differ across technologies, and uniform emission standards cannot accommodate this by design.

Ex Post Optimal Regulation
Perfect anticipation of the new technology is certainly an unrealistic assumption. It is more likely that the regulator will react to the adoption of some new technology. We assume the regulator follows the Pigouvian rule and sets the tax rate equal to marginal damage. After observing the share of firms $\tilde{\chi}$ adopting the new technology, the regulator sets the tax rate according to

$$\tau(\tilde{\chi}) = D'\left(\tilde{\chi}e_I + (1-\tilde{\chi})e_0\right), \tag{11.55}$$

where e_0 and e_I satisfy the optimal abatement rules $-C_0'(e_0) = \tau(\tilde{\chi})$ and $-C_I'(e_I) = \tau(\tilde{\chi})$, respectively. If all firms with fixed cost parameters $\chi \le \tilde{\chi}^*$ adopt the new technology, the regulator will set the tax rate equal to τ^* in (11.48). This is an adoption equilibrium since a firm with $\chi > \tilde{\chi}^*$ will not want to change its first stage decision, and adopt the new technology. Suppose instead that a higher share of firms $\hat{\chi} > \tilde{\chi}^*$ adopt the new technology. Then the regulator will respond by setting the tax such that

$$\hat{\tau} = D'\left(\hat{\chi}e_I(\hat{\chi}) + (1-\hat{\chi})e_0(\hat{\chi})\right) < D'\left(\tilde{\chi}^* e_I^* + (1-\tilde{\chi}^*)e_0^*\right) = \tau^*. \tag{11.56}$$

With this tax rate, however, adoption is not profitable for some of the adopting firms and so this cannot be an adoption equilibrium. Specifically, in anticipating the tax rate $\hat{\tau}$, firms with parameter $\chi > \tilde{\chi}^*$ will not invest in adoption in the first stage. An analogous argument holds if a smaller share of firms adopt the new technology in the first stage. This also cannot be an adoption equilibrium, because it would pay off for more firms to adopt the new technology in the first stage. We summarize our findings as follows.

Proposition 11.9

Under ex post regulation, where firms decide on technology adoption in the first stage and a regulator adjusts the level of her policy instrument in a second stage, the socially optimal rate of adoption and socially optimal setting of an emission tax rate or an emission cap for tradable permits is a sub-game perfect equilibrium.

Sub-optimality of Long-Term Pre-commitment

In most instances, regulators neither have sufficient information to anticipate future technologies, nor are they able adjust their policy instruments immediately to the current degree of technology. Instead, they make long-term commitments to both the choice of their policy instrument and their levels. For example, under the CAAA 1990, the US Environmental Protection Agency (EPA) made an indefinite commitment to a total emission cap of 8.9 million tons of sulfur dioxide emissions. Sweden has committed to an NO_X tax of around €4,000 per ton (see example 3.4). While these commitments can lead to static cost effectiveness for given emission targets and/or static efficiency for fixed technologies, they may not produce dynamically efficient outcomes. The basic insight comes from proposition 11.8. We have seen that investment incentives will be optimal if the regulator sets the emission tax or the emission cap at the socially optimal level, taking into account both abatement costs for the old and the new technology including fixed adoption cost. From this result it follows that if the regulator makes a long-term commitment to a higher tax rate, or a lower number of permits, there will be more investment in the new technology than is optimal. The opposite is true when the tax is lower or the emission cap is higher than optimal. A special case is the situation where the regulator completely disregards the possibility of future technology, and makes a long-term commitment to an emission policy that is optimal only with respect to currently installed technology base. In this case, we will have over-investment under taxes and under-investment with tradable permits.

11.4   ENVIRONMENTAL R&D AND LICENSING

Up to this point we have considered situations where the new technologies have been given exogenously, and we have concentrated on optimal and private behavior of the adopting firms. We now broaden our analysis to include the behavior of an innovator, as well as the social and private values of an environmental innovation. For this it is useful to first examine the difference between social and private innovation values for a general process innovation, and then the particular case of environmental innovations.

11.4.1 Value of a General Process Innovation

Suppose that a good is initially produced by many firms, each producing one unit at identical unit cost c_0. An innovator develops a new technology that makes it possible to produce the good at lower unit cost $c_I < c_0$. The new technology can be deployed by all firms, including new entrants. The industry output for the good is denoted by X, and consumers' valuation of X is represented by the downward sloping inverse demand function $P(X)$, similar to what we used in Chapter 5. The market price of the good is p, and we denote the aggregate demand function by $X(p)$. Given either technology, an efficient allocation requires that the product is sold to consumers at unit cost. Thus the *social value of innovation* is given by the difference in consumer surplus when we replace the old technology with the new, i.e.

$$V_S(c_I) = \int_{X(c_0)}^{X(c_I)} P(t)dt. \tag{11.57}$$

This is illustrated by area $a+b$ in Figure 11.8.

Suppose that the industry is perfectly competitive, so that prior to the introduction of the new technology, the price of the good is $p_0 = c_0$, and that a single innovator can license the new technology to the firms for a per output unit fee denoted by φ. Since the producers of X make zero profits before the innovation, the innovator can extract all of the surplus from the new technology by setting the fee such that $\varphi = c_0 - c_I$. The

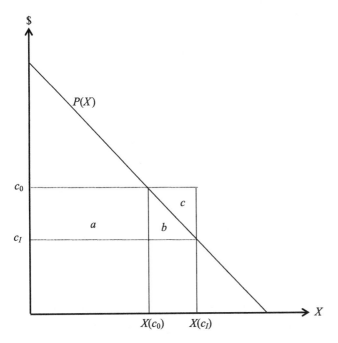

Figure 11.8 Social and private value of a process innovation under constant marginal cost

new output price will therefore be equal to the old output price, and the *private* value of innovation achieved by the innovator is given by

$$V_P(c_I) = [c_0 - c_I]X(c_o) < V_S(c_I). \tag{11.58}$$

The private value of innovation is shown as area a in Figure 11.8. This allocation is clearly not ex post optimal, since there is a welfare loss given by area b. It would be welfare improving to issue more licenses at zero cost. However, if the innovator were forced to issue licenses for free, he would have no incentive to engage in R&D in the first place.

How can a regulator encourage the optimal technology adoption? One possibility is to reimburse the license fee to firms that adopt the new technology – i.e. provide a subsidy for adoption in the amount of $\varsigma = \varphi = c_0 - c_I$. In this case the competitive market price will be $p_I = c_I$ and demand will be $X(c_I)$. The value of the new technology for the innovator is now

$$V_P^\varsigma(c_I) = [c_0 - c_I]X(c_I) > V_S(c_I), \tag{11.59}$$

which exceeds the social value. The value to the innovator with the adoption subsidy is shown as area $a + b + c$ in Figure 11.8. Note that the subsidy may provide excess R&D incentives, and possibly excess profits for the R&D firm. A solution to this problem is a profit tax, which we return to below.

11.4.2 A Model of R&D

We turn attention now to the behavior of the innovator and ask how much will be, and should be, invested in R&D effort. There are two simple prototype R&D models that we can use for our purposes: a probabilistic framework with exogenously given technology, and a deterministic framework with endogenous technology choice. In what follows we focus on the probabilistic model.

Following the previous subsection, we assumed that the unit cost for the new technology is exogenously given by c_I, but the technology itself is not yet discovered by the innovator. The innovator invests an amount κ in an effort to discover the technology. The probability of successful discovery is given by $pr(\kappa) \le 1$, and we assume that the probability of success is increasing in R&D expenditures at a decreasing rate, so that $pr'(\kappa) > 0$ and $pr''(\kappa) < 0$. The objective for both the social planner and the private innovator is to choose κ to maximize the expected return on R&D effort. Formally, the objective function is

$$W_i(\kappa) = pr(\kappa) \cdot V_i(c_I) - \kappa, \quad i = S, P, \tag{11.60}$$

where $V_S(c_I)$ and $V_P(c_I)$ are given by equations (11.57) and (11.58), respectively. The first-order condition for determining the first best and the private levels of R&D investment is then given by

$$pr'(\kappa) \cdot V_i(c_I) = 1, \quad i = S, P. \tag{11.61}$$

Thus the marginal expected benefit from innovation is equal to the marginal cost of increasing R&D success, which in this simple model is equal to one.

We use κ_S and κ_P to denote the solutions to (11.61), corresponding to the socially optimal and private investment levels, respectively. In the absence of regulation (e.g. without an adoption subsidy) we have seen that $V_S(c_I) > V_P(c_I)$, which implies that $\kappa_S > \kappa_P$. That is, the private R&D firm invests less in discovering a cost-reducing process innovation than is socially optimal. This market failure can be addressed either by subsidizing R&D effort or by setting up a research prize. The drawback of the first proposal is that subsidizing an input does not guarantee that the probability of success will increase. There is a moral hazard issue in that firm managers may simply declare ordinary workers to be innovators, in order to capture the subsidy. A research prize, by contrast, is awarded contingent on success. It has to be set up in a way that equates the social and private returns to innovation effort.

We saw in the previous subsection that an adoption subsidy can lead to optimal deployment of the new technology by raising $V_P(c_I)$ to $V_P^\zeta(c_I)$. In this case, there is excess R&D effort, since $V_P^\zeta(\cdot) > V_S(\cdot)$, where $V_P^\zeta(\cdot)$ is defined in Eq. (11.59). In order to align the private and social R&D incentives under an adoption subsidy, a profit tax is also needed. Under a profit tax rate T, the expected profit for the innovator is

$$E\Pi = \Pr(\kappa) \times (1-T)V_P^\zeta(c_I) - \kappa. \tag{11.62}$$

If the profit tax is set according to

$$T = 1 - \frac{V_S(c_I)}{V_P^\zeta(c_I)}, \tag{11.63}$$

it is easy to verify that the innovator will choose the socially optimal R&D investment level.

11.4.3 A Model of Environmental Innovation

In this subsection we adapt the ideas developed above for the general case to the context of an environmentally beneficial technological improvement. Suppose once again that a good X is produced at constant marginal cost c, and that emissions are proportional to output at a rate δ_0, such that $E = \delta_0 \cdot X$. Consumer demand for the good is again denoted by $X(p)$. For convenience we assume that the damage function is $D(E) = d \cdot E$ – i.e. there is constant marginal damage from emissions. Prior to the availability of the new technology, the optimal emission tax is $\tau_0 = d$, and the competitive market price of X is $p_0 = c + \delta_0 \cdot \tau_0$.

Suppose that an innovator offers a new technology that reduces the pollution intensity of production in a way that provides a new emission coefficient δ_I, where $\delta_I < \delta_0$. If the emission tax rate does not change, the per unit cost reduction provided to polluting firms by the new technology is $[\delta_0 - \delta_I] \times \tau_0$. As was the case for a general production cost reduction, the monopolistic innovator can capture competitive firms' adoption benefits by charging a license fee per unit of output $\varphi = [\delta_0 - \delta_I] \times \tau_0$. The private benefit of innovation in the environmental case is therefore

$$V_P(\delta_I; \tau_0) = [\delta_0 - \delta_I] \times \tau_0 \times X(c + \delta_0 \tau_0), \tag{11.64}$$

where $X(c + \delta_0 \tau_0)$ is the consumer demand for the good, at the initial price. The social value of innovation, in contrast, is given by

$$V_S(\delta_I) = \int_{c + \delta_I \tau_0}^{c + \delta_0 \tau_0} X(p)dp > V_P(\delta_I ; \tau_0). \tag{11.65}$$

Under the original tax, there is too little licensing of the new technology and, based on the probabilistic model derived above, too little R&D incentive. As in the general case, a solution for insufficient adoption is to subsidize adoption at the rate $\varsigma = \varphi = [\delta_0 - \delta_I] \times \tau_0$, so that the private innovation value is

$$V_P^\varsigma(\delta_I ; \tau_0) = [\delta_0 - \delta_I] \times \tau_0 \times X(c + \delta_I \tau_0) > V_S(\delta_I). \tag{11.66}$$

To align the private and social incentives for R&D investment we also need a tax on expected profits defined by

$$T = 1 - \frac{V_S(\delta_I)}{V_P^\varsigma(\delta_I ; \tau_0)}. \tag{11.67}$$

We summarize these analytical results in the following proposition.

Proposition 11.10

If there is a monopolistic innovator an environmental regulator needs a mix of three instruments to obtain the first-best outcome:

(a) *a Pigouvian tax set equal to marginal damages;*
(b) *an adoption subsidy that increases the private returns to licensing the new technology;*
(c) *a gross profit tax on the innovator that aligns the private and social incentives to engage in R&D expenditure.*

The environmental innovation case is displayed in Figure 11.9, which shows area $a + b$ as the social value of the innovation and area a as the pre-subsidy private value. With an adoption subsidy in place, the private value of the new technology to the innovating firm is shown as area $a + b + c$. Area c is the excess value to the innovator beyond the social benefit, which motivates the need for a gross profit tax.

If for some reason subsidies are ruled out, a second-best policy is to increase R&D incentives by raising the emission tax above the Pigouvian level. This increases the cost savings from the new technology, and with it the potential license fee $\varphi = [\delta_0 - \delta_I] \times \tau$. In principle, it is possible to raise the tax to a level such that the private innovation value is exactly equal to the social innovation value. However, such a policy comes at the expense of a too-high commodity price and hence too little consumer surplus. A second-best optimal tax policy would trade off the inefficient R&D incentive against the additional consumer surplus loss.

Increasing Marginal Damage

In this section we have assumed that marginal damage is constant, i.e. the optimal tax will be the same before and after innovation. If the marginal damage function is

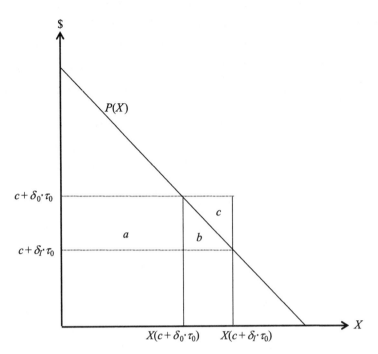

Figure 11.9 Social and private value of an environmental process innovation under constant marginal cost and constant marginal damage

increasing, however, the marginal damage will decrease if emissions fall, so the optimal tax rate after technology adoption should be adjusted to a lower level. If the regulator can anticipate the new technology, the optimal policy mix is similar to the one referred to in proposition 11.10, except, as we know from section 11.3.4, the tax rate should immediately be set at a level that corresponds to the new optimal marginal damage. Hence even in the case of increasing marginal damage, a policy mix of an ex-post optimal emission tax, an adoption subsidy, and an R&D subsidy or tax can induce the first-best allocation. If such a policy mix is not feasible, a tax at the Pigouvian level may no longer be optimal. In the next section, we use a richer model to study such second-best scenarios.

11.5   A COMPREHENSIVE MODEL OF R&D AND TECHNOLOGY ADOPTION

The previous sections developed the various components of a comprehensive model of R&D and technology adoption. In this section we complete the analysis by combining all of the components. We assume there is one innovator who has monopoly power over his new technology, which he sells to a competitive sector of initially identical downstream polluting firms. These downstream firms sell a commodity in a competitive market, and are individually too small to exercise non-competitive influences on prices and policy actions.

The innovator invests an amount κ in an effort to discover the new technology. As described previously, $pr(\kappa)$ is the probability of discovery success, where $pr'(\kappa) > 0$. We also assume there is a constant marginal cost mc incurred by the innovator to produce and sell one unit of the new technology. Using the continuum model of technology adoption from section 11.3, the expected social cost from the pollution, innovation, and abatement components is given by

$$ESC = pr(\kappa)\left\{(1-\tilde{\chi})C_0(e_0) + \tilde{\chi}C_I(e_I) + \int_0^{\tilde{\chi}} F(\chi)d\chi + mc\tilde{\chi} + D\big(\tilde{\chi}e_I + (1-\tilde{\chi})e_0\big)\right\}$$
$$+ \big[1 - pr(\kappa)\big]\{C_0(e_0) + D(e_0)\} - \kappa. \tag{11.68}$$

11.5.1 Socially Optimal Allocation

The socially optimal allocation is found by minimizing (11.68) with respect to e_0, e_I, $\tilde{\chi}$, and κ. For the first two of these, the optimal emission levels must satisfy the familiar conditions from (11.38):

$$-C_0'(e_0) = D'(E) \tag{11.69}$$

$$-C_I'(e_I) = D'(E), \tag{11.70}$$

where total emissions are given by $E = \tilde{\chi}e_I + (1-\tilde{\chi})e_0$ in the case of R&D success, and by $E = \tilde{\chi}e_0$ in the case of R&D failure. In the latter case (11.70) is superfluous. The optimal adoption rate is determined by

$$C_I(e_I) + F(\tilde{\chi}) + mc - C_0(e_0) = D'(E)[e_0 - e_I], \tag{11.71}$$

which is equivalent to (11.39), except that we have now added the variable production cost of the new technology, mc. This condition is also superfluous in the case of R&D failure. We use e_0^*, e_I^*, and $\tilde{\chi}^*$ to denote the optimal values for these choice variables in the case of R&D success, and e_{00}^* to denote the optimal value for the lone endogenous outcome, in the case of R&D failure. Note that in the failure case, Eq. (11.69) is the only relevant condition. Note too that $e_0^* \neq e_{00}^*$, since the position of the aggregate marginal abatement cost curve will be different under the R&D success and failure outcomes, and hence the optimal pollution levels will differ.

To derive the optimal condition for κ, it is useful to define the ex post optimal social cost, conditional on R&D success or failure. In the case of success, the social cost of pollution is

$$SC_I^* = (1-\tilde{\chi}^*)C_0(e_0^*) + \tilde{\chi}^*C_I(e_I^*) + \int_0^{\tilde{\chi}^*} F(\chi)d\chi + mc\tilde{\chi}^* + D(\tilde{\chi}^*e_I^* + (1-\tilde{\chi}^*)e_0^*), \tag{11.72}$$

and in the case of R&D failure we simply have

$$SC_0^* = C_0(e_{00}^*) + D(e_{00}^*). \tag{11.73}$$

With this notation, we can determine the optimal level for R&D investment by differentiating (11.68) with respect to κ:

$$pr'(\kappa)[SC_0^* - SC_I^*] = 1. \tag{11.74}$$

11.5.2 Decentralized Decision-Making and First-Best Regulation

To understand the potential for a suite of policy instruments to produce the first-best outcome, we need to first describe the order of moves among the different private entities. We assume that there is a first stage in which the innovator engages in R&D effort, which leads to the discovery of a new technology (R&D success), or continued availability of only the old technology (R&D failure). Conditional on success or failure, firms make their decisions as follows.

- In the case of R&D failure, downstream firms engage in emission reductions depending on the type of environmental policy they face.
- In the case of R&D success, the innovator first sets the price (or quantity sold) of the new technology. The downstream firms decide whether or not to adopt the new technology, and then engage in emission reductions, depending on the type of environmental policy they face.

The four different private decision levels – R&D effort, technology pricing, technology adoption, and emissions – cause three potential market imperfections. In the absence of regulation, downstream firms pollute too much. Innovators exercise monopoly power and charge too high a price for their new technology, leading to inefficiently low technology adoption. Finally, and despite market power in pricing the technology, the value to the innovator of the new technology is smaller than its social value. To achieve a decentralized first-best outcome, these three market imperfections call for three separate policy instruments.

To begin, the regulator needs to price the environmental externality using an emission tax or tradable permits. If the other market failures are internalized, equations (11.69) and (11.70) show that the emission price must follow the Pigouvian rule. For an emissions tax this is $\tau^* = D'(E^*)$, where E^* is the aggregate level of emissions. Under R&D success, we have $E^* = \tilde{\chi}^* e_I^* + (1 - \tilde{\chi}^*) e_0^*$, and under R&D failure, $E^* = e_{00}^*$. For a tradable permit program the regulator issues $L = E^*$ permits, leading to a price $\sigma^* = D'(E^*)$.

Second, the regulator needs to correct for the smaller deployment of the new technology that arises from the innovator's use of his market power. We have seen that she can do this by subsidizing the adoption of the new technology. As we discuss below, the size of the corrective subsidy depends on the elasticity of the inverse demand for the new technology among the downstream firms. Determining this elasticity is not an easy task in practice, as it depends on the instrument chosen to deal with pollution.

Suppose the regulator has chosen a tax instrument, and is able to commit to the level of the tax rate, before the innovator decides on his technology price and output. Define the inverse demand function faced by the innovator in this case by $\varphi(\tilde{\chi}, \tau, \zeta)$. This is the marginal willingness to pay by the polluting industry, for a marginal increase in $\tilde{\chi}$. Inverse demand is a function of $\tilde{\chi}$ because the quantity sold by the innovator is determined by the firm that is indifferent between adopting and not adopting the technology. In other words, for the indifferent firm, the total cost incurred with the new technology (including the fixed cost F, the license fee φ, and the adoption subsidy ς) is equal to the total cost incurred when it stays with the old technology:

$$C_I\left(e_I(\tau)\right) + \tau e_I(\tau) + \underbrace{F(\tilde{\chi}) + \varphi - \varsigma}_{\text{adoption payment}} = C_0\left(e_0(\tau)\right) + \tau e_0(\tau). \tag{11.75}$$

Since φ affects the marginal adopting firm in this way – and thus the share of adopting firms – we can derive the inverse demand function by solving (11.75) for ϕ :

$$\varphi(\tilde{\chi}, \tau, \varsigma) = C_0\left(e_0(\tau)\right) - C_I\left(e_I(\tau)\right) - F(\tilde{\chi}) + \tau\left[e_0(\tau) - e_I(\tau)\right] + \varsigma. \tag{11.76}$$

Equation (11.76) implies that the innovator's profit, conditional on R&D success, is

$$\Pi(\tilde{\chi}, \tau, \varsigma) = [\varphi(\tilde{\chi}, \tau, \varsigma) - mc]\tilde{\chi}. \tag{11.77}$$

Differentiating the profit function with respect to $\tilde{\chi}$ yields the innovator's first-order condition for the technology licenses it will sell:

$$\begin{aligned} 0 &= \varphi(\tilde{\chi}, \tau, \varsigma) - mc + \varphi_{\tilde{\chi}}(\tilde{\chi}, \tau)\tilde{\chi} \\ &= \varphi(\tilde{\chi}, \tau, \varsigma) - mc - F'(\tilde{\chi})\tilde{\chi}. \end{aligned} \tag{11.78}$$

Note that the second line follows from (11.76), where we see that $\varphi_{\tilde{\chi}}(\tilde{\chi}, \tau) = -F'(\tilde{\chi})$.

An efficient allocation requires that the innovator licenses his technology at its marginal cost, meaning the subsidy needs to be set so that the innovator's decision results in $\varphi(\tilde{\chi}, \tau, \varsigma) = mc$. Equation (11.78) and the form of $\varphi(\tilde{\chi}, \tau, \varsigma)$ imply that the optimal subsidy is

$$\varsigma^* = F'(\tilde{\chi}^*)\tilde{\chi}^* = -\varphi_{\tilde{\chi}}(\tilde{\chi}, \tau, \varsigma)\tilde{\chi}^*. \tag{11.79}$$

The formula for the optimal subsidy can be further transformed so it reads

$$\varsigma^* = \varphi(\tilde{\chi}^*; \tau^*, \varsigma)\frac{-\varphi_{\tilde{\chi}}(\tilde{\chi}^*; \tau^*, \varsigma)}{\varphi(\tilde{\chi}^*; \tau^*, \varsigma)}\tilde{\chi}^* = \varphi(\tilde{\chi}^*; \tau^*, \varsigma)\varepsilon_{\varphi}, \tag{11.80}$$

where ε_φ is the elasticity of the inverse demand function for the new technology. Note that the magnitude of ε_φ is large when the fixed cost of adoption increases quickly with an increase in χ. Thus a larger subsidy is needed to induce the optimal adoption, when the fixed cost of adoption increases rapidly with more adoption.

Finally, the regulator needs to correct for the difference between the social and the private value of innovation. In the absence of regulation the private value is smaller than the social value. We have seen that an adoption subsidy to correct for monopoly power can, however, increase private innovation value such that the regulator needs to tax the income from innovation, to prevent over-investment in new technology development. This income tax T has to be chosen according to

$$T^* = 1 - \frac{SC_0^* - SC_I^*}{[\varphi(\tilde{\chi}^*; \tau^*, \varsigma) + \varsigma^* - mc]\tilde{\chi}^*}. \tag{11.81}$$

11.5.3 Second-Best Analysis: Environmental Policy Only

An optimal policy mix as discussed above may not be feasible for several reasons. Usually, individual profit taxes to correct for insufficient R&D incentives are not legally feasible. Adoption subsidies can create politically unpopular windfall profits, and may also be in conflict with agreements governing international trade, which often prohibit such instruments. We therefore study second-best environmental policy, such as an emission tax or tradable permits, when the other instruments needed for efficiency are not available. We focus mainly on the case of an emission tax, and briefly outline the differences that arise under a permit regime. We begin by noting that second-best policy is not unambiguously defined. Rather, it depends crucially on what information is available, and the regulator's ability to make long-term commitments.

There are several points in time at which the regulator can step in and make a commitment to a fixed tax rate, or respond in a flexible way to the firms' decisions. These possibilities are displayed in Figure 11.10. In principle the regulator can:

(a) fix a single tax rate prior to R&D, taking into account the new technology and the demand for it (ex ante regulation before R&D);
(b) fix a menu of tax rates prior to R&D (ex ante regulation before R&D);
(c) fix a single tax rate after R&D success/failure, but prior to pricing and adoption of the new technology (ex ante regulation after R&D);
(d) fix a single tax rate simultaneously with the innovator's pricing decision (simultaneous move game);
(e) fix a single tax rate after the innovator announces his price, but before the downstream firms adopt the new technology (ex ante regulation after R&D and technology pricing);
(f) fix a single tax rate after adoption of the new technology (ex-post regulation).

In what follows we will examine cases (b), (c), and (f) in detail. The other cases are discussed in the appendices. For ease of exposition, we look at the last of these first, and then work backwards.

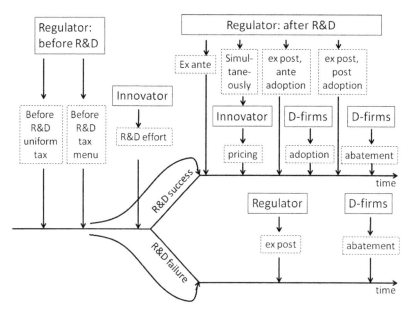

Figure 11.10 Possible timing paths for regulator actions

Ex Post Regulation – Timing (F)

The case of ex-post regulation after adoption is relevant because this is the only regime where environmental policy is time-consistent. The optimal emission price must be equal to marginal damage, and since all technology adoption decisions are made prior to regulation, the optimal tax and permit instruments are equivalent. That is, the regulator defines her instrument such that

$$\tau = \sigma = D'\left(\tilde{\chi}e_I + (1 - \tilde{\chi})e_0\right).$$
(11.82)

From this it is clear that

$$\tau'(\tilde{\chi}) = \sigma'(\tilde{\chi}) = D''(E)[e_I - e_0] < 0$$
(11.83)

for increasing marginal damage, and zero for constant marginal damages, meaning the optimal emission price is non-increasing in the adoption rate.

The interesting case is for increasing marginal damage. Within the emission tax context, the innovator will take into account that the regulator will lower the tax rate as a response to higher output of the new technology. That is, more adoption shifts the aggregate marginal abatement cost curve to the left, and the optimal tax down. The polluting industry inverse demand function (marginal willingness to pay) that arises from the equality of compliance costs under the new and old technologies for the indifferent firm is now

$$\varphi\left(\tilde{\chi}, \tau(\tilde{\chi})\right) = C_0(e_0) - C_I(e_I) - F(\tilde{\chi}) + \tau(\tilde{\chi})[e_0 - e_I].$$
(11.84)

The profit function for the innovator conditional on R&D success therefore becomes

$$\Pi(\tilde{\chi}, \tau(\tilde{\chi})) = \left[\varphi(\tilde{\chi}, \tau(\tilde{\chi})) - mc \right] \tilde{\chi}, \tag{11.85}$$

and the profit maximization condition with respect to $\tilde{\chi}$ (taking into account its effect on the tax rate) is

$$\varphi - mc + \left[\varphi_{\tilde{\chi}} + \varphi_{\tau} \tau'(\tilde{\chi}) \right] \tilde{\chi} = 0. \tag{11.86}$$

Differentiating (11.84), we see that the slopes of the inverse demand function with respect to $\tilde{\chi}$ and τ are given by

$$\varphi_{\tilde{\chi}}(\cdot) = -F'(\tilde{\chi}) + \tau'(\tilde{\chi})[e_0 - e_I] < 0 \tag{11.87}$$

and

$$\varphi_{\tau}(\cdot) = e_0 - e_I > 0, \tag{11.88}$$

respectively. Thus the inverse demand function is more elastic with respect to $\tilde{\chi}$ under the tax only regime than under the first best. In addition, a lower tax rate lowers the demand for the new technology.

Ex Ante Regulation After R&D – Timing (C)

We now turn to the case where the regulator can commit to the tax rate before the innovator decides on output (or the license fee). Working backwards to solve this game between the regulator and the innovator, we first look at the problem faced by the innovator, who now takes the tax rate as given. The inverse demand function for the new technology is

$$\varphi(\tilde{\chi}, \tau) = C_0(e_0) - C_I(e_I) - F(\tilde{\chi}) + \tau[e_0 - e_I], \tag{11.89}$$

which differs from (11.84) in that the tax rate does not depend on the innovator's output. The objective function conditional on R&D success for the innovator is

$$\Pi(\tilde{\chi}, \tau) = [\varphi(\tilde{\chi}, \tau) - mc]\tilde{\chi}, \tag{11.90}$$

with first-order condition

$$\begin{aligned} 0 &= \varphi - mc + \varphi_{\tilde{\chi}} \tilde{\chi} \\ &= \{ C_0(e_0) - C_I(e_I) - F(\tilde{\chi}) + \tau[e_0 - e_I] \} - mc - F'(\tilde{\chi})\tilde{\chi}. \end{aligned} \tag{11.91}$$

Differentiating with respect to τ, it is easy to see that the innovator's response to a tax increase is given by

$$\frac{d\tilde{\chi}}{d\tau} = \frac{e_0 - e_I}{2F'(\tilde{\chi}) + F''(\tilde{\chi})\tilde{\chi}} > 0. \tag{11.92}$$

Thus a higher tax induces a larger deployment of the new technology.

Taking into account the innovator's reaction, the regulator selects a tax rate to minimize total social cost. In appendix A we show that the second-best optimal tax rate is characterized by:

$$\tau = D'(E) - [\varphi - mc]\frac{d\tilde{\chi}/d\tau}{dE/d\tau} > D'(E). \tag{11.93}$$

We see that in this example of ex ante regulation (i.e. before the innovator's pricing or output decision), the regulator raises the tax rate above marginal damage, in order to push up demand for the new technology, and thus compensate for the output reduction stemming from the monopolist innovator's pricing strategy. Note that the innovator's profit margin $(\varphi - mc)$ in (11.93) can also be written as $(\varphi - mc) = -\varphi_{\tilde{\chi}}\tilde{\chi} = F'(\tilde{\chi})\tilde{\chi}$, and is therefore determined by the curvature of the adoption cost, depending on the firm specific parameter χ. The innovator's overall expected profit is dependent on his R&D effort, and the extent to which this R&D effort is higher or lower than under the ex post regulation case is ambiguous.

Note further that instead of working with the inverse demand function defined by (11.89), we could work with the direct demand function $\tilde{\chi}(\varphi, \tau)$, which through (11.89) is implicitly defined by

$$\varphi = C_0(e_0) - C_I(e_I) - F(\tilde{\chi}(\varphi, \tau)) + \tau[e_0 - e_I]. \tag{11.94}$$

In this case (11.93) reads:

$$\tau = D'(E) - [\varphi - mc]\frac{\tilde{\chi}_\varphi \dfrac{d\varphi}{d\tau} + \tilde{\chi}_\tau}{dE/d\tau}, \tag{11.95}$$

where $\tilde{\chi}_\varphi \cdot d\varphi/d\tau$ is the strategic effect, since the regulator has a first mover advantage.

To close our discussion on this regulation regime, we note that under such a commitment policy, taxes and tradable permits are no longer equivalent. The straightforward reasoning is as follows. Under a tax policy, the innovator can lower emissions by inducing the sale of more units of the new technology. Under commitment to a permit regime, by contrast, there is by definition no effect on emissions. As we have seen in section 11.3, more adoption leads to a lower permit price, which in turn lowers the demand for the new technology. The innovator will therefore act to counter the resulting lower permit price by reducing sales of his new technology. The effective inverse demand function is

$$\varphi(\tilde{\chi}, L) = C_0(e_0) - C_I(e_I) - F(\tilde{\chi}) + \sigma(L, \tilde{\chi})[e_0 - e_I], \tag{11.96}$$

where $\sigma(\tilde{\chi}, L)$ is the equilibrium permit price when the total number of permits is L, and the innovator supplies $\tilde{\chi}$ units of the new technology. The innovator's first-order condition for profit maximization is now

$$(\varphi - mc) + \left[\varphi_{\tilde{\chi}} + \varphi_\sigma \sigma'(L, \tilde{\chi})\right]\tilde{\chi} = 0, \tag{11.97}$$

which is different from (11.91) but has a similar structure to (11.86). Under tradable permits, the inverse demand function is more elastic than with an emission tax, and the monopolistic innovator will reduce output more than he would under the tax regime. This implies that the tax regime is more efficient.

Other Regimes – Timing (E) and (D)

As discussed above, there are in principle other timing options open to the regulator. The innovator could commit to a price, and the regulator could decide the level of her policy instrument thereafter (timing (e) above). Mathematically, this case is different in its handling, because one has to work with the direct demand function instead of inverse demand. In appendix B, we show that here too the second-best optimal tax rate exceeds marginal damage, because the innovator wants to increase demand for the new technology. Alternatively, the case might arise where neither the innovator nor the regulator can make a commitment (timing (d) above), meaning we have a simultaneous move game. We show in appendix C that, once again, the second-best optimal tax rate exceeds marginal damage.

To Commit or Not to Commit?

Which of the above regimes is best from a welfare point of view? The answer can be identified from a diagram depicting the innovator's iso-profit lines, the regulator's iso-social-cost lines, and both players' reaction curves, as in Figure 11.11. In both panels, the solid U-shaped curves represent the regulator's iso-social-cost lines. To the "north" we have lower iso-cost lines since – in the relevant range – more output of the new technology leads to lower social costs (too much adoption can also raise social costs; this region lies outside the diagram). The cost minima are connected by the regulator's reaction curve (dotted dashed line). The dashed curves opening to the right represent the innovator's iso-profit lines. Higher tax rates boost demand, and are therefore preferred by the innovator. Accordingly, the iso-profit lines are increasing to the right. The innovator's reaction curve connects the vertical parts of the iso-profit lines. In the simultaneous-move game, the two reaction functions intersect. Ex ante regulation and

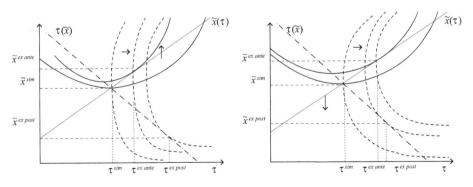

Figure 11.11 Isoprofit curves, iso-social-cost lines, and the innovator's and regulator's reaction curves

ex-post regulation can also be depicted in that figure. Under ex ante regulation, the regulator chooses a tax rate on the innovator's reaction curve that touches the lowest iso-cost curve. Under ex-post regulation, the innovator chooses an output level on the regulator's reaction curve (grey and downward-sloping) that touches the highest iso-profit curve. We see that the regulator is always best off if she can make an ex ante commitment. For the innovator, by contrast, the situation is ambiguous. Depending on cost and demand elasticities, the innovator may prefer ex ante or ex-post regulation. This is shown on the left- and right-hand panels of Figure 11.11. We also see that in the left-hand panel, the innovator prefers tax commitment over all other regimes. Thus there is no conflict of interest between the innovator and the regulator with respect to timing and commitment. In the right-hand panel, by contrast, the innovator is best off under ex-post regulation. That is also where the social costs are at their highest.

Ex Ante Regulation Prior to R&D – Timing (B)

In the regimes discussed so far, the regulator has enacted policy after R&D success, but has ignored the impact on R&D effort. To end this section, we investigate the case where the regulator makes an ex ante commitment before the innovator engages in R&D activity. As discussed above, such a commitment can be conditional or unconditional on R&D success. A contingent commitment to a menu of tax rates welfare dominates an unconditional commitment to a uniform tax, since it provides more flexibility. We examine the contingent commitment with two tax rates τ_0 and τ_I (timing case (b) above).

If there is no R&D success, the emission tax will be set equal to the marginal social damage that results when there is no new technology. In the case of R&D success, the regulator establishes the tax rate τ_I. To understand its structure, we first look at the innovator's problem. He maximizes expected profit given by

$$E\Pi(\tilde{\chi}, \kappa) = \Pr(\kappa)\left[\varphi(\tilde{\chi}, \tau_I) - mc\right]\tilde{\chi} - \kappa, \tag{11.98}$$

where the inverse demand function is the same as in (11.89), and the first-order condition with respect to output is given by (11.91). Let the solution be denoted by $\tilde{\chi}_{\tau_I}$. The first-order condition with respect to κ is then

$$\Pr'(\kappa)\left[\varphi(\tilde{\chi}_{\tau_I}, \tau_I) - mc\right]\tilde{\chi}_{\tau_I} = 1. \tag{11.99}$$

By differentiating this first-order condition with respect to the tax rate, it is easy to see that $\partial\kappa/\partial\tau_I > 0$. A higher tax rate increases demand by downstream firms for the new technology, thus increasing both the innovator's profit and the private value of innovation.

Taking the innovator's reaction as given, the regulator minimizes expected social costs

$$ESC(\tau_0, \tau_I) = \Pr(\kappa)SC(\tau_I) + \left(1 - \Pr(\kappa)\right)SC(\tau_0) - \kappa, \tag{11.100}$$

where $SC_I(\tau_I)$ is the social cost after innovation under tax rate τ_I and

$$SC_0(\tau_0) = C_0\left(e_0(\tau_0)\right) - D(e_0(\tau_0)) \tag{11.101}$$

is the social cost in the case of R&D failure. In appendix D, we show that the optimal menu of tax rates satisfies $\tau_0 = D'(e_0)$ and

$$\tau_I = D'(E) - \left(\frac{F'(\tilde{\chi})\tilde{\chi}}{dE_t/d\tau_I}\right)\frac{d\tilde{\chi}_{\tau_I}}{d\tau_I} + \left(\frac{\Pr'(\kappa)\big(SC_I(\tau_I) - SC_I(\tau_I)\big) - 1}{\Pr(\kappa)dE_t/d\tau_I}\right)\frac{d\kappa_{\tau_I}}{d\tau_I}. \quad (11.102)$$

The first two terms in (11.102) are the same as in (11.93), while the last term takes into account the deviation of R&D effort from its first-best level. In principle, this deviation can go in either direction, becoming too low or too high. We summarize these findings as follows.

Proposition 11.11
In a second-best world in which environmental policy is the only available instrument:

(a) *Among all the second-best scenarios (a) through (f) with an emission tax only, a menu of R&D success/failure conditional tax rates dominates all other regimes.*
(b) *If the regulator can only enact policy after R&D success, an ex ante commitment to a tax policy welfare dominates all other regimes, including commitment to a fixed amount of tradable permits.*

11.6 EXPERIMENTAL EVIDENCE

There are relatively few empirical studies comparing the influence of policy instruments on technology adoption. However, laboratory experiments have been used to test how different institutional settings impact polluters' incentives to adopt new technology. In an experimental setting, it is easier to simulate technology adoption than innovation (due to uncertain outcomes with the latter), and so experiments have focused on the adoption of existing technologies rather than innovation.

The experimental study from Camacho-Cuena et al. (2012) is closest to the theoretical model outlined in section 11.3. The authors ask if the allocation scheme in an emissions trading system (grandfathering versus auctioning) affects the incentives to adopt a new (marginal) abatement cost-reducing technology. In their experiment, emissions are abated in discrete steps, with marginal abatement cost given by stepwise weakly decreasing constants. Subjects were assigned one of five initial abatement technologies, which differed in the level of maximum (default) emissions, and therefore marginal abatement costs, since the slopes were all normalized to one. Subjects took two actions in each of six rounds. They first decided whether or not to adopt the new technology at a fixed investment cost, and then participated in a permit trading market. The authors explore three treatments related to free versus costly allocation: a pure (ascending clock) auction, grandfathering with intra-group reallocation via a single-unit double auction, and grandfathering with intra-group reallocation via an ascending clock auction.

Camacho-Cuena et al. (2012) find that outcomes under all three treatments differed significantly from the first-best investment decisions, but there was no significant difference in investment behavior across the three allocation schemes. Also, conditional on investment behavior, there was too little net trading in all treatments, relative to the first best. Despite these deviations, total investment efficiency in the experiments was around 92 percent, while total market efficiency was 83–85 percent. The results largely confirm the theoretical prediction that allocating permits freely provides the same incentives for technology adoption as auctioning.

There are other studies that investigate incentives to invest in environmentally friendly technologies. For example, Ben-David et al. (1999) consider an emission permit market where firms produce by employing emissions-generating capital. Subjects in the experiment choose one of three production technologies, where permit market spending and capital costs are inversely related. In each round, firms can make an irreversible investment to become cleaner. Somewhat surprisingly, the authors find that heterogeneity lowers market efficiency, likely due to the additional noise that heterogeneity introduces into trading. Gangadharan et al. (2013) examine the interaction between permit banking and investment in cleaner technology. Playing as firms, subjects have asymmetric technologies that differ in production capacity and cleanness. Similar to the set-up used by Camacho-Cuena et al. (2012), dirty firms gain more from investing than firms that are already relatively clean. Different from Camacho-Cuena et al., Gangadharan et al. provide participants with information about the other players' investment decisions. The authors find that under this setting, subjects tend to over-invest and over-bank, leading to sub-optimal market performance. Finally, Jones and Vossler (2014) study water quality trading, where firms (experimental subjects) can create tradable credits through upfront investments in a "baseline-and-credit" program. Comparing investment decisions under this institutional regime to both a cap-and-trade and a tax-subsidy scheme, the authors find that the latter performs best regarding efficiency, while the baseline-and-credit performs worst. The main reason for this is uncertainty about the total permit supply in the baseline-and-credit regime. Taken as a group, the studies reviewed here provide mixed evidence on the efficiency of different institutional frameworks. However, the results largely confirm the theoretical prediction on the equivalence of free and costly permits, as regards adoption incentives for cleaner technologies.

11.7 SUMMARY

In this chapter we have focused on behavior and policies related to the development and adoption of new, less-polluting technology. We have seen that the regulatory environment is made complex by multiple, overlapping market imperfections related to pollution damages and incentives for private firms to innovate. We explored individual firms' incentives and behavior, and considered the portfolio of policy actions the regulator would need to implement first-best outcomes. Recognizing that the use of multiple policy levers is typically not feasible, we also explored second-best approaches that attempt to address the multiple market imperfections with single environmental policy instruments. These efforts provided a number of relevant insights.

First, we saw that in the simplest case when innovation is purely private, meaning one firm's R&D investment efforts to reduce its abatement costs do not affect other firms' abatement costs, the ability of single instruments such as an emission tax or cap and trade program to provide the first-best allocation is unaffected. In this case, the optimal policy continues to be to price the externality at its Pigouvian level. When investment has public good-like attributes, such that R&D effort reduces costs for investing firms as well as other firms in the industry, a second market failure exists in the form of inefficiently low R&D expenditures. This can be addressed by subsidizing investment in addition to pricing emissions or, in a second-best context, by setting the emission price above its Pigouvian level. In the latter case the higher-than-marginal-damages emission price serves to indirectly encourage additional R&D effort by the polluting industry.

Second, we examined the discrete adoption decision, whereby polluting firms gauge the merit of paying a fixed cost in order to deploy a new technology, which serves to reduce their abatement and marginal abatement cost functions. We saw that an individual firm's adoption decision depends on the size of the fixed cost of adoption vis-à-vis the compliance-related savings that the new technology provides. Not surprisingly, we found that the strength of the adoption incentive depends on the stringency of environmental policy, regardless of the policy mechanism. However, when comparing the adoption incentives provided by different policy instruments from a common environmental starting point, we demonstrated that an emission tax will induce a higher proportion of polluting firms to adopt the new technology than a cap and trade program. This is because adoption by multiple firms shifts the aggregate marginal abatement cost curve to the left, thereby reducing the per emission price with cap and trade, but not with an emission tax. This result notwithstanding, we argued that the more relevant question is whether or not the various policy instruments induce the optimal level of technology adoption, which depends on pollution damages as well as fixed adoption costs and variable abatement costs. Here we saw that if the regulator anticipates the new technology, or is able to optimally react to firms' technology adoption choices, the Pigouvian rule alone provides sufficient incentives to decentralize the efficient allocation of abatement effort and technology adoption.

Third, we examined the behavior of a private innovator, who invests in R&D in order to discover a new technology and market it to the polluting industry. This is relevant because there is a socially optimal level of R&D investment that arises based on the likelihood of R&D success and the social benefits that the innovation can provide. In addition, achieving the socially optimal level of technology adoption amongst the downstream polluting firms requires that the innovator licenses his new technology at its marginal provision cost. We saw that for each of these, the private innovator's incentives do not perfectly align with those of the regulator. Our analysis suggested that the private value of the innovation is smaller than the social value, meaning too little R&D expenditure is provided by the innovator. Subsidizing adoption in order to raise the private value accordingly, however, creates excess profits for the innovator. Finally, the innovator's ability to exercise monopoly power when selling his technology to downstream firms means there will be too few technology licenses made available.

To close the chapter we presented a comprehensive model that integrated industry adoption and innovator behavior. We saw that obtaining the socially optimal levels of R&D effort and technology adoption rate required a suite of policy actions that include pricing emissions, subsidizing technology adoption, and taxing the innovator's excess profits. We also demonstrated that the structure of second-best policies depends on the timing over which investment, adoption, and policy stringency decisions are made. In most cases we saw that the regulator needs to set the emission price at a level higher than the Pigouvian rate, and that there is no equivalence between the tax and quantity instruments.

11.8   FURTHER READING

Kneese and Schultze (1975) were among the first to emphasize the long-term incentives of environmental policy instruments. The first contributions dealing with adoption of a new abatement technology are by Downing and White (1986), Milliman and Prince (1989), and Malueg (1989). Both Kennedy and Laplante (1999) and Requate and Unold (2003) criticize these authors' approach by pointing out that equilibrium considerations should be taken into account when studying the incentives to adopt new technology, and that the number of firms that adopt the new technology is determined endogenously. Laffont and Tirole (1996) study the innovation incentives under tradable permits, taking account of the marginal costs of public funds. Biglaiser and Horowitz (1995) and Parry (1995) were the first to rigorously combine the issues of innovation and adoption. Papers that investigate specific aspects of innovation incentives under tradable permits include Montero (2002a, 2002b) and Perino (2008, 2010). Denicolò (1999) was the first to explicitly compare ex ante and ex-post regulation for both emission taxes and tradable permits in a model with an upstream monopolistic R&D firm and many polluting downstream firms. Requate (2005) extends this approach; section 11.5 draws heavily on that article. Perino and Requate (2012) extend the analysis from section 11.3 by relaxing the assumption that innovation consists in a left-shift of the marginal abatement cost curve. Hoel (2010) discusses special features of environmental innovations.

Fischer and Newell (2008) and Reichenbach and Requate (2012) theoretically examine incentives to adopt renewable energy sources (RES), while Popp et al. (2011) empirically study the effects of RES diffusion policies.

There is a further branch of literature that discusses pollution in endogenous growth models. We have not addressed it here, since it requires more advanced methods of optimal control. Seminal contributions came from Bovenberg and Smulders (1995) and Bovenberg and de Mooij (1997). An important recent contribution is Acemoglu et al. (2012), which draws on the idea of directed technical change developed in Acemoglu (2002). Much as in our discrete time model, Acemoglu et al. (2012) find that even in a very long-term perspective, a policy mix consisting of emission taxes and adoption subsidies plus R&D subsidies is necessary to induce optimal R&D incentives and technology adoption. This is consistent with our findings from the simpler model.

Finally, there is an empirical literature that uses patent counts to understand how aspects of environmental policy affect technology. Popp (2010a) reviews some of this literature, and Johnstone et al. (2010) examine how renewable energy policies affect innovation. Similarly, Popp (2003) examines how the 1990 Clean Air Act Amendments affected innovation in flue gas desulfurization technologies. In more general applications, Popp (2002, 2010b) quantifies the relationship between energy prices and energy efficiency innovations.

APPENDIX A: DERIVATION OF (11.92)

Recall that the innovator's first-order condition for profit maximization is given by (11.91). In the case of R&D success, the regulator selects τ_I to maximize

$$
\begin{aligned}
SC_I(\tau_I) = &\tilde{\chi} C_I(e_I) \\
&+ \int_0^{\tilde{\chi}} F(\chi) d\chi + mc\tilde{\chi} + (1 - \tilde{\chi})C_0(e_0) + D(\tilde{\chi} e_I + (1 - \tilde{\chi})e_0),
\end{aligned} \tag{A11.1}
$$

treating the choice variables e_0, e_I, and $\tilde{\chi}$ as functions of the tax rate. Emissions are determined by firms' behavior according to

$$
-C'_{e_i}(e_i) = \tau, \qquad i = 0, I, \tag{A11.2}
$$

while the share of technology-adopting firms is determined by (11.91). Differentiating (A11.1) with respect to the tax rate we have

$$
\begin{aligned}
&\tilde{\chi} C'_I(e_I)\frac{de_I}{d\tau} + (1-\tilde{\chi})C'_0(e_0)\frac{de_0}{d\tau} + D'(E)\left[\tilde{\chi}\frac{de_I}{d\tau} + (1-\tilde{\chi})\frac{de_0}{d\tau}\right] + \\
&\left\{C_I(e_I) + F(\tilde{\chi}) + mc - C_0(e_0) + D'(E)\left[e_I - e_0\right]\right\}\frac{d\tilde{\chi}}{d\tau} = 0.
\end{aligned} \tag{A11.3}
$$

By substituting in (A11.2) as well as using the innovator's first-order condition

$$
C_I(e_I) + F(\tilde{\chi}) + mc - C_0(e_0) = -F'(\tilde{\chi})\tilde{\chi} - \tau(e_I - e_0) \tag{A11.4}
$$

from (11.91), we can rewrite (A11.3), after some rearrangement, as

$$
[D'(E) - \tau] \times \underbrace{\left[\tilde{\chi}\frac{de_I}{d\tau} + (1-\tilde{\chi})\frac{de_0}{d\tau} + (e_I - e_0)\frac{d\tilde{\chi}}{d\tau}\right]}_{dE/d\tau} - F(\tilde{\chi})\tilde{\chi}\frac{d\tilde{\chi}}{d\tau} = 0, \tag{A11.5}
$$

where $dE/d\tau$ (the terms in brackets) is the aggregate change in emissions when the tax rate changes. Isolating the tax rate on the left-hand side yields (11.93).

APPENDIX B: EX ANTE REGULATION AFTER R&D AND TECHNOLOGY PRICING

Here we study a timing context in which the innovator has committed to his price, but the regulator can set the tax before downstream firms adopt the new technology. In this case, we need to work with the demand function $\tilde{\chi}(\varphi, \tau)$ as well as with the inverse demand function $\varphi(\tilde{\chi}, \tau)$, where the latter is again implicitly defined by the indifferent firm $\tilde{\chi}$ according to

$$\varphi = C_0(e_0) - C_I(e_I) - F(\tilde{\chi}) + \tau(e_0 - e_I). \tag{A11.6}$$

The regulator minimizes the social cost

$$SC(\tau) = \tilde{\chi}C_I(e_I) + \int_0^{\tilde{\chi}} F(\chi)d\chi + mc\tilde{\chi} + (1 - \tilde{\chi})C_0(e_0) + D(\tilde{\chi}e_I + (1 - \tilde{\chi})e_0), \tag{A11.7}$$

by selecting the emission tax rate, taking as given the price for new technology ϕ, where the private choice variables $\tilde{\chi}$, e_0, and e_I are implicit functions of the tax rate. Differentiating (A11.7) with respect to the tax rate yields

$$\tilde{\chi}[C_I'(e_I) + D'(E)]\frac{de_I}{d\tau} + (1 - \tilde{\chi})[C_0'(e_0) + D'(E)]\frac{de_0}{d\tau} +$$
$$[C_I(e_I) - C_0(e_0) + F(\tilde{\chi}) + mc + D'(E)(e_I - e_0)]\frac{d\tilde{\chi}}{d\tau} = 0. \tag{A11.8}$$

Using the behavioral conditions from (A11.2), the shorthand notation

$$\frac{dE}{d\tau} = \tilde{\chi}\frac{de_I}{d\tau} + (1 - \tilde{\chi})\frac{de_0}{d\tau} + (e_I - e_0)\frac{d\tilde{\chi}}{d\tau} \tag{A11.9}$$

for the expression for φ in (A11.6), and rearranging, we can isolate φ according to

$$\tau(\varphi) = D'(E) - \frac{(\varphi - mc)}{dE/d\tau}\frac{d\tilde{\chi}}{d\tau}. \tag{A11.10}$$

Differentiating (A11.6) implicitly with respect to τ we obtain

$$\frac{d\tilde{\chi}}{d\tau} = \frac{e_0 - e_I}{F'(\tilde{\chi})}. \tag{A11.11}$$

Using this in (A11.10) we arrive at

$$\tau(\varphi) = D'(E) - \frac{(\varphi - mc)(e_0 - e_I)}{F'(\tilde{\chi}) \cdot dE/d\tau}. \tag{A11.12}$$

Given the reaction of the regulator, the innovator selects his price to maximize

$$\Pi(\varphi) = (\varphi - mc) \times \tilde{\chi}(\varphi, \tau(\varphi)), \tag{A11.13}$$

with first-order condition

$$\tilde{\chi}(\varphi, \tau(\varphi)) + (\varphi - mc)\left[\frac{\partial \tilde{\chi}(\varphi, \tau(\varphi))}{\partial \varphi} + \frac{\partial \tilde{\chi}(\varphi, \tau(\varphi))}{\partial \tau}\frac{d\tau}{d\varphi}\right] = 0. \tag{A11.14}$$

One can show that $d\tau/d\varphi > 0$ if $d^2E/(d\tau)^2 > 0$, which is the case if the third derivatives of the abatement cost functions are not numerically large. By differentiating (A11.6) implicitly with respect to τ, one can show that $d\tilde{\chi}/d\tau > 0$. That is, the demand for the new technology increases with a higher tax rate. Thus the demand function $\tilde{\chi}(\varphi, \tau(\varphi))$ is less elastic with the strategic manipulation of the tax rate than without, which in turn means that the inverse demand function is more elastic than without strategic manipulation.

APPENDIX C: SIMULTANEOUS DECISIONS ON THE TAX RATE AND TECHNOLOGY PRICE

We next look at the situation where neither the regulator nor the innovator is able to make a commitment. In this case, the inverse demand function is written as $\tilde{\chi}(\varphi, \tau)$ – instead of $\tilde{\chi}(\varphi, \tau(\varphi))$ – where, in equilibrium, the price for the technology φ and the tax rate τ are chosen simultaneously by the innovator and the regulator, respectively. The outcome can be obtained by combining our considerations from the previous appendices. For profit maximization of the innovator, instead of (A11.14) we obtain simply

$$\tilde{\chi}(\varphi, \tau) + (\varphi - mc)\frac{\partial \tilde{\chi}(\varphi, \tau)}{\partial \varphi} = 0. \tag{A11.15}$$

To maximize social welfare the regulator differentiates (A11.7) with respect to the tax rate, yielding

$$\tilde{\chi}[C'_I(e_I) + D'(E)]\frac{de_I}{d\tau} + (1 - \tilde{\chi})[C'_0(e_I) + D'(E)]\frac{de_0}{d\tau} +$$
$$[C_I(e_I) - C_0(e_0) + F(\tilde{\chi}) + mc + D'(E)(e_I - e_0)]\frac{\partial \tilde{\chi}}{\partial \tau} = 0, \tag{A11.16}$$

where, in contrast to (A11.8), we now have to use the partial tax effect $\partial \tilde{\chi}/\partial \tau$ instead of the total effect $d\tilde{\chi}/d\tau$. Once again using the behavioral equations in (A11.2), and the expression for φ in (A11.6), we get

$$\tilde{\chi}[-\tau + D'(E)]\frac{de_I}{d\tau} + (1 - \tilde{\chi})[-\tau + D'(E)]\frac{de_0}{d\tau}$$
$$- [\varphi - mc - \tau(e_0 - e_I) + D'(E)(e_0 - e_I)]\frac{\partial \tilde{\chi}}{\partial \tau} = 0, \tag{A11.17}$$

or

$$\tau\left[\tilde{\chi}\frac{de_I}{d\tau} + (1 - \tilde{\chi})\frac{de_0}{d\tau} + (e_I - e_0)\frac{d\tilde{\chi}}{d\tau}\right] =$$
$$D'(E)\left[\tilde{\chi}\frac{de_I}{d\tau} + (1 - \tilde{\chi})\frac{de_0}{d\tau} + (e_I - e_0)\frac{\partial \tilde{\chi}}{\partial \tau}\right] - (\varphi - mc)\frac{\partial \tilde{\chi}}{\partial \tau}. \tag{A11.18}$$

Isolating the tax rate, we obtain

$$\tau = D'(E) - (\varphi - mc)\frac{\partial \tilde{\chi}/\partial \tau}{dE/d\tau} > D'(E), \qquad (A11.19)$$

which is similar to (11.93) and (11.95), but the strategic term $\tilde{\chi}_\varphi \cdot d\varphi/d\tau$ is now missing, since in contrast to the case of ex ante commitment, the regulator cannot impact the innovator's price (and thus output), but she can anticipate the price in equilibrium, and therefore correct for the distortion.

APPENDIX D: DERIVATION OF (11.101)

The regulator's problem is to minimize (11.100) with respect to τ_0 and τ_I. Observe first that the innovator's expected profit in (11.98) is independent of τ_0, and therefore we have $d\kappa^*/d\tau_0 = 0$. Differentiating (11.100) with respect to τ_0 yields

$$\left(C'_0(e_0) + D'(e_0)\right)\frac{de_0}{d\tau} = \left(-\tau + D'(e_0)\right)\frac{de_0}{d\tau} = 0, \qquad (A11.20)$$

leading to $\tau = D'(e_0)$. Next, we differentiate (11.100) with respect to τ_I to obtain

$$\left\{\Pr'(\kappa)\left[SC_I(\tau_I) - SC_0(\tau_0)\right] - 1\right\}\frac{d\kappa}{d\tau} + \Pr'(\kappa)SC'_I(\tau_I) = 0. \qquad (A11.21)$$

Note that $SC'_I(\tau_I)$ is given by (A11.5). Solving for the tax rate τ_I, we obtain (11.102).

EXERCISES

11.1 * Consider an abatement cost function $C(e,\kappa) = (a - be - \kappa)^2/2b$, where κ is the amount of private investment to reduce abatement costs. There are J identical firms. The social damage function is $D(E) = d \cdot E^2/2$.
   (a) Determine the socially optimal allocation, including the level of investment for each firm. Determine also the socially optimal tax rate and the optimal number of emission permits.
   (b) Repeat for the cost function $C(e,\kappa) = a \cdot (e/\kappa)$.
   (c) Assume now that the firm has joint costs for producing output and abating emissions, given by $C(x,e,\kappa) = (ax - be - \kappa)^2/2b + cx^2/2$, and there are again J identical firms. The inverse demand for output is $P(X) = A - BX$, where $X = xJ$ is total output. Repeat part (a).
11.2 * Assume there is a single firm producing the output with a general cost function $C(x,e,\kappa)$.
   (a) Set up some reasonable assumptions on $C(x,e,\kappa)$.
   (b) Determine the socially optimal allocation, given a convex (linear) damage function.

(c) What instrument(s) does the regulator need to induce the first-best allocation?

(d) Derive a rule for the second-best optimal tax when the regulator only has an emission tax as her instrument.

(e) Now assume $C(x,e,\kappa)=(ax-be-\kappa)^2/2b+cx^2/2$, and repeat (a) through (d) for the specific functional form.

11.3 ** Consider an abatement cost function of the type

$$C^j(e_j,\kappa_j,\kappa_i^{-j}) = \left(a - be_j - \kappa_j - \varepsilon\sum_{i \neq j}\kappa_i\right)^2 / 2b$$

where $0<\varepsilon<1$ is a technological spillover parameter.

(a) Determine the socially optimal allocation.

(b) Determine the socially optimal policy mix, including optimal levels.

(c) Now assume the regulator may only use a single instrument. Determine the second-best optimal tax rate and the second-best optimal amount of tradable permits, respectively.

11.4 ** Consider abatement cost curves of the type $C_0(e)=(a_0-b_0e)^2/2b_0$ and $C_I(e)=(a_I-b_Ie)^2/2b_I$ with $a_0>a_I$ and $a_0/b_0>a_I/b_I$. The social damage function is $D(E)=d\cdot E^2/2$ and the adoption cost for technology I is denoted by F. The total number of firms is J, while J_I denotes the number of firms adopting the new technology.

(a) Determine the socially optimal allocation, including emissions and the optimal number of firms adopting the new technology.

(b) Determine the boundaries $\underline{F}$ and $\overline{F}$ of fixed costs for which complete adoption, partial adoption, and no adoption is socially optimal.

(c) For each case, determine the formula for the socially optimal emission tax rate and the optimal quantity of emission permits.

(d) Determine the second-best optimal emission standard.

11.5 *** Now consider the continuum-of-firms model as suggested in section 11.3. The conventional and new technologies are again given by $C_0(e)=(a_0-b_0e)^2/2b_0$ and $C_I(e)=(a_I-b_Ie)^2/2b_I$ with $a_0>a_I$ and $a_0/b_0>a_I/b_I$. The fixed cost is given by $F(\chi)=\gamma\chi^2/2$.

(a) Determine the socially optimal allocation, including emissions and the optimal share of firms adopting the new technology.

(b) Determine the optimal emission tax and the number of tradable permits. Assume now that the new technology is produced by a monopolist.

(c) Derive the inverse demand function for the new technology. Determine the profit-maximizing price for the monopolist when the tax rate is given.

(d) Derive formulas for the optimal policy mix.

(e) Assume that the regulator may only use an emission tax. Derive a formula for the ex ante second-best-optimal tax rate.

(f) Alternatively, assume that the regulator may only issue emission permits, and derive a formula for the ex ante second-best-optimal number of emission permits to provide.

(g) Assume that the regulator may only set a tax, and she has to set the tax rate ex post. Determine a formula for the ex-post optimal tax rate.

11.6 ** Consider the model from section 11.3. Assume now that the cost of new technology is $C^I(e,v)$ with $C_v^I(e,v)>0$, $C_{vv}^I(e,v)>0$, and $-C_{ev}^I(e,v)>0$, where v

is a technology parameter impacting the variable abatement cost function. Assume
further that $[e_0(\tau) - e_v(\tau)]$ is decreasing in τ, where $e_v(\tau)$ is firm v's optimal
emission choice with the new technology.

(a) Show that all the results from section 11.3 follow through under this assumption.

(b) Alternatively, assume that the old technology depends on v and is written as
$C^0(e, v)$, with $C_v^I(e, v) < 0$, $C_{vv}^I(e, v) > 0$, and $-C_{ev}^I(e, v) < 0$. Assume further that $[e_v(\tau) - e_I(\tau)]$ is decreasing in τ, where $e_v(\tau)$ is firm v's optimal
emission choice under the old technology. Proceed as in (a).

11.7 ** Consider a firm whose cost function is given by $c(x) = c \cdot x^2/2$. The output price
is fixed and denoted by p. Emissions are proportional to output according to
$e = \alpha_0 \cdot x$. The firm is subject to an emission tax τ.

(a) Calculate the optimal output and determine the firm's profit function.

(b) Determine the firm's marginal abatement cost function (as a function of emissions), when output is the only option to reduce emissions.

(c) Assume now that the firm can adopt a new technology with emissions coefficient $\alpha_1 < \alpha_0$. Determine the new marginal abatement cost function. Draw a
diagram with the marginal abatement cost functions resulting from the old and
from the new technology.

(d) Determine the cost savings from adopting the new technology. How does this
change with the tax rate? At which tax rate are the cost savings maximized?

(e) Assume now there is a continuum of firms represented by the unit interval.
A firm is denoted by $x \in [0,1]$. Adoption costs are identical and denoted by F
(alternatively: adoption costs are firm specific, and given by $F(x) = x^2/2$). The
social damage is given by $D(E) = d \cdot E^2/2$. Determine the socially optimal allocation as a function of the damage slope parameter d. What do you observe?
In which case can we decentralize the social optimum by an emission tax (or
by tradable permits)? Determine the optimal tax rate (the optimal amount of
tradable permits).

(f) Proceed as in (e), assuming constant marginal damage, i.e. $D(E) = d \cdot E$.

11.8 ** Consider a firm that produces output at constant marginal cost $c > 0$, and emissions are proportional to output so that $e = \alpha x$, where x is output and e is emissions.
The output price is normalized to 1. Assume that the firm has a technology with
emission coefficient α_0 and that a new technology is available that leads to a lower
emission coefficient $\alpha_1 < \alpha_0$. There is no adoption cost.

(a) Show that there is a switching tax rate where the regulator wants to adopt the
new technology for low tax rates, and stays with the old technology for high
tax rates.

(b) Assume there is a social damage function $D(E) = d \cdot E^2/2$. Determine the
socially optimal allocation as a function of the damage slope parameter d.

(c) How do the answers in (a) and (b) change if there is a positive adoption
cost $F > 0$?

CHAPTER 12

International Environmental Problems

To this point of the book we have ignored explicitly international aspects of environmental problems and policy. While the partial equilibrium models used in Chapters 3 through 6 do not rule out international trade, they abstract from issues that are specific to international pollution, policy contexts, and trade. An example of the first of these is transboundary pollution, whereby air and water emissions originating in one country are transported via wind, river, or marine systems to affect residents of other countries. This creates an environment in which the country suffering pollution damages does not have the legal authority to regulate emissions at their source. For this reason, unilateral national environmental policy usually fails to internalize the full consequences of domestic emissions, meaning that international cooperation is necessary to achieve an efficient outcome. One of the most prominent examples of transboundary pollution is climate change resulting from carbon dioxide and other greenhouse gas emissions. In sections 12.1 and 12.2 of this chapter we examine the transboundary pollution problem using a simple two-country, one commodity model without proper trade. We will see that it is relatively easy to describe efficient outcomes and policy initiatives for global pollutants. However, absent a single globally empowered regulator, countries' voluntary participation in these policy initiatives may require international transfers in order to assure that individual welfare under the cooperative outcome is higher for all countries than under the non-cooperative outcome.

A second topic that we cover in this chapter is the interaction between environmental policy and international trade. Unilateral environmental policy in one country can have consequences for pollution in another country, in that more stringent domestic environmental policy may trigger the migration of production and mobile inputs to countries with laxer policies. This is known as emission leakage, and it has become a major focus of research and policy debate in the twenty-first century, particularly as regards the potential for "pollution havens" to develop. In sections 12.3 and 12.4, we study the problem of environmental policy when there is free international trade. We distinguish between small and large open economies, and study the differences between unilateral and cooperative environmental policy, within the two contexts. We will see that an environmental regulator needs to consider several adjustment margins when setting her policy. These include, for example, domestic damage from domestic emissions; the effect domestic policy might have on foreign emissions and hence domestic damage from incoming transboundary pollution; and interactions with imports and exports.

This latter adjustment margin relates to how environmental and trade policy overlap. In sections 12.3 and 12.4 we also examine how environmental policy can masquerade as trade policy, to manipulate the terms of trade governing levels of imports and exports. Surprisingly, in our competitive markets model we see that the terms of trade effect will cause large exporting nations to *over-internalize* domestic externalities, all else being equal, in order to raise the price of the exported commodity and thereby increase export revenues. In contrast, a large importing nation will *under-internalize* domestic externalities, all else being equal, in order to keep the price of imports relatively low for its domestic consumers. These results are in contrast to the usual concern that exporting nations will use lax environmental policy in order to maintain the competitiveness of its export sector. In section 12.5 we address this by considering a model of imperfect competition, whereby oligopolistic firms compete for international market share. Here we will see that it may be optimal for a domestic regulator to under-internalize domestic damages, though this can occur for reasons not fully related to subsidizing the export sector.

In section 12.6 we turn to topics related to interactions between emissions and global energy markets. The concern we address here is that, in the context of climate change, efforts to reduce energy consumption (and hence carbon emissions) by a subset of countries will lower the global energy price, and hence lead to increased energy use (and higher carbon emissions) in the remainder of the world. This is a type of spatial emissions leakage operating through changes in energy demand. We also examine an intertemporal version of leakage, which occurs when fossil fuel-based emission reductions are planned in the future. We will see that energy providers move their supply of fossil fuel energy forward, in anticipation of the future regulation, thereby accelerating emissions into the present time. This has become known as the "green paradox".

A topic that has received a substantial amount of attention in the recent literature relates to the formation of international coalitions of countries to address international environmental problems, via international environmental agreements (IEAs). Prominent examples of IEAs include the Kyoto and Montreal protocols on climate change and ozone depletion, respectively. Researchers have used game theory models to characterize the properties of the coalitions, and to assess the likelihood that IEAs can provide solutions to transboundary pollution problems. The game-theoretic tools used in this literature are beyond the scope of our analysis here, and so in section 12.7 we simply describe some of the concepts that have been investigated, and note some of the main conclusions from this literature. We then continue in section 12.8 with an examination of elements of the Kyoto agreement such as the clean development mechanism (CDM), which were designed to enable wider participation in carbon emission abatement. We close the chapter in section 12.9 by presenting a stylized model that examines whether or not trade liberalization should be viewed as pro- or anti-environmental. We will see that the theoretical effect of expanded international trade is in fact ambiguous, meaning the trade-environment relationship is largely an empirical question.

12.1 TRANSBOUNDARY POLLUTION IN AN AUTARKY MODEL

In order to focus on the transboundary pollution in isolation, we start by examining an autarky model with two countries, where the transfer of commodities between countries is not possible. Nonetheless, pollution emitted from one country can affect the other through wind or other environmental media. The no-transfer abstraction allows us to derive several useful insights, and sets the stage for a richer examination to follow.

12.1.1 Model

Each country produces a commodity that generates pollution, part of which is transmitted to the other country. We use y and y_f to denote the maximum level of production (and hence consumption) for the home and foreign countries, respectively, and denote the baseline emissions associated with maximum production by $\hat{E}$ and $\hat{E}_f$. To reduce its emissions, a country must forgo some production. Let $C(E)$ denote the home country's abatement cost of moving to an emissions level $E < \hat{E}$, and similarly let $C_f(E_f)$ denote abatement costs for the foreign country. These costs are measured in terms of forgone production. The abatement functions satisfy the usual assumptions from Chapter 3, so that $C'(E) < 0$ and $C''(E) > 0$ for emission levels lower than the baseline.

Welfare in each country is generated by consumption and diminished by pollution according to the representative consumer utility functions $U(z,E,E_f)$ and $U_f(z_f,E,E_f)$ for the home and foreign countries, respectively, where z and z_f are consumption levels defined by $z = y - C(E)$ and $z_f = y_f - C_f(E_f)$. Note that in the general case, emissions from both countries affect both consumers. By substituting out for consumption, the utility functions can be expressed as a function of emissions only:

$$u = U\left(y - C(E), E, E_f\right)$$
$$u_f = U^f\left(y_f - C(E_f), E, E_f\right). \tag{12.1}$$

We assume that the home country utility function satisfies $U_z > 0$, $U_E < 0$, and $U_{E_f} < 0$, and make similar assumptions for the foreign utility function.

The utility functions in (12.1) nest two special cases. For the case of a *homogeneous global pollutant* such as greenhouse gasses, for which the location of emissions does not matter, we have

$$u = U\left(y - C(E), E + E_f\right)$$
$$u_f = U^f\left(y_f - C(E_f), E + E_f\right). \tag{12.2}$$

If, in contrast, the pollutant is non-uniform mixing, such that one country is only partially affected by the other's emissions, we can write

$$u = U\left(y - C(E), \alpha E + \beta E_f\right)$$
$$u_f = U^f\left(y_f - C(E_f), \alpha_f E + \beta_f E_f\right), \tag{12.3}$$

where (α, β) and (α_f, β_f) are transmission coefficients indicating how much domestic emissions and emissions from abroad affect domestic utility, for both countries.

12.1.2 Non-cooperative Behavior

We first consider the case where the two countries do not communicate, so that each can do no better than maximizing its own welfare, while taking the emissions of the other country as given. Since the welfare in each country depends on its own as well as its counterpart's activities, the two countries play a non-cooperative game whereby the players solve the following problems:

$$\max_E \{U(y - C(E), E, E_f)\}$$
$$\max_{E_f} \{U^f(y_f - C_f(E_f), E, E_f)\}. \tag{12.4}$$

The Nash equilibrium of this game is determined by the first-order conditions

$$-C'(E) \cdot U_z(z, E, E_f) + U_E(z, E, E_f) = 0$$
$$-C'_f(E_f) \cdot U^f_{z_f}(z_f, E, E_f) + U^f_{E_f}(z_f, E, E_f) = 0, \tag{12.5}$$

where the top condition describes the home country's choice, and the bottom equation describes the foreign country's choice. Upon rearranging, we obtain

$$-C'(E) = -\frac{U_E(z, E, E_f)}{U_z(z, E, E_f)} \tag{12.6}$$

and

$$-C'_{E_f}(E_f) = -\frac{U^f_{E_f}(z_f, E, E_f)}{U^f_{z_f}(z_f, E, E_f)}. \tag{12.7}$$

These conditions tell us that for each country, a unilaterally motivated social planner selects emissions such that domestic marginal abatement cost is equal to the domestic marginal rate of substitution between pollution reduction and consumption. We denote the resulting non-cooperative emission levels by (E^N, E^N_f) and the non-cooperative utility levels by

$$u^N = U\left(y^N - C(E^N), E^N, E^N_f\right)$$
$$u^N_f = U^f\left(y^N_f - C(E^N_f), E^N, E^N_f\right). \tag{12.8}$$

12.1.3 Cooperative Behavior

Non-cooperative behavior is typically not efficient, since each country ignores the damage it imposes on the other country. In this subsection, we characterize a cooperative (efficient) outcome by maximizing the utility of the home country, subject to the foreign country reaching a level of utility denoted by $\bar{u}_f$. This is analogous to the Pareto problem we examined in Chapter 1. Assuming an interior solution for emissions in both countries, the maximization problem is given by

$$\max_{E,E_f} L = U\left(y - C(E), E, E_f\right) + \lambda\left[U^f\left(y_f - C_f(E_f), E, E_f\right) - \bar{u}_f\right], \tag{12.9}$$

and the first-order conditions are

$$-C'(E) \cdot U_z + U_E + \lambda U_E^f = 0$$
$$-\lambda C_f'(E_f) \cdot U_{z_f}^f + \lambda U_{E_f}^f + U_{E_f} = 0. \tag{12.10}$$

Rearranging the top condition yields

$$-C'(E) = \frac{-\left(U_E + \lambda U_E^f\right)}{U_z} \tag{12.11}$$

for the home country and, equivalently, rearranging the bottom condition leads to

$$-C_f'(E_f) = \frac{-\left(U_{E_f} + \lambda U_{E_f}^f\right)}{\lambda U_{z_f}^f} \tag{12.12}$$

for the foreign country. We see that in a cooperative solution, each country sets emissions based on the weighted sum of the marginal disutility in both countries. In other words, the disutility from pollution both domestically and abroad should enter into each country's decision. However, even if the welfare weight between the countries is equal (i.e. $\lambda = 1$), the marginal abatement cost in the two countries need not be equal, since the sum of marginal damages is divided by different marginal utilities of income. If we assume, as usual, that marginal utility of consumption is decreasing, a rich country will have lower marginal utility of consumption than a poor country. This implies that, when welfare weights are approximately equal, at the efficient allocation, a rich country should incur higher marginal abatement costs than a poor country.

This said, it is important to note that it is not possible to directly compare the marginal abatement costs across the two countries, since abatement costs are measured in units of the production good for the respective countries, which need not be the same in both places. Since by assumption no trade or transfer of goods between the countries takes place, there is no common yardstick to measure and compare marginal abatement costs.

Limits to Cooperation

If we maintain the assumption that the two countries are not able to transfer commodities, but nevertheless can communicate, a cooperative outcome that obeys the efficiency conditions (12.11) and (12.12) is possible. However, to be feasible, the cooperative outcome must also satisfy participation (or individual rationality) constraints. To see this, define (E^C, E_f^C) as the solution to (12.11) and (12.12), and let the resulting utility levels be given by

$$
\begin{aligned}
u^C &= U\left(y^C - C(E^C), E^C, E_f^C\right) \\
u_f^C &= U^f\left(y_f^C - C(E_f^C), E^C, E_f^C\right).
\end{aligned}
\tag{12.13}
$$

The participation constraints then require that

$$
\begin{aligned}
u^C &\geq u^N \\
u_f^C &\geq u_f^N
\end{aligned}
\tag{12.14}
$$

are jointly satisfied. This means that utility for the representative individual in both countries should be higher under cooperation than under non-cooperation, if the former is to be feasible. This is not a trivial condition, in that if there is sufficient asymmetry between the countries, a Pareto-improvement through cooperation may not be possible, and negotiations over joint emission reductions will necessarily fail. In the utility structure in (12.3), for example, if $\alpha = 0$ and $\beta = 0$, while $\alpha_f > 0$ and $\beta_f > 0$, the foreign country is affected by its own pollution and pollution from the home country, but not vice versa. The foreign country would like the home country to reduce pollution, whereas the home country would not benefit from abatement efforts by the foreign country. That is, a pollution reduction by the home country beyond the non-cooperative outcome will create a cost that cannot be reciprocated by an emission reduction from the forcign country. Since transfers are not possible by assumption, mitigation of the asymmetric externality cannot be accomplished by payment from the foreign to the home country. To address this type of externality, we therefore need to extend our transboundary pollution model to include commodity transfer and, ultimately, proper trade.

12.2   COMMODITY TRANSFER

We extend our model by assuming that the output goods from the two countries can be measured by a common yardstick, so that commodity transfer is possible. If the goods are identical, we have a one commodity model, and there are no gains from trade in the classic commodity exchange sense. However, there are potential gains from exchanging emission reductions against the common commodity. We interpret such a bargain as one country compensating the other country for additional abatement effort by transferring some of its aggregate commodity.

To find a Pareto optimal allocation with possible commodity transfer between the countries we solve

$$
\max_{z, z_f, E, E_f} L = U\left(z, E, E_f\right) \quad s.t. \quad U^f\left(z_f, E, E_f\right) \geq \bar{u}_f,
\tag{12.15}
$$

subject to the feasibility constraint

$$z + z_f = y + y_f - C(E) - C_f(E_f). \tag{12.16}$$

Note that the single feasibility constraint here relaxes the problem in (12.9), where the separate constraints $z = y - C(E)$ and $z_f = y_f - C(E_f)$ needed to be satisfied under autarky. In other words, the feasibility of consumption and abatement effort needs to hold only in aggregate rather than for each country separately.

The Lagrangian for the Pareto problem now reads

$$\max_{z, z_f E, E_f} L = U(z, E, E_f) + \lambda \left[U^f(z, E, E_f) - \bar{u}_f \right]$$
$$- \mu \left[z + z_f - y - y_f + C(E) + C_f(E_f) \right], \tag{12.17}$$

and first-order conditions are

$$\frac{\partial L}{\partial z} = U_z - \mu = 0$$
$$\frac{\partial L}{\partial z_f} = \lambda U^f_{z_f} - \mu = 0, \tag{12.18}$$

and

$$\frac{\partial L}{\partial E} = U_E + \lambda U^f_E - \mu C'(E) = 0$$
$$\frac{\partial L}{\partial E_f} = U_{E_f} + \lambda U^f_{E_f} - \mu C'_f(E_f) = 0. \tag{12.19}$$

Eliminating μ from (12.18) we obtain $\lambda = U_z / U^f_{z_f}$. Substituting this expression for λ into (12.19) and using $\mu = U_z$ from (12.18) we obtain, after some rearranging,

$$-C'(E) = -\frac{U_E}{U_z} - \frac{U^f_E}{U^f_{z_f}} \tag{12.20}$$

for the home country and, likewise,

$$-C'_f(E^*) = -\frac{U_{E_f}}{U_z} - \frac{U^f_{E_f}}{U^f_{z_f}} \tag{12.21}$$

for the foreign country. These conditions tell us that, in both countries, the marginal abatement cost could equal the sum of the two representative individuals' marginal rates of substitution between emissions reduction (the public good) and private consumption. This is the familiar Lindahl-Samuelson condition from Chapter 1. Note that the marginal abatement costs need not be equal across countries, if the mutual impacts of pollution are sufficiently asymmetric. For example, if we take the specification given by

(12.3) and assume $\beta \gg \alpha_f$, the home country will suffer more from the foreign country's emissions than vice versa. The home country therefore has an incentive to offer a contract to the foreign country stipulating that the foreign country engages in a relatively higher abatement effort, and in return the home country pays compensation, by transferring some aggregate output.

In the special case of a homogeneous global pollutant we have

$$
\begin{aligned}
U_E &= U_{E_f} \\
U_E^f &= U_{E_f}^f,
\end{aligned}
\tag{12.22}
$$

meaning the marginal disutility of pollution is equal, irrespective of where the emission originates. In this case, the right-hand sides of (12.20) and (12.21) are identical, and at the efficient allocation, the marginal abatement costs should be equal across countries. Nevertheless, compensation from one country to the other may be necessary to guarantee that the participation constraints for all countries are satisfied.

The intuition for equal marginal abatement costs across countries is as follows. As long as, say, the foreign country has to give up fewer units of the consumption good to reduce one unit of the pollutant than the home country, the latter can offer the former some units of the good to compensate it for further emission mitigation, while at the same time emitting more but keeping total emissions constant. Both countries enjoy a higher consumption level while keeping emissions constant.

There are several reasons why compensation payments may be needed. The countries' preferences concerning the environment and the extent to which they are affected by emissions may be similar, but one country may be poorer than the other, and hence have a larger marginal utility of income (consumption). In this case the right-hand side of (12.6) and (12.7) is small for the poor and large for the rich country, meaning the poor country would abate less in a non-cooperative context. Differences in the right-hand sides of (12.6) and (12.7) can also arise when preferences or damages from pollution are different for the two countries, even if the countries are similarly wealthy.

During the course of negotiations over emission levels, countries may attempt to hide their "true" preferences by claiming environmental indifference, or by stating low damages from pollution, in order to bear a lower share of the abatement burden. This is an application of the more general notion that the Coase Theorem fails to induce an efficient outcome under incomplete information. It also relates to the real-world difficulty associated with securing international environmental agreements.

Decentralization Through Policy Instruments

It is natural to ask how the cooperative and non-cooperative solutions can be decentralized by policy instruments. This is relatively easy to address when product markets are competitive. To proceed, let E^C and E_f^C be the solutions to (12.20) and (12.21). These can be achieved when the two countries set emission taxes according to the generalized Pigouvian rules

$$
\tau = -\frac{U_E(z^C, E^C, E_f^C)}{U_z(z^C, E^C, E_f^C)} - \frac{U_E^f(z_f^C, E^C, E_f^C)}{U_{z_f}^f(z_f^C, E^C, E_f^C)}
\tag{12.23}
$$

for the home country, and

$$\tau_f = -\frac{U_{E_f}(z^C, E^C, E_f^C)}{U_z(z^C, E^C, E_f^C)} - \frac{U_{E_f}^f(z_f^C, E^C, E_f^C)}{U_{z_f}^f(z_f^C, E^C, E_f^C)} \tag{12.24}$$

for the foreign country. That is, the home tax rate is set equal to the aggregate marginal willingness to pay to reduce an emission originating from the home country, and correspondingly the foreign tax rate is set equal to the aggregate marginal willingness to pay to reduce an emission originating from the foreign country. Since a representative producer in each country sets its marginal abatement cost equal to the tax rate, we have $-C'(E) = \tau$ and $-C_f'(E_f) = \tau_f$, and the conditions in (12.20) and (12.21) are satisfied. As an alternative, the two countries can initiate cap and trade programs with emission permits given by $L = E^C$ and $L_f = E_f^C$.

For a homogeneous global pollutant, the optimal emission taxes must be equal across the countries. This may be difficult in practice, however, when exchange rates fluctuate or political motives intervene. In this case, a global cap and trade system may be easier to implement, where the total permit supply must satisfy $L + L_f = E^C + E_f^C$.

Distributional Issues

Note that by free allocation of permits, international distributional issues can be addressed. In particular, the participation constraint for each country can be solved by giving a sufficiently high number of permits to a country which, otherwise, would not participate in an international environmental agreement. With emission taxes or auctioned permits, participation may require direct international transfers. From Chapter 7 we know that, when there are pre-existing distortions in the public finance system, emission taxes or auctioned permits outperform freely distributed permits, since the revenues can be used to reduce other, distorting taxes. From a political economy point of view, however, freely distributed permits may be easier to agree on since the size of implicit international transfers from shifting emission allowances is less apparent than direct money transfers. Wealthy countries may agree to a relatively large endowment of emission permits for developing countries, while refusing to transfer tax revenues to those countries. On the other hand, pure redistribution of permits may not always suffice, meaning additional financial transfers may be necessary to guarantee individual rationality for each country.

12.3 MULTIPLE COMMODITIES AND PROPER TRADE

The model with a single aggregate consumption good can be generalized to a multiple commodity model in two ways. One approach is to set up a fully general equilibrium model with production functions for two or more goods, and representative consumer utility functions describing preference orderings over the consumption goods and emissions from both countries. A second approach, which we pursue here, takes a "partial" general equilibrium approach that extends the model from Chapter 5 to the case of an open economy. We refer to this as "partial" general equilibrium because, while we will accommodate trade flows, the quasi-linear preference function eliminates income effects.

12.3.1 Model Extension

We assume there is a representative firm in the home and foreign countries that produces a polluting good along with emissions. The home country firm has cost function $C(x,e)$, where x is output of the polluting good and e is emissions, which satisfies the properties described in Chapter 5. We assume here and in section 12.4 that output markets are competitive.

Because we are now considering open economies, we need to distinguish production of the good from its consumption. In our open economy with transboundary pollution the utility of the representative consumer in the home country is given by

$$U(c,z,e,e_f) = u(c) + z - D(e,e_f)$$
$$\equiv \int_0^c P(t)dt + z - D(e,e_f), \quad (12.25)$$

where c is consumption of the polluting good, $P(t) = U_c$ is the home country inverse demand function for that good, and $z = y - C(x,e) + p \cdot [x-c]$ is consumption of the numeraire good z, with initial income y. Moreover, e_f is emissions from the foreign firm, and p is the world market price for the polluting good. Finally, $p \cdot [x-c]$ is the value of exports of the polluting good if the term is positive, and spending on imports if negative. Substituting z into (12.25), we can write the welfare function for the home country as

$$W(x,c,e,e_f) \equiv \int_0^c P(t)dt - C(x,e) - D(e,e_f) + p \cdot [x-c], \quad (12.26)$$

where we have dropped the constant value y from the expression. By similar function definitions and logic, we can write the welfare function for the foreign country as

$$W^f(x_f,c_f,e,e_f) \equiv \int_0^{c_f} P_f(t)dt - C^f(x_f,e_f) - D^f(e,e_f) + p \cdot [x_f - c_f]. \quad (12.27)$$

12.3.2 Efficient Allocation

By virtue of our quasi-linear preference function, we can characterize a Pareto optimal solution by maximizing the sum of the welfare functions for the two countries. Carrying out this exercise establishes that an efficient allocation must satisfy two sets of conditions. First, for consumption and production levels of the polluting commodity, we have the usual rule

$$P(c) = P_f(c_f) = C_x(x,e) = C^f_{x_f}(x_f,e_f). \quad (12.28)$$

That is, consumers' marginal willingness to pay for the polluting good must be equal to the marginal cost of production, and the latter must be equal across countries.

For emission levels, the familiar Lindahl-Samuelson conditions must hold for each of countries' emission choices:

$$-C_e(x,e) = D_e(e,e_f) + D_e^f(e,e_f) \tag{12.29}$$
$$-C_{e_f}^f(x_f,e_f) = D_{e_f}(e,e_f) + D_{e_f}^f(e,e_f).$$

This means that a country's marginal abatement cost level, measured in units of its numeraire, must be equal to the sum of domestic marginal damages and marginal damages abroad, which arise from production. Note that (12.29) is simpler than (12.20) and (12.21), since the marginal utility of income is equal to one in our "partial" general equilibrium framework.

If the pollutant is not homogeneous, and one country is more affected by pollution than another, marginal abatement costs in the cooperative solution may be different across countries. If, by contrast, the pollutant is globally homogeneous, the damage functions can be written as

$$D(e,e_f) = D(E) \tag{12.30}$$
$$D^f(e,e_f) = D_f(E),$$

where $E = e + e_f$, and the right-hand sides of (12.29) both become $D'(E) + D_f'(E)$. Thus, for a globally homogeneous pollutant such as carbon dioxide or other greenhouse gasses, marginal costs should be equal across countries, since the location of an individual emission is irrelevant.

Decentralization

It is conceptually straightforward to define policy instruments to decentralize the efficient allocation. For heterogeneous pollutants, differentiated emissions taxes are set according to

$$\tau = D_e(e,e_f) + D_e^f(e,e_f) \tag{12.31}$$
$$\tau_f = D_{e_f}(e,e_f) + D_{e_f}^f(e,e_f),$$

implying the profit functions for the home and foreign firms are $\Pi(x,e) = px - C(x,e) - \tau e$ and $\Pi_f(x_f,e_f) = px_f - C^f(x_f,e_f) - \tau_f e_f$, respectively. Profit maximization by both firms leads to

$$p = C_x(x,e) = C_{x_f}^f(x_f,e_f) \tag{12.32}$$
$$\tau = C_e(x,e)$$
$$\tau_f = C_{e_f}^f(x_f,e_f),$$

and utility maximization by consumers in both countries results in $P(c) = P_f(c_f) = p$. Putting these equations together, we see that the socially optimal solution is achieved when the emission taxes are set according to (12.31). Alternatively, the countries can establish individual cap and trade programs, whereby L and L_f are permit endowments that correspond to the optimal solutions for e and e_f in (12.29).

EXAMPLE 12.1 (POLICY) The Kyoto Protocol reflects the fact that carbon dioxide and other greenhouse gasses are homogeneous, and that it does not matter for climate change where the gasses are emitted or abated. This is why the Protocol included flexible mechanisms for abating, where it is least costly to do so. Under the Protocol, 37 Annex I countries committed to reducing emissions of four major greenhouse gasses (carbon dioxide, methane, nitrous oxide, and sulfur hexafluoride) by 5.2 percent below their 1990 emission levels. The Protocol allows for the exchange of emissions across national borders, in addition to provisions such as the clean development mechanism (CDM) and joint implementation (JI). The latter provisions allow Annex I countries to meet their emission targets by purchasing reduction credits, which are generated outside the Annex I territories. We will study CDM and JI in more detail in section 12.8.

12.3.3 Unilateral Environmental Policy in a Small Open Economy

Having characterized the internationally efficient allocation of emissions as a baseline, we now examine countries' unilateral decisions and compare the outcomes to the efficient allocation. We distinguish the two cases of a small and a large open economy, though in our context the difference may be less sharp than in a purely trade context. In the latter, an economy is small when its domestic trade policy cannot affect relative world prices, and it is large when it does. In our situation, with transboundary environmental externalities, small and large may also refer to the relative impact of emissions on other countries. In what follows, we maintain the trade theory terminology, and refer to a small country as one in which changes in its trade patterns do not affect world prices, and a large country as one whose trade patterns do affect world prices. In this subsection, we study the small economy context. Since the large economy situation is more complicated, and requires distinguishing different cases, we delay its consideration until section 12.4.

To begin, we assume that the home government regulates pollution by an emission tax, and write welfare as a function of the domestic tax rate

$$W(\tau) = \int_0^c P(t)dt - C(x,e) + p \cdot [x-c] - D(e,e_f), \tag{12.33}$$

where x and e are endogenous outcomes that respond to the tax rate, according to the behavioral equations $\tau = C_e(x,e)$ and $p = C_x(x,e)$.[1] Home consumption c does not depend on the tax, since the world price of the polluting good p is exogenously given for the small open economy. To determine the unilaterally optimal home country emission tax, we differentiate (12.33) with respect to τ and obtain

$$W'(\tau) = \left(\underbrace{P(c) - p}_{0} \right) \underbrace{\frac{dc}{d\tau}}_{0} + \left(\underbrace{p - C_x(x,e)}_{0} \right) \frac{dx}{d\tau} + \left[\underbrace{-C_e(x,e) - D_e(e,e_f)}_{\tau} \right] \frac{de}{d\tau}$$

$$- D_{e_f}(e,e_f) \underbrace{\frac{de_f}{d\tau}}_{0} = 0, \tag{12.34}$$

---

[1] To avoid notational clutter, we write x instead of $x(\tau)$.

where the first and second terms are zero by the conditions for utility and profit maximization, respectively, as well as the fact that consumption c does not respond to the tax rate. In addition, $de_f/d\tau = 0$, because the foreign firm does not respond to the home country's domestic tax rate, and since it does not affect world market prices, there is no indirect effect on foreign emissions.[2] Therefore, (12.34) reduces to

$$\left(\tau - D_e(e,e_f)\right)\frac{de}{d\tau} = 0, \tag{12.35}$$

since $-C_e(x,e) = \tau$ from the profit maximization conditions. Because $de/d\tau < 0$, we obtain $\tau = D_e(e,e_f)$. The main conclusion from this analysis is summarized in the following proposition.

Proposition 12.1

In a small open economy with only home pollution, such that $D_{e_f}(e,e_f) = 0$ and $D_e^f(e,e_f) = 0$, a unilaterally optimal emission tax fully internalizes the externality. When there is transboundary pollution, such that $D_{e_f}(e,e_f) > 0$ and/or $D_e^f(e,e_f) > 0$, the unilaterally optimal emission tax internalizes all domestic environmental damage, but does not account for the externalities imposed on foreign countries, or the impact of foreign emissions on the home country.

The main insight here is that, as in the case of a closed economy, each country balances its producers' marginal abatement costs against the domestic marginal damage caused by the domestic pollution. Notably, this rule also holds if the domestic industry competes with other firms on the international market. Even if the foreign country sets a lower-than-optimal emission tax, perhaps for political or institutional reasons, the welfare maximizing home country government should still fully internalize its domestic pollution. Put differently, international competition in this model does not provide a rational reason to "race to the bottom" in domestic environmental stringency.

With this we can see that, for the case of transboundary pollution, unilaterally optimal emission taxes are not globally efficient, since they do not account for the damage imposed on foreign countries. The gap between the globally efficient tax rate and the unilaterally optimal tax rate is likely to be large in the case of greenhouse gasses, where the contribution of domestic pollution to the domestic damage is likely to be low for a small country. Therefore, it is not unilaterally rational to engage in greenhouse gas abatement, unless it is coordinated with other countries' efforts.

12.4 LARGE OPEN ECONOMIES

We now turn our attention to the large open economy case. As noted above, an open economy is large if it is able to affect world market prices by its domestic trade or

---

[2] Strictly speaking, there is a small effect on foreign emissions since the home producer produces less and, since the price stays constant, the home consumer buys more from the foreign producer. We ignore this small effect.

environmental policy. The channel for this is a domestic output change in response to, for example, a change in an environmental policy instrument, which is large enough to affect the world price. Depending on the structure of environmental policy in the foreign country – i.e. prices or quantities – the domestic environmental policy may also have an indirect effect on foreign emission. As we will see, the choice of optimal unilateral domestic environmental policy therefore depends on how the foreign country manages its emissions. In what follows, we consider two major cases: (a) the foreign country uses an emission tax (with a zero tax rate as a special case); and (b) the foreign country sets an emissions cap.

12.4.1 Optimal Unilateral Policy with a Foreign Emission Tax

As a step towards characterizing the optimal unilateral policy for the home country, we first describe the competitive equilibrium in an economy, without trade-limiting tariffs or quotas. While maintaining the assumption that the foreign country uses an emission tax, we look at equilibria when the domestic country uses a tax, and when it uses a quantity instrument.

Equilibrium When Both Countries Use an Emission Tax

The competitive market equilibrium of our stylized world economy is determined by utility maximization of home and foreign consumers, so that

$$
\begin{aligned}
P(c) &= p \\
P_f(c_f) &= p,
\end{aligned}
\tag{12.36}
$$

and profit maximization by the home and foreign firms:

$$
\begin{aligned}
p &= C_x(x,e) \\
\tau &= -C_e(x,e),
\end{aligned}
\tag{12.37}
$$

and

$$
\begin{aligned}
p &= C^f_{x_f}(x_f,e_f) \\
\tau_f &= -C^f_{e_f}(x_f,e_f).
\end{aligned}
\tag{12.38}
$$

In addition, the market for the polluting good must clear, so that

$$
x + x^f = c + c^f.
\tag{12.39}
$$

This is a system of seven endogenous variables c, c_f, x, x_f, e, e_f, and p, which are implicit functions of the domestic and foreign tax rates. Note that market clearing for the numeraire good is guaranteed by Walras' law.

To examine the optimal home country tax rate, the comparative static effects of a change in the home country tax rate need to be derived. We do this by differentiating the equation system (12.36) through (12.39) implicitly with respect to the home tax rate τ, and solving the resulting linear equation system for the derivatives of interest. In distinguishing effects we use, for example, $dx/d\tau$ to denote the total effect of a home country tax change on domestic production, and $\partial x/\partial\tau$ to denote the partial effect, whereby output price is kept constant. The signs of the various responses to a domestic tax change are summarized as follows.

Proposition 12.2
The responses of the equation system (12.36) through (12.39) to a change in the home emission tax rate are:

$dc/d\tau < 0, \quad dc_f/d\tau < 0;$
$dx/d\tau < 0, \quad dx_f/d\tau > 0;$
$de/d\tau < 0, \quad de_f/d\tau > 0;$ and
$dp/d\tau > 0.$

We present the algebra establishing these signs in the appendix, and describe here the channels through which the comparative statics operate. The home country tax increase has a direct impact on home pollution and thus, through output adjustment, also on the home production level. From this we know that, even if prices were not affected, the partial effect $\partial x/\partial\tau < 0$ would be negative, making the polluting commodity scarcer on the world market. If the domestic country is large, the output reduction pushes up the world market price, so that we also have $dp/d\tau > 0$. Although this price increase mitigates the output reduction, the total effect remains negative – i.e. $dx/d\tau < 0$ – as shown in the appendix. The increased price leads to decreased consumption in both countries, resulting in $dc/d\tau < 0$ and $dc_f/d\tau < 0$. On the other hand, the higher world market price increases supply in the foreign country, so that $dx_f/d\tau > 0$, and through this there are higher foreign emissions – i.e. $de_f/d\tau > 0$. The latter is often referred to as the "leakage" effect, meaning that an emission reduction at home is partially (or even totally) offset by increasing pollution abroad. While total output on the world market is decreasing in response to the unilateral emission tax increase, total emissions can in principle go up if the foreign technology is considerably more pollution-intensive than the domestic technology. In other words, the leakage effect can be more than 100 percent.

EXAMPLE 12.2 (EMPIRICAL) Fischer and Fox (2012) use a CGE model of global trade to simulate the effect of a unilateral carbon dioxide tax of $14 per ton on several energy and manufacturing sectors in the United States. They report leakage rates for each sector, where leakage is defined as the change in the foreign sector's emissions as a share of the domestic sector reduction. Fischer and Fox show that the largest emissions reductions occur in the electricity sector, and that leakage is modest – about 5 percent. This is because there is relatively little trade in electricity. In energy-intensive manufacturing, however, leakage is more substantial, given the exposure of these industries to international competition. For example, the iron and steel sector leakage rate is 58 percent, nonferrous metals (aluminum and copper smelting) is 57 percent, and nonmetallic minerals is 26 percent. While these industry-specific leakage rates are large, the overall leakage rate from the carbon dioxide tax is 7 percent, since most of the baseline emissions are in the energy sector, where import competition is lower than in manufacturing.

EXAMPLE 12.3 (EMPIRICAL) Aichele and Felbermayr (2012) econometrically examine carbon leakage in the context of the Kyoto agreement. For a panel of 40 countries, they compare two main outcomes, before and after the period when a subset of the countries ratified the Kyoto Protocol: carbon emissions, and the carbon footprint. A nation's carbon footprint measures its implicit consumption of CO_2 emissions, by adding emissions embodied in imports and subtracting emissions embodied in exports, from emissions generated in the country. This is important, because international trade drives a wedge between emissions and footprint, meaning that countries with low emissions can still be high consumers of carbon if their imports are based on carbon intensive production. Using newly assembled data, Aichele and Felbermayr show that 16 percent of the world's carbon emissions were embodied in cross-country trade in 1995, and that by 2007, this had increased to 21 percent. For their analysis, the authors define the years 1997 to 2000 as the "pre Kyoto" period, and the years 2004 to 2007 as the "post Kyoto" period. This choice is based on the observation that countries that ratified the agreement generally did so during the 2001 to 2003 period. Comparing these periods using a difference in differences model, and instrumenting for Kyoto ratification using membership in other (non-environmental) international agreements, they find on average that membership in Kyoto caused a 7 percent reduction in emissions in signatory countries. However, Kyoto ratification caused no change in a nation's carbon footprint, meaning the decrease in emissions was offset by an increase in the carbon intensity of imports. More specifically, the ratio of net carbon imports over total domestic emission increased 14 percent. These findings suggest leakage was nearly total: emission reductions within the Kyoto countries relocated to non-Kyoto countries, and the overall consumption of carbon emissions remained unchanged.

The Unilaterally Optimal Tax Rate

We now turn to deriving the unilaterally optimal tax rate. As in section 12.3.3, we write welfare as

$$W(\tau) = \int_0^c P(z)dz - C\left(x,e\right) + p \cdot [x - c] - D\left(e,e_f\right), \tag{12.40}$$

where once again we need to account for the response of the endogenous variables to the domestic tax rate. Differentiating with respect to τ yields

$$W'(\tau) = \left(\underbrace{P(c) - p}_{0}\right)\frac{dc}{d\tau} + \left(\underbrace{p - C_x(x,e)}_{0}\right)\frac{dx}{d\tau}$$

$$+ \left(\underbrace{-C_e(x,e) - D_e(e,e_f)}_{\tau}\right)\frac{de}{d\tau} - D_{e_f}(e,e_f)\frac{de_f}{d\tau} + \frac{dp}{d\tau}[x - c] = 0. \tag{12.41}$$

Using the behavioral conditions for utility and profit maximization, this expression reduces to

$$\left(\tau - D_e(e, e_f)\right)\frac{de}{d\tau} - D_{e_f}(e, e_f)\frac{de_f}{d\tau} + \frac{dp}{d\tau}[x - c] = 0, \tag{12.42}$$

from which we can characterize the optimal unilateral domestic tax as

$$\tau = D_e(e, e_f) + D_{e_f}(e, e_f)\frac{de_f / d\tau}{de / d\tau} - \frac{dp / d\tau}{de / d\tau}[x - c]. \tag{12.43}$$

This analysis demonstrates that the unilaterally optimal tax rate can be decomposed into three effects. The first part is $D_e(e, e_f)$, which accounts for the marginal damage to the domestic consumer, caused by domestic emissions. The second term accounts for the fact that foreign pollution is affected indirectly by domestic environmental policy, through the channel of the market price of the polluting good. Foreign pollution goes up when the market price increases, and some of the foreign pollution crosses the border to affect the home country, so the optimal tax contains the correction term $D_{e_f}(e, e_f)$. The additional damage from foreign pollution is weighted by the ratio of the change in foreign emissions, over the change in domestic emissions, where the former is positive and the latter negative, making the entire second term negative. This effect is referred to as the "not-in-my-backyard (NIMBY)" effect. It reflects the desire on the part of the domestic regulator to avoid simply replacing damages from the home country's emissions with damages from foreign emissions.

The third term in (12.43) is the terms-of-trade effect, which captures the impact on net exports/imports. As noted above, more stringent domestic environmental policy reduces domestic output. This causes a price increase for the polluting good. Thus, if the home country is an exporter of the polluting good, the terms of trade effect is positive, in that the home country can increase its export revenues by using environmental policy to increase the price it receives for selling the commodity abroad. If the home country is an importer of the polluting good, the terms of trade effect is negative. In this case, the domestic emission tax under-internalizes domestic pollution, in exchange for comparatively inexpensive imports of the polluting good. Note that, in the home country importer case, the emission tax is smaller than both the globally efficient level *and* the domestic Pigouvian level. It is often argued that international export competition forces governments to engage into a "race to the bottom" regarding environmental regulation. For this model, we see that the contrary is true when we consider the terms of trade motive in isolation: if there is no transboundary pollution, exporting countries have motivation to over-internalize their domestic pollution in order to improve their terms of trade. The contrary is true if the country is an importer, in which case a lower domestic tax rate causes the world price to fall, to the benefit of domestic consumers. In addition, the domestic industry faces less competition from foreign firms, since it does not pay the socially optimal price for pollution. As we will see in section 12.4.4, this abuse of environmental policy is not necessary if the domestic government has separate instruments to address the terms of trade.

Domestic Cap and Trade

We saw in Chapters 3 and 5 that under perfect information, price and quantity instruments are equivalent. This is also the case here, so long as the foreign country maintains its emission tax policy. In other words, conditional on the foreign tax policy, the home country can choose either a price or quantity instrument to achieve the same result. Formally verifying this is left as an exercise (see exercise 12.4).

12.4.2 Optimal Unilateral Policy with a Foreign Emission Standard

We now consider the case in which the foreign country sets an upper bound on its emissions, which in our representative producer model we denote using the emission standard $\bar{e}_f$. We once again consider in detail the context of the home country using an emission tax, and then briefly consider the case when both countries use an emission standard.

The Competitive Equilibrium

The competitive equilibrium when the foreign country sets an emission standard consists of the utility maximization conditions

$$P(c) = p$$
$$P_f(c_f) = p, \tag{12.44}$$

the home country profit maximization conditions

$$p = C_x(x,e)$$
$$\tau = -C_e(x,e), \tag{12.45}$$

and the output choice condition for the representative firm in the foreign country

$$p = C^f_{x_f}(x_f, \bar{e}_f). \tag{12.46}$$

Note that the emission standard in the foreign country means that the foreign firm does not freely select its emissions. Finally, the market clearing condition

$$x + x_f = c + c_f \tag{12.47}$$

closes the model.

Similar to proposition 12.2, one can derive the following comparative statics effects:

- $dc/d\tau < 0$, $dc_f/d\tau < 0$;
- $dx/d\tau < 0$, $dx_f/d\tau > 0$;
- $de/d\tau < 0$; and
- $dp/d\tau > 0$.

Note that, although foreign production goes up because the world market price increases, foreign pollution is not affected if the foreign government sets an emission cap and does not change its policy.

The Unilaterally Optimal Emission Tax

The unilateral optimal emission tax is now easy to characterize by proceeding as in the previous section. The only difference is that in the optimal tax formula, the NIMBY effect does not appear since there is no change in foreign emissions. Thus instead of (12.43), the optimal unilateral tax contains only two terms, and is given by

$$\tau = D_e(e, \bar{e}_f) - \frac{dp/d\tau}{de/d\tau}[x - c]. \tag{12.48}$$

From this it is clear that domestic damage resulting from domestic pollution is always over-internalized when the country is an exporter of the polluting good, and under-internalized when it is an importer.

In addition, the home country can achieve the same allocation by setting an emission standard $\bar{e}$, which satisfies

$$-C_e(x, \bar{e}) = D_e(\bar{e}, \bar{e}_f) - \frac{dp}{d\bar{e}}[x - c] = 0. \tag{12.49}$$

In this case we have $dp/d\bar{e} < 0$, since increasing the standard means relaxing environmental policy. The terms of trade effect is, therefore, still positive for an exporting country. If we interpret the emission standard as the emission cap in a cap and trade system, the condition can also be written in terms of the emission permit price:

$$-C_e(x, \bar{e}) = \sigma = D_e(\bar{e}, \bar{e}_f) - \frac{dp}{d\bar{e}}[x - c] = 0. \tag{12.50}$$

Policy Choice/Policy Game

Our discussion thus far in section 12.4 has shown that, given a particular policy choice by the foreign country, the home country is indifferent between the price and quantity instruments in our full certainty model. However, if both countries commit to a quantity instrument rather than an emission tax, they can provide mutual protection against leakage and the NIMBY effect, and therefore set their domestic policies more stringently than with price instruments. If a prearrangement about policy choice can be made, in the full certainty case they are therefore better off both implementing a quantity policy. Of course, other factors, such as uncertainty about abatement costs or revenue recycling needs, might favor an alternative choice.

If the countries play a two-step game, in which they decide the *type* of policy instrument in the first step and the *level* of stringency in a second, matters are more complicated. If countries are sufficiently symmetric, choosing quantity instruments in the first stage is a weak Nash equilibrium, in the sense that countries are indifferent between the quantity and tax instruments, but once having agreed on quantities, they have no incentive to deviate. If countries are sufficiently asymmetric, however, many different outcomes can occur and little can be said to predict what countries will do in such a case.

12.4.3 Internationally Mobile Factors

We have seen that domestic strengthening of environmental policy in a large open economy shifts production from the domestic to the foreign country and thus, other things equal, increases emissions abroad. The pathway for this effect is an increase in the world market price. Matters are similar when capital is mobile. To show this briefly, we revert to our model with one consumption good, which is now produced using a polluting input e and capital k, where the latter is mobile between countries. Domestic output is produced according to the production function $x=f(k,e)$; we assume $f_{ek}(k,e)=f_{ke}(k,e)>0$, so that capital improves the marginal product of the polluting input, and vice versa. When capital flows out to the foreign country, domestic households consume domestic production plus imports, where imports are financed using the interest earned on domestic capital that is employed in the foreign country. If the domestic country borrows from abroad, some of the domestic production must be transferred to the foreign country.

With such a model, one can show that a domestic emission tax lowers domestic emissions, and by virtue of $f_{ke}(k,e)>0$, also lowers demand for capital at home. This lowers the return on capital at home, and makes investment in the foreign country correspondingly more attractive. Thus capital migrates from home to foreign, and by the complementarity of emissions and capital in the foreign country, emissions also increase abroad. The main result is that also with mobile capital, strengthening domestic environmental policy shifts production from home to foreign, through shifting capital abroad. Derivation of the full comparative statics is left as an exercise. The unilaterally optimal domestic emission tax can be decomposed in a way similar to (12.43), with the commodity price p and export value $p[x-c]$ replaced with the rental price of capital and capital exports, respectively. See Rauscher (1994, 1997) for a detailed analysis of this model. In a two or more commodity world, things are more complicated, in that the comparative statics depend on whether the polluting or the non-polluting good is more capital intensive. In different cases, increasing the domestic emissions tax can cause capital to flow in or flow out of the domestic economy.

The notion of internationally mobile factors has given rise to concerns about "pollution havens", whereby production (and hence jobs and capital) migrates to places with lax environmental regulation. There is a sizeable amount of empirical literature investigating the existence and size of pollution haven effects. See Levinson and Taylor (2008) for an analysis finding a comparatively large pollution haven effect, and Jaffe et al. (1995) for a survey of earlier studies that did not find an effect.

12.4.4 Separation of Instruments

In this section, we have seen that environmental policy can be used as a substitute for trade policy aimed at improving the terms of trade, when free trade agreements do not allow direct use of import tariffs or export taxes. If such instruments are available to domestic policy makers, they can in principle be used to adjust the terms of trade, so that environmental policy instruments need only be used to manage emissions. Indeed, one can show that in the absence of transboundary pollution, the two objectives of inter-nalizing domestic pollution externalities and optimally manipulating the terms of trade to the domestic country's advantage are fully separable. In this case, the emission tax should be set at the Pigouvian level, while an import tariff or export tax is set based on import demand or export supply elasticities. Since it is not a core theme of this chapter we leave formal derivation of this as an exercise. We do note, however, that this is a further example of the Tinbergen (1952, 1956) principle that a policy maker generally needs as many instruments as there are variables to target.

Matters are more complicated when there is transboundary pollution. Since both environmental and trade policy affect foreign emissions, the formulas for unilaterally optimal taxes and tariffs are rather involved, and hence left to the advanced reader as an exercise (see exercise 12.7). In that case, the optimal combination of environmental and trade policy instruments will address three targets: the domestic marginal damage, the terms of trade, and the NIMBY effect. Note that there exists no straightforward policy instrument to target foreign emissions, and thus the NIMBY effect, directly. Even new instruments discussed recently in the literature such as border-tax adjustments cannot achieve this, and therefore can never be fully efficient. For a discussion see Helm and Schmidt (2015).

12.5 IMPERFECT COMPETITION AND ENVIRONMENTAL DUMPING

We saw in the previous section that, in the absence of tariffs, an exporting country would like to over-internalize environmental damage in order to improve its terms of trade. This result cannot explain what both environmentalists and economists have referred to as "environmental dumping", whereby exporting countries are said to use lenient environmental policy, so as to increase their share of the export market. To study this we need to develop a model that departs from the perfect competition assumption, which has characterized our discussion until now.

In an important paper, Brander and Spencer (1985) initiated a new research agenda on trade theory by showing that under imperfect (quantity) competition, the opti-mal unilateral trade policy involves making exports cheaper via subsidies rather than improving the terms of trade via export taxes. Thus, under imperfect competition, trade policy seeks to increase market share by worsening the terms of trade. In environmen-tal economics, Conrad (1993), Barrett (1994b), and Kennedy (1994) were among the first to show that, in the presence of imperfect competition, environmental policy can therefore be used to indirectly subsidize exports, by under-internalizing even domes-tic environmental damage. Given these results, it is common to hear accusations of environmental dumping, whenever a country fails to fully internalize its domestic pollution externalities. In what follows we adapt the arguments from Rauscher (1994) and Duval and Hamilton (2002) to examine the accuracy of this sentiment.

12.5.1 Extension of the Basic Model to Imperfect Competition

We again use the "partial general equilibrium model" developed in the previous sections. We use X to denote total world output of the polluting good, which consists of production x and x_f from the home and foreign countries, respectively, so that $X = x + x_f$. The world inverse demand function is denoted by $P_w(X)$, and we again use $P(c)$ and $P_f(c_f)$ to represent the home and foreign inverse demand functions, where c and c_f are the corresponding consumption levels. For simplicity we assume there is only one firm in each country, which produce emissions e and e_f.

The two firms engage in Cournot competition (quantity competition with a homogeneous good) on the world market, so that the home firm's profit function, when subject to an emissions tax, is

$$\Pi(x, x_f) = P_w(x + x_f) \cdot x - C(x, e) - \tau e. \tag{12.51}$$

The first-order conditions for the firm's profit maximization problem then read

$$P_w'(x_d + x_f) \cdot x + P_w(x + x_f) - C_x(x, e) = 0$$
$$-C_e(x, e) = \tau. \tag{12.52}$$

Cooperative Environmental Policy

We first study the benchmark case, where governments agree on their environmental policies in a cooperative way. In order to avoid problems of imperfect competition in the permit market, we assume that the governments use taxes as policy instruments. We further assume that transfer payments between governments are possible, which allows us to ignore participation constraints. In this case, the collective objective is to select the tax rates τ and τ_f to maximize

$$\int_0^{x + x_f} P_w(t) dt - C(x, e) - C^f(x_f, e_f) - D(e, e_f) - D^f(e, e_f). \tag{12.53}$$

Taking the first-order conditions, treating output and emissions as functions of the tax rate, and substituting in the behavioral conditions from (12.52), we characterize the cooperative tax rates as

$$\tau^c = D_e(e, e_f) + D_e^f(e, e_f) + P_w'(X) \cdot x \cdot \frac{\partial x / \partial \tau}{\partial e / \partial \tau}$$
$$\tau_f^c = D_{e_f}(e, e_f) + D_{e_f}^f(e, e_f) + P_w'(X) \cdot x_f \cdot \frac{\partial x_f / \partial \tau_f}{\partial e_f / \partial \tau_f}. \tag{12.54}$$

These equations show that, under a cooperative regime, each country taxes its emissions to account for the marginal damage inflicted by its domestic industry in both the home and foreign countries. Each country also adjusts its tax rate down from the Pigouvian level, based on the oligopolistic distortion caused by its own industry on the world market. These formulas are essentially equivalent to Eq. (6.33) in Chapter 6, and can also be found in Duval and Hamilton (2002).

Non-cooperative Environmental Policy

We now turn to the more interesting case of a non-cooperative policy setting. The institutional context is that domestic and foreign firms compete imperfectly à la Cournot in an international market, which may also include third-country markets. We assume the governments are not allowed to directly subsidize their firms' output, and so they will attempt to use environmental policy as trade policy. Taking into account the domestic firm's behavioral functions in (12.52), the objective for the domestic government is to choose a tax rate to maximize

$$W = \int_0^c P(t)dt - C(x,e) + P_w(X_w) \cdot [x-c] - D(e,e_f), \qquad (12.55)$$

where we have now included the market value of net exports/imports in domestic welfare. Differentiating welfare with respect to the tax rate, setting the derivative equal to zero, using the firm's behavioral responses, and isolating the tax rate, yields the following formula for the unilaterally optimal (non-cooperative) domestic tax rate:

$$\tau^{NC} = D_e(e,e_f) + D_{e_f}(e,e_f)\frac{\partial e_f / \partial \tau}{\partial e / \partial \tau}$$

$$- P_w'(X) \cdot x \cdot \frac{\partial x_f / \partial \tau}{\partial e / \partial \tau} + P_w'(X) \cdot c \cdot \frac{\left[\dfrac{\partial x}{\partial \tau} + \dfrac{\partial x_f}{\partial \tau}\right]}{\partial e / \partial \tau}. \qquad (12.56)$$

This decomposition consists of four parts. The first term represents the domestic marginal damage caused by the domestic firm. If the home and foreign firms are not too different, we can show that $\partial e / \partial \tau < 0$ and $\partial x / \partial \tau < 0$. The latter causes the world price to rise, leading to $\partial x_f / \partial \tau > 0$ and thus $\partial e_f / \partial \tau > 0$. The second term in (12.56) is therefore negative, and it describes the leakage/NIMBY effect – i.e. the domestic marginal damage caused by the change in foreign emissions, adjusted by the ratio of the foreign firm's increase and the domestic firm's decrease in emissions, following the tax change.

The third term can be interpreted as the rent shifting effect. For example, a lower domestic emission tax induces lower cost for the domestic firm, which then causes it to gain market share. This term is negative, meaning the regulator raises domestic welfare by increasing the domestic firm's market share, by adjusting the tax below its Pigouvian level. The last term reflects the negative impact of imperfect competition on domestic consumers. Similar to the second-best tax formulas in Chapter 6, this is also negative, since the regulator wants to encourage additional production by setting the tax rate lower than in the competitive market case.

We can now comment further on the frequently heard accusation of environmental dumping. From (12.56), we can see that there are two observationally equivalent reasons that countries may do this: to implicitly subsidize their exports, and to address the output-reducing consequences of imperfect competition. Only the former represents environmental dumping.

12.6 INTERACTIONS WITH ENERGY MARKETS

Thus far in the chapter we have characterized the leakage effect in NIMBY terms, whereby an individual country's unilateral environmental policy accounts for the indirect effect its actions have on emissions from abroad. In this section, we analyze additional leakage phenomena that arise based on interactions between energy markets and environmental policy. Leakage of this type is especially relevant for efforts to regulate carbon emissions. In particular, there are concerns that efforts by a coalition of countries to reduce carbon emissions by reducing energy demand will decrease energy prices, thereby stimulating energy use in non-coalition countries. The resultant increase in non-coalition emissions may partially (or fully) offset the reductions obtained by the coalition. This is the spatial leakage problem. A temporal version of the leakage problem is that plans to implement an emissions cap at some future date will cause energy supplies to move production forward in time, thereby increasing current emissions relative to the no-policy baseline. This effect has been popularized by Sinn (2008) as the "green paradox".

In this section we illustrate the mechanics of these effects using a simple two-region model in the spatial context, and a two-period model in the temporal context. We continue to use the "home" and "foreign" country labels for the two-region model. However, for this analysis it is better to think of "home" as a coalition of countries that has collectively agreed to reduce emissions (e.g. the Annex I countries that ratified the Kyoto Protocol), and "foreign" as the group of remaining, non-coalition countries.

12.6.1 Model Adjustments

We adjust the model in two ways. First, we assume that emissions are proportional to fossil fuel energy inputs. Leaving aside carbon capture and storage technologies, carbon dioxide emissions are roughly proportional to the amount of fossil fuel used, where the proportionality depends on the specific fuel. Here we imagine a single representative fuel, and denote both emissions and per-emission energy input using e and e_f for the home and foreign countries, respectively. Second, we assume abatement costs, spending on energy inputs, and production costs are separable for the representative firm in each country. We will focus on the first two of these, so that the opportunity cost of emission abatement plus energy inputs to the home economy is $C(e) + \psi e$, where ψ is the world factor price for energy, measured in emission-equivalent units. Likewise, we denote aggregate emission costs for the foreign country by $C_f(e_f) + \psi e_f$. In both countries, we interpret these expressions as the total opportunity cost of meeting a given emission/energy input target.

If the home country's firm is subject to an emission tax τ, its costs become $C(e) + (\psi + \tau)e$. In addition, we use $\Gamma(E)$ to denote the worldwide cost of extracting energy, where $E = e + e_f$ is the total amount of energy (and emissions) produced. We abstract from the fact that there are different fossil fuels with different extraction costs, and also ignore for the moment the effect of stock dependencies on $\Gamma(E)$. We assume that the marginal extraction cost (energy supply) $\Gamma'(E)$ is constant or upward sloping, so that $\Gamma''(E) \geq 0$. Special cases include perfectly elastic supply ($\Gamma''(E) = 0$), and perfectly inelastic supply in the relevant range ($\Gamma'(E) = \infty$).

12.6.2 Spatial Leakage

We assume for the spatial analysis that the energy supply function (marginal extraction cost) is strictly upward sloping, so that $\Gamma''(E) > 0$. If the foreign country does not implement environmental policy, the behavioral and market equilibrium conditions for energy and emissions are given by

$$
\begin{aligned}
-C'(e) &= \psi + \tau \\
-C_f'(e_f) &= \psi
\end{aligned}
\tag{12.57}
$$

for the two firms, and

$$
\Gamma'(E) = \psi, \quad E = e + e_f,
\tag{12.58}
$$

for the energy supplier. Rearranging the first expression in (12.57) for the home country, we obtain

$$
-C'(e) - \psi = \tau.
\tag{12.59}
$$

Note that the left-hand side is the marginal opportunity cost of reducing a carbon emission, where the net effect consists of the abatement cost less savings on the energy input. Thus, as the world price of energy increases, the marginal opportunity cost to the home country of carbon reduction falls.

To study the effect of a unilateral increase of the domestic emission tax, we differentiate (12.57) and (12.58) implicitly with respect to the domestic emission tax rate τ, and solve for the endogenous responses, which yields:

$$
\frac{de}{d\tau} = \frac{-C_f''(e_f) - \Gamma''(E)}{Det} < 0, \quad \frac{de_f}{d\tau} = \frac{\Gamma''(E)}{Det} > 0,
\tag{12.60}
$$

and

$$
\frac{dE}{d\tau} = \frac{-C_f''(e_f)}{Det} < 0, \quad \frac{d\psi}{d\tau} = \frac{-C_f''(e_f)\Gamma''(E)}{Det} < 0,
\tag{12.61}
$$

where

$$Det = C''(e) \cdot C_f''(e_f) + \left(C''(e) + C_f''(e_f)\right) \cdot \Gamma''(E) > 0 \qquad (12.62)$$

is the determinant of the linear equation system resulting when we differentiate (12.57) and (12.58). The signs of the comparative statics are intuitive. If the slope of the marginal energy cost function is finite – that is, $0 < \Gamma''(E) < \infty$ – then emissions fall in the regulated home country, but increase in the (unregulated) foreign country. The latter is triggered by the decreasing world market price for energy, making its use more attractive. While total emissions do fall, the size of the effect depends critically on the energy supply elasticity. For example, if energy supply is perfectly elastic, so that $\Gamma''(E) = 0$, neither the energy price nor foreign emissions are affected by the domestic policy, and so there is no leakage. If instead energy supply is perfectly inelastic, so that $\Gamma''(E) = \infty$, we obtain $de/d\tau = -1$, $de_f/d\tau = 1$, and $dE/d\tau = 0$. In other words, there is 100 percent leakage.

The spatial leakage problem has led environmental activists to argue that the world community should agree on a single worldwide tax on carbon emissions, such that $\tau = \tau_f = \tau_w$. In this case the first-order conditions for the firms' profit maximization become

$$\begin{aligned}
-C'(e) &= \psi + \tau_w \\
-C_f'(e_f) &= \psi + \tau_w.
\end{aligned} \qquad (12.63)$$

Differentiating the equation system in (12.63) and (12.58) with respect to τ_w leads to

$$\frac{dE}{d\tau_w} = \frac{-[C''(e) + C_f''(e_f)]}{Det} < 0. \qquad (12.64)$$

Note, however, that if energy supply is quite inelastic this effect will be small, given the form of the determinant in (12.62). In this case, a cap and trade system may be preferable to an emission tax, as it offsets the leakage effect induced by decreasing energy prices.

12.6.3 Intertemporal Leakage and the Green Paradox

Consider now a context in which the world community has reached agreement on a coordinated carbon emissions reduction strategy, which will become binding at some future date.[3] We now interpret $C_t(e_t) + \psi_t e_t$ as the global opportunity cost of reducing emissions/energy use in period t, where ψ_t is the time-indexed energy input price. We assume there are two time periods $t = 1, 2$, and that δ is the discount factor that converts period 2 costs into the present time.

To proceed we need to distinguish two cases. In the first, fossil fuel resources are sufficiently abundant that they will not be used up in the two periods. In the second,

---

[3] In this section we borrow model features from Eichner and Pethig (2011).

there is a finite amount of the fossil fuel resource that will be exhausted during the two periods. When fossil fuels are abundant enough that they can be used indefinitely, the two periods are independent, and a commitment to reduce emissions in the future will not affect the present.

The more interesting and realistic case is when the fossil fuel resource becomes depleted over time. We denote the total stock of available energy (embodied emissions) by E, so that over the two periods it must be the case that $e_1 + e_2 = E$. For convenience, we consider one representative, competitive firm that extracts the resource; our results do not change if many small competitive firms each own part of the total stock. Given this assumption, the competitive energy supplier selects e_1 and e_2 to maximize

$$\Pi(e_1, e_2) = \psi_1 e_1 - \Gamma(e_1) + \delta\left(\psi_2 e_2 - \Gamma(e_2)\right) \quad s.t. \quad E = e_1 + e_2. \tag{12.65}$$

With the binding resource constraint, the shadow value of the resource (the Lagrange multiplier in the maximization problem) is positive, and so the firm's first-order conditions collapse to

$$\psi_1 - \Gamma'(e_1) = \delta\left(\psi_2 - \Gamma'(e_2)\right). \tag{12.66}$$

Under zero extraction costs, this condition boils down to familiar Hotelling rule $\psi_1 = \delta\psi_1$.

We now assume that worldwide emission taxes rates τ_1 and τ_2 in periods 1 and 2, respectively, are agreed to. With these, the first and second period emissions/energy input conditions are

$$-C_1'(e_1) = \psi_1 + \tau_1 \tag{12.67}$$
$$-C_2'(e_2) = \psi_2 + \tau_2.$$

The inter-temporal equilibrium in the energy market is therefore determined by Eq. (12.67), along with the emissions constraint $E = e_1 + e_2$.

Consider a scenario in which the first period tax is $\tau_1 = 0$, but that the future tax is positive so that $\tau_2 > 0$. To determine the effect of τ_2 on first and second period emissions, we differentiate (12.67) and the emissions constraint with respect to τ_2, and solve for the endogenous responses to obtain

$$\frac{de_1}{d\tau_2} = \frac{\delta}{Det} > 0, \quad \frac{de_2}{d\tau_2} = -\frac{de_1}{d\tau_2} = -\frac{\delta}{Det} < 0 \tag{12.68}$$

for emissions and

$$\frac{d\psi_1}{d\tau_2} = \frac{-\delta C_1''(e_1)}{Det} < 0, \quad \frac{d\psi_2}{d\tau_2} = \frac{-\left(C_1''(e_1) + \Gamma''(e_1) + \delta\Gamma''(e_2)\right)}{Det} < 0 \tag{12.69}$$

for prices, where

$$Det = C_1''(e_1) + \Gamma''(e_1) + \delta\big(C_2''(e_2) + \Gamma''(e_2)\big) > 0. \tag{12.70}$$

Note that (12.68) implies $de_1/d\tau_1 + de_2/d\tau_1 = 0$. The introduction of an emissions tax lowers the energy price in both periods, and shifts emissions from period 2 to period 1, so that the damages from emissions occur earlier. In the case of carbon emissions, climate change is accelerated. The reverse effect is also true. If there is a positive emission tax in period 1, and no emission tax in period 2, climate change would be delayed until period 2, but will still occur.

If instead the world community acted immediately and implemented a total emission cap, such that $L < E$, aggregate emissions would be reduced over time. However, past experience related to the failure of the post-Kyoto conferences suggest this is an unlikely outcome. Thus, the paradox of our simple model accounting for the response of energy suppliers, is that it may be preferred to take no action rather than implementing moderate environmental policy now, and increasing its stringency over time. These basic effects also occur in richer models with stock-dependent extraction cost, continuous time, many countries, and so on. In particular, extraction costs are likely to be stock dependent, as easily available energy sources are first exploited, with more costly-to-obtain reserves being used later. Even in this case, so long as the resource constraint remains binding, the full leakage green paradox emerges. If, instead, the total resource constraint is not binding, so that the total amount of the resource used is determined by extraction costs, a leakage effect from the future to the present will still occur. The size of this leakage effect is based on the slope of the stock-dependent marginal extraction cost function, and will be stronger when this slope rises faster.

Clearly these are not encouraging results. We stress, however, that the temporal leakage effect only refers to policy measures that aim to reduce fossil fuel energy use, and does not affect carbon sequestration. If one country unilaterally engages in sequestration, other countries may still want to free ride on this, and there may be spatial leakage because of increasing marginal cost in the sequestering country. However, the leakage effect via the energy market does not occur. Therefore, sequestration measures such as afforestation and carbon capture and storage are likely to play an important role in the future.

12.7 INTERNATIONAL COALITION FORMATION

In our stylized two-country models, cooperation is always better than non-cooperative, unilateral welfare maximization. In other words, in a two-country world, countries are always better off agreeing to a binding cooperative contract when side payments guaranteeing that participation constraints are satisfied occur. In a world with more than two countries this need not always be the case. There is a lot of literature in environmental economics that uses game theory to analyze the prospects for successful international agreements amongst many countries. Here we introduce a few of the concepts that have been discussed in this area.

If there are a total of N countries, and a coalition of $J < N$ countries has signed a binding agreement to reduce their emissions, it may be rational for non-coalition countries to free ride on the emission reduction efforts of the coalition. In order to investigate incentives to join or leave a coalition, the concepts of *external* and *internal stability* have been coined in the literature. In the typical model, it is assumed that countries outside the coalition seek to unilaterally maximize their domestic welfare. In the climate change context, for a small country this generally means it should not engage in any emission reductions. By contrast, the models assume that the coalition maximizes the total welfare of its members, allowing for possible side payments amongst members. Under these conditions, a coalition is *internally stable* if is not beneficial for any of the coalition members to leave, and instead unilaterally maximize its own welfare. By contrast, a coalition is *externally stable* if it is not beneficial for any countries outside the coalition to join rather than unilaterally maximizing welfare. In a seminal paper, Barrett (1994a) shows that under rather general conditions, the maximum size of an internally and externally stable coalition is three. Subsequent theoretical research has generally shown that international environmental agreements (IEAs) cannot be expected to deliver more pollution reduction than member countries would be willing to unilaterally provide. In spite of these discouraging results, several IEAs such as the Montreal and the Kyoto protocols included much larger collections of signatory countries, though the extent to which they have delivered genuine environmental improvements is unclear. More recent research on coalition formation has examined concepts beyond internal and external stability. Most of these models are static in nature, however, and ignore the links between environmental policy and the temporal mechanics of energy supply and energy prices.

EXAMPLE 12.4 (EMPIRICAL) There are a handful of studies that attempt to empirically test whether IEAs provide environmental improvements beyond what would have occurred absent the agreement. A recent example is Kellenberg and Levinson (2014), who study the Basel Convention on the Control of Transboundary Movements of Hazardous Waste ('the Convention'). The idea of an agreement arose out of concerns about the volume of hazardous waste being shipped from wealthy countries to developing countries, where disposal may be subject to laxer environmental regulations. In the early 1990s, the Convention required signatories to disclose details about their waste shipments. In 1995 a ban was added, whereby wealthy countries (Annex VII signatories) were prohibited from shipping waste to developing countries (non-Annex VII signatories). Kellenberg and Levinson observe bilateral waste shipments among 117 countries over 21 years that bracket the Convention's requirements, as well as indicators for countries that ratified the Convention and enacted the ban. They use these data to examine how the trend in hazardous waste shipments between Annex VII and non-Annex VII countries was affected by aspects of the agreement. Consistent with theoretical predictions, they find no evidence that the original Convention or the 1995 ban altered pre-existing trends in signatory countries' hazardous waste shipments to developing countries.

12.8 KYOTO MECHANISMS: JI AND CDM

In this section we briefly discuss two flexible mechanisms that were part of the Kyoto agreement, which were designed to reduce emissions while helping to smooth marginal abatement costs across countries. As mentioned in example 12.1, the Kyoto Protocol divides the world into Annex I countries, which have committed to explicit carbon emission reduction targets, and the rest of the countries, which have not made commitments. The protocol allows international emissions trading amongst Annex I countries, subject to an aggregate emissions cap. The European Union, as a subset of Annex I countries, has implemented emissions trading, where additional Annex I countries such as Iceland, Norway, and Liechtenstein have joined. These systems can, in principle, minimize the abatement costs borne by trading system members as they seek to meet their collective emission cap. Trading by subsets of Annex I countries, however, does not provide abatement cost smoothing between Annex I countries that are not in the same emission trading block. In addition, the absence of emission reductions targets in non-Annex I countries means the world's emission trading systems are not able to take advantage of inexpensive abatement opportunities in developing countries.

Two auxiliary mechanisms were included in the Kyoto Protocol to address these latter two limitations. The Joint Implementation (JI) mechanism provides a means of coordinating abatement efforts between an Annex I country participating in an emissions trading program, and another Annex I country that is not, say between Germany and the Ukraine. The Clean Development Mechanism (CDM) provides a means of achieving emission reductions in a non-Annex I country via a partnership with an Annex I country, say between Norway and China. The JI and CDM are referred to as "project-based mechanisms", because they generate emission reductions from specific, targeted activities that occur outside of a country's normal participation in its domestic emissions reduction policy. Emission reductions resulting from such projects can be certified and, under certain conditions, converted into domestic emission reduction credits. An important condition for certification is that these reductions are *additional* to business-as-usual reductions. For this purpose, a baseline for business-as-usual reductions has to be defined. Setting such a baseline is one of the largest challenges in making operational the ideas inherent in JI and the CDM.

In the following, we formalize the JI and CDM mechanisms using our simple model. We use $C(e)$ to denote the abatement cost function for a domestic firm in an Annex I country, and $C_f(e_f)$ to denote the corresponding function in a foreign country, which we also refer to as the host country. To fix ideas, we assume the domestic firm is subject to an emission constraint $\bar{e}$, and that a foreign facility has business-as-usual baseline emissions $\hat{e}_f$. The domestic firm can lower its abatement costs by paying for emission reductions at the foreign facility, while increasing its own emissions by the same amount. The objective function for the domestic firm can then be written as

$$\min_{e_f} C(\bar{e} + e_f) + C_f(\hat{e}_f - e_f),$$

(12.71)

where e_f represents the emission reductions at the foreign (host) facility. In case of JI, these reductions have been labelled *emission reduction units* (ERUs); in case of CDM, they are *certified emission reductions* (CERs). It is clear from the objective function that the domestic firm chooses the emission reduction such that marginal abatement costs between its own and the host facility are equal:

$$-C'(\bar{e} + e_f) = -C'_f(\hat{e}_f - e_f).$$

(12.72)

Often, however, certifying these reductions involves transactions costs that we denote by $tr \cdot e_f$. In this case (12.72) becomes

$$-C'(\bar{e} + e_f) = -C'_f(\hat{e}_f - e_f) + tr, \qquad (12.73)$$

and the marginal abatement cost for the domestic firm will be larger than at the host facility.

If there is a market for emission allowances, the project manager does not need to compare the marginal abatement cost of a particular facility in the host country with those of his domestic firm. He can instead use the domestic allowance price as a point of reference. If there are transaction costs for certification, the project manager's objective function will be

$$\min_{e_f} C_f(\hat{e}_f - e_f) - (\sigma - tr)e_f, \qquad (12.74)$$

where σ is the price of a domestic emission allowance. The domestic firm will then choose the amount of foreign emission reductions e_f according to

$$-C'_f(\hat{e}_f - e_f) = \sigma - tr, \qquad (12.75)$$

which, due to the transaction costs of certifying emission reductions in the host country, is not fully efficient.

Note that in both JI and CDM, emissions are moved from the host country into the region where emission trading is operating. In other words, the emission cap in the emission trading region will be increased by the same amount as emissions are reduced in the host country. There is one crucial difference between JI and CDM, however: emission reductions produced in an Annex I host country reduce the allowable emissions in the host country, as ERUs must be subtracted from the emission target of the host country. By contrast, CERs do not reduce any emission budget in non-Annex I host countries. This difference means that regulatory agencies of Annex I host countries have an incentive to make sure that emission reductions are genuine. They also have an incentive to prevent foreign project hunters from implementing low-cost emission reductions, which sooner or later would have been achieved by the host country's own efforts. In non-Annex I countries these incentives do not exist, since regulators are not bound to an emission target. Therefore, the verification of the baseline is much more difficult for international agencies, and the risk of spurious emission reductions that would have occurred anyway is much greater under CDM than under JI.

Environmental activists often criticize JI and CDM on the basis that companies in industrialized countries simply buy themselves out of their moral obligation to reduce their emissions at home. They also argue that a large number of certified projects can flood the domestic emissions market with surplus allowances, thereby pushing down emission prices, and providing lower incentives to engage in domestic emission reduction efforts. The latter is certainly true. However, if true emission reductions can be achieved abroad at a low cost, it would be economically inefficient to forgo the opportunity. Falling emission prices and thus incentives to further reduce emissions can be mitigated by governments issuing a lower number of permits in the future, or even buying back permits at guaranteed prices.

12.9   DOES TRADE LIBERALIZATION INDUCE MORE OR LESS POLLUTION?

The integration of global economies through trade is often thought to be associated with higher local and global pollution. From a theoretical viewpoint it is, however, not clear whether trade liberalization causes pollution to rise or fall. There are different channels of effects which may work in opposite directions. More international trade tends to increase world production, and to the extent that production and pollution are positively related, this increases pollution. At the same time, trade causes countries to specialize in production areas where they have a comparative advantage. Thus some countries will specialize in pollution-intensive goods, while others will focus on producing cleaner goods. In total, pollution may increase or decrease through international specialization. In addition, international trade encourages the diffusion of production and abatement technologies, thereby allowing cleaner technology to be more widely adopted. The opposite may also be the case if pollution-intensive goods have other features that worldwide consumers like. A good example of this is the increased international sales of US-style sport utility vehicles (SUVs). Also, global increase in trade-related transport enhances pollution, since transport is energy intensive, and most transport vehicles are fossil fuel driven. Finally, over the long term, international trade tends to increase wealth, which may ultimately create an increase in demand for environmental quality in previously low-income countries.

In this section we demonstrate, using a stylized Ricardian trade model, that the overall impact of trade liberalization is in fact ambiguous. The extent to which trade liberalization leads to a net increase or decrease in worldwide pollution is therefore an empirical question.

12.9.1 A Stylized Ricardian Model

We consider a two-country model with home and foreign countries. Both produce goods X and Z. The quantities produced in the home country are denoted x and z, and those in the foreign country by x_f and z_f. Each country is endowed with one unit of labor, but they have different installed technologies, so that the marginal product of labor differs for the two goods across the two countries. In particular, we assume that

- $x = 1 \times l$ and $x_f = 2 \times l_f$
- $z = 2 \times l$ and $z_f = 1 \times l_f$

where l and l_f are labor inputs for the home and foreign countries, respectively. Thus the home country requires 1 unit of labor to produce a unit of X, and 0.5 units to produce a unit of Z, while the foreign country requires 0.5 units of labor to produce a unit of X, and 1 unit to produce a unit of Z.

The preference function for the representative consumer in the two countries is Cobb-Douglas, so that $U(x,z) = x^{0.5}z^{0.5}$ and $U^f(x,z) = x_f^{0.5}z_f^{0.5}$. In both countries, X is the polluting good, and we consider two variants of the relative emission coefficients, which translate production in the two countries into emissions e and e_f:

- Variant I: $e=x$ and $e_f=x_f$. That is, both countries have equal pollution intensities.
- Variant II: $e=3x$ and $e_f=0.33x_f$. That is, the home country's production of X is more pollution intensive.

For simplicity, in what follows we assume that consumers are not affected by emissions.

Autarky

We first consider a no-trade world. In this case, the home country's utility is maximized with production and consumption given by $(x^a, z^a) = (0.33, 0.66)$, and emissions $e^{a,I} = 0.33$ under variation I, and $e^{a,II} = 1$ under variant II. By contrast, the foreign country's solution is $(x^a_f, z^a_f) = (0.66, 0.33)$, with emissions $e^{a,I}_f = 0.66$ and $e^{a,II}_f = 0.22$ for variants I and II, respectively. Note that world emissions are $E^{a,I} = 1$ and $E^{a,II} = 1.22$ under the two scenarios.

Free Trade

We now consider outcomes under free trade. The home country has a comparative advantage in producing Z, while the foreign country has a comparative advantage in producing X, which leads to full specialization in this simple setup. Specifically, production in the home country is $(x^t, z^t) = (0, 2)$ and production in the foreign country is $(x^t, z^t) = (2, 0)$. Since relative prices are equal to one, both countries consume the bundle (1, 1), and are better off in terms of pure consumption.

In terms of emissions, in both parameter variants there is zero pollution in the home country, since no production of the polluting good occurs there. In the foreign country, where 2 units of X are produced, emissions are $E^{t,I} = e^{t,I}_f = 2$ and $E^{t,II} = e^{t,II}_f = 0.66$. Thus under variant I, worldwide emissions double from 1 to 2, while under variant II, emissions fall from 1.22 to 0.66. In variant I, the pollution intensity of the technologies is the same in both countries, and the increase in pollution is driven by an increase in total production. In variant II, the foreign country has a comparative advantage in producing X with respect to both labor input and the emission coefficient. Even though pollution triples domestically from $e^{a,II}_f = 0.22$ to $e^{t,II}_f = 0.66$, worldwide pollution falls, because production shifts to the country with the less pollution-intensive technology.

Composition, Scale and Technique Effect

In a more general theoretical approach, it is possible to separately identify three different channels affecting pollution when trade is liberalized. First, with trade, relative prices change in both countries. In our example, under autarky the relative price in the home country of good Z in terms of good X is two, while the opposite ratio holds in the foreign country. After trade liberalization, the relative price is one in both countries. This induces a *composition effect* in production, which shifts production of the clean good to the home country, and the dirty good to the foreign country. Thus, other things equal, pollution decreases at home and increases abroad, while the total effect – which is only of relevance when there is transboundary pollution – is in general ambiguous.

The second channel consists of increased output levels for both goods, through liberalized trade. This effect is referred to as the *scale effect* which, other things equal, increases worldwide pollution. Finally, the composition effect also induces a shift of production to a country that has a worse or better abatement technology. This effect is known as the *technique effect*.

The composition, scale, and technique effects were first identified by Copeland and Taylor (1994) in a more general model with a continuum of commodities. In our stylized model, the composition and the technique effect cannot be fully separated since there is a shift from one technology to another. In a model with incomplete specialization in the manner of Heckscher and Olin, the composition and the technology effect are more pronounced. Since in all countries, relative prices change through trade liberalization, the economies shift production to the good that has become relatively more expensive on the world market. This also induces a change in demand for polluting inputs. In such a model, the composition effect is more attenuated than in the simple Ricardo model presented here. Nonetheless, the simple example presented here conveys the main intuition of the three channels.

EXAMPLE 12.5 (EMPIRICAL) Antweiler et al. (2001) empirically investigate whether increased international trade is good or bad for the environment by empirically decomposing the environmental impacts of trade into the composition, scale, and technique effects. They examine the case of sulfur dioxide across 108 urban areas in 43 developing and developed countries, for the time period 1971 to 1996. The main empirical task is to identify proxies for the scale, composition, and technique effects, and compare them to sulfur dioxide concentrations. To measure pollution, the authors use the Global Environmental Monitoring System (GEMS) to compute the median concentration of SO_2 for each year in each urban area. For scale, gross domestic product (GDP) per kilometer squared in each urban area/year is computed. A country's capital to labor ratio is used to measure the composition effect. Finally, to proxy for the technique effect, the authors use a moving average of lagged income. The motivation behind this is that, as nations become richer, their governments will respond, with some delay, to increasing SO_2 damage by tightening emissions standards. Industries in turn react to tightening emission standards by installing more advanced abatement technology. Antweiler et al. present panel regressions of SO_2 concentrations on the scale, composition, and technique proxies, as well as interactions of these variables with the ratio of exports plus imports over GDP (as a measure of trade openness and intensity) and other controls. They find positive scale and negative technique effects, and that a higher capital to labor ratio is positively associated with pollution. Across different specifications, at the mean of the data, the scale elasticity ranges from 0.10 to 0.40, and technique elasticities are between −0.9 and −1.6. For composition, the authors find that a 1 percent increase in the capital to labor ratio causes pollution to increase 0.6 to 1 percent. Finally, a 1 percent increase in trade intensity causes pollution to fall by 0.4 to 0.9 percent.

The Antweiler et al. results suggest that, on net, trade does not harm the environment. Combining the scale and technique effects, and holding the capital to labor rate fixed, a 1 percent increase in output and income causes pollution to fall by approximately 1 percent. If the 1 percent growth in income is instead driven by an increase in capital accumulation, then the net effect is a small increase in pollution. Filtering the three effects through a 1 percent increase in income induced by more open trade, the net effect is a 0.8 to 0.9 percent decrease in pollution.

12.10 SUMMARY

In this chapter we have examined several topics that relate to international aspects of environmental problems. Our discussion here and in the related literature from which it was drawn can roughly be organized around three main topics: how to address the problem of transboundary pollution; what are the relationships and spillover aspects of environmental policy and international trade, and environmental and trade policies; and what are the environmental consequences of expanding international trade. We have seen that each of these major areas nests several sub-areas, including, for example, the differences between cooperative and unilateral policy approaches, the role of negotiations in environmental agreements, and the importance of linkages between environmental policy and energy markets.

Several important insights emerged from our discussion. To begin with, addressing transboundary pollution is challenging because of the need to accommodate the potentially asymmetric interests of different countries in a voluntary context. We saw that cooperative solutions are relatively easy to characterize, but it may be that international transfers are necessary to assure participation in joint efforts to reduce emissions. In addition, different solutions are possible when countries' welfare outcomes are differently weighted, meaning there is a significant equity component that needs to be addressed within the context of any agreement. These results help illustrate the challenges the world community has experienced in addressing, for example, global climate change. Some of these difficulties were illustrated via our discussions of specific mechanisms that are part of the Kyoto agreement on climate change, and international environmental agreements more generally.

We also saw that there are significant overlaps between environmental policy and international trade flows. Depending on whether the domestic economy is large or small, domestic environmental policy can affect the terms of international trade and lead to the outward migration of production and factor inputs. Thus, as we saw in Chapter 5, there is a pollution/production trade-off, but in the context of open economies, production and emissions may "leak" to other countries. Thus emissions may not be completely eliminated, but rather only shifted in location. We saw that if emissions have a transboundary effect, a domestic regulator needs to consider the extent to which leaked emissions may contribute to domestic damages. That is, there is a NIMBY effect to be considered.

Related to this, we saw that trade and environmental policy can become intermingled under free trade agreements, whereby environmental policy may also provide an indirect means of manipulating trade parameters to a country's advantage. We characterized how the optimal approach to using environmental policy for trade policy depends on the market structure of the export/import industry. Specifically, the common concern voiced by environmental activists that exporting countries pursue lax environmental policy in order to enhance their export sector requires imperfect competition in the export market to rationalize. In the case when domestic firms compete for export market share of the polluting good with their foreign counterparts, it may be optimal for the domestic government to under-internalize domestic environmental damage in order to help obtain market share for its firms. In contrast, when the export market for the polluting good is competitive, an exporting country may want to over-internalize pollution in order to increase export revenues. The main lesson from this analysis was that the domestic regulator needs to balance several effects when setting environmental policy, some of which will work in opposite directions.

The leakage effect that we saw operating through trade channels was shown to also have a counterpart related to energy markets. When energy markets are global, efforts by groups of countries to reduce emissions by reducing energy demand can create an indirect effect that operates through the price of energy. We saw that a spatial leakage problem can occur when falling energy prices from one group's reduction in energy demand causes an increase in energy use by another group. Thus we characterized the *spatial leakage* problem as operating through energy demand channels. We also saw that an *inter-temporal leakage* problem can operate through energy supply channels, whereby energy providers move supply forward in response to an announced future environmental policy.

Finally, we saw that the effect of expanded international trade on environmental quality is theoretically ambiguous. This has caused a large, still active empirical literature to develop that seeks to measure the magnitudes of the various channels through which trade and the environment are related.

12.11   FURTHER READING

Markusen (1974) was one of the first to study environmental policy in a large open economy with and without trade policy, finding in particular that the terms-of-trade effect can induce governments to set their unilaterally optimal emission taxes higher than marginal damage. Markusen also characterizes the optimal combination of environmental and trade policy instruments. Conrad (1993) was the first to study environmental policy as trade policy, when polluting firms engage in imperfect competition on a third market. Barrett (1994b) and Kennedy (1994) extend this analysis. Barrett in particular highlights the differences between quantity and price competition. Duval and Hamilton (2001) generalize the Cournot model to a market with several domestic and foreign firms, while Hamilton and Requate (2004) show that if Cournot firms can engage in two-part tariff contracts with upstream firms, government need not under-internalize the damage, but can instead apply the Pigouvian rule.

Rauscher (1997) was the first to introduce continuous mobile capital, while Markusen et al. (1995) study discretionary firm relocation as a reaction to more stringent environmental policy. Sinn (2008) identified the problem of inter-temporal leakage, out of which grew the label "green paradox". See also Konrad et al. (1994) for related early ideas, and Eichner and Pethig (2011) and van der Ploeg (2016) for recent extensions. Barrett (1994a) is the seminal paper on international environmental agreements (IEAs) and the concepts of internally and externally stable environmental agreement coalitions. Finus and Pintassilgo (2012, 2013) as well as Finus et al. (2013) address problems with implementing IEAs under different kinds of uncertainty. Finus and Caparros (2015) give an excellent survey on the recent developments on IEAs.

Copeland and Taylor (1994, 1995) introduce the decomposition of trade-related pollution changes into the composition, scale and technique effect channels. The theory of trade and the environment is fully developed in the book by Copeland and Taylor (2003), who address many topics not covered in this chapter. See also Copeland and Taylor (2004). One issue omitted here is the Environmental Kuznets Curve (EKC) hypothesis, stating that growth of an economy leads to an inverse U-shaped relationship between national income and pollution.

In recent years, a rich empirical literature on trade and the environment topics has emerged. Additional examples of papers investigating the pollution haven hypothesis include Ederington et al. (2005) and Millimet and List (2004). The problem of transboundary spillover effects, in the context of international rivers, was examined by Sigman (2002) and Olmstead and Sigman (2015). Since Antweiler et al. (2001), many papers have sought more refined estimates of the composition and technique effects; examples include Levinson (2009, 2015) and Cole (2000). The empirical literature on the EKC began with Grossman and Krueger (1995), and is reviewed and critiqued by Carson (2010).

APPENDIX: PROOF OF PROPOSITION 12.2

The global equilibrium is determined by the following equation system

$$
\begin{aligned}
&P(c) = p, \quad P_f(c_f) = p \\
&C_x(x,e) = p, \quad C^f_{x_f}(x_f, e_f) = p \\
&-C_e(x,e) = \tau, \quad -C^f_{e_f}(x_f, e_f) = \tau_f \\
&x + x_f = c + c_f.
\end{aligned}
\tag{A12.1}
$$

Differentiating this system with respect to the tax rate τ yields:

$$
\begin{aligned}
&P'(c)\frac{dc}{d\tau} = \frac{dp}{d\tau} \\
&P'_f(c^*)\frac{dc_f}{d\tau} = \frac{dp}{d\tau} \\
&C_{xx}(x,e)\frac{dx}{d\tau} + C_{xe}(x,e)\frac{de}{d\tau} = \frac{dp}{d\tau} \\
&C^f_{x_f x_f}(x_f, e_f)\frac{dx_f}{d\tau} + C^f_{x_f e_f}(x_f, e_f)\frac{de_f}{d\tau} = \frac{dp}{d\tau} \\
&-C_{xe}(x,e)\frac{dx}{d\tau} - C_{ee}(x,e)\frac{de}{d\tau} = 1 \\
&-C^f_{x_f e_f}(x_f, e_f)\frac{dx_f}{d\tau} - C^f_{e_f e_f}(x_f, e_f)\frac{de_f}{d\tau} = 0 \\
&\frac{dx}{d\tau} + \frac{dx_f}{d\tau} = \frac{dc}{d\tau} + \frac{dc_f}{d\tau},
\end{aligned}
\tag{A12.2}
$$

or in matrix form $M \cdot a = b$, where

$$
M = \begin{bmatrix}
P'(c) & 0 & 0 & 0 & 0 & 0 & -1 \\
0 & P_f'(c_f) & 0 & 0 & 0 & 0 & -1 \\
0 & 0 & C_{xx}(x,e) & 0 & C_{xe}(x,e) & 0 & -1 \\
0 & 0 & 0 & C_{x_f x_f}^f(x_f,e_f) & 0 & C_{x_f e_f}^f(x_f,e_f) & -1 \\
0 & 0 & -C_{xe}(x,e) & 0 & -C_{ee}(x,e) & 0 & 0 \\
0 & 0 & 0 & -C_{x_f e_f}^f(x_f,e_f) & 0 & -C_{e_f e_f}^f(x_f,e_f) & 0 \\
-1 & -1 & 1 & 1 & 0 & 0 & 0
\end{bmatrix},
$$

$$(A12.3)$$

$$
a' = \left(\frac{dc}{d\tau}, \frac{dc_f}{d\tau}, \frac{dx}{d\tau}, \frac{dx_f}{d\tau}, \frac{de}{d\tau}, \frac{de_f}{d\tau}, \frac{dp}{d\tau} \right),
\tag{A12.4}
$$

and $b' = (0,0,0,0,1,0,0)$. We write

$$
\begin{aligned}
H(C) &= C_{xx}C_{ee} - C_{xe}^2 > 0 \\
H(C^f) &= C_{x_f x_f}^f C_{e_f e_f}^f - \left(C_{x_f e_f}^f \right)^2 > 0
\end{aligned}
\tag{A12.5}
$$

to denote the Hessian matrices of the domestic and the foreign firm's cost functions. Then the determinant of the matrix M is given by

$$
Det(M) = (P' + P_f')\left(H(C) + H(C^f) \right) - P'P_f'\left(C_{ee}H(C^f) + C_{e_f e_f}^f H(C) \right),
\tag{A12.6}
$$

which by inspection is negative. Then, omitting function arguments for the sake of brevity, the remaining expressions are as follows:

$$
\begin{aligned}
\frac{dc}{d\tau} &= \frac{C_{xe}H(C^f)P_f'}{Det(M)} < 0 \\[4pt]
\frac{dc_f}{d\tau} &= \frac{C_{xe}H(C^f)P'}{Det(M)} < 0 \\[4pt]
\frac{dx}{d\tau} &= \frac{C_{xe}\left(H(C^f)(P' + P_f') - C_{ee}^* P'P_f' \right)}{Det(M)} < 0 \\[4pt]
\frac{dx_f}{d\tau} &= \frac{C_{xe}C_{e_f e_f}^f P'P_f'}{Det(M)} > 0 \\[4pt]
\frac{de}{d\tau} &= \frac{-(P' + P_f')H(C^f)C_{xx} + P'P_f'\left(H(C^f) + C_{xx}C_{e_f e_f}^f \right)}{Det(M)} < 0 \\[4pt]
\frac{de_f}{d\tau} &= \frac{P'P_f'C_{xe}C_{x_f e_f}^f}{Det(M)} > 0 \\[4pt]
\frac{dp}{d\tau} &= \frac{P'P_f'C_{xe}H(C^f)}{Det(M)} > 0
\end{aligned}
\tag{A12.7}
$$

The signs can be verified by inspection.

EXERCISES

12.1 ** Consider the model from section 12.1, where the countries' utility functions are

$$U(z,E,E_f) = z - \frac{\gamma_1}{2}E^2 - \frac{\gamma_2}{2}E_f^2$$

$$U^f(c_f,E,E_f) = z_f - \frac{\gamma_1^f}{2}E^2 - \frac{\gamma_2^f}{2}E_f^2.$$

The abatement cost functions are given by

$$C(E) = \frac{(d-gE)^2}{2h}$$

$$C_f(E_f) = \frac{(d_f - g_f E_f)^2}{2h_f}.$$

(a) Determine the efficient allocations.
(b) Determine the unilateral optimal emission choices (i.e. the emissions Nash equilibrium).
(c) Assume goods transfer is possible. Under what circumstances does one country have to pay compensation to the other country, to incentivize that country to sign an emission-reducing contract?
(d) Carry out the same exercise for utility functions

$$U(z,E,E_f) = z - \frac{\gamma}{2}(E+E_f)^2$$

$$U^f(c_f,E,E_f) = z_f - \frac{\gamma_f}{2}(E+E_f)^2.$$

12.2 ** Repeat exercise 12.1, but now use

$$U(z,E,E_f) = az - \frac{b}{2}a^2 - \frac{\gamma_1}{2}E^2 - \frac{\gamma_2}{2}E_f^2$$

for the domestic utility function, and a corresponding expression for the foreign utility function.

(a) What are the maximum consumption levels for z and z_f?
(b) Assume now that pollution is proportional to consumption so that $e = \phi z$ and $e_f = \phi_f z_f$. Repeat (a) through (d) in exercise 12.1, adjusting the utility function for (d) accordingly.

12.3 ** Consider utility functions

$$U(z,E,E_f) = z^\eta - \frac{1}{2}(\alpha E + \beta E_f)^2$$

$$U^f(z_f,E,E_f) = z_f^\eta - \frac{1}{2}(\alpha_f E + \beta_f E_f)^2.$$

with $\alpha,\beta > 0$, and $0 < \eta < 1$, and correspondingly for the foreign country. Production (income) is a function of energy input, scaled so that the energy input is equal to emissions. The production functions are given by $y = E^\chi$ with $0 < \chi < 1$, and $y_f = E_f^{\chi_f}$ with $0 < \chi_f < 1$. Repeat exercise 12.1, parts (a) through (c).

12.4 * Consider the model of section 12.4.1. Show that if the foreign country maintains its emission tax, domestically emission taxes and tradable permits are equivalent.

12.5 *** Extend the model from section 12.4 by assuming that there are J (not necessarily symmetric) domestic and J_f (not necessarily symmetric) foreign firms.

(a) Derive the unilaterally optimal emission tax formula for this case. Assume that both countries issue tradable permits, and that the permit markets of the two countries are separate.

(b) Set up the equation system that describes the world market equilibrium.

(c) Derive a formula for the optimal quantity of permits to be issued domestically. Assume now that the pollutant is homogeneous and an international emission trading system is implemented.

(d) Set up the equation system that describes the world market equilibrium.

(e) Derive a formula for the totally optimal quantity of permits to be issued world-wide.

(f) Assume now that the pollutant is homogeneous, but permit markets are separate. Assume again there is only one representative firm in each country. Determine the optimal domestic response when the foreign government relaxes its environmental policy (i.e. if the foreign number of permits increases).

(g) Assume again both countries charge emission taxes. Determine the optimal domestic response to a foreign emission tax increase.

12.6 *** Consider the model with mobile capital sketched in section 12.4.3.

(a) Set up the equation system that characterizes the international competitive equilibrium for the commodity and the capital markets.

(b) Conduct a full comparative statics analysis for a domestic tax increase.

(c) Derive a formula for the unilaterally optimal domestic emission tax rate.

12.7 *** Consider the model from section 12.4.4.

(a) Derive the second-best optimal combination of an emission tax and import tariff (export tax) for the case when there is no transboundary pollution.

(b) Derive the comparative static effects of an import tariff (export tax) increase.

(c) Assume now that the foreign country has issued tradable permits to regulate emissions, and repeat (a) and (b).

(d) Assume now that there is transboundary pollution. Derive the second-best optimal combination of an emission tax and import tariff (export tax).

12.8 *** Consider the inter-temporal leakage problem from section 12.6.3. Assume the extraction cost depend on the remaining stock – i.e. in the second period the extraction cost function is given by $\Gamma(e_2, S - e_1)$, where $\Gamma_2 < 0$, so that a higher remaining stock leads to lower extraction costs. Determine the impact of a second period emission tax increase. Distinguish the cases where the resource is fully depleted and where it is not.

CHAPTER 13

Accumulating Pollutants

In the previous chapters we studied pollution problems mainly in a static framework. With noise pollution, for example, the externality results directly from the instantaneous flow of noise. Many other pollutants, however, accumulate, and the externality results from the stock of the pollutant rather than from its flow. This is in particular the case for greenhouse gasses such as carbon dioxide. It is also relevant for air pollutants such as sulfur dioxide and nitrogen oxides, as well as for liquid pollutants that accumulate in groundwater reservoirs. This is not to say that our analysis so far is valid only for noise or other non-accumulating externalities, in that we can interpret our earlier findings as steady-state results. In this chapter, however, we focus directly on the dynamic consequences of accumulating pollutants. Although we do not deal in depth with resource economics in this book, pollution abatement for accumulating pollutants has parallels to the exploitation and management of renewable resources. In the case of climate change, for example, the atmosphere can be thought of as a sink for pollutants, and as such as a renewable resource.

To analyze accumulation dynamics, we need additional analytical tools from dynamic systems analysis. When conducting analysis in continuous time, we typically apply methods from dynamic optimization and optimal control. A full introduction to optimal control theory is beyond the scope of this book. Nonetheless, in appendix A to this chapter we briefly define the main concepts of optimal control theory, and lay out in a recipe-like fashion the corresponding optimality conditions.

This chapter is organized as follows. In section 13.1 we set up a dynamic version of our Chapter 3 model, with environmental damage resulting from accumulated pollution. We start by briefly presenting a discrete time version of the model to derive the optimality conditions via the familiar Lagrange method. In section 13.2 we then analyze the continuous time model in detail by first setting up the optimality conditions and looking at the optimal steady state, and then turning attention to the optimal path into the steady state. We do this analytically and using phase diagram analysis. In section 13.3 we link the problem of an exhaustible resource to the problem of an accumulating pollutant. We start by briefly recalling the Hotelling model of exploitation of an exhaustible resource and then present a model with an accumulating pollutant resulting from the exhaustible resource, and analyze its findings in the context of the climate change problem. The chapter closes with our usual summary and further readings sections.

13.1 THE ACCUMULATING POLLUTANT COST-DAMAGE MODEL

In a dynamic model we need to distinguish between flow and stock variables, also called *control* and *state variables*. In particular, we interpret emissions as the flow or control variable, and the ambient pollution stock as the state variable. Environmental policy can affect emissions directly, but we have less control on the stock of pollutants. Specifically, the regulator can only affect the stock by influencing emissions over time.

In the following, we use E_t to denote aggregate emissions in an economy, where t is the time index. We abstract from different pollution sources and the allocation of emissions among them. We use S_t to denote the *stock* of the pollutant at a point in time t. For the main part of this chapter we develop our models in continuous time, since it is analytically more convenient than discrete time models. For pedagogical reasons it is useful, however, to start by setting up the equation of motion and the relationship between flow and stock variables in discrete time periods.

13.1.1 Stock Dynamics

In discrete time, the relationship between the emissions E_t and the pollution stock S_t can be written as

$$S_{t+1} = (1-\beta)S_t + E_t. \tag{13.1}$$

Here β represents the natural *decay rate* (sometimes also called *disintegration rate*) of the pollutant. This means that a share β of the pollution stock decays from period t to period $t+1$, while a share $(1-\beta)$ survives. From this we see that the pollution stock shrinks from one period to the next through natural decay, but increases through additional emissions. We can rewrite (13.1) as a difference equation according to

$$S_{t+1} - S_t = E_t - \beta S_t. \tag{13.2}$$

In continuous time, the equation of motion for the pollution stock is the linear differential equation

$$\dot{S}_t = E_t - \beta S_t, \tag{13.3}$$

where β is now the instantaneous decay rate in continuous time, and $\dot{S}_t = dS_t/dt$ denotes the time derivative of the pollution stock.

13.1.2 Abatement Cost and Damage

We now consider the economic aspects of our dynamic model by drawing on concepts from Chapter 3. We use $C(E_t)$ to denote the aggregate abatement cost that results when emissions in time t are restricted to an aggregate level E_t. We assume the abatement cost function has the same properties as in Chapter 3, so that $C'(E_t) < 0$ and $C''(E_t) > 0$ for $E_t \leq \hat{E}$, where $\hat{E}$ is the maximum or "business as usual" emissions level. For convenience (to rule out corner solutions) we additionally assume $\lim_{E \to 0}\{-C'(E_t)\} = \infty$. Finally, we write the damage in period t resulting from the pollution stock as $D(S_t)$, where, as in Chapter 3, we assume $D'(S_t) > 0$ and $D''(S_t) \geq 0$.

The regulator's aim is to minimize the sum of total social costs over time periods running from the present to some endpoint T, which may be finite or infinite. In discrete time, the social objective function is to select E_t to minimize

$$\sum_{t=0}^{T} \delta^t \left(C(E_t) + D(S_t) \right), \tag{13.4}$$

subject to (13.2) and an initial condition $S(0) = S_0$. With a finite time horizon there may also be a terminal condition $S(T) = S_T$. In addition, $\delta = 1/(1+r)$ is the discount factor and $r \geq 0$ is the social discount rate, which adjusts for society's preference for current costs (or benefits) over future costs (or benefits). For $T = \infty$, we assume $\delta < 1$ to guarantee convergence of the sum in (13.4).[1]

In continuous time, an integral substitutes for the sum. With an infinite time horizon, the social objective function is given by

$$\min_{E_t} \int_0^\infty \left(C(E_t) + D(S_t) \right) e^{-rt} dt, \tag{13.5}$$

subject to (13.3), where r is once again the (instantaneous) social discount rate and e^{-rt} is the discount factor converting time t costs and benefits into present period values. To minimize (13.5) subject to the equation of motion and an initial condition for the pollution stock $S(0) = S_0$, we need to apply methods of dynamic optimization. We introduce this in the following section.

13.2 DYNAMIC OPTIMALITY

With our ideas and notation fixed, we are now ready to examine the optimality conditions. We begin with the discrete time model, since here we can apply the familiar Lagrange method and readily obtain the main optimality conditions, which can be directly interpreted. Then we proceed with the continuous time model, which will be useful for our more general examination to come.

13.2.1 Discrete Time

In discrete time, we minimize (13.4) with respect to (13.2). To set up the Lagrange function it is convenient to rewrite (13.2) as

$$\delta^{t-1} \left(S_{t+1} - (1-\beta)S_t - E_t \right) = 0. \tag{13.6}$$

---

[1] For reasons of simplicity and time consistency, we assume a time invariant discount rate. In Chapter 21, we discuss the discount rate in more detail, including the possibility of a decreasing-over-time discount rate.

That is, we discount the dynamic constraint to the current value of the objective function in period t. We can therefore write the present value Lagrangian as

$$L = \sum_{t=1}^{T} \delta^{t-1} \left(C(E_t) + D(S_t) - \lambda_t \left[S_{t+1} - (1-\beta)S_t - E_t \right] \right). \tag{13.7}$$

Differentiating with respect to E_t yields

$$C'(E_t) + \lambda_t = 0, \tag{13.8}$$

or

$$-C'(E_t) = \lambda_t. \tag{13.9}$$

This equation tells us that in each period, the current marginal abatement cost should be equal to shadow cost of the current period's dynamic constraint, which is the shadow social cost of the future pollution stock. In continuous time, this Lagrange multiplier is called the *co-state variable*. Note that we can interpret this shadow price as the optimal tax (or price for tradable permits), in that in a decentralized world the optimal tax must equal marginal abatement cost.

Next we differentiate (13.7) with respect to the pollution stock S_t to obtain

$$D'(S_t) - \frac{1}{\delta} \lambda_{t-1} + \lambda_t (1-\beta) = 0, \tag{13.10}$$

where the λ_{t-1} appears because S_t is part of the summation in the $t-1$ part of the summation. By using $\delta = 1/(1+r)$, and moving forward one time unit, we can rearrange this to obtain

$$D'(S_{t+1}) + \lambda_{t+1}(1-\beta) = (1+r)\lambda_t. \tag{13.11}$$

The last equation characterizes the optimal dynamics of the co-state variable. Along the optimal emission path, increasing emissions today by one unit, and saving the avoided marginal abatement cost, defined by $\lambda_t = -C'(E_t)$, yields a payoff of $(1+r)\lambda_t$ tomorrow (the right-hand side of (13.11)). This amount is equal to the resulting marginal damage from forgoing abatement, plus the added abatement cost in the next period from the extra emission, adjusted by the reduction due to the decay rate (the left-hand side of (13.11)).

Finally, we ask what happens when the time horizon goes to infinity. Do emissions, and thus the pollution stock, converge to zero, or does the pollution stock become infinitely large, or do both emissions and the pollution stock converge to positive but finite values? Regarding the first of these possibilities, it is clear that it will not be optimal to let emissions converge to zero, because the marginal abatement cost grows to infinity, while the marginal social damage converges to zero, as emissions – and thus eventually the pollution stock – approach zero. Similarly, the pollution stock cannot converge to infinity, since an infinitely increasing pollution stock would imply infinitely increasing emissions, which cannot be the case as $E_t \leq \hat{E}$. Therefore, in an infinite time horizon the system must converge to a *stationary state*, or for short *steady state*, with $\lim_{t\to\infty} E_t = E^*$, $\lim_{t\to\infty} S_t = S^*$, and $\lim_{t\to\infty} \lambda_t = \lambda^*$. The last condition implies that $\lim_{t\to\infty}(\lambda_t - \lambda_{t-1}) = 0$ also holds. Using the steady state values in (13.11) and substituting using (13.9), we obtain

$$-C'(E^*) = \frac{D'(S^*)}{r+\beta}. \tag{13.12}$$

This means that the marginal abatement cost is equal to the discounted sum of marginal damages, where the effective discount rate is the time discount rate plus the natural decay rate.

13.2.2 Continuous Time

In continuous time, there are at least two methods for analyzing dynamic optimization problems. The first is the recursive Bellman-Jacobi principle, and the second is Pontryagin's maximum (or minimum) principle. Here we mainly work with the latter. The key tool of Pontryagin's maximum principle is the Hamiltonian, which is a generalization of the Lagrange function to continuous time. The optimality conditions for the Hamiltonian approach are outlined in appendix A to this chapter. The Hamiltonian is the sum of the current objective (social cost in our context), plus the marginal future cost or benefit of increasing the stock variable by a marginal amount. The Hamiltonian therefore takes into account the consequences of a change in the stock variable for all points in time into the future. In the literature it is common to distinguish between the *current* value Hamiltonian and the *present* value Hamiltonian. The current value Hamiltonian assesses the instantaneous objective at some point in time t, as if we are starting from $t=0$. The present value Hamiltonian, by contrast, assesses the objective at some later point in time t from the present perspective, and therefore the objective is multiplied by the discount factor e^{-rt}. The approaches are equivalent in their analytical results. In models that converge to a steady state with a long run positive state variable (pollution stock in our case), it is convenient to work with the current value Hamiltonian, whereas in models with a stock that vanishes in the long run (as may be the case with exhaustible resources), it is often more convenient to work with the present value Hamiltonian.

In models with accumulating pollutants that have a natural decay, the system usually converges to a steady state with a positive stock of pollution, and so we will work with the current value Hamiltonian

$$H(E_t, S_t, \lambda_t) = [C(E_t) + D(S_t)] + \lambda_t [E_t - \beta S_t]. \tag{13.13}$$

The first term in brackets is the current social objective function. The variable λ_t is the co-state variable, which measures the marginal social cost arising in all future periods, if the pollution stock is increased by one unit. The co-state variable can also be interpreted as society's current marginal willingness to pay to avoid one more unit of the pollutant. This latter interpretation implies that the co-state variable depends on the discount rate.

To avoid lengthy mathematical expressions, it is conventional to omit the time sub-scripts in the Hamiltonian. We should always keep in mind, however, that all variables are functions of time. We therefore rewrite our Hamiltonian as

$$H(E, S, \lambda) = C(E) + D(S) + \lambda[E - \beta S]. \tag{13.14}$$

The first-order necessary conditions for the optimal emission path are then characterized by the following two equations:

$$\frac{\partial H}{\partial E} = 0 \quad \rightarrow \quad -C'(E) = \lambda, \tag{13.15}$$

$$-\frac{\partial H}{\partial S} = \dot{\lambda} - r\lambda \quad \rightarrow \quad D'(S) - \lambda\beta + \dot{\lambda} = r\lambda, \tag{13.16}$$

and the transversality (or terminal) condition

$$\lim\nolimits_{t \to T} e^{-rt} \lambda_t S_t = 0, \tag{13.17}$$

which is equivalent to $\lim_{t \to \infty} e^{-rt} \lambda_t = 0$ in a steady state with infinite horizon. Equation (13.15) states that the current marginal abatement cost should equal the future marginal social cost, represented by the co-state variable. Equation (13.16) characterizes the optimal dynamics of the co-state variable. It is similar to the discrete time version (13.11), and states that the social planner should be indifferent between (a) increasing the pollution stock by a marginal unit to earn the interest on saved marginal abatement costs; and (b) reducing the pollution stock by a marginal unit to get the social benefit of this reduction. This consists of three terms: the saved marginal damage costs, an adjustment for the natural decay, and the increase (or decrease) of the shadow price of pollution.

There can be infinitely many solution paths $\{E_t, S_t\}_{t \geq 0}$ that solve (13.15) and (13.16). Not all of them, however, are optimal. We therefore need to use the boundary conditions on the state and co-state variables to determine the optimal solution. One boundary condition is that the initial pollution stock is given, and the other is a transversality condition. For finite horizon problems, transversality conditions are typically terminal conditions that impose a final value on the state variable. In infinite horizon problems, the transversality condition is given by (13.17). This condition is satisfied in a steady state, where λ_t is constant over time. Therefore, it is usually sufficient to look for paths $\{E_t, S_t\}_{t \geq 0}$ that satisfy (13.15) and (13.16), and converge to a steady state.

13.2.3 The Steady State

Before we study the optimal emission path, it is convenient to first study the steady state the system will converge to along the optimal path. In the steady state, the variables converge to constants over time. This translates into time derivatives being zero – i.e. $\dot{E} = 0$, $\dot{S} = 0$ and $\dot{\lambda} = 0$. The steady state values are written as (E^*, S^*, λ^*). Setting $\dot{S} = 0$ in (13.3), we obtain $E^* = \beta S^*$. This means that at the steady state, emissions in the current period are equal to the amount that decays naturally. Setting $\dot{\lambda} = 0$ in (13.16), using (13.15), and rearranging we obtain:

$$-C'(E^*) = \lambda = \frac{D'(S^*)}{r + \beta}. \tag{13.18}$$

Equation (13.18) tells us that, at the optimal steady state, the marginal abatement cost is equal to the present value of all future damages arising by one more unit of emissions. The discount rate for emissions is then the sum of the discount rate for costs and benefits, plus the natural decay rate.

Comparative Statics for the Steady State

It is instructive to study how the different parameters affect the steady state variables. We are particularly interested in the influence of both the discount and the decay rates on the steady state. For this purpose, we rewrite (13.18) as

$$-C'(E^*)(r + \beta) = D'(S^*), \tag{13.19}$$

and differentiate the equation system consisting of $E^* = \beta S^*$ and (13.19) with respect to r, yielding

$$\frac{\partial E^*}{\partial r} = \beta \frac{\partial S^*}{\partial r}$$

$$-C''(E^*)(r + \beta)\frac{\partial E^*}{\partial r} - C'(E^*) = D''(S^*)\frac{\partial S^*}{\partial r}. \tag{13.20}$$

Solving this system (using Cramer's Rule) yields

$$\frac{\partial E^*}{\partial r} = \frac{-\beta C'(E^*)}{D''(S^*) + \beta(r + \beta)C''(E^*)} > 0$$

$$\frac{\partial S^*}{\partial r} = \frac{-C'(E^*)}{D''(S^*) + \beta(r + \beta)C''(E^*)} > 0. \tag{13.21}$$

We see that a higher discount rate implies higher emissions, and a higher steady-state pollution stock. This is intuitive, in that if society cares less about the future (reflected by a higher discount rate), it will leave a higher pollution stock to future generations. This also implies higher emissions at each point in time.

Doing the same exercise with respect to the decay rate, we obtain

$$\frac{\partial E^*}{\partial \beta} = \frac{-\beta C'(E^*) + S^* \cdot D''(S^*)}{D''(S^*) + \beta(r + \beta)C''(E^*)} > 0$$

$$\frac{\partial S^*}{\partial \beta} = \frac{-C'(E^*) - S^* \cdot (r + \beta) \cdot C''(S^*)}{D''(S^*) + \beta(r + \beta)C''(E^*)}. \tag{13.22}$$

Whereas the sign of $\partial E^*/\partial \beta$ is unambiguously positive – a faster decay allows for higher emissions – the sign of $\partial S^*/\partial \beta$ is ambiguous. The last result should not be surprising since we observe two opposing effects: higher emissions contribute to a higher pollution stock, whereas a faster decay lets the pollution stock shrink. If we substitute S^* into the numerator of the second equation in (13.22) using $S^* = E^*/\beta$, we obtain

$$\frac{\partial S^*}{\partial \beta} > 0 \quad \leftrightarrow \quad \frac{-C'(E^*)}{E^* \cdot C''(E^*)} > \frac{r + \beta}{\beta}. \tag{13.23}$$

This means that the pollution stock increases with the decay rate, if and only if the elasticity of the aggregate marginal abatement cost curve is sufficiently small (in other words, the demand-elasticity for emissions at a hypothetical price is sufficiently large), and vice versa.

13.2.4 Optimal Path to the Steady State

We now study the optimal emission/abatement path to the steady state, when starting from an arbitrary stock of pollution. For this purpose we differentiate (13.15) with respect to time to obtain

$$-C''(E) \cdot \dot{E} = \dot{\lambda}. \tag{13.24}$$

We can now use (13.15) and (13.24) to eliminate λ and $\dot{\lambda}$ from (13.16), yielding the equation of motion for emissions as

$$\dot{E} = \frac{D'(S) + (r + \beta)C'(E)}{C''(E)}, \tag{13.25}$$

or by rearranging

$$\dot{E} = \frac{\dfrac{D'(S)}{r + \beta} - \left(-C'(E)\right)}{\dfrac{C''(E)}{r + \beta}}. \tag{13.26}$$

This equation tells us that the evolution of emissions is driven by the difference between the present discounted value of marginal damage, and marginal abatement cost. This difference is zero in the steady state – i.e., for $\dot{E} = 0$, the equation of motion reduces to (13.18). From (13.26) we can see that if the stock is low, such that the marginal damage is low, E is decreasing, while for a high pollution stock, and thus for high marginal damage, E is increasing. This might seem counterintuitive. The reason is that emissions as a control variable are chosen optimally from the beginning of the planning period, and therefore can jump when switching from some non-optimal policy to the optimal path. Starting from an initially low pollution stock (lower than the optimal steady-state stock), society can afford to initially release more emissions than in the steady state, but over time has to run a more stringent environmental policy by reducing emissions. If, by contrast, the initial stock exceeds the optimal steady-state stock, society must restrict emissions immediately to a level below the steady state, so that environmental quality can recover. It can then gradually relax environmental policy, and approach the steady state from above. We will come back to the monotonicity of the optimal emission path in the next subsection.

13.2.5 Phase Diagrams

The dynamic system given by (13.3) and (13.16), or by (13.3) and (13.25), is an *autonomous system* where the control, state, and co-state variables do not directly depend on time, but only on the current state. Autonomous systems can be nicely illustrated and analyzed using phase diagrams, which depict the dynamics of the control and state variables in a control/state variable diagram, or alternatively, the dynamics of the co-state and state variables in a corresponding co-state/state variable diagram. We examine these in turn.

Phase Diagram in Control/State Space

To construct the control/state diagram we use equations (13.3) and (13.25), combined and rewritten as

$$\dot{S} = E - \beta S$$
$$\dot{E} = \frac{D'(S) + (r + \beta)C'(E)}{C''(E)}.$$

(13.27)

Setting $\dot{S} = 0$ in the first equation and $\dot{E} = 0$ in the second, we obtain two implicit relationships that determine emissions as a function of the pollution stock. The $\dot{S} = 0$ curve (also called isocline), which is driven by the *natural* decay process in (13.3), can be written as $E_N(S) = \beta S$, whereas the *control* equation for $\dot{E} = 0$ can be written as

$$E_C(S) = C_E^{-1}\left(-D'(S) / (r + \beta)\right),$$

(13.28)

where $C_E^{-1}(\cdot)$ is the inverse function to $C'(\cdot)$. The intersection point of the two curves defines the steady state of the dynamic system. Moreover, we see that the $\dot{S} = 0$ curve is increasing, since $E_N(S)$ is increasing in S, while $E_C(S)$ is decreasing in S, because $D'(S)$ is increasing (and thus $-D'(S)$ is decreasing) and $C_E^{-1}(\cdot)$ is increasing.

   In order to determine the optimal path into the steady state, starting from an arbitrary given initial pollution stock, we again consider the two equations of motion in (13.27) to construct a phase diagram. Such a diagram uses arrows to mark the direction of any path satisfying the equations of motion in the control/state variable plane. First consider the equation of motion for the pollution stock. If E exceeds βS, then $\dot{S}$ is positive. This implies that, above the $\dot{S} = 0$ curve, the phase diagram arrows will show S moving to the right (increasing). The opposite is true below the $\dot{S}-0$ – or $E_N(S)$ – curve, where E is smaller than βS. In this case, the phase diagram arrows will show S moving to the left (decreasing).

Next consider the equation of motion for the control variable. To the left of (or below) the $\dot{E}=0$ – or $E_C(S)$ – curve, the present value of marginal damage, given by $D'(S)/(\beta+r)$, is smaller than $-C'(E)$, the marginal abatement cost. Thus the phase diagram arrows for emissions point downwards, to indicate that E is decreasing. To the right of the $\dot{E}=0$ curve, the opposite is true. Therefore, the phase diagram arrows will point upwards, to indicate that E is increasing.

In Figure 13.1a we have labeled the four areas defined by the $\dot{S}=0$ and $\dot{E}=0$ curves. We see that all paths starting in areas I and III must move away from the steady state. In areas II and IV, by contrast, we find paths moving into the steady state. In fact, there is exactly one path in area II and one path in area IV leading into the steady state. All other paths above or below the bold arrowed path also move away from the steady state. Recall that the stock of pollution S is the state variable, while emissions E is the control variable. Therefore, for any given stock S, the bold arrowed path indicates how to choose emissions optimally. We can therefore consider the optimal path into the steady state as a function $E(S)$, which gives us the optimal emissions for any given pollution stock, implicitly assuming that from that point forward we keep on moving along the optimal path. Note further, that while all paths in the entire E/S diagram satisfy the equations of motion (13.3) and (13.25), only the two paths leading into the steady state – in II from the right, and in IV from the left – satisfy the transversality condition (13.17).

We now return to the monotonicity properties of the optimal path. Figure 13.1a tells us that if we start with an initial pollution stock lower than the steady state level, the optimal path approaches the steady state from above. If the initial pollution stock exceeds the optimal steady state level, so that we start to the right of S^*, emissions approach the optimal steady state from below. Note that the monotonicity of the optimal path is a particular property of this simple model with one control and one state variable. In models with several control and state variables, optimal paths can be non-monotonic over time. For example Moslener and Requate (2007, 2009) consider models with several pollutants, which may differ in their decay speed. They find that, depending on where the system starts, optimal emission paths can exhibit non-monotonic behavior. Note

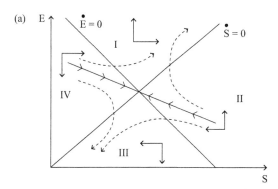

(a)

Figure 13.1a   The phase diagram in the S/E -space

also that if an economy faces adjustment costs it might not be optimal to approach the steady state immediately from below. It is generally the case, however, that if the initial stock is above the steady state, the optimal emission path must eventually approach the steady state from below, since otherwise it would not be possible for the pollution stock to recover.

Phase Diagram in State/Co-state Space

We now turn to the phase diagram in the state/co-state-variable plane. This is important, since the co-state variable can be interpreted as the shadow price for emissions, and so is also the optimal emission tax (or the optimal market price for tradable emission permits) in a regulated competitive economy.

We examine the two crucial equations of motion given by (13.3) and (13.16). Rearranging (13.16) yields:

$$\dot{\lambda} = \lambda(r + \beta) - D'(S). \tag{13.29}$$

To eliminate the control variable E from by (13.3), we use (13.15) to solve for E, yielding $E = C_E^{-1}(-\lambda)$, where once again $C_E^{-1}(\cdot)$ is the inverse function of $C'(E)$. Substituting into (13.3) we obtain

$$\dot{S} = C_E^{-1}(-\lambda) - \beta S. \tag{13.30}$$

From (13.29) and (13.30), respectively, we can see that the $\dot{\lambda} = 0$ curve is

$$\lambda = \frac{D'(S)}{r + \beta}, \tag{13.31}$$

and the $\dot{S} = 0$ curve is

$$\lambda = -C'(\beta S). \tag{13.32}$$

Since $D'(\cdot)$ is increasing in its argument, the $\dot{\lambda} = 0$ curve must also be increasing in S. By contrast, $-C'(\cdot)$ is decreasing and therefore the $\dot{S} = 0$ curve must be decreasing in the S/λ plane. The diagram is depicted in Figure 13.1b. To the right of the $\dot{S} = 0$ curve, we see from (13.30) that $\dot{S} < 0$, and the horizontal arrows point to the left. The opposite is true to the left of the $\dot{S} = 0$ curve. From (13.29), we see that to the right of the $\dot{\lambda} = 0$ curve, we have $\dot{\lambda} < 0$. The vertical arrows therefore point downwards, while the opposite is true to the left of the $\dot{\lambda} = 0$ curve.

From these arrows it follows that if the initial pollution stock exceeds the steady state level, the corresponding shadow price of emissions (and thus the optimal emission tax) must be larger than its steady state level. The optimal path in the state/co-state plane must therefore approach the steady state from above. The opposite is true if the initial pollution stock is smaller than its steady state level. This shape of the optimal path is similar to the optimal path in the control/state plane. To the right of the steady state

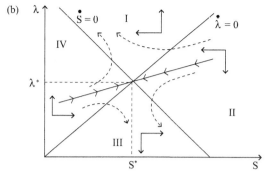

Figure 13.1b   The phase diagram in the S/λ -space

pollution stock level, emissions must be lower than the steady state level, meaning the shadow price must exceed its corresponding steady state level. The opposite is true for pollution stocks below the steady state level.

Optimal Feedback Strategy

As we can see from the phase diagram, the optimal path into the steady state can be described as a function relating emissions to the accumulated stock of pollution – i.e. $E = E(S)$. Since our dynamic process under consideration is an autonomous process, which does not depend on time directly, we can further use the optimality conditions (13.3), (13.15) and (13.16) to characterize the optimal feedback strategy $E(S)$. For this purpose, we differentiate (13.15) with respect to time to obtain

$$-C''(E) \cdot E'(S) \cdot \dot{S} = \dot{\lambda}. \tag{13.33}$$

Using (13.3) to eliminate $\dot{S}$ from (13.33) and using (13.15) and (13.33) to eliminate λ and $\dot{\lambda}$ from (13.16), we obtain a differential equation for the feedback strategy $E(S)$ as

$$-D'(S) - (\beta + r)C'(E) + C''(E)E'(S)(E - \beta S) = 0, \tag{13.34}$$

or

$$E'(S) = \frac{D'(S) + (\beta + r)C'(E)}{C''(E)(E - \beta S)}, \tag{13.35}$$

which is similar to (13.25). For specific functional forms of the damage and the abatement cost function, this differential equation can be solved in closed form.

EXAMPLE 13.1 (NUMERICAL/ANALYTICAL) We illustrate our results for quadratic abatement cost and damage functions

$$C(E) = \frac{(a - bE)^2}{2b}$$
$$D(S) = d\frac{S^2}{2}, \tag{13.36}$$

for which the steady state stock is straightforward to calculate as

$$S^* = \frac{(r+\beta)a}{d+(r+\beta)b\beta}.$$

(13.37)

From this we can also determine the steady emissions level as $E^* = \beta S^*$, and the co-state variable steady state level as $\lambda^* = a/b - E^*$.

In appendix B, we show how to solve for the optimal emission, pollution and co-state variable paths for this case. For our linear marginal abatement cost and marginal damage curves these can be presented as a function of time in closed form:

$$S(t) = S^* + (S_0 - S^*) \cdot K_S \cdot e^{\mu t}$$

(13.38)

$$E(t) = E^* - (S_0 - S^*) \cdot K_E \cdot e^{\mu t}$$

(13.39)

$$\lambda(t) = \lambda^* + (S_0 - S^*) \cdot K_\lambda \cdot e^{\mu t}$$

(13.40)

where K_S, K_E, and K_λ are positive constants, and μ is a negative number. As we will see, μ is an eigenvalue of the linearized dynamic system, and the constants K_S, K_E, and K_λ are components of the associated eigenvectors. We see nicely from these expressions that all variables converge to the steady state as t goes to infinity. We also see that if the initial stock exceeds the steady state level so that $S_0 > S^*$, the path $S(t)$ approaches S^* from above, and in the opposite case from below. The same holds true for the path of the co-state variable, and the opposite holds for the emissions path. For specific parameter values (see appendix B), the optimal time paths for the pollution stock, emissions, and the co-state variable are displayed in Figures 13.2a to 13.2c for the case of an initial pollution stock exceeding the steady state, and in Figures 13.2d to 13.2f for the case of an initially low pollution stock.

We can also look at the optimal feedback strategy. For our functional forms, (13.35) becomes

$$E'(S) = \frac{d \cdot S - (\beta + r)(a - bE)}{b(E - \beta S)}.$$

(13.41)

Solving this equation (for example by guessing a linear solution and comparing coefficients), we obtain the simple feedback rule, where optimal emissions are a linear function of the pollution stock:

$$E(S) = \frac{a}{b} - \frac{d}{b(\beta + r)} S.$$

(13.42)

(a)   S

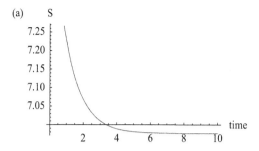

Figure 13.2a The optimal time path of the pollution stock, starting with an initial pollution stock exceeding the steady-state value

(b)   E

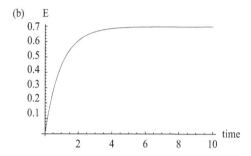

Figure 13.2b The optimal time path of emissions (with an initial pollution stock exceeding the steady-state value)

(c)   lambda

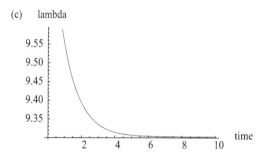

Figure 13.2c The optimal time path of the co-state variable (the Pigouvian tax rate) over time (with an initial pollution stock exceeding the steady-state value)

(d)   S

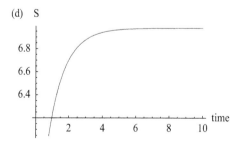

Figure 13.2d The optimal evolution of the pollution stock over time, starting with an initial pollution stock below the steady-state value

(e)   E

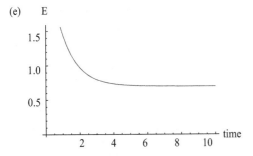

Figure 13.2e   The optimal evolution of emissions over time (with an initial pollution stock below the steady-state value)

(f)   lambda

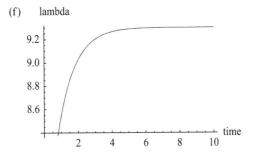

Figure 13.2f   The optimal evolution of the co-state variable (the Pigouvian tax rate) over time (with an initial pollution stock below the steady-state value)

13.2.6 Policy Instruments and Decentralized Decision-Making

We now briefly discuss decentralized decision-making under different policy instruments. We start with emission taxes, where a representative firm's total cost is given by

$$TC(E) = C(E) + \tau E. \tag{13.43}$$

If the regulator sets a tax path $\{\tau_t\}_{t \geq 0}$, the firm's objective function over the total planning horizon is

$$\min_{E_t} \int_0^\infty \left(C(E_t) + \tau_t E_t \right) dt. \tag{13.44}$$

Since the firm's profit or cost does not depend on the pollution stock, it is sufficient to minimize its current cost at each point in time. This yields

$$-C'(E_t) = \tau_t, \tag{13.45}$$

and since the first-order condition for the social optimum requires $-C'(E_t) = \lambda_t$, the regulator has to set the tax rate equal to the optimal shadow price for pollution in order to induce the first-best emissions path. That is, we have $\tau_t = \lambda_t$. From this it follows that the tax rate increases over time when the initial pollution stock is lower than the steady-state stock, and decreases when the initial pollution stock exceeds its optimal steady-state level.

Under a regime of tradable emission permits, the optimal amount of permits has to be set equal to the optimal level of emissions, resulting in $L_t = E_t^*$. If permit markets are competitive, the equilibrium permit price must be equal to the optimal shadow price of emissions, so that $\sigma_t = \lambda_t$.

EXAMPLE 13.2 (POLICY) In the climate change context, the marginal damage from an additional ton of carbon dioxide emitted is often referred to as the social cost of carbon (SCC). Equation (13.18) shows that the SCC is the discounted present value of the sum of all future damages from an emission, given in our model by $SCC_t = D'(S_t)/(r+\beta)$ for a reference stock S_t. Since the SCC is equivalent to the optimal tax on CO_2, research and policy analysis have focused on measuring it in a variety of contexts. Greenstone et al. (2013) describe the findings of an interagency working group in the United States that was tasked with developing "a transparent and economically rigorous way to value reductions in CO_2 emissions [from] federal regulations" (p.24). The group relied on three well-known integrated assessment models (IAMs – see Chapter 21) to produce a distribution of SCC estimates under a range of discount rates (2.5, 3, and 5 percent), socio-economic scenarios, and assumptions on the temperature effects of changing atmospheric carbon stocks. The group's central estimate, using a 3 percent discount rate, is $21 per ton of CO_2 emitted in 2010 (in 2007 dollars), and they advise using $5, $35, and $65 per ton in sensitivity analysis.

13.2.7 Final Remarks

Our extension of the simple model from Chapter 3 has ignored the output market. Doing so is valid as long as there is perfect competition in that market. Matters are more complicated when there are additional market/institutional failures, such as imperfect competition, unilateral policy in a world with transboundary pollution, strategic interaction amongst firms and policy makers, and so on. There are dozens of papers in the literature addressing these more advanced issues. With strategic interactions, control theory alone is not sufficient to analyze behavior. Additional tools from dynamic game theory (in continuous time) are necessary, which is beyond the scope of this book. However, the simple dynamic model presented here delivers important insights on the dynamic properties of optimal emission paths in a world with accumulating pollutants. One important extension, the link to fossil fuels as a source of an accumulating pollutant, is addressed in the following section.

13.3 EXHAUSTIBLE RESOURCES AND POLLUTION CONTROL

In this section we discuss accumulating pollutants and pollution control within the context of the related consumption of non-renewable fossil fuels. This is important, since these two issues are at the heart of the climate change debate, and policy discussions are often imprecise regarding the potentially distinct objectives of reducing emissions, versus reducing the use of fossil fuel. With this as motivation, we start with the simplest model describing the exploitation of an exhaustible resource, and then combine the two issues of pollution control and exhaustible resource management.

13.3.1 Pure Resource Extraction Model

We consider a model in which a representative household consumes a small fraction of some finite, exhaustible resource at each point in time. The consumption at time t is denoted by x_t and $u(x_t)$ is the utility drawn from resource consumption, where $u(\cdot)$ is an increasing and strictly concave function. Besides the resource, there is numeraire consumption denoted by z_t, so that total consumer utility is written as $U(x_t, z_t) = u(x_t) + z_t$. Furthermore, we assume there is constant marginal cost of extraction $c \geq 0$, measured in units of the numeraire commodity, and the household is endowed with income y_t. Finally, let R_t be the stock of the remaining resource stock in situ, where $R_0 = R(0)$ is the initial stock at point in time $t = 0$.

To characterize the socially optimal extraction of the resource, we assume that the representative household owns the resource stock, and consider its utility maximization problem

$$\max_{x = \{x_t\}} \int_0^\infty \left(u(x) + y - cx\right)e^{-rt}dt \tag{13.46}$$

subject to

$$\dot{R} = -x, \tag{13.47}$$

and the initial condition $R_0 = R(0)$, where r is the social discount rate and $z = y - cx$ is consumption of the numeraire. The equation of motion (13.47) shows that the resource stock in situ (i.e. in the ground) diminishes at each point in time, based on the extraction rate per unit of time, and there is no renewal of the stock. To solve this problem, we set up the current value Hamiltonian, omitting time indices, as

$$H(x, R, \varphi) = u(x) - cx - \varphi x, \tag{13.48}$$

where φ is the co-state variable with the respect to resource stock, and we have dropped the constant y. The first-order conditions are then

$$\frac{\partial H}{\partial x} = u'(x) - c - \varphi = 0 \quad \rightarrow \quad u'(x) = c + \varphi \tag{13.49}$$

$$-\frac{\partial H}{\partial R} = 0 = \dot{\varphi} - r\varphi \quad \rightarrow \quad \dot{\varphi} = r\varphi \tag{13.50}$$

$$\lim_{t \to \infty} \varphi e^{-\delta t} = 0. \tag{13.51}$$

From (13.50), we conclude that the co-state variable, which is the shadow value of the resource, must increase over time; by (13.49) this is likewise the case for the marginal utility of consuming the resource. Thus, if $u'(0) = \infty$, it will be optimal to use up the resource in infinite time, with $\lim_{t \to \infty} x_t = 0$. If, by contrast, $u'(0) < \infty$, it will be optimal to use up the resource in finite time.

The Competitive Market Solution

We next consider decentralized allocation. For simplicity, we abstract from the problem that the social discount rate may differ from the market interest rate, and assume that r represents both. We use p to denote the market price of the resource, which is a function of time. Also for simplicity, we assume that a representative firm owns the resource stock, but behaves as a price taker. Note that this means that the firm takes the whole time path of the price as given. The representative firm solves

$$\max_{x = \{x_t\}} \int_0^\infty (p - c) \cdot x \cdot e^{-rt} dt, \tag{13.52}$$

subject to

$$\dot{R} = -x, \tag{13.53}$$

and once again the initial condition $R_0 = R(0)$.

The current value Hamiltonian for this problem is now

$$H(x, z, \varphi) = (p - c)x - \varphi x, \tag{13.54}$$

and the derivative with respect to the control variable is $\partial H / \partial x = p - c - \varphi$, which is independent of x. Thus there is no proper interior solution for the output decision x. Nevertheless, we can draw some useful conclusions from (13.54). If $p - c - \varphi > 0$, the firm wants to supply infinitely many units, and deposit its earnings in an interest-earning account, thereby driving down the price. If $p - c - \varphi < 0$, the firm does not want to supply any of the resource, and the resulting excess demand would bid up the price. Therefore, the only candidate for an equilibrium price is $p = c - \varphi$. The additional first-order conditions are the same as the utility maximization case, provided that the market interest rate coincides with the social discount rate

$$\dot{\varphi} = r\varphi \tag{13.55}$$
$$\lim_{t \to \infty} \varphi_t e^{-rt} = 0.$$

Moreover, the utility maximizing consumer sets $u'(x) = p$.

From this, we see that the market price for the extracted resource consists of two parts: the marginal cost of extraction, and a part that is known as the resource royalty, which can also be interpreted as a scarcity rent. Since the household sets its demand according to $u'(x) = p$, we can recover the consumer's demand function $x(p)$ by inverting the first-order condition $u'(x) = p$. The market then has a unique equilibrium at each point in time, provided that we know the initial price p_0. That initial price is difficult to determine in general (see Dasgupta and Heal, 1979, for a detailed discussion). If, however, we assume that markets have perfect foresight such that the resource is used up completely, meaning that

$$\int_0^\infty x_t(p_t)dt = R_0,$$
(13.56)

the initial price can be uniquely determined. By the equality $u'(x) = p = c - \varphi$, we see that the decentralized market solution is socially optimal. The royalty part of the resource price increases exponentially, and thus slows down exploitation as the resource gets scarcer. From this we can conclude that scarcity of the resource is not a motivation for a government to correct for overexploitation if property rights are well defined.[2]

13.3.2 Optimal Extraction of a Polluting Resource

We are now ready to extend the fossil fuel resource extraction model to account for accumulating (greenhouse gas) emissions resulting from fossil fuel consumption. For this purpose, we assume that emissions from combustion E are proportional to resource extraction x, with an emission coefficient equal to one. In other words, we identify the flow of extraction with emissions, so that $E = x$. This implies that instead of (13.46), our objective function is now

$$\max_{x=\{x_t\}} \int_0^\infty \left(u(x) + y - cx - D(S)\right)e^{-rt}dt,$$
(13.57)

subject to the dynamics of resource depletion

$$\dot{R} = -x,$$
(13.58)

and the dynamics of emission accumulation

$$\dot{S} = x - \beta S.$$
(13.59)

In addition, we have initial conditions for the stock of the resource in situ $R_0 = R(0)$, and for the initial stock of pollution $S_0 = S(0)$. We set up the optimality conditions for this problem in appendix C, and report here the most important characteristics of the optimal path. These are summarized in the following proposition, which was originally proved by Tahvonen (1997).

---

[2] There is an extensive discussion in the literature about whether and why the market interest rate may differ from the social discount. See Gollier and Weitzman (2010) for a discussion, and Chapter 21 for additional discussion. A divergence between the two may provide a justification for government regulation of resource markets.

Proposition 13.1

Under the conditions of the model:

(a) *If the initial stock of pollution S_0 is sufficiently low, both the pollution stock and the co-state variable – i.e. the instantaneous shadow price – are inverted U-shaped.*

(b) *If the initial stock of pollution S_0 is sufficiently high, both the pollution stock and the co-state variable are decreasing along the optimal extraction/emission path.*

(c) *If $D'''(\cdot) \geq 0$, and the initial stock of pollution S_0 is sufficiently low (high), the optimal extraction path for x converges monotonically towards zero (is inverted U-shaped at the beginning and then eventually converges to zero).*

A detailed proof of the result is given in appendix C. Here, we interpret the findings for the three different cases. Condition (a) is relevant for a situation in which optimal pollution control begins in an early stage of the industrial process. The pollution stock has not yet accumulated in a substantial way. If the stock of the exhaustible resource is abundant, and exhaustion is not yet an issue, the situation is parallel to the model in section 13.2, in which the initial pollution stock S_0 is on the left-hand side of the steady state level S^* shown in Figures 13.1a and 13.1b. We know from Figure 13.1b that in that situation, both the pollution stock and the shadow price are increasing. This means that, as the pollution stock accumulates, environmental policy has to be tightened. Thus the situation in condition (a) is consistent with the findings in section 13.2. However, the system does not stay in this stage forever, because there is no constant flow of emissions in the long run. As the resource stock diminishes, extraction slows down, and emissions decrease. If the marginal damage function is increasing, this implies that the shadow price for pollution, and thus also the Pigouvian tax rate in a competitive economy, go down. This creates the inverted U-shape of both the pollution stock and the shadow price that are referred to in part (a) of the proposition. These are illustrated in Figures 13.3a and 13.3c. What does a low initial stock of the pollutant mean for the extraction path of the resource? Since society controls its pollution early on, it also sets the price for emissions optimally early on, meaning the early consumer price is higher, vis-à-vis the no regulation case. However, the price path increases according to $\dot{p} = \dot{\varphi} + \dot{\lambda}$. In the early stage of resource exploitation, both parts of the price are increasing. If the resource is abundant, $\dot{\varphi}$ may be close to zero for a long time. As the resource becomes scarcer, the effect of $\dot{\varphi}$ on the price increase gets stronger, while $\dot{\lambda}$ becomes negative due to part (a). As this continues, $\dot{\varphi}$ will eventually dominate, so that the price of the resource is increasing and extraction ceases. Thus the optimal extraction path starts relatively high and then is decreasing (see Figure 13.3e as an example).

When pollution control starts at a late stage, where the inherited pollution stock is already high, optimal action involves immediate emissions reduction, and a jump up in the co-state variable. As the stock of the pollutant slowly decays, the co-state variable and thus the optimal Pigouvian tax in a competitive economy fall. Figures 13.3b and 13.3d show the optimal time path of the pollution stock, and the corresponding shadow price, in this case. As the resource becomes scarcer, there is a reduced need for a high tax, and so both the co-state variable and the pollution stock go to zero. The optimal extraction path, by contrast, is now different. Note that S_0 can be high, and the resource stock nevertheless still abundant. Therefore, slowing down emissions calls for reducing resource extraction immediately (even if it is still abundant). As soon as the

(a) $S(t)$

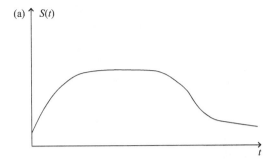

Figure 13.3a Optimal time path of the *pollution stock*, starting with an initially *low* pollution stock

(b) $S(t)$

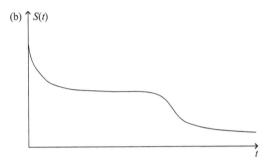

Figure 13.3b Optimal time path of the *pollution stock*, starting with an initially *high* pollution stock

(c) $\lambda(t)$

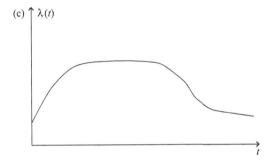

Figure 13.3c Optimal time path of the pollution stock's *shadow price* starting with an initially *low* pollution stock

(d) $\lambda(t)$

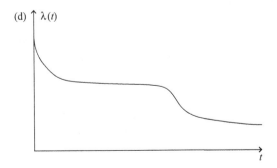

Figure 13.3d Optimal time path of the pollution stock's *shadow price* starting with an initially *high* pollution stock

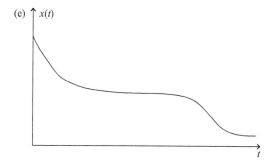

Figure 13.3e   The optimal *extraction path* over time, starting with an initially *low* pollution stock

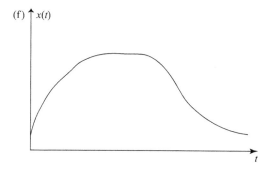

Figure 13.3f   The optimal *extraction path* over time, starting with an initially *high* pollution stock

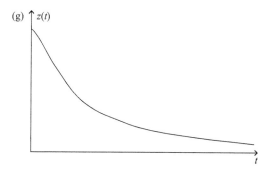

Figure 13.3g   The optimal time path of the remaining *resource stock* (all cases)

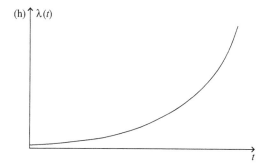

Figure 13.3h   The optimal time path of the *resource shadow price* (all cases)

pollution stock decays, emissions and thus the extraction constraint can be relaxed. As the resource becomes increasingly scarce, extraction goes down, and the pollution stock and the co-state variable (the Pigouvian tax) fall. This is displayed in Figures 13.3d and 13.3f.

Note that the meaning of sufficiently high or low in proposition 13.1 parts (a) and (b) can be quite different than the similar conditions in part (c). More precisely, it can be the case that for a particular initial pollution stock S_0 and some initial stock of the resource in situ R_0, the stock and the co-state are monotonically decreasing, while the extraction path is inverted U-shaped. It can also be the case that all three variables S, x, and λ are monotonically decreasing. Finally, it can of course be the case that for particular initial conditions S_0 and R_0, the variables S and λ are inverted U-shaped while x is monotonically decreasing (Figures 13.3a, 13.3c, and 13.3e). It can be ruled out, however, that all three variables are inverted U-shaped. In all cases, the time path of the resource stock is decreasing, while the corresponding shadow price of the resource stock is always increasing.

Finally, note that the condition $D'''(\cdot) \geq 0$ is satisfied for linear and quadratic damage functions, as is often assumed in the literature. This condition is sufficient, but by no means necessary, to produce the decreasing or inverted U-shaped looking extraction paths, respectively. Tahvonen (1997) shows by numerical examples that, even for functions with $D'''(\cdot) < 0$, extraction paths can have the above described properties. No examples are known where in this kind of model structure, U-shaped parts of one or the other variables occur.

From this discussion, we see that the stock externality slows down optimal extraction. In discussions about fossil fuel consumption and the climate change problem, the latter is often confused with resource scarcity. Subsidies for renewable energy are often defended for the reason that the world is running out of resources. However, as we have seen in this chapter, scarcity of the resource drives up the consumer price of the resource, and thereby slows down consumption such that, if we assume that backstop technologies are not available, consumption and extraction asymptotically approach zero. Indeed, under the threat of climate change, the consumption of fossil fuel resources should be slowed down not because there is too little, but because there is too much of those resources, and thus too much of an externality.

13.4 SUMMARY

In this chapter we have studied pollutants that accumulate over time. In contrast to previous chapters, we introduced fully dynamic aspects of the externality. Our simple framework at the start used both discrete and continuous time representations to characterize the dynamic optimality conditions for the pollution/abatement path, and the steady state. The most important insight from the steady state analysis was that, at the steady state, the marginal abatement cost of reducing the last unit of emissions must be equal to the discounted sum of all future marginal damages. The marginal damage is discounted by the sum of the pure rate of time preference, and the decay rate of the pollutant.

We then studied the optimal path into the steady state. We found that if the initial pollution stock exceeds (falls short of) the optimal steady state stock, the optimal emission path will approach the steady state emission level from below (above), while the co-state variable, which can also be interpreted as the shadow price for emissions (and thus the optimal Pigouvian tax rate), approaches its steady state level from above (below). We illustrated these optimal paths using phase diagrams. We also looked at the optimal feedback rule, which in the case of our model provided a rule for emissions as a function of the pollution stock, independently of time.

In a final step, we considered a stylized greenhouse problem by linking the pollution accumulation to the problem of exploiting a non-renewable resource, which generates emissions through consumption over an infinite time horizon. We argued that, depending on the initial pollution stock, the optimal emission path can be decreasing or inverted U-shaped. We also argued that the need for slowing down emissions is not driven by the scarcity of the resource, but rather by the externality through consumption.

13.5   FURTHER READING

One of the seminal papers looking at optimal abatement over time for accumulating pollutants is Falk and Mendelsohn (1993). Krautkraemer (1998a) gives an early survey of non-renewable resource models.[3] Farzin and Tahvonen (1996), Tahvonen (1997), and Döpke and Requate (2014) link the issue of accumulating pollutants to the problem of a non-renewable, emission-generating resource. Moslener and Requate (2007, 2009) study optimal emission and abatement paths when there are multiple pollutants interacting in the medium, or through joint abatement costs. There is, meanwhile, a large literature on dynamic pollution control under uncertainty, which is particularly important in the climate change context. Hoel and Karp (2001, 2002) study pollution control of an accumulating pollutant under different kinds of uncertainty, and Karp (2005) was among the first to deviate from the constant discount rule by studying the normative consequences of hyperbolic discounting. There is also a large literature on abatement of greenhouse gasses under uncertainty, both theoretically and numerically within integrated assessment models, and an extensive discussion on the appropriate way of discounting possible damages arising in the far distant future (Arrow et al., 2014; Cropper et al., 2014; Gollier and Weitzman, 2010). We will return to these issues in Chapter 21.

For methodological issues concerning optimal control theory, useful sources include Seierstad and Sydsaeter (1987) and Chiang (1992). For strategic interaction in continuous time, a topic that is beyond the scope of this book, see Dockner et al. (2000).

APPENDIX A: INTRODUCTION TO THE CALCULUS OF OPTIMAL CONTROL

In this appendix, we present some basic elements of dynamic optimization within the rubric of optimal control theory. Since this book does not generally focus on dynamic methods, we are brief. To understand principles of dynamic optimization and control

---

[3] Krautkraemer (1998a) studies the resource exploitation problem when the resource has an amenity value for society.

theory in detail, we refer the reader to the many excellent books on the subject, such as Seierstad and Sydsaeter (1987) and Chiang (1992).

The basic idea in dynamic optimization is that a sequence of decisions has to be made that ultimately results in the optimization of some objective function. Examples in economics are profit, utility, cost, welfare, and the like, where the objective is a sum of payoffs per period of time. The decisions are related to each other, as they impact some "state variable". A state variable can be a capital stock, a remaining amount of some renewable or exhaustible resource in situ, or a stock of an accumulating pollutant in the environmental medium. This means that payoffs depend not only on an agent's current decision, but also on what she has decided in the past. In a similar way, the current decision also affects future payoffs.

To formalize our ideas, we start with the current value objective function $F(c_t, S_t, t)$, which we interpret as the current period payoff at a point in time t. In general, the objective function may depend directly on the control variable c_t, the state variable S_t, and also on the point in time t. The state variable follows a law of motion, which in discrete time is a difference equation:[4]

$$S_t - S_{t-1} = g(c_t, S_{t-1}, t),$$ (A13.1)

while in continuous time is a differential equation written as

$$\dot{S} \equiv \frac{dS}{dt} = \tilde{g}(c_t, S_t, t).$$ (A13.2)

The overall objective or value function is then given by

$$V(t_0, T) = \int_{t_0}^{T} F(c_t, S_t, t) w(t) dt,$$ (A13.3)

where t_0 and T are the initial and final points in the planning horizon, and $w(t)$ is a function that puts a weight on the payoff at time t. In economics this is usually a discount factor. With a constant discount rate r, the discount factor (in continuous time) is then given by $w(t) = e^{-rt}$. Usually, the planning horizon is infinite, such that $T = \infty$, and the initial point in time is typically normalized to zero. Finally, in most models, both the present value objective function $F(\cdot)$ and the function that describes the equation of motion $g(\cdot)$ do not depend on time directly. When this is the case, we have a time invariant (or autonomous) control problem, and time indices are typically omitted, such that the current value objective function and the equation of motion are simply written $F(c, S)$ and $\dot{S} = g(c, S)$, respectively.

Keeping in mind that all variables change over time, the optimization problem can now be written as

$$\max_{c=\{c_t\}} \int_0^{\infty} F(c, S) e^{-rt} dt$$ (A13.4)

---

[4] If the control variable impacts on the stock at the beginning of some period, the difference equation can also take the form $S_t - S_{t-1} = g(c_{t-1}, S_{t-1}, t)$.

subject to

$$\dot{S} = g(c, S) \tag{A13.5}$$

and an initial condition for the inherited value of the state variable $S_0 = S(0)$. For optimization purposes we use the so-called Hamiltonian, which is a generalization of the Lagrangian function known from static optimization problems. The Hamiltonian takes into account the constraints between the time periods given by the equation of motion (A13.5). One can distinguish between the current value Hamiltonian

$$H = F(c, S) + \lambda g(c, S) \tag{A13.6}$$

and the present value Hamiltonian

$$H = F(c, S)e^{-rt} + \tilde{\lambda} g(c, S), \tag{A13.7}$$

where $\tilde{\lambda} = \lambda e^{-rt}$. The current value Hamiltonian optimizes the current value of the instantaneous objective function $F(c,S)$ at each point in time t, taking into account the impact on future periods. The present value Hamiltonian optimizes the function $F(c,S)$ at a point in time t, evaluated at the baseline time $t_0 = 0$. Therefore, $F(c,S)$ is multiplied by the weight or discount factor e^{-rt}. The variables λ and $\tilde{\lambda}$ are the co-state variables. They can be interpreted as shadow values of the state variables. The co-state variables in the objective function serve to ensure that the decision-maker correctly accounts for her choice of the control variable on all future periods. The current and the present value Hamiltonian approaches are equivalent in that they lead to the same solution of the optimal control path. It is a matter of convenience which approach to apply in what situation. In situations where the economic system optimally approaches a non-trivial stationary (steady) state, the current value Hamiltonian is more suitable, while in problems where both the control and the state variable approach zero in the limit (such as in problems with exhaustible resources), the present value Hamiltonian may be more convenient to work with.

Note that instead of (A13.6) and (A13.7), the Hamiltonians could also be written as $H = F(c,S) - \lambda g(c,S)$ and $H = F(c,S)e^{-rt} - \tilde{\lambda} g(c,S)$, respectively. Switching signs here induces opposite signs for λ and $\tilde{\lambda}$. Ultimately, the form of the objective function depends on the interpretation one wants to give to the co-state variables.

The Pontryagin maximum principle is a calculus that provides first-order optimality conditions for a control problem. We set up these conditions for the current value Hamiltonian in (A13.6). These are given by a condition on the control variable

$$H_c \equiv F_c(c, S) + \lambda g_c(c, S) = 0, \tag{A13.8}$$

a condition on the state variable

$$-H_S(c, S) \equiv -F_S(c, S) - \lambda g_S(c, S) = \dot{\lambda} - r\lambda, \tag{A13.9}$$

and by a transversality condition:

$$\lim_{t \to \infty} \lambda e^{-rt} S(t) = 0. \tag{A13.10}$$

The transversality condition in more general problems is a terminal condition. In economic systems approaching a steady state, with $\lim_{t \to \infty} S(t) > 0$, the second condition in (A13.10) will be satisfied if $\lim_{t \to \infty} \lambda e^{-rt} = 0$ is satisfied. The transversality condition can therefore be substituted by the steady-state condition.

In addition, the second-order conditions for the control variable should be checked. These are more complicated than in a static model. For details we refer to Seierstad and Sydsaeter (1977).

APPENDIX B: LINEAR MARGINAL DAMAGE AND MARGINAL ABATEMENT COST CURVES

Usually it is not possible to give closed form solutions for optimal control problems, notably for optimal emission paths in dynamic environmental economics problems. For the linear marginal abatement cost and linear marginal damage curves, however, closed form solutions can be calculated. In this appendix section we demonstrate this using the damage and abatement cost functions

$$D(S) = d\frac{S^2}{2} \tag{A13.11}$$
$$C(E) = \frac{(a - bE)^2}{2b}.$$

The equation of motion for the pollution stock is

$$\dot{S} = E - \beta S, \tag{A13.12}$$

and the optimality conditions in the state/co-state variable space are

$$a - bE = \lambda \tag{A13.13}$$

and

$$\dot{\lambda} = \lambda(r + \beta) - d \cdot S. \tag{A13.14}$$

Solving (A13.13) for E we have $E = (a - \lambda)/b$. Substituting this into (A13.12), we can write the system consisting of (A13.12) and (A13.14) in matrix form as

$$\begin{pmatrix} \dot{\lambda} \\ \dot{S} \end{pmatrix} = A\begin{pmatrix} \lambda \\ S \end{pmatrix} + B, \tag{A13.15}$$

where

$$A = \begin{pmatrix} (r + \beta) & -d \\ -\frac{1}{b} & -\beta \end{pmatrix}, \qquad B = \begin{pmatrix} 0 \\ a/b \end{pmatrix}. \tag{A13.16}$$

To solve the system, we calculate the characteristic roots (or eigenvalues) of the matrix A, which are given by

$$\mu_{1,2} = \frac{1}{2}\left(r \mp \frac{\sqrt{4d + b(2\beta + r)^2}}{\sqrt{b}} \right).$$

(A13.17)

Note that the smaller eigenvalue is always negative. Without loss of generality, we choose $\mu_1 < 0$ and $\mu_2 > 0$. The eigenvectors, where the second component is normalized to 1, are then given by

$$v_{1,2} = \begin{pmatrix} \frac{1}{2}\left(-b(r + 2\beta) \pm \sqrt{\beta(4d + b(r + 2\beta)^2)} \right) \\ 1 \end{pmatrix}.$$

(A13.18)

We denote $v_1^{(1)}$ and $v_2^{(1)}$ as the first component of each eigenvector. To find a special solution of the inhomogeneous system we solve

$$0 = A\bar{y} + B,$$

(A13.19)

which is simply the steady-state condition. This yields

$$\bar{y} = \begin{pmatrix} \lambda^* \\ S^* \end{pmatrix} = \begin{pmatrix} \dfrac{ad}{b\beta(\beta + r) + d} \\ \dfrac{a(\beta + r)}{b\beta(\beta + r) + d} \end{pmatrix},$$

(A13.20)

where λ^* and S^* are the steady-state values of $\lambda(t)$ and $S(t)$. We know from the theory of linear differential equations that the whole solution can be described by

$$\lambda(t) = \lambda^* + c_1 v_1^{(1)} e^{\mu_1 t} + c_2 v_2^{(1)} e^{\mu_2 t}$$

(A13.21)

$$S(t) = S^* + c_1 e^{\mu_1 t} + c_2 e^{\mu_2 t},$$

(A13.22)

where c_1 and c_2 are constants still to be determined. Since the larger eigenvalue is positive, saddle-point stability of the system requires $c_2 = 0$. To determine c_1, we exploit the fact that we have given an initial condition for the pollution stock $S_0 = S(0)$. Therefore, we obtain from (A13.22) the expression $c_1 = S_0 - S^*$. Substituting this value into (A13.21), we obtain the initial value for the co-state variable

$$\lambda_0 = \lambda(0) = \lambda^* + c_1 v_1^{(1)}.$$

(A13.23)

We can therefore write (A13.21) and (A13.22) as:

$$\lambda(t) = \lambda^* + (S_0 - S^*)K_\lambda e^{\mu_1 t}$$

(A13.24)

$$S(t) = S^* + (S_0 - S^*)K_S e^{\mu_1 t}, \tag{A13.25}$$

where $K_\lambda = v_1^{(1)}$ and $K_S = 1$ are positive constants. Finally, using $E = (a - \lambda)/b$, we can determine the optimal path for the control variable

$$E(t) = E^* - (S_0 - S^*)\frac{K_\lambda}{b}e^{\mu_1 t} = E^* - (S_0 - S^*)K_E e^{\mu_1 t}, \tag{A13.26}$$

with $K_E = K_\lambda/b$ again being a positive constant.

For special values of the parameters we can plot the optimal solution. We choose $a = 10.0$, $b = 1.0$, $\beta = 0.1$, $r = 0.05$, and $d = 0.2$. In the plots displayed in Figures 13.2a through 13.2f, we set $S_0 = 1.0 \cdot S^*$. Note that saddle-point stability of the system is guaranteed, since one eigenvalue is positive and one is negative, implying a negative determinant of the matrix A.

APPENDIX C: PROOF OF PROPOSITION 13.1

The proof follows closely Tahvonen (1997). We first set up the optimality conditions for the optimal extraction/pollution problem in (13.57). The Hamiltonian is given by

$$H = u(x) - cx - D(S) - \varphi x - \lambda(x - \beta S), \tag{A13.27}$$

and the optimality conditions for the control variable are

$$\frac{\partial H}{\partial x} = u'(x) - c - \varphi - \lambda \le 0 \tag{A13.28}$$

and the complementary slackness condition

$$(u'(x) - c - \varphi - \lambda)x = 0. \tag{A13.29}$$

For an interior solution this reduces to

$$u'(x) - c - \varphi - \lambda = 0. \tag{A13.30}$$

For the state variables, the optimality conditions read

$$-\frac{\partial H}{\partial z} = 0 = \dot{\varphi} - r\varphi \quad \rightarrow \quad \dot{\varphi} = r\varphi \tag{A13.31}$$

$$-\frac{\partial H}{\partial S} = -D'(S) + \lambda\beta = \dot{\lambda} - r\lambda \quad \rightarrow \quad \dot{\lambda} = -D'(S) + \lambda(r + \beta). \tag{A13.32}$$

Finally, the transversality conditions are given by:

$$\lim_{t \to \infty} e^{-rt} \lambda(t) = 0 \tag{A13.33}$$

$$\lim_{t \to \infty} e^{-rt} \varphi(t) \geq 0 \tag{A13.34}$$

$$\lim_{t \to \infty} e^{-rt} \varphi(t) z(t) = 0. \tag{A13.35}$$

We divide our proof of the proposition into several steps.

Step 1: Some observations

Observation 1: Since the resource stock is finite, extraction must approach zero in finite or infinite time.

Observation 2: Since extraction goes to zero, emissions must go to zero as time goes to infinity. Since the pollution stock decays and since $D'(0) = 0$, (A13.32) approaches $\dot{\lambda} = \lambda(r+\beta)$, which will either be satisfied if λ goes to zero or if λ eventually grows to infinity at rate $r+\beta$. But the latter contradicts (A13.33), and hence $\lim_{t \to \infty} \lambda(t) = 0$.

Observation 3: If $u'(0) = \infty$, then $x(t)$ goes to zero in infinite time. If $u'(0) < \infty$, then $x(t)$ goes to zero in finite time. This follows from (A13.28) and (A13.31).

Observation 4: At an interior solution for $x(t)$, in particular if $u'(0) = \infty$ holds, by using (A13.31) the time derivative of (A13.30) is

$$\dot{x} = \left(r\varphi + \dot{\lambda}\right) / u''(x). \tag{A13.36}$$

Step 2

The second step is to show that $\lambda(t)$ has a unique maximum, possibly at $t=0$. To show this, note that if $\dot{\lambda} \geq 0$, then (A13.36) implies immediately that $\dot{x} < 0$. Now assume that after a decreasing phase λ starts to increase again. By observation 2 we know that λ goes to zero, and so it must eventually decrease again. Therefore there must exist a point in time T_1 with $\dot{\lambda}(T_1) = 0$, where $\dot{\lambda}$ switches from negative to positive, and a point in time T_2 with $\dot{\lambda}(T_2) = 0$, where $\dot{\lambda}$ switches from positive to negative. From (A13.32) we have

$$\ddot{\lambda}(T_1) = -D''(S(T_1))\dot{S}(T_1) + \dot{\lambda}(T_1)(r+\beta) = -D''(S(T_1))\dot{S}(T_1) > 0, \tag{A13.37}$$

and $\ddot{\lambda}(T_2) = -D''(S(T_2))\dot{S}(T_2) < 0$. But this implies that $\dot{S}(t)$ switches its sign in the time interval (T_1, T_2), say at $t = \hat{T}$, so that $\dot{S}(\hat{T}) = 0$. Now $\dot{S} = x - \beta S$ and $\dot{S}(\hat{T}) = 0$

imply $\ddot{S}(\hat{T}) = \dot{x}(\hat{T}) - \beta \dot{S}(\hat{T}) = \dot{x}(\hat{T})$. Therefore $\dot{x} > 0$ for some $t \in (T_1, T_2)$, and therefore $x(\hat{T}) = \beta S(\hat{T}) > 0$. However, by our initial assumption we have $\dot{\lambda}(t) \geq 0$ for $t \in (T_1, T_2)$, and we have seen that for $\dot{\lambda} \geq 0$, Eq. (A13.36) implies $\dot{x} < 0$. This is a contradiction, and therefore the optimal time path of $\lambda(t)$ cannot have a minimum. Rather, it must have a unique maximum, possibly at the corner for $t = 0$.

Step 3

The third step is to show that if the initial stock S_0 is sufficiently high, then $\lambda(t)$ must be monotonically decreasing. To show this observe that $\lambda(0) > 0$ and $\varphi(0) > 0$. Therefore the optimality condition for the control variable, shown in (A13.29), requires $x(0) < \infty$. But then the equation of motion for S, $\dot{S} = x - \beta S$, implies $\dot{S}(0) = x(0) - \beta S(0) < 0$ for $S(0)$ sufficiently high.

Now assume, to the contrary, that $\dot{\lambda}(0) > 0$, but $\dot{\lambda}(t) < 0$ for some $t > 0$. By (A13.32) this is only possible for $S > S_0$. Now differentiating (A13.32) with respect time we obtain

$$\ddot{\lambda}(t) = -D''(S(t))\dot{S}(t) + \dot{\lambda}(t)(r + \beta). \tag{A13.38}$$

Since $\lambda > 0$ and $\lambda \to 0$ as $t \to \infty$, then if $\dot{\lambda}$ switches sign, there must be a turning point $\hat{T}_1$ with $\dot{\lambda}(\hat{T}_1) > 0$ and $\ddot{\lambda}(\hat{T}_1) = 0$. If so, then $0 = \ddot{\lambda}(\hat{T}_1) = -D''(S(\hat{T}_1))\dot{S}(\hat{T}_1) + \dot{\lambda}(\hat{T}_1)(r + \beta)$ implies $\dot{S}(\hat{T}_1) > 0$.

At the maximum $\lambda(\hat{T})$, it must hold that

$$\ddot{\lambda}(\hat{T}) = -D''(S(\hat{T}))\dot{S}(\hat{T}) + \dot{\lambda}(\hat{T})(r + \beta) = -D''(S(\hat{T}))\dot{S}(\hat{T}) < 0, \tag{A13.39}$$

which implies $\dot{S}(\hat{T}) > 0$. Since $\dot{S}(0) < 0$ for $S(0)$ sufficiently high as we have observed above, $\dot{S}$ must switch sign at some point in time $\hat{T}_2 < \hat{T}$. But this implies $\ddot{S}(\hat{T}_2) > 0$. Further, we have $0 < \ddot{S}(\hat{T}_2) = \dot{x}(\hat{T}_2) - \beta \dot{S}(\hat{T}_2) = \dot{x}(\hat{T}_2)$. But this contradicts the observation that for $\dot{\lambda} > 0$ (which is the case for $t = \hat{T}_2$) Eq. (A13.36) implies $\dot{x}(\hat{T}_2) < 0$. Therefore, if $\dot{\lambda}(0) > 0$, then $\dot{\lambda}$ must be positive for all t. However, since extraction goes to zero, $D'(S(t))$ goes to zero as t goes to infinity. But if $\dot{\lambda}$ is increasing, λ must approach $\exp((r + \beta)t)$ as t goes to infinity, and therefore $\lim_{t \to \infty} e^{-rt} e^{(r+\beta)t} = \infty$, contradicting the transversality condition (A13.34). Thus, if S_0 is sufficiently high, $\dot{\lambda}(0) < 0$ must hold, and by step 2, $\dot{\lambda}(t) < 0$ for all t.

Step 4

Our fourth step is to show that if S_0 is sufficiently low, then $\lambda(t)$ is inverted U-shaped. To prove this we begin by noting that for $S_0 = 0$ we have $D'(S_0) = 0$, and (A13.32) implies $\dot{\lambda}(0) > 0$. By continuity $\lambda(t)$ must also be increasing for S_0 sufficiently low. By observation 2, $\lambda(t)$ goes to zero when t goes to infinity and by step 2, $\lambda(t)$ has a unique maximum. Therefore $\lambda(t)$ must be inverted U-shaped. This completes the proof of the shape of $\lambda(t)$ in proposition 13.1, conditions (a) and (b).

Step 5

Our fifth step is to show that the optimal path of the pollution stock $S(t)$ cannot have a U-shaped element. To see this, we rewrite (A13.36). Substituting $\lambda = u'(x) - c - \varphi$ from (A13.30) into (A13.32) gives $\dot{\lambda} = -D'(S) + (u'(x) - c - \varphi)(r + \beta)$, and substituting this expression into (A13.36) yields

$$\dot{x} = \left[(u'(x) - c)(r + \beta) - \beta\varphi - D'(S) \right] / u''(x). \tag{A13.40}$$

Now assume $S(t)$ has a U-shaped element. Then, by a similar argument as in step 2, at the turning point $\hat{T}$, we have $\ddot{S}(\hat{T}) = \dot{x}(\hat{T}) > 0$. Since $S(t)$ and $x(t)$ are continuous and continuously differentiable, we must have $\dot{S}(t) > 0$ and $\dot{x}(t) > 0$ for $t > \hat{T}$ and sufficiently close to $\hat{T}$. Since $\dot{\varphi} = r\varphi$ holds by (A13.31), φ must be increasing, and as long as $\dot{x} \geq 0$ and $\dot{S} \geq 0$, both $u'(x)$ and $-D'(S)$ are decreasing, and the numerator of (A13.40) remains negative for all t larger than the assumed turning point $\hat{T}$. Since the resource eventually will be used up, a new turning point $\hat{T}$, where $\dot{S}$ switches back to negative, must exist and require $\ddot{S}(T) < 0$. But since $\ddot{S}|_{\dot{S}=0} = \dot{x} > 0$ holds, this is impossible. Thus U-shaped parts of S are ruled out. Note that the "trick" of our argument was to show that once we have passed a local minimum of x, there is no way to switch back along the optimal path since then $\ddot{S}|_{\dot{S}=0} = \dot{x} > 0$.

Step 6

We are now ready to characterize the optimal shape of $S(t)$. If $S(0) = 0$, $S(t)$ must be increasing first, and since $\lim_{t \to \infty} S(t) = 0$, the pollution stock $S(t)$ must have a unique maximum by step 5. Thus by continuity for $S(0) > 0$, but sufficiently small, the argument must hold, and if $S(0)$ is sufficiently high, such that $\dot{S}(0) < 0$, by step 5 the stock must be decreasing all the time again.

Step 7: Proof of (C)

Denote the numerator of (A13.40) by N. Differentiating (A13.40) with respect to time we obtain

$$\ddot{x} = \{[[U''(x)\dot{x}(r + \beta) - \beta\dot{\varphi} - D''(S)\dot{S}] / u''(x) - N \cdot u'''(x)\dot{x}\} / [u''(x)]^2, \tag{A13.41}$$

which for $\dot{x} = 0$ reduces to:

$$\ddot{x}|_{\dot{x}=0} = [-\beta\dot{\varphi} - D''(S)\dot{S}] / u''(x). \tag{A13.42}$$

Step 7a: First we consider the case where the initial stock S_0 is low. We show that in this case the optimal extraction path must be decreasing, meaning that $\dot{x} < 0$. Assume the contrary, so that $\dot{x} > 0$ in the initial phase of extraction, where the pollution stock is still increasing. Then there must be some point in time $\hat{T}$ where $\dot{x}$ switches from positive to negative – i.e. $\dot{x}(\hat{T}) = 0$ and $\ddot{x}(\hat{T}) < 0$. However, by (A13.42), and since $\dot{\varphi} > 0$ by (A13.31), $\ddot{x}(\hat{T}) < 0$ can only be the case if $\dot{S}(\hat{T}) < 0$. But this means that $\dot{S}$ must have turned from positive to negative for some $t < \hat{T}$. But as in step 5, we have $\ddot{S}\,|_{\dot{S}=0} = \dot{x} > 0$, which is a contradiction. Thus if $\dot{x} > 0$ all the time when $\dot{S} > 0$, it must increase until the resource is exhausted and then jump to zero, which cannot be optimal. Thus when $\dot{S} > 0$, it must be the case that $\dot{x} < 0$.

Step 7b: Next we consider the case where the initial pollution stock S_0 is sufficiently high, so that $\dot{S} < 0$. We will show again that the extraction path x cannot have a U-shaped part. We assume the contrary, meaning there must exist a moment in time $\hat{T}_1$ where $\dot{x}$ switches from negative to positive – i. e. $\dot{x}(\hat{T}_1) = 0$ and $\ddot{x}(\hat{T}_1) > 0$ – and a second moment in time $\hat{T}_2$ where $\dot{x}$ switches from positive to negative, given by $\dot{x}(\hat{T}_2) = 0$ and $\ddot{x}(\hat{T}_2) < 0$. But then (A13.42) implies

$$\left[-\beta\dot{\varphi}(\hat{T}_1) - D''\left(S(\hat{T}_1)\right)\dot{S}(\hat{T}_1) \right] / u''(x(\hat{T}_1)) > 0$$
$$> \left[-\beta\dot{\varphi}(\hat{T}_2) - D''\left(S(\hat{T}_2)\right)\dot{S}(\hat{T}_2) \right] / u''\left(x(\hat{T}_2)\right), \tag{A13.43}$$

and therefore

$$\beta\dot{\varphi}(\hat{T}_1) + D''\left(S(\hat{T}_1)\right)\dot{S}(\hat{T}_1) > 0 > \beta\dot{\varphi}(\hat{T}_2) + D''\left(S(\hat{T}_2)\right)\dot{S}(\hat{T}_2) \tag{A13.44}$$

or

$$G \equiv \left[\dot{\varphi}(\hat{T}_1) - \dot{\varphi}(\hat{T}_2) \right]\beta + D''\left(S(\hat{T}_1)\right)\dot{S}(\hat{T}_1) - D''\left(S(\hat{T}_2)\right)\dot{S}(\hat{T}_2) > 0. \tag{A13.45}$$

Since $\dot{\varphi} = r\varphi$, we have $\ddot{\varphi} = r\dot{\varphi} > 0$ and therefore the first term of G, i.e. $[\dot{\varphi}(\hat{T}_1) - \dot{\varphi}(\hat{T}_2)]\beta$, must be negative. Thus, to guarantee $G > 0$, it must be that

$$D''\left(S(\hat{T}_1)\right)\dot{S}(\hat{T}_1) - D''\left(S(\hat{T}_2)\right)\dot{S}(\hat{T}_2) > 0. \tag{A13.46}$$

Since $\dot{x}$ switches from positive to negative at $\hat{T}_1$ and from negative to positive at $\hat{T}_2$, the point $\hat{T}_1$ is a local minimum followed by a local maximum at $\hat{T}_2$, and therefore $x(\hat{T}_1) < x(\hat{T}_2)$ must be the case. Since S is decreasing it must also be the case that $S(\hat{T}_1) < S(\hat{T}_2)$. Now the equation of motion $\dot{S} = x - \beta S$ implies $\dot{S}(\hat{T}_1) - \dot{S}(\hat{T}_2) = x(\hat{T}_1) - x(\hat{T}_2) - \beta[S(\hat{T}_1) - S(\hat{T}_2)] < 0$. Thus, $\dot{S}(\hat{T}_1) < \dot{S}(\hat{T}_2) < 0$, and $D''(S(\hat{T}_1))\dot{S}(\hat{T}_1) - D''(S(\hat{T}_2))\dot{S}(\hat{T}_2) > 0$ can only hold if $D''(S(\hat{T}_1)) < D''(S(\hat{T}_2))$. But this can only hold if $D'''(\cdot) < 0$ for some levels $S \in [S(\hat{T}_1), S(\hat{T}_2)]$. Thus to invert the argument, when S has an inverted U-shape, $D'''(\cdot) > 0$ is a sufficient condition to guarantee that x is monotonically decreasing.

Step 7c: Therefore, there can be only two different shapes for the resource extraction path $x(t)$. When the initial pollution stock S_0 is sufficiently low, such that initially $\dot{S} > 0$, then $x(t)$ is monotonically decreasing. If the initial pollution stock S_0 is sufficiently high, such that initially $\dot{S} < 0$, then $x(t)$ is inverted U-shaped.

EXERCISES

13.1 ** Consider the discrete time model with two (and then three) periods.
   (a) For linear marginal abatement cost $-C'(E) = a - bE$ and linear marginal damage $D'(S) = d \cdot S$ calculate the optimal emission path.
   (b) Distinguish the two cases where S_T is bounded, and where there is no constraint on S_T. Assume that $a = 10$, $b = 1$, $d = 0.10$, $r = 0.05$, and $\beta = 0.05$. Let $S_0 = 5$ (and then $S_0 = 15$). Calculate the optimal emission paths for $T = 10$ (and then $T = 100$), for unconstrained S_T as well as for $S_T = 10$.

13.2 ** Consider the pollution model with linear marginal abatement cost $-C'(E) = a - bE$ and constant marginal damage $D'(S) = d$.
   (a) Determine the steady state.
   (b) Solve for the optimal feedback strategy.
   (c) Derive the optimal time paths for emissions, the pollution stock, and the optimal emission tax.
   (d) Draw a phase diagram.

13.3 ** Consider a parameterized damage function $D(S, \eta)$ where η is a damage parameter shifting up the damage and the marginal damage so that $D_\eta(S, \eta) > 0$ and $D_{S\eta}(S, \eta) > 0$.
   (a) Investigate how emissions and steady-state stock change when η increases.
   (b) Investigate how the optimal feedback strategy changes with increasing η.

13.4 *** Consider a pollution accumulation problem with two pollutants where E_1 and E_2 denote emissions and S_1 and S_2 the stocks of pollution for the two pollutants. The abatement cost functions of the two pollutants are given by $C_i(E_i) = \gamma_i [\bar{E}_i - E_i]^2 / 2$ while the damage function is given by $D(S_1, S_2) = d_1 [\alpha_1 S_1 + \alpha_2 S_2] + d_2 [\alpha_1 S_1 + \alpha_2 S_2]^2$.
   (a) Set up the dynamic optimality conditions.
   (b) Determine the steady state.
   (c) Carry out the comparative statics with respect to r and β_i.
   (d) Determine a general closed form solution for the optimal emission and co-state variable paths, and for the pollution stocks. Assume now the parameters are: $d_1 = 0$, $d_2 = 0.1$, $\gamma_1 = \gamma_2 = 2$, $\bar{E}_1 = \bar{E}_2 = 10$, $r = 0.06$.
   (e) Consider first the fully symmetric case with $\alpha_1 = \alpha_2 = 1$, $\beta_1 = \beta_2 = 0.1$. Simulate the dynamics of the system. Draw the time paths for optimal emissions co-state variables and the pollution stocks. Using a suitable software (Mathematica, Mathlab or the like), plot a 3D-picture of the optimal emission (co-state variable) path on the S_1/S_2 plane using different initial values for the pollution stocks.
   (f) Repeat (d) for asymmetric α's by choosing $\alpha_1 = 1$, $\alpha_2 = 1.1$.
   (g) Repeat (d) for asymmetric β's by choosing $\beta_1 = 0.9$, $\beta_2 = 1.1$.
   (h) To simulate the system with more realistic values choose a more flexible abatement cost function according to $C_i(E_i) = \gamma_{i1}[\bar{E}_i - E_i] + \gamma_{i2}[\bar{E}_i - E_i]^2 / 2$, $i = CO_2$, CH_4. For the parameters choose $d_1 = -0.352$, $d_2 = 4 \cdot 10^{-13}$, $\gamma_{CO_2,1} = -3.483$, $\gamma_{CH_4,1} = -0832$, $\gamma_{CO_2,2} = 6.08 \cdot 10^{-9}$, $\gamma_{CH_4,2} = 7.87 \cdot 10^{-6}$, $\bar{E}_1 = 30 \cdot 10^9$, $\bar{E}_2 = 112 \cdot 10^6$ (measured in tons of CO_2 equivalents) and finally $r = 0.02$. Determine the optimal paths, the steady states, and the shadow price

ratio between the optimal price for CO_2 and CH_4. How does that ratio vary over time?

13.5 *** Similar to the previous exercise, consider a pollution accumulation problem with two pollutants. But now the damage functions are additively separable such that $D_i(S_i) = d_i S_i^2$, while abatement costs are interdependent with $C(E_1, E_2) = \gamma_1[\bar{E}_1 - E_1]^2/2 + \gamma_2[\bar{E}_2 - E_2]^2/2 + \omega[\bar{E}_1 - E_1][\bar{E}_2 - E_2]$. If $\omega > 0$ we say the two pollutants are substitutes in abatement, while if $\omega < 0$ they are complements. Assume $|\omega| < \gamma_i$.

(a) Set up the dynamic optimality conditions.

(b) Determine the steady state.

(c) Carry out the comparative statics with respect to ω.

(d) Determine a general closed form solution for the optimal emission, the co-state variable paths and for the pollution stocks. Assume now the parameters are given as follows: $d_1 = d_2 = 1$, $d_2 = 0.1$, $\gamma_1 = \gamma_2 = 2$, $\bar{E}_1 = \bar{E}_2 = 10$, $r = 0.06$, $\beta_1 = \beta_2 = 0.1$, $\omega = 1$, and alternatively $\omega = -1$.

(e) Simulate the dynamics of the system. Draw the time paths for optimal emissions, the co-state variables and for the pollution stocks. Using suitable software (Mathematica, Mathlab or the like), plot a 3D-picture of the optimal emission (co-state variable) path on the S_1/S_2 plane using different initial values for the pollution stocks.

Valuing the Environment

Throughout Parts I and II of this book we have referred to damage, abatement cost, profit, and other economic functions in our discussion of environmental policy. As we have seen, these functions arise from household preferences and firm production technologies, and are therefore usually not directly observable. Nonetheless, to this point we have assumed regulators and other agents possess knowledge of these functions or estimates thereof, and conditional on this, we have proceeded with our mostly theoretical discussion of policy design. In Part III, we turn our attention to methods that have been developed to estimate the damage and cost functions needed to implement policy. With this, our emphasis switches to examining models of individual and household behavior, since the measurement concepts of interest usually arise out of individuals' interactions with the environment. Furthermore, Part III of the book has a greater emphasis on econometrics, since our discussion will also examine ways that these models can be brought to data to produce empirical results.

The themes we discuss in Part III are usually referred to collectively as the sub-field of non-market valuation. The general problem of non-market valuation is to compute a monetary value for environmental resources or services that, in the general setup of market economies, are not subject to exchange, and therefore do not have an observable market price. For example, we might be interested in knowing the monetary value of preserving a wooded area in an urban landscape, relative to its value in a residential use. Likewise, large-scale biodiversity preserves usually preclude extractive use, such as mining and timber harvest, within the boundaries of the preserve. What is the monetary value of the biodiversity protection relative to the market value of the forgone minerals and lumber? To answer this and similar questions, conceptual models that connect the environmental resource to people's preferences (or in some cases firm profits), and econometric approaches that connect data to the conceptual models, are needed.

For this our starting point is neoclassical welfare theory, as it was when we started the book. This helps us to stress that the valuation problem should not be viewed as separate from the policy design problem in Part II, since they are two sides of the same coin. Policy design involves using neoclassical welfare theory to derive optimal policy rules, while valuation uses the theory to suggest measurement methods needed to implement the policy rule. The externality example from Chapter 1 illustrates this nicely: when emissions result from production of a good, a Pareto optimal outcome can be obtained using an emission tax (equal to the marginal damage from pollution), but the socially optimal tax rate depends on the structure of individuals' preferences. Actual implementation therefore requires empirically examining people's behavior in order to learn something about their preferences, from which the correct tax rate can be computed. More generally, much of non-market valuation is concerned with estimating behavioral functions that are sufficiently revealing about preferences, to allow calculation of the monetary value of marginal or discrete changes in environmental conditions.

We begin in Chapter 14 by developing a general model of household behavior, which allows us to formally define useful concepts of value that arise from neoclassical welfare theory. We distinguish the theory and empirical methods that are available for analyzing the welfare effects of exogenous price changes for market goods, from those that are needed for examining changes in exogenously given quantities. We show that the latter is made challenging by the absence of markets for environmental goods. This motivates our discussion in Chapter 15, where we examine three revealed preference models that are used for valuing environmental outcomes. The three models are defined by the different ways that an environmental good can be related to a private good: as a complement, substitute, or as an attribute of a quality-differentiated market good. The models motivate specific empirical strategies in different application areas, which we explore individually in subsequent chapters. Before doing so, however, we devote Chapter 16 to discrete choice econometric models, given the importance of this class of analysis technique in applied non-market valuation.

In Chapter 17 we turn to applications, by examining how the complements revealed preference model is used in the context of recreation behavior. We present models of recreation behavior, and discuss in detail econometric approaches for measuring the role of environmental quality in generating economic value through recreation. This is followed in Chapter 18 by an in-depth discussion of property value models, which make use of the quality-differentiated market good framework. We explore the conceptual basis for hedonic property value and residential sorting models, and examine econometric methods that allow us to measure the value of local environmental amenities. Chapter 20 explores both the quality-differentiated goods and substitute goods revealed preference models, as they are applied to the valuation of health-influencing changes in environmental quality. This includes changes that affect fatality risks, as well as changes related to non-fatal illnesses. Before exploring the health applications, however, we discuss the broad area of stated preference methods in Chapter 19. While revealed preference methods rely on an interaction between the environment and a private good to measure welfare, stated preference approaches rely on survey questions to solicit values directly. This alternative paradigm has many advantages and several challenges, which are discussed in detail in the chapter.

Part III of the book is more empirically themed than the early parts, and as such there is more emphasis on applied examples and exercises. End-of-chapter exercises often make use of datasets, which are available for download on the book's website.

CHAPTER 14

Theory of Applied Welfare Analysis

In this chapter we present the conceptual basis for applied welfare analysis. We begin with a review of consumer welfare theory, and how economists have used the theory to develop standard empirical techniques for measuring the welfare effects of changes in private good prices. We present the well-established duality results linking estimable demand functions to preferences, and ultimately to monetary measures of economic value. Since most of non-market valuation involves examining the welfare impacts of changes in quasi-fixed goods (such as the level of an environmental indicator), we then discuss how the standard price-change techniques must be modified when we consider quantity changes. We show that while duality can still be used to link demand for the quasi-fixed good to the preference function, the absence of market exchange rules out the use of observed behavior to directly estimate a demand function. Instead, extra-market information is needed to infer individuals' monetary values for these goods, the sources of which we consider in subsequent chapters. We close this chapter by discussing generalizations needed to define welfare measures that are appropriate for use under state of the world uncertainty, and then by examining the conceptual relationship between different types of welfare measures.

It is useful at the outset to carefully define what we mean by monetary value, since it plays such a large role in the discussion. As described at the book's outset, the concept of value that we rely on is individualistic and based on consumer sovereignty, so that a person's preferences determine how outcomes (e.g. consumption levels, states of the environment, or his own health) translate to value. Outcomes can, of course, change through any number of channels. Prices can adjust, indirectly shifting consumption levels, or policy might directly alter environmental quality, thereby impacting the level of well-being that a person obtains. Establishing a monetary value for any action that directly or indirectly changes outcomes involves (a) defining a baseline state and an ending state, and (b) computing the person's *willingness to pay* (*WTP*) to secure the ending state, or his *willingness to accept* (*WTA*) to forgo it. The key points here are twofold. First, reference to monetary value is for something specific. We cannot define a person's monetary value for a generality like "clean drinking water", but we can define the health effects value of a specific (small or large) reduction in carcinogen contaminants, relative to current conditions. Second, *WTP* and *WTA* are income equivalents that link the starting and ending states to preferences. Consider, for example, a reduction in the price of a private good. The price reduction expands the range of consumption outcomes the person can obtain, and thereby potentially increases well-being. The starting point is the original price and the ending point is the new price. *WTP* is the amount of money the person would give up to have the new price, and hence the higher level of well-being. *WTA* is the amount of money the person would need to be given in lieu of the price decrease, and therefore reflects an equivalent way of obtaining the higher level of well-being. *WTP* and *WTA* are useful concepts because they convert information on preferences, which is inherently unquantifiable, into money equivalents. As we will see, substitutability among elements in an individual's preference function is a key determinant of *WTP* and *WTA*. For the price decrease example, if abundant and inexpensive alternatives to the now-cheaper good are already available, the reduction in its price is less valuable to the person than if the good were relatively unique. In establishing the monetary value of environmental goods, the notion of substitutability between market goods and environmental goods turns out to be critical. Non-market valuation is largely about measuring a person's *WTP* or *WTA* (often referred to collectively as "welfare measures" or "welfare effects") for changes in environmental variables. As such, references to *WTP* and *WTA* are ubiquitous throughout this and later chapters.

14.1   GENERAL SETUP

The traditional goal of applied welfare analysis is to use observed behavior to characterize the structure of preferences needed to calculate welfare measures. A necessary first step for this is to describe a model that gives rise to the observed behavior. Consider a generalization of the consumer problems given in earlier chapters. The utility function is now $U(x,z,q)$ where x is a J dimensional vector of private market goods, z is a numeraire good with price normalized to one, and q denotes a vector or scalar of environmental goods and services. In this generalization, q can represent a wide range of human interactions with the environment. This can include health effects, residential and recreational amenities, aesthetic impacts, ecosystem services, and public goods in general. In actual applications, the specific definition of q will depend on the nature of the problem, and pragmatic considerations such as the availability of data. For purposes of exposition here, we assume that q is a scalar quantity measured and expressed in known units, and that it generates positive marginal utility (i.e. q is a "good").

The consumer's problem is to choose amounts of x and z to maximize utility, given the fixed level of q and market prices p, subject to an exogenous income level y. The formal problem is given by

$$\max_{x,z} \left\{ U(x,z,q) + \lambda \left[y - z - p'x \right] \right\},$$ (14.1)

where λ is the Lagrange multiplier. The first-order conditions for this problem are

$$\partial U / \partial x_j = \lambda p_j, \quad j = 1,...,J,$$
$$\partial U / \partial x = \lambda,$$ (14.2)

and assuming an interior solution to the problem, we can solve for the ordinary demand functions $x_j(p,y,q)$, the Lagrange multiplier $\lambda(p,y,q)$, and the level of the numeraire.

Note that the ordinary demand functions are directly estimable, since they depend on the observable quantities p, y, and q. If we substitute the demand functions into the direct utility function, we obtain the indirect utility function $V(p,y,q)$. It is worth emphasizing that q appears in both the direct and indirect utility functions, due to the fact that its level is not chosen by the consumer. Finally, via the Envelope Theorem, $\lambda(p,y,q)$ can be interpreted as the marginal increase in realized utility due to a small change in the income constraint. This is often referred to as the marginal utility of income, and it will become important in later discussions.

The consumer's behavior can also be represented by the expenditure minimization problem

$$\min_{x,z}\left\{p'x+z+\mu\left[\bar{u}-U(x,z,q)\right]\right\}, \tag{14.3}$$

where $\bar{u}$ is a reference level of utility. The first-order conditions for this problem are

$$\begin{aligned}
\partial U/\partial x_j &= p_j/\mu, \quad j=1,...,J, \\
\partial U/\partial z &= 1/\mu \\
U(x,z,q) &= \bar{u},
\end{aligned} \tag{14.4}$$

and assuming an interior solution, we obtain the compensated demand functions $h_j(p,\bar{u},q)$ for each x_j and $h_z(p,\bar{u},q)$ for z. Note that, in contrast to the ordinary demand functions, the compensated demand functions are not directly estimable since they depend on a particular level of utility rather than income. By substituting the compensated demand functions into (14.3) we obtain the expenditure function $E(p,\bar{u},q)$, which is the smallest amount of income a person would need to reach utility level $\bar{u}$.

Duality relationships are critical in applied welfare analysis, and none is more so than the identity that connects the ordinary and compensated demands at the point of consumption. Suppose that u^0 is the utility level that is obtained in the utility maximization problem in (14.1), and that $E(p,u^0,q)$ is the expenditure needed to obtain u^0. By construction $y=E(p,u^0,q)$, and the solutions to the utility maximization and expenditure minimization problems are linked at the observed point of consumption by

$$x_j\left(p,E(p,u^0,q),q\right)\equiv h_j\left(p,u^0,q\right) \quad \forall j. \tag{14.5}$$

The identity allows us to state the relationship between the price responses for the ordinary and compensated demand functions. Differentiating both sides with respect to p_j leads to the Slutsky equation

$$\begin{aligned}
\frac{\partial x_j(p,y,q)}{\partial p_j} &= \frac{\partial h_j(p,u^0,q)}{\partial p_j} - \frac{\partial x_j(p,y,q)}{\partial y}\times\frac{\partial E(p,u^0,q)}{p_j} \\
&= \frac{\partial h_j(p,u^0,q)}{\partial p_j} - \frac{\partial x_j(p,y,q)}{\partial y}\times x_j(p,y,q),
\end{aligned} \tag{14.6}$$

where the second equality follows from Shephard's Lemma and the identity in (14.5). Equation (14.6) is important for two related reasons. It shows that the price effect for ordinary and compensated demand functions differs by an income gradient, so that if there is no income effect – i.e. $\partial x_j(\cdot)/\partial y = 0$ – then the two demand functions are equivalent. It also makes clear that utility is held constant for movements in price along the compensated demand curve, while movements in price along the ordinary demand curve confound two effects: the pure price effect, and an implicit income effect (the so-called substitution and income effects). Because of the latter, movements along the ordinary demand curve do not hold utility constant. This difference is important in distinguishing between the types of measures typically employed in applied welfare analysis.

14.2   PRICE CHANGE WELFARE MEASURES

Equations (14.1) through (14.6) provide the building blocks for defining measures that reflect the value consumers have for changes in prices, income, or the level of quasi-fixed goods. As noted above, these have come to be known as "welfare measures", although in general we are not able to measure individual utility changes. Rather, we are interested in measuring a person's willingness to pay for, or willingness to accept, the proposed change. In this section we review techniques that have been developed specifically for the case of price changes.

14.2.1   Compensating and Equivalent Variation

Consider a change in the price of a private consumption good, and suppose we are interested in assessing how the price change may impact the well-being of a person or group of people. For example, we may be interested in knowing how subsidized tuition for vocational training (an effective tuition price decrease) affects low income households. There are two related concepts that we can use to measure the effect, which differ by their choice of reference point. The first of these is *compensating variation*, which is summarized in the following definition.

Definition 14.1
Given a price decrease, the compensating variation (CV) is the amount of money that would need to be taken from a person to restore the original utility level. For a price increase, CV is the amount of money that would need to be given to the person to allow him to reach the original utility level.

As is clear from the definition, *CV* uses the pre-change level of utility as a reference point, and is the income offset that would, following the change, restore the original utility level. Analytically, it is easiest to see the definition of *CV* using the indirect utility function. For a change in prices from p^0 to p^1, the compensating variation is implicitly defined by the equation

$$V(p^0, y, q) = V(p^1, y - CV, q). \tag{14.7}$$

The left-hand side of the equation is the utility level obtained at baseline price conditions, denoted by p^0. The right-hand side summarizes the optimal behavioral outcome under the new conditions, with price p^1, but with an income adjustment to maintain the original utility level. As written here, $CV>0$ for a price decrease (money is taken away), and $CV<0$ for a price increase (income is augmented). Importantly, the equation also shows that CV can be interpreted as a willingness to pay or willingness to accept measure. For a price decrease, CV is the maximum amount of money a person would pay to have the lower price, since any smaller payment would provide a well-being improvement and the actual amount CV leaves him indifferent. For a price increase, CV is the minimum amount a person would be willing to accept in compensation for agreeing to the increase; anything less would leave him worse off.

The second welfare measure, *equivalent variation*, is defined based on the ex post utility level, and it is summarized in the following definition.

Definition 14.2
For a price decrease that provides a higher utility level, the equivalent variation (EV) is the payment that allows the person to reach the new utility level, without the price change. For a price increase leading to a lower utility level, EV is the amount that would need to be taken from the person to move him down to the lower utility level, without the price change.

EV differs from CV in that it uses the post-change level of utility as its reference point, and it is the income adjustment that moves the person to the new level of well-being, without the actual change. The indirect utility function is again useful for providing an analytical definition:

$$V(p^1, y, q) = V(p^0, y + EV, q). \tag{14.8}$$

The left-hand side shows the utility level that is reached given the new price vector. The right-hand side summarizes behavior at the original price vector, but with an income adjustment to maintain utility at the reference level. As written, $EV>0$ for a price decrease since more income is needed to obtain the new (higher) utility level. In contrast, $EV<0$ for a price increase, since money needs to be taken away to move utility to its new (lower) level.

Like compensating variation, EV has a clear *WTP/WTA* interpretation. For a price decrease, equivalent variation is the willingness to accept compensation to forgo the decrease. For a price increase, equivalent variation is the willingness to pay to prevent the increase. The link between EV and CV and WTP and WTA is central to applied welfare analysis. To begin the chapter, we argued that consumer sovereignty implies that the appropriate measure of value for an exogenous change is a consumer's willingness to pay to have the change, or his willingness to accept to forgo the change. This suggests that the operational goal of applied welfare analysis is to estimate a sufficient component of preferences to allow calculation of compensating or equivalent variation.

Two additional analytical expressions for CV and EV help move us in the direction of an operational strategy. The measures can be expressed using the expenditure function by

$$
\begin{aligned}
CV &= E(p^0, u^0, q) - E(p^1, u^0, q) \\
&= y - E(p^1, u^0, q), \\
EV &= E(p^0, u^1, q) - E(p^1, u^1, q) \\
&= E(p^0, u^1, q) - y,
\end{aligned}
\tag{14.9}
$$

where u^0 and u^1 are the original and new levels of utility, respectively. Recalling that Shephard's Lemma implies

$$h_j(p,u,q) = \frac{\partial E(p,u,q)}{\partial p_j}, \quad j = 1,...,J, \tag{14.10}$$

the expressions in Eq. (14.9) for the specific case of a change in p_j can also be expressed by the definite integrals

$$CV = \int_{p_j^1}^{p_j^0} h_j(p_j, p_{-j}, u^0, q) dp_j = E(p^0, u^0, q) - E(p^1, u^0, q)$$

$$EV = \int_{p_j^1}^{p_j^0} h_j(p_j, p_{-j}, u^1, q) dp_j = E(p^0, u^1, q) - E(p^1, u^1, q), \tag{14.11}$$

where p_{-j} denotes the vector of prices without p_j. From this we see the familiar result that CV or EV for a price change can be computed by measuring the area under the appropriate compensated demand curve, between the two price levels. If we know or can estimate the compensated demand curves, this calculation is straightforward. Normally, however, we estimate ordinary demand curves and the integrals in (14.11) cannot be directly computed. We discuss this apparent dilemma in detail below.

Figure 14.1 summarizes graphically the three equivalent ways of expressing EV and CV for the case of a single good and a numeraire, when the price decreases and the good is normal. Panel A illustrates behavior and the welfare measures in utility space. Income is shown as y_0 along the vertical axis showing consumption of z, the budget constraint for the initial price is labeled p_0, and the person chooses initial consumption amount x_0 and obtains utility level u^0. The price decrease results in the new budget constraint labeled p_1, which expands the feasible choice set. With the new price the person chooses consumption level x_1 and reaches a new, higher level of utility at u^1. Compensating variation is calculated by finding the expenditure needed to reach u^0, given the new price. In the Figure, the dashed line p_1' is a hypothetical budget line drawn for price p_1, but with income that is only sufficient to reach u^0. This income level is $E(p_1, u^0, q)$, and the graph shows that $CV = y_0 - E(p_1, u^0, q)$. Likewise, equivalent variation is found using the hypothetical budget line p_0', which is drawn for the original price p_0 but with the income needed to reach u^1. This is the expenditure level $E(p_0, u^1, q)$, from which we can see that $EV = E(p_0, u^1, q) - y_0$.

Panel B illustrates the same measures in indirect utility space, where income is on the vertical axis and price is on the horizontal axis. Recall that indirect utility is non-decreasing in income and non-increasing in price. Point a shows the initial outcome, where the person obtains utility $V^0 = u^0$ given y_0 and p_0. The price decrease leads to the new outcome at point b, where $V^1 = u^1$ is reached, given y_0 and p_1. The willingness to pay for the price decrease (CV) is the vertical distance between point b and hypothetical point c, which sits on the original utility curve V^0, but at the new price. The willingness to accept to forgo the price decrease (EV) is the vertical distance from point a to the hypothetical point d, which sits on the new utility curve V^1, but at the old price. The

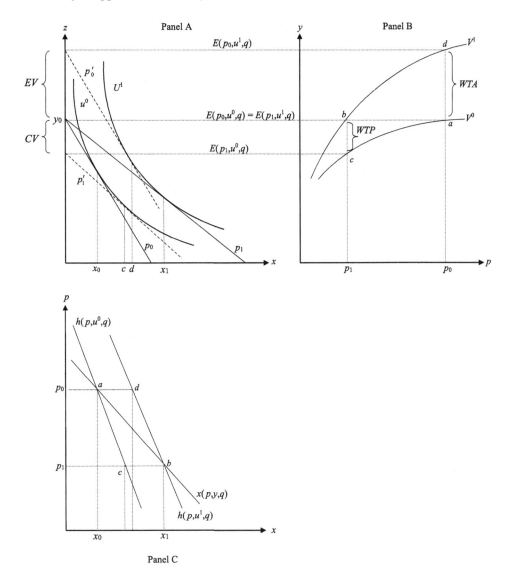

Figure 14.1   Price change welfare measures

hypothetical outcome points c and d are also shown on panel A, where they mark the unobserved compensated consumption levels.

Panel C connects utility space to demand space. The price change from p_0 to p_1 traces out the ordinary demand curve $x(p,y,q)$, with points a and b once again representing the initial and final observable outcomes, respectively. Reference to panels A and B reinforces the notion that the utility level changes as we move along the ordinary demand curve. The two compensated demand curves, in contrast, show fixed-utility responses to the price change. The budget lines p_0 and p'_1 trace out the response to the price change along u^0, shown as the movement from a to c, resulting in the compensated demand curve $h(p,u^0,q)$. Likewise, the budget lines p_1 and p'_0 trace out $h(p,u^1,q)$ via the movement from *b* to *d*. The fact that the compensated demand curves are based on hypothetical outcome points reinforces the notion that they are not directly observable. In panel C, compensating and equivalent variation are given by the change in the areas behind the appropriate compensated demand curve. In particular, *CV* is the area traced out by the points $p_0 a c p_1$, and *EV* is the area given by $p_0 d b p_1$.

14.2.2 Consumer Surplus

Equation (14.11) implies that *EV* and *CV* can be computed using the compensated demand curve, and as such they can be linked to a behavioral function for the good that has a price change. Typically, of course, it is ordinary rather than compensated demands that are estimated, and the integrals as given cannot be directly computed. A consequence is that consumer surplus has often been used in place of *EV* or *CV*, which is defined as follows.

Definition 14.3

Consumer surplus is the integral under the ordinary demand curve for a good, computed between a reference price and the point where the demand curve intersects the price axis (i.e. the choke price). The change in consumer surplus (C) for a good j is the integral under the ordinary demand curve between an initial and new price level, analytically given by

$$C = \int_{p_j^0}^{p_j^1} x_j(p, y, q) dp_j. \tag{14.12}$$

Since the integral in (14.12) is based on the ordinary demand curve, it can be readily computed using an estimate of consumer demand. Consumer surplus and its relation to *EV* and *CV* are shown graphically in panel C of Figure 14.1, where $C = p_0 a b p_1$. Although it can be readily calculated, using *C* in place of *CV* or *EV* begs the questions of what is being measured, and how it relates to willingness to pay or willing to accept. Hundreds of pages in dozens of journals have been devoted to this question, since Marshall introduced the concept of consumer surplus early in the last century. Here we summarize the differences that are most important for applied welfare analysis, focusing on the welfare theoretic interpretation of *C*, its uniqueness, and its performance as an approximation.

Interpretation of Consumer Surplus

In the most general case, consumer surplus has no meaningful *WTP* or *WTA* interpretation. Unlike a movement along a compensated demand curve, a price change along an ordinary demand curve implies a utility change. This was shown in Figure 14.1, where the change from p_0 to p_1 leads to an increase in utility from u^0 to u^1. Since utility is changing, the area behind the ordinary demand curve cannot be a utility-constant measure of willingness to pay or accept in the sense that *EV* and *CV* are. At best we can hope that *C* is something else – perhaps a measure that transforms a change in utility into a money-based (and hence quantitatively meaningful) reflection of the well-being change. To examine this possibility, it is useful to rewrite the expression for consumer surplus using Roy's Identity as

$$C = \int_{p_j^0}^{p_j^1} -\frac{V_{p_j}(p,y,q)}{V_y(p,y,q)} dp_j$$
$$= \int_{p_j^0}^{p_j^1} -\frac{V_{p_j}(p,y,q)}{\lambda(p,y,q)} dp_j, \tag{14.13}$$

where subscripts on V denote partial derivatives. By the Envelope Theorem, we know that $V_y(\cdot) = \lambda(p,y,q)$, and hence the second equality follows, where $\lambda(\cdot)$ is the marginal utility of income that arose from the solution to (14.1). Note as well that the numerator reflects the marginal (dis)utility of price. Finally, if $\lambda(p,y,q)$ is *not* a function of p_j – i.e. $\partial\lambda(\cdot)/\partial p_j = 0$ – then the denominator in Eq. (14.13) can be moved outside the integral, and consumer surplus rewritten as

$$C = \frac{1}{\lambda(p_{-j},y,q)}\int_{p_j^0}^{p_j^1} V_{p_j}(p,y,q) dp_j$$
$$= \left[V(p^1,y,q) - V(p^0,y,q)\right]\frac{1}{\lambda(p_{-j},y,q)}. \tag{14.14}$$

This is an important result. *If* the marginal utility of income is constant with respect to p_j (i.e. $\lambda(\cdot)$ is not a function of p_j), consumer surplus is indeed a money-metric reflection of the change in utility, and therefore has quantitative meaning. In particular, we can see from the second equality in (14.14) that C consists first of a utility change, which is then monetized by scaling it times a term that reflects the money value of a unit of utility change. This implies the measurement unit of C is the change in money that is implied by a change in utility, when $\partial\lambda(\cdot)/\partial p_j = 0$.

Consumer theory does not generally imply that $\partial\lambda(\cdot)/\partial p_j = 0$; instead, it is an extra assumption that needs to be maintained if C is to have the desired interpretation. To see how strong or weak this assumption might be, note that Roy's Identity for good j implies that

$$x_j(p,y,q) = \frac{-V_{p_j}(p,y,q)}{V_y(p,y,q)} \tag{14.15}$$
$$x_j(p,y,q) \times V_y(p,y,q) = -V_{p_j}(p,y,q).$$

If we differentiate both sides of the second equality with respect to y, we can derive the expression

$$x_j(\cdot) \times V_{yy}(\cdot) + \frac{\partial x_j(\cdot)}{\partial y} V_y(\cdot) = -V_{p_j y}(\cdot). \tag{14.16}$$

If the marginal utility of income $V_y(\cdot)$ is not a function of p_j, then $V_{yp_j}(\cdot) = 0$. By Young's theorem this implies $V_{p_j y}(\cdot) = 0$, and so it is the case that

$$\frac{\partial x_j(\cdot)}{\partial y} = \frac{-x_j(\cdot)V_{yy}(\cdot)}{V_y(\cdot)}, \qquad (14.17)$$

and after some manipulation,

$$\frac{\partial x_j(\cdot)}{\partial y} \frac{y}{x_j(\cdot)} = \eta_j = -\frac{y \times V_{yy}(\cdot)}{V_y(\cdot)}. \qquad (14.18)$$

This has ramifications for how the demand for good j responds to income changes. Note that η_j, the income elasticity for good j, is the same for all j in which $\partial\lambda(\cdot)/\partial p_j = 0$. Thus, for consumer surplus to have a meaningful interpretation, the income elasticity of demand must be a priori set equal, for all the goods whose price may change as part of the analysis. The restrictiveness of this condition depends on the context. If a subset of the prices is held constant throughout, the income elasticities for the goods with price changes must be equal, but the common elasticity can be any magnitude. For some applications this may be intuitively acceptable, even if statistical tests do not support the restriction. In instances when the analysis involves changing most or all of the prices, the assumption becomes more tenuous. To see why this is, we can differentiate the consumer's budget constraint with respect to y, and rearrange to obtain the Engle aggregation condition:

$$y \equiv \sum_{j=1}^{J} p_j \cdot x_j(p, y, q) + z(p, y, q)$$

$$1 \equiv \sum_{j=1}^{J} p_j \cdot \frac{\partial x_j(\cdot)}{\partial y} + \frac{\partial z(\cdot)}{\partial y} = \sum_{j=1}^{J} p_j \cdot \frac{\partial x_j(\cdot)}{\partial y} \frac{y \cdot x_j}{x_j \cdot y} + \frac{\partial z(\cdot)}{\partial y} \frac{y \cdot z}{z \cdot y} \qquad (14.19)$$

$$y = \sum_{j=1}^{J} \eta_j \cdot p_j \cdot x_j(\cdot) + \eta_z \cdot z(\cdot).$$

Note that to impose the constraint $\eta_j = \eta$ for all goods $j = 1,\ldots,J$, it must be the case that $\eta = \eta_z = 1$, which is unlikely to be a supportable restriction econometrically, or intuitively.

Uniqueness of Consumer Surplus

An additional difficulty with consumer surplus is that, absent restrictions, it is generally not unique for multiple price changes. When more than one price change is part of the analysis, consumer surplus is a line integral defined by

$$C = \int_L \sum_{k \in \omega} \frac{V_{p_k}(p, y, q)}{V_y(p, y, q)} dp_k, \qquad (14.20)$$

where ω is the set of goods for which prices changes in the analysis, and L is the path of integration. A line integral consists of a sum of interdependent definite integrals, and a path of integration that indicates the order in which the variables change. For example, if prices p_1 and p_2 in a two-good system change, we need to decide the order in which we calculate C. We could first change p_1, and calculate the consumer surplus change from the movement along $x_1(\cdot)$. To this we would add the consumer surplus change from the subsequent change in p_2, based on the movement along the (now shifted) $x_2(\cdot)$ curve, to obtain C. Analytically this is

$$C = \int_{p_1^0}^{p_1^1} x_1(p_1, p_2^0, y, q)dp_1 + \int_{p_2^0}^{p_2^1} x_2(p_2, p_1^1, y, q)dp_2. \tag{14.21}$$

We could, however, perform these calculations by first changing p_2 and then p_1, which is

$$C = \int_{p_2^0}^{p_2^1} x_2(p_2, p_1^0, y, q)dp_2 + \int_{p_1^0}^{p_1^1} x_1(p_1, p_2^1, y, q)dp_1. \tag{14.22}$$

The problem is that these two calculations will lead to different answers if certain restrictions do not apply, which casts further doubt on the usefulness of consumer surplus as a welfare measure.

Formally, a line integral has a unique value only if the integrand is an exact differential of a function, which the expression in (14.20) is not. However, *if* income and the prices of goods not included in ω remain constant, then the integral in (14.20) can be rewritten as

$$C = \frac{1}{V_y(p_{-\omega}, y, q)} \int_L \sum_{k \in \omega} V_{p_k}(p, y, q)dp_k, \tag{14.23}$$

since $V_y(\cdot)$ does not change within the path of integration L. With this restriction, the integrand in (14.23) is an exact differential of $V(p,y,q)$, and the resulting measure C is unique. From this we see that the restriction needed for uniqueness is equivalent to the restriction that provides C with a meaningful welfare interpretation for price changes. In general, consumer surplus can only be a meaningful welfare measure under potentially restrictive assumptions on how income affects demand. In particular, all income elasticities for the goods being analyzed must be set equal. An equivalent condition is that the ordinary demand cross price effects need to be equal (see exercise 14.2). The restrictiveness of this assumption will vary with the application, but is nonetheless unlikely to hold in many empirical applications.

Consumer Surplus As an Approximation

While we have seen that consumer surplus has disadvantages as a measure of well-being change, it has the notable advantage of being based on a directly estimable behavioral function. Because of this, applied welfare economists have long relied on consumer surplus in spite of its theoretical shortcomings. Given this, it is reasonable to ask how large the error will be when C is used in place of CV or EV. Figure 14.1 provides a hint at the answer. Note that for the case of a normal good, C is bound by the preferred measures, in that $CV<C<EV$. This observation suggests consumer surplus may be an acceptable approximation, in some circumstances. In an influential paper, Willig (1976) rigorously confirms this intuition for the single good case. Willig shows that the difference between C and the *WTP/WTA* measures is dependent on the magnitude of the good's income elasticity, and that in many cases the difference will be small. Specifically, if the income elasticity is small, or the change in consumer surplus is small relative to the overall budget (which seems likely for most price change analyses), the error from using C will be of second order importance, compared with errors in measurement, specification, and estimation. Willig goes so far as to derive analytical bounds on the error that suggest, for income elasticities falling in plausible ranges, only trivial differences between *WTP* and *WTA* can be expected to arise.

Subsequent research has also examined the quality of C as an approximation for multiple price changes, particularly as regards the issue of uniqueness. Just et al. (2004) show that, while a line integral as shown in Eq. (14.20) is not unique, any path of integration will lead to an estimate of C that lies between CV and EV for multiple price changes. Thus the bounding results derived by Willig carry over to multiple good cases. Based on this, the title of Willig's article – "Consumer surplus without apology" – seems appropriate, and changes in consumer surplus for price changes can, with confidence, be applied. But need they be?

14.2.3   Towards Measurement

Willig's paper provided legitimacy to applied economists who relied on consumer surplus measures for evaluating the welfare effects of price changes. However, influential work by Hausman (1981), appearing shortly after Willig's paper, presented the contemporary techniques used to directly calculate measures of compensating and equivalent variation for price changes, and made reliance on approximations unnecessary. The fundamental insight is that ordinary demand curves, if specified to be consistent with a well-defined utility maximization problem, contain sufficient information to recover the portion of the underlying preference function generating the observed behavior. Sufficient conditions for behavioral consistency are summarized by the "integrability" conditions. These in essence require that the functional form for the ordinary demand equations obey the curvature conditions implied by theory, and that the matrix of Slutsky substitution effects (i.e. the price gradients of the compensated demand curves) is symmetric and negative semi-definite.

Two identities from consumer theory are central to showing how the integrability conditions are operationally relevant for applied welfare analysis. The first is shown in (14.5), which says that the observed demand level represents the solution to both the utility maximization problem and the expenditure minimization problem. The second identity is

$$\bar{u} \equiv V\big(p, E(p,\bar{u},q),q\big), \tag{14.24}$$

which connects the indirect utility function to the expenditure function, for a reference level of utility $\bar{u}$. Differentiating (14.24) with respect to p_j leads to

$$\frac{\partial V(\cdot)}{\partial p_j} + \frac{\partial V(\cdot)}{\partial y}\frac{\partial E(\cdot)}{\partial p_j} = 0. \tag{14.25}$$

We can rewrite this expression as

$$\begin{aligned}\frac{\partial E(p,\bar{u},q)}{\partial p_j} &= -\frac{\partial V(\cdot)/\partial p_j}{\partial V(\cdot)/\partial y}\\ &= x_j(p,y,q),\end{aligned} \tag{14.26}$$

where the second equality holds by Roy's Identity. This can be interpreted as a differential equation relating income and p_j, which can in principle be solved to obtain $E(\cdot)$. Specifically, suppose we specify $x_j(\cdot)$ and estimate its parameters using consumption and price data. With a known parameterization of $x_j(\cdot)$, we can solve the differential equation

$$\frac{\partial y(p_j)}{\partial p_j} = x(p_j, p_{-j}, y, q) \tag{14.27}$$

to obtain

$$y\big[p_j, k(p_{-j}, q)\big], \tag{14.28}$$

where p_{-j} is the price vector absent p_j, and k is the constant of integration that lumps together all terms outside of p_j. If p_{-j} and q remain fixed in the analysis (so that $k(\cdot)$ remains fixed) it is possible to interpret (14.28) as a "quasi" expenditure function, and compute welfare measures using it. Specifically, because utility is ordinal – only comparisons, not levels, matter – we can, without loss of generality, normalize the constant of integration to the baseline level of utility, so that $u^0 = k(p_{-j}, q)$, and the expenditure function is denoted by $\hat{E}(p_j, u^0)$. This expenditure function is referred to as quasi, since it is only possible to recover the component of preferences related to the demand for good j. Anything else appearing in the full expenditure function is, by construction, assumed to be fixed. So long as only changes in p_j are considered, and the constant levels of p_{-j} and q can be subsumed into the normalization, it is simple to calculate compensating variation using $\hat{E}(p_j, u^0)$, which is fully characterized by the estimated parameters for the demand curve.

An example adapted from Freeman (2003, p.70) helps to show the power of this "integrating back" technique.

EXAMPLE 14.1 (NUMERICAL/ANALYTICAL) Suppose we are analyzing the demand for a single good and a numeraire, and we specify a linear demand equation by $x = \alpha - \beta p + \gamma y$, where (α, β, γ) are parameters that we estimate econometrically, and the other notation follows from above. Using Eq. (14.27), we have the differential equation

$$\frac{dy(p)}{dp} = \alpha - \beta p + \gamma y, \tag{14.29}$$

which is a common form with a known analytical solution, given by

$$y(p) = k\exp(\gamma p) - \frac{1}{\gamma}\left[\alpha - \beta p - \frac{\beta}{\gamma}\right]. \qquad (14.30)$$

If we normalize the constant of integration such that $k = u^0$ (the baseline level of utility), then the quasi expenditure function is

$$\hat{E}(p, u^0) = u^0 \exp(\gamma p) - \frac{1}{\gamma}\left[\alpha - \beta p - \frac{\beta}{\gamma}\right], \qquad (14.31)$$

from which, by substituting $y = \hat{E}(p_j, u^0)$, we can derive the indirect utility function as

$$u^0 = V(p, y) = \exp(-\gamma p)\left\{y + \frac{1}{\gamma}\left[\alpha - \beta p - \frac{\beta}{\gamma}\right]\right\}. \qquad (14.32)$$

This exercise shows that with estimates of the demand function parameters, the structural functions that are needed to compute welfare measures for a price change are also known.

There are two generalizations to the Hausman logic that deserve elaboration. First, the techniques described here are based on a demand equation that has a closed form solution for the differential equation, and thus an analytical expression for the quasi expenditure function. This limits options to a handful of functional forms that may not, for reasons of econometric fit and flexibility, be the best choice. Vartia (1983) describes a numerical algorithm that enables computation of welfare effects when there is no closed form for the expenditure function, and so in principle researchers have available a wide range of specifications whose only requirement is consistency with utility maximization conditions. Second, the discussion thus far has focused on a single demand curve. In many cases, x is a vector, and we are interested in recovering components of the preference function related to all of the goods under analysis. For this the techniques of integrating back need to be generalized to a system of demand context.

LaFrance and Hanemann (1989) rigorously examine how the one-dimensional differential equation in (14.26) generalizes to a system of partial differential equations, for the multi-good case. While the notation and mathematical techniques are substantially more involved than for the single good case, the basic intuition carries through. First, the analyst specifies a functional form for the system of demand equations in the analysis. As in the single good case, the specification needs to obey certain properties in order to be consistent with a well-defined utility maximization problem; these restrictions are the integrability conditions defined above. As we show in an example below, the restrictions needed in the system context can be quite severe. Second, the parameters of the J dimensional demand system are estimated using data on prices and quantities consumed for the collection of goods. Integrating back the J partial differential equations provides expressions for the quasi expenditure and indirect utility functions, which are then known based on the demand system parameter estimates. Finally, welfare analysis proceeds using the estimated functions. The following example helps to show how this method operates in practice.

EXAMPLE 14.2 (NUMERICAL/ANALYTICAL) Suppose we specify a system of J demand equations using a log-linear functional form

$$\ln x_j = \alpha_j + \beta_{jj} p_j + \sum\nolimits_{k \neq j} \beta_{jk} p_k + \gamma_j y, \quad j = 1, ..., J, \tag{14.33}$$

where $(\alpha_j, \beta_{jk}, \gamma_j)$ are parameters to be estimated. For this system to be consistent with utility maximization – i.e. for it to obey the integrability conditions – several restrictions are needed. These include $\beta_{jk} = 0$ for all $k \neq j$ and $\gamma_j = \gamma$ for all j. Note the severity of these restrictions, which imply that all ordinary demand cross price effects are zero, and the income coefficient is equal for all of the goods. With the integrability conditions imposed, the system in (14.33) can be integrated to obtain a closed form solution for the preference functions. For example, the indirect utility function corresponding to the log-linear system is

$$V(p, y) = \frac{-\exp(-\gamma y)}{\gamma} - \sum\nolimits_{j=1}^{J} \frac{\exp(\alpha_j + \beta_{jj} p_j)}{\beta_{jj}}. \tag{14.34}$$

Von Haefen (2002) discusses how a large variety of functional forms used in systems estimation need to be restricted in order to recover expenditure and indirect utility function parameters from their estimation.

While the usual challenges associated with any empirical measurement task apply, the main takeaway message concerning applied welfare analysis for price changes is that the techniques are well established, understood, and accepted. Whether a single or a set of goods is considered, the procedure for exact welfare analysis is the same. A properly restricted demand curve/system is specified and estimated, and the parameters that are recovered characterize the quasi expenditure and indirect utility functions. The ordinal nature of utility allows the terms not related to prices to be normalized away in the constant of integration. In instances when the integrating back strategy is not applied, Willig and his followers have shown that consumer surplus changes can often provide an acceptable approximation to compensating and equivalent variation. The ideas discussed in this section are nicely reviewed by Slesnick (1998), and studied in much greater detail in Just et al. (2004). As we show below, however, the operational techniques that are so effectively applied in price change analysis do not directly transfer to the quantity change case.

14.3 QUANTITY CHANGE WELFARE MEASURES

In environmental economics we are usually more concerned with measuring the well-being effects of changes in quasi-fixed quantities related to the environment rather than price changes for private goods. This problem requires that we define welfare measures for these changes, and consider operational strategies for quantifying them. In the following two subsections we begin to address these tasks.

14.3.1 Compensating and Equivalent Variation

The definitions of compensating and equivalent variation for quantity changes follow logically from their price change counterparts.[1] Using the indirect utility function, the compensating variation for a change in q from q^0 to q^1 is given by

$$V(p, y, q^0) = V(p, y - CV, q^1),$$ (14.35)

and equivalent variation is analogously defined as

$$V(p, y, q^1) = V(p, y + EV, q^0).$$ (14.36)

For an increase in the quantity of the quasi-fixed good, $CV > 0$ can be interpreted as the willingness to pay to have the improvement, and $EV > 0$ is the willingness to accept to forgo the improvement. When analyzing changes in fixed quantities, the distinction between *WTP* and *WTA* is perhaps of greater importance than for private good price changes. Here, the choice of CV or EV as a welfare measure is associated with an implicit assignment of property rights for the quasi-fixed good. The use of *WTP* implies the person is not entitled to the improvement. The person may, however, choose to purchase the improvement. In contrast, the use of *WTA* implies the person is entitled to the improvement, and any outcome that does not provide it must be met with appropriate compensation. If in practice the difference between *WTP* and *WTA* is not large, the choice is of little importance. We return to this point in section 14.4 below.

As in the price change case, we can also define CV and EV using the expenditure function by

$$\begin{aligned}
CV &= E(p, u^0, q^0) - E(p, u^0, q^1) \\
&= y - E(p, u^0, q^1), \\
EV &= E(p, u^1, q^0) - E(p, u^1, q^1) \\
&= E(p, u^1, q^0) - y.
\end{aligned}$$ (14.37)

Finally, we can define the valuation measures using demand curves. Because q is fixed from the perspective of the individual, however, we need to examine *inverse* demand functions, which in general track the prices a person would pay for different fixed quantities of a good. Define the compensated inverse demand for q function by

$$\pi^q(p, u, q) = -\frac{\partial E(p, u, q)}{\partial q},$$ (14.38)

and note that $\pi^q(\cdot)$ is also the marginal willingness to pay for q function, since it is the change in income that holds utility constant following a marginal change in q. We will

---

[1] Some use the terms "compensating surplus" and "equivalent surplus" to distinguish welfare measure for quality changes from their price change counterparts.

use the terms inverse demand and marginal willingness to pay function interchangeably. With knowledge of $\pi^q(\cdot)$, we can calculate EV and CV by computing the areas under the appropriate inverse demand curve:

$$
\begin{aligned}
CV &= \int_{q^0}^{q^1} \pi^q(p,u^0,q)dq \\
&= \int_{q^0}^{q^1} -\frac{\partial E(p,u^0,q)}{\partial q}\,dq = E(p,u^0,q^0) - E(p,u^0,q^1), \\
EV &= \int_{q^0}^{q^1} \pi^q(p,u^1,q)dq \\
&= \int_{q^0}^{q^1} -\frac{\partial E(p,u^1,q)}{\partial q}\,dq = E(p,u^1,q^0) - E(p,u^1,q^1).
\end{aligned}
\tag{14.39}
$$

Figure 14.2 illustrates these concepts graphically. The important difference between the behavior shown here and that in Figure 14.1 is that q is fixed from the perspective of the individual, and it does not have a market price. Total spending on private goods therefore does not change when q changes. Panel A shows the behavior and welfare measures in utility space, where spending on private goods (income) is on the vertical axis and q is on the horizontal axis. At observed income y_0 and initial quantity level q_0, the person obtains utility level u^0. This is shown as point a in the figure. An exogenous increase in quantity to q_1 allows the person to reach a higher utility level u^1, while maintaining private good spending y_0; this is shown as point b. The welfare measures are shown on the y axis. Compensating variation is the vertical distance between u^1 and u^0 at q_1. Note that this is the amount of money the person would pay for the increase, since it would move him to the hypothetical point c on the original utility curve. Equivalent variation is the vertical distance between u^1 and u^0 at q_0. To reach the new utility level without the quantity increase (point d), the person would need an increase in income equal to $E(p,u^1,q_0) - y_0$.

Tracing out the inverse demand curves for q is more involved than for the price case, since there is no market price, budget constraint, or choice related to q. However, we can identify *virtual* prices and income, which would lead the person to freely choose a given level of the quasi-fixed good if it were exchanged in markets. Several of these thought-experiment price and income level budget constraints are shown via the dashed lines in panel A, each labeled $\pi_0(\tilde{y}_0)$, $\pi_1(\tilde{y}_1)$, and $\pi_2(\tilde{y}_2)$. Consider for example $\pi_0(\tilde{y}_0)$, which is tangent to the initial outcome a. At point a, the person consumes q_0, but does not pay anything to do so. If q were instead exchanged in a market, at price π_0 and income $\tilde{y}_0 > y_0$ the person would, by construction, purchase q_0. Note that virtual income $\tilde{y}_0$ is greater than actual income in this case, since the budget must allow for expenditures on q.

The virtual prices are useful because, like market prices, they identify the marginal willingness to pay for q at different points in the indifference map. These allow us to trace out the compensated inverse demand curves shown in panel B. For example, the virtual prices π_0 and π_2 give us two points a and c on $\pi^q(p,u^0,q)$; likewise, π_1 and π_3 provide points d and b on the compensated inverse demand curve $\pi^q(p,u^1,q)$. The curves are compensated because as q changes, the amount of private good spending adjusts up or down to maintain the reference level of utility. The calculations shown in Eq. (14.39) are

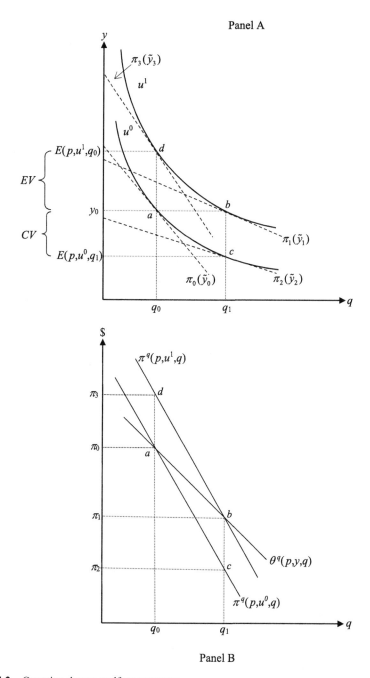

Figure 14.2   Quantity change welfare measures

illustrated in panel B by the area under the appropriate inverse demand curve. Compensating variation is the area q_0acq_1, and equivalent variation is the area q_0dbq_1.

The information in panel A also allows us to trace out an ordinary inverse demand for q curve, which we denote $\theta^q(p,y,q)$. By definition, ordinary demands are uncompensated, in that they maintain the initial income level while allowing utility to change.

Compensated demands are so named because they adjust income to maintain utility. The same idea applies to inverse demands. In panel A, the initial and final outcomes are shown as points a and b, respectively. At these two points, $(\pi_0, \tilde{y}_0)$ and $(\pi_1, \tilde{y}_1)$ show the marginal willingness to pay and virtual income needed, to maintain private good spending y_0, while utility changes. Note that $\tilde{y}_0 = y_0 + q_0 \pi_0$, and $\tilde{y}_1 = y_0 + q_1 \pi_1$, which allows the person to "purchase" q without changing spending on private goods. Connecting points a and b in panel B allows us to trace out $\theta^q(p,y,q)$ – the uncompensated marginal willingness to pay for q function.

Equations (14.35) through (14.39) are fairly intuitive extensions of the price change definitions given above, and there is an appealing symmetry between the expressions in (14.11) and those in (14.39). In particular, both seem to point to a link between the welfare measures of interest, and a well-defined behavioral function. Figures 14.1 and 14.2 further reinforce the symmetry, in that ordinary and compensated demand curves are shown to intersect at the observed consumption outcomes. The similarities, unfortunately, do not extend beyond these conceptual parallels. For the price change case, the intersection of compensated and ordinary demand curves was critical, since estimates of $x_j(p,y,q)$ based on observed choices could be used to recover sufficient information about preferences to allow computation of welfare measures. A parallel idea would be to similarly use estimates of $\theta^q(p,y,q)$. However, with no market for q, there is no mechanism through which people reveal their marginal values for q, and hence it is not possible to estimate the inverse demand curve by observing individual behavior. This is the crux of the problem, and does much to explain why it is notably more difficult to estimate the welfare effects of changes in the level of quasi-fixed goods than prices for private goods.

14.3.2 The Fundamental Challenge of Measurement

To best understand the challenge of welfare measurement for quantity changes, recall the fundamental role that Eq. (14.26) played in the price change case. Then it was possible to relate observed behavior to the expenditure function, and solve a differential equation to recover the necessary component of the preference function. The analytics are identical for the quantity change case. If we differentiate the identity in (14.24) with respect to q and rearrange we recover the relationship

$$- \frac{\partial E(p,u,q)}{\partial q} = \frac{\partial V(p,y,q)/\partial q}{\partial V(p,y,q)/\partial y} = \theta^q(p,y,q), \tag{14.40}$$

where $\theta^q(\cdot)$ is the ordinary inverse demand (willingness to pay function) for q, shown in Figure 14.2. If it were possible to estimate the inverse demand for q, the techniques described above would be relevant here. Solving the differential equation in (14.40) would allow recovery of the quasi expenditure function for q and, following estimation of $\theta^q(p,y,q)$, welfare measurement could proceed as usual. As noted, however, $\theta^q(\cdot)$ cannot be estimated using observed behavior, and so the integrating back strategy is not operationally useful.

A comparison of equations (14.27) and (14.40) nicely summarizes the fundamental challenge of welfare measurement for quantity changes. In the former, information on the observable demand for private goods allows recovery of the quasi expenditure function, but the normalization needed to eliminate the constant of integration $k(p_{-j}, U^0, q)$ requires that q remains fixed in the subsequent analysis. In the latter equation, information is not available to estimate the parameters entering the differential equation, and the quasi expenditure cannot be recovered. The main conclusion we draw from this is clear: without additional assumptions on specific aspects of the preference function, or information beyond individuals' observed behavior, quantity change welfare analysis is not possible. We return to this theme in detail throughout subsequent chapters in Part III of the book.

14.4 WTP AND WTA

Thus far in the chapter we have used *WTP* and *WTA* more or less interchangeably, having only noted with little elaboration that the choice of one or the other for applied welfare analysis has associated with it an implicit assumption on the distribution of property rights. For many environmental applications this distinction can matter in principle, since it determines (a) whether agents suffering the consequences of pollution are endowed with the right to demand pollution reduction or compensation for losses; or (b) they have no such right, and therefore must implicitly "buy" a reduction. The *WTP* versus *WTA* distinction therefore relates to the perennial ethical debate regarding the rights and responsibilities of polluters versus those suffering pollution's consequences. It can have practical ramification as well. For example, if the willingness to accept compensation by a neighborhood association for the development of adjacent open space is substantially larger than its willingness to pay to prevent development, the choice of measure may influence whether development or preservation is the cost/benefit analysis winner. For these reasons, studies of how *WTP* and *WTA* can differ – and the extent to which they actually do differ – have occupied environmental economists for nearly 40 years. Research on this topic includes theoretical and empirical work, as well as laboratory and field experiments. In this section we discuss how the basic model of behavior we have developed thus far can be used to identify one path to understanding when and how measures of *WTP* and *WTA* might converge or diverge. As such we do not attempt to review the enormous literature in this area. Instead, our aim is to continue the theme of this chapter by exploring how our simple model of behavior gives rise to valuation concepts that are critical for applied welfare analysis.

Early theoretical work by Willig (1976) and Randall and Stoll (1980) suggested that willingness to pay and willingness to accept should be close in most contexts. However, actual measurements in survey and experimental studies have persistently found *WTA* to be larger than *WTP*. For example, Horowitz and McConnell (2002) survey 45 studies on the subject, and report that, on average, *WTA* is seven times larger than its comparable *WTP* measure. In their meta-analysis updating Horowitz and McConnell, Tunçel and Hammitt (2014) confirm a gap has persisted in more recent studies. This empirical evidence has stimulated a large volume of work, both within and without the neoclassical paradigm, dedicated to identifying the sources of this divergence. Here we examine in detail Hanemann's (1991) explanation, which is noteworthy because it isolates an intuitive effect within the context of the static, neoclassical model we have developed thus far.

At the most basic level, *WTP* and *WTA* can diverge based on the budget constraint in that *WTP* is constrained by the person's income, while *WTA* is unbounded from above. By showing that *C* is a good approximation for *CV* or *EV*, however, Willig (1976) demonstrates that the difference ought to be small in practice for price changes given moderate income effects. In panel C of Figure 14.1, Willig's argument implies the area *adbc* will be small, and *CV≈EV*. Randall and Stoll (1980) consider the difference between *CV* and *EV* in the context of a quasi-fixed good (e.g. a public good), which consumers take as given. Using techniques similar to Willig, they show that a consumer surplus-type measure for a change in the good's quantity is bounded by *EV* and *CV*, and that the difference will be small for small income effects. Specifically, using the notation from Figure 14.2, if the income elasticity of $\theta^q(p,y,q)$ is small, then *CV≈EV*. Their argument is shown in panel B of the Figure. The consumer surplus-type measure is abq_1q_0, and *acbd* is predicted to be small if $\partial\theta^q(\cdot)/\partial y$ is small. From Willig and Randall and Stoll, the conventional wisdom emerged that theory predicts small differences in *WTP* and *WTA* for both price *and* quasi-fixed good quantity changes.

Taking this as his starting point, Hanemann shows that the difference between *WTP* and *WTA* depends implicitly on the degree of substitution between the quasi-fixed good, and the set of available private goods. His reasoning is fairly technical but ultimately quite intuitive. Rather than replicating the detailed derivation, we provide a heuristic sketch of the argument, based on the virtual prices and income described in the context of Figure 14.2. Consider first panel A. Although q is fixed in actuality, we have seen that it is possible to define a hypothetical price and income that *would* lead the person to freely choose the level of q in a market situation. Consider for example point a. At income y_0, a virtual price of π_0 and virtual income of $\tilde{y}_0=y_0+q_0\pi_0$ would cause the person to choose q_0 in a market situation. A similar argument can be made for point b, for which the virtual price and income π_1 and $\tilde{y}_1=y_0+q_1\pi_1$ would lead the person to choose q_1. These examples suggest a thought experiment in which we define an ordinary demand for q function

$$q = q(p, \pi, y + q\pi), \tag{14.41}$$

which summarizes the specific virtual price and virtual income that would lead to a particular choice of q.

The virtual price concept can also be used to derive a compensated demand function for q, based on a hypothetical expenditure minimization problem. Given the (virtual) price π_0, there is a minimum level of expenditure needed to reach u^0. The amount q_0 is the solution to this problem. Likewise, for the price π_1, reaching u^1 with minimum expenditure implies a choice of q_1. Points a and b in the upper panel of Figure 14.2 show these solution points. From these two examples, we can imagine a compensated demand for q function

$$q = h_q(p, \pi, u), \tag{14.42}$$

which, like its ordinary counterpart, is purely hypothetical. Nonetheless, the standard demand properties that relate the two functions, including the Slutsky relationship

$$\frac{\partial h_q(p,\pi,u)}{\partial \pi} = \frac{\partial q(p,\pi,y+q\pi)}{\partial \pi} + \frac{\partial q(p,\pi,y+q\pi)}{\partial y}q, \tag{14.43}$$

continue to hold. Inverting the ordinary demand equation in (14.41) connects us back to the ordinary inverse demand curve $\pi = \theta^q(p,y,q)$, as shown in Figure 14.2.

Hanemann's argument begins with the Randall and Stoll result. Define the income elasticity of the ordinary marginal willingness to pay function by

$$\xi = \frac{\partial \theta^q(p,y,q)}{\partial y}\frac{y}{\theta^q(\cdot)}, \tag{14.44}$$

and recall the prediction that for small values of ξ (i.e. small income effects), the difference between *WTP* and *WTA* will be small. While this result is correct, it masks a subtle point. The income elasticity in (14.44) imbeds two pieces: a pure income effect, and a pure substitution effect. To see this, implicitly differentiate (14.41) with respect to y to obtain:

$$0 = \frac{\partial q(p,\pi,y+\pi q)}{\partial \pi} \times \frac{\partial \pi}{\partial y} + \frac{\partial q(p,\pi,y+\pi q)}{\partial y} \times \left[1 + \frac{\partial \pi}{\partial y}q\right]. \tag{14.45}$$

Note that $\partial \pi/\partial y$ is the derivative of the virtual price – i.e. the marginal willingness to pay – with respect to income, which is by construction equal to $\partial \theta^q(\cdot)/\partial y$. Making this substitution and rearranging (14.45), we arrive at

$$\frac{\partial \theta^q(\cdot)}{\partial y} = -\frac{\partial q(p,\pi,y+q\pi)/\partial y}{\partial q(p,\pi,y+q\pi)/\partial \pi + \partial q(p,\pi,y+q\pi)/\partial y \times q}, \tag{14.46}$$

which, using the Slutsky relationship in Eq. (14.43), we can rewrite as

$$\frac{\partial \theta^q(p,y,q)}{\partial y} = -\frac{\partial q(p,\pi,y+q\pi)/\partial y}{\partial h_q(p,\pi,u)/\partial \pi}. \tag{14.47}$$

This is the key result. The income derivative that must be small for $WTP \approx WTA$ is on the left-hand side of the equation. The right-hand side shows, however, that it consists of two components. The numerator is an income effect measuring the ordinary demand for q response to changes in income. The denominator is a substitution effect, measuring how the compensated demand for q changes with its price. The latter will be small if $h_q(p,\pi,u)$ is price inelastic. That is, the denominator of (14.47) will be small if there are relatively few substitutes for q. From this we can see that, while it is indeed the case that the difference between *WTA* and *WTP* will be small if $\partial \theta^q(\cdot)/\partial y$ is small, income is not the only determinant. If q is relatively unique, or otherwise has few close substitutes, $\partial \theta^q(\cdot)/\partial y$ will be large *regardless* of the size of the income effect.

To complete the argument, we can restate the result in elasticity form by first rewriting (14.47):

$$\frac{\partial \theta^i(p,y,q)}{\partial y}\frac{y}{\pi} = -\frac{y}{\pi}\frac{\left[\partial q(p,\pi,y+q\pi)/\partial y\right]\left[(y+q\pi)/q\right]}{\left[\partial h_q(p,\pi,u)/\partial \pi\right]\left[(y+q\pi)/q\right]} = $$
$$\xi = -\frac{\eta_q \cdot y}{\varepsilon_q \cdot (y+q\pi)} = -\frac{\eta_q(1-s_q)}{\varepsilon_q},$$

(14.48)

where η_q is the income elasticity of the ordinary demand for q, ε_q is the compensated own-price elasticity for q, and s_q is the share of adjusted income $y+q\pi$ that is spent on q. Finally, denote the Allen-Uzawa elasticity of substitution between q and spending on market goods by σ_{qy}. Hanemann shows that the Allen-Uzawa elasticity can be related to ε_q by the relationship $\varepsilon_q = -\sigma_{qy}(1-s_q)$, from which the fundamental result in elasticity form can be stated as

$$\xi = \frac{\eta_q}{\sigma_{qy}}.$$

(14.49)

From this we see that if q cannot be readily substituted for with market goods (i.e. σ_{qy} is small), then *WTP* and *WTA* can diverge based on the uniqueness of q. Referring again to Figure 14.2, the decomposition of ξ shows that two criteria must be met for area *acbd* in panel B to be small: an income effect must be small, and the substitution possibilities between q and other commodities must be large. To the extent that non-market environmental goods are relatively unique, which is to say they are not easily replaced by purchased private goods, our simple model is consistent with the often observed divergence between the two measures. Whether or not this is a first order explanation for the observed phenomena continues to be the subject of debate, with support from some studies (e.g. Shogren et al., 1994) and more favored explanations emerging in others (e.g. Morrison, 1998).

14.5   WELFARE ANALYSIS UNDER UNCERTAINTY

Our discussion to this point has implicitly assumed individuals act with full information about the future availability of environmental goods, their own preferences, and a number of other factors that in the real world cannot be fully known. In many instances, ignoring background uncertainty is sensible from a modeling perspective. In other cases, when uncertainty is a defining feature of the problem, welfare measurement concepts that accommodate uncertainty are needed. For example, a person may not know if he will want to visit a public wildlife refuge in the future, yet he may need to decide now whether or not to vote yes in a referendum that will determine its future existence. How should we define the value upon which his choice is based? Perhaps more importantly, people face risks from carcinogens present in the ambient environment, yet a person cannot know if he will one day succumb to cancer. Individuals and governments must nonetheless make decisions on devoting resources to reducing cancer risk. How should we value these risk reductions? These two examples illustrate the need for models of behavior and welfare measures that accommodate broadly defined notions of risk and uncertainty. In particular, we are often interested in measuring individuals' *WTP* to secure a favorable outcome, before the state of the world is known.

The literature in economics on risk and uncertainty is large, and much has been written on the many specific ways that risk and uncertainty affect behavior and policy outcomes in environmental economics. It is beyond the scope of this section to discuss this literature generally. Instead, we present a model of individual behavior that allows us to define valuation concepts that parallel those that we examined in the certainty case. Specifically, we summarize how the expected utility maximization model can be used to define the concept of option price, and we summarize its relationship to compensating variation. At this point, we do not explore contemporary research themes related to risk perceptions and non-expected utility maximization. We return in Chapter 20 to the topic of risk and uncertainty, and related research, within the context of valuing reductions in mortality risk.

Expected utility maximization is an essentially static modeling framework. The important assumptions of the model are that multiple states of the world are possible, individuals make some resource commitments before the state of the world is revealed, and they know their preferences *and* the probability distribution governing the likelihood of seeing different states. The timing of events is referenced only by its relation to the resolution of uncertainty – decisions and outcomes occur either before or after the point when the state of the world becomes known. In this sense, expected utility maximization does not focus on the temporal dimensions of choice, but instead uses time as a sequencing metaphor.

These assumptions abstract from a host of interesting topics, many of which have been the basis for important research. However, they do provide a means for gaining valuable insights. Consider a generalization of the problem in (14.1). Suppose now that the level of q is uncertain from the perspective of current decisions. For simplicity, we assume q can take one of two values, each corresponding to unique states of the world L and H. Denote q_L and q_H as the values that q takes in states L and H, respectively. The variable q can represent several dimensions of human/environment interaction. It can denote the occurrence/non-occurrence of illness or death due to exposure to an environmental risk, or a stochastic measure of quality of an environmental resource. In keeping with the notation already established, we assume that q has positive marginal utility. For the discussion that follows, we also assume $q_L < q_H$, and that $U(x,z,q_L) < U(x,z,q_H)$. That is, all else being equal, the person realizes higher ex post utility when there is a higher level of q. Denote the probability that state L occurs by ρ, and the probability that state H occurs by $(1-\rho)$.

Expected utility maximization postulates that a person maximizes his ex ante expected utility according to

$$\max_{x,z} \rho U(x,z,q_L) + (1-\rho)U(x,z,q_H) \quad s.t. \quad y = p'x + z, \quad (14.50)$$

which gives rise to behavioral functions that determine actions and outcomes, conditional on the state of the world. Though the structure of $U(\cdot)$ is the same in both states of the world, the ex post levels of x and z, and their marginal utilities, are governed in part by the level of q. Based on this, we can define the ex post utility levels that arise once the state of the world is revealed. Specifically, define $V^H(p,y,q_H)$ as the indirect utility function that summarizes realized utility when state H arises, and $V(p,y,q_L)$ as the indirect utility function that does so when state L arises. By construction, the person is better off when state H occurs, and so $V^H(p,y,q_H) > V^L(p,y,q_L)$.

Using this setup, we first consider an ex post welfare measure. Suppose the uncertainty is resolved, and state of the world results in q_L. A person's *WTP* (compensating variation) to reverse the outcome, and instead have q_H, is implicitly defined by the expression

$$V^L(p,y,q_L) = V^H(p,y-CV,q_H).$$ (14.51)

This is a measure of the damages actually suffered when q_L occurs. However, it is arguably not the welfare measure we are interested in, since as an ex post concept, it does not reflect attitudes towards risk held by the individual. Indeed, for extreme definitions of q such as $q_H = survival$ and $q_L = death$, the ex post willingness to pay is the entire budget. In such cases, *CV* is neither interesting, nor is it a particularly useful measure for public policy.

A more useful measure is one based on an ex ante perspective that reflects the payment a person would make before the uncertainty is resolved, to secure a particular level of well-being ex post. Consider a measure of *WTP* defined by

$$\rho V^L(p,y,q_L) + (1-\rho)V^H(p,y,q_H) = V^H(p,y-OP,q_H),$$ (14.52)

where *OP* denotes option price. The left-hand side is the utility level the person expects to receive ex ante, under baseline uncertainty. The right-hand side denotes the level of ex post utility obtained conditional on the high state of nature, less an income offset to make it equal to the ex ante expected utility. With this setup, option price is defined as follows.

Definition 14.4
The option price (OP) is the reduction in income needed to equate the ex ante expected utility under baseline risk with the ex post actual utility under the favorable state – i.e. it is the ex ante willingness to pay to hold expected utility constant in either state of the world. Equivalently, OP is the amount the person would be willing to pay before the resolution of uncertainty to secure with certainty the favorable state (i.e. to make $\rho = 0$).

In general, *OP* is not equal to expected damages ($OP \neq \rho \cdot CV$); indeed, it is only in the special case when the person is risk neutral that option price and expected damages are equal. Thus *OP*, by construction, imbeds the individual's attitudes towards risk into the welfare measure. Conceptually it resembles an insurance premium, in that it is a payment that the person would make ex ante, to avoid the extreme consequences of either state of the world ex post. In most uncertainty cases, *OP* is more relevant than *CV* for policy analysis. Policy can often influence the level of q or the probability that a state of the world occurs; rarely can it reduce the uncertainty completely. Thus we are usually interested in the monetary value of efforts to influence states of the world, before the actual state is known. Option price provides one such measure.

There are also instances when we may be interested in measuring the ex ante marginal willingness to pay for changes in q or ρ. We assume now that q varies continuously, and that the well-being the person gets from q is in some way dependent on the state of the world. We first derive an expression for a person's marginal willingness to pay for an incremental increase in q. Starting with a reference level of expected utility given by

$$\bar{v} = \rho V^L (p, y, q) + (1 - \rho) V^H (p, y, q),$$ (14.53)

we differentiate with respect to q and y to get

$$\frac{dy}{dq} = \frac{\rho V_q^L (p, y, q) + (1 - \rho) V_q^H (p, y, q)}{\rho V_y^L (p, y, q) + (1 - \rho) V_y^H (p, y, q)},$$ (14.54)

where subscripts denote partial derivatives. This expression is similar to the marginal willingness to pay function for q under certainty, shown in (14.40). The main difference here, of course, is that the marginal utilities in the numerator and denominator are scaled by their respective probabilities, to reflect the uncertainty about the state of the world. We can also obtain an expression for the marginal willingness to pay to decrease the probability of state L by differentiating (14.53) with respect to ρ and y. Taking derivatives and rearranging we obtain

$$\frac{dy}{d\rho} = \frac{V^H (p, y, q) - V^L (p, y, q)}{\rho V_y^L (p, y, q) + (1 - \rho) V_y^H (p, y, q)}.$$ (14.55)

This equation has a familiar interpretation as well. The numerator is the utility improvement if the favorable state occurs, and the denominator is the expected marginal utility of income. Intuitively, the expression shows the monetized value of the utility change resulting from the probability change, properly scaled to account for the uncertainty in the state of the world.

14.6 SUMMARY

All non-market valuation applications, and indeed all of applied welfare economics, share the same basic structure. A behavioral model is needed that gives rise to the theoretically relevant valuation measures, and an empirical strategy is needed to connect observed behavior and other available information to operationally feasible valuation measures. Our focus in this chapter has been on the former, and how the specifics of the problem condition options for the latter. Through this several key insights have emerged. First, a general model of household behavior when one of the goods is quasi-fixed allows us to define several welfare measurement concepts. These include compensating and equivalent variation, consumer surplus, and option price. In differing ways, and under different assumptions, these concepts can be linked to willingness to pay or willingness to accept for a well-defined change in market good prices, or the level of the quasi-fixed good. Since the measurement of *WTP* or *WTA* is the primary objective in applied welfare analysis, our discussion suggests that empirical models must, at a minimum, shed light on a sufficient component of the preference function to allow estimation of *CV*, *EV*, *C*, or *OP*, and/or the marginal value of changes in q. Furthermore, though we tend to use the concepts *WTP* and *WTA* interchangeably, our model suggests that, when q is sufficiently unique, the two valuation measures can diverge by large amounts.

Regarding options for linking welfare measurement theory to empirical practice, we have seen that there is an intuitive symmetry between the conceptual basis for using ordinary demand curves to value price changes, and ordinary inverse demand curves to value quantity changes. In both cases, a well-defined demand function can be related to the underlying preference function, suggesting that knowledge of the demand function allows recovery of underlying preferences. The symmetry breaks down in practice, since ordinary private good demands are estimable from market transactions data, while by definition, no transactions exist upon which to base estimates of the inverse demand for the quasi-fixed good. This is the fundamental challenge of welfare analysis for changes in the level of quasi-fixed goods, and it can only be solved by using extra-market information. This can come in the form of assumptions about how the quasi-fixed good enters preferences, or from survey data not arising from market transactions. In the remainder of Part III of the book, we examine how the two general strategies are applied in a number of specific areas to estimate *WTP* or *WTA*, within both certainty and uncertainty contexts.

14.7 FURTHER READING

Our discussion in this chapter summarizes a collection of related ideas that are individually examined in greater detail in other works. For example, Just et al. (2004) provide a comprehensive treatment of both the theory and practice of welfare measurement for price changes. This includes a much more detailed discussion of consumer surplus as it relates to contemporary "integrating back" techniques. Bockstael and McConnell (2007, Chapter 2) provide a brief but informative overview of applied welfare analysis for price changes. Their style of description motivates much of how we have presented this material. Important original references on price change welfare measurement include Willig (1976) and Hausman (1981); see also Hanemann (1980). Slesnick (1998) discusses the empirical literature on price change welfare analysis. Our graphical treatment of the symmetry between price and quantity change welfare measurement is motivated by Hanemann (1991), whose analysis we have also borrowed from in describing an explanation for the willingness to pay/accept divergence. See also Hanemann (1999a) for a more detailed discussion of the theory of WTP and WTA. The empirical divergence between WTP and WTA is examined by Horowitz and McConnell (2002) and Tunçel and Hammitt (2014). Freeman (2003) and Freeman et al. (2014) provide full chapters on uncertainty themes that include topics such as option value and non-expected utility maximization, which are not covered here. We have drawn particularly on the Freeman discussion for our definition of option price and marginal willingness to pay under uncertainty. Useful references on welfare measurement under uncertainty include Jones-Lee (1974) and Graham (1981). Jindapon and Shaw (2008) and Shaw and Woodward (2008) discuss welfare measurement under non-expected utility maximization.

EXERCISES

14.1 * Consider evaluating the welfare effect of a change in an environmental quantity q. Recall that CV and EV have different implied property right implications and, depending on the direction of change, have either willingness to pay or willingness to accept interpretations. Based on these differences, complete the following table by indicating when each welfare measure is a WTP or WTA:

Welfare Measure	Increase in q	Decrease in q
CV – person entitled to status quo	WTP or WTA?	WTP or WTA?
EV – person entitled to the change	WTP or WTA?	WTP or WTA?

14.2 ** In section 14.2.2 we showed that for consumer surplus to be a unique, money-metric measure of utility change for price increases or decreases, the marginal utility of income must be constant with respect to the prices that change. We saw that this implies the income elasticities of demand for goods whose price change must be equal. Use the Slutsky equation relationship for any two goods j and k whose prices change in the analysis to show that a constant marginal utility of income also implies equality of the ordinary demand cross price effects.

14.3 ** Consider a demand equation of the form

$$x = \alpha - \beta p + \gamma y,$$

where p is price and y is income. Suppose we have estimated the parameters of this equation using market data on prices and quantities, so that $\alpha = 2$, $\beta = 0.65$, and $\gamma = 0.0002$. Assume that the initial market price is $10, and that we are interested in examining the welfare effects for a person with income of $50,000.

  (a) Compute the baseline demand, price elasticity, and income elasticity for this person. Is the income effect "large" or "small" according to your intuitive understanding?

  (b) Consider a price increase to $20. Compute the change in consumer surplus, as well as compensating and equivalent variation for this change. What is the percentage error in this case when we use C rather than CV as our measure of welfare?

14.4 *** Consider the following three incomplete demand system specifications for goods indexed $j = 1, \ldots, J$:

$$x_j = \alpha_j + \sum\nolimits_{j=1}^{J} \beta_{jk} p_k + \gamma_j y$$

$$\ln x_j = \alpha_j + \sum\nolimits_{j=1}^{J} \beta_{jk} p_k + \gamma_j y$$

$$x_j = \alpha_j + \sum\nolimits_{j=1}^{J} \beta_{jk} \ln p_k + \gamma_j \ln y$$

Using the results derived in von Haefen (2002), for each system state:

(a) the parameter restrictions needed for consistency with the integrability conditions;

(b) the quasi-indirect utility and quasi-expenditure functions.

14.5 *** In section 14.4 we presented the "substitutability" argument as one of several candidate explanations for the persistently observed gap between willingness to pay and willingness to accept. Other explanations are described, for example, in Morrison (1998), Zhao and Kling (2001), Kolstad and Guzman (1999), and Plott and Zeiler (2005). Examine the *WTP* vs. *WTA* literature to complete the following:

(a) Describe the different conceptual explanations for the *WTP/WTA* gap. Which do you find most compelling?

(b) Briefly summarize the empirical and experimental evidence for the different explanations. Has the research converged to consensus explanation for the gap? Which explanation is leading?

CHAPTER 15

Revealed Preference Models

In Chapter 14 we presented a general model of consumer preferences in the presence of a quasi-fixed good. We saw that it is relatively straightforward to define welfare measures for changes in exogenous variables faced by consumers – be they price or quasi-fixed good changes. We also saw how observation of behavior in private good markets reveals sufficient information on preferences to construct exact (compensating and equivalent variation) or approximate (consumer surplus) welfare measures for private good price changes. Welfare measurement for changes in exogenously given quantities, however, turned out to be considerably more complicated. The fundamental challenge of welfare measurement for changes in quasi-fixed quantities is based on the fact that, by definition, no markets exist for quasi-fixed goods such as environmental quality. Thus there is no observable behavior from which to construct a demand curve, and hence no direct window through which preferences can be observed. We concluded from this that extra-market information is needed to estimate the welfare effects of changes in quasi-fixed goods. In this chapter we focus on one potential source of extra information: assumptions on how the demand for a private good interacts with the quasi-fixed good. These assumptions give rise to the so-called revealed preference models for non-market valuation.

Revealed preference methods are based on the premise that, though there are no direct markets for environmental goods, people interact with the environment in a variety of observable ways. For example, there is no market that determines the population of orcas in Washington's Puget Sound, but visitors to the area purchase whale-watching tours to see them. If there are fewer animals available we are likely to observe fewer people booking tours. Air quality in many urban areas is highly variable due to geography and wind patterns. Though there is no market for air quality, people are often observed choosing their place of residence based in part on where air quality is higher. Likewise, people who are sensitive to episodic changes in ground-level ozone may alter their schedules so as to spend less time outdoors during pollution spikes. Other examples abound: fishermen go where the fish are, beach visitors favor areas with clean water, homebuyers like to locate near protected open space, and pregnant women avoid eating fish with mercury contaminants. The idea behind revealed preference analysis is that these points of interaction with the environment allow us to analyze the demand for private goods or actions related to the environment – for whale-watching trips, residential location, outdoor leisure activities, and types of food – in order to indirectly learn something about the value of a specific environmental characteristic. Through their participation in private good markets that interact with the environment, people often leave "behavioral footprints" that reveal information about their environmental preferences. What we need to exploit these behavioral footprints is an assertion about how a private and an environmental good are related, data on consumption choices, prices for the private good, and measurements for the relevant environmental good. Examination of three different assertions one can make about private/environmental good relationship, and the behavioral models appropriate for these assertions, is the main topic in this chapter. Specifically, in section 15.2 we will examine a model that is appropriate when the private and environmental good are complements, which is often appropriate when the environmental good contributes to recreation opportunities. In section 15.3 we will examine a substitutes model, in which the private and environmental goods are substitutable inputs in producing a utility generating service flow. This framework is often useful for valuing health-related environmental attributes. Finally, in section 15.4 we present a model of quality-differentiated market goods that can accommodate contexts when environmental quality is directly related to the price of a private good. As we will see, this provides, among other things, the theoretical basis for using property values to understand the demand for local environmental quality. Before examining these specific models, we begin in section 15.1 by reviewing the theoretical challenges associated with welfare measurement for quasi-fixed goods.

15.1   THE FUNDAMENTAL CHALLENGE REVISITED

Our starting point is the general model of preferences that was presented in detail in Chapter 14. Recall that a consumer has a direct utility function defined by $U(x,z,q)$, where the J dimensional vector x and scalar z are levels of private market and numeraire goods, respectively, and q is the level of a quasi-fixed environmental good that the person takes as given. Throughout this chapter we will refer to q as a scalar, though in actual applications q is often a vector. Given income y and the vector of market prices p, utility maximization leads to ordinary demand equations denoted by $x_j(p,y,q)$ and $z(p,y,q)$, where the subscript j denotes a specific element of x. Given a reference level of utility u, expenditure minimization leads to compensated demand equations denoted by $h_j(p,u,q)$ and $h_z(p,u,q)$. The ordinary and compensated demand functions are then used to obtain the indirect utility function $V(p,y,q)$ and expenditure function $E(p,u,q)$. Furthermore, the Envelope Theorem allows us to express the marginal utility of income as $V_y(\cdot)=\lambda(p,y,q)$, where $\lambda(\cdot)$ is the Lagrange multiplier from the utility maximization problem. We saw in Chapter 14 that knowledge of $V(\cdot)$ or $E(\cdot)$ allows us to compute the welfare measures suitable for valuing changes in prices p or quantity q. The empirical task when welfare measurement is the objective is therefore to estimate the components of $V(\cdot)$ and/or $E(\cdot)$ that are necessary to compute willingness to pay or willingness to accept, for the price or quantity change of interest.

For this purpose, the identity

$$V\left(p, E(p, u^0, q), q\right) \equiv u^0, \tag{15.1}$$

where u^0 is baseline utility, was found to be critical. For example, differentiating the identity with respect to p_j provides the result that is the basis for much of applied price change welfare analysis:

$$h_j(p, u^0, q) = \frac{\partial E(p, u^0, q)}{\partial p_j} \equiv -\frac{\partial V(p, y, q)/\partial p_j}{\partial V(p, y, q)/\partial y} = x_j(p, y, q). \tag{15.2}$$

At the observed consumption point, compensated and ordinary demands are equal, and they relate to the preference function via Shephard's Lemma and Roy's Identity, respectively. Since utility maximizing behavior generates $x_j(p,y,q)$, observation of this behavior in the form of market outcomes provides a direct window on the consumer's preferences. Estimation of ordinary market demand equations is therefore the applied task.

For the case of changes in the quantity of the quasi-fixed good, differentiating (15.1) with respect to q leads to

$$\pi^q(p, u^0, q) = -\frac{\partial E(p, u^0, q)}{\partial q} \equiv \frac{\partial V(p, y, q)/\partial q}{\partial V(p, y, q)/\partial y} = \theta^q(p, y, q), \tag{15.3}$$

where $\pi^q(\cdot)$ is the compensated inverse demand for q function, and $\theta^q(\cdot)$ is the corresponding uncompensated inverse demand function (see section 14.3 in Chapter 14). As in the price change case, estimation of either $\theta^q(\cdot)$ or $\pi^q(\cdot)$ provides sufficient information about preferences to estimate the welfare impacts of changes in q. This would seem to define the applied task. However, since the quasi-fixed good is not exchanged in markets, there is no directly observable behavior from which an inverse demand function can be estimated. This is the fundamental challenge of welfare measurement for quasi-fixed quantities that we defined in Chapter 14, and there are two general strategies for confronting it: a direct method, and an indirect method.

15.1.1 A Direct Approach

Suppose our objective is to estimate a person's willingness to pay (*WTP*) for an improvement in the level of q from q^0 to q^1. We can define this measurement objective analytically by

$$\begin{aligned} WTP &= \int_{q^0}^{q^1} \pi^q(p, u^0, q)dq \\ &= y - E(p, u^0, q^1), \end{aligned} \tag{15.4}$$

where u^0 is the baseline level of utility for a particular person. One possible route for learning the value of *WTP* is through direct questioning of individuals. To this end, imagine a household survey in which a respondent is first informed about the environmental good in question, and then queried on the value he holds for a well-defined change in the environmental good. Heuristically, questions could be of the form: "*How much would you be willing to pay to have the change?*" or: "*Would you be willing to pay $B to have the change?*" If people answer truthfully with their own well-being in mind, an answer to the former provides a sample of data WTP_i for $i = 1, \ldots, I$, where I is the number of respondents. Responses to the latter question format provide bounds on WTP_i of the form $WTP_i \geq B$ if the person answers "yes", and $WTP_i \leq B$ if the person answers "no". As we discuss later in the book, data of either type are relatively easy to analyze and can provide value estimates for a wide range of environmental goods. Techniques of this type that rely on direct questioning of individuals are known as stated preference (SP) methods. In Chapter 19 we discuss specific SP techniques and their performance in detail.

15.1.2 An Indirect Approach

A second option for measuring WTP as defined by Eq. (15.4) is to infer it indirectly by observing behavior in a related private good market, and estimating demand functions based on this behavior that depend in some way on q. For this we need a plausible assumption on how the private good and the environmental good interact. In general there are three possible assumptions, and the assumption that is chosen conditions the type of model we use and the analysis that is done.

The first possibility is a complementary relation, in which the environmental good is viewed as a quality attribute of one of the private goods, so that a change in q shifts the demand curve for the related private good. In this context the goal is to estimate the demand function for the private good, including the demand response to environmental quality. An example of when the complements assumption is plausible is when x_j is trips to a recreation site, p_j is the price of using the site, and q describes an attribute of the site that affects the recreation experience. Trips to the site and the site's quality are complements in the sense that a higher quality level increases the demand for trips, all else being equal.

The second potential assumption is that the private and environmental goods are substitutes. In this case it is useful to view x_j and q as inputs into the household production of a final consumption commodity, where both x_j and q have positive marginal products, and $H = f(x_j, q)$ describes the technology used to produce H units of the commodity. An example of when the substitutes assumption is plausible is when H is potable water consumed by the household, x_j is units of bottled water, and q reflects the amount of water obtained freely from a public source at a given quality level. In this context, an improvement in public water quality may allow the household to spend less on bottled water, while still maintaining a comparable level of H.

The final possibility is that q is a component of a quality-differentiated market commodity that is defined by a vector of product characteristics, as in Lancaster (1966). In this case the price of the market commodity adjusts with the level of q and the other characteristics. This is an important departure from the complements and substitutes frameworks, where q *does not* affect the purchase price of the related private good. Here, a higher level of q implies a higher price for the bundled commodity, of which it is a component. The housing market provides an example of how environmental quality can be linked to a private purchase in this way. If, for example, homebuyers value access to undeveloped areas that support populations of songbirds, prices of homes that sit in close proximity are likely to be higher, all else being equal. In this case we can describe home values using the hedonic price model, in which property prices are summarized by a function $P(x,q)$. In this context, x denotes everything else that people care about in a residential location (e.g. structure and lot size, commuting distance, local school quality, etc.), and q denotes a measure of distance to the preserved area. Understanding residential home values, in particular the role of q in determining market prices, can in this circumstance inform us about how households value q.

These three structures – complements, substitutes, and quality-differentiated market good models – are the main examples of ways that a private good and an environmental good could be related. Revealed preference (RP) approaches to non-market valuation rely on an assertion that a particular structure holds for the environmental good of interest, and that data with enough variability to estimate behavioral functions for the related private good are available. As such our objective is to formally examine how such an assertion, coupled with additional assumptions and model structure, can be used to link observed consumption of the private good to non-market values for the environmental good. More generally throughout this chapter, we want to explore how specific models and plausible assumptions lead us to behavioral functions that (a) can be estimated with realistically available data; and (b) once estimated, allow us to compute or approximate the welfare measures we are interested in. In their book-length treatment of RP models, Bockstael and McConnell (2007, p.5) nicely summarize our objectives here by noting:

> The essence (of revealed preference) is figuring out what sort of behavior will reveal welfare measures when the levels of (quasi-fixed goods) change. Another way of looking at the problem is to ask what kinds of restrictions on preferences will allow a given type of behavior to reveal these values. Of course, it is always possible to make assumptions about preferences that enable [us] to capture welfare measures from a given behavioral observation. The challenge is not so much the theoretical issue of whether there exists an assumption that will work. Rather, are there plausible and intuitively attractive stories about preferences that provide restrictions leading to the appropriate welfare measures?

It is useful to keep this quote in mind as we explore different model structures and empirical strategies for RP-based non-market valuation.

15.1.3 Why Revealed Preference?

The three possible assumptions described above for relating private and environmental goods give rise to the three main models for revealed preference analysis of non-market values. Each relies on assumptions that may be plausible but are fundamentally not testable. As we will see, the path from estimating the demand for the private good to measuring the value of the non-market good can also be serpentine, and data requirements substantial. In contrast, stated preference methods seem relatively straightforward. Why bother with revealed preference?

The answer lies in the long tradition in economics of basing inference on what people do rather than what they say. This is based on the notion that behavior has consequences. Revealed preference methods have the advantage of being based on behavior that has actually occurred. The person paid for and obtained the product or service, knowing he would have to live with the consequences of his choice. If the person is rational, the opportunity costs of the choice will have been considered, meaning the net benefits of the observed outcome were positive from the decision-maker's perspective. Answers to stated preference questions, in contrast, do not have direct consequences in the sense that there is not a real resource cost of hypothetical commitments. Without the market discipline, it is hard to know a priori if information obtained from surveys reflects actual notions of willingness to pay in particular, and resource trade-offs generally, or if they simply reflect attitudes people have towards the environmental good.

There is a large research agenda dedicated to investigating the extent to which answers to stated preference questions can be used to measure economic values. SP methods and research on their validity will occupy our attention later in the book. For now, it suffices to say that inference based on actual decisions continues to have considerable appeal. Because of this, many analysts prefer a revealed preference approach to valuation when it is feasible and a stated preference approach only when it is not. For this reason, research using revealed preference methods will always have a large role to play in non-market valuation.

15.2 COMPLEMENTS

We begin by considering the case when it is plausible to assume that the quasi-fixed good is a quality attribute of the private good. The leading example of this is in recreation, where environmental conditions at a destination affect the experience one has when visiting. In this context the private good is trips to a site, and the demand for trips is conditional on – i.e. shifts with – characteristics of the site. Our objective in this section is to derive the complements model, and to examine the conditions that are needed to link consumption of the private complement to theoretically appropriate measures of value for the environmental good.

To simplify our discussion, we assume for now that the private good x is a scalar, and that x and q are the complementary goods. It is useful to first consider expenditure minimization. An individual's compensated demand function for the private good is $h(p,u,q)$, where changes in q shift the demand curve. Suppose we are interested in measuring the willingness to pay for an increase in q from q^0 to q^1, which by definition is the difference in expenditure functions $CV = E(p,u^0,q^0) - E(p,u^0,q^1)$, where u^0 is the initial utility level. Since the change in q shifts out the compensated demand function from $h(p,u,q^0)$ to $h(p,u,q^1)$, a candidate measure of compensating variation is the change in the area behind the compensated demand curve resulting from the change in q. This is given by

$$a = \int_{p^0}^{\bar{p}(q^1)} h(p,u^0,q^1)dp - \int_{p^0}^{\bar{p}(q^0)} h(p,u^0,q^0)dp, \tag{15.5}$$

where p^0 is the price the person faces for the private good, $\bar{p}(q_1)$ is the price that would drive demand for the good to zero when $q = q^1$, and $\bar{p}(q_0)$ is the corresponding price for $q = q^0$. These latter prices are commonly referred to as "choke prices", and they generally depend on the specific value for q. To explore when this expression is equal to CV we examine the following proposition.

Proposition 15.1
If the condition

$$E\left[\bar{p}(q^1), u^0, q^1\right] - E\left[\bar{p}(q^0), u^0, q^0\right] = 0 \tag{15.6}$$

holds, then $a = CV$.

Showing that (15.6) implies $a = CV$ involves evaluating the definite integrals in (15.5) to obtain

$$
\begin{aligned}
a &= \left\{E\left[\bar{p}(q^1), u^0, q^1\right] - E\left[p^0, u^0, q^1\right]\right\} - \left\{E\left[\bar{p}(q^0), u^0, q^0\right] - E\left[p^0, u^0, q^0\right]\right\} \\
&= \left\{E\left[p^0, u^0, q^0\right] - E\left[p^0, u^0, q^1\right]\right\} \\
&\quad + \left\{E\left[\bar{p}(q^1), u^0, q^1\right] - E\left[\bar{p}(q^0), u^0, q^0\right]\right\}.
\end{aligned}
\tag{15.7}
$$

From this we can see that the last term in brackets needs to be zero for the quantity a to match the definition of CV.

Proposition 15.1 shows that under some (but not all) conditions, the change in the area behind the compensated demand curve is a theoretically valid measure of the compensating variation for a change in q. To interpret when the conditions are likely to hold, note that Eq. (15.6) says that if the private good is not consumed because its purchase price is at or above the choke price, then changes in q do not affect the expenditure needed to reach utility level u^0. In this case, q is said to have only *use value*, because its value is derived solely from its role in generating the utility provided by the consumption (or use) of the private good. Thus absent use of the private good, the environmental attribute q has no value. Continuing the recreation example, the stock of fish at a lake has only use value if its size matters to an angler only if he fishes at the lake. This seems intuitive for many otherwise unremarkable angling destinations. Less plausible is the notion that a person values the bison population at a unique site such as Yellowstone Nation Park only if he visits the park to view them. We might in this case suppose that Yellowstone's bison provide more than use value, and Eq. (15.6) is unlikely to hold. Assuming that q has only use value implies a restriction on preferences as described in the following definition.

Definition 15.1
Suppose that an individual's preference function is such that (a) x is non-essential, and (b)

$$\frac{\partial U(0, z, q)}{\partial q} = 0 \quad \leftrightarrow \quad U(0, z, q^1) = U(0, z, q^0).$$

Then x and q are said to be weak complements, *and the preference function exhibits the property of* weak complementarity. *The concept of weak complementarity was introduced by Mäler (1974).*

Formally, a good is non-essential when there is a choke price $\bar{p}(q^0)$, which in turn implies that

$$\int_{p^0}^{\bar{p}(q^0)} h(p, u^0, q^0) dp \tag{15.8}$$

is also finite. In words, non-essentiality of x means there is a finite amount of compensation that the person would accept for its elimination; it also means the optimal choice of x can be zero. This is sensible for most private goods, particularly if they are defined with enough specificity, since the ability to compensate is based on the presence of substitutes. The second condition is more critical, and has an intuitive interpretation. If $x=0$, then changes in q result in no change in utility, so the person's well-being can only be impacted by q when $x>0$. Equivalently, the person's utility level is the same regardless of the level of q if $x=0$. This is consistent with the notion of use value that we described above.

The top panel of Figure 15.1 illustrates a single indifference curve when weak complementarity holds. Smith and Banzhaf (2004) use this diagram to show how the non-essentiality of x implies the indifference curves must intersect the vertical axis, and how the different levels of q for a constant level of utility u^0 cause a fan-shaped indifference map, which lies in a single indifference hyper-plane. In the diagram $q^0 < q^1 < q^2$, and each segment of the fan is associated with a particular level of q. For $x>0$, each segment traces out the amounts of x and z that maintain utility u^0, conditional on the particular level of q. A change in q causes a change in the relevant segment; higher levels of q are associated with the lower segments of the fan, since as q increases less x and/or z are needed to maintain u^0. This becomes more apparent when we add a price line for the private good, labeled p^0. We have specified the price of x so that, at the reference point $q=q^0$ and $p=p^0$, none of the private good is consumed when utility is held fixed at u^0. As q increases and price stays fixed, less income is needed to maintain the utility level and consumption of the weak complement – the private good x – increases. Based on this we are able to define *WTP* for a change in q using the reduction in z that maintains utility. The lower panel shows the three compensated demand curves, all for utility level u^0 but at different levels of q. The initial curve $h(p, u^0, q^0)$ has a choke price $\bar{p}(q^0)$, and so we see again that at the reference point (p^0, q^0), none of the private good is consumed. An increase in q to q^1 or q^2 shifts the compensated demand curve to $h(p, u^0, q^1)$ or $h(p, u^0, q^2)$, respectively. Given weak complementarity, we can define the *WTP* for the increase in q as the change in the area under the demand curve and above the reference price. For the change from q^0 to q^1 this is shown as area a, and for q^0 to q^2 it is area $a+b$. These areas correspond directly to the measures of *WTP* shown along the vertical axis in the top panel.

15.2.1 Ordinary Demand Functions

We now turn our attention to utility maximization. Though our discussion of weak complementarity has thus far relied on compensated demand curves, it is ordinary demand

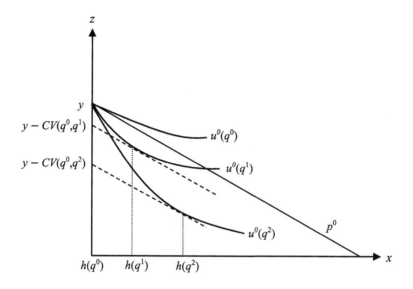

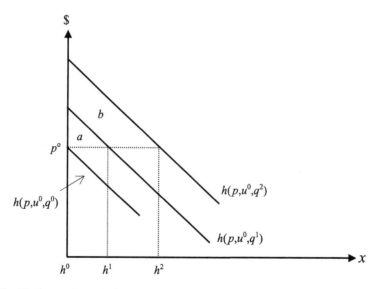

Figure 15.1   Weak complementarity

curves that we are able to directly estimate. In this subsection we examine the connection between the observable outcome of utility maximization on one hand, and the
welfare measure defined above on the other, where the latter depends on unobservable
expenditure minimization.

We have seen that if q has only use value (i.e. if weak complementarity holds), then

$$CV = \int_{q^0}^{q^1} \pi^q(p,u^0,q)dq = E(p,u^0,q^0) - E(p,u^0,q^1)$$

$$= \int_{p^0}^{\bar{p}(q_1)} h(p,u^0,q^1)dp - \int_{p^0}^{\bar{p}(q_0)} h(p,u^0,q^0)dp.$$

(15.9)

However, unless there are no income effects, in which case ordinary and compensated demands are the same, this expression is not of operational value. Instead, we are likely to estimate an ordinary demand function $x(p,y,q)$. With an estimate of $x(\cdot)$ in hand, we can readily compute the expression

$$c = \int_{p^0}^{\tilde{p}(q_1)} x(p,y,q^1)dp - \int_{p^0}^{\tilde{p}(q_0)} x(p,y,q^0)dp, \qquad (15.10)$$

where $\tilde{p}(\cdot)$ is the ordinary demand choke price for the private good x, and in general it is the case that $\tilde{p}(\cdot) \neq \bar{p}(\cdot)$. A natural question for applied welfare analysis is the extent to which the observable measure c given in (15.10) is a good approximation for the preferred measure CV in (15.9). The bounding arguments from Willig (1976) and Randall and Stoll (1980) that were discussed in Chapter 14 would seem to suggest that c is a good approximation – i.e. it is bounded in predictable ways by the theoretically appropriate CV and EV measures. However, due to some important subtleties, this turns out not to be the case.

The failure of the standard bounding argument is best seen from Figure 15.2, which is based on Bockstael and McConnell (1993, 2007). Note that at the original point of consumption x^0 with price p^0, the ordinary and compensated demand equations intersect, as is implied by the familiar identity

$$h(p^0,u^0,q) \equiv x\left(p^0, E(p^0,u^0,q),q\right). \qquad (15.11)$$

However, the shifts in $x(\cdot)$ and $h(\cdot)$ due to the change in q need not in general be the same size, so $x(p^0,y,q^1) \neq h(p^0,u^0,q^1)$. We can see this by differentiating (15.11) with respect to q, resulting in

$$\begin{aligned}
\frac{\partial h(p^0,u^0,q)}{\partial q} &\equiv \frac{\partial x(p^0,y,q)}{\partial q} + \frac{\partial x(p^0,y,q)}{\partial y} \times \frac{\partial E(p^0,u^0,q)}{\partial q} \\
&\equiv \frac{\partial x(p^0,y,q)}{\partial q} - \frac{\partial x(p^0,y,q)}{\partial y} \times \pi^q.
\end{aligned} \qquad (15.12)$$

From this Slutsky-like relationship it is clear that the compensated and ordinary demand derivatives with respect to q differ by an income effect. If the private good is normal, so that its income derivative is positive, the compensated demand response to a change in q is smaller than the ordinary demand response. This is the case that we have shown in Figure 15.2, where $x^1 > h^1$. Importantly, note that CV (area $d+e$) and c (area $b+d+f$) are indeterminate in their comparative magnitudes, and so we cannot say anything about the relationship between the two measures in general. This is in contrast to the private good price change case examined in Chapter 14, where we saw that the change in consumer surplus is predictably bounded by the compensating and equivalent variation measures. Therefore, for changes in the quasi-fixed good q, the quantity in Eq. (15.10) is not a useful approximation from an applied welfare standpoint, without further restrictions. To make it useful, additional structure needs to be added to the problem.

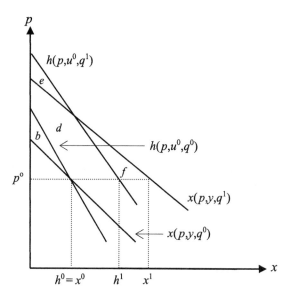

Figure 15.2   Ordinary vs. compensated demands

To explore the structure that is needed, recall from Chapter 14 (Figure 14.2 in particular) that the area under the ordinary inverse demand for q curve is a good approximation for the *WTP* for a change in q. Specifically,

$$C = \int_{q^0}^{q^1} \theta^q(p, y, q)dq = \int_{q^0}^{q^1} \frac{\partial V(p, y, q)/\partial q}{\partial V(p, y, q)/\partial y} \, dq \tag{15.13}$$

is related in predictable ways to the compensating and equivalent variation for a change in the quasi-fixed good. This is of little use directly, since we are not able to estimate $\theta^q(\cdot)$ nor compute C from observed behavior. However, if c from (15.10) is equal to the area under the ordinary inverse demand function in (15.13), then C in the latter can be indirectly computed from observed behavior using the former. The condition that is needed is summarized in the following proposition and subsequent discussion.

Proposition 15.2

If the preference function V(p,y,q) is such that the income elasticity of demand for x is equal to the income elasticity of the ordinary inverse demand for q, which is to say that

$$\eta \equiv \frac{\partial x(\cdot)}{\partial y} \frac{y}{x(\cdot)} = \frac{\partial \theta^q(\cdot)}{\partial y} \frac{y}{\theta^q(\cdot)} \equiv \xi, \tag{15.14}$$

then c = C as given in equations (15.10) and (15.13).

We provide a derivation of this result in appendix A. The proposition shows that for the expression in (15.10) to be useful for applied welfare analysis, we need to maintain an assumption regarding how income affects both the demand for x and the marginal willingness to pay for q. This has two ramifications. First, we are not able to independently investigate how the willingness to pay for q responds to income changes, since this effect is tied directly to the private good. Second (and related to this), our discussion of Hanemann's explanation for the *WTA/WTP* gap in Chapter 14 showed that ξ consists of two components: a pure income effect, and an effect that reflects the substitutability between q and spending on market goods generally. Specifically, we found that $\xi = \eta_q/\sigma_{qy}$, where η_q is the income elasticity of demand for q, and σ_{qy} is the Allen-Uzawa elasticity of substitution between q and spending on market goods. Thus, by restricting $\eta = \xi$ we are also implicitly restricting how much (or how little) substitutability exists between q and income. For applications when q is not particularly unique (such as when it is a recreation site attribute with wide availability) we might expect that $\sigma_{qy} \approx 1$ so that $\eta \approx \eta_q$, implying (15.14) is quite sensible.

The form in which we have expressed the restriction in (15.14) is due to Palmquist (2005a), who uses it to illustrate the intuition of a restriction referred to more generally by Bockstael and McConnell (1993) as the "Willig condition". The Willig condition is so named based on an influential paper from Willig (1978) that examines how demand equations can be specified to include quality attributes, and how quality changes can be measured as price change equivalents. In applications of the complements model, the Willig condition serves as a restriction that makes integrating over price changes as in (15.10) equivalent to integrating over quality changes as in (15.13), thereby allowing us to rely on ordinary demand functions to approximate the theoretically preferred welfare measures. As we show in the next subsection, Willig (1978) is also useful for the practical task of specifying demand equations and preferences functions that are consistent with weak complementarity.

15.2.2 Specifying Ordinary Demand Equations

In this subsection we close our discussion of the complements model by examining how estimable demand equations need to be specified, when recovery of a preference function exhibiting weak complementarity is the objective. As we will see, there is a close correspondence between the restrictions that are needed for exact welfare analysis using the indirect utility function, and approximate welfare analysis using ordinary demand functions.

In a general sense, neoclassical theory provides results that guide how prices and income should be related to quantity in empirical demand equations, and how both should enter preference functions generally. The theory is silent on how quality (and non-price attributes generally) should enter the specification. Absent theory, intuition has been the primary tool for deciding how to include quality variables in an empirical specification, and we have seen that weak complementarity is often a plausible starting point. Given this, researchers have investigated several ways that weak complementarity can be incorporated into standard demand and preference specifications. The most useful for applied work is the "repackaging" approach, whereby we fold quality effects into price effects, so that demand is specified as a function of a quality-adjusted price. In what follows, we describe repackaging generally and then illustrate with an example.

Repackaging involves redefining the utility-generating commodity to be a function of both x and q, so that the private good is "repackaged" in a way that functionally binds it to q. Two types of repackaging approaches are commonly used in empirical work: simple and cross-product. Simple repackaging involves augmenting a general utility function so that the maximization problem takes the form

$$\max_{x,z} U\left(x \cdot \delta(q), z\right) \quad s.t. \quad y = px + z, \tag{15.15}$$

where in this example, x and q are scalars, and $\delta(q)$ is a strictly positive function of q, which falls out of $U(\cdot)$ when $x = 0$, so that the specification is consistent with weak complementarity. Note that the utility-generating argument in the utility function is $x \cdot \delta(q)$ rather than x alone – i.e. we have functionally combined q and x into a reconstituted, or repackaged, commodity.

By writing out the first-order conditions with respect to x and z, substituting out for z using the budget constraint, and rearranging, we arrive at the following behavior-generating expression:

$$\frac{\partial U\left(x \cdot \delta(q), y - \dfrac{p}{\delta(q)} \delta(q) \cdot x\right)\Big/\partial x}{\partial U\left(x \cdot \delta(q), y - \dfrac{p}{\delta(q)} \delta(q) \cdot x\right)\Big/\partial z} = \frac{p}{\delta(q)}. \tag{15.16}$$

From this first-order condition we can solve for the ordinary demand function $x \cdot \delta(q) = g\left(p / \delta(q), y\right)$, or equivalently $x = g\left(p / \delta(q), y\right) / \delta(q)$, where the structure of $g(\cdot)$ is inherited from $U(\cdot)$. Thus, under simple repackaging, the quality-adjusted price is given by $p/\delta(q)$. From a practical point of view, simple repackaging folds the quality effect into the price effect – i.e. we have made quality act as a price modifier.

Under cross-product repackaging, a standard utility function is augmented so that the maximization problem reads

$$\max_{x,z} U\left(x, z + x \cdot \delta(q)\right) \quad s.t. \quad y = px + z, \tag{15.17}$$

where $\delta(q)$ is once again a strictly positive function of q. Note that when $x = 0$, q falls out of $U(\cdot)$, and so (15.17) is consistent with weak complementarity. By substituting out for z using the budget constraint, we can rewrite the maximization problem as

$$\max_{x} U\left(x, y - \left(p - \delta(q)\right)x\right), \tag{15.18}$$

which immediately shows the specific way that quality is folded into price under cross-product repackaging.

Moving forward with the first-order conditions, the behavior-generating expression implied by cross-product repackaging is

$$\frac{\partial U\left(x, y - \left[p - \delta(q)\right] \cdot x\right)\Big/\partial x}{\partial U\left(x, y - \left[p - \delta(q)\right] \cdot x\right)\Big/\partial z} = p - \delta(q). \tag{15.19}$$

Solving for x leads to a demand equation of the form $x = g\left(p - \delta(q), y\right)$, and substitution into $U(\cdot)$ implies an indirect utility function of the form $V\left(p - \delta(q), y\right)$. The structure of the ordinary demand and indirect utility functions suggests we should interpret $p - \delta(q)$ as a quality-adjusted price. By repackaging x according to (15.18), we have once again folded the role of quality into the price term.

Using either simple or cross-product repackaging, we can start with any familiar utility or demand function and add a quality effect by including $\delta(q)$ in the specification. In most instances cross-product repackaging is the more plausible from a behavioral perspective. Note, for example, that under simple repackaging the person is indifferent between an equal scaling of x or $\delta(q)$, since the two terms are multiplicative in the utility function. If x is trips to a hiking area and q is visibility at the vistas, this means there is a proportional relationship between utility generated via more trips or better visibility. In contrast, under cross-product repackaging an increase in q causes the price of a hike to be smaller in quality-adjusted terms without rescaling the way that a trip generates utility. Thus in most instances, it will be preferable to estimate demand equations that use the cross-product repackaging approach for including quality in the specification.

EXAMPLE 15.1 (ANALYTICAL/NUMERICAL) As an example of how we might use cross-product repackaging, consider the log-linear demand equation augmented to include quality

$$
\begin{aligned}
\ln x &= \alpha + \beta p + \theta q + \gamma y \\
&= \alpha + \beta\left(p + \frac{\theta}{\beta}q\right) + \gamma y,
\end{aligned}
\tag{15.20}
$$

where $(\alpha, \beta, \theta, \gamma)$ are parameters to be estimated. Note that this specification is consistent with cross-product repackaging, where $\delta(q) = (-\theta/\beta) \cdot q$. In Chapter 14 we examined this demand specification in the context of "integrating back" to obtain an indirect utility function. With q included as a price modifier, the same logic applies for deriving an indirect utility function that is consistent with (15.20). In particular, one can show that

$$
V(p, y, q) = \frac{\exp(-\gamma y)}{\gamma} + \frac{\exp(\alpha + \beta p + \theta q)}{\beta}.
\tag{15.21}
$$

This illustrates a specific example of the point that we made at the outset. Cross-product (and simple) repackaging involve folding quality effects into price effects, or said another way, specifying demand as a function of a quality-adjusted price. When this is done, the welfare effects of quality changes can be analyzed as if they were price changes, and all the tools we developed for price-change welfare analysis in Chapter 14 are applicable. This is an important point, and a notable advantage of the two repackaging strategies. It does not come without a cost, however. In exercise 15.2 we outline how to show that $V(p,y,q)$ in (15.21) is consistent with the Willig condition in (15.14). More generally, specifications that use simple and cross-product repackaging impose the Willig condition by construction, thereby restricting income effects in the way described in the previous subsection.

15.2.3 Application Preview

By way of summary, the complements model is appropriate when: (a) the quasi-fixed good can be interpreted as a quality attribute of a private good, (b) quality does not affect the price of the private good, and (c) there is only use value associated with the quasi-fixed good. In situations where we can argue that these conditions are reasonable, weak complementarity and the Willig condition provide the analytical structure that is needed to link ordinary demand curve estimates to exact or approximate welfare measures. From there the problem becomes one of econometrics and data availability. As we have alluded to, recreation behavior is an area that fits the assumptions of the complements model, and it is likely to generate outcomes with enough variability to estimate the demand functions that are needed. Thus while the complements model is general, easily its most important use is in examining the interaction between outdoor recreation and the environment.

There is a large empirical literature devoted to studying the demand for recreation visits, how environmental conditions at recreation destinations affect the demand, and the welfare consequences of changes in environmental conditions. Most of this literature uses survey data on visits individuals have made to particular destinations to estimate demand functions for trips. Because access to recreation sites is usually free or involves only a nominal fee, the cost of visiting a site is not a market price in the usual sense. Instead, the price of a visit is implicit, and it is based on the person's cost of getting to the site (travel expenses) and the value of time he must spend in transit (opportunity cost of time). Thus trip demand is a function of travel costs – the money and time costs of travel – and the attributes of the recreation site. Since the price of a recreation visit is non-market, it is not related in an equilibrium sense to the environmental attributes of the site. Thus recreation fits well with the complements model: trips to a recreation site are non-essential, we can argue that environmental conditions at a site (the quasi-fixed good) provide mainly use value via site visits, and quality levels at the site are independent of the price of a trip (the private good). The applied task is to use data on people's past recreation trips, travel costs, and measured site quality to estimate demand equations for site visits. The equations are then used to recover a sufficient component of preferences to measure the welfare effects of access to recreation sites and/or changes in the environmental conditions at the sites. In Chapter 17, we discuss specific ways of using recreation data to estimate environmental values, focusing on conceptual, econometric, and applied topics.

15.3 SUBSTITUTES

In this section we consider situations in which we can view the private and environmental goods as intermediary inputs into the production of a final consumption good. A few examples help motivate our discussion. The health status of an individual with asthma is determined in part by private interventions such as medication and inhaler use, as well as ambient air quality. Health is what the person cares about, and medicine and air quality are intermediate to the final health outcome. As a second example, households consume potable water as a final commodity, but the way in which it is obtained can depend on private inputs such as filtration devices or bottled water, as well as the quality of water from a public source. Subsistence fishing in a developing country context is a final example. When the utility-generating commodity is fish caught for consumption, both fishing trips (more trips lead to more fish) and fish stock at the destination (a higher stock implies more fish on a given trip) matter for the final outcome. In each of these cases, we can imagine there is a "production technology" that maps quantities of the "inputs" into units of the final consumption "commodity". When the environmental good of interest can be cast in this framework, the household production model is a useful organizing principle. In what follows, we examine the household production model with the goal of understanding when estimates of the private input demand and/or the household production technology can be used to estimate non-market values for the quasi-fixed good.

15.3.1 Technology and Behavior

We begin by describing the production technology. Consider a production function $H = f(x,q)$ that relates units of a private good x and a quasi-fixed environmental good q to a final consumption commodity H. In what follows we will continue to think of x as a scalar for simplicity of explanation. In this setup, we assume that both x and q have positive marginal product, so that $f_x(\cdot) > 0$ and $f_q(\cdot) > 0$. It is in this sense that x and q are substitutes, since an increase in H can be brought about by an increase in either input. The sign of $f_{xq}(\cdot)$, however, depends on the specific application. In the subsistence fishing example it is likely that $f_{xq}(\cdot) > 0$, since the addition to total catch from a given fishing trip is likely to be higher when the fish stock is larger. For the drinking-water example, when x is a private filtration device it seems likely that $f_{qx}(\cdot) < 0$. If q is high, the marginal contribution of the filtration device to drinking-water quality is likely to be small. Finally, it may be that $f_{xq}(\cdot) = 0$, which is a special case that we examine below.

As in a standard firm problem, we can summarize the production technology by deriving a cost function. Specifically, the minimum cost to the household of obtaining a particular level of H given technology, the price of x, and the level of q is

$$C(p,q,H) = \min_{x} \left\{ px + \mu \left[H - f(x,q) \right] \right\}. \tag{15.22}$$

We can use the cost function to describe actual behavior. In the household production framework, an individual chooses x and z according to

$$\max_{x,z} U(H,z) \quad s.t. \quad y = C(p,q,H) + z, \quad H = f(x,q). \tag{15.23}$$

Note two important assumptions that are implicit in (15.23). First, by substituting the cost function into the budget constraint we have assumed cost-minimizing behavior on the part of the household as regards the production of H. This is relatively innocuous. More importantly, we have assumed that q and x enter utility only through their effect on H, which rules out any "side benefits" of x or q.

The solution to (15.23) provides ordinary demand functions $x(p,y,q)$ and $z(p,y,q)$, and substitution of $x(\cdot)$ into $f(\cdot)$ allows us to state the implied level of the produced commodity as

$$H(p, y, q) = f\big(x(p, y, q), q\big). \tag{15.24}$$

These are observable outcomes in the sense that utility maximizing behavior generates their quantities, and we can in principle measure the demand level x, and the variables p, y, and q. With appropriate data and econometric methods, $x(\cdot)$, $f(\cdot)$, and $C(\cdot)$ are therefore potentially estimable functions.

For welfare measurement it is useful to also derive the expenditure function, which can be usefully stated in two equivalent forms. The first is

$$E(p, u, q) = \min_{H,z} \big\{C(p, q, H) + z \quad s.t. \quad U(H, z) = u\big\}, \tag{15.25}$$

the solution to which provides compensated demand functions for H and z. We denote these $h_H(p,u,q)$ and $h_z(p,u,q)$. Note that two distinct minimization problems are implicit in (15.25): cost minimization that initially produces $C(\cdot)$, and expenditure minimization that subsequently produces $E(\cdot)$. The second way of stating the problem combines these in a single step as

$$E(p, u, q) = \min_{x,z} \big\{xp + z \quad s.t. \quad U(H, z) = u, \quad H = f(x, q)\big\}, \tag{15.26}$$

which leads to an explicit compensated demand function for the private input, denoted $h(p,u,q)$. Since $h(p,u,q)$, $h_H(p,u,q)$ and $h_z(p,u,q)$ are all based on expenditure minimization, they are not in general quantities that we observe in the data.

For welfare analysis, our interest centers on the extent to which the behavior generated by (15.23) and the technology imbedded in $f(\cdot)$ and $C(\cdot)$ are useful for measuring the value of marginal or discrete changes in q. In this sense our objective is to measure

$$CV = E(p, u^0, q^0) - E(p, u^0, q^1), \tag{15.27}$$

where u^0 is the baseline utility level and q^0 and q^1 are the initial and changed levels of q. What can we say about CV from estimation of $x(p,y,q)$, $f(x,q)$ and/or $C(p,q,H)$?

Consider first marginal changes. Note that the Envelope Theorem applied to (15.25) implies

$$MWTP = -\frac{\partial E(p, u, q)}{\partial q} = -\frac{\partial C(p, q, H)}{\partial q} \tag{15.28}$$

for a fixed level of H. Likewise, from (15.22) we obtain $\partial C(x,q)/\partial q = -\mu \cdot \partial f(x,q)/\partial q$, and the first-order conditions for cost minimization imply $p = \mu \cdot \partial f(x,q)/\partial x$. Combining these two results allows us to also express the marginal willingness to pay as

$$-\frac{\partial C(p,q,H)}{\partial q} = p\frac{\partial f(\cdot)/\partial q}{\partial f(\cdot)/\partial x}. \tag{15.29}$$

We can add to this by differentiating (15.24) with respect to q while holding H fixed, so that

$$0 = \frac{\partial f(\cdot)}{\partial q} + \frac{\partial f(\cdot)}{\partial x}\frac{\partial x(\cdot)}{\partial q}, \tag{15.30}$$

which can be rearranged to obtain

$$-p\frac{\partial x(\cdot)}{\partial q} = p\frac{\partial f(\cdot)/\partial q}{\partial f(\cdot)/\partial x}. \tag{15.31}$$

We see that the marginal willingness to pay for q can be computed using the cost function as in (15.28), the production technology as in (15.29), or by using the input demand function for x as given by the left-hand side of (15.31). Thus for small changes in q that hold utility and H fixed we can use estimates of technology, costs, or private good behavior to compute welfare measures.

Consider next values for non-marginal changes in q. Estimates of $x(p,y,q)$ and $C(p,q,H)$ allow computation of two quantities that are useful building blocks for discrete change welfare analysis. These are given in the following two definitions.

Definition 15.2
Given the ordinary demand function $x(p,y,q)$, the actual savings (AS) in spending on the private input x resulting from a change in q from q^0 to q^1 is

$$AS = C(p,q^0,H^0) - C(p,q^1,H^1) = p\left[x(p,y,q^0) - x(p,y,q^1)\right]. \tag{15.32}$$

Note that AS is the change in spending on x from a change in q that has occurred, or the predicted change in spending from a hypothetical change in q. As we discuss below, its sign is formally indeterminate, though intuitively we might expect that $AS>0$ when q increases and $AS<0$ when q falls. In either case, this measures a behavioral response to the change in q.

Definition 15.3
Given the cost function $C(p,q,H)$, the potential savings (PS) in spending on the private input following a change in q from q^0 to q^1 is

$$PS = C(p,q^0,H^0) - C(p,q^1,H^0), \tag{15.33}$$

which is the change in spending that holds H constant at its original level, following the change in q.

Note that $PS>0$ when q increases, and $PS<0$ when q falls. PS is not a quantity generated by a behavioral response. Rather, it is a technical relationship based on the cost function, which can be computed without knowing anything about the person's actual preference function or input demand equation.

From their definitions it is apparent that neither *AS* nor *PS* is equal to *CV* for a discrete change in *q*, as defined by (15.27). For *AS*, note that $x(p,y,q^0)$ and $x(p,y,q^1)$ summarize the individual's utility maximizing behavior before and after a change in *q*, and therefore reflect different final levels of *H* and different utility levels. *AS* computed using $x(\cdot)$ imbeds re-optimization to a new utility level, and therefore by construction cannot be equal to a compensated, utility-constant welfare measure. At the other extreme, *PS* cannot be a measure of welfare because it does not reflect a behavioral measure, compensated or otherwise. This illustrates a general point, which is that the substitutes model as presented thus far does not provide a direct link between estimable functions and the theoretically appropriate welfare measures. Nonetheless, given additional assumptions that are reasonable in many cases, such a link can be made. In cases when the additional assumptions are not tenable, bounding results that depend on *PS* and *AS* are available that allow us to approximate the welfare measures. In what follows, we first discuss the assumptions allowing exact welfare analysis, and then turn our attention to the bounding results.

15.3.2 Exact Welfare Measures

There are two instances in which it is possible to compute or approximate exact welfare measures using estimates of $x(p,y,q)$ and/or $C(p,q,H)$. For both a restriction on technology needs to be maintained. The possibilities include assuming *x* is an essential input into the production of *H*, or assuming $f(x,q)$ is separable in its inputs.

Consider first the case when *x* is an essential input. Formally this means that $f(0,q)=0$, so that consumption of the produced commodity *H* must be zero when *x* is not purchased. That is, when $x=0$ the utility function $U(H,z)$ becomes $U(0,z)$, implying the environmental good does not enter utility, and so changes in *q* do not matter. Note that the consequence of *x* being essential in the production of *H* is similar to weak complementarity, in that *q* does not affect utility unless $x>0$. Here, however, the restriction operates through technology rather than preferences. Nonetheless, the assumption that *x* is an essential input is useful in the same way that weak complementarity was in the complements model, since it allows us to compute welfare measures by looking at the change in the area behind the demand curve for the purchased input.

To see this, we use the version of the expenditure function given in (15.26). Note that Shephard's Lemma implies $\partial E(p,u,q)/\partial p = h(p,u,q)$. By an argument identical to what we used for proposition 15.1, the fact that *x* is an essential input implies the welfare measure for an increase in *q* from q^0 to q^1 is

$$CV = \int_{p^0}^{\bar{p}(q^1)} h(p,u^0,q^1)dp - \int_{p^0}^{\bar{p}(q^0)} h(p,u^0,q^0)dp, \tag{15.34}$$

where $\bar{p}(q^0)$ and $\bar{p}(q^1)$ are the choke prices that cause the purchase of the essential input to be zero, and p^0 is the market price of the private input. We can see that this is the case by writing out the definite integral, similar to how we did in the complements case:

$$CV = \int_{p^0}^{\bar{p}(q^1)} h(p,u^0,q^1)dp - \int_{p^0}^{\bar{p}(q^0)} h(p,u^0,q^0)dp$$

$$= \left\{ E\left[\bar{p}(q^1),u^0,q^1\right] - E\left[p^0,u^0,q^1\right] \right\} - \left\{ E\left[\bar{p}(q^0),u^0,q^0\right] - E\left[p^0,u^0,q^0\right] \right\}.$$

(15.35)

Recall by definition of the choke price that

$$h\left(\bar{p}(q^1),u^0,q^1\right) = h\left(\bar{p}(q^0),u^0,q^0\right) = 0, \tag{15.36}$$

and that, because x is assumed to be an essential input into the production of the home produced commodity, we have $H=0$ at both choke prices $\bar{p}(q^0)$ and $\bar{p}(q^1)$. With $H=0$ in both cases, the expenditure needed to reach the reference utility level is the same, regardless of the level of q. More formally, we have $E\left[\bar{p}(q^1),u^0,q^1\right] - E\left[\bar{p}(q^0),u^0,q^1\right] = 0$. Making this substitution into (15.35), we see that the essential input assumption implies that the change in the area behind the compensated demand curve for the private input is equivalent to $CV = E(p^0,u^0,q^0) - E(p^0,u^0,q^1)$.

Since the level of q matters only insofar as it affects the production of H, changes in q do not affect the expenditure needed to reach u^0 when $x=0$ (and $H=0$). Thus knowledge of $h(p,u,q)$ allows us to exactly compute CV, while an estimate of the observable function $x(p,y,q)$ allows us to approximate CV using the change in consumer surplus, as we discussed in the complements case in section 15.2.1.

Consider now the case when the production function for H is separable in x and q, so that $f_{xq}(\cdot)=0$. For illustration, recall the example in which H is drinking water, x is units of bottled water and q measures the volume of publicly provided potable water available to the household per unit of time. In this case, x and q are perfect substitutes, and we could express the production technology as $f(x,q)=x+q$. With this, the cost function is derived according to

$$\min_{x} px + \mu(H - x - q), \tag{15.37}$$

and assuming an interior solution, the first-order conditions can be expressed as $p=\mu$ and $x=H-q$. Note that the cost function in this special case is therefore $C(p,q,H)=p\cdot(H-q)$, the form of which provides notable advantages when the objective is to measure the non-market value of q. Specifically, for this technology, the budget constraint in (15.23) becomes $y=p\cdot(H-q)+z$, and the problem can be written as

$$\max_{x,z} U(f(x,q),z) \quad s.t. \quad y + p\cdot q = p\cdot f(x,q) + z. \tag{15.38}$$

This makes clear that $p\cdot q$ acts as an income modifier, so that $\tilde{y}=y+p\cdot q$ is the effective income level, with the restriction that the augmentation $p\cdot q$ must be spent on H. Recall that the willingness to pay for an increase or decrease in income is simply the amount by which income changes. Thus for this special case, the amount $p \cdot (q^1 - q^0)$ is the effective change in income from a change in q, and is therefore the willingness to pay for the change. Note that only knowledge of $C(\cdot)$ is needed to compute the welfare measure in this special case.

15.3.3 Bounding Results

Assumptions on technology as given above are plausible in some cases, but not others. In the example when H is fish caught for subsistence consumption, it makes sense to assume that the private input – fishing trips – is essential. In other cases, such as when H is a health outcome and x is a medical service, this is less clear. Similarly, separable production technologies are likely to be the exception rather than the norm. To complete our discussion of the empirical usefulness of the substitutes model, it is therefore necessary to develop welfare bounds, which can be used in a wider range of situations. We first focus on the usefulness of PS, as summarized in the following proposition.

Proposition 15.3
Suppose we have an estimate of $C(p,q,H)$, and that H^0 denotes the choice of H at the initial level of the environmental good q^0. The quantity $PS = C(p,q^0,H^0) - C(p,q^1,H^0)$ is related to the welfare measure $CV = E(p,u^0,q^0) - E(p,u^0,q^1)$ according to

$$
\begin{aligned}
0 \leq PS \leq CV, \quad q^1 > q^0, \\
0 \geq CV \geq PS, \quad q^1 < q^0.
\end{aligned}
\tag{15.39}
$$

The proof of this proposition is given in appendix B, and the basic result is drawn from Bockstael and McConnell (2007). Note from the proposition that when q increases, PS is positive since less spending on x is needed to maintain H^0. In this case, PS is a lower bound on the willingness to pay (welfare gain) for the change in q. Correspondingly, when q decreases, PS is negative, since more spending on x is needed to maintain H^0. Since it is more negative than CV, in this case PS is an upper bound on the willingness to accept (welfare loss) for the change in q. These bounds are general in the sense that they do not depend on particular assumptions about technology. They are also independent of preferences and behavior, and therefore can be computed using only an estimate of $C(p,q,H)$. However, the applied usefulness of the two statements in (15.39) is asymmetric. For an increase in q, PS has empirical relevance as a lower bound on gains, since if it is greater than zero, evidence exists that there is a positive welfare effect from the change. In contrast, PS as an upper bound on loss in the case of a decline in q is less relevant, since a zero or small *WTA* value cannot be ruled out from its observation. Given this, we might ask if our bounding results can be improved by considering the role of *AS*.

To examine this, note first that

$$
\begin{aligned}
AS - PS &= \left\{ C(p,q^0,H^0) - C(p,q^1,H^1) \right\} - \left\{ C(p,q^0,H^0) - C(p,q^1,H^0) \right\} \\
&= C(p,q^1,H^0) - C(p,q^1,H^1).
\end{aligned}
\tag{15.40}
$$

If $\partial H(p,y,q)/\partial q > 0$ – a point to which we return below – then $H^1 > H^0$ when q increases and $H^1 < H^0$ if q decreases. From this we can deduce that $AS < PS$ for an increase in q and $AS > PS$ for a decrease in q, since more H costs more to produce. Thus, if $\partial H(\cdot)/\partial q > 0$ we are able to expand our bounding result for an increase in q to include $0 \le AS \le PS \le CV$. From this we can see that AS is in fact a *less* informative lower bound for CV than PS when q increases. Nonetheless, if a prediction for AS is more readily available and $\partial H(p,y,q)/\partial q > 0$ can be reasonably assumed, this expanded result may be of practical use. Furthermore, when $\partial H(p,y,q)/\partial q > 0$, we can get more from AS, as summarized in the following proposition.

Proposition 15.4

Suppose we have an estimate of $x(p,y,q)$ and that q^0 and q^1 denote the initial and changed levels of the quasi-fixed good. Suppose as well that $\partial H(p,y,q)/\partial y > 0$ and $C_{Hq}(\cdot) < 0$, where $H(\cdot)$ is the ordinary demand for the household produced commodity. Then $\partial H(p,y,q)/\partial q > 0$, and the quantity $AS = p \cdot [x(p,y,q^0) - x(p,y,q^1)]$ is related to the welfare measure $CV = E(p,u^0,q^0) - E(p,u^0,q^1)$ and PS according to

$$
\begin{aligned}
0 \le AS \le PS \le CV, \quad q^1 > q^0, \\
0 \ge AS \ge CV \ge PS, \quad q^1 < q^0.
\end{aligned}
\tag{15.41}
$$

A proof of this proposition is given in appendix C. Note that $\partial H(p,y,q)/\partial y > 0$ and $C_{Hq}(\cdot) < 0$ are relatively intuitive assumptions. The first says that H is a normal good, and the second says that the marginal cost of producing H falls when q increases. If these assumptions are maintained, propositions 15.3 and 15.4 are useful in slightly different situations. In particular, 15.4 can provide evidence of a non-zero welfare loss from a decrease in q if $AS \ne 0$, while 15.3 can provide evidence of a non-zero welfare gain from an increase in q if $PS \ne 0$. These results, along the expressions for marginal willingness to pay and the special cases when exact measurement is possible, provide the basis for welfare measurement in the substitutes model.

15.3.4 Application Preview

Our discussion of the substitutes model reveals three general conclusions. First, discrete change welfare measures do not generally fall out of the model based on the estimable functions $x(p,y,q)$, $C(p,q,H)$, and $f(x,q)$. However, if specific assumptions about technology can be maintained, we can compute or approximate welfare measures for non-marginal changes in q from these functions. Second, for marginal changes in the environmental good, $-\partial C(\cdot)/\partial q$ provides a general measure of marginal willingness to pay. This can be computed using either $C(\cdot)$, $f(\cdot)$, or $x(\cdot)$. Finally, bounding arguments based on $C(\cdot)$ and $x(\cdot)$ allow us to approximate welfare measures for non-marginal changes in q under more general technologies. Thus, estimation of some or all of the functions $x(p,y,q)$, $f(x,q)$, and $C(p,q,H)$ defines the empirical task in applications of the substitutes model.

One of the primary uses of the substitutes model is for studying the relationship between health outcomes and the environment, in order to value environmental improvements as they are reflected in improved health. This is a topic we take up more completely in Chapter 20. By way of preview, when used in this way the substitutes model is often cast as an *averting behavior* or *defensive expenditure* model. In these cases the environment is usually measured as a "bad" – e.g. particulate matter or ground-level ozone for air quality applications – and $C(\cdot)$ is referred to as the "defensive expenditure function." This label is appropriate since the person spends resources related to the private activity to defend against (or mitigate) the effects of exposure to pollution. In actual applications to health, it is necessary to define and measure H, x, and q. In some instances symptom diaries or objective health assessments are used for H; in other cases, proxies such as missed work or school days are used instead. For the private activity, consumption of health services (e.g. doctor's visits, purchases of devices or services) is a commonly examined input. Recently, researchers have also collected data on how time spent outdoors by people with pulmonary diseases is affected by air pollution (see Mansfield et al., 2006, or Graff Zivin and Neidell, 2009). Finally, q is often measured directly using, for example, ambient particulate matter or counts of ground-level ozone violations. In other cases proxies based on information releases, such as ozone alert announcements, are used.

In health applications, the estimation of $H = f(x,q)$ bears resemblance to epidemiologists' efforts to estimate dose-response functions, which map exposure to ambient pollution to specific health effects for different populations. The difference is that the health production function has an explicit role for behavior, and so the health outcome depends on people's choices as well as ambient conditions. Thus estimating $H = f(x,q)$ requires epidemiological and behavioral data, and it is made challenging by the fact that x is a choice variable, and is therefore likely to be endogenous in estimation. Estimating $x(p,y,q)$ in a health context requires establishing a causal link between the environment and private behavior – i.e. establishing that people do indeed defend themselves against pollution.

15.4   QUALITY-DIFFERENTIATED MARKET GOODS

The complements and substitutes models described above are appropriate when the quasi-fixed good does not influence the price of the related private good. In instances when the level of q influences a market price, an alternative model motivates most empirical work. In these cases, q can be viewed as a public or private characteristic of a bundled, attribute-differentiated market good. Residential housing markets are a good example of this. The commodity – a residential property – is best thought of as a bundle of attributes that includes private characteristics such as the size and layout of the structure, and public characteristics such as the quality of local schools. In some instances local environmental conditions, such as air quality near the property, may also be a defining feature of the commodity. It is intuitive that attributes like the number of rooms and lot size determine a home's market price; in a similar way it is plausible that local environmental conditions may also be reflected in the property's value. A second example relevant to environmental economics is wage rates. The compensation a person can earn from a particular job depends on the pecuniary and non-pecuniary characteristics of the workplace. The latter includes the physical surroundings, attractiveness of the area in which the job is located, the unpleasant-ness of expected duties, and health or safety risks borne while performing the work. Thus it is sensible to describe a job by the bundle of attributes that characterize the work environment, and in equilibrium the market wage will reflect compensation for these attributes. This includes compensation for job-related mortality risk, which is useful for understanding the value of mortality risk reductions more generally. A final example is when q is a private attribute of a bundled commodity, which none-theless has relevance for environmental policy. For example, a vehicle's safety rating (e.g. inclusion of airbags or anti-lock brakes) is a private characteristic produced by the manufacturer and purchased by the consumers as part of choosing a vehicle. Nonetheless, understanding people's willingness to pay for reduced mortality in traf-fic accidents via increased vehicle safety can also be useful for understanding the value of mortality risk reductions from environmental policy.

What distinguishes these three examples from those considered earlier in the chap-ter is that the environmental (or safety) good is indirectly priced and exchanged in the marketplace. If a person chooses to buy a home that is expensive due to its placement in a high environmental quality area, he has effectively purchased the environmental quality and consumes it along with the other attributes of his home. If a person accepts a job with a high risk of job-related fatality, he has indirectly agreed to bear the risk in exchange for the additional compensation that goes with it. If a person pays more money to own a Volvo, a vehicle known for its high safety rating, he has purchased a reduction in his risk of dying in a car accident. Situations such as these, in which people implicitly buy or sell levels of quasi-fixed goods through their participation in differentiated goods markets, are good sources of behavioral footprints for revealed preference analysis.

In this section we develop a model of behavior that will guide our use of observa-tions on quality-differentiated good choices to estimate non-market values. In particular, we examine the hedonic model of household and firm behavior in differentiated goods markets. Our goal is to examine how assumptions on behavior in this model allow us to (a) characterize a market equilibrium in the form of a hedonic price function; (b) link an empirical estimate of the market equilibrium to individuals' marginal willingness to pay for q; and (c) define concepts related to individual demand for q functions that can, in some instances, be estimated.

15.4.1 Hedonic Model

Rosen (1974) originally laid out the hedonic price model describing consumer and firm behavior, and market equilibrium conditions for a quality-differentiated commodity. Its defining assumptions are threefold. First, the commodity – a house, job, or car – can be completely described by a finite length vector of product characteristics. In non-market valuation, the characteristics include a J dimensional vector x that reflects the private characteristics of the bundle (e.g. the size of a home and the quality of its construction), and a term q that holds the attached environmental or safety good (e.g. air quality at the property). Second, household preferences and firm costs are defined over x and q rather than the commodity as a whole, so choices are with respect to attribute levels. Finally, the market price of a unit of the commodity with attribute levels x and q is summarized by $P(x,q)$, where we refer to $P(\cdot)$ as the equilibrium price schedule or hedonic price function. In what follows we examine consumer and producer behavior under these assumptions.

Consider first consumer's behavior. The utility function is defined as $U(x,q,z)$, and an individual chooses the levels of the attributes, along with the level of spending on other goods z, to maximize utility. Assuming that consumers are price schedule takers and consume just one unit of the bundled commodity, the formal problem is

$$\max_{x,q,z} U(x,q,z;s) \quad s.t. \quad y = P(x,q) + z, \tag{15.42}$$

where s denotes characteristics of the person, which cause preferences to be heterogeneous. Note two important assumptions in this formulation. First, q is a choice variable in that the person seeks out the amount of q as part of determining the composition of the bundled commodity consumed. Second, there is a continuum of levels of x and q that can be consumed in any combination. Given these two assumptions, the first-order conditions for utility maximization are

$$\frac{\partial U(x,z,q;s)}{\partial x_j} = \lambda \frac{\partial P(x,q)}{\partial x_j}, \quad j = 1,...,J,$$

$$\frac{\partial U(x,z,q;s)}{\partial q} = \lambda \frac{\partial P(x,q)}{\partial q}, \tag{15.43}$$

$$\frac{\partial U(x,z,q;s)}{\partial z} = \lambda,$$

where λ is the Lagrange multiplier (and the marginal utility of income). From (15.43), we can see that the marginal condition for q implies

$$\frac{\partial U(\cdot)/\partial q}{\lambda} = \frac{\partial U(\cdot)/\partial q}{\partial U(\cdot)/\partial z} = \frac{\partial P(x,q)}{\partial q}, \tag{15.44}$$

so that at the optimum, the person selects q to equate the marginal rate of substitution between q and z – i.e. the marginal willingness to pay for q – to the marginal implicit price of q. There is therefore a trade-off between the value of consuming a high level of q, and the cost of obtaining it.

To derive results that have a more direct connection to an empirical task, consider a reference level of utility $\bar{u}$, so that $\bar{u} = U(x,q,z;s)$, and note for subsequent use that we can write $z = U^{-1}(x,q,\bar{u};s)$, since utility is monotonically increasing in z. Define an amount b and attribute levels x and q so that

$$U(x,q,y-b;s) = \bar{u}. \tag{15.45}$$

This expression implicitly defines a bid function $b(x,q,y,s,\bar{u})$, which measures the maximum amount that a consumer would (and could) pay for a commodity unit, with attribute levels x and q, while holding utility fixed at $\bar{u}$. With the bid function so defined, y, z, and $b(\cdot)$ are related by the identity

$$b(x,q,y,s,\bar{u}) \equiv y - U^{-1}(x,q,\bar{u};s). \tag{15.46}$$

Implicitly differentiating (15.45) with respect to q allows us to obtain

$$0 = \frac{\partial U(\cdot)}{\partial q} - \frac{\partial U(\cdot)}{\partial z}\frac{\partial b(\cdot)}{\partial q}, \tag{15.47}$$

which we can rearrange to define

$$\pi^q(x,q,s,\bar{u}) = \frac{\partial b(x,q,y,s,\bar{u})}{\partial q} = \frac{\partial U(\cdot)/\partial q}{\partial U(\cdot)/\partial z}. \tag{15.48}$$

Note from (15.46) that $\partial b(\cdot)/\partial q$ is not a function of y, and so we have written $\pi^q(\cdot)$ without y as an argument, as is consistent for a compensated function. More importantly, the derivative of the bid function with respect to q is equal to the marginal willingness to pay for q, at a reference level of utility (while holding fixed the levels of the other attributes x), which by definition is the compensated inverse demand for q function. Thus obtaining an understanding of $\pi^q(x,q,s,\bar{u})$, from which welfare measures can be computed, is the applied objective in the hedonic model. Towards this end, note that combining (15.44) and (15.48) shows that, at the consumer's optimal choice, we have

$$\frac{\partial b(x,q,y,s,u^0)}{\partial q} = \frac{\partial P(x,q)}{\partial q}, \tag{15.49}$$

where u^0 is the level of utility obtained at the baseline choice. Estimation of an individual's marginal willingness to pay for q at baseline conditions – i.e. learning a single point on $\pi^q(x,q,s,u^0)$ – can therefore be achieved by estimating $\partial P(x,q)/\partial q$. The first empirical task suggested by the hedonic price model is therefore to use data on transactions prices for sales of the commodity, along with the associated levels of x and q chosen by individuals, to estimate the structure of $P(x,q)$.

Since estimation of $P(x,q)$ is a primary empirical objective, it is useful to examine further how the equilibrium price schedule arises in the model. In instances when q is public (i.e. provided by nature and/or the government) and the supply of the other attributes is effectively fixed, $P(x,q)$ is determined solely by consumer's preferences and their characteristics. In instances when q is private (produced in the marketplace), both the supply and demand side of the market are important.

To consider supply, suppose a firm produces one unit of the commodity, and that its cost per unit is $C(x,q;v)$, where v denotes characteristics of the particular firm that lead to heterogeneity among firms in the market. Note that $C(\cdot)$ depends on attribute levels x and q, suggesting production costs can in general vary with the amount of q provided. For example, if housing is the application and q is the amount of subdivision open space preserved during construction, it is likely that $C_q(\cdot) > 0$. In a different case, q could reflect safety or health risk mitigation characteristics of the structure, in which case q once again has positive marginal cost.

Assuming the firm is a price schedule taker, it maximizes profit by selling a single unit according to the objective function

$$\max_{x,q} \Pi = P(x,q) - C(x,q;v), \tag{15.50}$$

where q and the elements of x are the choice variables. The first-order conditions are

$$\frac{\partial P(\cdot)}{\partial q} = \frac{\partial C(\cdot)}{\partial q}, \quad \frac{\partial P(\cdot)}{\partial x_j} = \frac{\partial C(\cdot)}{\partial x_j}, \quad j = 1,...,J. \tag{15.51}$$

Similar to the consumer's case, define o as the amount of money the firm would accept to supply a unit of the commodity, with characteristics x and q, while maintaining a profit level of $\bar{\Pi}$, so that

$$\bar{\Pi} = o - C(x,q;v). \tag{15.52}$$

This allows us to implicitly define a firm's offer function as $o(x,q,\bar{\Pi},v)$, which summarizes the firm's willingness to accept to supply a unit of the commodity, conditional on reaching a reference level of profit. Differentiating (15.52) with respect to q allows us to derive the firm's marginal willingness to accept for q as

$$\frac{\partial o(x,q,\bar{\Pi},f)}{\partial q} = \frac{\partial C(x,q)}{\partial q}. \tag{15.53}$$

Finally, at the point of optimum choice by the firm, equations (15.51) and (15.53) show that the slope of the offer function is equal to the marginal implicit price of q

$$\frac{\partial o(x,q,\Pi^0,f)}{\partial q} = \frac{\partial P(x,q)}{\partial q}, \tag{15.54}$$

where Π^0 is the level of profit the firm obtains.

Equations (15.49) and (15.54) are central to understanding market equilibrium in the hedonic model. The way in which $P(x,q)$ arises is shown in the top panel of Figure 15.3, where we have depicted two consumers labeled s_1 and s_2, and two firms labeled v_1 and v_2. The consumers have utility functions that give rise to collections of bid functions, and the firms have cost functions that give rise to offer functions. For firm 1, three different offer curves are shown via dashed lines, each conditional on a different profit level, where $\Pi^1 > \Pi^0 > \Pi^2$. Note that profits are higher for firms as we move up the vertical axis, since a higher price is received for provision of a given quantity of q. For person 2, three different bid curves are shown via solid lines, each conditional on a different utility level, where $u^1 > u^0 > u^2$. Note that utility is higher for consumers as we move down the vertical axis, since a lower price is paid for a given quantity of q, thereby leaving more of the budget for the composite commodity. To reduce clutter, only one offer curve is shown for firm 2, and one bid curve for consumer 1.

The heavy line labeled $P(x,q)$ is the equilibrium price function, and it is traced out by the continuum of buyers and sellers finding each other in the market and conducting transactions. For example, note that at $q=q_1$ person 1 and firm 1 simultaneously satisfy their optimization conditions as given by (15.49) and (15.54), respectively, when the price is $P(x,q_1)$. This is a transaction. Likewise, at $q=q_2$ and $P(x,q_2)$ person 2 and firm 2 simultaneously satisfy their optimization conditions, and another transaction results. The equilibrium price schedule results from the double envelope of all the bid and offer functions held by consumers and producers in the market, and their meetings to conduct transactions. When supply is exogenous there are no offer curves, and $P(x,q)$ arises only from consumers bidding for the available units of the bundled commodity. In this case the equilibrium is traced out by the single envelope of bid functions that match to successful transactions.

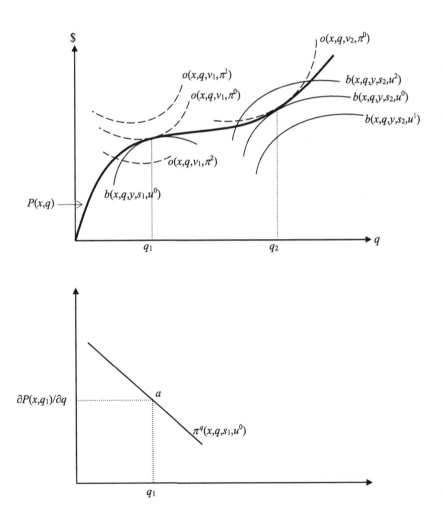

Figure 15.3 Hedonic equilibrium

As noted, the first empirical task defined by the hedonic model is to estimate the relationship between sales prices and attribute levels, which is to say we want to characterize the form of $P(x,q)$. This alone provides useful information, since we have seen that the marginal willingness to pay for any level of q is simply $\partial P(x,q)/\partial q$. This does not, however, provide more than a single point on a given household's inverse demand for q function. This is shown in the lower panel of Figure 15.3, where we have drawn the inverse demand curve for consumer 1 by tracing out the slope of the bid function $b(x,q,y,s_1,u^0)$. By computing $\partial P(x,q^1)/\partial q$, we obtain the height of the curve at q^1, and thereby locate point a. However, estimation of equilibrium price function $P(\cdot)$ does not provide any additional (out of equilibrium) points of the inverse demand curve. Thus, the second empirical task suggested by the hedonic price model is to seek ways of estimating $\pi^q(\cdot)$ in a subsequent step. We delay discussion of this more difficult task until Chapter 18, when we consider the hedonic model in the context of property values.

15.4.2 Application Preview

The hedonic model plays a particularly large role in two areas of environmental economics: analyzing the relationship between property values and the environment, and quantifying risk/income trade-offs. In the context of property value studies, the objective is to measure how variation in local environmental conditions causes housing price differentials, which we can use to measure the value of environmental changes. A common application is to air quality, for which an analyst collects data on property sales and locally varying ambient pollution levels. For the former, transaction information recording sales prices, the characteristics of the property (e.g. the size of the structure), and its position in the landscape is needed. Monitors recording the level of particulate matter at different points across the landscape are an example source for the latter. From this, a measure of air quality can be attached to each of the properties in the transactions data. A regression analysis of sales price on property characteristics and the air quality level provides an estimate of $P(x,q)$, and from this we can compute $\partial P(x,q)/\partial q$ to estimate marginal willingness to pay for changes in air quality. In Chapter 18 we will examine in greater detail application of the hedonic model to property values, including an analysis of when the available data allows us to recover an estimate of the full inverse demand for q function.

The second use of the hedonic model is to analyze workers' willingness to accept incremental changes in workplace mortality risks for additional wages. As we saw in Chapter 14, we are often interested in measuring the willingness to pay for small changes in the likelihood of an adverse event, such as death resulting from exposure to ambient carcinogens. In cases like this, we need to know a person's willingness to trade income off against the risk of death from environmental exposure. For such a measurement task, it is often sensible to examine how people make similar risk/money trade-offs in their private consumption and labor supply decisions. A wage hedonic model that regresses a sample of workers' wages onto a broad collection of job characteristics that includes mortality risk, is one way to measure a private risk/money trade-off. In Chapter 20 we discuss this type of analysis in greater detail, within the context of examining the health-related benefits and pollution reductions.

15.5   SUMMARY

As discussed in Chapter 14, applied welfare analysis for changes in quasi-fixed goods is difficult vis-à-vis the price change case, primarily due to a lack of observable market outcomes. While it is easy to define an inverse demand function for the quasi-fixed quantity, and to derive the duality conditions linking it to preferences, the behavior of individuals does not provide information that can be used to estimate it. Given this, we must look elsewhere when the objective is to understand preferences for the environment. The strategy we have discussed in this chapter is based on identifying observable behavior that is in some way linked to the quasi-fixed good, and then estimating functions based on this behavior. The general idea is that through interactions with the environment, people leave behavioral footprints which, in some circumstances and under some assumptions, provide the information needed to estimate welfare measures for changes in the environment. Because this approach is based on observing behavior that has occurred and for which the consequences have been borne, it is known generally as revealed preference. The primary advantage of revealed preference is that it is consistent with the tradition in economics of basing normative inference on choices people are observed to have made while acting in their own self-interest.

We have seen that a private good or activity can be related to the environment in one of three ways: as complements, substitutes, or quality-differentiated market goods. If they are complements, it is often sensible to view the quasi-fixed good as a shift factor in the demand curve for the private good. In this case, weak complementarity and the Willig condition are useful maintained assumptions. These preference restrictions allow us to link the measurable area under the estimable private good demand curve to exact welfare measures for changes in the quasi-fixed good. In contrast, if the environmental and private goods are substitutes in the home production of a final consumption commodity, then the household production framework is a useful organizing principle. In this case specific assumptions about technology allow us to link estimates of the input demand function or underlying production technology to exact welfare measures. In situations when more generality is needed, these same estimates allow us to compute bounds on the welfare measures of interest. Finally, when the environmental good influences the market price of a purchased differentiated commodity, the hedonic model applies. Because people effectively choose the level of the environmental good by participating in the market for the private good, an estimate of the equilibrium price function for the differentiated good provides a link to preferences and the marginal value of the environmental good.

All three of these models use maintained assumptions to derive results that are useful for applied welfare analysis. Thus, a key aspect of revealed preference analysis is the use of intuition and judgment to decide when the necessary assumptions are appropriate, and when other strategies should be pursued. Through several examples and application previews we have suggested (though not yet fully developed) areas in which RP analysis is often feasible. These examples also illustrate the close relationship that exists between the development of behavioral models on one hand, and practical considerations regarding data availability and sources of variability on the other. Thus, while this chapter has not been about empirical models per se, it has proceeded with the objective of describing models of behavior that lead to functions that can be estimated with available data, which in turn can be used to compute welfare measures. In subsequent chapters dedicated to examining recreation behavior, property markets, and health outcomes, we will discuss in more detail application of RP methods to these specific areas. Along the way, the attractiveness of revealed preference, when it is feasible, will become apparent. We will also see that there are many instances when revealed preference is not possible, either due to a lack of private interactions with the environment, or just as likely, insufficient variability in behavior or levels of environmental quality. In these instances we need to rely on stated preference methods, which we examine in detail in Chapter 19.

A final point concerns econometrics. Throughout this chapter we have referred to the estimation of private good demand functions, but we have had little to say about how to approach this problem. In some instances standard techniques based on a continuous demand function with strictly positive consumption quantities are appropriate. In many other instances, however, household behavior gives rise to lumpy data in which discrete choices, zero demand levels, and integer outcomes predominate. For this type of data, the tools of micro-econometrics are needed, and none is more important in environmental economics than discrete choice models. In the following chapter, we examine discrete choice models from both behavioral and econometric perspectives, thereby setting the stage for their use in several of the applied chapters to follow.

15.6   FURTHER READING

An excellent book-length treatment of revealed preference methods is provided by Bockstael and McConnell (2007), and much of our discussion in this chapter has drawn on their careful dissection of the many subtleties underlying the behavioral models. See also Bockstael and Freeman (2005). Important contributions in the development of the weak complementarity model include the original work by Mäler (1974), Bockstael and McConnell (1993), Smith and Banzhaf (2004, 2007), and Palmquist (2005a). Von Haefen (2007) provides a useful discussion of how one specifies empirical models that are consistent with weak complementarity. Other noteworthy papers focusing on weak complementarity include Larson (1991), Herriges et al. (2004), and Bullock and Minot (2006). See also Neill (1988) and Larson (1992). Key developments in the substitutes (household production) model include Bockstael and McConnell (1983) and Bartik (1988a), where the latter first suggested the bounds developed in section 15.3.3. For a nice discussion of how the substitutes model is applied to the problem of valuing health outcomes, see Dickie (2003). McConnell and Bockstael (2005) describe the related issue of the environment as a factor of production. The key paper describing the hedonic price model in general is Rosen (1974). Key papers discussing the second-stage hedonic model (see Chapter 18) include Brown and Rosen (1982), Bartik (1987a, 1987b, 1988b), Epple (1987), and Mendelsohn (1985). Nice overviews in the environmental economics literature are contained in Palmquist (1991, 2005b) and Taylor (2003).

APPENDIX A: PROOF OF PROPOSITION 15.2

We follow the derivation in Palmquist (2005a). To show that Eq. (15.14) implies c from (15.10) is the same as C from (15.13) and vice versa, begin by rewriting the expression for c using Roy's Identity as

$$
\begin{aligned}
c &= \int_{p^0}^{\tilde{p}(q^1)} -\frac{\partial V(p,y,q^1)/\partial p}{\partial V(p,y,q^1)/\partial y}\, dp - \int_{p^0}^{\tilde{p}(q^1)} -\frac{\partial V(p,y,q^0)/\partial p}{\partial V(p,y,q^0)/\partial y}\, dp \\
&= \int_{p^0}^{\tilde{p}(q^1)} -\frac{\partial V(p,y,q^1)/\partial p}{\lambda(p,y,q^1)}\, dp - \int_{p^0}^{\tilde{p}(q^1)} -\frac{\partial V(p,y,q^0)/\partial p}{\lambda(p,y,q^0)}\, dp,
\end{aligned}
\tag{A15.1}
$$

where the second equality follows from the fact that the denominator in the integrands is $V_y(\cdot)=\lambda(p,y,q)$, which is the marginal utility of income. Suppose that the marginal utility is not a function of p or q, so that $\lambda(p,y,q)=\lambda(y)$. We return to this point below. For now, note that this allows us to move the function $\lambda(\cdot)$ outside of the integrals as

$$
c = \frac{1}{\lambda(y)} \int_{p^0}^{\tilde{p}(q^1)} -\frac{\partial V(p,y,q^1)}{\partial p}\, dp - \frac{1}{\lambda(y)} \int_{p^0}^{\tilde{p}(q^1)} -\frac{\partial V(p,y,q^0)}{\partial p}\, dp.
\tag{A15.2}
$$

Evaluating the definite integrals allows us to write

$$
\begin{aligned}
c &= \frac{1}{\lambda(y)}\left\{ -V(\tilde{p}(q^1),y,q^1) + V(p^0,y,q^1) + V(\tilde{p}(q^0),y,q^0) - V(p^0,y,q^0) \right\} \\
&= \frac{1}{\lambda(y)}\left\{ V(p^0,y,q^1) - V(p^0,y,q^0) \right\} + \frac{1}{\lambda(y)}\left\{ V(\tilde{p}(q^0),y,q^0) - V(\tilde{p}(q^1),y,q^1) \right\}.
\end{aligned}
\tag{A15.3}
$$

Recall that weak complementarity implies that $U(0,z,q)=0$, and that $x(\tilde{p}(q^0),y,q^0) = x(\tilde{p}(q^1),y,q^1) = 0$ by definition. Plugging these demand functions evaluated at their choke prices into $U(x,z,q)$, we obtain

$$
V(\tilde{p}(q^0),y,q^0) - V(\tilde{p}(q^1),y,q^1) = 0
\tag{A15.4}
$$

by weak complementarity. Therefore, when $\lambda(p,y,q)=\lambda(y)$, the expression in (A15.3) for c reduces to

$$
c = \frac{1}{\lambda(y)}\left\{ V(p^0,y,q^1) - V(p^0,y,q^0) \right\}.
\tag{A15.5}
$$

This is familiar from Chapter 14 as a money-metric measure of the utility change, arising from the change in q. Therefore, under the assumption that the marginal utility of income is independent of p and q, Eq. (15.10) is a measure of consumer surplus change that also has a valid welfare interpretation.

We can conduct a similar exercise using Eq. (15.13) to obtain

$$
C = \int_{q^0}^{q^1} \frac{\partial V(p,y,q)/\partial q}{\partial V(p,y,q)/\partial y}\, dq = \int_{q^0}^{q^1} \frac{\partial V(p,y,q)/\partial q}{\lambda(p,y,q)}\, dq.
\tag{A15.6}
$$

Given the assumption from above that $\lambda(p,y,q)=\lambda(y)$, we can move the marginal utility of income outside of the integral to derive

$$C = \frac{1}{\lambda(y)} \int_{q^0}^{q^1} \frac{\partial V(p,y,q)}{\partial q} \, dq = \frac{1}{\lambda(y)} \left\{ V(p,y,q^1) - V(p,y,q^0) \right\}. \tag{A15.7}$$

This too is a money-metric measure of the utility change arising from the change in q, and inspection of (A15.5) and (A15.7) suggests $c=C$. Thus $\lambda(p,y,q)=\lambda(y)$ implies $c=C$.

Consider now the condition $\lambda(p,y,q)=\lambda(y)$, which is equivalent to the restriction that $V_{yq}(\cdot)=V_{yp}(\cdot)=0$. To establish (15.14), we use Roy's Identity to write

$$x(p,y,q) \times V_y(p,y,q) = -V_p(p,y,q), \tag{A15.8}$$

which we differentiate with respect to y to obtain

$$x(\cdot) \times V_{yy}(\cdot) + \frac{\partial x(\cdot)}{\partial y} V_y(\cdot) = -V_{py}. \tag{A15.9}$$

By the same process we can use the Roy's Identity-like formula in (15.3) for the ordinary inverse demand for q to write

$$\theta^q(p,y,q) \times V_y(p,y,q) = V_q(p,y,q), \tag{A15.10}$$

and differentiating with respect to y leads to

$$\theta^q(\cdot) \times V_{yy}(\cdot) + \frac{\partial \theta^q(\cdot)}{\partial y} V_y(\cdot) = V_{qy}. \tag{A15.11}$$

Define the income elasticity of demand for x (η) and the income elasticity of the inverse demand for q (ς) by

$$\eta = \frac{\partial x(\cdot)}{\partial y} \frac{y}{x(\cdot)}$$

$$\xi = \frac{\partial \theta^q(\cdot)}{\partial y} \frac{y}{\theta^q(\cdot)}. \tag{A15.12}$$

Note from the expressions in (A15.9) and (A15.11) that η and ξ are equal only when $V_{yq}(\cdot)=V_{yp}(\cdot)=0$:

$$\frac{\partial x(\cdot)}{\partial y} \frac{y}{x(\cdot)} = \eta = -\frac{y \times V_{yy}(\cdot)}{V_y(\cdot)}$$

$$\frac{\partial \theta^q(\cdot)}{\partial y} \frac{y}{\theta^q(\cdot)} = \xi = -\frac{y \times V_{yy}(\cdot)}{V_y(\cdot)}. \tag{A15.13}$$

Thus $\eta = \xi$ implies that $\lambda(p,y,q) = \lambda(y)$, which our analysis above shows implies $c = C$ from (15.10) and (15.13), respectively.

APPENDIX B: PROOF OF PROPOSITION 15.3

Bartik (1988a) provides the key result relating CV and PS. The main insight is to define a conditional expenditure function of the form:

$$E(p,u,q \mid H = \hat{H}) = \min_{z} \left\{ z + C(p,q,\hat{H}) \quad s.t. \quad U(\hat{H},z) = u \right\}, \tag{A15.14}$$

where $\hat{H}$ is an arbitrary fixed level of the produced commodity, and the solution gives the amount of spending on z that is needed to reach utility level u while constraining $H = \hat{H}$. We use $h_z(p,u,q \mid H = \hat{H})$ to denote compensated demand function for z that results from this problem.

Based on this, consider the expression

$$\begin{aligned} E(p,u^0,q^0) &- E(p,u^0,q^1 \mid H = H^0) \\ &= \left[C(p,q^0,H^0) + h_z(p,u^0,q^0) \right] - \left[C(p,q^1,H^0) + h_z(p,u^0,q^1 \mid H = H^0) \right], \end{aligned} \tag{A15.15}$$

where u^0 and H^0 are the original levels of utility and the produced commodity, respectively. Note that $h_z(p,u^0,q^0) = h_z(p,u^0,q^1 \mid H = H^0)$ in both the conditional and unconditional expenditure minimization problems, since both end with $H = H^0$ and we need to maintain $u^0 = U(z^0,H^0)$ in both problems. This allows us to rewrite (A15.15) as

$$E(p,u^0,q^0) - E(p,u^0,q^1 \mid H = H^0) = C(p,q^0,H^0) - C(p,q^1,H^0) = PS. \tag{A15.16}$$

Finally, note that optimizing behavior implies

$$E(p,u^0,q^1) \leq E(p,u^0,q^1 \mid H = H^0), \tag{A15.17}$$

since the minimum expenditure needed to reach u^0 when H is free to adjust cannot be greater than the expenditure needed when H is restricted. Combining (A15.16) and (A15.17) gives us Bartik's result

$$\begin{aligned} CV &= E(p,u^0,q^0) - E(p,u^0,q^1) \\ &\geq E(p,u^0,q^0) - E(p,u^0,q^1 \mid H = H^0) = PS, \end{aligned} \tag{A15.18}$$

upon which Eq. (15.39) is based.

APPENDIX C: PROOF OF PROPOSITION 15.4

The following is based on the derivation in Bockstael and McConnell (2007). To begin, we recall the identity $h_H(p,u,q) \equiv H[p,E(p,u,q),q]$ and Slutsky-type relationship

$$\frac{\partial H(p,y,q)}{\partial q} \equiv \frac{\partial h_H(p,u,q)}{\partial q} - \frac{\partial H(p,y,q)}{\partial y} \times \frac{\partial E(p,u,q)}{\partial q},$$ (A15.19)

where the latter is derived by differentiation with respect to q. Note that the last term is positive if H is a normal good. To sign $\partial h_H(\cdot)/\partial q$, we examine the first-order conditions for the expenditure minimization problem in (15.25):

$$\begin{aligned} C_H(p,q,H) - \mu U_H(H,z) &= 0 \\ 1 - \mu U_z(H,z) &= 0 \\ u - U(H,z) &= 0. \end{aligned}$$ (A15.20)

Differentiating the equation system with respect to q leads to

$$C_{Hq}(p,q,H) + C_{HH}(p,q,H)\frac{\partial h_H}{\partial q} - \mu U_{HH}(H,z)\frac{\partial h_H}{\partial q} - \mu U_{Hz}(H,z)\frac{\partial h_z}{\partial q} - U_H(H,z)\frac{\partial \mu}{\partial q} = 0$$

$$-\mu U_{zH}(H,z)\frac{\partial h_H}{\partial q} - \mu U_{zz}(H,z)\frac{\partial h_z}{\partial q} - U_z(H,z)\frac{\partial \mu}{\partial q} = 0$$

$$-U_H(H,z)\frac{\partial h_H}{\partial q} - U_z(H,z)\frac{\partial h_z}{\partial q} = 0,$$ (A15.21)

or in matrix form

$$\begin{bmatrix} C_{HH} - \mu U_{HH} & -\mu U_{Hz} & -U_H \\ -\mu U_{zH} & -\mu U_{zz} & -U_z \\ -U_H & -U_z & 0 \end{bmatrix} \begin{bmatrix} \dfrac{\partial h_H}{\partial q} \\[4pt] \dfrac{\partial h_z}{\partial q} \\[4pt] \dfrac{\partial \mu}{\partial q} \end{bmatrix} = \begin{bmatrix} -C_{Hq} \\ 0 \\ 0 \end{bmatrix}.$$ (A15.22)

Using Cramer's Rule to solve for $\partial h_H(\cdot)/\partial q$ one can show that

$$\frac{\partial h_H(p,u,q)}{\partial q} = \frac{C_{Hq} \times (U_z)^2}{\Delta},$$ (A15.23)

where Δ is the determinant of the 3×3 matrix in (A15.22), which is negative by the second-order conditions for expenditure minimization. Thus the sign of $\partial h_H(\cdot)/\partial q$ is dependent on technology, and opposite to the sign of $C_{Hq}(\cdot)$. When $C_{Hq}(\cdot) < 0$, it follows that $\partial h_H(\cdot)/\partial q > 0$. Therefore, a sufficient condition for $H(p,y,q)/\partial q > 0$ is $C_{Hq}(\cdot) < 0$ and

$\partial H(\cdot)/\partial y > 0$. We showed in the text that $H(p,y,q)/\partial q > 0$ implied $0 \leq AS \leq PS \leq CV$ for an increase in q.

To examine the case when q decreases, rewrite CV as

$$
\begin{aligned}
CV &= E(p,u^0,q^0) - E(p,u^0,q^1) \\
&= C(p,q^0,H^0) + h_z(p,u^0,q^0) - C\left(p,q^1,h_H(p,u^0,q^1)\right) - h_z(p,u^0,q^1),
\end{aligned}
\tag{A15.24}
$$

and AS as

$$
AS = C(p,q^0,H^0) - C\left(p,q^1,H(p,y,q^1)\right).
\tag{A15.25}
$$

Based on this we can express $CV - AS$ as

$$
\begin{aligned}
CV - AS &= \left\{ C\left(p,q^1,H(p,y,q^1)\right) - C\left(p,q^1,h_H(p,u^0,q^1)\right) \right\} \\
&\quad + h_z(p,u^0,q^0) - h_z(p,u^0,q^1).
\end{aligned}
\tag{A15.26}
$$

To sign $CV - AS$, we need to sign the term in curved brackets as well as $h_z(p,u^0,q^0) - h_z(p,u^0,q^1)$. For the former, note from (A15.19) that $H(p,y,q^0) = h_H(p,u^0,q^0)$ and $H(p,y,q^1) < h_H(p,u^0,q^1)$ when q decreases, since the gradient of the ordinary demand for H with respect to q is greater than the compensated demand gradient – i.e. there is a larger shift back in $H(\cdot)$ than in $h_H(\cdot)$ when q falls. This implies the term in curved brackets is negative, since $C(\cdot)$ is increasing in H. Also, it must be the case that $h_z(p,u^0,q^0) - h_z(p,u^0,q^1) < 0$ when q decreases, since a decrease in H needs to be offset by an increase in z to maintain utility. Thus when q decreases, $CV < AS$, which is to say that CV is more negative than AS. This result implies that $0 \geq AS \geq CV \geq PS$.

EXERCISES

15.1 * Which of the following utility functions are consistent with weak complementarity?

(a) $U(x,z,q) = \Psi \times \ln(x \cdot \delta(q) + \theta) + \ln z$, $\quad \Psi, \theta > 0$, $\quad \delta(q) > 0$

(b) $U(x,z,q) = \delta(q) \times \ln(x + \theta) + \ln z$, $\quad \theta > 0$, $\quad \delta(q) > 0$

(c) $U(x,z,q) = \delta(q) \times \ln(x + \theta) + \ln z$, $\quad \theta = 1$, $\quad \delta(q) > 0$

(d) $U(x,z,q) = \delta(q) \times \ln(x + \theta) - \delta(q) \times \ln \theta + \ln z$, $\quad \theta > 0$, $\quad \delta(q) > 0$

(e) $U(x,z,q) = \Psi \times \ln(x + \theta) + \ln(z + x \cdot \delta(q))$, $\quad \Psi, \theta > 0$, $\quad \delta(q) > 0$

15.2 ** Show that the indirect utility function given in Eq. (15.21) is consistent with the Willig condition by demonstrating that Eq. (15.14) holds. (*Hint*: first use $V(\cdot)$ to derive $\theta^q(\cdot)$, and then state the relevant elasticities.)

15.3 ** Consider a demand equation for a private good x of the form

$$
x = \alpha - \beta p + \kappa q + \gamma y,
$$

where p is price, y is income, and q is a quasi-fixed quality attribute of x. Suppose we have estimated the parameters of this equation and found that $\alpha = 2$, $\beta = 0.65$,

$\kappa = 1.50$ and $\gamma = 0.0002$. Assume that the baseline price and quality are $p = \$10$ and $q = 1$, respectively, and that we are interested in examining the welfare effects for a person with income of $\$50,000$.

(a) Compute the baseline demand level, income elasticity, ordinary demand price and quality elasticities, and choke price for this person. At the baseline, is demand more sensitive to changes in quality or price?

(b) State the indirect utility function $V(p,y,q)$ for this demand equation. (*Hint*: see Eq. (14.32) in Chapter 14 and note that quality enters here via cross-product repackaging.) Use $V(\cdot)$ to derive the ordinary inverse demand for q function. Compute the income elasticity for the ordinary inverse demand for q at baseline conditions. How does it compare to the income elasticity for x?

(c) Consider a quality increase from $q = 1$ to $q = 2$. Compute the change in consumer surplus from this using the expression in Eq. (15.10), and then using the expression in Eq. (15.13). How do they compare? Also compute the compensating and equivalent variations for the change in q. What is the percentage error when we use C rather than CV as our welfare measure?

15.4 ** Consider the substitutes model in which utility is $U(H,z)$ and the production technology is $H = f(x,q)$. Assume the baseline price of the private input x is $p = \$10$ and that the baseline level of the environmental good is $q = 2$.

(a) Suppose $H = x + (1 - \phi)q$, where $\phi = 0.3$. Compute the exact willingness to pay for an increase in q from $q = 2$ to $q = 4$.

(b) Suppose $H = x^\phi q^{1-\phi}$, where $\phi = 0.3$. Assume we have estimated an ordinary demand for x curve given by $x = \alpha - \beta p + \kappa q$, where $\alpha = 10$, $\beta = 0.65$, and $\kappa = 2$. What is the baseline level of H? Noting that x is an essential input for the production of H, compute an approximation to the exact willingness to pay for an increase in q from $q = 2$ to $q = 4$. What is the level of H after the increase in q?

(c) Suppose once again that $H = x^\phi q^{1-\phi}$ and $x = \alpha - \beta p + \kappa q$, where the parameter values are as given above. Derive the cost function $C(p,q,H)$. Use $C(\cdot)$ to compute a lower bound on the willingness to pay for an increase from $q = 2$ to $q = 4$, using proposition 15.3.

(d) Using the function and parameter values from (c), compute bounds on the willingness to accept for a decrease in q from $q = 2$ to $q = 1$.

CHAPTER 16

Discrete Choice Models

In Chapter 15 we emphasized that revealed preference analysis often involves estimating the demand function for a private activity, which in some way relates to a quasi-fixed environmental good. In particular, we discussed how specific assumptions about an individual's preference function $U(x,z,q)$ allow us to infer the value of an environmental good q from an estimate of the ordinary demand function $x(p,y,q)$, which was assumed to be continuous and strictly positive. In actual applications, however, data at the individual level often consist of yes/no outcomes, small integers, and consumption levels equal to zero. For example, in a recreation application it is not unusual to observe a person making only one trip during the study period, and so the relevant decision is which site he visited rather than how many trips he made. Similarly, understanding the demand for water filtration in a household production application might involve analyzing whether or not a household has installed the necessary equipment. In these two contexts the data do not support estimation of a continuous demand equation, nor is the behavior generating the data well described by a continuous model. Instead, we need to use discrete choice analysis to frame the behavioral problem and estimate the relevant demand parameters. Other types of behavior are more explicitly discrete. For example, a person votes yes or no on a referendum, does or does not donate money to environmental causes, and accepts or refuses an offer of compensation for damages suffered. As these contexts illustrate, discrete outcomes are ubiquitous in environmental economics, and a working knowledge of discrete choice econometrics is essential for many areas of applied research. In this chapter we provide an overview of discrete choice models as they are used in the field, focusing on both conceptual and econometric topics.

The departure point for discrete choice analysis is the recognition that for many household decisions, the "which one" component of choice is more relevant than the quantity purchased. For example, most households buy only one automobile at a time, yet they select from dozens of different models at the time of purchase. Durable appliances such as washing machines are one-unit purchases, but there are usually a large number of different types available. In cases like these, a model is needed that describes how attributes of the choice alternatives and characteristics of the purchaser influence which option is chosen. In the automobile example, the seating capacity and prices of the available vehicles are likely to affect choices, based in part on household size and income. A discrete choice econometric model allows an analyst to write the probability that an option will be chosen by an individual, as a function of these types of variables. In addition, the framework we will explore allows us to link the probability of choice to a theoretically consistent model of behavior, which we can use to conduct welfare analysis as described in Chapters 14 and 15. The combination of discrete choice econometrics and a structural model of behavior results in the random utility maximization (RUM) model, which is an essential tool in many applied microeconomic fields, including environmental economics.

We begin this chapter by considering the conceptual basis for the RUM model. We examine the assumptions that need to be added to our familiar behavioral framework, and discuss when these assumptions are plausible. The bulk of the chapter is then spent discussing econometric aspects of RUM models, and their use for applied welfare analysis with quasi-fixed goods. Our objective is narrow, in that we aim to provide details sufficient for readers to see how discrete choice econometric models are used in the recreation, property value, stated preference, and health valuation applications described in later chapters. Thus as we proceed it is worth keeping in mind that the literature on discrete choice econometrics and their applications is enormous, and we only scratch the surface here. We emphasize nonetheless that there is a large payoff to becoming an expert in the use of RUM models and their generalizations within and outside of environmental economics, and we encourage readers to also consult other sources, particularly the book-length treatment by Train (2009) and the references included therein.

16.1 CONCEPTUAL BASIS

Our goal in this section is to examine the behavioral assumptions that lead to a discrete choice situation. We begin with an individual's utility function $U(x,z,q)$, where as usual x is a J dimensional vector of private goods, z is the scalar numeraire, and q is a vector or matrix of quasi-fixed goods. For expositional purposes we treat q as a J dimensional vector, so that x_j and q_j are private and public goods, respectively, that are related in one of the three ways discussed in the previous chapters – i.e. they are substitutes, complements, or components of a bundled market good. As described in previous chapters, the household's problem in this setup is to maximize utility by selecting x and z in strictly positive quantities, given the budget constraint $y=px+z$ and conditional on the values in q. The utility maximizing solution describes *intensive margin* outcomes for the elements of x and the amount z.

16.1.1 Theoretical Discrete Choice Model

To arrive at the conceptual basis for a purely discrete choice model, we add two restrictions to this setup. In particular, the choice problem is given by

$$\max_{x,z} U(x, z, q) \quad s.t. \quad y = px + z, \quad x_j x_k = 0 \quad \forall k \neq j, \quad x_j \in \{0, c\} \forall j, \qquad (16.1)$$

where c is a fixed constant. Via the constraint $x_j x_k = 0$, the person chooses one and only one element of x to consume, in the exogenously given amount c.[1] It is customary to set

---

[1] The model could also include the option to not select any of the elements of x.

$c = 1$, which can be accomplished without losing generality by adjusting the units of x. In this choice context the solution describes only an *extensive margin*, since there is no quantity aspect to the problem. The person simply chooses which one from among the available goods to consume, and the selected alternative describes the utility maximization outcome. This greatly simplifies the derivation of an indirect utility function, since there is no ordinary demand system to solve for. Instead, the utility the person receives when x_j is chosen is

$$V_j(y - p_j, q) = U(x_1 = 0, ..., x_j = 1, ..., x_J = 0, y - p_j, q), \tag{16.2}$$

where we have substituted out for z using the budget constraint $z = y - p_j$. We refer to $V_j(\cdot)$ as the *conditional* indirect utility function, since it is the utility level attained conditional on the person choosing x_j. If we assume that weak complementarity holds, so that $\partial V_j(\cdot)/\partial q_k = 0$ for $k \neq j$, we can further simplify the conditional indirect utility function to $V_j(y - p_j, q_j)$.

To place this model in context, consider a vehicle choice situation. A household usually shops for one vehicle at a time, and so reducing the problem by asserting that $x_j \cdot x_k = 0$ (the household does not buy both vehicle j and vehicle k) and $x_j = 0$ or 1 (the household buys only one of the selected vehicle) is sensible. The utility that the household receives from purchasing vehicle j depends on its price and non-price attributes p_j and q_j, but does not depend on the attributes of vehicles not purchased.

The utility maximizing decision rule can also be written using the (unconditional) indirect utility function, which is the maximum of the full set of conditional indirect utilities:

$$V(p, y, q) = \max \left[V_1(y - p_1, q_1), ..., V_J(y - p_J, q_J) \right]. \tag{16.3}$$

Equations (16.1) and (16.3) are dual representations of the same preference structure. Since working with the indirect utility function is less cumbersome in this case, we proceed by focusing on $V(p, y, q)$.

Note that Roy's Identity does not play a central role in this representation, since we are not interested in an ordinary demand equation per se. Instead, utility maximizing behavior implies the consumer selects option j if and only if $V_j(\cdot) \geq V_k(\cdot)$ for all $k \neq j$, which is to say that he selects the alternative that provides the greatest level of utility from the choice opportunity. As part of selecting alternative j, he pays p_j and spends $y - p_j$ on other goods during the choice timeframe.

Characterizing $V(p, y, q)$ as given in (16.3) is useful for welfare analysis in the same way that the indirect utility function was useful in earlier chapters. For example, if a person chooses option j he obtains a level of utility given by $V_j(y - p_j, q_j) = \bar{u}$. To obtain an expression for his marginal willingness to pay for a small change in q – i.e. a change that does not alter the extensive margin outcome – we take the total differential while holding utility constant at $\bar{u}$:

$$\frac{\partial V_j(\cdot)}{\partial y} dy + \frac{\partial V_j(\cdot)}{\partial q_j} dq = 0, \tag{16.4}$$

from which we see that the marginal willingness to pay for q is

$$\frac{dy}{dq} = -\frac{\partial V_j(\cdot)/\partial q_j}{\partial V_j(\cdot)/\partial y}. \tag{16.5}$$

Likewise, the compensating variation for a discrete improvement in q from q^0 to q^1 is implicitly defined by

$$\max \left\{ V_1(y - p_1, q_1^0), ..., V_J(y - p_J, q_J^0) \right\} = \\ \max \left\{ V_1(y - p_1 - CV, q_1^1), ..., V_J(y - p_J - CV, q_J^1) \right\}. \tag{16.6}$$

Estimation of the welfare effects in (16.5) and (16.6) is a prime motivation for using discrete choice models in environmental economics. For example, in a recreation application the conditional indirect utility function measures the utility payoff to visiting a recreation site, and the welfare expression in (16.6) can be used to measure the value of a change in an attribute at one or more of the sites.

16.1.2 Towards an Empirical Model

Moving from a conceptual to an empirical discrete choice model involves first introducing a stochastic term to the problem. The way in which this is done is the defining feature of a RUM model. In particular, we assume that the individual knows his preference function with certainty, but that it is imperfectly known by an observer. This is sensible in that an individual knows all the many drivers of his decisions, while an outside observer can only measure a fraction of these. To reflect this uncertainty from the observer's perspective we specify the conditional indirect utility function as consisting of systematic and random components, so that

$$V_j(y - p_j, q_j, s, \varepsilon_j) = v_j(y - p_j, q_j, s) + \varepsilon_j, \quad j = 1, ..., J, \tag{16.7}$$

where $v_j(\cdot)$ is a function of measured variables, including household specific characteristics denoted by s, and ε_j is a random variable. Importantly, $\varepsilon = (\varepsilon_1, ... \varepsilon_J)'$ has a structural interpretation. It is an integral part of the utility function whose value is known to the decision-maker, and hence affects his choices, but unobserved by the analyst. For this reason the random variable in a RUM model is often referred to as unobserved heterogeneity, since it accounts for drivers of decisions not accounted for by the measured variables. Effective accommodation of unobserved heterogeneity is critical in analyses using individual level data, since people who are equivalent in their observed characteristics often make different choices. Likewise, the same person may make different selections when multiple-choice outcomes are observed.

The operational assumption in the application of RUM models is that, although the analyst does not observe the J dimensional random vector $\varepsilon = (\varepsilon_1, ... \varepsilon_J)'$, she knows the distribution from which it is drawn. Thus, while the analyst cannot predict outcomes ahead of time, she can state the ex ante probability of observing a choice conditional on $v_j(\cdot)$. In particular, the person will choose alternative j if and only if $V_j(\cdot) \geq V_k(\cdot)$ for all

$k \neq j$, and so we are interested in an expression for the probability of that choice occurring. We denote this by Pr_j. For the case of $j = 1$ the probability is

$$
\begin{aligned}
\text{Pr}_1 &= \text{Pr}\left[v_1(y - p_1, q_1, s) + \varepsilon_1 \geq v_k(y - p_k, q_k, s) + \varepsilon_k, \forall k \neq 1\right] \\
&= \text{Pr}\left[v_1(y - p_1, q_1, s) - v_k(y - p_k, q_k, s) \geq \varepsilon_k - \varepsilon_1, \forall k \neq 1\right] \qquad (16.8) \\
&= \text{Pr}\left[\tilde{\varepsilon}_k^1 \leq v_1(y - p_1, q_1, s) - v_k(y - p_k, q_k, s), \forall k \neq 1\right],
\end{aligned}
$$

where $\tilde{\varepsilon}_k^1 = \varepsilon_k - \varepsilon_1$.

The discussion thus far suggests a general empirical strategy for estimating a parameterization of individuals' utility functions, which we denote by $V_{ij}(y_i - p_j, q_j, s_i, \varepsilon_{ij}, \beta)$. The script i is now included to indicate a specific individual, and β is a vector of parameters to be estimated. To proceed we first need to observe choice outcomes by a sample of $i = 1, \ldots, I$ decision-makers, each of whom selects a single alternative from the J mutually exclusive options. We refer to the J options as the "choice set", which is defined by the analyst according to the purposes of the study. We also need to observe values for the relevant explanatory variables, such as p_j, q_j, y_i, and s_i. Then, we write down a functional form for $v_{ij}(y_i - p_j, q_j, s_i, \beta)$ and assume a distribution for $\varepsilon_i = (\varepsilon_{i1}, \ldots \varepsilon_{iJ})'$. With these, we can derive statements for Pr_{ij}, conditional on values for β; by matching observed outcomes to their respective probability expressions, we derive a likelihood function and use maximum likelihood to estimate values for β. Finally, we can use resulting predictions of individuals' indirect utility functions for applied welfare analysis. In the following sections we discuss each of these steps in detail.

16.1.3 A Running Example

Since RUM models are best understood within the context of a specific example, we will use an automobile purchase application to illustrate concepts. Understanding automobile purchase decisions has long been of interest to environmental economists, since vehicle demand is a key input into understanding the performance of gasoline taxes, fuel consumption standards, hybrid vehicle subsidies, and other policies. The data we use are a small subset of what was analyzed by Bento et al. (2009), simplified and reconfigured for pedagogical purposes. We have information on $I = 3,216$ new vehicle purchases by US households, obtained from the 2001 National Household Travel Survey. Our set of available alternatives consists of $J = 55$ manufacturer/vehicle class aggregates, so that examples of choice elements in the models we look at include "midsize Ford", "full-size Toyota", and "Honda minivan". All told, we consider six classes of manufacturers (Ford, General Motors, European, Honda, Toyota, other East Asian) and ten vehicle classes (compact, luxury compact, midsize, full size, luxury mid/full size, small SUV, large SUV, minivan, small truck, large truck). Combinations that do not exist in the marketplace or are not purchased by households in our sample are not represented in the choice set.

We have attached three vehicle attributes to each of the 55 manufacturer/class aggregates. Definitions, means (standard deviations), and units for these variables are:

- *operating cost* (*oper*) – cost in US cents of a gallon of gasoline divided by miles per gallon: 6.98 (1.12) US cents.

- *wheelbase* (*wb*) – distance in inches from front to rear axle: 111.00 (9.01) inches.
- *MSRP* (*price*) – manufacturer suggested retail price in $1,000s: $27.27 (13.66).

Each of these variables is computed using market share weighted values of the individual vehicle models included in the make/class aggregates. Because the price of gasoline is different at different locations across the US, *oper* varies both over households and choice elements. In contrast, the variables *wb* and *price* vary only over the choice elements.

We have also attached one household characteristic to each of the 3,216 decision-makers in our sample:

- *household size* (*hhsize*) – number of people in the household: 2.77 (1.27) people.

The models we examine below generally focus on estimating how these alternative-varying and household-varying attributes affect which vehicle is selected on a given purchase occasion. Of particular interest is households' response to the *operating cost* variable, since this has ramifications for several environmental and energy-related policies. For example, in their full application Bento et al. (2009) examine the efficiency and distributional impacts of gasoline taxes. In our simple models we focus instead on the welfare effects of improved fuel efficiency. Importantly, our use of the data here is for pedagogical rather than policy purposes, and as such we have taken a number of simplifying steps. Readers interested in a complete analysis and discussion of preferences for new car purchases, and the ramification of policies that interact with these preferences, should consult Bento et al. (2009).

16.2   BASIC ECONOMETRICS

In this section we examine the workhorse model of discrete choice analysis in environmental economics: the linear in parameters, conditional logit model. To derive this model, note from (16.8) that the probability of observing the choice of alternative *j* by person *i* depends on a $J-1$ dimension random vector of error differences, defined in general as

$$\tilde{\varepsilon}_i^j = \left[(\varepsilon_{i1} - \varepsilon_{ij}),(\varepsilon_{i2} - \varepsilon_{ij}),...,(\varepsilon_{ij-1} - \varepsilon_{ij}),(\varepsilon_{ij+1} - \varepsilon_{ij}),...,(\varepsilon_{iJ} - \varepsilon_{ij})\right]'$$
$$= \left[\tilde{\varepsilon}_{i1}^j,...,\tilde{\varepsilon}_{ij-1}^j,\tilde{\varepsilon}_{ij+1}^j,...,\tilde{\varepsilon}_{iJ}^j\right]'. \tag{16.9}$$

Since we know the distribution of the *J* dimensional random vector $\varepsilon_i = (\varepsilon_{i1},...\,\varepsilon_{iJ})'$ by assumption, we know (or can derive) the distribution for $\tilde{\varepsilon}_i^j$, which we denote by $f(\tilde{\varepsilon}_i^j)$. With this, the probability of observing person *i* choosing option *j* is

$$\text{Pr}_{ij} = \int_{-\infty}^{v_{ij}(\cdot)-v_{i1}(\cdot)} \int_{-\infty}^{v_{ij}(\cdot)-v_{i2}(\cdot)} \cdots \int_{-\infty}^{v_{ij}(\cdot)-v_{iJ}(\cdot)} f(\tilde{\varepsilon}_i^j)d\tilde{\varepsilon}_i^j, \tag{16.10}$$

which is equivalent to (16.8) for $j=1$, rewritten using the probability distribution function $f(\tilde{\varepsilon}_i^j)$. This is a general statement for the probability that holds for any error distribution that we might assume.

For specific values of the explanatory variables and utility function parameters β, we can in principle compute Pr_{ik} for any person i and choice alternative k using (16.10). For estimation, the likelihood function is constructed by matching observed choice outcomes to the corresponding value of Pr_{ik} for each person in the sample. Estimates for β are recovered by numerically maximizing the likelihood function, which requires repeated computation of (16.10) for each observed choice outcome, as the numerical routine iterates over different parameter values. The computational burden of this depends critically on the size of J and what is assumed about the error distribution. For example, if we assume the errors are multivariate normal so that $\varepsilon_i \sim N(0, \Sigma)$, where Σ is a $J \times J$ dimensional variance/covariance matrix, the multivariate probit model emerges. Computation of (16.10) in the probit case involves integrating a multidimensional normal density function in $J-1$ dimensions, which usually requires simulation techniques when J is larger than five. Other assumptions lead to more tractable, albeit less flexible, models such as the conditional logit model. We examine the conditional logit model in detail in the following subsections.

16.2.1 Conditional Logit Model

If we assume ε_{ij} is distributed independent and identical type I extreme value, so that standardized the probability density function is

$$f(\varepsilon_{ij}) = \exp(-\varepsilon_{ij}) \times \exp\left[-\exp(-\varepsilon_{ij})\right], \tag{16.11}$$

the multivariate (or conditional) logit model emerges. Under this assumption for the error terms, Pr_{ij} has the closed form expression

$$\text{Pr}_{ij} = \frac{\exp\left(v_{ij}(\cdot)\right)}{\sum_{k=1}^{J} \exp\left(v_{ik}(\cdot)\right)} = \frac{1}{1 + \sum_{k \neq j}^{J} \exp\left(v_{ik}(\cdot) - v_{ij}(\cdot)\right)}, \quad j = 1, \ldots, J, \tag{16.12}$$

which is simple to compute for given values of β. In particular, the integral in (16.10) has an analytical solution when the unobserved heterogeneity is distributed extreme value, meaning estimation does not need to rely on simulation of the choice probabilities. Train (2009, p.36) provides a derivation of (16.12), beginning with the cumulative distribution function for the extreme value distribution.

The conditional logit model is the most commonly applied discrete choice model when agents have multiple choice alternatives, owing to its ease of estimation. To see this, suppose we observe I agents' choice outcomes, where we denote $d_{ij}=1$ if person i chose alternative j, and $d_{ij}=0$ otherwise. The log-likelihood for the sample when the errors are independent type I extreme value has the closed form

$$LL(\beta) = \sum_{i=1}^{I} \sum_{j=1}^{J} d_{ij} \ln \text{Pr}_{ij}$$

$$= \sum_{i=1}^{I} \sum_{j=1}^{J} d_{ij} \left\{ v_{ij}(\cdot) - \ln\left[\sum_{k=1}^{J} \exp(v_{ik}(\cdot))\right]\right\}, \tag{16.13}$$

where the independence of the I choice outcomes allows us to write the function as a sum of logged probabilities. Maximizing $LL(\beta)$ with respect to the elements of β is straightforward using a numerical search routine, since $LL(\beta)$ is globally concave and it has continuous, closed form derivatives with respect to the elements of β. Thus we can use maximum likelihood to recover estimates of β, given a specific choice of functional form for $v_{ij}(\cdot)$. From the perspective of contemporary computers and software, application of this model is easy and can be completed with virtually any commercial or publicly available econometric software.

16.2.2 Specification

Given that ε_{ij} is distributed extreme value, all that remains to complete the specification of our simple RUM model is selection of a specific form for $v_{ij}(\cdot)$. This depends on the nature of the study and the available data, but two important features of RUM models condition the choice: (a) the scale of utility is irrelevant; and (b) only utility differences matter. Both conditions are based on the ordinal nature of utility. Since behavior will be the same if each of the conditional indirect utility functions is multiplied by a constant, their absolute magnitudes cannot have meaning. Likewise, since behavior is based on a comparison of utility levels, only utility differences matter for behavior and therefore have empirical relevance. To explore what these features of discrete choice models mean for specification, we define W_{ij} as a K dimensional vector of covariates used to parameterize $v_{ij}(\cdot)$. For example, W_{ij} includes specific variables such as $y_i - p_j$ and q_j as defined above, as well as variables constructed from elements of s_i. We assume that W_{ij} enters utility linearly, so that $v_{ij} = \beta' \cdot W_{ij}$, where β is a K dimensional parameter vector that will be estimated.

Note from Eq. (16.10) and the second expression in (16.12) that the utility difference $V_{ij} - V_{ik}$, rather than the level utility, is what enters the probability expressions and hence the likelihood function. For the specific parameterization $v_{ij} = \beta' \cdot W_{ij}$, we observe person i choosing option j if and only if $\varepsilon_{ik} - \varepsilon_{ij} \le \beta' \cdot (W_{ij} - W_{ik})$ for all $k \ne j$. Importantly, only variables that remain in the differenced terms $(W_{ij} - W_{ik})$ have a role to play in explaining behavior. In addition, adding a fixed constant to each of the v_{ij} functions does not affect outcomes, since the constant will fall away in the difference.

To understand the consequences of these features of RUM models, consider our vehicle purchase application. A simple specification allowing us to learn something about how the attributes of a vehicle affect the utility it provides is

$$V_{ij} = \beta_0 (y_i - price_j) + \beta_1 oper_{ij} + \beta_2 wb_j + \varepsilon_{ij}, \quad j = 1,...,55, \tag{16.14}$$

where y_i is household income. Note three things about V_{ij} as it is written here. First, the signs of the elements of β have a clear economic meaning. For example, if $\beta_2 > 0$, we can conclude that an increase in wheelbase (a proxy for the size of the vehicle) increases the utility payoff for an alternative, and therefore the likelihood of its purchase. Likewise, $\beta_0 > 0$ suggests a smaller price is preferred, all else being equal. Second, the magnitudes of parameters such as $\beta_2 = \partial V / \partial wb$ and $\beta_0 = \partial V / \partial y$ – the marginal utility of operating cost and income, respectively – do not have a quantitative interpretation, since the scale of an ordinal utility function is irrelevant for behavior. Finally, this specification for V_{ij} does not allow income to affect choices. To see this, note that when utility for alternative j is differenced against alternative k we obtain

$$V_{ij} - V_{ik} = \beta_0 y_i - \beta_0 y_i - \beta_0 (price_j - price_k) + \beta_1 (oper_{ij} - oper_{ik})$$
$$+ \beta_2 (wb_j - wb_k) + \varepsilon_{ij} - \varepsilon_{ik}, \quad k \neq j. \tag{16.15}$$

Because *price*, *oper*, and *wb* vary between alternatives j and k, they remain when utility is differenced. In contrast, y_i is the same in V_{ij} and V_{ik}, since it is a characteristic of the decision-maker that does not change across the choice alternatives. Thus $\beta_0 y_i$ drops out of (16.15), and a household's income does not affect its choice when utility is linear in the budget constraint. Nonetheless, we can still estimate the marginal utility of income β_0, since the price difference remains in $V_{ij} - V_{ik}$. Because income falls out of the utility difference, it is customary to write linear-in-income utility functions without explicit reference to y_i:

$$V_{ij} = -\beta_0 price_j + \beta_1 oper_{ij} + \beta_2 wb_j + \varepsilon_{ij}, \quad j = 1,...,55. \tag{16.16}$$

EXAMPLE 16.1 (EMPIRICAL) We estimate this model using the Bento et al. data, and obtain the following results:

$$V_{ij} = \underset{(18.90)}{-0.051 \cdot} price_j + \underset{(1.61)}{0.038 \cdot} oper_{ij} + \underset{(8.50)}{0.021 \cdot} wb_j + \varepsilon_{ij}, \tag{16.17}$$

where z-statistics are given in parentheses below the estimates. Note that we find intuitive signs for the attributes *price* and *wb* – i.e. people like lower prices and bigger vehicles. However, the sign on *oper* is positive, suggesting vehicles with higher operating expenses are more attractive than those that cost less to run. As we discuss in detail below, this counterintuitive result is likely due to omitted variable bias, since there are many other attributes of vehicles that affect choices.

As described earlier, the estimates of the marginal utility of income ($\beta_0 = 0.051$) and the marginal utility of wheelbase ($\beta_2 = 0.021$) do not have quantitative interpretations. However, the expression in (16.5) demonstrates that the ratio of parameters does have an economic interpretation. In particular, $\beta_2/\beta_0 = 0.021/0.051 = 0.418$ is the marginal willingness to pay (in \$1,000s) for a one inch increase in vehicle length. Thus, on average, the estimates show that new vehicle purchasers value an additional inch of vehicle length at \$418. More generally, the ratio of the parameter on a non-monetary attribute over the marginal utility of income provides an estimate of the marginal willingness to pay for a unit of that attribute.

The specification in (16.14) includes two types of variables. The terms *price* and *wb* vary only across the $J = 55$ alternatives and so estimates of β_0 and β_2 arise based on a maximum of 55 different values for the explanatory variables. The term *oper* varies over both the $J = 55$ alternatives and the $I = 3,216$ decision-makers, meaning more data are contributing to the estimate of β_1. A third type of variable is not included in (16.14).

Characteristics of decision-makers are not present in the specification, though it is intuitive that household size, for example, might affect utility levels of different vehicle classes, and hence purchase decisions. In RUM models, decision-maker characteristics need to be included as interaction variables. There are two possible ways to do this. One is to allow decision-maker characteristics to affect the utility of some alternatives relative to others, meaning the interaction is between the household characteristic and a choice alternative indicator. An example of this is

$$
\begin{aligned}
V_{ij} &= -\beta_0 price_j + \beta_1 oper_{ij} + \beta_2 wb_j + \gamma_1 hhsize_i + \varepsilon_{ij}, \quad j \in large \\
V_{ij} &= -\beta_0 price_j + \beta_1 oper_{ij} + \beta_2 wb_j + \varepsilon_{ij}, \quad j \notin large,
\end{aligned}
\tag{16.18}
$$

where "large" is the set of vehicle alternatives that have space for six or more passengers. Note that γ_1 is the additional utility provided by "large" vehicles, relative to not-large vehicles, for each additional person in the household. We can estimate γ_1 because it remains in the utility difference

$$
\begin{aligned}
V_{ij} - V_{ik} &= -\beta_0 (price_j - price_k) + \beta_1 (oper_{ij} - oper_{ik}) \\
&\quad + \beta_2 (wb_j - wb_k) + \gamma_1 hhsize_i + \varepsilon_{ij} - \varepsilon_{ik},
\end{aligned}
\tag{16.19}
$$

when j is an element of "large" and k is not. By way of contrast, we cannot estimate both γ_1 and γ_2 in

$$
\begin{aligned}
V_{ij} &= -\beta_0 price_j + \beta_1 oper_{ij} + \beta_2 wb_j + \gamma_1 hhsize_i + \varepsilon_{ij}, \quad j \in large \\
V_{ij} &= -\beta_0 price_j + \beta_1 oper_{ij} + \beta_2 wb_j + \gamma_2 hhsize_i + \varepsilon_{ij}, \quad j \notin large,
\end{aligned}
\tag{16.20}
$$

since the utility difference

$$
\begin{aligned}
V_{ij} - V_{ik} &= -\beta_0 (price_j - price_k) + \beta_1 (oper_{ij} - oper_{ik}) \\
&\quad + \beta_2 (wb_j - wb_k) + (\gamma_1 - \gamma_2) hhsize_i + \varepsilon_{ij} - \varepsilon_{ik}
\end{aligned}
\tag{16.21}
$$

does not isolate γ_2 separately from γ_1. Thus the normalization $\gamma_2 = 0$ is needed, which reduces the specification to (16.18).

In general, household characteristics can be used to estimate the change in utility relative to an excluded alternative. Thus, we can include a decision-maker characteristic in up to $J-1$ of the alternatives, and estimate up to $J-1$ coefficients for that characteristic. For example, we could estimate the specification

$$
\begin{aligned}
V_{ij} &= -\beta_0 price_j + \beta_1 oper_{ij} + \beta_2 wb_j + \gamma_j hhsize_i + \varepsilon_{ij}, \quad j = 1,\ldots,54, \\
V_{ij} &= -\beta_0 price_j + \beta_1 oper_{ij} + \beta_2 wb_j + \varepsilon_{ij}, \quad j = 55,
\end{aligned}
\tag{16.22}
$$

in order to learn how household size makes the different vehicle alternatives more or less attractive, relative to each other and the left out alternative. With the normalization, comparisons between γ_j and γ_k are meaningful. For example, if we find that $\gamma_j > \gamma_k$, where j is "Honda minivan" and k is "Honda compact", we can conclude that the former becomes relatively more attractive with increases in household size, all else being equal.

A second way to introduce decision-maker characteristics is via interactions with the characteristics of alternatives. Rather than specifying the role of household size as in (16.18), we can instead use

$$V_{ij} = -\beta_0\, price_j + \beta_1 oper_{ij} + \beta_2 wb_j + \gamma_1 wb_j \times hhsize_i + \varepsilon_{ij}, \quad \forall j. \tag{16.23}$$

Note that the marginal utility of wb is now $\partial V/\partial wb = \beta_2 + \gamma_1 \times hhsize_i$. Thus the contribution of vehicle size to utility depends on the number of people in the household. We can estimate γ_1 in this specification, since the utility difference is

$$
\begin{aligned}
V_{ij} - V_{ik} = &-\beta_0(price_j - price_k) + \beta_1(oper_{ij} - oper_{ik}) \\
&+ \beta_2(wb_j - wb_k) + \gamma_1 hhsize_i(wb_j - wb_k) + \varepsilon_{ij} - \varepsilon_{ik},
\end{aligned}
\tag{16.24}
$$

which contains γ_1.

EXAMPLE 16.2 (EMPIRICAL) Estimation results for the specification in (16.23) are given by

$$
\begin{aligned}
V_{ij} = &-\underset{(18.81)}{0.051} \cdot price_j + \underset{(1.39)}{0.033} \cdot oper_{ij} + \underset{(0.22)}{0.0009} \cdot wb_j \\
&+ \underset{(6.07)}{0.0075} \cdot wb_j \cdot hhsize_i + \varepsilon_{ij}.
\end{aligned}
\tag{16.25}
$$

From this specification we can see the relationship between the number of people in the household, and the attractiveness of larger cars generally. For example, the marginal willingness to pay for a larger wheelbase by a household with two people is $(0.0009 + 0.0075 \times 2)/0.051 = 0.31$, while the corresponding figure for a household with six is $(0.0009 + 0.0075 \times 6)/0.051 = 0.90$. Converting these back to dollars, the comparison is $310 versus $900 per extra inch of length for households with two and six people, respectively.

A final specification topic concerns the use of alternative specific constants (ASCs) – alternative fixed effects – in the conditional utility functions. As we discuss below, this can be an effective way of accounting for attributes of choice alternatives that are not measured by the analyst, in the same way that time fixed effects are used in panel data applications to control for unobserved time effects. Two points bear mention regarding the use of ASCs. First, we cannot estimate J separate constants in a model with J alternatives, since this would imply estimation of the magnitude of level utility for all alternatives. Instead we can estimate at most $J-1$ constants, so that the magnitudes of the ASCs are interpreted relative to the left out alternative. In our car example we can estimate

$$
\begin{aligned}
V_{ij} &= \delta_j + \beta_1 oper_{ij} + \gamma_1 wb_j \times hhsize_i + \varepsilon_{ij}, \quad j = 1,...,54 \\
V_{ij} &= + \beta_1 oper_{ij} + \gamma_1 wb_j \times hhsize_i + \varepsilon_{ij}, \quad j = 55,
\end{aligned}
\tag{16.26}
$$

where δ_j is the average utility (after accounting for $oper$ and the interaction of wb and $hhsize$) for vehicle j relative to vehicle $j = 55$. Note that with this normalization, comparisons between ASCs are meaningful – i.e. if we find that $\delta_j > \delta_k$, we can conclude that alternative j is on average more attractive than k, controlling for the other covariates.

The specification in (16.26) illustrates the second point regarding the use of ASCs. In particular, it is not possible to estimate both a full set of $J-1$ ASCs *and* the effect of attributes that vary only over alternatives. This is because δ_j in Eq. (16.26) captures the overall utility difference between alternatives, while β_0 in Eq. (16.23) captures the part of the utility difference attributable to one factor. Since the latter is nested within the former, we cannot separate out β_0 from δ_j. Said another way, in our vehicle choice application it is not possible to estimate

$$
\begin{aligned}
V_{ij} &= \delta_j - \beta_0 price_j + \beta_1 oper_{ij} + \beta_2 wb_j + \gamma_1 wb_j \times hhsize_i + \varepsilon_{ij}, \quad j \neq 55 \\
V_{ij} &= \quad\;\; - \beta_0 price_j + \beta_1 oper_{ij} + \beta_2 wb_j + \gamma_1 wb_j \times hhsize_i + \varepsilon_{ij}, \quad j = 55,
\end{aligned}
\tag{16.27}
$$

since the ASCs and attribute variables are confounded – i.e. they do not separately vary. This is analogous once again to time fixed effects in a linear panel data model, where individual invariant variables (e.g. macro-economic shocks) are swallowed up by the time fixed effects, and therefore cannot be independently estimated.

EXAMPLE 16.3 (EMPIRICAL) Estimation results for the vehicle choice model with ASCs are given by

$$
V_{ij} = \delta_j \underset{(-22.42)}{-0.437 \cdot} oper_{ij} + \underset{(9.83)}{0.0072 \cdot} wb_j \times hhsize_i + \varepsilon_{ij},
\tag{16.28}
$$

where we have not written out the 54 ASCs that were also estimated. Note that we now find a negative and significant coefficient for operating costs, suggesting that people do indeed prefer vehicles that are less costly to operate, holding fixed all other attributes. The omitted variable bias alluded to above is less of a concern in (16.28), since the other attributes of vehicles that may be correlated with operating costs (e.g. engine size) are accounted for by δ_j. However, since *price* is subsumed into the ASC, we are not able to estimate the marginal utility of income directly – a point to which we return in the next subsection.

16.3 IDENTIFICATION

Our discussion on specification in the previous section was largely mechanical, in that we focused on how different types of variables need to be specified in order to estimate their coefficients. We had little to say about the actual reliability of the estimates we obtained. In this section we turn our attention to "identification" – determining the circumstances in which we are able to consistently estimate (reliably identify) the role of attributes in the utility function. This is a topic that has received increasing attention as the use of RUM models has proliferated throughout applied microeconomics. To a great extent identification in RUM models (as in standard linear models) depends on how we treat unmeasured determinants of behavior. For this reason it is useful to expand our notation to distinguish between attributes of choice alternatives that are measured by the analyst, and attributes that affect choice but are not measured. Specifically, define $(p_j, q_j, w_{ij}, \xi_j)$ as the collection of attributes of alternative j, where w_{ij} contains attributes that vary over both alternatives and people and the remaining terms vary only over alternatives. The price variable p_j and the variables included in q_j and w_{ij} are measured by the analyst – i.e. available in the data – and the scalar ξ_j represents characteristics of alternative j that she cannot observe. For example, in a recreation application where alternatives are freshwater lakes, ξ_j could reflect the presence/absence of noise levels from nearby roadways, the thickness of subsurface weed beds, or general congestion levels. Importantly, ξ_j is known by decision-makers, and so it enters the utility function and influences people's choices. Thus, in referring to ξ_j as an unobserved attribute of alternative j, it is from the perspective of the analyst.

The idea that there are attributes of alternatives that are perceived by the decision-maker but unmeasured by the analyst is intuitive in other applications besides recreation. Suppose we are considering which residential neighborhood a household will select as its primary residence. Intangibles such as the general upkeep of structures and quality of landscaping are observed by potential buyers, but they are difficult to measure objectively by the analyst. In a vehicle choice application, the available models may differ in their reputations for reliability, but the analyst is unlikely to possess a variable reflecting this. As this and the other examples suggest, ξ_j often contains intangible or difficult to measure quality aspects of the choice alternatives. With ξ_j now included, a general way to write the conditional indirect utility function for person i is

$$V_{ij} = -\beta_0 p_j + \beta' q_j + \beta'_w w_{ij} + \xi_j + \sum_{m=1}^{Q} \gamma_m \times s_i \times q_{jm} + \varepsilon_{ij}, \qquad (16.29)$$

where the βs measure the "main" effects of the attributes, and the γs capture the "interaction" effects that are included in the model. For purposes of exposition it is useful to group together factors that only vary over alternatives, and so we rewrite the indirect utility function as

$$V_{ij} = \delta_j + \beta'_w w_{ij} + \sum_{m=1}^{Q} \gamma_m \times s_i \times q_{jm} + \varepsilon_{ij}, \quad j = 1, \ldots, J, \quad i = 1, \ldots, I, \qquad (16.30)$$

where

$$\delta_j = -\beta_0 p_j + \beta' q_j + \xi_j, \quad j = 1, \ldots, J. \qquad (16.31)$$

Expressed this way, we can view the alternative specific constant δ_j as a fixed effect that subsumes all main effects that are constant over people for alternative j – both measured and unmeasured.

Our task is to examine how different assumptions about the relationship between ξ_j and the observed attributes imply different estimation and identification strategies. In particular, it will be critical to judge the extent to which ξ_j varies across alternatives, and whether or not ξ_j is correlated with p_j and/or elements of q_j and w_{ij}. All RUM models employ one of two assumptions in this regard, either explicitly or implicitly. The first is to assume that ξ_j is constant for all j so that $\xi_j = c$, in which case the specification reduces to

$$V_{ij} = c - \beta_0 p_j + \beta' q_j + \beta'_w w_{ij} + \sum_{m=1}^{Q} \gamma_m \times s_i \times q_{jm} + \varepsilon_{ij}. \qquad (16.32)$$

Since c is constant across all alternatives, and therefore falls away in differencing, this is equivalent to assuming that $\xi_j = 0$, so

$$V_{ij} = -\beta_0 p_j + \beta' q_j + \beta'_w w_{ij} + \sum_{m=1}^{Q} \gamma_m \times s_i \times q_{jm} + \varepsilon_{ij}. \qquad (16.33)$$

This assumption says that an alternative is fully characterized by (and hence fully differentiated from the other alternatives by) the observed attributes contained in p_j, q_j, and w_{ij}. That is, other than ε_{ij}, there is nothing unobserved or unmeasured by the analyst that systematically affects people's choices. In instances where high-quality data containing many variables are available, this may be reasonable.

In the event that the levels of unmeasured attributes do vary across the choice alternatives, so that in reality $\xi_j \neq \xi_k$, the specification in (16.33) will result in inconsistent parameter estimates. For example, our vehicle choice specification in (16.23) implicitly used the assumption that $\xi_j = 0$. This is to say that vehicles in our choice set are fully characterized by their price, size, and operating cost variables. This is unlikely to be true, implying there are attributes of vehicles that matter to buyers, but which are excluded in the simple specification. As evidence of this, recall that we found an unexpectedly positive coefficient on *oper* when we estimated the parameters in (16.23). We speculated that this resulted from operating expense being correlated with aspects of vehicles that are not included in the specification, such as engine size. People therefore do not prefer vehicles that are more costly to operate. Instead, it is more plausible that, holding all else constant, vehicle consumers care about engine size, which is positively correlated with operating expense, since larger engines consume more fuel. Omitting engine size from the specification created an omitted variable bias that led to the perversely signed coefficient on *oper*.

The second assumption is to explicitly allow $\xi_j \neq \xi_k$, which is closely related to using a full set of alternative specific constants. When $\xi_j \neq \xi_k$, we would ideally estimate a specification as in (16.29), with the objective of recovering estimates of the βs, γs, and $\xi_1, ..., \xi_{J-1}$, where ξ_J is normalized to zero. As discussed in the previous section, however, this is equivalent to estimating a full set of alternative specific constants *and* the main effects simultaneously, which cannot be accomplished in a single step due to the nesting of individual main effects in the overall utility average δ_j. We could nonetheless proceed with a specification as in (16.30), which allows us to recover β_w (the coefficients on variables that vary across both people and alternatives), as well as the γs and the ASCs $\delta_1, ..., \delta_{J-1}$. This strategy is equivalent to using a fixed effect to control for all attributes of alternative j, which provides consistent estimates of β_w and the γs, since the problematic unmeasured variables are subsumed into the fixed effect. An example of this is our vehicle choice specification in (16.26), where we used ASCs to control for all person-constant attributes of the choice alternatives. More specifically, the effect of engine size (and all other attributes of vehicle j) was captured by the alternative specific constant δ_j, which allowed us to recover an estimate of the coefficient on *oper* that was intuitively signed and plausibly consistent. However, we were not able to estimate the marginal utility of income, since price, along with the other factors varying only over alternatives, was subsumed into the fixed effect.

When fixed effects are used to consistently estimate β_w and the γs, additional effort is needed if we want to decompose the coefficients $\delta_1,...,\delta_{J-1}$ and $\delta_J = 0$ into their observable (β_0 and β) and unobservable ($\xi_1,...,\xi_J$) components. In some instances it is possible to do this using a second stage, linear regression defined by (16.31).

EXAMPLE 16.4 (EMPIRICAL) The vehicle choice model in (16.30) provided a full set of ASCs, which we can use in a second step to estimate the linear regression

$$\delta_j = \delta - \beta_0 \, price_j + \beta_2 wb_j + \xi_j, \quad j = 1,...,55. \tag{16.34}$$

The results when we use OLS to recover $(\delta, \beta_0, \beta_2)$ are

$$\delta_j = \underset{(-3.47)}{-5.63} - \underset{(2.96)}{0.028} \cdot price_j + \underset{(3.01)}{0.042} \cdot wb_j + \xi_j, \quad j = 1,...,55, \tag{16.35}$$

and the residuals from this regression provide estimates of $\xi_1,...,\xi_J$. Thus for the vehicle choice example, we are able to estimate *all* of the components of preferences shown in Eq. (16.29).

There are two final points regarding identification when $\xi_j \neq 0$. First, by using OLS to estimate the second stage regression we have assumed that the observed variables are uncorrelated with ξ_j. In our vehicle choice example, this is to say that $price_j$ is not correlated with aspects of vehicle quality not included in the regression, and hence residing in ξ_j. This seems unlikely in reality, since quality will be reflected in market prices, inducing positive correlation between $price_j$ and ξ_j. Thus the coefficient on price will be biased towards zero – it will be too small in absolute value – since $price_j$ in (16.35) reflects something unattractive (a larger amount of the budget is needed for purchase) and something attractive (higher price also reflects higher quality). Ideally we would like to purge the latter from our estimate of β_0, which can often be accomplished using instrumental variables (IV) rather than OLS to estimate (16.34). Though we do not pursue this here, IV regression in this context uses the same methods and imbeds the same challenges as with any linear model. The second point concerns when a second stage regression is feasible. Note that the number of observations in the linear regression is J – the number of choice alternatives. Thus this approach to identification requires a moderate to large choice set to be feasible.

Our discussion here and in the previous section highlights that the effective use of RUM models requires an understanding of two complementary topics. The first is mechanical, and has to do with how factors that vary over alternatives, people, and/or alternatives and people can be included in the model, and how estimates should be interpreted. The second is more subtle, and has to do with the interaction between determinants of behavior that we can measure, and those that we cannot. The latter is critical for judging the reliability of estimates, and it requires intuition and introspection. Explicitly considering the role of ξ_j in the specification is a useful vehicle for focusing attention on identification, even if we ultimately need to assume that $\xi_j = 0$ for all alternatives, in order to estimate the marginal utilities of specific, varying-over-alternative variables. When the choice set is large enough to accommodate a two-stage estimation approach, we have seen that the use of ASCs recasts the identification problem into a familiar, linear regression context.

16.4   FEATURES OF THE LOGIT MODEL

The linear-in-parameters conditional logit model that we have thus far examined has two defining features. The first is its ease of estimation, which explains its widespread use in applied analysis. The second is the assumption that ε_{ij} is independent from ε_{ik} for all $j \neq k$, which arises from the independent and identical type I extreme value distribution. As we discuss in this subsection, this latter feature implies restrictive and in some cases implausible behavioral patterns. This has motivated alternative distributions for the unobserved heterogeneity in RUM models, which we discuss subsequently.

Recall that ε_{ij} plays a key role in RUM models, in that it represents aspects of person i's preferences that affect choices but are not observed by the analyst. Thus in the conditional logit model, the underlying assumption is that the unobserved components of utility are uncorrelated across choice alternatives. To understand the ramifications of this, consider again our vehicle choice application. It is sensible to suppose that larger households will prefer larger vehicles, all else being equal. Indeed, we found evidence of this in one of our empirical examples. Suppose, however, that the data do not contain information on household size. In this case the role of household size resides in the error term – i.e. household size is an unobserved determinant of utility for each alternative. For a household i with many people, this implies that ε_{ij} is bigger for any vehicle j within the subset of "large" vehicles. This in turn suggests there is positive correlation between ε_{ij} and ε_{ik} when alternatives j and k are both "large." However, the conditional logit model does not allow this correlation to arise, due to its assumption of independent errors. This is just one example of how the complexity of human behavior might be expected to induce correlation among the elements of $\varepsilon_i = (\varepsilon_{i1}, \ldots, \varepsilon_{iJ})$ in a RUM model. Other examples from our vehicle choice application include an upper middle-class preference for imports, young males' tendency to prefer vehicles with larger engines, and parents' interest in safety features. If these factors are systematic in the population of buyers – and variables reflecting wealth, age and gender, and the presence of young children are not included in the specification – then the conditional logit model results in a misspecification.

To understand how such a misspecification might matter for inference, consider the *independence of irrelevant alternatives* (IIA) property of logit models. Note in particular that the ratio of two choice probabilities in the conditional logit model is given by

$$\frac{\Pr_{ij}}{\Pr_{ik}} = \frac{\exp\left(v_{ij}(\cdot)\right)}{\sum_{m=1}^{J} \exp\left(v_{im}(\cdot)\right)} \bigg/ \frac{\exp\left(v_{ik}(\cdot)\right)}{\sum_{m=1}^{J} \exp\left(v_{im}(\cdot)\right)} = \frac{\exp\left(v_{ij}(\cdot)\right)}{\exp\left(v_{ik}(\cdot)\right)}. \tag{16.36}$$

Thus the ratio Pr_{ij}/Pr_{ik} depends *only* on the attributes of alternatives j and k, implying the relative odds of selecting j over k is the same, regardless of what other alternatives are available, or what their attribute levels are. This has fairly strong ramifications for how the conditional logit model computes substitution patterns among the available alternatives. To see this consider the log odds ratio

$$\ln\left(\frac{\mathrm{Pr}_{ij}}{\mathrm{Pr}_{ik}}\right) = v_{ij}(\cdot) - v_{ik}(\cdot), \tag{16.37}$$

and differentiate with respect to one of the attributes in alternative k (say price p_k) to obtain

$$\frac{\mathrm{Pr}_{ik}}{\mathrm{Pr}_{ij}}\frac{\partial\left[\mathrm{Pr}_{ij}/\mathrm{Pr}_{ik}\right]}{\partial p_k} = -\frac{\partial v_{ik}(\cdot)}{\partial p_k} \quad \rightarrow \quad \frac{\partial\left[\mathrm{Pr}_{ij}/\mathrm{Pr}_{ik}\right]}{\partial p_k} = -\frac{\partial v_{ik}(\cdot)}{\partial p_k}\frac{\mathrm{Pr}_{ij}}{\mathrm{Pr}_{ik}}. \tag{16.38}$$

Note that $\partial v_{ik}(\cdot)/\partial p_k$ is the proportional change in the odds that the decision-maker chooses j relative to k, when an attribute of alternative k changes. Importantly, the proportional change is *not* a function of $v_{ij}(\cdot)$. Thus the same proportional change in Pr_{ij} occurs for all $j \neq k$, when an attribute in k changes. For example, if there is an increase in the price of alternative k, the probabilities for all the remaining alternatives will increase by the same proportion. This can be a significant limitation of the conditional logit model. To see an example of this, consider a vehicle choice context in which the choice set includes three vehicle classes: small gas engine cars, large gas engine cars, and small electric engine cars. Furthermore, suppose we want to predict the effect on choice of a cash rebate following purchase of an electric engine vehicle. This decrease in the price of electric engine cars will reduce the choice probabilities for the other vehicle classes. Due to the IIA property of the conditional logit model, the predicted probabilities for the large gas and small gas vehicles must fall by the same proportion, in response to the small electric vehicle price reduction. In reality, however, we would expect a lower purchase price for small electric cars to reduce the choice probability for small gas cars by a larger proportion than it would for large gas cars. This is because the two small car classes are likely closer substitutes than the large car class is with either of the small car classes. Using the conditional logit model, we are likely to over-predict the change in choice probability for large gas engine cars.

Train (2009) uses examples of this type to discuss how the IIA property of the conditional logit model is both a strength and weakness. If the model is richly specified with alternative specific constants and several interactions between decision-makers and alternative characteristics, independent errors (and hence IIA) may be an appropriate property, since it implies that the unexplained variation in choices is just white noise. In other circumstances, however, IIA represents a clear limitation of the conditional logit model.

16.5 ADVANCED ECONOMETRICS

The potential limitations of the IIA property of the conditional logit model have long been recognized, and for an equally long period of time researchers have therefore sought more flexible alternatives. For example, as noted above, the multinomial probit model arises when we assume that the unobserved component of preferences $\varepsilon_i = (\varepsilon_{i1}, \ldots, \varepsilon_{iJ})$ is distributed $N(0, \Sigma)$, where $N(\cdot)$ denotes the normal distribution and Σ is a J-dimensional covariance matrix with non-zero diagonal elements. This latter feature allows the probit model to capture very general patterns of correlation among the unobserved components of preferences, and so it is in principle an attractive alternative to the conditional logit model. Until recently, however, computational challenges have limited the applicability of the probit model. In particular, we saw from Eq. (16.10) that calculation of the choice probabilities in a discrete choice model, which is necessary for estimation, requires computation of a $J - 1$ dimensional integral. The difficulty with the probit model is that no analytical solution exists for (16.10) when $\varepsilon_i \sim N(0, \Sigma)$, and so some type of numerical approximation is needed. Limitations in computing power and numerical methods effectively meant that, throughout the 1970s and 1980s, probit models could not be estimated with more than a handful of alternatives in the choice set.

This began to change in the 1990s with the arrival of powerful and widely distributed desktop computing resources. Probability expressions as in (16.10) no longer needed to be numerically approximated, but could instead be simulated using newly developed algorithms, such as the GHK simulator for multivariate normal probability integrals (see Train, 2009, p.129). With computational limitations relaxed, applied researchers began to investigate the performance of strategies for relaxing the IIA assumption in conditional logit models, while maintaining some of their attractive features. An important development in this area, which has been widely applied in environmental economics, is the mixed logit model. In what follows we sketch the basic structure and intuition of the mixed logit model, and describe its capabilities. Readers interested in a full treatment should consult Train (2009, Chapter 6).

The motivating idea behind the mixed logit model is that utility is given by

$$V_{ij} = \beta_i' W_{ij} + \varepsilon_{ij}, \quad i = 1, \ldots, I, \quad j = 1, \ldots, J, \tag{16.39}$$

where W_{ij} is the collection of covariates, β_i is a vector of utility function parameters specific to person i, and ε_{ij} is distributed type I extreme value. Note that, aside from the subscript on the parameter vector, this is identical to the conditional logit model. The generalization comes from assuming that β_i is known by person i, but that it is a random variable (drawn from a known distribution) from the perspective of the analyst. A common assumption is that $\beta_i \sim N(b, \Omega)$, where b is a vector of mean marginal utilities in the population associated with the variables in W_{ij}, and the variance matrix Ω describes how much preferences for attributes vary in the population. Thus the parameters in the utility function are themselves random from the observer's perspective, and unobserved heterogeneity enters the model both via ε_{ij} and β_i. This has considerable appeal, in that it allows for the possibility that the intensity of like or dislike for different attributes of the J alternatives varies within the population. Indeed, it is even possible that some elements of β_i are positive for some decision-makers, and negative for others. It may also be that elements of β_i are constant in the population (i.e. have a degenerate distribution).

The probability of observing person i choosing alternative j conditional on β_i is simply the conditional logit probability as given in (16.12). Since we do not know β_i, however, it is the unconditional probability that we need to compute in order to construct the likelihood function. This is given by

$$\Pr_{ij} = \int \frac{\exp(\beta_i' W_{ij})}{\sum_{k=1}^{J} \exp(\beta_i' W_{ik})} f(\beta_i) d\beta_i, \quad j = 1,...,J, \tag{16.40}$$

where $f(\beta_i)$ is the probability density function (PDF) for β_i, and the integral is evaluated over the full support of the PDF. Thus $\Pr_{ij}$ is a weighted average of the logit probability evaluated at the different values that the coefficients can take, where the weights are determined by how likely the different values for β_i are. In the mixed logit model, we use (16.40) to compute the choice probabilities and construct the likelihood function, and the objective of estimation is to recover the parameters of the PDF for β_i. For example, when $\beta_i \sim N(b, \Omega)$, we are interested in obtaining estimates for b and Ω so as to measure both mean preferences (via b) and how variable preferences are (via Ω).

An important advantage of the mixed logit model is that it does not exhibit the IIA property. To see this, note that the log odds that person i selects alternative j over alternative k is

$$\ln\left(\frac{\Pr_{ij}}{\Pr_{ik}}\right) = \ln\left(\int \frac{\exp(\beta_i' W_{ij})}{\sum_{k=1}^{J} \exp(\beta_i' W_{ik})} f(\beta_i)\right) - \ln\left(\int \frac{\exp(\beta_i' W_{ik})}{\sum_{k=1}^{J} \exp(\beta_i' W_{ik})} f(\beta_i)\right), \tag{16.41}$$

and that the mixed logit analog to Eq. (16.38) is

$$\frac{\Pr_{ik}}{\Pr_{ij}} \frac{\partial \left[\Pr_{ij} / \Pr_{ik} \right]}{\partial p_k} = \frac{1}{\Pr_{ij}} \frac{\partial \Pr_{ij}}{\partial p_k} - \frac{1}{\Pr_{ik}} \frac{\partial \Pr_{ik}}{\partial p_k}. \tag{16.42}$$

Thus the response of the probability that a person selects alternative j when an attribute in alternative k changes depends on the full range of substitution possibilities, as reflected in $\Pr_{ij}$, $\Pr_{ik}$, and their derivatives.

The cost of these capabilities is that (16.40) does not have a closed form analytical solution, and so estimation is more complicated than in the conditional logit case. In particular, maximizing the likelihood function requires that we compute (16.40) across the entire sample, for candidate values of the unknown parameters, and nest these computations within the maximum likelihood numerical search routine. As it turns out, this is a comparatively easy simulation problem. Heuristically, for a particular individual and particular values of the parameters of the distribution function $f(\beta_i)$, we simulate R realizations of β_i from its distribution $f(\beta_i)$. Each realization β_i^r is then used to compute the closed form conditional logit probability, and the average of the resulting R probabilities provides an approximation to the true probability. Estimation of the mixed logit model proceeds by using the simulated probabilities for all sample members to construct the likelihood function, and estimating the unknown parameters – that is, the parameters of the probability distribution function $f(\beta_i)$ – via simulated maximum likelihood.

To illustrate the mixed logit model we examine the following specification for the vehicle choice application:

$$V_{ij} = -\beta_0 \, price_j + \beta_1^i oper_{ij} + \beta_2^i wb_j + \varepsilon_{ij}, \quad j = 1,...,55, \tag{16.43}$$

where β_0 is a constant and the parameters on $oper_{ij}$ and wb_j vary across the population. Specifically, we assume that $\beta_1^i \sim N(b_1, \sigma_1^2)$ and that $\beta_2^i \sim N(b_2, \sigma_2^2)$, where b_1 and b_2 are the population average marginal utilities, and σ_1^2 and σ_2^2 are the respective variances. Note that this specification assumes that β_1^i and β_2^i are independent.

It is useful for interpretation to write β_1^i and β_2^i as

$$\begin{aligned}
\beta_1^i &= b_1 + \sigma_1 \times \eta_1^i \\
\beta_2^i &= b_2 + \sigma_2 \times \eta_2^i,
\end{aligned} \tag{16.44}$$

where η_1^i and η_2^i are independent standard normal random variables. This makes it clear that the marginal utilities consist of a mean component that is shared by all individuals, and a random component whose potential distance from the mean is governed by the standard deviation. Substituting the marginal utilities in (16.44) into (16.43) allows us to rewrite the conditional indirect utility function as

$$V_{ij} = -\beta_0 \, price_j + b_1 oper_{ij} + b_2 wb_j + \psi_{ij}, \quad j = 1,...,55, \tag{16.45}$$

where

$$\psi_{ij} = \sigma_1 \times \eta_1^i \times oper_{ij} + \sigma_2 \times \eta_2^i \times wb_j + \varepsilon_{ij}. \tag{16.46}$$

EXAMPLE 16.5 (EMPIRICAL) Estimating the model in (16.45) and (16.46) via simulated maximum likelihood results in the following parameter estimates:

$$\begin{aligned}
V_{ij} = &-\underset{(13.56)}{0.041} \, price_j - \underset{(-3.53)}{0.123} \, oper_{ij} + \underset{(5.72)}{0.025} \, wb_j \\
&+ \underset{(15.18)}{0.634} \times \eta_1^i \times oper_{ij} + \underset{(0.682)}{0.014} \times \eta_2^i \times wb_j + \varepsilon_{ij},
\end{aligned} \tag{16.47}$$

where z-statistics are given in parentheses underneath the parameter estimates. Using this specification we find, in contrast to the conditional logit model using only these three variables, that the population average marginal utility for operating cost is negative. However, the large standard deviation ($\sigma_1 = 0.634$) for the distribution shows that there is substantial heterogeneity in the population, and that the distribution of marginal utility for operating costs includes a substantial area of support where the marginal utility is positive. In contrast, the marginal utility for wheelbase is positive, though with little heterogeneity in the population, since the estimate of σ_1 is not significantly different from zero.

Using the conditional logit model for this specification we found that the marginal willingness to pay for an additional inch of vehicle length was $418. Here, the population average marginal willingness to pay is $1000 \times (0.025/0.041) = \$609$. The difference arises primarily from the smaller marginal utility of income with the mixed logit model. Turning to the marginal willingness to pay for an improvement in operating cost, recall from the earlier summary statistics that a 1 percent improvement in operating costs corresponds to a reduction of approximately 0.07 cents per mile. According to the mixed logit estimates, the population average marginal willingness to pay in purchase price for this improvement is $1000 \times (0.123/0.041) \times 0.07 = \$210$.

16.6   WELFARE COMPUTATION

Recall that our objective in applied welfare analysis is to recover enough of individuals' preference functions to allow welfare analysis of changes in prices and/or quasi-fixed goods. Our emphasis thus far in the chapter has been on obtaining estimates of the parameters of the indirect utility function in a RUM framework. In this section, we turn our attention to how we use these estimates to measure the willingness to pay for or accept exogenous changes in attributes of the alternatives. Our starting point is Eq. (16.6), which provides an implicit definition for compensating variation (CV) in a discrete choice situation. We can link this to an empirical RUM model by defining CV_i for an increase in q from q^0 to q^1 for a specific person i as

$$\max_{j \in J}\left\{V_{ij}(y_i - p_j - CV_i, q_j^1, \beta) + \varepsilon_{ij}\right\} = \max_{j \in J}\left\{V_{ij}(y_i - p_j, q_j^0, \beta) + \varepsilon_{ij}\right\}, \tag{16.48}$$

where we have left out s_i and ξ_j to reduce clutter. This definitional statement echoes our discussion in Chapter 14, and simply says that CV_i is the amount of money we need to take from individual i to assure that the maximum utility available from the J alternatives with the new level of q in place, is equal to the maximum utility the person obtained from the choice set at the original level of q. This definition for compensating variation makes clear that CV_i is a function of the parametric components of the utility function, as well as the components that are unobserved by the analyst, making CV_i a random variable from the analyst's perspective. Thus the inference task is to calculate $E(CV_i)$ for each person in the sample, given the functional form for $v_{ij}(\cdot)$, distribution of ε_{ij}, and estimates of the utility function parameters β. As with much in discrete choice analysis, this is a relatively easy task when the model is linear in income and the errors are distributed type I extreme value.

16.6.1   The Linear in Parameters Logit Model

For the linear-in-income model, the implicit definition for CV_i simplifies to

$$\max_{j \in J}\left\{\beta_0(y_i - p_j - CV_i) + \beta q_j^1 + \varepsilon_{ij}\right\} = \max_{j \in J}\left\{\beta_0(y_i - p_i) + \beta q_j^0 + \varepsilon_{ij}\right\}, \tag{16.49}$$

or

$$-\beta_0 CV_i + \max_{j \in J}\left\{-\beta_0 p_j + \beta q_j^1 + \varepsilon_{ij}\right\} = \max_{j \in J}\left\{-\beta_0 p_j + \beta q_j^0 + \varepsilon_{ij}\right\}, \tag{16.50}$$

where $-\beta_0 CV_i$ can come outside of the maximum function because it is constant for all j. From this, we can write CV_i as

$$CV_i = \frac{1}{\beta_0}\left[\max_{j \in J}\left\{-\beta_0 p_j + \beta q_j^1 + \varepsilon_{ij}\right\} - \max_{j \in J}\left\{-\beta_0 p_{ij} + \beta q_j^0 + \varepsilon_{ij}\right\}\right] \qquad (16.51)$$

which, as a utility change scaled by the constant inverse of the marginal utility of income, is the definition of consumer surplus (see section 14.2.2 in Chapter 14). Thus, as we know to be the case when there are no income effects in demand equations, compensating variation and consumer surplus are the same for linear-in-income RUM models. Still, we cannot directly calculate CV_i, since it depends on the individual's unobserved heterogeneity outcomes $(\varepsilon_{i1}, \ldots, \varepsilon_{iJ})$. Thus we need to compute

$$E(CV_i) = \frac{1}{\beta_0}\left[E\left(\max_{j \in J}\left\{-\beta_0 p_j + \beta q_j^1 + \varepsilon_{ij}\right\}\right) - E\left(\max_{j \in J}\left\{-\beta_0 p_j + \beta q_j^0 + \varepsilon_{ij}\right\}\right)\right], \quad (16.52)$$

where we refer to the expectations inside the square brackets as the "expected maximum utility", evaluated at the relevant values for p_j and q_j. Note that the sign of $E(CV_i)$ depends on the nature of the change we are analyzing. If there is an improvement in an attribute, so that $q_j^1 \geq q_j^0$ for all j, then the expected maximum utility under the changed conditions is higher, and since the marginal utility of income β_0 is positive, $E(CV_i) > 0$. In this case the welfare measure is a willingness to pay. In contrast, if $q_j^1 \leq q_j^0$, the expected maximum utility under the changed conditions in lower, $E(CV_i) < 0$, and the welfare measure is a willingness to accept. These two interpretations are most apparent from inspection of (16.49).

Note that the welfare measures in (16.51) and (16.52) reflect the possibility of re-optimization following a change. Thus the alternative chosen under the changed conditions need not be the same as was chosen under the original conditions. The underlying welfare measures therefore reflect the degree of substitutability among the alternatives at both the baseline and new levels of q.

With type I extreme value errors, Small and Rosen (1981) show that the expected maximum utility has a closed form expression given by

$$E\left(\max_{j \in J}\left\{-\beta_0 p_{ij} + \beta q_j + \varepsilon_{ij}\right\}\right) = \int \max_{j \in J}\left\{-\beta_0 p_{ij} + \beta q_j + \varepsilon_{ij}\right\} f(\varepsilon_i) d\varepsilon_i$$

$$= \ln\left[\sum\nolimits_{j=1}^{J} \exp(-\beta_0 p_{ij} + \beta q_j)\right] + C, \qquad (16.53)$$

where $f(\varepsilon_i)$ is the joint probability distribution for $\varepsilon_i = (\varepsilon_{i1}, \ldots, \varepsilon_{iJ})$ and C is a constant reflecting the ordinal nature of utility. This log-sum expression is ubiquitous in applied welfare analysis with RUM models. With it, we can see that $E(CV_i)$ for a change in site quality levels reduces to

$$E(CV_i) = \frac{1}{\beta_0}\left\{\ln\left[\sum\nolimits_{j=1}^{J} \exp(-\beta_0 p_j + \beta q_j^1)\right] - \ln\left[\sum\nolimits_{j=1}^{J} \exp(-\beta_0 p_j + \beta q_j^0)\right]\right\}, \quad (16.54)$$

which, given estimates of the utility function parameters, is simple to calculate for any values of q^1, q^0, and the other variables in the model.

EXAMPLE 16.6 (EMPIRICAL) We illustrate welfare analysis in the linear-in-income, conditional logit model using our vehicle choice application. Consider the results summarized in equations (16.28) and (16.35), which together provide a characterization of preferences given by

$$
\begin{aligned}
V_{ij} = &-\underset{(2.96)}{0.028} \cdot price_j -\underset{(-22.42)}{0.437} \cdot oper_{ij} +\underset{(3.01)}{0.042} \cdot wb_j \\
&+\underset{(9.83)}{0.0072} \cdot wb_j \times hhsize_i + \xi_j + \varepsilon_{ij}, \quad j=1,...,55,
\end{aligned}
\tag{16.55}
$$

where the values for ξ_j are recovered via the residuals in (16.35). Among the 55 alternatives, six fall within the popular vehicle class "minivan", which typically uses more fuel to operate than passenger vehicles. With this as motivation, we consider the welfare effect of a 5 percent improvement in fuel efficiency for minivans, which we proxy by decreasing operating costs for these six alternatives. We use Eq. (16.54) to compute the willingness to pay by each of the 3,216 households in our sample, where the changed value of $oper_{ij}$ is 5 percent smaller for $j=4$, 13, 22, 30, 38, and 46. The average in the sample is $470. This is to say that, on average, vehicle purchasers would pay $470 for this improvement in the set of vehicles available to them at the time of purchase. This is an unconditional measure, in the sense that it is calculated based on the preferences of all buyers – not only those who ultimately select a minivan option.

The formula in (16.54) illustrates the critical role that β_0 plays in calculating welfare effects, and so its identification deserves special scrutiny. In the vehicle choice example, recall that our estimate of β_0 is probably biased towards zero due to omitted variables, which implies we may have overestimated the value to consumers of improved minivan gas mileage. Nonetheless, the example serves to illustrate how the linear-in-income RUM model can be easily used for welfare analysis.

16.6.2 The Role of Income

Our discussion in this chapter has focused almost entirely on the linear-in-income specification. This has been motivated by two factors – one conceptual, and the other computational. Consider first the conceptual reason. In a choice occasion model the role of income is fundamentally different than in a demand system model, in which behavior unfolds over a given period of time. In this context income influences the quantity of purchase, which gives us the familiar concepts of income elasticity and normal/inferior goods. The definition of income corresponds to the amount of time the model covers – often a year, so that income is annual income. In a choice occasion model the timeframe is often less clearly defined. For example, recreation choice occasions can occur frequently throughout a year, making the definition of choice occasion income somewhat arbitrary. A residential home purchase occurs only a few times in a lifetime, which again complicates the definition of income available for purchase. In addition, since there is no quantity component, an income effect in a choice occasion model must describe how the same individual would select a different alternative when his income changes. For large budget items such as homes, vehicles, or durable goods, this could occur via the budget constraint. Even here, however, it seems more likely that a person's income would condition the makeup of his choice set rather than marginally affect his choice probabilities. For example, in our vehicle choice application it may be better practice to eliminate expensive luxury alternatives from the choice set faced by low income households rather than modeling choice as a function of income. Finally, measured income is a proxy for other variables, such as wealth, education, and the sophistication of tastes, which might affect choices through an avenue other than the budget constraint. Given this, it is sometimes better empirical practice to use income (or a qualitative variable based on income, such as income quartile dummies) as a socio-economic indicator rather than as part of a non-linear budget constraint effect.

This conceptual discussion suggests that, before including a non-linear income effect in a RUM model, we should have some intuition about the potential role of income in the choice we are modeling, and there should be variability in the proportion of the budget that needs to be committed to purchase the different options. When this is the case, a specification such as

$$V_{ij} = \beta_0 \ln(y_i - p_j) + \beta' q_j + \varepsilon_{ij}, \quad j = 1, ..., J \tag{16.56}$$

will maintain y_i in the utility difference, and therefore make the choice outcome dependent on $y - p_j$ rather than just p_j. In general, a specification like (16.56) does not imply any major difficulties for estimation, provided $y_i - p_j > 0$. Rather, the challenge is in conducting welfare analysis, since the marginal utility of income is no longer constant – i.e. it is $\beta_0 \cdot (y_i - p_j)^{-1}$ in this example. Thus, we are not able to look at a simple difference in expected utility levels as the basis for computing welfare effects, since our analysis in Chapter 14 showed that this does not correspond to a well-defined welfare concept, when the marginal utility of income is not constant.

The problem when income enters utility non-linearly is related to the computation of welfare effects. Continuing with (16.56) as an example, consider calculating $E(CV_i)$, where CV_i for an increase in q from q^0 to q^1 is implicitly defined by

$$\max_{j \in J} \left\{ \beta_0 \ln(y_i - p_j - CV_i) + \beta' q_j^1 + \varepsilon_{ij} \right\} = \max_{j \in J} \left\{ \beta_0 \ln(y_i - p_j) + \beta' q_j^0 + \varepsilon_{ij} \right\}. \tag{16.57}$$

Note that, unlike in the linear case, we cannot take CV_i outside of the brackets, and so there is no closed form expression for $E(CV_i)$. Thus some combination of numerical and/or simulation analysis is needed. One approach uses Monte Carlo integration, whereby R realizations of the vector $\varepsilon_i = (\varepsilon_{i1}, ..., \varepsilon_{iJ})$ are simulated for person i, and the value CV_i^r calculated for each draw using (16.57). Note that, given the simulated value for ε_i, all the components of (16.57) are known, and a numerical algorithm can be used to solve for CV_i^r. The welfare effect $E(CV_i)$ is then estimated as the average over the R values for CV_i^r. The law of large numbers implies that as R grows, the simulated approximation to $E(CV_i)$ converges to its true expectation.

16.7 SUMMARY

Discrete outcomes are ubiquitous in environmental economics. In the following chapters, for example, we will consider recreation site choice, residential location, and voting on referenda, all within the context of discrete choice models. Our objective in this chapter therefore has been to introduce the modeling and econometric background needed for these types of problems. In particular, we have seen that discrete choice econometrics combined with a model describing behavior when agents face a discrete set of alternatives leads to the random utility maximization (RUM) model. This empirical model is appropriate when the interesting aspect of behavior is the "which one" decision rather than "how many," as in the examples discussed throughout. As such, a RUM model's focus is on a single-choice situation in which a person consumes one unit of the commodity. Since there is no quantity aspect to the decision, we do not use demand equations in RUM models. Instead, the relevant behavioral function (and objective of estimation) is the conditional indirect utility for each alternative.

We saw that the defining feature of a RUM model is its treatment of the stochastic error term. An agent knows his preference function with certainty, and on a given choice occasion, he selects a single option that provides the highest utility level. An observer cannot know all the factors that drive a person's decisions, and so from her perspective, utility consists of two components: one that is made up of observable factors and another that is unobservable. We referred to the latter as unobserved heterogeneity, and by knowing its distribution the analyst can derive a statement for the probability of observing a particular choice. Different RUM models arise from different assumptions on how the stochastic elements are distributed, and where they reside in the utility function. The conditional logit model uses type I extreme value errors, the multinomial probit model assumes the errors are normal, and the mixed logit model adds random parameters to the basic logit specification. These different RUM models vary in how easy or difficult they are to estimate, and how capable they are of capturing the rich patterns of correlation among the unobserved components of utility.

Our discussion of specification and identification in RUM models stressed two points. Mechanically, we saw that only variables that remain when utility is differenced can be estimated in a RUM model. This conditions the way that different variables types – i.e. those that vary over people, alternatives, and alternatives and people – can be entered into the specification. It also conditions how we should interpret estimates from the model, and the extent to which we can use alternative specific constants to characterize average conditional indirect utility for each alternative. We saw that identification requires a careful consideration of the drivers of behavior that we can and cannot measure. Obtaining reliable estimates in RUM models requires judgment and care that is akin to the familiar tools used in linear models. Indeed, the use of alternative fixed effects in some instances allows us to recast the non-linear identification problem into one for which we can use the familiar tool of linear regression and instrumental variables.

Welfare measurement is almost always the objective when RUM models are used in environmental economics, and we saw in this chapter that it is relatively straightforward for conditional logit models that are linear in the budget constraint.

This chapter completes our three-chapter discussion of the primary analytical and applied tools that are used in non-market valuation. In the following chapters we turn our attention to specific areas of non-market valuation, where RUM models will play a prominent role.

16.8   FURTHER READING

The literature on the development and application of discrete choice models in economics is large and diverse. The best pedagogical source on applying discrete choice models is Train (2009), which covers logit-based models as well as more advanced approaches. Greene's (2011) text also contains a detailed treatment of discrete choice models, and McFadden's (2001) Nobel Prize lecture traces the history of discrete choice analysis, and highlights early contributions. See also McFadden (1973). Bockstael and McConnell (2007, Chapter 5) provide a thorough review of the theory underlying welfare measurement in discrete choice models. Hanemann (1984a) presents a useful discussion of the relationship between continuous and discrete choice contexts, and Hanemann (1983) derives the expression for marginal willingness to pay in a RUM model. See also Hanemann (1999b) and Small and Rosen (1981) for discussion on welfare analysis with discrete choice models. More recently, Phaneuf and von Haefen (2009) and Phaneuf (2013) describe RUM models in the context of estimating the demand for quality-differentiated goods. Notable advances in discrete choice methods applied in industrial organization, which have become important in environmental economics, include Berry (1994) and Berry et al. (1995, 2004).

EXERCISES

16.1   ** A useful feature of the conditional logit model with a specification including a full set of alternative specific constants is that

$$
s_j = \frac{1}{I} \sum_{i=1}^{I} \frac{\exp(v_{ij})}{\sum_{k=1}^{J} \exp(v_{ik})}, \quad j = 1, \ldots, J, \tag{*}
$$

where s_j is the proportion of times in the data that alternative j is selected, and the right-hand side is the average predicted probability for alternative j. Using the log-likelihood function in (16.13) and the specification $v_{ij} = \delta_j + \beta X_{ij}$ for $j = 1, \ldots, J-1$ and $v_{iJ} = \beta X_{iJ}$ for $j = J$, show that the first-order conditions with respect to $\delta_1, \ldots, \delta_{J-1}$ for maximum likelihood estimation lead to (*) for all alternatives.

16.2   ** For the specification in exercise 16.1, derive expressions for the elasticities of the probability of alternative j with respect to a change in X_{ij} and a change in X_{ik}, for k not equal to j.

The following exercises are based on data describing the choice of residential home heating systems in newly constructed homes in California. The dataset *home_heating* (available on the book's website) was provided by Prof. Kenneth Train, and it forms the basis for homework assignments in his discrete choice econometrics course at UC-Berkeley. We observe 900 single-family homes that were newly built and have central air conditioning. Five types of home heating systems were considered feasible in these homes:
- central gas heating ($j=1$)
- room gas heating ($j=2$)

- central electrical heating ($j=3$)
- room electrical heating ($j=4$)
- heat pump ($j=5$).

In addition to an indicator for choice, the dataset includes the following variables:

id – unique identifier for each household

ic_1, ic_2, ic_3, ic_4, ic_5 – installation cost (in 100s of USD) for each of the $J=5$ alternatives

oc_1, oc_2, oc_3, oc_4, oc_5 – annual operating cost (in 100s of USD) for each of the $J=5$ alternatives

income – annual income for the household (in 1,000s of USD)

age – age of household head

rooms – number of rooms in the house

r_1, r_2, r_3, r_4 – dummy variables for the region of the state where the home is located. Regions include northern coast (r_1), southern coast (r_2), mountain region (r_3), and central valley (r_4). The installation and operating cost variables vary over both households and alternatives, while the income, age, region, and room count variables vary only over households.

16.3 ** Suppose you have estimated a model that includes only the installation and operating cost variables. The results are

$$v_{ij} = -0.6231 \times ic_{ij} - 0.4580 \times oc_{ij}, \quad j = 1,...,5.$$

In addition, the data for three of the observations are as follows:

IC					OC				
ID $j=1$	$j=2$	$j=3$	$j=4$	$j=5$	$j=1$	$j=2$	$j=3$	$j=4$	$j=5$
3 5.9948	7.8305	7.1986	9.0011	10.483	1.6558	1.378	4.3906	4.0474	1.7147
14 5.6844	6.1743	6.8718	7.1872	7.7554	1.1945	1.1168	3.6592	3.9514	1.7353
21 6.5757	8.9216	7.8807	7.9952	10.831	1.7615	1.4893	4.4099	2.8629	2.0387

(a) The negative of the coefficient on oc_{ij} can be interpreted as the marginal utility of a dollar of annual income. Given this, interpret the ratio of the coefficient on ic_{ij} over the coefficient on oc_{ij}.

(b) Using a spreadsheet, compute the probability of choice for each alternative/person combination.

(c) Using a spreadsheet and the formula derived in exercise 16.2, compute for each person the elasticity of the probability of alternative 1, with respect to the installation cost for each of the five alternatives (i.e. compute one own- and four cross-cost elasticities).

(d) Once again using the negative of the coefficient on oc_{ij} as the marginal utility of annual income, use a spreadsheet to compute the one-time *WTP* for a 15 percent reduction in the installation cost of alternative $j=5$, for each of the three people (recall that the cost variables are measured in 100s of USD, and adjust accordingly).

16.4 *** Using the *home_heating* data, complete the following.

(a) Estimate a model that includes only the installation and operating cost variables, and check that you are able to replicate the estimates shown in exercise 16.3.

(b) Estimate a model that includes the operating and installation cost variables, as well as the full set of $J-1$ alternative specific constants (ASCs). Comment on the differences in the estimates relative to part (a). How does inclusion of the ASCs affect the estimate of the marginal willingness to pay for a change in installation cost? What is the likely explanation for the differences?

(c) Now consider the role of income in explaining choices. Specify a model that allows you to test whether higher income households are more or less likely to install a central (as opposed to room) heating system (i.e. more likely to select options $j=1,3,5$). Run your model with and without ASCs, and comment on the differences.

(d) Consider a situation in which a 15 percent of installation cost rebate is being offered when a heat pump is selected. Using the model with oc_{ij}, ic_{ij}, and the full set of ASCs, predict how the average probability of a household selecting the heat pump changes due to the rebate.

(e) Using the same model as in (d), calculate the sample average willingness to pay for the rebate program. Compare your predictions for observations 3, 14, and 21 to what you derived in exercise 16.3. Which of the two calculations do you find most plausible? Explain your reasoning.

CHAPTER 17

Recreation

One of the more ubiquitous uses of the natural environment is for outdoor leisure activities. Natural features such as lakes, rivers, beaches, forests, and mountains provide the places people visit to participate in a large variety of outdoor activities. Less overtly natural areas such as local parks, trails, and designated recreation areas also provide infrastructure that facilitates spending time outdoors. In many cases these types of resources are officially designated as parks or other public use areas; in other instances they simply exist and are used by the public. In some situations access to outdoor recreation areas is rationed by markets (alpine skiing is a good example), but in most cases recreation is a non-market, open access good in the sense that entry is free (or involves only a nominal fee), and generally unrestricted. Several examples of recreation uses of the environment fitting this description were given in prior chapters; these included obvious activities such as high-altitude hiking, lake angling, and ocean swimming. Establishing the dollar value of the existence of mountains, lakes, and beaches that support such activities usually requires the tools of non-market valuation.

Prior chapters also provided examples of how environmental conditions at places supporting recreation determine, to a large degree, the quality of a visit to the area. When people visit lakes for recreation fishing, the number of fish caught depends on the fish stock and the underlying ecology of the lake. The attractiveness of a high-altitude hiking trail depends to a large extent on the mountain flora and fauna that one sees along the way, together with the quality of vistas encountered. Beach visits are more enjoyable when the water is clean and the sand free of debris. In these examples, better environmental conditions enhance the use of a recreation resource. Often we are interested in measuring the value of changes in environmental conditions as they relate to natural areas used for outdoor leisure. This too requires the tools of non-market valuation, since the environmental conditions at a recreation site are even less likely to be market determined than access to the site itself.

Measuring the value of access to recreation resources, and the value of potential changes in environmental conditions at specific sites, is important in many contexts. Several types of environmental policies are designed primarily to improve conditions that are important for outdoor recreation. A good example is the US Clean Water Act, which directs state governments to designate the primary use of freshwater lakes and streams, and sets quality criteria that allows these uses to be obtained. The use criteria include recreation-relevant descriptions such swimmable, fishable, and suitability for non-contact uses such as boating. As such, many of the past and future benefits of Clean Water Act enforcement are thought to accrue primarily through recreation uses of water resources. Park systems provided by national and regional governments, and open space preservation by local governments, are motivated in part by constituents' interest in recreation opportunities. In these examples, estimates of the value of recreation opportunities are used for project evaluation and cost-benefit analysis. In addition, lost recreation benefits are often a major component of damages from environmental accidents. In natural resource damage assessment the welfare impacts of lost or degraded recreation opportunities are used to estimate compensation owed to resource trustees.

In this chapter we discuss ways that the complements revealed preference model described in Chapter 15 is used for valuing recreation services provided by the environment. At the outset we need to be clear on what we mean by recreation services. Outdoor leisure that depends on the environment is a broad category of consumption activity. It includes privately provided goods such as access to golf courses and alpine skiing areas. It also overlaps with the tourism industry, in that many types of vacations include natural features as a primary attraction. Ecotourism – travel to an exotic destination to experience rare or exceptional landscapes and animal populations – is a further example. These points of interaction with the environment are market based, and/or involve the purchase of supporting market goods that constitute the bulk of expenditures. The demand for these types of commodities is not a primary focus of our discussion here, since it falls more within the realm of market good analysis. Instead, we focus on smaller-scale recreation uses of the environment that involve trips from home to a specific destination, where the primary purpose is to visit the site and engage in an activity. Although this type of outdoor leisure is less dramatic, the large volume of activity that occurs makes it a critical component of the overall demand for environmental services.

A natural starting point for examining the link between recreation and the environment is a model of individual recreation behavior, in which we derive the demand for visits to a destination as a function of the access price and characteristics of the destination. The challenge, of course, is that access to most recreation sites is not rationed by the market, and so there is no market price in the usual sense. In a letter to the US National Park Service, Hotelling (1947) suggested that the price of consuming a recreation visit is the resources a person must part with to reach the site, usually via road transport. The travel cost model grew out of this suggestion, in which the price of a recreation visit is the money and time costs borne while traveling to the destination. Today's travel cost models use individual-level data on trips, employ a high level of spatial resolution to measure travel distances and time, and rank among the more sophisticated uses of structural micro-econometric techniques. Gaining an understanding of contemporary recreation demand analysis therefore requires consideration of modeling, econometric, and data issues. We begin in the next section by providing a stylized model of recreation behavior, and use this to describe the main assumptions, data needs, and econometric problems that all empirical models must, to some degree, confront. We then describe the three primary empirical frameworks used for recreation demand analysis: demand system models, discrete choice models, and corner solution models. Our discussion in this empirical section introduces several econometric models, though our emphasis throughout is on the behavioral motivations for the particular techniques. Finally, we turn our attention to several generic issues, such as the opportunity cost of time and choice set definition, which all recreation applications must address.

17.1 THEORETICAL MODEL

To set the stage for what follows, suppose we are interested in understanding the demand for trips to a single recreation site in order to value access to the site or changes in its characteristics. Following our established notation, let x denote the number of recreation trips a person makes to the site and let q denote a (scalar) quality attribute of the site. Suppose that the money cost of travel and access (i.e. fuel, vehicle depreciation, and entry fees) that the person must pay to reach and use the site is c. By way of an example from the US, in 2013 the American Automotive Association (AAA) estimated the average cost per road mile to be nearly \$0.61, so the money cost of travel would be $0.61 \cdot mi$, where mi is the round-trip travel distance in miles.[1] Since this also includes fixed costs per mile, a smaller unit cost is normally used in applications. Define t as the round-trip travel time to the destination plus the time needed to complete the activity, where the latter is fixed and exogenous, and suppose the person is endowed with a time budget denoted T. Out of this budget he can supply labor at a wage rate of w, the earnings from which are used to pay the money cost of recreation and to purchase other, non-recreation goods. As usual, consumption of non-recreation market goods is denoted by the numeraire z. To this we add a time numeraire good l, which is the consumption of non-recreation leisure time. Given these definitions, the utility maximization problem is subject to both income and time constraints. Drawing on Phaneuf and Smith (2005) and Freeman et al. (2014), we can write the problem as

$$\max_{x,z,l} U(x,z,l,q) \quad s.t. \quad wH = cx + z, \quad T = H + l + tx, \tag{17.1}$$

where H is hours of labor supplied, which produces money income wH. Note that the two constraints can be combined by solving the time constraint for H and substituting it into the money constraint. Once we make this substitution, the problem reduces to a single constraint that does not include H. After some manipulation, it is given by

$$\max_{x,z,l} U(x,z,l,q) \quad s.t. \quad wT = z + (c + wt)x + wl. \tag{17.2}$$

We can consolidate notation by letting $Y = wT$ and $p = (c + wt)$, where we refer to p as the "full price" of a visit to the site and Y as "full income." These terms are so-labeled because they include the monetized value of time as well as nominal dollar amounts. With this, the formal problem becomes the familiar looking

$$\max_{x,z,l} U(x,z,l,q) + \lambda(Y - z - px - wl), \tag{17.3}$$

---

[1] Information on driving costs in the US is available from AAA at http://exchange.aaa.com/automobiles-travel/automobiles/driving-costs/#.VquufFn-l_M.

which gives rise to the ordinary demand and indirect utility functions $x(p,w,Y,q)$, $z(p,w,Y,q)$, $l(p,w,Y,q)$, and $V(p,w,Y,q)$. Since we do not usually model the demand for residual leisure explicitly, we will often drop reference to the price of leisure in these solutions, and simply refer to $x(p,Y,q)$ and $V(p,Y,q)$ as the functions of interest.

The model described by equations (17.1) to (17.3) fits well with the complements model that we examined in Chapter 15. In particular, a recreation trip is the private good and q is the weak complement. Because the price of x – the full price or "travel cost" of getting to the site – is not a market price, it is not systematically related to the level of q. We can readily make the model operational by observing trips to the site for a sample of people, measuring their travel costs, and estimating a trip demand equation that includes p, Y, and q as explanatory variables (variation in q is a topic we take up below). If q enters the specification as a price modifier, say by cross-product repackaging, then the standard price and quality change welfare measurement techniques we examined in Chapters 14 and 15 can be used to assess the willingness to pay for changes in q. Specific econometric strategies for carrying out this type of analysis will occupy us later in the chapter. For now, we continue to focus on the conceptual aspects of this model by noting the assumptions (explicit and implicit) that are inherent in its description.

17.1.1 Underlying Assumptions

The model described thus far is the canonical travel cost model that developed out of Hotelling's original idea. There are several assumptions inherent in it that condition how the model is used and its results interpreted. These assumptions have also motivated contemporary research seeking to generalize features of the model structure, and so we review them carefully here.

First consider aspects related to time. The opportunity cost of time is an important component of the implicit price of a recreation visit – arguably the most important for households that are more constrained by time than modest road expenses. The baseline model uses a simple depiction of labor supply to arrive at the value of time, resulting in the price of leisure being the market wage rate. This assumes people earn wages rather than a fixed salary, and that they are able to freely exchange time for money by optimally adjusting work hours at the margin. In fact, a person may face a fixed work schedule (or may not work at all), which prevents the smooth exchange of labor and leisure time. In this case, time and money are not perfectly fungible, the time and money constraints cannot be collapsed into one, and the opportunity cost of time is not the wage rate. To this we can add the observation that there are no dynamics in this problem. We imagine a timeframe over which the demand for trips unfolds, but behavior is essentially static. Thus the model does not accommodate the potential role of state variables such as knowledge about destinations acquired through repeated visits, or allow decisions to depend on lagged outcomes due to variety seeking or habit formation. Finally, trips of different durations are in some respects different commodities, in that longer trips cost more in the way of time resources but presumably provide greater enjoyment. By assuming visits have a fixed and exogenous duration, our canonical model does not admit this component of behavior.

Next, consider aspects of how the commodity is defined. By examining the demand for just one site, we account for potential substitute sites only indirectly through their role in the composite commodity. Since many recreation sites are likely to have close substitutes (e.g. fishermen can choose from multiple lakes in many areas), the non-market value of a site of interest will hinge heavily on the existence and characteristics of substitute sites, the effect of which is not well captured by a single-site model. Also, because we impute the cost of a recreation trip using the resources given up to travel to the site, and ultimately derive the non-market value of the site based on these resource costs, we need to assume that the sole purpose of travel is to consume a visit to the site. Of course, in reality trips occur for multiple reasons that can include activities at the site, spending time with family and friends, or visiting multiple destinations. Related to the assumption of single-purpose trips, we also assume there is no utility or disutility from travel to the site.

Finally, consider how the choice problem is framed. We have assumed people choose a continuous number of trips, which results in a strictly positive demand for visits. In reality trips are not divisible and must therefore be consumed in non-negative integer amounts, so there is an element of discreteness in recreation behavior. More importantly, the canonical model abstracts from participation versus non-participation decisions in which a person can decide *not* to visit the site of interest if he so chooses. Indeed, actual decisions include an extensive margin component on which sites to visit during a season, and an intensive margin decision on the frequency of visit. As a practical matter, variation in participation/non-participation aspects of recreation decisions is often richer than the variation in the number of trips observed by participants alone, and so models that admit discreteness and non-participation are important in applied analysis.

To summarize, the standard assumptions in the travel cost model outlined thus far include single-purpose trips, static optimizing behavior, an opportunity cost of time based on flexible labor market decisions, exogenous onsite time, and the absence of utility/disutility of travel. To this we can add features of the problem such as a limited accounting for substitute sites, non-participation, and the discreteness of behavior, though these are more related to early econometric limitations than modeling assumptions per se. When these assumptions approximately hold, estimation of $x(p,Y,q)$ and $V(p,Y,q)$ provides the behavioral basis for welfare analysis using the techniques described in Chapters 14 and 15.

17.1.2 Some Generalizations

Though we have noted the potential limitations of the canonical model, many of its assumptions are reasonable or good approximations in specific cases. Others, such as the role of time constraints, substitute sites, and non-participation, are arguably less tenable. A substantial proportion of research in recreation demand has therefore been directed at developing models and econometric methods which generalize the baseline model in these dimensions. To motivate our subsequent discussion of these topics we close this section by presenting a generalization of the canonical model, which includes two additional features. Suppose now that x is a J dimensional vector that records trips by an individual to J recreation sites, where we refer to the collection of available sites as the choice set. Likewise define the J dimensional vectors c, t, and q as the money costs, time costs, and quality levels for the J sites, respectively. Finally, suppose that the individual's labor market status is predetermined via a long-term decision, and that this decision endows the person with money income (wage and non-wage) y and net-of-work time L for allocation over the short term (e.g. a recreation season). As previously, the utility function is $U(x,z,l,q)$, where z and l are the numeraire goods for the income and time budgets, respectively. The person chooses the elements of x along with z and l to maximize utility, subject to the money constraint $y=z+c'x$ and the time constraint $L=l+t'x$.

A formal statement of the new problem is summarized by the two-constraint problem

$$\max_{x,z,l} U(x,z,l,q) + \lambda\left(y - z - c'x\right) + \mu\left(L - t'x - l\right), \tag{17.4}$$

where λ is the Lagrange multiplier for the money constraint, and μ is an additional multiplier for the constraint on time. The first-order conditions for this problem are

$$\frac{\partial U(\cdot)}{\partial x_j} = \lambda c_j + \mu t_j, \quad j = 1,...,J, \quad \frac{\partial U(\cdot)}{\partial z} = \lambda, \quad \frac{\partial U(\cdot)}{\partial l} = \mu, \tag{17.5}$$

and we can use these expressions to derive

$$\frac{\partial U(\cdot)/\partial l}{\partial U(\cdot)/\partial z} = \frac{\mu}{\lambda},$$

$$\frac{\partial U(\cdot)/\partial x_j}{\partial U(\cdot)/\partial z} = c_j + \frac{\mu}{\lambda} t_j, \quad j = 1,...,J. \tag{17.6}$$

Written this way, the first-order conditions illustrate an important point. Note that by the Envelope Theorem, the solutions for the money and time Lagrange multipliers, $\lambda(c,t,y,L,q)$ and $\mu(c,t,y,L,q)$, measure the marginal utility of money and time, respectively, at the optimal solution. Taking this a step further, we can define the implied shadow value of time as $\phi(c,t,y,L,q)=\mu(\cdot)/\lambda(\cdot)$, which is the money-denominated value of an incremental increase in time. Unlike the simple model in which the wage rate is the opportunity cost of time, here an individual's shadow value of time arises endogenously with the other resource allocation decisions, and it depends on exogenous parameters such as the person's income and time budgets, as well as the money and time costs of recreation. Thus the first-order conditions show that the marginal rate of substitution between recreation trips and spending on other goods is equal to the implicit price of a recreation trip as usual, but the time component of the price is codetermined with other aspects of the decision. In this sense the short-term opportunity cost of time is at least partially decoupled from the long-term labor market decision, which is sensible for many types of recreation decisions.

We can make further progress in describing the solution to the problem by rewriting the expression in (17.4). Having defined the solution for the shadow value of time by

$\phi(\cdot) = \mu(\cdot)/\lambda(\cdot)$, it is helpful to also re-express the multiplier on the time constraint as $\mu = \phi \cdot \lambda$. If we substitute this for μ into the original problem, we have

$$\max_{x,z,l} U(x, z, l, q) + \lambda (y - z - c'x) + \phi \cdot \lambda (L - t'x - l).$$ (17.7)

Collecting terms in λ and rearranging leaves us with

$$\max_{x,z,l} U(x, z, l, q) + \lambda \left[(\phi L + y) - z - (c + \phi t)'x - \phi l \right].$$ (17.8)

While this is still a two constraint model formally (we have done nothing more than redefine terms), writing it so it resembles a single constraint problem is useful for intuition. As in the simple model, we define $p = (c + \phi t)$ as the vector of "full prices" for recreation trips, with the only difference being that the opportunity cost of time is now endogenously determined rather than exogenously given by the wage rate. Likewise, define the scalar $Y = (\phi L + y)$ as "full income." Given this we can write the solution to (17.8) as including the J dimensional ordinary demand system $x(p,Y,q)$, the scalar $z(p,Y,q)$, the demand for leisure $l(p,Y,q)$, and the opportunity cost of time $\phi(c,t,y,L,q)$. The latter term is the shadow value of leisure time as well as a component of the travel cost vector p and full income Y. From these we can express the indirect utility function as $V(p,Y,q)$, dropping as above explicit reference to residual leisure demand. This writing of the model suggests a more general operational task, which is to simultaneously estimate a J dimensional system of site demand equations $x(p,Y,q)$ *and* an expression for the opportunity cost of time $\phi(c,t,y,T,q)$. This allows us to explicitly address (a) the role of substitute sites and site characteristics in the analysis, and (b) the common observation that time and money are imperfectly fungible for most people.

The baseline model and its generalizations illustrate several assumptions and decisions that are the building blocks for empirical models. All travel cost models use a combination of road and travel time costs to characterize the implicit price of accessing a site; the way in which the opportunity cost of time is computed varies with the objectives and sophistication of the study. Some accounting for the presence of substitute sites in an analysis is generally needed; studies vary in the extent to which trips to substitute sites are explicitly modeled. In the following sections we discuss the different empirical approaches that arise out of the general model, stressing how each characterizes different aspects of behavior.

17.2   DATA STRUCTURES

Much of the discussion that follows is econometric, so it is useful to keep in mind characteristics of recreation data and the analysis objectives as we proceed. The majority of datasets used are at the micro level, with records on individual trips taking behavior obtained from intercept, telephone, mail, or internet surveys. Usually, information on visits is collected for multiple recreation sites, though studies occasionally focus only on a single site. In all cases visits are recorded as non-negative integers, since trips are not divisible. The frequency of visits observed for a typical individual to a particular site is usually low (e.g. observing only two trips in a 12-month period is not unusual), though the presence of avid visitors in the sample often skews the empirical distribution of trips to the right. Finally, "corner solutions" dominate in multiple-site databases in that, depending on the number of destinations under study, most people visit only a small fraction of the available sites over the analysis period, but they visit these multiple times.

The use of micro level data allows for the estimation of individual level demand functions, with which we can derive individual welfare measurements from the estimated functions. While this is a notable advantage, micro data based recreation studies also exhibit several practical challenges. First, sampling can be complicated. A general population survey conducted by phone or mail may provide relatively few people who have actually visited the sites of interest. Intercepting people on site is a more efficient way to gather information about actual visitors, but it results in a selected sample that, by construction, includes only site users. Onsite sampling is also likely to over-represent avid users, since avid users are more likely to be on site at the time of sampling. The latter is referred to as endogenous stratification. Second, zero and small integer trip outcomes mean recreation data requires the use of econometric methods that go beyond the familiar regression paradigm.

The non-behavioral components of a recreation database include travel costs, site characteristics, and socio-economic data on the sampled individuals. Travel costs depend on the road distance and travel time from a person's residence to the sites. In the past these were either self-reported or manually approximated by analysts using maps. Today, global information system (GIS) software linking zip codes with latitude/longitude coordinates for recreation sites enables highly accurate, automated measurement of the distance and time components of travel cost. Information on site characteristics varies in availability and quality, and is usually incomplete in the sense that the features of a site are not fully described by the available measures. Ideally, an analyst would be able to measure a wide range of environmental features (e.g. ambient water quality for swimming beaches) and non-environmental features (e.g. the presence of boat ramps at a lake) of recreation sites, but inevitably some variables are lacking. Finally, socio-economic and attitude information about recreation participants can be obtained via the same point of contact that provides the behavioral data.

These descriptions are general, and characteristics of individual databases can and do vary greatly. Nonetheless, these basic features of recreation data are the dominant explanation for how empirical modeling techniques have evolved in recreation demand. The analysis objective is usually to estimate trip demand equations and/or indirect utility functions that are suitable for welfare analysis, within the constraints and opportunities conveyed by the nature of the available data.

17.2.1 A Running Example

In later sections we use data from the Iowa Lakes Valuation Project to illustrate several empirical recreation demand models. As part of the project, researchers at Iowa State University conducted annual surveys of state residents between 2002 and 2005, which gathered data on sampled individuals' use of the 135 major lakes in the American state of Iowa. During the same time period and for the same lakes, Iowa State University limnologists conducted annual measurements of water quality conditions. The overall goal of the project was to assess lake usage in the state, and to measure the contribution of water quality to the non-market benefits provided by the lakes.

We use a cross-section of respondents from the 2002 version of the survey. The sample consists of 2,489 Iowa residents who made at least one recreation trip to a lake in the state during the year. Information on visits by each individual to 127 of the major lakes is available. In addition, the travel distance and time for each person to each of the lakes was calculated and used to impute travel costs for the sample. On average, respondents made ten trips to lakes in the state during 2002. The median number of trips is six, and the standard deviation is nearly 11. Thus the distribution of observed trips is skewed to the right. Travel costs were imputed using a per mile cost of $0.28,[2] and the opportunity cost of time is assumed to be exogenous and equal to one-third of the individual's average wage rate (this decision is discussed in more detail below). With these a unique value for travel cost to each of the 127 lakes is computed for the 2,489 members of the sample. The 127 sample averages for travel cost to the lakes range from $123 to $305. This variability arises from the spatial distribution of both lakes in the choice set and sampled respondents' homes. For example, a popular destination is Saylorville Lake, which is located near Des Moines, the state's largest city. The sample average travel cost for this destination is $124.

Most recreation users visit only a small fraction of the 127 lakes in a given year. Indeed, the median sample member visited only two of the available lakes during 2002, and so an alternative summary of cost is to compute the average travel cost across trips observed in the sample – i.e. the travel costs that were actually borne. The figure for this is $74, which suggests that people on average tend to visit lakes that are close to home, and hence have lower travel costs. This is most apparent when we examine a single lake. Consider once again Saylorville Lake, which was visited by 21 percent of people in the sample. Amongst these the average travel cost is only $55.

Nutrient pollution from non-point sources is the main environmental concern in Iowa lakes, and so we model decisions as a function of ambient nutrient concentrations in the lakes. In the examples that follow, we use the average of three chlorophyll a (CHL) concentration readings taken at each of the 127 lakes during the 2002 summer recreation season. Chlorophyll is a useful measure because it reflects the amount of algae and other plant growth responding to nutrient enrichment. Across the lakes the average CHL concentration is 40.44 micrograms per liter (μg/l), and the median is 28.44 μg/l. The standard deviation of 38.06 μg/l implies there is large variation in water quality conditions across the state, with very clean lakes (CHL < 10 μg/l) and much polluted lakes (CHL > 100 μg/l) represented.

17.3 EMPIRICAL MODELS

In this section we trace the development of three types of empirical models: single equation and demand systems, discrete choice models, and corner solutions. To varying degrees all of these are important contemporary tools for non-market valuation, and so

---

[2] The AAA average national rate in 2002 was approximately $0.50 per mile. The figure of $0.28 per mile is intended to reflect operating and depreciation costs, net of fixed ownership costs.

our focus is on presenting the current state of art for each model. In subsequent sections we describe additional modeling and data issues that continue to occupy researchers, and which tend to be relevant for all three of the empirical approaches that we examine.

17.3.1 Demand Systems

To fix ideas we begin by presenting an empirical model that is suitable for analyzing the demand for trips at a single recreation site. Models employing probability distributions that take non-negative integers, such as the Poisson and negative binomial, are the workhorses of single-site recreation demand analysis. We refer to these as count or count data models. To understand how count models work, define the scalar $x_i \in 0,1,2...$ as the number of trips a person indexed i makes to a single site. Suppose the process that generates the trip outcome is uncertain to the analyst, in the sense that she knows the probability distribution generating trip outcomes, but she cannot perfectly predict the actual outcome due to incomplete observation of agents' preferences. Suppose further that the distribution of trips from the analyst's perspective is described by the random variable X_i, where X_i is distributed Poisson with $E(X_i) = \delta_i > 0$ so that

$$\Pr(X_i = x_i) = \frac{\exp(-\delta_i)\delta_i^{x_i}}{x_i!}, \quad x_i = 0,1,2,... \tag{17.9}$$

Thus far this is only a statistical model. It becomes an economic model through the parameterization of δ_i as the expected demand equation for trips. Since the expected value of a Poisson random variable must be strictly positive, the most common specification has a log-linear form. For illustration, suppose

$$E(X_i) = \delta_i = \exp(\alpha + \beta p_i + \gamma Y_i), \quad i = 1,...,I, \tag{17.10}$$

where $i = 1,...,I$ is the sample of people for whom we observe trip, travel cost, and income data, and we have suppressed the site quality attribute for the moment. The demand equation parameters (α, β, γ) are the objects of estimation. These are obtained via maximum likelihood using probabilities of the form shown in (17.9), which results in a sample log-likelihood that is well behaved and easy to maximize numerically. Almost all econometric software packages contain prepared routines for estimating this model.

  The Poisson count model has a number of attractive features. First, as a discrete distribution it matches the integer nature of the data in that it admits probability mass only at integer outcomes. This is likely to be important when visit frequencies are low, since continuous distributions may poorly approximate small integers. Also, since $\Pr(X_i=0) = \exp(-\delta_i) > 0$ implies the Poisson distribution has probability mass at zero, it accommodates observation of zero trips in the data. Second, it can be readily manipulated for different sampling regimes. For example, if the data are gathered by onsite intercept questioning the sample is truncated, since no one will be observed consuming zero trips, even though this is a permissible outcome in the population. If X_i in the population (non-visitors as well as visitors) is distributed Poisson, then the outcome for a given person in the sample is distributed truncated Poisson, where $\Pr(X_i = x_i | x_i > 0)$ is the expression that enters the likelihood function for person i:

$$\Pr(X_i = x_i \mid x_i > 0) = \frac{\exp(-\delta_i)\delta_i^{x_i}}{(1 - \exp(-\delta_i))x_i!}, \quad x_i = 1, 2, 3, \ldots \tag{17.11}$$

This is a relatively straightforward change to make in the log-likelihood function, and again, most econometric software packages support a version of this model. Finally, although the Poisson distribution itself is relatively inflexible due to the equality of its mean and variance (i.e. $E(X_i) = VAR(X_i) = \delta_i$), it can be readily generalized to a negative binomial distribution, which allows the variance of X_i to be decoupled from its mean.[3] This is of practical importance, since recreation data often exhibit over-dispersion – i.e. the empirical distribution of trips has a large spread relative to the size of its mean, due to the large variation in behavior among infrequent, average, and avid visitors. From this discussion we can see that the statistical properties of the Poisson count model and its negative binomial generalization are attractive for single-site recreation data analysis. This and their general accessibly explain the wide use of count models in applied analysis.

Count models are also attractive in that recovering an estimate of the demand equation and its associated preference function by the methods described in Chapter 14 is relatively straightforward. For example, we have seen in previous contexts (see section 14.2.3) that a log-linear demand equation leads to the indirect utility functions

$$E(V_i) = \frac{\exp(-\gamma Y_i)}{\gamma} - \frac{\exp(\alpha + \beta p_i)}{\beta}, \quad \gamma > 0, \tag{17.12}$$

and

$$E(V_i) = Y_i - \frac{\exp(\alpha + \beta p_i)}{\beta}, \quad \gamma = 0. \tag{17.13}$$

These formulas can also be verified using Roy's Identity, and they are useful for conducting welfare analysis over price changes. We have labeled the utility function $E(V_i)$ to stress that it is the *expected* indirect utility function, since it is derived using the expected demand equation. With an estimate of $E(V_i)$ we can, for example, calculate the value of access to the site for person i by analyzing the welfare impact of pushing his travel cost to infinity, which is equivalent to the elimination of the site.

EXAMPLE 17.1 (EMPIRICAL) To illustrate the single-site model we estimate the parameters in (17.10) for Saylorville Lake, which, as noted above, was visited by 21 percent of the sample. Its average chlorophyll a concentration of 2.45 µg/l makes it the cleanest site in our choice set. Those who visited Saylorville Lake during 2002 did so on average 3.75 times (the median is 2). Using the full sample of survey respondents, which

---

[3] It is worth noting that estimates of the parameters in the Poisson model are still consistent when the mean/variance equality is violated. Estimates of conventional standard errors are inconstant, however.

includes the 79 percent of people who did not visit Saylorville Lake, results in the following estimates:

$$\ln \delta_i = \underset{(8.17)}{1.23} - \underset{(-11.68)}{0.027} \cdot p_i + \underset{(4.39)}{0.007} \cdot Y_i, \tag{17.14}$$

where Y_i is measured in 1,000s of dollars, and z-statistics are shown in parentheses. Although the coefficient on income is statistically significant, it is economically near zero (i.e. it is zero out to five decimal places when income is measured in dollars), and so a potentially preferable specification constrains the income effect to be zero:

$$\ln \delta_i = \underset{(14.93)}{1.61} - \underset{(-12.05)}{0.028} \cdot p_i, \tag{17.15}$$

meaning that (17.13) is the relevant expected indirect utility function. To predict the value of access to the site, we can calculate compensating variation (CV) according to

$$Y_i - \frac{\exp(1.61 - 0.028 p_i)}{-0.028} = Y_i + CV_i - \underbrace{\frac{\exp(1.61 - 0.028 \cdot \infty)}{-0.028}}_{0} = Y_i + CV_i, \tag{17.16}$$

which defines CV_i as the amount of income adjustment needed to restore utility to the original level after the site has been eliminated (i.e. the travel cost is set to infinity). Solving for the income adjustment leads to $CV_i = E(X_i)/0.028$. Across the full sample (which includes the many people who did not visit the lake), the average welfare loss is nearly \$28. For the 20 percent of the sample that did visit the lake, the average welfare loss from eliminating the site is \$134.

The zero income effect demand equation implies we can, for this special case, compute the "value of a trip" to the site using only our estimate of β. Specifically, when $E(X_i) = 1$ the welfare loss from eliminating the site is simply $-1/\beta$, which is equivalent to the lost consumer surplus from a single trip (recall that the change in consumer surplus and compensating variation are the same when there is no income effect). For our example, the net consumer benefit per trip to Saylorville Lake is 1/0.028, or nearly \$36.

Multiple Sites

There are a variety of reasons we may want to generalize the single-site model to a system context. Three are particularly important. First, the value of the services provided by a particular site depends critically on the extent to which close substitutes are available, yet a specification as in (17.10) does not allow us to account for this effect directly. Second, we are often interested in the role that attributes of recreation sites (q in our notation) play in behavior and site valuation. However, site attributes are in many cases constant for a particular site. For example, in the single-site analysis above, all visitors to Saylorville Lake in 2002 experienced the same average water quality during the year. Thus the variability that is needed to estimate how changes in site-constant quality variables affect trip demand is not available when we observe trips and characteristics for only one site. Finally, non-market values are often needed for interventions that affect the availability or characteristics of multiple sites. For these reasons, multiple-site models are usually preferred to their single-site counterparts.

Generalizing count data models to include multiple sites is conceptually straightforward. For example, let x_{ij} be the number of trips person i makes to site j, where $j=1,\dots,J$ is the index of available sites, and let X_{ij} be the corresponding random variable whose distribution summarizes the stochastic nature of trip demand from the analyst's perspective. If X_{ij} is distributed Poison with $E(X_{ij})=\delta_{ij}$, then

$$\Pr(X_{i1}=x_{i1},\dots,X_{iJ}=x_{iJ})=\prod_{j=1}^{J}\frac{\exp(-\delta_{ij})\delta_{ij}^{x_{ij}}}{x_{ij}!},\quad i=1,\dots,I. \tag{17.17}$$

This statistical model says that the distribution of trips to site j places probability mass only on the non-negative integers, and that it is independent of trips to all other sites. As in the single-site case, this becomes an economic model via a parameterization for δ_{ij}, where the usual functional form is

$$E(X_{ij})=\delta_{ij}=\exp\left(\alpha+\sum_{k=1}^{J}\beta_{jk}p_{ik}+\gamma_{j}Y_{i}+\theta q_{j}\right),\quad j=1,\dots,J. \tag{17.18}$$

There are three points to note about (17.18). First, travel costs p_{ij} vary over both dimensions i (since people live in different places) and j (since sites are located in different places). However, the site characteristic level is constant for all visitors to a particular site, and so variability in q_j arises only through the multiple sites. Thus the parameter θ needs to be constant for all J equations, and it is identified by the variability in trip allocation among the available sites, after travel costs are controlled for. For this reason, variation in site characteristic levels across the extent of the choice set is crucial for estimating the role of site quality in system models. Second, the specification is consistent with cross-product repackaging (quality enters as an effective price modifier) and weak complementarity. Regarding the latter, $E(X_{ij})$ is strictly positive, but in the limit there is a finite amount of compensation the person would accept for the site's elimination, as is apparent from the single-site case in (17.16). Also, because $E(X_{ij})$ is strictly positive, q_j never drops out of the preference function. Finally, the demand system as written does not satisfy the integrability conditions, and so restrictions are needed to derive an indirect utility function. In particular, recall from Chapter 14 that for the log-linear system, $\beta_{jk}=0$ for all $j\neq k$, and $\gamma_j=\gamma$ for all j. Thus the system we estimate using a likelihood function derived from (17.17) is

$$E(X_{ij})=\delta_{ij}=\exp\left(\alpha+\beta_{jj}p_{ij}+\gamma Y_{i}+\theta q_{j}\right),\quad j=1,\dots,J, \tag{17.19}$$

which implies an indirect utility function given by

$$E(V_{i})=\frac{\exp(-\gamma Y_{i})}{\gamma}-\sum_{j=1}^{J}\frac{\exp(\alpha+\beta_{jj}p_{ij}+\theta q_{j})}{\beta_{jj}}, \tag{17.20}$$

for $\gamma > 0$ and

$$E(V_i) = Y_i - \sum_{j=1}^{J} \frac{\exp(\alpha + \beta_{jj} p_{ij} + \theta q_j)}{\beta_{jj}}, \tag{17.21}$$

for $\gamma = 0$ (see section 14.2.3). With these restrictions, we can use the expected indirect utility function $E(V_i)$ for the full range of price and quality change welfare analysis.

Estimation of the parameters in (17.19) is slightly more challenging than in the single-site case, owing primarily to the fact that cross-equation restrictions are needed to assure that θ is identified. Nonetheless, most econometric packages support system estimation of this type.

EXAMPLE 17.2 (EMPIRICAL) As an example of the multiple-site model, we estimate the parameters in (17.19) using visits to all of the 127 lakes in the Iowa dataset, setting $\gamma = 0$ as in the single-site case (estimation with income results in a coefficient estimate that is once again zero out to five decimal places). Thus we recover estimates for α and θ as well as 127 unique values for β_{jj}:

$$E(X_{i,99}) = \delta_{i,99} = \exp\left(\underset{(15.38)}{1.34} - \underset{(-15.54)}{0.024} \cdot p_{i,99} - \underset{(-3.34)}{0.005} \cdot q_j\right), \tag{17.22}$$

where we have shown the price coefficient for site $j = 99$, which is Saylorville Lake. The other 126 price coefficient estimates range from -0.18 to -0.01. Note that the negative coefficient on q_j implies that higher levels of chlorophyll a result in fewer visits to a lake.

The parameter estimates can be used in conjunction with Eq. (17.21) to compute counterfactual welfare analyses. In general, the compensating variation (change in consumer surplus with $\gamma = 0$) for a change in q_j from q_j^0 to q_j^1 across the choice set is

$$CV_i = \sum_{j=1}^{J} \frac{\exp(\alpha + \beta_{jj} p_{ij} + \theta q_j^1)}{\beta_{jj}} - \sum_{j=1}^{J} \frac{\exp(\alpha + \beta_{jj} p_{ij} + \theta q_j^0)}{\beta_{jj}}. \tag{17.23}$$

As a specific example, consider the willingness to pay for a 50 percent reduction in chlorophyll a concentration at Clear Lake, an important recreation destination in the north-central part of the state. At observed conditions the average concentration in the lake is 30.23 µg/l. Across the full sample the average welfare gain from this improvement is $1.16 per year, and amongst the subset of people who visited the lake the average welfare gain is $4.17. As a point of reference, the average consumer surplus loss from eliminating Clear Lake from the choice set is $24 for the full sample and $193 for the 12 percent of people who visited the lake. As a second example, consider the willingness to pay for a 50 percent reduction in chlorophyll a concentration at all 127 lakes in the choice set. Using Eq. (17.23) we find that the average per person welfare gain from this change is $23.82 per year.

Advantages and Disadvantages

As noted above, count data models in both their single and multiple equation form convey numerous advantages from a statistical and econometric perspective. Their performance from an economic perspective is more equivocal. Count distribution approaches characterize the expectation of an individual's demand and indirect utility functions, and this has implications for how we interpret estimates from the model. Note in particular that $E(X_{ij})$ is positive by construction, so the economic interpretation of the model is strictly one of interior solutions. This greatly simplifies welfare analysis in the sense that there is no extensive margin decision to consider; all demand responses to changes in prices or qualities are continuous, divisible, and bounded away from zero. However, this also means we are unable to explore the extent to which changes in site availability or characteristic levels may induce discrete adjustments, such as changes in the portfolio of sites visited. This is an important point. Although the Poisson model and its generalizations accommodate zero demands and integer outcomes from an econometric perspective, economic inference from the model focuses only on the continuous, "how many" aspect of the recreation decision. There is not a behavioral explanation for why corner solutions occur, nor does the structure of the model effectively exploit variation in the discrete, "which ones" dimension of choice.

17.3.2 RUM Models

We now turn our attention to discrete choice models of recreation choice. In its simplest form, recreation represents a straightforward application of the discrete choice methods we discussed in Chapter 16. When faced with a decision on where to go for a recreation outing, a person considers the portfolio of options – the choice set in our current terminology. He maximizes his well-being by first considering the conditional utility available from a visit to each site, and then selecting the site that delivers the highest utility. His conditional utility function for each site depends on measurable variables such as travel cost and site characteristics, along with unobserved (to the analyst) preference and site heterogeneity. The econometric objective is to estimate a sufficient component of the indirect utility function to allow comparisons of utility across sites, and ultimately the computation of welfare measures. In this subsection we examine features of random utility maximization (RUM) model analysis that are particularly relevant for recreation applications.

The use of RUM models in recreation is based on methodological work by McFadden (1973; see also McFadden, 2001), and Hanemann's (1978) dissertation, which first applied the method to recreation data. Since then RUM models have become the dominant paradigm in modeling recreation preferences. For this reason alone they are deserving of careful discussion. However, RUM models also provide an excellent contrast to the system perspective examined above. There, the economic model described visits to J destinations over a timeframe sufficiently long to allow multiple visits to several sites. An interior solution for the J available sites was the primary analytical tool used to derive welfare measures. In this sense the model focused on the frequency of visits – i.e. variability in how many trips a sample of individuals made to the available sites. RUM models, by contrast, shrink the time dimension of the decision to a single choice outcome. By construction one trip is consumed, so no variability in the frequency of visits is used. Instead, we observe trade-offs that people make between travel costs and site attributes as they select the site that maximizes utility on a choice occasion. In this sense RUM models focus only on the extensive margin of choice – i.e. the "which one" component of the overall decision. The analytical tool we use for welfare analysis is a discrete comparison of the utility available to a person from each of the J available sites.

In this subsection we continue our discussion of RUM models that began in Chapter 16, with specific focus on issues related to recreation applications. To this end suppose we are interested in modeling choices among J recreation sites in order to understand the value of individual sites and their attributes. Recall that the basic assumption of a RUM model is that on a given choice occasion, a person selects a single alternative among J available options to maximize his utility level. The person knows his preferences with certainty and so the choice from his perspective is deterministic. An observer, however, cannot know all of the features of a person's utility function, and so preferences are at least partially random from the perspective of the analyst. To reflect this we write the utility a person i can receive from a visit to site j as consisting of observable and unobservable components, so that

$$U_{ij} = V_{ij}(Y_i - p_{ij}, q_j, \xi_j; \beta) + \varepsilon_{ij}, \quad j = 1, ..., J, \tag{17.24}$$

where q_j and ξ_j are attributes of site j, $V_{ij}(\cdot)$ is a known functional form characterizing the observable component of utility, β is a vector of parameters, and ε_{ij} is a random variable with known distribution that summarizes the component of utility that is unobserved by the analyst. The two attribute variables q_j and ξ_j are separately included to explicitly distinguish between attributes that are observed by the analyst (q_j) and those that are known by the decision-maker but not the analyst (ξ_j). To maximize utility, the person chooses to visit site j if and only if $U_{ij} \geq U_{ik}$ for all $k \neq j$.

The model is made operational via assumptions on the functional form for $V_{ij}(\cdot)$ and the distribution of ε_{ij}. Almost all recreation applications have assumed that U_{ij} is linear in $Y_i - p_{ij}$, so that income drops out of the model when utility is differenced (see section 16.2.2). Though there are notable exceptions, most applications have also not distinguished between q_j and ξ_j, and thereby have effectively assumed $\xi_j = 0$ for all j. Finally, we typically start out by assuming ε_{ij} is independently and identically distributed type I extreme value. Under this assumption, the conditional logit model arises. Thus the canonical RUM model specification is something akin to the following:

$$U_{ij} = -\beta p_{ij} + \theta q_j + \varepsilon_{ij}, \quad j = 1, ..., J, \quad i = 1, ..., I, \tag{17.25}$$

where β is the marginal utility of income, ε_{ij} is distributed independent and identical type I extreme value.

We will use this version of the model to discuss several topics of particular importance for RUM models in recreation demand. To begin our illustration, the following example presents estimates of the parameters in (17.25), using the Iowa lakes data.

EXAMPLE 17.3 (EMPIRICAL) In the Iowa lakes data, if we only include the most recent visit made to each lake by each survey participant (a point to which we return below), we observe 7,818 visits to the 127 lakes by the 2,489 survey respondents (individuals can visit multiple lakes). We assume that each observed trip is the outcome of an independent choice situation, in which the person selected a lake to maximize utility from a single trip. With travel cost and chlorophyll a concentration in the model, this results in the following parameter estimates:

$$U_{ij} = \underset{(43.95)}{-0.026} \cdot p_{ij} - \underset{(-18.87)}{0.0091} \cdot q_j + \varepsilon_{ij}, \tag{17.26}$$

where z-statistics computed using robust (sandwich) standard errors are shown in parentheses. Recall from Chapter 16 that the ratio $-\theta/\beta$ is the marginal willingness to pay for a reduction in chlorophyll concentration. Thus conditional on taking a trip, and holding the conditional indirect utility level constant, respondents are willing to pay $0.0091/0.026 \approx \$0.35$ per trip for a 1 µg/l reduction. In addition, we can use (17.26) to predict the welfare effect of a discrete change in phosphorus concentration. Consider once again a decrease in chlorophyll a at Clear Lake, where a 50 percent reduction from the 30.23 µg/l baseline is equivalent to a concentration of 15.11 µg/l. *Conditional* on the choice of Clear Lake, the dollar value of the utility change from this improvement is $0.0091 \cdot (15.11)/0.026 \approx \$5.28$ per trip. An alternative, ex ante welfare measure considers the per choice occasion value based on a comparison of the expected utility from a trip opportunity before and after the quality improvement. The formula for expected maximum utility described in section 16.6 is needed for this, whereby

$$E(CV_i) = \frac{1}{0.026}\left\{\begin{array}{l} \ln\left[\sum_{j=1}^{127}\exp(-0.026\cdot p_{ij}-0.0091\cdot q_j^1)\right] \\ -\ln\left[\sum_{j=1}^{127}\exp(-0.026\cdot p_{ij}-0.0091\cdot q_j^0)\right] \end{array}\right\}, \tag{17.27}$$

and q_j^0 and q_j^1 are the baseline and new quality levels, respectively. Applying this formula we find that the per-choice occasion welfare value is \$0.16 across the entire sample, and \$0.85 for the sub-sample of people who visited Clear Lake. The difference between these estimates and the ex post, conditional-on-visit estimate reflects the role of substitution across the entire choice set: changing the characteristics at a single recreation site has a smaller welfare impact, when the full range of available alternatives is accounted for in the model and welfare concept.

Why Are RUM Models So Successful?

By almost any measure, RUM models have become the dominant empirical approach in recreation demand. This is the case both for applications and for methodological explorations of more general issues. There are several reasons why this is so. Perhaps most importantly, the behavioral data requirements are mild relative to system-type models. In the simplest case, gathering information on where a sample of people went on their most recent trips – which requires only a single question on a survey – can provide sufficient data to estimate a RUM model. Indeed we have thus far illustrated the model using only a subset of the actual trip records that are available from the Iowa lakes survey. In such a case the choice set can be defined ex post after observing the distribution of trips in the data, thereby allowing considerable flexibility in model specification. In contrast, system-type models require a full history of trip-taking behavior over a given time period. Usually this information is gathered by presenting survey respondents with an ex ante defined choice set, and asking people to recall their trip counts to each site. This type of question places a larger burden on the respondent and it is more subject to recall error than simply asking about the most recent trip. While either solicitation approach can be completed with good surveying techniques, it is generally true that data for RUM modeling can be obtained at higher accuracy and lower cost than data for system-type modeling.

Other reasons have to do with the overlap between the capabilities of RUM models and the main needs of recreation analysis. Although the frequency of visits to particular sites undeniably has an important role to play, welfare measurement in recreation applications hinges most heavily on the substitutability of options available to visitors. RUM models focus directly on this feature, providing a transparent means of quantifying the trade-offs people are willing to make between the available sites and their attributes. Indeed, one way to view a RUM model is as a vehicle through which we observe people choosing the site attribute levels that they most value. If, for example, the spatial distribution of these choices shows people traveling further to obtain higher levels of q, we have strong evidence of the role of q in determining how similar or dissimilar different sites are. Abstracting from the frequency of visits allows this feature of preferences to clearly emerge.

A further point related to the capabilities of RUM models concerns specification. First, RUM models are well designed for specifying preferences that are consistent with weak complementarity, in that one only needs to include quality variables for site j in the utility function for site j, and nowhere else. Also, as we saw above for the Iowa example and in Chapter 16, welfare measurement in linear-in-income logit type models is relatively simple, owing to the constant marginal utility of income. In many applications (vehicle and residential home choices are good examples) abstracting from income effects is counterintuitive, but in recreation analysis it is less so. While income levels may influence the types of activities people engage in, it seems unlikely that income plays an appreciable role in determining which among the available sites a person visits to engage in that activity. Thus good arguments can be made for specifying simple, linear-in-price RUM models for use when welfare analysis is the objective.

Econometric Identification of Site Characteristics

A defining characteristic of many RUM models is their parsimony in the number of parameters that need to be estimated. This is an advantage in the sense that we can often characterize substitution patterns among sites with relative ease. In the Iowa lakes example, we examined the welfare effects of water-quality changes after estimating only two parameters. However, it also means that a lot is expected of the error term in a RUM model. It must account for the role of unobserved preference heterogeneity, unmeasured household variables, and site attributes that are not available for inclusion in q. Methodological research on RUM models has suggested that the single additive, independent error term is often not up to the task. A good example of this was discussed in Chapter 16, in which we identified the independence of irrelevant alternatives (IIA) property of the conditional logit model. Our discussion suggested there are good reasons for seeking specifications that allow non-zero correlation among the random variables $\varepsilon_{i1},...,\varepsilon_{iJ}$, as well as methods that can accommodate observed and unobserved preference heterogeneity. We also discussed the role of unobserved attributes of alternatives, and how failure to explicitly consider varying values for ξ_j in Eq. (17.24) could lead to biased results. In this subsection we consider this latter point in the context of recreation site choice RUM models.

As defined above, let ξ_j be an index that captures everything about site j that visitors observe and care about, but which the analyst cannot measure. In this case the utility function from (17.25) is generalized to

$$U_{ij} = -\beta p_{ij} + \theta q_j + \xi_j + \varepsilon_{ij}, \quad i = 1,...,I, \quad j = 1,...,J. \tag{17.28}$$

As was discussed in Chapter 16, many applications implicitly assume $\xi_j = 0$. To see why this might be a problem, suppose some values of ξ_j are large for certain sites relative to others, and as such the proportion of observed visits to those sites is large for reasons not related to the corresponding value of q. In the context of the Iowa lakes application, for example, suppose Saylorville Lake ($j=99$) is frequently visited and has high water quality (both of which we observe) *and* other attractive features (which we do not), so that ξ_{99} is large relative to other sites. In the model presented above, which constrained $\xi_j = 0$ for all sites in the choice set, the estimator sought parameters β and θ to predict a comparatively large value for

$$\text{Pr}_{i,99} = \frac{\exp(-\beta p_{i,99} + \theta q_{99})}{\sum_{k=1}^{J} \exp(\beta p_{ik} + \theta q_k)}, \quad i = 1,...,I. \tag{17.29}$$

Intuitively, the variability arising from the unmeasured attributes of sites must "find a place to go" – even though ξ_j is not in the model. This will result in estimates of β and θ that adjust accordingly, and hence do not accurately reflect the role of p and q in individuals' choices. As discussed in general in Chapter 16, this results in omitted attributes bias.

An approach to accommodating unobserved recreation site attributes was examined by Murdock (2006). It starts with a specification as in (17.28), which can be usefully rewritten as

$$U_{ij} = \delta_j - \beta p_{ij} + \varepsilon_{ij}, \quad i = 1,...,I, \quad j = 1,...,J, \tag{17.30}$$

where

$$\delta_j = \theta q_j + \xi_j, \quad j = 1,...,J. \tag{17.31}$$

Writing the utility function this way suggests a solution in which we first include a full set of alternative specific constants – i.e. recreation site fixed effects – which control for both observed *and* unobserved site attributes nonparametrically in a single term. Maximum likelihood estimation is then used to recover estimates of $\delta_1,...,\delta_{J-1}$ and β, where δ_J is normalized to zero for identification. A second stage of estimation is then carried out to recover θ, which makes use of a linear regression based on (17.31). Once θ is estimated, ξ_j can be computed as a residual from (17.31). In this way, both observed and unobserved site attributes are accounted for in the utility function, which is ultimately used for welfare analysis. Note, however, that this solution is only operational when J is large enough for θ to be identified in a regression context.

EXAMPLE 17.4 (EMPIRICAL) We present an illustration of the two-step estimation approach using the Iowa lakes data, with the 7,818 observed trips. In the first stage, we find our estimate for the marginal utility of income is unchanged from the earlier approach ($\beta = 0.0275$). However, our estimate for the coefficient on chlorophyll a is now small and insignificant, with $\theta = -0.0009$ (z-statistic -0.352). This finding, which contrasts with the estimate shown above, has two possible explanations. First, it may be that the strongly negative effect found using the more parsimonious model is biased by the absence of other, potentially correlated, site characteristic variables in the specification. Second, it may be that there is insufficient variation in water quality across the choice set to estimate an effect with any precision.

The estimates from the first stage are nonetheless useful for measuring the value of access to a site on a given trip-taking occasion. Applying once again the formula described in section 16.6, the value of access to Saylorville Lake ($j = 99$) is given by

$$E(CV_i) = \frac{1}{0.0275} \left\{ \begin{array}{l} \ln\left[\sum_{j=1}^{127} \exp(\delta_j - 0.0275 \cdot p_{ij}) \right] \\ -\ln\left[\sum_{\forall k \neq 99} \exp(\delta_k - 0.0275 \cdot p_{ik}) \right] \end{array} \right\}. \tag{17.32}$$

The sample average estimate is $1.07, and the average for sample members who visited Saylorville Lake is $3.08.

Repeated Choices

RUM models by their nature are designed to analyze a single-choice situation, and as we have seen, they are particularly useful for analyzing substitution patterns among available sites. A limitation of RUM models is that by focusing on a single-choice outcome, they do not address observation of repeated visits over the course of a recreation season. A solution to this is to treat each observed trip as the outcome of a separate choice occasion. In this way, a person contributes data points equal to the number of his total observed trips. In the simplest models multiple-choice outcomes from the same person are stacked and treated independently, so there is effectively no difference between a large sample of single-trip taking individuals, and a smaller sample of multiple-trip taking individuals.

This does not, however, provide a behavioral explanation for why multiple choices are observed in the first place, since even when multiple-trip outcomes per person are included, RUM models of site choice operate at the choice occasion level. This leads to challenges for welfare analysis, in that compensation measures are produced at the level of a choice occasion. This is somewhat odd in the world of applied welfare analysis. For example, using the parsimonious model above (i.e. without alternative specific constants), we found that a 50 percent decrease in chlorophyll a at a single site was worth $0.16 per trip to a lake in the choice set. To be useful for policy, this number needs to be aggregated in two dimensions: over people and over trips. The former is a familiar, if not always straightforward, problem. The latter requires an assumption on the total number of trip-taking occasions affected by the improvement. While the total demand for trips would likely increase with the quality improvement, the basic RUM specification does not provide a means of estimating this change. A common solution is to multiply the per trip willingness to pay by the baseline total trips (or a population estimate thereof), which constrains the total trip response to a change in quality to zero. For example, the average survey respondent in 2002 took ten trips to the major lakes in Iowa, and so an estimate of the annual welfare gain from the Clear Lake improvement is $1.60 per person. While multiplying by the baseline number of observed trips can provide a useful bound on the aggregate willingness to pay for a change in site quality levels, it serves to illustrate the limitation inherent in models that do not explain trip frequency along with site choice.[4]

Repeated RUM models that also include a no-trip option are a partial solution to this limitation. In this approach there are $J+1$ choice alternatives: J recreation sites, and a no-trip option. To add a frequency of choice component, the analyst assumes there are a fixed number of choice opportunities over the timeframe of interest. For a calendar year, $T=50$ is a common assumption (corresponding approximately to one choice per week). Observation of the total number of trips to all J sites over the timeframe determines the number of times the no-trip option is selected. In this way each person in the sample contributes T choices to the analysis, and the total number of trips (i.e. the number of times the no-trip option is *not* selected) is endogenous to the model. Under this framework, the analyst can predict, for example, how the probability of the no-trip option falls when quality improves at the recreation sites, and thereby predict the change in the number of times the no-trip option is selected. By this method, the RUM model framework can be adapted to account for the change in the total demand for trips, though somewhat awkwardly relative to using a demand equation.

EXAMPLE 17.5 (EMPIRICAL) As an illustration of the repeated RUM method, we generalize the parsimonious Iowa lakes model to include a no-trip option according to

$$
\begin{aligned}
U_{i0t} &= \delta_0 + \varepsilon_{i0t}, \quad j = 0, \\
U_{ijt} &= -\beta p_{ij} + \theta q_j + \varepsilon_{ijt}, \quad j = 1,...,127, \quad i = 1,...,I, \quad t = 1,...,50,
\end{aligned}
\tag{17.33}
$$

where now the constant δ_0 captures the utility from not making a trip on choice occasion t, relative to visiting one of the $J=127$ lakes. Since travel cost and site quality in this dataset do not change over time, we have only included a choice occasion subscript on the error term. The estimates from this model are $\delta_0 = 2.69$ (23.85), $\beta = 0.0329$ (16.54), and $\theta = -0.0092$ (−11.04), where z-statistics are shown in parenthesis and estimates are based on observation of $50 \times 2,489$ outcomes (50 for each sample member). Consider, using this model, the behavioral and welfare effects of reducing chlorophyll concentrations by 50 percent at all 127 lakes in the choice set. The average willingness to pay per choice occasion for this improvement is nearly $0.89, which when multiplied by $T=50$ annual choice occasions, implies an annual willingness to pay per person of nearly $45. This figure reflects both the improved

---

[4] Taking the Iowa example further, there are 2.35 million adult residents of Iowa, and over 50 percent report visiting a lake each year. Thus an annual lower bound estimate of the statewide welfare improvement from the Clear Lake scenario is approximately $1.88 million.

quality of existing trips, as well as additional trips. In particular, the average probability of the no-trip alternative is given by

$$\text{Pr}_0 = \frac{1}{I} \sum_{i=1}^{I} \frac{\exp(\delta_0)}{\sum_{k=1}^{J} \exp(-\beta p_{ij} + \theta q_j)}, \tag{17.34}$$

which falls from 0.796 to 0.774 following the quality improvement. This implies that the average number of "no trip" choice outcomes falls from $50 \times 0.796 = 39.8$ to $50 \times 0.774 = 38.7$, which translates to an average increase of 1.1 trips per person during the year following the quality improvement.

17.3.3 Corner Solution Models

The two empirical models we have examined thus far focus on the intensive margin (systems) and extensive margin (RUM models) aspects of behavior, respectively. We have seen that observed behavior is a mix of these two components, and a model that blends aspects of the system and RUM approaches therefore seems desirable. Exploiting both types of variability may also provide advantages in identifying the role of site quality variables. Corner solution models attempt to do this. These models take their name from the notion that a person's optimal consumption of a commodity may be zero, in which case the outcome is often referred to as a "corner solution", in order to differentiate it from an "interior solution" with positive consumption. A distinguishing characteristic of corner solution models is the integration of the theory of consumer choice under binding non-negativity constraints with a structural econometric model. The basic econometric framework for such an empirical model was described by Wales and Woodland (1983) and Lee and Pitt (1986), though applications were slow to follow due primarily to the computational limitations of the era. Phaneuf et al. (2000) present the first full application of corner solution models in recreation demand, and their approach was refined by von Haefen et al. (2004). As we discuss below, there are clear advantages to pursuing corner solution models in recreation applications. However, realizing these advantages involves coming to terms with methods that are more complicated than we have examined to this point. In what follows, we discuss corner solution models by first presenting a stylized conceptual baseline. We then describe intuitively how such a model can be made empirical. Only then do we present the model generally and move on to a discussion of how it has been used in practice. Since there are few accessible descriptions of this model elsewhere, our pace in this subsection is more deliberate than in our discussion of other purely econometric techniques.

Conceptual Description

Corner solution models – or Kuhn-Tucker models, as they are also called – are most appropriate for multiple-site analysis. To gain intuition, however, consider a single-site model in which utility is given by $U(x,z,q,\varepsilon)$, where for the moment x is a scalar recording trips to the site. As usual, z and q are numeraire consumption and site quality, respectively, and ε is the component of preferences known to the individual but not observed by the analyst. The individual chooses x and z subject to budget and non-negativity constraints, so that the formal problem is

$$\max_{x,z} U(x, z, q, \varepsilon) + \lambda(Y - px - z) + \kappa(x - 0). \tag{17.35}$$

The first-order conditions take the form of Kuhn-Tucker conditions as described in the first section of this chapter, which are given by

$$\frac{\partial U(x, z, q, \varepsilon)}{\partial x} = \lambda p - \kappa, \quad x \geq 0, \quad \kappa \cdot x = 0$$

$$\frac{\partial U(x, z, q, \varepsilon)}{\partial z} = \lambda. \tag{17.36}$$

It is useful for interpretation to rewrite these conditions as

$$\frac{\partial U(x, Y - px, q, \varepsilon)/\partial x}{\partial U(x, Y - px, q, \varepsilon)/\partial z} = \zeta = p - \frac{\kappa}{\lambda}, \tag{17.37}$$

where we have substituted out for z using the budget constraint, and we refer to $\varsigma = p - \kappa/\lambda$ as the virtual price of x. In what follows, it will be useful to also define the virtual price at the solution, which we write as $\varsigma(x, p, Y, q, \varepsilon) = p - \kappa(\cdot)/\lambda(\cdot)$. Note that there are two types of solutions to (17.35). When $\kappa > 0$, we have $x = 0$ (a corner solution); when $\kappa = 0$, we have $x > 0$ (an interior solution). The distinction between these is discrete: utility is higher *either* at a corner solution *or* an interior solution, and the person lands at one or the other based on a discrete comparison. This allows us to consider the two types of solutions in turn.

Consider first an interior solution. In this case (17.37) collapses to

$$\frac{\partial U(x, Y - px, q, \varepsilon)/\partial x}{\partial U(x, Y - px, q, \varepsilon)/\partial z} = \zeta(x, p, Y, q, \varepsilon) = p. \tag{17.38}$$

As with any interior solution, the marginal willingness to pay for x is equal to the price of x. Equation (17.37) shows that the virtual price is another way of expressing the marginal willingness to pay for x, and so it is not surprising that it equals the price in this instance. The solution in the interior case is therefore familiar, and includes the ordinary demand function $x(p, Y, q, \varepsilon)$ arising from (17.38), and the conditional indirect utility function $V_{in}(p, Y, q, \varepsilon)$, where the subscript *in* denotes the interior solution. We have called this "conditional", and used the *in* subscript, to stress that this is the maximum utility obtained when $x > 0$.

Consider next a corner solution. In this case we have

$$\frac{\partial U(0, Y, q, \varepsilon)/\partial x}{\partial U(0, Y, q, \varepsilon)/\partial z} = \zeta(Y, q, \varepsilon) \leq p, \tag{17.39}$$

and it is *not* the case that the marginal willingness to pay for x is its price. Instead, at the point $x = 0$ the person values a unit of the good at the level $\varsigma(Y, q, \varepsilon)$, which is less than the actual price p. In this case the virtual price represents two things. It is the marginal willingness to pay for x at $x=0$ and it is the endogenous reservation price for the person. To appreciate the latter, note that if the price were to drop below $\varsigma(\cdot)$, the person would consume some x. The solution in the corner solution case is perhaps less familiar, in that we have $x(\varsigma,Y,q,\varepsilon)=0$ and $V_{co}(\varsigma,Y,q,\varepsilon)$, where the former arises from (17.39), the latter via substitution of $x=0$ into $U(\cdot)$, and the subscript co indicates the corner solution.

To see how these concepts work with a specific utility function, consider a specification given by

$$U(x,z,q,\varepsilon) = \Psi \cdot \ln\left[x\cdot\delta + \theta\right] + \ln(z)$$
$$\Psi = \exp(\alpha + \varepsilon) \qquad\qquad (17.40)$$
$$\delta = \exp(\gamma \cdot q),$$

where δ is a simple repackaging index, and (α,θ,γ) are parameters. The first-order Kuhn-Tucker conditions with respect to x and z can, for this example, be manipulated to arrive at

$$(Y - px)\cdot\frac{\Psi\cdot\delta}{x\cdot\delta + \theta} = p, \quad x > 0 \qquad\qquad (17.41)$$

for an interior solution, and

$$\zeta(Y,q,\varepsilon) = \frac{Y\cdot\Psi\cdot\delta}{\theta} \leq p, \quad x = 0 \qquad\qquad (17.42)$$

for a corner solution. In the case of an interior solution, we can solve (17.41) to obtain the demand function for x as

$$x(p,Y,q,\varepsilon) = \frac{\Psi\cdot Y}{p(1+\Psi)} - p\left(\theta/\delta\right). \qquad\qquad (17.43)$$

Note that when $p=\varsigma(\cdot)$ from (17.39) is plugged into $x(\cdot)$ in (17.43), the result is $x(\varsigma,Y,q,\varepsilon)=0$. Plugging $x=0$ into (17.40) gives us $V_{co}(\cdot)$, and likewise plugging (17.43) into the direct utility function gives us $V_{in}(\cdot)$.

Having considered the two possible outcomes, it is now possible to describe the overall solution to (17.35) as one of extensive and intensive margins. In particular, the unconditional indirect utility function is

$$V(p,Y,q,\varepsilon) = \max\left\{V_{in}(p,Y,q,\varepsilon), V_{co}(\zeta,Y,q,\varepsilon)\right\}, \qquad\qquad (17.44)$$

which bears resemblance to a RUM model in its inclusion of discrete options. If V_{in} is highest, there is also a frequency of visit component given by $x(p,Y,q,\varepsilon)$, which bears resemblance to the system model in its use of an actual demand equation. The form of (17.44) suggests an empirical strategy that considers both the choice of demand regime – i.e. an interior or corner solution in this one site example – and intensity of site use. It also hints at what we might hope to accomplish when conducting welfare analysis. Note, for example, that a change in q can have two types of effects. It could result in a movement from corner to interior status, or vice versa, which we refer to as a regime change. This is a pure discrete response, which is the type of welfare measurement the RUM model is designed to capture. It could also lead to a marginal adjustment in the quantity of x, which is the type of welfare measurement the system model quantifies. The corner solution model nests both of these adjustments and welfare impacts into a single, theoretically consistent description of behavior.

The two types of solutions possible in this stylized example are shown via the two identical indifference maps in Figure 17.1. Because x is allowed to be zero (i.e. it is non-essential), the indifference curves intersect the vertical axis, thereby allowing corner solutions. In both panels the person has full income Y available to spend on x and z, but the budget constraints are drawn so that the price of x is greater in panel B than in panel A. In panel A, the price p^0 results in an interior solution for x, and the person reaches utility level U^0 at the point labeled a. In panel B, the slope of the budget constraint is everywhere greater in absolute value than the slope of the indifference curves. Thus the person reaches the maximum utility level U^1 ($<U^0$) at a corner solution, shown via point b, which corresponds analytically to Eq. (17.39). Importantly, the marginal rate of substitution between x and z does not equal p^1 at point b. Instead, the slope of the indifference curve (and the marginal willingness to pay for x) at b is the virtual price ς. Note that at the solution, ς rather than p^1 is the behaviorally relevant price. If p rises above p^1 there are no behavioral or welfare changes for the person. However, if p were to drop below ς the person would adjust to an interior solution, and there would be welfare effects from the change. Note as well that $\varsigma(Y,q,\varepsilon)$ is a quality-adjusted virtual price, since at the point of solution it is a function of q. If a quality attribute of the site improves, ς may increase, potentially causing a person originally at a corner solution to switch to an interior solution. In this quality-adjusted sense as well, ς is the behaviorally relevant price for a person at a corner solution.

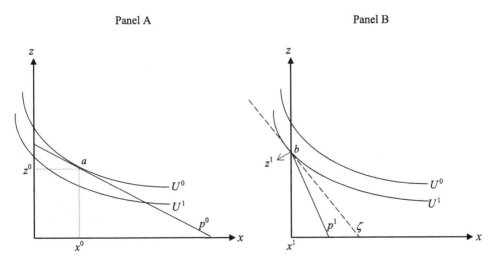

Figure 17.1 Corner solution outcome

Figure 17.1 also serves to further illustrate the differences between the three models we have examined. The demand system approach relies on solutions such as point a, and uses variability in price, the number of trips, and quality to trace out the curvature of the indifference map via marginal concepts. In the process it abstracts from outcomes such as point b and does not address discrete concepts such as regime switching. RUM models use a comparison of utility levels between discrete points such as a and b, but ignore variability in the number of trips made by different people. Instead, variability in price and quality alone are used to quantify level values for U^0 and U^1. Corner solution models combine these two concepts, using variability in x, p, and q to trace out the shape of indifference curves while also exploiting regime switching to assess level differences.

The price of this is a more difficult empirical task. To see what is required, assume we have chosen a parametric form for utility and a distribution for the random variable ε_i, which is the component of person i's preference function known by him but unobserved to the analyst. For person i in the data, we observe if he has chosen a corner or interior solution, and if it is the latter, we observe the number of trips. Estimating equations are derived from the first-order conditions, which gives the Kuhn-Tucker model its name. In particular, if we observe an interior solution for person i we derive a probability statement based on

$$\frac{\partial U(x_i, Y_i - p_i x_i, q, \varepsilon_i)/\partial x}{\partial U(x_i, Y_i - p_i x_i, q, \varepsilon_i)/\partial z} = p_i \quad \rightarrow \quad \varepsilon_i = g(x_i, q, Y_i, p_i). \tag{17.45}$$

For a corner solution we derive

$$\frac{\partial U(0, Y_i, q, \varepsilon_i)/\partial x}{\partial U(0, Y_i, q, \varepsilon_i)/\partial z} \le p_i \quad \rightarrow \quad \varepsilon_i \le g(q, Y_i, p_i), \tag{17.46}$$

where in both cases "$\rightarrow$" denotes algebraically solving for ε_i as a function of the other variables, and $g(\cdot)$ is the form the function takes, which is based on $U(\cdot)$. If person i is observed at an interior solution, he contributes $\Pr[\varepsilon_i = g(\cdot)]$ to the likelihood function; if he is observed at a corner solution he contributes $\Pr[\varepsilon_i \le g(\cdot)]$. Assumptions on the form of $U(\cdot)$ and the distribution for ε_i provide the structure needed to estimate β by maximum likelihood. This is best seen by returning to our specific utility function in (17.40). When we observe an interior solution for person i, the condition in (17.41) can be rearranged to arrive at

$$\begin{aligned} \varepsilon_i &= \ln\left[\frac{p_i(x_i \cdot \delta + \theta)}{\delta(Y_i - p_i x_i)}\right] - \alpha \\ &= \ln p_i + \ln(x_i \cdot \delta + \theta) - \ln(\delta) - \ln(Y - px) - \alpha = g(x_i, q, Y_i, p_i). \end{aligned} \tag{17.47}$$

When we observe a corner solution for person i, the condition in (17.42) is rearranged as

$$\begin{aligned} \varepsilon_i &\le \ln\left[\frac{p_i \theta}{Y_i \delta}\right] - \alpha \\ &\le \ln p_i - \ln \theta - \ln Y_i - \ln \delta - \alpha = g_i(q, Y_i, p_i). \end{aligned} \tag{17.48}$$

The probabilities that enter the likelihood function are

$$\Pr\left[\varepsilon_i = g(x_i, q, Y_i, p_i)\right] = f\left[g(\cdot)\right]\left|\frac{dg(\cdot)}{dx}\right|$$

$$\Pr\left[\varepsilon_i \leq g(q, Y_i, p_i)\right] = F\left[g(\cdot)\right], \tag{17.49}$$

where $f(\cdot)$ and $F(\cdot)$ are the probability density and cumulative distribution functions for ε_i, respectively, and $|dg(\cdot)/dx|$ is the absolute value of the derivative of (17.47) with respect to x.[5]

The way that the estimate for β and the distribution of ε_i are used for welfare analysis is best seen by looking at the form that the indirect utility takes, as shown in (17.44). Recall from Chapter 14 that compensating variation CV can be defined implicitly using the indirect utility function by $V(p, Y-CV, q^1, \varepsilon) = V(p, Y, q^0, \varepsilon)$, where in this case $CV > 0$ is the initial and new quality levels are such that $q^1 > q^0$. In the specific case of our stylized Kuhn-Tucker model, CV_i is implicitly given by

$$\max\left\{V_{i,in}(p_i, Y_i - CV_i, q^1, \varepsilon_i, \beta), V_{i,co}(\zeta_i, Y_i - CV_i, q^1, \varepsilon_i, \beta)\right\}$$
$$= \max\left\{V_{i,in}(p_i, Y_i, q^0, \varepsilon_i, \beta), V_{i,co}(\zeta_i, Y_i, q^0, \varepsilon_i, \beta)\right\}. \tag{17.50}$$

Two things are apparent from this definition. First, the compensating variation will depend on the arguments of the indirect utility function, so we can write $CV_i(p_i, Y_i, q^0, q^1, \varepsilon_i, \beta)$. This implies CV_i is a random variable, since it depends on the unknown value for ε_i. Second, even if we were to observe the value of ε_i, there is in general no analytical solution for CV_i, and so it must be solved using a numerical approach. These two features suggest that having estimated β, we need an algorithm that nests simulation of values for ε_i and a numerical solver for CV_i, to compute values for $E(CV_i)$. The requirement that we simulate values for ε_i is identical to the problem we examined when income enters a RUM model non-linearly, which required the use of Monte Carlo integration. The need to solve for CV numerically, however, is unique to the Kuhn-Tucker model and has been a barrier to its broader use.

General Statement

The discussion given above was intended to illustrate the conceptual and empirical features of the Kuhn-Tucker model. Usually we are interested in using this model for cases when $J > 1$, and so we now turn our attention to discussing the model in this more general case. Suppose now that the utility function is $U(x, z, q, \varepsilon, \beta)$, where x, q, and ε are J dimensional vectors of trips to the available sites, quality attributes at the sites, and

---

[5] This latter point follows from the transformation of random variables theorem. Similar to our case, suppose ε is a continuous random variable with probability density function $f(\varepsilon)$ and that $x = h(\varepsilon)$ is a one-to-one transformation. Define $\varepsilon = h^{-1}(x) = g(x)$ as the inverse transformation function. Then the probability density function for x is given by $f(g(x)) \times |dg(x)/dx|$. This formula is used to construct the probability of observing recreation trips x, which enters into the likelihood function.

unobserved heterogeneity, respectively. As usual z is the scalar numeraire, and β is a vector of parameters to be estimated. The consumer's problem is given by

$$\max_{x,z} U(x_i, z_i, q, \varepsilon_i, \beta) + \lambda_i (Y_i - p_i' x_i - z_i) + \sum_{j=1}^{J} \kappa_{ij} (x_{ij} - 0), \tag{17.51}$$

and the first-order Kuhn-Tucker conditions, after substituting out for z using the budget constraint, are

$$\frac{\partial U(x_i, Y_i - p_i' x_i, q, \varepsilon_i, \beta)/\partial x_j}{\partial U(x_i, Y_i - p_i' x_i, q, \varepsilon_i, \beta)/\partial z} = p_{ij} - \frac{\kappa_{ij}}{\lambda_i} \leq p_{ij}, \quad x_{ij} \geq 0, \quad \kappa_{ij} \cdot x_{ij} = 0, \quad j = 1, ..., J. \tag{17.52}$$

Estimating equations are derived using the first-order conditions, which gives rise to the label Kuhn-Tucker model. In particular, suppose the utility function is chosen so that it is possible to rearrange the first-order conditions as

$$\varepsilon_{ij} \leq g_j(x_i, Y_i - p_i' x_i, q, p_i, \beta), \quad x_{ij} \geq 0,$$
$$x_{ij} \cdot \left[\varepsilon_{ij} - g_j(x_i, Y_i - p_i' x_i, q, p_i, \beta) \right] = 0, \quad j = 1, ..., J, \tag{17.53}$$

where, as above, the form that the function $g_j(\cdot)$ takes is inherited from $U(\cdot)$. Stating the first-order conditions in this way facilitates transition to an empirical model. Suppose we observe a value for x_i for person i in the data. Furthermore, without loss of generality suppose we observe an interior solution for sites $j = 1, ..., m$ and a corner solution for goods $j = 1 + m, ..., J$. Using (17.53) and an assumption for the distribution of ε_i, we can state the probability of observing the outcome as

$$\Pr(x_{i1}, ..., x_{im}, 0_{i,m+1}, ..., 0_{iJ})$$
$$= \Pr\left[\varepsilon_{i1} = g_{i1}(\cdot), ..., \varepsilon_{im} = g_{im}(\cdot), \varepsilon_{i,m+1} \leq g_{i,m+1}(\cdot), ..., \varepsilon_{iJ} \leq g_{iJ}(\cdot) \right]$$
$$= \int_{-\infty}^{g_{i,m+1}} \cdots \int_{-\infty}^{g_{iJ}} f(g_{i1}, ..., g_{im}, \varepsilon_{i,m+1}, ..., \varepsilon_{iJ}) |JA_m| d\varepsilon_{i,m+1} ... d\varepsilon_{iJ}, \tag{17.54}$$

where $f(\cdot)$ is the probability density function for ε and $|JA_m|$ is the Jacobian of transformation from $x_1, ..., x_m$ to $\varepsilon_1, ..., \varepsilon_m$. Deriving a similar probability statement for all individuals in the sample allows estimation of β by maximum likelihood.

There are two things to note about this more general statement of the problem. First, calculation of the probability in (17.54) requires that we evaluate a $J - m$ dimensional probability integral. Depending on the specific distributional assumption, this may be computationally challenging. For example, if ε_i is distributed multivariate normal, it is not possible to calculate (17.54) directly when $J - m$ is larger than four. Other distributions, such as independent extreme value, provide a closed form expression for the probability. Second, estimation of β allows us to characterize an indirect utility function that has a form similar to our stylized example, in that it is a maximum function over conditional indirect utility functions defined at the demand regime level. However, when $J > 1$ the demand regimes become much more numerous. For example, if $J = 2$ the possible site visitation combinations include $\{12\}$, $\{1\}$, $\{2\}$, and $\{\varnothing\}$, so there are four possible regimes. If $J = 3$ we have $\{123\}$, $\{12\}$, $\{13\}$, $\{23\}$, $\{1\}$, $\{2\}$, $\{3\}$, and $\{\varnothing\}$, so that are eight possible regimes. In general there are J^2 possible demand regimes, which we denote $\omega = 1,\ldots,J^2$, and we refer to the set of possible demand regimes using Ω. Given this notation, the indirect utility function has the form

$$V(p_i, Y_i, q, \varepsilon_i, \beta) = \max_{\omega \in \Omega} \left\{ V_{i\omega}(p_{i\omega}, Y_i, q, \varepsilon_i, \beta) \right\}. \tag{17.55}$$

This is the function that we ultimately use for welfare analysis.

Empirical Uses

To apply the Kuhn-Tucker model in actual applications, two computational challenges must be overcome. The first we alluded to above, which relates to estimation difficulties for particular distribution choices for ε_i. When ε_{ij} is distributed independent extreme value a closed form exists for the probability in (17.54), and estimation of the utility function parameters is relatively straightforward. As in RUM models, however, simple distributions can imply unrealistic relationships among the unobserved components of preferences. This aside, in some ways a larger challenge occurs post-estimation, when welfare analysis is done. From (17.55), we can see that the compensating variation for a change from q^0 to q^1 is implicitly defined by

$$\max_{\omega \in \Omega} \left\{ V_{i\omega}(p_{i\omega}, Y_i - CV_i, q^1, \varepsilon_i, \beta) \right\} = \max_{\omega \in \Omega} \left\{ V_{i\omega}(p_{i\omega}, Y_i, q^0, \varepsilon_i, \beta) \right\}. \tag{17.56}$$

We have already seen that computing $E(CV_i)$ requires Monte Carlo integration coupled with a numerical solving strategy to find CV_i for given values of the errors. Note, however, that even when J is of modest size, the latter requires that we compute and compare a potentially enormous number of functions to determine the maximum utility.

The solution to this problem has been to use functional forms for utility that allow for computational tricks to get around the direct computation of the 2^J functions at each iteration of the algorithm. Von Haefen et al. (2004) and von Haefen and Phaneuf (2005) discuss these tricks, which rely on the use of a preference function that is additively separable in the elements of x. To date the most commonly used utility function is

$$U(x_i, z_i, q, \varepsilon_i) = \sum_{j=1}^{J} \Psi_j \cdot \ln\left[x_{ij} \cdot \delta_j + \theta \right] + \frac{1}{\rho} z^\rho,$$

$$\Psi_j = \exp(\alpha + \varepsilon_{ij}) \tag{17.57}$$

$$\delta_j = \exp(\gamma \cdot q_j),$$

which, when ε_{ij} is distributed independent extreme value with freely estimated (non-normalized) scale parameter, can be used to complete estimation and welfare computations for arbitrarily large choice sets.

EXAMPLE 17.6 (EMPIRICAL) To illustrate the corner solutions model with the Iowa lakes data, we use maximum likelihood estimation to recover the parameters in (17.57) for the full sample, with chlorophyll *a* concentration as the quality variable. Our estimates are as follows (z-statistics in parentheses): $\alpha=0.971$ (6.67), $\theta=0.903$ (50.40), $\gamma=-0.0048$ (−18.95), and $\rho=0.80$ (18.95). With the exception of ρ, the magnitudes of these estimates do not have an intuitive interpretation, though in some cases their signs do. Specifically, $\gamma<0$ implies that higher concentrations of chlorophyll *a* negatively affect the utility of trips via the simple repackaging parameter. The utility function parameters can be used to simulate the welfare effects of site availability or changes in quality conditions at select recreation sites. For example, consider once again the benefits of a 50 percent reduction in chlorophyll concentration at Storm Lake. The average per-person annual willingness to pay for this quality improvement is $1.73. Consider as well the benefits of reducing chlorophyll concentrations by 50 percent at all 127 lakes in the choice set. The average per-person annual willingness to pay for this scenario is $41.06. Finally, the annual value of access to Saylorville Lake can be estimated by examining the welfare impacts of setting the travel cost to the site for all people to an arbitrarily large number. The annual per-person average welfare loss (i.e. willingness to pay for access) from eliminating Saylorville Lake is $17.45.

17.3.4 Summary of Empirical Models

Our review of empirical models used in recreation analysis suggests that three distinct approaches are available to practitioners. Although all three exploit similar databases, they approach the problem of estimation and welfare analysis from very different perspectives. Each has its unique strengths and weaknesses. System-type models using count data distributions provide a basis for welfare analysis that is closest to the interior solution, duality-based methods we examined in Chapter 14. The Poisson (and negative binomial) distributions that are used in applications match well with the small integer nature of most recreation visit outcomes. In their simplest form these models are quite accessible, in that they can usually be estimated using provided routines in most econometric software packages. The limitation of count models is their lack of a mechanism for explaining or exploiting the behavioral reasons for non-visitation by sampled individuals to some sites. In contrast, discrete choice models excel at explaining the "which one" aspect of recreation behavior that system-type models do not. The ability of RUM models to reveal the substitutability among available sites and their attributes is one of their main selling points. In addition, welfare measurement in linear-in-price models is relatively simple. These strengths of RUM analysis notwithstanding, their limited ability to explain multiple trip-taking behavior has motivated the development of corner solution models, which combine the best aspects of both systems and RUM type models. Corner solution models, however, are currently less accessible and transparent than their counterparts, and by and large require more restrictive functional specifications.

17.4 MODELING ISSUES

The three modeling approaches described above provide different ways of exploiting recreation data to estimate preferences, and ultimately the value of recreation opportunities and amenities. Although they have different strengths and weaknesses, they share a common reliance on modeling decisions related to how the choice set is defined, how variables are measured and included, the role that time and time budgets play, and other assumptions. In many instances decisions on these aspects of a specific application matter as much as the choice of econometric model. For this reason understanding the importance of basic model assumptions is important, and this task continues to occupy researchers to this day. In this section, we examine a small number of issues that are of perennial importance and/or have received current attention. Though many of these themes have been researched within the context of a specific empirical model – usually RUM approaches – we describe them generally, linking discussion to a specific model when it is useful for exposition. There are many additional topics that we do not cover, which are nonetheless important in applied modeling. A non-exhaustive list of general issues, and references to relevant research, is provided in Table 17.1, which is adapted from Phaneuf and Smith (2005).

17.4.1 Choice Set Definition

All recreation demand models begin with a decision on which recreation sites to include in the analysis. In multiple-site analysis this decision is particularly relevant, since it determines the J sites that constitute the choice set. There is little theoretical guidance on how a choice set should be constructed, outside of the notion that a model of day-trip behavior places natural constraints on the geographical extent of the study area. Like much with empirical work, the construction of the choice set requires judgment and assumptions. Here, we briefly discuss specific issues related to these judgments.

At its core, defining the choice set is about defining the extent of substitutes that are available for recreation activities. For some types of specialized activities, such as stream angling for wild (as opposed to hatchery-reared) trout in North Carolina, the list of possible locations may be relatively small. For others, such as walleye fishing in Minnesota or alpine hiking in Austria, the number of sites can run into the thousands. In a narrow sense a larger choice set is desired, since it is less likely to leave out important substitutes. Furthermore, case study research (see Phaneuf and Smith (2005) for discussion of specific examples) seems to indicate that including irrelevant sites in the choice set results in less bias than excluding relevant sites. Finally, a larger J can provide more useable variation in site attributes levels that are constant for a given site. These comments notwithstanding, a large choice set must be balanced against the increasing computational and data demands that come with it. For example, site characteristics need to be gathered for all sites included in the choice set. This may be prohibitively expensive for arbitrarily large choice sets, or the data may simply not exist. Large choice sets can also lead to estimation and computation challenges. For some models – particularly systems and some types of corner solution models – the number of parameters to be estimated grows with the number of sites included in the model. Even for RUM models, which tend to be more parsimonious in parameters, large choice sets can present challenges in computing probabilities for estimation and welfare calculation. Each of these observations suggests there are pragmatic reasons for balancing the desire for a large number of available substitutes with the modeling costs of doing so.

Table 17.1 Selected modeling issues

Issue	Comment	Selected References
Defining the choice set	• What is the spatial extent of the available sites? • Is the choice set exogenous or endogenous to the individual?	Parsons et al. (2000) Haab and Hicks (1999) Hicks and Schnier (2010)
Defining a recreation site/destination	• What are the ramifications of defining a recreation site based on a specific feature (e.g. a single lake), a spatial boundary (e.g. a census block), or environmental boundaries (e.g. a watershed)?	Haener et al. (2004) Lupi and Feather (1998)
Measuring the opportunity cost of time	• Appropriateness of wage rate and fraction of the wage rate proxies • Use of more sophisticated labor market models • Decoupling the opportunity cost of time from labor market choices	Feather and Shaw (1999) Palmquist et al. (2010) Fezzi et al. (2014) Larson and Lew (2014)
Measuring site attribute variables	• Use of objective (measured) versus subjective (visitor believed) measures of quality • Use of technical (specialist assessed) versus descriptive (lay language) variables • The role of unobserved site attributes • Specifying driving costs	Murdock (2006) Hagerty and Moeltner (2005) Bateman et al. (1996)
Welfare measurement	• Partial versus general equilibrium welfare measurement • Computational issues	Phaneuf et al. (2000) von Haefen (2003) Phaneuf et al. (2009) Timmins and Murdock (2007)
Agent heterogeneity	• Use of observed variables versus random parameters to account for heterogeneity in preferences for environmental attributes	Phaneuf (2013) von Haefen and Phaneuf (2008)
Dynamics	• State dependence, habit formation and variety seeking • Time-dependent site-quality variables • Forward-looking behavior, dynamically evolving constraints	Baerenklau and Provencher (2005)
Sampling and data collection	• Onsite, mail, telephone, internet surveys • Participants vs. non-participants • Econometric consequences of different sampling regimes	Egan and Herriges (2006) Shaw (1988)

By referring to *the* choice set we have abstracted from the notion that choice sets may differ over people. Sometimes sites can be exogenously excluded from a person's choice set based on distance, or perhaps the non-ownership of equipment needed to access certain alternatives. These are relatively easy adjustments to make. What is more challenging is to model the process by which a person accumulates information and experience that subsequently determine the portfolio of alternatives he considers. This could be important if, for example, changes in environmental conditions cause knowledge stocks about affected destinations to become more or less valuable. While the dynamics of this process have not been formally modeled, researchers have gathered data on sites that people have considered, and used this information to model the likelihood that a given site is in a person's choice set. These approaches notwithstanding, the process by which people arrive at the set of alternative sites to consider is still an area of open research.

17.4.2 Opportunity Cost of Time

Research examining the opportunity cost of time is ubiquitous in the recreation demand literature. Recall that the baseline model postulates that individuals can smoothly trade time for money at the market wage rate, which implies that the wage rate is the appropriate opportunity cost of travel (and onsite) time. In a generalization we examined how the opportunity cost of time arises endogenously, and is decoupled from the wage rate, when people face an inflexible work schedule (or do not work at all). These two results beg the question of how we should compute travel costs in recreation demand applications, and research on this topic has long occupied analysts working in non-market valuation. For the most part, applications have relied on rules of thumb that stipulate the opportunity cost of time is an exogenous fraction of the average wage rate; this was the case in our examples using the Iowa lakes data. Nonetheless, in recent years increasingly sophisticated alternatives to this practice have become available.

To illustrate how thinking on the opportunity cost of time has evolved, consider a stylized single-equation count data model of the type described in the previous section

$$
\begin{aligned}
E(X_i) &= \exp\left[\alpha + \beta(c_i + \phi_i t_i)\right] \\
       &= \exp\left[\alpha + \beta c_i + \beta\phi_i t_i\right],
\end{aligned}
\tag{17.58}
$$

where i denotes a particular person, ϕ_i is his opportunity cost of time, and for simplicity we have not included an income effect in the equation. In the baseline model $\phi_i = w_i$, where w_i is the wage rate (or average hourly salary) for the individual. The model is made operational simply by computing w_i from information on a person's earnings. If earnings are zero, then $\phi_i = 0$. Researchers recognized early on that this was not a fully satisfactory approach to including time costs. McConnell and Strand (1981), continuing work that began with Cesario (1976), were among the first to examine a simple alternative. Rather than assuming $\phi_i = w_i$, they specified a trip demand equation in which $\phi_i = \varphi \cdot w_i$, where φ is an additional parameter to be estimated. In our context, this would imply a demand equation of the form

$$
E(X_i) = \exp\left[\alpha + \beta c_i + \beta(\varphi \times w_i) t_i\right],
\tag{17.59}
$$

and estimation proceeds as usual, except that φ is estimated along with α and β. In this way the opportunity cost of time is determined by the data to be some proportion of the person's wage rate. In early applications, estimates of φ seemed to cluster in the range of 0.33 to 0.66, which gave rise to the common practice of assuming the opportunity cost of time is one-third the average hourly wage rate. To this day, most applications of the travel cost model – including the examples presented above – rely on these early results and assume that time is valued using an asserted proportion of the average wage rate, usually ranging from one to two thirds.

There are two main alternatives to the common practice of asserting a fraction of the wage rate. The first starts with the basic framework in (17.58), but then seeks alternative sources of variability in money and time costs of a trip, for use in identifying φ_i as distinct from the wage rate. More specifically, an empirical challenge in specifications similar to (17.58) is that c_i and t_i are highly collinear, in that both are determined by the distance from the person's home to the recreation site. Thus even when the conceptual basis for the model allows the opportunity cost of time to arise endogenously via trade-offs between the time and money costs of a trip, the limited amount of independent variation between c_i and t_i makes empirical estimation of an endogenous opportunity cost of time difficult. A recent solution to this challenge makes use of the fact that, in some areas, visitors to a recreation destination can travel to the site by using or avoiding toll roads. Routes using major, higher-speed toll roads are more expensive but faster, while routes using lower-speed side roads are cheaper but slower. Observation of an individual's route choice provides information on how he traded off money and time costs, which is decoupled from the simple distance to the destination from his home. In an application to beach recreation travel in northern Italy, Fezzi et al. (2014) find that visitors trade off travel time and money at a rate close to three-quarters of their average annual wage rate.

A second alternative to measuring the opportunity cost of time considers the labor market more directly. A good example of this is Feather and Shaw (1999), which uses an extension of Heckman's (1974) labor supply model to derive time values that need not be equal to the average wage rate. The idea is best seen by returning to our two-constraint baseline model,

$$\max_{x,z,l} U(x,z,l,q) + \lambda(wH - z - cx) + \mu(T - l - tx), \tag{17.60}$$

where we have not collapsed the two constraints, and for simplicity we revert back to the case in which x is a scalar. Regardless of whether or not we can collapse the two constraints, the first-order conditions for this problem (assuming an interior solution for x) are

$$\frac{\partial U(\cdot)}{\partial x} = \lambda c + \mu t, \quad \frac{\partial U(\cdot)}{\partial z} = \lambda, \quad \frac{\partial U(\cdot)}{\partial l} = \mu, \tag{17.61}$$

from which we can state the shadow value of time as

$$\frac{\partial U(\cdot)/\partial l}{\partial U(\cdot)/\partial z} = \frac{\mu}{\lambda} = \phi(\cdot). \tag{17.62}$$

As we saw above, *if* the person has a flexible work schedule that provides for the free adjustment of work hours, the two constraints can be collapsed, and $\phi(\cdot) = w$; that is, the market wage is the opportunity cost of time. Denote the optimal work time in the case of free adjustment by H^*, which leads to optimal values for market spending and non-work time, which we denote by y^* (i.e. the optimal $z + cx$) and L^* (i.e. optimal $T - H$), respectively.

Consider now cases in which the person either decides not to work ($H^* = 0$), or is not able to optimally adjust work hours, perhaps due to a fixed hours offer of employment. For the former we know that $\phi(\cdot) \geq w$, since choosing not to work implies the shadow value of leisure time is larger than the market wage rate for all positive values of H. The latter case nests two possibilities. Denote the fixed work hours by $\hat{H}$, and the implied money income and non-work time by $\hat{y}$ and $\hat{L}$, respectively. If $\hat{H} > H^*$ then the fixed work schedule implies the person is working more than he considers optimal, and so his leisure time is smaller than optimal, so that $\hat{L} < L^*$. In this case the person is *over-employed*. When $H^* < \hat{H}$ and $\hat{L} > L^*$, the person is working less than he considers optimal, and hence he is *under-employed*.

Examples of optimal, under-, and over-employment outcomes are shown in Figure 17.2, which also illustrates the link between employment status and the shadow value of time. The budget constraint with slope w, drawn for a given time budget, shows the feasible combinations of income y and non-work time L. The indifference curves summarize trade-offs the person is willing to make between money and time. When work hours and leisure time are freely chosen, the solution is the tangency shown at L^*, and the marginal rate of substitution between time and money is the wage rate:

$$\frac{\partial U(\cdot)/\partial l}{\partial U(\cdot)/\partial z} = \frac{\mu}{\lambda} = \phi(L^*) = w. \tag{17.63}$$

If instead the person is constrained to be at $\hat{L}^o$ he is over-employed (consuming too little leisure) and reaches a lower level of utility relative to the flexible situation. In this case the absolute value of the slope of the indifference curve is greater than the wage rate, which is to say that

$$\frac{\partial U(\cdot)/\partial l}{\partial U(\cdot)/\partial z} = \frac{\mu}{\lambda} = \phi(\hat{L}^o) > w. \tag{17.64}$$

The shadow value of time relative to the wage rate is shown in the Figure as a dashed line. If free to adjust, the person would consume more leisure and fewer market goods, decreasing work hours until the value of leisure time falls to the wage rate. Finally, if the person is constrained to be at $\hat{L}^u$ he is under-employed (consuming too much leisure). In this case the slope of the indifference curve is less than the wage rate, which is to say that

$$\frac{\partial U(\cdot)/\partial l}{\partial U(\cdot)/\partial z} = \frac{\mu}{\lambda} = \phi(\hat{L}^u) < w. \tag{17.65}$$

Once again we have shown the value of leisure time relative to the wage rate by a dashed line. If free to adjust in this case, the person would consume less leisure by increasing work hours until the value of leisure time increases to the wage rate.

Figure 17.2 and the three associated expressions relating w and ϕ show that identifying a person's labor market status – optimal, under-, or over-employed – is useful

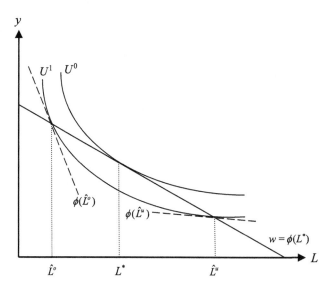

Figure 17.2   Labor market outcomes

because it places bounds on the person's shadow value of time vis-à-vis his market wage rate. Feather and Shaw suggest that simple questioning of people to determine (a) their weekly work hours, and (b) if they would like to increase, decrease, or keep their work hours unchanged, can reveal the relationship between a person's market wage rate and his shadow value of time. Their empirical strategy is to use this information to estimate a predictive equation for the shadow value of time. In particular, for a sample of individuals $i = 1,\ldots,I$ they specify the two empirical equations

$$\phi_i = \beta s_i^s + \beta_H H_i + \varepsilon_i \tag{17.66}$$
$$w_i = \theta s_i^m + \eta_i,$$

where ϕ_i and w_i are the shadow value of time and market wage rate equations for individual i, respectively. The former depends on a vector of person-specific covariates s_i^s, the current work hours H_i, and an error term ε_i, where s_i^s can include a variety of factors such as non-wage income and preference indicators. The market wage equation includes standard wage determinant variables such as age, education, experience, and gender as well as an error term η_i. Feather and Shaw assume ε_i and η_i are disturbed bivariate normal, from which they derive the following probability statements conditional on the different employment status outcomes:

$\Pr(\phi_i = w_i)$ $\rightarrow$ flexible work schedule
$\Pr(\phi_i \geq w_i | H_i = 0)$ $\rightarrow$ unemployed
$\Pr(\phi_i \geq w_i)$ $\rightarrow$ under-employed
$\Pr(\phi_i \leq w_i)$ $\rightarrow$ over-employed

By matching people in the sample to one of these four employment status/probability statements, Feather and Shaw construct a likelihood function and use maximum likelihood to estimate (β, β_H, θ). The parameter estimates provide a characterization of the shadow wage equation, which can then be used to predict the shadow value of time for all individuals in the sample, including those who are not working or have an inflexible work schedule. The predictions $\hat{\phi}_1, ..., \hat{\phi}_I$ are then used to construct travel costs and full income estimates for subsequent use in estimating the recreation demand model.

The Feather and Shaw approach to estimating the shadow value of time is intuitively appealing, its data requirements are mild, and the analytical techniques used are generally accessible. Nonetheless, it has not seen wide application compared to the simple habit of using a fraction of the average wage rate. One potential reason for this is that its predictions are ultimately tied to the labor market and a person's average wage rate, since the value of time equation is identified by its relationship to w. A consequence of this is that the qualitative nature of time value estimates from the Feather and Shaw model are often not dramatically different from fraction of the wage rate assumptions. This suggests one of two conclusions. Either ad hoc uses of the average wage rate are a good way to approximate the opportunity cost of time, or alternative models that look at time/money trade-offs that are decoupled from the labor market, such as the toll road example described above, are needed. Either way, the limitations of the "one-third the wage rate" consensus notwithstanding, the recreation literature has yet to settle on an alternative approach predicting the shadow value of travel time.

17.4.3 Onsite Time

Onsite time is a topic that has had some lack of clarity in the methodological and applied recreation demand literature. This stems from the fact that, in the most general case, onsite time confounds two partially competing factors. On one hand it is a quality attribute of a trip, in that more time on site presumably leads to greater enjoyment of the resource. On the other hand, onsite time has scarcity value, since time budgets are usually a binding constraint. The dual role played by onsite time therefore raises challenges, since if time onsite is a choice variable, the resource cost of consuming a visit is no longer exogenous to the decision. While this is manageable from a modeling perspective, it may cause difficulty for estimation and welfare computation, since travel cost becomes an endogenous choice variable, and the normal link between exogenous prices and preferences falls away. In this subsection we present a model generalization that addresses this issue.

As we noted above, one solution to this difficulty is to assume that onsite time is exogenous to the person's decision. Effectively we assume that a given amount of time is needed to complete a visit, and all the utility benefits of time on site are bundled with the benefits of consuming a trip; onsite time therefore only needs to be reckoned as a cost. In many instances this is true, or the variation in onsite time is small enough that it is sufficiently close to true. Even in these cases some confusion remains. First, there is the issue of what the shadow value of onsite time is, though most analysts are comfortable assuming it is the same as the opportunity cost of travel time. Second, data describing the duration of a visit is often more costly to obtain, and generally of lower quality than counts of visits (since time on site is probably subject to more recall bias). Due to the latter, many applications simply ignore onsite time, and compute the implicit price of a visit using only road costs and the opportunity cost of travel time. In the dominant linear-in-income RUM model paradigm this matters little, since if the amount of onsite time is constant for the person across the choice set, the shadow value of onsite time is constant, and drops out when utility is differenced. In system and corner solution models the decision to ignore onsite time may be more consequential, and so in what follows we briefly discuss onsite time in the system context.

Recall our model from section 17.1, in which we used t to denote the amount of round trip travel time *and* exogenous onsite time that was needed to complete a trip to a single recreation site. To distinguish travel time from onsite time here, we let $t = t^r + t^d$, where t^r is the round trip travel (road) time that is needed, and t^d is the onsite (visit duration) time. In the simple model with one recreation site and exogenous onsite time we used $U(x,z,l,q)$ to denote the utility function, which implicitly implied that the utility provided by onsite time is bundled with the utility from a trip. As a generalization consider the utility function $U(x,t^d,z,l,q)$, where t^d is the endogenously selected time spent onsite during each of the x trips. With this the household choice problem is a generalization of (17.2), which we write as

$$\max_{x,t^d,z,l} U(x,t^d,z,l,q) \quad s.t. \quad wT = z + (\underbrace{c + wt^r}_{p})x + wt^d x + wl. \tag{17.67}$$

For simplicity we assume that the wage is the opportunity cost of travel and onsite time, and note that the parametric price of a trip $p = c + wt^r$ now only includes the round trip travel time. The first-order conditions for an optimal interior solution are

$$\frac{\partial U}{\partial x} = \lambda p + \lambda wt^d$$

$$\frac{\partial U}{\partial t^d} = \lambda wx, \quad \frac{\partial U}{\partial l} = \lambda w, \quad \frac{\partial U}{\partial z} = \lambda, \tag{17.68}$$

where λ is the Lagrange multiplier.

The solution to (17.68) consists of the optimal levels of x, t^d, l, and z, given as a function of the parametric prices and resource budgets. In particular, we can solve the four first-order conditions for $x(p,w,T,q)$ and $t^d(p,w,T,q)$, as well as the optimal levels of leisure and spending on other goods. Importantly, the demand for trips is conditional on the opportunity cost of onsite time (w in this example), but the price of a trip depends only on the exogenously given time (t^r) and money (c) round trip road costs. Therefore, when onsite time is endogenously selected, estimating equations for trip demand should not include the amount of onsite time in the calculation of trip costs, since onsite time is "optimized out" of the problem. Thus, in a fortuitous finding originally pointed out by McConnell (1992), the practice of ignoring onsite time when estimating trip demand equations is correct under a plausible interpretation of the underlying behavior. Furthermore, the indirect utility function derived by integrating $x(p,w,T,q)$ back over the range of values for p provides a valid platform for welfare analysis. For this reason, most applied studies of recreation behavior, including the Iowa lakes example used in this chapter, do not consider onsite time in calculating the resource cost of a trip.

17.4.4 Dynamics

The final topic that we discuss focuses on the role that dynamic behavior plays in recreation demand analysis. By its nature, introducing dynamic behavior takes us away from the purely static environment in which we have conducted most of our discussion. This departure from static analysis has two potentially large costs. First, the empirical techniques needed to analyze dynamic behavior when it also has a spatial aspect (such as choice among multiple sites) are complicated, and fully general methods are incompletely developed and difficult to apply. Second, the data needs are much more demanding, in that summaries of behavior in diary form, and time-specific constraint information and site quality variables, are needed. While it is the richness of data needs that is ultimately more constraining, both have contributed to limiting the integration of dynamic aspects into models of recreation behavior. Examples of ad hoc dynamics are more numerous, but these too are often limited by data constraints. For these reasons dynamic analysis is not commonly undertaken in recreation demand modeling, though there are notable exceptions (see, for example, Provencher and Bishop, 1997). As such, in what follows we do not derive formal models of dynamic behavior or their approximations. Instead, we limit our attention to describing the types of dynamic behavior that may be important for non-market valuation, thereby providing motivation for future efforts aimed at expanding the stock of models that can accommodate specific types of dynamic effects.

There are three behavioral motivations for including dynamic aspects of behavior in recreation models. The first concerns learning. As noted above, the set of sites a person considers as viable options likely depends on past experience and past effort he has made to learn about the features of these sites. It may also depend on past equipment investments that are needed at some destinations. Thus the formation of a person's choice set is effectively a dynamic process that involves the accumulation of experience and investment in learning about choice options. Second, there are issues of temporal adjustment. Conditions at a recreation site tend not to be static. Instead, they change over the course of a decision horizon due to natural and human-caused variation. It is plausible that people adjust to these changing circumstances, either by changing the temporal distribution of trips or by changing the frequency of trips. For many policy questions – such as the damages caused by a temporary beach closure or quality decrease due to an oil spill – the type of temporal adjustment matters for measurement. A related example is how people's constraint sets adjust over time. Although time is not perfectly fungible, it is partially so in that a person can adjust commitments and work duties to assemble time for a future outing. It may be that the dynamic process of leisure time adjustment and allocation, and the shadow costs of these adjustments, is an important determinant of non-market values. Finally, dynamic aspects of preferences themselves may matter for how a person values recreation sites and their attributes. For example, habit formation and variety seeking are specific examples of a general phenomenon in which current decisions depend on a past stock of behavior. Because habit formation and variety seeking affect how the substitutability among available sites is understood by the individual, they can legitimately affect how an individual values a site or its attributes.

17.5 SUMMARY

In this chapter we have reviewed models and empirical approaches that are used to estimate the value of recreation services that are provided by the natural environment. The motivation for the development and use of this large array of sophisticated tools stems from the seemingly quaint notion that people use lakes, forests, streams, mountains, trails, parks, and the like for outdoor leisure. The sheer volume of such activity, however, suggests that recreation uses of natural areas are a primary point of contact between households and environmental quality, and hence human welfare and the environment. As such, recreation is an obvious place to look for the behavioral footprints that we previously identified as necessary for revealed preference analysis. It is also an important consideration in examining the efficiency of many environmental initiatives, including examples as far reaching as the US Clean Water Act. For these reasons the need for recreation demand analysis, and research on suitable methods, are likely to continue.

Our discussion highlighted the role that the travel cost paradigm plays in estimating the demand for recreation. The basic notion is simple. Travel is costly in money and time, both are scarce resources, and to give them up to visit a recreation site is to reveal that the visit is worth, at the margin, at least the value of the forgone resources. From this we derived demand equations for visits to sets of sites that depend on travel costs and site quality variables, where the former include both road costs and the opportunity cost of a person's time. Importantly, we saw that behavior can consist of discrete decisions on which sites to visit, and intensity of use decisions on the number of trips to make. Trip outcomes typically observed in multiple-site recreation databases therefore are integers, display zero trips to many of the available sites, and mix low-frequency use for some people with higher use by more avid visitors. The objective of analysis is to use this data and an empirical framework to estimate demand equations and/or indirect utility functions, which allow us to apply the methods described in Chapters 14, 15, and 16 to compute welfare effects for changes in sites' attributes or availability. Weak complementarity and cross-product repackaging of quality terms are usually the starting point for model specification.

The econometric approaches used in recreation demand span three classes of microeconometric models, each of which has different strengths and limitations. RUM models are ubiquitous, and their increasing sophistication allows us to characterize the substitutability among available sites with confidence, though they are limited in the extent to which they accommodate multiple-choice outcomes. Systems models combine probability distributions that accommodate micro level data with a direct connection to the interior solution welfare methods that are most familiar from duality theory. Both RUM and system models are accessible econometrically and are well understood. Corner solution models, which combine the attractive features of RUM and systems analysis, are currently less accessible and require more in the way of restrictive assumptions than their counterparts. All three modeling frameworks have roles to play in contemporary applications, and all three continue to be the subject of methodological research. The model used for a particular application depends largely on the type of data that is available, the size of the choice set, the objectives of the analysis and uses of its results, and the tastes of the researcher.

In this chapter we have also noted that, in some cases, the choice of econometric framework is less important than modeling and specification decisions that include choice set definition, the opportunity cost of time and time on site, and other assumptions, such as those listed in Table 17.1. We also discussed the potential role that dynamic factors can play, and noted that the research in this area is underdeveloped vis-à-vis modeling and econometric techniques used in static cases. As such, the area of dynamics is likely to be a fruitful topic for future research.

17.6 FURTHER READING

There are several surveys of the recreation literature that provide historical context, additional how-to detail, and summaries of empirical findings. Phaneuf and Smith (2005) provide a high-level discussion of modeling and econometric topics, while Parsons (2003) presents the steps needed to execute a travel cost analysis in a more hands-on fashion. Bockstael and McConnell (2007) provide a detailed discussion of welfare measurement in recreation models, with particular attention paid to discrete choice models. Haab and McConnell (2002) discuss several topics related to the econometrics of recreation demand modeling, and Moeltner and von Haefen (2011) review the most recent innovations in the microeconometrics of recreation demand models. Finally, Freeman et al. (2014) provide an additional textbook treatment of the topic.

The references listed in Table 17.1 provide examples of literature in specific topical areas. For modeling approaches, examples of single equation count data analysis include Shaw (1988) and Englin and Shonkwiler (1995). Herriges et al. (2008), Egan and Herriges (2006), and von Haefen and Phaneuf (2003) estimate demand system models with count distributions. Von Haefen and Phaneuf (2003) also compare count data estimates to estimates from a corner solutions model. Other applications of Kuhn-Tucker style models include Phaneuf et al. (2000), von Haefen et al. (2004), Phaneuf et al. (2009), and Kuriyama et al. (2010). Examples of discrete choice analysis in recreation demand are ubiquitous. A sampling includes Train (1998), Herriges and Phaneuf (2002), Murdock (2006), and Egan et al. (2009). Examples of studies that incorporate dynamics, either formally or by accounting for habit formation/variety seeking, include Baerenklau and Provencher (2005), Provencher and Bishop (1997), and Moeltner and Englin (2004).

EXERCISES

17.1 ** The chapter made extensive use of empirical examples from the Iowa Lakes Project. Using these examples complete the following:

(a) Summarize the range of welfare estimates for similar scenarios from the three different models. Note the places where the predictions are similar and different, and speculate on what could be driving these differences. Imagine different uses for these estimates, and discuss how the differences in predictions may or may not be important for the different uses.

(b) Examine the suite of models and results, and distinguish the findings that you find credible and those that you do not. In particular, consider the identification assumptions needed for each model and discuss potential threats to the validity of the estimates.

17.2 *** Empirical practice in the recreation demand literature continues to rely on fraction-of-the-wage-rate assumptions to account for the opportunity cost of travel time. Using papers referenced in the chapter and any others you find relevant, complete the following:

(a) Inventory the different approaches researchers have used to measure the shadow value of time, both within and without the environmental economics literature. Provide an example citation for each.

(b) Based on your review propose an answer to the following question, and support it with findings from the literature: what fraction of the average wage rate should applied researchers use to best represent the opportunity cost of time in recreation models?

17.3 *** This exercise is based on data describing recreation visits to 17 beaches in the American state of North Carolina by a sample of residents from the eastern part of the state. The dataset *NC_beach* (available on the book's website) was collected by John Whitehead and colleagues, and an analysis based on these data is provided by Whitehead et al. (2010). Here we use a configuration of the data that is designed to examine single and multiple equation count data models. We observe 610 people who made at least one trip to visit a beach (and no more than 50 trips) in the southeastern part of North Carolina in 2003. The dataset contains the following variables:

id – unique identifier for each household

inc – annual household income

tr_1, tr_2,... – trips to each of the 17 beaches

pr_1, pr_2,... – travel costs for each of the 17 beaches

$width_1$, $width_2$,... – width (in feet) of each of the 17 beaches

$park_1$, $park_2$,... – number of parking spaces (in 100s) available at each of the 17 beaches.

   Travel costs were computed using $0.37 per mile for out-of-pocket costs, and one-third the average wage rate for the opportunity cost of travel time. The *width* and *park* variables are site attributes that are constant across individuals. Data files are also available that link the names of the beaches to an index number, which references each beach to its trip, travel cost, and site attribute variables. Using these data complete the following:

(a) Wrightsville Beach (#10) is the most frequented destination. Estimate a single-demand equation for trips to this beach using the Poisson model, exploring versions that include and then exclude income as an explanatory variable. Depending on your findings, use the indirect utility function in Eq. (17.12) or (17.13) to estimate the average welfare loss in the sample if the site were eliminated. Then estimate the average annual welfare loss from a $5 per person beach access fee.

(b) Consider now a system of 17 demand equations for trips. Estimate models of the form

$$E(tr_{ij}) = \exp\left(\alpha + \beta pr_{ij} + \gamma inc_i + \theta_1 width_j + \theta_2 park_j\right)$$

and

$$E(tr_{ij}) = \exp\left(\alpha + \beta_j pr_{ij} + \gamma inc_i + \theta_1 width_j + \theta_2 park_j\right)$$

Report the coefficient estimates, their statistical significance, and interpret their signs and magnitudes. Note any differences you find when you estimate a single price coefficient versus 17 different price coefficients. What might explain these differences?

(c) Repeat part (b) using the natural log of *width*. Interpret the coefficient estimate and comment on the differences you find with the linear in *width* specification. Use the model with the separate price coefficients and log specification to estimate the welfare effects in increasing beach width 50 percent at Wrightsville and Carolina Beaches.

(d) Note that a model of the form

$$E(tr_{ij}) = \exp\left(\alpha_j + \beta_j pr_{ij} + \gamma inc_i\right)$$

can be estimated, but it does not allow direct inclusion of the site-varying characteristics. Estimate this model to recover $\alpha_1,...,\alpha_J$, and then examine the correlation between the constants and beach width by running the regression

$$\alpha_j = \alpha_0 + \theta_1 width_j + \xi_j.$$

Consider also a similar regression using the log of *width*. Compare your point estimates to what you find in parts (b) and (c), and discuss the extent to which you think the estimates of the site attribute coefficients in the earlier models are well identified.

17.4 *** This exercise is based on a subset of the data analyzed by Murdock (2006), and describes 2,404 trip outcomes to 100 angling destinations in the American state of Wisconsin. The data set *WI_100* is available on the book's website. It is organized around the following worksheets:

choice – person id and site chosen on each of 2,404 observed trip outcomes;
price – travel costs to each of the 100 sites for each of the 2,404 outcomes;
household – decision-maker characteristics *boat* and *kids*, where *boat*=1 if the person owns a boat and *kids*=1 if there are children in the household;
attributes –site quality/attribute variables labeled and ordered *ramp*, *bath*, *walleye*, *salmon*, and *pan fish*.

The attribute variables are as follows: an indicator if the site has a paved boat ramp (*ramp*), an indicator if the site has public restrooms (*bath*) and catch rates per trip for the sport fishing species walleye, salmon, and pan fish.

(a) Using these data, estimate a RUM model that includes only the fish catch rate as explanatory variables. Calculate the marginal willingness to pay for a change in expected walleye catch rate.

(b) Estimate the model again, but this time include the site attributes *ramp* and *bath* in the specification as well as interactions between *ramp* and the household attribute *boat*, and *bath* and the household attribute *kids*. Once again calculate the marginal willingness to pay for a change in walleye catch rate, and explain any differences you find from (a).

(c) Identify the ten sites with the highest share of aggregate visits. Calculate the per choice occasion willingness to pay for a policy that increases the walleye catch rate at these ten sites by 30 percent. Identify the site with the highest share of aggregate visits. Calculate the per choice occasion value of access to the site.

(d) Now estimate the model with a full set of alternative specific constants, in addition to the interactions between *boat* and *ramp* and *bath* and *kids*. Use a second-stage regression to estimate the main effects for *ramp* and *bath* as well as the three catch rate variables. Describe any differences you see from part (b) and explain what might drive these differences.

(e) Repeat the welfare calculations from part (c) using the model with the full set of alternative specific constants and describe any differences in your findings.

CHAPTER 18

Property Value Models

As described in previous chapters, the fundamental challenge of environmental valuation stems from the fact that environmental amenities are not, in general, exchanged in markets. With no directly observed transactions available to infer value, revealed preference analysis relies on observation of behavior in a related private good market, coupled with assumptions on how the environmental and private good are related. One example of this is when the environmental good is assumed to be a component of a bundled or quality-differentiated market good, in which the attributes of the good (including the environmental attribute) determine its price. By choosing a particular bundle to purchase, individuals indirectly choose – and pay for – a given level of the environmental good. In these cases the hedonic or discrete choice models for quality-differentiated market goods apply, and observation of sales for the differentiated good can in principle be used to infer the value of the environmental good. In environmental economics one of the most common applications of these models is to property values. In this chapter we discuss specific modeling and econometric approaches for using property values to measure environmental values.

In several respects, real estate markets provide an ideal circumstance for measuring environmental value from market behavior. In urban areas real estate markets are usually competitive with a large flow of transactions, and the notion that property prices should reflect attributes of the location and structure is intuitive and non-controversial. Property purchases are sizeable investments that condition many other aspects of life for long periods of time, and so market participants are likely to be well informed about the many attributes that affect home prices and the services a home provides. This can include local environmental conditions. For example, nearby landscape amenities such as nature trails often attract buyers, while others may try to avoid living near contaminated industrial sites. Thus residential home purchases are a promising window through which to view households' environmental preferences. There are, however, challenges and limitations to be recognized and overcome. First, the scope of public and environmental goods that can be valued via housing markets is limited by geography and information. Only local amenities that vary across the landscape and are observed by consumers will influence housing prices. Thus property value techniques are well-suited for valuing environmental goods such as local (monitored) air quality or permanent open space; they are not useful for larger-scale issues such as biodiversity preservation.

Second, property purchases are dynamic decisions, since a home provides both current residential services and long-term investment opportunities. Thus property markets include both consumption and asset management features, which complicates their use for inferring non-market values. Finally, though the data requirements and modeling techniques needed for measuring marginal environmental values are generally mild, measuring values for non-marginal changes requires that we confront several conceptual, econometric, and data availability issues.

Property value models have always been important in environmental economics, but their use has expanded since the 1990s due to the increased availability of databases linking information on residential home sales to spatially explicit variables such as school quality, neighborhood characteristics, transportation networks, and landscape descriptions. In the United States, for example, many assessors' offices (usually a county-level function) maintain digital databases of property transactions that can include a decade or more of sales information. Global information system (GIS) technology and software has allowed analysts to merge multiple data layers, so that a particular property can be referenced to physical and jurisdictional features of the landscape, with potentially large variation in spatial scale among the variables. For example, one can often obtain summaries of land use patterns (e.g. forested, paved, low-density residential) down to the city block level, or distances to bodies of water measured in meters, while also tracking larger aggregates such as school district and municipality boundaries. Contemporary property-value databases can include tens of thousands of records on sales prices and property characteristics over several years, and multiple layers of referenced spatial data. This increased data quality has helped spur several modeling and econometric innovations.

In what follows, we examine the different ways that environmental economists have used property value information to measure the non-market values of environmental quality. We begin with a discussion of the well-established hedonic property value models that have dominated the literature. We then turn our attention to two alternative classes of models that emphasize comparatively more structural and reduced form analysis, respectively. In particular, we examine how discrete choice models can be used in a property value context, and then explore how quasi-experimental techniques have recently been exploited to better understand the causal effect of environmental variables on property values.

18.1 HEDONIC PROPERTY VALUE MODELS: THEORY

We begin by reviewing the theory of hedonic models within the context of residential property value applications. As in Chapter 15, we assume that a unit of the quality-differentiated good – a residential house in this context – is completely characterized by the vectors x and q, where x is a J dimensional vector of property characteristics that is broadly defined to include structural, parcel, and neighborhood attributes. Elements of x may include, for example, the size of the house, the age of the structure, distance to employment centers, local school quality, and the demographic makeup of the neighborhood, to name but a few. The vector q contains the quasi-fixed environmental or public goods that are the object of study. Examples include local air quality, access to parks or lakes, water quality, and proximity to hazardous waste sites. For the purposes of exposition, in what follows we assume that q is a scalar, though this need not be the case in actual applications. The price of a particular house is determined by an equilibrium price schedule (or hedonic price function) that we denote $P(x,q)$. The hedonic price function provides a mapping between values of the characteristics x and q and the market value of the property, so that for a particular house k the market price is given by $p_k = P(x_k, q_k)$, where x_k and q_k are the characteristic levels for property k. The price schedule arises in equilibrium via the interaction of all buyers and sellers in the market, as was described generally in Chapter 15. In most hedonic property value applications, the supply of houses is assumed to be fixed in the short run, so that the equilibrium price schedule arises from homebuyers bidding for a fixed supply of houses. In this section, we examine how these assumptions about the housing market are used to derive expressions for households' willingness to pay for environmental attributes, and begin to discuss how the theoretical model motivates the use of data on housing transactions to measure environmental values.

18.1.1 Consumer's Choice Problem

Homebuyers participate in the market by purchasing one residential property, conditional on their budget constraint and preferences. Rather than choosing a specific house from an available set as in a discrete choice setting, in the hedonic model consumers maximize utility by choosing the levels of all the individual attributes, which together result in a specific home purchase. Formally, a representative homebuyer solves the problem

$$\max_{x,q,z} U(x,q,z;s) \quad s.t. \quad y = z + P(x,q), \tag{18.1}$$

where z is the strictly positive numeraire good, y is annual income, and s summarizes the household's characteristics, such as family size and composition. Three points regarding this problem require additional commentary. First, a maintained assumption is that consumers have available a continuum of all the attributes in x and q, and that they can be readily chosen in any combination. In reality many attributes are discrete, and others are not available in particular combinations. For example, it is unlikely that one could purchase a small home in a dense urban area with a large lot surrounded by forest. Second, the level of environmental quality q is a choice variable. In this setting the quasi-fixed good is not imposed on consumers as is the case for a pure public good; rather, it is endogenous to the consumer's problem. Thus, the hedonic model is based to a large degree on Tiebout's (1956) notion that mobile households choose a location in part to obtain the desired level of a local public good. Related to this, the level of q is assumed to vary across the landscape, so that different households can and do choose different levels of environmental quality. This is a key feature of the model, in that spatial variability in q is essential for everything that we discuss in this chapter. Finally, we need to clarify the temporal dimension of the consumer's problem. It is best to think of $P(\cdot)$ as the property's annual rental rate rather than its asset price. In this way annual income is the relevant budget constraint, and the problem can be viewed as a static (and annually repeated) choice of consumption levels rather than a dynamic problem related to asset allocation and wealth management. For renting households this interpretation is intuitive. For home-owning households, an abstraction in which we separate the landlord (or asset owning) role of the household from its home consuming (or rent paying) role is necessary, though not always realistic. In this case we effectively assume that the household rents the home from itself each year, at the market rental rate of $P(\cdot)$.

Continuing with the consumer's problem, the first-order conditions for an interior solution to (18.1) are readily derived by setting up the Lagrangian, and taking partial derivatives to obtain the first-order conditions

$$\frac{\partial U(\cdot)}{\partial x_j} = \lambda \frac{\partial P(\cdot)}{\partial x_j}, \quad j = 1, ..., J,$$

$$\frac{\partial U(\cdot)}{\partial q} = \lambda \frac{\partial P(\cdot)}{\partial q}, \tag{18.2}$$

$$\frac{\partial U(\cdot)}{\partial z} = \lambda, \quad y = z + P(x, q),$$

where λ is the Lagrange multiplier on the budget constraint. Focusing on the condition for q and substituting out for λ (the marginal utility of income) we obtain

$$\frac{\partial U(\cdot)/\partial q}{\lambda} = \frac{\partial U(\cdot)/\partial q}{\partial U(\cdot)/\partial z} = \frac{\partial P(\cdot)}{\partial q}. \tag{18.3}$$

This implies that, at the optimum, the consumer chooses the level of q to equate the marginal rate of substitution between q and z to the marginal implicit cost of q. Because z is the numeraire good with price equal to one, the left and middle terms in (18.3) both equal the marginal willingness to pay for q, which at the household's optimum is equal to the marginal price of obtaining q, as given by the right-hand side. This result is by itself useful, since it suggests that knowledge of the hedonic price function alone can, in equilibrium, reveal a particular household's marginal willingness to pay for q at its chosen level of q.

We gain further insight into the consumer's problem by considering a reference utility level $\bar{u}$ given by

$$U(x, q, z; s) = \bar{u}. \tag{18.4}$$

Following Rosen's (1974) original formulation, define a bid function $b(x, q, y, s, \bar{u})$ so that

$$U[x, q, y - b(x, q, y, s, \bar{u}); s] = \bar{u}. \tag{18.5}$$

In this expression, $b(\cdot)$ is by definition the maximum amount that the consumer would (and could) pay for a house with attributes (x, q), given his income and characteristics, while holding utility fixed at $\bar{u}$. For subsequent use, note as well that Eq. (18.4) can be inverted to solve for z such that

$$z = U^{-1}(x, q, \bar{u}, s). \tag{18.6}$$

This is possible because utility is a monotonically increasing function of z. Finally, note that income, the bid function, and z are related by the identity

$$b(x, q, y, s, \bar{u}) \equiv y - U^{-1}(x, q, s, \bar{u}). \tag{18.7}$$

With these preliminaries, we are now able to derive a marginal willingness to pay function for q that relates to the general expressions we presented in Chapter 14. In particular, if we implicitly differentiate $b(\cdot)$ with respect to q in (18.5), we obtain

$$\frac{\partial U(\cdot)}{\partial q} - \frac{\partial U(\cdot)}{\partial z} \frac{\partial b(\cdot)}{\partial q} = 0, \tag{18.8}$$

which, after rearranging, results in

$$\frac{\partial b(x, q, y, s, \bar{u})}{\partial q} = \frac{\partial U(\cdot)/\partial q}{\partial U(\cdot)/\partial z}. \tag{18.9}$$

Note from Eq. (18.7), however, that the bid function is additively separable in y, which implies that $\partial b(\cdot)/\partial q$ is not a function of income. This allows us to rewrite the derivative as

$$\pi^q(x, q, s, \bar{u}) = \frac{\partial b(x, q, y, s, \bar{u})}{\partial q} = \frac{\partial U(\cdot)/\partial q}{\partial U(\cdot)/\partial z}. \tag{18.10}$$

Conditional on values for the attributes x, Eq. (18.10) is the household's compensated willingness to pay (inverse demand) function for q, which we derived for the general case in Chapter 14. Here, by assuming q is part of a bundle of residential services, we are able to characterize the demand for q via its relationship to the larger housing market. As in the general case, knowledge of the inverse demand for q allows us to measure the value of marginal *or* discrete changes in q.

The primary objective of empirical applications of the hedonic model is to obtain an estimate of all or parts of $\pi^q(x, q, s, \bar{u})$ for individual households. Figure 18.1 motivates the link between the theory and empirical applications for a representative consumer. The top panel shows a cross-section of the hedonic price function relating q to property prices conditional on values for x. Three bid functions for a single household, with different reference utility levels u^0, u^1, and u^2, are also shown. Note that higher levels of utility are associated with lower bids, since the same level of q can be obtained while allowing a higher consumption of z; thus in the Figure we have $u^1 > u^0 > u^2$. According to equations (18.3) and (18.10), the optimal choice occurs at a tangency of the hedonic price and bid functions, resulting for this example in observed consumption level q_0, a transaction price of $P(x, q_0)$, and realized utility u^0 for the household. The point labeled a can be observed via housing transactions data that record sales prices and the attributes of properties that are exchanged, including the environmental attribute.

The middle panel shows the compensated marginal willingness to pay function that is associated with $b(x, q, y, s, u^0)$. According to (18.10), it is traced out as the slope of the bid function as q varies. Point b in this graph is observable if an estimate of $P(x, q)$ – and hence its derivative – can be obtained. This is an important point. As we discuss in the

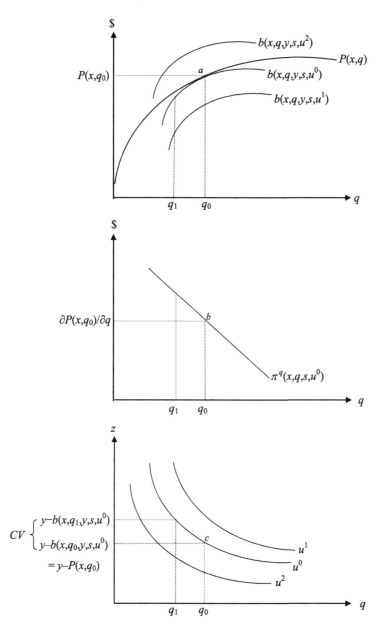

Figure 18.1   Household choice outcome

next section, estimation of $P(x,q)$ in specific applications can be readily accomplished using a sample of observed sale prices and their associated attribute and environmental quality levels. The outcome labeled a in the top panel is an example of a single data point observed in such a sample. An estimate of $P(x,q)$ is useful because the household's optimal choice of q implies the slope of the hedonic price function and marginal willingness to pay for q are equal. From this we can identify a single point on the consumer's inverse demand for q function simply by estimating the hedonic price function. In the graph this corresponds to

$$\frac{\partial P(x,q_0)}{\partial q} = \pi^q(x,q_0,s,u^0).\tag{18.11}$$

The bottom panel of Figure 18.1 provides a reinterpretation of the bid function as an indifference curve. Here, we have used (18.5) to draw the indifference surfaces for u^0, u^1, and u^2 in (z,q) space, conditional on values for x. Each indifference curve maps to a single bid function, since for a given level of q the bid function determines the amount of z needed to achieve the reference utility level, and vice versa. Specifically, z is directly linked to the bid function and income via (18.7). In equilibrium the amount of z that is consumed is also linked to the hedonic price function by the budget constraint, so the observed point a in the top panel corresponds directly to the observed point c in the bottom panel. Thus, an estimate of $P(x,q_0)$ and observation of q_0 gives us a point on the bid function, a point on the marginal willingness to pay function, and a point on an indifference curve for the household. It does not, however, tell us anything about the height of these curves at an alternative point, such as q_1.

The middle and bottom panels of Figure 18.1 mirror Figure 14.2 in Chapter 14, which we used to define compensating variation (CV) generally for a change from q_0 to q_1. Here CV is defined as the difference in bid function amounts

$$\begin{aligned}CV &= b(x,q_0,y,s,u^0) - b(x,q_1,y,s,u^0)\\ &= P(x,q_0) - b(x,q_1,y,s,u^0),\end{aligned}\tag{18.12}$$

which we can also express as the area under the compensated inverse demand curve:

$$CV = \int_{q1}^{q_0} \pi^q(x,q,s,u^0)dq.\tag{18.13}$$

This suggests that, with an estimate of the inverse demand for q function, we can compute welfare measures for individual households for discrete changes in q.

Our discussion thus far helps to define two specific empirical tasks. First, a characterization of $P(x,q)$ can provide point estimates of all market participants' marginal willingness to pay for q at their baseline level of q. We can estimate $P(x,q)$ using data on home prices and property attributes only. This is referred to as the first stage of hedonic estimation, and in some instances this may be sufficient for the measurement needs of a study. In other instances, when a fuller understanding of the demand for q is needed (perhaps for computing welfare measures for non-marginal changes in q), it is necessary to also estimate $\pi^q(x,q,s,u^0)$ or a suitable approximation thereof. This is referred to as the second stage of hedonic estimation, and it is more data intensive than the first stage, in that information about the households that purchased the homes is needed. We delay detailed discussion of these two empirical tasks until section 18.2. We complete this section by first describing an example that we will use throughout the remainder of the chapter, and then discussing how different welfare measurement concepts are derived using the hedonic price and inverse willingness to pay functions.

18.1.2 A Running Example

Much of the discussion that follows is necessarily abstract. To better connect the general concepts to how they are used in actual applications, we will refer throughout the following sections to a common example, which we describe here. Suppose we are interested in understanding households' willingness to pay for drinking water quality in an urban area. Specifically, in our example drinking water is provided by private wells attached to the individual properties, and that the quality of the water (as measured by contaminant levels, taste, and appearance) varies across the landscape. Part of this variability is due to the location of several manufacturing sites, which release effluent that is known to impact groundwater quality and ultimately the characteristics of water from nearby private wells. We are interested in households' inverse demand functions for drinking water quality as it is reflected in real estate markets, perhaps as an input to decisions being made regarding regulation of the local manufacturers. Though drinking water quality is usually assessed by measuring the level of contaminants, we will maintain our convention of denoting the quasi fixed quantity as a good. Thus we refer to q_i as the quality of drinking water at property i, where a higher level of q_i implies better drinking water. The data environment that we imagine when referring to this example will vary with the topic, but we can note a few common features. At a minimum, we have a sample of I home transactions, for which we observe the sale price p_i, the vector of property characteristics x_i, and the quality level q_i, for $i=1,\ldots,I$. We also refer to a vector describing the household living in house i, which we denote s_i. This includes variables such as income, the size and age composition of the household, and the education level of the household head.

18.2 HEDONIC PROPERTY VALUE MODELS: WELFARE MEASUREMENT

Welfare measurement in the hedonic model involves using estimates of $P(x,q)$, $\partial P(x,q)/\partial q$ and/or $\pi^q(x,q,s,u)$ to calculate the marginal or non-marginal willingness to pay for changes in q. Conditional on having the actual estimates, this is in some respects straightforward since equations (18.3) and (18.13) provide definitions that directly link to our earlier discussion of theoretically consistent welfare measures. Two features of the problem deserve further attention, however. First, it is useful to know when an estimate of $P(x,q)$ alone can provide both marginal *and* discrete change welfare measures for q, since estimates of the marginal willingness to pay function may not always be available. Second, large enough changes in q may induce location changes among households in the market, resulting in a new equilibrium and a shift in the hedonic price schedule. In this case a conceptual question arises. Should the welfare measure be conditional on holding households at their original location, as is implicitly implied by Eq. (18.13)? Or should it reflect the fact that households can adjust via relocation, in which case the welfare measure needs to account for changes in the hedonic price schedule and location outcomes, as well as moving costs? We refer to the conditional on-location measure as a partial equilibrium welfare measure; others (e.g. Bockstael and McConnell, 2007) have labeled this the "pure willingness to pay" for an environmental change. We refer to welfare measures that include relocation, moving costs, and price schedule changes as general equilibrium measures.

18.2.1 Localized Changes in Quality

Consider first instances when an estimate of $P(x,q)$ may be sufficient for discrete change welfare measurement. Suppose we are interested in examining the welfare impact of a localized, non-marginal change in q. By localized we mean a change that is limited to a small number of properties relative to the full extent of the market, which therefore does not induce landscape-wide readjustment and a new equilibrium price schedule. In our running example, this could correspond to a single small manufacturing plant shutting down, and thereby improving drinking water quality in a single nearby neighborhood. It is sensible that this type of local change would not impact housing prices across the entire urban area. As a thought experiment, suppose the change increases the level of q, affects only one property, and that households have no moving or other transactions costs.[1] Since a continuum of homes and home renters is present in the market, and the price schedule has not changed, by the free mobility assumption the household living in the affected house can move to a new house that provides the original level of x and q at an unchanged price. Thus the original renter of the affected home has no change in consumption or utility. The owner of the affected house, however, now receives increased rent in the amount $P(x,q_1) - P(x,q_0)$, where q_1 is the new, higher level of the amenity and q_0 is the original level. In this story, all of the renters in the market experience no utility change (and hence no welfare effect), while the owner realizes an annual increase in income from the increased rent. This increase in income is exactly the amount the owner would be willing to pay to secure the improvement, and therefore is the welfare measure of interest. Thus, with no moving costs and localized environmental shocks that do not shift the equilibrium hedonic price function, we only need to predict the change in prices at the affected homes to construct a theoretically consistent welfare measure. This can be done using *only* the hedonic price function.

The idea is illustrated by the upper panel of Figure 18.2, where a representative household originally locates at point a, consumes q_0, and reaches utility level u^0. If an exogenous shock increases quality at the original home from q_0 to q_1, the household moves without cost to re-establish itself at another location that is identical to point a. Nothing changes for the renting household, but the owner of the original house now receives the higher rent $P(x,q_1)$. When moving is not free, the affected household bears a one-time cost if it relocates. We denote these moving costs by tc. If quality improves at the property and the renting household relocates, society's annual welfare gain is $P(x,q_1) - P(x,q_0) - tc$. That is, the owner's gain less the renter's loss due to costly relocation is the welfare measure of interest. In this case the predicted price change provides an upper bound on the welfare gain for a quality improvement. Finally, if relocation is costly enough that the renting household does not move, a disequilibrium results. In the top panel of Figure 18.2 this is shown as point b, where the renting household consumes the improved quality q_1, pays the higher rent $P(x,q_1)$, and is no longer at a point of tangency between the hedonic price function and a bid function. The latter persists due to the transaction costs of adjustment. Thus the renting household may benefit to some degree from the quality improvement, but it pays more in rent and consumes more q than it would under free mobility. In this case the Figure demonstrates that the predicted

---

[1] These ideas are based on Palmquist (1992a, 1992b).

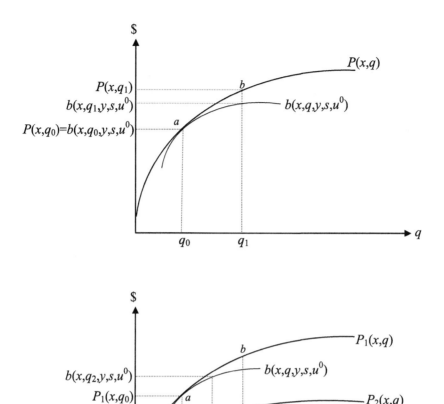

Figure 18.2   Partial and general equilibrium welfare measurement

price change is once again an upper bound on the welfare gain for an improvement. Specifically, the household's willingness to pay for the improvement is shown as

$$
\begin{aligned}
WTP &= b(x, q_1, y, s, u^0) - b(x, q_0, y, s, u^0) \\
&= b(x, q_1, y, s, u^0) - P(x, q_0) \\
&\leq P(x, q_1) - P(x, q_0),
\end{aligned}
\tag{18.14}
$$

where the inequality follows from the standard convexity of preferences assumption. If $\pi^q(x,q,s,u^0)$ is known we can compute WTP directly. If we don't know $\pi^q(x,q,s,u^0)$, we can say that the gain to the household from the improvement lies somewhere between zero and the size of the price change, and the actual amount depends on the shape of the bid function. Thus, when households do not move, the rent increase from an improvement is a transfer payment from renting households to home owners, and society's welfare improvement is the dollar-denominated benefit to the household for the improvement from q_0 to q_1. In all of these cases, the price change provides an upper bound on the welfare gain (and correspondingly a lower bound on welfare loss from a quality decrease), though its proximity to the true value will depend on specific features of the application, such as the size of the change in q, typical moving costs, and the preferences of households in the affected homes.

Consider this strategy in the context of our drinking water example. Suppose we want to analyze the welfare effects of a potential improvement in quality that is limited to a single neighborhood, and is relatively small in the sense that the water quality improves on average by only a fraction of its original level. Suppose as well that we have an estimate of $P(x,q)$ in hand, and that $i = 1, \ldots, S^s < I$ is the sub-sample of houses that experience an improvement. In this case the willingness to pay by household i for the improvement is likely to be well approximated by

$$WTP_i = P(x_i, q_i^1) - P(x_i, q_i^0), \quad i = 1, \ldots, S^s, \tag{18.15}$$

where q_i^0 and q_i^1 are the original and improved levels of drinking water quality at property i, respectively.

We have made these arguments for when knowledge of $P(x,q)$ alone is sufficient for discrete change welfare analysis under the assumption that changes in q are localized enough that no shift in the hedonic price function occurs. However, the same arguments apply when one is interested in partial equilibrium welfare measures that are conditional on households staying in their original home. In this case the change in q being analyzed may be widespread enough to induce relocation and a shift in the hedonic price schedule, but consideration of these effects is not relevant for the welfare measure. Instead, the correct welfare measure is again given by Eq. (18.13), which as discussed will be smaller than the predicted price change (using the original equilibrium price schedule) for an improvement, and greater in absolute value than the predicted price change for a quality decrease. As in the case of a localized change, the extent to which bounds based on predicted price changes are a good approximation for partial equilibrium welfare measures will depend on the specifics of the application.

18.2.2 General Equilibrium Effects

General equilibrium welfare measurement adds additional complexity to the analysis. In this case we are interested in a household's willingness to pay for an improvement (or willingness to accept a decrease) in quality, when it can move in response to the quality change and the equilibrium price schedule can shift. The components of the general equilibrium adjustment are shown in the bottom panel of Figure 18.2 for a specific example. As previously, the household begins at point a, where it consumes quality level q_0, pays the rental price $P_1(x,q_0)$, and obtains its baseline utility level u^0. The subscript 1 on the hedonic price function denotes the initial equilibrium. Suppose an exogenous shock changes the level of environmental quality at the original house to q_1. With no change in the price schedule and no mobility, the household would find itself at point b. However, the household may wish to move in response to the change, and if the shock affects many properties and induces an equilibrium shift, a new price schedule such as $P_2(x,q)$ emerges. In this example we have drawn $P_2(\cdot)$ so it lies below the original schedule, though in general any type of movement is possible. The household's re-optimization leads in this example to a new outcome at the point labeled c, where it consumes a new quality level q_2, pays a new rental rate $P_2(x,q_2)$, and reaches a new utility level u^2. After the adjustment the household's rental rate is lower, its consumption of q is higher, and it reaches a higher utility level, though the direction of these movements is specific to our example and need not hold in general. These multiple adjustments complicate welfare analysis for the household, in that we need to consider the quality change, the location change, and the price change. Using the baseline utility u^0 as the reference level, the welfare gain from the change in quality from the baseline q_0 to the final level q_2 is $b(x,q_2,y,s,u_0) - P_1(x,q_0)$. However, in this example the household also pays a smaller rental rate, so the general equilibrium willingness to pay for the improvement by the household shown in Figure 18.2 is:

$$CV^{GE} = \int_{q_0}^{q_2} \pi^q(x,q,s,u^0)dq + \left[P_1(x,q_0) - P_2(x,q_2)\right]. \tag{18.16}$$

From the perspective of society, all changes in rents in a fixed-supply landscape represent transfers among renting households and home owners, since all of the existing houses are occupied before and after the shock. The gains to society, therefore, are found by summing the definite integral in (18.16) over all renting households in the market. This integral, and the gross measure that also includes the price change, are difficult if not impossible to calculate in practice. Forecasts of counterfactual equilibrium price schedules and new household location choices (and thus new consumption levels for q), along with the estimate for $\pi^q(x,q,s,u)$, are needed to construct the welfare measure. Recognizing the difficulty of this, Bartik (1988b) discusses how an estimate of $\pi^q(x,q,s,u)$ alone can be used to construct a lower bound on the aggregate general equilibrium welfare measure. Bockstael and McConnell (2007, p.173) describe Bartik's thought experiment in three steps as follows. Following an improvement in q, each renting household stays in its original house and enjoys a partial equilibrium benefit that is measurable using (18.13). This is step one. In a hypothetical second step, the equilibrium price schedule shifts to its new position, but we imagine this has happened while households stay in their original homes. This causes a change in rents across the landscape, which from the perspective of society is a transfer between renters and home-owners. Though some individuals will gain and others will lose via the rent changes, in aggregate the transfers sum to zero and are therefore welfare neutral. In the final step, each household adjusts its location if it desires to do so. Adding this mobility step can only be welfare improving, since households are free to stay in their original location if a move does not improve well-being. Thus, from the perspective of society, the aggregation of partial equilibrium welfare measures computed using (18.13) is a constrained measure, and therefore must be a lower bound on society's general equilibrium willingness to pay for a quality improvement. By similar reasoning, the partial equilibrium welfare loss arising from a decrease in quality is an upper bound on the size of the general equilibrium welfare loss. Of course, these arguments treat changes in rents as transfers, though there may be circumstances in which we would like to understand the distributional effect of changes on households, in which case the gross general equilibrium measure from (18.16) is more appropriate. To obtain this type of measure a forecast of the new equilibrium price schedule must be obtained.

18.3 HEDONIC PROPERTY VALUE MODELS: ESTIMATION

In the previous section we identified two empirical tasks related to estimating the hedonic property value model. We now turn our attention to the econometric approaches that are specific to each of the two steps.

18.3.1 First Stage Estimation

The objective of first stage hedonic estimation is to use data on home prices and their characteristics to estimate the equilibrium price schedule $P(x,q)$. As was noted above, these type of data are increasingly available at a high level of spatial resolution. Micro data – observations on actual home sales and the characteristics of the property – are generally used for first stage estimation, though in some instances self-reported values obtained from census data have been used. In either case, the estimation task is essentially an exercise in reduced form econometrics. Specifically, we want to use a sample of size I to estimate the parameters β in

$$p_i = f(x_i, q_i, \beta, \varepsilon_i), \quad i = 1, ..., I, \tag{18.17}$$

where p_i is the observed price of property i, $f(\cdot)$ is a functional specification for the hedonic price schedule, q_i and x_i are the observed environmental and non-environmental characteristics of property i, respectively, and ε_i is a disturbance term that captures the determinants of price not accounted for by the explanatory variables. Ideally, our estimates of β will allow us to (a) explain a large amount of the variability in property prices; (b) establish a causal relationship between environmental quality and home prices; and (c) obtain an unbiased estimate of the marginal implicit price of q_i for household i, which is defined as

$$\hat{p}_{q_i} = \partial \hat{f}(x_i, q_i, \beta) / \partial q_i, \quad i = 1, ..., I. \tag{18.18}$$

If (b) and (c) in particular are accomplished, our discussion from above indicates that we can measure households' marginal willingness to pay for q in equilibrium directly from our estimate of the hedonic price schedule. As we discuss below, the first stage estimates are also a crucial building block for obtaining estimates of the marginal willingness to pay function.

There are several decisions to be made when estimating (18.17). For example, theory provides little guidance on the form that $f(\cdot)$ takes, since it summarizes an equilibrium outcome in an entire market rather than a specific behavioral function. Other considerations are described in Table 18.1, which provides a non-exhaustive list of issues related to the estimation of the hedonic price function. Much of this is adapted from the careful surveys by Palmquist (1991, 2005b) and Taylor (2003). In what follows, we provide discussion on

Table 18.1 Examples of first stage hedonic estimation issues

Issue	Comment	Selected References
Extent of the market	• What is the spatial extent of the market: city, county, metropolitan area with multiple counties; a larger region? • What is the length of time over which the equilibrium price function is stable?	Palmquist (1991, 2005b), Taylor (2003)
Functional specification	• What is the functional relationship between p_i and (x_i, q_i)? Simple or flexible forms? Liberal or limited use of spatial fixed effects? Selection of structural explanatory variables.	Cropper et al. (1988), Kuminoff et al. (2010)
Unbiased estimation of $\partial P(\cdot)/\partial q$	• Omitted variable bias. • Endogenous household sorting and sample selection. • Use of quasi-experimental techniques.	Chay and Greenstone (2005), Bockstael and McConnell (2007), Parmeter and Pope (2012)
Variable measurement	• Observed transactions, self-reported values, professionally assessed values for p_i? • Asset (purchase) price or rental rate? • Objective (e.g. monitored air quality) or subjective (e.g. residents' impression of air quality) measurements of environmental attributes?	Taylor (2003), Kiel and Zabel (1999), Palmquist (1991, 2005b)
Spatial econometrics	• Are the disturbances spatially autocorrelated? • Do prices exhibit spatial lag dependence?	Bell and Bockstael (2000) Kim et al. (2003), LeSage and Pace (2009)
Timing of impacts	• When can we expect changes in environmental conditions to capitalize into property values? What is the role of information dissemination?	Pope (2008a, 2008b), Gayer et al. (2000)

a subset of topics that are particularly important, and/or have been explored in literature subsequent to the Palmquist and Taylor reviews. We encourage the reader to consult the cited works or the recent reviews for additional coverage of the remaining points.

Extent of the Market

The hedonic price function is an equilibrium outcome that results from the aggregate behavior of all participants in a market. Implicit in its definition are important notions of spatial and temporal stability. Specifically, the spatial dimension of the market should include only locations over which participants in the market could potentially choose to reside. It need not be the case that every participant would consider every location; rather, enough participants need to consider sufficiently overlapping locations so that arbitrage forces the marginal implicit prices of property characteristics to be equal across the market area. The spatial extent of the market is generally not something that can be formally tested, and instead is based on the judgment of the researcher. Often large urban and suburban areas with common geography and an integrated labor market can sensibly be considered a single housing market. It seems unlikely, however, that distant and geographically distinct areas – particularly as related to the environmental variable of interest – should be included in the same market. There are, however, some trade-offs inherent in defining the spatial extent of the market. Most importantly, spatial variability in environmental conditions of interest is necessary for estimation, which, other things equal, favors a larger study area.

The temporal extent of the market is defined as the length of time over which the property market stays in the equilibrium summarized by a single hedonic price schedule. This is not to say that property values cannot move with normal macroeconomic trends. It does, however, mean that shocks which shift the supply or demand functions for specific attributes do not occur. For example, if there are structural disruptions in an area's labor market, or major transportation networks are altered, the housing market will likely adjust to a new equilibrium, and the hedonic price function will shift. In this case estimation of a single hedonic price function should not be based on data from both temporal sides of the shock. Like its spatial counterpart, it is difficult to formally test the temporal extent of the market. Once again judgment, and knowledge of the specific circumstances in the area under study, needs to be used to decide how many years of transaction data can sensibly be included in the same regression. Like its spatial counterpart, the temporal extent of the market needs to be balanced against the partially competing objective of including sufficient variability in environmental conditions. For example, it is often desirable to use a long study period so as to temporally bracket any shocks to environmental conditions that occur over time.

Specification

Specification of the hedonic price function requires choice of a functional form $f(\cdot)$, and decisions on which variables to include in the regression. Typically the specification is linear in the disturbance term. Options for $f(\cdot)$ include simple choices such as linear, log-linear (semi-log) and log-log relationships. More flexible options include quadratic specifications, a variety of variable transformations (e.g. Box-Cox transformations), and nonparametric approaches. Some examples of different parametric specifications are shown in Table 18.2, which is based on Taylor (2003), along with the marginal implicit prices that are implied by each. The simple specifications are straightforward to estimate, usually via some type of least squares approach, and their coefficients are easy to interpret. For example, in the log-linear model the marginal willingness to pay is βp_i, implying that β is the constant proportion of price that people are willing to pay for additional q. In the log-log model β is the elasticity of price with respect to q.

Table 18.2 Functional forms for first stage estimation[a]

Name	Example relationship	Implicit price
Linear	$p_i = \cdots + \beta q_i + \cdots + \varepsilon_i$	$\partial \hat{P}/\partial q_i = \beta$
Log-linear	$\ln p_i = \cdots + \beta q_i + \cdots + \varepsilon_i$	$\partial \hat{P}/\partial q_i = \beta p_i$
Log-log	$\ln p_i = \cdots + \beta \ln q_i + \cdots + \varepsilon_i$	$\partial \hat{P}/\partial q_i = (p_i/q_i)\beta$
Linear Box-Cox	$p_i = \cdots + \beta q_i^{\phi_q} + \cdots + \varepsilon_i$	$\partial \hat{P}/\partial q_i = \phi_q \beta q_i^{\phi_q - 1}$
Quadratic Box-Cox	$p_i = \cdots + \beta q_i^{\phi_q} + \sum_{j=1}^{J} \delta_j x_{ij}^{\phi_x} q_i^{\phi_q} + \cdots + \varepsilon_i$	$\partial \hat{P}/\partial q_i = \phi_q \beta q_j^{\phi_q - 1} + \phi_q \sum_{j=1}^{J} \delta_j x_{ij}^{\phi_x} q_i^{\phi_q - 1}$

[a] Unknown parameters for estimation include β, ϕ_q, δ_j, and φ_x.

Transformations that are non-linear in parameters are not as easy to interpret and they typically require maximum likelihood for estimation; they do, however, allow greater flexibility in the curvature properties of $P(\cdot)$ as related to q_i. Researchers have also pursued nonparametric and semi-nonparametric approaches to estimating the hedonic price function. On this point Palmquist (2005b) notes that years of experience with home appraisals have provided researchers with substantial guidance on how major attributes such as structure and lot size should enter $f(\cdot)$. As such, semi-parametric approaches in which major attributes enter parametrically and environmental amenities in more flexible ways are likely to produce the best results.

There is some literature investigating which of the parametric specifications performs best under what circumstances. Most analysts agree, for example, that $f(x_i, q_i, \beta, \varepsilon_i)$ should be non-linear in q_i and x_i, since attributes cannot usually be perfectly "repackaged". Indeed, Ekeland et al. (2004) suggest there are sound theoretical reasons to expect a non-linear function. Distinguishing among the several non-linear options is more challenging. Using a simulation-based experimental design, Cropper et al. (1988) examine how common functional forms perform under ideal and omitted variable scenarios. Their study involved simulating collections of equilibrium outcomes using parameterizations of household utility functions, and then using the generated data to estimate a suite of hedonic price functions and implicit attribute prices. "Good" estimates are those that are close to the known marginal values implied by the choice of utility function. Cropper et al. find that the flexible parametric approaches perform well when all the explanatory variables are used in the regression, but that if a variable is omitted, the flexible forms exacerbate bias relative to the simple specifications. This finding has been influential, leading analysts since the 1990s to favor simple semi-log and log-log forms for the hedonic price function.

Kuminoff et al. (2010) revisit the question of functional form, and update the Cropper et al. experimental design to include more features of contemporary hedonic analysis. Their simulation study is more explicitly spatial in that correlation across space in environmental-type variables is introduced in their data-generating process. They also consider larger datasets, allow for the potential use of spatial fixed effects (area dummy variables) in their models, and examine a wider range of estimators. Their results suggest that for contemporary property value databases with many observations, and enough variation in q_i to allow for the use of spatial fixed effects, the more flexible functional forms outperform their simple counterparts under both the full specification and omitted variable scenarios.

Consistent Estimation

Most property value databases are single or repeated cross-sections (repeat sales analysis is an exception that we discuss below), so in spite of their spatial richness, the challenges of causal inference in cross-sectional analysis remain. In practical terms this means one must be concerned about omitted variable bias, and the effect this can have on the estimates for marginal implicit prices. Although omitted variable bias has always been a concern, attention to its consequences in property value models has intensified with recent broader emphasis in applied analysis on "clean identification" – i.e. considering all the ways that causal inference may be compromised by the imperfections of non-experimental data. The basic problem is that unbiased estimation of the effect of environmental quality on housing prices requires that the regressors – x_i and q_i in our case – are not correlated with the disturbance term. To see that this is a strong assumption, consider a log-linear specification of the "true" relationship

$$\ln p_i = x_i \beta + \theta q_i + \xi_i + \eta_i, \tag{18.19}$$

where ξ_i is a determinant of price not included among the observed regressors x_i and q_i, and η_i is a random disturbance term. Because we do not observe ξ_i the specification we estimate is

$$\ln p_i = x_i \beta + \theta q_i + \varepsilon_i, \tag{18.20}$$

where the disturbance term now consists of two parts so that $\varepsilon_i = \xi_i + \eta_i$. Our estimates will only be unbiased if $E(\varepsilon_i | x_i, q_i) = 0$, which is to say that the unmeasured attribute ξ_i needs to be uncorrelated with x_i and q_i. As an example of when this can fail, consider the drinking water quality application. We noted that private wells are of lower quality if the property is located near a manufacturing facility. However, the manufacturing facilities themselves may be unattractive, and therefore proximity to one may be associated with lower home prices due to the disamenity effect attached to this type of surrounding land use. If variables for surrounding land use (e.g. dummy variables for residential, industrial, retail, etc.) are not included in the regression, their effect on price resides in ξ_i, and the condition $E(\varepsilon_i | x_i, q_i) = 0$ is violated. In our example the estimate of θ will be biased up (i.e. more positive) since it reflects two positive aspects of a location being distant from a manufacturing facility: a drinking water effect and a surrounding land use effect. The estimate of θ confounds these two determinants of home prices.

Problems with endogenous explanatory variables can and have been addressed using the traditional method of puzzling out important omitted variables and taking steps to minimize their detrimental effects. As Kuminoff et al. (2010) show, the use of spatial fixed effects (e.g. census tract indicators, county dummy variables, or neighborhood fixed effects) can often reduce bias, since the fixed effects nonparametrically account for any unmeasured determinants of housing prices within the spatial area. This strategy has limits, however, since including spatial fixed effects at too fine a level removes variation in q_i that is necessary for estimating the effect of the environmental amenity in the first place. Addressing the challenges of consistent estimation in property value models has led researchers to consider quasi-experimental methods of inference. We review these in section 18.5 below.

Purchase Price Versus Rental Rate

The theory that motivates the first stage regression is based on interpreting $P(\cdot)$ as an annual rental rate, while it is typically the property purchase price or asset value that is available for analysis. Standard economic theory holds that the market price of a durable asset such as a home is the present value of the stream of services provided over the life of the asset. Thus there is a direct relationship between the sales price of a home and the rental rate of the service it provides each year:

$$p_i = \sum_{t=1}^{T} \frac{rent_{it}}{(1+r)^t}, \tag{18.21}$$

where $rent_{it}$ is the annual rental rate, r is the interest rate, and T is the expected life of the property. If the inflation-adjusted rent is constant over the life of the asset, or if rents and prices simultaneously adjust to shocks, then the purchase price and rental rate differ only by a factor of proportionality. In many cases this is a reasonable approximation. If there is an expectation of a future change in environmental quality, however, this change will be reflected in the purchase price but *not* the current rental rate. Palmquist (2005b) cites beachfront property as a good example of this. Proximity to the ocean may imply a high current rental rate if visitors want easy access to the beach, though the expectation that a future storm will wash away the property will depress its asset value. In this and similar circumstances, asset prices are a poor substitute for the rental rates described in the model.

18.3.2 Second Stage Estimation

The objective of the second stage hedonic estimation is to use the results of the first stage estimation, coupled with data on the characteristics of households occupying the individual homes, to estimate an inverse demand function for q. For many reasons this is a difficult task relative to first stage estimation. First, the data needs are substantially more demanding. Unlike the first stage of estimation, which uses only information on prices and characteristics of the property, second stage estimation requires data on household characteristic, such as income and family size. The former is usually public and often readily available, whereas the latter is private information generally available only via surveys. This reason alone explains why first stage hedonic applications are ubiquitous, while second stage applications remain relatively rare. Beyond the issue of data availability, however, there remain several challenges that must be addressed if one hopes to obtain estimates of $\pi^q(x,q,s,u)$.

The idea of a second stage of estimation arose in Rosen's (1974) original treatment of the formal model. If $f(x_i,q_i,\beta,\varepsilon_i)$ is non-linear in q_i, then the marginal implicit price of q

(marginal willingness to pay) as defined in (18.18) varies with the level of q. As different households choose different levels of q, variability in $(\hat{p}_{q_i}, q_i, s_i)$ arises within the cross-section. Thus estimating the parameters γ in

$$\frac{\partial \hat{f}(x_i, q_i, \beta)}{\partial q_i} = \hat{p}_{q_i} = g(q_i, s_i, \gamma) + \eta_i, \quad i = 1, ..., I, \tag{18.22}$$

where $g(\cdot)$ is a functional form for the inverse demand curve and η_i is a disturbance term, could provide a suitable approximation for the marginal willingness to pay for q function. Beginning with Brown and Rosen (1982), however, research has focused on problems inherent within this approach. The largest of these has become known as the "identification" problem, and it is best seen by looking at Figure 18.3. The top and middle panels replicate the curves displayed in Figure 18.1, but do so for two distinct households, denoted s_1 and s_2. The top panel shows the individual bid functions and the observed outcomes, labeled as points a and b for households s_1 and s_2, respectively. Estimates of the hedonic price function allow us to locate point c on the s_1 inverse demand curve, and point d on the inverse demand curve for s_2. For this example with $I = 2$, points c and d represent the sample of data referred to in Eq. (18.22).

The identification problem arises because the regression in Eq. (18.22) fits a function such as the dashed line in the middle panel, which is *not* the inverse demand curve for either of the sampled households. Said another way, the data used in the regression do not represent I points on a single person's inverse demand curve, but are instead a collection of I points on I *different* inverse demand curves. Without additional assumptions, the regression in (18.22) has no economic interpretation. This should not be surprising. To estimate a curve, we need to observe at least two unique points on that curve. Observation of a single home purchase by a single household does not, by construction, provide enough information to estimate a household-specific curve.

This becomes clearer when we compare the data-generating process from the hedonic model to something more akin to a standard demand model. For the latter, prices are parametric and decoupled from quantity. It is therefore possible to observe different consumption amounts by different households at the same parametric price, along with the price/quantity variation. This allows us to identify both demand shifters and the price/quantity gradient, and thereby characterize the full demand function. In contrast, the hedonic price schedule provides consumption quantities that vary *only* when the implicit price varies; as such we cannot observe different quantity outcomes for different households at the same implicit price. Thus the variability needed to estimate the price/quantity gradient is available – this is exploited in the first stage regression – but we are not able to characterize factors that shift the inverse demand function.

To see when the dashed line in the middle panel is a valid inverse demand curve, consider the bottom panel. Here we have assumed that both people have the same inverse demand function, so that points c and d correspond to two points on a single curve. A single inverse demand curve can only arise, however, when the households have identical preferences. This is best seen by reference to the top panel, where the hedonic price function must coincide with a universally held bid function that is independent of household characteristics, if a single inverse demand function is to be derived by tracing out its slope. But if this is the case, a second stage regression is not needed, since all of

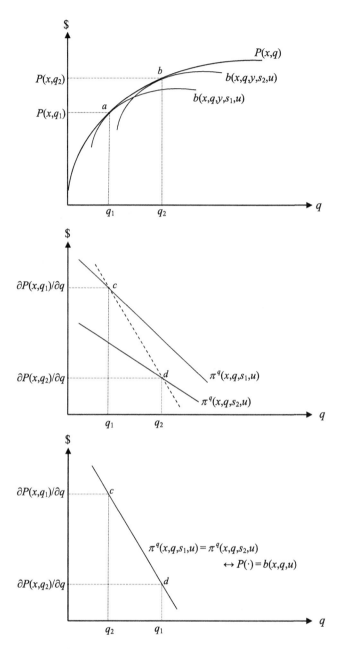

Figure 18.3   Second stage identification problem

the information in the sample is contained in the first stage regression characterization
of $P(x,q) = b(x,q,u)$.

Since Brown and Rosen's paper, researchers have considered two ways of obtaining
estimates of inverse demand functions. The first makes use of restrictions on household
preferences, or exclusion restrictions in the inverse demand functions, to achieve identification. Mendelsohn (1985) provides an example of this as well as a critique of the
strong assumptions that must be used. In essence, the specific non-linearity assumptions

in the hedonic price schedule, implicit price function, and the inverse demand curve are used to back out the demand parameters. Different assumptions lead to different demand parameters, the accuracy of which cannot be gleaned from the data or statistical tests. If reasonably flexible functional forms are used (e.g. Chattopadhyay, 1999) we may have more confidence in the resulting estimates; nonetheless efforts to identify demand parameters using specific functional assumptions (and assumed forms of non-linearity generally) have fallen out of favor in the environmental economics literature.[2]

The second approach to second stage estimation involves taking steps to obtain multiple observations of the marginal implicit price and consumption outcome for the same household. Specifically, we would like to have

$$\left(\hat{p}_{q_{it}}, q_{it}, s_i \right), \quad i = 1, \dots, I, \quad t = 1, \dots, T, \tag{18.23}$$

where T is the number of observed choices for each household i. If $T \geq 2$ it is possible to say something about household i's inverse demand function. To obtain multiple outcomes for the same literal household, however, we would need to observe multiple transactions from the household within the same market. Such rich panel data on the movement of people over time, with accompanying housing transaction information, is almost never available. Instead, researchers have tried to approximate this type of data using a multiple-market approach, which works as follows. First, we assume that households in different spatial or temporal markets with the same observable characteristics (e.g. income, family size) have the same preferences, and hence the same marginal willingness to pay for q function. For distinct markets $t = 1, \dots, T$ we then estimate distinct hedonic price functions $f_t(x_{it}, q_{it}, \beta_t, \varepsilon_{it})$. The different markets can be different areas across space, the same area across time, or some combination thereof. With the estimated hedonic price functions, we then compute $\hat{p}_{q_{it}}$ for all households in each market. Finally, we run the second stage regression using the collection of data points over people and markets. By using the assumption of identical preferences for households with the same socio-economic profile, the pooled data contain up to T observations for each household type. The multiple market data provide variation in implicit price across the markets for a given household type, and variation in quantity for different household types within each market. With these data the resulting estimates can be interpreted as an inverse demand for q curve that shifts with changes in socio-economic variables.

The multi-market strategy is shown graphically in Figure 18.4. The top panel shows an equilibrium price schedule for market 1, and the middle panel shows a price schedule for market 2. Note the equilibrium price functions are different in the two markets. We would expect this to arise for any number of reasons, including differences in the housing stocks in the two areas, varying levels of q across the two landscapes, or other geographical differences. Because they face different price schedules, the same household will consume different levels of q in the two markets. This is shown for two unique

---

[2] A challenge to this view has emerged outside of environmental economics. Ekeland et al. (2004) show that non-linearity of the price schedule and the implicit price for attributes follows from the theory. They claim that a flexible, nonparametric characterization of this non-linearity can (and should) be used to estimate preference parameters. This literature is in its infancy and has not yet provided operational solutions for estimating preferences, though it seems to have considerable potential.

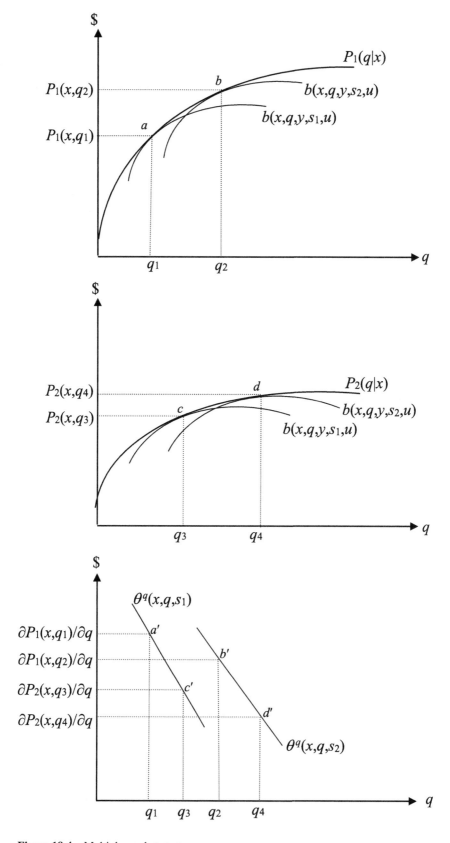

Figure 18.4 Multiple market strategy

households, once again denoted s_1 and s_2. In market 1 s_1 chooses consumption level q_1, while in market 2 the same household chooses q_3. Likewise, s_2 chooses consumptions levels q_2 and q_4 in markets 1 and 2, respectively. Thus the same preference structure results in different outcomes in the two markets, providing variability in q and the implicit price of q for a single household. In the multi-market empirical approach, s_1 and s_2 are not the same literal households in the two markets, but rather different households that are observationally equivalent and assumed to have the same preferences. With this assumption we observe points a and c on two different bid functions for household type s_1, and similarly points b and d for type s_2. As shown in the lower panel, estimation of the two hedonic price functions allows us to locate points a' and c' on an inverse demand curve for s_1, and points b' and d' on a different curve for s_2. Estimation using these four points allows us to trace out the curves labeled $\theta^q(x,q, s_1)$ and $\theta^q(x,q,s_2)$.

Given the necessary data, these mechanical aspects of estimating the second stage hedonic model are relatively straightforward. Consider again our drinking water example, which focused on a single urban area. Suppose, however, that we have also assembled a property sales database for two additional markets, and that the additional databases include information on the quality of drinking water at each transacted home. Using these data we can estimate three separate first stage hedonic regressions using, for example, log-linear specifications

$$
\begin{aligned}
\ln p_i^1 &= x_i^1 \beta^1 + \theta^1 q_i^1 + \varepsilon_i^1, \quad i = 1,...,I^1 \\
\ln p_i^2 &= x_i^2 \beta^2 + \theta^2 q_i^2 + \varepsilon_i^2, \quad i = 1,...,I^2 \\
\ln p_i^3 &= x_i^3 \beta^3 + \theta^3 q_i^3 + \varepsilon_i^3, \quad i = 1,...,I^3,
\end{aligned}
\tag{18.24}
$$

where superscripts now denote data and parameters from the three distinct markets and I^t is the sample size in markets $t=1,2,3$. Via the estimates from the first stage equations we can construct estimates of the marginal implicit prices (marginal willingness to pay) for all observed households at baseline conditions. For the log-linear functional form these are given by

$$
\hat{p}_{q_i^t} = \beta^t \times p_i^t, \quad t = 1, 2, 3, \quad i = 1,...,I^t.
\tag{18.25}
$$

The marginal implicit price estimates are then used as the left-hand side variables in the second stage regression, which pools all the data points from the three markets. An example specification is

$$
\hat{p}_{q_i^t} = \gamma_0 + \gamma_1 q_i^t + \gamma_2 y_i^t + \gamma_3 kids_i^t + \eta_i^t, \quad i = 1,...,I^t, \quad t = 1, 2, 3,
\tag{18.26}
$$

where we have included income and the number of children in the household as example shift variables in the marginal willingness to pay function, along with the baseline level of water quality. Note that the data required for estimating this second stage regression is substantial, in that we need to observe transactions in multiple markets, the amenity we are interested in (private well quality in our example) must be present and relevant in all the markets, and household-specific information for households living in the transacted homes must be available in all the markets. However, the multiple markets provide decoupled variation in implicit prices and consumption amounts, so that the pooled data contain variation of the type we usually see in standard demand estimation applications. This allows us to identify γ_1 (the price/quantity gradient), as well as the demand shift parameters γ_2 and γ_3.

While this example shows that the multi-market approach can in principle solve the identification problem, it leaves many issues unresolved. To begin, note that we have labeled the inverse demand curves in Figure 18.4 by $\theta^q(x,q,s_i)$ rather than by $\pi^q(x,q,s_i,u)$ as in Figure 18.3. This reflects an important distinction. We are primarily interested in characterizing the compensated inverse demand function $\pi^q(x,q,s_i,u)$, since integrating under this curve provides a theoretically consistent, utility-constant welfare measure. The functions shown in Figure 18.4, however, are uncompensated inverse demand curves. For each household, the two observed outcomes lie on different bid functions, and hence are associated with different utility levels. This implies that movements along $\theta^q(x,q,s_i)$ result in different utility levels, and integrating under this curve does not provide a utility-constant welfare measure. Also, q is only one of the attributes in (q, x) for which equations such as $\theta^q(x,q,s_i)$ or $\pi^q(x,q,s_i,u)$ can be written. To be completely general we would need to estimate a system of inverse demand equations to describe households' preferences. Palmquist (2005b) discusses how separability assumptions allow us to focus only on $\theta^q(x,q,s_i)$, and how fairly complex duality techniques in principle allow us to recover $\pi^q(x,q,s_i,u)$ from estimates of $\theta^q(x,q,s_i)$. As a practical matter, the consumer surplus measure calculated from $\theta^q(x,q,s_i)$ is often a good approximation for the constant utility welfare measure, as was discussed in general in Chapter 14.

A more difficult problem lies in the econometrics of consistently estimating (18.22), once the multi-market outcomes have been assembled. Because the hedonic price function is non-linear, households' choices reflect a simultaneous selection of q and its implicit price $\partial P(x,q)/\partial q$. This economic simultaneity translates to econometric endogeneity, in that q_i will by construction be correlated with η_i in the second stage regression in (18.22). Bartik (1987a, p.178) notes that the residual η_i contains unobserved household tastes. A household with higher than average taste for q – i.e. positive η_i – will choose a lower level of $\partial P(x,q)/\partial q$ and a higher level of q, introducing in this case positive correlation between q_i and η_i. Estimation of (18.22) must therefore be by instrumental variables, and an instrument for q is needed. Bartik (1987b) and Epple (1987) show that elements of x_i that are excluded from the regression and might therefore be natural instruments, are in fact also correlated with η_i. Thus the nature of the second stage regression conspires to limit analysts' options in defining a general instrument strategy, so solutions to the endogeneity problem tend to be application specific. Palmquist and Israngkura (1999) and Zabel and Kiel (2000) provide examples of second stage regression in environmental economics.

18.4   STRUCTURAL MODELS

The hedonic model we have described thus far is ubiquitous in environmental economics. Data needed for first stage estimation are readily available and often of high quality. With relatively few assumptions and careful econometric work, one can obtain estimates of the marginal willingness to pay for a variety of local environmental goods. For all its success, however, the hedonic model is quite limited in the types of measurements it can provide. Once we move beyond marginal values to focus on discrete change welfare analysis, we need to rely on approximations of unknown quality or second stage regression. Even when we can obtain data needed for the latter, conceptual and practical challenges remain. This has led researchers to consider alternative approaches for using property value data to measure non-market values.

A distinguishing feature of the hedonic model is its focus on an aggregate market outcome (i.e. the hedonic price schedule) rather than individual optimizing behavior. In this section we consider how discrete choice models that focus on individual household decisions are applicable in property value contexts. We label the approach examined here a structural model, since it starts with a parameterization of households' utility functions, and then uses utility maximizing behavior to derive estimating equations. As we will see, structural models require more in the way of assumptions than their hedonic counterparts, but are in turn capable of providing a wider range of measurement options using similar data requirements.

In what follows we first examine how standard discrete choice models as described in Chapter 16 have been used with property value data. We then discuss how a newer class of sorting models, based in large part on innovations in the empirical industrial organization literature, has evolved out of the discrete choice paradigm.

18.4.1 Discrete Choice Models

Discrete choice approaches to modeling housing demand differ from their hedonic counterpart in how the household's choice is described. Rather than choosing attribute levels in continuous space, households select a single house to purchase from a discrete set of available properties. Each individual property constitutes a bundle of attributes that includes its market price p, as well as its non-price characteristics x and q. The household optimizes by selecting and paying for the home that provides the highest utility level. This assumption does not require attributes to be continuously available in all combinations, as the hedonic approach does. More realistically, it simply postulates that there is a set of homes for sale that differ in prices and the attributes, and that each participating household purchases one of these homes.

We formalize this setup using the random utility maximization (RUM) model that was described generally in Chapter 16. Specific to the property market context, we observe $i = 1, ..., I$ consumers participating in the market, each of whom purchases one home. A household i considers a set of J^i houses that are affordable given its income y_i. The indirect utility available to the household from house j is:

$$U_{ij} = V_{ij}(y_i - p_j, x_j, q_j, \xi_j, s_i; \beta) + \varepsilon_{ij}, \quad j = 1, ..., J^i, \quad i = 1, ..., I. \quad (18.27)$$

In the equation, p_j is the price of house j, we used the budget constraint $y_i = z_i + p_j$ to substitute out the numeraire good, x_j, q_j, and s_i are the observed property, environmental, and household attributes, respectively, and β is a parameter vector. The random variable ε_{ij} represents idiosyncratic aspects of the preference function known to the individual but unobserved by the analyst. Finally, for later reference we have explicitly included the term ξ_j, which denotes unobserved (to the analyst) attributes of property j.

Household i maximizes utility by selecting house j if and only if $U_{ij} \geq U_{ik}$ for all $k \neq j$. Thus the household balances spending on a home against spending on other goods to obtain the optimal bundle of residential services.

Recall that a defining feature of RUM models is that household preferences are random from the perspective of the analyst due to ε_{ij}, which has a known distribution. This means the analyst cannot determine which house a consumer will choose ex ante; rather, she can only state the probability that a particular choice will occur. As a specific example, when ε_{ij} is distributed type I extreme value the conditional logit model arises, and the probability has a closed form given by

$$\text{Pr}_{ij} = \frac{\exp\left[V_{ij}(y_i - p_j, x_j, q_j, \xi_j, s_i; \beta)\right]}{\displaystyle\sum_{k=1}^{J^i} \exp\left[V_{ik}(y_i - p_k, x_k, q_k, \xi_k, s_i; \beta)\right]}. \tag{18.28}$$

Note that Pr_{ij} is in general a function of the attributes of *all* properties in the choice set, which allows us to write $\text{Pr}_{ij} = \text{Pr}_{ij}(p, x, q, \xi, y_i, s_i; \beta)$, where the variables without subscripts are vectors of attribute levels for all properties in the landscape. This is particularly obvious for the conditional logit case, since $V_{ik}(y_i - p_k, x_k, q_k, \xi_k, s_i; \beta)$ appears in the denominator for all the properties in the choice set.

Estimation of the utility function parameters contained in $V_{ij}(\cdot)$ is by maximum likelihood. Households' choices are observed in the data ex post, and these outcomes are matched to their respective ex ante probabilities to construct the likelihood function. With a characterization of $V_{ij}(\cdot)$ in hand, the welfare measurement techniques for RUM models described in Chapter 16 can be used to analyze the household-level willingness to pay for changes in q. As in the hedonic model, however, a distinction needs to be drawn between measurements that allow/do not allow location changes, and include/ do not include the effects of price changes. Housing choice RUM models can readily accommodate either version of the former. However, the standard RUM model does not include a description of how equilibrium home prices are determined. That is, the model does not include a market equilibrium condition, and so it is not possible to predict how prices change when the system is shocked. Thus, although households can change their location, all welfare measurement in housing choice RUM models must be conditional on fixed housing prices across the landscape.

As described thus far, discrete choice models applied to property values are similar to other applications of the RUM model method, including the recreation applications described in Chapter 17. There are, however, two considerations that complicate matters relative to other areas in which discrete choice models are commonly applied. The first is a version of the extent of the market issue, as described for the hedonic model. As in that case, the researcher needs to decide on the spatial and temporal dimensions of the analysis. However, because the discrete choice model focuses on individuals, she must also determine the set of alternatives available to each decision-maker at the time of purchase. Two possibilities for this have been used. As implied by (18.27), one alternative defines choice elements $j = 1, \ldots, J^i$ as literal houses. For this choice set definition it is not appropriate to assume that all decision-makers have the same set of homes available to choose from, since households conduct searches at different times and are differentially constrained by income to different price ranges. Ideally we would like to know when a household was actively engaged in a search and what its target price range was, to which we would match appropriately priced homes on the market at the same time to construct J^i. This type of information is, of course, rarely available. Instead, the analyst needs to use judgment to construct individuals' choice sets, often by including homes sold within a particular time before and after a household's observed purchase, while excluding unaffordable homes based on rules of thumb. Banzhaf and Smith (2007) provide one of the few systematic examinations of how these decisions affect estimates of environmental values arising from discrete choice housing models, when individual houses are the units of choice.

An alternative is to define the unit of choice as a spatial neighborhood rather than an individual house. A neighborhood can be defined in a variety of ways, including jurisdictional boundaries, school districts, natural divisions caused by transportation networks, or geological boundaries such as air- or watersheds. Depending on the specific application, it may be reasonable to assume that all decision-makers face the same set of neighborhood options, so that $J^i = J$ for all households. This can simplify the analysis and, as we discuss below, has potential modeling and econometric advantages as well. However, since a choice element is not a specific house but rather a spatial area containing many properties, the variables p_j, x_j, and q_j must be imputed from the collection of properties in neighborhood j, and interpreted as an index. This adds additional assumptions and degrees of analyst judgment to the empirical exercise.

The second consideration is computational. In recreation, transportation, and other areas where discrete choice models are commonly applied, the size of the choice set has natural limits. In housing applications, however, decision-makers may have thousands of alternatives from which to choose. Many discrete choice models become empirically intractable when such large choice sets are used. Simpler models, including the conditional logit, can usually be used with large choice sets, since consistent estimation can be accomplished using a randomly selected sub-set of alternatives in J^i to compute a decision-maker's probability. For this reason almost all discrete choice housing applications have relied on the conditional (or in some cases, nested) logit model. Even with logit-type models, however, computational challenges remain. Recall from Chapter 16 that when $V_{ij}(\cdot)$ is linear in $(y_i - p_j)$, income y_i drops out of the expression when utility is differenced. This implies $\text{Pr}_{ij}(\cdot)$ is *not* a function of income, suggesting the probability that a person purchases a house with price p_j is independent of his income level. It seems unlikely that this is a valid assumption for a large-scale decision such as purchasing a home. Thus, in housing choice applications, it is usually desirable to use a specification for $V_{ij}(\cdot)$ that is non-linear in income, such as $\ln(y_i - p_j)$. This does not cause much in the way of difficulties for estimation. As we saw in our general discussion of welfare measurement in RUM models in Chapter 16, however, it does imply that simulation algorithms are needed to compute willingness to pay estimates for changes in the environmental good.

It is relatively straightforward to describe how a discrete choice model could be used to estimate preferences in our drinking water quality example. Suppose that the landscape in our urban area can be divided into J complete and mutually exclusive neighborhoods that are defined, for example, based on attendance zones for the area's public elementary schools. By construction, each of the observed sales $i = 1, \ldots, I$ occurred in one of the $j = 1, \ldots, J$ neighborhoods. The empirical objective is to characterize the utility a household receives from locating in a particular neighborhood. An example specification is

$$V_{ij} = \alpha \ln(y_i - p_j) + x_j' \beta + \theta q_j + \gamma q_j \times kids_i + \varepsilon_{ij}, \quad j = 1, \ldots, J, \quad i = 1, \ldots, I, \quad (18.29)$$

where p_j and x_j describe the price and non-environmental attributes of neighborhood j, q_j measures the drinking water quality a household obtains if it locates in neighborhood j, and ε_{ij} is distributed type I extreme value. Recall that the price and non-price attributes are in fact measured at the level of the property (i.e. p_i, x_i, q_i), so an aggregation strategy is needed to compute the explanatory variables that enter the utility function. For example, we might use

$$
\begin{aligned}
p_j &= \text{median}\left\{p_i, \forall i \in j\right\} \\
x_j &= \text{median}\left\{x_i, \forall i \in j\right\} \\
q_j &= \text{median}\left\{q_i, \forall i \in j\right\},
\end{aligned}
\tag{18.30}
$$

where $i \in j$ indicates that property i lies within the boundaries of neighborhood j. Estimation proceeds by using the I observed neighborhood choices to estimate the parameters $(\alpha, \beta, \theta, \gamma)$ by maximum likelihood, which provides a characterization of preferences that can be used to value changes in drinking water quality. For example, the indirect utility function in (18.29) implies that the marginal willingness to pay for q is

$$\frac{\partial V_{ij}(\cdot)/\partial q}{\partial V_{ij}(\cdot)/\partial y} = \frac{(\theta + \gamma \times kids_i) \times (y_i - p_j)}{\alpha}. \tag{18.31}$$

Furthermore, we can use the techniques described in Chapter 16 to estimate the value to household i of a non-marginal change in water quality in any of the neighborhoods across the urban area.

Note that equations (18.26) and (18.31) represent different expressions based on different modeling approaches for the same underlying behavioral function, in the same application. In both instances estimation of the unknown parameters provides the ability to measure the willingness to pay for a non-marginal change in drinking water quality. However, the discrete choice model allows us to estimate the preference parameters using data from a single market, while the second stage hedonic model requires data from multiple markets. In this sense focusing on optimizing behavior allows us to get more out of the same data; doing so, however, requires additional assumptions, the reasonableness of which depends on the specific application.

18.4.2 Sorting Models

The term "sorting model" grew out of local public finance research describing households self-selecting, or sorting themselves, into local jurisdictions à la Tiebot to obtain a desired level of a spatially differentiated local public good. A family choosing a community based on local school quality is the classic example of this behavior. However, the concepts of sorting and spatial equilibria arising due to sorting have also been used to explain persistent differences in observed property values, poverty and crime rates, and the racial composition of communities, to give but a few examples. In the late 1990s researchers began to consider empirical versions of these models, in which parametric assumptions about preferences and the nature of equilibria across space were combined with data on home prices and quasi-fixed good levels to estimate utility function parameters. To date, two types of empirical sorting models have been examined in environmental economics: a *vertical* sorting model (Sieg et al., 2004), and a *horizontal* sorting model (Bayer et al., 2009), where the terms vertical and horizontal are borrowed from the industrial organization literature describing how differentiated products are ranked by consumers. Here, we focus attention on the horizontal sorting model, since it is a direct extension of the discrete choice models we have discussed here and in other chapters.

Chris Timmins and his co-authors have been particularly active in developing horizontal sorting models for use in environmental economics. Their approach has been to begin with a discrete choice model, add an equilibrium concept to the analysis (prices and/or social interactions), and address the resulting endogeneity of particular variables in estimation. A general description of this strategy is given in Bayer and Timmins (2007). As in a RUM model, the landscape of interest is divided into J neighborhoods, each of which contains a fixed supply of houses. A household takes the attributes of neighborhoods as given (including the attribute ξ_j, which is unobserved to the analyst but known to consumers), so that its utility from neighborhood j depends parametrically on p_j, x_j, q_j, ξ_j, and the characteristics of household members. A household demands (chooses) a location j if the utility from that location is its highest option, conditional on what other market participants do. To add an equilibrium concept, we assume the aggregate demand for location j is the summation over all individual household demands for location j. A Nash equilibrium in the landscape is then characterized by three related features: housing supply equals aggregate housing demand for all neighborhoods, a set of equilibrium prices $p_1,...,p_J$ arises that clears the housing market, and all households have chosen a neighborhood out of which, conditional on the other households' choices, they do not wish to move.

To construct an empirical model based on this logic, we first assume that the prices and individual location decisions observed in a typical property value database were generated by an equilibrating process as just described. We then assume a stochastic form for utility, as in Eq. (18.27), and derive statements for the probability of each household's choice. To proceed further, it is useful to think of the probability $\text{Pr}_{ij}=\text{Pr}_{ij}(p,x,q,\xi; y_i,s_i,\beta)$ as an expression of the household's *expected* demand for location j, where p, x, q, and ξ are vectors representing attributes of all the locations such that $p=(p_1,...,p_J)$, $x=(x_1,...,x_J)$, $q=(q_1,...,q_J)$, and $\xi=(\xi_1,...,\xi_J)$. Under this interpretation, the collection of probabilities $\text{Pr}_{i1},...,\text{Pr}_{iJ}$ summarizes the demand for all neighborhoods in the landscape by household i. To obtain an expression for market demand for each neighborhood j, we need to aggregate up the individual demands. For this let $g(y_i,s_i)$ denote the density function summarizing the distribution of household characteristics y_i and s_i in the population. The aggregate demand share for neighborhood j is the expectation of Pr_{ij} in the population with respect to y_i and s_i:

$$s_j^D(p,x,q,\xi,\beta) = \int \text{Pr}_{ij}(p,x,q,\xi;y_i,s_i,\beta)g(y_i,s_i)dy_ids_i, \quad j=1,...,J. \tag{18.32}$$

Note that $s_j^D(\cdot)$ is the proportion of market participants who are expected to select neighborhood j, given a set of prices and attributes, and that as a market-level concept it is not a function of household characteristics. From this we can define the equilibrium in the model based on

$$s_j^D(p,x,q,\xi,\beta) = s_j^S, \quad 1,...,J, \tag{18.33}$$

where s_j^S is the exogenous supply of homes in neighborhood j, written as a share of the total supply of houses in the landscape. Note that for given vectors of x, q, and ξ across the landscape, Eq. (18.33) implicitly determines the equilibrium set of prices $p = (p_1,...,p_J)$.

Estimation is based on finding the utility function parameters that optimize an econometric objective function (e.g. the likelihood function) based on matching Pr_{ij} to observed individual choices, while also satisfying the equilibrium conditions in (18.33). Estimates of these parameters provide a characterization of household preferences *and* the equilibrium structure in the landscape. Thus, the empirical sorting model differs from a standard discrete choice model through its explicit characterization of an equilibrium condition. As we discuss below, this conveys both econometric and inference advantages related to (a) consistent estimation, and (b) simulating new equilibrium prices following a shock.

The model is made operational with assumptions for the utility function and error distribution. For exposition purposes, consider again our drinking water example in which utility is now

$$U_{ij} = x_j'\beta + \theta_i q_j + \alpha p_j + \xi_j + \varepsilon_{ij}, \quad j = 1,...,J,$$
$$\theta_i = \theta + \gamma kids_i, \quad i = 1,...,I, \tag{18.34}$$

and ε_{ij} is distributed type I extreme value, so that the probability expression in (18.28) arises. This example allows for preference heterogeneity through the household-specific parameters θ_i. In particular, the marginal utility of drinking water quality is $\theta + \gamma kids_i$, which includes the person-constant effect θ and a component that varies with the number of children in the household, based on the sign and size of γ. Preferences for other attributes contained in x_j can also exhibit heterogeneity, though we ignore this here for ease of exposition. The specification also includes the alternative-specific "fixed effect" ξ_j, which nonparametrically controls for the unobserved-to-the-analyst attributes for choice j. The role of household- versus alternative-specific effects becomes clearer when we rewrite utility as

$$U_{ij} = \delta_j + \gamma kids_i \times q_j + \varepsilon_{ij}, \quad j = 1,...,J, \quad i = 1,...,I, \tag{18.35}$$

where

$$\delta_j = x_j'\beta + \theta q_j + \alpha p_j + \xi_j, \quad j = 1,...,J. \tag{18.36}$$

Note that this specification differs from (18.29) in two ways. First, price enters linearly into utility, and therefore there is no income effect in the model. This is mainly for expositional purposes, though non-linear income effects do affect estimation more directly in a sorting framework than in the standard discrete choice model. A more important difference is the presence of ξ_j, and the role it plays in the model.

In (18.35), δ_j is the population mean utility level for neighborhood j, and since it depends only on the observed and unobserved attributes of neighborhood j, it is the same for all households. The other terms in U_{ij} serve to differentiate utility away from the mean for households based on observed (i.e. $kids_i$) and unobserved (i.e. ε_{ij}) household-specific terms. Equations (18.35) and (18.36) demonstrate how both individual heterogeneity and the intensity of average tastes in the population are relevant for estimating preferences. The latter is reflected in the comparative magnitudes of the alternative specific constants $\delta_1,...,\delta_{J-1}$ and $\delta_J=0$ (without loss of generality, recall that one of these must be normalized for estimation).

The alternative specific constants (ASCs) play multiple roles in the horizontal sorting model. First, recall that the equilibrium condition from (18.33) requires expected aggregate demand shares to equal the exogenous supply shares. In a model with type I extreme value errors and the utility function as in (18.35), this implies

$$s_j^S = \frac{1}{I}\sum_{i=1}^{I} \frac{\exp(\delta_j + \gamma kids_i \times q_j)}{\sum\limits_{k=1}^{J} \exp(\delta_k + \gamma kids_i \times q_k)} = s_j^D(\cdot), \quad j=1,...,J. \tag{18.37}$$

Thus, from the perspective of the economic model, the alternative specific constants $\delta_1,...,\delta_{J-1}$ are estimated in a way that assures that the J equilibrium conditions from the sorting model are met. Coincidentally, it is a property specific to the conditional logit econometric model that (18.37) holds when the expression is evaluated at the maximum likelihood estimates for $\delta_1,...,\delta_{J-1}$ and γ. The conditional logit model therefore allows the analyst to first estimate $\delta_1,...,\delta_{J-1}$ and γ by maximum likelihood, which by construction imposes the equilibrium condition implied by the sorting model. This is referred to as the first stage of estimation. To decompose each δ_j into its observable and unobservable components, a second stage of estimation is used in which the linear model shown in (18.36) is estimated using the first stage estimates of $\delta_1,...,\delta_{J-1}$ and $\delta_J=0$ as the dependent variables, and p_j, x_j, and q_j as the independent variables. The two steps together provide estimates of all the parameters in (18.34) – including the fixed effect ξ_j, which is computed using the residuals from the second stage regression.

Use of a first and second stage regression in this class of model grew out of work in the mid 1990s in empirical industrial organization. Influential articles on modeling the demand for quality-differentiated goods by Berry (1994) and Berry et al. (1995, 2004) provided the main motivation for this approach. These articles provided a computational device for estimating the alternative specific constants in the first stage when J is large. Heuristically, we define (18.37) as a contraction mapping that allows one to concentrate out the ASCs from the likelihood function and compute them as a residual, thereby avoiding a numerical search for their values. Since J can number in the thousands (in which case gradient-based searches are infeasible) this device is critical for making horizontal sorting models operational.

In Berry (1994) the second stage of estimation is a linear model, which allows analysts to employ the familiar suite of regression tools to recover estimates of β, θ, and α in Eq. (18.36). This is a notable advantage, since intuition suggests the variables x_i, p_i, and q_i are likely to be correlated with the unmeasured attributes ξ_j. This is particularly so for price, since the equilibrating process implies that attributes of neighborhoods – including those that are not measured by the analyst – determine neighborhood prices. Thus p_j is endogenous from both the economic *and* econometric perspectives of the sorting model. If p_j and ξ_j are positively correlated (i.e. higher levels of unmeasured neighborhood quality imply a higher price) then an OLS estimate of α will be biased towards zero from the left (and perhaps even positive), and it will appear as though households prefer higher prices when in fact they prefer higher neighborhood quality. The linear second stage regression allows one to employ the full suite of instrumental variables and other identification strategies to consistently identify the parameters in (18.36). Thus the primary econometric advantage of the sorting model vis-à-vis a standard discrete choice approach is that it provides a mechanism for addressing the related issues of unobserved neighborhood attributes and econometrically endogenous explanatory variables.

The second advantage of the sorting model lies in our ability to use the model to predict new equilibrium prices in response to an exogenous shock to q. With estimates of the utility function parameters in hand, including values for $\xi_1, \ldots \xi_J$, Eq. (18.33) generally or (18.37) for our specific example can be used to solve for $p_1, \ldots, p_J$ given any values of $q_1, \ldots, q_J$. For example, we can specify hypothetical changes in the level of the environmental goods, and predict new equilibrium prices based on the change. In principle this means the sorting model can be used to compute the full range of welfare measures that we identified above: marginal *WTP*, fixed location *WTP*, fixed price *WTP* with relocation, and *WTP* with relocation and a new price equilibrium.

18.4.3 Advantages and Disadvantages of a Structural Approach

As we have seen, discrete choice models and their sorting generalizations provide econometric and inference capabilities that go beyond what we can usually accomplish using first and second stage hedonic regression. These capabilities, however, come at a cost. Discrete choice models generally, and sorting models in particular, require numerous non-testable assumptions for implementation. They are highly specification dependent in the sense that inference arises both from the data and from the assumptions on functional forms and distributions. This is most apparent for the sorting model's ability to simulate new equilibria, since the predictions are based on a very specific characterization of the equilibrium process. Thus it is not always obvious if the extra capabilities of the sorting model in particular are based on the added assumptions, or a better use of the available data. Research in this area is still in its infancy, and ongoing work will likely help determine the extent to which discrete choice sorting models represent a genuine alternative to the elusive second stage hedonic regression.

18.5   QUASI-EXPERIMENTAL APPROACHES

Since the early 1990s, literature in applied economics has increasingly emphasized the use of natural experiments to establish causal relationships between variables. The key step in these so-called "quasi-experimental" approaches is the identification of an unexpected event caused by nature or policy, which induces a change in behavior related to the phenomenon of interest. In property value applications quasi-experiments have typically involved isolating exogenous information disclosures or policy interventions, and then comparing market prices before and after the shock. An example of an information-based quasi-experiment is Davis (2004), who examines the relationship between home prices and environmental health risks using the announcement of a cancer cluster. Specifically, for an isolated county in Nevada that experienced a sudden and dramatic increase in pediatric leukemia, he examines home prices in and around the affected area before and after the spike became known. The cancer cluster provided an unanticipated, exogenous shock to environmental health risks within the county, from which it was possible to observe home prices reacting. A second example based on a policy intervention comes from Chay and Greenstone (2005). These authors noted a peculiarity in the structure of federal air quality regulation in the United States, which causes counties to be designated as non-attainment areas if the concentration of a regulated air pollutant exceeds a legislated threshold. Pollution sources in non-attainment counties are subject to stricter regulation relative to those in attainment counties, causing larger relative pollution reductions over time in non-attainment counties. Therefore, counties with similar initial pollution levels lying just below or just above the threshold experienced quite different subsequent pollution paths due to the designation. Chay and Greenstone compare changes in home prices over time between counties on either side of the threshold, to see how home values respond to improvements in air quality.

A defining feature of quasi-experimental research in environmental economics and the broader economics literature is the application of experimental language and techniques to problems that have traditionally been examined using non-experimental, observational data. Approaching inference from this perspective has several advantages, but it requires familiarity with terms and concepts that, until recently, have not been part of the environmental economist's econometric toolkit. As such we begin this section with an overview of the experimental paradigm within the context of property value questions. We then discuss techniques that are often used with property value data, and more generally in environmental economics.

18.5.1 Background and Motivation

The main motivation for quasi-experimental approaches in housing market studies is concern for omitted variables, and the bias they induce in estimates of marginal willingness to pay for q. For this reason most studies have focused narrowly on estimating the equivalent of the marginal implicit price as derived from the hedonic price function. However, the path to this end is quite different than was described above. The point of departure is the Rubin Causal Model (RCM), which is nicely described by Imbens and Wooldridge (2009). The RCM is a framework for conceptualizing a causal measurement objective. Two key concepts in this framework are *potential outcomes* and *assignment mechanisms*. We consider these in the context of understanding how an environmental variable q affects the sale price of a home. For illustration, suppose that q takes one of two values, so the observed level at house i is either $q_i = q^h$ or $q_i = q^l$, where h and l denote high and low levels of the amenity, respectively. For a specific house i there are two potential outcomes: the price the house would sell for if $q_i = q^h$, and the price it would sell for if $q_i = q^l$. We denote these by (p_i^h, p_i^l), where superscripts indicate the level of q. The objective is to measure

$$ATT = E(p_i^h - p_i^l \mid q_i = q^h), \tag{18.38}$$

which is the expected difference in house prices attributable solely to a location having the high amenity level. The acronym *ATT* indicates that our objective is to estimate the "average treatment effect on the treated", where the term treated refers to a property that has (is "assigned") the high amenity value of q.

The fundamental challenge is that we cannot observe both potential outcomes for a single property. Instead, for each property in a sample of data we observe the actual sale price p_i, which will be equal to either p_i^h or p_i^l, depending on the value of q_i. Therefore, to estimate *ATT* we need to compare different houses that have different levels of q. For example, ignoring for the moment the property's non-environmental attributes, we can with these data readily estimate the quantity

$$\theta = E(p_i \mid q_i = q^h) - E(p_i \mid q_i = q^l), \tag{18.39}$$

which may or may not be equal to the average price differential we hope to measure. Judging the accuracy of θ as an estimate for *ATT* requires consideration of the assignment mechanism, which in this example is the process through which a house receives either q^l or q^h as its quality level. More generally, the assignment mechanism is the process through which different units are assigned to different "treatment" status – i.e. the value of the explanatory variable of interest.

To understand the importance of the assignment mechanism it is helpful to rewrite θ with the non-observable (or counterfactual) term $E(p_i^l \mid q_i = q^h)$ added and subtracted, so that

$$\begin{aligned} \theta &= E(p_i \mid q_i = q^h) - E(p_i^l \mid q_i = q^h) + \left\{ E(p_i^l \mid q_i = q^h) - E(p_i \mid q_i = q^l) \right\} \\ &= ATT + SE. \end{aligned} \tag{18.40}$$

Note that the counterfactual term $E(p_i^l \mid q_i = q^h)$ is the price we expect a treated house would have sold for, had it not been treated. In (18.40), the term in brackets must be zero if what we are able to measure (θ) is equal to what we hope to measure (*ATT*). We refer to the term in brackets as the *selection effect* (*SE*). The *SE* is fundamentally non-observable, and so it is only based on understanding the assignment mechanism that we can intuit when it will or will not be zero. A non-zero selection effect often arises when the assignment mechanism is not random, as is the case with observational data. This is the primary impediment to causal inference with observational data. Obtaining an intuitive grasp of non-random assignment is central to understanding strategies for minimizing its impact.

To this end, consider a thought experiment based on our drinking water example in which all I homes have a baseline level of low (q^l) drinking water quality. To begin the experiment, we randomly select $M < I$ homes. For large enough I and M it is sensible that the average price of the M selected homes is essentially the same as the average price of the $(I - M)$ non-selected homes. Next, we "treat" each of the M randomly selected homes – perhaps with some type of water filtration system – so that drinking water quality at the property increases to q^h. Based on the sample of M treated and $(I-M)$ untreated houses, we then observe prices $p_1,\ldots,p_I$ and the associated quality levels $q_1,\ldots,q_I$. In this story it is safe to assume that

$$SE = E(p_i^l \mid q_i = q^h) - E(p_i \mid q_i = q^l) = 0, \qquad (18.41)$$

though we cannot directly measure SE, since we do not observe what houses receiving q^h would have sold for absent the treatment. That $SE=0$ is a sensible assumption in this case is apparent from the fact that there is nothing a priori special about a house being among the M randomly selected houses that receive $q_i = q^h$, and hence no reason to believe that, absent the treatment, it would have a different mean price. This type of randomized treatment is the basis for designed experiments in many experimental disciplines, including case/control studies in medical research.

Consider now how drinking water quality is actually assigned to houses in our market of size I. Suppose we once again observe sales prices for M houses that have $q_i = q^h$, and $I-M$ houses that have $q_i = q^l$, but that the differences do not arise from a thought experiment. Instead, they arise from the real world interaction of geography, the spatial distribution of manufacturing facilities, market behavior, policy, and any number of other factors. In this alternative story, it is generally *not* safe to assume that (18.41) holds. To do so is to say that the high drinking water quality houses are not systematically distinct from the low drinking water quality houses, aside from the different level of q. This can fail for any number of reasons. The disamenity example from above is one case in point. If properties with low drinking water quality are near manufacturing facilities, and the presence of these facilities causes the surrounding landscape to be comparatively less attractive, then the $I-M$ homes observed with low drinking water quality would have a smaller average sales price due to the unattractive surrounding landscape, even if there had never been differences in drinking water quality. For this example, $SE>0$ and θ will overstate the role of water quality in determining home prices. This example shows that concerns about a non-zero selection effect in an experimental context are identical to concerns about omitted variables in a regression context.

One common strategy for addressing the selection problem in observational data is to condition on observables x_i, which further connects the experimental perspective to the regression approach shown in Eq. (18.17). Imbens and Wooldridge (2009) refer to the case when

$$SE = E(p_i^l \mid q_i = q^h, x_i) - E(p_i \mid q_i = q^l, x_i) = 0 \qquad (18.42)$$

as *unconfounded* assignment. An unconfounded assignment mechanism says that, once we have conditioned on measured covariates x_i, there is no systematic difference between high and low amenity properties, other than the difference in environmental quality. Continuing our example, if surrounding land use is a variable included in x_i and D_i is a dummy variable equal to one when $q_i = q^h$, the regression equation

$$\ln p_i = x_i'\beta + \theta \times D_i + \varepsilon_i \qquad (18.43)$$

will capture the influence of nearby industrial land use (and the other covariates) on price, so that any price differences that remain can be captured by θ. If x_i and D_i are not correlated with ε_i, that is, if the usual exogeneity assumptions hold, then $\theta = ATT$ and the regression will provide valid inference on the quantity of interest. An approach to inference that assumes the assignment mechanism is unconfounded – i.e. an approach that assumes (18.42) holds – is known as a selection on observables approach.

18.5.2 Alternative Identification Strategies

Greenstone and Gayer (2009) argue that the selection on observables strategy is generally unreliable, and advocate the use of natural or quasi-experiments to cleanly identify the relationship between property values and environmental quality. The econometric methods used for this purpose are straightforward. The challenge instead is to find a natural experiment that provides variation related to the phenomenon of interest, and to isolate its potential effect on property prices. This involves searching for potential sources of exogenous variability generated by policies, weather events, information disclosures, accidents, and so on. Once the potential experiment is located, considerable care is needed to determine how baseline circumstances and the shock combine to provide exogenous variation. These steps by their nature are context-specific. However, most natural experiments can be classified as one of a small number of types, which conditions how we think about estimating the effect of interest. In what follows, we examine two common approaches, or experimental designs: the difference in differences (DD) design, and the regression discontinuity (RD) design.

Difference in Differences

The difference in differences model is appropriate in the following, often-observed circumstance. Suppose we observe multiple years of home sales that overlap an exogenous shock, such as the cancer cluster analyzed by Davis (2004). Suppose as well that the housing market can be divided into two spatial components, only one of which experienced the shock. In the cancer cluster example, the event was recorded in one county, while the neighboring counties experienced no increase in sickness rates. These two sources of variation in "treatment" – spatial and temporal – allow the analyst to compare the change in housing prices over time in the affected area to the change over time in the unaffected area. The difference in these differences is an estimate of the causal effect of the shock.

More formally, suppose we observe sales in years $t=0$ and $t=1$, and that the shock occurs after the first year. For continuity from our earlier examples, suppose the shock changes the value of q from q^l to q^h. Denote p_{it} as the price of a property i that sold in year t, and define the spatial dummy variable $S_{it}=1$ if the property is in the affected area, and $S_{it}=0$ otherwise. Consider the regression equation

$$\ln p_{it} = x_{it}'\beta + \delta_1 S_{it} + \delta_2 T_{it} + \theta^{DD} \times T_{it} \times S_{it} + \varepsilon_{it}, \tag{18.44}$$

where the temporal dummy variable $T_{it}=1$ indicates that the sale occurred in year 1, and $T_{it}=0$ indicates the sale occurred in year 0. In this regression, θ^{DD} captures the price differential attributable to a property being sold in the affected area, after the shock. That θ^{DD} is a difference in differences estimate is best seen by noting that the expected change in log price for non-affected properties between $t=0$ and $t=1$ is δ_2, while the expected change in price for affected properties is $\delta_2+\theta^{DD}$. The difference between these is θ^{DD}, and if certain conditions hold, it will reflect the causal impact on property values of the change in q.

The conditions under which $\theta^{DD}=ATT$ are milder than for the selection on observables case, which explains its popularity. Specifically, the selection effect in a DD estimator is

$$SE^{DD} = \left\{ E(p_{it}^l \mid x_{it}, S_{it}=1, T_{it}=1) - E(p_{it} \mid x_{it}, S_{it}=1, T_{it}=0) \right\} \\ - \left\{ E(p_{it} \mid x_{it}, S_{it}=0, T_{it}=1) - E(p_{it} \mid x_{it}, S_{it}=0, T_{it}=0) \right\}. \tag{18.45}$$

The first difference in brackets cannot be observed; it is a counterfactual describing how average prices in the affected area would have changed between $t=0$ and $t=1$, had there been no shock. The second term in brackets can be observed; it describes how average prices in the unaffected area did change between $t=0$ and $t=1$. The formula shows that for SE^{DD} to be zero, these two terms need to be the same. Thus the two areas can be systematically different in areas outside the environmental effect, so long as their time trends are similar. This is important because the presence of unobserved attributes that are correlated with x_{it} or q_{it} need not in this design invalidate causal inference. Of course, in specific examples it can be that $SE^{DD}\neq 0$, which invalidates the causal inference. An understanding of the shock from every possible angle is needed to argue that this is not the case.

Repeat Sales

The difference in differences approach as described thus far is based on repeated cross-sectional observation of sales rather than a true panel. Thus the cross-time comparisons are between different houses, and the comparison is conditioned on values of the other covariates x_{it}. A special case of the DD estimator arises when sales of the same house are observed in different periods bracketing the exogenous shock. In this case the repeat sales model, introduced by Palmquist (1982), is appropriate. The repeat sales model allows considerable flexibility in controlling for unobserved attributes of homes, though by its nature it limits the number of observations available for analysis relative to repeated cross-sections. A stylized version of the model begins with a specification of the hedonic price equation as

$$p_{it} = B_t \exp\left(v(x_i)\right)\exp(\theta^{RS} q_{it})\exp(-\delta A_{it})\exp(\eta_{it}), \tag{18.46}$$

where B_t is a real estate price index at time t, $v(x_i)$ is an unspecified function of the non-environmental attributes that are constant over time, and A_{it} is the age of the house at time t. For simplicity, suppose we observe a sale for each house i at consecutive time periods $t=0$ and $t=1$. We can form the ratio of the prices as

$$\frac{p_{i1}}{p_{i0}} = \frac{B_1}{B_0}\exp\left[\theta^{RS}(q_{i1}-q_{i0})\right]\exp\left[-\delta(A_{i1}-A_{i0})\right]\exp\left[\eta_{i1}-\eta_{i0}\right]. \tag{18.47}$$

Taking the natural log of both sides, we obtain the regression equation

$$\begin{aligned}
\ln(p_{i1}/p_{i0}) &= \beta_1 - \beta_0 - \delta(A_{i1}-A_{i0}) + \theta^{RS}(q_{i1}-q_{i0}) + \eta_{i1} - \eta_{i0} \\
&= \alpha + \theta^{RS}(\Delta q_i) + \varepsilon_i,
\end{aligned} \tag{18.48}$$

where the intercept nonparametrically controls for appreciation and age effects, and θ^{RS} measures the difference in log prices attributable to the change in q. The repeat sales estimator can take one of two forms. If the sample does not include distinct "treatment" and "non-treatment" groups – i.e. distinct spatial areas where a shock did and did not occur – then θ^{RS} is a linear fixed effects panel estimator. If there is an exogenous shock of the type described above, so that $\Delta q_i = 0$ for the non-treated properties, then the repeat sales model is a difference in differences estimator with a selection effect given by (18.45).

Regression Discontinuity

A second experimental situation is when the value of an observed covariate effectively assigns a house to either a "treated" group or an "untreated" group. In the Chay and Greenstone (2005) air quality example, the ambient level of total suspended particulates (*TSP*) determined whether a county was in attainment or non-attainment status based on a discrete cutoff point. Non-attainment status was effectively a pollution-reducing treatment, since it triggered additional regulation of emissions in the county. Thus counties with *TSP* levels on either side of the discrete cutoff started with only marginally different baseline pollution levels, but received dramatically different pollution reduction treatments. This type of discontinuity can, in some instances, be used to mimic a random assignment mechanism.

A regression discontinuity (*RD*) design uses only observations that bracket the threshold to estimate the effect of interest. Continuing with our drinking water quality example, suppose we observe a cross-section of sale prices p_i for $i=1,\ldots,I$ properties and that we are interested in measuring how $q_i\in(q^h,q^l)$ affects price. As in Eq. (18.43), estimating θ in the relationship

$$\ln p_i = x_i'\beta + \theta \times D_i + \varepsilon_i, \quad i=1,\ldots,I, \tag{18.49}$$

is the primary objective, where $D_i = 1$ indicates the house has $q_i = q^h$ and $D_i = 0$ otherwise. Assume now that there is also a continuous variable d_i which contains a discrete threshold th so that if $d_i < th$ the house has $q_i = q^h$, and if $d_i > th$ we observe $q_i = q^l$. In our example we imagine d_i is the distance in miles from a manufacturing facility to property i, and that homes located less than th miles from the facility receive water filtration devices that assure high-quality drinking water (q^h). Homes more than th miles away receive no such assistance. Suppose that $M < I$ homes have values of d_i that are "close" to the threshold – i.e. just under (so the treatment occurs) or just over (so it does not). An *RD* approach uses the regression

$$\ln p_i = x_i' \beta + \theta^{RD} \times D_i + \varepsilon_i, \quad i = 1, ..., M, \tag{18.50}$$

to estimate the effect of interest, where the only difference is that the sample has been limited to the set of properties that border the threshold. The idea is that D_i and ε_i should *not* be correlated in (18.50), since the value of D_i is effectively random via the accident of being on one or the other side of th among a collection of houses with near identical values of d_i. When this type of natural experiment exists, it can be an effective way to estimate *ATT*. However, there is some concern that the estimate is only accurate for properties near the threshold (i.e. the ones included in the regression), and that it is less relevant for the majority of properties in the full sample of size I that were not included in the analysis.

18.5.3 Structural Versus Quasi-experimental Analysis

There is an ongoing intellectual debate in applied economics concerning the relative merits of structural versus reduced quasi-experimental approaches to estimation. The latter focuses on establishing causality among variables, but usually does so at the expense of limiting the extent of the inference that is possible from the analysis. Structural analysis aims to estimate the parameters of theory-based functions such as utility, cost, and profit functions, and usually does so using data, theoretical results, and specific functional forms. Because behavioral functions are recovered, structural approaches provide greater flexibility in the answers they provide. However, there are always questions about the extent to which conclusions are based on the researcher's assumptions and choices rather than the available data. Regardless of one's ultimate persuasion, this debate has been tremendously informative. A good general discussion on the debate from a structuralist perspective is provided by Nevo and Whinston (2010) and Angrist and Pischke's (2009) book provides a nice summary of an experimentalist approach to econometrics.

Property value applications as we have examined here provide an excellent illustration of the general debate. The strengths and weaknesses of the structural approach were described in the previous section. Here, we complete the discussion by examining how quasi-experimental approaches fare when the objective is to measure non-market values. Intuitively, this objective requires two things. First, we need to establish that market prices are affected by changes in the environmental variable. This is the question of causality and the existence of a price/quality relationship. Second, we need to link the estimated price/quality relationship to a conceptual welfare measure, such as marginal willingness to pay or compensating variation. For this the empirical estimate needs to connect to an economic model. The quasi-experimental methods we have described are designed for the first task. What is less clear, however, is the extent to which the measurements that emerge from a well-executed experiment – i.e. the average treatment effect on the treated (*ATT*) – relate to theoretically consistent welfare measures.

Kuminoff and Pope (2014) look at this issue for the case of housing prices. Using the hedonic model as their theoretical basis, they consider the conditions under which the *ATT* is equal to the average marginal willingness to pay (*AMWTP*) for a change in the amenity. In general they show that *ATT≠AMWTP*. This can occur for several reasons, but the most intuitive is based on the fact that wide spatial and temporal variability – and non-marginal changes in *q* – are usually used to estimate *ATT*. It is likely that a single, temporally stable hedonic price schedule, to which marginal values are linked, does not exist within the range of the data. Furthermore, the discrete change in *q* that results from most natural experiments usually does not provide a good approximation to a marginal change. Kuminoff and Pope suggest that in many cases, *ATT* is better interpreted as a capitalization rate rather than a welfare measure. Under assumptions that are unlikely to hold in most cases, this capitalization rate is equal to *AMWTP*. Thus, to some degree, quasi-experimental methods relax the assumptions needed to establish causality, but strengthen the assumptions needed to link estimates to marginal values. Like the first stage hedonic model that it is related to, quasi-experimental approaches also cannot provide more than approximations for the welfare effects of discrete changes in *q*. Thus it is difficult to pick a winner among experimental and structural approaches to using property values to measure non-market values. Both have important roles to play and both are likely to continue to be at the forefront of research using property value data.

18.6   SUMMARY

The literature on using property values to infer values for environmental goods is enormous, and as the previous two sections suggest, it continues to grow. The basic idea that the large and consequential purchase of a residential location ought to reveal something about consumer preferences for the surrounding environment is compelling enough to have supported a continuously active research agenda over multiple decades. If anything, interest in property value approaches has intensified as researchers have pursued structural and quasi-experimental alternatives to the traditional hedonic model. This expanding interest has been enabled by the increasing availability (particularly in the United States) of high-quality, spatially explicit data on property sales and landscape characteristics.

Four general lessons have emerged from our discussion in this chapter. First, the hedonic model is well-suited for examining the marginal willingness to pay for an environmental good as it relates to residential services. The data requirements for the first stage hedonic model are comparatively mild, and the economic assumptions needed to link estimates to a consistent concept of value are generally plausible. To a large degree, these two features explain why applications of the model are ubiquitous in environmental economics. Nonetheless, recent research from an experimentalist perspective has expressed doubt about the econometric assumptions needed for identification in many first stage hedonic applications. In particular, concern about omitted variables in cross-sectional regressions has motivated a quasi-experimental approach to estimating the relationship between home prices and environmental quality. This literature has encouraged a greater emphasis on identification in first stage hedonic models generally – from both experimental and non-experimental perspectives – and thereby helped cement the model as one of the workhorses of non-market valuation.

Second, the first stage hedonic model is limited in the extent to which it can provide information on the value of discrete changes in an environmental good. This is a non-trivial concern, since most environmental policy involves discrete rather than small adjustments in environmental quality. To conduct valuation of discrete changes within the hedonic model, a second stage regression is needed that recovers estimates of households' inverse demand curves. This aspect of the hedonic model, however, has proved difficult to make operational. As a result, researchers have investigated alternative approaches based on discrete choice models. This research has taken a structural perspective that focuses on individual household location decisions. Direct parameterizations of household utility functions are estimated by observation of the price and property attribute trade-offs people make in selecting a place to live. Standard discrete choice models can recover utility function estimates, while the newer sorting models also characterize the price equilibrium arising out of households' behavior. These structural approaches have considerable appeal, in that discrete change welfare analysis can be readily conducted using the tools that are familiar from other RUM model applications. However, more in the way of assumptions relative to the hedonic model are needed to realize these advantages, and the extent to which the structural approaches provide better data-driven inferences remains an area of active research.

Third, welfare measurement concepts in property value models are complicated by the ability of homeowners to move in response to environmental or other shocks, and the fact that the price equilibrium in the landscape can shift due to shocks and households' relocation. To some extent this affects all facets of valuation. For marginal changes in an amenity it is usually reasonable to assume a stable equilibrium, and so marginal willingness to pay is in principle easy to measure. However, many identification strategies – particularly the experimental approaches – rely on large spatial and temporal extents of the market and comparatively large changes in the amenity to estimate the price/quality gradient. In such cases, the empirical estimate may not relate well to the concept of value implied by the theoretical model. For discrete change welfare analysis, one must assume a stable equilibrium, predict a new equilibrium, or rely on bounding arguments of unknown quality. Traditional hedonic models do not readily accommodate prediction of a new equilibrium. While the sorting models do provide this capability, they do so for quite specific parameterizations that may or may not be a good approximation of reality. Thus, for many reasons, discrete change welfare analysis remains challenging in property value applications.

Finally, analysis of property values in environmental economics provides a good example of the general debate in applied economics of the relative merits between structural and reduced form approaches. Our discussion makes clear that both approaches have their strengths and weaknesses, and that it is difficult to unequivocally say that one is better than the other. Rather, our sense is that studying this debate is tremendously informative, regardless of one's ultimate persuasion. Indeed, we advise that attention to the source of identification in empirical models should always be discussed and made explicit, even when structural assumptions based on a reasonable model of behavior are perhaps valid means of getting more out of the data.

18.7 FURTHER READING

There are many treatments in the general and environmental economics literature of the theory and econometrics of hedonic property value models. In this chapter we have relied heavily on the conceptual discussion from Bockstael and McConnell (2007) in describing the theory, and Palmquist (1991, 2005b) and Taylor (2003) for the econometrics. Our treatment of quasi-experimental methods draws heavily on Parmeter and Pope (2012), who discuss this class of econometric model in the context of property values. Kuminoff et al. (2013) provide a review of sorting models in the housing market context that includes discussion of environmental, urban, and public economic applications. Timmins and Schlenker (2009) review the general debate between reduced form and structural modeling approaches in environmental economics.

There are a large number of papers addressing specific methodological topics related to property values in environmental economics. Cropper et al. (1988) present an influential discussion of functional form choices for first stage hedonic models; their analysis has been updated and expanded by Kuminoff et al. (2010). Roback (1982) is an often-cited paper that focuses on how local amenities capitalize into both property and labor markets. Bajari et al. (2012) address the issue of consistent estimation in the presence of both time-fixed and time-varying unobserved determinants of prices, when the objective is to recover the implicit price of air pollution. Bell and Bockstael (2000) examine estimation approaches for models with spatial lags and spatially correlated errors. Additional references on topics specific to first stage hedonic models are shown in Table 18.1.

A sampling of recent empirical studies examining environmental impacts in housing markets includes Taylor et al. (2016), Currie et al. (2015), Mastromonaco (2015), and Gamper-Rabindran and Timmins (2013) for hazardous waste; Gopalakrishnan and Klaiber (2014) and Muehlenbachs et al. (2015) for proximity to mining activity; and Bento et al. (2015) and Bajari et al. (2012) for air quality. Other examples of amenities/disamenities that have been studied include flood risk (Bin and Landry, 2013), noise (Pope, 2008a), protected landscapes (Gibbons et al., 2014), and water quality (Phaneuf et al., 2008).

As noted above, studies implementing second stage estimation are rare. Examples include Zabel and Kiel (2000), Boyle et al. (1999), and Chattopadhyay (1999). Several influential papers have discussed the econometric problems involved with estimating the second stage hedonic model. Examples include Brown and Rosen (1982), Bartik (1987a, 1987b), and Mendelsohn (1985). See also the papers cited in Chapter 15. Recent examples of papers focused on second stage hedonic topics include Bajari and Benkard (2005), Heckman (2010), Kuminoff and Pope (2012), and Zhang et al. (2015).

In lieu of second stage hedonic models, sorting models have recently been used to quantify preferences for local environmental amenities. Key methodological contributions include Epple and Sieg (1999), Sieg et al. (2004), and Bayer et al. (2007). Example applications include Bayer et al. (2009) and Hamilton and Phaneuf (2015) for air quality, and Klaiber and Phaneuf (2010) for open space.

EXERCISES

The property value database *wake_exercise* is available for download on the book's website, along with documentation on the variables. Versions of these data were analyzed by

Phaneuf et al. (2008) and Pope (2008a), among others. The file holds records of sales of 38,817 single family homes in Wake County, NC, during 1998 and 1999. The following empirical exercises make use of these data.

18.1 * Familiarize yourself with the database by examining summary statistics, data plots, and basic regressions. In particular, use ordinary least squares to estimate the parameters of the baseline model

$$\ln p_i = \beta_0 + \beta_1 \times living\_area_i + \beta_2 \times baths_i + \beta_3 \times age_i$$
$$+ \beta_4 \times fireplace_i + \beta_5 \times garage\_area_i + \sum_{k=A}^{C} \beta_{6k} condk_i + \varepsilon_i.$$

Interpret your estimates. According to this regression, what is the marginal implicit price of an additional square foot of living area?

18.2 ** The Wake County database contains a variable *lakedist*, which measures the distance (in hundreds of meters) from the property to the nearest lake. Consider using this variable to proxy the value of access to lake-based amenities by including it in a first stage hedonic regression.

(a) Examine specifications that add *lakedist* and the natural log of *lakedist* to the baseline specification. Interpret the coefficient estimates and report the sample mean prediction for marginal willingness to pay for access to a lake. Does the functional form for distance matter?

(b) This specification includes no variables that account for other spatial aspects, such as school quality, access to employment centers, or access to other landscape amenities. How might this affect the estimates of the implicit price of lake access?

(c) Using the level distance variable, examine regressions that first add a control for commuting time (*median_commute*), and then spatial fixed effects (submarket dummy variables *zone1*,...,*zone18*). How does this affect your coefficient and marginal implicit price estimates?

(d) We might hypothesize that lake proximity is a highly local driver of home prices, in which case we would no longer expect to see an economically significant effect on property values beyond a certain distance or cutoff point. With this as motivation, Phaneuf et al. (2008) use a transformation of distance given by

$$tr\_dist_i = \max \left\{ 1 - \left(\frac{lakedist_i}{maxd} \right)^{1/2}, 0 \right\},$$

where *maxd* is a hypothesized cutoff distance. Note that $0 \le lakedist \le 1$, and that if $lakedist_i > maxd$ the variable codes to zero. Since *tr_dist* is a decreasing function of *lakedist* we expect a positive sign when it is included in the regression. Examine a regression that includes this transformed variable for $maxd = 10$ (i.e. 1 km). What is the average implicit price of distance for homes that are less than 1 km away from a lake? Note that you do not want to calculate the marginal implicit price of *tr_dist* per se, but instead want to consider the marginal effect of *lakedist* operating through the non-linear transformation.

CHAPTER 19

Stated Preference Methods

In Chapter 14 we established the conceptual basis for non-market valuation and defined what we referred to as the fundamental challenge of welfare measurement. In particular, we noted that the absence of observable demand behavior for most environmental and other public goods requires additional assumptions or extra-market information to measure their value. Up to this point in Part III of the book we have focused on additional assumptions as a solution to the fundamental challenge. We have seen that in many instances, assertions about the relationship between the environmental or public good and a related private commodity can be used to link behavioral functions, which are estimable from actual behavior, to values for environmental goods. Examples of this type of revealed preference approach were discussed in Chapter 17 for recreation and Chapter 18 for property markets.

In this chapter, we turn our attention to an alternative strategy that uses surveys to obtain the data needed for welfare measurement. Stated preference (SP) methods use information on how respondents say they would behave in carefully constructed hypothetical situations, and so in contrast to revealed preference (RP) methods, there is no need to observe actual behavior. Stated preference methods are in fact quite general and have been used for decades in a variety of social science fields. Carson and Louviere (2011, p.541) present a definition that is almost a tautology when they note that "a stated preference survey is a survey that asks agents questions that embody information about preferences". Seen in this light, familiar classes of surveys used in marketing (which of these would you buy?) and political polling (who will you vote for?) are examples of stated preference applications. Our interest is specifically in stated preference valuation methods in which answers to questions lead directly or indirectly to measures of economic value for a commodity that is being studied.

Stated preference valuation surveys in environmental economics typically focus on a well-defined environmental commodity, and usually present questions using one of the following three stylized formats, where B denotes an amount of money:

- *Would you be willing to pay $B to have this improvement in resource quality?*
- *Which from among the following three resource quality and cost combinations would you select?*
- *How would your use of the resource change if the quality was improved to this level?*

As we discuss in greater detail below, these are examples of contingent valuation, discrete choice experiment, and contingent behavior questions, respectively. All three are designed to quantify a trade-off between a change in resource quality and some aspect of the person's constraint set. If value elicitation questions in SP surveys are incentive compatible in the sense that people answer accurately and truthfully, they provide the basis for estimating preference functions and non-market values for the environmental good.

If incentive compatibility holds, then SP methods have several attractive features. Most importantly, SP methods allow researchers to expand the range of variability in environmental and economic variables, beyond what is observed at baseline conditions. The importance of this cannot be overstated. For many environmental goods there is little variation in the conditions people face at the status quo, and hence little variability in how people respond to different provision levels. For example, all the visitors to a particular lake at a particular time experience the same water quality, and so we cannot observe behavior over a range of quality conditions without expanding the temporal or spatial dimension of the problem. Indeed some people who do not visit the lake at current conditions may do so if quality was better, but nature does not provide the means to test this. Furthermore, for many environmental goods, it is difficult to observe interactions with private behavior at any useful frequency. For example, while the willingness among people to invest public funds in protecting endangered species can be inferred via a referendum on a specific proposal, such things are not often put to the ballot. With SP methods we can mimic a referendum, vary the level of an environmental commodity, present different provision prices to different households, and control the institutional environment in which decisions are made – all without having to depend on chance or natural variability to provide these things. Finally, when nonuse value – which we define below – needs to be measured, SP is the only approach available to researchers.

When RP methods are feasible there may still be subtle advantages to an SP approach. Reliance on observational outcomes in RP models means we have to be concerned about confounders in the data that may make identification difficult, and any inference is conditional on the specific institutional features of the market from which the data are drawn. In contrast, SP methods provide the analyst with the ability to experimentally design the variability and institutional features she needs for her valuation task. Thus, conditional on our ability to secure accurate answers via a survey, threats to econometric identification ought to be smaller with SP approaches than with their RP counterparts. The main disadvantage of SP approaches is their reliance on answers provided to hypothetical scenarios. For this reason, many economists are skeptical that SP methods can deliver useful information on preferences. Concerns include the belief that respondents do not consider their income and other constraints when answering questions, that they may answer strategically rather than honestly, or that they may not take the exercise seriously. Some have gone so far as to assert that the survey itself may influence or even produce the values that it seeks to measure. For many, therefore, doubts about the accuracy of an SP approach trump the potential advantages described above. For this reason stated preference methods have remained somewhat controversial, particularly outside the community of non-market valuation researchers.

Our objective in this chapter is to describe how stated preference methods are used in environmental economics, and how their accuracy has been assessed.[1] In the first section we review the different types of stated preference methods and connect the specific types of questions that are used to our underlying model of behavior. In the second section we discuss econometric models that are used to analyze stated preference data. Together these two sections, and the examples therein, provide a general sense of how SP is done in practice. Sections 19.3 and 19.4 discuss research that has been done to assess the accuracy of SP methods; we then draw on the findings from this research when we discuss best practice and experimental design for SP studies in section 19.5. Section 19.6 provides a brief discussion of combining RP and SP data sources, and section 19.7 summarizes.

19.1   STATED PREFERENCE APPROACHES

In this section our objective is to provide a general description of the three main types of stated preference methods used in non-market valuation. This allows us to introduce several of the defining features of stated preference analysis generally, including the types of resource values we can measure, and it leads naturally into a discussion of empirical models that are commonly used for stated preference data.

To begin, however, we provide a listing of the features that all SP valuation surveys share in some form, roughly in the order in which they are presented to the survey respondent. A main component of the survey is usually devoted to defining the environmental commodity. This includes describing its physical features, geographic scope, uses, threats to its quality or existence, and other relevant details. An effective survey defines the commodity with a high level of specificity in a way that is both scientifically correct and understandable to the lay respondent. Importantly, the description also includes a clear definition of the current state of the resource. Once the commodity is defined, the respondent is given information about how some aspect(s) of it can change, and how the change arises. For contingent valuation, this usually comes from an explicit government program that improves or protects the resource. Next, the respondent receives information on how changes in the commodity may affect him. In many SP scenarios, a payment for the change is proposed, and so the respondent is made aware of how the payment would be made (e.g. higher property taxes, higher electricity bill, contribution to a private foundation, higher prices for a private good). Finally, the person answers questions soliciting how he would respond to specific situations involving a trade-off between levels of the environmental commodity, and some aspect of his constraint set. It is in this final step that the various SP methods differ in what types of decisions are solicited.

It will be useful to keep in mind the analytical framework we have used throughout Part III of the book. We assume that a person has a direct utility function defined by $U(x,z,q,s)$, where x is a scalar or vector that records the quantity of a private good or

---

[1] Though our focus is environmental economics, it is worth noting that SP methods are relevant for many fields in applied economics. Thus researchers and practitioners in areas such as transportation, health, and marketing have also been key contributors to the literature.

activity related to the environmental resource, z is spending on other market goods, q is a scalar or vector reflecting the quality/quantity of the resource, and s denotes characteristics of the individual. Given income y and a scalar or vector of prices p for the private good, utility maximization leads to ordinary demand equations denoted by $x_j(p,y,q,s)$, where j indexes elements of the vector x. From this we can state the indirect utility level that a person with characteristics s receives from a given quality/price/income level as $V(p,y,q,s)$. We can also consider the expenditure minimization problem to derive the expenditure function $E(p,q,s,u)$, where u is a reference level of utility.

Finally, it is important to note at the start that stated preference methods are unique in their ability to measure *nonuse* benefits from a resource. In Chapter 15 we defined use value as the contribution of the environment to the economic benefits a person receives from consuming a related private good. We saw that this type of value only arises if there is positive consumption of the private good. In contrast, nonuse value can arise if a person benefits from an environmental commodity, without directly interacting with it.

Recall from Chapter 14 that compensating variation (CV) for an increase in q from q^0 to q^1 is given by

$$CV = E(p, u^0, q^0) - E(p, u^0, q^1), \tag{19.1}$$

where we have suppressed s to reduce clutter. To formally define nonuse value, we return to the analysis from Chapter 15. Specifically, in proposition 15.1 we noted that

$$E\left[\bar{p}(q^0), u^0, q^0\right] - E\left[\bar{p}(q^1), u^0, q^1\right] = 0 \tag{19.2}$$

must hold for the change in the area behind a related private good's compensated demand function to equal CV, where $\bar{p}(q^k)$, $k=0,1$, is the "choke" price driving consumption of the related private good to zero. We will refer to the expression on the left-hand side in (19.2) as NUV, for *nonuse value*. Inspection of (19.2) shows that both expenditure levels are computed for the case when there is no consumption of the private good. Therefore, $NUV>0$ implies that value is generated by the improvement in q even in the absence of the use of x. The ramification of this is best seen by rearranging Eq. (15.7) in Chapter 15 so that

$$\begin{aligned} CV &= a + E\left[\bar{p}(q^0), u^0, q^0\right] - E\left[\bar{p}(q^1), u^0, q^1\right], \\ &= UV + NUV, \end{aligned} \tag{19.3}$$

where $a = UV$ is the change in the use value for q, and NUV is the change in the nonuse value associated with q. Thus, for pedagogical purposes, we can think of the value of an environmental resource as potentially consisting of both use and nonuse value.

There are several reasons that nonuse value could be nonzero. One example is the fact that people may have a positive willingness to pay to preserve endangered species that they are unlikely to ever encounter in the wild or even see in a zoo. Another is the benefit a person receives from government efforts to preserve his country's ecological heritage through a system of national parks, even if he himself never intends to visit one of the parks. In these cases economic value is generated by aspects of a person's preferences that might relate to bequest motives, the desire to preserve a future option to use the resource, or simply knowing the resource exists. The common thread in these examples is that economic value exists, but for practical purposes no observable actions accompany or reflect it. Therefore, when the objective is to measure values for natural resources that include the various types of passive use values, a stated preference of the types described below is usually the only option.

19.1.1 Contingent Valuation Method

The contingent valuation method (CVM) is an approach that is designed to solicit a person's value for an environmental commodity, often without reference to a specific behavior or use of the resource. Its virtue is its conceptual simplicity. After presentation of the environmental commodity, its baseline condition, a program or scenario that changes something about the commodity, and the means of payment, the person answers a question about how much he would be willing to pay or willing to accept for the change. In what follows we frame our discussion in willingness to pay terms, since this is the most commonly used format.

The way that a survey asks the willingness to pay question is particularly important, and there are many strategies that have been used to solicit a person's valuation within the CVM. The strategies that we discuss here include: (a) open ended, (b) payment card, (c) dichotomous choice (single binary choice), and (d) double-bounded dichotomous choice.

The *open-ended* format is straightforward to explain, since the person is simply asked to state the maximum amount he would be willing to pay to have a proposed change. If he answers truthfully (a point to which we return in section 19.3), the person's response provides a direct estimate of his willingness to pay, defined formally as the compensating variation (*CV*) in

$$V(p, y - CV, q^1, s) = V(p, y, q^0, s), \tag{19.4}$$

where q^1 is the improved level of quality, and q^0 is the baseline level of quality. An advantage of the open-ended format is that responses can be directly compared across individuals with different income and socio-economic characteristics. A disadvantage is that it places survey respondents in an unfamiliar context. Consumers are generally accustomed to judging a posted price rather than naming the price they would pay, and so the cognitive burden of responding to this format can be high.

Payment card and dichotomous choice formats were designed to limit the cognitive burden on survey takers of the open-ended format. In a typical *payment card* approach, the respondent is shown a card containing a range of money values. He selects the option corresponding to his maximum willingness to pay, or answers "yes" and "no" to several possible bids presented on the card.

In the *dichotomous choice* format, the person is presented with a single price for a change in the environmental commodity, and simply asked to respond yes or no. A stylized version of this format involves a question such as *"would you be willing to pay $B to have the improved level of the resource?"* where *B* is the presented bid amount that is varied across individuals. This format places respondents in a familiar decision context – i.e. responding to a posted price – and therefore minimizes the cognitive burden of answering. As we discuss below, in some circumstances it also has favorable incentive properties. These two features have caused the dichotomous choice format to be the most widely used value elicitation method in CVM surveys. Among our four options, however, it provides the smallest amount of information on willingness to pay. In particular, if the person answers yes to the question we only know that $CV \geq B$, and if he answers no we can only conclude that $CV < B$. From the definition of compensating variation (see Chapter 14), these can be equivalently written as

$$
\begin{aligned}
y - E(p, q^1, s, u^0) &\geq B \\
y - E(p, q^1, s, u^0) &< B,
\end{aligned}
\tag{19.5}
$$

where u^0 is the baseline level of utility, and the first expression holds for a "yes" answer and the second for a "no." Finally, we can also conclude from the person's answer that one of the following holds:

$$
\begin{aligned}
V\left((y - B), q^1, s\right) &\geq V(y, q^0, s) \\
V\left((y - B), q^1, s\right) &< V(y, q^0, s),
\end{aligned}
\tag{19.6}
$$

where again the first expression is consistent with a "yes" answer and the second is implied by a "no."

A *double-bounded dichotomous choice* format is an extension of the single binary choice. After the person responds to the initial bid, he is presented with a follow-up question. If the initial answer was "yes" the bid is higher, and if the initial answer was "no" the bid is lower. Under this approach, the person ultimately responds to two bid amounts, B^1 and B^2, where the superscripts 1 and 2 denote the bids faced on the initial and follow-up questions, respectively. Use of a follow-up question provides additional information of the following form:

- $B^1 \leq CV < B^2$ for a yes-no response
- $B^1 > CV \geq B^2$ for a no-yes response
- $CV \geq B^2$ for a yes-yes response
- $CV < B^2$ for a no-no response.

EXAMPLE 19.1 (EMPIRICAL) To provide an example of contingent valuation in practice, we use a study undertaken by Phaneuf et al. (2013[2]; see also Van Houtven et al., 2014) to measure the non-market value of lake water quality in the southeastern United States. Specific interest centered on nitrogen and phosphorus pollution with the objective of measuring (a) how the general population valued lake water quality for any purpose, and (b) how visitors to lakes valued water quality for recreation purposes. Lake water quality q was defined over five levels such that $q \in (A, \ldots, E)$, where $q = A$ corresponds to the best lake water quality and $q = E$ corresponds to the worst. Table 19.1 provides a summary

---

[2] www.epa.gov/sites/production/files/2015-10/documents/final-report-stated-preferences-surveys.pdf

Table 19.1 Abbreviated water quality descriptions from Phaneuf et al. survey

CATEGORY	A	B	C	D	E
COLOR	Blue	Blue/brown	Brown/green	Brown/green	Green
CLARITY	Can see 5 feet deep or more	Can see 2–5 feet deep	Can see 1–2 feet deep	Can see at most 1 foot deep	Can see at most 1 foot deep
FISH	Abundant game fish and a few rough fish	Many game fish and a few rough fish	Many rough fish and a few game fish	A few rough fish but no game fish	A few rough fish but no game fish
ALGAE BLOOMS	Never occur	Small areas near shore; some years, 1–2 days	Small areas near shore; most years, 1 week	Large areas near shore; once a year, 2–3 weeks	Large, thick areas near shore; every year, most of summer
ODOR	No unpleasant odors	1–2 days a year, faint odor	1–2 days a year, faint odor	3–4 days a year, noticeable odor	Several days a year, noticeable odor

Source: Authors' files.

of how these qualitative levels were linked to descriptions of physical and perceptible water quality dimensions for lakes in the region. Baseline quality levels in much of the study region are between $q = B$ and $q = C$.

Contingent valuation was used to measure the willingness to pay among residents of individual states, for statewide improvements in lake water quality. The environmental commodity for the CVM question was defined as the distribution of lake water quality levels within the person's home state, expressed as the proportion of the state's lakes falling into each of the five categories shown in Table 19.1. The survey was conducted via an online protocol, and in the CVM section respondents received information of the following type (abbreviated, and presented here without specific context or supporting graphics):

Information about water quality at public lakes is often collected and reported by state agencies. This information can be used to show the percentage of lakes in North Carolina that are in each of the five water quality categories:

- *5% (1 out of every 20 lakes) are in category A*
- *15% (3 out of every 20 lakes) are in category B*
- *55% (11 out of every 20 lakes) are in category C*
- *20% (4 out of every 20 lakes) are in category D*
- *5% (1 out of every 20 lakes) are in category E.*

Imagine that state agencies in charge of water resources in North Carolina are considering a program to improve lake water quality. If the program is implemented it is expected that water quality throughout the state would improve such that

- *10% (2 out of every 20 lakes) are in category A*
- *25% (5 out of every 20 lakes) are in category B*
- *50% (10 out of every 20 lakes) are in category C*
- *15% (3 out of every 20 lakes) are in category D*
- *0% (0 out of every 20 lakes) are in category E.*

The changes required by the program would have a cost for all North Carolina house-holds. Some of the basic things people spend money on would become more expensive. For example, for homeowners, water bills or costs for maintaining septic systems would go up. For renters, rent or utility bills would go up. Imagine that for households like yours, starting next year, the program would permanently increase your cost of living by $B per year.

In the online version of the survey, respondents viewed a graphical representation of the baseline and counterfactual distributions of water quality in their state. The bid amount B was randomly assigned to the respondent from the collection of possible levels $B \in (24, 120, 216, 360)$. Note that this question is designed to solicit the total value for lake water quality, including any nonuse values that might underlie a person's response. The payment vehicle is a general increase in the cost of living in the person's home state, expressed at the annual level, which was presented as unavoidable by the household, should the program go forward. A dichotomous choice value elicitation format was used, whereby respondents voted "yes" or "no" on a hypothetical referendum to launch the program.

19.1.2 Discrete Choice Experiments

A discrete choice experiment (DCE) is a stated preference method in which survey respondents report their preferences by selecting a favored option from among a discrete set of alternatives. The defining feature of a DCE is that the choice elements are described by a finite number of attributes that can take on different levels. That is, the commodity is characterized by a bundle of individual attributes. The specific choice alternatives are distinguished by different levels of the attributes, and a choice task involves selecting from among two or more alternatives that differ in their attribute levels. In most cases, respondents complete multiple-choice tasks as part of the survey.

DCEs can be viewed as an alternative elicitation technique under the more general contingent valuation method rather than a separate category of SP approach. Indeed, the distinction between the two formats is somewhat artificial, and it has been suggested by Carson and Louviere (2011) that we update our nomenclature to reflect this. We agree with this sentiment, and urge readers to avoid seeing DCEs as conceptually unique, vis-à-vis contingent valuation. Nonetheless, for organizational purposes, it is useful to distinguish the survey design, analysis methods, and model interpretations that are used in the DCE format, and so we describe DCEs separately from the other contingent valuation sections.

As an example of a simple choice experiment, the Phaneuf et al. (2013) lake water quality study included a scenario in which the commodity was a lake that a person might visit for recreation. Each lake was characterized by two explicitly designed attributes – the travel time from the person's home and its water quality – and respondents selected their preferred destination from two lakes with different travel time/quality configurations. Figure 19.1 provides a stylized example of the type of question used in the online survey. A second, richer example is the DCE described in Mansfield et al. (2008). The objective of this study was to examine preferences for winter recreation visits to Yellowstone National Park in the United States. The commodity was a winter visit to the park, which was defined via the following attributes: activity, entrance point, guide status,

		LAKE 1	LAKE 2
WATER QUALITY	WATER QUALITY CATEGORY	**C**	**B**
	COLOR	Brown/green	Blue/brown
	CLARITY	Can see 1–2 feet deep	Can see 2–5 feet deep
	FISH	Many rough fish and a few game fish	Many game fish and a few rough fish
	ALGAE	Small areas near shore; most years, 1 week	Small areas near shore; some years, 1–2 days
	ODOR	Faint odor, 1–2 days a year	Faint odor, 1–2 days a year
ONE-WAY DISTANCE FROM YOUR HOME		[40-minute drive]	[120-minute drive]
Which lake would you choose? (check one box)		☐ LAKE 1	☐ LAKE 2

Figure 19.1   Example DCE question from Phaneuf et al. survey
Source: Authors' files.

snowmobile traffic, park road conditions, snowmobile noise and exhaust levels, and cost. Figure 19.2 provides an example of the question format used in the mail survey. An advantage of the DCE elicitation format is that it allows the analyst to individually examine and value the attributes that define the commodity.

Discrete choice experiments do not provide a direct estimate of the monetary value of the resource. Instead, they provide information on how the person ranks the available alternatives. In Figure 19.1, a person selects from two alternatives (labeled 1 and 2) that differ in their water quality level and travel time; a follow-up question asks if the person would make a trip or do something else, given these are his only options. In selecting his preferred alternative, a person provides a partial ranking of the utility levels associated

22. CHOICE 1: Which do you prefer—Trip A, Trip B or "Not Visit"?

Please check ONE box at the bottom of the table to indicate whether you prefer Trip A, Trip B or Not Visit. If you choose Trip A or Trip B, write the number of days you spend on a trip doing only that activity.

Note that we shaded the boxes that are the same for both trips. The conditions and prices described in this question may be different than what the parks are like today.

		Trip A	Trip B	Not Visit
Activity		Take a guided snowcoach tour to see park sights in Yellowstone starting at the South entrance (near Flagg Ranch)	Take an unguided snowmobile trip in Yellowstone starting from the West entrance (near West Yellowstone)	**I would not enter Yellowstone or Grand Teton National Park if these were my only choices**
Conditions during trip	Daily snowmobile traffic at the entrance where you started	High (800 to 1,500 snowmobiles)	Moderate (300 to 600 snowmobiles)	
	Snowmobile traffic at most crowded part of the trip	High (800 to 1,500 snowmobiles)	Moderate (300 to 600 snowmobiles)	
	Condition of snow on the road or trail surface for all or most of the trip	Smooth	Bumpy and rough	
	Highest noise level experienced on trip	Loud (Like a gas-powered lawn mower or a busy highway)	Loud (Like a gas-powered lawn mower or a busy highway)	
	Exhaust emission levels	Very noticeable	Very noticeable	
	Total Cost for DAY per person	$230	$50	
I would choose... (check only one)		☐ If you planned a trip doing just this activity, how many days would you spend on the trip?_____days	☐ If you planned a trip doing just this activity, how many days would you spend on the trip?_____days	☐ go to Question 22b below

22b. Answer this question if you chose "Not Visit": What would you likely do instead?

☐ Stay at home; I would not travel to the Greater Yellowstone Area.

☐ Travel to the Greater Yellowstone Area to cross-country ski outside the Parks.

☐ Travel to the Greater Yellowstone Area to downhill ski at Big Sky or one of the ski areas near Jackson Hole.

☐ Other, please describe activity_____

location _____

Figure 19.2 Example DCE Question from Mansfield et al. survey
Source: Authors' files.

with each alternative. For example, if the person indicates that 2 is his preferred alternative and he would make a trip rather than stay home, we can infer that

$$V(y - p_2, q_2, s) \geq V(y - p_1, q_1, s),$$
$$V(y - p_2, q_2, s) \geq V(y, s),$$

(19.7)

where p_j is the monetized value of travel time and the "something else" option is not a function of water quality. That is, the person's utility from 2 is higher than what he would get by not making a trip, or from the price/quality level given by 1. Note, however, that we cannot make any statements concerning the ranking of alternative 1 to the no-trip alternative. As we discuss in the next section, choices of this type allow us to use the discrete choice econometric methods described in Chapter 16 to estimate the parameters of $V(\cdot)$ and conduct welfare analysis.

EXAMPLE 19.2 (EMPIRICAL) As noted, the Phaneuf et al. (2013) study included a DCE section that recreation users of lakes in the southeastern US completed using the qualitative rankings shown in Table 19.1. In particular, respondents were presented with an online version of the following:

Sometime next summer, the weather forecast for the weekend looks good so you begin thinking about a day trip *to enjoy your favorite lake recreation activity. On each of the next few screens, you will be asked to compare two lakes and to select the one you would most likely visit. In each case, please imagine that the two lakes are your* only *options for the day trip. The* only *differences between these two lakes are the travel time and water quality; otherwise they are exactly the same in every other way.*

After this prompting, people answered eight questions of the type shown in Figure 19.1. Later in the chapter, we discuss analysis methods that are used to estimate utility function parameters with this type of data.

19.1.3 Contingent Behavior

The final class of SP method that we define asks people to report what their behavior would be in a given situation, generally relative to their actual or stated behavior at the status quo. For example, in the Phaneuf et al. survey respondents were asked to report the number of visits they made to specific lakes in their area during the previous year, which provides a revealed preference data point on visitation behavior at the status quo quality conditions. Though the study did not do so, a follow-up question could have asked people about their expected visits to local lakes in the next season, and how this would change if water quality conditions at the lakes became better or worse. Answers to questions like these provide a second and third data point on visitation behavior, which can be used to measure the effect of a quality change away from the status quo. Thus, we have observations of behavior (one actual, two contingent) for a person with characteristics s that correspond to the behavioral functions $x_j(p^0,y,q^0,s)$ and $x_j(p^1,y,q^1,s)$, where the superscript 1 indicates the new conditions, 0 indicates the status quo, and j indexes the specific lake that the person is asked about. With these three data points available for a sample of people, it is possible to estimate how trip demand changes with changes in water quality, even without actual variability in quality at the status quo. Contingent behavior (CB) is often employed in situations when an RP approach is theoretically possible but not practical, usually due to insufficient variability in the environmental conditions that exist in nature. As such, the CB approach provides the variation needed to estimate behavioral functions that in other circumstances might have been estimated using RP data only.

19.2   EMPIRICAL MODELS FOR STATED PREFERENCE DATA

SP methods all share the feature that respondents report something about their preferences by responding to survey questions. The elicitation methods described in the previous section differ in how the choices they record link to the preference function. We saw that in most cases, a person's answers do not provide a point estimate of his value for the resource. Instead, the data that are generated need to be filtered through an empirical model that rationalizes the person's answers according to a theoretically consistent econometric specification. Estimation of the model's parameters provides a characterization of the relevant preference or behavioral function, which can then be used to predict non-market values. In this sense, analysis of stated preference data often occurs in two steps: the survey data are used to estimate an econometric model, and then the estimated model is used to predict non-market values. In this section we focus on empirical models for estimation and welfare calculation in the binary choice CVM and DCE elicitation contexts; models for contingent behavior tend to be specific to the behavior under analysis, and therefore are more similar to the RP econometric models described in previous chapters. Since the literature on the econometrics of SP data is enormous, our coverage of specific CVM and CDE models is by necessity limited. Our objective is to present models that demonstrate how SP-generated variability is used to estimate specific types of model parameters, and how parameters in the different model types are interpreted and used for welfare analysis.

19.2.1 Binary Choice

The binary choice elicitation format is the dominant paradigm in contingent valuation, and so we focus on describing models for this type of data. Two basic strategies for data analysis exist: the utility function approach as described by Hanemann (1984b) and the expenditure function approach from Cameron and James (1987).

Hanemann Model

For Hanemann's model, we take (19.6) as our starting point and assume that the binary choice response reflects a comparison between two utility levels. Given this, the random utility maximization (RUM) model described in Chapter 16 provides the underlying basis for analysis. Recall that the RUM model begins with a specification for the utility that is available from each alternative, where the utility function consists of an observable component, and a component that is unknown to the researcher but known to the decision-maker. In the binary choice CVM context, the utility available to person i from the two alternatives is

$$V_{i1}(y_i - B_i, q_1, s_i, \varepsilon_{i1}) = v_{i1}(y_i - B_i, q_1, s_i) + \varepsilon_{i1}$$
$$V_{i0}(y_i, q_0, s_i, \varepsilon_{i1}) = v_{i0}(y_i, q_0, s_i) + \varepsilon_{i0},$$

$$(19.8)$$

where the subscript 1 denotes the counterfactual scenario and subscript 0 denotes the status quo. In (19.8), B_i is the bid amount that was presented to person i in the survey, $v(\cdot)$ is a parametric specification for the observable component of utility, and ε_{ij} is a random variable with known distribution, such as normal or extreme value for the binary probit and logit models, respectively. In either case, we assume the person answers "yes" if and only if $V_{i1}(\cdot) \geq V_{i0}(\cdot)$. It is convenient to express this condition for a "yes" answer as the utility difference

$$
\begin{aligned}
v_{i1}(y_i - B_i, q_1, s_i) + \varepsilon_{i1} &\geq v_{i0}(y_i, q_0, s_i) + \varepsilon_{i0} \\
\varepsilon_{i0} - \varepsilon_{i1} &\leq v_{i1}(y_i - B_i, q_1, s_i) - v_{i0}(y_i, q_0, s_i) \\
\varepsilon_i &\leq v_{i1}(y_i - B_i, q_1, s_i) - v_{i0}(y_i, q_0, s_i),
\end{aligned}
\tag{19.9}
$$

where $\varepsilon_i = \varepsilon_{i0} - \varepsilon_{i1}$ is symmetric with a mean of zero, and normalized scale. From this we can see that the probability of observing a "yes" answer by person i is

$$
\Pr(yes_i) = \Pr\left[\varepsilon_i \leq v_{i1}(\cdot) - v_{i0}(\cdot)\right].
\tag{19.10}
$$

The parameters included in $v_{ij}(\cdot)$ are estimated via maximum likelihood, where the likelihood function is constructed by matching the "yes" and "no" answers contained in the sample $i = 1, \ldots, I$, to their appropriate probability expressions. Standard econometric software routines are available for this task.

To proceed with estimation, a functional form must be chosen for $v_{ij}(\cdot)$. The simplest approach is to assume that all the variables enter linearly. A stylized example of a linear specification is

$$
\begin{aligned}
v_{i1} &= \alpha + \beta(y_i - B_i) + \gamma q_1 + \eta q_1 \times s_i \\
v_{i0} &= \beta y_i + \gamma q_0 + \eta q_0 \times s_i,
\end{aligned}
\tag{19.11}
$$

where in this context s_i is a scalar variable measuring a household characteristic (e.g. the presence of children) and $(\alpha, \beta, \gamma, \eta)$ are parameters to be estimated. Note that the value of s_i and the bid amounts B_i vary over individuals, and the value of q varies between the two alternatives. It is these three sources of variability – two that arise from the experimental design and one from the population – that allow us to estimate the utility function parameters. Recall also from Chapter 16 that in the linear specification, income falls out in the utility difference and β is the marginal utility of income. Thus in the linear specification, a person's income does not affect his choices or his value for the environmental good, and the marginal utility of money is constant for all people.

Once the utility function parameters are estimated, calculating willingness to pay for the linear specification is straightforward. By definition, willingness to pay – compensating variation (*CV*) in the case of an improvement in q – is the reduction in income that leaves the person indifferent between the baseline and improved level of q. Using (19.11), *CV* is therefore defined by

$$
\alpha + \beta(y_i - CV_i) + \gamma q_1 + \eta q_1 \times s_i + \varepsilon_{i1} = \beta y_i + \gamma q_0 + \eta q_0 \times s_i + \varepsilon_{i0}.
\tag{19.12}
$$

Solving for CV we find that the value for person i of the change from q_0 to q_1 is

$$CV_i = \frac{\alpha + (\gamma + \eta s_i)\Delta q}{\beta} - \frac{\varepsilon_i}{\beta}, \tag{19.13}$$

where $\Delta q = q_1 - q_0$ and, as above, $\varepsilon_i = \varepsilon_{i0} - \varepsilon_{i1}$. This expression illustrates the important point that CV_i is a random variable from the perspective of the analyst, in that the unobserved component of preferences carries over into the formula for CV_i. A measure of central tendency is therefore needed to obtain a point estimate of CV_i. As the difference between two identically distributed random variables, ε_i has a symmetric distribution with mean zero, and so the expected compensating variation for person i is $E(CV_i) = (\alpha + (\gamma + \eta s_i)\Delta q)/\beta$. Furthermore, the median and mean of ε_i are equal due to the symmetry of its distribution, and so the median compensating variation for person i is equal to $E(CV_i)$.

EXAMPLE 19.3 (EMPIRICAL) In the Phaneuf et al. water quality study, 302 people from the southeastern US answered the version of the survey that included the question shown in example 19.1; 55 percent answered "yes" to the bid amount they were presented with. Among the respondents there were 81 people who were presented with $B = \$24$, of whom 73 percent answered yes. This falls to 51 percent, 50 percent, and 44 percent for the 78, 75, and 68 people who were presented with the bid amounts $120, $216, and $360, respectively. Using a binary logit model, the estimated parameters for the simplest possible specification are

$$v_{i1} = -0.0032 \times B_i + 0.769 \times q_i, \tag{19.14}$$
$$\phantom{v_{i1} = }(-3.31) (3.78)$$

where $q_i = 1$ indicates the program is in place, $q_i = 0$ indicates the status quo, and asymptotic t-statistics are given in parenthesis. For this specification, a typical member of the target population has expected willingness to pay for the quality improvement of 0.769/0.0032, or $241 per year. Estimates for a slightly richer specification are

$$v_{1i} = -0.0033 \times B_i + 0.648 \times q_i + 0.396 \times q_i \times recreate_i, \tag{19.15}$$
$$\phantom{v_{1i} = }(-3.42) (2.97) (1.60)$$

where $recreate_i = 1$ indicates the person has visited a lake for recreation in the past 12 months. Using conventional tests, the coefficient on the interaction term is not statistically significant, though its magnitude suggests it may be economically important, in the sense that people who visit lakes are willing to pay more for quality improvements. Specifically, from the parameter point estimates the willingness to pay for non-recreators is $196 (computed as 0.648/0.0033), while the willingness to pay for lake recreators is (0.654 + 0.384)/0.0032, or $316 per year.

Cameron Model

The Cameron expenditure function approach takes (19.5) as its starting point. Rather than interpreting a person's answer as reflecting a utility level comparison, we interpret the answer directly as a lower or upper bound on the person's willingness to pay. The link to a theoretical concept comes from recognizing that (19.5) provides a willingness to pay function that we denote $CV(y,q^0,q^1,s,u^0)$, where u^0 is the baseline level of utility. The empirical strategy is to assume a specification for $CV(\cdot)$, and estimate its parameters using the bounds implied by respondents' answers. A common empirical approach is to use an exponential specification, so that in this case our stylized specification reads

$$CV_i = \exp\left[\gamma(q_1 - q_0) + \eta s_i (q_1 - q_0) + \varepsilon_i\right], \tag{19.16}$$

where ε_i is a random variable with known distribution that again arises due to the analyst's inability to fully observe a person's preferences. Note that this specification implies there is an underlying, but unspecified, utility function giving rise to the willingness to pay function. Since each person is presented with a bid B_i, we know from his answer that $CV_i < B_i$ or $CV_i \geq B_i$. The probability of observing a "yes" answer for person i is therefore

$$\begin{aligned}
\Pr(yes_i) &= \Pr\left[CV_i \geq B_i\right] \\
&= \Pr\left[\ln CV_i \geq \ln B_i\right] \\
&= \Pr\left[\gamma(q_1 - q_0) + \eta s_i(q_1 - q_0) + \varepsilon_i \geq \ln B_i\right] \\
&= \Pr\left[\varepsilon_i \geq \ln B_i - \gamma(q_1 - q_0) - \eta s_i(q_1 - q_0)\right].
\end{aligned} \tag{19.17}$$

A common assumption when the willingness to pay function is used is to assume that $\varepsilon_i \sim N(0,\sigma^2)$, which allows us to convert the probability in (19.17) into a binary probit problem, by normalizing on the standard deviation of ε_i. In particular,

$$\begin{aligned}
\Pr(yes_i) &= \Pr\left[\frac{\varepsilon_i}{\sigma} \geq \frac{1}{\sigma}\ln B_i - \frac{\gamma}{\sigma}(q_1 - q_0) - \frac{\eta}{\sigma}s_i(q_1 - q_0)\right] \\
&= \Pr\left[\varepsilon_i^* \geq \frac{1}{\sigma}\ln B_i - \gamma^*(q_1 - q_0) - \eta^* s_i(q_1 - q_0)\right] \\
&= \Pr\left[\varepsilon_i^* \leq -\frac{1}{\sigma}\ln B_i + \gamma^*(q_1 - q_0) + \eta^* s_i(q_1 - q_0)\right],
\end{aligned} \tag{19.18}$$

where the last line follows from the symmetry of the normal distribution, and $\Pr(no_i) = 1 - \Pr(yes_i)$. Maximum likelihood estimation provides estimates of the unknown parameters γ^*, η^*, and $-1/\sigma$. Transformation of these estimates provides a characterization of the unknown parameters in (19.16).

With a characterization of the willingness to pay function in hand, welfare analysis is straightforward, in that we can directly predict the mean or median using (19.16). For example, the expected compensating variation for person i is

$$E(CV_i) = \exp\left[\gamma(q_1 - q_0) + \eta s_i(q_1 - q_0)\right] \times E\left[\exp(\varepsilon_i)\right]. \tag{19.19}$$

The random variable $\exp(\varepsilon_i)$ is log-normally distributed with a mean of $\exp(0.5\sigma^2)$, and so

$$E(CV_i) = \exp\left[\gamma(q_1 - q_0) + \eta s_i(q_1 - q_0) + 0.5\sigma^2\right]. \tag{19.20}$$

Note that for large values of σ^2, the expected value can become implausibly large. This is known as the "fat tails" problem that can occur when CV_i is log-normally distributed. The median of CV_i, in contrast, is given by $\exp(\gamma(q_1-q_0)+\eta s_i(q_1-q_0))$. Thus for the log-linear willingness to pay function, the mean and median of the distribution for CV_i differ by an adjustment factor related to the right-skewed nature of the distribution – i.e. the log-normal distribution admits strictly positive values and has a long right tail. This can lead to an unreliable estimate of the mean, when the estimated standard deviation is large.

EXAMPLE 19.4 (EMPIRICAL) We use the same 302 responses to the Phaneuf et al. water quality study referred to in example 19.3 to estimate a willingness to pay function. The simplest illustrative specification is $\ln(CV_i)=\gamma q+\varepsilon_I$, and we recover estimates (t-statistics) of the parameters $\gamma^*=1.449$ (4.05) and $1/\sigma=0.275$ (3.77). These estimates imply the transformed parameter estimate is $\gamma=(0.275)^{-1}\times1.449=5.27$. With this, we can predict the median willingness to pay in the population as $\exp(5.27)=\$194$ per year. The mean willingness to pay is $\exp(5.27+0.5\times3.63^2)$, which is inflated far above the median, due to the large standard deviation (i.e. $\sigma=3.63$). This is an example of the fat tails problems and it illustrates why the median is usually a preferred measure of central tendency for log-normal distributions.

A richer specification is $\ln(CV_i)=\gamma q+\eta\times q\times recreate_i+\varepsilon_i$, for which we recover estimates (t-statistics) of the parameters $\gamma^*=1.394$ (3.88), $\eta^*=0.240$ (1.57) and $1/\sigma=0.282$ (3.87). From these estimates we conclude that, like with the utility difference model, there is no statistically significant difference between recreators' and non-recreators' willingness to pay. Nonetheless, there may be economic differences, in that the median point estimate values for the program are \$140 for non-recreators, and \$328 for recreators.

Which Analysis Strategy?

The Hanemann and Cameron approaches to analyzing dichotomous choice data both serve to highlight the notion that a person's willingness to pay is a random variable from the perspective of the analyst. Conceptually, the stochastic feature of CV_i is inherited from the fact that preferences are incompletely known to an outside observer. Operationally, this means we are interested in understanding the distribution of willingness to pay in the population of interest. The parametric models in (19.8) and (19.16) serve as a vehicle for linking the stochastic nature of preferences to a probabilistic response model that relates to a person's survey answers. In this sense, the utility difference and willingness to pay function approaches are motivated by the same underlying model of behavior, and the same operational objective. McConnell (1990) discusses in detail how their differences are empirical, in that they imply different functional specifications for preferences and how the error term enters the specification, and so one approach is not inherently preferred. The choice will usually depend on the specifics of the study and the tastes of the analyst, and it is often useful to examine more advanced models. Haab and McConnell (2003) provide several chapters dedicated to the econometrics of dichotomous choice contingent valuation.

Double-Bounded Dichotomous Choice

Researchers recognized early on that more information can be obtained about the distribution of willingness to pay if survey participants responded to additional bid amounts. It was out of this realization that the double-bounded dichotomous choice format arose.

Analyzing data from a double-bounded elicitation format requires an important specification decision. This is best seen using the Cameron approach, with the specification shown in (19.16). In a purely statistical sense, we can think of the two binary choices as reflecting two *CV* functions, which we denote as

$$CV_i^k = \exp\left[\gamma^k(q_1 - q_0) + \eta^k s_i(q_1 - q_0) + \varepsilon_i^k\right], \quad k = 1, 2, \tag{19.21}$$

where *k* denotes the willingness to pay function attached to each binary choice. We have labeled this "purely statistical," since the underlying behavioral function should not vary with the order of the bids. Maintaining for the moment this separation we can, for example, express the probability of a yes-no answer as

$$\Pr(yes_i, no_i) = \Pr\left[CV_i^1 \geq B_i^1, CV_i^2 \leq B_i^2\right]. \tag{19.22}$$

Expressions for the remaining three answer configurations can be similarly written. If we assume that the two-dimensional random variable $(\varepsilon_i^1, \varepsilon_i^2)$ is normally distributed, the bivariate probit model arises. With this, maximum likelihood is used to estimate the structural parameters $(\gamma^1, \eta^1, \sigma_1, \gamma^2, \eta^2, \sigma_2, \rho)$, where σ_k is the standard deviation for choice *k*, and ρ is the correlation coefficient between ε_i^1 and ε_i^2.

Since the responses to the first and second bids are presumably based on the same underlying preference structure, it may make sense to constrain the specification so the underlying distributions are the same – i.e. maintain (19.16) as the specification, and use the additional bounds to specify probabilities of the form

$$\begin{aligned}
\Pr(yes_i, no_i) &= \Pr\left[B_i^2 > CV_i \geq B_i^1\right] \\
\Pr(no_i, yes_i) &= \Pr\left[B_i^2 \leq CV_i < B_i^1\right] \\
\Pr(yes_i, yes_i) &= \Pr\left[CV_i \geq B_i^2\right] \\
\Pr(no_i, no_i) &= \Pr\left[CV_i < B_i^2\right],
\end{aligned} \tag{19.23}$$

where $\gamma^1 = \gamma^2 = \gamma$ and $\eta^1 = \eta^2 = \eta$. This results in the highest level of estimation precision, but if statistical tests demonstrate that the two distributions are different, it might raise concerns about accuracy and robustness. Indeed, starting with Cameron and Quiggin (1994), researchers noted an empirical regularity with double-bounded approaches, in which the willingness to pay function for the follow-up question implied a smaller estimated value for the resource. As we discuss in section 19.3, one explanation for this is that the follow-on question is not incentive compatible, in the sense that the respondent may have strategic reasons for misrepresenting his true value during the second question. For this reason, many analysts present a follow-on bid, but use it mainly for robustness and supporting analyses rather than for primary inference. Exercise 19.2 provides an opportunity to explore this using the Phaneuf et al. (2013) data.

19.2.2 Discrete Choice Experiments

The data that are generated from discrete choice experiments fit well into the RUM paradigm from Chapter 16. In particular, when faced with a set of alternatives indexed $c = 1,...,C$ in the context of a DCE question, we assume the person selects the option that provides the highest utility. Thus the empirical model begins with a specification for the conditional indirect utility function for the set of alternatives a person faces in the experiment. For illustration, suppose the experiment includes a price attribute p and a vector of non-price attributes $q = (q^1,...,q^K)$, so that in total there are $K + 1$ attributes that define the commodity. A simple specification for the utility available to person i from selecting an alternative c is

$$V_{ic}(p_{ic}, q_{ic}, s_i, \varepsilon_{ic}) = \alpha_c + \beta(y_i - p_{ic}) + \gamma' q_{ic} + \varepsilon_{ic}, \tag{19.24}$$

where β is the marginal utility of income, γ is a K-dimensional vector of utility function parameters, p_{ic} and q_{ic} denote the designed attribute levels that define alternative c for person i, α_c captures everything about alternative c that is not explicitly described by q, and ε_{ic} is the unobserved component of utility. This is known as a *main effects specification*, and the elements of the vector γ are called the main effects since they measure the contribution to utility of an attribute independent of the level of the other attributes. A richer model is a *main and interaction effects specification*, given by

$$V_{ic}(p_{ic}, q_{ic}, s_i, \varepsilon_{ic}) = \alpha_c + \beta(y_i - p_{ic}) + \gamma' q_{ic} + \sum_{\forall k \neq j} \sum_{j=1}^{K} \delta_{kj} q_{ic}^k q_{ic}^j + \varepsilon_{ic}, \tag{19.25}$$

where the δs are called interaction effects, since they measure how the utility from an attribute depends on the levels of other attributes. The marginal utility for attribute k in this richer specification is:

$$\frac{\partial V_c(\cdot)}{\partial q^k} = \gamma^k + \sum_{j=1}^{K} \delta_{kj} q_c^j. \tag{19.26}$$

In contrast, for the main effects specification, the marginal utility of attribute k is simply γ^k. As with any RUM model, estimation of the utility function parameters proceeds based on a specific assumption for the distribution of ε_{ic}.

Equations (19.24) and (19.25) are useful for illustrating several general properties of applied DCE models. First, discrete choice experiments can be either *labeled* or *generic*. A labeled experiment presents people with alternatives that are already familiar in some way. For example, we might be interested in understanding how people value the characteristics of low-emission vehicles sold by Honda and Toyota. In this case, each alternative has a brand – the manufacturer – as well as levels for the designed attributes. Respondents are likely to have different likes and dislikes for the two brands, that are outside the control of the experiment. In a labeled experiment these are captured by different values for α_c. In a generic experiment, the alternatives are described only by the designed attributes. The Phaneuf et al. (2013) DCE described in example 19.2 is generic, in that the commodity (a lake for recreation) does not correspond to a specific named location. In a generic experiment, we assume that everything about the commodity that is not described by the designed attributes is constant across all alternatives, and survey respondents are explicitly reminded of this during the elicitation process. In the model specifications shown above, this implies $\alpha_c = \alpha$ for all the alternatives; the constant terms therefore fall out of the model upon estimation.

Second, the variability needed for estimation comes from the *experimental design*. This is the process by which the analyst selects (a) the definition and range of values that p and q can take (i.e. the attribute levels); (b) how the attribute levels are combined to create choice alternatives; and (c) how the choice alternatives are grouped to create choice tasks. An example of these decisions is shown in Figure 19.1, where two attributes were used: travel time to a lake, and water quality at the lake. For each alternative, the water quality attribute could take one of the five levels shown in Table 19.1, and the one-way travel time attribute was 20, 40, 60, or 120 minutes. The alternatives labeled 1 and 2 show two of several possible combinations of attribute levels that could define the commodity, and the Figure itself shows one possible choice task. The survey presented each respondent with six choice tasks, each of which contained two commodity configurations varying in their attribute levels. Different respondents answered different collections of choice tasks. Together the decisions on attributes, their levels, and how different combinations are presented provide the variation needed to estimate specifications such as (19.24) or (19.25). There is a large and sophisticated literature dedicated to studying the design of discrete choice experiments, which we touch on briefly in section 19.5.

Finally, DCEs provide substantial flexibility for welfare analysis. The marginal willingness to pay for a small change in attribute k is easily computed as

$$\frac{\partial V(\cdot)/\partial q^k}{\partial V(\cdot)/\partial y} = \frac{\gamma^k + \sum_{j=1}^{K} \delta_{kj} q_c^j}{\beta} \tag{19.27}$$

for the main and interaction effects specification, or simply as γ^k/β for the main effects only specification. Likewise, it is straightforward to compute the willingness to pay for a discrete change in some of the attributes. For example, with the main effects specification and a generic experiment, the per choice occasion expected willingness to pay for an improvement in the resource from a baseline denoted by q_0 to a counterfactual level q_1 is

$$E(CV_i) = \frac{\sum_{j=1}^{K} \gamma^k (q_1^k - q_0^k)}{\beta}. \tag{19.28}$$

Importantly, this assumes that everything else about the resource stays constant.

Equations (19.24) and (19.25) also illustrate the econometric issues that arise in DCE applications. Most importantly, as written, these specifications assume respondents are homogeneous in their valuation of the K attributes. Many of the econometric innovations in choice modeling focus on accounting for heterogeneity in people's preferences. A relatively simple way to account for heterogeneity is to include interactions with observable household characteristics, so that marginal utilities and marginal values are functions of these characteristics. For example, a richer version of the main effects specification in (19.24) is

$$V_{ic}(p_{ic}, q_{ic}, s_i, \varepsilon_{ic}) = a_c + \beta(y_i - p_{ic}) + \gamma' q_{ic} + \eta' q_{ic} \times s_i + \varepsilon_{ic}, \qquad (19.29)$$

where s_i is again a scalar variable measuring household characteristics, and η is a K dimensional vector of parameters. In this specification, the marginal willingness to pay for attribute k is $(\gamma^k + \eta^k s_i)/\beta$, which shows that the value of this attribute is heterogeneous, in the sense that it depends on s_i. In many instances, however, there is heterogeneity in preferences beyond what can be accounted for with measured variables. To model unobserved heterogeneity researchers have used the newer classes of discrete choice models, such as mixed logit and latent class specifications, which allow preference parameters to have a distribution in the population. See Train (2009) for a discussion of these more advanced discrete choice econometric models.

EXAMPLE 19.5 (EMPIRICAL) In the Phaneuf et al. (2013) study, 810 respondents each completed six choice tasks of the type shown in Figure 19.1; they were also given the opportunity to "opt out" of taking a trip if they did not like either of the generic lake alternatives offered. The lake water quality levels varied according to the five definitions in Table 19.1, and the one-way travel time possibilities included 20, 40, 60, and 120 minutes. For analysis, the one-way travel times were converted to round-trip travel costs using the methods from Chapter 17, whereby assumptions on the out-of-pocket costs per mile and the opportunity cost of time were used to derive dollar-based visit prices for each of the two alternatives.

In this example, we are interested in estimating main effects utility functions of the form

$$V_{ict} = \beta price_{ict} + \sum_{k=A}^{E} \gamma_k D_{ict}^k + \varepsilon_{ict}, \quad c = 1, 2$$
$$V_{i0t} = \varepsilon_{i0t}, \qquad (19.30)$$

where $c = 1, 2$ denotes the generic lakes, $c = 0$ denotes the opt-out option, $price_{ict}$ is the travel cost for person i to visit option c on choice task t (constructed from the travel time), and $D_{ict}^k = 1$ if lake c on choice task t takes quality level k, for $k = A, \ldots, E$ shown in Table 19.1. We assume that the error terms are distributed type I extreme value, so that the conditional logit model arises.

Our estimates (t-statistics) are summarized as follows:

$$V_{ict} = \underset{(-16.19)}{-0.016} price_{ict}$$
$$+ \underset{(24.82)}{2.56} D_{ict}^A + \underset{(20.56)}{1.93} D_{ict}^B + \underset{(12.48)}{0.98} D_{ict}^C + \underset{(2.21)}{0.17} D_{ict}^D - \underset{(-1.37)}{0.11} D_{ict}^E + \varepsilon_{ict}. \qquad (19.31)$$

Note that each of the coefficients on the quality level dummy variables should be interpreted relative to the opt-out option, and to each other. Thus on average, a trip to a lake with quality levels A through D is preferred to not making a trip, while not making a trip is preferred to visiting a lake with quality level E (the lowest). In addition, the estimates are such that $\gamma_A > \gamma_B > \ldots > \gamma_E$, so that conditional on travel cost, trips to higher-quality lakes are preferred over trips to lower-quality lakes.

Using a version of Eq. (19.28), we can predict the per trip willingness to pay for an improvement in quality from level k to level j as $-(\gamma_j - \gamma_k)/\beta$. This implies the following per trip average values for incremental quality improvements:

- Level E to Level D: $18.38
- Level D to Level C: $52.05
- Level C to Level B: $61.55
- Level B to Level A: $40.16

19.3   INCENTIVE PROPERTIES OF STATED PREFERENCE SURVEYS

We now turn our attention to describing research that has aimed to assess the accuracy of stated preference methods. We do this in two sections, beginning here with a discussion of what economic theory tells us about how people behave when they are asked to complete a stated preference survey. For this we use the tools of mechanism design to understand the circumstances in which we expect people to devote cognitive energy to the survey, reveal their true preferences, and in general answer the questions as the analyst intended. In section 19.4 we build on this theory to define different concepts of validity for stated preference valuation measures, and the types of approaches researchers have used to establish or refute the accuracy of different SP approaches.

Much of what we discuss in this section stems from the recent efforts by Richard Carson and colleagues to establish a theoretical framework for predicting how self-interested people ("agents") approach the task of filling out an SP survey administered by a government or other organization (the "agency"). A key concept in their framework is the extent to which a survey is viewed by respondents as consequential or inconsequential. Specifically, the following definitions are taken from Carson and Groves (2007, p.183):

Definition 19.1
A survey is consequential *if its results are seen by the agent as potentially influencing an agency's actions and the agent cares about the outcomes of those actions. In this case, the agent views the survey as an opportunity to influence the agency's decisions and hence his own welfare. In contrast, a survey is* inconsequential *if its results are not seen as having any influence on the agency's actions or if the agent is indifferent among all possible outcomes the agency might select. In this case the survey has no potential to influence the agent's welfare.*

Carson and Groves (2007) claim that when a survey is consequential, standard models of self-interested behavior apply, so that responses from agents can be interpreted using mechanism design theory that examines the incentive structures inherent in the survey questions. They further claim that economic theory has little to say about how people answer inconsequential surveys. Viewed in this light, a necessary condition for establishing that SP results are accurate is to ensure that the survey vehicle is consequential, since this suggests agents have the incentive to invest the cognitive effort needed to complete the exercise.

Once consequentiality is established, the issue becomes whether or not the agent has the incentive to answer the survey questions truthfully. To analyze this we add the following definition (Carson and Groves, p.184):

Definition 19.2

A *survey question is* incentive compatible *if a truthful response to the actual question asked constitutes an optimal strategy for the agent.*

In the following two subsections, we examine the incentive properties of CVM and DCE elicitation formats, respectively. For CVM we examine the extent to which different elicitation formats and payment vehicles cause the agent's strategic response to diverge or overlap with his preference revealing response. We continue this theme for DCE, and also examine the extent to which different information processing strategies might be optimal when respondents are faced with a cognitively difficult task.

19.3.1 Incentive Properties of CVM

We begin with the binary choice response format. Early theory on voting behavior demonstrated that certain types of referenda are incentive compatible. In particular, if the vote is a take-it-or-leave-it, binary choice over a single issue, and the majority outcome is coercive (in the sense that the population must follow its conditions and pay its costs), then the dominant voting strategy is for a person to select his preferred alternative. From this we can conclude that a binary choice CVM elicitation format can be incentive compatible if it is sufficiently similar to a single issue voting referendum. This result is the starting point for considering how incentive compatibility can be obtained in practice, given the practical constraints of a survey vehicle. Four dimensions are worth noting. First, a CVM survey may not be able to plausibly mimic a binding referendum, since the hypothetical nature shows it clearly is not. Instead, it might be more plausible to construct the survey-based vote using the language of an advisory poll, in which the likelihood of action on the part of the agency increases with the proportion of people who vote in favor. Carson and Groves cite evidence that this type of advisory referendum format is demand revealing. This is an appealing result, since a survey can be made more consequential and plausible by describing the exercise as advisory to the agency on future decisions. Second, a CVM survey uses a sample of the population rather than the full voting ranks. Since Green and Laffont (1978) show that replacing the full population with a random sample does not change the incentive properties of a mechanism, the sampling nature of a CVM survey should also not affect its incentive compatibility. Third, the advantage of SP methods generally is that they allow the researcher to expand the values for key variables outside the range that occurs naturally at the status quo. There are, however, limits to how far this can be taken. If the levels for the payment amount, the commodity, or other experimentally designed variables are viewed as being implausible by the respondent, he may implicitly substitute a value he sees as more plausible when answering. This constitutes a failure of demand revelation, because the agent has not answered the question the agency intended.

Finally, to avoid the aversion that many respondents have about tax increases or other coercive payments, researchers have on occasion used a voluntary payment vehicle – e.g.

donating voluntarily to a fund managed by a non-government organization – as a way that survey respondents pay for the proposed commodity or program. This departure from a coercive payment causes the incentive compatibility of binary choice CVM to break down, since it provides an opportunity for a type of free riding. When offered the chance to hypothetically pledge to the fund, a rational agent has incentive to do so, even if his true willingness to pay is smaller than the bid he is presented with. This is because his yes vote in a consequential survey will increase the likelihood that the actual fund-raising will take place, and he will have the opportunity to subsequently enjoy the commodity – even if in the actual event he decides not to contribute. As described by Carson and Groves, the voluntary contribution format gives agents "an incentive to over-pledge, in order to obtain the opportunity to underpay" (p.188). We summarize these properties of the single choice, binary response format in the following proposition.

Proposition 19.1

A CVM survey that is (a) consequential; (b) uses a single binary choice binding or advisory-type referendum format, with coercive payment and provision point that increases with the proportion voting yes; and (c) presents price and other variable levels that are plausible to respondents, is incentive compatible in the sense that an agent's best strategy is to answer the agency's questions truthfully.

Vossler et al. (2012) present a proof of this proposition. The favorable properties of the binary choice format as described in proposition 19.1 suggest it is the standard against which other approaches are measured. It is not without its drawbacks, however. As noted in section 19.2, the single question binary choice format provides relatively little information about preferences, and so a large sample size is usually needed to obtain statistically precise estimates. Other elicitation formats can extract more information from a respondent. Early CVM surveys used the open-ended format, for the obvious reason that it delivers the highest information content. This format, however, contributed to early skepticism about stated preference, with the supposition being that people would report unrealistically high values. Interestingly, this has often been found not to be the case. Rather, surveys contained an unusually large number of zero bids, item non-response, and protests that centered on the fact that no information was given on what the good would cost the household. Furthermore, a casual empirical regularity is that binary choice formats lead to higher estimates of value than open-ended formats. One explanation for this is that, absent any information on the actual cost to the household, the respondent makes his own guess. If his willingness to pay is smaller than his estimate of his share of the cost, his optimal strategy is to bid zero – thereby hoping to influence the agency not to provide the good. This suggests the open-ended format may be both cognitively difficult and incentive incompatible.

While the open-ended format is not often used today, other formats that are designed to extract more information from respondents often are. The best example of this is the double-bounded approach described in section 19.2, where we indicated that the second question was not incentive compatible. There are several potential explanations for why, in general, a sequence of binary choices may lead to strategic answers. The belief structure that the person forms in response to the new information contained in the follow-up question is particularly important. Carson and Groves (2007) describe several respondent belief structures that might lead to strategic answers, which include: (a) the actual cost to the household is uncertain; (b) the second price signals the agency's willingness to bargain over cost; (c) the actual cost will be a weighted average of the two prices; and (d) the change in price signals is interpreted to include a concurrent change in the quantity and/or quality. The main point is that, whatever the belief structure that is at play, the appearance of a second cost figure signals to the rational agent that something is going on, and this triggers a response to the subsequent question that is conditional on the updated information set.

19.3.2 Incentive Properties of Discrete Choice Experiments

Recall from our discussion above that DCEs typically present people with multiple-choice tasks involving comparisons between two or more alternatives. At one level it is straightforward to conclude from this that DCEs are in general not incentive compatible. For a pure public good in which all agents consume the same quantity, this stems in part from the implied provision mechanism. Consider the analogy of a three-candidate election, in which the single person who receives a plurality of votes wins. If a voter thinks his genuinely preferred candidate does not have a chance of winning, it is in his interest to vote for an alternative candidate among the set of those that do have a chance of winning. This is because a vote for his true preference cannot influence his utility, while a vote in favor of a less-preferred candidate, who could win, can have an impact on his well-being. The same logic suggests a person may not select his preferred option in a multinomial-choice experiment setting over multiple levels of a pure public good. Though he is still reporting his preferences, incentive compatibility fails because he is not providing the information the analyst intended. Things are less dire when the commodity is quasi-public, in the sense that multiple provision levels are possible. For example, in the water quality study discussed above, different actual lakes can have different quality and travel time configurations. In this case, the person does not decrease the likelihood of receiving his second-best outcome by selecting his first best, even if his favorite is unlikely to overlap with others' choices. In these types of cases incentive compatibility can hold in that the person's utility maximizing choice is to select his highest-ranked alternative.

Even for the quasi-public good case, however, incentive compatibility of DCEs may still be compromised by the use of repeated choice tasks. We noted above that multiple-choice tasks signal to the respondent that "something is going on", and under several belief structures this can lead to strategic behavior. If the person answers the multiple questions independently, then incentive compatibility is not violated in DCEs. There are, however, plausible ways that task independence may fail. For example, respondents may become better at sorting through their preferences as they move through a sequence of tasks. Alternatively, fatigue may cause the quality of answers to decrease later in the sequence. Perhaps more problematically, people may use the initial choice as a reference point when completing later tasks, causing responses to depend on the order in which choices occur. While there is evidence suggesting that ordering effects exist in DCEs (see Day et al., 2012), there is still uncertainty about the extent to which incentive incompatibility from multiple-choice tasks is an empirically relevant concern.

There is an additional incentive-related consideration with DCEs that comes from the attribute processing strategies used by respondents. By their nature, choice experiments impose a larger cognitive burden on people than other types of SP questions. The implicit assumption used to analyze DCE data is that people process and respond to all of the information provided in the survey, and all the attributes that define an alternative. There are, however, alternative information processing strategies that a rational agent might use. A survey respondent might reduce the cognitive cost of completing a sequence of tasks by ignoring certain attributes, or by focusing on a single attribute he considers most important. For example, in Figure 19.2, a respondent may base decisions only on his interest in a single activity (e.g. riding a snowmobile), and so would ignore the values for road condition, and noise and exhaust levels. Several recent empirical studies (e.g. Scarpa et al., 2010; Balcombe et al., 2011; Cameron and DeShazo, 2010) have identified different types of "attribute non-attendance" in repeated discrete choice experiment applications, and proposed methods for recovering estimates that account for respondents' different information processing strategies. These rely on direct approaches, such as asking respondents if they considered the full information set, and indirect approaches, based on using the pattern of responses to detect evidence of reduced- or non-relevance of certain attributes.

19.4 VALIDITY

We now turn our attention to the framework and tools that researchers have used to assess the validity of estimates from stated preference surveys. By validity we mean the extent to which an SP approach provides unbiased estimates of the true underlying value it is designed to measure. There is a large literature centered on the theme of stated preference validity, and the history of its development – summarized in Carson and Hanemann (2005) – is among the more interesting subplots in the story of environmental economics. For our purposes it is useful to identify the 1989 *Exxon Valdez* oil spill as the point of departure for the contemporary validity literature. Around this time, US law began to admit lost nonuse values into the damages that defending companies may be liable for in natural resource damage cases. This transformed the validity debate – particularly for contingent valuation and its ability to measure nonuse values – from an academic endeavor into a high stakes legal issue. Following the Exxon accident, the state of Alaska sought damages in the amount of $2.8 billion based mainly on lost passive use value; Exxon in return countered that only lost use values should be considered. Both sides hired consultants and funded research to argue their perspective concerning the use of CVM in the Exxon case. The competing viewpoints and early post-Exxon findings are summarized in Hanemann (1994) and Diamond and Hausman (1994).[3] This influx of attention and resources led to a large expansion of interest in stated preference research among academic economists, and helped define the research agenda for the next decade. A large part of this agenda has focused on testing – empirically, theoretically, and experimentally – the validity of SP methods.

In this section we describe the validity concepts that have been investigated, discuss the strategies used to carry out validity tests, and summarize what the literature has

---

[3] The studies used to support the damage claims are described in Carson et al. (2003) and Hausman et al. (1995).

taught us about the accuracy of stated preference methods. Four validity concepts have been used to assess the accuracy of SP estimates. Tests of *criterion validity* involve comparing an estimate obtained using SP to an observed benchmark. Tests of *convergent validity* involve comparing estimates obtained from SP to those gleaned from other sources – usually an RP method, when the valuation problem allows estimation from both perspectives. *Construct validity* involves assessing the extent to which SP estimates are consistent with theoretical predictions. Finally, *content validity* involves assessing the extent to which an SP estimate was obtained using generally accepted best practices. In what follows we discuss each of the validity concepts in turn.

19.4.1 Criterion Validity

By definition, non-market values that we use SP to measure are not directly observable. Tests of criterion validity have therefore relied on indirect means of establishing a value, to which the estimated SP value is compared. Typically this has been done using experiments (both laboratory and field), though in some instances, SP surveys have been fielded prior to an actual preference-revealing local referendum. One style of laboratory experiment uses an induced value approach in which participants are assigned an individual value for a public good, where both the good and its value to subjects are defined and controlled within the experimental context. In contrast to participants' actual underlying (or home grown) values, the experimentally induced value for the good is known by the researchers, and so it provides an observed criterion. A typical experiment involves multiple sessions, in which participants vote on a posted bid amount that represents their contribution to the public good. In some sessions, the vote is binding in that actual payment and provision of the good occurs; in other sessions, the vote is hypothetical. Data from the different experimental treatments allow the analyst to compare how willingness to pay distributions obtained from the real and hypothetical votes compare to the underlying distribution of induced values. If convergence in the distributions is observed, the experiment provides support for criterion validity. Evidence from induced value experiments (e.g. Murphy et al., 2010; Vossler and McKee, 2006) generally suggests that the aggregate distribution of willingness to pay obtained from a hypothetical vote is close to the distribution of experimentally designed values.

A second type of laboratory experiment uses respondents' "home grown" (actual) values. In this approach, a public good for which participants are likely to have preexperiment values, such as a tree-planting program, is introduced in an experimental setting. The criterion is the distribution of actual values held by participants for the program. These values are measured using a binding vote in the experimental session, for which payment is made and the good is provided, if a majority votes in favor. The distribution of values from the binding vote sessions is compared to the distribution of values gleaned from similar, but nonbinding hypothetical, votes. Most home grown value experiments of this type find that values obtained from the hypothetical vote are larger than those obtained from the binding vote (e.g. Cummings et al., 1995; Harrison and Rutström, 2008). This supports a finding of criterion invalidity for stated preference. The two styles of laboratory experiments – induced and home grown values – therefore provide conflicting evidence.

The limitation of laboratory experiments is that they do a poor job of mimicking the conditions under which a typical SP survey is fielded. For this reason, researchers have also used field experiments to assess the criterion validity of SP methods. One of the earliest examples of this approach is Bishop and Heberlein (1979), who recruited two samples of Wisconsin hunters holding special goose-hunting permits. One group was offered actual cash payments to relinquish their permits, while the other was offered the same, but non-binding, opportunity in a hypothetical survey. In general Bishop and Heberlein find that the hypothetical group had a higher willingness to accept than the real group. More recent field experiments have also found evidence that hypothetical elicitation leads to higher-value estimates. For example, Blumenschein et al. (2008) examine hypothetical and real sales of a diabetes management system, and find that the hypothetical willingness to pay is higher than actual willingness to pay. List (2001) conducted real and hypothetical auctions for sports memorabilia using participants at a sports card convention as subjects. He finds that the hypothetical auction leads to higher estimates of participants' willingness to pay for sports cards. A limitation of field experiments, however, is that they tend to be more feasible for private goods (e.g. hunting permits, health care, and sports cards) than for public goods, which are the usual focus in environmental economics.

To compare SP estimates to actual, rather than experimental, outcomes for public goods, researchers have on occasion fielded hypothetical surveys that were designed to mirror a subsequent binding referendum. An example of this approach is Johnston (2006), who uses a binding referendum on public water provision in a New England town as his criterion. His survey was fielded before the referendum was approved or scheduled, and it was framed as an exploratory exercise. Johnston finds a very close correspondence between his SP survey predictions and the results of the actual referendum.

Hypothetical Bias

As the examples given above suggest, many tests of criterion validity – particularly those that use home grown values for the criterion – find that non-market values obtained from hypothetical questioning are larger than their real counterparts. This phenomenon has enough empirical regularity that it has become known as *hypothetical bias*, and research has been devoted to understanding its causes, and designing mechanisms to mitigate its effect. Two bias-reducing mechanisms deserve mention. The first has become known as "cheap talk," because survey respondents are given a script that details the tendency in hypothetical situations for people to overstate what they would be willing to pay, relative to a real situation. The script also urges people to be cognizant of this when filling out the survey. Laboratory experiments by Cummings and Taylor (1999) have shown that cheap talk scripts can reduce hypothetical bias, though subsequent lab and field experiments have been less conclusive.

The second approach involves the use of certainty questions following elicitation. After answering a willingness to pay question, survey respondents are asked to rate the level of confidence that they have in their answer. This information provides the analyst with the option of down-weighting uncertain responses in estimation, or recoding uncertain yes answers to no. Evidence of how the uncertainty information can be used to mitigate hypothetical bias is provided by Champ et al. (1997). In a field experiment that involved real and hypothetical donations to a public good, the authors asked hypothetical respondents to rate the level of certainty they felt about answering the donation question. They found evidence of hypothetical bias in general, but that the bias disappeared when uncertain "yes" votes were changed to "no" votes. Subsequent investigations have usually confirmed this original finding.

What can we conclude about the criterion validity of SP methods from the evidence to date? First, hypothetical bias is a real phenomenon and as such we cannot simply conclude that SP as a general methodology always passes the criterion validity test. This, however, is probably too high a standard to apply. A more realistic standard is to ask what features of SP study design lead to estimates that are sufficiently free of hypothetical bias to serve their intended purpose. On this, recent research has made progress. The idea that surveys need to be consequential for valid inference is a relatively new notion in the stated preference literature. Since many of the earlier studies establishing the existence of hypothetical bias used explicitly inconsequential surveys in their comparisons, some authors have suggested that the evidence on hypothetical bias should be reassessed. Specifically, real payment experiments should be compared to consequential non-payment experiments, to draw comparisons between a real payment criterion and methods practitioners are likely to use in the field. Recent studies from Carson et al. (2014), Vossler et al. (2012), and Vossler and Evans (2009) have shown using field experiments that, when survey respondents believe their responses have some possibility of influencing an outcome they care about, differences between real payment and non-payment treatments disappear. However, when respondents know the exercise is purely hypothetical, in the sense that there is no chance a response can influence an outcome of interest, hypothetical bias returns. Though the research on consequentiality is still in its early stages, the results to date suggest hypothetical bias stems from the nature of the home grown value experiments, which lends more support to the idea that well-designed SP studies can achieve criterion validity.

19.4.2 Convergent Validity

In some instances it is possible to use both SP and RP (or different types of SP) approaches to estimate the same underlying value or behavioral response for an environmental change. For example, the willingness to pay for air quality improvements can be measured using hedonic price models, discrete choice experiments, or contingent valuation. The value of recreation resources can be measured using the travel cost model, contingent valuation, discrete choice experiments, or contingent behavior. Thus a natural validity exercise is to see if the estimates obtained from different data sources converge (or diverge for expected reasons). In the past an SP estimate was considered criterion valid if it matched the RP estimate. However, the more recent literature has acknowledged that both RP and SP estimates may contain biases, and so neither can be considered a true criterion. The notion of convergent validity is now used, whereby both estimates are considered more valid if they converge to a common value. An example of a large-scale, systematic investigation of convergent validity is Carson et al. (1996). For their analysis the authors collected information from 83 different studies that provided RP and SP estimates for a wide variety of quasi-public good (e.g. access to fishing sites, landscape preservation, and estuary water quality). Using meta-analysis, they find that the RP and SP approaches are highly correlated and provide values that converge on average; there are, however, substantial differences in individual cases. Thus there is evidence that many early SP and RP values were generally convergent.

The more recent literature comparing RP and SP estimates has been case-study focused. In instances when researchers are building a new survey-based dataset, it is now common to include questions that support both RP and SP analysis of the same environmental commodity in a way that allows careful comparison of preference parameters, behavioral predictions, and value estimates. For example, Whitehead et al. (2010) compare predictions on how beach recreation changes when the width of beaches on North Carolina's coast change due to erosion or beach nourishment policies. Using contingent behavior data and records of actual trip taking, they find that predictions of behavioral changes from the RP and SP models converge, but willingness to pay estimates for width increases are different. One of the lessons from the recent studies is that the assumptions used to build the RP and SP models often influence the extent to which their predictions match. More generally, the extent to which the individual case studies exhibit convergent validity depends to a large extent on how the standard is defined. In many instances, analysis of comparable RP and SP data provides qualitatively similar characterizations of preferences and underlying resource values estimates, but formal statistical tests reject the hypothesis of the same underlying data-generating process. One explanation for this is that both data sources are informative, but their different underlying strengths and limitations cause their estimates to diverge. This has led researchers to begin thinking of RP and SP data as complements rather than substitutes. Research that focuses on combining RP and SP data is our focus in section 19.6.

19.4.3 Construct Validity

A third type of validity involves assessing the extent to which an SP approach delivers findings that are consistent with theoretical predictions. In the development of this literature, an important element has been debate on what constitutes the appropriate theory. In the 1980s and early 1990s, most of the intuition that was used to judge SP estimates came from theoretical results derived for private market commodities. For example, environmental goods are often assumed to be luxury goods, and so it was expected that the income elasticity of willingness to pay should be larger than one. Likewise, results from Willig (1976) and Randall and Stoll (1980) suggested that the difference between willingness to pay and willingness to accept for environmental goods should be small. Other intuition came from the law of demand. Analysts expected that SP respondents should be responsive to price, and they should be willing to pay more to have a larger quantity of the commodity. These predictions were used to formulate several tests that SP studies needed to pass before they were considered construct valid. Two that have received a large amount of attention are income effect tests and scope tests.

Income effects are tested by looking at the sensitivity of willingness to pay estimates (or the probability of voting yes to a given bid amount) to a person's income. For this, casual intuition suggests the income elasticity of willingness to pay should be greater than one – i.e. willingness to pay should be elastic with respect to income if the environment is a "luxury" good. In contrast, an empirical regularity with SP studies that estimated income effects are positive but not large – apparently suggesting environmental commodities are essential "normal" goods rather than luxury goods. Based on this, many SP studies were judged by skeptical commentators to be invalid. In response, researchers began looking more closely at the theory that was being applied. An important insight was that the relevant theory needed to account for quantity-rationed public good commodities, in addition to the freely chosen levels of non-rationed private goods. This is because the environmental goods that individuals consume are quantity-fixed, so the marginal willingness to pay for the good, rather than the quantity of it, is the endogenous outcome. Flores and Carson (1997) show that the income elasticity of willingness to pay for an exogenously determined quantity of a good is a different theoretical concept than the income elasticity of demand for a private good. It is the former of these that drives income effect estimates in most contingent valuation applications. Using methods similar to Hanemann's (1991) analysis of the WTP/WTA gap (see Chapter 14), Carson and Flores show that an income elasticity of demand for an environmental commodity that is greater than one can, in many plausible circumstances, imply the income elasticity of willingness to pay is less than one. This reinterpretation of the relevant theory suggests that most income effect tests do not imply SP estimates are construct invalid.

A scope test examines the extent to which an SP study predicts that people are willing to pay more to have more of the environmental commodity. Sensitivity to scope has long been considered important as a vehicle for sorting out whether or not SP surveys value the actual commodity under study, or instead a more abstract notion of "caring about the environment." For example, it may be that a stated preference study measuring a population's willingness to pay to preserve an endangered sea turtle is in fact measuring its concern for endangered species generally. If the latter is true, then the level of provision is merely a symbol, and people's reported values should not respond to changes in the level. An early proponent of this viewpoint is Kahneman and Knetsch (1992), who suggested that CVM respondents' lack of scope sensitivity meant they were purchasing the moral satisfaction of contributing to a cause rather than purchasing the actual commodity. In this sense, scope tests became an important litmus test for SP validity. Though it is easy to find examples of SP survey vehicles that fail scope tests, the empirical consensus today is that well-designed SP studies (see section 19.5) do in general exhibit sensitivity to scope (see, for example, Lew and Wallmo, 2011).

The findings on income effects and scope sensitivity in recent studies illustrate how the validity literature has evolved. In early debates on contingent valuation, construct validity was used as a tool for assessing the overall efficacy of the CVM method, and failure of construct validity in example cases was used as evidence that the approach in general was suspect. Today construct validity is assessed on a case-by-case basis, with the general expectation that well-designed studies will be construct-valid according to the specific study context.

19.4.4 Content Validity

The final type of validity that we consider is based on the extent to which an SP survey adheres to best practice. Clearly this is a subjective notion of validity, but it is nonetheless a critical concept in that it reflects the role of accumulated experience in applied SP studies. For discussion purposes, we divide the notion of content validity into four subareas. The first concerns the extent to which a new survey considers the lessons that are available from examining previous, similar surveys. The success of a stated preference study often hinges on the way that the commodity, choice situation, payment vehicle, etc. are described. The history of SP studies is one of trial and error, as analysts have examined different mechanisms for communicating salient features of the hypothetical market. A new study that replicates design problems identified in past literature is considered content invalid. For example, past experience suggests that effective SP surveys include commodity definitions that avoid the use of generalities and vague descriptions. If different survey respondents perceive the environmental commodity differently owing to a lack of specificity, the survey is content invalid, in that experience suggests such designs often fail scope and other construct validity tests.

The second category of content validity relates to the extent to which an SP survey avoids several well-known design problems. Carson (1991, pp.138–39) catalogs several sources of bias that can arise from common design problems. Among these are *implied value cues*, *context misspecification*, and *amenity misspecification*; the latter two can be grouped under the more general heading of *scenario misspecification*. Implied value cues are elements of a survey that suggest to respondents what the "correct" value of the environmental commodity is. These can come in many forms. For example, if the environmental commodity is control of a destructive invasive species, and the commodity description includes information on control costs for the invasive, people may base their valuation answers on provision costs rather than their actual willingness to pay. Context misspecification occurs when elements of the survey are perceived differently than the researcher intended, causing people to respond in unintended ways. A common worry is that people will answer valuation questions conditional on a perceived property right. For example, a survey seeking to measure the willingness to pay for improved health outcomes arising from better air quality may elicit a response based on the belief that people are entitled to clean air, and therefore should not have to pay to obtain it, rather than one based on preferences for health outcomes. Amenity misspecification occurs when the respondent perceives the good to be different than was intended by the analyst. For example, if the intent of the study is to value the preservation of blue whales, but the commodity description mixes specific information on blue whales with information on whale populations more generally, the person may perceive that the program is focused on the latter, and answer from that perspective.

The third type of content validity relates to the process used to design and administer the survey. As we discuss in the next section, the effective design of SP surveys involves the use of focus groups, one-on-one cognitive interviewing, pre-testing, and peer commentary before it is fielded. A systematic process of this type provides the analyst with multiple opportunities to incrementally evaluate and adjust the survey vehicle. Effective administration of the survey means following standard survey protocol to maximize response rates, minimize item non-response, and guard against selected samples. Designing and fielding an SP survey that follows these suggestions is expensive in time and money. Inevitably, trade-offs need to be made between the resources that are available for a project and the commitment of funds to survey development.

The final type of content validity is based on the extent to which the survey design reflects the current state of knowledge on avoiding theoretical pitfalls. Based on our previous discussion, we might ask the following: does the elicitation method avoid the potential for incentive incompatibility? Is the survey consequential? Does the survey provide tools for assessing the information processing strategies used by respondents? What steps have been taken to minimize the potential for hypothetical bias? Data analysis choices can also determine the content validity of a study. Our discussion in section 19.3 stressed the importance of carefully investigating how the parametric assumptions used to characterize the distribution of willingness to pay in CVM studies affect inference. Likewise, we noted the important connection between experimental design and parameter identification in DCE models. Failure to appreciate the connection between design, analysis, and prediction can also jeopardize the content validity of a study.

19.5 BEST PRACTICE AND EXPERIMENTAL DESIGN

In this section we provide additional discussion on how stated preference studies are actually carried out. We divide our coverage into two main subsections. We first examine how the theoretical and applied research on the accuracy of SP methods has been translated into practice. As with other areas of SP methodology, entire books have been written on this theme, and so our objective is not to provide a comprehensive survey of the details of best practice; fuller treatments on several SP topics are given in the Champ et al. (2003) and Kanninen (2007) edited volumes. Our goal instead is to give readers a flavor of the types of issues that SP practitioners need to be cognizant of, in order to carry out effective studies. For this we attempt to link the insights gained from the research described in sections 19.3 and 19.4 to the present discussion. Our second emphasis in this section is on experiment design. Recall from above that experimental design is the process by which the various moving parts in an SP survey are set, so as to provide the variability needed to estimate a given behavioral function. We discuss how SP researchers have thought about experimental design, as well as the practical issues that must be addressed.

As was the case with validity, modern discussions of SP best practice start with the *Exxon Valdez* case. During the legal battle concerning the inclusion of nonuse values in the damages that Exxon would be liable for, it became apparent that a careful assessment of the suitability of stated preference methods (CVM in particular) for use in natural resource damage cases was needed. The US National Oceanic and Atmospheric Administration (NOAA) commissioned a panel of experts, chaired by Kenneth Arrow and Robert Solow, to study the CVM methodology and make recommendations on the features that a study should exhibit if it is to be useable for litigation. The panel's report was published in the US government's *Federal Register* (Arrow et al., 1993), and it quickly became the de facto early standard for best practice in CVM research. Key elements of the panel's recommendation included the use of a WTP rather than WTA format, dichotomous choice referendum-style elicitation, inclusion of explicit budget constraint and substitute resource reminders, careful pretesting of the policy/commodity description (including photos and graphics), and the generous use of follow-up questions to understand the motivation for people's choices (and potentially to trim the sample). Though there was disagreement on many of the specifics, the NOAA panel's report helped to set the early research agenda on what constitutes best practice in SP studies.

19.5.1 Best Practice

A discussion of best practice in stated preference research requires that we define the specific tasks associated with executing a study, and then describe how past research and accumulated experience have resulted in guidelines and methodologies that are applicable to the specific task. We begin our discussion by noting a set of preliminaries that are needed for any survey-based project, such as defining the relevant population, designing and executing a sampling plan, and choosing the survey mode (e.g. in-person, telephone, mail, or internet). While these are standard tasks, the specific needs of stated preference research often condition which options are feasible. Several examples of this are given in what follows.

A preliminary task that is specific to non-market valuation survey studies is to define the valuation objective. This includes identification of the environmental resource and its spatial extent, as well as ways of objectively and subjectively measuring its quality and/or quantity. In addition, an understanding of the possible ways that human and natural forces affect characteristics of the resource should be sought. Best practice on this task involves marshalling the relevant environmental or ecological expertise – either directly via collaborating researchers, or indirectly via literature surveying – to assure that the study is well grounded in basic environmental science. Once defined, the valuation objective is a key input into determining the relevant survey population. For studies related to local environmental goods, such as lake water quality, the spatial distribution of the resource may overlap with the spatial distribution of the population. In other contexts, such as when the resource is a remote wilderness preserve, the population and environmental resource may be geographically separate.

Survey design begins after the valuation objective is defined, and the tasks mirror the major sections contained in any stated preference survey. To begin, an information section sets the context for the valuation task. It defines and describes the resource and sets the baseline quality against which counterfactual changes will be compared. The information section also presents any background, resource characteristics, and measurement units that are needed for an informed response. Best practice in designing the first part of the information section involves balancing several partially competing objectives. The information should be scientifically accurate but accessible to non-experts. It should be complete but presented in a way that does not overwhelm participants. The importance of the resource should be made clear, but the presentation should be neutral in tone. The use of photos, graphs, and figures is usually critical for meeting these objectives, which eliminates the possibility of using a telephone survey mode in most contexts. In a state-of-the-art survey, the information section is developed using an iterative (and often time-consuming) process of drafting, testing using focus groups, redrafting, and so on.

Many stated preference surveys – particularly contingent valuation surveys – contain a subsequent component of the information section that describes a counterfactual change in the environmental resource, which provides the context for an elicitation question. This may be the result of a policy intervention, an accident, or some other shock. Best practice here requires specificity. The change should be presented as the result of a well-defined and plausible event, which alters an aspect of the resource in a way that can be understood using information presented earlier in the survey.

Contingent valuation and discrete choice experiment surveys vary in how the information section is structured, but the same basic principles apply. Respondents need to understand the specific environmental good, how its level or quality can vary, and what causes the variability. For CVM, the variability is usually the result of a policy, while with DCEs the variability is often linked to naturally occurring differences, such as different water quality levels at different lakes in the study area. For both methods, the baseline and changes in resource quality levels should be concrete enough so as to preclude different interpretations by different respondents.

An elicitation section follows the information section in most stated preference surveys. This section contains the questions whose answers provide the basis for estimating preferences. Here the differences between CVM and DCE are more pronounced. With DCEs, the respondent completes a series of choice tasks over two or more configurations of the commodity. In designing the choice tasks it is considered best practice to include an "opt out" option among the alternatives. Depending on the context, this could allow the person to express a preference for a cost neutral status quo, relative to the costly counterfactual alternatives. Alternatively, it could allow the person to forgo purchasing a good or participating in an activity. More generally, since "do nothing" is usually an option in real choices, it should also be an option in stated preference DCEs. Other decisions related to elicitation in DCEs include the number of attributes used to characterize the commodity, the different levels of the attributes, and the number of choice tasks a respondent should complete. The first two of these overlap closely with the information section, in that the attributes and their levels need to be communicated before choices over them can be presented. All three require considering trade-offs between the information gathered from each respondent and the cognitive burden each person faces. As noted in the validity section, when faced with complex choices respondents may seek out coping strategies, such as ignoring less salient attributes or triaging alternatives based on a threshold level of a particular attribute. For example, in Figure 19.2 (the Mansfield et al. Yellowstone Park example), people interested in only one winter activity, such cross-country skiing, may ignore other attributes and select only alternatives that include the preferred activity in the configuration. As with many things related to survey design, focus groups and one-on-one interviews with respondents over early survey drafts are necessary for balancing the "maximizing information" and "minimizing cognitive burden" objectives with DCEs.

As we have seen, the most common elicitation method in contingent valuation is the dichotomous choice referendum approach. Given the program description and statement of the respondent's costs if the program proceeds, he casts a vote. As noted above, this setup can be incentive compatible, in the sense that a person's best choice from a strategic perspective is to select the option he most prefers, though other assumptions must also hold. As such, meeting best practice standards on the elements of the dichotomous choice elicitation requires attention to several details. In the run-up to the elicitation, best practice requires reminding the person that he would be required to make payment if a majority votes in favor and the environmental commodity is provided. A specific vehicle should be presented that describes how the person would make payment. Examples of payment vehicles include higher property taxes, a surcharge on a utility bill, or a onetime direct payment. The payment vehicle should make sense in the context of the good being valued. For example, a property tax or rental property surcharge is appropriate in the context of a local public good operating at the level of the taxing jurisdiction. The payment vehicle should also be coercive, in the sense that a person cannot avoid payment while still enjoying the outcome of the program. For this reason, voluntary payment mechanisms, such as contributions to a nonprofit organization, are usually not used.

At the stage of elicitation, a state-of-the-art SP survey will also present information that helps to increase the quality of respondents' answers. For example, when a vote is solicited, survey participants are reminded that they should answer as if real payment were being made. This is a type of "cheap talk" that attempts to mitigate any tendencies people might have to ignore their budget constraint, and the possibility of substitutes for the program on offer. At the same time respondents should be reminded that the survey and their answers are important for something they care about. The goal of this consequentiality reminder is to increase the willingness of people to devote cognitive energy to their answer. Finally, it is useful to remind survey participants that there is not a right or wrong response, so as to deflect any tendency among respondents to answer in a way that is thought will please the researcher, rather than based on their preferences and constraints. All of these are designed to promote a sense of realism and importance, so as to encourage answers that can be interpreted as genuine economic choices.

After elicitation, a follow-on questions section of the survey is presented, which serves multiple purposes. First, researchers often include a certainty scale question that allows respondents to indicate the degree of confidence they have in their answer. Debriefing questions are also presented, which help the researcher to gauge the motivation for respondent's answers. These types of questions can be used in multiple ways. For example, certainty scale information can be useful for identifying yes or no responses that are not firm, and therefore could change if the vote were real. A common robustness check is to reanalyze the data after recoding uncertain "yes" votes to "no." Debriefing questions are useful for identifying "protest votes" or "feel good" votes, which may say more about a person's general attitudes towards taxes, the government, or the overall environment than their actual budget constrained non-market value. Debriefing questions can also be used to understand the extent to which people believe the proposed policy is feasible, or if they believe the survey could possibly impact something they care about. If answers to these questions suggest the person rejected the feasibility of the policy, did not understand aspects of the survey, or answered in a way suggesting a non-truthful response, the observation could be removed from the estimation sample in robustness checks. Finally, follow-on questions are used to gather conditioning variables, such as household income and structure, general attitudes and interests, and other characteristics of people relevant for the study.

Once the survey is fully drafted, it is often useful to request a review from an outside expert who can provide remarks on its structure from the perspective of someone not intimately involved with its development. From there the survey vehicle should be pretested using a small sample from the relevant population, and the data analyzed with an eye towards assessing the effectiveness of the experimental design and the variation in people's answers. Conditional on its satisfactory performance, the survey then goes to the field.

Most of the important decisions regarding a stated preference study are made at the stage of study and survey design. Nonetheless, there are aspects of data analysis and interpretation that help define best practice research. For example, summary statistics should be presented that demonstrate construct validity. Are people less likely to select an alternative that is more costly? Do the data exhibit sensitivity to scope, if indeed sensitivity is expected in the context of the study? The form of these summaries statistics and graphics will be context specific, but they should in general illustrate the variation in the data, without parametric modeling assumptions.

Analysis should then proceed in a way that transparently informs the valuation question, beginning with the simplest model and then adding necessary complexity based on the needs of the study. It should also demonstrate the extent to which the findings are robust to alternative modeling or analysis decisions and assumptions. Finally, the study should be clear on the aspects we might judge to be externally valid – i.e. insights that transfer generally – and the aspects that are specific to the context under study. The fact that best practice in contingent valuation requires a high degree of specificity in the program, including its payment vehicle and provision method, means that the final nonmarket value that is estimated is conditional on these characteristics. Since economic value is always context specific, this is desirable from an accuracy perspective, but it does require careful interpretation of what the findings mean for other contexts.

What can be taken away from this brief survey of best practice stated preference research? The themes that connect the various tasks include attention to detail, a premium on a high level of specificity, frequent testing and retesting of proposed approaches on representative survey takers, and proceeding at a deliberative pace. Application of these general principles, along with familiarity with the expanding stock of applications and accumulated wisdom, will increase the likelihood that a stated preference study meets content validity standards, and is judged reliable by observers.

19.5.2 Experimental Design

A major advantage of stated preferences approaches to non-market valuation is that the researcher is able to generate the variation that she needs for her study, rather than relying on happenstance or nature to provide it. As a practical matter, this means that the variation in conditions faced by respondents needs to be determined as part of the study, and presented during the course of the survey. Experimental design is the term used to describe the process of setting up the variation in the dimensions over which survey participants make choices via the elicitation questions. Like best practice, much has been written about experimental design in contingent valuation and discrete choice experiment contexts, and so our aim here is not to present all of the specifics. Rather, we will briefly describe the basic tasks and knowledge areas that are needed to construct state of the art designs for stated preference research.

We divide discussion into design needs for CVM and DCE approaches. The former is usually much simpler due to the smaller number of moving parts. For example, with dichotomous choice referendum formats, survey participants vote yes or no to a posted bid. The design task is to select a range of bids, which are then randomly assigned to each respondent during the elicitation stage. A good bid design spans the population distribution of willingness to pay for the program. In addition, experience (e.g. Alberini, 1995) has shown that designs with five to eight values clustered around the population median, with large and small bid values not too far into the left and right tails of the distribution, perform best in terms of the statistical efficiency of estimates. For example, if the median willingness to pay in the population is \$30 and the standard deviation in the population is \$15, a candidate collection of bids is (\$5, \$10, \$20, \$30, \$40, \$50, \$60).

Of course, this suggests that the optimal bid design requires knowledge of the object of estimation, and so actual implementation requires some prior knowledge on the likely range of values in the population. This is usually obtained during the survey design stage, via focus groups and pretest results. This challenge notwithstanding, so long as the range of bids overlaps with the population willingness to pay distribution, the consequences of sub-optimal bid designs tend to be in the precision of estimates rather than the ability to obtain estimates.

Experimental design in DCE is, by contrast, more complex and central to the success of the enterprise. With DCEs there are four dimensions that need to be considered: the number of attributes used to characterize the commodity, the number of levels each attribute takes, the number of alternatives a person selects from on a given choice occasion, and the total number of choices the person will face. Recall from Eq. (19.25) that the objective is to estimate a set of utility function parameters which includes main effects (how an attribute affects utility independent of other attributes), or main effects and interaction effects (how an attribute's contribution to utility depends on the levels of other attributes). Experimental design decisions condition the combination of main and interaction effects that can be estimated from the resulting data, as well as the precision of the estimates.

To appreciate this, consider a situation in which the commodity is described using four attributes, and that each attribute can take on three levels. This means there are $3^4 = 81$ different versions of the commodity. This is referred to as the *full factorial* – i.e. the full listing of possible combinations of attribute and attribute levels. To estimate the full set of main and interaction effects, choice tasks need to be designed so that, across the sample, all 81 different combinations are represented. If the choice task involves selecting from among three designed alternatives, a single person would need to complete 27 choices to see all the combinations. If we limit the number of choice tasks for a single person to (say) nine, three survey respondents would be needed to obtain readings on the full factorial. By similar logic, nine respondents completing three choice tasks each would also provide information needed to estimate the main and interaction effects.

Covering the full factorial becomes more difficult with more complex designs. For example, if there are five attributes each taking four levels, there are $4^5 = 1,024$ unique commodities. For this and larger experiments, it may not be possible to present the full factorial via a reasonable combination of choice tasks and choice set blocks within the sample. In these instances a *fractional factorial* design is used. This involves presenting a subset of the commodity definitions in the survey. The choice of which combinations to present is important, since it determines which of the main and interaction effects we will be able to estimate, with the resulting choice data.

The distinction between a full and fractional factorial design is important because it illustrates an important trade-off: full factorial designs are needed to estimate a fully general model, but they are usually not feasible in practice. Fractional factorial designs must be used in practice, but by their nature they do not provide full generality. This dilemma has motivated research on the best way to construct a fractional factorial design, given the specific needs of a study.

The technical aspects of optimal fractional factorial designs are beyond our scope here; useful references include Johnson et al. (2007) and Hensher et al. (2005). We note, however, that the starting point is usually a main effects design, whereby attention is limited to the utility function parameters in Eq. (19.24). This reduces the number of coefficients to estimate (i.e. coefficients on interactions among the attributes are left out), which dramatically reduces the fraction of the full factorial that needs to be presented in the sample. An optimal main effects design involves selecting the subset of choice pairs to present to the sample in a way that maximizes the precision (minimizes the variances) of the main effects coefficient estimators. Similarly, when a subset of the attribute interaction terms are thought to be important, a design is sought that selectively increases the fraction of the full factorial that is contained in the survey. Specifically, choice pairs are presented that provide the variability needed to estimate the full set of main effects, as well as the selected set of interaction effects.

19.6 COMBINING SP AND RP DATA

Throughout Part III of the book we have presented RP and SP methods for non-market valuation as separate paradigms. An alternative perspective, however, is to view the two as complementary sources of information, which can be simultaneously useful for estimating preferences. The case for this is best made by noting that RP and SP have strengths and weaknesses that line up as opposites. For example, the primary strength of RP approaches is that estimation is based on choices that actually occurred, while the primary weakness of SP is that decisions do not have real consequences for sampled individuals. In contrast, the main advantage of SP methods is that a researcher can exploit variation and contexts outside of the range observed at the status quo, while the main disadvantage of RP methods is their reliance on specific behavioral contexts and naturally occurring variation. These characterizations of SP and RP methods suggest there may be advantages to exploiting multiple data types according to their specific strengths. This sentiment has led analysts to explore methods for combining multiple data sources in the same model, and to examine questions related to when the different data sources should be combined. In this section we review key concepts and ideas that have emerged from this research.

19.6.1 Methodological Topics

In their book-length treatment on combining RP and SP data, Whitehead et al. (2011) categorize three classes of data-combining models that can arise, based on the specific types of RP and SP data that are being used. The first we consider is *frequency models*, which arise when both the RP and SP data provide quantity (frequency) information for the same underlying function. The best example of this is when individual-level data on annual visits to a recreation site are combined with contingent behavior data, which also describe visits to the same recreation site. This provides multiple data points that can be used to fit the same model – i.e. a demand equation in the recreation example – and so the data can be "stacked" in a single dataset. The stacking of like data types means that combining SP and RP frequency data presents no special challenges as regards model estimation. The advantage of combining the data is that the RP data are, by definition, generated by status quo environmental conditions, while the SP data can provide information on behavior in counterfactual circumstances. Thus, conditional on the SP and RP data reflecting the same underlying data-generating process (a point to which we return below), the combined model can be useful for a wider range of measurement objectives.

The second class of combined model makes use of the discrete choice paradigm, and so we label it *discrete models*. This class arises when the RP and SP data both record discrete choices from a set of alternatives, where there is overlap in the available options and/or the attributes that influence choices. Adamowicz et al. (1994) provide an early example of this in a recreation context. Revealed preference data on recreation destination choices are combined with a discrete choice experiment, where the SP data describe the role of recreation site attributes. Joint use of the two data sources was possible because the attributes examined in the SP data were also measured for (and relevant to) the destinations included in the RP application. A second example is housing choice (e.g. Earnhart, 2002), where we can observe actual location choices as a function of observed neighborhood characteristics. These RP data could be combined with a discrete choice experiment, which examines how neighborhood attributes that overlap with the RP data affect housing choices amongst homebuyers. Under the conditions of both these examples, the choice outcomes data can be stacked, and the same discrete choice econometric routine used to estimate utility function parameters.

To see this more clearly, consider a conditional indirect utility function for an RP recreation site choice model

$$V_{ij} = -\beta p_{ij} + \gamma' q_j + \xi_j + \varepsilon_{ij}, \quad j = 1, ..., J, \tag{19.32}$$

where i indexes the person, p_{ij} is the travel cost to site j, q_j is a vector of person-constant observable site characteristics, and ξ_j captures things about site j that are constant over people, but which we cannot measure. Suppose that we observe $i = 1, ..., I$ people who have each made one destination choice. In Chapters 16 and 17, we discussed the methods and challenges associated with estimating both γ and ξ_j in this purely RP data environment. Consider now a situation in which we also have a DCE that presented the same sample of I respondents with non-labeled choices over recreation sites, in which the designed attributes match the variables p_{ij} and q_j. That is, the same variables that are measured for the RP application sites are presented in the DCE. Similar to Eq. (19.24), the conditional indirect utility function for a main effects, non-labeled design that we would estimate using the DCE data is

$$V_{ict} = -\beta p_{ict} + \gamma' q_{ict} + \varepsilon_{ict}, \quad c = 1, ..., C, \quad t = 1, ..., T, \tag{19.33}$$

where c denotes an alternative in the SP choice task set C, and we have included the subscript t to reflect the fact that most DCE surveys include multiple-choice tasks per person. Note that, unlike in the RP data where the values in q_j did not vary over people, in the SP data we are able to present different people with different attribute levels q_{ict}, both within and across choice tasks. Stacking the I revealed preference outcomes with the $I \times T$ stated preference choice outcomes per person, we are able to estimate a single discrete choice model that provides estimates of β, γ, and the net-of-q alternative specific constants $\xi_1, ..., \xi_{J-1}$. The additional variability from the DCE therefore allows us to more readily estimate the role of observed site characteristics of interest. Thus, once again conditional on the SP and RP data reflecting the same underlying data-generating process, the combined model can be useful when there is insufficient natural variation in attribute levels to support RP-only estimation.

The final data-combining model identified by Whitehead et al. (2011) is referred to as a *mixed model*. This is needed when the RP and SP data provide information on a common resource, but reflect different behavioral outcomes. Here there are two types of dependent variables, and so the data cannot be easily stacked. The first analysis of this type is Cameron (1992), who considered a recreation example starting with RP information on the number of trips people take to a specific site. She also conducted a CVM study that asked people if they would still visit the site if there was an additional cost per trip (e.g. an entry fee per trip). The trip fee amount was randomly assigned to survey respondents. With these data, there are two endogenous outcomes: the number of recreation trips at the baseline, and a yes/no answer to a hypothetical price increase. Conceptually these are related, in that both outcomes can be described using a single functional specification for utility. Estimation is operationalized by choosing a parametric form for utility and distributions for stochastic terms, and deriving conditions that correspond to the two outcomes. These include (a) the functional form for demand; and (b) a comparison of utility with trips equal to zero, and utility with a positive number of trips and the price increase. The RP data on baseline demand is matched to (a), and the answer to the yes/no question determines the direction of comparison for (b). Both conditions for an individual are expressed probabilistically (e.g. Poisson for the recreation trips, and logit for the utility comparison), and entered into a likelihood function. Maximum likelihood is then used to estimate the underlying preference parameters, as a function of both the RP and SP outcomes.

19.6.2 When Should RP and SP Data Be Combined?

The preceding discussion focused on the methods used to combine multiple data sources. It was implicitly asserted that the RP and SP data sources were generated from the same underlying preference function, and that as such it made sense to combine them. An alternative approach is to test whether the underlying data-generating processes are in fact the same. This is possible in the frequency and discrete models defined in the previous subsection, since in principle both data types can be used to estimate the same underlying model parameters. Statistical tests of parameter equality are then used to assess the convergent validity of the underlying behavioral models.

A large research literature is devoted to examining when and why parameter estimates converge or diverge for discrete and frequency-type models. One area that has proven important in this literature is the general idea that SP data may be less precise than their RP counterparts in the sense that the cognitive challenges associated with answering unfamiliar SP questions may lead to "noisier" data, and that this needs to be explicitly accounted for when assessing the convergent validity of RP and SP estimated parameters. While attention to this detail has increased the likelihood of convergent validity from a statistical perspective, it is still often the case that formal tests reject the hypothesis of parameter equality. In this case, context-specific judgment is needed to determine the source of discrepancy, decide if it is economically important, and if there are reasons to prefer SP only, RP only, or a combined model.

19.7 SUMMARY

Our goal in this chapter has been to provide a discussion of stated preference methods that has enough breadth to convey an understanding of the different aspects of the sub-field, and enough depth to illustrate the subtle issues involved with credibly executing SP studies. We saw that there are three classes of stated preference approaches: contingent valuation, discrete choice experiments, and contingent behavior. Contingent valuation elicits resource values by asking people to respond to posted bids for a program, which affects an environmental outcome. Discrete choice experiments rely on observing choices from different configurations of a quality-differentiated commodity, which differ according to the levels of their attributes. Contingent behavior elicits how a particular type of behavior would change in response to a counterfactual scenario. Although these three classes differ in many of their underlying details, they all rely on answers people provide to experimentally designed, survey-conveyed scenarios, which provides substantial flexibility in the types of resources and contexts that can be valued.

Since most types of stated preference elicitation methods do not provide direct observation of resource values, we saw that it is usually necessary to estimate econometric models of behavior using data generated from SP surveys. In the case of contingent valuation, the objective is typically to characterize the distribution of willingness to pay in the population. With discrete choice models, discrete choice random utility maximization (RUM) models are used to estimate the marginal utilities of individual attributes. Contingent behavior data are often used to estimate models that are similar to the revealed preference models reviewed in previous chapters. More generally, stated preference applications, like many of their revealed preference counterparts, make use of state-of-the-art structural discrete choice modeling to recover estimates of utility function parameters, which are then used for welfare analysis.

A major area of research, and a source of considerable debate, relates to the accuracy of stated preference methods. In this chapter we discussed the current framework for this debate by describing the important concepts of consequentiality and incentive compatibility. We saw that SP surveys need to be presented in a way that assures the respondent that his answers have some chance of influencing an outcome that he cares about, and that the elicitation question needs to be demand revealing. When this is so, the necessary conditions for an SP exercise to reflect real economic choices are met, in that it is in the person's interest to answer truthfully and carefully. After establishing these necessary conditions, we discussed the empirical, experimental, and theoretical literature devoted to assessing the validity of stated preference methods. We saw that the literature can be divided into four validity areas that assess: (a) criterion – the extent to which SP estimates match their real payment counterparts; (b) convergent – the extent to which an SP estimate matches an RP or different SP estimate of the same item; (c) construct – the extent to which SP estimates are consistent with theoretical predictions; and (d) content – the extent to which an SP estimate was derived according to best practice. The evidence concerning the overall accuracy of SP based on these validity concepts is favorable but not universally so, and while work continues, one conclusion is that validity can be achieved by well-designed stated preference surveys that adhere to the consequentiality paradigm.

Research on the validity of stated preference and its overall efficacy has produced a large body of knowledge on what works and does not work in applied studies. This stock of knowledge conveys several best-practice notions, which we identified over the course of the chapter. Importantly, contemporary stated preference research places a large emphasis on specificity, plausibility and realism, and a deliberative process of survey design that makes use of extensive focus group and other respondent-feedback mechanisms. We also saw that the experimental design phase, during which the scenario configurations that respondents will respond to are generated, is a key aspect of executing stated preference surveys.

Finally, we saw that the extensive research on both RP and SP methods in environmental economics has led to a sizeable literature dedicated to developing methods that can simultaneously exploit both sources of data. This notion has been employed both as a means of harnessing complementary strengths of the two paradigms, as well as a sophisticated means of assessing convergent validity of RP and SP models alone.

We close this chapter by noting several additional points that do not fit cleanly into the various sections of the main chapter. First, stated preference research is relevant for many fields of applied economics. Thus researchers and practitioners in fields such as transportation, health, and marketing have been key contributors to the literature. We have focused on the environmental economics literature here, but it needs to be stressed that much can be learned about the topic reviewed here by also reading literature in related fields. Second, though we have focused mainly on the role of environmental economists in executing SP surveys, actual studies are often multidisciplinary in the sense that environmental scientists and ecologists are key contributors to the descriptions of environmental resources and the changes. Likewise, statisticians and cognitive psychologists have made contributions to experimental design and decision sciences that are relevant to SP. Finally, very few of our examples in this chapter have focused on health outcome valuation, which is a key area of application in environmental economics. In Chapter 20 we discuss health valuation more generally, and present several ways that stated preference methods have been used specifically.

19.8   FURTHER READING

The literature on stated preference in environmental economics and other fields is enormous, and the excellent primary and secondary sources available to readers are too numerous to list here. As such we provide a categorization of different readings and example references. Useful top-level overviews are contained in Carson and Louviere (2011), Carson (2000), and Whitehead and Haab (2013). Early examples of influential book-length treatments on research and best practice in stated preference include Mitchell and Carson (1989) and Cummings et al. (1986). The history of stated preference research, with an emphasis on contingent valuation, is provided by Carson and Hanemann (2005) and Smith (2006). Carson and Hanemann is also the most recent and comprehensive chapter-length survey of stated preference research. The earlier review by Carson (1991) is also useful. Finally, Freeman et al. (2014) contains an additional textbook treatment of stated preference.

Stated preference methods generally, and contingent valuation in particular, have long been controversial, and so the literature has also produced a number of debate pieces. The early literature was critiqued in a 1994 *Journal of Economic Perspectives* (*JEP*) symposium that included articles by Hanemann (1994) and Diamond and Hausman

(1994), as well as an overview from Portney (1994). A 2012 *JEP* symposium provided opposing critiques of the stated preference literature that developed subsequently. Papers from Carson (2012) and Hausman (2012) provide advocacy perspectives, while Kling et al. (2012) attempt a neutral assessment of the validity research. Haab et al. (2013) provide a response to the review by Hausman (2012).

The literature on best practice has evolved to include several high-quality contributions. The edited volume by Champ et al. (2003) presents several chapters devoted to the hands-on practice of stated preference research. We have relied heavily on the chapter from Kevin Boyle in writing the best practice section here. In addition, Kanninen (2007) includes several chapters devoted to the how-to of discrete choice experiments, and Haab and McConnell (2002) provide an accessible treatment of stated preference econometrics. Finally, the edited volume from Bateman and Willis (1999) provides a European and world perspective on the theory and practice of contingent valuation.

Research on the accuracy of stated preference methods has appeared in hundreds of journal articles over the past two decades, and key contributions are too numerous to list. A sampling of individual researchers who have worked on validity topics, and whose work we have relied on for this chapter, includes Ian Bateman, Richard Carson, Nick Flores, Glenn Harrison, Robert Johnston, John List, James Murphy, Gregory Poe, Kerry Smith, Laura Taylor, Christian Vossler, and John Whitehead. In addition, Loomis (2011) provides an overview of hypothetical bias, and Vossler and Poe (2011) present a useful framing of the role of consequentiality in explaining hypothetical bias. This list is far from exhaustive, and is only intended to provide a starting point for literature searches on validity topics.

The literature on combining revealed and stated preference data is nicely summarized in the Whitehead et al. (2011) edited volume. An article-length survey of this literature is provided by Whitehead et al. (2008). Example applications include von Haefen and Phaneuf (2008), Phaneuf et al. (2013), Whitehead et al. (2010), and Adamowicz et al. (1994).

EXERCISES

The data used in examples 19.1, 19.3, and 19.4 are drawn from a more detailed dataset that presented different versions of the quality change. Specifically, while all respondents were given the same baseline, there were four different versions of the quality change:

- Version I – A = 10%, B = 25%, C = 50%, D = 15%, E = 0%
- Version II – A = 15%, B = 35%, C = 40%, D = 10%, E = 0%
- Version III – A = 20%, B = 45%, C = 30%, D = 5%, E = 0%
- Version IV – A = 10%, B = 55%, C = 30%, D = 5%, E = 0%

The 302 respondents used in the chapter examples responded to version I. Note that in expectation, the quality levels increase from version I to version III. In the full dataset, there are 1,327 respondents divided across the four treatments. The full data set phaneuf_cvm is available for download on the website, along with variable definitions. The following exercises use these data.

19.1 *Consider the Hanemann and Cameron specifications shown in examples 19.3 and 19.4.

(a) For the full dataset, summarize the proportion of people who vote "yes" in the referendum for each of the four bid levels. Does the proportion of yes votes respond to bid levels in the way you would expect?

(b) Replicate the example 19.3 and 19.4 estimates by running the specifications shown in the chapter, using only the individuals who responded to version I. Note that the predictions for willingness to pay are random variables since they are functions of estimated parameters. Predict the standard errors and confidence intervals for the welfare measures, using a bootstrap or alternative strategy.

(c) Run the same models using only the individuals who responded to version III. Comment on any differences in the estimates you recover for the value of the program.

(d) Now run models that pool observations from version I and version III. Modify your specifications so that you are able to distinguish differences in the willingness to pay for programs I and III. Do you find a statistically significant difference? What do your findings suggest about sensitivity to scope?

(e) Survey respondents answered a follow-on question in which they reported the level of confidence they had in their answers to the referendum questions. Based on this, individuals are classified as *very certain*, *certain*, or *uncertain*. Repeat part (c), but this time drop respondents who report they are uncertain. Does this change your findings on sensitivity to scope? Rather than dropping uncertain respondents, change their votes to "no" (if they voted yes). Explain how this changes your value estimates and findings on scope.

19.2 ***The survey included a follow-on choice (double bound), whereby individuals responded to a second bid. The bid was lower if the first vote was "no," and higher if the first vote was "yes." For the original bids $B_0 \in (24, 120, 216, 360)$, the following patterns were used:

- $B_0=24$: $B_1=120$ if "yes," $B_1=12$ if "no"
- $B_0=120$: $B_1=216$ if "yes," $B_1=24$ if "no"
- $B_0=216$: $B_1=360$ if "yes," $B_1=120$ if "no"
- $B_0=360$: $B_1=480$ if "yes," $B_1=216$ if "no"

(a) Using the Cameron model, estimate a bivariate probit model using the two choice outcomes and the two bid amounts, limiting your sample to version III respondents. Allow the coefficient estimates to differ across the two choices, and predict the median willingness to pay separately using the choice 1 and choice 2 findings. Comment on their similarities or differences, and discuss potential reasons for any discrepancies. Repeat the exercise for the other survey versions. Do you find similar patterns?

(b) Return to the version III sample. Estimate the bivariate probit model again, but this time constrain the parameter estimates to be equal across the two choices. Predict median willingness to pay from this model, and compare it to your findings from (a). Explain any differences. Repeat the exercise for the other survey versions. Do you find similar patterns?

19.3 **Van Houtven et al. (2014) use these data as part of an analysis linking stated preference with expert elicitation to value water quality. Their Table 7 presents estimates from several models and several configurations of the data, including a continuous version of the water quality indicator. Replicate as many of the six model estimates as you can.

19.4 ***In Phaneuf et al. (2013), the authors use a discrete choice experiment to measure the value of remediating the Lower Buffalo River in Buffalo, New York, which was classified as an Area of Concern (AOC) due to past contamination. A sample of recent homebuyers completed choice tasks in which their actual purchase was compared to an alternative home that differed in the following attributes (attribute levels):

- home size (+25%, +15%, no change, −15%);
- AOC condition (full cleanup, partial cleanup, no change, more pollution);
- distance to AOC (2 miles closer, 1 mile closer, no change, 2 miles further);
- home price (+30%, +15%, no change, −10%).

The full data set *ptb_dce* is available for download on the website, along with variable definitions. The data are based on a sample of 281 people, each of whom completed eight choice tasks that compared their actual home to one designed alternative.

(a) Using these data, estimate a main effects model using log transformations for the home size and distance to AOC variables, and individual dummy variables for the environmental conditions. Make sure you also include an intercept term to distinguish the real from the designed alternative. What is the marginal willingness to pay in home purchase price for one additional square foot of home size, for a representative 1,500 square foot structure? What is the marginal willingness to pay for an additional 0.10 miles distance from the AOC, for a representative home 1.5 miles away from the river? Predict the average willingness to pay in home purchase price for remediating the river from its current state, to full cleanup.

(b) Repeat the exercise in (a), but now include interactions between the distance to AOC and environmental condition attributes, as well as the main effects. Compare your estimates and willingness to pay predictions from this to a specification that excludes the main effects for the environmental conditions (while maintaining the interactions with the distance to the AOC).

(c) Return to the main effects specification in (a). Examine the extent to which preferences for the distance and environmental condition attributes depend on household characteristics, such as income, presence of children, and age of respondent.

19.5 ***In their survey of stated preference validity, Kling et al. (2012) note that past literature using "home grown" values tended to find evidence of hypothetical bias. However, more recent studies have postulated that the absence of "consequential" questioning in laboratory experiments may be responsible for the persistence of this finding. Using literature cited in Kling et al. and any additional/newer studies, evaluate the following general statement: *Stated preference methods are likely to pass criterion validity tests if the survey is consequential and incentive compatible.*

CHAPTER 20

Health Valuation

In many instances, pollution affects human well-being primarily through its impact on human health. For example, diesel exhaust, benzene in fuel oils, arsenic in drinking water, and radiation from power plants are known carcinogens that can increase the risk of premature death from cancer. Conventional air and water pollutants can also cause elevated mortality risks from cardiovascular and intestinal conditions, respectively. This is particularly so for the elderly, young, and individuals with pre-existing health problems. Thus regulatory efforts to decrease pollution can increase well-being by reducing mortality risks for the affected population. Indeed in the United States, the primary justification for far-reaching statutes such as the Safe Drinking Water Act and the Clean Air Act lies in protecting human health. At the same time, reductions in pollution can decrease the incidence of some types of illnesses. For example, exposure to ground-level ozone causes non-fatal (and fatal) respiratory problems for people with asthma, and food and waterborne pathogens can lead to gastrointestinal sickness. Thus regulatory efforts that limit air, land, and water pollution can increase well-being by reducing morbidity. Each of these pathways suggests that non-market benefits from pollution control can arise from the subsequent improvement in human health. In this chapter we describe the approaches that economists have used to measure these benefits.

We begin by noting that tools from several disciplines are in fact needed to measure the value of changes in health outcomes stemming from pollution reductions. It is first necessary to estimate the physical links between a pollutant and health outcomes in a population. Viscusi and Gayer (2005) discuss this process in some detail, listing steps that include (a) establishing a biological link between a compound and an outcome; (b) estimation of an exposure-response function linking different ambient exposure levels to a quantitative measure of the outcome, while accounting for any behavioral adjustments; and (c) assessing the ambient levels experienced by a population at baseline and counterfactual conditions. These steps are not historically done by economists, though in recent years economists have contributed to estimating exposure-response functions. Rather, they provide the input for an economic analysis of how people value the changes in health outcomes brought about by a policy-induced reduction in exposure. For example, to measure the benefits of cleaning up a hazardous waste site containing cancer-causing compounds, we first need to know how exposure to the compound in general elevates the risk of cancer. We then need to know how the level of exposure affects outcomes in the surrounding population. With this information, we can assess the mortality risk decrease that the policy would provide to the exposed population, and then measure the population's willingness to pay for the risk reduction. A morbidity example is the measurement of benefits a person with asthma receives from a reduction in ground-level ozone. An exposure-response function in this case needs to relate the frequency and duration of asthma symptoms to ozone exposure, taking account of any defensive actions he undertakes. For example, this requires mapping a person's symptoms to the ambient pollution level, his time spent outdoors, and his use of medical inputs. This mapping is often referred to as a health production function. With this, the non-market valuation task is to measure the person's willingness to pay for a reduction in asthma symptoms from a given reduction in pollution, accounting for changes in his time spent outdoors, use of medical services, and other mitigating activities.

Our objective in this chapter is to focus primarily on the last steps in the two examples given above. Specifically, we will separately examine models used to measure the value of changes in *mortality risk* and *morbidity outcomes*. This organization follows the traditional division of these two topics in environmental economics, though many pollutants clearly cause both sickness- and fatality-based externalities. Likewise, valuation tasks can involve measuring changes in morbidity risk as well as morbidity outcomes. The division is nonetheless convenient, in that our mortality discussion will be framed around the issue of the willingness to pay for small fatality risk reductions, while our morbidity discussion will abstract from risk and focus on the direct links between pollution exposure and specific illnesses or symptoms.

The two literatures also have different organizational characteristics. Since mortality risk is a clearly defined outcome there is more overlap in the objectives of non-market valuation research in this area. As we will see, the intent is almost always to measure the "value of a statistical life" or VSL – i.e. an individual specific marginal willingness to pay, which can be aggregated to measure how much a population would be willing to pay ex ante to prevent the death of a single unknown person in a given time period. By contrast, morbidity studies have tended to be more case specific, and the outcomes examined are much more heterogeneous. As such this research typically produces estimates of value for specific symptoms or illnesses that are context dependent.

We begin our discussion of mortality valuation in section 20.1 by examining models of behavior that help us link valuation concepts to empirical methods. Our point of departure is the simple static model of behavior under an exogenous fatality risk as was presented in Chapter 14. We generalize this model to allow some types of risk to arise from individual decisions, which motivates the main revealed preference (RP) approaches to valuing mortality risk. We then look at a richer life cycle model that illustrates the importance of temporal factors when we are specifically interested in environmental mortality risks. This model serves as the motivation for much of the stated preference (SP) work in this area. In section 20.2 we examine the empirical RP and SP approaches that researchers have used, focusing specifically on hedonic wage models as described in Chapter 15 and survey methods applied to health. Our objective in this section is to provide an overview of how applied research in this area is carried out, and we illustrate the two approaches with examples from the literature. In section 20.3 we discuss morbidity valuation. The starting point for this area is the household production, or substitutes, model presented in Chapter 15. We present a version of this model that is tailored to the morbidity valuation problem, and then discuss how both RP and SP methods have been used to link empirical estimates to its theoretical predictions.

20.1 MORTALITY RISK VALUATION – MODELING

In this section we focus on describing models that motivate the various empirical approaches to measuring the willingness to pay for mortality risk reductions. Our intent is to derive theoretical expressions for willingness to pay, and then to consider what types of behavior and data might allow us to construct empirical estimates that are theoretically valid. For this we first consider a simple static model that provides two relatively straightforward links to observable behavioral margins. We then generalize the model to include dynamic considerations, which allows us to more fully consider the assumptions needed to implement the empirical models described later in the chapter.

20.1.1 Static Model

We begin with a simple static model that allows us to express conditions that define a person's marginal willingness to pay for a mortality risk reduction. Recall that in Chapter 14 we considered a model with two states of the world, where individuals were uncertain about which state would occur. The probability of a given state was exogenous to the individual and governed by a known probability distribution. With this setup, we were able to derive an expression for the person's marginal willingness to pay for a reduction in the probability of the bad state (see Eq. (14.55) in Chapter 14). For our analysis here we again apply the two-state framework, and label the good state as "survival" and the bad state as "death." Let ρ_e be the exogenous probability of death from exposure to an environmental contaminant. This could, for example, be the risk of fatality from exposure to a carcinogen at a toxic waste site. Define the direct utility function when a person is alive by $U(z;s)$, where z is consumption of a composite commodity, with price normalized to one, on which all income y is spent, and s denotes characteristics of the person. If we normalize utility to zero when the person is not alive, the expected utility from consumption is $\bar{U} = (1 - \rho_e) \cdot U(y;s)$, where we have substituted out $z = y$. This normalization is a special case in that it eliminates any bequest motive, which might imply the marginal utility of wealth is positive upon death. Nonetheless, it is an analytically convenient normalization that we maintain throughout this section. Taking the total differential of expected utility leads to $d\bar{U} = (1 - \rho_e)U_z(y;s)dy - U(y;s)d\rho_e$, and by holding expected utility constant, so that $d\bar{U} = 0$, we can derive the marginal willingness to pay for a change in ρ_e as

$$\frac{dy}{d\rho_e} = \frac{U(y;s)}{\pi \times U_z(y;s)}, \tag{20.1}$$

where $\pi = (1 - \rho_e)$ is the survival probability and $U_z(\cdot)$ is the marginal utility of income. This expression is equivalent to the one derived in Chapter 14. From it we see that, in the face of a strictly exogenous mortality risk, the person's marginal willingness to pay for a risk reduction is based on his income, survival probability, and the specifics of his preference function and personal characteristics. No obvious link to a private decision regarding risk/income trade-offs arises from this simple setup.

The model thus far has used a single exogenous fatality risk, but in reality the full collection of fatality risks that a person faces in his day-to-day life is not strictly exogenous. Fatality risks are present due to accidents or illness at home or in the workplace, and can arise from the private consumption and activity choices we make. For example, we accept a small fatality risk when we travel in a car or drive a motorcycle. The magnitude of the fatality risk when we travel in a car can be altered by selecting an automobile that has optional safety equipment. The magnitude of the fatality risk when we drive a motorcycle can be reduced by wearing a helmet. Home safety equipment such as smoke detectors and water filters reduce the risk of fatality from fires and water-borne pathogens, respectively. Products such as alcohol and cigarettes provide consumption benefits that come with an elevated fatality risk. Risky professions such as firefighting, commercial fishing, and law enforcement often pay more than jobs that require similar skills; in choosing these professions, people reveal a willingness to accept a higher mortality risk in exchange for more income. The point of these examples is to stress that trade-offs between private choices and small ex ante probabilities of death are a common part of most people's day-to-day decisions. To reflect these possibilities – and to motivate a class of revealed preference empirical models – we need to generalize the model to allow endogenous levels for some types of mortality risk.

To this end, suppose there is a private commodity x with price p, which reduces the probability of dying from an accident or illness. Denote $\rho(x)$ as the specific mortality risk that depends on x, where $\rho'(x)<0$ implies an increase in x decreases the risk of dying in a given time period. Adding to the list of examples given above, x might be consumption of preventative medicine. Suppose as well that a person's labor market income depends in part on the level of mortality risk that he is willing to accept in the workplace. To reflect this, we generalize the model so that occupation – and hence job-related mortality risk – is a choice variable, and income is endogenous. We denote income earned in the labor market by the hedonic price function $y(\rho_y;s)$, where ρ_y is the workplace mortality level, and s is included as a conditioning variable to stress that earnings also depend on a worker's characteristics. We assume that $dy(\cdot)/d\rho_y>0$, meaning that all else being equal, there is a positive wage differential available to someone who is willing to take on a higher risk of dying on the job. For example, it is intuitive that the wage rate for someone who cleans windows in a high-rise building is larger than the wage rate for someone who cleans windows at ground level. With these three types of mortality risks, ρ_e (exogenous), $\rho(x)$ (endogenous through the choice of defense measures), and ρ_y (determined by occupational choice), the probability of survival in a given time period, if the three risks are independent, is

$$\pi = (1-\rho_e)\times(1-\rho(x))\times(1-\rho_y)$$
$$\approx 1-\rho_e-\rho(x)-\rho_y, \tag{20.2}$$

where the second line follows from the fact that mortality risks of the type considered here are small enough that their products are of second order importance. If we assume that x does not generate utility in its own right, then the expected utility for a person facing these three risks is

$$\bar{U} = (1 - \rho_e - \rho(x) - \rho_y) \times U\left(y(\rho_y; s) - px; s\right),$$ (20.3)

where x and ρ_y are the choice variables, and we have used the budget constraint $y(\rho_y; s) = px + z$ to substitute out for z.

To see how this generalization affects the expressions for marginal willingness to pay, we examine the first-order conditions. In particular, the first-order condition for expected utility maximization with respect to ρ_y – the occupation choice – is

$$(1 - \rho_e - \rho(x) - \rho_y) U_z(z; s) \frac{dy(\rho_y; s)}{d\rho_y} - U(z) = 0.$$ (20.4)

Rearranging this expression we have

$$\frac{dy(\rho_y; s)}{d\rho_y} = \frac{U(z; s)}{\pi \times U_z(z; s)},$$ (20.5)

which shows that the marginal willingness to pay for a change in fatality risk (the right-hand side) is equivalent in equilibrium to the change in labor market income stemming from a small change in risk. Thus Eq. (20.5) provides motivation for an empirical strategy that uses the first-stage hedonic model to estimate how wages respond to changes in workplace fatality rates, holding constant all other determinants of a person's earnings. We discuss the specifics of this in section 20.2. The first-order condition for expected utility maximization with respect to x is

$$-(1 - \rho_e - \rho(x) - \rho_y) \times U_z(z; s) p - \rho'(x) U(z; s) = 0.$$ (20.6)

Rearranging leads to

$$-\frac{p}{\rho'(x)} = \frac{U(z; s)}{\pi \times U_z(z; s)},$$ (20.7)

which shows that the person purchases x up to the point that the effective cost of a marginal change in fatality risk arising from x (the left-hand side) is equal to his marginal willingness to pay for a risk reduction. Thus Eq. (20.7) provides motivation for an empirical strategy that focuses on understanding how the demand for a range of safety products or risky consumption activities reveals people's private risk-income trade-offs.

This model – particularly Eq. (20.5) – has been a key motivation for the revealed preference empirical methods used to measure income/risk trade-offs. Because of this, it is useful to look in more detail at the characteristics of the model, and the assumptions that are needed to transfer estimates based on workplace risks and safety products, to environmental risk cases. Regarding the model, the presence of s in each of the formulas serves to stress that there is heterogeneity in how people trade off risk and money. For example, someone who is elderly or in poor health might value risk reductions differently from someone who is young or in good health; these can be reflected in how a person sorts into the labor market or consumes risk-altering products. In environmental economics the relationship between age and willingness to pay has been particularly important, since the lives saved from environmental policy tend be among older adults and, to a lesser extent, young children. Our static model does not predict how willingness to pay changes with age, but it can reflect heterogeneity related to age (or health status, wealth, etc.). We discuss this topic in more detail below. Regarding assumptions, our static model implies that the risk of accidental death in the workplace and death from exposure to a pollutant are perfect substitutes. More specifically, the person is indifferent between an improvement in survivability that comes about from a reduction in environmental, workplace, or private activity risks. In reality, the type of death may matter to the person. Accidental deaths tend to be instantaneous events, while death from exposure to a carcinogen is usually accompanied by a long period of painful illness. People may also have different attitudes towards freely chosen versus exogenously imposed risks. A model that reflects these potential differences would need to account for more than two states of the world. For example, we would need to include states for survival, death from an accident, and death following a protracted illness. If the state-dependent utility relationships are different for the latter two, then the equality of the marginal willingness to pay expressions in (20.5), for example, breaks down. Ultimately it is an empirical question regarding how accurately the willingness to pay to decrease the risk of accidental death reflects the willingness to pay for decreases in environmentally related fatality risks.

Two final points concern the continuity of risk levels available from the product and labor markets, and the lack of a temporal dimension in the model. The opportunity to buy safety-enhancing products is often discrete, meaning that the marginal conditions shown in Eq. (20.7) may not be obtainable. Similarly, there may not be a continuum of risk levels available for the occupations available to a person with a given stock of human capital and job-specific skills. These are issues that any hedonic-style analysis needs to confront, and once again the extent to which the model provides a reasonable approximation is an empirical question. More specific to environmental policy is the issue of latency. The static model implicitly assumes that the payment and risk reduction provision occur simultaneously, when expressions for willingness to pay are derived. Many environmental fatalities, however, are characterized by a period of latency – i.e. there is a lag between exposure and the onset of symptoms and ultimately death. This may occur because of latency inherent in the exposure, or because the exposure will not affect a person until he reaches a later, more vulnerable age. Thus the relevant willingness to pay measure might be the amount a person would part with now, to reduce his probability of dying sometime in the future. In this case, we would expect temporal variables like rates of time preference and savings behavior to influence willingness to pay. With this as motivation, we turn attention now to a generalization of the model that includes these features.

20.1.2 Life Cycle Model

To introduce a temporal dimension we assume the person's lifetime stream of expected utility from consuming z is additively separable in years. We also revert back to the case of strictly exogenous mortality risk. Following the framework from Cropper and Sussman (1990), this allows us to write the stream of utility obtained by the person from age a onward as

$$U_a = \sum_{t=a}^{T} \pi_{at} (1+\delta)^{a-t} u_t(z_t), \tag{20.8}$$

where T is the maximum possible length of life, δ is the person's subjective rate of time preference (utility discount rate), π_{at} is the conditional probability that the person is alive at time t, given that he has survived to age a, and $u_t(z_t)$ is the utility at time t from consuming the composite commodity z_t. Note that $\pi_{aa} = 1$, and define ρ_k as the conditional probability of dying at age k, given the person has reached this age. From this we can see that

$$\pi_{at} = (1-\rho_{a+1}) \times (1-\rho_{a+2}), ..., (1-\rho_{t-1}) \tag{20.9}$$

for $t > a$. This expression shows that the probability that an age a person survives to age t is the product of the conditional survival probabilities for each subsequent year of life, beginning at the reference age a and continuing until age $t-1$. From this expression, it is apparent that a change in mortality risk in year k changes π_{at} according to

$$\frac{\partial \pi_{at}}{\partial \rho_k} = -(1-\rho_{a+1}) \times (1-\rho_{a+2})...(1-\rho_{k-1}) \times (1-\rho_{k+1})...(1-\rho_{t-1})$$

$$= -\frac{1}{(1-\rho_k)} \pi_{at} < 0. \tag{20.10}$$

Suppose the person has exogenous lifetime earnings given by $y_a, ..., y_T$, and that he can smooth consumption over time by saving and borrowing. A convenient way to model consumption smoothing is to assume annuity markets are well functioning. Specifically, a person can invest one currency unit at the beginning of year k, and receive $(1+R_k)$ at the end of the year with probability $(1-\rho_k)$, and nothing with probability ρ_k. Likewise, he can borrow one currency unit at the interest rate R_k. If r is the risk-free interest rate for borrowing and saving – i.e. the rate when there is no risk of death causing a loan default or unspent savings – a competitive and actuarially fair annuity market implies R_k is determined according to

$$(1+R_k) \times (1-\rho_k) = 1+r, \tag{20.11}$$

so that $R_k > r$. Thus a saver receives a premium for accepting the risk that he will not survive to enjoy the return on his investment, and a borrower pays an interest premium based on the probability that he will not survive to repay the loan. Using R_k as the consumption discount rate, the present value at time a of consumption z_t in period t is

$$\frac{z_t}{\prod_{s=a}^{t-1}(1+R_s)}. \tag{20.12}$$

This expression is useful for deriving an intertemporal budget constraint. In particular, the present value of all future consumption must equal the present value of all future income, plus wealth in the current period. Formally this is given by

$$\sum_{t=a}^{T}\left[\frac{z_t}{\prod_{s=a}^{t-1}(1+R_s)}\right] = \sum_{t=a}^{T}\left[\frac{y_t}{\prod_{s=a}^{t-1}(1+R_s)}\right] + W_a, \qquad (20.13)$$

where W_a is wealth in the reference period a, which has accumulated from past borrowing and saving decisions.

It is useful for what follows to rewrite the budget constraint in terms of survival probabilities and the risk-free interest rate. For this note that

$$\prod_{s=a}^{t-1}(1+R_s) = \prod_{s=a}^{t-1}\frac{(1+r)}{(1-\rho_s)}$$
$$= \frac{(1+r)^{t-a}}{\pi_{at}}, \qquad (20.14)$$

where the first equality follows from (20.11) and the second from the definition of π_{at} in (20.9). Using (20.14) we can write the budget constraint for the allocation of consumption over time as

$$\sum_{t=a}^{T} \pi_{at}(1+r)^{a-t} z_t = \sum_{t=a}^{T} \pi_{at}(1+r)^{a-t} y_t + W_a. \qquad (20.15)$$

This shows that at time a, the expected consumption over a person's remaining life years should be equal to his remaining expected earnings plus current wealth, where all future consumption and income amounts are discounted to time a values.

The individual's objective is to maximize (20.8) at age a subject to (20.15), by selecting the stream of consumption $z_a, ..., z_T$. Formally, the problem is given by

$$V_a = \max_{z_a, ..., z_T} L_a = \sum_{t=a}^{T} \pi_{at}(1+\delta)^{a-t} u_t(z_t) + \lambda \left(W_a + \sum_{t=a}^{T} \pi_{at}(1+r)^{a-t}(y_t - z_t) \right). \qquad (20.16)$$

The first-order condition for z_t is

$$\pi_{at}(1+\delta)^{a-t} u_t'(z_t) - \lambda \pi_{at}(1+r)^{a-t} = 0, \qquad (20.17)$$

which we rearrange to show that

$$\frac{\lambda}{(1+r)^{t-a}} = \frac{u_t'(z_t)}{(1+\delta)^{t-a}}. \qquad (20.18)$$

Equation (20.18) has a useful interpretation. By the Envelope Theorem, λ is the marginal utility of one unit of wealth in time a. In a future year t, a unit of wealth needs to be discounted at the rate of interest r to be comparable with year a wealth. Thus the left-hand side of (20.18) is the marginal utility of future wealth, expressed in year a terms. The right-hand side is the marginal utility of consumption in year t, expressed in year a terms by discounting back using the person's rate of time preference δ. At the optimum allocation, the marginal utility of the consumption that wealth can purchase is equal to the marginal utility of wealth itself. From this, we can see that consumption allocation depends on the interest rate, the rate of time preference, and how the age-dependent utility function evolves as the person moves through life.

We are interested in the marginal willingness to pay at age a, for a change in the probability of dying at age k. That is, we want to evaluate the benefit a person receives from a small decrease in ρ_k. For this we need to come to terms with the fact that willingness to pay is in the *current* time a for a *future* benefit, and that a change in the probability of surviving during year k changes the conditional probability of survival in all future years as well. The relationship that we need is

$$MWTP_{ak} = \frac{-\partial V_a / \partial \rho_k}{\partial V_a / \partial W_a}, \tag{20.19}$$

where the denominator is equal to λ in Eq. (20.16) by the Envelope Theorem. Differentiating (20.16) with respect to ρ_k, and using (20.10), leads to

$$\frac{\partial V_a}{\partial \rho_k} = -(1-\rho_k)^{-1}\left(\sum_{t=k+1}^{T} \pi_{at}(1+\delta)^{a-t}u_t(z_t) + \lambda \sum_{t=k+1}^{T} \pi_{at}(1+r)^{a-t}(y_t - z_t)\right). \tag{20.20}$$

By dividing by λ and then substituting out for λ using (20.18), we can write the marginal willingness to pay for a change in time k risk – i.e. Eq. (20.19) – as

$$MWTP_{ak} = (1-\rho_k)^{-1}\sum_{t=k+1}^{T} \pi_{at}(1+r)^{a-t}\left(\frac{u_t(z_t)}{u_t'(z_t)} + y_t - z_t\right). \tag{20.21}$$

This expression shows that the marginal value of a reduction in the probability of dying in year k depends on the survival probability-weighted stream of utility that occurs from year $k+1$ onwards, scaled to currency units by dividing by the marginal utility of income. To convert the value of these future utility benefits to period a wealth, the expression is discounted to the present value at the rate of interest r. Finally, (20.21) contains a budget constraint component that adjusts willingness to pay, based on future saving and borrowing levels.

Equation (20.21) can also be compared to the static model result on the right-hand side of (20.1). If we set $T=1$, $a=1$, $z_1=y_1$, use $k=0$ to denote an instantaneous change in the mortality risk, and recall that $\pi_{11}=1$, then the two expressions are equivalent. From the comparison we see that in the more general case, willingness to pay depends on the time structure of a person's preferences, the interest rate, the evolution of mortality probabilities over time, and borrowing and saving behavior. These additional features allow us to examine several questions that are relevant to environmental policy.

Consider first how the willingness to pay for a risk reduction changes with a person's age. An age $a-1$ person's marginal willingness to pay for a risk reduction at age a is

$$MWTP_{a-1,a} = (1-\rho_a)^{-1} \sum_{t=a+1}^{T} \pi_{at} (1+r)^{a-t} \left(\frac{u_t(z_t)}{u'_t(z_t)} + y_t - z_t \right), \tag{20.22}$$

which can be increasing or decreasing in a. To derive an unambiguous prediction, suppose that $u_t(z_t) = u(z_t)$, so that the utility function does not depend on time, and that there is no saving or borrowing, so that $z_t = y_t$ in all periods. Suppose as well that income is equal across years, so that $y_t = y$. Finally, let $\rho_a = \rho$, so that the conditional probability of dying does not depend on age. In this special case we have

$$MWTP_{a-1,a} = (1-\rho)^{-1} \sum_{t=a+1}^{T} \pi_{at} (1+r)^{a-t} \left(\frac{u(y)}{u'(y)} \right), \tag{20.23}$$

which is decreasing in a by the simple fact that there are fewer years remaining until T, when a is larger. This special case implies that the willingness to pay for a risk reduction is smaller for older individuals – a result that has some intuitive appeal, and has occasionally been asserted to hold.

Note, however, that there is no theoretical reason to constrain the structure of preferences to be constant over time, and so the prediction on the relationship between marginal willingness to pay and age is ambiguous, even if the other special conditions in (20.23) approximately hold. Given the importance for environmental policy of risk reductions for older members of the population, who are often a main benefactor group from pollution reduction, this theoretical ambiguity has motivated an active empirical literature.

Equation (20.21) is also useful for examining the role of latency. To see this, note from (20.21) that

$$
\begin{aligned}
MWTP_{a+1,k} &= (1-\rho_k)^{-1} \sum_{t=k+1}^{T} \pi_{a+1,t} (1+r)^{a+1-t} \left(\frac{u_t(z_t)}{u'_t(z_t)} + y_t - z_t \right) \\
&= \frac{(1+r)}{(1-\rho_{a+1})} (1-\rho_k)^{-1} \sum_{t=k+1}^{T} \pi_{a,t} (1+r)^{a-t} \left(\frac{u_t(z_t)}{u'_t(z_t)} + y_t - z_t \right),
\end{aligned}
\tag{20.24}
$$

which implies

$$MWTP_{ak} = \frac{(1-\rho_{a+1}) MWTP_{a+1,k}}{(1+r)}. \tag{20.25}$$

Repeated use of this expression allows us to state the willingness to pay at age a for a change in risk at age k as

$$MWTP_{ak} = \pi_{ak} (1+r)^{a-k} MWTP_{kk}. \tag{20.26}$$

Equation (20.26) shows that the marginal willingness to pay today for a decrease in risk at age k (e.g. $k = 75$) is lower when the probability of surviving to age k is lower. It also shows that the marginal willingness to pay for a decrease in risk at age k increases with current age. Thus a latency period has multiple effects on the willingness to pay for a future risk reduction. In general, people's willingness to pay now for a future risk reduction, is not the same as the willingness to pay for a current reduction. Latency also introduces heterogeneity effects. For example, an older person in poor health might be willing to pay less than a similarly aged healthy person, but the unhealthy older person might be willing to pay more than a healthy younger person.

20.1.3 Lessons from Theory

The static and dynamic models allow us to examine slightly different behavioral phenomena, and they have somewhat different ramifications for how we might approach empirical measurement. The static model provides a clean link to easily observable behavior in labor and product markets. Thus it motivates a revealed preference approach, in which actual risk/income trade-offs are used to infer people's marginal values of risk reductions. However, the static model and most of the applied methods that follow from it abstract from many of the specific details of environmental policy – particularly as related to the nature and timing of fatality risks, as well as the types of people who are most likely to benefit from policy. The life cycle model suggests there are more complexities in how people trade off risk and income through time. This, combined with the context-specific types of risks that are of interest, suggests that a stated preference approach in which the valuation scenario is completely under the control of the researcher might be warranted. In the following section we discuss the typical RP and SP approaches used for measuring the benefits of mortality risk reductions in environmental policy.

20.2   MORTALITY RISK VALUATION – EMPIRICAL MODELS

In this section we examine both revealed and stated preference approaches to measuring the willingness to pay for reductions in mortality risks. Before doing so, however, it is useful to define a few concepts that are commonly used in empirical studies. For illustration, suppose we measure annual fatality risk from an environmental contaminant in deaths per 10,000 people, and that $\rho_e = 10/10{,}000$ (or 0.0010) is the baseline risk. Suppose a person is willing to pay $500 for a 1/10,000 reduction in the baseline risk; we refer to this as his *value of risk reduction* (VRR). From this we know that the person's marginal WTP for risk reduction is $500. If there were 10,000 identical people, and each had a VRR of $500, then as a group they would be willing to pay $500 × 10,000, or $5 million dollars in total, for the risk reduction. We have summed the individual VRRs to reflect the fact that the ex ante risk reduction is non-rival. Statistically, the group expects one less fatality during the year, but at the time of payment the specific person is not known. Thus the group of identical individuals is willing to pay $5 million during the year to prevent a single statistical death. A convenient way to compute this aggregate willingness to pay is to divide the VRR for a one-unit reduction by the unit reduction size. In our example, this would be $500/(0.0001) = \$5{,}000{,}000$.

The aggregation of individuals' marginal WTPs into a population willingness to pay is the basis for defining the *value of a statistical life* (VSL). Since this term has played an influential role in environmental economics and policy, we summarize it formally in the following definition.

Definition 20.1
The value of a statistical life (VSL) is the amount of money a population would pay ex ante to prevent the death of a single unknown member of the population, during a given time period. It is an aggregate concept that arises from the summation of individuals' marginal willingness to pay for small fatality risk changes.

The concept of VSL has been controversial, since it seems to imply there is a dollar value that we can assign to a specific human life. Cameron (2010) discusses some of the communication problems that have arisen from this terminology; she also proposes alternative language that focuses on marginal WTP rather than the aggregate concept of VSL. We refer the reader to Cameron's well-argued article for more detail on this debate. An additional problem with the VSL language is related to heterogeneity. Much of the applied literature has focused on estimating *the* VSL – i.e. a measure of central tendency that can be used to value each statistical life that is expected to be saved by a specific intervention. It has been argued, however, that the concept of a single VSL precludes accounting for the types of heterogeneity that were discussed above, and which are likely to be important in practice. Given this, it is sensible to focus on VSL measures that are more type specific, and perhaps context specific. For example, if the typical 70-year-old in good health has a willingness to pay of $600 for a 1/10,000 reduction in risk arising from a policy initiative, then the expected number of avoided fatalities among 70-year-olds in good health should be valued using a VSL of $6 million.

20.2.1 Hedonic Wages

The hedonic wage method has dominated the revealed preference literature on estimating risk/income trade-offs. The basic theoretical background for this model was covered in Chapter 15, and so we only sketch its intuition here. In the labor market context, firms hire workers and households provide labor. Firms try to attract workers by offering a compensation package that includes wages as well as non-wage aspects of the job. Among the latter are things like workplace amenities (e.g. onsite daycare facilities) and occupational safety measures. It is costly for firms to provide these amenities, and firms participating in a particular labor market segment have differential cost structures. A worker provides his labor to firms by selecting the combination of wages and workplace amenities that maximize his utility, subject to the job opportunities he is qualified for. Workers participating in a labor market sector have heterogeneous preferences for workplace attributes, such as risks to health and life. Equilibrium in a labor market segment is reached when all workers and firms are matched at particular wage and amenity levels, away from which no party wants to deviate. The hedonic wage function is the locus of these pairings that relates wages to the non-wage aspects of the workplace, conditional on workers' skills and other industry/job-specific attributes. The empirical objective in hedonic wage studies is to estimate the hedonic wage function so as to understand the extra compensation a worker requires to voluntarily take on additional fatality risk at the workplace, holding all else fixed. Linking things to the model shown above, the intent is to estimate the left-hand side of (20.5) using labor market observations, so as to obtain an estimate of the value of risk reduction, as given by the right-hand side.

The basic estimation problem is to identify the parameter γ in the regression equation

$$\ln y_i = \beta X_i + \gamma \rho_i^y + \varepsilon_i, \tag{20.27}$$

where y_i is usually measured as hourly earnings for worker i, ρ_i^y is the workplace fatality risk that worker i faces in the time period (usually a year), and X_i is a vector of additional controls. We expect that $\gamma > 0$, meaning a higher annual fatality risk should imply a higher hourly wage, holding all else fixed. Since (20.27) is a wage regression, many of the insights from labor economics are relevant for its specification. For example, X_i should include variables reflecting workers' productivity and characteristics of their industry and occupation. It is particularly important to control for the fact that many high-paying jobs are also very safe, since this tends to be the result of labor market segmentation rather than risk/income trade-offs per se. Thus hedonic wage regressions need to account for differences in productivity, as well as industry, geographic, and qualification-based segmentation.

Estimation of (20.27) is relatively straightforward regarding the steps that need to be taken. First, data on workers' wages, characteristics (e.g. age, education, experience, and marital status), occupation, and industry are needed. In the United States – where the literature is large and mature – a small number of data sets have formed the basis for hedonic wage estimation since the 1990s. These include the Panel Study of Income Dynamics (PSID), Current Population Survey (CPS), Health and Retirement Survey (HRS), and the Survey of Income and Program Participation (SIPP). Although these data sets are relatively complete, they do not contain information on the injury and fatality risks that workers face on the job. The second step is therefore to gather data on workplace injuries and fatality rates, and match them to the workers in the income sample. Currently in the United States, the best source for this information is the Bureau of Labor Statistics (BLS) Census of Fatal Occupational Injuries (CFOI) data. This is a census of annual workplace fatalities linked to occupation and industry categories, based on the US Census' North American Industry Classification System (NAICS). Using the CFOI information, it is possible to link the labor market and fatality data across 720 unique industry/occupation categories.

EXAMPLE 20.1 (EMPIRICAL) The hedonic wage literature focused on applications outside of the United States is somewhat limited. The small number of European studies have used similar data, and followed similar procedures, to those of the US studies. For example, in a German application Schaffner and Spengler (2010) use labor market data from a 1 percent random sample of West German contributors to the state pension system. Workplace accident data were assembled from a separate public source, and reported at the level of an occupational code, which is also used to classify workers in the labor market data. By combining the two data sources, variation in fatality rates and wages across 275 occupation categories was available for analysis. A Polish application

from Giergiczny (2008) relied on a similar data environment. Wage and worker characteristics were drawn from an annual survey conducted by the central government, and
workplace fatality rates were separately assembled from National Labor Inspectorate
records. Once again, the data sources were linked by occupation and industry categories, providing variation across 156 occupation categories for use in estimation.

With the earnings and fatality risk data sources collected and merged, the applied
task is to run models as in (20.27) and assess their reliability. Researchers using hedonic
wage models to measure marginal values for risk reduction have needed to confront
several econometric challenges, as well as issues related to the validity of the underlying
assumptions. The econometric challenges relate to standard issues of unbiased estimation of γ in (20.27). Three related issues in particular have drawn attention: measurement error, omitted variables, and the endogeneity of risk. The main measurement error
problem relates to the fact that an individual worker's fatality risk is not known, in that
we are not able to observe plant-level fatality rates and match them to specific workers
in the sample. Instead, as described above, an industry/occupation or similar aggregate
average is matched to each person. For example, Viscusi (2004) uses the CFOI data in
a US application to break out fatality rates by 72 industry and 10 occupation categories,
meaning that workers in his sample are assigned to one of the 720 average risk levels
noted above. If the actual conditions at the worker's place of employment deviate randomly from this average then the estimate of γ will suffer from attenuation bias based
on classical measurement error. At the same time, if actual conditions deviate from the
average in a systematic way, then the resulting estimate of γ will suffer from omitted
variable bias. For example, if safer-than-average plants also tend to have better onsite
amenities that are unrelated to safety, the compensating wage differential attributed to
fatality risk in the regression actually reflect other aspects of the workplace.

Other omitted variable problems in regressions such as (20.27) can pose threats to the
validity of fatality risk effect estimates. The general issue is that data on worker and job
characteristics are usually limited in availability, and their omission from X_i in (20.27)
will lead to biased estimates if they are correlated with fatality risks. The concern related
to omitted variables on workers is that the workforce risk a person faces is endogenous,
in the sense that people select themselves into occupations based on qualifications and
risk attitudes. People also differ in their ability to manage workplace risk. Panel datasets
have on occasion been used to control for fixed worker characteristics (e.g. Kniesner
et al., 2012), but problems with omitted job characteristics remain, even within this
richer data environment. Factors such as the non-fatal injury rate, injury compensation
plans, and the overall quality of management are likely to be correlated with the fatality
rate, and are in many cases not observed. In such cases one would ideally use occupation and industry dummy variables to somewhat control for unmeasured job characteristics. Use of these dummy variables, however, often leaves little variability in risk
rates with which to estimate γ, since fatality risks are only measured at the occupation/
industry level.

Econometric challenges of the types described here are not unique to wage/fatality
risk reductions, and as this is still an active area of research, progress on obtaining
unbiased estimates of the coefficient on fatality risk in wage regressions seems likely.
Laying aside the econometric issues, however, a number of conceptual assumptions

must also hold for estimation of (20.27) to provide an accurate measure of the value of risk reduction. First, workers need to be well informed about the distribution of risks among the different occupations from which they select. Related to this, they must also be able to compare small differences in risks. For example, while most people intuitively know that working in a mine is more dangerous than working in an office, they may not appreciate the different risks associated with being a miner relative to being a firefighter. Finally, the assumption of labor market equilibrium may be more tenuous in this context than in the property market context. In the latter case, we examined recent purchases in which observation of optimal outcomes is a reasonable assumption. Labor market studies generally rely on observing a sample of workers rather than a sample of workers who have recently moved jobs. For many, it may be that the current job is no longer optimal in the hedonic model sense, but that transactions costs have prevented an adjustment. In this case, the slope of the hedonic wage function need not correspond to the marginal willingness to pay for risk. Bockstael and McConnell (2007) highlight this argument as part of a critical critique of hedonic wage models.

If the value of risk reduction in a labor market context is properly identified, there still may be concerns with using it for environmental policy. These relate to the fact that most of the inference from hedonic wage regressions arises from working-age males in blue-collar industries facing the risk of accidental death. It may be that values recovered in this context do not transfer well to deaths from illness suffered primarily by older individuals, as is most often the relevant population for environmental policy. For these reasons, many researchers have come to prefer a stated preference approach, which we discuss in the next subsection.[1]

EXAMPLE 20.2 (EMPIRICAL) Viscusi (2004) provides an example of a well-executed hedonic wages study using data in the United States. His sample is drawn from the 1997 Current Population Survey (CPS), and contains information on 99,033 full-time workers between the ages of 18 and 65. Fatality risks are computed using the US BLS Census of Fatal Occupational Injuries (CFOI) database, which, for example, recorded 6,217 US workplace fatalities in 1992 and 6,238 in 1997. Viscusi uses the sum of fatalities in each of 72 industry and 10 occupation combinations, divided by BLS estimates of employment totals for each industry/occupation cell, to compute average fatality risks. His table 1 (p.33) illustrates the variation in risk across occupations and industries. For example, machine operators in mining and construction suffer 24.31 and 30.41 fatalities per 100,000 workers, respectively, while the figure for machine operators in manufacturing is 2.15. The average across all occupations and industries is 4.02 deaths per 100,000, or an annual fatality probability of 0.00004.

Viscusi presents regression results that include variables for worker characteristics such as age, gender, racial groups, marital status, and education. Job characteristics include the union status of the worker, a dummy variable for a public industry, nine occupational category dummies, injury and illness rates, and injury compensation rates as well as the fatality risk. The dependent variable is the log of the average hourly wage. In his table 2 (p.37), Viscusi reports a full sample estimate of $\hat{\gamma} = 0.0017$ for the

---

[1] Our presentation of the empirical and conceptual challenges associated with wage hedonics is based to a large extent on the discussion in Cropper et al. (2011).

coefficient on annual fatality risk in (20.27), and an average VSL of $4.7 million aris-
ing from this estimate. In particular, the VSL in the semi-log specification is computed
according to

$$VSL = (0.0017 \times wage) \times 2000 \times 100,000,$$

                                                                                   (20.28)

where the term in parenthesis is the change in the sample mean hourly wage caused by
a one-person decrease in fatalities per 100,000 workers. The last two terms are included
to convert the change to annual income (assuming 40 working hours and 50 working
weeks implies 2,000 working hours in a year), and to sum the value over the 100,000
people who share the risk reduction, respectively.

20.2.2 Stated Preference

As was discussed in Chapter 19, a primary advantage of stated preference (SP) methods
is the flexibility they afford the researcher to examine questions in specific contexts
using designed experiments fully under the control of the investigator. Our discussion
of the conceptual and empirical challenges inherent in using wage hedonic models to
value environmental fatality risks suggests there are likely to be gains from the flexibility provided by SP in this context. In this subsection we describe how SP techniques can
be deployed for the purpose of measuring context-specific environmental fatality risks,
and discuss the challenges that researchers must confront when doing so.

   Though a variety of SP models have been used to value mortality risks, they generally
share a common structure. First, the relevant population is defined. In most instances
this has been a general population, but in some studies researchers have focused on a
particular segment, such as children or the elderly. Second, a specific fatality that can
arise from exposure to a particular pollutant is described. For example, a survey might
look at cancer deaths from exposure to pesticide residues or hazardous waste, or heart-
related deaths from exposure to conventional air pollutants such as particulate matter.
Third, the baseline risk for the person is communicated. This is often conditional on age,
to reflect the fact that different cohorts of people face different risks from similar levels
of ambient pollution. Next, an intervention is described that changes the risk faced by
the person to a lower level. This risk reduction is the commodity the person will be
asked to value, and it can be tailored to the policy context. For example, the scenario
might describe a current reduction in pollution that will affect a person's mortality risk
at some time in the future. In other cases the commodity is a medical intervention.
Finally, a choice situation is presented in which the person has the opportunity to give
something up – usually money – to have the decreased mortality risk. Answers to the
choice questions allow the analyst to examine money/risk trade-offs in the specific context described by the survey, for the target population, and conditional on the age and
other characteristics of the person.

   Stated preference models typically used for mortality risk analysis include mixtures
of contingent valuation and discrete choice experiment approaches. The experimental
design often presents respondents with options that vary some or all of the following
attributes: fatality risk, cause of fatality (e.g. cancer, car accident, etc.), length/intensity

of illness before death, age of symptom onset and death, length of time between exposure and illness (e.g. latency), and the private or public nature of the risk reduction. This flexibility allows the features of the life cycle model presented above – particularly the role of time preferences, age-dependent utility functions, and age-specific conditional survival figures – to be incorporated into the empirical analysis. Therefore, most stated preference exercises rely at least implicitly on the life cycle model and exogenous risks for motivation.

There are two main challenges associated with stated preference approaches. The first relates to the non-binding nature of people's answers, and therefore corresponds to the general discussion on hypothetical bias presented in Chapter 19. The second is more specific to risk valuation. It is an empirical regularity that people have a difficult time understanding and comparing probabilities for unlikely events. For example, although fatality probabilities of 1/10,000 and 2/100,000 differ substantially, without careful presentation respondents in an SP survey may fail to distinguish between them, or may rank the latter as a higher risk than the former. Thus the key attribute in stated preference studies related to valuing mortality risks is also the most difficult to describe, and present alternative values for.

This problem can manifest itself in estimates of willingness to pay that are insensitive to the magnitude of the risk reduction (see Hammitt and Graham, 1999 for detailed discussion). Using the terms from the last chapter, SP studies of mortality risk have often failed scope tests regarding the size of risk reductions. Thus, while respondents are generally willing to pay to have *a* risk reduction, the amount is similar for different *sizes* of reductions. In response to this, researchers have invested considerable energy in designing effective risk communication approaches. As an example of this, Corso et al. (2001) systematically examined the performance of risk ladders and dot/grid visual aids on the sensitivity of willingness to pay to reduce risk levels, relative to no visual aid. A risk ladder provides a vertical graphic illustrating a progression of low- to high-risk occurrences (see Corso et al., p.183). On the bottom are events such as being struck by a falling aircraft (6 in 100 million); the top events include the risk of death from heart disease for someone over 65 (2 in 100). A dot/grid approach presents respondents with a rectangular grid with dots filled in to illustrate different risk probabilities. Krupnick et al. (2002, p.167) provide an example of this. Corso et al. (2001) find that the use of both visual aids leads to improved scope performance, relative to no visual aid. More generally, the lesson from studies of this type is that the survey needs to devote considerable time to educating people on how to think about risks; visual aids combined with different written or verbal presentations are critical for this. For example, in a state-of-the-art, computer-executed study related to mortality risks, Cameron and DeShazo (2013) employed four different communication strategies: the grid/dot graphic, a written description, and two different numerical presentations. These are accompanied by exercises that test people's ability to comprehend risk differences, and provide additional instruction for respondents who incorrectly perceive the differences.

EXAMPLE 20.3 (EMPIRICAL) Cameron and DeShazo (2013) present a stated preference analysis of mortality risks from different causes, using a choice experiment. Though not explicitly linked to environmental causes, it is an excellent example of the flexibility provided by SP. The basic objective is to examine trade-offs individuals are willing to make among different health profiles, which unfold from the current period over the course of the person's remaining life. Each profile is defined by an illness, the probability it will occur, treatment options, the timing of symptom onset, recovery, and/or death, and the severity of pain from the illness. People have the opportunity to purchase treatment options via co-payments that reduce the risk that the profile will occur, relative to the status quo. Figure 20.1 provides an example of the types of choices individuals in the study were asked to make.

A representative sample of 2,400 US adults completed the survey. The survey was administered online, which allowed for the development of personalized illness profiles, conditional on the respondent's gender and current age. The experimental design includes a continuum of values for lost life years, latency period, associated pain, and time spent sick, as well as several different causes of death. With this Cameron and DeShazo are able to predict risk reduction values in a wide range of specific circumstances. To report their results, the authors use a small change in risk known as a "microrisk" (μr), which is a reduction of 1/1,000,000 in the risk of dying. For comparison to the hedonic wage literature, they estimate that a 45-year-old with $42,000 in household income would pay $6.74 in the current year to reduce his chance of sudden

Choose the program that reduces the illness that you most want to avoid. But think carefully about whether the costs are too high for you. If both programs are too expensive, then choose Neither Program.

If you choose "neither program", remember that you could die early from a number of causes, including the ones described below.

	Program A for Respiratory Disease	Program B for Colon Cancer
Symptoms/ Treatment	Get sick when 65 years old No hospitalization Minor surgery Moderate pain for 1 month	Get sick when 68 years old 1 month of hospitalization Major surgery Severe pain for 18 months Moderate pain for 2 years
Recovery/ Life expectancy	Recover at 65 Die of something else at 68 instead of 88	Recover at 71 Die of something else at 73 instead of 88
Risk Reduction	75% From 4 in 1,000 to 1 in 1,000	50% From 4 in 1,000 to 2 in 1,000
Costs to you	$18 per month [= $216 per year]	$4 per month [= $48 per year]
Your choice	◯ **Reduce my chance of respiratory disease**	◯ **Reduce my chance of colon cancer**
	◯ **Neither Program**	

Figure 20.1   Example choice card from Cameron and DeShazo
Source: Cameron, T.A. and J.R. DeShazo. 2012. *Handbook to accompany "Demand for health risk reductions" and related papers.* Permission for use granted by the authors.

accidental death by 1µr. Multiplying this by 1 million implies a VSL equivalent of $6.74 million, which is close to the median of estimates from the various US wage hedonic studies.

The value of the Cameron and DeShazo research, however, is that we can examine the willingness to pay for more environmentally relevant risks, conditional on individual heterogeneity. For example, the authors find that a person who is 35 today would be willing to pay $3.55 in current dollars per year for a 1µr reduction in the probability of getting sick at age 50 and dying one year later. This can be compared to a 60-year-old, who would be willing to pay $0.98 in current dollars per year to reduce the probability of a similar illness profile beginning at age 80.

20.3   VALUING CHANGES IN MORBIDITY

Morbidity effects from pollution arise because many types of emissions cause sickness or exacerbate the symptoms from existing illnesses. Prominent examples noted above include the effect of ground-level ozone on people with asthma, and the gastrointestinal problems caused by bacteria in drinking water. Thus environmental improvements can convey benefits via a reduction in pollution-related illnesses. In this section we discuss the challenges and methods used to measure the value of these benefits.

The literature on valuing morbidity is not as well organized or developed as the mortality literature. There are several reasons for this. First, with morbidity there is substantial heterogeneity in outcomes that need to be addressed. While fatalities and fatality risks are relatively straightforward concepts, there are several dimensions to morbidity. Sickness can be either acute or chronic, illnesses have start and end dates, symptoms can be intense or mild, and there is variation in how people respond to treatment and how symptoms limit day-to-day activities. As such, applied morbidity studies tend to focus on specific contexts, and there is no single dominant valuation objective, like mortality risk, that the literature is organized around. Second, morbidity presents a more challenging data environment than mortality. In most instances, deaths and their causes are reported, while most pollution-related illnesses are not recorded. For example, while we may be able to observe emergency room visits for pulmonary and cardiovascular problems, we cannot easily observe illnesses that do not require treatment. Finally, the morbidity literature in and beyond environmental economics has pursued a wider range of measurement objectives. Researchers have, for example, looked at the medical costs associated with treatment, lost wages or school attendance owing to sickness, private resources spent on preventative behavior, and the actual disutility from symptoms. A theoretically correct welfare measure would account for all of these channels. In practice, however, applied work has often focused on subsets of these measurement objectives.

Cameron (2014) elaborates on these points in detail, and describes the general state of morbidity reduction benefits research. In this section our objective is to first organize thinking on morbidity valuation by presenting a simple conceptual model, which is followed by examples of RP and SP approaches that derive from it. We close the section by briefly considering the role of quality-adjusted life years (QALYs) in environmental economics.

20.3.1 A Model of Health Production

Most efforts at valuing the morbidity effects of pollution rely either explicitly or implicitly on the substitutes model discussed in Chapter 15. The basic idea is that health outcomes are produced by individuals via a combination of purchased inputs (e.g. medical services), lifestyle choices (e.g. nutrition), time inputs (e.g. exercise), and the ambient environment. Individuals select levels of the private inputs, taking as given environmental conditions, and so behavioral functions for the inputs depend on environmental conditions. The empirical task is therefore to use either RP or SP methods to estimate the relevant behavioral functions, and link them to the environment. In this subsection we present a formal model of health production and behavior, which is useful for framing the different types of empirical studies.

Suppose that the number of healthy days in a time period is denoted by H, and that healthy days are produced according to the production function $H=f(x,a,q;s)$, where x is a purchased input, a is a time input, q is ambient environmental quality, and we have conditioned the function on the person's characteristics vector s. In what follows, we will often drop the explicit dependence on s in order to reduce notational clutter. We assume all three inputs have positive marginal product, meaning that q is measured as environmental quality rather than pollution. Implicit in this function is the notion that the effect of the pollution that the person is exposed to is determined jointly by the levels of q, x, and a, and that the dose and the person's characteristics (e.g. genetic makeup) jointly determine H.

It is worth noting that our model is already context specific. The health commodity per day is a healthy/not healthy binary outcome rather than a gradation of health levels. In addition, we have not distinguished utility effects by the type of illness or specific symptoms. This means the person experiences utility from being healthy or disutility from sickness, but the specific profile of illness or symptoms does not matter. As we show below, this is useful for motivating different classes of models, though perhaps less useful for designing specific empirical studies.

Given the health production function $H=f(x,a,q;s)$, the person derives utility from consuming a numeraire good z and leisure l, and disutility from being sick. The utility function is given by $U(z,l,S)$, where $S=T-H$ is the number of days sick and T is the number of days in the time period. The individual can spend his healthy days earning income at the wage rate w, consuming leisure, or investing time in health production. Earned income can be used to purchase units of x at price p, or it can be consumed as z. The person's utility maximization problem is

$$\max_{z,l,a,x} L = U\left(z,l,T - f(x,a,q)\right) + \lambda\left(wf(x,a,q) - wl - wa - px - z\right). \tag{20.29}$$

The first-order conditions for z and l are simply $\partial U(\cdot)/\partial z = \lambda$ and $\partial U(\cdot)/\partial l = \lambda \cdot w$, respectively, and so the marginal value of time is the wage rate w. The first-order conditions for a and x are

$$-\frac{\partial U(\cdot)}{\partial S}\frac{\partial f(\cdot)}{\partial a} = \lambda\left[w - w\frac{\partial f(\cdot)}{\partial a}\right] \quad \rightarrow \quad w\lambda - \frac{\partial U(\cdot)}{\partial S} = \frac{w\lambda}{\partial f(\cdot)/\partial a} \tag{20.30}$$

and

$$-\frac{\partial U(\cdot)}{\partial S}\frac{\partial f(\cdot)}{\partial x}=\lambda\left[p-w\frac{\partial f(\cdot)}{\partial x}\right] \quad\rightarrow\quad w\lambda-\frac{\partial U(\cdot)}{\partial S}=\frac{p\lambda}{\partial f(\cdot)/\partial x}, \tag{20.31}$$

respectively. The first-order conditions give rise to ordinary input demand functions that we denote by $x(p,w,q)$ and $a(p,w,q)$. Plugging these expressions into the technology function allows us to write the number of healthy days that the person has available as

$$H = f\left(x(p,w,q),a(p,w,q),q\right) = H(p,w,q). \tag{20.32}$$

We note in passing that (20.30) and (20.31) imply $(\partial f(\cdot)/\partial a)/(\partial f(\cdot)/\partial x)=w/p$, which tells us that the marginal rate of transformation between health-improving activity a and expenditure on commercially available defense measures x equals the price ratio between the two. Put differently, we have $(\partial f(\cdot)/\partial x)/p=(\partial f(\cdot)/\partial a)/w$, so that one dollar lost in terms of wages through spending time on health activity has the same marginal effect on health as one dollar spent on other defensive measures available in the market. This equality is useful for measuring private responses to changing environmental quality.

20.3.2 Revealed Preference Approaches

Revealed preference applications of the health production model have, in practice, usually focused on the marginal willingness to pay for q. To derive an expression for this based on the time or private good input, we differentiate (20.29) with respect to q to obtain

$$\begin{aligned}\frac{\partial L}{\partial q} &= -\frac{\partial U(\cdot)}{\partial S}\frac{\partial f(\cdot)}{\partial q}+\lambda w\frac{\partial f(\cdot)}{\partial q}=\frac{\partial f(\cdot)}{\partial q}\left(\lambda w-\frac{\partial U(\cdot)}{\partial S}\right)\\ &=\frac{\partial f(\cdot)/\partial q}{\partial f(\cdot)/\partial a}w\lambda\\ &=\frac{\partial f(\cdot)/\partial q}{\partial f(\cdot)/\partial x}p\lambda,\end{aligned} \tag{20.33}$$

where the second and third lines follow from equations (20.30) and (20.31), respectively. To derive the marginal willingness to pay for q, we divide through by the marginal utility of income, λ. With this, we can express the marginal willingness to pay for q in two ways:

$$MWTP(q) = \frac{\partial f(\cdot)/\partial q}{\partial f(\cdot)/\partial x}p = \frac{\partial x(p,w,q)}{\partial q}p, \tag{20.34}$$

and

$$MWTP(q) = \frac{\partial f(\cdot)/\partial q}{\partial f(\cdot)/\partial x}w = \frac{\partial a(p,w,q)}{\partial q}w. \tag{20.35}$$

These expressions are equivalent to those derived in Chapter 15, where we showed that knowledge of the demand for the private good substitute provided sufficient information to estimate the marginal willingness to pay for environmental quality.

This logic suggests an empirical strategy in which we gather data on private behavior such as changes in time spent outdoors or consumption of health services, and attempt to identify the causal effect of changes in environmental quality on these activities. We illustrate this type of approach with the following example.

EXAMPLE 20.4 (EMPIRICAL) Graff Zivin et al. (2011) examine how the demand for bottled drinking water responds to changes in tap water quality by matching data on bottled water sales at specific supermarkets, to violations of drinking water standards in the areas served by the supermarkets. They take advantage of the fact that the US Safe Drinking Water Act requires that water utilities monitor levels of specific contaminants and provide public notification when standards are exceeded. Violations between 2001 and 2005 by utilities in Northern California and Nevada were matched to the zip codes that the utilities serve. Data on weekly bottled water sales at major grocery stores in the same zip codes for the same time period were also obtained. The matched data allow the authors to examine how weekly bottled water consumption at the zip code level responds to spatially and temporally varying announcements of tap water quality violations. The authors show, for example, that a 22 percent increase in weekly bottled water sales occurs when a "microorganism" violation is announced – i.e. a bacteria-based violation that may cause immediate gastrointestinal health threats. They also show that a "chemicals" violation – i.e. elevated levels of chemical compounds such as arsenic – leads to a 17 percent increase in sales. Extrapolating the California and Nevada estimates to the entire US (and employing several other assumptions), Graff Zivin et al. estimate that in 2005 people spent $11.34 million on bottled water in response to microorganism violations and $47.15 million in response to chemical violations.

It is worth emphasizing here that the aggregate figures reported by Graff Zivin et al. (2011) are not based on marginal changes, but rather are estimates of the actual change in expenditures on bottled water that resulted from announced violations in 2005. As such, the bounding arguments described in Chapter 15 are needed to formally relate the change in expenditures to a theoretically valid welfare measure. For the context here, proposition 15.4 is relevant, in that the increase in expenditures on bottled water provide a lower bound on the welfare loss associated with the quality violations.

Epidemiology-Style Approaches

A recent trend in the revealed preference literature has taken a step back from estimating the structural equations needed for welfare analysis, and has instead focused on providing credible causal evidence that people's private choices regarding health are indeed influenced by environmental quality. This has shifted the focus away from explicit household production models, and more towards reduced form analysis of behavioral responses, which are then used to approximate welfare measures. The motivation for this trend is that epidemiology studies seeking to estimate the response of health to pollution often do not control for the potential behavioral responses emphasized by economists.

To illustrate this, note that we can obtain an expression for the total response of healthy days to a change in the environment by differentiating (20.32) with respect to q:

$$\frac{dH}{dq} = \frac{\partial f(\cdot)}{\partial x}\frac{\partial x(\cdot)}{\partial q} + \frac{\partial f(\cdot)}{\partial a}\frac{\partial a(\cdot)}{\partial q} + \frac{\partial f(\cdot)}{\partial q}. \tag{20.36}$$

The left-hand side is the overall response of healthy days to environmental quality that we would observe simply by comparing health outcomes data to pollution data. The right-hand side shows that this full effect nests indirect behavioral responses in x and a, as well as the direct effect of the environment on health. Thus a simple regression of the form $H = \beta_0 + \beta_1 q + \varepsilon$ is unlikely to recover an estimate of the direct effect $\partial f(\cdot)/\partial q$, because of omitted variable bias. Specifically, the level of q is likely to be negatively correlated with the level of the omitted variables x and a, since during lower-quality events people are likely to use more of the private inputs. An ordinary least squares estimate of β_1 will therefore be biased towards zero. Use of this estimate will lead one to understate the welfare loss from a decrease in environmental quality, since it will not account for the costly increase in the use of x and a, to mitigate the negative health consequences of the decrease in q. With this as motivation, recent empirical work has used quasi-experimental and instrumental variables approaches to more precisely distinguish $\partial f(\cdot)/\partial q$ from dH/dq. This is illustrated by the following example.

EXAMPLE 20.5 (EMPIRICAL) Moretti and Neidell (2011) examine how ozone levels cause respiratory-related hospitalizations in the Los Angeles area. The empirical challenge they face is illustrated by Eq. (20.36). Specifically, to identify the all-else-held-equal effect of ozone on hospital visits (i.e. $\partial f(\cdot)/\partial q$), it is necessary to account for the fact that during high ozone pollution days, which are publicly announced, people engage in avoidance behavior by staying indoors. Moretti and Neidell address this by using an instrumental variables (IV) approach. They assemble data on daily respiratory-related hospital visits at the level of patients' zip code for the Los Angeles area between 1993 and 2000. These data are spatially and temporally matched to daily air pollution readings from 35 ozone monitors and 20 carbon monoxide/nitrogen dioxide monitors located across the city. Weather controls are also included, and regressions for the April to October ozone season are examined.

To establish a point of comparison, Moretti and Neidell regress hospital visits on daily ozone concentration, using ordinary least squares (OLS). They find that a 0.01 parts per million (ppm) increase in ozone – 20 percent of the mean concentration in the sample – is associated with 1.16 percent increase in hospital visits. This figure likely includes omitted variable bias, and therefore provides an estimate of dH/dq rather than $\partial f(\cdot)/\partial q$. This is because people stay inside more on high ozone days, which decreases the number of hospital visits, meaning that there is an unobserved determinant of visits that is correlated with ozone levels. To address this problem, the authors use daily boat traffic at the Port of Los Angeles as an instrument for ozone in an IV regression, since freight traffic at the port is a large contributor to air pollution in the area. The authors demonstrate that boat traffic is positively correlated with ozone concentrations, and argue that avoidance behavior (e.g. staying indoors) is unlikely to be correlated with boat traffic at the port. In their IV regression, Moretti and Neidell find that a 0.01 ppm increase in ozone concentration causes a 4.54 percent increase in hospital admissions, supporting the notion that the OLS regression is biased downwards by the failure to account for people's optimizing response to known pollution levels.

To understand the welfare impacts of ozone pollution, Moretti and Neidell assemble data on the average bill and length of stay for respiratory related hospital admissions. They value the opportunity cost of a hospital stay via the average wage earnings in the Los Angeles area. Using the hospital bill and wage data along with the biased OLS estimate implies that a 0.01 ppm reduction in ozone is worth \$2.8 million per year. With the IV estimate the value increases to \$11.2 million annually.

Cost of Illness

An alternative expression for the marginal willingness to pay can be derived that allows us to link the concept of willingness to pay to the notion of the opportunity cost of an illness. Following Freeman et al.'s (2014, p.218) derivation, note that we can rearrange (20.36) to obtain:

$$\frac{\partial f(\cdot)}{\partial q} = \frac{dH}{dq} - \frac{\partial f(\cdot)}{\partial x}\frac{\partial x(\cdot)}{\partial q} - \frac{\partial f(\cdot)}{\partial a}\frac{\partial a(\cdot)}{\partial q}. \tag{20.37}$$

Multiplying both sides by the first-order conditions shown in (20.30) and (20.31) leaves us with

$$\left(\frac{w\lambda}{\partial f(\cdot)/\partial a}\right)\frac{\partial f(\cdot)}{\partial q} = \frac{dH}{dq}\left(w\lambda - \frac{\partial U(\cdot)}{\partial S}\right)$$
$$- \frac{\partial f(\cdot)}{\partial x}\frac{\partial x(\cdot)}{\partial q}\left(\frac{p\lambda}{\partial f(\cdot)/\partial x}\right) - \frac{\partial f(\cdot)}{\partial a}\frac{\partial a(\cdot)}{\partial q}\left(\frac{w\lambda}{\partial f(\cdot)/\partial a}\right), \tag{20.38}$$

where we have used alternative versions of the equalities in the first-order conditions strategically across the four components. Dividing both sides by the marginal utility of income λ, distributing terms, and carrying out the cancelations leads to

$$MWTP(q) = \left\{\frac{dH}{dq}w - \frac{\partial x(\cdot)}{\partial q}p - \frac{\partial a(\cdot)}{\partial q}w\right\} - \frac{\partial U(\cdot)/\partial S}{\lambda}\frac{dH}{dq}, \tag{20.39}$$

which has a useful interpretation. The term in brackets is the direct pecuniary benefit of a marginal increase in q, in that it includes: (a) the value of the time provided by the change in H, and (b) the savings from the reduced expenditures on x and a. When cast in terms of a decrease in q, this is often labeled the "cost of illness," because it reflects the observed monetary losses that the change causes. Since the term in brackets can often be calculated from lost wages and increased medical expenses, the cost of illness is commonly used to approximate the theoretically desirable willingness to pay. Equation (20.39) shows that the accuracy of the cost of illness as an approximation depends on the component of willingness to pay that reflects the disutility from sickness. It also shows that the cost of illness will generally be a lower bound on the marginal willingness to pay for a change in q.

EXAMPLE 20.6 (EMPIRICAL) Our Moretti and Neidell (2011) example can also be used to illustrate the difference between a cost of illness and a willingness to pay estimate. One interpretation of their OLS coefficient estimate is that it is the total change in hospital visits from a change in ozone rather than an all-else-held-constant partial effect. In this regard it is akin to dH/dq in Eq. (20.36), rather than effect $\partial f(\cdot)/\partial q$, which is identified by the IV estimator. Equation (20.39) shows that the total change in expenditure from the change in pollution is a lower bound, cost of illness estimate of the welfare effects. Thus we can interpret the $2.8 million per year estimate from Moretti and Neidell as reflecting a cost of illness approximation. In this example, the cost of illness approximation is too low by a factor of four.

20.3.3 Stated Preference Approaches

SP approaches to valuing morbidity effects typically use the health production model to motivate a direct focus on symptoms or sickness management. A common experimental design presents respondents with the opportunity to purchase a medical intervention that eliminates sickness or controls symptoms in a specified way. In terms of the substitutes model from Chapter 15, the intervention – which is typically hypothetical and tailored to the needs of the study – is a perfect substitute for a reduction in pollution exposure. For example, a person's willingness to pay for a product that will reduce asthma symptoms in a given time period is plausibly equal to their willingness to pay for the same reduced symptoms resulting from a decrease in pollution. Thus SP studies related to pollution and morbidity tend to be focused on characterizing the relationship between illness or symptoms and an experimentally designed private good. Often the link to the environment is not part of the actual survey, even if the intent is to use the results for environmental policy.

EXAMPLE 20.7 (EMPIRICAL) Cropper et al. (2004) examine the value of malaria prevention in Ethiopia. They surveyed 848 heads of households across 18 villages in an area of the country that experiences seasonal malaria outbreaks. Among those questioned, 78 percent had been ill with malaria sometime in their lifetime, while 58 percent had been ill sometime during the last two years. Since lost productivity is a substantial cost of malaria in Africa, Cropper et al. were interested in comparing the cost of illness and willingness to pay approaches to valuing a reduction in malaria incidence. For a point of reference, the authors calculate that a malaria episode suffered by an adult costs the household 21 workdays, distributed among the sick person and the caregiver. The lost wages plus money spent on treatment for such a case is estimated to be between $7 and $24 in 1997 US dollar prices. With average incomes of around $200 per year, this is a large fraction of a household's resources. The cost, however, does not reflect the disutility of illness for the person suffering from the disease or the utility costs on caregivers (particularly when the sick person is a child).

To obtain a more accurate estimate of the willingness to pay for malaria prevention, Cropper et al. solicited households' willingness to pay for a vaccine that would prevent malaria with certainty for one year. Since no such malaria vaccine exists, the authors described the product hypothetically, and asked the decision-maker to respond to an experimentally designed bid. The person indicated whether or not they would buy any vaccines, and if so, how many and to whom they would be administered. The person was allowed to buy as many vaccines as there were people in his household. Using the designed bids and quantity responses, Cropper et al. are able to estimate a demand curve for household vaccines, which reflects the full welfare cost of the illness for a household. They find that the household head is, on average, willing to pay $36 to vaccinate all members of his household. This suggests that, if the expected incidence of malaria in the household is one case per year, the willingness to pay measure is in the neighborhood of twice as large as the cost of illness measure.

20.3.4 Quality-Adjusted Life Years

In health economics, it is common to use the concept of quality-adjusted life years (QALYs) to quantify changes in an individual's health status. The basic idea is that a change in health status can be described along two dimensions: how it affects the quality of life, and how it affects the length of life. For example, if an intervention provides two additional years of life in perfect health, it is worth 2 QALYs. If the intervention provides two additional years, but only at half of a person's perfect health, it is worth 1 QALY. A variety of methods have been developed to predict the quality dimension – i.e. the fraction of perfect health implied by a larger set of symptoms and capabilities. For example, in a comparison of QALYs and willingness to pay measures, von Stackelberg and Hammitt (2009) use sophisticated survey methods to develop weights for their QALY calculations. Nonetheless, while QALYs are a useful tool for collapsing the many dimensions of health into a simple index that can be aggregated across people, they have not often been used by environmental economists. Cameron (2014) describes the potential reasons for this, which largely boil down to the different tasks assigned to researchers in the two fields. Environmental economists are usually interested in valuation, which requires identification of a plausible link to preferences. Absent strong assumptions, however, there is no general link between QALYs and individual preferences, and so the applied usefulness of the former is limited in the field. In contrast, health economists are often interested in non-monetary comparisons across different, and often complex, health outcomes. For this, QALYs provide a useful metric.

20.4 SUMMARY

In this chapter we have examined approaches that economists use to value reductions in mortality risks and morbidity outcomes that arise from environmental policy. We divided our discussion by first reviewing models and empirical methods used for mortality risk, and then turned to the smaller and less-developed literature on morbidity. In both cases the motivation for studying health and environment interactions arises from the fact that many environmental policies are primarily designed to protect human health. Thus, though it has occasionally led to controversy and accusation of debasing human life by putting it at the level of a commodity, understanding the trade-offs people are willing to make between money, small changes in mortality risks, and symptoms of illness is critical for efficient policy design.

We saw that two models of behavior are useful for motivating empirical approaches to valuing mortality risk reductions. A simple static model of expected utility maximization demonstrated that, when some private mortality risks are endogenous to people's decisions, it is possible to link the value of risk reduction in an environmental context to labor and product market outcomes. Linking private choices about occupational fatality risks to environmental risks is shown to be particularly useful, since it motivates hedonic wage regressions in which the objective is to measure the compensating differential a worker receives for accepting a higher on-job fatality risk. Models of this type have long served as the basis for estimating the Value of Statistical Life (VSL) in the United States, though in recent years more attention has been paid to the potential econometric and conceptual problems that may jeopardize the validity of this approach.

After exploring the static model, we discussed how the realities of environmental risks might require the use of a dynamic life cycle model. Environmental risks often involve a lag between exposure and impacts, and risk can differentially affect people of different ages. Thus the theoretically desired willingness to pay concepts may have a temporal dimension based on latency, age effects, saving and borrowing behavior, and the structure of preferences through time. These complications make it difficult to directly link private decisions on endogenous instantaneous mortality risks, to the willingness to pay for environmental health risks. This has motivated an alternative class of empirical approaches using stated preference methods.

Health applications provide a good example of how stated preference can be used to examine the specific contexts that are relevant for environmental policy. For example, it is possible to solicit values for reducing the risk of fatality from particular causes, such as cancer, for different classes of people, such as the elderly. These advantages come with the usual suite of SP challenges, however, including the need to communicate concepts related to small changes in risks to a survey audience.

Methodological and applied research for valuing mortality risk reductions continues to this day, with much exciting work dedicated to addressing the omitted variables problems in wage hedonic regressions, and designing stated preference protocols for communicating risk and the complex contexts that characterize environmental mortality risks. This said, research on the value of mortality risk reduction is well developed and organized, relative to research on valuing morbidity reduction. We saw that this stems in large part from the more challenging data environment – illnesses are not cataloged in the same way that fatalities are – and the large number of different health outcomes that can be linked to the environment. This means it is difficult to both write down general models and to assemble data sources that are externally valid, outside the specific context of the application. Nonetheless, researchers have made progress in understanding how the behavioral responses of optimizing individuals require that care be taken when estimating the relationship between health outcomes and pollution. In addition, we have seen examples of ways that the demand for private inputs in household production models can inform us about the willingness to pay for pollution changes. Finally, an example stated preference study was used to show how the method can be tailored to the specific context at hand, to derive estimates of the value of changes in morbidity outcomes.

By focusing only on two major topics we have left many important topics uncovered. For example, there is an important empirical literature that explores how the heterogeneity in the value of risk reductions varies with age. Issues related to risk and uncertainties are also relevant for morbidity; we have nonetheless presented our morbidity discussion in a certainty framework. More generally, our discussions have been cast in terms of private willingness to pay for health-related outcomes, when in fact there may be substantial altruism motivations for protecting human health. We have also said little about differences across countries, or between developed and developing country populations. We encourage the reader to explore these topics using the references provided in the following section.

20.5   FURTHER READING

There are many useful treatments of health- and environment-related topics, serving different purposes. The Freeman et al. (2014) chapter on health models contains useful historical and policy context, as well as models and derivations drawn from some of the same sources as we have used here. An article-length overview of the theory and practice of valuing mortality risk is given by Hammitt (2000); see also the citations therein. A more detailed review of the literature on valuing environmental health outcomes is contained in the *Handbook of Environmental Economics* chapter from Viscusi and Gayer (2005). See also Banzhaf (2014) for an historical perspective on the VSL label. Finally, Cropper et al. (2011) provide a critical assessment of the mortality risk valuation literature, documenting both the successes and challenges of RP and SP approaches.

The applied literature on valuing fatality risk reductions is enormous. A review of early empirical results is provided by Viscusi (1993). More recent meta-analyses of VSL findings include Kochi et al. (2006) and Dekker et al. (2011), where the latter focuses on SP studies. Recent examples of risk valuation studies using wage regressions include Scotton and Taylor (2011) and Evans and Schaur (2010). A recent product market study is Rohlfs et al. (2015), who use the demand for vehicle air bags to infer the value of risk reductions. Examples of stated preference studies of mortality risk valuation are Alberini et al. (2006) and Alberini and Ščasný (2011). See also the *Review of Environmental Economics and Policy* (*REEP*) symposium on risk valuation and age, which includes papers from Aldy and Viscusi (2007), Hammitt (2007), and Krupnick (2007).

Turning to the morbidity sources, Cameron (2014) presents a thoughtful overview of current empirical research and research needs. A review of environment and health topics that focuses on human capital and productivity is Graff Zivin and Neidell (2013). Examples of empirical papers in this literature area include Currie et al. (2009), and Graff Zivin and Neidell (2009, 2012). Mansfield et al. (2006) use stated preference to measure parents' willingness to pay to avoid restrictions on children's outdoor time during high ozone days. Other examples of studies valuing pollution-related morbidity costs include Alberini et al. (1997), Alberini and Krupnick (1998) for a developing country, and Blomquist et al. (2011) and Adamowicz et al. (2011) for developed countries. The latter study also explores issues related to private versus altruistic valuation of health improvements. Related to this, Adamowicz et al. (2014) study how health risk reductions are valued within a family unit.

EXERCISES

20.1 ***We saw that there are several ways to measure the value of mortality risk reductions. Search the recent empirical literature to locate three different studies measuring the VSL: a wage hedonic, a product market study, and a stated preference study. Compare and contrast the studies according to the following:

(a) What is the specific context that gives rise to the risk/income trade-off in each paper? Discuss the plausibility of each study's use for informing environmental policy with reference to the static and dynamic models described in the chapter.

(b) Discuss the magnitudes of the three VSL estimates, and explain (or speculate) on what drives any differences you see.

(c) Describe any limitations in the three studies, being careful to explain how this might affect the VSL estimate. Suggest steps you might take if you were going to redo one of the studies.

20.2 **Consider the following indirect utility functions for the states "alive" (A) and "dead" (D), where m is non-labor income and w is the wage:[2]

$$V_A = \frac{-\exp(-\mu m)}{\mu} + \frac{\exp(\alpha + \beta)}{\beta}$$

$$V_D = \frac{-\exp(-\mu m)}{\mu}.$$

Let ρ denote the person's risk of a job-related fatality, and assume there is no other source of risk.

(a) Derive an expression for the marginal willingness to pay for a change in the fatality risk.

(b) Derive the comparative statics of the marginal willingness to pay with respect to ρ, m, and w. Interpret the signs.

(c) Suppose that you have data on hours of work h, as well as wage w and non-wage income m for a sample of people. In addition, suppose that ρ is measured in fatalities per 100,000 workers. Describe how you would estimate the marginal willingness to pay, and present a formula for the VSL based on your estimates (*hint*: you can derive the labor supply function from the indirect utility function).

20.3 ***The data file *evans_wage* is available on the website, along with descriptions of the included variables. In contains information on hourly wages for a sample of individuals, along with variables describing workers' education, gender, age, average hours per week and weeks per year, and race. In addition, the fatality risk for the worker's industry, measured in deaths per 10,000 workers, is available. Finally, there is a variable indicating the person's occupation from among 16 possible categories.[3]

---

[2] This question is courtesy of Christian Vossler.
[3] Parts of this question and the data file are courtesy of Mary Evans.

(a) Estimate a semi-log hedonic wage model, including covariates for age, education, race, gender, fatality risk, and the full set of occupational fixed effects. Do you find evidence of a compensating wage differential for risk? Calculate the VSL implied by your estimates.

(b) Describe any threats that might exist to the validity of your estimate, using the discussion in the chapter and any other sources. How does your point estimate (in 2004 dollars) compare with other estimates in the VSL literature?

   The data file also contains variables for the person's height (in meters) and weight (in kilograms). A person's body mass index (BMI) is defined as weight divided by height squared. A BMI ≥ 25 is considered overweight.

(c) Write out a model that allows you to test the hypothesis that an overweight person has a different marginal value of risk reduction than someone with healthy weight. What direction do you think the difference will be, and why? Estimate the model and test the hypothesis. Are the results consistent with your intuition? Calculate the average VSL for overweight people in the sample.

(d) Discuss how the exclusion of an age/fatality risk interaction might lead you to misinterpret your findings in (c).

The Practice of Environmental Economics

Parts I, II, and III thus far have presented the theory, methods, and policy examples that have historically defined the field of environmental economics. The order of topics has largely followed the intuitive division of the field into the subfields of environmental policy design and non-market valuation. While this organizational scheme was pedagogically useful, it left several important areas heretofore uncovered. Many of these topics fall roughly under the rubric of the "doing" of environmental economics, and so in Part IV we begin by discussing a handful of loosely related topics organized around the theme of cost-benefit analysis (CBA), and then close the book with a wide-ranging discussion of current practice in the field.

Cost-benefit analysis is in some sense the quintessential applied task for environmental and other economists. However, there are important theoretical aspects that need to be understood – particularly when the task involves comparing costs and benefits over long periods of time. We therefore begin in Chapter 21 with a detailed discussion of discounting. We note the common practice of using the market interest rate to compare costs and benefits across time, and present the conceptual basis for this choice, based on the classic result from Ramsey (1928). We then discuss different viewpoints on discounting the distant future, when there are market failures and/or uncertainty about future interest rates. We note how this is particularly relevant for CBA of climate change policies, where the choice of a discount rate is of first order importance.

Climate change CBA is also the primary motivation for our second topic in Chapter 21: integrated assessment models (IAMs). An IAM in general is any modeling system that combines compatible modules from multiple disciplines for the purposes of conducting policy simulations. IAMs are best known for their role in climate change policy, whereby a model of the world economy is paired to a climate system model, and connections between the climate and economic systems are calibrated. As an example of this type of research, we present the analytical aspects of William Nordhaus's DICE model, and show how his stylized representation allows experimentation with different policy scenarios. A general lesson from this is that IAMs are not truth machines, but they are useful for comparing how different policies interact with the economic and climate systems to produce different future outcomes.

In Chapter 22 we turn to two applied topics in environmental CBA. We saw throughout Part III that the measurement of environmental values often requires sophisticated conceptual and empirical techniques. In the real world of policy analysis, however, money budgets and timelines usually preclude the use of an original valuation study to measure the non-market benefits of proposed environmental policies. In these instances an alternative, pragmatic method of assessing benefits is needed. The body of research and practice dedicated to this has become known as "benefits transfer." In the first part of Chapter 22, we present the basic concepts and applied tools for benefit transfer, and discuss the state of the science and practice in the area. In the second half of Chapter 22, we turn to the cost side of CBA. Though it is often said that measuring the costs of environmental policies is comparatively straightforward, we show in our discussion that it still requires high-quality data and careful econometric work, and that the former can often be a limiting factor. In addition, we note from Part II that abatement costs are properly viewed as reflecting society's opportunity costs, meaning costs may extend beyond the firms in the regulated industry. Nonetheless, since most of the discussion on estimating abatement costs in environmental economics focuses on regulated firms, we present empirical methods suitable for measuring these costs under different data and institutional contexts.

In Chapter 23 we end the book by highlighting several aspects related to current and future work in environmental economics. One point we emphasize is the increasingly empirical nature of research in the field. To illustrate, we describe research and results related to a number of applied questions. We also discuss a range of important topics that we have not addressed in the book, and the skill sets useful for research in the field. We then close by calling on our experience as environmental economics journal editors to identify future research needs and trends in the field.

CHAPTER 21

Cost-Benefit Analysis: Modeling

Cost-benefit analysis (CBA) is a technique economists use to assess the desirability of some action, be it investment in a local highway project or an economy-wide reduction in carbon emissions. On the surface the idea is straightforward: we measure the benefits and costs of the action in a common unit of account (usually money), and if the sum of the benefits is greater than the costs then the project is "worth it." This simple statement, of course, masks the practical challenges of applying the technique, and arguably misrepresents the way that cost-benefit analysis can best contribute to policy debates. A more nuanced view of CBA is that it provides an organizational framework for identifying the range of potential costs and benefits of an action, and for considering the extent to which they can be meaningfully compared. The requirement that benefits and costs be explicitly listed imposes discipline on the process and encourages concrete discussion. The final decision is then informed (though not necessarily determined) by a comparison of those costs and benefits that can be expressed in comparable terms, along with qualitative consideration of the costs and benefits that cannot.

The intellectual roots of cost-benefit analysis lay in the desire among early twentieth-century economists to make interpersonal comparisons on the well-being effects of policy prescriptions. At issue was the fact that almost any intervention involves winners and losers, implying that a criterion requiring that everyone be made better off would always lead to the status quo. Avoiding this meant making judgments about the relative gains and losses as they are spread out over many people, yet most agreed it was not possible to make meaningful interpersonal comparisons of utility levels. Kaldor (1939) and Hicks (1939) solved this dilemma by proposing that a policy was justified on efficiency grounds if the winners from the intervention could compensate the losers – meaning that the willingness to pay to have the policy among those that gain exceeds the willingness to accept compensation for damages among those who are made worse off. Whether or not the compensation actually takes place is immaterial for the basic efficiency outcome; if the political process deems it desirable, the equity issues can be addressed with suitable income transfers. Cost-benefit analysis today relies on the Kaldor-Hicks compensation criterion to make statements about the efficiency of specific actions without necessarily addressing issues of income distribution. As we have seen in other contexts, this has allowed economists to stay silent on issues of equity and fairness, while focusing on the relatively familiar task of measuring economic costs and benefits.

The basic analytical structure of cost-benefit analysis is useful for motivating the topics we will address in this chapter. Suppose some private investment opportunity will provide a person with certain benefits in year t equal to B_t, where $t=0,\ldots,T$ indexes time from the present until the end of the planning horizon. Similarly, suppose the investment involves certain costs given by C_t, and that r denotes the interest rate on risk-free savings bonds. Given the availability of risk-free savings, a person is always able to save one currency unit today and receive with certainty $(1+r)$ units in a year's time. With $r=0.05$, for example, a dollar today will be worth \$1.05 a year from today. By similar logic, a dollar delivered a year into the future is worth only $1/(1+r)$ dollars today – or approximately \$0.95 in our example. Thus costs and benefits occurring at different points in time need to be *discounted* to a common point in time using an appropriate interest rate if meaningful comparisons are to be made. Typically all costs and benefits are discounted to their *present value* equivalents. Thus the present value of one dollar delivered in one year with an interest rate of $r=0.05$ is \$0.95. More generally, the present value of an amount B delivered t years in the future is $B/(1+r)^t$. This suggests that the investment opportunity should be evaluated according to

$$
\begin{aligned}
NPV &= B_0 - C_0 + \frac{(B_1 - C_1)}{(1+r)} + \frac{(B_2 - C_2)}{(1+r)^2} + \ldots + \frac{(B_T - C_T)}{(1+r)^T} \\
&= \sum_{t=0}^{T} \frac{(B_t - C_t)}{(1+r)^t}.
\end{aligned}
\tag{21.1}
$$

If the net present value (NPV) is positive, the investment is worthwhile for the individual; if $NPV<0$, he is better off saving the investment costs at the interest rate r. This example is quite stylized, in that the opportunity applies to a single person, a relatively short and finite time period is assumed, and costs, benefits, and the appropriate interest rate are known with certainty.

Suppose instead that the investment opportunity is a public policy that will involve aggregate taxpayer costs C_t and convey total public benefits B_t in year t. The basic logic for determining the sign of NPV is the same as in the individual's case, but issues related to the distribution of costs and benefits are more complicated. In particular, an efficient outcome in which $NPV>0$ may be associated with an undesirable income distribution outcome. This is one of the challenges that CBA practitioners must confront when using the technique to evaluate public policy. For the case of environmental policy, there are a number of other issues. First, we have stressed throughout that the benefits of environmental policy are almost always non-market, meaning that the methods described in Part III are needed to estimate $B_1,\ldots,B_T$. Second, the flow of costs $C_1,\ldots,C_T$ can also be challenging to estimate – particularly when the timeframe is long enough that technology (and hence abatement costs) may change, or when a policy itself might induce technological change. Third, the flow of costs and benefits may be uncertain, which introduces issues related to decisions under uncertainty. Finally, the choice of discount rate often is of first order importance in determining the sign of NPV, yet there is little agreement on what it should be for public investments. The problem is even more acute when the issue is one of discounting the distant future as, for example, is the case for evaluating the costs and benefits of climate change policy. The issues of uncertain future interest rates and conceptualizing intergenerational transfers become important in this context. All of these issues – pragmatic estimation of costs and benefits, selecting discount rates, dealing with uncertainties, applying CBA – fall under the rubric of the practice of environmental economics.

In this chapter we begin our discussion by examining modeling topics. Specifically, in the next section we present a theoretical examination of discount rates, which allows us to highlight an active area of research aimed at identifying which discount rate is appropriate for use in integrated assessment modeling of climate change policy. Following this, in section 21.2, we discuss integrated assessment modeling as a tool for comparing costs and benefits of environmental policies. Though a full consideration of integrated assessment models (IAMs) is beyond the scope of this book, our sense is that some familiarity with their workings is useful for applied environmental economists, and so we devote a section to the theme. We close the chapter with our usual summary and suggestions for further reading.

21.1 DISCOUNTING

Discounting future costs and benefits is fundamentally related to how an individual or society is willing to trade off consumption in the present versus consumption in the future. In the stylized example above, we used the interest rate as an intuitive starting point for understanding this trade-off by an individual. Here we take a step back, and initially consider the willingness to engage in inter-temporal consumption swaps apart from the interest rate. The goal is to understand the structural determinants of the discount rate by looking at first principles.[1] To this end, define z_t as the amount of consumption that some action will provide in time period t. Throughout this section it will be convenient to think of z_t as consumption of a numeraire good for a representative person (or the aggregate of a number of identical people) in period t, which provides utility $U(z_t)$. Let $\{z_1, z_2, z_3, \ldots\}$ be a stream of consumption outcomes that we denote by $\{z_t\}$. The consumption discount rate describes the rate at which a person would be willing to swap one unit of consumption between two adjacent periods. Specifically, for a consumption discount rate ρ, the person would give up one unit of z in period t to receive $(1+\rho)$ units in period $t+1$. Equivalently, the person sees a unit of consumption next year to be the equivalent of $1/(1+\rho)$ units today. It is usually thought that $\rho > 0$ for two reasons. First, an individual might be impatient, meaning he would rather have the benefits of consumption now rather than in the future. Second, he might expect to be wealthier in the future, meaning the marginal utility of an additional unit of consumption will be smaller in the future than in the present, assuming that marginal utility $U'(z_t)$ falls with additional consumption – i.e. $U''(z_t) < 0$. These same arguments for $\rho > 0$ can apply when $\{z_t\}$ represents consumption for a single generation in a society over a number of years, or when it is the consumption level for many generations over a number of centuries. In the following subsection we discuss the underlying determinants of ρ, using the Ramsey (1928) optimal growth framework.

---

[1] This section draws heavily on the ideas and exposition in Dasgupta (2008).

21.1.1 Intergenerational Welfare

Consider the case in which z_t is consumption by a representative member of a generation indexed by t. Define δ as the utility discount rate, which measures the amount by which the utility of a future generation will be discounted in welfare calculations relative to the utility of the current generation. With this we can define the present value of the stream of utility for a given consumption trajectory $\{z_t\}$ by

$$W_0 = \sum_{t=0}^{\infty} \frac{U(z_t)}{(1+\delta)^t}, \tag{21.2}$$

where we use W_0 to denote the welfare level that $\{z_t\}$ provides. The utility discount rate is also referred to as the pure rate of time preference; it implies, for example, that a generation consuming z today and receiving $U(z)$ in utility is welfare equivalent to next year's generation receiving $U(z)/(1+\delta)$ in utility for the same consumption amount. There is a long history of debate on what the value of δ is or ought to be, given that it is not directly observable. Writers such as Ramsey (1928) and Dietz and Stern (2008) have asserted that $\delta \approx 0$ is the only ethically defensible choice for normative analysis, in that it weights the utilities of the current and future generations equally. Writers such as Nordhaus (2007b) argue that actual observation of the consumption growth rate and savings behavior implies that $\delta > 0$, meaning that a positive rate of time preference such as $\delta = 0.02$ is an appropriate baseline for welfare comparisons between different consumption trajectories. We return below to the topic of how different analysts have selected values for δ in intergenerational cost-benefit analysis.

It is important to stress that $\{z_t\}$ leading to welfare level W_0 in (21.2) is a generic consumption trajectory that need not be optimal in the sense of maximizing welfare. We will use it to formally derive the consumption discount rate. To this end, let Δz_t and Δz_{t+1} be small consumption changes that leave the overall value of W_0 unchanged, so that

$$U'(z_t)\Delta z_t + \frac{U'(z_{t+1})\Delta z_{t+1}}{1+\delta} = 0. \tag{21.3}$$

We denote the *consumption discount rate* at time t by ρ_t and note that it is defined according to

$$\Delta z_t = \frac{-\Delta z_{t+1}}{1+\rho_t}. \tag{21.4}$$

More specifically, ρ_t is the rate at which we can move consumption between periods t and $t+1$ while keeping welfare at the fixed level W_0. From (21.3) it is clear that in the generic case, ρ_t depends on the preference function, the pure rate of time preference δ, and the levels of z_t and z_{t+1}.

Two additional definitions are needed to proceed with the analysis. First, let $g(z_t)$ be the rate of change in consumption between periods t and $t+1$, so that $1+g(z_t)=z_{t+1}/z_t$. Note that this rate of change can be positive or negative, though we are used to thinking of it as positive if a society grows wealthier over time, in which case we refer to $g(z_t)$ as the growth rate. Second, the elasticity of the marginal utility of consumption is described as follows.

Definition 21.1

The elasticity of the marginal utility of consumption is

$$\eta = -z \frac{U''(z)}{U'(z)},$$ (21.5)

which measures how $U'(z)$ – the marginal utility of z – changes with the level of z. For example, $\eta = 2$ implies that a 1 percent increase in consumption decreases the marginal utility by 2 percent.

One interpretation of η is that it measures a society's preference for consumption equality, or equivalently, its aversion to consumption inequality. If η is large, the marginal utility of income (consumption) falls quickly with additional income. From the perspective of the social welfare function given by (21.2), this means welfare is higher if income is relatively equally distributed across the generations.

Additional insights on the role of η for discounting can be obtained when we use a specific functional form for utility. In particular, let $U(z)$ have iso-elastic marginal utility so that

$$U(z) = \begin{cases} z^{(1-\eta)}/(1-\eta) & \eta > 0, \ \eta \neq 1 \\ \ln z & \eta = 1, \end{cases}$$ (21.6)

where the elasticity of marginal utility η is a constant. Using this functional form Dasgupta (2008, p.152) provides the following example to illustrate the welfare implications of different values of η. Suppose two representative people have the preference function in (21.6) with $\eta = 2$, but that person 1 consumes \$360 per year and person 2 consumes \$36,000 per year. A 50 percent reduction in income for person 2 in this case produces the same utility loss as a 1 percent consumption reduction for person 1, meaning that reductions of \$3.60 and \$18,000 for persons 1 and 2, respectively, are welfare equivalent. When $\eta = 1$, there is less aversion to consumption inequality, and like percentage reductions in consumption cause a like percentage decrease in utility. Thus the \$18,000 reduction for person 2 is equivalent to a \$180 reduction for person 1. When $\eta = 3$, the aversion to consumption inequality is high enough that the \$3.60 (1 percent) decrease in consumption by person 1 is welfare equivalent to a \$33,480 (93 percent) decrease by person 2. Thus different values for the elasticity of marginal utility have strikingly different implications for the welfare level associated with a consumption trajectory $\{z_t\}$.

The utility function in (21.6) is also useful for deriving a compact expression for the consumption discount rate. In appendix A, we show that this specific form implies that

$$1 + \rho_t = (1 + \delta)\left(1 + g(z_t)\right)^{\eta}$$ (21.7)

for a generic consumption trajectory $\{z_t\}$. Taking the natural log of both sides results in

$$\ln(1 + \rho_t) = \eta \ln\left(1 + g(z_t)\right) + \ln(1 + \delta),$$ (21.8)

which can be approximated as

$$\rho_t \approx \delta + \eta g(z_t), \qquad\qquad (21.9)$$

since for a small number u, it is the case that $\ln(1+u) \approx u$. Thus for a given consumption trajectory, the implied intergenerational consumption discount rate (the willingness to swap consumption across time periods) is a function of three fundamental parameters: the pure rate of time preference δ, the consumption growth rate $g(\cdot)$, and the curvature of the preference function η.

Equation (21.9) provides a useful illustration of the normative and equity issues associated with the intergenerational discount rate. The most obvious of these is δ, since it reflects the degree to which the current generation is favored based purely on a preference for the presence. From an ethical perspective it is often compelling to consider situations in which δ is close to zero, so that there is minimal favoring of the current generation based on "selfish" motives. In this case we can see that the consumption discount rate is positive if there is positive growth. Its magnitude is driven by the rate of growth, as well as the degree of aversion to consumption inequality that is reflected by η. A robust rate of growth – meaning that future generations are wealthier – combined with $\eta > 1$ can imply a fairly large consumption discount rate, conditional on the trajectory $\{z_t\}$. If, however, the rate of growth is negative – perhaps owing to disruptions in production occurring because of climate change – the consumption discount rate could be negative. The key insight is that the consumption discount rate can be derived without reference to a specific interest rate, can be positive or negative, and it need not be constant over time for an arbitrary consumption trajectory.

21.1.2 Optimal Growth

Equation (21.9) was derived for a generic, and not necessarily optimal, consumption trajectory. Further insights on the discount rate can be gleaned when we introduce the idea of an optimized economy in which savings can be used to shift consumption over time. For this we need to introduce ideas related to investment and capital accumulation.

We use the simplest available notion of capital for our analysis. Specifically, we assume that K_t is a stock of wealth at time t that is broadly defined to include all reproducible human and physical capital. At time t, the economy can consume its wealth or forgo consumption in favor of additional wealth accumulation. The accumulation process is given by

$$K_{t+1} = (K_t - z_t)(1+r), \qquad\qquad (21.10)$$

where r is the exogenously given return on investment (forgone consumption). The residual wealth available at time t (after consumption) therefore grows at the rate r, to produce the wealth that is available in the following period. The optimal outcome is found by selecting $\{z_t\}$ to maximize the social welfare function in (21.2), subject to (21.10) and with the initial wealth stock K_0 exogenously given.

With r deterministic and known, one unit of forgone consumption in period t can provide $(1+r)$ additional units of consumption in period $t+1$. Thus r is the rate that the economy can physically shift consumption through time; the role of capital in the model is merely to provide a vehicle for this. Recall from our discussion in the previous subsection that ρ_t is the rate at which a society is willing to swap consumption between periods t and $t+1$, holding welfare constant. When the economy is on its optimal consumption trajectory, it must therefore be the case that $r=\rho_t$. This is Ramsey's (1928) classic result. The reason for this is best seen by experimenting with situations in which $\rho_t \neq r$. Suppose, for example, that at the current $\{z_t\}$ we have $\rho_t < r$ for some time period t. In this case, a forgone unit of consumption in period t will provide additional consumption in period $t+1$ that exceeds the amount society is willing to swap into the future. Thus it will be optimal to increase the amount of savings – i.e. send more consumption forward – which is equivalent to adjusting ρ_t up. Suppose instead that $\rho_t > r$ for the current $\{z_t\}$, so that the return on savings provides additional consumption in period $t+1$ that is smaller than the current willingness to move consumption forward one period. In this case, it is optimal to reduce savings and consume more in the current period, which implies an adjustment down in ρ_t as we move towards the optimum. From these examples, it is apparent that $\{z_t\}$ needs to adjust such that $\rho_t = r$ for the economy to reach its optimum, in which no further reallocation of consumption is desired. With r, δ, and η fixed, this also implies that a constant rate of growth g is optimal, and it arises endogenously based on preferences and the exogenous real rate of return on investment. Putting these pieces together we have

$$
\begin{aligned}
r &= \rho_t \\
&= \delta + \eta g(z_t) \\
&= \delta + \eta g.
\end{aligned}
\tag{21.11}
$$

Thus for an optimized economy, the interest rate is equivalent to the consumption discount rate, and observation of r, g, and η can provide a revealed behavior estimate of δ. We will refer to the expression in (21.11) as the "Ramsey equation."

Equation (21.11) provides a useful baseline that arises in a full certainty, perfect competition, and complete-markets economy. From a normative perspective, it suggests that the interest rate is a good choice for the consumption discount rate when these conditions are approximately met. This is most likely to be the case with short time horizon projects that are too small to influence capital markets or the overall productivity of the economy. Thus Eq. (21.11) is the formal justification for using the interest rate in the simple CBA example presented in the introduction to this chapter.

21.1.3 Uncertainty

There are many reasons that an existing consumption/investment trajectory may be socially sub-optimal, such as the presence of externalities or missing markets. In addition, over longer timeframes, the growth rate of the economy is likely to be unknown, perhaps due to uncertainty about how climate change will affect future productivity.

This has given rise to an active area of research debating, for example, how the future benefits and costs of carbon emissions abatement should be discounted. The simplest way to conceptualize the problem is based on Weitzman (1998, 2010). Suppose that the future growth rate $g(z_t)$ is constant over time, but uncertain at the moment when the optimal consumption trajectory is chosen. For this exposition, suppose there is a finite number S of possible values, so that g_s occurs with probability π_s for $s = 1, \ldots, S$, and $\sum_{s=1}^{S} \pi_s = 1$. Equation (21.9) suggests that π_s is also the probability that ρ_s is the correct discount rate, where

$$\rho_s = \delta + \eta g_s. \tag{21.12}$$

From this we can see that the discount factor at time t for state of the world s is

$$A_t(\rho_s) = (1 + \rho_s)^{-t}, \quad s = 1, \ldots, S, \tag{21.13}$$

where $A_t(\rho_s)$ is the weight that the net benefits occurring at time t would receive in a net present value calculation, conditional on state s occurring. The expectation of $A_t(\rho_s)$ over the different states of the world can be interpreted as the ex ante, time t effective discount factor, which we denote by A_t. The expectation in our specific context is the sum of probability weighted, state-specific discount factors:

$$A_t = \sum_{s=1}^{S} \pi_s \times (1 + \rho_s)^{-t}, \quad t = 1, \ldots, T. \tag{21.14}$$

We can use (21.14) to derive the time t effective consumption discount rate R_t, and with it establish some useful properties. Specifically, we define R_t according to

$$(1 + R_t)^{-t} = \sum_{s=1}^{S} \pi_s \times (1 + \rho_s)^{-t}, \quad t = 1, \ldots, T, \tag{21.15}$$

so that R_t is the certainty equivalent discount rate to use at time t. Taking the log of both sides of this expression leads to

$$\ln(1 + R_t) = -\frac{\ln\left[\sum_{s=1}^{S} \pi_s \times (1 + \rho_s)^{-t}\right]}{t}, \quad t = 1, \ldots, T, \tag{21.16}$$

and once again applying the approximation $\ln(1 + u) \approx u$, we arrive at

$$R_t \approx -\frac{\ln\left[\sum_{s=1}^{S} \pi_s \times (1 + \rho_s)^{-t}\right]}{t}, \quad t = 1, \ldots, T. \tag{21.17}$$

Expressed this way, R_t is the ex ante effective consumption discount rate. It has two important properties, which we list in the following proposition.

Proposition 21.1

The ex ante effective consumption discount rate defined by equations (21.16) and (21.17) has the following properties:

(a) $R_0 = \sum_{s=1}^{S} \pi_s \rho_s$

(b) $R_\infty = \min\{\rho_1, ..., \rho_S\}$.

Parts (a) and (b) imply that R_t eventually decreases from R_0 as time increases.

A proof of the proposition is included in appendix B. It suggests that when future productivity is uncertain, cost-benefit analysis practitioners should use discount rates that decline over time. Furthermore, the distant future should be discounted at the lowest possible rate. This conclusion, however, has been the subject of some debate, over what became known as the Gollier/Weitzman puzzle. To see the puzzle, recall that Weitzman's effective consumption discount rate evaluates the future benefits of an environmental program in the current period ($t=0$). If at $t=100$ a project is to deliver $100 in benefits, an investment today of $37 today is worth it if the growth rate is 1 percent, while the break-even amount falls to $0.76 if the growth rate is 5 percent. We have seen that as the time horizon increases, the lowest potential growth rate determines the effective growth rate for use in the calculation. In a series of papers, Gollier (2004, 2009) takes the opposite approach. He asks if it is worth it to invest a fixed amount today in an environmental project, knowing that different realizations of the growth rate would produce different future returns on an alternative investment. For example, an investment of $37 today produces $100 in 100 years if the growth rate is 1 percent, but $6,271 if the growth rate is 5 percent. Gollier shows the effective discount rates viewed from this perspective imply using the highest possible value, as the time horizon increases. In a joint paper, Gollier and Weitzman (2010) attempt to solve the puzzle, and conclude that when agents optimize their consumption plans, Weitzman's dictum is the correct approach. This notwithstanding, other authors have continued to wrestle with the seemingly opposite findings regarding uncertainty in the discount rate (e.g. Traeger, 2013).

21.1.4 Empirical Calibration

Though the analytical structure of discount rates is relatively straightforward to derive, there is little in the way of consensus on the actual numbers that should be used for evaluating particular projects. For cost-benefit analyses that operate over relatively short time periods, this can usually be solved by conducting robustness checks in which a variety of discount rates are used to assess how sensitive the sign of the *NPV* is to alternative assumptions. In many cases the recommendation is invariant to the choice of a range of discount rates. For projects that operate at longer time scale, however, the choice of discount rate is often the key determinant of the sign of the *NPV*. This is because at a relatively high discount rate even large benefits occurring in the distant future provide little in the way of present value returns. For example, using a discount rate of 0.06, the present value of $100 delivered in 100 years is only $0.25. Using this discount rate, it would *not* be worthwhile to invest one dollar today in abatement costs to secure a future $100 in avoided damages. If, however, we use a discount rate of 0.02, the present value of $100 delivered in 100 years is $13.53, which easily supports investing one dollar today.

These examples make clear that practical cost-benefit analysis of the distant future requires judgments on what discount rate to use and these judgments can matter for the recommendation. The usual method for rationalizing a discount rate is to calibrate based on the Ramsey equation, which can take either a positive or normative approach. The positive approach views the world as it currently is as the appropriate baseline, and selects a discount rate based on observed rates of return on capital – i.e. the *left-hand* side of the Ramsey equation. No case is made for the social desirability of the discount rate, or the extent to which the implied pure rate of time preference and aversion to consumption inequality make ethical sense. Under this approach, a real rate of return on capital of 6 percent is often used for the discount rate. The normative approach selects ethically attractive values for the parameters on the *right-hand* side of the Ramsey equation. For example, a near-zero pure rate of time preference is usually asserted, along with a modest growth rate and a value of η that ranges from 1 to 1.5. The latter is an ethical choice intended to imbed some preference for consumption equality without the seemingly extreme redistribution implications of values greater than two (as illustrated by the example above). Thus if the growth rate is forecast to be approximately 2 percent, the implied consumption discount rate is at or somewhat above 2 percent. The examples given above show how these two approaches to rationalizing a discount rate based on the Ramsey equation can have large effects on the outcome of a cost-benefit analysis.

Weitzman (2001) provides an interesting take on these differences of opinions. He suggests that discounting the distant future is a topic about which different experts can reasonably disagree, given the uncertainties associated with predicting future rates of return on capital, and the different viewpoints on the ethical foundations of intergenerational welfare comparisons. These differences of opinions imply that the discount rate is a random variable whose subjective distribution summarizes the non-reducible uncertainty about what rate should be used for practical cost-benefit analysis. With this as motivation, Weitzman surveyed over 2,000 professional economists about their discount rate beliefs. In particular, individuals were asked to state their belief on what the discount rate should be for evaluating the future net benefits of climate change mitigation. Using the responses, Weitzman conducted an empirical analysis motivated by the framework in the previous subsection.

In describing Weitzman's analysis, we follow our earlier notation and use ρ_s to denote the discount rate suggested by an expert indexed s. We assume that ρ_s is a realization from a continuous subjective probability distribution given by $f(\rho)$, which summarizes the range of beliefs held by the expert panel. This is the continuous counterpart to our use of S discrete possibilities, with probabilities $\pi_1, \ldots \pi_S$, presented in the previous subsection. For analytic convenience, we also switch to exponential discounting, so that the discount factor at time t suggested by expert s is

$$A_t(\rho_s) = \exp(-\rho_s t). \tag{21.18}$$

For small time intervals, (21.18) is equivalent to the similar expression in (21.13).

We further assume that $f(\cdot)$ is the gamma distribution, so that

$$f(\rho) = \frac{\beta^\alpha}{\Gamma(\alpha)} \rho^{\alpha-1} \exp(-\beta\rho), \tag{21.19}$$

where Γ denotes the gamma function, and α and β are the parameters whose specific values define the distribution.[2] The mean of the gamma distribution is $\mu = \alpha/\beta$ and the variance is $\sigma^2 = \alpha/\beta^2$. Using his survey data to estimate the parameters of the gamma distribution, Weitzman finds that $\mu \approx 4$ and $\sigma \approx 3$. Thus the subjective distribution of discount rates among the sample of experts is centered at 4 percent, with a standard deviation of 3 percent.

The combination of exponential discounting and the gamma distribution provides analytical tractability in computing the implied, certainty equivalent discount rates over time. Under these specific assumptions, Weitzman shows that the counterparts to (21.14) and (21.17) are

$$A_t = \int_0^\infty \exp(-\rho t) f(\rho) d\rho$$
$$= \left(1 + t \frac{\sigma^2}{\mu} \right)^{-\frac{\mu^2}{\sigma^2}}, \tag{21.20}$$

and

$$R_t = \frac{\mu}{1 + t \dfrac{\sigma^2}{\mu}}, \tag{21.21}$$

respectively. Consistent with proposition 21.1, which was derived under more general conditions, the effective discount rate under gamma discounting is the mean of the distribution when $t=0$, and declines to zero over time. Weitzman (p.261) uses (21.21) to summarize his main empirical findings as follows:

- The immediate future (1 to 5 years) should be discounted at 4 percent per year.
- The near future (6 to 25 years) should be discounted at 3 percent per year.
- The medium future (26 to 75 years) should be discounted at 2 percent per year.
- The distant future (76 to 300 years) should be discounted at 1 percent per year.
- The far distant future (<300 years) should be discounted at 0 percent per year.

Returning to the example we used to start the subsection, these findings suggest that $100 delivered 100 years in the future should be discounted using a rate of 0.03, meaning the present value is $5.20. Thus Weitzman's analysis supports the proposition that

---

[2] The gamma function is given by $\Gamma(\alpha) = \int_0^\infty t^{\alpha-1} e^{-t} dt$ for $\alpha > 0$.

investing $1 today in climate mitigation, which provides $100 at a point 100 years from today, is worthwhile.

When examined from the perspective of individual behavior, this kind of non-constant discounting is also referred to as hyperbolic discounting. A drawback of this is that it leads to recommendations or plans that may not be time consistent. For example, if decision-makers in 6, 26, or 76 years from now have the same preferences as current decision-makers, and look at the plans suggested and executed by present decision, they are likely to revise the plans, and use a discount rate of 4 percent for the next five years instead of the prescribed 3, 2, or 1 percent. A temporal plan made by present decision-makers that binds future generations may therefore be of little value.

21.2   INTEGRATED ASSESSMENT MODELING

Analysis of environmental policy almost always requires input from multiple disciplines. For example, economics provides the tools necessary to assess the benefits of improved ambient water quality, and the costs of land use changes that can reduce pollution loadings. Connecting land use changes to changes in actual emissions, and translating emissions into ambient concentrations, requires expertise in landscape and hydrological modeling. Thus cost-benefit analysis of a particular ambient pollution target needs to incorporate knowledge from the environmental sciences as well as economics. Climate change is a second example. Economics can be used to measure the costs of reducing carbon emissions. Experts from a variety of earth sciences focus on how emissions over time map into changes in temperature, precipitation, and sea level. Additional disciplines are then needed to predict how these climatic changes will affect agricultural systems, disease vectors, terrestrial and marine ecosystems, and other managed and natural systems that affect human well-being. Finally, economists can measure how climate change affects human well-being, via the predicted impacts on natural and managed systems. Cost-benefit analysis of a proposed carbon reduction trajectory therefore requires input from a large and varied number of disciplines in addition to economics. Models that nest expertise from multiple disciplines for policy purposes, with components that are connected via spatially and temporally compatible inputs and outputs, are known as integrated assessment models (IAMs). In this section we provide an overview of the important role that IAMs play in environmental cost-benefit analysis.

In recent years, integrated assessment models have been closely associated with climate change policy, and indeed the best-known IAMs focus on climate. Nonetheless, we use the term generally, and stress that IAMs can display a variety of features. For example, the economic component can operate at the partial or general equilibrium level, and the environmental component can be local, regional, or global in scale. Uses of IAMs include policy optimization, evaluation of competing policies, and descriptive analysis. IAMs can also serve as pedagogical tools. In general, the purpose of IAM research is to combine the various disciplines in a way that simplifies each component as much as the ultimate use of the model allows. Thus the scientific contribution of IAMs is generally not disciplinary. Rather, a good IAM provides insights that are greater than the sum of the model's parts, and helps shed light on big-picture questions that cannot otherwise be addressed. In the following two subsections we use the water quality and climate change examples to illustrate these features of contemporary IAM analysis in more detail.

21.2.1 A Small-Scale Partial Equilibrium Example

Evaluating local or regional nutrient surface water pollution policy requires expertise on hydrology, water quality monitoring and modeling, and economics. Policy goals are usually expressed in terms of the ambient concentration of a criterion pollutant, such as total phosphorus (TP). Users of surface waters are affected by the concentration of TP via a function $q = f(TP)$, where $f(\cdot)$ maps the concentration level into a vector q of perceptible water body characteristics that affect the uses the water body supports. The economic value of changes in TP is determined by the preference function $U(q)$, where q might influence recreation and residential location decisions. Parameterization of the functions $f(TP)$ and $U(q)$ provides the basis for understanding the benefits side of policies that change ambient pollution concentrations.

The relationship between pollution sources and ambient concentrations is summarized by a model $TP = a(e_1, \ldots, e_J)$, where e_j is emissions of phosphorus in the reference time period from polluter j. The J polluters in the nutrient context could include municipal wastewater treatment facilities, crop and animal agriculture, storm water runoff from impervious surfaces, and fertilizer runoff from golf courses and residential landscaping. A spatially explicit hydrological model of the loadings, fate, and transport of emissions is needed to relate pollution e_j occurring at a particular point in the landscape, to the concentration of TP in a specific water body. In instances where e_j is from a non-point source (and hence not directly observable), models of land use are needed to estimate e_j via a function of the type $e_j = h(L_j)$, where L_j is a vector describing land use decisions at location j. Parameterizations for the functions $a(\cdot)$ and $h(\cdot)$ contribute an understanding of how ambient pollution levels arise from potential targets of regulation, such as observable emissions and/or land uses.

The abatement cost side of nutrient pollution policy evaluation requires an understanding of the abatement cost functions $c_j(e_j)$, which may involve looking at point source abatement technologies and/or estimating the opportunity costs of alternative agricultural land use practices. The latter requires the expertise of agronomists, who are able to determine the yield ramifications of pollution-reducing production alternatives. An integrated assessment model for evaluating nutrient pollution management combines elements of each of these individual models, with the spatial and temporal scales of analysis coordinated, so that outputs from the physical models are useable as inputs to the economic models. A model of the type sketched here could be used to determine the optimal concentration of TP in a water body. Alternatively, it could be used to conduct a cost-benefit analysis of a proposed ambient concentration standard. The latter task might differentiate the analysis based on the use of abatement cost minimizing policies, or policies that are politically convenient but not cost effective.

IAMs of this type are partial equilibrium because they usually take the prices of inputs and outputs as given. In addition, feedback mechanisms are usually not emphasized – i.e. a model of this type will usually ignore any effects on water quality that arise from end users' interactions with the resource.

EXAMPLE 21.1 (POLICY) Van Houtven et al. (2014) present an analysis that combines three distinct modules to value improvements in lake water quality in the US state of Virginia. Policies to reduce nutrient pollution into the Chesapeake Bay watershed are expected to improve surface water quality throughout the region. To analyze the effects of the proposed policy, Van Houtven et al. first use the SPARROW hydrological model (Moore et al., 2011) to map policy-induced changes in nutrient loads in the Bay region to changes in ambient pollution concentrations in lakes throughout Virginia. Predictions on changes in concentrations for pollutants such as total nitrogen, total phosphorus, and chlorophyll were then linked to an expert elicitation model. Using data from a survey of water quality scientists in the southeastern US, the expert elicitation model allowed the authors to translate changes in chemical pollutant measures into changes in perceptible characteristics of water bodies over which individuals have preferences. Specifically, the experts' opinions were used to parameterize a model that takes a lake's chemical quality measures as inputs, and produces a prediction corresponding to an index of narrative quality levels (see Table 19.1). Finally, a stated preference approach was used to value the policy-induced quality changes in lakes throughout Virginia – one component of the benefits expected from the policy. Van Houtven et al. consider the improvements predicted to arise from the Chesapeake Bay Total Maximum Daily Load (TMDL), established in 2010. Limiting attention to Virginia lakes, the authors find that households in the state are willing to pay $60 per year on average for the improvement. Aggregating over all households, the component of the policy benefits considered in the study totals $184 million per year (2010 dollars).

21.2.2 A Large-Scale General Equilibrium Example

Integrated assessment models have become closely associated with climate policy research due to the scale and complexity of the problem. No single area of science is equipped to examine the entire climate-human system within the bounds of its own discipline. While progress on understanding specific aspects of the system needs to take a disciplinary perceptive, understanding the overall ramifications of individual discoveries for policy requires an integrated approach. The purpose of climate IAMs is to aggregate knowledge from the individual disciplines into a coherent, albeit relatively simplified, illustration of the entire system. To use a cliché, IAMs help us see the climate policy forest without having our view blocked by the vast number of disciplinary trees.

Most economics-themed climate change IAMs share a common overall structure. Their foundation is a long time horizon model of the world economy, often disaggregated into several regions. Production, consumption, capital investment, and abatement activities by populations at points in time (and space in the regional resolution models) lead to flows of greenhouse gas emissions. Emissions feed into a model of atmospheric carbon concentrations, which in turn feeds into a model predicting global temperatures and possibly other climatic characteristics. Temperature levels are connected to productive features of the economy, so that climate change damages materialize as diminished future consumption. Technological progress decreases the emission intensity of consumption/production. Policy interventions – e.g. a proportionate reduction in emissions – lead to alternative consumption and emission trajectories, and greenhouse gas concentrations and climate regimes. In most economic IAMs, the present discounted value of the flow of costs and benefits from different policy interventions are compared, or the optimal emissions trajectory is found by optimizing the system.

Within this general structure, climate change IAMs vary significantly in their underlying details. Some models are "large" in the sense that they track thousands of endogenous and policy variables such as commodity prices, regional trade flows, taxes on factors of production, tariffs on imports, and renewable energy mandates. Other models are "small" in the sense that economic activity is represented by a few stylized aggregates such as consumption and investment, defined for broad regions of the world. Large models are useful for detailed policy analysis in a specific region – e.g. for looking at the net consequences for different industries or classes of consumers in the United States of different carbon abatement levels and policies. Their complexity, however, means it is difficult to dissect how the underlying assumptions and calibrations affect the policy predictions. Small models cannot provide spatially resolute or nuanced predictions, but their comparative transparency facilitates discussion on the major assumptions used to assess the big-picture questions. Integrated assessment models also differ in their solution concepts, incorporation of uncertainty, computational intensity, underlying programing language, portability amongst users, the extent to which technological progress is endogenous or exogenous, data sources for calibration, and other dimensions. Importantly, the main IAMs constructed by economists use optimization as the solution concept in the sense that time paths for the relevant endogenous variables arise based on maximization of a welfare function. Decentralization of the socially optimal consumption, investment, and emission trajectories is then usually studied within a competitive market economy by choosing optimal levels of suitable policy instruments, such as Pigouvian taxes. The business as usual (i.e. pre-policy) consumption and emission trajectories in this type of setup provide the market baseline, which can be compared to welfare levels under proposed and/or fully optimal emissions control.

Arguably the best-known integrated assessment model for climate policy is the DICE (Dynamic Integrated model of Climate and the Economy) model developed by William Nordhaus. DICE is a deterministic, globally aggregated model with a small number of endogenous variables. The economic component is a neoclassical growth model in which the global population consumes a portion of its wealth today, and invests the remainder in emissions abatement and productive capital to improve consumption in the future. The climate system is included as a type of natural capital that diminishes with emissions or grows with abatement. DICE appeared in its current form in the early 1990s and has been upgraded several times, culminating in the 2013 version described in Nordhaus and Sztorc (2013). In what follows, we provide a sketch of the DICE model as a pedagogical vehicle for demonstrating the structural components of climate IAMs and their uses.

Economic Component

The economic component of the DICE model begins with utility and social objective functions that are similar to those described in the previous section:

$$W = \sum_{t=1}^{T_{\max}} L_t \frac{z_t^{1-\eta}}{1-\eta} (1+\delta)^{-t}. \tag{21.22}$$

Per capita world consumption is denoted by z_t, and δ and η are the pure rate of time preference and elasticity of marginal utility, respectively. The exogenous world population at time t is denoted by L_t, so that social welfare is the discounted stream of population-weighted utility arising from per capita consumption. Nordhaus calibrates δ and η descriptively via the Ramsey equation, using observed market rates of return. In the baseline DICE 2013 model, the values for these parameters are $\delta = 0.02$ and $\eta = 1.45$. The consumption growth rates that emerge from the baseline model are described below. On average, they imply consumption discount rates of $\rho = 0.05$ in the immediate term and $\rho = 0.0425$ in the longer term. The time path for L_t is calibrated to grow over time according to United Nations projections until the year 2100, at which point a population steady state of 10.5 billion people is reached.

Economic output in year t (measured in 2005 dollars) is denoted by the single aggregate commodity Y_t, which can be used for consumption, or saved and invested in the capital stock. Thus $Y_t = Z_t + I_t$, where I_t is savings (investment), Z_t is total consumption, and per capita consumption is defined by $z_t = Z_t/L_t$. The capital stock evolves according to

$$K_t = I_t + (1-v)K_{t-1}, \tag{21.23}$$

where $v = 0.10$ is the annual depreciation rate used in the baseline calibration of the model. Net output in the world economy is produced according to the constant returns to scale Cobb-Douglas production function

$$\begin{aligned} Y_t &= \frac{[1-\Lambda_t]}{[1+\Omega_t]} A_t K_t^{0.30} L_t^{0.70} \\ &= \frac{[1-\Lambda_t]}{[1+\Omega_t]} Y_t^G. \end{aligned} \tag{21.24}$$

In this expression, Λ_t and Ω_t represent emission abatement costs and economic damages from climate change, respectively, and A_t accounts for general technological change (the evolution of total factor productivity). Together these three terms translate the capital and labor inputs into net output. Said another way, the capital and labor inputs produce gross output Y_t^G, which is scaled by the abatement and damage functions to obtain net output Y_t. The specific forms for abatement costs and climate change damages are described below.

The initial values A_{2010} and K_{2010} are calibrated to match gross world product in the base year of 2010. From there, A_t grows exogenously over time at a decreasing rate. In the DICE model, solutions for variables are derived at five-year increments, and so for computational convenience, growth rates are often expressed in five-year blocks. For example, from 2010 to 2015, total factor productivity grows according to

$$A_{2010} = A_{2015}\left(1 + g_{2015}^A\right), \tag{21.25}$$

where $g_{2015}^A = 0.079$. Therefore, total factor productivity grows 7.9 percent during the five years from 2010 to 2015. After 2015, the growth in total factor productivity decreases by 0.6 percent every five years. These assumptions imply that consumption per capita increases on average by 1.9 percent per year through 2100, and 0.90 percent afterwards.

The equations for population, consumption and investment, capital growth, net output, and productivity growth are familiar components of neoclassical growth models. To connect the growth model to climate change, however, we need to link output to emissions. In the DICE model, carbon emissions E_t are proportional to gross production, so that

$$\begin{aligned} E_t &= \sigma_t\left(1 - \mu_t\right)A_t K_t^{0.30} L_t^{0.70} \\ &= \sigma_t\left(1 - \mu_t\right)Y_t^G. \end{aligned} \tag{21.26}$$

In this expression, μ_t is a policy variable recording the proportion of emissions that are abated, and σ_t is the carbon intensity of output. In the baseline calibration, $\sigma_{2010} = 0.549$ tons of carbon dioxide per \$1,000 of output. The carbon intensity of output then changes each year according to

$$\sigma_t = \sigma_{t-1}\left(1 + g_t^\sigma\right). \tag{21.27}$$

For the five years from 2010 through 2015, the carbon intensity decreases by 1 percent per year. The size of the decrease falls thereafter, so that on average, the carbon intensity of output falls by 0.95 percent per year through 2100, and 0.87 percent per year in later years. These assumptions about the rate of technological change are specific to the emissions sector, and therefore distinct from the general growth in total factor productivity.

The DICE model includes a constraint on the total carbon emissions that are available to the economy, so that

$$\bar{E} \geq \sum_{t=1}^{T_{\max}} E_t. \tag{21.28}$$

This implies that scarcity in fossil fuel energy use is implicitly induced via the scarcity of carbon emissions. The value of the constraint is calibrated to an assessment of the stock of fossil fuels available in the world economy as of 2010. Note from Eq. (21.26) that emissions and/or abatement are necessary for production, and that if the emissions limit is reached, output can only be produced if $\mu_t = 1$ – i.e. all emissions are abated. To allow for this, DICE includes a backstop technology that can be thought of as a replacement for the energy content of emissions. In the 2013 vintage of the model, the initial cost of the backstop technology is $BS_{2010} = \$344$ per ton of CO_2 avoided. The cost of the backstop, denoted BS_t, then declines at a rate of 0.50 percent per year thereafter. These points imply that Eq. (21.26) is the implicit energy input constraint, in the sense that a given level of output requires a given level of emissions, abatement, or the replacement of emissions via the backstop technology.

Returning now to the abatement and damage functions, DICE is parameterized so that abatement proportionately reduces output, where

$$\Lambda_t = \theta_t \mu_t^{\theta_2} \tag{21.29}$$

is the proportion of gross output spent on abatement, and θ_t and θ_2 are parameters that characterize the shape of the function. Nordhaus uses $\theta_2 = 2.80$ in the baseline calibration, so that the cost function is convex – i.e. Λ_t increases quickly with a higher emission reduction rate μ_t. In addition, θ_t is the fraction of output needed to completely eliminate carbon emissions in year t (i.e. when $\mu_t = 1$). Its path is therefore calibrated based on the evolution of the cost of the backstop technology. Specifically, in appendix C we show that

$$\theta_t = \frac{BS_t \cdot \sigma_t}{1000 \cdot \theta_2}. \tag{21.30}$$

We also show that the marginal abatement cost implied by (21.29) is

$$MAC_t = BS_t \mu_t^{\theta_2 - 1}. \tag{21.31}$$

Note that the latter provides the optimal carbon price for a given proportion reduction in emissions. For example, for $\mu_{2010} = 0.20$, $MAC_{2010} \approx \$19$ is the optimal price for a ton of carbon dioxide.

The way that climate damages enter is a crucial ingredient in any IAM. In DICE, output is reduced by climate change according to the damage function Ω_t, which depends on how much higher the year t temperature is, relative to the baseline. Climate change damage is proportional to output as shown in Eq. (21.24). The 2013 version of DICE uses a simple damage function generally, and in comparison to previous versions of the model, that is given by

$$\Omega_t = \varphi_1 T_t^{AT} + \varphi_2 \left(T_t^{AT} \right)^2. \tag{21.32}$$

In the expression, T_t^{AT} is temperature change at the earth surface from the given global mean temperature baseline, at time t. The parameter values $\phi_1 = 0$ and $\phi_2 = 0.00267$ are chosen in part based on Tol (2009), who surveys the literature on the economic damages from climate change. However, Nordhaus' value for ϕ_2 includes a 25 percent upward adjustment from the Tol calibration, to account for damage categories not included in his survey.

The damage function in (21.32) implies that the economic impacts of small temperature changes are modest, but rise non-linearly for larger temperature changes.

For example, an average temperature increase of 1.5° Celsius reduces global output by 0.6 percent, while warming in the range of 3° Celsius reduces global output by 2.4 percent. Climate damages in DICE are therefore simple and transparent, but the parameterization is limited in many respects. The model does not accommodate the potential for thresholds or tipping points, nor does it allow for the existence of low probability, catastrophic climate disruptions. Finally, the damage function is calibrated based on estimates for small to medium-size temperature changes, and so is unlikely to be accurate for increases above 3° Celsius.

Geophysical Component

To link temperature to emissions and greenhouse gas concentrations, the geophysical component of the DICE model describes (a) the carbon cycle, and (b) the radiative forcing process, where the latter links atmospheric carbon stocks to temperature changes. For the carbon cycle, DICE distinguishes among three carbon reservoirs: the atmosphere (AT), the upper oceans and life-supporting areas of the planet (UP), and the lower and deep ocean layers (LO). The carbon held in each of these reservoirs at time t is denoted by MT_t^{AT}, MT_t^{UP}, and MT_t^{LO}, respectively. Stocks are measured in gigatons (Gt) of carbon, where 1 Gt is one billion metric tons.

Additions to and movements amongst these reservoirs determine the amount of carbon in the atmosphere at any given time. For example, the atmospheric carbon stock is determined by

$$M_t^{AT} = E_t + E_t^{land} + \phi_{11} M_{t-1}^{AT} + \phi_{21} M_{t-1}^{UP}, \tag{21.33}$$

where E_t^{land} denotes emissions into the atmosphere from land use changes (e.g. deforestation), which is exogenous in the DICE model. Land emissions are set to 3.3 Gt of carbon dioxide in 2010, and then decrease exogenously over time. The positive values of ϕ_{11} and ϕ_{21} govern the rate of persistence of carbon in the atmosphere, and the rate of transfer from the upper oceans to the atmosphere, respectively. The calibrated values imply, for example, that a 100 Gt carbon pulse today leaves 35 Gt of additional carbon in the atmosphere in 100 years. Similar equations describing persistence and mixing for MT_t^{UP} and MT_t^{LO} are included in the model, though without emission terms.

The concentration of carbon in the atmosphere affects "radiative forcing" in the earth system, which describes the planet's energy balance. Energy flows in from the sun and is either absorbed or radiated back to space. If the amounts of energy being absorbed in and radiated out are equal, the system is in equilibrium – i.e. there is no warming or cooling impetus, and radiative forcing is zero. A higher carbon concentration increases the absorption capability of the planet, meaning less energy is radiated out than is kept in. In this case, radiative forcing is positive and the resulting energy imbalance causes warming. The DICE model includes the following equation describing radiative forcing:

$$F_t = \omega \left\{ \log_2 \left[M_t^{AT} / M_{1750}^{AT} \right] \right\} + F_t^{EX}. \tag{21.34}$$

This expression maps the change in energy balance in year t, relative to the pre-industrial year 1750, due to carbon changes in the atmosphere (the first term), and adds to it the forcing attributable to non-carbon influences (the second term). The latter is exogenous in DICE. The specification for F_t assumes that carbon-based radiative forcing was in its pre-industrial equilibrium in the year 1750, and that industrial era carbon emissions have pushed the balance in the positive direction since then.

Mean temperature at the earth's surface (T_{AT}) and in the deep ocean (T_{LO}) evolve based on the level of radiative forcing according to the following general equations of motion:

$$T_t^{AT} = T^{AT}\left(F_t, T_{t-1}^{AT}, T_{t-1}^{LO}\right) \tag{21.35}$$

and

$$T_t^{LO} = T^{LO}\left(T_{t-1}^{AT}, T_{t-1}^{LO}\right). \tag{21.36}$$

Note that the temperature at the earth surface in period t is determined by the present radiative forcing, as well as lagged values of the atmospheric and low ocean temperatures. Relatively simple linear representations are used in DICE for the specific forms of (21.35) and (21.36), with parameter values that are chosen to mimic predictions from the more complicated general circulation models described in the IPCC Fifth Assessment (IPCC, 2013). The calibration implies that a doubling of carbon dioxide in the atmosphere leads to a 2.9° Celsius temperature increase.

Using the Model

The equation structure of the DICE model illustrates how the economic system influences the climate system via emissions, and the climate system influences the economic system via temperature. Thus the two systems are consistently linked and feed back on each other, which allows simultaneous determination of the endogenous economic and climate variables. This is accomplished by "running" the model – i.e. numerically finding the consumption trajectory that maximizes the social welfare function, subject to the production and climate equations and an emission control regime. One type of scenario analysis involves choosing the consumption trajectory subject to a specified emission control rate (e.g. a 5 percent reduction in 2015 growing over time to 50 percent in 2050). The consumption trajectory is associated with an emissions trajectory, changes in concentrations of carbon dioxide in the atmosphere, the evolution of temperature, and annual proportions of gross output that are spent on abatement and lost to damages. These outcomes can be compared for different control rates, including the baseline case of no emissions control. A second type of scenario analysis maximizes welfare by finding the socially optimal emissions reduction rate. The implied trajectories from the optimum can then be compared with the trajectories from alternative, non-optimal control rates.

By way of example, the DICE model predicts business as usual (i.e. existing 2010 emission control regimes stay unchanged) per capita consumption in 2020 of $8,768 and $16,600 in 2050. These are relative to the 2010 baseline of $6,886. The three consumption levels are associated with atmospheric concentrations of carbon dioxide of 390 ppm, 425 ppm, and 560 ppm in 2010, 2020, and 2050, respectively. Over this same period, temperatures are 1.06 degrees higher in 2020, and 2.01 degrees higher in 2050 (all temperature changes are in Celsius and relative to the year 1900).

These baseline figures can be compared to the optimal paths for the same variables. Under the optimal solution near-term consumption changes little from the baseline ($8,756 in 2020 and $16,567 in 2050). Emission control rates – the proportion of overall emissions abated as given by μ_t in Eq. (21.26) – are 22 percent and 39 percent in 2020 and 2050, respectively. This translates to carbon dioxide concentrations of 421 ppm in 2020 and 513 ppm in 2050. Finally, the optimal trajectory implies carbon prices of $22.20 in 2020, which rises to $51.50 in 2050.

The DICE model has been used to examine many other proposed emission reductions. However, a defining and lasting prediction from the model is that emission reductions should be initially small and then ramp up in the future. Regardless of its literal truth, this finding illustrates the usefulness of IAMs for framing policy debate and clarifying the important questions. Given the relatively transparent structure of DICE, we can initiate research on what features of the model lead to the slow ramp-up prediction, and the extent to which alternative representations might lead to different predictions. For example, the DICE model includes only crude notions of uncertainty or risk aversion as reflected in the parameter choices for the damage function. Technological change is exogenous (meaning there is no scope for R&D subsidies as a policy option), and the choice of consumption discount rate is higher than some have advocated. Other IAMs have incorporated these dimensions and produced baseline and optimal predictions that deviate from the DICE predictions. This variation illustrates that IAMs should not be viewed as truth machines, nor should the output from any one model run be given much policy influence. Indeed an alternative way of viewing the merits of IAMs is to reverse the analysis direction: a policy idea should make economic sense when evaluated using *some* IAM for it to be discussed in the policy arena. Once this necessary condition is met, the features of the IAM that gave the favorable rating can be dissected and critiqued as part of the overall evaluation.

21.3 SUMMARY

Cost-benefit analysis (CBA) is a tool used by economists to assess the efficiency of some proposed action. At its most basic level, the technique involves adding up and comparing the time-adjusted economic costs and benefits of the action, and seeing if the difference is positive or negative. If net benefits are positive, the step is worth it from an efficiency perspective, though this does not say anything about the equity or other characteristics of the project. Thus economists usually see cost-benefit analysis as one step in the policy assessment process rather than the single criterion. Nonetheless, when applied with suitable care, most economists believe CBA provides a systematic and disciplined tool for evaluating policy.

While the basic intuition of CBA is simple, actual implementation for environmental policy requires attention to several conceptual and applied details. In this chapter we have examined two of the larger conceptual topics: discounting, and the need for integrated assessment. We saw that discounting is used to convert benefits or costs occurring in the future into present time values. For short time horizon analyses, the choice of a specific discount rate from amongst a range of possibilities can be immaterial for the qualitative result. For long horizon problems, however, the choice of discount rate is often of first order importance in determining whether an action produces positive net benefits. This has motivated research and debate on how to select a discount rate for evaluating multigenerational issues such as climate change. We saw that, in a model with full certainty, the discount rate depends on the consumption growth rate, the pure rate of time preference, and the elasticity of the marginal utility of consumption. Therefore, for an arbitrary consumption path, the discount rate must be selected based on ethical arguments, a forecast for consumption growth, and an understanding of intergenerational preferences for consumption smoothing. When a discount rate is selected based on consideration of these three inputs, it is referred to as a "prescriptive" approach, since it relies on normative judgments rather than market outcomes. When the economy is on its welfare-maximizing optimal consumption path, as it would be under full certainty and completely competitive markets, we saw that the consumption discount rate is equal to the real interest rate (rate of return on capital). If the discount rate is selected based on observation of the market interest rates, it is referred to as a "descriptive" approach, since it uses revealed behavior rather than normative judgments as a criterion. The "prescriptive" and "descriptive" perspectives provide bookends defining a vigorous intellectual debate on intergenerational discounting.

The rate of return on capital and the consumption growth rate are difficult to predict for intermediate and long-term time horizons, and so research on intergenerational discounting has sought to incorporate uncertainty in these parameters into the analysis. We saw that, within the Weitzman framework, this implies that the certainty-equivalent discount rate used for long time horizon projects should decline over time. Furthermore, distant future net benefits should use a discount rate that approaches zero. This paradigm has been advocated by many economists as the best approach for climate change policy analysis (e.g. Arrow et al., 2013), though substantial disagreement on discounting remains.

Our examination of integrated assessment was motivated by the reality that most environmental policy questions require the expertise of multiple scientific disciplines. Our main example was climate change. Cost-benefit analysis of a proposed reduction in greenhouse gas emissions requires predictions about the economic costs of reductions, the impact of emission changes on atmospheric stocks of greenhouse gasses, the relationship between atmospheric stocks and climate change, and the economic costs of climate change damages. An integrated assessment model (IAM) combines individual models for each of these components, which operate at compatible temporal and spatial scales. The individual components work together to quantify the relationships and feedback loops between the economic and climate systems, thereby providing a platform for understanding the net economic benefits (and geophysical consequences) of different policy paths.

We used the DICE model from William Nordhaus to illustrate the usefulness and limitations of integrated assessment modeling. We saw that there is a trade-off between transparency, and the realism that can be included in a model. DICE is a "small" model that seeks to characterize the most important phenomena using the simplest possible representations of the economic and climate systems. Its parsimonious structure allows relatively simple identification of the main drivers of policy predictions that emerge from its model runs. However, this means DICE is limited in its ability to capture real-world complexities related to threshold effects in the earth systems, or the role of low probability, high consequence events. More generally, the DICE model's strengths and limitations illustrate that IAMs are not likely to be truth machines, but instead serve as useful tools for organizing discussions on the potential cost, benefit, and climate consequences of different greenhouse gas emission trajectories.

21.4 FURTHER READING

The basic cost-benefit analysis task is well described in undergraduate environmental economics texts and graduate public policy books. Wheelan (2011) is a good example of the latter. Atkinson and Mourato (2008) provide an article-length review of environmental CBA. In writing this chapter we have drawn heavily on Dasgupta's (2008) accessible, discrete-time analysis of discounting for climate change. Sections 21.1 and 21.2 are largely based on his presentation. The material on discounting under uncertainty is based on Weitzman's (1998, 2001, 2010) work on the topic. Gollier (2002, 2009) has also made important contributions. Papers on the "Weitzman-Gollier" puzzle include Weitzman and Gollier (2010) and Traeger (2013). There is a large literature exploring other theoretical aspects of discounting; examples include Traeger (2014) and Karp (2005). Commentaries on discounting in the context of climate change are also numerous. Useful discussions are provided by Sterner and Persson (2008), Dietz and Stern (2008), Nordhaus (2007b), and Weitzman (2007). Arrow et al. (2013, 2014) present an argument aimed at policy makers for the use of a Weitzman-style discount rate that declines over time.

For our discussion of integrated assessment modeling, we have relied on the *DICE User Manual* from Nordhaus and Sztorc (2013), as well as Nordhaus (2013a). Examples of applications and generalizations of the DICE modeling framework include Popp (2004), Jensen and Traeger (2014), Dietz and Stern (2015), and Nordhaus (2014). There are numerous other IAM frameworks. Pindyck (2013) provides critical assessments of integrated assessment modeling generally. Clarke et al. (2009) introduce a study using ten leading IAMs to consider similar climate change policies. A special issue of *Energy Economics* (volume 31, 2009) identifies the models and presents the results of the study.

APPENDIX A: DERIVING THE RAMSEY EQUATION

To show this, recall that by definition

$$\frac{U'(z_t)\Delta z_t}{(1+\delta)^t} + \frac{U'(z_{t+1})\Delta z_{t+1}}{(1+\delta)^{t+1}} = 0. \tag{A21.1}$$

Also by definition we have

$$\rho_t = -\left(\Delta z_{t+1} / \Delta z_t\right) - 1 \tag{A21.2}$$

and

$$\frac{z_{t+1}}{z_t} = 1 + g(z_t). \tag{A21.3}$$

We then rearrange (A21.1), and plug in the specific utility functional form for marginal utility:

$$\left(\frac{z_{t+1}}{z_t}\right)^\eta (1 + \delta) = -\frac{\Delta z_{t+1}}{\Delta z_t}. \tag{A21.4}$$

Plugging in (A21.2) and (A21.3) we have

$$\left(1 + g(z_t)\right)^\eta (1 + \delta) = 1 + \rho_t. \tag{A21.5}$$

Finally, taking log of both sides and using the fact that for a small number u $\ln(u + 1) \approx u$, we obtain

$$\begin{aligned}
&\eta \ln\left(1 + g(z_t)\right) + \ln(1 + \delta) = \ln(1 + \rho_t) \\
&\approx \eta g(z_t) + \delta \approx \rho_t.
\end{aligned} \tag{A21.6}$$

APPENDIX B: PROOF OF PROPOSITION 21.1

To prove both parts, we start with expression:

$$\ln(1 + R_t) = -\frac{\ln\left[\sum_{s=1}^{S} \pi_s \times (1 + \rho_s)^{-t}\right]}{t}, \quad t = 1, ..., T. \tag{A21.7}$$

For (a), we apply L'Hopital's rule, which requires that we derive the derivative with respect to t for both the numerator and denominator of (A21.7). For the numerator we have

$$\frac{d\left\{-\ln\left[\sum_{s=1}^{S} \pi_s \times (1 + \rho_s)^{-t}\right]\right\}}{dt} = \frac{\sum_{s=1}^{S} \pi_s \times (1 + \rho_s)^{-t} \ln(1 + \rho_s)}{\sum_{s=1}^{S} \pi_s \times (1 + \rho_s)^{-t}}, \tag{A21.8}$$

and for the denominator simply $d[t]/dt = 1$. The limit of the derivative of the denominator as t tends to zero is a constant equal to one. The limit of (A21.8) as t tends to zero is

$$\sum_{s=1}^{S} \pi_s \times (1 + \rho_s). \tag{A21.9}$$

Using the approximation $\ln(u+1) \approx u$ for a small number u, we obtain the result.

For (b), we need to take limit of (A21.7) as t tends to infinity. For this, it is useful to rewrite (A21.7) as follows:

$$
\begin{aligned}
\ln(1 + R_t) &= -\frac{\ln\left[\sum_{s=1}^{S} \pi_s \times (1 + \rho_s)^{-t}\right]}{t} \\
&= -\frac{\ln\left[\left\{\sum_{s=1}^{S} \pi_s \times \left(\frac{1 + \rho_s}{1 + \rho_{\min}}\right)^{-t}\right\} \times (1 + \rho_{\min})^{-t}\right]}{t} \\
&= -\frac{\ln\left[\left\{\sum_{s=1}^{S} \pi_s \times \left(\frac{1 + \rho_s}{1 + \rho_{\min}}\right)^{-t}\right\}\right]}{t} - \frac{\ln\left[1 + \rho_{\min}\right]^{-t}}{t} \\
&= -\frac{\ln\left[\left\{\sum_{s \neq s_{\min}}^{S} \pi_s \times \left(\frac{1 + \rho_s}{1 + \rho_{\min}}\right)^{-t} + \pi_{s_{\min}}\right\}\right]}{t} - \frac{\ln\left[1 + \rho_{\min}\right]^{-t}}{t} \\
&= \frac{\ln\left[\left\{\sum_{s \neq s_{\min}}^{S} \pi_s \times \left(\frac{1 + \rho_s}{1 + \rho_{\min}}\right)^{-t} + \pi_{s_{\min}}\right\}\right]}{t} + \ln\left[1 + \rho_{\min}\right].
\end{aligned}
\tag{A21.10}
$$

Note that $(1 + \rho_s)/(1 + \rho_{\min}) > 0$, and so the first term is defined as t gets large. As t tends to infinity, the first term is zero, so that

$$\ln(1 + R_\infty) = \ln(1 + \rho_{\min}). \tag{A21.11}$$

Using the approximation $\ln(u+1) \approx u$ for a small number u, we obtain the result.

APPENDIX C: DERIVING (21.30) AND (21.31)

In the DICE model, total abatement cost is

$$TAC_t = Y_t^G \theta_t \mu_t^{\theta_2}. \tag{A21.12}$$

In addition, emissions are proportional to gross output, so that

$$E_t = \frac{Y_t^G \sigma_t}{1000} \quad \rightarrow \quad Y_t^G = \frac{E_t 1000}{\sigma_t}. \tag{A21.13}$$

Substituting out for Y_t^G in (A21.12), we have

$$TAC_t = \frac{E_t 1000}{\sigma_t} \theta_t \mu_t^{\theta_2}. \tag{A21.14}$$

The derivative of TAC_t with respect to μ_t measures the addition to total abatement cost from an incremental increase in the proportion of emissions abated. Taking this derivative and setting $\mu_t = 1$, as needed for the complete elimination of emission, we have

$$\frac{\partial TAC_t}{\partial \mu_t}\Big|_{\mu_t=1} = \frac{\theta_2 E_t 1000 \theta_t}{\sigma_t}. \tag{A21.15}$$

The derivative of (A21.15) with respect to E_t measures the marginal cost of the last emission eliminated, when all emissions are abatement. By definition this is BS_t, so that

$$\frac{\theta_2 \cdot 1000 \cdot \theta_t}{\sigma_t} = BS_t. \tag{A21.16}$$

Solving for θ_t, we obtain the result in (21.30).

Plugging the expression for θ_t into (A21.14) allows us to express the total abatement cost at time t as

$$TAC_t = E_t \frac{BS_t}{\theta_2} \mu_t^{\theta_2}. \tag{A21.17}$$

As noted, the addition to total abatement cost from a change in μ_t is the derivative of TAC, given in general by

$$\frac{\partial TAC_t}{\partial \mu_t} = E_t BS_t \mu_t^{\theta_2-1}. \tag{A21.18}$$

The derivative of (A21.18) with respect to E_t measures the marginal cost of the last emission eliminated, when the abatement proportion is μ_t, given by (21.31).

EXERCISES

21.1 *Consider an environmental policy that provides no benefits in the first ten years after implementation, but costs $10,000 per year. In years 11 through 40 the benefits are $30,000 per year, while the costs are still $10,000 per year. During years 41 through 100, there are no costs, and the benefits remain constant at $30,000 per year.

(a) Calculate the net present value of the policy using constant discount rates of 1, 5, and 7 percent.

(b) Find the discount rate that makes the net present value exactly zero.

(c) Calculate the net present value using discount rates that decline over time according to the Weitzman suggestion described above.

21.2 **A 2008 symposium in *Review of Environmental Economics and Policy* (volume 2, issue 1) contains a collection of articles debating elements of climate change policy. Much of the discussion in the papers and the references cited focuses on how future costs and benefits should be discounted. Summarize the different perspectives, and comment on the extent to which more recent research has made progress on settling the discounting debate.

21.3 ***Three of the better-known IAMs for climate change policy are DICE (William Nordhaus), FUND (Richard Tol), and PAGE (Chris Hope). Greenstone et al. (2013) and the references contained therein (see in particular Mastrandrea, 2009) present various summaries of the features of these models. Key assumptions in climate IAMs include the climate response (how changes in CO_2 stocks affect temperature and other climate variables), the structure of the damage function, the potential for adaptation, and discounting. Using overview and/or technical literature, compare and contrast these the IAMs along these dimensions, and any others you think are important, and comment on how they condition typical predictions from the model.

CHAPTER 22

Cost-Benefit Analysis: Empirical

We saw in Chapter 21 that cost-benefit analysis (CBA) is a technique used to assess whether a project is "worth it" from an efficiency perspective. As the name implies, a critical step in cost-benefit analysis is the estimation of the economic costs and benefits of the proposed action. In this chapter, we continue our discussion of CBA for environmental policy by focusing on two estimation-related topics: benefits transfer, and the empirical characterization of abatement cost functions.

We have noted that the benefits of environmental policy outcomes are usually non-market, meaning the methods presented in Part III of this book are critical inputs for executing at least part of an environmental cost-benefit analysis. In the context of an original study, however, non-market valuation methods require a non-trivial commitment of resources and often the skills of a specialist. This observation often presents policy analysts with a two-fold dilemma. First, in some instances deadlines and institutional constraints make execution of an original valuation study in support of a specific policy analysis infeasible. Second, many decisions – particularly those taken at more localized levels – are too limited in scope to justify expenditure on original research. In these cases, practitioners of CBA need some method of assessing non-market benefits without resorting to an original study. That is, the benefits of the proposed policy need to be measured using previous studies and secondary sources of information. The art and science of doing this is known in environmental economics as "benefits transfer."

In contrast to benefits, it is often thought that the costs of environmental policy are relatively straightforward to estimate. For example, observation of accounting records on what regulated entities spend to comply with a policy should provide the data needed to tally the cost side of cost-benefit analysis. While this may be a useful first step, our discussion in Chapter 5 demonstrated that abatement cost, when properly viewed as the opportunity cost of reducing emissions, is a broader concept than firms' compliance costs. Thus far in the book, however, we have said little about how to translate the conceptual aspects of abatement cost functions into empirical strategies for measuring the costs of environmental policies.

In this chapter, we review current thinking in environmental economics on benefits transfer, and estimating abatement costs, beginning in section 22.1 with a review of benefits transfer concepts and methods. In section 22.2 we review abatement cost estimation, focusing primarily on methods for estimating polluting firms' abatement cost functions.

22.1   BENEFITS TRANSFER

A description of the benefits transfer context is as follows. Suppose an analyst is interested in assessing the benefits of a proposed intervention at a *policy* site. As a specific example, the US state of Wisconsin might be considering a new ambient water quality standard at a specific inland lake within its borders. The measurement needs are time, space, and context specific in that they depend on the existing environmental conditions in the lake, the size of the proposed environmental improvement, the way that environmental quality is measured (e.g. ambient concentration of nutrients), and how the lake is used by the surrounding population. Suppose as well that the analyst has information available from one or more candidate *study* sites – i.e. water bodies that have been the subject of an original non-market valuation study. The estimates of environmental quality values from the study sites are also time, space, and context specific, and they depend on the choices the original researchers made in carrying out their study. For example, a published study might provide information from a stated preference survey on the willingness to pay by residents of the state of North Carolina to have water quality in a lake improve from "unsafe for swimming" to "safe for swimming." A second study might provide estimates from a recreation lake choice model in the state of Minnesota, in which one of the site attributes included in the specification is total phosphorus concentration. The benefits transfer task is to credibly use information from these study sites to estimate the benefits of the proposed action at the policy site.

To a large degree, the benefits transfer task is a specific example of the general method of using existing knowledge to inform a pending decision, and in this sense it differs little from other techniques used in applied policy analysis. For example, labor supply and product demand elasticities from specific studies are often used to predict behavioral responses to policy shocks in other contexts. The non-market nature of environmental benefits, however, presents a number of unique challenges that have defined the research agenda on benefits transfer and conditioned how it is used in practice. We have seen in other contexts that non-market values arise via the combination of preferences among the relevant population, and physical characteristics of the environmental resource. While we can think of these heuristically as the demand and supply sides, respectively, it is important to recall that there are not always equilibrating forces that serve to make marginal resource values equal across space. Thus the estimated economic value for water quality in North Carolina and Minnesota might differ from that in Wisconsin due to a different range of available substitute sites, different baseline values of environmental quality, different non-environmental characteristics of the water bodies, and/or different preferences among the residents. In what follows, we discuss how these features of the policy task have conditioned the evolution of thinking on benefits transfer.

22.1.1 Terms and Concepts

The science and practice of contemporary benefits transfer grew out of a set of pragmatic needs that pre-dated careful evaluation of the method. Environmental economists usually trace the beginning of systematic study of benefits transfer to a 1992 symposium published in *Water Resources Research*. These papers began the process of defining relevant concepts, outlining methodological issues, suggesting best practice, and identifying validity criteria. Since that time, researchers and practitioners have converged on a common nomenclature, which we review in this subsection.[1]

As indicated above, the benefits transfer literature uses the term *policy site* to denote the place or resource for which a non-market value is needed. Though the label evokes images of a specific geographical feature (e.g. a lake), it is worth emphasizing that the policy site should be carefully defined over several dimensions, including its spatial scale, its value-receiving population, and the physical effects of any proposed policy. The benefits transfer literature uses the term *study site(s)* to denote resources that have been the subject of a primary study, and which may have relevance for the valuation task at hand. The study sites are defined over the same dimensions as the policy site, in addition to features of the original study, such as the methodology applied and the nature of the sample. At the most basic level, good benefits transfer practice starts with the idea that the policy and study sites should be similar in as many dimensions as possible.

Once the policy and study sites have been identified, two general methods have been identified for carrying out a benefits transfer: *unit value* and *benefit function* transfers. The former involves the direct transfer of values "as is" from the study sites. Turning again to the Wisconsin example, the analyst might survey the applied literature to locate estimates of the per-trip recreation value of improvements in water quality that mirror the proposed improvement at the policy site. If a single suitable study is located, the unit value approach would use the single estimate directly. If multiple studies were located, the mean or median across estimates could be used. Given this, the unit value approach implicitly assumes that the study and policy sites are identical in all relevant dimensions. For the Wisconsin example, we would need to assume that the study and policy sites have similar underlying ecological characteristics and a similar set of available substitutes, and that the characteristics and preferences of the benefiting populations were the same.

In some instances, the conditions needed for unit value transfer may be reasonable for the task at hand, but often they represent strong and unrealistic assumptions. The benefit function approach instead seeks a parameterized relationship between a non-market value, and characteristics of the sites and populations associated with the value. In this way, the site and benefiting population characteristics at the policy site can be "plugged into" the benefit function to predict a transfer value that reflects the specific conditions at the policy site. For the Wisconsin example, the analyst might seek studies that allow her to understand how the per-trip recreation value of a water quality improvement depends on the distance to the nearest alternative lake, the types of game fish available in the lake, the presence of sand beaches, the percentage of rural versus urban users of the water body, and other conditioning variables. She could then perform the transfer exercise conditioning on the values of these variables at the policy site.

As we discuss in more detail below, it is generally thought that the benefit function approach is more reliable than the unit value approach, though errors can occur in either case. To gauge quality, the benefits transfer literature distinguishes between two potential sources of error: *measurement error* and *generalization error*. Measurement error in

---

[1] The basic terms and concepts described here are drawn from Johnston et al. (2015), Chapter 2.

the benefits transfer context refers to problems with the study sites, whereby the original studies fail to measure the resource value at the study site correctly. Generalization error refers to problems in transferring the study site value to the policy site context. These concepts allow us to differentiate between a *reliable* (or accurate) transfer, which means generalization error is minimized, and *transfer validity*, which means the transferred value is equal to the true underlying value. In practice, the true underlying value for the policy site is unknown, and so transfer validity is difficult to test. Instead, research on benefits transfer usually assesses validity via *convergent validity*, which requires both transfer and original study estimates for the same site. Specifically, convergent validity is achieved when the transfer value is found to be equal to the value obtained from a subsequently conducted original study at the policy site.

22.1.2 Benefit Function Approaches

Most of the academic literature on benefits transfer has focused on developing and testing different approaches for calibrating benefit functions. Two general categories exist: reduced form approaches, and structural approaches. In this subsection we introduce the two strategies, and discuss their advantages and disadvantages.

Meta-analysis

The reduced form approach to benefit function transfer has relied to a great extent on meta-analytic summaries of the existing valuation literature. Meta-analysis is an area of statistics that is used to summarize what a group of studies on a particular phenomenon collectively tell us. Meta-analysis was originally developed for use in medical research, but has subsequently spread to other areas of study, including economics.

While there are several analytic techniques that fall under the rubric of meta-analysis, the most commonly used method in economics is meta-regression. In a meta-regression, a sample of primary studies is assembled, and the common outcome from each is recorded in a consistent and comparable way. For example, an analyst might review studies that quantify the value of a statistical life (VSL) in order to assemble a sample of VSL point estimates. Converting each estimate to a base year currency allows the different estimates to be compared, and their variability analyzed. A linear regression is usually used to examine the variability in estimates, whereby characteristics of the individual studies are coded and used as explanatory variables. For the VSL example, this might include sample characteristics (working age versus full population), study method (revealed versus stated preference), and the private risk attribute (at-work fatality versus ambient pollution exposure). By regressing the VSL estimates onto characteristics of the individual studies, we can measure how aspects of the study context, or decisions on how the study was executed, systematically affect the findings. More generally, a meta-regression can be used to estimate a literature-mean outcome, characterize the distribution of literature findings, identify outliers, explain systematic variation in previous studies, and make out-of-sample predictions. The latter two capabilities are particularly relevant when meta-regression is used for benefit function transfer.

Meta-regression for benefit function transfer is a conceptually simple idea. The analyst first identifies all suitable studies that predict the value of interest. She then constructs a predictive function by regressing the sample of assembled values on a set of explanatory variables. The explanatory variables differentiate the assembled study values along observable, site- and study-specific dimensions. The transfer is constructed by forecasting the value of interest, using policy-site specific values for the explanatory variables. In this way, the disadvantages of unit value transfers, which do not condition on observable policy and study site heterogeneity, can be avoided.

While the idea of meta-regression for benefit function transfer is simple, the actual implementation requires attention to a number of details. Perhaps the largest challenge involves translating estimates from the sample of primary studies into a consistent definition of the dependent variable in the meta-regression. Consider again the water quality example, where an analyst was interested in the value of quality improvements in a Wisconsin lake. Different ways of describing surface water quality include chemical (e.g. concentration of total phosphorus), biological (e.g. abundance indicator species), perceptive (e.g. visual clarity), and narrative (e.g. safe for swimming). Thus even when the commodity definition is clear – the recreation value of a water quality improvement in our example – different studies may employ different concepts as a means of defining and valuing quality changes. Specifying the dependent variable in a benefits transfer meta-regression involves making judgments on how these different quality concepts can be reconciled.

To some degree, heterogeneity in study site value concepts can be reduced by conducting a narrow literature review. This relates to the general topic of how primary studies are selected for inclusion in the metadata. A narrow definition for inclusion can result in a sparse sample, while a broad criterion may require more reconciling of different commodity or quality measurement concepts, and/or a greater need for understanding heterogeneity in predicted values. Analysts also need to make decisions on how to triage studies based on quality, study year, and publication status. For example, meta-regressions in environmental economics often include unpublished estimates drawn from grant and consulting reports and agency analyses (sometimes referred to as "gray" literature), as well as peer-reviewed journal articles. The gray literature can be useful because a wider range of estimates are usually presented in reports, relative to journal articles. However, gray literature sources may be of uneven quality due to the absence of peer review.

A third set of judgments is needed to define the set of explanatory variables in the meta-regression. The range of categories over which the original studies can be distinguished includes: (a) physical characteristics of the resource under examination; (b) characteristics of the change to the resource that is valued; (c) context variables, such as characteristics of the population whose values are measured; and (d) methodological descriptors (e.g. stated versus revealed preference) for the original studies. The first three of these can in principle have counterparts in the policy site, and so estimates of their influence on values provide the basis for the benefit function. The role of the latter category is less obvious, since by definition methodological variables are not defined for the policy site. Nonetheless, experience has shown that methodological variables often do explain some of the systematic variation in value estimates, and so they should be included in the meta-regression (see Stapler and Johnston, 2009, for detailed discussion).

An additional challenge that bears mention is that the primary studies forming the valuation metadata were not necessarily published with their subsequent use in benefits transfer in mind. When the original intent of the journal article was to investigate a methodological topic, for example, the data description and summary statistics may not be detailed enough to support inclusion in a benefit function calibration. Thus in addition to selecting suitable studies, practitioners often need to add an additional level of triage, based on the existence of sufficient documentation to enable construction of consistent dependent variable values, as well as conditioning variables. The occasional mismatch between what is reported in published articles, and what is needed for benefits transfer, has motivated efforts to establish reporting protocols for applied studies that are consistent with benefits transfer needs (e.g. Loomis and Rosenberger, 2006). This challenge notwithstanding, the valuation literature contains a large number of meta-analyses that were designed to provide a platform for benefit function transfers. In the following example we describe a surface water quality value meta-analysis.

EXAMPLE 22.1 (EMPIRICAL) Ge et al. (2013) conduct a meta-analysis over the willingness to pay for a change in surface water quality. They assemble 332 estimates from 38 distinct studies of annual household willingness to pay for (or willingness to accept) a water quality increase (or decrease). Their metadata include a mixture of travel cost, hedonic property, and contingent valuation studies drawn from peer-reviewed journal articles (69 percent), PhD/Master's theses (13 percent), and other sources (18 percent). To facilitate translation of value estimates to a common quality change metric, the authors sought studies that used one of three water quality descriptions: water clarity, chemical/biological pollutant concentrations, and an index known as a "water quality ladder." Water clarity is usually assessed using a secchi disk; the measure is the deepest level that a black-and-white disk remains visible when placed below the surface. Chemical and biological indicators include measures such as phosphorus and nitrogen concentration, dissolved oxygen levels, pH, and fecal coliform presence. The water quality ladder used by Ge et al. is an index taking values 0 to 100, where the values correspond to a hierarchical list of uses that the water body supports. Examples include drinkable (95), swimmable (70), fishable (50), boatable (25), suitable for outings (15), and supporting no activities (5).

In its original formulation, the 100 point water quality index was used to aggregate multiple chemical and biological indicators into a one-dimensional ordinal index, where each individual indicator was assigned a weight in the index. Ge et al. use updated versions of the original weights to translate quality changes in the studies that used water clarity and chemical/biological indicators, into changes in the water quality index. Thus all quality changes in the metadata are represented as water quality index changes, making the associated willingness to pay estimates comparable across studies.

The authors run a meta-regression of annual household willingness to pay on the quality change, baseline quality level, and controls for the water-body type (lake, river, estuary, other), water-body size, and region of the US (northeast, Midwest, etc.). They also include controls for average income in the original sample, and the size (in square miles) of the sampled region. To examine the role of study characteristics, a dummy variable is coded to distinguish estimates that reflect "total value" from those that only measure "use value"; indicators for methodology (travel cost, hedonic, contingent valuation) are also included.

The meta-regression coefficients provide the basis for constructing a benefit function for use in forecasting the value of a quality change at a policy site. Specifically, the results show that willingness to pay is increasing in the size of the quality improvement and the size of the water body, and decreasing in the baseline index value. Estimates of total value are on average 25 percent higher than estimates reflecting only use value, and quality improvements in estuaries are valued more than quality improvements in lakes and rivers. Household income was not a significant predictor of value. These findings imply, for example, that a household living less than 225 miles from a 100 square mile lake would be willing to pay $64 per year to have an improvement in the index level from 70 to 80.

Structural Benefit Functions

The meta-analysis, reduced form approach to benefit function calibration has been the dominant method to date, but it is not without limitations. The most prominent of these is the absence of a formal connection to consumer theory. As a purely empirical exercise, meta-regression transfers are not constructed in a way that is consistent with utility maximizing agents interacting with the policy site. This has at least two consequences. First, as we have seen in previous chapters, primary studies in non-market valuation are usually conducted using structural methods derived from constrained utility maximization. Value estimates are therefore conditional on the population's underlying constraint set, including, for example, income, time, experience, health, and/or equipment ownership constraints. In structural estimation, the income constraint enters the empirical specification according to theoretical curvature conditions, which are unlikely to be well represented by the population variables used as controls in a meta-regression. Transfers based on meta-regression may therefore admit measures that are inconsistent with constraints among the benefiting population at the policy site. Second, the restrictions from consumer theory provide an additional source of information that can be exploited in calibrating the benefit function. The a-theoretic meta-analysis approach may therefore ignore useful information in an estimation context that, in many cases, is data sparse to begin with.

Structural benefit function transfer addresses these limitations by starting with a parametric specification for the policy site structural function that is needed for the valuation exercise. For example, the analyst interested in water quality in Wisconsin might write down a parametric demand function for a recreation site that shifts with water quality, and which integrates back to an indirect utility function. In a separate context, she might specify an indirect utility function that captures a person's optimal trade-off between mortality risk and a private good, which could be used to measure the value of a risk reduction. By this choice, the policy site preference function can be made to include as much detail as needed for the policy analysis.

The analytical task in structural benefits transfer is to use the existing literature to calibrate the parameters of the policy site structural function. Heuristically, this is done in two ways. First, in some cases, the parameters of the structural function have direct counterparts in existing studies. For example, for some demand function specifications, the parameter on own price is the uncompensated own price elasticity of demand. Thus the analyst could calibrate an own price elasticity for her policy site structural function, using information on conceptually similar elasticities, gleaned from the literature. Second, economically meaningful quantities such as marginal willingness to pay and the willingness to pay for discrete resource changes are often non-linear functions of the policy site structural function parameters. For example, for many demand function specifications, the welfare loss from forcing consumption of the commodity to zero has a closed form analytical expression. Information about the set of parameters lumped into the expression can be sought from other studies. Specifically, the analyst can match conceptually similar welfare estimates from existing studies of a similar commodity to the policy site expression for the welfare loss.

Implementation of the calibration logic can occur in several ways. As a simple example, consider again the water quality valuation task for a Wisconsin lake. Suppose the analyst is interested in parameterizing a demand function for the number of trips x to the policy site lake, and she selects the following functional form for a representative visitor:

$$x = \exp\left(\alpha + vD + \beta p + \gamma y + \delta q\right), \tag{22.1}$$

where p is the travel cost for the person, y is income, D is a dummy variable equal to one if the person owns a boat, and q is the measure of water quality. Recall that for log-linear demand functions such as this, the coefficients can be interpreted as proportionate changes. For example,

$$\frac{\partial x}{\partial D} = \exp\left(\alpha + vD + \beta p + \gamma y + \delta q\right) v$$
$$= vx. \tag{22.2}$$

If $v > 0$, then v is the proportionate increase in trips when the person owns a boat. By similar logic, the income elasticity of demand is

$$\frac{\partial x}{\partial y} \frac{y}{x} = \exp\left(\alpha + vD + \beta p + \gamma y + \delta q\right) \gamma \frac{y}{x}$$
$$= \gamma y. \tag{22.3}$$

In addition, the consumer surplus loss when the travel cost approaches infinity is

$$CS = \int_{p_0}^{\infty} \exp\left(\alpha + vD + \beta p + \gamma y + \delta q\right) dp$$
$$= -\frac{1}{\beta} \exp\left(\alpha + vD + \beta p_0 + \gamma y + \delta q\right)$$
$$= -\frac{x}{\beta}. \tag{22.4}$$

This implies that the consumer surplus per trip is simply $-1/\beta$. As discussed in Chapters 14 and 15, we can integrate the ordinary demand function to derive the associated indirect utility function, which for the functional form in (22.1) is

$$V = \frac{\exp(-\gamma y)}{\gamma} + \frac{\exp(\alpha + \beta p + vD + \delta q)}{\beta}, \tag{22.5}$$

with $\beta < 0$. Finally, using the indirect utility function, we can derive the marginal willingness to pay for q as

$$\frac{\partial V/\partial q}{\partial V/\partial y} = -\frac{\delta}{\beta}\exp(\alpha + vD + \beta p + \gamma y + \delta q)$$

$$= -\frac{\delta}{\beta}x. \tag{22.6}$$

Each of the expressions in (22.1), (22.2), (22.3), (22.4), and (22.6) are economic concepts whose values are often reported in empirical studies. Their functional forms follow from the analyst's choice of a parametric specification; different specifications will lead to different expressions. For example, use of $\ln(y)$ in place of y in (22.1) would imply a different assertion about how income affects the demand for recreation trips.

The benefits transfer task is to calibrate the parameters $(\alpha, v, \beta, \gamma, \delta)$ to represent visitor demand for trips to the policy site. To this end, suppose the analyst surveys the literature, and locates the following estimates from primary studies of sites that are similar to the policy site:

- Consumer surplus per trip: $35.
- Per-trip marginal willingness to pay for quality: $0.75.
- Income elasticity of demand for trips: 0.15.
- Average number of trips per year per visitor: 5.
- Percent increase in trips taken by boat-owning households: 20 percent.

In addition, suppose the analyst calculates that the average visitor to the policy site has annual income of $40,000, owns a boat, and pays $75 in travel costs to visit the site. She also measures the baseline water quality at the policy site using the 100-point index described in example 22.1, and finds that $q = 70$. With this information in hand, the calibration proceeds by solving the following system of five equations in five unknowns:

$$0.20 = v$$
$$35 = -\frac{1}{\beta}$$
$$0.15 = \gamma y$$
$$0.75 = -\frac{\delta}{\beta}$$
$$5 = \exp(\alpha + vD + \beta p + \gamma y + \delta q). \tag{22.7}$$

This results in a policy site, parameterized demand function given by

$$x = \exp\left(1.90 + 0.20D - 0.0285p + 0.375 \times 10^{-5} y + 0.0214q\right). \tag{22.8}$$

The parameterized demand function can be used to estimate the per-person welfare effects needed to support the policy analysis. Specifically, the indirect utility function in (22.5) implies that the compensating variation (CV) for a quality change at the policy site from q_0 to q_1 is implicitly defined by

$$\frac{\exp(-\gamma y)}{\gamma} + \frac{\exp(\alpha + \beta p + vD + \delta q_0)}{\beta}$$
$$= \frac{\exp\left(-\gamma(y - CV)\right)}{\gamma} + \frac{\exp(\alpha + \beta p + vD + \delta q_1)}{\beta}. \tag{22.9}$$

Solving for *CV* we obtain

$$CV = \frac{1}{\gamma} \ln\left[1 - \frac{\gamma}{\beta}(x_1 - x_0)\right]$$
$$= \frac{1}{\gamma} \ln\left[1 - \frac{\gamma}{\beta}\{\exp(\alpha + vD + \beta p + \gamma y + \delta q_1) - \exp(\alpha + vD + \beta p + \gamma y + \delta q_0)\}\right]. \tag{22.10}$$

Using the parameter values shown in (22.8), the willingness to pay for an increase in quality from $q_0 = 70$ to $q_1 = 80$ is \$41.81.

Kerry Smith and his co-authors have been the main developers of structural benefits transfer, and they have labeled the approach shown in the example as "prudential algebra for policy."[2] They have also considered more complex cases. Our linear example is just-identified, meaning that the number of parameters to calibrate is equal to the number of conditions. If the parameters enter the expressions non-linearly, they need to be solved numerically using a software package such as GAMS or Mathematica. In some cases, the system may be over-identified, in the sense that there are more conditions available than parameters to calibrate. For example, suppose the literature review in the Wisconsin case also provided an estimate of the willingness to pay for an alternative discrete change in water quality from q_0 to q_1, equal to \$25. According to this literature finding and the formula in (22.10), we have

$$CV = \frac{1}{\gamma} \ln\left[1 - \frac{\gamma}{\beta}(x_1(q_1) - x_0(q_0))\right] = 25. \tag{22.11}$$

Expressed this way, Eq. (22.11) can be used as an additional condition for calibrating the demand function parameters.

---

[2] See Smith et al. (2002, 2006).

Along with those in (22.7), there are now six conditions available to identify five parameters, meaning the system is over-identified. Calibration in this case requires a minimum distance solution. To show this, suppose in general that there are G conditions and K parameters, denoted by the K-dimensional vector θ, to calibrate. In our example, we have $G=6$, $K=5$, and $\theta=(\alpha,\nu,\beta,\gamma,\delta)$. Define each condition by the general statement

$$m_g(\theta) = v_g - f_g(\theta), \quad g = 1,...,G, \tag{22.12}$$

where $f_g(\theta)$ is the expression derived from the structural function (e.g. willingness to pay for a discrete quality change), and v_g is its value, gleaned from the literature. In (22.11), for example, $v_g=25$ and $f_g(\theta)$ is the expression for CV. The objective of the calibration in the over-identified case is to find values for θ that make each $m_g(\theta)$ as close to zero as possible, for all g. To proceed, denote $m(\theta)$ as the $G\times 1$ vector with individual elements $m_g(\theta)$. The calibrated parameters are implicitly defined according to

$$\begin{aligned}
\theta_{BT} &= \arg\min_{\theta} \left[m(\theta)' \cdot I_G \cdot m(\theta) \right] \\
&= \arg\min_{\theta} \left[\sum_{g=1}^{G} \left(v_g - f_g(\theta) \right)^2 \right],
\end{aligned} \tag{22.13}$$

where I_G is the $G\times G$ identify matrix. The parameters defining the policy site structural function can be found by carrying out the minimization via a numerical routine.

The research literature on structural benefits transfer is much less developed than the literature investigating reduced form, meta-regression approaches. In addition, the skills needed for implementing the former are more advanced than the latter, which has limited its use in actual policy contexts. Thus the small amount of accumulated experience in both research and policy contexts means it is too early to assess the advantages and limitations of structural benefit transfer vis-à-vis the more ubiquitous reduced form approaches.

22.1.3 Defining and Assessing Benefits Transfer Quality

Benefits transfer is a pragmatic tool for policy analysis that, by its nature, produces estimates that are likely to be of lower quality than what a well-executed primary study would provide. Criteria for determining if a transfer meets a minimum quality threshold therefore need to admit the possibility of some error, and evaluation of the quality of a particular transfer exercise needs to be conditional on its intended use. These features mean that the research literature has not produced a one-size-fits-all list of quality metrics or best practices. Nonetheless, much has been written on the subject of benefits transfer reliability and validity. In this subsection, we review several of the key ideas that have emerged.

As defined above, generalization error in the benefits transfer context refers to inaccuracies that occur when using information from an existing study to estimate a value at a policy site. A transfer is considered reliable when the generalization error is minimized, and so authors have sought criteria for selecting study sites that will produce reliable estimates at the policy site. These have by and large been descriptive. For example, Loomis and Rosenberger (2006) include *commodity consistency*, *market consistency*, and *welfare measure consistency* in a list of criteria to consider when selecting policy sites. Commodity consistency implies that the study and policy resources should be similar physically and in their surrounding populations. Market consistency refers to similarity in own- and cross-price effects, and overlap in expected behavioral responses to quality changes. Welfare consistency means that estimates of benefits from the study sites should be conceptually the same as the welfare measure being sought at the policy site. For example, ordinary consumer surplus changes should not be compared to measures based on compensated demands. Likewise, benefits measures from the literature need to reflect similar quality descriptions and magnitude changes, to be comparable. To this list we might add *temporal consistency*, to reflect the fact that population average non-market values are often stable over short periods of time, but may shift in the long run as income levels and sociodemographic profiles in the population shift. Thus studies should be drawn from time periods that are not too distant from the policy context.

These four consistency concepts mirror basic common sense, and their necessity has been implicit in much of our discussion thus far. In addition, it is difficult to objectively measure the commodity and market consistency between study and policy sites, and so an analyst's judgment is necessary to decide what constitutes "close enough." Also, analyst judgment is needed to assure welfare measure consistency among even closely related studies when different quality measurement concepts are used. Thus the narrative guidelines serve mainly as an organizing vehicle for the decisions that need to be made, in an actual transfer context.

Narrative guidelines have nonetheless been useful for understanding tests of convergent validity for benefits transfer. A number of studies have constructed estimates of value at policy sites using benefits transfer, and then compared the estimates to values obtained from a simultaneous or subsequent primary study. For example, Kaul et al. (2013) identify 31 empirical studies providing 1,071 estimates of transfer errors, where the percent benefit transfer error (%*BTE*) is

$$\%BTE = \left[\frac{WTP_{BT}}{WTP} - 1\right] \times 100, \tag{22.14}$$

WTP is the estimate from the original study, and WTP_{BT} is the corresponding benefits transfer estimate. The authors report that the median benefit transfer error in the data they analyze is 33 percent (the mean transfer error is 42 percent). Analysis of the distribution of transfer errors confirms, for example, that function transfers outperform value transfers on average. Related to this, errors are smaller when multiple pre-existing studies are used rather than when a single study site is identified. Geographic proximity of study and policy sites also reduces errors – perhaps due to the fact that nearby sites have greater similarity in unobserved characteristics. Finally, transferred value estimates for changes in environmental quality have larger percentage errors than transferred value estimates for quantity changes. Thus, for example, we should expect a larger error rate when looking at the value of an improvement in water quality at a lake used for recreation than when valuing a recreation trip at that lake.

The use of *%BTE* as a quality metric requires a decision on how large an error is acceptable. An alternative concept is to test the statistical equivalence of transfer estimates and primary study estimates. In a reduced form context this usually occurs by comparing the actual estimates of value, where the null hypothesis is that the transfer and original study values are equal. In structural benefits transfer, convergent validity hypothesis tests can also be carried out for model parameters, or ratios of parameters. In summarizing validity tests from several studies (including a large overlap with those used in Kaul et al.), Rosenberger (2015) finds that statistical hypothesis tests of value equivalence are rejected the majority of the time. He notes, however, that statistical rejection of a transfer value's equality with its original study counterpart is only weakly correlated (*corr* = 0.26) with the size of the *%BTE* outcome. Thus small transfer errors and formal convergent validity are somewhat distinct ways of assessing transfer quality.

22.1.4 Benefits Transfer in Practice

Estimates from the benefits transfer validity literature suggest that transfer errors may be large, but that careful judgment and application of a function transfer methodology can reduce errors. While acceptable error rates will vary with the specific context, a positive view of developments is that the research community has made progress in understanding what types of approaches are likely to perform best in actual policy contexts. Continued progress, as well as the ongoing accumulation of high-quality primary studies, will therefore provide benefits transfer practitioners with the methods and data needed for credible policy analysis.

If true, research and improved practice in benefits transfers has the potential to make a large contribution to social welfare. In the United States, via executive orders dating to the Reagan and Clinton administrations, all proposed federal regulations having impacts beyond a given threshold must include a cost-benefit analysis. For the US Environmental Protection Agency (EPA), this means that most of its rulemaking procedures need to include estimates of the value of the ecological and human health benefits that are expected to arise. Given time and resource constraints, EPA analysts usually apply benefits transfer to obtain the needed estimates. Likewise, the US Forest Service has a long history of transferring estimates of forest recreation benefits, to assess the non-market value of different timber management approaches.

Benefits transfer is also widely used in Europe. For example, in 2000 the European Commission's Directorate-General for the Environment hosted a workshop and commissioned studies designed to identify a unit value VSL, which could be used for cost-benefit analysis of new European Union directives aimed at reduced environmental mortality risks. As a second example, the UK National Ecosystem Assessment uses benefits transfer to value the flow of market and non-market services provided by the nation's natural capital. Other examples from the US, Europe, and Australia/New Zealand are provided in Loomis (2015), Brouwer and Navrud (2015), and Rolfe et al. (2015), respectively.

In spite of the large use of benefits transfer by the world's environmental agencies, at the time of writing there remains a gap between the academic literature and how benefits transfer is practiced. Though there are important exceptions, the majority of analyses rely on unit value transfers from single studies. This persists for several reasons. The construction of a benefit function using meta-regression requires experience with regression methods, and access to/familiarity with a large amount of literature and data on primary studies. This latter requirement is often the binding constraint for agency analysts working on short time budgets, and who are reluctant to stray from practices that have been judged satisfactory in the past. A non-specialist charged with carrying out a cost-benefit analysis may also lack the statistical background needed for benefit function transfer using meta-analysis. Likewise, the modeling and numerical skills necessary for structural benefits transfer are somewhat advanced, even for PhD economists. Without evidence that the approach produces better results, analysts working in environmental agencies are understandably hesitant to invest in the needed expertise. Thus there are ongoing opportunities to improve both the theory and practice of benefits transfer for environmental cost-benefit analysis.

22.2   ESTIMATING ABATEMENT COSTS

We turn now to examining how costs are estimated for cost-benefit analysis. At the start, we need to be clear in defining whose costs we seek to measure, the types of costs to be included, and the mechanisms through which the costs arise. In earlier chapters we saw that abatement costs are properly viewed as the opportunity cost of reducing emissions. This broad perspective can include a combination of polluting firms' compliance costs and profit losses, households' lost consumption benefits, and the effects brought about by interactions with other policies and pre-existing distortions. The task of empirical cost estimation therefore relates, in principle, to many of the theoretical topics discussed in Part II of the book. Nonetheless, when practical abatement cost estimation is discussed in the literature, the usual emphasis is on quantifying firms' regulatory compliance costs, and so in this section we largely focus on firms' costs. As motivation, we begin in the next subsection by reviewing the abatement cost concepts developed in Chapter 5, and relating these to different applied measurement objectives. We then discuss specific empirical methods that environmental economists have used to estimate cost functions for polluting firms.

22.2.1 Measurement Objectives and Contexts

In Chapter 5 (see section 5.5), we presented a discussion of abatement costs along three dimensions. We denoted a competitive, polluting firm's cost function by $C(x,e)$, where x is output and e is emissions, and its profit function by $\Pi = px - C(x,e)$, where p is the output price. We also used $\hat{e}^x$ to denote the pre-regulation emission level associated with an output level x. With these, we first defined

$$\breve{C}(x,e) = C(\overline{x},e) - C(\overline{x},\hat{e}^{\overline{x}}) \tag{22.15}$$

as the technical cost of reducing emissions from $\hat{e}^{\overline{x}}$ to e, while holding output fixed at a reference level $\overline{x}$. We noted that this is not in general a correct characterization of the firm's opportunity cost of achieving emissions level e, since it does not allow the firm to adjust output in response to the regulation. Nonetheless, we saw that

$$-\breve{C}_e(\overline{x}, e) = -C_e(\overline{x}, e) = MAC, \tag{22.16}$$

implying that we can use an understanding of the technical cost of reducing emissions, to measure the marginal abatement cost, for specific values of x and e.

To derive the firm's abatement cost function, we then considered the polluting firm's profit maximizing condition $C_x(x,e) = p$, from which we expressed its optimal output level, given an emissions target e, as $x(e)$. With this, we defined a firm's abatement cost for emissions level e, when price stays fixed, as the difference between profit levels pre- and post-regulation:

$$AC(e) = \left[p \cdot x(\hat{e}^x) - C\left(x(\hat{e}^x), \hat{e}^x\right) \right] - \left[p \cdot x(e) - C\left(x(e), e\right) \right]$$
$$= C\left(x(e), e\right) - C\left(x(\hat{e}^x), \hat{e}^x\right) + p\left[x(\hat{e}^x) - x(e) \right]. \tag{22.17}$$

Comparison with (22.15) shows that the technical cost does not in general equal a firm's opportunity cost of reducing emissions, though the two are equal when output does not change in response to the new regulatory regime.

Finally, we noted that *society's* abatement costs are equal to the sum of *firms'* abatement costs when the output price stays fixed. In this case, households do not change consumption levels, meaning that output reductions in the regulated sector are offset by an increase in output elsewhere in the economy. If, in contrast, the regulation is large enough to affect the industry supply curve, price will change, and society's abatement costs are shared among the polluting firms and consumers of the polluting good. In this case, abatement costs include both profit losses and a decrease in households' consumption benefits.

Figure 22.1 illustrates when firms' abatement costs are (and are not) equivalent to society's abatement costs, and hence correspond to empirical measurement objectives. In each panel we have drawn two industry marginal cost curves: one that is conditional on the pre-regulation industry level of emissions $\hat{E}^X$, and another for a regulated level of emissions E. Panel A shows a vertical demand curve at X^0, so that the quantity of production and consumption stays fixed pre- and post-regulation. Area a is the increase in firms' costs from reducing emissions, holding output fixed at X^0. In this special case, area a also corresponds to society's abatement cost. Therefore, when output does not change, the empirical objective is to measure technical costs for the regulated firms, as defined by (22.15).

Panel B includes a perfectly elastic inverse demand function $P(X)$, so that the regulated sector's output falls from X^0 to X^1 following the emissions reduction. In this case, the firms' opportunity cost of reducing emissions is area $b + c$, which also corresponds to society's abatement cost. Therefore, when price does not change, measurement requires observation (or estimation) of the change in production cost and the change in output. Importantly, knowledge of the additional cost of producing X^1 due to the regulation (area b) is not sufficient to characterize abatement costs, though it can be interpreted as a lower bound.

Panel A

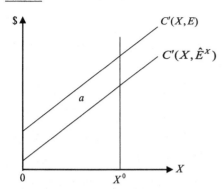

Panel B

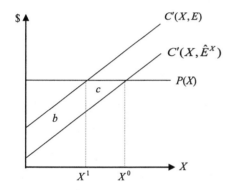

Panel C

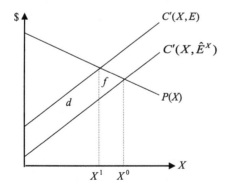

Figure 22.1 Abatement cost concepts

Panel C illustrates the general case in which both price and quantity change following regulation, due to households' imperfectly elastic inverse demand curve. The social cost of regulation in this context arises from the reduction in output from X^0 to X^1 and the increase in firms' costs, so that society's abatement cost is given by area $d+f$. Note that area d is the added cost to firms of producing X^1 under the emissions reduction policy regime, relative to what X^1 would cost in the absence of regulation. It does not, however, reflect firms' share of society's abatement costs. As in panel B, the additional cost of producing X^1 under the regulation does not account for the decreased output. In contrast to panel B, however, the price increase shifts some of the cost of abatement to consumers. Nonetheless, area d in panel C provides a lower bound on abatement costs, though how informative this is depends on the slope of the inverse demand function.

Figure 22.1 suggests an organizational structure in which we first examine empirical contexts where either price or quantity remains fixed, which allows us to focus only on firms' abatement costs, before turning to more general cases. This mirrors Pizer and Kopp (2005), whose review of research on pollution abatement cost estimation proceeds along three overlapping dimensions: partial versus general equilibrium cost estimates, retrospective versus prospective data environments, and empirical versus engineering modeling approaches. Partial equilibrium in this context means a focus on a single regulated industry with output price or quantity fixed (panels A and B), while general equilibrium includes the price change case (panel C), as well as consideration of spillover effects to the wider economy.

A retrospective data environment refers to a context in which data are available that describe agents' choices under the regulatory regime being analyzed. In contrast, a prospective data environment is one in which the regulation has not been implemented, meaning there is no historical data record of behavior under the regulatory regime of interest. Estimates from this latter perspective are often referred to as ex ante cost estimates. The data environment conditions the type of analysis that can be conducted. When there is a historical record of behavior under conditions similar to the policy being evaluated, it is possible to use an empirical model to parametrically estimate abatement and marginal abatement cost functions. This is often referred to as a "revealed behavior" approach, since it is based on observation of firms' presumably optimal decisions, given the regulatory environment. Absent the requisite historical data record, an engineering model needs to be constructed by a process expert, who designs a way to comply with the emissions reduction, and predicts the material, capital, and labor costs needed for the compliance strategy. Engineering cost estimates are also referred to as "bottom up" cost estimates, and they are the typical source of ex ante abatement cost function estimates. In the following subsections we discuss these three dimensions in specific contexts.

22.2.2 Partial Equilibrium – Retrospective Analysis

When a project is small or localized, it is often reasonable to evaluate its costs and benefits in a partial equilibrium framework. As noted above, partial equilibrium in this context refers to a situation when output price or quantity does not change. For local regulations targeting a subset of an industry's firms, the number of polluting entities may be small relative to the overall industry, meaning output price will not change following the regulation. This may also be true for internationally traded goods. In other cases, such as for the electricity sector, demand is highly inelastic in the short run, meaning a fixed quantity assumption may be appropriate. In these cases abatement cost estimation can focus only on firms' costs.

In retrospective analyses, data describing behavior while the regulation was in place are available for empirical modeling. A large literature in production economics has focused on estimating cost functions and production functions, given observation of output and input quantities, production costs, and/or input prices. For example, in a review from three decades ago, Jorgenson (1986) notes that "the objective of econometric modeling [of production] is to determine the nature of substitution among inputs, the character of differences in technology, and the role of economies of scale." These ideas have been adapted and applied to estimating abatement cost functions and abatement technologies.

Cost Functions

To illustrate cost function estimation, consider the following idealized data environment. We observe a panel of $j = 1, \ldots, J$ firms in an industry across $t = 1, \ldots, T$ time periods, with variation in the regulatory regime existing across time and/or firms in the panel. That is, the study period spans times when at least some firms are subject to the regulation, and when they are not. For each firm/time period combination, we observe total production costs $cost_{jt}$, output x_{jt}, emissions e_{jt}, and the regulatory regime that was in place when output and emissions were generated. We also observe a vector of firm characteristics Z_{jt}, where individual variables can be time varying or time fixed. With these data, an econometric model of the form

$$cost_{jt} = \beta' Z_{jt} + f(x_{jt}, e_{jt}, Z_{jt}, D_{jt}, \gamma) + c_j + \tau_t + \varepsilon_{jt} \tag{22.18}$$

could be used to characterize the cost function, where $f(\cdot)$ is a specific empirical functional form such as

$$f(x_{jt}, e_{jt}, Z_{jt}, D_{jt}, \gamma) = \gamma_1 x_{jt} + \gamma_2 e_{jt} D_{jt} + \gamma_3 x_{jt} e_{jt} D_{jt} + \frac{1}{2} \gamma_4 e_{jt}^2 D_{jt} + \gamma_5' Z_{jt} e_{jt} D_{jt}, \tag{22.19}$$

c_j and τ_t are firm and time-fixed effects, respectively, and D_{jt} is a dummy variable equal to one if firm j was subject to emissions limits in period t. Note that in this specification, the marginal abatement cost curve is derived from

$$\frac{\partial \cos t_{jt}}{\partial e_{jt}} = \gamma_2 D_{jt} + \gamma_3 x_{jt} D_{jt} + \gamma_4 e_{jt} D_{jt} + \gamma_5' Z_{jt} D_{jt}, \tag{22.20}$$

which is conditional on firms' production scale, current emissions, and other characteristics.

This stylized data and econometric model provides the basis for predicting each of the cost concepts shown in panels A and B in Figure 22.1. For example, if output and input prices do not change, observation of $cost_{jt} - cost_{js}$ provides an estimate of area a in panel A for firm j, when the regulation is active in period t and inactive in period s. When output changes, estimates from (22.18) and (22.19) can be used to predict area b

in panel B. Likewise, observation of the change in output, and predictions for marginal cost before and after the regulation, can be used to approximate area c. Thus for partial equilibrium analysis, historical data and careful econometrics allows estimation of the abatement and marginal abatement cost levels from a previously implemented policy.

This discussion has taken a reduced form approach to specifying the cost function. Much of the applied production literature, however, uses a structural approach to estimating the cost function. For example, the costs for firm j could instead be empirically specified as

$$
\ln cost_{jt} = \alpha_j + \alpha_x \ln x_{jt} + \alpha_e \ln e_{jt} + \sum_{k=1}^{K} \alpha_k \ln w_k^{jt} + \beta_{xe} \ln x_{jt} \ln e_{jt} +
$$
$$
\sum_{m=1}^{K} \sum_{k=1}^{K} \beta_{mk} \ln w_m^{jt} \ln w_k^{jt} + \sum_{k=1}^{K} \beta_{kx} \ln w_k^{jt} \ln x_j + \sum_{k=1}^{K} \beta_{ke} \ln w_k^{jt} \ln e_j + \varepsilon_{jt},
$$

(22.21)

where K is the number of inputs, $w = (w_1, \ldots, w_K)$ is the vector of input prices, ε_{jt} is an econometric error, and the vectors α and β are parameters to be estimated. The theoretical properties of a cost function are usually imposed by restricting the parameter values so that

$$
\sum_{k=1}^{K} \alpha_k = 1
$$
$$
\sum_{j=1}^{K} \beta_{jk} = \sum_{j=1}^{K} \beta_{jx} = \sum_{j=1}^{K} \beta_{je} = 0.
$$

(22.22)

With this, differentiating $cost_{jt}$ in Eq. (22.21) with respect to one of the input prices leads to

$$
\frac{1}{cost_{jt}} \frac{\partial cost_{jt}}{\partial w_k^{jt}} = \frac{l_k^{jt}}{cost_{jt}} = \frac{1}{w_k^{jt}} \left(\alpha_k + \beta_{kx} \ln x_{jt} + \beta_{ke} \ln e_{jt} + \sum_{m=1}^{K} \beta_{mk} \ln w_m^{jt} \right), \quad (22.23)
$$

where l_k^{jt} is the factor input level for factor k, and the first equality follows from Shephard's Lemma. This gives rise to the factor cost share equation

$$
s_k^{jt} = \alpha_k + \beta_{kx} \ln x_{jt} + \beta_{ke} \ln e_{jt} + \sum_{m=1}^{K} \beta_{mk} \ln w_m^{jt} + \eta_k^{jt}, \quad k = 1, \ldots, K,
$$

(22.24)

where η_k^{jt} is an econometric error term. Observation of total production costs and the share of costs associated with each input allows joint estimation of the cost function (22.21) and the K factor share equations in (22.24), to recover the vectors α and β. While it is possible to estimate α and β without the cost share data, cost shares provide additional information that is useful for estimating the model.

With estimation complete, the marginal abatement cost function for a representative firm is derived by differentiating (22.21) with respect to e_{jt} to obtain

$$
\frac{\partial \ln cost_{jt}}{\partial e_{jt}} = \frac{1}{e_{jt}} \left(\alpha_e + \beta_{xe} \ln x_{jt} + \sum_{k=1}^{K} \beta_{ke} \ln w_k^{jt} \right),
$$

(22.25)

implying that

$$MAC_{jt} = -\frac{C_{jt}}{e_{jt}}\left(\alpha_e + \beta_{xe}\ln x_{jt} + \sum_{k=1}^{K}\beta_{ke}\ln w_k^{jt}\right). \qquad (22.26)$$

Note that the marginal abatement cost function depends on the full vector of input substitution possibilities, as reflected in the values for the β_{ke} terms, as well as the scale of production.

EXAMPLE 22.2 (EMPIRICAL) Carlson et al. (2000) provide an example of cost function estimation, based on a version of the structural specification in (22.21). They assembled cost data for coal-fired electricity plants in the US, with the goal of estimating marginal abatement costs for sulfur dioxide emissions. The econometric model focuses on the 260 plants that used fuel switching to comply with reductions required under the 1990 US Clean Air Act Amendments (firms that scrubbed emissions were examined separately). Inputs include labor units, generating capital, and the volume of low- and high-sulfur coal; input prices faced by each plant were also obtained. Emissions were computed based on the sulfur content of the coal used in electricity production. The authors jointly estimate the cost function and input cost share equations to recover estimates of the structural parameters. The estimates are then used to predict plant-specific marginal abatement costs for sulfur dioxide in 1985 and 1994 in order to measure the potential gains from trade under the sulfur dioxide cap and trade program that began in 1995. They find that both average marginal abatement cost and emissions declined between 1985 and 1994, and show substantial heterogeneity across firms. For example, in 1994 the phase I plants – the largest and dirtiest plants – had a mean marginal abatement cost of $121. In contrast, the phase II plants – generally with lower baseline emission rates – had a mean of $1,092.

In practice, the data needed to estimate the parameters in (22.18) and (22.19) or (22.21) and (22.24) are often difficult to obtain. Private firms' cost information is usually proprietary, and even with access to confidential records, key variables are often missing, including emissions levels. This challenge can be partially mitigated by fielding surveys that solicit polluting firms' environmental regulation compliance expenditures. Indeed, many governments collect data on spending by firms in polluting industries for environmental compliance. For example, the US Census Bureau periodically administers the Pollution Abatement Costs and Expenditures (PACE) survey, which queries manufacturing plant managers on their capital and operational spending needed to comply with air, land, and water pollution regulations. Use of self-reported data like the PACE survey for estimating abatement cost functions requires that the reported environmental spending is "additional to" costs that would have occurred in the absence of regulation. Users of the data also need to interpret reported expenditures based on one of two possible assumptions on firms' output:

$$PACE^1(x,e) = C\big(x(e),e\big) - C\big(x(\hat{e}^x),\hat{e}^x\big)$$

$$PACE^2(x,e) = C\big(\overline{x},e\big) - C\big(\overline{x},\hat{e}^{\overline{x}}\big). \qquad (22.27)$$

In $PACE^1$, the assumption is that managers' answers reflect the difference between costs at the no-regulation level of output and emissions, and costs at the regulated output and emission levels. For $PACE^2$, the assumption is that the manager uses a reference level of output – i.e. the current period output – and reports how the regulation increases the cost of producing that quantity. Neither of these is, in general, equal to the firm's opportunity cost of reducing emissions, though in special cases they may be. When output is not affected by the regulation, $PACE^1 = PACE^2$, and the reported expenditures are equivalent to area a in panel A of Figure 22.1. When output is affected, $PACE^1$ corresponds to a component of the costs shown in Eq. (22.17), and so it understates the firm's opportunity cost of reducing emissions. Likewise, when the reference quantity is current production, $PACE^2$ corresponds to area b in panel B of the figure, and once again understates society's abatement costs.

Morgenstern et al. (2001) describe several conceptual reasons that both interpretations in (22.27) may fail to hold, which mainly derive from the difficulties that survey respondents are likely to face when queried about specific spending categories. For example, if pollution control requirements reduce operating flexibility and thereby raise production costs, accounting records on pollution-related expenditures may not accurately reflect abatement costs. In contrast, if there are complementarities between environmental compliance and the production process, reported abatement expenditures may overstate firms' abatement cost. Morgenstern et al. (2001) test the accuracy of survey-based abatement cost information by comparing reported abatement spending to firms' total production costs. The intuition of their approach is that there should be a one-to-one relationship between reported abatement expenditures and total costs, if either version in (22.27) holds, in the sense that one additional dollar of abatement spending should translate to one dollar of increased total cost. On average, they find some evidence that reported abatement expenditures overstate actual abatement costs, and no evidence that reported expenditures understate actual abatement costs. This contrasts somewhat with Becker (2005), who used the PACE data to examine air pollution abatement costs under the Clean Air Act for US manufacturers. He finds that reported expenditures by plants located in federally-designated "non-attainment" counties are, on average, higher than for plants located in "attainment" counties. This qualitatively supports the efficacy of the PACE survey's measurements, since plants in non-attainment counties are subject to stricter regulations, and therefore should have higher abatement costs. Analysis of abatement expenditures for specific pollutants such as NO_X, however, revealed insignificant differences in capital and operating expenses between firms subject to higher and lower regulatory scrutiny. Becker (2005) concludes from this that abatement expenditures associated with changes in production processes, as are needed for NO_X reductions, are more difficult for plant managers to quantify than end-of-pipe abatement expenditures. This suggests that the accuracy of self-reported abatement expenditure may depend on the mechanisms through which the cost arises.

EXAMPLE 22.3 (EMPIRICAL) Hartman et al. (1997) provide an example of how the PACE survey data can be used to estimate marginal abatement cost functions. The authors examine air pollution abatement expenditures during the period 1979 to 1985, for 37 US manufacturing sectors and seven different air pollutants. By merging abatement expenditure data from the PACE survey with information from the US Census of Manufacturers, Hartman et al. assemble information on 100,000 facilities for use in their analysis. In sector-specific regressions, they regress reported plant-specific total air pollution abatement spending on abatement quantities and abatement quantities squared, for each of the seven pollutants. The authors then predict pollutant- and sector-specific marginal and average abatement cost levels. They use their estimates to illustrate the non-cost minimizing nature of the command and control policies that dominated US air pollution regulations during their study period. They find large heterogeneity in marginal abatement costs across sectors for the same pollutants, showing, for example, that the four highest-cost sulfur dioxide abating sectors had marginal abatement costs ranging from \$53 (industrial chemicals) to \$146 (pulping).

Technology Functions

There is a long tradition in applied economics of estimating parametric production and technology functions (see the many citations in Jorgenson, 1986). In general, production functions describe how quantities of inputs relate to outputs, conditional on the underlying technology, and so estimation uses observation of physical quantities to characterize input and output substitutability. This is useful when costs are not observed, since results from production theory can, in some instances, be used to link technical substitution possibilities to marginal values.

This possibility underlies a large empirical literature on abatement cost estimation, dating to Färe et al. (1993), that begins with the characterization of a polluting firm's output and emissions as joint products. In Chapter 5, we defined a vector of inputs $l = (l_1, \ldots, l_K)$ and the technology relationships that mapped the input vector l to the firm's output x and emissions e. Here we assume that the technology is denoted T, and that it maps l to a joint output vector $y = (x, e)$ according to

$$T = \{(l, y) : l \to y\}. \tag{22.28}$$

In words, T describes the set of production pairs x and e that can be produced using l, where we refer to x as a desirable output, and emissions e as an undesirable output. With this we can define the production possibility relationship for a specific input level as

$$T(l) = \{y : (l, y) \in T\}. \tag{22.29}$$

Figure 22.2 shows an example relationship between x and e, conditional on an input level l. Since e is an undesirable output, at the boundary of $T(l)$ the quantity of x needs to be reduced in order to reduce the output of e. This is consistent with the assumption of weak disposability, which means that the polluting firm cannot dispose of undesirable outputs without cost. Specifically, weak disposability says that if l can produce y, it can also produce a proportionate reduction in y, so that if $y \in T(l)$, then $\phi y \in T(l)$ for $\phi \in [0,1]$. Weak disposability can be contrasted with strong disposability, whereby e can be decreased without reducing x, for a given input level.

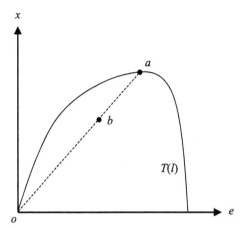

Figure 22.2   Production possibility set for output and emissions given an input vector

With joint products, it is conceptually and empirically convenient to represent technology with the output distance function (see Färe and Primont, 1995), which is formally given by

$$D(l, y) = \min_{\theta} \left\{ \theta : \left(l, \frac{y}{\theta} \right) \in T(l) \right\}. \tag{22.30}$$

This representation of technology is useful because it is scalar-valued, even for the case of joint outputs. In particular, $D(l,y)$ measures the distance from the reference output vector y to the efficient production frontier. If y is on the boundary of $T(l)$, then $D(l,y) = 1$ and the inputs are being efficiently used. If y is in the interior of $T(l)$, then $D(l,y) < 1$ and production is inefficient. In Figure 22.2, the output pair at point a is on the frontier, and the line segment oa has distance one, so that $D(l,y_a) = 1$. In contrast, the output pair at point b is in the interior, and the line segment ob has distance $D(l,y_b) < 1$.

It is possible to empirically estimate a parametric distance function for the firm, given observation of the physical quantities of its inputs and outputs. For example, one parametric representation of (22.30) is

$$\ln D(l, y) = \alpha_0 + \alpha_1 \ln x + \alpha_2 \ln e + \sum_{k=1}^{K} \beta_k \ln l_k + \sum_{k=1}^{K} \sum_{m=1}^{K} \beta_{km} \left(\ln l_k \right) \left(\ln l_m \right)$$
$$+ \sum_{k=1}^{K} \gamma_{xk} \left(\ln l_k \right) \left(\ln x \right) + \sum_{k=1}^{K} \gamma_{ek} \left(\ln l_k \right) \left(\ln e \right),$$

$$\tag{22.31}$$

where $\ln D(l, y) \le 0$, and restrictions on the parameters (α, β, γ) are imposed so as to maintain the theoretical properties of the distance function, including homogeneity of degree one in outputs. Empirical implementation requires observation of the physical quantities of outputs and inputs for a sample of J firms. Färe et al. (1993) and Coggins and Swinton (1996) show how, in the most basic case, estimation is not by econometrics, but instead uses linear programing to find the parameters that maximize

$$\sum_{j=1}^{J} \ln D_j(l_j, y_j) \quad s.t. \quad \ln D_j(l_j, y_j) \leq 0 \forall j. \tag{22.32}$$

Note that this is consistent with selecting parameter values that make output from the sample of firms as close to the efficient production frontier as possible, given the data and functional form.

Estimation of the distance function is useful because duality theorems can be used to link the distance function to marginal values. Specifically, the revenue function conditional on an input vector l and marginal values $r = (p, \tau)$ is defined by

$$R(l, r) = \max_{y} \left\{ px + \tau e : D(l, y) \leq 1 \right\}, \tag{22.33}$$

where p is the market price for x and $\tau \leq 0$ is the "shadow price" of emissions. The latter is equivalent to the negative of firm's marginal abatement cost, and the object of estimation. If the firm is subject to environmental regulation, weak disposability implies that there is an opportunity cost in x from reducing e, conditional on the input level l. The shadow price of emissions in (22.33) reflects the lost revenue from this reduction in x.

Note that the revenue function describes how the firm selects x and e to maximize revenue, subject to technical feasibility, and conditional on the input level. Thus if we observe an input vector, we can use revenue maximization to describe the remainder of the firm's profit maximizing choice. This choice is derived according to

$$\max_{x, e} px + \tau e + \lambda \left(1 - D(l, y) \right), \tag{22.34}$$

with first-order conditions

$$p = \lambda \frac{\partial D(l, y)}{\partial x}$$
$$\tau = \lambda \frac{\partial D(l, y)}{\partial e}. \tag{22.35}$$

These conditions are key for estimating the shadow cost of emissions, since they imply that

$$\frac{\tau}{p} = \frac{\frac{\partial D(l, y)}{\partial e}}{\frac{\partial D(l, y)}{\partial x}} \quad \rightarrow \quad \tau = p \frac{\partial D(l, y) / \partial e}{\partial D(l, y) / \partial x}. \tag{22.36}$$

From this we see that observation of the market price and estimation of the distance function is sufficient to estimate firms' shadow price of emissions, and hence marginal abatement cost. More generally, we are able to use an empirical representation of the firm's technology to obtain a single point on its marginal abatement cost function, at its observed output and emission levels. This is equivalent to the conceptual representation in Eq. (22.16).

EXAMPLE 22.4 (EMPIRICAL) An example of marginal abatement cost estimation via the distance function is provided by Coggins and Swinton (1996). The authors examine abatement costs for sulfur dioxide emissions at 14 non-scrubbing coal-burning electricity plants in the US state of Wisconsin during the years 1990–92 (prior to the start of the sulfur dioxide cap and trade program). For each year, they observe sulfur dioxide emissions and electricity and model them as joint outputs, given observation of sulfur content, energy, labor, and capital as inputs. The distance function shown in (22.31) is estimated via linear programing. Using the derivatives of the distance function and the market price of electricity, the authors predict the marginal abatement cost of a ton of sulfur dioxide for each of the 14 plants in their sample. They report an average marginal abatement cost of $293, and median of $112.

22.2.3 Partial Equilibrium – Prospective Analysis

As defined above, prospective analysis occurs when cost estimates are needed for a regulatory intervention that has not yet occurred, meaning the historical data record cannot be used to measure firms' responses to the new policy regime. Cost estimates in this case are obtained via engineering models, whereby a process expert designs a compliance strategy, and predicts the cost of the additional inputs needed for implementation. Estimates obtained in this way are often referred to as "ex ante," and by definition they are not derived based on firms' optimal real-time response to the regulation.

The main analytic task in prospective analysis is to design the compliance strategy, and so environmental economists have historically not been major contributors to ex ante abatement cost estimation. Nonetheless, in some instances economists have used detailed engineering studies to comment on, for example, the potential ex ante cost effectiveness of proposed regulations. The following example illustrates this type of analysis.

EXAMPLE 22.5 (EMPIRICAL) Fowlie et al. (2012) study the cost effectiveness of NO_X regulations in the US, which are separately aimed at controlling emissions from power plants and mobile sources. For this they need to predict marginal abatement cost (MAC) functions for both sources. If the MACs are not equal across the two sectors at given abatement levels, cost savings are possible via reallocation. The amount of available cost savings depends on the actual MAC curves for the two sources. The authors take an ex ante approach to their analysis in order to mimic the considerations of policy makers prior to implementation, when decisions on sector coordination/non-coordination needed to be taken. They first use the results of an engineering study that detailed 15 emission-reducing strategies available to coal-burning electricity plants in the eastern US. For each strategy, abatement possibilities and plant specific costs were predicted based on over 60 unit- and plant-level operating characteristics, fuel types, boiler specifications, etc. (p.107). With this, the minimum ex ante costs of achieving various abatement levels for 632 generating units were computed, and the individual curves were horizontally summed to derive an aggregate marginal abatement cost curve. Similarly, the authors report the US EPA's predictions of per-vehicle costs of achieving a given level of NO_X reduction, for different combinations of vehicle class and engine size. This information is used to construct an aggregate marginal abatement cost curve for NO_X reductions by new vehicle manufacturers. Fowlie et al. then use their MAC function estimates to analyze the joint cost effectiveness of two NO_X control programs: the federal "Tier 2" passenger vehicle emissions reduction program, and the "NO_X Budget" program, where the latter uses a cap and trade approach to reduce NO_X emission from electricity plants in the eastern US. They find that, under the program parameters, the MAC for point sources is more than double the MAC for mobile sources, which results in $1.6 billion in excess costs due to the failure to coordinate across sources.

22.2.4 General Equilibrium

We now briefly turn to the problem of general equilibrium abatement cost estimation. In our organizational scheme this includes instances in which there is a price change in the regulated market, and cases in which spillover effects to other markets may have indirect welfare consequences. We saw in Chapter 7 that, if there are no distortions in related markets, optimal environmental policy design can focus only on the direct effects in the regulated market. For example, in the Chapter 7 model, the shift in labor supply that occurs when the price of the polluting good increases does not affect the optimum emission tax rate, so long as there is no pre-existing distortionary income tax. This logic carries through to the calculation of costs. For example, area $d+f$ in panel C of Figure 22.1 is the total (direct) abatement cost from the regulation in the market for X, and it is equal to society's total abatement cost if the related final good and factor input markets are distortion free. Measurement in this case requires attention to firms' costs, as discussed above, as well as an estimate of the demand for the polluting good.

Things are more complicated when there are pre-existing distortions in related markets. For example, in Chapter 7 we saw that the opportunity cost of reducing emissions depended on demand and supply in the market for the polluting good, as well as the labor supply elasticity, the marginal tax rate on income, the degree of substitutability between leisure and the polluting good, and the government's budget needs. Prediction of the gross abatement costs in the simple model from Chapter 7 therefore would require empirical measurement of several diverse phenomena. Furthermore, the model in Chapter 7 was simplified for analytical tractability; actual analysis of specific policies in real-world contexts requires more attention to institutional detail. All of this is to say that estimation of abatement costs when policy impacts are large, and spillovers to multiple markets occur, is not possible with analytical models and reductionist empirical approaches. Rather, large-scale, multiple equation numerical models that operate at the level of a national or the global economy are needed to accomplish the cost-benefit analysis. Models of this type are known as computable general equilibrium (CGE) models, and they are distinct from most of what we have discussed in this book.

22.3 SUMMARY

Completion of a cost-benefit analysis in environmental economics usually requires estimates of the non-market benefits or damages of the proposal, and the abatement costs
associated with its implementation. In this chapter we focused on these empirical tasks.
We began by noting that regulatory timelines and budgets often preclude the use of
an original study for measuring the non-market benefits of a proposal. In these cases,
benefits transfer is used to obtain estimates of the proposal's benefits based on existing
results gleaned from the literature. We saw that this involves collecting information
from a set of study sites, and using it to formulate an estimate for the policy site. We distinguished between unit value transfers and benefit function transfers, where the former
simply uses the study site estimates directly, at the study site. Benefit function transfer
is a more sophisticated approach, which adjusts information from the study sites for
systematic differences in the policy site's population and/or environmental characteristics. The academic research on benefit functions has mainly focused on using meta-
analysis of existing studies to forecast values at a policy site. An alternative approach to
benefit function transfer uses study site estimates to calibrate structural functions (e.g.
indirect utility, demand, or expenditure functions), which can be used to predict values
at the policy site. We saw that researchers have made progress in using both of these
approaches, and that convergent validity studies suggest that they can often provide
estimates that are sufficiently accurate for use in many policy contexts. We noted, however, that the practice of benefits transfer has lagged behind the research, and that there
remain many opportunities for research that helps to bridge this gap.

  In the second half of the chapter we examined the estimation of abatement costs.
Focusing on regulated firms, we saw that the type of estimate and method of application
depends on several institutional and data aspects. We defined a retrospective analysis as
one in which regulated firms have already operated under the constraints of the policy,
meaning cost, production, and emissions outcomes can be observed before and after the
policy change. In this case, econometric methods can be used to estimate costs, subject
to data availability. We described how the large literature from production economics
provides guidance on estimating cost or production functions, which allow prediction
of marginal abatement costs. We saw, however, that estimation of level (non-marginal)
abatement costs requires we pay attention to market responses. In cases where the output price or quantity does not change, we saw that it is relatively straightforward to use
an estimate of the abatement cost function to predict society's gross abatement costs.
However, when price and quantity change, abatement costs are shared between producers and consumers, and information beyond firms' costs will be needed.

  Cost estimates are often needed as part of a prospective evaluation of a proposed policy. In this context, potentially regulated firms have not yet operated under the constraints
of the policy, and so there is no record of cost, output, or emissions responses. Cost estimates must therefore be obtained via the efforts of a process expert, who designs a means
of compliance, and tracks the labor and capital costs associated with the strategy. We saw
that engineering estimates of this type are referred to as bottom-up approaches, and that
they play a critical role in the ex ante evaluation of proposed policies.

  We closed our discussion of abatement costs by noting that, for large-scale analyses,
estimation of firms' abatement costs may not be the primary measurement objective. We

saw in Chapter 5 that the opportunity cost of emissions reduction is ultimately based on the gross welfare cost to society, which is assessed via households' utility functions. As such, CGE models of the entire economy are often used to evaluate the costs (and benefits) of large-scale, economy-wide interventions.

22.4 FURTHER READING

Contemporary work on benefits transfer is usually traced to a special issue of *Water Resources Research* (volume 28, issue 3, 1992), which introduced terms and concepts that are still used today. Key papers in the issue include Boyle and Bergstrom (1992), Smith (1992), and Loomis (1992). A subsequent special issue in *Ecological Economics* (volume 60, 2006) provides an updated and wider-ranging survey of both methods and practice. Johnston and Rosenberger (2010) and Boyle et al. (2010) present article-length surveys of benefits transfer, and the edited volume by Johnston et al. (2015) is an authoritative summary of the theory, empirics, and practice of benefits transfer.

On specific aspects of benefits transfer, Bergstrom and Taylor (2006) provide a discussion of meta-analysis for benefits transfer, and Nelson and Kennedy (2009) offer a more general summary and critique of meta-analysis, as used in environmental economics. Colombo et al. (2007) and Johnston (2007) discuss the use of discrete choice experiments in the context of benefits transfer. Smith et al. (2002, 2006) provide structural benefits transfer examples, and Kaul et al. (2013) survey evidence on convergent validity in benefits transfer. Leon-Gonzalez and Scarpa (2008), Moeltner et al. (2007), and Phaneuf and Van Houtven (2015) explore Bayesian econometric methods for benefits transfer.

Our discussion of abatement cost estimation has relied heavily on Pizer and Kopp (2005) for organization and concepts. Färe and Primont (1995) contains a useful overview of production theory, and Färe et al. (1993) provide the initial application of the distance function approach to measuring marginal abatement costs. Zhou et al. (2014) provide a recent review of literature in this area. Examples of estimation where costs are observed include Carlson et al. (2000), McClelland and Horowitz (1999), and Mérel and Wimberger (2012). Examples of estimation based on survey data include Hartman et al. (1997), Höglund Isaksson (2005), and Becker (2005). Bergman's (2005) overview of CGE modeling in environmental applications contains topics relevant for using these models to predict abatement costs for economy-wide policies, and Böhringer et al. (2015) present an application to carbon tariffs. Goulder et al. (1999) and Parry et al. (1999) are further examples of analytical/numerical modeling frameworks for comparing costs across different policy choices.

EXERCISES

22.1   **There are several online databases of non-market values that are used for benefit transfers. A good example is the *Recreation Use Values* database, maintained by Randy Rosenberger.[3]

---

[3] See http://recvaluation.forestry.oregonstate.edu/.

(a) Examine the database and describe its main features, including its potential uses for benefits transfer practice and research. Summarize the findings from one published paper making use of this database.

(b) Suppose you are interested in measuring the value of a freshwater angling day at an inland lake in the US state of Wisconsin. Use the database to construct a unit value transfer, based on "study" site entries that seem suitably similar to your policy site context.

(c) Suppose you are interested in knowing how SP, RP, and combined RP/SP measurement methods produce systematically different (i.e. higher or lower) estimates of unit values. Conduct a meta-analysis of the database values to answer this question, making sure you take care to control for any other variables you think are necessary.

22.2 ***Consider now a structural benefits transfer approach for valuing aspects of freshwater recreation. Using the example specification beginning in Eq. (22.1), search for studies that will help you parameterize the function in the context of single-day angling and swimming trips at Lake Mendota in Madison, Wisconsin. Use your model to predict the value of an angling trip, and compare this to your findings from the Recreation Use Values database. Then use your model to predict the benefits of a 25 percent reduction in phosphorus concentrations in the lake.

CHAPTER 23

Final Thoughts

Via the 22 previous chapters in this book we have tried to tell the story of environmental economics, beginning with its roots in neoclassical welfare theory and the environmental movements of the 1960s, and through to the sophisticated theoretical and applied research that today defines the field. We have attempted to integrate in a single volume the conceptual, empirical, and policy aspects of the field, without compromising on the depth of coverage. This, more than anything, explains the length of the book and the amount of time it has taken to write. Even with this, there are many topics that deserve discussion which we have elected not to cover in the book. In this chapter we will briefly discuss some of the important omissions and offer some closing thoughts.

We begin in the next section by noting that environmental economics, like many other fields in microeconomics, has experienced a flowering of empirical research. This is due to several simultaneously occurring factors, including greater appreciation for careful applied work in the economics profession, advances in applied econometric methodology, and the increased availability of high-quality behavioral and environmental data. Many of the questions being pursued do not fit cleanly into the standard canon of the field, which has served as the organizing principle of the book. To highlight this increasingly important aspect of the field, in section 23.1 we summarize a handful of recent papers that illustrate the range of empirical research questions that have occupied environmental economists.

In addition to specifically empirical topics, there are several other areas that we have not covered or have discussed only briefly. Examples include the large economic literature on climate change, topics at the nexus of energy and environmental economics, and political economy/environment issues related to interest group activities, alternative regulator objective functions, and voting. We have also omitted traditional resource economics, and topics that combine elements of environmental policy and natural resource management. In section 23.2 we catalog these topics, discuss their omission in the context of the book's organization and intent, and provide references for further reading.

Finally, we note that this book has largely focused on the field's history and its current state. While we hope study of the basic tenets will help students to identify and carry out novel research, we have not explicitly sought to define the research frontier in the field, or discussed the analytical toolkits needed for conducting research in its various subareas. In section 23.3 we break from this and identify specific tools that are particularly important for specific areas, to help guide students in seeking out the relevant training. In section 23.4 we then discuss research topics that we think will be important in the future. Finally, we close the book in section 23.5 by briefly sharing some final thoughts.

23.1   AN INCREASINGLY EMPIRICAL FIELD

The structure of this book has followed the traditional order and division of topics in graduate environmental economics courses. Parts I and II were more theoretically focused on policy design, while Parts III and IV had a larger emphasis on empirical methodology and implementation. While we have attempted throughout to use examples to highlight empirical research that was motivated by theoretical results, our organizational structure did not easily lend itself to the discussion of purely applied questions, or questions that fall outside of the traditional theoretical structure in the field. This leaves some important topics uncovered, and more importantly, does not do justice to the wide range of compelling empirical research that is occurring in the field. In this section we present three examples of largely empirical research areas in order to highlight the trend towards this style of inquiry in environmental economics.

23.1.1 Voluntary Pollution Reduction Mechanisms

A fundamental premise of the theory developed in this book is that pollution reduction is costly, and because of this, polluters will not reduce emissions unless they are compelled to do so. In spite of this, polluting firms do on occasion act in a socially desirable way, and there has been a large increase in the use of "voluntary" pollution reduction mechanisms in both developed and developing countries. This has set up theoretical questions on why firms might undertake costly actions absent explicit regulation, and empirical questions on whether or not voluntary mechanisms actually lead to emission reductions below the status quo. A related topic is the extent to which public information campaigns encouraging pro-social behavior are effective substitutes for outright regulation. In this subsection we highlight examples of empirical research in these areas.

One of the most studied voluntary programs is the 33/50 program from the US EPA. The initiative was launched in 1991 to encourage firms in the chemical and other industries to reduce emissions of a number of toxic chemicals. The goal was to reduce emissions into all environmental media by 33 percent in 1992 and 50 percent by 1995. In joining the program, firms pledged to reduce their emissions by an amount and means of their choosing. The goals of the program were largely reached by 1994, though it needs to be emphasized that there was a downward trend in emissions prior to the program. As such a large empirical literature has examined the 33/50 program's efficacy by comparing eligible firms' participation status to their toxic releases, as well as financial performance indicators.

Khanna and Damon (1999) provide an early and influential contribution to this literature (we have drawn our description of the program from their paper). Though participating firms did indeed reduce emissions more than non-participating firms, they note that this may be due to firms selecting into the program based on firm-specific reduction trends that are independent from the program. If this is the case, emission reductions from the program are not additional. Establishing the causal effect of the 33/50 program therefore requires construction of a counterfactual describing what participating firms' emissions would have been, absent the program. In their early paper, M. Khanna and Damon take steps to partially address the non-random assignment into the program, and find that it was effective in reducing emissions. Several subsequent papers have analyzed the 33/50, with each using a somewhat different approach to controlling for selection effects. This has led to somewhat mixed results. For example, in two recent studies, Bi and M. Khanna (2012) report estimates supporting the effectiveness of the program, while Vidovic and N. Khanna (2012) report estimates suggesting the program was not effective.

Cutter and Neidell (2009) study an alternative voluntary mechanism that is aimed at households rather than firms. The "Spare the Air" program in the San Francisco Bay area issues advisories on days when ground-level ozone concentration is predicted to be above national standards. The intent of the program is to reduce ozone-increasing automobile trips by encouraging greater use of ride sharing and public transit on days forecast to have poor air quality. The authors assess the program's efficacy by comparing administrative data on highway traffic volume and public transit ridership for alert and non-alert days, while controlling for a number of potentially confounding effects. They find small reductions in traffic counts are attributable to "Spare the Air" on announcement days, and some evidence that mass transit ridership increases.

The 33/50 and Spare the Air programs are just two examples of a large and increasing number of voluntary-type programs in both developed and developing countries. A related area is the impact of product labeling and disclosure regulations on consumer choices, and the potential for environmentally friendly choices to be a private provision alternative to the public provision of environmental quality. For example, researchers have examined how product labels certifying environmentally friendly production affect demand (Teisl et al. 2002), energy efficiency labels affect purchases of consumer durables (Newell and Siikamäki, 2014), and environmental disclosure laws affect housing choices (Pope, 2008a, 2008b).

23.1.2 Environmental Justice

It is an empirical regularity in the US and other countries that lower income households are exposed to higher levels of local pollutants. In urban areas, for example, low income neighborhoods are more likely to be near hazardous waste facilities. In the US it has been reported that nearly 44 percent of residents living within 1 km of a hazardous waste site were Hispanic or African-American, but only 19 percent of residents outside a 5 km buffer were members of these groups.[1] Correlations of this type have given rise to an area of study known as "environmental justice," which is concerned with understanding the causes and potential solutions to what is widely regarded as an inequitable distribution of the consequences of industrial pollution.

---

[1] From United Church of Christ, "Toxic waste and race at twenty: 1987–2007". www.ucc.org/environmental-ministries.

Environmental economists have been interested in understanding the underlying mechanisms driving the observed correlations. Discriminatory explanations include the inequitable siting of polluting facilities in poor areas, and the disproportionate allocation of enforcement actions. Other possibilities arise from residential location choices, and include "coming to the nuisance" and "fleeing the nuisance" explanations. The former means that lower income individuals sort into areas that have higher pollution (and more generally, lower-quality local amenities) due to lower home prices and rental rates. The latter means that wealthier, mobile households leave higher-pollution areas for neighborhoods with better local amenities. The sorting explanations are neither mutually exclusive nor exhaustive, but they are plausible starting points for understanding the role of differential demand for local residential amenities in explaining observed outcomes.

In a recent example, Depro et al. (2015) use an analysis of residential location choices in Los Angeles to show that mobility plays an important role in explaining race/income/ pollution exposure correlations. Using a sorting model (see Chapter 18), they first show that Hispanics have a lower marginal willingness to pay to avoid exposure to cancer risks from hazardous waste sites than whites. The authors then conduct a counterfactual experiment, whereby they assume equal preferences among Hispanics and whites for cancer risk reductions, and then simulate an alternative pattern of residential sorting across the landscape, given the change. This simple change in preferences leads to dramatically reduced Hispanic/pollution correlation. The finding is consistent with differences in economic circumstances giving rise to lower demand among poor and minority households for local residential amenities, and leading to observed correlations between income/race and pollution exposure. The finding also suggests that environmental injustice is at least to some degree a consequence of earnings gaps between minority and other groups, and is therefore best addressed by policies aimed at improving earnings among the poor rather than direct environmental policy. Further research on the topic is needed to confirm sorting as an explanation, and to measure the contributions of other mechanisms.

23.1.3 Productivity and the Environment

In Chapter 15 we described a conceptual model in which environmental quality was a factor input in the production of a household commodity. Chapter 20 focused on this and other models to describe the relationship between health outcomes and pollution. The specific theoretical and empirical models we examined relate broadly to the notion that environmental quality can have impacts on productivity in a variety of contexts. Other examples include the relationships between agricultural output, human capital acquisition, and worker productivity and a variety of pollution and climate outcomes. An influential empirical literature has arisen that seeks to identify causal relationships between the environment, and a range of productivity-related outcomes.

Graff Zivin and Neidell (2013) provide a systematic review of economic research examining the links between human capital – e.g. labor supply, productivity, and cognition – and the environment. In a specific study, the same authors (Graff Zivin and Neidell, 2012) examine how the productivity of agricultural workers is impacted by ground-level ozone pollution. They assemble data from a central California berry and grape farm that records the daily harvest levels for individual farm workers, who are paid on a harvest volume basis. The daily harvest data are merged with daily fluctuations in ambient ozone concentrations. The average ozone concentration is nearly 50 parts per billion (ppb) over the days of study, with a standard deviation of 13 ppb. The authors find that a 10 ppb decrease in ozone concentration increases workers' productivity by 5.5 percent, which is roughly equivalent to a $700 million saving in labor expenditure.

A second area examining productivity and the environment concerns agriculture and climate/weather fluctuations. This literature focuses on understanding the potential ramifications of climate change – e.g. changes in temperature and precipitation – on agricultural productivity, where productivity is measured using farmland values, profits, or crop yields. Two broad strategies have been used for this type of research. The first examines the relationship between farmland values and climatic conditions using cross-sectional variation in land prices, temperature, precipitation, and other controls across a large geographic area. This is known as the Ricardian model, since it is based on the insight from Ricardo (1817) that the price of an acre of farmland derives from the discounted sum of its expected future returns. An early application of the Ricardian model is Mendelsohn et al. (1994), and Fezzi and Bateman (2015) provide a recent analysis and commentary. Alternative approaches use panel data to better account for place-specific, time-constant, unobserved productivity drivers. Since climate does not vary at points in space across time (or does so only slowly), these models use year-to-year fluctuations in weather at specific locations (i.e. in a county), to estimate how changes in temperature and precipitation affect crop yields or farm profits. Examples of this approach include Schlenker and Roberts (2006, 2009), and Deschênes and Greenstone (2007, 2012).

The empirical literature on agricultural productivity and climate is noteworthy both for its importance in understanding climate change damages, and for the distinct strengths and limitations that the two competing methodologies exhibit. In general, Ricardian models account for adaptation to different climate conditions, since the estimates are derived using climatic variation and observed productivity indicators, which are optimally adapted to the specific climate. However, their reliance on cross-sectional data makes concerns about omitted variables hard to dismiss. Panel models lead to estimates that are well identified, but their reliance on short-term weather fluctuations at points in the landscape means the estimates are conditional on current input and cropping decisions. As such they do not capture potential adaptations to slow-changing climate conditions. The distinction is important, since many panel models (e.g. Schlenker and Roberts, 2009) predict dramatic decreases in crop yields due to temperature increases, while Ricardian models (e.g. Mendelsohn and Reinsborough, 2007) often suggest relatively small impacts on agricultural productivity. This suggests the empirical literature has yet to reach consensus on the direction and magnitude of the damages to agriculture from climate change.

23.2   OTHER OMISSIONS

We noted in the introduction to this chapter that, despite the book's length, there are many topics that we do not address. Indeed, environmental economics is a growing field, and over the time it has taken us to write this book, new areas of inquiry have emerged and/or become more important. For example, in Part I of the book we connected the field to its roots in the environmental awareness that arose in wealthy countries in the 1960s and 1970s. The problems in those years were local and regional in scale, and demand for action came from populations whose basic needs had largely been met. As such, the outlines of the field emerged within the context of national and sub-national issues in wealthy economies. Today, many of the issues we grapple with are global and involve developing countries. Nonetheless, as the variety of environmental contexts examined by economists expanded, the core ideas related to efficient policy design and measuring costs and benefits remained salient. We believe this is still the case today, and hope that our presentation of the field's core ideas will serve as a useful point of entry for people interested in all aspects of environmental economics.

That said, like most scientific disciplines, there are sub-areas of environmental economics that are increasingly specialized. Our coverage in this book has touched on several of the major specialties, but it has not delved deeply into them. The best example is climate change economics. In Chapter 13 we briefly presented a simple dynamic model that was designed to illustrate the basic characteristics of optimal policy for accumulating pollutants, such as carbon dioxide and other greenhouse gasses. However, treatment of the many complexities related to uncertainty, intergenerational equity, international cooperation, and non-linear damage functions was beyond the scope of our discussion. In addition, much of the research in climate change economics requires familiarity with dynamic theory and optimization, numerical models, computational techniques, and earth sciences. Thus readers who are interested in further study on climate change economics should consult additional sources, such as Nordhaus (2013b) or Tol (2014).

A second area we have not explicitly covered is the energy-environment nexus, of which climate change is only one component. Energy economics is usually seen as a separate field from environmental (and resource) economics, though many topics discussed under the umbrella of energy economics relate to the environment. Examples include the emission consequences of time-of-day electricity pricing (Holland and Mansur, 2008), subsidies designed to encourage the deployment of renewable electricity generation (Hughes and Podolefsky, 2015), the effectiveness of demand-side conservation measures (Gillingham et al., 2006), the role of smart technologies in reducing demand (Gans et al., 2013), the energy efficiency gap (Allcott and Greenstone, 2012), and so on. Our sense is that the concepts discussed in this book are necessary prerequisites for considering environmental issues related to energy, and many of the examples cited throughout are based on externalities from energy production and consumption. Nonetheless, the institutional and policy contexts surrounding the energy sector are important and unique, and we have not attempted to provide the comprehensive background discussion that links features of the energy sector to specific concepts and questions in environmental economics.

To the list of topics not explicitly covered we can add a number of dual-name subfields, including, for example, environmental and development economics, economic growth and the environment, macroeconomics and the environment, and agricultural economics and the environment. These are areas that have their roots in a separate primary field (e.g. development economics), but focus on questions that relate to the environment (e.g. health consequences of water pollution). The intersection between development and environmental economics is a particularly important area in that, unlike most developed country cases, pollution and resource quality problems in developing countries are often of first order importance for income and human health outcomes. The context in which environmental problems are examined is also quite different. For example, institutional realities such as ineffective governance, incomplete property rights, common pool resources, and low levels of human capital need to be considered when researching the causes of environmental problems and their solutions. Income disparities are also important – particularly as regards global public goods such as tropical forests that also provide income for local residents. These institutional details distinguish environmental and development economics from what we have generally called environmental economics, and have led to specialization by researchers. The edited volume from Barrett et al. (2014) honoring Partha Dasgupta (a leader in environment/development research) provides an overview of past and current research. Perrings (2014) also provides a historical perspective on the intersection between development and environmental issues.

Finally, there is the (separate) field of resource economics. Classical resource economics focuses on the efficient private use of renewable and non-renewable resources, identifying, for example, the optimal extraction rate of a finite stock of copper, and the basic causes of fishery over-exploitation. In writing a text on environmental economics it was easy to exclude these topics given the existence of several excellent treatments of dynamic resource allocation (e.g. Clark, 1990; Conrad, 2010). We did briefly discuss the link between climate change and fossil fuel abundance in Chapter 13, which illustrates a recent trend in resource economics towards consideration of the optimal social use of natural resources, accounting for both private benefits from extraction as well as external benefits and costs from the resource or its exploitation. A further example of this is forestry, where models describing the profit maximizing harvest time for timber have been generalized to include the non-market habitat and recreation services provided by the standing forest. Consideration of the broader social costs and benefits requires attention to external effects and the measurement of non-market costs and benefits.[2] In this regard, the ideas discussed in this book on environmental economics are also relevant for contemporary resource economics, though we have not attempted to survey the specifics of how the two contemporary fields overlap. Likewise, there are several topical areas that occupy the space somewhere between resource and environmental economics. Examples include biodiversity preservation, land conservation, and the effects of pollution on renewable resource stocks. Again, the ideas we have presented are relevant for these areas, but their specific contexts were not discussed in detail in the book.

23.3 TOOLKITS

We have tried to write this book at an advanced level, while being cognizant of the fact that different readers will have different levels of analytical skills. Our hope is that, even when a core skill is not fully developed, the basic insights from each chapter will be accessible to students with a basic background in microeconomic theory and applied

---

[2] See Anderson and Parker (2013) for a more general discussion of this theme.

econometrics. This is different, however, from possessing the skillsets needed for original research in the different areas we have covered. In this section we briefly connect the major themes in the book to the types of research that produced the key results, and the analytical techniques that should be acquired for further research motivated by those results. We also identify other fields in economics that are potential complements to environmental economics, given their reliance on similar skillsets and/or inclusion of cross-over themes.

23.3.1 Theoretical Models

In Part I and the early chapters in Part II of the book we examined environmental policy in a static and partial equilibrium context. For this we used basic results from microeconomic theory, and most of our findings were derived by exploiting first-order conditions for static optimization, and deriving comparative statics. In instances when "second best" policies were derived, such as for the optimal taxation of a polluting monopolist (Chapter 6), we often relied on response functions, whereby the regulator or a competing firm would take account of the polluter's behavioral response when designing policy and making a choice. The analytical skills needed for replication and extension of these analyses are part of the typical training for most PhD and many Master's students in economics. In some instances, however, theoretical research on environmental policy – particularly with imperfect information and/or strategic interactions – uses more sophisticated game theory concepts that go beyond the comparatively simple methods used in this book. For example, the theoretical literature on international environmental agreements uses advanced game theory models describing the complex cost, benefit, and strategic environments in which countries negotiate. As such, we did not cover this literature in detail in Chapter 12. More generally, our sense is that most PhD students (but few Master's students) are exposed to these methods in their core training, but full competency is achieved only when the student has a specific interest in modeling strategic interactions. Thus original research examining nuanced features of environmental regulation in non-competitive contexts may require additional investment in game theory and related techniques.

In Chapter 7 we extended our basic conceptual model to allow consideration of spillover effects into other markets, when pre-existing distortions are present. The research basis for this chapter has its roots in the public finance literature on optimal taxation, and many of the techniques used to isolate the determinants of second-best policies are taught in public economics courses. For example, Auerbach and Hines (2002) in the *Handbook of Public Economics* is usually found on graduate public economics syllabi; it provides a systematic review of taxation and economic efficiency. An additional, classic reference on the topic is Diamond and Mirrlees (1971). These topical and toolkit overlaps suggest that students interested in the interactions between environmental policy and the broader fiscal system should consider seeking a co-field in public economics.

Other chapters in Part II have used models that include uncertainty and asymmetric information. In the simplest cases this required the use of expected values in formulating optimal policy or agent responses, so as to maximize expected welfare/profit/ utility. In the more advanced topics, such as mechanism design (Chapter 4), aspects of ambient pollution control (Chapter 9), and liability (Chapter 10), more attention was paid to the information that different agents possess, and how information asymmetries affect behavior and optimal environmental policy. These topics took us in the direction of principle-agent models, various adverse selection issues, and more generally the economics of information. In *The Economics of Uncertainty and Information*, Laffont (1989) provides a general overview and synthesis of this field of study, while Tirole and Laffont (1993) apply the ideas to regulatory contexts. The history of study on information topics, and an inventory of many of its applications, are described in the Nobel lectures by Stiglitz (2002), Spence (2002), and Akerlof (2002).

Most of the topics in Part II were developed using static models, or in some instances using simple two-period specifications (e.g. for the study of bankable emission permits in Chapter 8). In our brief examination of climate policy (Chapter 13) we switched to using dynamic optimization to describe the optimal policy for a stock pollutant. In addition, our discussion of discounting and integrated assessment models (Chapter 21) involved modeling more explicitly dynamic behavior. As noted above, however, more advanced study of dynamic topics requires expertise in optimal control, dynamic programing, stochastic dynamic programing, and differential games, which are well beyond the scope of this book. Expertise in computational economics is also necessary for exploring dynamic phenomena that cannot be analytically characterized. Students interested in original research in climate economics and resource/environment overlap topics should therefore seek expertise in economic dynamics. A sampling of textbooks in this area includes Caputo (2005) for optimal control, Stokey et al. (1989) for dynamic programing, and Miranda and Fackler (2002) for numerical dynamic programing (and general computational topics). The explicitly dynamic aspects of environmental and resource economics are typically covered in a graduate resource economics course, which is often paired with an environmental economics course to constitute a field sequence.

23.3.2 Structural Econometrics

Many elements of Parts III and IV had an explicitly empirical component that required familiarity with different econometric techniques. This was also the case for several of the examples in Part II. Core graduate study in economics typically provides students with the applied econometric skills needed to appreciate the discussion and applied examples making use of linear model variations (e.g. OLS, panel methods, instrumental variables). This is perhaps less so for contexts using discrete choice econometrics. Our hope is that the overview provided in Chapter 16 will help readers to understand the basics of discrete choice econometric models, and appreciate the connection between behavioral function ("structural") estimation, and discrete choice empirical models. However, conducting original research in non-market valuation, and other areas of applied environmental economics as well, requires expertise in non-linear econometric models that goes beyond the overview we have provided. Good starting points for obtaining this expertise include the books by Train (2009) on discrete choice methods, and Cameron and Trivedi (2013) on count data methods. In addition, the structural discrete choice models that were developed in industrial organization applications (e.g. Berry et al., 1995) are seeing fruitful use in environment economics (Bayer and Timmins, 2007).

Thus a co-field in empirical industrial organization can be useful for students who are interested in non-market valuation, as well as applied topics in environmental economics with an industrial organization overlap. Examples of the latter include studies of the automobile industry (Beresteanu and Li, 2011), and resource extraction (Lin, 2013).

23.3.3 Reduced Form Econometrics

There is an ongoing debate in applied econometrics concerning the relative merits of "structural" versus "reduced form" empirical analysis. The former seeks to estimate behavioral specifications that have a direct link to economic models, such as utility or cost functions. In doing so, analysts are often willing to make non-testable assumptions on agents' objective functions, empirical functional forms, and error term distributions. The payoff to this is the ability to conduct counterfactual analysis – i.e. predict outcomes for contexts outside the range of past observations. Reduced form approaches seek to identify the existence and size of a phenomenon using a minimum of assumptions. As the name implies, research designs of this type are more reductionist in nature. The payoff here is that the findings are based only on the data, and therefore possess a high degree of credibility. Our sense is that the two paradigms are more complements than substitutes, and much can be learned by combining elements from both. As such, possession of empirical skills related to "quasi" experimental analysis is useful in empirical environmental economics. Most of these methods were developed in labor economics, and this continues to be the field where many of the advances in reduced form econometrics are discussed. Because of this, a co-field in labor economics can be a useful investment for students interested in empirically oriented environmental economics. Angrist and Pischke (2009) provide an accessible yet authoritative treatment of many of the key econometric ideas that are broadly classified as "reduced form."

23.3.4 Experiments

The use of laboratory experiments in economics is a relatively recent development, though the methodology has matured to the point that lab experiments are no longer considered novel simply for being experiments. Rather, experiments have become a tool occupying the space between theoretical and applied economics. The evolution of their use in environmental economics illustrates this. We saw in our stated preference discussion (Chapter 19) that lab and field experiments have been critical tools for assessing the validity of different stated preference approaches. They have also helped illustrate the different ways that insights from behavioral economics can inform our discussion of the general efficacy of stated preference. In other areas, experiments have been used to test the predictions from theory, or to examine the potential performance of policy mechanisms that have not been used in practice. Examples of this latter use were described in the context of non-point source pollution (Chapter 9). The prevalence of experiment-based contributions in these two areas illustrates that acquisition of skills in designing and running laboratory experiments is valuable in environmental economics. This insight is valid for both theoretically and empirically inclined researchers.

The term "field experiment" in economics has come to mean an experimental setup that incorporates the realism and institutional context present in the topic of interest. This can be contrasted with lab experiments, which by design are highly stylized and controlled, and usually use undergraduate university students as subjects. Harrison and List (2004) summarize the distinguishing features of field experiments as arising from the dual interest among researchers of obtaining exogenous variability for causal inference, and observing behavior in its natural context. Field experiments in environmental economics have been used in ways complementary to lab experiments (e.g. assessing stated preference validity). They have also been used in developing-country contexts, such as for understanding common pool resource management and assessing the efficacy of health-improving interventions. The use of field experiments is part of a trend in applied economics towards using randomized controlled trials (RCTs), whereby treatment and control groups are designated as part of an effort to identify the causal impact of an intervention. Many of the examples of RCTs in environmental economics are in energy-overlap topics, where researchers have partnered with electricity utility companies to present electricity customers with randomly assigned price or use monitoring interventions. In seems likely, however, that the explicit use of RCTs in environmental economics will expand into other areas of the field.

23.3.5 Other Skills

There are of course many other skills that are useful in environmental economics, which we have not listed above. To finish this section, we briefly list a few of these. As we complete this book, the concept of "big data" has entered the nomenclature. This refers to the massive amounts of information that are available through constant monitoring of environmental and other natural phenomena, devices that track decisions in real time, social media, etc. Researchers have begun to consider techniques suitable for exploiting information of this form, which may not fit with traditional statistical approaches. There will undoubtedly be opportunities for environmental economists to engage in big data projects in the near future. Currently, the wide availability of fine-scale spatial and temporal data on environmental outcomes, coupled with the increasing ability to access detailed behavioral data, means many empirical questions can be answered by assembling data from multiple sources and building spatially/temporally referenced databases. This requires skills in the use of GIS software, as well as competency in managing complex data environments.

Another useful skillset is survey design and administration. Though rarely glamorous, small decisions made during the process of fielding surveys can substantially affect the usefulness of the resulting data. Acquiring some knowledge of best practice survey methods is therefore helpful for applied environmental economists.

Finally, we mentioned above that computable general equilibrium (CGE) models have been an important tool in climate economics. In fact, their usefulness goes beyond climate change, in that numerical simulations can be a useful complement to analytical modeling. A good example of this is optimal second-best taxation (see Chapter 7), where a common strategy is to explore a concept analytically for intuition and clarity, and then measure its magnitude using a richer numerical model (e.g. Bovenberg and Goulder, 1996). In other instances a numerical model provides the primary tool for exploring an issue in its full contextual richness (e.g. Goulder et al., 2012). Research of this type requires skills in modeling, as well as the ability to solve for and simulate model outcomes using computational software packages like GAMS (e.g. Rutherford, 1995).

23.4 FUTURE RESEARCH

Our objective in this book has been to provide a narrative synthesis of the historical and contemporary topics that have defined the field of environmental economics. This is distinct from a survey of ongoing research and knowledge gaps. Thus while we have tried to use both recent and historical examples to illustrate developments in the field, we have not in general attempted to identify the research frontier. Nonetheless, as this book goes to press, Phaneuf serves as the editor in chief for the *Journal of the Association of Environmental and Resource Economists* (*JAERE*), and Requate is the managing editor for the *Journal of Environmental Economics and Management* (*JEEM*). Via these positions we have the privilege of seeing much of the field's research output, which gives us a useful perspective from which to comment on the state of research in the field, and its future directions. In this section, we briefly combine our experience as textbook authors with our experience as editors to speculate on future research needs and directions in the field.

We begin by noting that much of the conceptual development in the field has been dedicated to developing policy instruments for achieving economically efficient (or cost effective) outcomes. Research has refined our understanding of the detailed workings of the portfolio of available instruments, and the increased use of economic incentive-based policies has provided practical experience. At the same time, policy debates often focus as much (or more) on the distributional and fairness properties of different initiatives. Our sense is that research on the theory and practice of environmental policy will increasingly focus on a broader set of criteria, including the incidence of costs and benefits, identifying heterogeneity in the types of agents who gain or lose from the policy, and equity-efficiency trade-offs. A larger focus on distributional aspects sets up positive political economy-type questions related to opposition or support among different groups for different policy approaches, as well as normative questions related to achieving given cost and benefit incidence objectives at least cost. Examples of recent research on distributional topics include Grainger and Kolstad (2010), Grainger (2012), and Fullerton (2011). See also Bento (2013) for a review.

Second, we see research in the field emphasizing developing country environment and resource problems to a much greater degree. As noted early in the text, the field grew out of wealthy country environmental problems, and most research has proceeded from the perspective of developed economies. The world today, however, is characterized by larger populations and rates of economic growth in developing and transition economies. This has led to large-scale landscape changes and air and water pollution problems that have had first order impacts on the health and productivity of populations in these countries. In addition, world-scale problems such as climate change, deforestation and biodiversity, and food security relate directly to the decisions by governments and residents of developing and transition economies, and overlap with issues of equity and fairness identified above. These trends suggest that research in environmental economics will continue evolving to reflect the wider variety of institutional contexts, scales of environment and resource problems, and population attributes that character-ize non-developed countries. At a more micro scale, developing country case studies on behavior-environment interactions are underrepresented in the empirical literature and likely to become increasingly important.

Our next area of further research derives from the increasing influence of "behavio-ral economics" in the discipline of economics. Behavioral economics is a broad con-cept that seeks to understand the complexities of human behavior by going beyond the caricature of people as perfectly rational and selfish utility maximizers. One strand of behavioral economics studies persistent optimization errors and other behavioral anom-alies not predicted by neoclassical theory. This line of work is often seen as a challenge to the neoclassical welfare theory that forms the background of much of environmen-tal economics. A second strand of behavioral economics maintains the assumption of rationality, but seeks to expand the range of variables and factors that enter utility or constrain choices. Findings from this line of study suggest that a wide range of usually non-monetary phenomena may be of first order importance for positive and normative analysis. Both types of research in behavioral economics suggest future research tasks in environmental economics. For example, evidence of irrationality casts doubt on the principle of consumer sovereignty – i.e. the notion that a person's actions are the best indicator of his well-being. Our sense is that conclusions of irrationality should be made only after a full accounting of explanations based on unmeasured constraints or a richer characterization of the objective function is complete. This implies that research on subtle drivers of behavior such as information acquisition costs and processing strate-gies, time budgets, cognitive energy budgets, and a range of social interactions will be needed.

These points overlap with the more general goal of expanding understanding of the range of monetary and non-monetary factors that drive and condition behavior. In envi-ronmental economics and other fields, researchers have begun to explore the role of networks, social norms, type-based sorting, and other social interactions on outcomes. It is clear that these topics are relevant for environmental outcomes and policies, in that endogenous networks and social norms may interact with a range of policies in differ-ent ways.

Distributional, development, and social interactions are broad areas that may influ-ence future research in a range of topics in environmental economics. There are also a handful of topic-specific areas with good opportunities for future research. Empirical work related to climate is a good example. Careful empirical work quantifying the rela-tionship between productivity and climate will continue to be important. This includes agriculture and other climate-sensitive industries, in developed and developing country contexts. In addition, relatively little is known about the market and non-market costs of adaptation to climate change. For example, research on the migration/climate/environ-ment nexus will continue to grow in importance.

Research on morbidity outcomes and the environment will also grow in importance. In Chapter 20 we noted that there is a large amount of work dedicated to valuing reduc-tions in mortality risk, but relatively little work on morbidity. As such, there are oppor-tunities in health valuation research for studies that systematically link environmental policy outcomes to changes in morbidity symptoms and values. In addition, averting behavior-type revealed preference models continue to be relatively rare, though the availability of spatially resolute, individual health outcomes data available through confidential and public sources provides opportunities for this style of inquiry.

Research on technology development and technology adoption is a third topical area of note. As we say in Chapter 11, models of technological progress tend to be stylized descriptions relating research and development expenditures to the stochastic appearance of new technologies. Our sense is that research aimed at opening up the black box of the creative process, particularly as regards clean energy and clean production, would help to push the technology-environment literature in a valuable new direction. Possibilities include exploiting "big data" and/or confidential records to disaggregate and better measure the inputs into public and private discoveries.

Finally, and perhaps surprisingly, our sense is that we know relatively little about abatement costs. The empirical literature has overwhelmingly focused on input and output substitution patterns among polluting firms, to characterize the traditional contribution of industrial, manufacturing, and energy firms to industry and aggregate abatement costs. However, many abatement costs are borne by households, and are partially non-market. Examples include the range of behavioral adjustments such as using public transit, sorting trash, learning about energy-saving technologies, and monitoring electricity use that have shadow costs, and result in better environmental outcomes.

23.5   CLOSING THOUGHTS

Two overarching themes have become clear to us during the process of writing this book. First, environmental economists have made impressive progress since the start of the field in the late 1960s and early 1970s. We have developed substantial admiration for the successive generations of economists who have continuously pushed forward our understanding of environmental policy and behavior related to the environment. Second, it is an exciting time to be working in the field. The range of interesting questions and policy needs continues to grow, and the tools and data we have available to work on these issues are likewise expanding. We hope this book has helped readers to appreciate the breadth and depth of the field, provided the core knowledge needed to work in the field, and helped students to identify specific interests that they may want to specialize in. More generally, we hope this book will help motivate the next generation of students to excel in the research, teaching, and policy analysis dimensions of environmental economics.

References

Acemoglu, D. 2002. "Directed Technical Change." *Review of Economic Studies*. 113: 1055–89.

Acemoglu, D., P. Aghion, L. Bursztyn, and D. Hemous. 2012. "The Environment and Directed Technical Change." *American Economic Review*. 102: 131–66.

Adamowicz, W.L. 1994. "Habit formation and variety seeking in a discrete choice model of recreation demand." *Journal of Agricultural and Resource Economics*. 19: 19–31.

Adamowicz, W., M. Dickie, S. Gerking, M. Veronesi, and D. Zinner. 2014. "Household Decision Making and Valuation of Environmental Health Risks to Parents and Their Children." *Journal of the Association of Environmental and Resource Economists*. 1: 481–19.

Adamowicz, W., D. Dupont, A. Krupnick, and J. Zhang. 2011. "Valuation of cancer and microbial disease risk reductions in municipal drinking water: An analysis of risk context using multiple valuation methods." *Journal of Environmental Economics and Management*. 61: 213–26.

Adamowicz, W., J. Louviere, and M. Williams. 1994. "Combining Revealed and Stated Preference Methods for Valuing Environmental Amenities." *Journal of Environmental Economics and Management*. 26: 271–92.

Adar, Z., and J.M. Griffin. 1976. "Uncertainty and the choice of pollution control instruments." *Journal of Environmental Economics and Management*. 3: 178–88.

Aghion, P., and P. Howitt. 1998. *Endogenous Growth Theory*. Cambridge, MA: MIT Press.

Aichele, R., and G. Felbermayr. 2012. "Kyoto and the carbon footprint of nations." *Journal of Environmental Economics and Management*. 63: 336–54.

Akerlof, G.A. 2002. "Behavioral macroeconomics and macroeconomic behavior." *American Economic Review*. 92: 411–33.

Alberini, A. 1995. "Optimal Designs for Discrete Choice Contingent Valuation Surveys: Single-Bound, Double-Bound, and Bivariate Models." *Journal of Environmental Economics and Management*. 28: 287–306.

Alberini, A., M. Cropper, T.-T. Fu, A. Krupnick, J-T. Liu, D. Shaw, and W. Harrington. 1997. "Valuing Health Effects of Air Pollution in Developing Countries: The Case of Taiwan." *Journal of Environmental Economics and Management*. 34: 107–26.

Alberini, A, M. Cropper, A. Krupnick, and N.B. Simon. 2006. "Willingness to pay for mortality risk reductions: Does latency matter?" *Journal of Risk and Uncertainty*. 32: 231–45.

Alberini, A. and A. Krupnick. 1998. "Air Quality and Episodes of Acute Respiratory Illness in Taiwan Cities: Evidence from Survey Data." *Journal of Urban Economics*. 44: 68–92.

Alberini, A. and M. Ščasný. 2011. "Context and the VSL: Evidence from a Stated Preference Study in Italy and the Czech Republic." *Environmental Resource Economics*. 49: 511–38.

Alberola, E. and J. Chevallier. 2009. "European carbon prices and banking restrictions: evidence from phase I (2005–2007)." *The Energy Journal*. 30: 51–80.

Aldy, J.E. and W.K. Viscusi. 2007. "Age Differences in the Value of Statistical Life: Revealed Preference Evidence." *Review of Environmental Economics and Policy*. 1: 241–60.

Allcott, H. and M. Greenstone. 2012. "Is There an Energy Efficiency Gap?" *Journal of Economic Perspectives*. 26: 3–38.

Alpízar, F., T. Requate, and A. Schramm. 2004. "Collective vs. random fining: an experimental study on controlling ambient pollution." *Environmental and Resource Economics*. 29: 231–52.

Anderson, T.L. and D.P. Parker. 2013. "Transaction Costs and Environmental Markets: The Role of Entrepreneurs." *Review of Environmental Economics and Policy*. 7: 1–17.

Anger, N., Böhringer, C., and A. Löschel. 2010. "Paying the piper and calling the tune? A meta-regression analysis of the double-divided hypothesis." *Ecological Economics*. 69: 1495–502.

Angrist, J.D. and J.S. Pischke. 2009. *Mostly Harmless Econometrics*. Princeton University Press.

Antweiler, W., B.R. Copeland, and M.S. Taylor. 2001: "Is Free Trade Good for the Environment?" *American Economic Review*. 91: 877–908.

Arrow, K.J., M.L. Cropper, C. Gollier, B. Groom, G.M. Heal, R.G. Newell, W.D. Nordhaus, R.S. Pindyck, W.A. Pizer, P.R. Portney, T. Sterner, R.S.J. Tol, and M.L. Weitzman. 2013. "Determining Benefits and Costs for Future Generations." *Science*. 341: 349–50.

Arrow, K.J., M.L. Cropper, C. Gollier, B. Groom, G.M. Heal, R.G. Newell, W.D. Nordhaus, R.S. Pindyck, W.A. Pizer, P.R. Portney, T. Sterner, R.S.J. Tol, and M.L. Weitzman. 2014. "Should Governments use a Declining Discount Rate in Project Analysis?" *Review of Environmental Economics and Policy*. 8: 145–63.

Arrow, K.J., R. Solow, P.R. Portney, E.E. Leamer, R. Radner, and H. Schuman. 1993. "Report of the NOAA panel on contingent valuation." *Federal Register* 58: 4601–14.

Atkinson, G. and S. Mourato. 2008. "Environmental Cost-Benefit Analysis." *Annual Review of Environment and Resources*. 33: 317–44.

Auerbach, A.J. and J.R. Hines. 2002. "Taxation and Economic Efficiency." In A.J. Auerbach and M. Feldstein, eds. *Handbook of Public Economics 3*. Amsterdam: Elsevier.

Baerenklau, K.A. and B. Provencher. 2005. "Static modeling of dynamic recreation behavior: Implications for prediction and welfare estimation." *Journal of Environmental Economics and Management*. 50: 617–36.

Bajari, P. and C.L. Benkard. 2005. "Demand Estimation with Heterogeneous Consumers and Unobserved Product Characteristics: A Hedonic Approach." *Journal of Political Economy*. 113: 1239–76.

Bajari, P., J.C. Fruehwirth, K.I. Kim, and C. Timmins. 2012. "A Rational Expectations Approach to Hedonic Price Regressions with Time-Varying Unobserved Product Attributes: The Price of Pollution." *American Economic Review*. 102: 1898–926.

Balcombe, K., M. Burton, and D. Rigby. 2011. "Skew and attribute non-attendance within the Bayesian mixed logit model?" *Journal of Environmental Economics and Management*. 62:446–61.

Balkenborg, D. 2001. "How Liable Should a Lender Be? The Case of Judgment-Proof Firms and Environmental Risk: Comment." *American Economics Review*. 91: 731–38.

Banzhaf, H.S. 2014. "The Cold War Origins of the Value of Statistical Life (VSL)." *Journal of Economic Perspectives*. 28: 213–26.

Banzhaf, H.S. and V.K. Smith. 2007. "Meta-analysis in model implementation: choice set and the valuation of air quality improvements." *Journal of Applied Econometrics*. 22: 1013–31.

Barnett, A.H. 1980. "The Pigouvian tax rule under monopoly." *American Economic Review*. 70: 1037–41.

Baron, D.P. and R.B. Myerson. 1982. "Regulating a monopolist with unknown costs." *Econometrica*. 50: 911–30.

Barrett, S. 1994a. "Self-Enforcing International Environmental Agreements." *Oxford Economics Papers*. 46: 878–94.

Barrett, S. 1994b: "Strategic Environmental Policy and International Trade." *Journal of Public Economics*. 54: 325–38.

Barrett, S., K.G. Mäler, and E.S. Maskin, eds. 2014. *Environment and Development Economics: Essays in Honor of Sir Partha Dasgupta*. Oxford University Press.

Bartik, T.J. 1987a. "Estimating hedonic demand parameters with single market data: the problems caused by unobserved tastes." *Review of Economics and Statistics.* 69: 178–80.

Bartik, T.J. 1987b. "Estimation of demand parameters in hedonic price models." *Journal of Political Economy.* 95: 81–8.

Bartik, T.J. 1988a. "Evaluating the benefits of non-marginal reductions in pollution using information on defensive expenditures." *Journal of Environmental Economics and Management.* 15: 111–27.

Bartik, T.J. 1988b. "Measuring the benefits of amenity improvements in hedonic price models." *Land Economics.* 64: 172–83.

Bateman, I.J., G.D. Garrod, J.S. Brainard, and A.A. Lovett. 1996. "Measurement Issues in the Travel Cost Method: A Geographical Information Systems Approach." *Journal of Agricultural Economics.* 47: 191–205.

Bateman, I.J. and K.G. Willis, eds. 1999. *Valuing Environmental Preferences: Theory and Practice of the Contingent Valuation Method in the US, UEEU, and Developing Countries.* Oxford University Press.

Baumol, W.J. 1972. "On Taxation and the Control of Externalities." *American Economic Review.* 62: 307–22.

Baumol, W.J. and W.E. Oates. 1971. "The Use of Standards and Prices for Protection of the Environment." *Swedish Journal of Economics.* 73: 42–54.

Baumol, W.J. and W.E. Oates. 1988. *The Theory of Environmental Policy.* Cambridge University Press.

Bayer, P., F. Ferreira, and R. McMillan. 2007. "A Unified Framework for Measuring Preferences for Schools and Neighborhoods." *Journal of Political Economy.* 115: 588–638.

Bayer, P., N. Keohane, and C. Timmins. 2009. "Migration and hedonic valuation: the case of air quality." *Journal of Environmental Economics and Management.* 58: 1–14.

Bayer, P. and C. Timmins. 2007. "Estimating equilibrium models of sorting across locations." *Economic Journal.* 117: 353–74.

Beard, T.R. 1990. "Bankruptcy and Care Choice." *The Rand Journal of Economics.* 21: 626–34.

Becker, R.A. 2005. "Air pollution abatement costs under the Clean Air Act: evidence from the PACE survey." *Journal of Environmental Economics and Management.* 50: 144–69.

Bell, K.P. and N.E. Bockstael. 2000. "Applying the Generalized-Moments Estimation Approach to Spatial Problems involving Microlevel Data." *The Review of Economics and Statistics.* 82: 72–82.

Ben-David, S., D.S. Brookshire, S. Burness, M. McKee, and C. Schmidt. 1999. "Heterogeneity, irreversible production choices, and efficiency in emission permits markets." *Journal of Environmental Economics and Management.* 38: 176–94.

Bennear, L.S., A. Tarozzi, A. Pfaff, S.H. Balasubramanya, K.M. Ahmed, and A. van Green. 2013. "Impacts of a Randomized Controlled Trial in Arsenic Risk Communication on Household Water-Source Choices in Bangladesh." *Journal of Environmental Economics and Management.* 65: 225–40.

Bento, A. 2013. "Equity impacts of environmental policy." *Annual Review of Resource Economics.* 5: 181–96.

Bento, A., M. Freedman, and C. Lang. 2015. "Who Benefits from Environmental Regulation? Evidence from the Clean Air Act Amendments." *The Review of Economics and Statistics.* 97: 610–22.

Bento, A.M., L.H. Goulder, M.R. Jacobsen, and R.H. von Haefen. 2009. "Distributional and efficiency impacts of increased US gasoline taxes." *American Economic Review.* 99: 667–99.

Bento, A.M. and M. Jacobsen. 2010. "Ricardian rents, environmental policy and the 'double-divided' hypothesis." *Journal of Environmental Economics and Management.* 53: 17–31.

Beresteanu, A. and S. Li. 2011. "Gasoline prices, government support, and the demand for hybrid vehicles in the United States." *International Economic Review.* 52: 161–182.

Bergman, L. 2005. "CGE Modeling of Environmental Policy and Resource Management." Chapter 24 in K.-G. Mäler and J.R. Vincent, eds. *Handbook of Environmental Economics 3.* Amsterdam: Elsevier.

Bergstrom, T. 1976. "Collective choice and the Lindahl allocation method." In S.A.Y. Lin, ed. *Theory and Measurement of Economic Externalities.* 4:107–31. New York: Academic Press.

Bergstrom, T. and R. Cornes. 1983. "Independence of allocative efficiency from distribution in the theory of public goods." *Econometrica.* 51:1753–65.

Bergstrom, J.C. and L.O. Taylor. 2006. "Using meta-analysis for benefits transfer: Theory and practice." *Ecological Economics.* 60: 351–60.

Bernauer, T. 1995. "The International Financing of Environmental Protection: Lessons from Efforts to Protect the River Rhine against Chloride Pollution." *Environmental Politics.* 4: 369–90.

Berry, S.T. 1994. "Estimating discrete choice models of product differentiation." *Rand Journal of Economics.* 25: 242–62.

Berry, S.T., J. Levinsohn, and A. Pakes. 1995. "Automobile prices in market equilibrium." *Econometrica.* 63: 841–90.

Berry, S.T., J. Levinsohn, and A. Pakes. 2004. "Differentiated products demand systems from a combination of micro and macro data: the new car market." *Journal of Political Economy.* 112: 68–105.

Bi, X. and M. Khanna. 2012. "Reassessment of the Impact of the EPA's Voluntary 33/50 Program on Toxic Releases." *Land Economics.* 88: 341–61.

Biglaiser, G. and J.K. Horowitz. 1995. "Pollution Regulation and Incentives for Pollution-Control Research." *Journal of Economics and Management Strategy.* 3: 663–84.

Bin, O. and C.E. Landry. 2013. "Changes in implicit flood risk premiums: Empirical evidence from the housing market." *Journal of Environmental Economics and Management.* 65: 361–76.

Bishop, R.C. and T.A. Heberlein. 1979. "Measuring Values of Extramarket Goods: Are Indirect Measures Biased?" *American Journal of Agricultural Economic.* 61: 926–30.

Blomquist, G.C., M. Dickie and R.M. O'Conor. 2011. "Willingness to pay for improving fatality risks and asthma symptoms: Values for children and adults of all ages." *Resource and Energy Economics.* 33: 410–25.

Blumenschein, K., G.C. Blomquist, M. Johannesson, N. Horn, and P. Freeman. 2008. "Eliciting Willingness to Pay without Bias: Evidence from a Field Experiment." *The Economic Journal.* 118: 114–37.

Bockstael, N.E. and A.M. Freeman III. 2005. "Welfare Theory and Valuation." Chapter 12 in K.-G. Mäler and J.R. Vincent, eds. *Handbook of Environmental Economics 2.* Amsterdam: Elsevier.

Bockstael, N.E. and K.E. McConnell. 1983. "Welfare measurement in the household production framework." *American Economic Review.* 79: 806–14.

Bockstael, N.E. and K.E. McConnell. 1993. "Public goods as characteristics of non-market commodities." *Economic Journal.* 103: 1244–57.

Bockstael, N.E. and K.E. McConnell. 2007. *Environmental and Resource Valuation with Revealed Preferences: A Theoretical Guide to Empirical Models.* Dordrecht: Springer.

Böhringer, C. and A. Lange. 2005a. "Economic Implications of Alternative Allocation Schemes for Emission Allowances." *The Scandinavian Journal of Economics.* 107: 563–81.

Böhringer, C. and A. Lange. 2005b. "Mission Impossible!? On the Harmonization of National Allocation Plans under the EU Emissions Trading Directive." *Journal of Regulatory Economics.* 27: 81–94.

Böhringer, C. and A. Lange. 2005c. "On the design of optimal grandfathering schemes for emission allowances." *European Economic Review.* 49: 2041–55.

Böhringer, C., A. Müller, and J. Schneider. 2015. "Carbon Tariffs Revisited." *Journal of the Association of Environmental and Resource Economists.* 2: 629–72.

Böhringer, C. and K. Rosendahl. 2010. "Green promotes the dirtiest: on the interaction between black and green quotas in energy markets," *Journal of Regulatory Economics.* 37(3): 316–25.

Bontems, P. and J.-M. Bourgeon. 2005. "Optimal environmental taxation and enforcement policy." *European Economic Review.* 49: 409–35.

Bovenberg, A.L. 1999. "Green tax reforms and the double dividend: an updated reader's guide." *International Tax and Public Finance.* 6: 421–43.

Bovenberg, A.L. and L.H. Goulder. 1996. "Optimal Environmental Taxation in the Presence of Other Taxes: General-Equilibrium Analyses." *The American Economic Review.* 86: 985–1000.

Bovenberg, A.L. and L.H. Goulder. 2002. "Environmental taxation and regulation." *Handbook of Public Economics 3*. 23: 1471–545. Amsterdam: North Holland.

Bovenberg, A.L. and R.A. de Mooij. 1994. "Environmental Levies and Distortionary Taxation." *American Economic Review*. American Economic Association. 84: 1085–89.

Bovenberg, A.L. and R.A. de Mooij. 1997. "Environmental Tax Reform and Endogenous Growth." *Journal of Public Economics*. 63: 207–37.

Bovenberg, A.L. and S.A. Smulders. 1995. "Environmental Quality and Pollution-Augmenting Technological Change in a Two-Sector Endogenous Growth Model." *Journal of Public Economics*. 57: 369–91.

Bovenberg, A.L. and F. van der Ploeg. 1994a. "Consequences of environmental reforms for involuntary unemployment and welfare." *Environmental and Resource Economics*. 12: 137–50.

Bovenberg, A.L. and F. van der Ploeg. 1994b. "Environmental policy, public finance and labour market in a second-best world." *Journal of Public Economics*. 55: 349–90.

Bovenberg, A.L. and F. van der Ploeg. 1996. "Optimal taxation, public goods and environmental policy with involuntary unemployment." *Journal of Public Economics*. 62: 59–83.

Bowen, H.R. 1943. "The interpretation of voting in the allocation of resources." *Quarterly Journal of Economics*. 58: 27–48.

Boyd, J. and D.E. Ingberman. 1994. "Noncompensatory Damages and Potential Insolvency." *The Journal of Legal Studies*. 23: 895–910.

Boyer, M. and J.J. Laffont. 1997. "Environmental Risks and Bank Liability." *European Economic Review*. 41: 1427–59.

Boyle, K. J. and J.C. Bergstrom. 1992. "Benefit transfer studies: myths, pragmatism, and idealism." *Water Resources Research*. 28: 657–63.

Boyle, K.J., N.V. Kuminoff, C.F. Parmeter, and J.C. Pope. 2010. "The Benefit-Transfer Challenges." *Annual Review of Resource Economics*. 2: 161–82.

Boyle, K.J., P.J. Poor, and L.O. Taylor. 1999. "Estimating the Demand for Protecting Freshwater Lakes from Eutrophication." *The American Journal of Agricultural Economics*. 81: 1118–22.

Brander, J. and B. Spencer. 1985. "Export subsidies and international market share rivalry." *Journal of International Economics*. 16: 227–42.

Brouwer, R. and S. Navrud. 2015. "The use and development of benefit transfer in Europe." Chapter 4 in R.J. Johnston, J. Rolfe, R.S. Rosenberger, and R. Brouwer, eds. *Benefit Transfer of Environmental and Resource Values: A Guide for Researchers and Practitioners*. Dordrecht: Springer.

Brown, J.N. and H.S. Rosen. 1982. "On the estimation of structural hedonic price models." *Econometrica*. 50: 765–8.

Buchanan, J.M. 1969. "External diseconomies, corrective taxes, and market structure." *American Economic Review*. 59: 174–7.

Buchanan, J.M. and W.C. Stubblebine. 1962. "Externality." *Economica*. 29: 371–84.

Bullock, D.S. and N. Minot. 2006. "On Measuring the Value of a Non-market Good Using Market Data." *American Journal of Agricultural Economics*. 88: 961–73.

Burtraw, D. and K. Palmer. 2004. "SO_2 Cap-and-Trade Program in the United States – A 'Living Legend' of Market Effectiveness." Chapter 2 in W. Harrington, R.D. Morgenstern, and T. Sterner, eds. *Choosing Environmental Policy – Comparing Instruments and Outcomes in the United States and Europe*. Washington, DC: Resources for the Future.

Camacho-Cuena, E. and T. Requate. 2012. "The Regulation of Non-Point Source Pollution and Risk Preferences." *Ecological Economics*. 73: 179–87.

Camacho-Cuena, E., T. Requate, and I. Waichman. 2012. "Investment Incentives under Emissions Trading: An Experimental Study." *Environmental and Resource Economics* 53: 229–49.

Cameron, T.A. 1992. "Combining Contingent Valuation and Travel Cost Data for the Valuation of Non-market Goods." *Land Economics*. 68: 302–17.

Cameron, T.A. 2010. "Euthanizing the Value of Statistical Life." *Review of Environmental Economics and Policy*. 4: 161–78.

Cameron, T.A. 2014. "Valuing Morbidity in Environmental Benefit-Cost Analysis." *Annual Review of Resource Economics*. 6: 249–72.

Cameron, T.A. and J.R. DeShazo. 2010. "Differential Attention to Attributes in Utility-Theoretic Choice Models." *Journal of Choice Modelling*. 3: 73–115.

Cameron, T.A. and J.R. DeShazo. 2013. "Demand for health risk reductions." *Journal of Environmental Economics and Management*. 65: 87–109.

Cameron, T.A. and M.J. James. 1987. "Efficient Estimation Methods for 'Closed-Ended' Contingent Valuation Surveys." *The Review of Economics and Statistics*. 69: 269–76.

Cameron, T.A. and J. Quiggin. 1994. "Estimation Using Contingent Valuation Data from a 'Dichotomous Choice with Follow-Up' Questionnaire." *Journal of Environmental Economics and Management*. 27: 218–34.

Cameron, A.C. and P.K. Trivedi. 2013. *Regression Analysis of Count Data*. Second edition. Cambridge University Press.

Caputo, M.R. 2005. *Foundations of Dynamic Economic Analysis: Optimal Control Theory and Applications*. Cambridge University Press.

Carlson, C., D. Burtraw, M. Cropper, and K.L. Palmer. 2000. "Sulfur Dioxide Control by Electric Utilities: What Are the Gains from Trade." *Journal of Political Economy*. 108: 1292–326.

Carlsson, F. 2000. "Environmental taxation and strategic commitment in duopoly models." *Environmental and Resource Economics*. 15: 243–56.

Carlton, D.W. and G.C. Loury. 1980. "The limitations of Pigouvian taxes as a long run remedy for externalities." *Quarterly Journal of Economics*. 95: 559–66.

Carlton, D.W. and G.C. Loury. 1986. "The limitations of Pigouvian taxes as a long run remedy for externalities: an extension of results." *Quarterly Journal of Economics*. 101: 631–4.

Carson, R. 1962. *Silent Spring*. Boston, MA: Houghton Mifflin.

Carson, R.T. 1991. "Constructed Markets." In J.B. Braden and C.D. Kolstad, eds. *Measuring the Demand for Environmental Commodities*. Amsterdam: North-Holland.

Carson, R.T. 2000. "Contingent valuation: a user's guide." *Environmental Science and Technology*. 34: 1413–18.

Carson, R.T. 2010. "The Environmental Kuznets Curve: Seeking Empirical Regularity and Theoretical Structure." *Review of Environmental Economics and Policy*. 4: 3–23.

Carson, R.T. 2012. "Contingent Valuation: A Practical Alternative when Prices Aren't Available." *The Journal of Economic Perspectives*. 26: 27–42.

Carson, R.T., N.E. Flores, K.M. Martin, and J.L. Wright. 1996. "Contingent Valuation and Revealed Preference Methodologies: Comparing the Estimates for Quasi-Public Goods." *Land Economics*. 72: 80–99.

Carson, R.T. and T. Groves. 2007. "Incentive and informational properties of preference questions." *Environmental Resource Economics*. 37: 181–210.

Carson, R.T., T. Groves, and J.A. List. 2014. "Consequentiality: A Theoretical and Experimental Exploration of a Single Binary Choice." *Journal of the Association of Environmental and Resource Economists*. 1: 171–207.

Carson R.T. and W.M. Hanemann. 2005. "Contingent valuation." Chapter 17 in K.-G. Mäler and J. Vincent, eds. *Handbook of Environmental Economics 2*. Amsterdam: Elsevier.

Carson, R.T. and J.J. Louviere. 2011. "A Common Nomenclature for Stated Preference Elicitation Approaches." *Environmental Resource Economics*. 49: 539–59.

Carson, R.T., R.C. Mitchell, M. Hanemann, R.J. Kopp, S. Presser, and P.A. Ruud. 2003. "Contingent Valuation and Lost Passive Use: Damages from the Exxon Valdez Oil Spill." *Environmental and Resource Economics*. 25: 257–86.

Cason, T.N. 1993. "Seller Incentive Properties of EPA's Emission Trading Auction." *Journal of Environmental Economics and Management*. 25: 177–95.

Cesario, F.J. 1976. "Value of time in recreation benefit studies." *Land Economics*. 52: 32–41.

Champ, P.A., R.C. Bishop, T.C. Brown, and D.W. McCollum. 1997. "Using Donation Mechanisms to Value Nonuse Benefits from Public Goods." *Journal of Environmental Economics and Management*. 33: 151–62.

Champ, P.A., K.J. Boyle, and T.C. Brown, eds. 2003. *A Primer on Non-market Valuation*. Dordrecht: Kluwer Academic Publishers.

Chattopadhyay, S. 1999. "Estimating the demand for air quality: new evidence based on the Chicago housing market." *Land Economics*. 75: 22–38.

Chay, K.Y. and M. Greenstone. 2005. "Does air quality matter? Evidence from the housing market." *Journal of Political Economy*. 113: 376–424.

Chevallier, J. 2012. "Banking and Borrowing in the EU ETS: a review of economic modeling, current provisions, and prospects for future design." *Journal of Economic Surveys*. 26: 157–76.

Chevallier, J. 2013. "Carbon Trading: past, present and future." In R. Fouquet *Handbook of Energy and Climate Change*. Cheltenham, UK & Northampton, MA: Edward Elgar. 471–89.

Chiang, A. 1992. *Elements of Dynamic Optimization*. New York: McGraw Hill.

Chichilnisky, G. 1994. "North-South Trade and the Global Environment." *The American Economic Review*. 84: 851–74.

Clark, C.W. 1990. *Mathematical Bioeconomics: The Optimal Management of Renewable Resources*. Second edition. Chichester, UK: Wiley.

Clarke, L., J. Edmonds, V. Krey, R. Richels, S. Rose, and M. Tavoni. 2009. "International climate policy architectures: Overview of the EMF 22 International Scenarios." *Energy Economics*. 31: 64–81.

Clemenz, G. 1999. "Adverse Selection and Pigou Taxes." *Environmental and Resource Economics*. 13: 13–29.

Coase, R. 1960. "The problem of social cost." *Journal of Law and Economics*. 3: 1–44.

Cochard, F., M. Willinger, and A. Xepapadeas. 2005. "The efficiency of non-point source pollution instruments: an experimental approach." *Environmental and Resource Economics*. 30: 393–422.

Coggins, J.S. and J.R. Swinton. 1996. "The Price of Pollution: A Dual Approach to Valuing SO_2 Allowances." *Journal of Environmental Economics and Management*. 30: 58–72.

Cole, M.A. 2000. "Air Pollution and 'Dirty' Industries: How and Why Does the Composition of Manufacturing Output Change with Economic Development?" *Environmental and Resource Economics*. 17: 109–23.

Colombo, S., J. Calatrava-Requena, and N. Hanley. 2007. "Testing choice experiment for benefit transfer with preference heterogeneity." *American Journal of Agricultural Economics*. 89: 135–151.

Conrad, J.M. 2010. *Resource Economics*. Second edition. Cambridge University Press.

Conrad, K. 1993. "Taxes and Subsidies for Pollution—Intense Industries as Trade Policy." *Journal of Environmental Economics and Management*. 25: 121–35.

Copeland, B.R. and M.S. Taylor. 1994. "North-South Trade and the Environment." *The Quarterly Journal of Economics*. 109: 755–87.

Copeland, B.R. and M.S. Taylor. 1995. "Trade and Transboundary Pollution." *American Economic Review*. 85: 716–37.

Copeland, B.R. and M.S. Taylor. 2003. *Trade and the Environment: Theory and Evidence*. Princeton and Oxford: Princeton University Press.

Copeland, B.R. and M.S. Taylor. 2004. "Trade, Growth, and the Environment." *Journal of Economic Literature*. 42: 7–71.

Cornes, R. and T. Sandler. 1996. *The Theory of Externalities, Public Goods, and Club Goods*. Cambridge: Cambridge University Press.

Corso, P., J.K. Hammitt, and J.D. Graham. 2001. "Valuing Mortality-Risk Reduction: Using Visual Aids to Improve the Validity of Contingent Valuation." *The Journal of Risk and Uncertainty*. 23: 165–84.

Costello, C. and L. Karp. 2004. "Dynamic taxes and quotas with learning." *Journal of Economic Dynamics and Control*. 28: 1661–80.

Cramton, P. and Kerr, S. 2002. "Tradeable carbon permit auctions: How and why to auction not grandfather." *Energy Policy*. 30: 333–45.

Cropper, M.L., L.B. Deck, and K.E. McConnell. 1988. "On the choice of functional form for hedonic price functions." *Review of Economics and Statistics*. 70: 668–75.

Cropper, M.L., M.C. Freeman, B. Groom, and W. Pizer. 2014. "Declining Discount Rates." *American Economic Review: Papers and Proceedings*. 104: 538–43.

Cropper, M.L., M. Haile, J. Lampietti, C. Poulos, and D. Whittington. 2004. "The demand for a malaria vaccine: evidence from Ethiopia." *Journal of Development Economics*. 75: 303–18.

Cropper, M., J.K. Hammitt, and L.A. Robinson. 2011. "Valuing Mortality Risk Reductions: Progress and Challenges." *Annual Review of Economics*. 3: 313–36.

Cropper, M.L. and F.G. Sussman. 1990. "Valuing Future Risks to Life." *Journal of Environmental Economics and Management*. 19: 160–74.

Cummings, R.G., D.S. Brookshire, and W.D. Schulze, eds. 1986. *Valuing Environmental Goods: An Assessment of the Contingent Valuation Methods*. Totowa: Rowman and Allanheld.

Cummings, R.G., G.W. Harrison, and E.E. Rutström. 1995. "Homegrown Values and Hypothetical Surveys: Is the Dichotomous Choice Approach Incentive-Compatible?" *The American Economic Review*. 85: 260–6.

Cummings, R.G. and L.O. Taylor. 1999. "Unbiased Value Estimates for Environmental Goods: A Cheap Talk Design for the Contingent Valuation Method." *The American Economic Review*. 89: 649–65.

Currie, J., L. Davis, M. Greenstone, and R. Walker. 2015. "Environmental Health Risks and Housing Values: Evidence from 1,600 Toxic Plant Openings and Closings." *American Economic Review*. 105: 678–709.

Currie, J., E.A. Hanushek, E.M. Kahn, M. Neidell, and S.G. Rivkin. 2009. "Does Pollution Increase School Absences?" *The Review of Economics and Statistics*. 91: 682–94.

Cutter, W.B. and M. Neidell. 2009. "Voluntary information programs and environmental regulation: Evidence from 'Spare the Air'." *Journal of Environmental Economics and Management*. 58: 253–65.

Dasgupta, P. 2008. "Discounting climate change." *The Journal of Risk and Uncertainty*. 37: 141–69.

Dasgupta, P., P. Hammond, and E. Maskin. 1980. "On imperfect information and optimal pollution control." *Review of Economic Studies*. 47: 857–60.

Dasgupta, P. and Heal, G.M. 1979. *Economic Theory and Exhaustible Resources*. Cambridge University Press.

Dasgupta, P. and K. Mäler. 2003. "The economics of non-convex ecosystems: introduction." *Environmental and Resource Economics*. 26: 499–525.

Day, B., I.J. Bateman, R.T. Carson, D. Dupont, J.J. Louviere, S. Morimoto, R. Scarpa, and P.W. 2012. "Ordering effects and choice set awareness in repeat-response stated preference studies." *Journal of Environmental Economics and Management*. 63: 73–91.

David, M. and B. Sinclair-Desgagné. 2005. "Environmental regulation and the eco-industry." *Journal of Regulatory Economics*. 28: 141–55.

David, M. and B. Sinclair-Desgagné. 2010. "Pollution abatement subsidies and the eco-industry." *Environmental and Resource Economics*. 45: 271–828.

Davis, L.W. 2004. "The effect of health risk on housing values: evidence from a cancer cluster." *American Economic Review*. 94: 1693–704.

Dekker, T., R. Brouwer, M. Hofkes, and K. Moeltner. 2011. "The Effect of Risk Context on the Value of a Statistical Life: a Bayesian Meta-model." *Environmental Resource Economics*. 49: 597–24.

Denicolò V. 1999. "Pollution-reducing innovations under taxes and permits." *Oxford Economics Papers*. 51: 184–99.

Depres, C., G. Grolleau, and N. Mzoughi. 2008. "Contracting for Environmental Property Rights: The Case of Vittel." *Economica*. 75: 412–34.

Depro, B., C. Timmins, and M. O'Neil. 2015. "White Flight and Coming to the Nuisance: Can Residential Mobility Explain Environmental Injustice?" *Journal of the Association of Environmental and Resource Economists*. 2: 439–68.

Deschênes, O. and M. Greenstone. 2007. "The Economic Impacts of Climate Change: Evidence from Agricultural Output and Random Fluctuations in Weather." *The American Economic Review*. 97: 354–85.

Deschênes, O. and M. Greenstone. 2012. "The Economic Impacts of Climate Change: Evidence from Agricultural Output and Random Fluctuations in Weather: Reply." *The American Economic Review*. 102: 3761–73.

Diamond, P.A. and J.A. Hausman. 1994. "Contingent Valuation: Is Some Number better than No Number?" *The Journal of Economic Perspectives*. 8: 45–64.

Diamond, P.A. and J.A. Mirrlees. 1971. "Optimal taxation and public production II: tax rules." *American Economic Review*. 61: 261–78.

Dickie, M. 2003. "Defensive behavior and damage cost methods." In P.A. Champ, K.J. Boyle, and T.C. Brown, eds. *A Primer on Non-Market Valuation*. Dordrecht: Springer.

Dietz, S. and N. Stern. 2008. "Why Economic Analysis Supports Strong Action on Climate Change: A Response to the *Stern Review*'s Critics." *Review of Environmental Economics and Policy*. 2: 94–113.

Dietz, S. and N. Stern, 2015. "Endogenous Growth, Convexity of Damage and Climate Risk: How Nordhaus' Framework Supports Deep Cuts in Carbon Emissions." *The Economic Journal*. 125: 574–620.

Dixit, A. and J. Stiglitz. 1977. "Monopolistic competition and optimal product diversity." *American Economic Review*. 67: 297–308.

Dockner, E., S. Jorgensen, N. van Long, and G. Sorger. 2000. *Differential games in economics and management science*. Cambridge University Press.

Döpke, L.K. and T. Requate. 2014. "The economics of exploiting gas hydrates." *Energy Economics*. 42: 355–64.

Dorfman, R. and P. Steiner. 1954: "Optimal Advertising and Optimal Quality." *American Economic Review*. 44: 826–36.

Downing, P. and W. Watson. 1974. "The economics of enforcing air pollution controls." *Journal of Environmental Economics and Management*. 1: 219–36.

Downing, P.B. and L.J. White. 1986. "Innovation in Pollution Control." *Journal of Environmental Economics and Management*. 13: 18–29.

Duval, Y. and S. Hamilton. 2002. "Strategic environmental policy and international trade in asymmetric oligopoly markets." *International Tax and Public Finance*. 9: 259–71.

Earnhart, D. 2002. "Combining Revealed and Stated Data to Examine Housing Decisions Using Discrete Choice Analysis." *Journal of Urban Economics*. 51: 143–69.

Ebert, U. 1992. "Pigouvian taxes and market structure: the case of oligopoly and different abatement technologies." *Finanzarchiv*. 49: 154–66.

Ebert, U. 1998. "Relative standards: a positive and normative analysis." *Journal of Economics*. 67: 17–38.

Ederington, J., A. Levinson, and J. Minier. 2005. "Footloose and Pollution-Free." *The Review of Economics and Statistics*. 87: 92–9.

Egan, K.J. and J.A. Herriges. 2006. "Multivariate count data regression models with individual panel data from an on-site-sample." *Journal of Environmental Economics and Management*. 52: 567–81.

Egan, K.J., J.A. Herriges, C.L. Kling, and J.A. Downing. 2009. "Valuing Water Quality as a Function of Water Quality Measures." *The American Journal of Agricultural Economics*. 91: 106–23.

EIA. 2011. "Average prices for spot sulfur dioxide emissions allowances at EPA auction set new lows." *Today in Energy, US Energy Information Agency*. www.eia.gov/todayinenergy/detail.cfm?id=1330

Eichner, T. and R. Pethig. 2011. "Carbon Leakage, The Green Paradox, And Perfect Future Markets." *International Economic Review*. 52: 767–805.

Ekeland, I., J.J. Heckman, and L. Nesheim. 2004. "Identification and estimation of hedonic models." *Journal of Political Economy*. 112: 60–109.

Ellerman, A.D., P.L. Joskow, R. Schmalensee, J.P. Montero, and E.M. Bailey. 2000. *Markets for Clean Air: The US Acid Rain Program*. Cambridge University Press.

Endress A. and B. Rundshagen. 2013. "Incentives to Diffuse Advanced Abatement Technology under the formation of international environmental agreements." *Environmental and Resource Economics*. 57: 177–210.

Englin, J. and J.S. Shonkwiler. 1995. "Estimating Social Welfare Using Count Data Models: An Application to Long Run Recreation Demand under Conditions of Endogenous Stratification and Truncation." *Review of Economics and Statistics*. 77: 104–12.

EPA (Ireland). Office of Environmental Enforcement. 2011. "Environmental Liability Regulations Guidance Document." Wexford, Ireland. http://ec.europa.eu/environment/legal/liability/pdf/eld_guidance/ireland.pdf

Epple, D. 1987. "Hedonic price and implicit markets: estimating demand and supply functions for differentiated products." *Journal of Political Economy.* 95: 59–80.

Epple, D. and H. Sieg. 1999. "Estimating Equilibrium Models of Local Jurisdictions." *Journal of Political Economy.* 107: 645–81.

European Commission (EC). 2003. "Directive 2003/87/EC of the European Parliament and of the council of 13 October 2003 establishing a scheme for greenhouse gas emission allowance trading within the Community and amending Council Directive 96/61/EC. *Official Journal of the European Union.*

European Commission (EC). 2011. "Document C (2011) 2772 (2011/278/EU): Commission decision of 27 April 2011 determining transitional Union-wide rules for harmonised free allocation of emission allowances pursuant to Article 10a of Directive 2003/87/EC." *Official Journal of the European Union.*

European Commission (EC). 2016. *EU ETS Handbook.* http://ec.europa.eu/clima/publications/docs/ets_handbook_en.pdf

Evans, M.F. and G. Schaur. 2010. "A quantile estimation approach to identify income and age variation in the value of statistical life." *Journal of Environmental Economics and Management.* 59: 260–70.

Falk, I. and R. Mendelsohn. 1993. "The Economics of Controlling Stock Pollutants: An Efficient Strategy for Greenhouse Gases." *Journal of Environmental Economics and Management.* 25: 76–88.

Färe, R., S. Grosskopf, C.A.K. Lovell, and S. Yaisawarng. 1993. "Derivation of Shadow Prices for Undesirable Outputs: A Distance Function Approach." *The Review of Economics and Statistics.* 75: 374–80.

Färe, R. and D. Primont. 1995. *Multi-Output Production and Duality: Theory and Applications.* Dordrecht: Kluwer Academic Publishers.

Farzin, Y. and O. Tahvonen. 1996. "The global carbon cycle and the optimal time path of a carbon tax." *Oxford Economic Papers.* 48: 515–36.

Feather, P. and W.D. Shaw. 1999. "Estimating the cost of leisure time for recreation demand models." *Journal of Environmental Economics and Management.* 38: 49–65.

Fees, E. and U. Hege. 2000. "Environmental Harm and Financial Responsibility." *The Geneva Papers of Risk and Insurance.* 25: 220–34.

Fees, E. and U. Hege. 2002. "Safety Regulation and Monitor Liability." *Review of Economic Design.* 7: 173–85.

Feldman, A.M. and R. Serrano. 2006. *Welfare Economics and Social Choice Theory.* Berlin: Springer.

Ferris, A.E., R.T. Shadbegian, and A. Wolverton. 2014. "The Effect of Environmental Regulation on Power Sector Employment: Phase I of the Title IV SO2 Trading Program." *Journal of the Association of Environmental and Resource Economists.* 1: 521–53.

Fezzi, C., I.J. Bateman, and S. Ferrini. 2014. "Using revealed preferences to estimate the Value of Travel Time to recreation sites." *Journal of Environmental Economics and Management.* 67: 58–70.

Fezzi, C. and I. Bateman. 2015. "The Impact of Climate Change on Agriculture: Non-linear Effects and Aggregation Bias in Ricardian Models of Farmland Values." *Journal of the Association of Environmental and Resource Economists.* 2: 57–92.

Finus, M., 2001. *Game Theory and International Environmental Cooperation.* Cheltenham: Edward Elgar.

Finus, M., C. Kotsogiannis, and S. McCorriston, 2013. "International coordination on climate policies." *Journal of Environmental Economics and Management.* 66: 159–65.

Finus, M. and A. Caparros. 2015. *Handbook on Game Theory and International Environmental Cooperation: Essential Readings.* Cheltenham, UK: Edward Elgar. (The International Library of Critical Writings in Economics Series).

Finus, M. and P. Pintassilgo, 2012. "International environmental agreements under uncertainty: Does the 'veil of uncertainty' help?" *Oxford Economic Papers.* 64: 736–64.

Finus, M. and P. Pintassilgo. 2013. "The role of uncertainty and learning for the success of international climate agreements." *Journal of Public Economics*. 103: 29–43.

Fischer, C. and A.K. Fox. 2012. "Comparing policies to combat emissions leakage: Border carbon adjustment versus rebates." *Journal of Environmental Economics and Management*. 64: 199–216.

Fischer, C. and R.G. Newell. 2008. "Environmental and technology policies for climate mitigation." *Journal of Environmental Economics and Management*. 55: 142–62.

Fischer C., I.W. Parry, and W.A. Pizer. 2003. "Instrument choice for environmental protection when environmental technological innovation is endogenous." *Journal of Environmental Economics and Management*. 45: 523–45.

Flores, N.E. and R.T. Carson. 1997. "The Relationship between the Income Elasticities of Demand and Willingness to Pay." *Journal of Environmental Economics and Management*. 33: 287–95.

Fowlie, M., C.R. Knittel, and C. Wolfram. 2012. "Sacred cars? Cost-effective regulation of stationary and nonstationary pollution sources." *American Economic Journal: Economic Policy*. 4: 98–126.

Fowlie, M. and J.M. Perloff. 2013. "Distributing Pollution in Cap-And-Trade Programs: Are Outcomes Independent of Allocation?" *The Review of Economics and Statistics*. 95: 1640–52.

Franckx, L. 2005. "Environmental enforcement with endogenous ambient monitoring." *Environmental and Resource Economics*. 30: 195–220.

Fraser, I. and R. Waschik. 2013. "The Double Dividend hypothesis in a CGE model: Specific factors and the carbon base." *Energy Economics*. 39: 286–95.

Freeman, A.M. 2003. *The Measurement of Environmental and Resource Values*. Second edition. Washington, DC: Resources for the Future.

Freeman, A.M., J.A. Herriges, and C.L. Kling. 2014. *The Measurement of Environmental and Resource Values*. Third edition. Washington, DC: Resources for the Future.

Friehe, T and A. Endress. 2011. "Incentives to Diffuse Advanced Abatement Technology under Environmental Liability Law." *Journal of Environmental Economics and Management*. 62: 30–40.

Fullerton, D. 2011. "Six Distributional Effects of Environmental Policy." *Risk Analysis*. 31: 923–9.

Fullerton, D. and R. Stavins. 1998. "How economists see the environment." *Nature*. 395: 433–4.

Gamper-Rabindran, S. and C. Timmins. 2013. "Does cleanup of hazardous waste sites raise housing values? Evidence of spatially localized benefits." *Journal of Environmental Economics and Management*. 65: 345–60.

Gangadharan, L., A. Farrell, and R. Croson. 2013. "Investment decisions and emissions reductions: experimental results in emissions permit trading." In M.K. Price and J.A. List, eds. *Handbook of Experimental Economics and the Environment*. Cheltenham, UK: Edward Elgar. 233–64.

Gans, W., A. Alberini, and A. Longo. 2013. "Smart meter devices and the effect of feedback on residential electricity consumption: Evidence from a natural experiment in Northern Ireland." *Energy Economics*. 36: 729–43.

Gayer, T., J.T. Hamilton, and W.K. Viscusi. 2000. "Private Values of Risk Trade-offs at Superfund Sites: Housing Market Evidence on Learning About Risk." *The Review of Economics and Statistics*. 82: 439–51.

Ge, J., C.L. Kling, and J.A. Herriges. 2013. "How Much is Clean Water Worth? Valuing Water Quality Improvement Using a Meta Analysis." *Working Paper No. 13016*. Department of Economics, Iowa State University.

Gersbach, H. and T. Requate. 2004. "Emission taxes and optimal refunding schemes." *Journal of Public Economisc*. 88: 713–25.

GFA-VO. 1983, 1990. Dreizehnte Verordnung zur Durchführung des Bundes-Immisionsschutzgesetzes (Verordnung über Großfeuerungsanlagen – 13. BImSchV) of June 22, 1983 (BGBl. I 1983, p.719, BGBl. III 2129-8-1-13, BGBl. I 1990, p.2106.) (13th Order for the implementation of the federal law on ambient air pollution [regulation on large firing installations].)

Gibbons, S., S. Mourato, and G.M. Resende. 2014. "The Amenity Value of English Nature: A Hedonic Price Approach." *Environmental Resource Economics*. 57: 175–96.

Giergiczny, M. 2008. "Value of a Statistical Life—the Case of Poland." *Environmental Resource Economics*. 41: 209–21.

Gillingham, K., R. Newell, and K. Palmer. 2006. "Energy Efficiency Policies: A Retrospective Examination." *Annual Review of Environment and Resources.* 31: 161–92.

Gollier, C. 2002. "Discounting an uncertain future." *Journal of Public Economics.* 85: 149–66.

Gollier, C. 2004. "Maximizing the expected net future value as an alternative strategy to gamma discounting." *Finance Research Letters.* 1: 85–9.

Gollier, C. 2009. "Should we discount the far-distant future at its lowest possible rate?" *Economics: The Open-Access, Open-Assessment E-Journal.* 3: article 25.

Gollier, C. and M.L. Weitzman. 2010. "How should the distant future be discounted when discount rates are uncertain?" *Economics Letters.* 107: 350–3.

Gopalakrishnan, S. and H.A. Klaiber. 2014. "Is the Shale Energy Boom a Bust for Nearby Residents? Evidence from Housing Values in Pennsylvania." *The American Journal of Agricultural Economics.* 96: 43–66.

Goulder, L.H. 1995. "Environmental taxation and the double dividend: a reader's guide." *International Tax and Public Finance.* 2: 157–83.

Goulder, L.H., M.R. Jacobsen, and A.A. van Benthem. 2012. "Unintended consequences from nested state and federal regulations: the case of the Pavley greenhouse-gas-per-mile limits." *Journal of Environmental Economics and Management.* 63: 187–207.

Goulder, L.H. and I.W.H. Parry. 2008. "Instrument Choice in Environmental Policy." *Review of Environmental Economists and Policy.* 2: 152–74.

Goulder, L.H., I.W.H. Parry, R.C. Williams III, and D. Burtraw. 1999. "The cost-effectiveness of alternative instruments for environmental protection in a second-best setting." *Journal of Public Economics.* 72: 329–60.

Graff Zivin, J.G. and M. Neidell. 2009. "Days of haze: environmental information disclosure and intertemporal avoidance behavior." *Journal of Environmental Economics and Management.* 52: 119–28.

Graff Zivin, J. and M. Neidell. 2012. "The Impact of Pollution on Worker Productivity." *American Economic Review.* 102: 3652–73.

Graff Zivin, J. and M. Neidell. 2013. "Environment, Health, and Human Capital." *Journal of Economic Literature.* 51: 689–730.

Graff Zivin, J., M. Neidell, and W. Schlenker. 2011. "Water Quality Violations and Avoidance Behavior: Evidence from Bottled Water Consumption." *American Economic Review: Papers and Proceedings.* 101: 448–53.

Graham, D.A. 1981. "Cost-Benefit Analysis under Uncertainty." *The American Economic Review.* 71: 715–25.

Grainger, C.A. 2012. "The distributional effects of pollution regulations: Do renters fully pay for cleaner air?" *Journal of Economics.* 96: 840–52.

Grainger, C.A. and C.D. Kolstad. 2010. "Who Pays a Price on Carbon?" *Environmental and Resource Economics.* 46: 359–76.

Gray, W.B. and J.P. Shimshack. 2011. "The Effectiveness of Environmental Monitoring and Enforcement: A Review of the Empirical Evidence." *Review of Environmental Economics and Policy.* 5: 1–23.

Green, J.R. and J.J. Laffont. 1978. "A sampling approach to the free rider problem." In A. Sandmo, ed. *Essays in Public Economics.* Lexington, MA: Lexington Books.

Greene, W.H. 2011. *Econometric Analysis,* 7th Edition. Upper Saddle River, NJ: Prentice Hall.

Greenstone, M. 2002. "The Impacts of Environmental Regulations on Industrial Activity: Evidence from the 1970 and 1977 Clean Air Act Amendments and the Census of Manufactures." *Journal of Political Economy.* 110: 1175–219.

Greenstone, M. and T. Gayer. 2009. "Quasi-experimental and experimental approaches to environmental economics." *Journal of Environmental Economics and Management.* 57: 21–44.

Greenstone, M., E. Kopits, and A. Wolverton. 2013. "Developing a Social Cost of Carbon for US Regulatory Analysis: A Methodology and Interpretation." *Review of Environmental Economics and Policy.* 7: 23–46.

Grigalunas, T.A. and J.J. Opaluch. 1988. "Assessing Liability for Damages under CERCLA: A new approach for providing incentives for pollution avoidance?" *Natural Resource Journal.* 28: 509–33.

Grossman, G.M. and Krueger, A.B. 1995. "Economic Growth and the Environment." *The Quarterly Journal of Economics.* 110: 353–77.

Haab, T.C. and R.L. Hicks. 1999. "Choice Set Considerations in Models of Recreation Demand: History and Current State of the Art." *Marine Resource Economics.* 14: 271–81.

Haab, T.C., M.G. Interis, D.R. Petrolia and J.C. Whitehead. 2013. "From Hopeless to Curious? Thoughts on Hausman's 'Dubious to Hopeless' Critique of Contingent Valuation." *Applied Economic Perspectives and Policy.* 35: 593–612.

Haab, T.C. and K.E. McConnell. 2002. *Valuing Environmental and Natural Resources: The Econometrics of Non-Market Valuation.* Northampton, MA: Edward Elgar.

Haener, M.K., P.C. Boxall, W.L. Adamowicz, and D.H. Kuhnke. 2004. "Aggregation Bias in Recreation Site Choice Models: Resolving the Resolution Problem." *Land Economics.* 80: 561–74.

Hagerty, D. and K. Moeltner. 2005. "Specification of Driving Costs in Models of Recreation Demand." *Land Economics.* 81: 127–43.

Hahn, R.W. 1984. "Market Power and Transferable Property Rights." *The Quarterly Journal of Economics.* 99: 753–65.

Hamilton, T.L. and D.J. Phaneuf. 2015. "An integrated model of regional and local residential sorting with application to air quality." *Journal of Environmental Economics and Management.* 74: 71–93.

Hamilton, S. and T. Requate. 2004. "Vertical Contracts and Strategic Environmental Trade Policy." *Journal of Environmental Economics and Management.* 47: 260–69.

Hammitt, J.K. 2000. "Valuing Mortality Risk: Theory and Practice." *Environmental Science & Technology.* 34: 1396–400.

Hammitt, J.K. 2007. "Valuing Changes in Mortality Risk: Lives Saved Versus Life Years Saved." *Review of Environmental Economics and Policy.* 1: 228–40.

Hammitt, J.K. and J.D. Graham. 1999. "Willingness to Pay for Health Protection: Inadequate Sensitivity to Probability?" *Journal of Risk and Uncertainty.* 18: 33–62.

Hanemann, W.M. 1978. *A Methodological and Empirical Study of the Recreation Benefits from Water Quality Improvement.* PhD Dissertation, Department of Economics, Harvard University, Cambridge, MA.

Hanemann, W.M. 1980. "Measuring the worth of natural resource facilities: comment." *Land Economics.* 56: 482–6.

Hanemann, W.M. 1983. "Marginal Welfare Measures for Discrete Choice Models." *Economics Letters.* 13: 129–36.

Hanemann, W.M. 1984a. "Discrete/Continuous Models of Consumer Demand." *Econometrica.* 52: 541–61.

Hanemann, W.M. 1984b. "Welfare evaluations in contingent valuation experiments with discrete responses." *American Journal of Agricultural Economics.* 66: 332–41.

Hanemann, W.M. 1991. "Willing to pay and willing to accept: how much can they differ?" *American Economic Review.* 81: 635–47.

Hanemann, W.M. 1994. "Valuing the Environment Through Contingent Valuation." *The Journal of Economic Perspectives.* 8: 19–43.

Hanemann, W.M. 1999a. "Neoclassical economic theory and contingent valuation." Chapter 3 in I.J. Bateman and K.G. Willis, eds. *Valuing Environmental Preferences: Theory and Practice of the Contingent Valuation Method in the US, EU, and Developing Countries.* Oxford University Press.

Hanemann, W.M. 1999b. "Welfare analysis in discrete choice models." In J.A. Herriges and C.L. Kling, eds. *Valuing Recreation and the Environment: Revealed Preference Methods in Theory and Practice.* Cheltenham, UK: Edward Elgar.

Harford, J. 1978. "Firm behavior under imperfectly enforceable pollution standards and taxes." *Journal of Environmental Economics and Management.* 5: 26–43.

Harford, J. 1984. "Relatively Efficient Pollution Standards under Perfect Competition." *Public Finance Quarterly.* 12: 183–95.

Harford, J. 1987. "Self-reporting of pollution and the firm's behavior under imperfectly enforceable regulations." *Journal of Environmental Economics and Management.* 14: 293–303.

Harford, J. and G. Karp. 1983. "The effects and efficiencies of different pollution standards." *Eastern Economic Journal.* 9: 79–89.

Harford, J. and S. Ogura. 1983. "Pollution taxes and standards: a continuum of quasi-optimal solutions." *Journal of Environmental Economics and Management.* 10: 1–17.

Harrington, W., R.D. Morgenstern, and T. Sterner, eds. 2004. *Choosing Environmental Policy: Comparing Instruments and Outcomes in the United States and Europe.* Washington, DC: Resources for the Future.

Harrison, G.W. and J.A. List. 2004. "Field experiments." *Journal of Economic Literature.* 42: 1009–55.

Harrison, G.W. and E.E. Rutström. 2008. "Experimental Evidence on the Existence of Hypothetical Bias in Value Elicitation Methods." Chapter 8 in C. Plott and V.L. Smith, eds. *Handbook of Experimental Economics Results.* Amsterdam: Elsevier B.V.

Hartman, R.S., D. Wheeler, and M. Singh. 1997. "The cost of air pollution abatement." *Applied Economics.* 29: 759–74.

Hausman, J.A. 1981. "Exact consumer's surplus and deadweight loss." *American Economic Review:* 71: 662–76.

Hausman, J. 2012. "Contingent Valuation: From Dubious to Hopeless." *The Journal of Economic Perspectives.* 26: 43–56.

Hausman, J.A., G.K. Leonard, and D. McFadden. 1995. "A utility-consistent, combined discrete choice and count data model. Assessing recreational use losses due to natural resource damage." *Journal of Public Economics.* 56: 1–30.

Heckman, J.J. 1974. "Shadow price, market wages, and labor supply." *Econometrica.* 42: 679–94.

Heckman, J.J. 2010. "Nonparametric Identification and Estimation of Nonadditive Hedonic Models." *Econometrica.* 78: 1569–91.

Helfand, G. 1991. "Standards versus standards: the effects of different pollution restrictions." *American Economic Review.* 81: 622–34.

Helfand, G.E., P. Berck, and T. Maull. 2003. "The theory of pollution policy." Chapter 6 in K.-G. Mäler and J.R. Vincent, eds. *Handbook of Environmental Economics 1.* Amsterdam: Elsevier.

Helm, C. and R.C. Schmidt. 2015. "Climate cooperation with technology investments and border carbon adjustment." *European Economic Review.* 75: 112–30.

Helm, C. and F. Wirl. 2014. "The Principal-Agent Model with Multilateral Externalities: An Application to Climate Agreements." *Journal of Environmental Economics and Management.* 67: 141–54.

Henry, C. 1989. *Microeconomics for Public Policy: Helping the Invisible Hand.* Oxford: Clarendon Press.

Hensher, D.A., J.M. Rose, and W.H. Greene. 2005. *Applied Choice Analysis: A Primer.* Cambridge University Press.

Hepburn, C. 2006. "Regulation by Prices, Quantities or Both: A Review of Instrument Choice." *Oxford Review of Economic Policies.* 22: 226–47.

Herriges, J.A., C.L. Kling, and D.J. Phaneuf. 2004. "What's the use? Welfare estimates from revealed preference models when weak complementarity does not hold." *Journal of Environmental Economics and Management.* 47: 55–70.

Herriges, J.A. and D.J. Phaneuf. 2002. "Inducing Patterns of Correlation and Substitution in Repeated Logit Models of Recreation Demand." *American Journal of Agricultural Economics.* 84: 1076–90.

Herriges, J.A., D.J. Phaneuf, and J.L. Tobias. 2008. "Estimating demand systems when outcomes are correlated counts." *Journal of Econometrics.* 147: 282–98.

Heyes, A. 1996. "Lender Penalty for Environmental Damages and the Equilibrium Cost of Capital." *Economica.* 63: 311–23.

Hicks, J.R. 1939. "The foundations of welfare economics." *The Economic Journal.* 49: 696–712.

Hicks, R.L. and K.E. Schnier. 2010. "Spatial regulations and endogenous consideration sets in fisheries." *Resource and Energy Economics.* 32: 117–34.

Höglund Isaksson, L. 2005. "Abatement costs in response to the Swedish charge on nitrogen oxide emissions." *Journal of Environmental Economics and Management.* 50: 102–20.

Hoel, M. 2010. *Environmental R&D*. Memorandum 12/2010. Oslo: Department of Economics, University of Oslo.

Hoel, M. and L. Karp. 2001. "Taxes and quotas for a stock pollutant with multiplicative uncertainty." *Journal of Public Economics*. 82: 91–114.

Hoel, M. and L. Karp. 2002. "Taxes versus quotas for a stock pollutant." *Resource and Energy Economics*. 24: 367–84.

Holland, M., S. Pye, P. Watkiss, B. Droste-Franke, and P. Bickel. 2005. "Damages per tonne emission of PM2.5, NH3, SO2, NOx, and VOCs from each EU25 Member State (excluding Cyprus) and surrounding seas." *Service contract (to the European Commission DG Environment) for carrying out cost-benefit analysis of air quality related issues, in particular in the clean air for Europe (CAFE) programme*. Reference number: AEAT/ED51014/CAFÉ CBA damage costs.

Holland, S.P. 2012. "Emissions taxes versus intensity standards: Second-best environmental policies with incomplete regulation." *Journal of Environmental Economics and Management*. 63: 375–87.

Holland, S.P. and E.T. Mansur. 2008. "Is Real-Time Pricing Green? The Environmental Impacts of Electricity Demand Variance." *The Review of Economics and Statistics*. 90: 550–61.

Horan, R.D. and J.S. Shortle. 2005. "When Two Wrongs Make a Right: Second Best Point Nonpoint Trading." *American Journal of Agricultural Economics*. 87: 340–52.

Horan, R.D., J.S. Shortle, and D. Abler. 2002. "Ambient Taxes Under m-Dimensional Choice Sets, Heterogeneous Expectations, and Risk-Aversion." *Environmental and Resource Economics*. 21: 189–202.

Horan, R.D., J.S. Shortle, and D.G. Abler. 2004. "Point-Nonpoint Trading Programs and Agri-Environmental Policies." *Agricultural and Resource Economics Review*. 33: 61–78.

Horowitz, J.K. and K.E. McConnell. 2002. "A review of WTA/WTP studies." *Journal of Environmental Economics and Management*. 44: 426–47.

Hotelling, H. 1931. "The economics of exhaustible resources." *Journal of Political Economy*. 39: 137–75.

Hotelling, H. 1947. Letter of June 18, 1947, to Newton B. Drury. Included in "The Economics of Public Recreation: An Economic Study of the Monetary Evaluation of Recreation in the National Parks." 1949. Mimeographed. Washington, DC: Land and Recreational Planning Division, National Park Service.

Howe, C. 1994. "Taxes Versus Tradeable Discharge Permits: A Review in the Light of the US and European Experience." *Environmental and Resource Economics*. 4: 151–69.

Hughes, J.E. and M. Podolefsky. 2015. "Getting Green with Solar Subsidies: Evidence from the California Solar Iniative." *Journal of the Association of Environmental and Resource Economists*. 2: 235–75.

Hutchinson, E. and K. van't Veld. 2005. "Extended Liability for Environmental Accidents: What you see is what you get." *Journal of Environmental Economics and Management*. 49: 157–73.

Icelandic Law on Fisheries Management. 2006, 2012. The Fisheries Management Act, 116/2006, with amendments from January 2012. Information Center of the Icelandic Ministry of Fisheries and Agriculture. http://althingi.is/lagas/140a/2006116.html

Imbens, G.W. and J.M. Wooldridge. 2009. "Recent developments in the econometrics of program evaluation." *Journal of Economic Literature*. 47: 5–86.

IPCC. 2013. *Climate Change 2013: The Physical Science Basis. Contribution of Working Group I to the Fifth Assessment Report of the Intergovernmental Panel on Climate Change*. T.F. Stocker and D. Qin, co-chair eds. Geneva, Switzerland: IPPC.

IPCC. 2014. *Climate Change 2014: Synthesis Report. Contribution of Working Groups I, II and III to the Fifth Assessment Report of the Intergovernmental Panel on Climate Change*. Core Writing Team, R.K. Pachauri and L.A. Meyer, eds. Geneva, Switzerland: IPPC.

Jacobs, B. and R.A. de Mooij. 2015. "Pigou meets Mirrlees: On the irrelevance of tax distortions for the second-best Pigouvian tax." *Journal of Environmental Economics and Management*. 71: 90–108.

Jaffe, A.B., S.R. Peterson, P.R. Portney, and R.N. Stavins. 1995. "Environmental Regulation and the Competitiveness of U.S. Manufacturing: What Does the Evidence Tell Us?" *Journal of Economic Literature*. 33: 132–63.

Jenkins, R.R., E. Kopits, and D. Simpson. 2009. "Policy Monitor—The Evolution of Solid and Hazardous Waste Regulation in the United States." *Review of Environmental Economics and Policy*. 3: 104–120.

Jensen, S. and C.P. Traeger. 2014. "Optimal climate change mitigation under long-term growth uncertainty: Stochastic integrated assessment and analytic findings." *European Economic Review*. 69: 104–25.

Jindapon, P. and W.D. Shaw. 2008. "Option price without expected utility." *Economics Letters*. 100: 408–10.

Johnson, F.R., B. Kanninen, M. Bingham, and S. Ozdemir. 2007. "Experimental design for stated choice studies." Chapter 7 in Kanninen, B.J., ed. *Valuing Environmental Amenities Using Stated Choice Studies: A Common Sense Approach to Theory and Practice*. Dordrecht: Springer.

Johnston, R.J. 2006. "Is hypothetical bias universal? Validating contingent valuation responses using a binding public referendum." *Journal of Environmental Economics and Management*. 52: 469–81.

Johnston, R.J. 2007. "Choice experiments, site similarity and benefits transfer." *Environmental and Resource Economics*. 38: 331–51.

Johnston, R.J., J. Rolfe, R.S. Rosenberger, and R. Brouwer, eds. 2015. *Benefit Transfer of Environmental and Resource Values: A Guide for Researchers and Practitioners*. Dordrecht: Springer.

Johnston, R.J. and R.S. Rosenberger. 2010. "Methods, Trends and Controversies in Contemporary Benefit Transfer." *Journal of Economic Surveys*. 24: 479–510.

Johnstone, N., I. Haščič, and D. Popp. 2010. "Renewable Energy Policies and Technological Innovation: Evidence Based on Patent Counts." *Environmental and Resource Economics*. 45: 133–55.

Jones-Lee, M. 1974. "The Value of Changes in the Probability of Death or Injury." *Journal of Political Economy*. 82: 835–49.

Jones, R.J. and C.A. Vossler. 2014. "Experimental tests of water quality trading markets." *Journal of Environmental Economics and Management*. 68: 449–62.

Jorgenson, D.W. 1986. "Econometric methods for modeling producer behavior." Chapter 31 in Z. Griliches and M.D. Intriligator, eds. *Handbook of Econometrics v. 3*. Amsterdam: Elsevier.

Jost, P.J. 1996. "Limited Liability and the Requirement to Purchase Insurance." *International Review of Law and Economics*. 16: 259–76.

Jotzo, F. and A. Löschel. 2014. "Emissions trading in China: Emerging experiences and international lessons." *Energy Policy*. 7: 3–8.

Jung, J. 1988. "Die Kosten der SO2 und NOX-Minderung in der deutschen Elektrizitätswirtschaft." *Elektrizitätswirtschaft*. 87: 267–70.

Just, R.E., D.L. Hueth, and A. Schmitz. 2004. *The Welfare Economics of Public Policy: A Practical Approach to Project and Policy Evaluation*. Northampton, MA: Edward Elgar.

Kahneman, D. and J.L. Knetsch. 1992. "Valuing Public Goods: The Purchase of Moral Satisfaction." *Journal of Environmental Economics and Management*. 22: 57–70.

Kanninen, B.J., ed. 2007. *Valuing Environmental Amenities Using Stated Choice Studies: A Common Sense Approach to Theory and Practice*. Dordrecht: Springer.

Kaldor, N. 1939. "Welfare propositions of economics and interpersonal comparisons of utility." *The Economic Journal*. 49: 549–52.

Kaplow, L. and S. Shavell. 2002. "Economic Analysis of Law." In A. Auerbach and M. Feldstein, eds. *Handbook of Public Economics*. 25: 1661–784. Amsterdam: Elsevier.

Karp, L. 2005. "Global warming and hyperbolic discounting." *Journal of Public Economics*. 89: 261–82.

Katsoulacos, Y. and A. Xepapadeas. 1995. "Pigouvian taxes under oligopoly." *Scandinavian Journal of Economics*. 97: 411–20.

Kaul, S., K.J. Boyle, N.V. Kuminoff, C.F. Parmeter, and J.C. Pope. 2013. "What can we learn from benefit transfer errors? Evidence from 20 years of research on convergent validity." *Journal of Environmental Economics and Management*. 66: 90–104.

Kellenberg, D. and A. Levinson. 2014. "Waste of Effort? International Environmental Agreements." *Journal of the Association of Environmental and Resource Economists*. 1: 135–69.

Kennedy, P. 1994. "Equilibrium Pollution Taxes in Open Economies with Imperfect Competition." *Journal of Environmental Economics and Management*. 27: 49–63.

Kennedy, P.W. and B. Laplante. 1999. "Environmental Policy and Time Consistency: Emission Taxes and Emissions Trading." In E. Petrakis, E.S. Sartzetakis, and A. Xepapadeas, eds. *Environmental regulation and market power: Competition, time consistency and international trade.* Cheltenham: Edward Elgar. 116–44.

Keohane, N. and S. Olmstead. 2007. *Markets and the Environment.* Washington, DC: Island Press.

Khanna, M. and L.A. Damon. 1999. "EPA's Voluntary 33/50 Program: Impact on Toxic Releases and Economic Performance of Firms." *Journal of Environmental Economics and Management.* 37: 1–25.

Kiel, K.A. and J.E. Zabel. 2009. "The Accuracy of Owner-Provided House Values: The 1978–1991 American Housing Survey." *Real Estate Economics.* 27: 263–98.

Kim, C.W., T.T. Phipps, and L. Anselin. 2003. "Measuring the benefits of air quality improvement: a spatial hedonic approach." *Journal of Environmental Economics and Management.* 5: 24–39.

Kittle, L.J. 1987. Marine Resource Damage Assessment Report for the Arco Anchorage Oil Spill. Seattle, WA: Washington Department of Ecology.

Klaiber, H.A. and D.J. Phaneuf. 2010. "Valuing open space in a residential sorting model of the Twin Cities." *Journal of Environmental Economics and Management.* 60: 57–77.

Kling, C.L., D.J. Phaneuf, and J. Zhao. 2012. "From Exxon to BP: Has Some Number Become Better than No Number?" *The Journal of Economic Perspectives.* 26: 3–26.

Kling, C. and J. Rubin. 1997. "Bankable permits for the control of environmental pollution." *Journal of Public Economics.* 64: 101–15.

Kneese, A.V. and R.C. d'Arge. 1974. "Editorial." *Journal of Environmental Economics and Management.* 1: 1.

Kneese, A.V. and C.L. Schultze. 1975. *Pollution, Prices and Public Policy.* Washington, DC: Brookings.

Kniesner, T.J., W.K. Viscusi, C. Woock, and J.P. Ziliak. 2012. "The Value of a Statistical Life: Evidence from Panel Data." *The Review of Economics and Statistics.* 94: 74–87.

Kochi, I., B. Hubbell, and R. Kramer. 2006. "An Empirical Bayes Approach to Combining and Comparing Estimates of the Value of a Statistical Life for Environmental Policy Analysis." *Environmental & Resource Economics.* 34: 385–406.

Kohn, R. 1992. "When subsidies for pollution abatement increase total emissions." *Southern Economic Journal.* 59: 77–87.

Koichi, K., W.M. Hanemann, and J.R. Hilger. 2010. "A latent segmentation approach to a Kuhn-Tucker model: An application to recreation demand." *Journal of Environmental Economics and Management.* 60: 209–20.

Kolstad, C.D. and R.M. Guzman. 1999. "Information and the divergence between willingness to accept and willingness to pay." *Journal of Environmental Economics and Management.* 38: 66–80.

Konrad, K.A., T.E. Olson, and R. Schöb. 1994. "Resource Extraction and the Threat of Possible Expropriation: The Role of Swiss Bank Accounts." *Journal of Environmental Economics and Management.* 26: 149–62.

Kornhauser, L.A. and R.L. Revesz. 1990. "Apportioning Damages among Potentially Insolvent Actors." *Journal of Legal Studies.* 19: 617–51.

Krautkraemer, J.A. 1998a. "Nonrenewable Resource Scarcity." *Journal of Economic Literature.* 36: 2065–107.

Krautkraemer, J.A. 1998b. "Resource Amenities and the Preservation of Natural Environments." *The Review of Economic Studies.* 52: 153–70.

Krupnick, A. 2007. "Mortality-risk Valuation and Age: Stated Preference Evidence." *Review of Environmental Economics and Policy.* 1: 261–82.

Krupnick, A., A. Alberini, M. Cropper, N. Simon, B. O'Brien, R. Goeree, and M. Heintzelman. 2002. "Age, Health and the Willingness to Pay for Mortality Risk Reductions: A Contingent Valuation Survey of Ontario Residents." *The Journal of Risk and Uncertainty.* 24: 161–86.

Krupnick, A., W. Oates, and E. van de Verg. 1980. "On marketable air pollution permits: the case for a system of pollution offsets." *Journal of Environmental Economics and Management.* 10: 233–47.

Kuminoff, N.V., C.F. Parmeter, and J.C. Pope. 2010. "Which hedonic models can we trust to recover the marginal willingness to pay for environmental amenities?" *Journal of Environmental Economics and Management.* 60: 145–60.

Kuminoff, N.V. and J.C. Pope. 2012. "A novel approach to identifying hedonic demand parameters." *Economics Letters*. 116: 374–76.

Kuminoff, N.V. and J.C. Pope. 2014. "Do 'Capitalization Effects' for Public Goods Reveal the Public's Willingness to Pay?" *International Economic Review*. 55: 1227–50.

Kuminoff, N.V., V.K. Smith, and C. Timmins. 2013. "The New Economics of Equilibrium Sorting and Policy Evaluation Using Housing Markets." *Journal of Economic Literature*. 51: 1007–62.

Kuriyama, K., W.M. Hanemann, and J.R. Hilger. 2010. "A latent segmentation approach to a Kuhn-Tucker model: An application to recreation demand." *Journal of Environmental Economics and Management*. 60: 209–20.

Kwerel, E. 1977. "To tell the truth: imperfect information and optimal pollution control." *Review of Economic Studies*. 44: 395–601.

Laffont, J.J. 1989. *The Economics of Uncertainty and Information*. Cambridge, MA: MIT Press.

Laffont, J.J. and J. Tirole. 1996. "Pollution permits and environmental innovation." *Journal of Public Economics*. 62: 127–40.

LaFrance, J.T. and W.M. Hanemann. 1989. "The dual structure of incomplete demand systems." *American Journal of Agricultural Economics*. 71: 262–74.

Lancaster, K.J. 1966. "A New Approach to Consumer Theory." *Journal of Political Economy*. 74: 132–57.

Lange, A. and T. Requate. 1999. "Emission Taxes for Price Setting Firms: Differentiated Commodities and Monopolistic Competition." In E. Petrakis, E. Sartzetakis, and A. Xepapadeas, eds. *Environmental Regulation and Market Power, Competition, Time Consistency and International Trade*. Cheltenham: Edward Elgar.

Lange, A. and T. Requate. 2000. "Pigouvian Taxes in General Equilibrium with a Fixed Tax Redistribution Rule." *Journal of Public Economic Theory*. 2: 25–42.

Larson, D.M. 1991. "Recovering Weakly Complementary Preferences." *Journal of Environmental Economics and Management*. 21: 97–108.

Larson, D.M. 1992. "Further Results on Willingness to Pay for Non-market Goods." *Journal of Environmental Economics and Management*. 23: 101–22.

Larson, D.M. and D.K. Lew. 2014. "The Opportunity Cost of Travel Time as a Noisy Wage Fraction." *American Journal of Agricultural Economics*. 96: 420–37.

Lee, D.R. 1975. "Efficiency of Pollution Taxation and Market Structure." *Journal of Environmental Economics and Management*. 2: 69–72.

Lee, L.F. and M.M. Pitt. 1986. "Microeconometric demand systems with binding non-negativity constraints: the dual approach." *Econometrica*. 54: 1237–42.

Lee, S.H. 1999. "Optimal Taxation for Polluting Oligopolists with Endogenous Market Structure." *Journal of Regulatory Economics*. 15: 293–308.

LeMarquand, D.G. 1977. *International Rivers: The politics of cooperation*. Vancouver: University of British Columbia, Westwater Research Center.

Leon-Gonzalez, R. and R. Scarpa. 2008. "Improving multi-site benefit functions via Bayesian model averaging: A new approach to benefit transfer." *Journal of Environmental Economics and Management*. 56: 50–68.

LeSage, J. and R.K. Pace. 2009. *Introduction to Spatial Econometrics*. Boca Raton, FL: Chapman and Hall.

Levin, D. 1985. "Taxation within Cournot oligopoly." *Journal of Public Economics*. 27: 281–90.

Levinson, A. 2009. "Technology, International Trade, and Pollution from US Manufacturing." *American Economic Review*. 99: 2177–92.

Levinson, A. 2015. "A Direct Estimate of the Technique Effect: Changes in the Pollution Intensity of US Manufacturing, 1990–2008." *Journal of the Association of Environmental and Resource Economists*. 2: 43–56.

Levinson, A. and M.S. Taylor. 2008. "Unmasking the Pollution Haven Effect." *International Economic Review*. 49: 223–54.

Lew, D.K. and K. Wallmo. 2011. "External Tests of Scope and Embedding in Stated Preference Choice Experiments: An Application to Endangered Species Valuation." *Environmental Resource Economics*. 48: 1–23.

Lewis, T.R. 1996. "Protecting the environment when costs and benefits are privately known." *RAND Journal of Economics*. 27: 819–47.

Lin, C.Y.C. 2013. "Strategic decision making with information and extraction externalities: a structural model of the multistage investment timing game in offshore petroleum production." *Review of Economics and Statistics*. 95: 1601–21.

Lindahl, E. 1958 (1919). "Just taxation—A positive solution." In R.A. Musgrave, and A.T. Peacock. London: Macmillan: *Classics in the Theory of Public Finance*. (Original German title: *Die Gerechtigkeit der Besteuerung*.)

List, J.A. 2001. "Do Explicit Warnings Eliminate the Hypothetical Bias in Elicitation Procedures? Evidence from Field Auctions for Sportscards." *The American Economic Review*. 91: 1498–507.

Loomis, J. 1992. "The evolution of a more rigorous approach to benefit transfer: benefit function transfer." *Water Resources Research*. 28: 701–705.

Loomis, J. 2011. "What's to Know about Hypothetical Bias in Stated Preference Valuation Studies?" *Journal of Economic Surveys*. 25: 363–70.

Loomis, J. 2015. "The use of benefit transfer in the United States." Chapter 3 in Johnston, R.J., J. Rolfe, R.S. Rosenberger, and R. Brouwer, eds. *Benefit Transfer of Environmental and Resource Values: A Guide for Researchers and Practitioners*. Dordrecht: Springer.

Loomis, J.B. and R.S. Rosenberger. 2006. "Reducing barriers in future benefit transfers: needed improvements in primary study design and reporting." *Ecological Economics*. 60: 343–350.

Lupi, F. and P.M. Feather. 1998. "Using partial site aggregation to reduce bias in random utility travel cost models." *Water Resources Research*. 34: 3595–603.

Mäler, K.-G. 1974. *Environmental Economics: A Theoretical Inquiry*. Baltimore, MD: Johns Hopkins University Press.

Malueg, D.A. 1989. "Emission Credit Trading and the Incentive to Adopt New Pollution Abatement Technology." *Journal of Environmental Economics and Management*. 16: 52–7.

Mansfield, C., F.R. Johnson, and G. Van Houtven. 2006. "The missing piece: valuing averting behavior for children's ozone exposures." *Resource and Energy Economics*. 28: 215–28.

Mansfield, C., D. Phaneuf, F.R. Johnson, J.-C. Yang, and R. Beach. 2008. "Preferences for Public Lands Management under Competing Uses: The Case of Yellowstone National Park." *Land Economics*. 84: 282–305.

Markusen, J.R. 1975. "International Externalities and Optimal Tax Structures." *Journal of International Economics*. 5: 531–51.

Markusen, J.R., E.R. Morey, and N. Olewiler. 1993. "Environmental Policy When Market Structure and Plant Locations Are Endogenous." *Journal of Environmental Economics and Management*. 24: 68–86.

Markusen, J.R., E.R. Morey, and N. Olewiler. 1995: "Competition in Regional Environmental Policies when Plant Locations Are Endogenous." *Journal of Public Economics*. 56: 55–77.

Mastrandrea, M. 2009. "Calculating the benefits of climate policy: examining the assumptions of integrated assessment models." Working paper. Pew Center on Global Climate Change.

Mastromonaco, R. 2015. "Do environmental right-to-know laws affect markets? Capitalization of information in the toxic release inventory." *Journal of Environmental Economics and Management*. 71: 54–70.

McClelland, J.D. and J.K. Horowitz. 1999. "The Costs of Water Pollution Regulation in the Pulp and Paper Industry." *Land Economics*. 75: 220–32.

McConnell, K.E. 1990. "Models for Referendum Data: The Structure of Discrete Choice Models for Contingent Valuation." *Journal of Environmental Economics and Management*. 18: 19–34.

McConnell, K.E. 1992. "On-site time in the demand for recreation." *American Journal of Agricultural Economics*. 74: 918–25.

McConnell, K.E. and N.E. Bockstael. 2005. "Valuing the Environment as a Factor of Production." Chapter 14 in K.-G. Mäler and J.R. Vincent, eds. *Handbook of Environmental Economics 2*. Amsterdam: Elsevier.

McConnell, K.E. and I. Strand. 1981. "Measuring the cost of time in recreation demand analysis: an application to sportfishing." *American Journal of Agricultural Economics*. 63: 153–6.

McFadden, D. 1973. "Conditional logit analysis of discrete choice behavior." In P. Zarembka, ed. *Frontiers of Econometrics*. New York: Academic Press.

McFadden, D.L. 2001. "Economic choices." *American Economic Review*. 91: 351–78.

McGartland, A. and W. Oates. 1985. "Marketable permits for the prevention of environmental deterioration." *Journal of Environmental Economics and Management*. 12: 207–28.

Medema, S.G. 2014. "The Curious Treatment of the Coase Theorem in the Environmental Economics Literature." *Review of Environmental Economics and Policy*. 8: 39–57.

Mendelsohn, R. 1985. "Identifying structural equations with single market data." *Review of Economics and Statistics*. 67: 525–9.

Mendelsohn, R., W.D. Nordhaus, and D. Shaw. 1994. "The impact of global warming on agriculture: a Ricardian analysis." *American Economic Review*. 84: 753–71.

Mendelsohn, R. and M. Reinsborough. 2007. "A Ricardian analysis of US and Canadian farmland." *Climatic Change*. 81: 9–17.

Meran, G. and U. Schwalbe. 1987. "Pollution control and collective penalties." *Journal of Institutional and Theoretical Economics*. 143: 616–29.

Mérel, P. and E. Wimberger. 2012. "Improving air quality in California's San Joaquin Valley: The role of vehicle heterogeneity in optimal emissions abatement." *Journal of Environmental Economics and Management*. 63: 169–86.

Metcalf, G. 2009. "Designing a carbon tax to reduce US greenhouse gas emissions." *Review of Environmental Economics and Policy*. 3: 63–83.

Milliman, S.R. and R. Prince. 1989. "Firm incentives to promote technological change in pollution control." *Journal of Environmental Economics and Management*. 17: 247–65.

Millimet, D.L. and J.A. List. 2004. "The Case of the Missing Pollution Haven Hypothesis." *Journal of Regulatory Economics*. 26: 239–62.

Millock, K. and T. Sterner. 2004. "NO_x Emissions in France and Sweden: Advanced fee schemes versus regulations." Chapter 5 in W. Harrington, R.D. Morgenstern, and T. Sterner, eds. *Choosing Environmental Policy – Comparing Instruments and Outcomes in the United States and Europe*. Washington, DC: Resources for the Future.

Milman, O. 2015. "James Hansen, father of climate change awareness, calls Paris talks 'a fraud'." *The Guardian*. December 12, 2015.

Miranda, M.J. and P.L. Fackler. 2002. *Applied Computational Economics and Finance*. Cambridge, MA: MIT Press.

Misiolek, W. 1980. "Effluent Taxation in Monopoly Markets." *Journal of Environmental Economics and Management*. 7: 103–07.

Misiolek, W.S. and H.W. Elder. 1989. "Exclusionary Manipulation of Markets for Pollution Rights." *Journal of Environmental Economics and Management*. 16: 156–66.

Mitchell, R.C. and R.T. Carson. 1989. *Using Surveys to Value Public Goods: The Contingent Valuation Method*. Washington, DC: Resources for the Future.

Moeltner, K, K.J. Boyle, and R.W. Paterson. 2007. "Meta-analysis and benefit transfer for resource valuation-addressing classical challenges with Bayesian modeling." *Journal of Environmental Economics and Management*. 53: 250–69.

Moeltner, K. and J. Englin. 2004. "Choice Behavior Under Time-Variant Quality." *Journal of Business & Economic Statistics*. 22: 214–24.

Moeltner, K. and R. von Haefen. 2011. "Microeconometric Strategies for Dealing with Unobservables and Endogenous Variables in Recreation Demand Models." *Annual Review of Resource Economics*. 3: 375–96.

Montero J.P. 2002a. "Permits, standards, and technology innovation." *Journal of Environmental Economics and Management*. 44: 23–44.

Montero, J.P. 2002b. "Prices versus quantities with incomplete enforcement." *Journal of Public Economics*. 85: 435–54.

Montero, J.P. 2008. "A simple auction mechanism for the optimal allocation of the commons." *American Economic Review*. 98: 496–518.

Montgomery, W.D. 1972. "Markets in Licenses and Efficient Pollution Control Programs." *Journal of Economic Theory*. 5: 395–418.

Moore, R.B., C.M. Johnston, R.A. Smith, and B. Milstead. 2011. "Source and delivery of nutrients to receiving waters in the northeastern and mid-Atlantic regions of the United States." *Journal of the American Water Resources Association.* 47: 965–90.

Mørch von der Fehr, N-H. 1993. "Tradable Emission Rights and Strategic Interaction." *Environmental and Resource Economics.* 3: 129–51.

Moretti, E. and M. Neidell. 2011. "Pollution, Health, and Avoidance Behavior. Evidence from the Ports of Los Angeles." *The Journal of Human Resources.* 46: 154–75.

Morgenstern, R.D., W.P. Pizer, and J.S. Shih. 2001. "The cost of environmental protection." *Review of Economics and Statistics.* 83: 732–8.

Morrison, G.C. 1998. "Understanding the disparity between WTP and WTA: endowment effect, substitutability, or imprecise preferences?" *Economics Letters.* 59: 198–94.

Moslener, U. and T. Requate. 2007. "Optimal Abatement in Dynamic Multi-Pollutant Problems when Pollutants are Complements or Substitutes." *Journal of Economic Dynamics and Control.* 31: 2293–316.

Moslener, U. and T. Requate. 2009. "The Dynamics of Optimal Abatement Strategies for Interacting Pollutants – An Illustration in the Greenhouse." *Ecological Economics.* 86: 1521–34.

Muehlenbachs, L., E. Spiller, and C. Timmins. 2015. "The Housing Market Impacts of Shale Gas Development." *American Economic Review.* 105: 3633–59.

Muehlenbachs, L., S. Staubli, and M.A. Cohen. 2016. "The impact of team inspections on enforcement and deterrence." *Journal of the Association of Environmental and Resource Economists.* 3: 159–204.

Muller, N.Z. and R. Mendelsohn. 2009. "Efficient pollution regulation: getting the prices right." *American Economic Review.* 99: 1714–39.

Muller, N.Z. and R. Mendelsohn. 2012. *Using Marginal Damages in Environmental Policy: A Study of Air Pollution in the United States.* Washington, DC: AEI (American Enterprise Institute) Press.

Murdock, J. 2006. "Handling unobserved site characteristics in random utility models of recreation demand." *Journal of Environmental Economics and Management.* 51: 1–25.

Murphy, J.J., T.H. Stevens, and L. Yadav. 2010. "A Comparison of Induced Value and Home-Grown Value Experiments to Test for Hypothetical Bias in Contingent Valuation." *Environmental Resource Economics.* 47: 111–23.

Murray, B.C., R.G. Newell, and W.A. Pizer. 2009. "Balancing cost and emissions certainty: an allowance reserve for cap and trade." *Review of Environmental Economics and Policy.* 3: 84–103.

Neill, J.R. 1988. "Another Theorem on Using Market Demands to Determine Willingness to Pay for Non-traded Goods." *Journal of Environmental Economics and Management.* 15: 224–32.

Nelson, J.P. and P.E. Kennedy. 2009. "The Use (and Abuse) of Meta-Analysis in Environmental and Natural Resource Economics: An Assessment." *Environmental and Resource Economics.* 42: 345–77.

Nevo, A. and M.D. Whinston. 2010. "Taking the Dogma out of Econometrics: Structural Modeling and Credible Inference." *Journal of Economic Perspectives.* 24: 69–82.

Newell, R.G. and W.A. Pizer. 2003. "Regulating stock externalities under uncertainty." *Journal of Environmental Economics and Management.* 45: 416–32.

Newell, R.G. and K. Rogers. 2004. "Leaded gasoline in the United States: the breakthrough of permit trading." Chapter 8 in W. Harrington, R.D. Morgenstern, and T. Sterner, eds. *Choosing Environmental Policy – Comparing Instruments and Outcomes in the United States and Europe.* Washington, DC: Resources for the Future.

Newell, R.G., J.N. Sanchirico, and S. Kerr. 2005. "Fishing quota markets." *Journal of Environmental Economics and Management.* 49: 437–62.

Newell, R.G. and J. Siikamäki. 2014. "Nudging Energy Efficiency Behavior: The Role of Information Labels." *Journal of the Association of Environmental and Resource Economists.* 1: 555–98.

Nordhaus, W. 2013a. "Integrated Economic and Climate Modeling." In P.B. Dixon and D.W. Jorgenson, eds. *Handbook of Computable General Equilibrium Modeling.* North Holland, Elsevier B.V. 1069–131.

Nordhaus, W. 2013b. *The Climate Casino: Risk, Uncertainty, and Economics for a Warming World.* New Haven, CT: Yale University Press.

Nordhaus, W. 2014. "Estimates of the Social Cost of Carbon: Concepts and Results from the DICE-2013R Model and Alternative Approaches." *Journal of the Association of Environmental and Resource Economists.* 1: 273–312.

Nordhaus, W.D. 2007a. "To tax or not to tax: alternative approaches to slowing global warming." *Review of Environmental Economics and Policy.* 1: 26–44.

Nordhaus, W.D. 2007b. "Review: A Review of the *Stern Review on the Economics of Climate Change.*" *Journal of Economic Literature.* 45: 686–702.

Nordhaus, W.D. and P. Sztorc. 2013. *DICE2013R: Introduction and User's Manual 2nd Edition.* Downloaded from www.econ.yale.edu/%7Enordhaus/homepage/documents/DICE_Manual_100413r1.pdf

Olmstead, S.M. and H. Sigman. 2015. "Damming the Commons: An Empirical Analysis of International Cooperation and Conflict in Dam Location." *Journal of the Association of Environmental and Resource Economists.* 2: 497–526.

Olsen, J.R. and J.S. Shortle. 1996. "The Optimal Control of Emissions and Renewable Resource Harvesting under Uncertainty." *Environmental and Resource Economics.* 7: 97–115.

Palmquist, R.B. 1982. "Measuring environmental effects on property values without hedonic regressions." *Journal of Urban Economics.* 11: 333–47.

Palmquist, R.B. 1991. "Hedonic methods." In J. Braden and C. Kolstad, eds. *Measuring the Demand for Environmental Quality.* Amsterdam: North-Holland.

Palmquist, R.B. 1992a. "Valuing Localized Externalities." *Journal of Urban Economics.* 31: 59–68.

Palmquist, R.B. 1992b. "A Note on Transactions Costs, Moving Costs, and Benefit Measurement." *Journal of Urban Economics.* 32: 40–44.

Palmquist, R.B. 2005a. "Weak complementarity, path independence, and the intuition of the Willig condition." *Journal of Environmental Economics and Management.* 49: 103–15.

Palmquist, R.B. 2005b. "Property value models." Chapter 16 in K.-G. Mäler and J. Vincent, eds. *Handbook of Environmental Economics 2.* Amsterdam: Elsevier.

Palmquist, R.B. and A. Israngkura. 1999. "Valuing air quality with hedonic and discrete choice models." *American Journal of Agricultural Economics.* 81: 1128–33.

Palmquist, R.B. and D.J. Phaneuf. 2010. "Short Run Constraints and the Increasing Marginal Value of Time in Recreation." *Environmental Resource Economics.* 46: 19–41.

Parmeter, C. and J.C. Pope. 2012. "Quasi-Experiments and Hedonic Property Value Methods" In J.A. List and M.K. Price, eds. *Handbook on Experimental Economics and the Environment.* Southampton: Edward Elgar.

Parry, I.W.H. 1995a. "Optimal pollution taxes and endogenous technological progress." *Resource and Energy Economics.* 17: 69–85.

Parry, I.W.H. 1995b. "Pollution Taxes and Revenue Recycling." *Journal of Environmental Economics and Management.* 29: 64–77.

Parry, I.W.H. and A.M. Bento. 2000. "Tax Deductions, Environmental Policy, and the 'Double Dividend' Hypothesis." *Journal of Environmental Economics and Management.* 39: 67–96.

Parry, I.W.H., J. Norregaard, and D. Heine. 2012. "Environmental Tax Reform: Principles from Theory and Practice." *Annual Review of Resource Economics.* 4: 101–283.

Parry, I.W.H., R.C. Williams III, and L.H. Goulder. 1999. "When Can Carbon Abatement Policies Increase Welfare? The Fundamental Role of Distorted Factor Markets." *Journal of Environmental Economics and Management.* 37: 52–84.

Parsons, G.R. 2003. "The travel cost model." In P.A. Champ, K.J. Boyle, and T.C. Brown, eds. *A Primer on Non-Market Valuation.* Dordrecht: Springer.

Parsons, G.R., A.J. Plantinga, and Kevin J. Boyle. 2000. "Narrow Choice Sets in a Random Utility Model." *Land Economics.* 76: 86–99.

Peirce, J., R.F. Weiner, and P. Vesilind. 1998. *Environmental Pollution and Control.* 4th edition. Woburn, MA: Butterworth-Heinemann.

Perino, G. 2008. "The merits of new pollutants and how to get them when patents are granted." *Environmental and Resource Economics.* 40: 313–27.

Perino, G. 2010. "Technology Diffusion with Market Power in the Upstream Industry." *Environmental and Resource Economics.* 46: 403–28.

Perino, G. and T. Requate. 2012. "Does more stringent environmental regulation induce or reduce technology adoption? When the rate of adoption is inverted U-shaped." *Journal of Environmental Economics and Management.* 64: 456–67.

Perrings, C. 2014. "Environment and development economics 20 years on." *Environment and Development Economics.* 19: 333–66.

Phaneuf, D.J. 2013. "Heterogeneity in environmental demand." *Annual Review of Resource Economics.* 5: 227–44.

Phaneuf, D.J., J.C. Carbone, and J.A. Herriges. 2009. "Non-price equilibria for non-marketed goods." *Journal of Environmental Economics and Management.* 57: 45–64.

Phaneuf, D.J., C.L. Kling, and J.A. Herriges. 2000. "Estimation and welfare calculations in a generalized corner solution model with an application to recreation demand." *Review of Economics and Statistics.* 82: 83–92.

Phaneuf, D.J. and T. Requate. 2002. "Incentives for Investment in Advanced Pollution Abatement Technology in Emission Permit Markets with Banking." *Environmental and Resource Economics.* 22: 369–90.

Phaneuf, D.J. and V.K. Smith. 2005. *Recreation demand models.* Chapter 15 in K.-G. Mäler and J. Vincent, eds. *Handbook of Environmental Economics 2.* Amsterdam: Elsevier.

Phaneuf, D.J., V.K. Smith, R.B. Palmquist, and J.C. Pope. 2008. "Integrating property value and local recreation models to value ecosystem services in urban watersheds." *Land Economics.* 84: 361–81.

Phaneuf, D.J., L.O. Taylor, and J. B. Braden. 2013. "Combining revealed and stated preference data to estimate preferences for residential amenities: A GMM approach." *Land Economics.* 89: 30–52.

Phaneuf, D.J. and G. Van Houtven. 2015. "Structural benefit transfer using Bayesian econometrics." Chapter 23 in Johnston, R.J., J. Rolfe, R.S. Rosenberger, and R. Brouwer, eds. *Benefit Transfer of Environmental and Resource Values: A Guide for Researchers and Practitioners.* Dordrecht: Springer.

Phaneuf, D.J. and R. von Haefen. 2009. "Estimating the demand for quality with discrete choice models." Chapter 12 in D. Slottje, ed. *Quantifying Consumer Preferences.* Bingley, UK: Emerald Group Publishing.

Phaneuf, D.J., R. von Haefen, C. Mansfield, and G. Van Houtven. 2013. "Measuring nutrient reduction benefits for policy analysis using linked non-market valuation and environmental assessment models." Report to the US EPA, Office of Water.

Pigou, A.C. 1920. *The Economics of Welfare.* London: Macmillan and Company.

Pigou, A.C. 1932. *The Economics of Welfare,* 4th edition. London: Macmillan and Company.

Pindyck, R.S. 2007. "Uncertainty in environmental economics." *Review of Environmental Economics and Policy.* 1: 45–65.

Pindyck, R.S. 2013. "Climate change policy: what do the models tell us?" *Journal of Economic Literature.* 51: 860–72.

Pitchford, R. 1995. "How Liable Should a Lender Be? The Case of Judgment-Proof Firms and Environmental Risk." *American Economics Review.* 85: 1171–86.

Pizer, W.A. and R. Kopp. 2005. "Calculating the Costs of Environmental Regulation." Chapter 25 in K.-G. Mäler and J.R. Vincent, eds. *Handbook of Environmental Economics 3.* Amsterdam: Elsevier B.V.

Plott, C.R. and K. Zeiler. 2005. "The willingness to pay-willing to accept gap, the endowment effect, subject misconceptions, and experimental procedures for eliciting valuations." *American Economic Review.* 95: 530–45.

Polinsky, A.M. and Shavell, S. 1991. "A Note on Optimal Fines When Wealth Varies Among Individuals." *American Economic Review.* 81: 618–21.

Pope, J.C. 2008a. "Buyer information and the hedonic: The impact of a seller disclosure on the implicit price for airport noise." *Journal of Urban Economics.* 63: 498–516.

Pope, J.C. 2008b. "Do seller disclosures affect property values? Buyer information and the hedonic model." *Land Economics.* 84: 551–72.

Popp, D. 2002. "Induced Innovation and Energy Prices." *The American Economic Review.* 92: 160–80.

Popp, D. 2003. "Pollution Control Innovations and the Clean Air Act of 1990." *Journal of Policy Analysis and Management.* 22: 641–60.

Popp, D. 2004. "ENTICE: endogenous technological change in the DICE model of global warming." *Journal of Environmental Economics and Management.* 48:742–68.

Popp, D. 2010a. "Innovation and Climate Policy." *The Annual Review of Resource Economics.* 2: 275–98.

Popp, D. 2010b. "Exploring links between innovation and diffusion: adoption of NOX control technologies at U.S. coal-fired power plants." *Environmental and Resource Economics*, 45: 319–52.

Popp, D., I. Hascic, and N. Medhi. 2011. "Technology and the diffusion of renewable energy." *Energy Economics*, 33: 648–62.

Portney, P.R. 1994. "The Contingent Valuation Debate: Why Economists Should Care." *The Journal of Economic Perspectives.* 8: 3–17.

Posner, R.A. 1972. *Economics Analysis of Law. 1st Edition.* Boston: Little, Brown, and Company.

Prasenjit, B. and J.F. Shogren. 2012. "Material interests, moral reputation, and crowding out species protection on private land." *Journal of Environmental Economics and Management.* 63: 137–49.

Provencher, B. and R.C. Bishop. 1997. "An estimable dynamic model of recreation behavior with an application to Great Lakes angling." *Journal of Environmental Economics and Management.* 33: 107–27.

Quirion, P. 2004. "Prices versus quantities in a second best setting." *Environmental and Resource Economics.* 29: 337–60.

Ramsey, F.P. 1928. "A Mathematical Theory of Saving." *The Economic Journal.* 38: 543–59.

Randall, A. and J.R. Stoll. 1980. "Consumer's surplus in commodity space." *American Economic Review.* 70: 449–55.

Rauscher, M. 1994. "On Ecological Dumping." *Oxford Economic Papers.* 46: 822–40.

Rauscher, M. 1997. *International Trade, Factor Movements and the Environment.* Oxford University Press.

Reichenbach, J. and T. Requate. 2012. "Subsidies for renewable energies in the presence of learning effects and market power." *Resource and Energy Economics.* 34: 236–54.

Reichhuber, A., E. Camacho, and T. Requate. 2009. "A framed field experiment on collective enforcement mechanisms with Ethiopian farmers." *Environment and Development Economics.* 14: 641–63.

Requate, T. 1993a. "Equivalence of effluent taxes and permits for environmental regulation of several local monopolies." *Economics Letters.* 42: 91–5.

Requate, T. 1993b. "Pollution Control under Imperfect Competition: Asymmetric Bertrand Duopoly under Linear Technologies." *Journal of Institutional and Theoretical Economics.* 149: 415–42.

Requate, T. 1993c. "Pollution Control in a Cournot Duopoly via Taxes or Permits." *Journal of Economics.* 58: 255–91.

Requate, T. 1997. "Green Taxes in Oligopoly if the Number of Firms Is Endogenous." *Finanzarchiv.* 54: 261–80.

Requate, T. 2005. "Timing and Commitment of Environmental Policy. Adoption of New Technology, and Repercussions on R&D." *Environmental and Resource Economics.* 31: 175–99.

Requate, T. 2006. "Environmental Policy under Imperfect Competition." In H. Folmer and T. Tietenberg, eds. *The International Yearbook of Environmental and Resource Economics 2006/2007.* Cheltenham: Edward Elgar.

Requate, T. 2013. "Prices versus Quantities." Chapter 27 in J.F. Shogren, ed. *Encyclopedia of Energy, Natural Resource, and Environmental Economics 3.* Amsterdam: Elsevier.

Requate, T. 2015. "Green tradable certificates versus feed-in tariffs in the promotion of renewable energy shares." *Environmental Economics and Policy Studies.* 17: 211–39.

Requate, T. and A. Lange. 2000. "Pigouvian Taxes in General Equilibrium with a Fixed Tax Redistribution Rule." *Journal of Public Economic Theory.* 2: 25–42.

Requate, T., and W. Unold. 2001. "On the incentives created by policy instruments to adopt advanced abatement technology if firms are asymmetric." *Journal of Institutional and Theoretical Economics.* 157: 536–54.

Requate, T. and W. Unold. 2003. "Environmental policy incentives to adopt advanced abatement technology: will the true ranking please stand up?" *European Economic Review.* 47: 125–46.

Ricardo, D. 1817. *On the Principles of Political Economy and Taxation.* London: John Murray.

Rico, R. 1995. "The US Allowance Trading System for Sulfur Dioxide: An Update on Market Experience." *Environmental and Resource Economics.* 5: 115–29.

Roback, J. 1982. "Wages, Rents, and the Quality of Life." *Journal of Political Economy.* 90: 1257–78.

Roberts, M.J. and M. Spence. 1976. "Effluent charges and licenses under uncertainty." *Journal of Public Economics.* 5: 193–208.

Rohlfs, C., R. Sullivan, and T. Kniesner. 2015. "New Estimates of the Value of a Statistical Life Using Air Bag Regulations as a Quasi-Experiment." *American Economic Journal: Economic Policy.* 7: 331–59.

Rolfe, J., J. Bennett, and G. Kerr. 2015. "Applied benefit transfer: an Australian and New Zealand policy perspective." Chapter 5 in Johnston, R.J., J. Rolfe, R.S. Rosenberger, and R. Brouwer, eds. *Benefit Transfer of Environmental and Resource Values: A Guide for Researchers and Practitioners.* Dordrecht: Springer.

Rosen, S. 1974. "Hedonic price and implicit markets: product differentiation in pure competition." *Journal of Political Economy.* 82: 34–55.

Rosenberger, R.S. 2015. "Benefit transfer validity and reliability." Chapter 14 in Johnston, R.J., J. Rolfe, R.S. Rosenberger, and R. Brouwer, eds. *Benefit Transfer of Environmental and Resource Values: A Guide for Researchers and Practitioners.* Dordrecht: Springer.

Rutherford, T.F. 1995. "Extension of GAMS for complementary problems arising in applied economics analysis." *Journal of Economic Dynamics and Control.* 19: 1299–324.

Salop, S. 1979. "Monopolistic Competition with Outside Goods." *The Bell Journal of Economics.* 10: 141–56.

Samuelson, P.A. 1954a. "The pure theory of public expenditures." *Review of Economics and Statistics.* 36: 387–9.

Samuelson, P.A. 1954b. "The Theory of Public Expenditure." *Review of Economics and Statistics.* 36: 386–9.

Sartzetakis, E.S. 1997. "Raising Rivals' Costs Strategies via Emission Permits Markets." *Review of Industrial Organization.* 12: 751–65.

Scarpa, R., M. Thiene, and D.A. Hensher. 2010. "Monitoring Choice Task Attribute Attendance in Non-market Valuation of Multiple Park Management Services: Does it Matter?" *Land Economics.* 86: 817–39.

Schaffner, S. and H. Spengler. 2010. "Using job changes to evaluate the bias of value of a statistical life estimates." *Resource and Energy Economics.* 32: 15–27.

Schlenker, W. and M.J. Roberts. 2006. "Nonlinear Effects of Weather on Corn Yields." *Review of Agricultural Economics.* 28: 391–8.

Schlenker, W. and M.J. Roberts. 2009. "Nonlinear temperature effects indicate severe damages to U.S. crop yields under climate change." *Proceedings of the National Academy of Sciences of the USA.* 106: 15594–98.

Schmalensee, R. and R. Stavins. 2013. "The SO2 Allowance Trading System: The Ironic History of a Grand Policy Experiment." *Journal of Economic Perspectives.* 27: 103–22.

Schwartz, A. 1985. "Products Liability, Corporate Structure, and Bankruptcy: Toxic Substances and the Remote Risk Relationship." *The Journal of Legal Studies.* 14: 689–736.

Schwartz, J. and R. Repetto. 2000. "Nonseparable Utility and the Double Dividend Debate: Reconsidering the Tax-Interaction Effect." *Environmental and Resource Economics.* 15: 149–57.

Schweizer, U. 1988. "Externalities and the Coase Theorem: hypothesis or result?" *Journal of Institutional and Theoretical Economics.* 144: 254–66.

Scotton, C.R. and L.O. Taylor. 2011. "Valuing risk reductions: Incorporating risk heterogeneity into a revealed preference framework." *Resource and Energy Economics.* 33: 381–97.

Segerson, K. 1988. "Uncertainty and the incentives for nonpoint pollution control." *Journal of Environmental Economics and Management.* 15: 87–98.

Seierstad, A. and K. Sydsaeter. 1977. "Sufficient Conditions in Optimal Control Theory." *International Economic Review.* 18: 367–91.

Seierstad, A. and K. Sydsaeter. 1987. *Optimal Control Theory with Economic Applications.* Amsterdam: North Holland.

Selden, T.M. and D. Song. 1994. "Environmental Quality and Development: Is there a Kuznets Curve for Air Pollution Emissions?" *Journal of Environmental Economics and Management.* 27: 147–62.

Shavell, S. 1980. "Strict Liability versus Neglience." *Journal of Legal Studies.* 9: 1–25.

Shavell, S. 1982. "On Liability and Insurance." *Bell Journal of Economics.* 13: 120–32.

Shavell, S. 1986. "The Judgment Proof Problem." *International Review of Law and Economics.* 6: 45–58.

Shavell, S. 1987. *Economic Analysis of Accident Law.* Cambridge, MA: Harvard University Press.

Shaw, D. 1988. "On-site sample regression: problems of non-negative integers, truncation, and endogenous stratification." *Journal of Econometrics.* 37: 211–23.

Shaw, W.D. and R.T. Woodward. 2008. "Why environmental and resource economists should care about non-expected utility models." *Resource and Energy Economics.* 30: 66–89.

Sheriff, G. 2008. "Optimal environmental regulation of politically influential sectors with asymmetric information." *Journal of Environmental Economics and Management.* 55: 72–89.

Shimshack, J. 2014. "The economics of environmental monitoring and enforcement." *Annual Review of Resource Economics.* 6: 339–60.

Shimshack, J.P. and M.B. Ward. 2005. "Regulator reputation, enforcement, and environmental compliance." *Journal of Environmental Economics and Management.* 50: 519–40.

Shogren, J.F., S.Y. Shin, D.J. Hayes, and J.B. Kliebenstein. 1994. "Resolving differences in willingness to pay and willingness to accept." *American Economic Review.* 84: 225–70.

Shortle, J.S. and J. Braden. 2013. "Economics of Nonpoint Pollution." In J. Shogren *Encyclopedia of Energy, Natural Resource, and Environmental Economics.* Amsterdam: Elsevier.

Shortle, J.S. and R.D. Horan. 2001. "The economics of nonpoint pollution control." *Journal of Economic Surveys.* 15: 255–89.

Siebert, H. 1995. *The Economics of the Environment, Theory and Policy.* Berlin, Heidelberg: Springer.

Sieg, H., V.K. Smith, H.S. Banzhaf, and R. Walsh. 2004. "Estimating the General Equilibrium Benefits of Large Changes in Spatially Delineated Public Goods." *International Economic Review.* 45: 1047–77.

Sigman, H. 2002. "International Spillovers and Water Quality in Rivers: Do Countries Free Ride?" *The American Economic Review.* 92: 1152–9.

Simpson, D. 1995. "Optimal Pollution Taxation in a Cournot Duopoly." *Environmental and Resource Economics.* 6: 359–69.

Sinn, H.W. 2008. "Public Policies against Global Warming: A Supply Side Approach." *International Tax and Public Finance.* 15: 360–94.

Slesnick, D.T. 1998. "Empirical approaches to the measurement of welfare." *Journal of Economic Literature.* 36: 2108–65.

Small, K.A. and H.S. Rosen. 1981. "Applied Welfare Economics with Discrete Choice Models." *Econometrica.* 49: 105–30.

Smith, V.K. 1992. "On separating defensible benefit transfers from smoke and mirrors." *Water Resources Research.* 28: 685–94.

Smith, V.K. 2006. "Fifty years of contingent valuation." Chapter 2 in A. Alberini and J.R. Kahn, eds. *Handbook on Contingent Valuation.* Northampton, MA: Edward Elgar.

Smith, V.K. and H.S. Banzhaf. 2004. "A diagrammatic exposition of weak complementarity and the Willig condition." *American Journal of Agricultural Economics.* 86: 455–66.

Smith, V.K. and H.S. Banzhaf. 2007. "Quality adjusted price indexes and the Willig condition." *Economics Letters.* 94: 43–8.

Smith, V.K., S.K. Pattanayak, and G.L. Van Houtven. 2006. "Structural benefit transfer: An example using VSL estimates." *Ecological Economics.* 60: 361–71.

Smith, V.K, C. Poulos, and K. Hyun. 2002. "Treating open space as an urban amenity." *Resource and Energy Economics.* 24: 107–29.

Smith, V.K., H. Sieg, H.S. Banzhaf, and R.P. Walsh. 2004. "General equilibrium benefits for environmental improvements: Projected ozone reductions under EPA's Prospective Analysis for the Los Angeles air basin." *Journal of Environmental Economics and Management.* 47: 559–84.

Smith, V.K., G. Van Houtven, and S.K. Pattanayak. 2002. "Benefit Transfer via Preference Calibration: 'Prudential Algebra' for Policy." *Land Economics*. 78: 132–52.

Spence, M. 2002. "Signaling in retrospect and the informational structure of markets." *American Economic Review*. 92: 434–59.

Spraggon, J. 2002. "Exogenous targeting instruments as a solution to group moral hazards." *Journal of Public Economics*. 84: 427–56.

Spraggon, J. 2004. "Testing ambient pollution instruments with heterogeneous agents." *Journal of Environmental Economics and Management*. 48: 837–56.

Spulber, D.F. 1985. "Effluent regulation and long run optimality." *Journal of Environmental Economics and Management*. 12: 103–16.

Stapler, R.W. and R.J. Johnston. 2009. "Meta-analysis, benefit transfer, and methodological covariates: implications for transfer error." *Environmental and Resource Economics*. 42: 227–46.

Starrett, D.A. 1972. "Fundamental non-convexities in the theory of externalities." *Journal of Economic Theory*. 4: 180–99.

Stavins, R.N. 1995. "Transaction Costs and Tradeable Permits." *Journal of Environmental Economics and Management*. 29: 133–48.

Stavins, R.N. 1996. "Correlated uncertainty and policy instrument choice." *Journal of Environmental Economics and Management*. 30: 218–32.

Stavins, R.N. 1998. "What Can we Learn from the Grand Policy Experiment? Lessons from SO2 Allowance Trading." *The Journal of Economic Perspectives*. 12: 69–88.

Sterner, T. and U.M. Persson. 2008. "An Even Sterner Review: Introducing Relative Prices into the Discounting Debate." *Review of Environmental Economics and Policy*. 2: 61–76.

Stiglitz, J.E. 2002. "Information and the change in the paradigm in economics." *American Economic Review*. 92: 460–501.

Stokey, N.L, R.E. Lucas, and E.C. Prescott. 1989. *Recursive Methods in Economic Dynamics*. Cambridge, MA: Harvard University Press.

Stranlund, J.K. 2007. "The regulatory choice of noncompliance in emissions trading programs." *Environmental and Resource Economics*. 38: 99–117.

Stranlund, J.K., C.A. Chávez, and M.G. Villena. 2009. "The optimal pricing of pollution when enforcement is costly." *Journal of Environmental Economics and Management*. 58: 183–91.

Stranlund, J.K. and K.K. Dhanda. 1999. "Endogenous monitoring and enforcement of a transferable emissions permit system." *Journal of Environmental Economics and Management*. 38: 267–82.

Suter, J.F., J.M. Spraggon, and G.L. Poe. 2013. "Thin and lumpy: an experimental investigation of water quality trading." *Water Resource and Economics*. 1: 36–60.

Suter, J.F. and C.A. Vossler. 2014. "Towards an Understanding of the Performance of Ambient Tax Mechanisms in the Field: Evidence from Upstate New York Dairy Farmers." *American Journal of Agricultural Economics*. 96(1): 92–107.

Suter, J.F., C.A. Vossler, and G.L. Poe. 2009. "Ambient-based pollution mechanisms: A comparison of homogeneous and heterogeneous groups of emitters." *Ecological Economics*. 68: 1883–92.

Suter, J.F., C.A. Vossler, G.L. Poe, and K. Segerson. 2008. "Experiments on damage-based ambient taxes for nonpoint source polluters." *American Journal of Agricultural Economics*. 90: 86–102.

Swierzbinski, J.E. 1994. "Guilty until proven innocent – regulation with costly and limited enforcement." *Journal of Environmental Economics and Management*. 27: 127–46.

Tahvonen, O. 1997. "Fossil Fuels, Stock Externalities, and Backstop Technology." *The Canadian Journal of Economics*. 30: 855–74.

Taylor, L.O. 2003. "The hedonic method." In P.A. Champ, K.J. Boyle, and T.C. Brown, eds. *A Primer on Non-Market Valuation*. Dordrecht: Springer.

Taylor, L.O., D.J. Phaneuf, and X. Liu. 2016. "Disentangling property value impacts of environmental contaminants from locally undesirable land uses: implications for measuring post-cleanup stigma." *Journal of Urban Economics*, in press.

Teisl, M.F., B. Roe, and R.L. Hicks. 2002. "Can Eco-Labels Tune a Market? Evidence from Dolphin-Safe Labeling." *Journal of Environmental Economics and Management*. 43: 339–59.

Tiebout, C.M. 1956. "A pure theory of local expenditures." *Journal of Political Economy*. 64: 416–24.

Tietenberg, T.H. 1980. "Transferable Discharge Permits and the Control of Stationary Source Air Pollution: A Survey and Synthesis." *Land Economics.* 56: 391–416.

Tietenberg, T.H. 2006. *Emissions Trading: Principles and Practice.* 2nd edition. Washington, DC: Resources for the Future.

Timmins, C. and J. Murdock. 2007. "A revealed preference approach to the measurement of congestion in travel cost models." *Journal of Environmental Economics and Management.* 53: 230–49.

Timmins, C. and W. Schlenker. 2009. "Reduced-Form Versus Structural Modeling in Environmental and Resource Economics." *Annual Review of Resource Economics.* 1: 351–80.

Tinbergen, J. 1952. "On the Theory of Economic Policy." 2nd edition. *Volume 1 of Contributions to Economic Analysis.* Amsterdam: North-Holland.

Tinbergen, J. 1956. *Economic Policy, Principles, and Design.* Amsterdam: North-Holland.

Tirole, J.J. and J. Laffont. 1993. *The theory of incentives in procurement and regulation.* Cambridge, MA: MIT Press.

Tol, R.S.J. 2009. "The economics effects of climate change." *Journal of Economic Perspectives.* 23: 29–51.

Tol, R.S.J. 2014. *Climate Economics: Economic Analysis of Climate, Climate Change, and Climate Policy.* Northampton, MA: Edward Elgar.

Traeger, C.P. 2013. "Discounting under uncertainty: Disentangling the Weitzman and the Gollier effect." *Journal of Environmental Economics and Management.* 66: 573–82.

Traeger, C.P. 2014. "Why uncertainty matters: discounting under intertemporal risk aversion and ambiguity." *Economic Theory.* 56: 627–64.

Train, K.E. 1998. "Recreation Demand Models with Taste Differences over People." *Land Economics.* 74: 230–9.

Train, K.E. 2009. *Discrete Choice Methods with Simulation*, 2nd edition. New York: Cambridge University Press.

Tunçel, T. and J.K. Hammitt. 2014. "A new meta-analysis on the WTP/WTA disparity." *Journal of Environmental Economics and Management.* 68: 175–87.

United Nations Treaty Collection. 2015. 7. d Paris Agreement, Paris, December 12, 2015.

Unold, W. and T. Requate. 2001. "Pollution control by options trading." *Economics Letters.* 73: 353–8.

van der Ploeg, F. 2016. "Second-best carbon taxation in the global economy. The Green Paradox and Carbon Leakage Revisited." *Journal of Environmental Economics and Management.* 78: 85–105.

Van Houtven, G., C. Mansfield, D.J. Phaneuf, R. von Haefen, B. Milstead, M.A. Kenney, and K.H. Reckhow. 2014. "Combining expert elicitation and stated preference methods to value ecosystem services from improved lake water quality." *Ecological Economics.* 99: 40–52.

van't Veld, K. 2006. "Hazardous-Industry Restructuring to Avoid Liability for Accidents." *International Review of Law and Economics.* 26: 297–322.

van't Veld, K. and E. Hutchinson. 2009. "Excessive Spending by Firms to Avoid Accidents: Is it a Concern of Practice?" *International Review of Law and Economics.* 29: 324–35.

Vartia, Y.O. 1983. "Efficient methods of measuring welfare change and compensated income in terms of ordinary demand functions." *Econometrica.* 51: 79–98.

Vidovic, M. and Khanna, N. 2012. "Is Voluntary Pollution Abatement in the Absence of a Carrot or Stick Effective? Evidence from Facility Participation in the EPA's 33/50 Program." *Environmental Resource Economics.* 52: 369–93.

Viscusi, W.K. 1993. "The Value of Risks to Life and Health." *Journal of Economic Literature.* 31: 1912–46.

Viscusi, W.K. 2004. "The Value of Life: Estimates with Risks by Occupation and Industry." *Economic Inquiry.* 42: 29–48.

Viscusi, W.K. and T. Gayer. 2005. "Quantifying and Valuing Environmental Health Risks." Chapter 20 in K.-G. Mäler and J.R. Vincent, eds. *Handbook of Environmental Economics 2.* Amsterdam. Elsevier B.V.

von Haefen, R.H. 2002. "A complete characterization of the linear, log-linear, and semi-log demand system models." *Journal of Agricultural and Resource Economics.* 27: 281–319.

von Haefen, R.H. 2003. "Incorporating observed choice into the construction of welfare measures from random utility models." *Journal of Environmental Economics and Management*. 45: 145–65.

von Haefen, R.H. 2007. "Empirical strategies for incorporating weak complementarity into consumer demand models." *Journal of Environmental Economics and Management*. 54: 15–31.

von Haefen, R.H. and D.J. Phaneuf. 2003. "Estimating preferences for outdoor recreation: a comparison of continuous and count data demand system frameworks." *Journal of Environmental Economics and Management*. 45: 612–30.

von Haefen, R.H. and D.J. Phaneuf. 2005. "Kuhn-Tucker demand system approaches to non-market valuations." In A.R. Scarpa and A. Alberini, eds. *Applications of Simulation Methods in Environmental and Resource Economics*. New York: Springer.

von Haefen, R.H. and D.J. Phaneuf. 2008. "Identifying demand parameters in the presence of unobservables: A combined revealed and stated preference approach." *Journal of Environmental Economics and Management*. 56: 19–32.

von Haefen, R.H., D.J. Phaneuf, and G.R. Parsons. 2004. "Estimation and welfare analysis with large demand systems." *Journal of Business and Economic Statistics*. 22: 194–205.

von Stackelberg, K. and J. Hammitt. 2009. "Use of Contingent Valuation to Elicit Willingness-to-Pay for the Benefits of Developmental Health Risk Reductions." *Environmental Resource Economics*. 43: 45–61.

Vossler, C.A., M. Doyon, and D. Rondeau. 2012. "Truth in Consequentiality: Theory and Field Evidence on Discrete Choice Experiments." *American Economic Journal: Microeconomics*. 4: 145–71.

Vossler, C.A. and M. Evans. 2009. "Bridging the gap between the field and the lab: Environmental goods, policy maker input, and consequentiality." *Journal of Environmental Economics and Management*. 58: 338–45.

Vossler, C.A. and M. McKee. 2006. "Induced-Value Tests of Contingent Valuation Elicitation Mechanisms." *Environmental & Resource Economics*. 35: 137–68.

Vossler, C.A. and G.L. Poe. 2011. "Consequentiality and Contingent Values: An Emerging Paradigm." Chapter 7 in J. Bennett, ed. *International Handbook on Non-Market Environmental Valuation*. Northampton, MA: Edward Elgar.

Vossler, C.A., G.L. Poe, W.D. Schulze, and K. Segerson. 2006. "Communication and Incentive Mechanisms based on Group Performance: An Experimental Study of Nonpoint Pollution Control." *Economic Inquiry*. 44: 599–613.

Wales, T.J. and A.D. Woodland. 1983. "Estimation of consumer demand systems with binding nonnegativity constraints." *Journal of Econometrics*. 21: 263–85.

Walker, M. and D.J. Storey. 1977. "The 'Standard-and-Prices' approach: Problems of Iteration." *The Scandinavian Journal of Economics*. 79: 99–109.

Walker, W.R. 2013. "The Transitional Costs of Sectoral Reallocation: Evidence from the Clean Air Act and the Workforce." *The Quarterly Journal of Economics*. 128: 1787–835.

Wätzold, F. 2004. "SO_2 Emissions in Germany, Regulations to Fight Waldsterben." Chapter 1 in W. Harrington, R.D. Morgenstern, and T. Sterner, eds. *Choosing Environmental Policy – Comparing Instruments and Outcomes in the United States and Europe*. Washington, DC: Resources for the Future.

Weitzman, M.L. 1974. "Prices versus quantities." *Review of Economic Studies*. 41: 477–91.

Weitzman, M.L. 1998. "Why the Far-Distant Future Should Be Discounted at Its Lowest Possible Rate." *Journal of Environmental Economics and Management*. 36: 201–08.

Weitzman, M.L. 2001. "Gamma Discounting." *American Economic Review*. 91: 260–71.

Weitzman, M.L. 2007. "A Review of 'The Stern Review on the Economics of Climate Change'." *Journal of Economic Literature*. 45: 703–24.

Weitzman, M.L. 2010. "Risk-adjusted gamma discounting." *Journal of Environmental Economics and Management*. 60: 1–13.

Weitzman, M. and C. Gollier. 2010. "How Should the Distant Future be Discounted When Discount Rates are Uncertain?" *Economics Letters*. 107: 350–3.

West, S.E. and Williams III, R.C. 2007. "Optimal taxation and cross-price effects on labor supply: Estimates of the optimal gas tax." *Journal of Public Economics*. 91: 593–617.

Wheelan, C. 2011. *Introduction to Public Policy*. New York: W.W. Norton.

Whitehead, J.C. and T. Haab. 2013. "Contingent valuation method." In J. Shogren, ed. *Encyclopedia of Energy, Natural Resource, and Environmental Economics*. Amsterdam: Elsevier.

Whitehead, J.C., T. Haab, and J.C. Huang. 2011. *Preference Data for Environmental Valuation: Combining Revealed and Stated Approaches*. New York: Routledge.

Whitehead, J.C., S.K. Pattanayak, G. Van Houtven, and B.R. Gelso. 2008. "Combining revealed and stated preference data to estimate the non-market value of ecological services: an assessment of the state of the science." *Journal of Economic Surveys*. 22: 872–908.

Whitehead, J.C., D.J. Phaneuf, C.F. Dumas, J. Herstine, J. Hill, and B. Buerger. 2010. "Convergent Validity of Revealed and Stated Recreation Behavior with Quality Change: A Comparison of Multiple and Single Site Demands." *Environmental Resource Economics*. 45: 91–112.

Williams, R.C. III. 2003. "Health effects and optimal environmental taxes." *Journal of Public Economics*. 87: 323–35.

Willig, R.D. 1976. "Consumer's surplus without apology." *American Economic Review*. 66: 589–97.

Willig, R.D. 1978. "Incremental consumer's surplus and hedonic price adjustment." *Journal of Economic Theory*. 17: 227–53.

World Bank. 2002. "Water – the essence of life." *Development News*, May 17.

World Bank. 2013. *World Development Indicators*. Washington, DC: World Bank.

Xepapadeas, A.P. 1991. "Environmental Policy under Imperfect Information: Incentives and Moral Hazard." *Journal of Environmental Economics and Management*. 20: 113–26.

Zabel, J.E. and K.A. Kiel. 2000. "Estimating the demand for air quality in four US cities." *Land Economics*. 76: 174–94.

Zhang, C., K.J. Boyle, and N.V. Kuminoff. 2015. "Partial identification of amenity demand functions." *Journal of Environmental Economics and Management*. 71: 180–97.

Zhang, D., V.J. Karplus, C. Cassisa, and X. Zhang. 2014. "Emissions trading in China: progress and prospects." *Energy Policy*. 75: 9–16.

Zhao, J. and C.L. Kling. 2000. "On the long run efficiency of auctioned vs. free permits." *Economics Letters*. 69: 235–8.

Zhao, J. and C.L. Kling. 2001. "A new explanation for the WTP/WTA disparity." *Economics Letters*. 73: 293–300.

Zhou, P., X. Zhou, and L.W. Fan. 2014. "On estimating shadow prices of undesirable outputs with efficiency models: A literature review." *Applied Energy*. 130: 799–806.

Author Index

Subject Index

Printed in the United States
by Baker & Taylor Publisher Services